# *Warman's*
# Americana & Collectibles

## 9TH EDITION

### EDITED BY ELLEN T. SCHROY

Published by

**krause
publications**

**700 E. State Street • Iola, WI 54990-0001**
**Telephone: 715/445-2214**


Please, call or write us for our free catalog of antiques and collectibles publications.
To place an order or receive our free catalog, call 800-258-0929.
For editorial comment and further information,
use our regular business telephone at (715) 445-2214.


Library of Congress Catalog Number: 84-643834
ISBN: 0-87341-699-6


Printed in the United States of America

# Table of Contents

## Part 1

Introduction . . . . . . . . . . . . . . . . . . . . . . . . . .4
Abbreviations . . . . . . . . . . . . . . . . . . . . . . . . .10
Board of Advisors . . . . . . . . . . . . . . . . . . . . . .11
Auction Houses . . . . . . . . . . . . . . . . . . . . . . . .13
Antiques and Collectibles Periodicals . . . . . . . . . . .18

## Part 2

Categories . . . . . . . . . . . . . . . . . . . . . . . . . . . .22

## Part 3

Index . . . . . . . . . . . . . . . . . . . . . . . . . . . . . .396

**One of the new categories in this year's guide is Star Wars Collectibles.**

# INTRODUCTION

Welcome to *Warman's Americana & Collectibles*, the cornerstone of the Warman's Encyclopedia of Antiques and Collectibles. In 1984, the first edition of *Warman's Americana & Collectibles* introduced the collecting community to category introductions featuring collecting hints, history, references, periodicals, and reproduction and copycat information complemented by detailed, accurate listings and values. As a result of the enthusiastic acceptance of this format, it was extended to *Warman's Antiques and Collectibles Price Guide* and ultimately to volumes in the Warman's Encyclopedia of Antiques and Collectibles.

*Warman's Americana & Collectibles* was a pioneering work, the first general price guide to mass-produced 20th-century objects. It helped define and solidify the modern collectibles market. As the collectibles market has matured, so has *Warman's Americana & Collectibles*. If you have a copy of the first edition, compare the categories listed in it to those found in this eighth edition. Times *have* changed. Perhaps this is why so many individuals find the collectibles market so exciting.

*Collectibles* are the things with which your parents, you, and your children have played and lived. The things that belonged to your grandparents are now *antiques*. The evolution of an object from new to desirable to collectible to antique within one's lifetime, i.e., an approximately 50-year span, is difficult for some to accept. However, it is reality.

*Warman's Americana & Collectibles* takes you on a nostalgic trip down memory lane. Sometimes it's sad to think back about things that have been passed on to others, perhaps have been broken or discarded. However, it's better to be thrilled by the value of the things that were saved. Do not hesitate to buy back the things from your childhood that evoke pleasant memories. As you do, you will find that the real value of objects is not monetary, but the joy that comes from collecting, owning, and, most importantly, playing and living with them once again.

As we embrace a new century, it's our philosophy that collectors should enjoy what they treasure so passionately and take the time to learn more about their specialties. *Warman's Americana & Collectibles* is based on the premise that it is acceptable to collect anything you wish. Remember one simple fact: All of today's antiques were collectibles in the past.

## What is a Collectible?

As the 20th century nears its end, the definition of an antique remains clear while what constitutes a collectible has become more confusing.

For the purpose of this book, an antique is anything made before 1945. A great many individuals in the antiques and collectibles field disagree with this definition, but with each passing year it becomes harder and harder to deny this premise. The key is the war years of 1942-1945. During this period, production switched from domestic to wartime products. When the war ended, things were different. American life and expectations were very different in 1948 than in 1938. New war technology modified for productive civilian use was partially responsible. However, the most-telling fact of all is that well over half the population living in America today was born after 1945 and approximately two-thirds grew up in the post-1945 era.

Keeping this in mind and seeking technical definitions, a collectible then becomes an object made between 1945 and 1965, and a "desirable" an object made after 1965. The difference between a collectible and a desirable is that a collectible has a clearly established secondary market, while a desirable exists in a market rampant with speculation.

Actually, the post-1945 era is broken down into three distinct collecting periods: 1945-1965, 1965-1980, and post-1980. Goods from the 1965 to 1980 period are moving out of their speculative mode into one of price stability.

Within the Warman's Encyclopedia of Antiques and Collectibles, *Warman's Americana & Collectibles* is the volume designed to deal with objects from the 20th century. Three criteria are applied when preparing the book: Was the object mass produced? Was it made in the 20th century, preferably after 1945? Do the majority of the items in the category sell for less than $200? The ideal collectible fits all three qualifications.

Since collecting antiques became fashionable in the early 20th century, there have been attempts to define certain groups of objects as the "true" antiques, worthy of sophisticated collectors, and to ignore the remaining items. Most museums clearly demonstrate this attitude. Where do early 20th-century tin toys, toy soldiers, or dolls fit? Those made before 1915 are antique. No one argues this any longer. Those made between 1920 and 1940 are in transition. We designate them "prestige" collectibles, objects changing in people's minds from collectible to antique.

In some collecting areas, such as advertising, dolls, and toys, *Warman's Americana & Collectibles* offers readers descriptions and values for 20th century items that might not be covered in *Warman's Antiques & Collectibles*. Other topics covered in *Warman's Americana & Collectibles* expand on the information found in that companion book. Areas like costume jewelry and Star Wars can better be addressed in *Warman's Americana & Collectibles*. When *Warman's Americana & Collectibles* was initially launched, it was hoped that this book could capture that segment of the market place that was missing from other price guides. Today, that fine tradition continues as *Warman's Americana & Collectibles* evolves again to respond to the collectibles marketplace.

To clarify the distinction between antique and collectible, consider Webster's definition of collectible: "an object that is collected by fanciers, especially one other than such traditionally collectible items as art, stamps, coins, and antiques."

## International Market

Collectibles began to draw worldwide interest at the end of the 1980s. All of a sudden, American buyers found themselves competing with buyers from Europe and Japan on their home turf. In head-to-head competition, the American buyers frequently lost. How can this be explained?

The largest portion of the 1990s collectibles market is made up of post-World War II material. During this period, the youth of the world fell under three dominant American influences: movies, music, and television. As the generations of the 1950s, 1960s, and even 1970s reached adulthood and started buying back their childhood, many of the things they remember and want have American associations.

America is the great mother lode of post-war collectibles. At the moment, it is packages and boxes of American collectibles that are being sent abroad. It will not be too much longer before the volume reaches container loads.

American collectors also are expanding their horizons. They recognize that many objects within their favorite collectible category were licensed abroad. They view their collections as incomplete without such examples. Objects are obtained by either traveling abroad or by purchasing from foreign sources through mail or auction.

The addition of the internet and it's auctions, dealer websites, and collector club websites has created additional buying opportunities. Collectors no longer have to set aside time to travel to their favorite haunts and search for hours for something to add to their collection. Sometimes it's as easy as sitting down at their computer and reading what's posted for sale. Some collecting areas are also benefiting from chat rooms dedicated to their specialties, allowing collectors to explore and learn from each other in ways and with speed only now available. This new openness is creating more savvy collectors and allowing information to flow globally.

## Price Notes

Prices in the collectibles field are not as firmly established as in the antiques area. Nevertheless, we do not use ranges unless we feel they are absolutely necessary.

Our pricing is based on an object being in

very good condition. If otherwise, we note this in our description. It would be ideal to suggest that mint, or unused, examples of all items do exist. In reality, objects from the past were used, whether they be glass, china, dolls, or toys. Because of this, some normal wear must be expected.

The biggest problem in the collectibles field is that an object may have more than one price. A George Eastman bubble gum card may be worth $1 to a bubble gum card collector but $35 to a collector of photographic memorabilia. I saw the same card marked both ways. In preparing prices for this guide we have considered the object in terms of the category in which it is included. Hence, a girlie matchcover may be valued at 25¢ to 50¢ in the matchcover category and $2 to $5 in pinup art. However, for purposes of making a sale, if all you can find are matchcover collectors, take the quarter and move on.

## Organization of the Book

**Listings:** We have attempted to make the listings descriptive enough so the specific object can be identified. Most guides limit their descriptions to one line, but not *Warman's*. We have placed emphasis on those items which are actively being sold in the marketplace. Nevertheless, some harder-to-find objects are included in order to demonstrated the market spread. A few categories in this book also appear in *Warman's Antiques and Collectibles Price Guide*. The individual listings, however, seldom overlap except for a few minor instances. We've tried to include enough objects to give readers a good base for comparison. After all, that is what much of the collectibles marketplace uses to establish prices: comparables. To properly accomplish this task, some overlapping between books is unavoidable. It is our intention to show objects in the low to middle price range of a category in *Warman's Americana & Collectibles* and the middle to upper range in our main antiques guide, *Warman's Antiques and Collectibles Price Guide*, thus creating two true companion lists for the general dealer or collector.

**Collecting Hints:** This section calls attention to specific hints as they relate to the category. We note where cross-category collecting and nostalgia are critical in pricing. Clues are given for spotting reproductions. In most cases, we

just scratch the surface. We encourage collectors to consult specialized publications.

**History:** Here we discuss the category, describe how the object was made, who are or were the leading manufacturers, and the variations of form and style. In many instances, a chronology for the object is established. Finally, we place the object in a social context—how it was used, for what purpose, etc.

**References:** Many general references are listed to encourage collectors to learn more about their objects. Included are author, title, most recent edition, publisher, and a date of publication. If published by a small firm or individual, we have included the address when known.

Finding many of these books may present a problem. The antiques and collectibles field is blessed with a dedicated core of book dealers who stock these specialized publications. You may find them at flea markets, antiques shows, or through their advertisements in leading publications in the field. Many dealers publish annual or semi-annual catalogs. Ask to be put on their mailing lists. Books go out-of-print quickly, yet many books printed more than 25 years ago remain the standard work in a field. Also, haunt used-book dealers for collectible reference material.

The reference list listed in *Warman's Americana & Collectibles* should be a good starting point, but don't assume we've listed every reference book pertaining to a particular topic. That would be a wonderful feature to offer, but would leave little room for price listings. We try to list the most current books to assist you in your search for information.

**Collectors' Clubs:** The large number of collectors' clubs adds vitality to the collectibles field. Their publications and conventions produce knowledge which often cannot be found anywhere else. Many of these clubs are short-lived; others are so strong that they have regional and local chapters. Many collector clubs are now going on-line, offering chat rooms and other benefits to their members.

**Periodicals:** In respect to the collectibles field, there are certain general monthly periodicals to which the general collector should subscribe:

*Antiques & Collecting Hobbies*, 1006 South Michigan Avenue, Chicago, IL 60605.

*Antique Trader Weekly*, P.O. Box 1050,

Dubuque, IA 52001; http://www.csmonline.com.

*AntiqueWeek*, P.O. Box 90, Knightstown, IN 46148; http://www.antiqueweek.com.

*Maine Antique Digest*, P.O. Box 358, Waldoboro, ME 04572; http://www.maineantiquedigest.com.

Several excellent periodicals and magazines relating to the collectibles marketplace are published by Krause Publications, 700 East State St., Iola, WI 54990-0001; http://www.krause.com. Check out these interesting publications:

*Coin Prices*
*Coins*
*eBay Magazine*
*Goldmine*
*Numismatic News*
*Sports Cards*
*Sports Collectors Digest*
*Toy Shop*
*Warman's Today's Collector*

Many of the categories included in *Warman's Americana & Collectibles* have listings of specialized periodicals and newsletters. Please refer to your specific collecting interest for these additional references.

**Museums:** The best way to study any field is to see as many documented examples as possible. For this reason, we have listed museums where significant collections are on display. Special attention must be directed to the Margaret Woodbury Strong Museum in Rochester, New York, and the Smithsonian Institution's Museum of American History in Washington, D.C.

**Reproduction Alert:** Reproductions are a major concern, especially with any item related to advertising. Most reproductions are unmarked; the newness of their appearance is often the best clue to uncovering them. Where the words "Reproduction Alert" alone appear, a watchful eye should be kept on all objects in the category.

Reproductions are only one aspect of the problem; outright fakes are another. Unscrupulous manufacturers make fantasy items which never existed, e.g., a Depression glass Sharon butter dish reproduced in Mayfair blue.

## Research

Collectors of objects in the categories found in this book deserve credit for their attention to scholarship and the skill with which they have assembled their collections. This book attests to how strong and encompassing the collectibles market has become through their efforts.

We obtain our prices from many key sources—dealers, publications, auctions, collectors, the internet, and field work. The generosity with which dealers have given advice is a credit to the field. Everyone recognizes the need for a guide that is specific and has accurate prices. We study newspapers, magazines, newsletters, and other publications in the collectibles and antiques fields, as well as spending more and more time on-line. All of them are critical to understanding what is available in the market. Special recognition must be given to those collectors' club newsletters and magazines which discuss prices.

Our staff is constantly monitoring the field, paying attention to all parts of the country. We accomplish this by reading trade publications and using the Internet and its vast resources to reach many places. Frequent visits to several different Web sites yield valuable information as to what is being offered for sale and what people are looking for, as well as insights into collecting clubs and new collecting interests. Our Board of Advisors provides regional as well as specialized information. More than 100 specialized auctions are held annually, and their results provided to our office. Finally, private collectors have worked closely with us, sharing their knowledge of price trends and developments unique to their specialties.

## Buyer's Guide, Not Seller's Guide

*Warman's Americana and Collectibles* is designed to be a buyer's guide, a guide to what you would have to pay to purchase an object on the open market from a dealer or collector. **It is not a seller's guide to prices.** People frequently make this mistake and are deceiving themselves by doing so.

If you have an object mentioned in this book and wish to sell it, you should expect to receive approximately 35% to 40% of the value listed. If the object cannot be resold quickly, expect to receive even less. The truth is simple: Knowing to whom to sell an object is worth 50% or more of its value. Buyers are very specialized; dealers work for years to assemble a list of collectors who will pay top dollar for an item.

Examine your piece as objectively as possible. If it is something from your childhood, try to step back from the personal memories in evaluating its condition. As an antiques' appraiser, I spend a great deal of my time telling people their treasures are not "gold," but items readily available in the marketplace.

In respect to buying and selling, a simple philosophy is that a good purchase occurs when both the buyer and seller are happy with the price. Don't look back. Hindsight has little value in the collectibles field. Given time, things tend to balance out.

## Where to Buy Collectibles

The collectible has become standard auction house fare in the 1990s. Christie's East (219 East 67th St., New York, NY 10021) and Sotheby's Arcade (1334 York Avenue, New York, NY 10021) and Skinner's Discovery (Bolton Gallery, 357 Main St., Boston, MA 01740) conduct collectibles sales several times each year. Specialized auction firms, e.g., James Julia, Inc. (P.O. Box 830, Fairfield, ME 04937) and Bill Bertoia Auctions (1881 Spring Road, Vineland, NJ 08360) in advertising, toys, and a host of other categories, have proven the viability of the collectible as a focal point.

The major collectibles marketing thrust has changed from the mail auction to internet auctions. Hake's Americana & Collectibles (P.O. Box 1444, York, PA 17405) is the leader in mail auctions. More and more collectible mail auctions are sprouting up all across the country. Add to this the excitement of buying online and even participating in online auctions, and you can see why so many expand their collections using these venues.

It is becoming easier and easier to buy and sell collectibles on-line. There are numerous auction sites, including e-bay.com, Collectoronline.com, etc. The same excitement of buying collectibles at a real auction can be achieved. However, this arena is growing quickly and is not yet regulated. Buyers need to be cautious, know what they are buying and learn to set limits on what to spend. Buyers should feel comfortable with the venue before jumping in on the bidding and should feel free to ask questions of the seller, just as they would in a more traditional selling setting. With on-line services and live auctioneers merging and forming new alliances, it will soon be possible to live bid on objects being auctioned off at a major auction house. This is a brand new area to explore and hopefully it will bring excitement and energy to the antiques and collectibles market as we enter the new millennium.

Direct-sale catalogs abound. Most major categories have one or more. These dealers and many more advertise in periodicals and collectors' clubs' newsletters. Most require payment of an annual fee before sending their catalogs.

Of course, there are an unlimited number of flea markets, estate and country auctions, church bazaars, and garage sales. However, if you are a specialized collector, you may spend days looking for something to add to your collection. If you add in your time, the real cost of an object will be much higher than the purchase price alone.

All of which brings us to the final source—the specialized dealer. The collectibles field is so broad that dealers do specialize. Find the dealers who handle your material and work with them to build your collection.

## Board of Advisors

Our Board of Advisors are dealers, authors, collectors, and leaders of collectors' clubs throughout the United States. All are dedicated to accuracy in description and pricing. If you wish to buy or sell an object in their field of expertise, drop them a note. Please include a stamped, self-addressed envelope with all correspondence. If time permits, they will respond.

We list the names of our advisors at the end of their respective categories. Included in the list at the front of this book are mailing address for each advisor and, when available, phone number and/or e-mail address.

## Comments Invited

*Warman's Americana & Collectibles* is a major effort dealing with a complex field. Our readers are encouraged to send their comments and suggestions to P.O. Box 392, Quakertown, PA 18951-0392; or via e-mail to schroy@voicenet.com.

# Acknowledgments

Since it's creation in 1984, *Warman's Americana & Collectibles,* this edition has grown and changed with the shifts of the antiques and collectibles marketplace. New categories are included that show what folks are collecting as the 1990s come to a close. Whether you collect them or not, the Beanie Baby phenomena has impacted the marketplace. It has drawn new collectors to flea markets and antique shops, taught folks how to collect, and encouraged them to be passionate about it. Will the collecting momentum associated with Beanie Babies continue into the next century - **certainly!** Will *every collector* continue to add new items to their collections - **probably not**. However, this is also typical of almost every other segment of the collectibles market. Perhaps it's living in a country and society where you are free to decide what to collect, how to spend your money, or perhaps my aging baby-boomer philosophy, but a Beanie Baby collector is a *true* collector and my hat is off to them for the dedication and enthusiasm. (Pssst, look for a new listing of Beanie Babies in this edition). Other new topics include: Advertising Watches, Griswold, Soakies, Star Wars, Wrestling, and a few other new categories tucked in here and there.

No edition of *Warman's* would ever be complete without a special thanks to the members of the Board of Advisors, a wonderful, dedicated group. Some new names have been added, helping to give this edition a very up-to-date and wide-geographical flavor, while providing some solid information about some hot topics, like collecting Holt Howard, Monsters, and Griswold. Through the mail, telephone, and now e-mail, I've been in contact with each and every one, heard about what's important to their collecting interests as well as what's new in their lives. Through these conversations and their warm wishes of support, we've created an even better *Warman's Americana & Collectibles.*

The fine staff of Krause Publications continues it's nurturing support of *Warman's.* Perhaps you have noticed some of the additional titles that now include "Warman's" in their titles, like *Warman's Dolls* and *Warman's Depression Glass.* As we head toward the new millennium, expect to see more titles including *Warman's Flea Market Price Guide,* and additional editions to some of the favorites. But, also be assured that every title that contains that familiar Warman's name is full of good information as well as solid, up-to-date pricing. So with a special thanks to Kris Manty, Jon Brecka and their talented co-workers in production, layout, and photography, we'll now offer you a new edition of *Warman's Americana & Collectibles.*

Here's hoping you enjoy it as much as we enjoy creating it for collectors and dealers like you.

**Ellen Tischbein Schroy**

**July 1999**

# ABBREVIATIONS

The following are standard abbreviations which we have used throughout this edition of *Warman's*.

3D = three dimensional
ADS = Autograph Document Signed
adv = advertising
ALS = Autograph Letter Signed
approx = approximately
AQS = Autograph Quotation Signed
b&w = black and white
C = century
c = circa
cov = cover
CS = Card Signed
d = diameter or depth
dec = decorated
dj = dust jacket
DS = Document Signed
ed = edition, editor
emb = embossed
ext. = exterior
ftd = footed
gal = gallon
ground = background
h = height
horiz = horizontal
hp = hand painted
illus = illustrated, illustration, illustrator
imp = impressed
int. = interior
irid = iridescent
j = jewels
K = karat
l = length
lb = pound
litho = lithograph
LS = Letter Signed

MBP = mint in bubble pack
mfg = manufactured
MIB = mint in box
MIP = mint in package
MISB = mint in sealed box
mkd = marked
MOC = mint on card
MOP = mother of pearl
n.d. = no date
No. = number
NRFB = never removed from box
opal = opalescent
orig = original
oz = ounce
pat = patent
pc = piece
pcs = pieces
pg = page
pgs = pages
pr = pair
PS = Photograph Signed
pt = pint
qt = quart
rect = rectangular
sgd = signed
SP = silver plated
SS = sterling silver
sq = square
TLS = Typed Letter Signed
vol = volume
w = width
yg = yellow gold
# = numbered

# BOARD of ADVISORS

**Franklin M. Arnall**
The Collector
P.O. Box 253
Claremont, CA 91711
(909) 621-2461
e-mail: Roksnlocks@aol.com
*Padlocks*

**Rick Botts**
2345 SE 60th Court
Des Moines, IA 50317
(515) 265-8324
*Jukeboxes*

**Lorie Cairns**
Cairns Antiques
P.O. Box 44026
Lemon Cove, CA 93244
(559) 564-2158
*Labels*

**Barry L. Carter**
Knightstown Antique Mall
136 West Carey St.
Knightstown, IN 46148
(765) 345-5665
e-mail: carterb@juno.com
*Soldiers, Dimestore; Soldiers, Toy*

**Tina M. Carter**
882 South Mollison Ave.
El Cajon, CA 92020
(619) 440-5043
e-mail: premos2@aol.com
*Cookie Cutters; Teapots*

**Jimer De Vries**
9740 Campo Road, #134
Spring Valley, CA 91977-1415
(935) 462-2333
*Swarovski Crystal*

**Marilyn Dipboye**
33161 Wendy Drive
Sterling Heights, MI 48315
(810) 264-0285
*Cat Collectibles*

**Bruce L. Flamm**
10445 Victoria Ave.
Riverside, CA 92503
e-mail: bflamm@ix.netcom.com
*Calculators*

**David J. and Deborah G. Folckemer**
RR2, Box 394
Hollidaysburg, PA 16648
(814) 696-0301
*Royal China*

**M. D. Fountain**
201 Alvena
Wichita, KS 67203
(316) 943-1925
*Swankyswigs*

**Ted Hake**
Hake's Americana & Collectibles
P.O. Box 1444
York, PA 17405
(717) 848-1333
*Disneyana; Political & Campaign Items*

**Doris & Burdell Hall**
B & B Antiques
210 West Sassafras Drive
Morton, IL 61550
(309) 263-2988
*Morton Potteries*

**Mary Hamburg**
20 Cedar Ave.
Danville, IL 61832
(217) 446-2323
*Pig Collectibles*

**Jon Haussler**
1806 Brownstone Ave., SW
Decatur, AL 35603
(256) 351-8567
e-mail: jhaus23985@aol.com
*Griswold*

**Tom Hoepf**
c/o Antique Week
P.O. Box 90, 27 North Jefferson
Knightstown, IN 46148
(800) 876-5133
e-mail: antiqueth@aol.com
*Cameras & Accessories*

**Tim Hughes**
P.O. Box 3636
Williamsport, PA 17701-8636
(570) 326-1045
(570) 326-7606 fax
e-mail: tim@rarenewspapers.com
website:
  www.rarenewspapers.com
*Newspapers, Headlines*

**Joan Hull**
1376 Nevada
Huron, SD 57350
(605) 352-1685
*Hull Pottery*

**Sharon Iranpour**
24 San Rafael Drive
Rochester, NY 14618
e-mail: siranpour@aol.com
*Advertising Watches*

**David & Sue Irons**
Irons Antiques
223 Covered Bridge Road
Northampton, PA 18067
(610) 262-9335
*Irons*

**Don Johnson**
5110 S. Greensboro Pike
Knightstown, IN 46148
e-mail: Djohnson@spitfire.com
*Uhl Pottery*

**Ellen G. King**
King's Antiques
102 North Main St.
Butler, PA 16001
(724) 894-2596
*Flow Blue China, American*

**Bob Levy**
The Unique One
2802 Centre St.
Pennsauken, NJ 08109
(609) 663-2554
*Slot Machines; Pinball
Machines; Vending
Machines*

**Patricia McDaniel**
Old Storefront Antiques
411 W. 28th St.
Connersville, IN 47331
(765) 825-6295
*Drugstore*

**Peter Meissner**
347 Threw Bridge Road
Nesnick, NJ 08853
(908) 369-1159
*Stangl*

**Nancy McMichael**
P.O. Box 53132
Washington, DC 20009
*Snowdomes*

**Gary L. Miller & K. M.
Scotty Mitchell**
Millchell
2112 Lipscomb
Fort Worth, TX 76110
(817) 923-3274
*Electrical Appliances*

**Thomas G. Morris**
P.O. Box 8307
Medford, OR 97504
e-mail: chalkman@cdsnet.net
*Carnival Chalkware*

**Jocelyn C. Mousley**
137 South Main Street
Quakertown, PA 18951
*Dog Collectibles*

**Joan Collett Oates**
685 South Washington
Constantine, MI 49042
(616) 435-8353
*Phoenix Bird China*

**Clark Phelps**
Amusement Sales
7610 South Main St.
Midvale, UT 84047
(801) 255-4731
*Punchboards*

**Evalene Pulati**
P.O. Box 1404
Santa Ana, CA 92702
*Valentines*

**Arthur Rein**
Lottery Collector's Society
2 Sherwood Terrace
Yonkers, NY 10704-3343
(914) 237-7417
e-mail Lotteryfan@aol.com.
*Lottery Tickets*

**Jim & Nancy Schaut**
7147 W. Angela Drive
Glendale, AZ 85308-8507
(602) 878-4293
e-mail: Jnschaut@aol.com
*Horse Collectibles*

**Kenneth E. Schneringer**
271 Sabrina Court
Woodstock, GA 30188
(707) 926-9383
*Catalogs*

**Virginia R. Scott**
275 Milledge Terrace
Athens, GA 30606
(706) 548-5966
*Candlewick*

**Richard Shields**
The Carolina Trader
P.O. Box 769
Monroe, NC 28112
(704) 289-1604
*Scouting*

**Judy Smith**
1702 Lamont St. NW
Washington, DC 20010-2602
(202) 332-3020
e-mail: Reamers@quiltart.com
*Reamers*

**Lissa Bryan-Smith and
Richard Smith**
17 Market St.
Lewisburg, PA 17837
(570) 523-3376
e-mail: lbs8253@ptd.prolog.net
*Christmas Items; Holiday
Collectibles; Santa Claus*

**Connie Swaim**
P.O. Box 331
Carthage, IN 46115
e-mail:TheLorax50@aol.com
*Dr. Seuss Collectibles*

**Dixie Trainer**
P.O. Box 70
Nellysford, VA 22958
(804) 361-1739
*Souvenir Buildings*

**Lewis S. Walters**
143 Lincoln Lane
Berlin, NJ 08009
(609) 589-3202
e-mail: lew69@erols.com
*Radios*

# AUCTION HOUSES

The following auction houses cooperate with *Warman's* by providing catalogs of their auctions and price lists. This information is used to prepare *Warman's Antiques and Collectibles Price Guide*, volumes in the Warman's Encyclopedia of Antiques and Collectibles. This support is truly appreciated.

**Albrecht & Cooper Auction Services**
3884 Saginaw Rd
Vassar, MI 48768
(517) 823-8835

**Sanford Alderfer Auction Company**
501 Fairgrounds Rd
Hatfield, PA 19440
(215) 393-3000
web site: http://
    www.alderfercompany.com

**American Social History and Social Movements**
4025 Saline St.
Pittsburgh, PA 15217
(412) 421-5230

**Andre Ammelounx**
The Stein Auction Company
P.O. Box 136
Palantine, IL 60078
(847) 991-5927

**Apple Tree Auction Center**
1616 W. Church St.
Newark, OH 43055
(614) 344-4282

**Arthur Auctioneering**
RD 2, P.O. Box 155
Hughesville, PA 17737
(717) 584-3697

**Auction Team Köln**
Jane Herz
6731 Ashley Court
Sarasota, FL 34241
(941) 925-0385

**Auction Team Köln**
Postfach 501168 D 5000
Köln 50, W. Germany

**Noel Barrett Antiques & Auctions, Ltd.**
P.O. Box 1001
Carversville, PA 18913
(610) 297-5109

**Robert F. Batchelder**
1 W Butler Ave.
Ambler, PA 19002
(610) 643-1430

**Bear Pen Antiques**
2318 Bear Pen Hollow Road
Lock Haven, PA 17745
(717) 769-6655

**Beverly Hills Auctioneers**
9454 Wilshire Blvd., Suite 202
Beverly Hills, CA 90212
(310) 278-8115

**Bill Bertoia Auctions**
1881 Spring Rd
Vineland, NJ 08360
(609) 692-1881

**Biders Antiques Inc.**
241 S. Union St.
Lawrence, MA 01843
(508) 688-4347

**Brown Auction & Real Estate**
900 East Kansas
Greensburg, KS 67054
(316) 723-2111

**Butterfield, Butterfield & Dunning**
755 Church Rd
Elgin, IL 60123
(847) 741-3483
web site: http://
    www.butterfields.com

**Butterfield, Butterfield & Dunning**
7601 Sunset Blvd.
Los Angeles, CA 90046
(213) 850-7500
web site: http://
    www.butterfields.com

**Butterfield, Butterfield & Dunning**
220 San Bruno Ave.
San Francisco, CA 94103
(415) 861-7500
web site: http://
    www.butterfields.com

**C. C. Auction Gallery**
416 Court
Clay Center, KS 67432
(913) 632-6021

**W. E. Channing & Co., Inc.**
53 Old Santa Fe Trail
Santa Fe, NM 87501
(505) 988-1078

**Chicago Art Galleries**
5039 Oakton St
Skokie, IL 60077
(847) 677-6080

**Childers & Smith**
1415 Horseshoe Pike
Glenmoore, PA 19343
(610) 269-1036
e-mail:
    harold@smithautionco.com

14

**Christie's**
502 Park Ave.
New York, NY 10022
(212) 546-1000
web site: http://
www.christies.com

**Christie's East**
219 E. 67th St.
New York, NY 10021
(212) 606-0400
web site: http://
www.christies.com

**Cincinnati Art Galleries**
635 Main St.
Cincinnati, OH 45202
(513) 381-2128

**Mike Clum, Inc.**
P.O. Box 2
Rushville, OH 43150
(614) 536-9220

**Cobb's Doll Auctions**
1909 Harrison Road
Johnstown OH 43031-9539
(740) 964-0444

**Cohasco Inc.**
Postal 821
Yonkers, NY 10702
(914) 476-8500

**Collection Liquidators
Auction Service**
Suite 407
341 Lafayette St.
New York, NY 10012
(212) 505-2455
website: http://
www.rtam.com/coliq/bid.html
e-mail: coliq@erols.com

**Collector's Sales and
Service**
P.O. Box 4037
Middletown RI02842
(401) 849-5012
website: http://
www.antiquechina.com

**Coole Park Books and
Autographs**
P.O. Box 199049
Indianapolis, IN 46219
(317) 351-8495
e-mail: cooleprk@indy.net

**Copeke Auction**
226 Route 7A
Cokepe, NY 12516
(518) 329-1142

**Samuel J. Cottonne**
15 Genesee St.
Mt. Morris, NY 14510
(716) 583-3119

**Craftsman Auctions**
1485 W. Housatoric
Pittsfield MA 01202
(413) 442-7003
web site: http://
www.artsncrafts.com

**Dargate Auction Galleries**
5607 Baum Blvd.
Pittsburgh, PA 15206
(412) 362-3558
web site: http://
www.dargate.com

**Dawson's**
128 American Road
Morris Plains, NJ 07950
(973) 984-6900
web site: http://
www.idt.net/-dawson1

**DeWolfe & Wood**
P.O. Box 425
Alfred, ME 04002
(207) 490-5572

**Marlin G. Denlinger**
RR3, Box 3775
Morrisville, VT 05661
(802) 888-2775

**Dixie Sporting Collectibles**
1206 Rama Rd.
Charlotte, NC 28211
(704) 364-2900
web site: http://
www.sportauction.com

**William Doyle Galleries,
Inc.**
175 E. 87th St.
New York, NY 10128
(212) 427-2730
web site: http://
www.doylegalleries.com

**Dunbar Gallery**
76 Haven St.
Milford, MA 01757
(508) 634-8697

**Early Auction Co.**
123 Main St.
Milford, OH 45150
(513) 831-4833

**Fain & Co.**
P.O. Box 1330
Grants Pass, OR 97526
(888) 324-6726

**Ken Farmer Realty & Auction Co.**
105A Harrison St.
Radford, VA 24141
(703) 639-0939
web site: http://kenfarmer.com

**Fine Tool Journal**
27 Fickett Rd
Pownal, ME 04069
(207) 688-4962
web site: http://
www.wowpages.com/FTJ/

**Steve Finer Rare Books**
P.O. Box 758
Greenfield, MA 01302
(413) 773-5811

**Flomaton Antique Auction**
207 Palafox St.
Flomaton, AL 36441
(334) 296-3059

**William A. Fox Auctions
Inc.**
676 Morris Ave.
Springfield, NJ 07081
(201) 467-2366

**Freeman\Fine Arts Co. of
Philadelphia, Inc.**
1808 Chestnut St.
Philadelphia, PA 19103
(215) 563-9275

**Garth's Auction, Inc.**
2690 Stratford Rd.
P.O. Box 369
Delaware, OH 43015
(740) 362-4771

**Greenberg Auctions**
7566 Main St.
Skysville, MD 21784
(410) 795-7447

**Green Valley Auction Inc.**
Route 2, Box 434
Mt. Crawford, VA 22841
(540) 434-4260

**Guerney's**
136 E. 73rd St.
New York, NY 10021
(212) 794-2280

**Hake's Americana &
Collectibles**
P.O. Box 1444
York, PA 17405
(717) 848-1333

**Gene Harris Antique
Auction Center, Inc.**
203 South 18th Ave.
P.O. Box 476
Marshalltown, IA 50158
(515) 752-0600

**Norman C. Heckler &
Company**
Bradford Corner Rd.
Woodstock Valley, CT 06282
(203) 974-1634

**High Noon**
9929 Venice Blvd.
Los Angeles CA 90034
(310) 202-9010

**Michael Ivankovich
Auction Co.**
P.O. Box 2458
Doylestown, PA 18901
(215) 345-6094
web site: http://www.nutting.com

**Jackson's Auctioneers &
Appraisers**
2229 Lincoln St.
Cedar Falls, IA 50613
(319) 277-2256
web site: http://
    www.jacksonauction.com

**James D. Julia Inc.**
Rt. 201 Skowhegan Rd
P.O. Box 830
Fairfield, ME 04937
(207) 453-7125

**J. W. Auction Co.**
54 Rochester Hill Rd
Rochester, NH 03867
(603) 332-0192

**Lang's Sporting
Collectables, Inc.**
31 R Turthle Cove
Raymond, ME 04071
(207) 655-4265

**La Rue Auction Service**
201 S. Miller St.,
Sweet Springs, MO 65351
(816) 335-4538

**Leonard's Auction
Company**
1631 State Rd.
Duncannon, PA 17020
(717) 957-3324

**Howard Lowery**
3818 W. Magnolia Blvd.
Burbank, CA 91505
(818) 972-9080

**Joy Luke**
The Gallery
300 E. Grove St.
Bloomington, IL 61701
(309) 828-5533

**Mapes Auctioneers &
Appraisers**
1729 Vestal Pkwy
Vestal, NY 13850
(607) 754-9193

**Martin Auctioneers Inc.**
P.O. Box 477
Intercourse, PA 17534
(717) 768-8108

**McMasters Doll Auctions**
P.O. Box 1755
Cambridge, OH 43725
(614) 432-4419

**Metropolitan Book Auction**
123 W. 18th St., 4th Floor
New York, NY 10011
(212) 929-7099

**Wm. Frost Mobley**
P.O. Box 10
Schoharie, NY 12157
(518) 295-7978

**Wm. Morford**
RD #2
Cazenovia, NY 13035
(315) 662-7625

**Neal Auction Company**
4038 Magazine St.
New Orleans, LA 7015
(504) 899-5329
web site: http://
    www.nealauction.com

**New England Auction
Gallery**
P.O. Box 2273
W. Peabody, MA 01960
(508) 535-3140

**New Orleans Auction St.
Charles Auction Gallery,
Inc.**
1330 St. Charles Avenue
New Orleans, LA 70130
(504) 586-8733
web site: http://
    www.neworleansauction.com

**New Hampshire Book
Auctions**
P.O. Box 460
92 Woodbury Rd
Weare, NH 03281
(603) 529-7432

**Norton Auctioneers of
Michigan Inc.**
50 West Pearl at Monroe
Coldwater MI 49036
(517) 279-9063

**Old Barn Auction**
10040 St. Rt. 224 West
Findlay, OH 45840
(419) 422-8531
web site: http://
    www.oldbarn.com

**Ohio Cola Traders**
4411 Bazetta Rd
Cortland, OH 44410

**Richard Opfer
Auctioneering Inc.**
1919 Greenspring Dr.
Timonium, MD 21093
(410) 252-5035

**Pacific Book Auction
Galleries**
133 Kerney St., 4th Floor
San Francisco, CA 94108
(415) 989-2665
web site: http://
    www.nbn.com/~pba/

**Pettigrew Auction
Company**
1645 S. Tejon St.
Colorado Springs, CO 80906
(719) 633-7963

**Phillips Ltd.**
406 E. 79th St.
New York, NY 10021
(212) 570-4830
web site: http://
www.phillips-auction.com

**Postcards International**
2321 Whitney Ave., Suite 102
P.O. Box 5398
Hamden, CT 06518
(203) 248-6621
web site: http://
www.csmonline.com/post-
cardsint/

**Poster Auctions International**
601 W. 26th St.
New York, NY 10001
(212) 787-4000

**Profitt Auction Company**
P.O. Box 796
Columbia, VA 23038
(804) 747-6353

**Provenance**
P.O. Box 3487
Wallington, NJ 07057
(201) 779-8725

**David Rago Auctions, Inc.**
333 S. Main St.
Lambertville, NJ 08530
(609) 397-9374
web site: http://
www.ragoarts.com

**Lloyd Ralston Toys**
173 Post Rd.
Fairfield, CT 06432
(203) 255-1233

**James J. Reeves**
P.O. Box 219
Huntingdon, PA 16652-0219
(814) 643-5497
website:
www.JamesJReeves.com

**Mickey Reichel Auctioneer**
1440 Ashley Rd
Boonville MO 65233
(816) 882-5292

**Sandy Rosnick Auctions**
15 Front St.
Salem MA 01970
(508) 741-1130

**Thomas Schmidt**
7099 McKean Rd.
Ypsilanti, MI 48197
(313) 485-8606

**Seeck Auctions**
P.O. Box 377
Mason City, IA 50402
(515) 424-1116
website: www.willowtree.com/
~seeckauctions

**L. H. Selman Ltd.**
761 Chestnut St.
Santa Cruz, CA 95060
(408) 427-1177
web site: http://www.selman.com

**Sentry Auction**
113 School St.
Apollo, PA 15613
(412) 478-1989

**Skinner Inc.**
Bolton Gallery
357 Main St.
Bolton, MA 01740
(978) 779-6241
web site: http://
www.skinnerinc.com

**Skinner, Inc.**
The Heritage on the Garden
63 Park Plaza
Boston MA 02116
(978) 350-5429
web site: http://
www.skinnerinc.com

**C. G. Sloan & Company Inc.**
4920 Wyaconda Rd
North Bethesda, MD 20852
(301) 468-4911
web site: http://
www.cgsloan.com

**Smith & Jones, Inc., Auctions**
12 Clark Lane
Sudbury MA 01776
(508) 443-5517

**Smith House Toy Sales**
26 Adlington Rd
Eliot, ME 03903
(207) 439-4614

**R. M. Smythe & Co.**
26 Broadway
New York, NY 10004-1710
(212) 943-1880
web site: http://
www.rm-smythe.com

**Sotheby's**
1334 York Ave.
New York, NY 10021
(212) 606-7000
web site: http://
www.sothebys.com

**Southern Folk Pottery Collectors Society**
1828 N. Howard Mill Rd.
Robbins, NC 27325
(910) 464-3961

**Stanton's Auctioneers**
P.O. Box 146
144 South Main St.
Vermontville, MI 49096
(517) 726-0181

**Stout Auctions**
11 W. Third St.
Williamsport, IN 47993-1119
(765) 764-6901

**Michael Strawser**
200 N. Main St., P.O. Box 332
Wolcottville, IN 46795
(219) 854-2859

**Swann Galleries Inc.**
104 E. 25th St.
New York, NY 10010
(212) 254-4710

**Swartz Auction Services**
2404 N. Mattis Ave.
Champaign, IL 61826-7166
(217) 357-0197
web site: http://www/SwartzAuc-
tion.com

**The House In The Woods**
S91 W37851 Antique Lane
Eagle, WI 53119
(414) 594-2334

**Theriault's**
P.O. Box 151
Annapolis, MD 21401
(301) 224-3655
web site: http://www.theri-
aults.com

**Toy Scouts**
137 Casterton Ave.
Akron, OH 44303
(216) 836-0668
e-mail: toyscout@sala-
mander.net

**Treadway Gallery, Inc.**
2029 Madison Rd.
Cincinnati, OH 45208
(513) 321-6742
web site: http://
www.a3c2net.com/treadwayg-
allery

**Unique Antiques & Auc-
tion Gallery**
449 Highway 72 West
Collierville, TN 38017
(901) 854-1141

**Venable Estate Auction**
423 West Fayette St.
Pittsfield, IL 62363
(217) 285-2560
e-mail: sandiv@msn.com

**Victorian Images**
P.O. Box 284
Marlton, NJ 08053
(609) 985-7711

**Victorian Lady**
P.O. Box 424
Waxhaw, NC 28173
(704) 843-4467

**Vintage Cover Story**
P.O. Box 975
Burlington, NC 27215
(919) 584-6900

**Bruce and Vicki Waasdorp**
P.O. Box 434
10931 Main St.
Clarence, NY 14031
(716) 759-2361

**Web Wilson Antiques**
P.O. Box 506
Portsmouth, RI 02871
1-800-508-0022

**Winter Associates**
21 Cooke St. Box 823
Plainville, CT 06062
(203) 793-0288

**Wolf's Auctioneers**
1239 W. 6th St.
Cleveland, OH 44113
(614) 362-4711

**Woody Auction**
Douglass, KS 67039
(316) 746-2694

**York Town Auction, Inc.**
1625 Haviland Rd
York, PA 17404
(717) 751-0211
e-mail: yorktownauction@cybe-
ria.com

# ANTIQUES and COLLECTIBLES PERIODICALS

The antiques and collectibles marketplace is fortunate to have some great publications in the form of weekly or monthly newspapers and magazines. Although many of these are regional publications, others are larger in scope. The periodicals listed below contain general information. For specialized material, please check the specific categories listed in Warman's Americana and Collectibles. Many of these publications can be found at your local news stand or book store. Frequently, complimentary copies can be obtained at flea markets. Look for them!

**American Collector**
225 Main St., Suite 300
Northport, NY 11768-1737
(516) 261-8337
http://www.tias.com/mags/IC/
  AntiqueDollWorld/

**American History
Illustrated**
741 Miller Drive
Harrisburg, PA 20175
(703) 771-9400
http://www.thehistorynet.com

**Americana Magazine**
29 W. 38th St.
New York, NY 10018
(212) 398-1550

**Antique Almanac, The**
P.O. Box 1613
Bowie, TX 76230-1613
(817) 872-6186

**Antique & Collectables**
P.O. Box 13560
El Cajon, CA 92022
(619) 593-2925

**Antique & Collectible
News**
P.O. Box 529
Anna, IL 62906-0529
(618) 833-2158

**Antique Collecting
Magazine**
Antique Collectors' Club Ltd.
5 Church St.
Woodbridge
Suffolk 1P12 1DS, UK
http://www.antiquecc.com/mag/
  magtoc.htm

**Antique Collector &
Auction Guide, The**
P.O. Box 38
Salem, OH 44480
(216) 337-3419

**Antique Dealer &
Collectors Guide, The**
200 Meacham Ave.
Elmont, NY 11003

**Antique Gazette**
6949 Charlotte Pike, Suite 106
Nashville, TN 37209-4200
(615) 352-0941

**Antique Press, The**
12403 N. Florida Ave.
Tampa, FL 33612
(813) 935-7577

**Antique Review**
P.O. Box 538
Columbus, OH 43085-0538
(614) 885-9757

**Antique Shoppe, The**
P.O. Box 2175
Keystone Heights, FL 32656
(352) 475-5326

**Antique Showcase**
103 Lakeshore Road
St. Catharines
Ontario L2N 2T6 Canada
(905) 646-7744

**Antiquer's Guide to the
Susquehanna Region**
P.O. Box 388
Sidney, NY 13838
(607) 563-8339

**Antique & Auction News**
P.O. Box 500
Mount Joy, PA 17552-0500
(717) 633-4300

**Antiques & Collectibles**
150 Linden Ave.
P.O. Box 33
Westbury, NY 11590
(516) 334-9650

**Antiques & Collecting
Magazine**
1006 S. Michigan Ave.
Chicago, IL 60605-9840
(312) 939-4767

**Antiques & Fine Art**
25200 La Paz Road
Laguna Hills, CA 92653-5135

**Antiques & The Arts
Weekly (The Newtown
Bee)**
5 Church Hill Road
P.O. Box 5503
Newtown, CT 06470-5503
(203) 426-3141

**Antiques Today**
977 Lehigh Circle
Carson City, NV 89705-7160
(702) 267-4600

**Antiques West**
3450 Sacramento St., Suite 618
San Francisco, CA 94118
(415) 221-4645

**Antiques!**
27 Queen St. East, Suite 707
Box 1860
Toronto M5C 2M6 Canada
(416) 944-3880

**Antiques-Collectibles**
P.O. Box 268
Greenvale, NY 11548
(516) 767-0312

**Antique Trader Weekly, The**
P.O. Box 1050
Dubuque, IA 52004-1050
(800) 334-7165
http://www.csmonline.com

**Antique Traveler, The**
P.O. Box 656
Mineola, TX 75773
(800) 446-3588

**AntiqueWeek**
Central or Eastern Edition
P.O. Box 90
Knightstown, IN 46148-0090
(765) 345-5133
http://www.antiqueweek.com

**Arizona Antique News & Southwest Antiques Journal**
P.O. Box 26536
Phoenix, AZ 85068-6536
(602) 943-9137

**Art & Antiques**
3 E. 54th St.
New York, NY 10022-3108
(212) 752-5557

**Auction Action News**
131 E. James St.
Columbus, WI 53925
(414) 623-3767

**Auction Price Check Newsletter**
8728 U.S. Highway 19
Port Richey, FL 34608
(813) 869-9114

**Brimfield Antique Guide, The**
RFD 1 Box 20
Brimfield, MA 01010-9802
(413) 245-9329

**Buckeye Marketeer, The**
P.O. Box 954
Westerville, OH 43086-0954
(614) 895-1663

**Cape Cod Antiques & Arts**
P.O. Box 400
Yarmouth Port, MA 02675-0400
(508) 362-2111

**Carolina Antique News**
P.O. Box 24114
Charlotte, NC 28224-4114

**Collectible Canada**
103 Lakeshore Road
St. Catharines
Ontario L2N 2T6 Canada
(905) 647-0995

**Collectibles/Flea Market Finds**
1700 Broadway
New York, NY 10019-5905
(212) 541-7100

**Collector Magazine**
436 W. Fourth St. #222 at Park Avenue
Pomona, CA 91766-1620
(909) 620-9014

**Collector Magazine & Price Guide**
P.O. Box 1050
Dubuque, IA 52004-1050
(800) 334-7165
http://www.csmonline.com

**Collector's Digest**
P.O. Box 23
Banning CA 92220-0023
(909) 849-1064

**Collectors Journal**
P.O. Box 601
Vinton, IA 52349-0601
(319) 472-4763

**Collector's Mart**
700 E. State St.
Iola, WI 54990-0001
(715) 455-2214

**Collectors News**
P.O. Box 156
Grundy Center, IA 50638-0156
(319) 824-6981
http://collectors-news.com

**Collectors' Classified**
P.O. Box 347
Hollbrook, MA 02343-0347
(617) 961-1463

**Collector's Marketplace, The**
P.O. Box 25
Stewartsville, NJ 08886-0025
http://www.4-collectors.com

**Collector, The**
P.O. Box 148
Heyworth, IL 61745-0158
(309) 473-2466

**Comic Buyer's Guide**
700 E. State St.
Iola, WI 54990-0001
(715) 455-2214

**Cotton & Quail Antique Trail**
P.O. Box 326
Monticello, FL 32344-0326
(800) 757-7755

**Depression Glass Daze, The**
P.O. Box 57
Otisville, MI 48463-0057
(810) 631-4593

**Elvin's Small Fortune**
P.O. Box 229
Rexford, NY 12148-0229
(518) 384-1182

**Georgian Antiques Digest**
P.O. Box 429
Tornbury
Ontario NGH 2P0 Canada
(519) 599-5017

**Goldmine**
700 E. State St.
Iola, WI 54990-0001
(715) 455-2214

**Great Lakes Trader**
132 S. Putnam
Williamstown, MI 48895
(517) 655-5621

**Hawaii Antiques**
P.O. Box 853
Honolulu, HI 96808-0853
(808) 591-0049

**Historic Traveler**
741 Miller Drive
Harrisburg, PA 20174
(703) 771-9400
http://www.thehistorynet.com

**Hudson Valley Antiquer, The**
P.O. Box 561
Rhinebeck, NY 12572-0561
(914) 876-8766

**Inside Antiques**
11912 Mississippi Avenue #E
Los Angeles, CA 90025
(310) 826-8583

**Journal America**
P.O. Box 459
Hewitt, NJ 07421-0459
(201) 728-8355

**Magazine Antiques, The**
575 Broadway
New York, NY 10012
(212) 941-2800

**Maine Antique Digest**
P.O. Box 1429
Waldoboro, ME 04572-1429
(207) 832-7534
http://mainantiquedigest.com

**MassBay Antiques**
P.O. Box 192
Ipswich, MA 01938-0192
(508) 777-7070

**Master Collector**
12513 Birchfalls Drive
Raleigh, NC 27614-9675
(800) 772-6673
http://www.mastercollector.com

**Memories**
1515 Broadway
New York, NY 10036
(212) 719-4000

**MidAtlantic Antiques Magazine**
P.O. Box 908
Henderson, NC 27536-0908
(919) 492-4001

**Mountain States Collector**
P.O. Box 2525
Evergreen, CO 80439-2525
(303) 987-3994

**New England Antiques Journal, The**
P.O. Box 120
Ware, MA 01082-0120
(413) 967-3505

**New Hampshire Antiques Monthly**
P.O. Box 546
Farmington, NH 03835-0546
(603) 755-4568

**News Antique Shopper, The**
37600 Hills Tech Drive
Farmington, MI 48331-5727

**New York Antique Almanac**
P.O. Box 2400
New York, NY 10021-0057

**New York-Pennsylvania Collector, The**
P.O. Box Drawer C
Fishers, NY 14453
(716) 924-8230

**Northeast Journal of Antiques & Art**
P.O. Box 635
Hudson, NY 12534
(518) 828-1616

**Numismatic News**
700 E. State St.
Iola, WI 54990-0001
(715) 455-2214

**Ohio Collectors' Magazine**
P.O. Box 1522
Piqua, OH 45356

**Old Cars Price Guide**
700 E. State St.
Iola, WI 54990-0001
(715) 455-2214

**Old Cars Weekly News & Marketplace**
700 E. State St.
Iola, WI 54990-0001
(715) 455-2214

**Old News is Good News Antiques Gazette, The**
P.O. Box 305
Hammond, LA 70403-1069
(504) 429-0575

**Old Stuff**
P.O. Box 1084
Meminnville, OR 97128-1084

**Old Times, The**
P.O. Box 340
Maple lake, MN 55350-0340
(800) 539-1810

**Renninger's Antique Guide**
P.O. Box 495
Lafayette Hill, PA 19444-0495
(610) 828-4614

**Southern Antiques**
P.O. Box 1107
Decatur, GA 30031-1107
(404) 289-0954

**Sports Cards**
700 E. State St.
Iola, WI 54990-0001
(715) 455-2214

**Sports Collectors Digest**
700 E. State St.
Iola, WI 54990-0001
(715) 455-2214

**Stamp Collector**
700 E. State St.
Iola, WI 54990-0001
(715) 455-2214

**Swap Meet Shopper, The**
P.O. Box 35123
Panama City, FL 32412
http://members.aol.com/
smshopper/index.html

**Toy Shop**
700 E. State St.
Iola, WI 54990-0001
(715) 455-2214

**Treasure Chest**
P.O. Box 245
North Scituate, RI 02847-0245
(212) 496-2234

**Unravel the Gavel**
9 Hurricane Road #1
Belmont, NH 03220-5603
http://www.the-forum.com/gavel

**Upper Canadian, The**
P.O. Box 653
Smiths Falls
Ontario K7A 5B8 Canada
(613) 283-1168

**Vintage Collector, The**
P.O. Box 764
Hotchkiss, CO 81419-0764
(970) 872-2226

**Vintage Times, The**
5692 Zebulon Road, #368
Macon, GA 31202
(912) 757-4755

**Warman's Today's Collector**
700 E. State St.
Iola, WI 54990-0001
(715) 455-2214

**Wayback Times, The**
RR #1, Rednersville Road
Belleville
Ontario K8N 4Z1 Canada
(613) 966-8749

**West Coast Peddler**
P.O. Box 5134
Whittier, CA 90607
(310) 698-1718

**Western CT/Western MA Antiquer, The**
P.O. Box 561
Rhinebeck, NY 12572-0561
(914) 876-8766

**Wonderful Things**
P.O. Box 2288
Winter Park, Fl 32790-2288
(406) 332-0954

**Yankee Magazine**
P.O. Box 37017
Bonne, IA 50037-0017
http://www.newengland.com/
store/store.YKsub.html

**Yesteryear**
P.O. Box 2
Princeton, WI 54968-0002
(920) 787-4808

# A

## Abingdon Pottery

**Collecting Hints:** Like wares from many contemporary potteries, Abingdon Pottery pieces are readily available in the market. The company produced more than 1,000 shapes and used more than 150 colors to decorate its wares. Because of this tremendous variety, it is advisable to collect Abingdon Pottery with particular forms and/or colors in mind.

Abingdon art pottery, with its vitreous body and semi-gloss and high-gloss glazes, is found at all levels of the market, from garage sales to antiques shows. For this reason, price fluctuations for identical pieces are quite common. Study the market carefully before buying. Learn to shop around.

While there is no price guide devoted exclusively to Abingdon Pottery, price listings can now be found in all the general antiques and collectibles price guides, as well as in several of the specialized ceramic and pottery guides. Pieces regularly appear for sale in classified advertisements in most trade papers, providing a good basis for pricing Abingdon wares.

Collectors and dealers are still in the process of defining the market relative to the most desirable shapes and colors. At the moment black (gunmetal), a semi-gloss dark blue, a metallic copper brown, and several shades of red are the favored colors. Decorated pieces command a premium of 15-20%.

**History:** The Abingdon Sanitary Manufacturing Company, Abingdon, Illinois, was founded in 1908 for the purpose of manufacturing plumbing fixtures. Sometime between 1933 and 1934, Abingdon introduced a line of art pottery. In 1945, the company changed its name to Abingdon Potteries, Inc. Production of the art pottery line continued until 1950 when fire destroyed the art pottery kiln.

After the fire, the company once again placed its emphasis on plumbing fixtures. Eventually, Abingdon Potteries became Briggs Manufacturing Company, a firm noted for its sanitary fixtures.

**Collectors' Club:** Abingdon Pottery Collectors' Club, 210 Knox Hwy. S., Abingdon, IL 61410.

| | |
|---|---|
| Ashtray, #456 | 36.00 |
| Bookends, pr, horse head, black, 6-1/2" h | 60.00 |
| Bowl, shell, #50 | 18.00 |
| Candleholders, pr, double scroll, white, gold trim | 38.00 |

Console Bowl
| | |
|---|---|
| 14" l, pink | 50.00 |
| 14" l, turquoise | 50.00 |
| 14" l, white, scroll | 40.00 |
| 14-1/2" l, blue, scroll | 40.00 |
| 15" l, blue, leaf shape, sq ink mark "Abingdon USA" | 40.00 |

| | |
|---|---|
| Console Set, blue, #532 and #575 | 25.00 |

Cookie Jar
| | |
|---|---|
| Hobby Horse | 250.00 |
| Little Miss Muffet, #622 | 200.00 |
| Sunflower | 40.00 |
| Train engine | 70.00 |
| Windmill, #678 | 250.00 |
| Cornucopia, double, white, orig paper label | 50.00 |

Figure
| | |
|---|---|
| Flamingo | 25.00 |
| Heron | 36.00 |
| Peacock, pink | 20.00 |

Planter
| | |
|---|---|
| Fan and bow | 10.00 |
| Sailing ship, raised dec, imp rope handles, sea green glaze | 24.00 |
| Salt and Pepper Shakers, pr, Little Bo Peep | 45.00 |

Vase
| | |
|---|---|
| 5-1/2" h, Classic #117, blue | 32.00 |
| 7" h, Abbey, yellow | 24.00 |
| 7" h, oval, shell, blue | 55.00 |
| 7" h, Sierra Blue, Acadia, glossy, white int., #516 | 30.00 |
| 7" h, ship, white | 58.00 |
| 9" h, swirl, pink | 62.00 |
| 9-1/2" h, 7" w, Art Deco, matte pink, two low handles, #911 | 25.00 |
| 10" h, double handles, blue | 55.00 |
| 10" h, 9" w, oval, scallop shape, beige, high gloss | 25.00 |
| 11" h, 5" w, salmon, white int., mkd "Abingdon USA #182" | 35.00 |
| 18" h, yellow | 150.00 |

Wall Pocket
| | |
|---|---|
| Butterfly, #601 | 70.00 |
| Flower, 7-5/8" l, gray sticker, imp "377" | 35.00 |

## Action Figures

**Collecting Hints:** This is one of the hot, trendy collecting categories of the 1990s. While there is no question that action figure material is selling—and selling well—much of the pricing is highly speculative. Trends change from month to month, as one figure or group of figures becomes hot and another cools off.

The safest approach is to buy only objects in fine or better condition and, if possible, with or in their original packaging. Any figure that has been played with to any extent will never have long-term value. This is a category with off-the-rack expectations.

Be extremely cautious about paying premium prices for figures less than ten years old. During the past decade, dealers have made a regular practice of buying newly released action figures in quantity, warehousing them, and releasing their stash slowly into the market once production ceases.

Also examine packaging very closely. A premium is placed on a figure in its original packaging, i.e., the packaging which was used when the figure was introduced into the market. Later packaging means a lower price.

**History:** An action figure is a die-cast metal or plastic posable model with flexible joints that portrays a real or fictional character. In addition to the figures themselves, clothing, personal equipment, vehicles, and other types of accessories are also collectible.

Collectors need to be aware of the following attempts to manipulate the market: 1) limited production—a deliberate act on the part of manufacturers to hold back on production of one or more figures in a series; 2) variations—minor changes in figures made by manufacturers to increase sales (previously believed to be mistakes, but now viewed as a deliberate sales gimmicks), and 3) prototypes—artists' models used during the planning process. Any prototype should be investigated thoroughly—there are many fakes.

The earliest action figures were the hard-plastic Hartland figures of popular television Western heroes of the 1950s. Louis Marx also included action figures in a number of playsets during the late 1950s. Although Barbie, who made her appearance in 1959, is posable, she is not considered an action figure by collectors.

G.I. Joe, introduced by Hassenfield Bros. in 1964, triggered the modern action figure craze. In 1965, Gilbert introduced action figures for James Bond 007, The Man from U.N.C.L.E., and Honey West. "Bonanza" figures arrived in 1966, along with Ideal Toy Corporation's Captain Action. Ideal altered the figures by simply changing heads and costumes. Captain Action and his accessories were the hot collectible of the late 1980s.

In 1972, Mego introduced the first six super heroes in what would become a series of 34 different characters. Mego also established the link between action figures and the movies when the company issued series for "Planet of the Apes" and "Star Trek: The Motion Picture." Mego's television series figures included "CHiPs," "Dukes of Hazzard," and "Star Trek." When Mego filed for bankruptcy protection in 1982, the days of eight- and twelve-inch fabric-clothed action figures ended.

The introduction of Kenner's Star Wars figure set in 1977 opened a floodgate. Action figures enjoyed enormous popularity, and manufacturers rushed into the market, with Mattel quickly following on Kenner's heels. Before long, the market was flooded, not only with a large selection but also with production runs in the hundreds of thousands.

Not all series were successful, just ask companies such as Colorform, Matchbox, and TYCO. Some sets were not further produced when initial sales did not justify the costs of manufacture. These sets have limited collector value. Scarcity does not necessarily equate with high value in the action figure market.

**References:** John Bonavita, *Mego Action Figure Toys*, Schiffer Publishing, 1996; Tom Heaton, *The Encyclopedia of Marx Action Figures, A Price Guide and Identification*, Krause Publications, 1999; Paris & Susan Manos, *Collectible Action Figures*, 2nd ed., Collector Books, 1996; John Marshall, *Action Figures of the 1980s*, Schiffer Publishing, 1998; Sharon Korbeck, *Toys & Prices, 1999*, 6th edition, Krause Publications, 1998; Stuart W. Wells, III, *Science Fiction Collectibles: Identification & Price Guide*, Krause Publications, 1999.

**Periodicals:** *Action Figure News & Review*, 556 Monroe Tpk., Monroe, CT 06468; *Tomart's Action Figure Digest*, Tomart Publications, 3300 Encrete Lane, Dayton, OH 45439.

**Collectors' Clubs:** Captain Action Collectors Club, P.O. Box 2095, Halesite, NY 11743; Captain Action Society of Pittsburgh, 516 Cubbage St., Carnegie, PA 15106.

**Additional Listings:** G.I. Joe Collectibles, Super Heroes, Star Wars, Star Trek.

**Ultimate Predator, white, $10.**

### Alien
| | |
|---|---|
| Arachnid | 20.00 |
| Bull | 20.00 |
| Gorilla | 20.00 |
| Killer Krab | 12.00 |
| Night Cougar | 12.00 |
| Panther | 12.00 |
| Queen, deluxe | 20.00 |
| Scorpion | 20.00 |
| Snake | 15.00 |
| Wild Boar | 12.00 |

### A-Team, Galoob, 6" h
| | |
|---|---|
| Amy Allen, MOC | 30.00 |
| Hannibal, MOC | 20.00 |
| Mr. T, © 1983, MIB | 38.00 |
| Murdock, MOC | 25.00 |
| Templeton Peck, MOC | 20.00 |
| Villians, 4 pack | 45.00 |

### Baseball, Starting Lineup, MBP
| | |
|---|---|
| Clemens, 1999 | 10.00 |
| Jeter, 1998 | 10.00 |
| McGwire, 1999 | 15.00 |
| Griffey Jr., 1999 | 10.00 |
| Ripkin, 1997 | 15.00 |
| Williams, 1998 | 10.00 |

### Basketball, Starting Lineup, MBP
| | |
|---|---|
| Bryant, 1998 | 10.00 |
| Bryant, extended, 1996 | 80.00 |
| Duncan, 1997 | 50.00 |
| Hill, 1996 | 10.00 |
| O'Neill, 1996 | 10.00 |
| Rodman, 1998 | 10.00 |
| Rodman, red, 1994 | 50.00 |
| Van Horn, 1997 | 50.00 |

### Battlestar Galactica
| | |
|---|---|
| Baltar, loose | 35.00 |
| Laserscope Fighter, Italy, loose | 195.00 |

### Black Hole
Dr. Alex Durant, 12-1/2" h, Mego, © 1979, WDP, MIB ........ 50.00

### Buck Rogers in the 25th Century
12-1/2" h, Mego, ©1979, MIB ....... 45.00

### Charlie's Angels
Jill, Farrah Fawcett, MIB .............. 75.00

### Clash of the Titans
Mattel, 1980, Charo, 3-3/4" h, MOC ........ 35.00

### Comic Book
| | |
|---|---|
| Mercy, Hobby Exclusive, gold edition, 7" h | 17.50 |
| Pandora, Bolt, MOC | 15.00 |
| Widow Variant, MOC | 15.00 |

### DC Direct
| | |
|---|---|
| Elvira, 7-1/2" h, regular (serpent and chainsaw) or witch variant, each | 13.00 |
| Supergirl, animated, Kenner exclusive, 5" h | 12.00 |
| Superman, animated, Kenner exclusive, 12" h | 25.00 |
| Usage Yojimbo, Antarctic Press, 5" h | 12.00 |
| Xena, 6-1/2" h, Series II, Harem | 9.00 |

### Defenders of the Earth, Galoob, 1985
| | |
|---|---|
| Flash Gordon, MOC | 35.00 |
| Garax, MOC | 35.00 |
| Garax Swordship, MIB | 45.00 |
| Lothar, MOC | 35.00 |
| Ming the Merciless, MOC | 35.00 |
| Phantom, MOC | 35.00 |

### Falcon
8" h, Mego .............. 40.00

### Happy Days, Mego
| | |
|---|---|
| Fonzie, loose | 35.00 |
| Fonzie, MOC | 75.00 |
| Potsie, MOC | 65.00 |
| Ralph, MOC | 65.00 |
| Ritchie, MOC | 65.00 |

### MAD Magazine, 6" h
| | |
|---|---|
| Alfred E. Neuman | 12.00 |
| Spy vs. Spy, white or black, each | 12.00 |

### Monster, Universal, 8" h, Mego
| | |
|---|---|
| Frankenstein | 90.00 |
| Mummy | 90.00 |
| Wolfman | 90.00 |

### Our Gang
Buckwheat, 6" h, MOC ........ 65.00

### Planet of the Apes, Kenner
| | |
|---|---|
| Cornelius | 30.00 |
| Dr. Zaius | 25.00 |
| General Ursus | 25.00 |

### Raiders of the Lost Ark
| | |
|---|---|
| Indiana Jones, Kenner, MOC | 325.00 |
| Sinthia, Princess of Hell, Skybolt Toys, Lightning Comics, MOC | 17.00 |

### Star Com, 2" h, Coleco, 1986, MOC
| | |
|---|---|
| Col. John Griffin | 17.50 |
| Cpl. Storm | 17.50 |
| General Vondar | 20.00 |
| Pfc. John Jefferson | 15.00 |
| Sgt. Hector Morales | 17.50 |
| Sgt. Red Baker | 15.00 |

**Star Trek,** see *Space Adventurers and Exploration Category*

**Star Wars,** see Star Wars Category

### Super Powers, Kenner, Canada, 1985
Batman, MOC ............ 65.00

Cyclotron, MOC ............................ 75.00
Darkseid, MOC ............................. 25.00
Darkseid Destroyer, MIB .............. 45.00
Delta Probe One, MIB .................. 30.00
Golden Pharaoh, MOC .............. 125.00
Kalibak's Boulder Bomber, MIB

......................................................... 30.00
Lex-Soar 7, MIB ........................... 25.00
Penguin, mint in orig bag ............. 65.00
Steppenwolf, mint in orig bag

......................................................... 10.00
Superman, MOC ........................... 45.00
Windsock, mail-in premium, MIP .. 25.00

**S.W.A.T.**
Hondo, LIN Toys, © 1975, MOC

......................................................... 35.00

**Visionaires, Hasbro, 1987**
Arzon, MOC ................................... 35.00
Cryotec, MOC ............................... 35.00
Darkstorm, MOC ........................... 35.00
Leoric, MOC .................................. 35.00
Lexor, MOC ................................... 40.00
Witterquick, MOC .......................... 35.00

# Advertising

**Collecting Hints:** Many factors affect the price of an advertising collectible—the product and its manufacturer, the objects or people used in the advertisement, the period and aesthetics of design, the designer and illustrator of the piece, and the form the advertisement takes. In addition, advertising material was frequently used to decorate bars, restaurants, and other public places. Interior decorators do not purchase objects at the same price level as collectors.

In truth, almost every advertising item is sought by a specialized collector in one or more collectible areas. The result is diverse pricing, with the price quoted to an advertising collector usually lower than that quoted to a specialized collector.

Most collectors seem to concentrate on the period prior to 1940, with special emphasis on the decades from 1880 to 1910. New collectors should examine the advertising material from the post-1940 period. Much of this material is still very inexpensive and likely to rise in value as the decorator trends associated with the 1950s through the 1970s gain importance.

**History:** The earliest advertising in America is found in colonial newspapers and printed broadsides. By the mid-19th century, manufacturers began to examine how a product was packaged. The box could convey a message and help identify and sell more of the product. The advent of the high-speed, lithograph printing press led to regional and national magazines, resulting in new advertising markets. The lithograph press also introduced vivid colors into advertising.

Simultaneously, the general store branched out into specialized departments or individual specialty shops. By 1880, advertising premiums such as mirrors, paperweights, and trade cards arrived on the scene. Through the early 1960s, premiums remained popular, especially with children.

The advertising character developed in the early 1900s. By the 1950s, endorsements by the popular stars of the day became a firmly established advertising method. Advertising became a lucrative business as firms, many headquartered in New York City, developed specialties to meet manufacturers' needs. Advertising continues to respond to changing opportunities and times.

**References:** Fred Dodge, *Antique Tin, Book II*, Collector Books, 1998; Sharon and Bob Huxford, *Huxford's Collectible Advertising*, 3rd ed., Collector Books, 1996; Ray Klug, *Antique Advertising Encyclopedia*, Vol. 1 (1978, 1993 value update), Vol. 2 (1985, 1990 value update), L-W Book Sales; Rex Miller, *The Investor's Guide to Vintage Character Collectibles*, Krause Publications, 1999; Robert Reed, *Bears and Dolls in Advertising*, Antique Trader Books, 1998; David and Micki Young, *Campbell's Soup Collectibles from A to Z*, Krause Publications, 1998; David L. Wilson, *General Store Collectibles*, Collector Books, 1994; David Zimmerman, *Encyclopedia of Advertising Tins*, published by author (6834 Newtonsville Rd., Pleasant Plain, OH 45162), 1994.

**Periodicals:** Advertising Collectors Express, P.O. Box 221, Mayview, MO 64071; Let's Talk Tin, 1 S. Beaver Lane, Greenville, SC 29605; National Assoc. of Paper and Advertising Collectors (P.A.C.), P.O. Box 500, Mt. Joy, PA 17552; Paper Collectors' Marketplace (PCM), P.O. Box 128, Scandinavia, WI 54977; Tin Fax Newsletter, 205 Brolley Woods Drive, Woodstock, GA 30188; Tin Type Newsletter, P.O. Box 440101, Aurora, CO 80044; Trade Card Journal, 143 Main St., Brattleboro, VT 05301.

**Collectors' Clubs:** Advertising Cup and Mug Collectors of America, P.O. Box 680, Solon, IA 52333; Antique Advertising Assoc. of America, P.O. Box 1121, Morton Grove, IL 60053; Ephemera Society of America, P.O. Box 37, Schoharie, NY 12157; Inner Seal Collectors Club, 6609 Billtown Rd., Louisville, KY 40299; Tin Container Collectors Assoc., P.O. Box 440101, Aurora, CO 80044; Trade Card Collector's Assoc., Box 284, Marlton, NJ 08053.

**Reproduction Alert.**

**Ashtray**
Blue Diamond Coal Co., metal, 6" d
......................................................... 20.00
Dobbs Hats, black glass, hat shape
......................................................... 27.50
Esso, clear glass, red and blue dealer inscription, 1950s, 4-1/4" sq .... 38.00
Evinrude, brass, circular, 1950s ... 65.00
Firestone Tires, copper ................. 20.00
John Deere, deer jumping over log, galvanized metal, 3-1/4" d ............ 35.00
Mountain States Telephone & Telegraph Directory Department, man in center wearing yellow pages uniform, holding telephone book, porcelain, 6" d
......................................................... 295.00
Pyrene Fire Extinguisher, figural, Bakelite ..................................... 50.00
Universal Studios, emb cameras and crew, metal .............................. 20.00
**Bill Hook,** Breakfast Cheer Coffee, Campbell & Woods, Pittsburgh, celluloid mounted to wire hanger loop, 4" stiff wire barbed hook, shows red package, early 1900s, 2" x 2-3/4"
......................................................... 40.00

**Blotter**
Eagle White Lead, York Hardware, 3" x 6" ...................................... 7.50
Levi's, full color art, black and white imprint of local dealer store, unused, 1960s, 2-3/4" x 6-1/4" ............... 20.00
Libby's Food Products, three cardboard ink blotters under celluloid cover, steer head plus six food packages, Libby, McNeill & Libby, Chicago, capped river with black and white portrait of gentleman, printed by F. F. Pulver Co., Rochester, early 1900s, 3" x 5-1/2" ................................. 45.00
Marble Granite Works, Westport, CT, "A Happy Future," fortune telling Mammy, Harry Roseland print, 1906, 6-1/2" x 3-1/2" .......................... 40.00
Morton's Salt, 3-1/2" x 6-1/8" .......... 7.00
Optimist Week, November 1955, yellow, 4" x 8" .......................................... 5.00
The Soap Suds Blues, dog being bathed in tub, Harry N. Johnson, Real Estate & Insurance, Highlands, NJ ................................................. 10.00
**Booklet,** *The Story of Rubber*, Hood Rubber Co., Watertown, MA, c1925, 39 pgs, 3-1/4" x 7" ................... 18.00

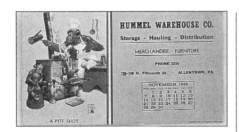

**Blotter, Hummel Warehouse, Allentown, PA, "A Pot Shot," monkeys in kitchen, November 1943 calendar, 6-1/8" x 3-3/8", $7.50.**

## Bookmark

Cameron Steam Pump, celluloid, multicolored, Scottish bagpiper, product text, New York City, blank reverse .................................................. 70.00
Eberhart & Miller, Shoes & Rubbers, Warren, PA, aluminum, emb floral design, attached silk cord ......... 7.50
Maltine, diecut thin celluloid, multicolored image, brown and white owl, lengthy text on reverse ............. 45.00
Morrell's Meats, heart-shaped diecut celluloid, slogan "Iowa's Pride Meats," black and white text on reverse ...................................... 42.00
Palmer Violets Bloom Perfume, gold trim .......................................... 15.00
Printzless, celluloid, multicolored image of lady in stylish white plumed hat, matching gown, brown fur accessories, black and white text ......... 75.00
Standard Publishing Co., Cincinnati, multicolored image of female cardinal, "Search The Scriptures" .... 25.00
Theo F. Siefert Furs, Philadelphia, celluloid, multicolored image of delivery truck .......................................... 40.00
United States Fidelity & Guarantee Co., brass, etched logo and "Home Office Baltimore USF & G" ......... 5.00

## Box

Andy Gump Sunshine Biscuits, cardboard, 5" x 3" x 2" ................... 425.00
Argo Starch, unopened, 1930s .................................................. 12.00
Baker's Chocolate, 12 lb size, wood .................................................. 25.00
Candy, Whitman's Pleasure Island Chocolates, cardboard, pirate scenes on 5 sides, map on bottom, 1924 ......................................... 28.00
Fairies Bath Perfume, unopened, 1920s .................................................. 12.00
King Brand Rolled Oats ............... 45.00
Ladies Favorite Polish, paper label, 4" ................................................. 10.00
National Lead Co., paint chip samples .................................................. 25.00
Regal Underwear, cardboard ....... 20.00
Ward Baking Co., wood .............. 100.00

## Brochure

Arm & Hammer, Cleansing Help for the Housewife, 1922 ......................... 4.50
Electrol Automatic Oil Heating, 1937 .................................................. 5.00

Larkin Soap, 1885 ........................ 17.50
Magic Yeast .................................... 7.50
Philco Radio, fold-out, 1936 ........... 9.00
Seymour-Smity & Son, Pruning, 1935 .................................................. 7.50
Westinghouse, Today's Ben Franklin, 1943 ............................................. 5.00

## Clip

Bengal Ranges, 1-1/2" l, multicolored celluloid, spring clip mkd "Ever Handy Letter Clip No. 2," made by C. H. Hunt Pen Co., 1920s ....... 40.00
Dold Food Products, oval celluloid log, blue, yellow, and red, 1920s ...... 25.00
Golden Blend Coffee, black, white, and red waiter bringing coffee cup, "Here You are Sir!" ............................. 48.00
Rochester Automatic Oiler, black, white, and red celluloid, red lettering ... 45.00

## Coffee Tin

Capitol Mills, 5-1/2" h, 5" d, Lincoln, Seyms & Co., small top, canister .................................................. 60.00
Comrade, 3-1/2" h, 5" d, J. A. Folger & Co., 1 lb, keywind .................. 170.00
Dining Car, 4" h, 5" d, scene of passengers eating in train's dining car, 1 lb, keywind ...................................... 95.00
Golden Wedding, 3-3/4" h, 5-1/4" d, old couple at breakfast table, The Ennis-Hanly-Blackburn Coffee Co., 1 lb, snap top ................................... 60.00

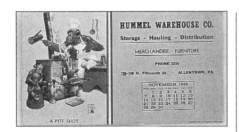

**Brochure, John Deere, No. 999 Corn Planter, 1917, 8 pgs, 4" x 9", $15.**

Lindley's Motor, 3-1/2" h, 5" d, images of electric motor on both sides, 1 lb, keywind ...................................... 50.00
Old Judge, 5-3/4" h, 4-1/4" d, titled "Settles the Question," David O. Evans Coffee Co., 1 lb, slip lid ........... 70.00
Seal of Minnesota, 6-1/4" h, 4" d, Philip B. Hunt & Co., Illinois Can Co., farmer working land, Indian warrior on horseback in background, 1 lb, missing slip lid ......................... 85.00
Universal, 6-1/2" h, 4" d, E. B. Miller & Co., Uncle Sam image, knob top, 1 lb, even wear ........................... 50.00
Wedding Breakfast, 4" h, 5" w, 1 lb, keywind ...................................... 50.00

## Display

Beech Nut Gum, tapered multi-tiered oak stand, two sided marquee with trademark and other Beech Nut products, 41" h .................... 1,550.00
Blue-Jay Corn Plasters, cardboard, two drawers, "Make hard roads easy," displays two hobos walking along railroad tracks while passing billboard for Blue-Jay Plasters, © 1903, 6-1/2" h, 9-1/4" l, 10-1/4" d ....... 50.00
Boston Garter, diecut tin, five orig boxes of garters, man examining garter on his left as he reads from back of box, 9" h, 4" w ............................... 425.00
Diamond Dye, wood cabinet, emb tin front showing children playing with Maypole, rusting and staining to fair condition tin panel, 30" h, 22-3/4" w, 10-1/4" d ............................... 550.00
Miller Lock, diecut cardboard, shows ship going thru Panama Canal, actual examples of Gatun Locks, easel back, patent 1905 Breuker & Kessler Co. litho, 16" h, 13" w .. 50.00

### Display Cabinet, counter top

Van Haagen's Fine Toilet Soaps, German silver, curved corners, front glass etched with name, some denting to moldings ..................... 525.00
Zeno Gum, wood, emb Zeno marquee with fancy filigree, 18" h, 10-1/2" w, 8" d ......................................... 575.00
**Egg,** Fleischmann's Egg Beaters, wood, red, wear to paint .................... 10.00

## Fan

Alva Hotel, Philadelphia, diecut cardboard, 5-1/2" l wood handle, full color of nude toddler holding thermometer in process of shattering from heat while talking on candlestick telephone, sweating puppy looks on, early 1900s, 9-1/2" h, 8" w ......................................... 60.00
Tip-Top Bread, diecut cardboard, full color stars artwork, reverse with six red, white, and blue illus of suggested snacks using bread, c1930, 7-1/4" x 9-1/4" ......................... 25.00

### Flipper Pin, diecut thin celluloid, 1-3/4" h

Blue Valley Creamery, milk can shape, scenes titled "The Old Way" and "Our Way," back text "Blue Valley Butter/Churned Fresh kin Chicago Every Day" ............................. 18.00

Eternal Range, black and white kitchen range, orange rim, white letters, slogan on back "Pull The Strong and Meet A Warm Member," orig fastener and pull string ............................ 25.00

Fansteel Electric Iron, gold pocket watch image on one side, inscribed "See The Woman In The Case," reverse black and white illus of woman using iron ..................... 20.00

Golden Orangeade, orange fruit, red and black inscription, slogan on back "Everybody Likes It-What?" ................................................ 30.00

Schaeffer Pianos, full color image of upright piano, inscribed "Schaeffer, Best in the West," black and white logo on reverse, ad text, 1905 patent date ....................................... 30.00

St. Charles Evaporated Milk, product miniature, slogan on back "Highest Award Everywhere," Meek Co., patent 1906 ............................ 15.00

Sunset Coffee, canister shape, sponsored by International Coffee Co. ................................................ 12.00

Ward's Bread, turkey shape, slogan on back "Serve Ward's Bread With Your Thanksgiving Dinner" .............. 18.00

**Hat Rack**, Johnson Hat Company, metal, celluloid plaque with adv, c1920, 6-1/2" l .......................... 75.00

**Keychain Fob,** Arm & Hammer, diecut celluloid panels, blue and white logo on one side, other side reads "Name & Address Of Owner Inside," unused, early 1900s ................. 55.00

**Key Holder,** celluloid disk, metal ring

Lion Milk, product illus on one side, other with holly sprig and "Compliments of Lion Brand Condensed Milk" ........................................ 25.00

New York Edison Co., silvered metal circular clip, black, white, red, and gold celluloid disk on both sides ..... 20.00

**Letter Opener,** Coshocton Glove Co., celluloid, work glove shape, some red accent striping at wrist, early 1900s, 8-1/2" l, 2" w at wrist ..... 48.00

**Lunch Box,** tin litho

Fashion Cut Plug Tobacco, 7-3/4" l, 5-1/4" w, 4" d, image of couple ................................................ 95.00

Hand Bag Tobacco, figural .......... 75.00

Round Trip Tobacco, 6-1/2" h, 5" l, 3-1/2" d ................................... 100.00

**Memo Booklet**

Associated Fraternities of America, celluloid cover, full color art of young lady model with long brown hair, white dress, drapery over one arm, back cover inscribed to annual meeting in Milwaukee, August 1905, printed by Whitehead & Hoag Co., 2-1/2" x 4-3/4" ............................ 45.00

Libby's Food Products, Libby, McNeill & Libby, celluloid cover, full color view of Chicago factory, six examples of packaged products, 14 pages, printed by Whitehead & Hoag Co., 2-1/2" x 4-1/2" ............................... 55.00

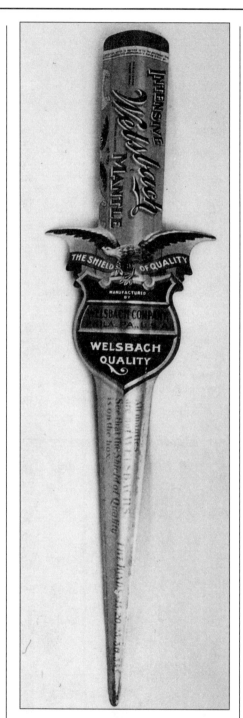

**Letter Opener, Welsback Co., Philadelphia, litho tin, $35.**

Sunbeam, celluloid cover with young lady, swirling hair, sheer fabric, pale yellow sun rays, published by Bastian Bros. Co., 2-1/2" x 4-3/4" ... 40.00

**Mirror, Pocket**

Angelus Marshmallows, multicolored winged cherub holding trumpet, announcing "A Message Of Purity," sponsor Rueckheim Bros. & Eckstein, Chicago .......................... 90.00

Brunswick Phonograph Record, black and white, figural record shape, Brunswick-Balke-Collender Co. label, 1920s ............................. 40.00

Buster Brown Shoes, multicolored portrait of Buster and Tige, lighted aged collet, traces of scratching .... 175.00

Fargo School Shoes, C. H. Fargo & Co., Chicago, silvered tin rim ......... 40.00

Horlick's Malted Milk, multicolored milkmaid and cow in wooded setting, gold rim .................................... 55.00

Jansen Bros. Dancing and Bowling, multicolored profile portrait of brunette young lady, wearing sheer pale green top, Covington, KY address ................................................ 80.00

Pennisular Stove Co., blue and white, ornate home heating stove ....... 60.00

Victrola Phonograph Record, black and white, figural record shape, red label for Victor Talking Machine Co., tiny Nipper and phonograph symbol, record titled "Her Bright Smile Haunts Me Still," by Edward Johnson, 1930s ...................... 55.00

**Model,** tooth, Crest Toothpaste, 1950s ................................................ 95.00

**Paperweight**

American Oil Products, Somerville, Mass, "We Want To Do Business With The Man On The Other Side," domed glass with silvered reverse, red on white design of elephant within circular title, 1920s, 3" d ................... 55.00

A. P. Smith Mfg. Co., East Orange, NJ, silvered white metal, figural 2-3/4" h fire hydrant, finely detailed raised aerial view of factory building, maker Van Gytenbeek Inc., New York City, inscribed on base, 1920s, 6" w, 3-1/2" h ................................... 60.00

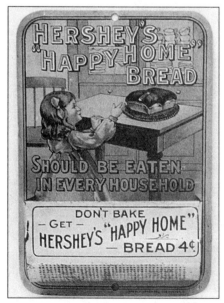

**Match Safe, Hershey's Happy Home Bread, gray, silver, black, white, and red, black lettering, blond girl in pink dress, yellow border, 5-1/4" h, $72.**

Badger Insurance, hollowed cast iron, replica of crouching badger on base, inscribed "The Badger Mutual Fire Insurance Co., engraved 1887-1937, dark luster, 2" x 3-1/2" h ..................................................... 75.00

Bon Ami, glass, color ad, 3" w, 4-1/4" l .. ..................................................... 85.00

Brown's Tested Seeds, Alfred J. Brown Seed Co., Grand Rapids, MI, clear glass, tinted color real photo of seed packets, patent dated June 14, 1917, 7/8" thick, 3" d ................ 55.00

Coates Clipper, Coates Clipper Mfg. Co., Worcester, Mass, glass, slogan "For Barbers and Horseman," 1" x 2-1/2" x 4", early 1900s................ 50.00

Derby & Kilmer desk Co., Boston and New York, glass, black and white illus of roll-to desk and flat-top desk, 7/8" x 2-1/2" x 4" ....................... 40.00

Fink, Bodenheimer & Co., Diamond Importers and Cutters, glass, chart listing prices for single and multiple sale units, 1" x 3-1/4" x 4-1/2" l, slight scratching to top ...................... 35.00

Kall-Zimmers Mfg. Co., Milwaukee, WI, Children's Shoes, glass, real photo of toddler in striped shirt, bib overalls, shoes, 1900s, 1" x 2-1/4" x 4" l ................................................... 50.00

Krag Brothers, Johnstown, NY, hollowed white metal boar, name and slogan "Originators Of Pigskin Leathers For Fine Gloves," felt underside, 1930s, 5" l, 3-1/2" h ............................. 70.00

James Hartley Brewing Co., Providence, RI, Prince Albert Race Horse, glass, black and white photo of horse, red lettering "Prince Albert 1.57/The World's Champion Harness Gelding," 3/4" x 2-1/2" x 4" l ................................................... 75.00

Leatherbee Lumber, Co., Boston, glass, two black and white lumber processing facilities, inscribed "Established 1821" and "Incorporated 1897," made by J. N. Abrams, New York City, early 1900s, 3/4" x 2-1/2" x 4" l ................................................... 50.00

Mathewson Hotel, glass, detailed view of "The New Mathewson Narragansett Pier, RI, Grandest Hotel Plaza in the World, maker American P. W. Co., Pittsburgh, 1890s, 1" x 2-1/2" x 4" ....................................... 60.00

Niagara Falls Lumber & Coal, glass, black and white engraved style scenic falls from US side, black inscriptions, red lettering, early 1900s, 3/4" x 2-1/4" x 4" l ...................... 45.00

Oriental Silk Co. Limited, Montreal, white metal bull dog figure, black luster finish, name and slogan "Never Loses Its Grip On The Seam," British empire motto "What We Have We Hold," maker name, Whitehead & Hoad Co., Montreal on underside, 4" l, 2-1/2" h, 3-1/2" d base .......................................... 75.00

Tuttle & Bailey, duck head, solid brass, oval base inscribed with sponsor's name, 3" x 5" x 3-1/4" h ........... 80.00

United States Asbestos Division of Raybestos-Manhattan, Inc., solid brass eagle position on 4-3/4" x 6" rounded oval steel tray, maker Hubley Mfg. Co., Lancaster, PA, on underside, 1920s, 6" w, 3" h..... 65.00

**Pencil Sharpener,** Baker's Cocoa Girl, figural ...................................... 45.00

**Pinback Button**

Acadia Butter, oval, yellow and brown package, red ground, c1920, orig back paper ............................. 30.00

Baltimore Canned goods, black and white, orange rim ..................... 32.00

Budd's Baby Shoes, tinted color real photo, brown rim, white letters. 20.00

Ceresota Flour, trademark figure, early 1900s, 1-3/4" d ......................... 27.50

Derby Refining Co., Petroleum Products, star, red, white, and blue, c1930 ................................... 15.00

Diamond C. Hams, Cudahy Packing Co., multicolored, dark green background, white lettering ............. 10.00

Dot Food Stores, red, white, and blue, "Individually Owned" grocery store, 1930s ........................................ 12.00

Edison Records, multicolored illus of hand holding early cylinder phonograph record inscribed "Make Music," white background, black letters ...................................... 60.00

Favorite Stoves and Ranges, multicolored , red rim ........................... 20.00

Fearman Hams, brown ham, pale blue ground, dark bleu rim, white letters, Thomas Wibby Co., Toronto, Canada issue........................................ 30.00

Fleischmann's Yeast Delivery Wagon, multicolored, horse pulling vendor wagon, red lettering "In Storm, In Sunshine, Rain Or Sleet, You See Our Wagons On The Street," c1900 . ................................................ 115.00

Forbes Coffee, dark purple, white lettering, "Bon-Ton & Splendid" brands ................................................ 10.00

Friedman Bros. Shoe Co., St. Louis, "Our Little Samson School Shoe," multicolored ............................. 45.00

Hostess Cake, red, white, and blue, 1940s ........................................ 22.00

Kennedy Mansfield Milk, yellow, brown, and white, early horse drawn delivery wagon, 1930s .................... 25.00

Koester's Bread, red, white, blue, and gold, 1930s............................. 25.00

Lehigh Stoves, red and white flame design .................................... 18.00

Maypo, black and white illus, slogan, 1960s ........................................ 25.00

Palmolive Health Club, red, white, blue, and fleshtones, youngster drying himself with towel, 1930s ......... 42.00

Patton's Sun-Proof Paint, orange and black design, yellow smiling sun face, 1920 ............................. 12.00

Red Cross Macaroni, red, white, and blue, Long Mac cartoon, 1930s ................................................ 37.50

Roberts, Johnson & Rand Shoes, "Tess and Ted School Shoes," multicolored, orig back paper insert.... 20.00

S.O.S. Magic Bunny, black, white, and yellow, litho, c1940 .................. 25.00

Van Camp's Pork & Beans............ 12.00

**Radio, figural**

Coors Beer Can........................... 25.00

Crayola Rocks, AM....................... 35.00

FS Super Lube Oil Can, unused.... 40.00

Grand Old Parr Scotch Whiskey, MIB ... ................................................ 50.00

Heinz .......................................... 85.00

Kraft Macaroni & Cheese Dinomac carton............................................ 35.00

Marathon Ultra-D SW-40, oil can shape ................................................ 45.00

Marlboro Cigarette Pack.............. 45.00

Oreo Cookie, Amico ................... 35.00

Yago Sangria Bottle, unused ....... 85.00

**Record Brush,** celluloid top, soft tufted bristles, c1925

Ellis Bookkeeping Machine, black and white image of bookkeeping machine, red lettering, 3-1/2" d ................20.00

Liberty State Bank, bluetone image of Wilkes-Barre, PA, bank building, dark blue inscriptions, 1924 patent date, maker Parisian Novelty Co., Chicago, 4" d ......................... 15.00

**Ruler,** Whitehead & Hoag Co., ivory white celluloid, printed with emblem of button maker and five inch markings, reverse with Philadelphia office and manager name ................. 20.00

**Sharpening Stone,** Pike Mfg. Co., Pike, NH, gold luster finish metal case, pike fish passing through letter "P," rect whetstone, some wear to stone and luster ................................. 45.00

**Shoe Horn**

Brown's 5-Star Shoes, St. Louis, litho metal, red and yellow dec, made by Chas W. Shonk Co., Chicago, 1920s, 4-1/2" l...................................... 45.00

T. G. Plant Co., Boston, Queen Quality Shoes, ivory white celluloid, full color portrait of young regal lady, curled top, regional info on reverse, 1920s, 6" l............................................ 50.00

**Sign**

Carter's Union Suits, tin, young man in only his union suit, framed, 10-3/4" h, 6-3/4" l .................................... 200.00

Continental Insurance, framed paper in three sections, left panel with Victorian Brooklyn, Continental Insurance Building with signage on front, right panel with New York Continental Insurance Building with multiple horse drawn carriages in front, center with Indian tribe watching as wild animals run out of burning forest, J. Ottoman litho, © 1895, some minor staining to orig matting, 34-1/2" h, 68-1/2" w .............................. 1,450.00

Elgin Watch, reverse painting on glass, trademark Father Time, gold on black, framed, 23-1/2" h, 17-1/2" w... ................................................ 500.00

G. E. Fans Buy Them Here, two sided flanged tin, shows table top rotating fan, 12" h, 16" l ........................ 300.00

Ghirardelli's Cocoa, diecut cardboard, baby in highchair, framed ...... 225.00

Gooch's Sarsaparilla - for the Blood, paper, showing upper Thames River scene, artist sgd "Bowers," framed, 7-1/2" h, 9-1/2" l ...................... 200.00

John P. Squire & Co., self framed emb tin, pig in center, titled "Squires Arlington, Hams-Bacon-Sausage," © 1906, 24" h, 20" w .................. 800.00

Kis-Me-Gum, 1emb cardboard diecut, lady in diaphanous top, © 1905, framed, 8" h, 13" w ................. 500.00

Korbel Sec Champagne, self framed tin over cardboard, lady admiring grapes, 13" h, 19" l ............... 175.00

Lotus Flower, paper, proud boy doing man's job, wearing man's clothing, matted and framed, 15-1/4" h, 11-1/2" w .................................... 75.00

Merkle's Blu-J Brooms, emb tin, shows Blu-J sitting atop broom, framed, some damage, 13" h, 9-1/2" w .................................................... 175.00

Monarch Paint, two-sided flanged porcelain, hand holding paint brush, 17" h, 15-1/2" l ........................ 225.00

Niagara Shoe, beveled tin over cardboard, American Art Works litho, 19" h, 8-3/4" w ....................... 150.00

Occident Flour, tin over cardboard, actual examples as it goes through cleaning, washing, and scouring process, 9" h, 13-3/4" w ........... 75.00

Purity Butter Pretzels, diecut cardboard, easel back, smiling blond boy carrying giant pretzel against black background, white lettering, early 1930s, 22" h, 12-1/4" w ..................... 70.00

Putnam Dyes, tin, trademark of British soldiers chasing George Washington, Shonk Works litho, framed, some loss to one corner, 10-1/2" h, 21-1/2" l ............................... 60.00

Railway Express Agency, porcelain, black ground, yellow border and letters, some fogging and staining, 12" h, 71-1/2" l .............................. 75.00

Royal Baking Powder, paper, Gingerbread Man pointing to can with one hand, pointing to book titled *The Little Gingerbread Man* with other hand, small tear at center, 30" h, 20-1/2" l ..................................... 125.00

**Sign, Rex Smoking Tobacco, emb tin litho, yellow ground, pocket tin, pipe, and cigarette, 19-1/2", $135.**

Simon Pure Baking Powder, reverse painting on mirror, showing Simon Pure, framed, some loss of paint and silvering, 17" h, 14" l ............ 225.00

Star Brand Shoes, self framed tin, bust of young lady with flowing hair, advertising "Women's Mayflower Shoe, $2.50," some overall spotting and inpainting, 26" h, 19" w ... 300.00

Woolworth's, fiberboard, diamond-shape, "Woolworth's, Satisfaction Guaranteed, Replacement or Money Refunded," white and black letters, red and white ground, some paint chipping and flaking ................ 35.00

W W W Rings, tin over cardboard, lady in vintage clothing at college football game, some damage, 9-1/4" h, 6-1/4" l .................................................... 100.00

Zenith Radios, enamel, bright blue and white letters on red field, yellow background, "Long Distance Radio," 60" l, 18" w ........................... 200.00

**Stamp Case**, book shape, early 1900s

By-Lo Breath Perfume, black, white, and red celluloid, spine lettered "Stamp And Court Plaster Edition" and sponsor's name ............... 55.00

North-Western Line, black and white illus of railway line, spine lettered "Postage And Revenue Stamps/Court Plaster/Nick Nacks" ....... 60.00

Scarritt Seats, horizontal formal, black, white, and red sides, illus of Scarritt Car Chairs & Seats, black cover reads 'For Steam and Streetcar' .................................................... 55.00

Tom Moore Cigar, black and white portrait on front, red and gold spine and corners, black and white portrait for "Henry George Cigar" on back, spine lettered "Postage And Revenue Stamps/Court Plaster/Nick Nacks" .................................... 60.00

**Stickpin,** Old Dutch Cleanser, enameled figure, brass pink, reverse "Old Dutch Cleanser Chases Dirt" slogan, 1920s ....................................... 35.00

**Store Bin**

Beech Nut Chewing Tobacco, slant front, 6" w, 10" l, 8" h, green ground, white lettering ......................... 400.00

Sweet Cuba Tobacco, slant front, tin litho, 10" l, 8" w ...................... 365.00

Tiger Chewing Tobacco, round, picture of pack on rear, 11-3/4" h, 8-3/4" d. .................................................... 300.00

**Stove,** 4-1/2" h, miniature, ceramic, pot bellied, "49 Nash Hotter Than A Depot Stove," mottled red and black stove ....................................... 35.00

**Stud**

All Tobacco Cigarettes, red, white, and blue celluloid, metal lapel stud, inscribed "Morgan Marshall's Red White & Blue All Tobacco Cigarettes," 1896, some yellowing .................................................... 25.00

High Admiral Cigarettes, multicolored celluloid, metal lapel stud, young girl dancer, ethic outfit, inscribed "Smoke

High Admiral Cigarettes And Dance For Joy," early 1900s ................. 40.00

**Tape Measure**, celluloid canister

Dr. Caldwell's Syrup Pepsin Cures Constipation, reverse slogan "Cures All Stomach Troubles," yellow product box on both sides ................... 40.00

Hawk Work Clothes, full color brown half holding red, white, and blue sign from beak, yellow background, blue rim, blue letter on reverse "Miller Co.," 1920s ............................. 35.00

Indian Head National Bank, blue lettering, white ground, one side with Indian profile, other side with slogan text, 1920s ............................. 30.00

**Telephone, figural**

Heinz Catsup Bottle..................... 45.00
Raid Bug................................. 120.00
7-Up Spot............................... 125.00
Tetley Tea................................ 50.00

**Tin**

Bauer & Black Baby Talc, sample size; 2-1/4" h, some wear to rim ..... 155.00

Bee Brand Insect Powder ........... 17.50

Dream Girl Talc............................. 35.00

Euclid Candy Co., Zingo Sweets Tin, racing car illus, Tindeco, 8-1/2" h, 10" d.................................... 100.00

Golden Bear Cookies, black and orange ...................................... 25.00

Johnson & Johnson Baby Powder .................................................... 20.00

Rich's Crystallized Canton Ginger, yellow and black .......................... 15.00

Runkel's Essence of Chocolate, small top, canister, 8-1/4" l, 6" w, 6" d, wrong lid ................................. 60.00

Sauer's Selected Spices, cream, red, and dark blue .......................... 9.00

**Tin, Bon-Ami Powder, 12 oz, $18.**

Sunshine Fruit Cake, Egyptian woman dec ........................................... 15.00

Wizard Carpet Clean, 1901 ......... 48.00

**Toothpick Holder**

Souvier Buchu-Gin, celluloid, multicolored image of product bottle, "For The Kidneys & Bladder," 3 swing-out celluloid toothpicks, early 1900s ............................................... 30.00

Sunlight Milk Plant, diecut celluloid, milk bottle shape, Indianapolis factory illus on one side, reverse inscribed "Polk's Best," 3 swing-out celluloid toothpicks ................................. 40.00

**Toy**

Cat's Paw, Foster Rubber Co., Boston, celluloid, center wooden spinner dowel, yellow and black, c1920 ............................................... 35.00

Nature's Remedy Tablets, celluloid, center wooden spinner dowel, brown and white, c1920 ...................... 20.00

N.C.R. Coffee, spinner top, celluloid, center wooden spinner dowel, red coffee package illus, white and black letters, c1920 .................. 30.00

Oscar Mayer Weinermobile, pop-up Oscar figure ........................... 155.00

PF Flyers, decoder ring ................ 50.00

Weatherbird Shoes, cardboard Indian bonnet ...................................... 25.00

**Tray**

Bartlett Spring Mineral Water, doe and fawn drinking from pure mountain spring, oversized bottle of mineral water in background, Kaufmann & Strauss Co. litho, 13" d ........... 150.00

Beamer Shoes, Victorian woman, c1900 ....................................... 75.00

CD Kenny Coffee Co., Santa Claus, 9-1/2" d ..................................... 70.00

Donaldson's Dept. Store ............... 48.00

Enterprise Brewing Co. Old Tap Ape, toothless happy old man, minor wear to rim, some staining to background ............................................... 175.00

Golden West Brewing Co., factory scene, early trolleys and horse drawn carts, American Art Works, some chipping and soiling ..... 300.00

Heck's Capudine Medicine ......... 215.00

Kaiser Willhelm Bitters Co., oversized bottle with trademark label, "For Appetite and Digestion" ........... 70.00

National Brewery Co. White Seal Beer, factory scene, horse drawn wagon, early blob top bottle, Griesedieck Bros., proprietors, chipping and scratching .............................. 185.00

Olympia Brewing Co., trademark Turnwater "It's the Water," Savage Manufacturing Co., 12" d, overall scratching, soiling, and light surface rust ..... 90.00

Pacific Brewing & Malting Co., Mt. Tacoma illus, orig 1912 work order from Chas. W. Shonk Co. on back ................................................. 50.00

Park Brewing Co., factory scene, early railroad, horse drawn carts, and automobilia, Chas. W. Shonk Co. litho, some inpainting, 12" d .............. 60.00

**Wall Pocket, diecut, two dogs, house, red roof, green door and grass, emb "Paul's Market, Saylorsburg, PA," 7-1/2" x 10", $17.50.**

Robinson's Pilsener Beer, factory scene, refrigerating room, gray dryer, bottling building, stables, wagon sheds, early railroad and multiple horse drawn wagons, Haeusermann litho, 12" d ............... 90.00

Ruhstaller Brewery, elderly man in Turkish outfit enjoying his pipe and stein of beer, H. D. Beach Co. litho, 16-1/2" l, 13-1/2" w, some rubbing and chipping to rim ................................ 300.00

Stahley's Flour, horse and girl, 1905 ............................................... 50.00

Stegmaier Brewing Co. factory scene, early railroad and automobilia, minor scratching and rubbing ........... 70.00

Wolverine Toy Co., c1920, 4" x 6" ............................................... 95.00

**Whistle**

Butter-Krust Bread, red and white celluloid, tin backing panel, 1930s ..... 20.00

Endicott Johnson Shoes, green litho tin, biplane shape, red lettering, mkd "Made In Germany," c1930 ........ 25.00

Golden Royal Milk, yellow and black ................................................. 7.50

Old Reliable Coffee ..................... 10.00

Oscar Meyer Weiner, painted ....... 15.00

Poll Parrot Shoes, tin litho, yellow, red, and green trademark, made by Kilchof Co., 1930s ................... 40.00

**Whistle, Agfa Film, black ground, red and blue box, white text, $24.**

# Advertising Characters

**Collecting Hints:** Concentrate on one advertising character. Three-dimensional objects are more eagerly sought than two-dimensional ones. Some local dairies, restaurants, and other businesses developed advertising characters. This potential collecting area has received little attention.

**History:** Americans learned to recognize specific products by their particular advertising characters. In the early 1900s, many immigrants could not read but could identify the colorful characters. Thus, the advertising character helped to sell the product.

Some manufacturers developed similar names for inferior-quality products, like Fairee Soap versus the popular Fairy Soap. Trade laws eventually helped protect companies by allowing advertising characters to be registered as part of a trademark.

Trademarks and advertising characters are found on product labels, in magazines, as premiums, and on other types of advertising. Popular cartoon characters also were used to advertise products.

Some advertising characters, such as Mr. Peanut and the Campbell Kids, were designed to promote a specific product. The popular Campbell Kids first appeared on streetcar advertising in 1906. The illustrations of Grace G. Drayton were originally aimed at housewives, but the characters were gradually dropped from Campbell's advertising until the television industry expanded the advertising market. In 1951, Campbell redesigned the kids and successfully reissued them. The kids were redesigned again in 1966. Other advertising characters (e.g., Aunt Jemima) also have enjoyed a long life; some, like Kayo and the Yellow Kid, are no longer used in contemporary advertising.

**References:** Warren Dotz, *Advertising Character Collectibles*, Collector Books, 1993; —, *What a Character*, Chronicle Books, 1996; David Longest, *Character Toys and Collectibles*, 1st Series (1984, 1992 value update), 2nd Series (1987, 1990 value update), Collector Books; Rex Miller, *The Investor's Guide to Vintage Character Collectibles,* Krause

Publications, 1999; Robert Reed, *Bears and Dolls in Advertising*, Antique Trader Books, 1998; David and Micki Young, *Campbell's Soup Collectibles from A to Z*, Krause Publications, 1998.

**Collectors' Clubs:** Campbell Kids Collectors, 649 Bayview Dr., Akron, OH 44319; Campbell's Soup Collector Club, 414 Country Lane Ct., Wauconda, IL 60084; Peanut Pals, 804 Hickory Grade Rd., Bridgeville, PA 15017; R. F. Outcault Society, 103 Doubloon Dr., Slidell, LA 70461.

**Reproduction Alert.**

**Additional Listings:** Advertising, Advertising Logo Watches, Black Memorabilia, Cartoon Characters, Fast Food, Planter's Peanuts.

**AC Spark Plug,** diecast, diecast horse in bathtub .............................. 250.00

**Alka Seltzer, Speedy**
Figure, 5-1/2" h, plastic, 1960s ..... 20.00
Paper Cup, 1977 .......................... 12.00
Sign, 10" w ................................. 65.00

**Aunt Jemima**
Button, "Aunt Jemima Breakfast Club," tin litho, 4" d, color image of smiling Jemima, red background, black text "Eat a Better Breakfast," Green Duck Co., Chicago, c1960 ............... 35.00
Cookbook, Aunt Jemima's Album of Secret Recipes, 1935, 33 pgs, soft cover, booklet form .................. 32.00
Hat, Aunt Jemima's Breakfast Club, paper, fold-out style ................ 20.00
Magazine Tear Sheet, Aunt Jemima Pancakes, 1949, 13" x 5" ......... 15.00
Place Mat, paper, full color, Story of Aunt Jemima, "Story of Aunt Jemima and her Pancake Days, ...has devoted her time to working with service clubs ...on her community Pancake Day Festivals...," unused, 1950s, 10-1/2" x 13-1/2" .......... 45.00
Restaurant Table Card, diecut face, full color, "Folks...It's a treat to eat out often...Bring the whole family...time for Aunt Jemima Pancakes," 1953, 4-3/4" x 3" ................................. 55.00

**Borden's, Elsie and Family**
Badge, white ground, blue lettering, 1-1/2" d .................................... 10.00
Cookie Cutter, Buelah, hard plastic, emb face, 2-1/14" d ................. 48.00
Drinking Glass, Elsie the Cow, Elmer, and Beauregard, 1776 garb, red, white, and blue ......................... 30.00
Fun Book, Elsie Fun Book, comic book style, coloring pages, dot games, safety games, etc., 20 pgs, unused, 1940s ...................................... 75.00
Postcard, Elsie and Elmer, color, traveling scene ................................. 25.00
Poster
    Borden's Egg Nog, portrait of Elsie, 20" x 14" ................................ 30.00

**Buster Brown, Froggie wiggle picture, $17.50.**

Welcome Home, "Join in the Celebration of June Dairy Month!" portrait of Elsie, smaller print reads, "Looking forward to our future, we salute our past," 1942, 5" x 15" .......... 15.00
Ring, dark gold luster plastic, center clear plastic dome over multicolored Elsie image, 1950 .................... 35.00
Salt and Pepper Shakers, pr, Elsie and Elmer, china, c1940 .............. 125.00
Serving Tray, shows whole family, 1950s ...................................... 85.00
Tab, diecut litho tin, red and yellow image, c1940 .......................... 10.00

**Buster Brown**
Book, *Buster Brown's Drawing Book*, 1906, 12 pgs, 3-1/2" x 5", full color cover, premium from Emerson Piano Co. ........................................ 350.00
Box, Buster Brown Stockings, c1905, 11" x 4" x 3" ........................... 150.00
Game
    Buster Brown Game and Play Box, Andy Devine photo, unused .... 80.00
    Pin-The-Tail, c1910, 24" x 30" color litho poster .......................... 110.00
    Pattern, stuffed doll, uncut, full color, makes 17" Buster Brown doll and 11" Tige, 42" x 18" sheet, 1924 .... 275.00
Pinback Button
    Buster Brown Hose Supporter, multicolored, 1920s ....................... 25.00
    Buster Brown Shoes, sepia letters, brown rim ............................. 20.00
Playing cards, copyright 1906, each card 1-3/4" x 2-1/4" ............... 180.00
Postcard, sgd by Outcault, dated 1903 ......................................... 20.00
Ring, sq flicker ring, 1950s .......... 50.00
**Cadbury Bunny,** stuffed rabbit, talking ........................................... 125.00

**Campbell Kids**
Bank, ceramic, 1970s .................. 70.00
Christmas Ornament .................... 25.00
Doll, boy and girl, vinyl, orig clothes, pr ............................................ 145.00

Radio, MIB ................................. 45.00
Soup Bowl, Campbell Girl on inside, alphabet and "Christine" on bottom, c1940 ..................................... 30.00
Truck, semi, chunky soup adv ...... 65.00

**Dutch Boy Paint, Dutch Boy**
Hand Puppet, 11" h, vinyl head, fabric body, orig cellophane bag, 1960s ........................................... 45.00
Marker, diecut thin cardboard inserted into slotted wooden base, front side with Dutch Boy Painter, reverse with black and white image of paint can, inscribed "Paint with Dutch Boy White Lead," c1930 ................. 20.00
Paint Book, Dutch Boy illus, 1907, unused .................................... 25.00
Pinback Button, multicolored trademark, red and blue rim inscription ........ 12.00
Sign, 49" h, 26-1/2" w, linen cloth, "Now for another good paint job!" painter getting into overalls next to Dutch Boy holding bucket of Dutch Boy White Lead, Sweeney Litho Co., artist Rundle, c1932 .................. 125.00
Statue, composition figure, holding full pail of paint, 36" h, some denting to base ........................................ 400.00

**Esso, Tiger**
Bank, tiger, figural, plastic ............ 35.00
Drinking Glass, Esso Tiger, "Put a Tiger in Your Tank," slogan printed on back in 8 different languages, 5" h ........................................... 18.00
**Fleischmann's Yeast,** John Dough, pinback, oval, multicolored, baker image formed by brown bread loaf body parts, blue background, c1915 ........................................... 90.00
**Frito Bandito,** eraser, figural ....... 15.00

**Green Giant**
Dancing Doll, cloth, mail away premium, 40" h ............................. 125.00
Figure, Sprout, vinyl ................... 20.00
Telephone, Little Sprout, 14" h ...... 65.00
**Hawaiian Punch,** Punchy, figure, hard plastic, blue or orange ............. 12.00
**Hush Puppy,** figure, Hush Puppies Shoes, composition, 8-1/4" h .... 40.00
**Joe Camel,** fishing lure, MIP ........ 40.00

**Keebler, Elf**
Bank, figural, ceramic ................. 65.00
Cookie Jar, cookie tree, raised figures ........................................... 95.00

**Campbell's Kid, sign, metal, 23-1/4" x 14-1/2", $80.**

Doll, Ernie, plush, talking mechanism not working .............................. 15.00

**Kellogg's, Tony the Tiger**

Bank, figural vinyl .......................... 40.00
Doll, Tony the Tiger, cloth ............. 25.00
Radio ............................................... 30.00
Spoon, SP, emb "Kellogg's" ......... 10.00

**Kool Cigarettes**

Figure, Dr. Kool, 4-1/2" h, black and white, painted plaster, full figure walking along carrying satchel with name on side, wearing stethoscope, late 1930s, professional repair to base chip .............................. 136.00
Pinback Button, Willie between donkey and elephant, 1930s ................. 25.00
Salt and Pepper Shakers, pr, Willie and Millie, figural, 3-1/2" h, black and white plastic, yellow accent beaks, red accent necklace and dark red hair bow on Millie, c1950 ......... 35.00
**Lee Jeans,** Lee Boy, bank, ceramic, 8" h, MIB ..................................... 150.00
**Michelin Man,** figure, plastic, 12" h ............................................. 100.00
**Mr. Bubble,** figure, plastic ............ 25.00
**Mr. Clean,** figure, plastic .............. 65.00

**Philip Morris, Johnny**

Pinback Button, black, white, red, and fleshtone, 1930s ....................... 35.00
Place Card, figural ........................ 17.50
Sign, emb tin, well worn, 12" x 14" ............................................... 95.00

**Pillsbury Co., Dough Boy**

Cookie Jar ..................................... 25.00
Doll, 7-1/4" h, vinyl, smiling full figure boy, blue accent eyes, button on cap, copyright 1971 Pillsbury Co. Minneapolis .............................. 18.00
Salt and Pepper Shakers, 4" h Poppin Fresh, 3-1/4" h Poppie, names on bases, blue accents, copyright 1974 ............................................... 28.00

**RCA Victor, Nipper**

Coffee Mug, plastic .......................... 8.00
Hanger Pin, His Master's Voice, diecut thin celluloid, black, white, and red, figural Nipper, inscribed "Owens Music Store Spencer, Ind." ...... 40.00
Pinback Button, 1-1/4" d, diecut celluloid, red, white, and blue, dealer's name on back .......................... 40.00
Snowdome .................................... 40.00

**Red Goose Shoes**

Bank ............................................. 150.00
Egg layer, 27" h, 22" w, plastic red goose sitting atop cardboard box, slight paint loss ..................... 200.00
Ring, secret compartment, glow, photo. ............................................... 150.00
String Holder, 15" h, 11" w, cast iron, wing emb "Red goose Shoes" ......... 150.00

**Reddy Kilowatt**

Cookie Cutter ................................ 25.00
Figure, 5" h plastic, 1/4" x 1-1/2" x 3" black plastic base, translucent pink body and white plastic heat, hands

and boots glow after being exposed to bright light, name on base, mid-1930s .................................... 300.00
Identification Badge, 3-3/4" sq, red and white paper envelope, 3" d still paper peel-off "E-Z Stick-On" badge with yellow upper and lower bands, red and white Reddy portrait, 1950s, unused .................................... 20.00
Magic Gripper, 5-1/4" sq red and white paper envelope, 4-3/4" d thin textured dark yellow rubber disk, printed on one side with title and image of Reddy the Chef, c1950 ............................................... 20.00
Pin, 1" h brass and red enamel figure, orig 2-1/4" x 2-3/4" diecut card with clear plastic window, c1950 .... 40.00
Pinback Button, red figure, white background, blue letters, c1940 ...... 20.00
Plate, 9" d, white china, 2-1/2" h smiling full figured Reddy at left, dark red accent rim, early 1950s ........... 60.00
Potholder, MIP ............................... 30.00
Sign, Public Service Co. of Oklahoma, porcelain, green ground, white with illus of running Reddy, 21-1/2" h, 71" l ............................................... 100.00
**7-Up,** Fresh-Up Freddy, ruler ....... 15.00
**Sinclair Oil,** Dinosaur, booklet, 1960s ............................................... 20.00

**Sunkist, Charlie Tuna**

Alarm Clock, 1969 ........................ 85.00
Doll, talking, Mattel, not working ............................................... 100.00
**Trix Rabbit,** figure, vinyl .............. 45.00
**Tropicana,** Orange Bird
Bank, 4-3/4" h orange vinyl, yellow accent, green leaf petal hair and wings, Hong Kong, c1960 ....... 35.00
Nodder ....................................... 150.00
Radio ............................................ 30.00
Squeeze Toy, figural, MIB ............. 95.00

# Advertising-Logo Watches

**Collecting Hints:** Advertising-logo watches are an increasingly popular collectible. They reflect popular culture, are interesting technically and artistically, and are possible to find. Numerous themes, subjects, and types create a high degree of cross-collectibility. Watches are often tie-ins to a trend, movie, or TV program.

Age and demand affect value; demand can change with an increase or decrease in popularity. Look for clean, complete watches in excellent condition; the newer the piece, the better the condition must be. Original mint packaging can double or triple value. Information regarding the source and the associated printed matter (original offers, boxes, enclosures, outer wrap/ mailer etc.) is important.

The earlier and scarcer pieces for popular companies and characters can have good value. Even a brand new ad-logo watch can be highly collectible if available for only a short time. An example is the watches being produced for the Millennium. Two are the M&M Millennium watch and The Pillsbury Doughboy Millennium watch with printed tin.

Copyright dates can lead to confusion about the year of issue and age of a watch. The date generally refers to when the character or logo was first "published" and cannot be relied upon to date a watch.

Look for watches in collecting publications, house and garage sales, rummage sales, flea markets, and antiques and collectibles shows. Knowledgeable collector friends/ dealers might be the most reliable way to acquire both watches and information. Internet sales and auctions are increa1singly popular, but the caveat "let the buyer beware" remains.

Collectible ad watches include:
Giveaways and premiums
Retail, catalog, website, store ad watches
Mechanical wind-up and battery-operated pocket and wrist watches
Digital and analog (with hands) watches, plastic and metal
Dress and sport watches
Company logo and characters,
Licensed characters and events
In-house awards, events, and commemoratives.

**History:** The earliest early ad-logo timepieces are pocket watches. Advertising on the pocket watch face first appeared around the turn of the 20th century. Earlier, 19th century pocket watches might feature a company name engraved on the case, but advertising watch fobs attached to the watch chain were more popular.

The internal movements and cases of the pocket watches were cheaply made; few early ones survive. The cases are usually chrome plate and the "crystals" often made from an early plastic, are yellowed with age. Only a company name is likely to appear on the face. Pocket watches were worn by men, and the ads have masculine orientation.

Wrist watches came into popular use in the 1920-30s, but pocket watches remained common through the 1950s and have experienced a resurgence in the 1990s.

The first documented trademark character wrist watch, featuring Twinkie the Brown Shoe Elf, was issued by the Hamilton Brown Company in the mid-'20s. A Twinkie pocket watch was released as well. Chevrolet issued a salesman's award wrist watch around the same time; it has a clever radiator shaped case.

A smattering of ad watches from the 1940-60s are known, but it wasn't until the 1970s that the constant visibility of wrist watches was recognized, and more and more were produced.

Watch Features By Decade:

**1970s:** Mechanical wind-ups with heavy metal cases, generally marked "Swiss Made." Wide leather or plastic straps with snaps. Earliest revolving disks and mechanical digitals. The value is from $75-$300.

**1980s:** Battery operated, both digital and analog. Slim, plastic cases common. New features include electronic hands only visible when the battery is good, clam shell case digitals, pop-up digitals, and printed plastic straps. Hanger cards and other elaborate packaging common. The value is from $10-$75 in mint condition.

**1990s:** New features include holograms, revolving sub-dials, "talking" features, water-filled cases and straps, game watches, stopwatches and timers, giga pet watches, and clip-on "clocks," clear printed resin straps and laser cut straps. Special boxes and printed tins important. Value is rarely above $25, and the plastic watches range from $10-$15.

**References:** Hy Brown, *Comic Character Timepieces*, Schiffer, 1992; Cooksey Shugart, *The Complete Guide to Watches,* Shugart & Gilbert, published annually.

**Periodical:** The Premium Watch Watch, 24 San Rafael Drive, Rochester, NY 14618, e-mail: siranpour@aol.com.

**Advisor**: Sharon Iranpour

**Reproduction Alert:** Watch faces can be color copied and old ones replicated or the copy can be put in the wrong cases. Familiarize yourself with the "right" look.

Campbell Soup Co., 1982 "Original Edition," Criterion, windup, set of four, each is marked on the back, clear plastic box has a slip cover printed with the Kids, MIB

Boy Kid, 1" goldtone case; face: red hat, jacket and school bag, black plastic strap ............................ 40.00
Boy Kid, 1-1/8" goldtone case; face: orange jacket, blue jeans, black plastic strap ............................ 40.00
Girl Kid, 1" goldtone case; face: red jacket and school bag, red plastic strap ...................................... 40.00
Girl Kid: 1-1/8" goldtone case; face: green dress, mirror in hand, black plastic strap ............................ 40.00
Captain Midnight, Ovaltine, 1988, digital, yellow plastic case; face: rocket takes off, "S.Q. Secret Squadron Member," blue plastic strap, yellow buckle, includes letter from Ovaltine, mint with letter ................. 40.00
Charlie the Tuna, Starkist, date on the face:
1971, heavy goldtone 1-1/2" case, blue leather double strap, mint with offer insert ............................... 50.00
1971, small lightweight goldtone 1-1/8" case, blue leather double strap, mint with offer insert ....... 50.00
1973, silvertone case, date window on face, blue plastic strap with four double sets of holes on each side ............................................... 45.00
1977, silvertone case, blue plastic strap with four double sets of holes on each side ........................... 40.00
1986, silvertone case, 25th Anniversary 1961-1986, black leather strap, brown box, MIB ........................ 30.00
1990, goldtone small 15/16" case, black leather strap, white box, MIB .. ............................................... 25.00
1992, black metal case, black leather strap, white box, red "StarKist," MIB ........................ 25.00
1998, blue plastic case, plastic strap, yellow upper, red lower, silver box, MIB................................ 15.00
Chuck Wagon Dog Food, Lafayette Watch Co., 1970s, goldtone case; face: chuck wagon, running dog on revolving disk, black suede strap, blue plastic box, red velvet lining, MIB....................................... 100.00
Coppertone 40th Birthday, 1980s, man's and woman's, goldtone case; face: classic girl and dog, balloons, "Happy 40th Birthday!" brown leather strap, mint, each ......... 25.00
Icee Bear, Hassis Watches, 1971, stainless steel case; face: red and blue Icee Bear holds drink in each hand, white strap with snaps, mint .................................................. 125.00
Keebler Elf, 1970s, Swiss wind-up, silvertone case; face: porcelain, Ernie stands with arms held to side, original strap unknown, VG............. 75.00
Little Hans, Nestle, Piet Israel, 1971, silvertone case; face: Little Hans in center, eyes that move side to side, VG ........................................... 60.00

Major Moon, Moonstone Cereal, 1970, silvertone case; face: character holds yellow "Moonstone" in his hands, plastic blue denim look strap with snaps, VG........................ 75.00
M & Ms, Mars Candy, plastic cases and straps, dated, front or back 1987, yellow case; face: yellow, orange, green and red Ms, red and green strap, yellow buckle and keeper, mint .......................................... 20.00
1990, 50th Birthday Watch, included in M & Ms Birthday Club pack, yellow case; face: red M, party hat, horn, confetti, red and green strap, yellow buckle and keeper, 9" x 12" printed envelope, MIP with all enclosures ....................................... 40.00
1993, red case; face: orange, red, green, and yellow Ms, yellow and green strap, red buckle and keeper, mint .......................................... 15.00
1994, Cool Moves Watch, red case; face: green ramp, an M on skateboard on revolving disk, brown strap printed with Ms, plastic case, printed sleeve, MIB .............................. 20.00
1996, New Blue M&M Watch, black case and strap, face: blue M plays saxophone, Ms on revolving disk, plastic case, printed sleeve, MIB .................................................. 20.00
1997, Fun Watch, black case; face: red circle with white M, black laser cut strap, plastic case, white sleeve, MIB ......................................... 15.00
1997, M&M Minis, yellow painted metal case; face: candy tube, Minis on revolving disk, purple laser cut strap, plastic case, white sleeve, MIB ......................................... 15.00
1998, Millennium Watch, brushed silvertone, silver under-printing "The Official Candy of the Millennium" on crystal; face: red M against starry sky, black leather strap with embossed "MM means 2000," mint .................................................. 15.00
Peter Pan Peanut Butter, S&M Inc., 1980s, red plastic case and strap; face: jar of peanut butter with feet, hands are the watch hands, MIB .................................................. 20.00
Punchy, Hawaiian Punch
1970s, Swiss digital wind-up, rectangular goldtone, face: Punchy, hours & minutes in separate windows, wide red strap with snaps, VG ......... 60.00
1971, goldtone case, Swiss wind-up, face: Punchy's arms are hands, shiny red strap with snaps, mint......... 50.00
1980s, blue plastic case; face: Punchy next to erupting volcano, feet and skateboard are printed on the white plastic strap, mint..... 15.00
Raid Bug Spray, Swiss wind up, 1970s, goldtone case; face: Raid can, hands on hips, a bug on revolving disk, black leather strap. VG ........... 150.00

Reddy Kilowatt Pocket Watch, Philadelphia Light & Electric, 1930s, silvertone case. "Compliments of Philadelphia Light & Electric" on face, several versions, VG ..................... 200.00
Ritz Cracker, Continental Watch Co., 1971, silvertone case; face: red and blue, crackers at hour marks, yellow "Ritz," black vinyl strap with snaps; box: black bottom, red velvet insert, elastic holders, white top, MIB ..................... 200.00
Scrubbing Bubble, Dow, Marcel, 1970s, goldtone case; face: Scrubbing Bubble in center, "Scrubbing Bubbles" at lower right, black plastic strap, VG .................. 50.00
Shell Golden Oil Pocket Watch, Girard-Perregaux, 1940s, clear front and back, Roman numerals, "Shell" on watch movement, the oil was so "pure" the watch could be filled with it, VG ...................... 150.00
Snickers Anniversary, Mars, Advance Watch Co., 1990, goldtone case; face: gold with embossed stars, Snicker's wrappers through time rotate on sub-dial, brown leather strap, mint ............... 35.00
Stanley Powerlock, Stanley Tools, 1980, black plastic case; face: yellow background, "Stanley Powerlock," yellow strap, printed like a tape measure, MIB ................. 25.00
Swiss Miss, Elam Watch Co., Swiss wind-up, 1981, goldtone case; face: Swiss Miss in blue dress and "Swiss Miss," brown leather strap, plastic box, MIB ................. 25.00
Tony The Tiger, Kellogg's Frosted Flakes, Swiss wind-up, 1976, silvertone case; face: striding Tony, black vinyl strap with snaps, box with shiny black bottom, shiny orange top, MIB ................ 200.00
Toppie the Elephant, Tip Top Bread, Ingraham, 1951, small size chrome case; face: pink polka dot elephant wearing cape with "Toppie," good ............ 100.00
Westinghouse Refrigerator Pocket Watch, New Haven Clock Co., 1940s, silvertone case; face: red with a yellow wedge between 10-12, "Westinghouse kitchen-proved refrigerator, 10 out of 12 hours it uses no current at all," green box, has yellow top with face art in black on cover, Form No. 8 DR-8005 MIB .............. 85.00

# Akro Agate Glass

**Collecting Hints:** The Akro Agate mark—"Made in USA"—often includes a mold number. Some pieces also have a small crow in the mark.

Akro Agate glass is thick; therefore, collectors should buy only mint pieces. The marbleized types of Akro Agate were made in many color combinations. The serious collector should look for unusual combinations.

**History:** The Akro Agate Co. was formed in 1911, primarily to produce marbles. In 1914, the owners moved from near Akron, Ohio, to Clarksburg, West Virginia, where they opened a large factory. They continued to profitably produce marbles until after the Depression. In 1930, the competition in the marble business became too intense, and Akro Agate Co. decided to diversify.

Two of its most successful products were the floral ware lines and children's dishes, first made in 1935. The children's dishes were very popular until after World War II when metal dishes captured the market.

The Akro Agate Co. also made special containers for cosmetics firms, such the Jean Vivaudou Co. and Pick Wick bath salts (packaged in the Mexicali cigarette jar). Operations continued successfully until 1948. The factory, a victim of imports and the increased use of metal and plastic, was sold to the Clarksburg Glass Co. in 1951.

**References:** Gene Florence, *Collectors Encyclopedia of Akro Agate Glassware*, revised ed., Collector Books, 1975, 1992 value update; Roger and Claudia Hardy, *Complete Line of the Akro Agate*, published by author, 1992.

**Collectors' Clubs:** Akro Agate Art Assoc., P.O. Box 758, Salem, NH 03079; Akro Agate Collector's Club, 10 Bailey Street, Clarksburg, WV 26301.

**Reproduction Alert:** Pieces currently reproduced are not marked "Made In USA" and are missing the mold number and crow.

**Children's Dishes, small unless otherwise noted**
Cereal Bowl
  Concentric Ring, blue, large.... 27.50
  Interior Panel, green, transparent, large ......................... 25.00
  Stacked Disk and Interior Panel, blue, transparent, large .......... 35.00
Creamer
  Chiquita, cobalt blue, baked-on ............... 10.00
  Interior Panel, topaz transparent ............... 20.00
  Octagonal, sky blue, open handle, large ......................... 25.00
  Stacked Disk, green ............... 10.00
  Stacked Disk, pink .................. 25.00
  Stippled Band, green, large .... 30.00
Cup
  Chiquita, opaque green............. 8.50
  Chiquita, transparent cobalt blue ............... 14.00
  Concentric Rib, green, opaque ....6.00

Interior Panel, green transparent, large......................... 15.00
J. Pressman, lavender ............ 32.00
Octagonal, closed handle, dark green, large ........................... 8.00
Stacked Disk, aqua blue .......... 5.00
Stacked Disk, green opaque..... 6.00
Stacked Disk, green transparent ............... 12.00
Stacked Disk Interior Panel, pumpkin ............... 38.00
Stippled Band, green, large ....... 20.00
Cup and Saucer
  Chiquita, green opaque............. 8.00
  Interior Panel, green and white marble......................... 37.50
  Stippled Band, cobalt blue, large ............... 35.00
  Stippled Band, green, large .... 30.00
  Stippled Band, green, small .... 30.00
Demitasse Cup and Saucer, J. Pressman, green......................... 22.00
Pitcher
  Interior Panel, blue transparent ..35.00
  Stacked Disk, blue opaque........ 15.00
  Stacked Disk and Panel, green transparent.............................. 45.00
  Stippled band, green transparent ............... 18.00
Plate
  Chiquita, opaque green............. 8.00
  Concentric Rib, opaque green ... 3.00
  Concentric Ring, dark blue........ 6.50
  Interior Panel, blue opaque, medium ............... 15.00
  Interior Panel, green opaque, large ............... 7.00
  Interior Panel, topaz transparent ............... 10.00
  J. Pressman, green, baked-on, 3-3/4" d ..................... 5.00
  Octagonal, green, large............. 8.00
  Octagonal, white, small ............ 8.00
  Stacked Disk, green ............... 10.00
  Stacked Disk, medium blue....... 6.00
  Stacked Disk and Panel, transparent cobalt blue, large ............... 22.00
  Stippled Band, green, small .... 15.00
  Stippled Band, topaz, large..... 10.00
Saucer
  Chiquita, opaque yellow .......... 12.00
  Concentric Rib, white ............... 3.00
  Concentric Ring, ivory ..... 4.50
  Interior Panel, medium blue, opaque, large ......................... 9.00
  Octagonal, dark pink ................. 8.00
  Octagonal, white, large ........... 12.00
  Stacked Disk, green ................. 7.00
  Stacked Disk and Panel, transparent green, small ..................... 12.00
Set
  Concentric Ring, green plates, green cups, white saucers, blue creamer and sugar, blue teapot with white lid, 16 pcs, orig box..................... 200.00
  Interior Panel, green cups and saucers, green creamer, pink sugar, pink teapot, white lid, small size ............... 290.00
  Interior Panel, topaz transparent, service for 4, cups, saucers, plates, creamer and sugar, teapot with lid ............... 215.00

Octagonal, closed handle, green plates and cups, white creamer, sugar, saucers, and teapot, large, 17 pcs ........................................ 165.00
Stippled Band, amber, 2 cups and saucers, 2 dinner plates, covered teapot ...................................... 60.00
Sugar, cov
Chiquita, green opaque ............. 8.00
Chiquita, transparent cobalt blue ............................................. 8.00
Stacked Disk, green ................. 10.00
Stacked Disc, pink ................... 50.00
Teapot, cov
Chiquita, green opaque ........... 18.00
Chiquita, transparent cobalt blue ........................................... 35.00
Interior Panel, green, white lid, large ............................................ 45.00
Interior Panel, green, white lid, small ............................................ 25.00
Interior Panel, medium blue opaque, lid missing, large ...................... 36.00
Stacked Disk, azure blue, white lid ............................................ 10.00
Stippled Band, green, small .... 35.00
Tumbler
Interior Panel, green transparent, 2" h ...................................... 12.00
Stacked Disk, beige ................. 12.00
Stacked Disk, white ................. 12.00
Stacked Disk and Interior Panel, transparent green, 2" h ........... 12.00
Water Set
Octagonal, open handle, blue pitcher, 2 dark and 2 light green tumblers ......................................... 70.00
Stacked Disk and Interior Panel, transparent green, 7 pcs ...... 70.00
Stippled Band, green, pitcher, six tumblers ................................ 110.00

**Tea Set, American Made, No. 325, 3 opaque colors, closed handles, orig box, $165.**

## Household Items
Ashtray
2-7/8" sq, blue and red marble ...... 8.50
4-1/2" w, hexagon, blue and white ................................................. 35.00
Basket, 2 handles, orange and white ................................................. 35.00
Cornucopia, orange and white ....... 8.00
Flowerpot
2-1/4" h, Ribbed, green and white ................................................. 10.00
2-1/2" h, Stacked Disk, green and white ................................... 12.00
4" h, Stacked Disk, blue and white ................................................. 25.00
5-1/2" h, Scalloped Top, blue ..... 32.00
Lamp
5-1/2" d, ribbed base, Housez ................................................. 115.00
12" h, brown and blue marble, 4" d black octagonal top, Globe Spec Co. ...................................... 75.00
Marbles, Chinese Checkers, set of 60, orig box ................................. 130.00
Mexicalli Jar, cov
Green and white ...................... 30.00
Orange and white ................... 40.00
Planter, 8-1/2" l, Graduated Dart, oval, scalloped, dark blue ................ 30.00
Powder Jar, Colonial Lady, yellow ................................................. 65.00
Vase
3-3/4" h, green, marble ............ 15.00
4-1/4" h, lily, marble ................. 17.50
4-5/8" h, 4-1/4" w, flared, green and white marble, rust streaks, raised flower on each side, mkd "Made in USA" with backwards S, crow over letter A ..................................... 28.00

# Aluminum, Hand Wrought

**Collecting Hints:** Some manufacturers' marks are synonymous with quality, e.g., "Continental Hand Wrought Silverlook." However, some quality pieces are not marked and should not be overlooked. Check carefully for pitting, deep scratches, and missing glassware.

**History:** During the late 1920s, aluminum was used to make many decorative household accessories. Although manufactured by a variety of methods, the hammered aluminum with repoussé patterns appears to have been the most popular.

At one time, many companies were competing for the aluminum giftware market. In order to be more competitive, numerous silver manufacturers added aluminum articles to their product lines during the Depression. Some of these aluminum objects were produced strictly as promotional items; others were offered as more afford-able options to similar silver objects. Many well-known and highly esteemed metalsmiths contributed their skills to the production of hammered aluminum. With the advent of mass-production and the accompanying wider distribution of aluminum giftware, the demand began to decline, leaving only a few producers who have continued to turn out quality work using the age-old and time-tested methods of metal crafting.

**References:** Marilyn E. Dragowlck (ed.), *Metalwares Price Guide*, Antique Trader Books, 1996; Dannie A. Woodard, *Hammered Aluminum Hand Wrought Collectibles, Book Two*, Aluminum Collectors' Books, 1993; —, *Revised 1990 Price List for Hammered Aluminum*, Aluminum Collectors' Books, 1990; Dannie Woodard and Billie Wood, *Hammered Aluminum*, published by authors, 1983.

**Periodical:** *Aluminist*, P.O. Box 1346, Weatherford, TX 76086.

**Collectors' Club:** Aluminum Collectors, P.O. Box 1346, Weatherford, TX 76086; Wendell August Collectors Guild, P.O. Box 107, Grove City, PA 16127.

Ashtray
3-1/4" d, Stanhome, Stanley Home Product, center relief dec of house ................................................. 5.00
4-3/4" d, Whirlpool, Open House, Oct 1965, Marion Division ................ 8.00
Basket
8" x 5-1/4", floral and leaf design, cut-out dec, Farbers & Shlevin Inc. Handwrought #1705 ................ 20.00
9" l, rose handle, mkd "Continental Trade Mark Hand Wrought Silverlook 754" .................................. 25.00
Bowl
8" d, Wendell August Forge, Pine Cone pattern ............................ 45.00
10" d, souvenir of Minnesota, center scene ......................................... 5.00
11-3/4" d, Continental Silverlook, Chrysanthemum pattern, applied leaves, #715 ............................ 20.00
Bread Tray, 13-1/4" l, 7-3/4" w, Continental, chrysanthemum decoration, #572 ........................................... 25.00
Butter Dish, Buenilum, round, domed cover, double-loop finish, glass insert ......................................... 35.00
Candleholder, 6" h, Buenilum, beaded edge base, aluminum stem with wood ball ................................. 10.00
Candy Tray, 8" d, chrysanthemum dec, unmarked ................................. 10.00
Casserole, cov
7-1/2" d, Everlast Forged Metal, rose dec, beaded knob ................... 28.00

10" d, 7-1/2" h, mkd "B. W. Buenilum" ................................................. 18.00
Coaster
Flying ducks and cattails, set of six ................................................. 12.00
Stanhome, Stanley Home Products .................................................. 3.00
State of Texas, various state symbols ................................................ 7.50
Compote, 5" h, Continental Hand Wrought Silverlook, wild rose dec, #1083 .......................................... 18.00
Creamer and Sugar, Continental hand Wrought Silverlook, Chrysanthemum pattern, grooved handles, applied leaves, matching tray .............. 30.00
Crumb Catcher Set, unmarked..... 10.00
Desk Set, Everlast Forge, Bali Bamboo pattern, price for 3 pc set ........ 45.00
Dish
4" l, leaf shape, 4" l ...................... 3.00
5" d, floral design ....................... 3.00
7-1/2" d, tulip design, raised sides, Buenilum ................................... 24.00
Ice Bucket, cov, 10" h, insulated, mkd "Krome Enduring Beautiful and Pat Pending," large knob on top, blister on bottom, use marks, plastic rim cracked .................................... 20.00
Ladle, 14-1/2" l, Argental Cellini Craft ................................................. 25.00
Lazy Susan, 16" d, Rodney Kent, covered glass dish, ribbon and flower trim .......................................... 35.00
Pitcher
Buenilum, ovoid, slender neck, twisted handle.......................... 35.00
Regal, some scratches and wear ................................................. 15.00
Plate, flying ducks and cattails, 5" d ................................................. 6.00
Scoop, 6-1/2" l, handle curled under ................................................. 6.00
Serving Dish, marine motif, shells and shrimp dec, 16-1/2" x 16-1/2", mkd "B & B, St. Paul, Minn., USA" .........65.00
Silent Butler
Flower design, unmarked ........ 18.00
Moon and star design, 6-1/2" x 11" ................................................. 24.00

**Coaster, Flying Geese, 3-1/4" d, $4.**

Tidbit Tray, 10" h, 13" d, 3 tiers, dogwood pattern, mkd "Wilson Specialties Co., Inc., Brooklyn, NY" .....................30.00
Tray
11-1/4" d, flower design, unmarked ................................................. 15.00
12" x 12", floral design, mkd "Hand Forged Everlast Metal," minor wear ................................................. 24.00
14" x 9-1/4" d, leaf design, mkd "Hand Forged Everlast Metal" with anchor and arm with hammer in hand, wear .............................. 15.00
14" x 20", Rodney Kent, tulip dec, handles, #425 ......................... 32.00
18" d, four flying ducks, mkd "Hand Wrought by Federal S. Co.," wrapped handles .................... 30.00

# American Bisque

**Collecting Hint:** When searching for American Bisque products, look for a mark consisting of three stacked baby blocks with the letters "A," "B," and "C." This common mark is readily found.

**History:** The American Bisque Company was founded in Williamstown, West Virginia, in 1919. Although the pottery's original product was china-head dolls, it quickly expanded its inventory to include serving dishes, cookie jars, ashtrays, and various other decorative ceramic pieces. B. E. Allen, founder of the Sterling China Company, invested heavily in the company and eventually purchased the remaining stock. In 1982 the plant was sold and operated briefly under the name American China Company. The plant closed in 1983.

Sequoia Ware and Berkeley are two trademarks used by American Bisque, the former used on items sold in gift shops, and the latter found on products sold through chain stores. Cookie jars produced by this company are marked "ABC" inside blocks.

**References:** Susan and Al Bagdade, *Warman's American Pottery and Porcelain*, Wallace-Homestead, 1994; Mary Jane Giacomini, *American Bisque*, Schiffer Publishing 1994.

**Periodical:** *Pottery Collectors Express*, P.O. Box 221, Mayview, MO 64071.

Bank
Elephant, gray, standing on circus platform, 6" h............................. 85.00
Popeye.................................. 250.00

Clothes Sprinkler, figural, cat, marbles for eyes ................................... 165.00
Cookie Jar
After School Cookies, bell in lid, chipped .................................. 55.00
Baby Elephant, bonnet .......... 165.00
Bear with Cookie, mkd "USA" ................................................. 80.00
Beehive, 11-3/4" h, mkd "USA" ................................................ 165.00
Coffee Pot, 9-1/2" h, mkd "USA" ................................................ 110.00
Cookie Truck, 11-1/2" h, mkd "USA 744" ........................................ 195.00
Dino, with golf clubs .................. 900.00
Donald Duck, standing.............. 385.00
Dutchboy with sailboat ............. 165.00
Jack-in-the-Box, 12" h, imp "USA" on back................................... 195.00
Kitten, 11-3/4" h, mkd "USA"........ 165.00
Milk Wagon, 9" h, mkd "USA 740" ................................................ 165.00
Rudolph the Red Nosed Reindeer ................................................ 650.00
Toy Soldier, Sentry, 11-1/4" h, mkd "USA 743" ....................................... 225.00
Yogi Bear ................................... 725.00
Food Mold
Fish, 10" l, white, red trim, ring for hanging, incised "ABC" .......... 15.00
Set, hand painted, round, red and white, rings for hanging, set of four, incised "ABC" ........................ 70.00
Pitcher, chick, gold trim ............... 48.00
Planter
Duck, wearing flower hat ......... 30.00
Flamingo, 7-1/4" x 10" l ............ 65.00
Lamb, 4-3/4" h, 6-1/2" l ............. 8.00
Rooster, 5" h............................. 24.00

**Bank, plaster, hand painted, incised "copyright ABCO" on back, coin slot between ears, rubber stopper, 8-5/8" h, $50.**

Salt and Pepper Shakers, pr, churn ................................................65.00
Teapot, Red Rose, 6-1/2" h, gold trim ................................................55.00
Vase
  6" h, white heart, blue bow.......28.00
  7-1/4" h, green, fern frond handles ................................................20.00

# Animation Art

**Collecting Hints:** A very specific vocabulary is used when discussing animation cels. The differences between a Courvoisier, Disneyland, master, key production, printed, production, and studio background can mean thousands of dollars in value. Sotheby's and Christie's East, the two major auction houses selling animation art, do not agree on terminology. Carefully read the glossary section of any catalog.

A second of film requires more than 20 animation cels. The approximate number of cels used to make that cartoon can be determined by multiplying the length of a cartoon in minutes times 60 times 24. The question that no one seems to be asking as prices reach the ten- and hundred-thousand dollar level is "What happened to all the other animation cels?" Vast quantities of cels are in storage.

There is no doubt that Walt Disney animation cels are king. Nostalgia, legend, and hype drive pricing more than historical importance or workmanship. The real bargains in the field lie outside the Disney material.

Although animation art has a clearly established track record, it also is an area that has been subject to manipulation, representational abuse, and shifting nostalgia trends. It is not the place for the casual collector.

Avoid limited-edition serigraphs—color prints made by silk screening. Although they may appear to be animation cels, they are not.

**History:** According to film historians, the first animated cartoon was Winsor McCay's 1909 "Gertie the Dinosaur." Early animated films were largely the work of comic strip artists. The invention of the celluloid process (a "cel" is an animation drawing on celluloid) is attributed to Earl Hurd. Although the technique reached perfection under animation giants such as Walt Disney and Max Fleischer, individuals such as Ub Iwerks, Walter Lantz, and Paul

Terry—along with studios such as Columbia, Charles Mints and Screen Gems, MGM, Paramount/Famous Studios, UPA, and Warner Brothers—did pioneering work.

Leonard Maltin's *Of Mice and Magic: A History of American Animated Cartoons* (A Plume Book/New American Library, revised and updated edition, 1987) is an excellent source for historic information.

**References:** Jeff Lotman, *Animation Art: The Early Years*, Schiffer Publishing, 1995, —, *Animation Art at Auction: Since 1994;* Schiffer Publishing, 1998; —, *Animation Art: The Later Years*, Schiffer Publishing, 1996; Jerry Weist, *Original Comic Art*, Avon Books, 1992.

**Periodicals:** *Animation Film Art*, P.O. Box 25547, Los Angeles, CA 90025; *Animation Magazine*, 4676 Admiralty Way, Ste. 210, Marina Del Ray, CA 90292; *Animato!*, P.O. Box 1240, Cambridge, MA 02238; *In Toon!*, P.O. Box 217, Gracie Station, New York, NY, 10028; *Storyboard/The Art of Laughter*, 80 Main St., Nashua, NH 03060.

**Collectors' Club:** Greater Washington Animation Collectors Club, 12423 Hedges Run Dr. #184, Lake Ridge, VA 22192.

**Museums:** Baltimore Museum of Art, Baltimore, MD; International Museum of Cartoon Art, Boca Raton, FL; Museum of Cartoon Art, Rye Brook, NY; Museum of Modern Art, New York, NY; Walt Disney Archives, Burbank, CA.

Donald Duck, orig layout drawing, Donald swinging ring on his finger, wearing straw hat....................650.00
Fat Albert and the Cosby Kids, Filmation Studios, 1970s, tempera background sheet, framed............950.00
Fred and Wilma Flintstone, Barney and Betty Rubble, orig production cel, multi-cel set mounted on full celluloid, framed, glazed, 16" x 19" ................................................450.00
Hercules, Walt Disney Productions, Pain running, wearing sandals, 12-1/2" x 17" sheet size, 1997, certificate of authenticity, matted................500.00
Jungle Book, Walt Disney, 1967, Baloo, 6-1/2" x 4", gouache on celluloid, cel trimmed, unframed ................900.00
Ludwig Von Drake, Walt Disney Studios, artist's field paper, 2-3/4" x 1-1/2" image size, matted ...................75.00
Peanuts, Charles Schulz, blue and colored graphite drawings on artist's field paper, 1980s
  Sally, 2-3/4" x 1-1/2" image size, matted....................................75.00

Snoopy, 3-1/2" x 2" image size, matted............................................45.00
Pink Panther, Depatie-Freleng Studio, gouache, 10-1/2" x 12-1/2", c1960 ................................................125.00
Pooh and Tigger, Walt Disney Productions, seri-cel, 5-1/2" x 7-1/2", Walt Disney silver seal...................145.00
Robin Hood, Walt Disney Productions, Sir Hiss, 10" x 13" sheet size, orig Walt Disney sticker, matted....480.00
Sleeping Beauty, Walt Disney Productions, King Hubert, 7-1/2" x 4-1/2" image size, matted ..................75.00
Smurf, 8" x 10" sheet size, matted ................................................40.00
Simpsons, Bart, dopey expression, black and orange pencil drawing, 4-1/2" x 1-1/2" image size, matted ................................................25.00
Sword in the Stone, Walt Disney Productions, production cel, #55 in sequence, Sir Ector drinking wine, 7" x 6-1/2" image size, certificate of authenticity, matted..................65.00
Sylvester, orig production cel, gouache on full celluloid, accompanied by orig layout drawing, c1960, 17" x 32", mounted, framed ...................450.00
Teenage Mutant Ninja Turtle, MWS Inc., 9-1/2" x 7-1/2" image size, framed ................................................65.00
Tom and Jerry Golfing, Turner Home Entertainment seal, 11" x 14" sheet size, matted ...........................115.00

# Autographs

**Collecting Hints:** The condition and content of letters and documents significantly influences value. Signatures should be crisp, clear, and located so that they do not detract from the rest of the item. Whenever possible, obtain a notarized statement of authenticity, especially for pieces worth more than $100.

Forgeries abound; copying machines compound the problem. Furthermore, many signatures of political figures (especially presidents), movie stars, and sports heroes were signed by machine or by a secretary rather than by the individuals themselves. Photographically reproduced signatures resemble originals. Use a good magnifying glass or microscope to check all signatures.

Presentation material, something marked "To_____," has less value than a non-presentation item. The presentation personalizes the piece and often restricts interest to someone with the same name.

There are autograph mills throughout the country run by people who write to noteworthy individuals requesting their signatures on large groups of material. They in turn sell this material on the autograph market. Buy an autograph of a living person only after the most careful consideration and examination.

**History:** Autograph collecting is an old established tradition. Early letters were few; hence, treasured in private archives. Municipalities, churches, and other institutions maintained extensive archives to document past actions.

Autograph collecting became fashionable during the 19th century. However, early collectors focused on the signatures alone, clipping off the signed portion of a letter or document. Eventually collectors realized that the entire document was valuable.

The popularity of movie stars and sports, rock 'n' roll, and television personalities brought about changes in the way autographs were collected. Fans pursued these individuals with autograph books, programs, and photographs. Collectors requested that autographs be signed on everything imaginable. Realizing the value of their signatures and the speculation that occurs, modern stars and heroes are often unwilling to sign material under certain circumstances.

**References:** Mark Allen Baker, *All Sport Autograph Guide*, Krause Publicties, 1994; —, *Collector's Guide to Celebrity Autographs*, Krause Publications, 1996; —, *Standard Guide to Collecting Autographs,* Krause Publications, 1998; Kevin Martin, *Signatures of the Stars*, Antique Trader Books, 1998; Kenneth W. Rendell, *Forging History: The Detection of Fake Letters and Documents*, University of Oklahoma Press, 1994; —, *History Comes to Life*, University of Oklahoma Press, 1996; George Sanders, Helen Sanders, and Ralph Roberts, *1994 Sanders Price Guide to Autographs*, No. 3, Alexander Books, 1994; —, *Sanders Price Guide to Sports Autographs*, Scott Publishing, 1993.

**Periodicals:** *All-Star Celebrity Address Book*, P.O. Box 1566, Apple Valley, CA 92307; *Autograph Collector*, 510-A S Corona Mall, Corona, CA 91720; *Autograph Dealer's Price Guide*, P.O. Box 63, Umpqua, CA 97486; *Autograph Quarterly & Buyers Guide*, P.O. Box 55328, Stockton, CA 95205; *Autograph Review*, 305 Carlton Rd., Syracuse, NY 13207; *Autograph Times*, 2302 N. 44th St.,

#225, Phoenix, AZ 85008; *Autographs & Memorabilia*, P.O. Box 24, Coffeyville, KS 67337; *Celebrity Access Directory*, 20 Sunnyside Ave., Ste. A241, Mill Valley, CA 94921; *Collector*, P.O. Box 225, Hunter, NY 12442; *John L. Raybin's Baseball Autograph News*, 527 Third Ave., #294-A, New York, NY 10016.

**Collectors' Clubs:** Manuscript Society, 350 N. Niagara St., Burbank, CA 91505; Universal Autograph Collectors Club, P.O. Box 6181, Washington, DC 20044.

**Libraries:** New York Public Library, New York, NY; Pairpoint Morgan Library, New York, NY.

### Autograph Letters Signed (ALS)

Fred Astaire, hand-written three page letter, c1958, accompanied by 8" x 10" black and white still from 1951 MGM movie "Royal Wedding" ............................................. 165.00
Doris Day, letter sgd ..................... 45.00
Marlene Dietrich, ten autographed letters to Stanley Hall, 1966 to 1978 ............................................. 165.00
Diana Dors, personal stationery, 1959 ............................................. 95.00
Edsel B. Ford fund-raising letter, typed, 8" x 10" ..................................... 85.00
Katherine Hepburn, 1 page 8" x 10", Oct. 18, 1973, typed, thank you note, orig envelope ......................... 185.00
Burl Ives ..................................... 38.00
Vivan Leigh, letter, sgd, personal stationery, 1959 ............................. 650.00
Peter Sellers, letter, sgd, personal stationery, 1959 ......................... 125.00
Gene Stratton Porter, author and poet, 1919, 8" x 10" ......................... 200.00

### Cards Signed (CS)

Louie Belson, real photo postcard, autographed 1948, several other signatures ............................... 65.00
Barbara Billingsley, 3" x 5" black and white card, sgd "Love, Barbara Billingsley" ................................... 8.00
Humphrey Bogart, framed with Warner Bros. promotional photo......... 820.00
Lloyd Bridges, 3" x 5" white card, inscribed "Best Wishes David, Lloyd Bridges" ................................... 35.00
Barbara Bush, First Lady, Blair House stationery, 3" x 2" ..................... 60.00
Gloria DeHaven, 3" x 5" black and white card, sgd "Best of luck always, Gloria DeHaven"........................... 20.00
Elinor Donahue, 3" x 5" card, sgd "Warmest regards Elinor Donahue" ............................................. 7.50
James Garner, black and white postcard......................................... 24.00
Dwayne Hickman, 3" x 5", sgd "To David, Best wishes, Dwayne Hickman "Dobie"............................... 5.00
Wally Schirra, 3" x 5" white card ............................................. 25.00

**Astronaut Donald K. Slayton, color photo, US Govt. Printing Office, 1974, $15.**

George Takei, Star Trek, 3" x 2" white card, dark blue Star Trek imprinted at top, blue Enterprise image ...... 75.00

### Document Signed (DS)

Julie Andrews, two sgd checks ............................................. 82.00
Thomas A. Edison, minutes from Board of Directors meeting, 12" x 16", 2 pgs, c1920......................... 295.00
Andrew Jackson, President, land grant to Palmer Eliot, IL, Jan. 3, 1832 60.00
David Niven, two sgd checks..... 164.00
Nolan Ryan, *Legends Magazine* cover ............................................. 150.00
Rod Sterling, writer and producer, bank check, June 1968 ................. 295.00
Mae West, theater playbill, 6" x 9" program for stage production of Kenley Players production of "Come On Up, Ring Twice," July 7, 1952, 12 pgs ............................................. 75.00
Eula Whitehouse, book, *Texas Flowers in Natural Colors,* first edition, 1936 ............................................. 40.00

### Equipment

Hank Aaron, baseball bat........... 120.00
Richie Ashburn, baseball cap...... 40.00
Yogi Berra, baseball cap.............. 50.00
Earl Campbell, football ............... 125.00
Jim Carey, hockey puck .............. 32.00
Jim Colbert, golf club .................. 75.00
Andre Dawson, baseball ............. 25.00
Steve Ellington, golf cap, US Open ............................................. 35.00
Reggie Jackson, baseball cap..... 10.00
Jim Kelly, football....................... 125.00
Joe Namath, official Jets helmet ............................................. 400.00
Ken Schroy, football.................... 80.00
Payne Stewart, golf cap .............. 45.00
Lawrence Taylor, official Giants helmet ............................................. 425.00

## First Day Covers (FDC)

Fred Astaire and Ginger Rogers, honoring the 50th Anniversary of Talking Pictures, canceled Hollywood, 1977 ........................................ 195.00

Janis Paige, Palmomar Mt. Observatory, postmarked 1948 ..................... 10.00

Prince Rainer, honoring Great American Presidents, Washington, Lincoln, FDR, and Eisenhower, canceled 1966, blue ink signature ........... 50.00

Chuck Yeager and Scott Crossfield, honoring Glenn Curtiss, canceled NY, 1980 ..................................... 50.00

## Photograph Signed (PS)

Tray Aikmen, black and white glossy, 11" x 14" ................................. 48.00

Muhammad Ali, black and white glossy, 8" x 10" .................................... 45.00

Gillian Anderson, color promo photo, 8" x 10", X-Files filing cabinet ....... 90.00

Michael Andretti, black and white glossy, 8" x 10" ........................... 30.00

Barbara Babcock, black and white photo, inscribed "Jeff, Peace, Barbara Babcock," slight crease one corner ................................................ 15.00

Ralph Bellamy, black and white photo, sgd "Ralph Bellamy 20/20" ...... 45.00

Nicholas Cage, black and white glossy, 8" x 10" .................................... 55.00

Cher, black and white glossy, 8" x 10" ............................................. 50.00

Eric Clapton, black and white glossy, 8" x 10" .................................... 55.00

Cindy Crawford, black and white glossy, 8" x 10" ........................... 55.00

Al DeNiro, black and white glossy, 8" x 10" ............................................ 55.00

Cecile Dion, black and white glossy, 8" x 10" .................................... 45.00

Joe DiMaggio, black and white glossy, 11" x 14" ................................. 175.00

Bob Feller, black and white promo action photo, 8" x 10" ............... 12.00

WC Fields, promotional 10" x 13" photo, as Poppy, playing cigar box cello ................................................ 90.00

George Foreman, black and white glossy photograph, 8" x 10" ..... 40.00

Vince Gill, black and white glossy, 8" x 10" ............................................ 35.00

Bob Hope, black and white, 8" x 10", inscribed "To David Stratton Thanks for the memory, Bob Hope" ..... 75.00

Helen Hunt, black and white glossy, 8" x 10" .................................... 50.00

Spike Jones, radio photo, sgd ...... 75.00

Winona Judd, black and white glossy, 8" x 10" .................................... 40.00

Jack Kemp, black and white glossy, 16" x 20" .................................... 60.00

Carol Lawrence, black and white photo, inscribed "God Love Ya Jeff! Carol Lawrence" ................................. 15.00

Al Martino, black and white promo, 8" x 20", inscribed "To Jeff, with best wishes, Al Martino" ............... 10.00

Virginia Mayo, black and white glossy, 8" x 10",. Inscribed "To George, Best wishes, Virginia Mayo," slight crease ................................................ 25.00

Joe McCarthy, black and white newspaper clipping photo sgd ............ 40.00

Joe Montana, black and white glossy, 8" x 10" .................................... 50.00

Jack Nicholson, black and white glossy, 8" x 10" ........................... 60.00

Greg Norman, black and white glossy, 8" x 10" ........................... 30.00

Arnold Palmer, Arnold, black and white glossy, 8" x 10" ......................... 50.00

Sam Rice, black and white newspaper clipping photo ......................... 40.00

Ginger Rogers, black and white photograph, 8" x 10" ..................... 70.00

Ruth Roland, silent film star, wedding photo, sgd, inscribed ............... 45.00

Ken Schrader, color photo, 8" x 10" ................................................ 20.00

Spielberg, Scheider, Dreyfuss, Jaws, black and white glossy, 8" x 10" ................................................ 140.00

Rod Stewart, Rod, black and white glossy, 8" x 10" ......................... 65.00

Shania Twain, black and white glossy, 8" x 10" .................................... 60.00

Al Unser Jr., color photo, 8" x 10" ..... 30.00

Bruce Willis, black and white glossy, 8" x 10" .................................... 55.00

Tiger Woods, black and white glossy, 8" x 10" .................................... 55.00

John Young, color astronaut photo ................................................ 125.00

# Aviation Collectibles

**Collecting Hints:** This field developed in the 1980s and is now firmly established. The majority of collectors focus on personalities, especially Charles Lindbergh and Amelia Earhart. New collectors are urged to look at the products of airlines, especially those items related to the pre-jet era.

**History:** Most of the income for the first airlines in the United States came from government mail-carrying subsidies. The first non–Post Office Department flight to carry mail was in 1926 between Detroit and Chicago. By 1930, there were 38 domestic and five international airlines operating in the United States. A typical passenger load was ten. After World War II, four-engine planes with a capacity of 100 or more passengers were introduced.

The jet age was launched in the 1950s. In 1955, Capitol Airlines used British-made turboprop airliners for domestic service. In 1958, National Airlines began domestic jet passenger service. The giant Boeing 747 went into operation in 1970 as part of the Pan American fleet. The Civil Aeronautics Board, which regulates the airline industry, ended control of routes in 1982 and fares in 1983.

Major American airlines include American, Delta, Northwest, Pan Am, TWA, United, and USAir. There are many regional lines as well. As a result of deregulation, new airlines are forming; some lasting longer than others.

**References:** *Air Transport Label Catalog,* Aeronautica & Air Label Collectors Club of Aerophilatelic Federation of America, n.d.; Stan Baumwald, *Junior Crew Member Wings,* published by author, n.d..

**Periodical:** *Airliners,* P.O. Box 52-1238, Miami, FL 33152.

**Collectors' Clubs:** Aeronautica & Air Label Collectors Club, P.O. Box 1239, Elgin, IL 60121; C.A.L./N-X-211 Collectors Society, 226 Tioga Ave., Bensenville, IL 60106; Gay Airline Club, P.O. Box 69A04, West Hollywood, CA 90069; World Airline Historical Society, 3381 Apple Tree Lane, Erlanger, KY 41018.

## Commercial

Book, *Official Guide of Commercial Aviation,* in Spanish, shows schedules of all companies operating in South America (Aerolineas Argentinas, Panair, Panagra, Pan American, Air France, etc., November 1957 ................................................ 25.00

Bowl, Delta Airlines, for VIP International flights, Mayer China ................. 20.00

Cup and Saucer, Delta Airlines, for VIP International flights, Mayer China ................................................ 25.00

Dinner Plate, Delta Airlines, for VIP International flights, Mayer China ................................................ 20.00

Cigar Cutter, pocket, Pan Am, 1901 ................................................ 70.00

Figure, Air-India, 4-1/2" h, painted plastic statuette, green flying carpet base, traditional red, white, and blue striped turban, green clasp, red jacket, white harem trousers, curled red shoes, orig label "Ameya Industries/Bombay, India," c1970 ......................... 35.00

Napkin Holder, American Airlines, 1" h, 1-1/2" d, open ended metal clasp, center with "AA" soaring eagle symbol, c1930 .................................. 15.00

Place Setting, United, china ......... 42.00

Playing Cards, 3/4" x 2-1/4" x 3-1/2" box, c1960-80

American Airlines, US mail plane ................................................ 10.00

Delta Airlines, white pyramid design ................................................ 8.00

Eastern/Ryder, text with logo design ................................................ 8.00

Ozark, snow covered Rockies design ................................................ 10.00

TWA Collectors Series, Douglas DC-9, 1966 .................................... 12.00

Postcard, unused
    Aerolineas Argentinas, 1950s, Carrasco Airport, Montevideo Uruguay, black and white .............. 10.00
    Air Canada preparing for takeoff, oversized .................................... 6.00
    Air Transat, Lockheed L1011, color, oversized ............................... 6.00
    Alitalia, Caravelle III S.E. 210, radio print on back ............................ 8.00
    Eastern, Constellation, color ...... 6.00
    Iberia, Spanish airline, airline issued ............................................... 6.00
    KLM Connie, Lockheed Super constellation 1049 G, airline issued .............................................. 8.00
    KLM, Douglas DC-6b, airline issued, slight crease ............................. 7.00
    Lufthansa DC10, airline issued.... 5.00
    Pan American, Super 6 Clipper, color ................................................... 8.00
    Pan American World Airways, advertising ............................................. 5.00
    Piedmont Airlines. Boeing 737-300 series, color, oversized ............. 6.00
    Pluna, Uruguayan Airline, Boeing 737, radio club .......................... 6.00
    Trans-Canada Airlines, airline issued, Viscount at Windsor Airport, Windsor, Ontario, Canada ......... 8.00
Stand-Up Display, TWA Flight Attendant, 1960s ............................. 45.00
Stewardess Wings, United Airlines, 2-1/2" x 3-1/4" orig black and white card, 2" w silver accent wings, red, white, and blue center logo, c1960, unused ........................................ 20.00
Toy Car, TWA Airlines, airport service car, tin friction, 11" l ................ 120.00
Toy Plane
    Corvair Inter-continental Jet, friction, 14" l, MIB ................................ 145.00
    Pan Am Boeing 747, battery operated, automatic stop and go auction, see thru cockpit, flashing jet engines, realistic sound, 13" l, MIB ......................................... 225.00
    Pan Am Boeing 747, friction, 7" l, MIB ......................................... 225.00
    Royal Dutch Airlines, KLM Corvair jet, friction, 14" l ...................... 95.00
Travel Bag, Pan Am World ............ 10.00

### General

Ashtray, Aviation Building, 1939 NY World's Fair, scene in center, ceramic ..................................... 30.00
Book, *Bombardment Aviation,* Keith Ayling, RAF pilot, copyright 1944, Military Service Publishing Co., 234 pgs, hard cover ........................... 15.00
Ashtray, Naval Aviation Museum, Pensacola, Florida, figural airplane, souvenir decal, gold lettering, incised "Japan," 7" l .................. 24.00
Cigarette Lighter, chrome plated, desk type, propeller, lighter compartment in wing, c1937.......................... 95.00
Comic Book, *Jim Ray's Aviation Sketchbook,* No. 2, 1946, ink stain on front cov, wear, yellowing, 64 pgs...... 18.00

Game, Wings, The Air Mail Game, Parker Brothers, 4" x 5-1/2", flying Air Mail plane, set of 99 cards, orig instruction sheet, copyright 1928 ................................................. 25.00
Magazine Tear Sheet, Bendix Aviation Corp, 1947, Saturday Evening Post ................................................... 2.00
Gum Cards, Aviation Pioneers, Hugo Junkers, Otto Lilienthal, Orville Wright, biographies in German, set of three ...................................... 15.00
Palm Puzzle, silvered rim, plastic cover, full color paper playing surface, Vosin box aircraft in flight, inscription "1908 80 Kahen/Frankreich," German, c1970 ............................. 35.00
Paperweight, copper colored metal, Sphere and Trylon, orange tag with plane on each end reads "Aviation Bldg, N.Y.W.F." ......................... 95.00
Plate, Martin Aviation, Vernon Kilns, brown illus of 5 aircraft, titles, c1940, 10-1/2" d ............................... 55.00
Postcard, unused
    Friendship Airport, Baltimore, MD, textured paper, tinted art, C. T. Art-Colortone, mid-1950s, 3-1/2" x 5-1/2", unused, set of four .................... 18.00
    Zeppelin flying over Montevideo, Uruguay, black and white ........ 28.00
Teaspoon, Aviation Building, NY World's Fair, 1939 ............................... 15.00
Sign, Texaco Aviation, enameled porcelain .......................................... 20.00

### Personalities

Autograph Charles Lindbergh, on Franc ................................................ 500.00
Book
    *Alone,* account of Richard Byrd in Antarctica, 1934, autographed .............................................. 125.00
    *That's My Story,* Douglas Corrigan, published by E P Dutton & Co.,

**Sign, Imperial Tobacco Co., Wills White Star, multicolored, cardboard back, 7-1/2" x 10", $65.**

1938, 5-1/2" x 8-1/4", hard cover, 221 pgs, 56 sepia photos .............. 20.00
Christmas Light Bulb, 3" h, Charles Lindbergh wearing aviation uniform ................................................ 65.00
Film, Lindbergh's Paris Flight, Pathex Motion Pictures ....................... 50.00
Game, Howard Hughes Game, 11" x 17" x 3", Family Games, Inc., thick brown plastic box designed as attaché case, orig cardboard label and shrink wrap, copyright 1972 .. 100.00
Money Clip, Spirit of St Louis, silvered brass, spring clip, finely detailed illus of Lindbergh aircraft, Anson Co ................................................ 125.00
Pinback Button
    7/8" d, Welcome Lindbergh, blue and white ............................... 75.00
    1-1/4" d
        Atlantic, Newfoundland to Wales, Amelia Earhart and passengers Lou Gordon and William Stultz, 1928 .................................. 325.00
        Bond Bread, Spirit of St Louis, dark red, black, and white, c1930 ......................................... 40.00
        Captain Lindbergh, black and white photo ......................... 25.00
        General Balbo portrait, sepia, leader of Italian air fleet visitation to Chicago World's Fair, 1933 ........................................... 50.00
    Welcome Wiley Post, black and white, aviator with patch over blinded eye, 1930s ............... 150.00
    1-3/8" d, red, white, and blue litho, photo of Lindbergh, eagle, Spirit of St Louis, Statue of Liberty, and Eiffel Tower, American flags........... 120.00
    2" d, Orville Wright, black, white, and buff litho, "Orville Wright-American/ First Man To Fly," 1930s ....... 20.00
Photograph, 31" x 41", Wright Bros. first flight, 1903, framed ............... 165.00
Plate, 8-1/2" sq, Lindbergh commemorative, yellow ground, multicolored transfer center, marked "Limoges China, Sterling, Golden Glow". 35.00
Pocket Mirror, 2-1/4" x 3-1/2", celluloid, Lindbergh and plane in flight, maroon and white ................. 125.00
Postcard, 3-3/4" x 5-1/2", air mail, black and white, issued to welcome Lindbergh, Milwaukee, August, 1927, back text endorses air mail ..... 30.00
Sheet Music, 9-1/4" x 12-1/4", *Lindy, Lindy,* Wolfe Gilbert and Abel Baer, 1927 copyright, black, white, and orange cov............................... 25.00
Tapestry, Charles Lindbergh, large center portrait, Spirit of St. Louis on left flying over New York skyscrapers, Statue of Liberty, right with Spirit of St. Louis flying over Paris, Eiffel Tower, 50" x 20", made in France ................................................ 400.00

# Avon Collectibles

**Collecting Hints:** Avon collectibles encompass a wide range of objects, including California Perfume Company bottles, decanters, soaps, children's items, jewelry, plates, and catalogs. Another phase of collecting focuses on Avon Representatives' and Managers' awards.

Avon products are well marked with one of four main marks. There is a huge quantity of collectibles from this company; collectors should limit their interests. Although they may be harder to find, do include some foreign Avon collectibles. New items take longer to increase in value than older items. Do not change the object in any way; this destroys the value.

**History:** David H. McConnell founded the California Perfume Co. in 1886. He hired saleswomen, a radical concept for that time. They used a door-to-door technique to sell their first product, "Little Dot," a set of five perfumes; thus was born the "Avon Lady," although by 1979 they numbered more than one million.

In 1929, California Perfume Co. became the Avon Company. The tiny perfume company grew into a giant corporation. Avon bottles began attracting collector interest in the 1960s.

**References:** Bud Hastin, *Bud Hastin's Avon Products & California Perfume Co. Collector's Encyclopedia*, 13th ed., published by author (P.O. Box 9868, Kansas City, MO 64134), 1994; —, *Bud Hastin's Avon Collectible Price Guide*, published by author (P.O. Box 9868, Kansas City, MO 64134), 1991.

**Periodical:** *Avon Times*, P.O. Box 9868, Kansas City, MO 64134.

**Collectors' Clubs:** National Assoc. of Avon Collectors, Inc., P.O. Box 7006, Kansas City, MO 64113; Shawnee Avon Bottle Collectors Club, 1418 32nd NE, Canton, OH 44714; Sooner Avon Bottle Collectors Club, 6119 S. Hudson, Tulsa, OK 74136; Western World Avon Collectors Club, P.O. Box 23785, Pleasant Hills, CA 94523.

**Museums:** Hagley Museum and Library, Wilmington, DE; Nicholas Avon Museum, Clifton, VA.

**Reproduction Alert.**

### Awards and Representative Gifts

Necklace, sterling silver, acorn, velvet pouch, Tiffany box and card, 1980 .................................................. 90.00
Order Book, 1968, Charisma, red pen .................................................. 7.50

Pin, Manager's, diamond crown, guard, 1961 .................................. 175.00
Plate, For Avon Representatives Only, 1977 .................................... 5.00
Tie Tac, telephone, gold tone, 1981 .................................................. 15.00

### California Perfume Company

Bath Salts, Ariel, ribbed glass jar, 1903 .................................. 135.00
Perfume, White Rose, clear glass jar, orig neck ribbon, 1918 .......... 145.00
Talcum, California Rose, 3-1/2 oz, 1921 .................................. 115.00
Toilet Water, Lily of the Valley, 2 oz, ribbed glass jar, 1923 .......... 115.00

### Children's Items

Bank, Humpty Dumpty, 5" h, ceramic, 1982 ................................ 18.50
Bubble Bath
  Freddy the Frog, mug, 5 oz, white glass, red top, 1970 ............ 9.00
  Mickey Mouse, plastic, 1969 ..... 7.50
  Snoopy, snow flyer, plastic, 1973 .................................................. 6.00
Comb and Brush Set, Hot Dog, yellow and red plastic, 1975 ............ 5.00

**Charisma Cologne, Rosepoint bell, cranberry colored glass base, gold colored plastic handle, 4 oz, 7-3/4" h, $8.50.**

Nail Brush, Happy Hippo, 3" l, pink, 1973 .......................................... 2.50
Set
  Cowboy Set, white box, two red leatherette cowboy cuffs, cream hair dressing, toothpaste, and toothbrush, c1950 .......................... 50.00
  Hair Trainer, 6 oz bottle, blue cap, red and white label, plastic comb, 1967 .................................... 25.00
Shampoo, Jet Plane, red, white, and blue plastic tube, white plastic wings, 1965 .............................. 3.00
Soap
  Artistocat Kitten Soap, orig box, 1970s ...................................... 65.00
  Christmas Children, girl holds doll, boy holds toy rocking horse, 1983 .................................................. 9.00
Soakie, Batmobile, MIB ................ 48.00
Toothpaste, Toofie, 3-1/2 oz, white tube, raccoon, pink cap, pink toothbrush, 1968 .......................................... 4.50

### Men's Items

After Shave, figural
  Golf Cart, green glass, 5-1/2" l, 1973 .................................................. 5.00
  Guns, set of seven, MIB .......... 35.00
  Pony Express, brown glass, copper man, 1971 ................................. 6.00
  US Mail Truck, plastic and glass, red, white, and blue ................... 6.50
Body Splash, tennis ball, 3 oz, light green flocking, green cap, 1977 .................................................. 4.00
Chess Piece, 3 oz, amber glass, silver colored top, each ....................... 6.00
Decanter, totem pole ..................... 7.00
Valet, maroon and ivory box, 4 oz after shave, shaving cream tube, talc can, smoker's tooth powder, 1945 .... 85.00

### Miscellaneous

Dish, Presidents Celebration Silverware, F. B. Rogers Silver Co., 7" d, 1-1/2" h, orig bag .................................. 20.00

**Charisma Foaming Bath Oil, white opaque clock shaped bottle, $15.**

Doll, Colorsnaps, Courtney, dated 1987, 14" h .......... 30.00
Egg Dish, cov, multicolored flowers and butterflies, gold trim, mkd "Produced Exclusively for Avon Products, Inc., Fine Porcelain decorated with 24K gold trim, Avon 1974 1979R .... 14.00
Figurine, Images of Hollywood series, MOB
   Dorothy, Wizard of Oz, 5-3/4" h, 1985 .......... 85.00
   Elvis Presley, 7" h, mkd "Copyright 1967 Elvis Presley Productions, Inc." .......... 125.00
   Scarlett O'Hara and Rhett Butler, 1985 .......... 135.00
   John Wayne, 7-1/2" h, 1985 ..... 90.00
Heritage Bowl, 1981, Independence Day, 6" d .......... 15.00
Plate
   Cardinal, North America Songbird, 1974, 10-1/2" d .......... 12.50
   Gentle Moments, Wedgwood, 1975, 8-1/2" d .......... 12.50

Sign, tin, Avon Polish for Boots & Leggings, 8" x 3" .......... 30.00

**Women's Items**

Bubble Bath, Christmas Sparkler, red, 1969 .......... 10.00
Candle
   Gingerbread House, brown and white, 1977 .......... 8.00
   Snowman, 5-1/2" h, white, green trim, 1981 .......... 5.00
Cologne
   Betsy Ross, glass, white, 1976 .......... 15.00
   Moodwind, dogwood flower design, paper label, 3" h .......... 15.00
Decanter, Skin So Soft, 5-3/4 oz, cylindrical carton, 1962 .......... 20.00
Foaming Bath Oil, cruet, amber, ribbed, 1973 .......... 6.00
Hand Lotion, rooster, 6 oz, milk glass, red plastic head, 1973 .......... 6.00
Lip Gloss, Lucky Penny, 2" d compact type, 1978 .......... 4.00

Perfume Glace, cameo ring, 1970, MIB .......... 20.00
Pomander
   Bountiful Harvest, spiced apple fragrance, orig box, c1973 .......... 25.00
   Heart, Wedgwood blue and white, plastic, white tassel, 1973 .......... 5.00
   Picture Hat, yellow and pink, plastic, yellow cord and tassel, 1975 ..... 5.00
   Pig, orig sticker .......... 5.00
Sachet, cream type
   Petit Point, purple glass base, cloth insert, 1 oz .......... 4.00
Salt Shaker, milk glass, yellow and white buttercups, yellow plastic cap, 1974 .......... 4.50
Set
   Fragrance Notes, writing paper, sealing wax, goldtone seal, 1977 .......... 7.00
   Winter Frolics Guest Soap, 6 oz, orig box, 1972 .......... 18.00
Thimble, porcelain, blue and red flowers, mkd "Avon" .......... 6.00

# B

# Banks, Still

**Collecting Hints:** The rarity of a still bank has much to do with determining its value. Common banks, such as tin advertising banks, have limited value. The Statue of Liberty cast iron bank by A. C. Williams sells in the hundreds of dollars. See Long and Pitman's book for a rarity scale for banks.

Banks are collected by maker, material, or subject. Subject is the most prominent, focusing on categories such as animals, food, mailboxes, safes, transportation, and world's fairs. There is a heavy crossover of buyers from other collectible fields.

Banks are graded by condition. Few banks are truly rare. Therefore, only purchase examples in very good to mint condition—those which retain all original paint and decorations.

**History:** Banks with no mechanical action are known as still banks. The first still banks were made of wood or pottery or from gourds. Redware and stoneware banks, made by America's early potters, are prized possessions of today's collectors.

Still banks reached their golden age with the arrival of the cast-iron bank. Leading manufacturing companies include Arcade Mfg. Co., J. Chein & Co., Hubley, J. & E. Stevens, and A. C. Williams. The banks often were ornately painted to enhance their appeal. During the cast-iron era, banks and other businesses used the still bank as a form of advertising.

The tin lithograph bank, again frequently a tool for advertising, was at its zenith between 1930 to 1955. The tin bank was an important premium, whether a Pabst Blue Ribbon beer can bank or a Gerber's Orange Juice bank. Most tin advertising banks resembled the packaging of the product.

Almost every substance has been used to make a still bank—die-cast white metal, aluminum, brass, plastic, glass, etc. Many of the early glass candy containers also converted to a bank after the candy was eaten. Thousands of varieties of still banks were made, and hundreds of new varieties appear on the market each year.

**References:** Don Cranmer, *Collectors Encyclopedia: Toys-Banks*, L-W Book Sales, 1986, 1994–95 value update; Don Duer, *Penny Banks Around the World*, Schiffer Publishing, 1997; Earnest and Ida Long and Jane Pitman, *Dictionary of Still Banks*, Long's Americana, 1980; Andy and Susan Moore, *Penny Bank Book*, Schiffer Publishing, 1984, 1994 value update; Tom and Loretta Stoddard, *Ceramic Coin Banks*, Collector Books, 1997; Vickie Stulb, *Modern Banks*, L-W Book Sales, 1997.

**Periodicals:** *Glass Bank Collector*, P.O. Box 155, Poland, NY 13431; *Heuser's Quarterly Collectible Bank Newsletter*, 508 Clapson Rd., P.O. Box 300, West Winfield, NY 13491.

**Collectors' Club:** Still Bank Collectors Club of America, 1456 Carson Ct., Homewood, IL 60430.

**Museum:** Margaret Woodbury Strong Museum, Rochester, NY.

**Reproduction Alert.**

### Ceramic

Barnaby Bee.................................. 50.00
Eagle, Emigrant Industrial Savings Bank.......................................... 18.00
Entenmann's Baker, unused ......... 40.00
ET.................................................. 25.00
Garfield, 6" h, 1981 ...................... 50.00
Pig, white body, pink rosebuds, green trim............................................ 25.00
Snoopy, figural
  Italy, c1969, 6" h...................... 75.00
  With Woodstock, 40th Anniversary, orig hang-tag, unused ............. 30.00
TP Thompson Products, Indian and Teepee, company logo on teepee, c1950, 5" x 6-1/4" x 6-3/4" ...... 140.00

### Metal

Atlas Storage, litho tin................... 24.00
Bank Building, litho tin, cupola, blue, red roof, c1870......................... 70.00
Barrel, litho tin, Happy Days, Chein
.................................................. 30.00
Cable Car, Citizens Federal Savings, orig key ................................... 27.50
Cat, cast iron, with ball ............... 175.00
Clock, cast iron, emb "A Money Saver," Arcade, c1910 ......................... 65.00
Elephant, cast iron, red blanket, wheels
.................................................. 90.00
Horse, cast iron, black, emb "Beauty"
.................................................. 65.00
Jack and Jill, diecast, dark bronze finish, holding pail, 5" h.............. 35.00
Lion, pot metal, Harris Trust and Savings, Chicago........................... 30.00
Lucas Paint, litho tin..................... 24.00
Ocean Spray Cranberry Juice, litho tin
.................................................. 24.00
Old Dutch Cleanser, litho tin......... 28.00
Pig, pot metal, painted gold, seated
.................................................. 65.00

**Elephant, painted cast iron, white shirt with red dots, blue pants, yellow hat with black trim, Hubley, 1930s, 3-7/8" h, $40.**

Rocking Horse, bronze finish, 4-1/2" h
.................................................. 30.00
Safe, cast iron, combination lock, emb "Security Safe Deposit," black.. 95.00
Superman, litho tin, dime register, opens at $5, DC Publications .. 85.00
Top Hat, cast iron, emb "Pass Around The Hat" ................................... 90.00

### Plastic and Vinyl

Barney Rubble, with bowling ball. 45.00
Bionic Man................................... 40.00
Bionic Woman............................... 42.00
Bozo the Clown, figural, 6" h ........ 35.00
Bullwinkle, 1973........................... 75.00
Bus, Greyhound Amercruiser, Jimson, Hong Kong, 10" l, MIB ............. 60.00
Esso Tiger.................................... 35.00
Garfield, Feed the Kitty, Enesco, MIB
.................................................. 45.00
Hitachi Panda .............................. 35.00
Hobo Joe, Dakin........................... 45.00
Hockhua Bank .............................. 35.00
Icee Bear..................................... 25.00
Ice Fire Jean Boy.......................... 35.00
Mr. Brasso.................................. 200.00
Nestle Chamyto ........................... 35.00
Political Senator, smiling reindeer, Taiwan ......................................... 50.00
Rountrees, adv ............................. 30.00
Shmoo, figural, 1948, orig card, cello wrapper .................................... 95.00
Snoopy, orange airplane, Flying Ace decals, Determined, © 1977 ... 45.00
Speedy Alka Seltzer ................... 150.00
Street Fighter, Capcom................. 25.00
Wonder Bread Fresh Guy, orig paper label and closure ................... 125.00

### Tin

Atomic, litho and diecut, Hobbyville Toy Co., 1950s, 10" h .................. 110.00
Mr. Zip, Ohio Art, mail box shape....70.00

# Barbershop and Beauty Collectibles

**Collecting Hints:** Many barbershop collectibles have a porcelain finish. If chipped or cracked, the porcelain is difficult, if not impossible, to repair.

Buy barber poles and chairs in very good condition or better. A good appearance is a key consideration.

Many old barbershops are no longer in business. The back rooms that often contained excellent display pieces are being dispersed and finding their way to the antiques and collectibles marketplace.

Collectors are also starting to appreciate the products used in early beauty parlors. Some collectors now include home beauty products in their collections. Watch for attractive packaging and endorsements by famous people.

**History:** The neighborhood barbershop was an important social and cultural institution during the 19th century and first half of the 20th century. Men and boys gathered to gossip, exchange business news, and check current fashions. "Girlie" magazines and comic books, usually forbidden at home, were available for browsing, as were adventure magazines and police gazettes.

In the 1960s, the number of barbershops dropped by half in the United States. Unisex shops broke the traditional men-only barrier. In the 1980s, several chains began running barber and hairdressing shops on a regional and national basis.

**References:** *Barbershop Collectibles*, L-W Book Sales, 1996; Lester Dequanine, *Razor Blade Banks: An Illustrated History and Price Guide*, published by author (39 W. Main St., Box 14, Meriden, CT 06451-4110); John Odell, *Digger Odell's Official Antique Bottle and Glass Collector Magazine Price Guide Series*, Vol. 1, published by author (1910 Shawhan Rd., Morrow, OH 45152), 1995; Robert Sloan and Steven Guarnaccis, *A Stiff Drink and a Close Shave*, Chronicle Books, 1995.

**Collectors' Clubs:** National Shaving Mug Collectors' Association, 320 S. Glenwood St., Allentown, PA 18104; Safety Razor Collectors' Guild, P.O. Box 885, Crescent City, CA 95531.

**Museum:** National Shaving and Barbershop Museum, Meriden, CT.

Advertising Trade Card, S. Kain for the Best Harrow, "Strict Attention to Business" as he cuts ear off patron, adv on back, 2-3/4" x 4-1/2" ........... 30.00
Antiseptic Container, 8" h, plated brass .................................................. 48.00
Barber Bottle
   Amber, white and blue florals, green leaves, orig top ...................... 100.00
   Milk Glass, sq, orig top ........... 75.00
Barber Chair, Koken, wood, emb filigree on sides, imitation leather reupholster, head rest, child's seat, 46" h to top of head rest, restored ...... 800.00
Blade Bank, figural
   Shaving Brush, ceramic, 6" h... 25.00
   Treasure Chest, Ever Ready adv, litho tin..................................... 25.00
Catalog
   Crown Hair Goods Co., New York, NY, 1920s, 48 pgs, 8" x 10-3/4", hair pieces, wigs, beauty parlor furniture .................................................. 82.00
   Theo. A. Kochs, Co., Chicago, IL, 1932, 16 pgs of professional chairs for beauty parlors, 8-1/2" x 11" .................................................. 65.00
Clippers, Andis, c1940 ............. 25.00
Comb Holder, Barbacide.............. 30.00
Counter Mat, 9" x 8", Wardonia Razor Blades, rubber ......................... 20.00
Display Case, West Hair Nets, 15" h, 6" w, 5" d, tiered display case, tin litho picture of flapper lady in touring car inside lid................................... 60.00
Facial Kit, Revlon, Moondrops at Home, orig packaging......................... 45.00
Flicker Pin, Clairol Hair Coloring, image changes between fleshtone face and hair image with slogan "Will She

**Battery Operated Toy, Barber Bear, orig box, 9-1/2" h, $495. Photo courtesy of McMasters Doll Auction.**

**Razor Blade Bank, World War II airplane, Bomb Tokyo, pottery, red, and green, "Buy A Bomber," 10-1/2" w wing span, 8" l, $35.**

Or Won't She" to full color image of blond, inscribed "Clairol Says She Will," early 1960s .................... 40.00
License, framed, c1960............... 10.00
Magazine Tear Sheet, Joe DiMaggio homers for Blue Brylcreem, from Men's Hairstylist and Barber's Journal, 1968 ................................... 4.00
Neck Duster, cherry handle.......... 30.00
Pole
   31-1/4" to top of porcelain, wall mounted, red and white striped glass, porcelain top and mount, heavy soiling, oxidation to aluminum ..... 550.00
   37" to top of porcelain, floor standing, porcelain, disassembled, glass cylinder, red and white insert, top globe missing, warped insert 375.00
   91" h, floor standing, porcelain, beige, green, red, and white, top cylinder rotates, round white top globe .......................................... 1,000.00
Razor, Burham Razor, 1-1/2" w, 3-3/4" l, 3/4" h, tin litho safety razor tin, orig razor, 3 blades in orig envelope, complete, unused, red ground, black lettering ....................... 160.00
Razor Tin
   Gem Cutlery Co., 5-3/8" h, 1-3/8" d, image of gentleman shaving on front, adv on back................. 300.00
   Yankee Blades, 1-1/4" w, 2-1/4" l, tin litho, eagles and center image of man shaving, red ground ...... 200.00
Shaving Brush, Every Ready, blue box, black celluloid handle, dark bristles, MIB ......................................... 15.00
Shaving Mug
   Ancient Order of United Workers, gold trim, monogram ............ 190.00
   Baker, delivery scene, gold trim .............................................. 225.00
   Floral, pink and yellow flowers, gold trim............................................ 70.00
   Horse, gold trim, maroon base .............................................. 185.00
   Milkman, milk wagon ............ 375.00
Shaving Mug Rack, 38" h, pine, holds 24 mugs................................. 200.00
Sign
   Barber, Bastian Bros., NY Allied Printing, Rochester, 15" x 6" ............ 155.00

Klondike Head Rub, 11" x 8-3/8", emb, blue letters, cardboard ... 22.00
Strop, 9" x 2-1/2" x 2", leather, 2-sided, mkd "Horse Hair Burl Finish" ..... 20.00
Tin
Sweet Georgia Brown Hair Dressing Pomade, Valmore Products Co., 1-1/8" d, black, white, and red, stylish male and female young blacks, instructions for use on back, c1930 .............. 35.00
Watkins Medical Co., Winona, MN, Watkins Tooth Powder, 5-1/2" h x 2-1/2" w, tin litho, cameo of woman on both sides .............................. 120.00

# Barbie

**Collecting Hints:** Never forget that a large quantity of Barbie dolls and related material has been manufactured. Because of this easy availability, only objects in excellent to mint condition with original packaging (also in very good or better condition) have significant value. If items show signs of heavy use, their value is probably minimal.

Collectors prefer items from the first decade of production. Learn how to distinguish a Barbie #1 doll from its successors. The Barbie market is one of subtleties. You must learn them.

Recently collectors have shifted their focus from the dolls themselves to the accessories. There have been rapid price increases in early clothing and accessories, with some of the prices bordering on speculation.

**History:** In 1945, Harold Matson (MATT) and Ruth and Elliott (EL) Handler founded Mattel. Initially the company made picture frames but became involved in the toy market when Elliott Handler began to make doll furniture from scrap material. When Harold Matson left the firm, Elliott Handler became chief designer and Ruth Handler principal marketer. In 1955, Mattel advertised its products on "The Mickey Mouse Club" and the company prospered.

In 1958, Mattel patented a fashion doll. The doll was named "Barbie" and reached the toy shelves in 1959. By 1960, Barbie's popularity was assured.

Development of a boyfriend for Barbie, named Ken after the Handlers' son, began in 1960. Over the years, many other dolls were added. Clothing, vehicles, room settings, and other accessories became an integral part of the line.

From September 1961 through July 1972, Mattel published a Barbie magazine. At its peak, the Barbie Fan Club was second only to the Girl Scouts as the largest girls' organization in the United States.

Barbie is now a billion-dollar baby, the first toy in history to reach this prestigious mark—that's a billion dollars per year, just in case you're wondering.

**References:** J. Michael Augustyniak, *Collector's Encyclopedia of Barbie Doll Exclusives and More*, Collector Books, 1997; —, *Thirty Years of Mattel Fashion Dolls, 1967 Through 1997: Identification and Value Guide*, Collector Books, 1998; A. Glenn Mandeville, *Doll Fashion Anthology & Price Guide*, 4th ed., Hobby House Press, 1993; Maria Martinez-Esguerra, *Collector's Guide to 1990s Barbie Dolls*, Collector Books, 1998; Marcie Melillo, *Ultimate Barbie Doll Book*, Krause Publications, 1996; Lorraine Mieszala, *Collector's Guide to Barbie Doll Paper Dolls*, Collector Books, 1997; Patrick C. Olds and Myrazona R. Olds, *Barbie Doll Years*, 2nd ed., Collector Books, 1997; Margo Rana, *Collector's Guide to Barbie Exclusives*, Collector Books, 1995; Jane Sarasohn-Kahn, *Contemporary Barbie*, Antique Trader Books, 1996; Beth Summers, *Decade of Barbie Dolls and Collectibles*, Collector Books, 1996; Marco Tosa, *Barbie: Four Decades of Fashion, Fantasy, and Fun*, Harry N. Abrams, 1998.

**Periodicals:** *Barbie Bazaar*, 5617 6th Ave., Kenosha, WI 53140; *Barbie Fashions*, 387 Park Ave. S., New York, NY 10016; *Barbie Talks Some More*, 19 Jamestown Dr., Cincinnati, OH 45241; *Collector's Corner*, 519 Fitzooth Dr., Miamisburg, OH 45342; *Miller's Price Guide & Collectors' Almanac*, West One Summer #1, Spokane, WA 99204.

Accessories, Skipper, shower cap, red ballet slippers, 2 mirrors, 2 combs, fitted case ................................ 15.00
Beauty Kit, 1961, MIB .................. 30.00
Bed, Starlight, canopy and bed linens, lamp, orig box, 1991, played-with condition ................................. 18.00
Book
*Barbie & Ken,* Random House, Mattel copyright, 1963, illus of Barbie and Ken talking on telephone on cover ....................................... 20.00
*Barbie's Fashion Success,* Mary Lou Maybee, 1962, 188 pgs .......... 20.00
Box
Barbie, for issue No. 850, brunette ponytail, 1962 ...................... 115.00
Ken, for issue No. 750, 1961 ... 115.00

Car, Corvette, 1968, MIB .............. 60.00
Case, Ken, vinyl, 1962 ................. 35.00
Christmas Ornament, Hallmark, 1993, red dress, 1st edition ............. 125.00
Colorforms Set ............................ 15.00
Cookbook, *Barbie's Easy-As-Pie Cookbook,* Cynthia Lawrence, 1964, 1st printing, 114 pgs ..................... 15.00
Diary, 1963, unused .................... 20.00
Doll
Barbie B Mine, ©1993 Mattel, MIB ......................................... 25.00
Blossom Beautiful Barbie, ©1992, Sears, orig outfit, shoes ...... 270.00
Camp Barbie Skipper, #11076, ©1993, Mattel, NRFB .............. 25.00
Dolls of the World Collection, 1st issue, ©1985 Mattel
German Barbie, MIB ........... 50.00
Greek Barbie, MIB .............. 40.00
Icelander, MIB ................... 50.00
Irish Barbie, MIB ............... 95.00
Japanese Barbie, MIB ........ 45.00
Korean Barbie, MIB ............ 50.00
Empress Bride, Bob Mackie, ©1992, orig cardboard shipping box .. 750.00
Fun to Dress Barbie, ©1988 Mattel, MIB ...................................... 25.00
Golden Dream Barbie, ©1980 Mattel, MIB ................................. 30.00
Graduation Barbie, Class of 1996, ©1995 Mattel .......................... 25.00
Great Shape Barbie, ©1983 Mattel, MIB ...................................... 35.00
Growing Hair Francie, 1970 ..... 75.00
Holiday Barbie, 10th Anniversary, African-American, ©1997 ........ 75.00
Holiday Dreams Barbie, Ready for Christmas, ©1994 Mattel, MIB .. 25.00

**Ponytail Barbie #4, blonde, 1960, $300.**

Hollywood Legends, Scarlett O'Hara, #13254, ©1994, NRFB 85.00

International Fashion Doll
  Canadian Barbie, 1st issue, ©1987 Mattel, MIB ............. 50.00
  Peruvian, 1st issue, ©1985 Mattel ........................................... 50.00

Island Fun Barbie, ©1907 Mattel, island wrap skirt, MIB ............. 25.00

Ken
  #1930, white pants, striped shirt, ©1979 ............................... 30.00
  #1932, beach cover-up, ©1980 ........................................... 25.00

My Fair Lady, #15501, pink dress, NRFB ...................................... 150.00

My First Barbie, ©1982 Mattel, MIB ................................................. 25.00

50th Anniversary Nascar, blond, ads for Hot Wheels, Coca-Cola, STP, Spree Racing, and Mac Tools, NRFB ................................................ 50.00

Porcelain Series, Barbie, stand, orig certificate, some wear to box
  Blue Rhapsody Barbie, No. 03220, 1986 ..................... 350.00
  Enchanted Evening Barbie, No. 0044986, 1987 ................. 200.00

Russell Stover Candies, ©1996, blond, multicolored dress, MIB.. 30.00

Skipper, ©1963 Mattel, Inc., orig red and white swimsuit ................... 60.00

Skooter, straight leg, lavender dress, attached slip, matching purse and shoes, cross necklace, played-with condition ..................................... 40.00

Solo In the Spotlight, #13820, ©1994 Mattel, NRFB ........................... 45.00

Sun Luvin Malibu Barbie, ©1978 Mattel, mirrored sunglasses, tan lines, MIB ..................................... 25.00

Teen Talk Barbie, #1612, ©1991 Mattel, Black, NRFB ...................... 55.00

Twist 'n' Turn Julia, 2 pc uniform, 1969 ........................................ 35.00

Skipper Twist 'n' Turn, ©1964 Mattel, flower girl outfit, white shoes, bent knee ........................................ 80.00

Walk Lively Barbie, ©1971, Mattel, NRFB ...................................... 175.00

Gift Set, Barbie, Stacie, and Skipper, 1991 Mattel, NRFB ................... 65.00

Lunch Box, World of Barbies, vinyl, 1972 ........................................ 30.00

Magazine, *Mattel Barbie Magazine*, March-April, 1969 ................... 15.00

Outfit
  Arabian Nights, #0874, 1963 ... 37.50
  Ballerina, #989, 1961 ............... 30.00
  Bride's Maid Dress, hat and lace leggings, tagged, played-with condition ................................................. 12.00
  Busy Gal, #981, 1958 ............... 42.00
  Coat, Francie, vinyl, tagged, 1965, loose ........................................ 25.00
  Coat, Ken, blue felt, double breasted, played-with condition ....... 22.00
  Coat, Skipper, pink, tagged, played-with condition ........................... 20.00
  Fur stole, 1960s ........................ 20.00
  Garden Tea Party, #1606, 1964 ................................................. 30.00

**Ponytail Barbie #5, brunette, 1961 Solo in the Spotlight outfit, $250.**

  School Teacher Dress, played-with condition ............................... 6.00
  Ship Ahoy, #1918, 1964 .......... 27.50
  Shirt, Skipper, hot pink, orig hanger, tagged ..................................... 5.00
  Trim Twosome, dress, Skipper, #1960, 1968, played-with condition ................................................. 40.00

Pencil Case, Skipper and Skooter, Standard Plastic, 1966 ................... 15.00

Pendant, Sweet 16 ........................ 20.00

Playset
  Barbie Pool Party, Mattel, 1973, orig box and contents, some wear to box and accessories ..................... 50.00
  Fashion Plaza, 1976 ................. 80.00

Record, 12-1/2" x 12-1/2", 33-1/3 rpm, sealed
  Birthday Album ......................... 6.50
  Sing-Along ................................ 6.00

Refrigerator, 11-3/4" h, Mattel, 1987, played-with condition .............. 12.00

Ring, 1962, MOC ........................ 175.00

Stand, black wire, mid-1960s ....... 15.00

Stickers, complete set of 216 stickers, album, display box, Topps, 1983 ................................................. 80.00

Viewmaster, talking, MIB .............. 70.00

Wonder Book ............................... 15.00

# Baseball Cards

**Collecting Hints:** Condition is a key factor—collectors should strive to obtain only cards in excellent to mint condition.

Concentrate on the superstars; these cards are most likely to increase in value. Buy full sets of modern cards. This way, you have the superstars of tomorrow on hand. When a player becomes a member of the Baseball Hall of Fame, the value of his cards and other memorabilia will increase significantly.

The price of cards fluctuates rapidly, often changing on a weekly basis. Spend time studying the market before investing heavily.

Reproduced cards and sets have become a fact of life. Novice collectors should not buy cards until they can tell the difference between the originals and reproductions.

The latest, highly speculative trend is collecting rookie cards, i.e., those from a player's first year.

**History:** Baseball cards were first printed in the late 19th century. By 1900, the most common cards, known as "T" cards, were those made by tobacco companies such as American Tobacco Co. The majority of the tobacco-related cards were produced between 1909 and 1915. During the 1920s, American Caramel, National Caramel, and York Caramel candy companies issued cards identified in lists as "E" cards.

During the 1930s, Goudey Gum Co. of Boston (from 1933 to 1941) and Gum Inc. (in 1939) were prime producers of baseball cards. Following World War II, Bowman Gum of Philadelphia (B.G.H.L.I.), the successor to Gum, Inc., lead the way. Topps, Inc., (T.C.G.) of Brooklyn, New York, followed. Topps bought Bowman in 1956 and enjoyed almost a monopoly in card production until 1981 when Fleer of Philadelphia and Donruss of Memphis became competitive. All three companies now produce annual sets numbering 600 cards or more.

**References:** *Baseball Card Price Guide*, 12th ed., Krause Publications, 1998; Jeff Kurowski and Tony Prudom, *Sports Collectors Digest Pre-War Baseball Card Price Guide*, Krause Publications, 1993; Mark Larson (ed.), *Baseball Cards Questions & Answers*, Krause Publications, 1992; —, *Sports Collectors Digest Minor League Baseball Card Price Guide*, Krause Publications, 1993; —, *Sports Collectors Digest: The Sports Card Explosion*, Krause Publications, 1993; Bob Lemke (ed.), *Sportscard Counterfeit Detector*, 3rd ed., Krause Publications, 1994; *101 Sports Card Investments*, Krause Publications, 1993; —, *Premium Insert Sports Cards*, Krause Publications, 1995; Alan Rosen, *True Mint*, Krause Publications, 1994; *Standard Catalog of Baseball Cards*, 6th ed., Krause Publications, 1996.

**Periodicals:** The following appear on a monthly or semi-monthly basis: *Baseball Update*, 220 Sunrise Hwy, Ste. 284, Rockville Centre, NY 11570; *Beckett Baseball Card Monthly*, 4887 Alpha Rd, Ste. 200, Dallas, TX 75244; *Beckett Focus on Future Stars*, 4887 Alpha Rd., Ste. 200, Dallas, TX 75244; *Card Trade*, 700 E. State St., Iola, WI 54990; *Diamond Angle*, P.O. Box 409, Kaunakakai, HI 96748; *Old Judge*, P.O. Box 137, Centerbeach, NY 11720; *Sports Cards*, 700 E. State St., Iola, WI 54990; *Sports Collectors Digest*, 700 E. State St., Iola, WI 54990; *Your Season Ticket*, 106 Liberty Rd., Woodsburg, MD 21790.

**Collectors' Clubs:** There are many local card collecting clubs throughout the United States. However, there is no national organization at the present time.

**Reproduction Alert.**

**Notes:** The prices below are for cards in excellent condition. The listings for cards after 1948 show the price for a complete set, common player, and superstars. The number of cards in each set is indicated in parentheses.

### Pre-Bowman/Topps Period

Barbeau, T206 .............................. 28.00
M. Brown, T206, Cubs on shirt ..... 70.00
Comorosky, #77, Goudey, 1933.... 40.00
Jennings, #77, Cracker Jack, 1915
.................................................. 28.00
Kiner, #91, Leaf, 1949 .................. 47.00
McGinnity, T206 ........................... 68.00
Terry, #21, Goudey, 1934 ............ 145.00
Triple Folder, T202l 1912, Just before the battle, Matthewson/Meyers
.................................................. 170.00
Williams, #82, 77, Goudey, 1933
.................................................. 40.00

### Bowman Era

1948 Bowman, black and white
  Complete Set (48) .............. 1,500.00
  Common Player (1-36) ............ 10.00
  Common Player (37-48) .......... 12.50
  6 Y. Berra ............................. 165.00
  36 S. Musial ......................... 340.00
1949 Bowman
  Complete Set (240) ............. 7,000.00
  Common Player (1-36) ............. 7.50

  Common Player (37-73) ............. 8.50
  Common Player (74-144) ............ 6.50
  Common Player (145-240) ....... 35.00
  85 J. Mize ............................. 125.00
  100 Gil Hodges ...................... 30.00
  157 Walt Masterson ................ 22.00
1950 Bowman
  Complete Set (252) ............. 2,850.00
  Common Player (1-72) ............ 12.00
  Common Player (72-252) .......... 8.00
  18 E. Robinson ...................... 10.00
  217 C. Stengel ....................... 35.00
  248 Sam Jethroe ..................... 6.50
1951 Bowman, color
  Complete Set (324) ............. 8,350.00
  Common Player (1-252) ............ 9.50
  Common Player (253-324) ......... 6.50
  134 W. Spahn ........................ 80.00
  143 T. Kluszewski ................... 36.00
  305 W. Mays ...................... 1,250.00
1952 Bowman, color
  Complete Set (252) ............... 900.00
  Common Player (1-216) ............ 2.50
  Common Player (217-252) ......... 4.00
  4 R. Roberts ......................... 24.00
  8 Pee Wee Reese ................... 80.00
  14 C. Chambers ...................... 5.00
  22 W. Ranmsdell ..................... 8.00
  44 R. Campanella ................... 55.00
  53 R. Ashburn ....................... 36.00
  100 S. Sisty .......................... 8.00
  159 D. Leonard ...................... 12.00
  200 K. Silvestri ..................... 12.00
1953 Bowman, color
  Complete Set (160) ............. 4,500.00
  Common Player (1-96) ............ 15.50
  Common Player (97-112) ......... 16.50
  Common Player (113-128) ........ 26.00
  Common Player (129-160) ....... 18.00
  40 L. Doby ........................... 24.00
  57 L. Boudeau ....................... 24.00
  59 M. Mantle ...................... 1,100.00

**Bowman, 1953, #10, Richie Asburn, $90.**

  125 F. Hatfield ....................... 35.00
  153 W. Ford ......................... 185.00
1954 Bowman
  Complete Set (224) ............... 850.00
  Common Player (1-128) ............ 4.00
  Common Player (129-224) ......... 4.50
  1 P. Rizzulo ......................... 60.00
  50 G. Keill .......................... 16.00
  74 J. Gillam ......................... 20.00
1955 Bowman, color
  Complete Set (320) ............. 2,900.00
  Common Player (1-96) ............. 6.50
  Common Player (97-224) ........... 7.50
  Common Player (225-320) ........ 14.00
  10 Rizzuto ........................... 13.00
  29 Schoendienst ..................... 18.00
  67 Lauren, poor condition ......... 3.00
  156 Hughes ........................... 6.00
  201 Reynolds ........................ 7.50

### Topps Era

1951 Topps, blue backs
  Complete Set (52) ................. 725.00
  Common Player (1-52) ............ 12.00
  3 R. Ashburn ........................ 22.00
  37 B. Doerr ......................... 20.00
  50 J. Mize ........................... 25.00
1951 Topps, red backs
  Complete Set (52) ................. 350.00
  Common Player (1-52) ............. 3.10
  1 Y. Berra .......................... 27.50
  31 G. Hodges ........................ 10.00
  38 D. Snider ......................... 20.00
1952 Topps
  Complete Set (407) ............. 4,850.00
  Common Player (1-80) ............ 14.00
  Common Player (81-252) ........... 6.50
  Common Player (253-310) ........ 12.00
  Common Player (311-407) ........ 25.00
  33 W. Spahn ......................... 20.00
  48 J. Page, error ................... 45.00
  88 B. Feller ......................... 20.00
  400 B. Dickey ...................... 225.00
1953 Topps
  Complete Set (280) ............. 5,000.00
  Common Player (1-165) .......... 11.50
  Common Player (166-220) ......... 7.50
  Common Player (221-280) ....... 42.50
  1 J. Robinson ...................... 175.00
  10 S. Burgess ....................... 16.00
  62 M. Irvin .......................... 8.00
  100 B. Miller ........................ 20.00
  149 D. DiMaggio ..................... 31.00
1954 Topps
  Complete Set (250) ............. 2,900.00
  Common Player (1-50) ............. 7.00
  Common Player (51-75) ............ 8.00
  Common Player (76-250) ........... 5.00
  3 Irvin ............................. 10.00
  30 Matthews ......................... 30.00
  63 Pesky ............................ 10.00
  66 Lepicio .......................... 37.50
  94 Banks ........................... 175.00
  177 Milliken ......................... 4.00
  222 Wilson .......................... 17.00
  248 Smith ........................... 10.00
1955 Topps
  Complete Set (210) ............. 3,600.00
  Common Player (1-160) ............ 6.00
  Common Player (161-210) ......... 7.50
  6 Hack .............................. 6.50
  31 Spahn ............................ 30.00

90 Spooner................................7.50
120 Kluszewski........................20.00
182 H. Robinson......................22.00
1956 Topps
Complete Set (340)............2,275.00
Common Player (1-180)..........2.50
Common Player (181-260).........3.50
33 R. Clemente.....................265.00
180 R. Roberts........................15.00
226 Giants Team.....................11.00
1957 Topps
Complete Set (407)............3,500.00
Common Player (1-88)..............3.50
Common Player (89-176)...........3.00
Common Player (177-264)........6.00
Common Player (265-352)........8.50
Common Player (353-407)........2.50
18 D. Drysdale......................110.00
20 H. Aaron............................85.00
120 B. Lemon..........................10.00
154 R. Schoendienst.................3.00
1958 Topps
Complete Set (495).............1,500.00
Common Player (1-110)..............3.50
Common Player (111-440)..........3.00
Common Player (441-495).........2.00
52 Clemente..........................165.00
70 Kaline................................50.00
310 Banks...............................50.00
440 Matthews..........................10.00
485 Williams............................50.00
1959 Topps
Complete Set (572)............2,350.00
Common Player (1-10)..............3.50
Common Player (11-198)...........2.75
Common Player (199-506)........2.50
Common Player (507-572)........7.50
8 Phillies Team.........................8.00
102 F. Alou, RC.......................11.00
317 Ashburn/Mays...................24.00
467 H. Aaron HR........................7.00
1960 Topps
Complete Set (572).............1,350.00
Common Player (1-506)............2.50
Common Player (507-572)........2.00
73 Gibson...............................17.00
136 Kaat.................................20.00
302 Phillies Team......................4.00
464 Braves Coaches................6.00
584 Mincher.............................8.00
1961 Topps
Complete Set (589).............1,650.00
Common Player (1-522)............1.00
Common Player (523-589).....7.00
2 R. Maris...............................25.00
35 R. Stato RC........................16.00
98 Checklist..............................7.50
1962 Topps
Complete Set (598)............4,600.00
Common Player (1-370)............3.50
Common Player (371-446)........5.00
Common Player (447-522)........7.50
Common Player (553-598).......20.00
5 S. Koufax...........................105.00
73 N. Fox..................................3.50
530 B. Gibson..........................85.00
1963 Topps
Complete Set (576).............1,200.00
Common Player (1-196)............2.50
Common Player (197-446)........2.00
Common Player (447-506)........2.00
Common Player (507-576)........1.50
10 Leaders...............................4.00

79 Checklist..............................4.00
128 Alou...................................6.00
138 Pride of NL.......................35.00
439 Zimmer.............................19.00
1964 Topps
Complete Set (587)...............750.00
Common Player (1-370)..............50
Common Player (371-522)...........75
Common Player (523-587).........1.25
5 Koufax/Drysdale....................5.00
125 P. Rose............................55.00
243 H. Aaron...........................35.00
1965 Topps
Complete Set (598)...............950.00
Common Player (1-506).............1.00
Common Player (507-598).........1.50
27 Mets Team............................7.00
87 Cardinals Team.....................8.00
232 Lopez.................................5.00
400 Spahn..............................32.00
573 Duffalo..............................24.00
1966 Topps
Complete Set (598)...............900.00
Common Player (1-506).............1.00
Common Player (507-598).........3.50
70 Yastrzemski........................20.00
194 Senators Team....................6.00
221 Leaders..............................5.00
420 Marichal...........................11.00
551 Purkey..............................30.00
1967 Topps
Complete Set (609)...............900.00
Common Player (1-533)..............75
Common Player (534-609)........2.00
103 Mantle Checklist.................6.00
480 W. McCovey.....................20.00
609 T. John............................25.00
1968 Topps
Complete Set (598)...............750.00
Common Player (1-457)..............75
Common Player (458-598)...........50
30 Torre....................................9.00
45 Seaver...............................17.50
144 Morgan...............................5.00
497 Cardinals Team...................7.00
571 La Russa..........................12.00
1969 Topps
Complete Set (664)...............600.00
Common Player (1-218)..............50
Common Player (219-327)...........30
Common Player (328-512)...........25
Common Player (513-664)...........30
7 Leaders.................................6.00
35 Morgan...............................11.00
107 Checklist..........................10.50
552 Dodge.................................7.00
657 Murcer.............................11.00
1970 Topps
Complete Set (720)...............450.00
Common Player (1-132)..............20
Common Player (133-459)...........20
Common Player (460-546)...........25
Common Player (547-633)...........35
Common Player (634-720)...........60
140 R. Jackson........................15.00
210 Juan Marichal.....................2.50
537 J. Morgan...........................2.25
712 N. Ryan...........................300.00
1971 Topps
Complete Set (752)...............365.00
Common Player (1-523)..............25
Common Player (524-643)...........35
Common Player (644-752)...........75

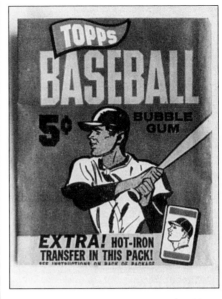

**Topps, 1965, waxed wrapper, $7.50.**

180 A. Kalkine........................10.00
709 D. Maylor.........................50.00
1972 Topps
Complete Set (787)...............365.00
Common Player (1-394)..............20
Common Player (395-525)...........20
Common Player (526-656)...........25
Common Player (657-787)...........65
26 B. Blyleven...........................5.00
595 N. Ryan............................75.00
588 Cardinals Team...................3.50
1973 Topps
Complete Set (660)...............225.00
Common Player (1-396)..............20
Common Player (397-528)...........40
Common Player (529-660)...........45
31 B. Bell................................1.75
193 C. Fisk...............................1.75
245 C. Yastrzemski....................5.00
615 M. Schmidt RC..................235.00
1974 Topps
Complete Set (660)...............175.00
Common Player (1-660)..............15
50 R. Carew..............................2.75
283 M. Schmidt........................25.00
456 D. Winfield........................30.00
1975 Topps
Complete Set (660)...............225.00
Common Player (1-660)..............50
61 D. Winfield..........................25.00
70 M. Schmidt.........................25.00
223 R. Young Mini RC...............65.00
370 T. Seaver............................7.00
1976 Topps
Complete Set (660)...............115.00
Common Player (1-660)..............10
19 G. Brett................................6.00
340 J. Rice................................6.00
480 M. Schmidt..........................6.25
1977 Topps
Complete Set (660)...............115.00
Common Player (1-660)..............10
110 S. Carlton............................2.25
400 S. Garvey............................1.75
473 Rookies Outfielders.............9.00

1978 Topps
Complete Set (726) .................. 95.00
Common Player (1-726) ............... .10
36 E. Murray ........................ 18.00
72 A. Dawson ........................ 2.00
360 M. Schmidt ...................... 2.50
1979 Topps
Complete Set (726) .................. 65.00
Common Player (1-726) ............... .06
39 D. Murphy ........................ 4.00
469 L. Parish ....................... 1.75
650 P. Rose ......................... 2.50
1980 Topps
Complete Set (726) .................. 65.00
Common Player (1-726) ............... .06
70 Gary Carter ...................... 1.25
77 D. Steib ......................... 1.00
482 R. Henderson .................... 15.00
1981 Topps
Complete Set (726) .................. 65.00
Common Player (1-726) ............... .06
315 K. Gibson ....................... 2.50
479 Expos Future Stars .............. 7.00
700 G. Brett ........................ 1.75
1982 Topps
Complete Set (792) .................. 60.00
Common Player (1-792) ............... .05
70 T. Raines ........................ 1.25
254 J. Bell ......................... 9.00
668 D. Murphy ....................... 1.50
1983 Topps
Complete Set (792) .................. 60.00
Common Player (1-792) ............... .05
49 W. McGee ......................... 2.00
163 C. Ripken ....................... 4.50
251 A. Wiggins ...................... .50

# Baseball Collectibles

**Collecting Hints:** Baseball memorabilia spans a wide range of items that have been produced since baseball became the national pastime more than 100 years ago. This variety has made it more difficult to establish reliable values, leaving it to the individual to identify and determine what price to pay for any particular item. This "value in the eye of the beholder" approach works well for the experienced collector. Novices should solicit the advice of a reliable dealer or an advanced collector before investing heavily. Fluctuating market trends are compounded by the emerging interest in—and inordinately high prices paid for—unique pieces, especially items associated with superstars such as Cobb, Ruth, and Mantle.

Because of the unlimited variety of items available, it is virtually impossible to collect everything. Develop a collecting strategy, concentrating on particular player(s), team(s), or type of collectible(s), such as Hartland Statues or Perez-

Steele autographed postcards. A special emphasis allows the collector to become more familiar with the key elements effecting pricing within that area of interest, such as condition and availability, and permits building a collection within a prescribed budget.

**History:** Baseball had its beginnings in the mid-19th century and by 1900 had become the national pastime. Whether sandlot or big league, baseball was part of most every male's life until the 1950s, when leisure activities expanded in a myriad of directions.

The superstar has always been the key element in the game. Baseball greats were popular visitors at banquets, parades, and, more recently, baseball autograph shows. They were subjects of extensive newspaper coverage and, with heightened radio and TV exposure, achieved true celebrity status. The impact of baseball on American life has been enormous.

**References:** David Bushing and Joe Phillips, *Vintage Baseball Bat 1994 Pocket Price Guide*, published by authors (217 Homewood, Libertyville, IL 60048), 1994; —, *Vintage Baseball Glove Pocket Price Guide, No. 4*, published by authors (217 Homewood, Libertyville, IL 60048), 1996; Larry Canale, *Mickey Mantel: The Yankee Years, The Classic Photography of Ozzie Sweet*, Tuff Stuff Books, 1998; Bruce Chadwick and David M. Spindel authored a series of books on major-league teams published by Abbeville Press between 1992 and 1995; Mark Larson, *Complete Guide to Baseball Memorabilia*, 3rd ed., Krause Publications, 1996; Michael McKeever, *Collecting Sports Memorabilia*, Alliance Publishing, 1996.

**Periodicals:** *Baseball Hobby News*, 4540 Kearney Villa Rd., San Diego, CA 92123; *John L. Raybin's Baseball Autograph News*, 527 Third Ave., #294-A, New York, NY 10016; *Sports Collectors Digest*, 700 E. State St., Iola, WI 54990; *Tuff Stuff*, P.O. Box 1637, Glen Allen, VA 23060.

**Collectors' Clubs:** Glove Collector, 14057 Rolling Hills Lane, Dallas, TX 75210; Society for American Baseball Research, P.O. Box 93183, Cleveland, OH 44101, members receive *Baseball Research Journal The SABR Bulletin* and *National Pastime*.

**Museum:** National Baseball Hall of Fame and Museum, Cooperstown, NY.

**Reproduction Alert:** Autographs and equipment.

Autograph
Album Page, sgd by Gehrig and Ruth .................................. 1,100.00
Check, sgd by J. Franklin Baker ........................... 2,640.00
Photograph, panoramic view, Philadelphia Athletics, 1929 ....... 5,500.00
Radio Script, Babe Ruth ..... 1,650.00
Will Codicil, Harry Wright, 1895, pertaining to creation of a "National Collection" of baseball artifacts ........................... 9,350.00
Baseball, autographed on sweet spot, certificate of authenticity
Steve Avery ........................... 25.00
Wilson Alvarez ...................... 20.00
Jermaine Allensworth ............. 20.00
Rich Becker ........................... 20.00
Jay Bell ................................. 25.00
Kevin Brown ........................... 48.00
Wade Boggs ........................... 40.00
A. J. Burnette ........................ 27.00
Dave Burba ........................... 25.00
Scott Elarton ......................... 25.00
Mike Frank ............................ 22.00
Brad Fulmer ........................... 27.50
Mark Gardner ........................ 25.00
Tom Gordon ........................... 25.00
Von Hayes ............................. 28.00
Glenn Hoffman ....................... 22.00
Todd Hundley ........................ 32.00
Quinton McCracken ................ 25.00
Minnie Minoso ....................... 28.00
Scott Morgan ......................... 25.00
Charles Nagy ......................... 30.00
Phil Nickro ............................. 30.00
Rich Nye ............................... 25.00
Ben Oglivie ........................... 25.00
Gaylord Perry ........................ 25.00
Darrell Porter ........................ 30.00
Steve Reed ............................ 25.00
Pee Wee Reese ...................... 75.00
Grant Roberts ........................ 20.00

**Autographed baseball, Hank Aaron signature, $25.**

Ken Ryan.................................. 20.00
Jeff Shaw................................. 25.00
Paul Sorrento........................... 28.00
Willie Stargell.......................... 30.00
Franklin Stubbs ....................... 20.00
Jim Tatum................................ 20.00
Ralph Terry.............................. 28.00
Bill Virdon ............................... 25.00
Mo Vaughn .............................. 40.00
Turk Wendell............................ 25.00
Mike Williams .......................... 20.00
Tony Womack........................... 30.00
Mosato Yoshi............................ 35.00
Kevin Young ............................ 25.00
Ed Yost ................................... 36.00

Bat, game-used
  Edgardo Alfonzo, Louisville Slugger, cracked ............................... 70.00
  Jay Bell, Louisville Slugger, cracked ................................... 600.00
  Rod Carew, H & B, uncracked, autographed .................................. 575.00
  Al Martin, Louisville Slugger, cracked ................................... 65.00
  Frank Thomas, 1996 Adirondack, cracked, autographed ........... 450.00

Book, *Dynasty: The New York Yankees, 1949-1964*, Peter Golenbock, Prentice-Hall, 1975, dj, 394 pgs...... 20.00

Calendar, 1941, Babe Ruth artwork ................................................ 275.00

Calling Card Stand, silverplated ................................................ 750.00

Cigar Box, Honus Wagner, fair condition ............................................ 9,900.00

Clothing
  Hat, Rockford Peaches, woman's league, used ...................... 1,650.00
  Warm-up jacket, Philadelphia Phillies, 1947-49...................... 4,300.00

Doll, San Francisco Giants, 7-1/2" h, celluloid head........................... 60.00

Game, Pro-Baseball, The Great American Game, P. M. Game Co., 1946, roulette wheel spinner, orig instructions, score sheets, 8" sq box dec as stadium ......................... 600.00

Glass Lantern Slide
  Group photo of vintage baseball stars ....................................... 690.00
  Mathewson............................. 415.00

Glove, softball, Sears Roebuck, 1933, orig box............................. 165.00

Hall of Fame Bat Display, First Five, Cobb, Johnson Mathewson, Ruth, Wagner, 1991 ......................... 995.00

Hartland Figurine
  Bat Boy, 25th Anniversary, MIB ................................................ 100.00
  Berra, 1 ................................. 350.00
  Drysdale, 2............................. 450.00
  Fox, 2 .................................... 200.00
  Killebrew, 25th Anniversary, MIB ................................................. 50.00
  Mantle, 4 ............................... 150.00
  Minor Leaguer, black base .... 250.00
  Minor Leaguer, white.............. 150.00
  Maris, 1 ................................. 600.00
  Matthews, 2............................ 150.00
  Musial, 1................................ 350.00
  Ruth, 2................................... 150.00
  Ruth, 25th Anniversary............. 25.00
  Spahn, 25th Anniversary.......... 20.00

Williams, 2............................. 150.00

Jersey, game-used
  Brian Downing, 1988 California Angels, road ......................... 250.00
  Tony Gwynn, 1997, San Diego Padres, home, autographed ............................................. 1,395.00
  Gregg Jeffries, 1990 NY Mets, home ............................................. 400.00
  Dick Schofield, 1987 California Angels, road ......................... 225.00

Lamp, Gone with the Wind style, sports dec shade and base........... 2,750.00

Locker Tag, Shibe Park, 1940s ................................................ 290.00

Magazine
  *Boy's Life,* Mickey Mantle cover ................................................. 85.00
  *Look,* Joe DiMaggio in uniform with children .................................. 50.00

Mirror, adv, Philadelphia A's, celluloid, 1910.................................. 2,640.00

Napkin Ring, silverplated, Victorian ................................................ 855.00

Nodder
  San Francisco '49, one white, other black face, pr......................... 500.00

**Match Book, St. Louis Cardinals, Universal Match Co., 1982, $.50.**

St. Louis Cardinals, plastic ...... 15.00
Pennant, Yankees, 1950 .............. 38.00

Photograph
  Advertising Premium, Philadelphia A's, 1906 ............................... 220.00
  Daguerreotype, 1/6 plate, young boy in uniform........................... 3,300.00
  Panoramic, Boston Braves, 1920 ............................................. 1,020.00
  Team Photo, Chester Giants African Americans, 1920................... 750.00
  Tintype, unidentified early player ................................................ 250.00

Plate, Philadelphia A's, 1911 ...... 855.00

Pocket Knife, Babe Ruth, bat shape ................................................. 90.00

Poster
Pittsburgh BBC, 1894, lithography, some professional restoration ............................................. 3,550.00
U. S. Coast Guard, 1930s........ 1,050.00

Press Pen and Original Artwork, used by Balfour Co., 1953 New York Yankees World Series ................. 995.00

Print
  A Stolen Base?, Prang & C., 1890, orig frame .......................... 3,740.00
  1889 Opening Game The Boston Baseball Club .................... 2,530.00
  King's Bohemian Beer adv, period frame................................. 1,100.00

Program
  World Series 1957, Yankees/Braves ................................................. 90.00
  World Series 1958, Yankees/Braves ................................................. 90.00

Record, Mickey Mantle, My Favorite Hits, RCA Victor, © 1958........ 120.00

Ring, Babe Ruth, baseball club ................................................ 165.00

Rules Book, D & M, 1919, illus ..... 80.00

Scorer, Payme Tobacco, celluloid watch fob, red, white, and blue image of tobacco pack on front, back with image of baseball game in progress, inner wheels to record runs, hits, innings, c1920 ...................... 125.00

Season Pass, NY Giants, sterling silver ................................................ 750.00

Shaving Mug, occupational..... 3,300.00

Trophy, Spaulding, fielder's, orig condition ....................................... 3,520.00

Wrist Watch, Montreal Expos, Bulova, Sportstime, quart, 1980s, MIB....95.00

# Basketball Collectibles

**Collecting Hints:** The National Basketball Association is trying hard to make collectors out of all its fans. Enjoy the hoopla, as more and more collectibles are being generated. Save those programs, promotional pieces, and giveaways.

Collectors should pay careful attention to the growing interest in women's collegiate basketball and the enthusiasm it's creating.

**History:** The game of basketball originated in Springfield, Massachusetts, in 1891, under the direction of Dr. James Naismith of the YMCA. Schools and colleges soon adopted the game, and it began to spread worldwide.

Basketball was added to the Olympic games in 1936. The NBA was founded in 1949 after professional teams became popular. Today the NBA consists of 27 teams in two conferences, each having two divisions.

Basketball is generally considered to be an indoor game, but almost every town in America has some place where locals gather to shoot a few hoops. Regulation games have two teams with five players each. Courts are 92 feet long and 50 feet wide and have a hoop attached to a backboard at each end.

**References:** David Bushing, *Sports Equipment Price Guide*, Krause Publications, 1995; *Standard Catalog of Football, Basketball & Hockey Cards*, 2nd edition, Krause Publications, 1996.

**Periodical:** *Sports Collectors Digest*, 700 E. State St., Iola, WI 54990.

**Museum:** Naismith Memorial Basketball Hall of Fame, Springfield, MA.

Advertising
    Dream Team, display, orig Dream Team 10 members, USA uniforms, orig shipping box .................. 350.00
    Keds, letter regarding star athlete, orig envelope, sgd by Pete Maravich ........................................ 85.00
Badge, 3-1/2" d, Harlem Globetrotters, celluloid, full color team photo, white ground, blue letters, small gold stars, c1970 ......................... 24.00
Basketball, autographed
    Red Auerbach, official Spaulding NBA leather ball ..................... 150.00
    Larry Bird, sgd and numbered limited edition, Spaulding leather all-star game ball ........................ 400.00
    Larry Bird and Red Auerbach, official Spaulding NBA leather ball ... 300.00
    Boston Celtics, 20 team autographs, official Spaulding NBA leather ball, numbered ......................... 2,500.00
    Julius Erving and Connie Hawkins, ABA 30th Year Reunion ball ... 400.00
    Grant Hill, Christian Laettner, Bobby Hurley, Duke University, Final four ball ................................. 275.00
    Scottie Pippen, Spaulding leather all-star game ball, 1994 ......... 375.00
    Rick Pitting, official Spaulding indoor/outdoor NBA ball .......... 85.00
Jersey, double tags
    Kobe Bryant, LA Lakers, Champion Pro, rookie year ..................... 250.00

John Havlicek, Boston Celtics, NBA ........................................ 250.00
    Keith Michale, Upper Deck authenticated .................................. 300.00
    Robert Parish, Upper Deck authenticated .................................. 200.00
Keychain, Chicago Bulls, #2203 .... 8.00
Lithograph
    Los Angeles Lakers, five greatest players, artist Ann Neilsen, hand signed by Wilt Chamberlain, Jerry West, Magic Johnson, Elgin Baylor, and Kareem Abdul-Jabbar, limited to 1992 pcs, 22" x 39" unframed ..695.00
    UCLA Legends, Coach John Wooden, Jabbar, Goodrich, Warren, Johnson, Walton, Erickson, action photos and portraits, sgd in blue underneath each player, 22" x 40" unframed ............................... 150.00
Magazine
    *Basketball Digest*, November 1980, Larry Bird cover ..................... 15.00
    *Maravich*, tribute for Pete Maravich, Pistol Pete action cover, 9" x 12", black and white, color cover, uncirculated ................................. 125.00
    *Sports Illustrated*, November 1977, Larry Bird and Cheerleaders cover ....................................... 45.00
Notebook, Spaulding Official NBA, unused .................................... 20.00
Photograph, autographed
    Kenny Anderson, 8" x 10" ........ 20.00
    Vic Baker, 8" x 10" ................... 15.00
    Kenny Carr, 8" x 10" ................ 15.00
    Wilt Chamberlain, 100 point game, 8" x 10" ................................ 125.00
    C. Fitzsimmons, 8" x 10" ......... 15.00
    George Gervin, 8" x 10" ........... 35.00
    Brian Grant, 8" x 10" ............... 20.00
    H. Grant, 8" x 10" ..................... 20.00
    Grant Hill, 8" x 10" .................. 45.00
    Juwan Howard, Univ. of Michigan, 8" x 10" ................................. 7.50
    Chris Jackson, 8" x 10" ........... 20.00
    Magic Johnson and Larry Bird, 1997 NCAA Finals, 15" x 19", signed only by Bird ................................. 165.00
    Magic Johnson and Larry Bird, Upper Deck, authenticated, 16" x 20", signed by both ............... 350.00
    K. C. Jones, 8" x 10" ................. 8.00
    Bob Knight and Steve Fisher, 11" x 14", signed by both ......... 75.00
    J. Lucas, 8" x 10" ..................... 25.00
    Moses Malone, 8" x 10" ........... 15.00
    Meadowlark Lemon, 8" x 10".... 25.00
    Theo Ratliff, Wyoming, 8" x 10" ....................................... 5.00
    N. Thurmond, 8" x 10" ............. 25.00
    Robert Traylor, Univ. of Michigan, 8" x 10" ............................... 12.00
    C. Webber, 8" x 10" .................. 25.00
Photograph, vintage, shows team, Grove City, OH, 5" x 7", 1930s .............. 32.00
Poster, Michael Jordan
    Caricature, uncirculated, 40" x 60" ....................................... 150.00
    Space Jam, unreleased, Nike, Looney tunes, 1992 ................. 55.00
Program
    1982 NCAA Final Four .......... 125.00

Retirement, Kevin McHale, January 1994, McHale vs. Lakers cover, full ticket, mini-replica banner ....... 50.00
St. Louis Hawks and Boston Celtics, 1982, autographed by Bill Russell, Bob Cousy, Sam Jones, Jim Loscutoff, Tom Sanders ................... 275.00
Seal and Diecut, Dennison, orig cellophane envelope, 4" h ................ 5.00
Shoes, game used, dual autograph
    Patrick Ewing ........................ 425.00
    Larry Johnson, Converse ....... 200.00
    Alonzo Mournng, Nike Air Force ........................................... 325.00
    Steve Smith, Reebok ............. 150.00
Soap, Shaq Shower Suds, 8 oz tube, orig contents ............................ 8.00
Tie-tac, chain, figural basketball player ........................................... 12.00
Trading Card
    Finest 1, 1998/99, MIB ............ 90.00
    Fleer, uncut sheet, 1990/91 ..... 18.00
    Fleer II Metal, 1996/97, MIB..... 35.00
    NBA Hoops, Michael Jordan
        #5, 1990-91, Most Valuable Player, good condition .......... 3.00
        #298, 1992-93, All Star Weekend ................................... 2.00
        #30l 1991-92, Most Valuable Player, good condition .......... 3.00
        #358, illus by Ken Goldammer, 1990 .................................. 2.00
        #536, 1991-92, All-Time Active Leader Scoring .................... 2.00
    Pacific Prism Draft, 1996/97, MIB ....................................... 40.00
    Skybox, 1990/91, hand collated ....................................... 20.00
    Stadium Club I, 1997/98, MIB ....................................... 45.00
    Stadium Premium I, 1998/99, MIB ....................................... 60.00
    Topps, 1980/81, wax pack ...... 55.00
    Upper Deck, 1991/92, factory sealed ................................... 20.00
    Upper Duck, 1992/93, Italian series, foil, wax, MIB ......................... 25.00
Uniform, autographed, Wilt Chamberlain, LA Lakers, double tagged, home ...................................... 450.00
Wire Service Photo
    Los Angeles Lakers Earvin Johnson and Miami Heat Sylvester Gray, 1989 ....................................... 3.50
    Los Angeles Lakers, Earvin Johnson, Supersonics Reynolds, 1989 ..... 3.50
    Los Angeles Lakers, Magic Johnson, 1989 ....................................... 3.50
    Los Angeles Lakers, Magic Johnson and Seattles Jerry Reynolds, 1989 ....................................... 3.50
    Los Angeles Lakers, Kareem Abdul Jabbar, A.C. Green, and Magic Johnson, 1989 ........................ 3.50
    Los Angeles Lakers, Magic Johnson and Phoenix Suns Tyrone Corbin, 1989 ....................................... 3.60
Yearbook
    Boston Celtics, 1974/75, Silas and Chaney on cover, Dick Raphael photos ....................................... 40.00
    Chicago Bulls, 1984/85, Orlando Woolridge and Michael Jordan on cover ...................................... 125.00

# Battery Operated Automata

**Collecting Hints:** Prices fluctuate greatly, but operating condition is a key factor. Many pieces were originally made with accessory parts; these must be present for full value to be realized. The original box, especially if it has a label, adds 10 to 20% to the price. Also, the more elaborate the action, the higher the value.

Many collectors live in Japan, and dealers must allow enough margin to ship pieces overseas.

**History:** Battery-operated automata began as inexpensive Japanese imports in the 1950s. They were meant for amusement only, many ending up on the shelves of bars in the recreation rooms of private homes. They were marketed through 5 and 10¢ stores and outlets.

The subjects were animals—bears being favored—and humans. Quality of pieces varies greatly, with Linemar items being among the best made.

Astro Dog, Japan, orig box......... 450.00
Batmobile, red, orig box ............. 275.00
Bartender, unused, MIB ................ 50.00
BMW 3.5 CSL turbo car, Dunlop and Bosch Electric advertising, tin, MIB ................................................... 120.00
Brainstorm Beany, blue felt beanie, yellow lettering and trim, orig 6" x 6" x 4" deep box, light bulb attached to top center of hat, back cord connects to cardboard and tin cylinder for battery, Electric Game Co., Inc., c1950 ......... 45.00

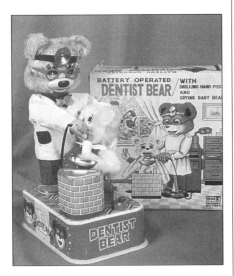

**Dentist Bear, orig box, 19" h, $450. Photo courtesy of McMasters Doll Auctions.**

Brave Eagle, beating drum, raising war hoop, MIB ............................. 145.00
Bubble Blowing Monkey, raises hand from pan on lap to mouth, MIB ............................................................. 195.00
Captain Robo and Space Transporter, 21st Century Toys, Japan, 1970s, plastic ..................................... 125.00
Choo Choo Train, tin, orig box ...... 60.00
Family Panda, panda pulls baby panda on carriage, 1970s................... 25.00
Fireman, multicolored litho tin, 3 small ladder sections, Sonsco, Japan, c1950 .................................... 165.00
F-14A Tomcat Jet Fighter, MIB...... 90.00
Happy Santa, Japan, 5 actions, 12" h ............................................... 235.00
Highway Patrol Police Car, blinking red light on top, MIB....................... 75.00
Indian Scout AT-11, Amar Toys, Indian , 1950s ...................................... 95.00
Juggling Monkey, orig box ......... 175.00
Kingsize Cadillac, red convertible, orig box ........................................... 85.00
Lambourhini Countach car, red, black, trim, MIB................................. 120.00
Loop the Loop Monkey, TN, Japan, orig box, 1970s .............................. 35.00
Love-Love Volkswagen Beetle, blinking light in back window, tin, orange, Mobil, Champion, Goodyear sayings, VW on hubcaps, MIB .... 145.00
Magic Snowman, white fabric, red facial accents and gloves, orig box with cellophane window, Modern Toys, Japan, c1960 ......................... 225.00
McGregor, Scotsman smoking cigar, raises up and down from pirates chest, MIB............................. 195.00
Mr. Magoo, some damage, orig box ............................................... 350.00
Musical rabbit, litho metal, beats drum, Japan, orig box........................ 50.00
My Fair Dancer, litho tin, dancer in naval outfit, seahorse graphics on base, 11" h, MIB............................. 225.00
Piggy Cook, flips tin ham and egg from pan over stove, MIB............... 225.00
Poodle, white plush, red, gray, and yellow plaid body, c1950.............. 95.00
Racing Camaro, Esso, Taiyo, Japan, MIB.......................................... 50.00
Rosko, bartender, shakes mixer, pours, and drink, smoke rises from ears, MIB.......................................... 75.00
Sandy the Seal, orig box ............ 175.00
Santa Claus, rings bell, large, MIB ............................................... 150.00
School Bus, tin litho, switch to open front and back doors, headlights light up ................................... 175.00
Taxi Cab, Andy Gard, yellow, remote control wheel steering, dome signal light, 10" l, MIB ...................... 250.00
Teddy the Drummer, orange bear, Alps, Japan, orig box........................ 50.00

# Bauer Pottery

**Collecting Hints:** Bauer pieces range in style from Art Deco to Streamlined Modern. Focus on highly stylistic, designer forms; interest in utilitarian redware and stoneware pieces is minimal.

Remember that jiggered and cast-production pieces were made in large quantities. Unfortunately, hand-thrown pieces by Matt Carlton and Fred Johnson, which were made in limited numbers, are not marked. Learn to identify them by studying photographs of known examples. Among the more desirable shapes are oil jars—the taller the jar, the higher the price.

Some colors of dinnerware are more highly prized than others. Premium prices are paid for burgundy, orange-red, and white pieces in all patterns.

**History:** In 1885, John Bauer founded the Paducah Pottery in Paducah, Kentucky, to manufacture stoneware and earthenware utilitarian pieces such as crocks and jugs. Bauer died in 1898, and John Andrew Bauer continued the business in Paducah until 1909, at which time the plant was moved to Los Angeles, California.

Bauer's initial California production consisted of redware flowerpots. Stoneware production did not resume immediately after the move to California because of the difficulty of locating suitable stoneware clay. Utilitarian ware such as bean pots and mixing bowls remained a company staple.

In 1913, Matt Carlton, an Arkansas potter, and Louis Ipsen, a Danish designer, developed an artware line of glazed bowls, jardinieres, and vases. The company won a bronze medal at the Panama-California Exposition of 1915-16, but within a short time period, the firm's artware was replaced by a line of molded stoneware vases.

In 1922, John Andrew Bauer died. Just prior to his death, he established a partnership with Watson E. Brockmon, his son-in-law. The firm prospered under Brockmon's leadership.

In the early 1930s, the company introduced a line of popular dinnerware designed by Ipsen and covered with glazes developed by Victor Houser, a ceramic engineer. In 1931, "ring" ware was introduced to contrast with the plain ware of the previous year. Eventually, over a hundred different shapes and sizes were manufactured in table and kitchenwares. Brusche Contempo (1948-61), La

Linda (1939-59), Monterey (1936-45), and Monterey Moderne (1948-1961) were some of the more successful tableware lines. Ipsen's Aladdin teapot design was part of the Glass Pastel Kitchenware series.

The company continued operations during World War II, reformulating the glazes to correspond to wartime restrictions. Wheel-thrown artware featuring the designs of Carlton and Fred Johnson was made, and cast forms were kept in production. Tracy Irwin, a designer, developed a modern line of floral containers.

Following the war, the company faced stiff competition in the national, as well as California market. A bitter strike in 1961 signaled the end, and in 1962, W. E. Brockmon's widow closed the plant.

**References:** Susan and Al Bagdade, *Warman's American Pottery and Porcelain*, Wallace-Homestead, 1994; Jack Chipman, *Collector's Encyclopedia of California Pottery*, 2nd ed., Collector Books, 1998, and *Collector's Guide To Bauer Pottery*, Collector Books, 1997; Lois Lehner, *Lehner's Encyclopedia of U.S. Marks on Pottery*, Porcelain & Clay, Collector Books, 1988.

Artware
  Model, cowboy hat, yellow..... 125.00
  Vase
    9" h, gold trim ...................... 45.00
    10" h, Matt Carlton............. 395.00
Atlanta
  Mixing Bowl, cobalt blue, No. 24
  ...................................................... 65.00
  Pot, 4" d, white ........................ 40.00
Kitchenware, Gloss Pastel
  Bowl, 11-1/2" l, 2-3/4" h, light green
  ...................................................... 25.00
  Casserole, cov
    1 qt..................................... 45.00
    1-1/2 pt.............................. 35.00
La Linda
  Ashtray, 4" sq, cobalt blue ....... 25.00
  Tumbler, chartreuse, price for set of six............................................. 95.00
Monterey
  Butter Dish, cov
    Ivory ................................... 65.00
    Red...................................... 85.00
  Teapot, cov, yellow................ 145.00
Plainware
  Carafe, jade ............................ 75.00
  Pudding Bowl, #3..................... 60.00
Ring-Ware
  Batter Bowl, yellow................... 35.00
  Bowl, 10" d, green.................... 50.00
  Butter Dish, cov
    Delph, light blue............... 135.00
    Green ................................ 130.00
    Red...................................... 165.00
  Candleholder, yellow................ 20.00

Canister, wooden lid, oval, orange, "Coffee"..................................... 80.00
Casserole, cov, individual size
  Green ..................................... 55.00
  Red, wooden frame............. 60.00
Chop Plate
  12" d, orange......................... 80.00
  14" d, green............................ 75.00
  14" d, orange....................... 140.00
Coffee Server, red, copper handle
  ...................................................... 65.00
Cookie Jar, cov, red .............. 695.00
Creamer
  Delph, light blue.................. 35.00
  Ivory ................................... 125.00
  Red...................................... 35.00
Jardiniere, white, 4" d, rim chip
  .................................................... 100.00
Mixing Bowl
  5" d, No. 36, yellow .............. 15.00
  7" d, No. 24, blue ................. 20.00
  8" d, No. 12, turquoise ........ 40.00
  10" d, No. 9, black............. 250.00
Mug, barrel
  Jade ................................... 300.00
  Yellow ................................ 300.00
Plate
  7-1/2" d, salad, mixed colors, set of six................................. 100.00
  9" d
    Red .................................. 20.00
    Yellow ............................... 15.00
  10-1/2" d, dinner
    Black................................. 75.00
    Red ................................... 50.00
    White................................ 75.00
Salt and Pepper Shakers, pr, black, short............................................. 95.00
Sherbet, ftd, yellow ................. 35.00
Spice Jar, red, 3 quart ........... 595.00
Sugar, cov, Ivory ..................... 125.00
Sugar Shaker, jade................. 350.00
Teapot, cov
  Cobalt blue......................... 135.00
  Cobalt blue, six cup .......... 350.00
  Red...................................... 150.00
  Rust, Hi-Fire line ................. 60.00
Tumbler, black, 6 oz, wooden handle
  ...................................................... 60.00
Water Set, carafe and six tumblers, wooden handles, red and yellow tumblers, price for set............ 250.00
S. D. Expo, carafe, no cup, 1935
  .................................................... 125.00

# Beanie Babies®

**Collecting Hints:** Here's a collecting category where much of the present-day value depends on the toy being in mint condition with the original tag. The collecting frenzy created by this toy has excited the collectibles marketplace and still continues.

A whole new set of abbreviations, such as MWMT, MWM3T, etc. have evolved, along with terms such as "tush tag" and "string tag." This kind of enthusiasm and creativity in ways to communicate about the collectibil-

ity of Beanie Babies will help foster continued interest, as will the Internet, where websites and chat rooms about Beanie Babies are numerous.

**History:** When H. Ty Warner founded Ty, Inc. in 1986, he hoped to make an impact on the toy market with his stuffed toys. By using good quality fabrics and interesting designs, plus stuffing them with beans and making them affordable to children, he was well on his way. The original set of nine Beanie Babies was released in late 1993. That set included: Chocolate the Moose, Cubbie the Brown Bear, Flash the Dolphin, Legs the Frog, Patti the Platypus, Pincher the Lobster, Splash the Whale, Spot the Dog, and Squealer the Pig. Several of these original nine have been retired and have since increased significantly in value from their original issue price of $5.

By the spring of 1994, a second generation of string tags was developed (today there are 5 generations) and also the second generation of tush tags (today there are 7 different types). Speculation in the market place was fueled by retiring animals, mistakes, changes in tag design, and other variations. By November of 1997, there were 78 releases of different animals and variations.

**References:** Shawn Brecka, *The Beanie Family Album and Collectors Guide,* Antique Trader Books, 1998; —, *The Bean Family Pocket Guide 1999 Values & Trends,* Antique Trader Books, 1998; Les and Sue Fox, *The Beanie Baby Handbook,* West Highland Publishing, 1957; Peggy Gallagher, *The Beanie Baby Phenomenon,* published by author, 1997; Sharon Korbeck, ed., *Toys & Prices, 1999,* 6th edition, Krause Publications, 1998; Rosie Wells, *Rosie's Price Guide for Ty's Beanie Babies,* Rose Wells Enterprises, 1997.

**Periodicals:** *Beanie Collector;* Mary Beth's Beanie World; *Mo's Beanie Baby News Magazine;* Toy Shop; *White's Guide to Collecting Beanie Babies,* plus more. Visit a local newsstand or book store for the latest publications.

**Abbreviations:** Here's a list of some of the new language which has evolved because of Beanie Babies and their dedicated collectors:

MWMT - mint with mint tag

MWM3T - mint with mint three tags (including Canadian tag)

MWCT - mint with creased tag

MWBT - mint with bent tag or mint with both tags

**Note:** Prices listed below are for toys in mint condition, with original tags.

### Advertising

A & W Rootbear Bear...................... 18.00
Caesar's Pizza, Christmas, 1997
..................................................... 15.00
Dairy Queen Cone ......................... 15.00
Energizer Bunny ............................ 15.00
Ernie the Keebler Elf..................... 15.00
Hawaiian Punch............................. 15.00
M & Ms, 4 pc set........................... 45.00
McDonald's, employee promo, 6" h, set of 3 ......................................... 35.00
Mr. Peanut, Planters...................... 10.00
NBC Studios, peacock .................. 25.00
Pillsbury Doughboy ....................... 15.00
Travel Lodge Sleep Bear .............. 15.00

### Retired

Ally the alligator ............................ 49.00
Ants the anteater............................. 6.00
Baldy the eagle............................. 10.00
Bernie the St. Bernard .................... 6.00
Bessie the cow.............................. 60.00
Bruno the terrier.............................. 6.00
Bubbles the fish........................... 145.00
Cubbie the bear............................ 19.00
Daisy the cow ................................. 6.00
Ears the bunny.............................. 12.00
Fetch the golden retriever............... 6.00
Flash the dolphin .......................... 95.00
Flip the cat.................................... 24.00
Goldie the goldfish........................ 55.00
Gracie the swan.............................. 7.00
Grunt the razorback..................... 160.00
Hoot the owl.................................. 39.00
Inch the worm ............................... 16.00
Lizzy the lizard .............................. 19.00

**Kuku the Cockatoo, Ty, $7.**

Manny the manatee..................... 150.00
Patti the platypus .......................... 15.00
Quackers the duck .......................... 8.00
Radar the bat............................... 160.00
Rover the dog................................ 16.00
Seamore the seal......................... 129.00
Sly the fox....................................... 6.00
Snort the bull................................... 6.00
Splash the whale .......................... 95.00
Sting the ray................................ 150.00
Tank the armadillo......................... 70.00
Waddie the penguin ...................... 17.00
Weenie the dog ............................ 18.00
Ziggy the zebra ............................ 10.00
Zip the cat..................................... 20.00

# Beatles

**Collecting Hints:** Beatles collectibles date from 1964 to the present. The majority of memorabilia items were produced from 1964-68. The most valuable items are marked "NEMS." Most collectors are interested in mint or near-mint items only, although some items in very good condition, especially if scarce, have considerable value.

Each year Sotheby's holds one or two auctions which include Beatles memorabilia, primarily one-of-a-kind items such as guitars and stage costumes. The average collector generally does not participate in these sales since the items command high prices.

**History:** The fascination with the Beatles began in 1964. Soon the whole country was caught up in Beatlemania. The members of the group included John Lennon, Paul McCartney, George Harrison, and Ringo Starr. The group broke up in 1970, after which the members pursued individual musical careers. Beatlemania took on new life after the death of John Lennon in 1980.

**References:** Jeff Augsburger, Marty Eck, and Rick Rann, *Beatles Memorabilia Price Guide*, 3rd ed., Antique Trader Books, 1997; Barbara Crawford, Hollis Lamon and Michael Stern, *The Beatles: A Reference & Value Guide, 2nd Edition,* Collector Books, 1998.

**Periodicals:** *Beatlefan*, P.O. Box 33515, Decatur, GA 30033; *Instant Karma*, P.O. Box 256, Sault Ste. Marie, MI 49783.

**Collectors' Clubs:** Beatles Connection, P.O. Box 1066, Pinellas Park, FL 34665; Beatles Fan Club, 397 Edgewood Ave., New Haven, CT 06511; Beatles Fan Club of Great Britain, Superstore Productions, 123 Marina,

St. Leonards on Sea, East Sussex, England TN38 OBN; Working Class Hero Club, 3311 Niagara St., Pittsburgh, PA 15213.

**Reproduction Alert:** Records, picture sleeves, and album jackets have been counterfeited. Sound quality may be poorer on the records, and printing on labels and picture jackets usually is inferior to the original. Many pieces of memorabilia have been reproduced, often with some change in size, color, or design.

Apron, paper, white, black pictures, name, and song titles .............. 75.00
Bag, 9-1/2" x 10", textured vinyl, red, portraits, black inscription and signatures, cord carrying strap, 1964 ......... 165.00
Bank, 7-1/2" h, plastic, Yellow Submarine, bust figures of each Beatle, 1960s, price for set of 4, minor damage........................................ 1,400.00
Banner, printed nylon, black images of four Beatles, blue printed "The Beatles," Memphis, 1966 ........... 1,150.00
Beach Towel, 34" x 57", terry cloth, Beatles in bathing suits, c1960....115.00
Billfold, red, four white signatures on one side, picture on other........ 90.00
Blanket, 62" x 80", wool, tan, printed black and red bust figures and instruments, "The Beatles" center, mfg by Whitney...................... 165.00
Bobbing Head, Ringo, 8" h, 1964
.....................................................90.00
Book, *Yellow Submarine,* Signet Book, October 1968, paperback, 128 pgs
..................................................... 20.00
Bubble Gum Cards, Topps, black and white, 1964 ................................ 2.00
Calendar, 12", spiral bound, 1969, Golden Press, orig brown paper envelope .................................. 65.00
Cake Decorating Kit, figurals, playing instruments, set of 4, MIB...... 195.00
Christmas Tree Ornament, 7" h, blown glass, figural, three in red, one in blue, three plastic guitars, c1960
................................................... 925.00
Coat Hangers, Yellow Submarine, set
................................................... 295.00
Coaster, 4" sq, Yellow Submarine, cardboard, set of 12....................... 65.00
Coloring Book, 8-1/4" x 11", Saalfield, 1964 Nems copyright, includes 8 black and white photos, unused
..................................................... 65.00
Doll, 5" h, Paul McCartney, Remco, 1962....................................... 85.00
Drum, 14" d, red sparkle finish, "The Beatles Drum" on skin, metal stand, mfg by Mastro........................ 325.00
Figure, 6-1/2" h, painted and glazed plaster, set of four, 1960s....... 150.00
Handkerchief, 8-1/2" sq................ 20.00
Hummer, 10-1/2" l cardboard tube, full color paper label of Beatles portraits against blue background, black text "Hum Along With Your Official Beatle

**Record Case, olive green and black, ©1966 NEMS Enterprises, Ltd., plastic, 8-1/4" h, $75.**

Hummer," Merrimaker, © 1964 NEMS Enterprises Ltd., yellow plastic cap, funnel end missing.....................20.00
Lunch Box
  Blue, rim wear ........................285.00
  Yellow Submarine, some edge wear ...................................................125.00
Magazine Cover and Story
  *Life,* Aug. 6, 1981, Yoko story .. 15.00
  *Pop Pics Super,* 1964...............12.00
  *Sixteen,* August 1966...............15.00
  *Teen World,* July 1965..............15.00
  *Time,* Dec. 22, 1980, John Lennon .................................................10.00
Mug, 4" h, 3" d, ceramic, bust photos of group wearing blue jackets, England, c1964.........................85.00
Notebook, three-ring binder, red vinyl cov, Standard Plastic Products ...................................................135.00
Paddle Ball Game........................100.00
Pencil Case, 8" x 3-1/2", vinyl, blue, group picture and facsimile autographs, zipper top, Standard Plastic Products....................................35.00
Pencil Tablet, 7-3/4" x 10", full color photo cover, facsimile signatures, Lewis F. Dow Co., ©NEMS Ltd. London, dated 1967.......................35.00
Pennant, 23" l, felt, white, red, and black, printed illus and facsimile signatures, red trim and streamers, "Official Licensee" copyright, c1964 .................................................80.00
Photograph, official, 8" x 10", printed in USA, set of 4 ............................45.00
Program, tour, Beatles pictured in playing cards, 1964 British tour, minor folds ......................................230.00
Puzzle, Yellow Submarine, MIB ....55.00
Ring, flasher type, 1960s, set of 4 ...........................................25.00
School Bag, 12" x 9" x 3-1/2", tan, "The Beatles" printed on flap, handle, and shoulder strap.........................215.00
Scrapbook, NEMS, 1964 ..............50.00

Soap Container, 10" h, plastic, Ringo, removable head, Colgate-Palmolive Co., 1965 Nems copyright........85.00
T-Shirt, Beatles '65, size large ...... 17.00
Tile, 6" sq, ceramic, group picture, "The Beatles," mfg by Carter Tiles... 85.00
Wallet, 3-1/2" x 4-1/2" tan vinyl, brown-tone photo, black facsimile signatures, Standard Plastics Products, ©Ramat & Co., Ltd., 1964........85.00
Wallpaper Section, 20-1/2" x 21", unused, four images, facsimile signatures, c1964 .........................20.00

# Beer Bottles

**Collecting Hints:** Beer bottles often are found by digging in old dumps or wells. Although these bottles may be discolored and flaked, the key is whether or not they are broken. Damage to the bottle is of greater concern in pricing than the discoloration.

Concentrate on the bottles from one brewery or area. When an example is sold in the area in which it originated, it is likely to command more money than when sold outside that local region

Over the years, breweries usually changed bottle styles several times. This also is true for the paper labels found on later bottles.

Early bottles had special closures, and a bottle is worth more if the closure is intact. Presence of the metal caps is not critical to the value of later bottles. However, collecting metal caps is a growing field.

**History:** Breweries began in America shortly after the arrival of the first settlers. By the mid-19th century, most farmsteads had a small brewery on them. Local breweries dominated the market until the arrival of Prohibition. The majority of breweries closed although a few larger ones survived.

When Prohibition ended, a much smaller number of local breweries renewed production. The advertising, distribution, and production costs of the 1950s and 1960s led to the closing of most local breweries and the merger of many other breweries into a few national companies.

In the 1960s, imported beers from Europe entered the American market. Some companies signed licensing agreements to produce these foreign labels in the United States. In more recent years, beers brewed in Canada and Mexico have been gaining popularity.

**References:** Donna S. Baker, *Vintage Anheuser-Busch, An Unofficial Collector's Guide,* Schiffer, 1999; Ralph and Terry Kovel, *Kovels' Bottles Price List,* 11th ed., Crown Publishers, 1999; Michael Polak, *Bottles,* 2nd ed., Avon Books, 1997.

**Collectors' Club:** American Breweriana Association, Inc., P.O. Box 11157, Pueblo, CO 81001.

**Embossed**

Buffalo Brewing Co., Sacramento, CA, cmb buffalo jumping through horse shoe, 12" h, amber, blob top.... 20.00
Cumberland Brew Co., Cumberland, MD, amber..............................10.00
Excelsior, 9-1/4" h, aqua ..............18.50
Hand Brew Co., Pawtucket, RI, aqua ...................................................15.00
Iroquois, Buffalo, Indian head, amber ...................................................12.00
Piel Bros., East New York Brewery, fancy logo, aqua.....................19.00
Royal Ruby, ABM, 9-1/2" h............28.00

**Painted Label**

Augusta Brewing Co., Augusta, CA, 7" h, aqua.......................................15.00
Rolling Rock Extra Pale, blue and white label, green label, unopened... 20.00
Schlitz Brewing Co., 9-1/2" h, amber ...................................................10.00

**Paper Label**

Central Brand Extra Lager Beer, 9-1/4" h, aqua.......................................8.00
Cooks 500 Ale, 9-1/2" h, aqua........5.00
Diamond Jim's Beer, 9-1/4" h, aqua ...................................................6.50
Pabst Extract, amber, two labels ...................................................12.00
Southern Brewing Co., machine made, 9-1/2" h, green .........................4.00

**Stoneware**

Biscomb's, 8-1/2" h, brown and tan ...................................................15.00
Ginger Beer, c1915 ......................35.00
Russell's.......................................40.00

# Beer Cans

**Collecting Hints:** Rusted and dented cans have little value unless they are rare examples in some respect. Most collectors remove the beer from the cans. Cans should be opened from the bottom to preserve the unopened top.

As beer can collecting became popular, companies issued special collectors' cans which never contained beer. Many were bought on speculation; value has been shaky.

**History:** Before Prohibition, beer was stored and shipped in kegs and dispensed in returnable bottles. When the Prohibition Act was repealed in 1933, only 700 of 1,700

breweries resumed operation. Expanding distribution created the need for an inexpensive container that would permit beer to be stored longer and shipped safely. Cans were the answer.

The first patent for a lined can was issued to the American Can Co. on Sept. 25, 1934, for its Keglined process. Gotfried Kruger Brewing Co., Newark, New Jersey, was the first brewery to use the can. Pabst was the first major company to join the canned-beer movement.

Continental Can Co. introduced the cone-top beer can in 1935, and Schlitz was the first brewery to use this type of can. The next major change in beer can design was the aluminum pop-top in 1962.

**Reference:** Thomas Toepfer, *Beer Cans*, L-W Book Sales, 1976, 1995 value update.

**Collectors' Clubs:** Beer Can Collectors of America, 747 Merus Ct., Fenton, MO 63026; Capitol City Chapter of the Beer Can Collectors of America, P.O. Box 287, Brandywine, MD 20613; Gambrinus Chapter of the Beer Can Collectors of America, 985 Maebelle Way, Westerville, OH 43081.

**Museum:** The Museum of Beverage Containers and Advertising, Goddlettsville, TN.

**Note:** The listings follow this order: name, type of beer, brewery location, top identification, price.

**Abbreviations:** The following abbreviations are used in the listings:
    CR - Crowntainer-type cone top
    CT - cone type
    FT - flat top
    ML - malt liquor
    PT - pull top

### 7 oz

Ace Hi M.L, Ace, Chicago, IL, FT ............................................. 115.00
Lucky Lager, Lucky Lager, San Francisco, CA, FT ............................ 12.00
Olympia Light, Olympia, Olympia, WA, PT ...................................... 8.50
Rolling Rock, Labrobe, Latrobe, PA, PT ............................................. 4.50

### 8 oz

Bantam, Goebel, Detroit, MI, FT ..... 27.50
Colt 45 M.L., National, 4 cities, PT ............................................. 2.00
Goebel Ale, Goebel, Detroit, MI, FT ............................................. 35.00
Pike's Peak M.L., Walter, Pueblo, COP, FT ............................................. 45.00
Tech Premium, Pittsburgh, Pittsburgh, PA, FT ...................................... 60.00

### 10 oz

Budweiser, Anheuser-Busch, 7 cities, PT ............................................. 5.00
Fabacher Brau, Jackson, New Orleans, LA, PT ...................................... 12.00
Schaefer, Schaefer, 3 cities, PT ...... 3.50

### 11 and 12 oz

ABC Ale, Wagner, Columbus, OH, PT ............................................. 4.00
Atles, National, Detroit, MI, FT ...... 40.00
Ballantine, P Ballantine, Newark, NJ, PT ............................................. 5.00
Berghoff, Berghoff, Ft Wayne, IN, FT ............................................. 75.00
Breuing's, Rice Lake, Rice Lake, WI, FT ............................................. 7.50
Butte Special, Butte, Butte, MT, FT ............................................. 25.00
Chief Oshkosh, Oshkosh, Oshkosh, WI, FT ............................................. 15.00
Dutch Treat, Dutch Treat, Phoenix, AZ, PT ............................................. 2.50
Eastside Old Tap, Pabst, Los Angeles, CA, FT ............................................. 15.00
Fisher Light, General, 2 cities, PT ......... 2.00
Gablinger's, Forrest, New Bedford, MA, PT ............................................. 6.50
Hamm's, Hamm, St Paul, MN, PT ... 4.00
Heidelbrau, Heileman, LaCrosse WI, PT ............................................. 2.50
Horlacher Pilsner, Horlacher, Allentown, PA, FT ............................................. 10.00
Kentucky M.L., Fehr, Louisville, KY, FT ............................................. 45.00
Manheim, Reading, Reading, PA, FT ............................................. 12.00
Milwaukee's Best, Miller, Milwaukee, WI, PT ............................................. 7.50
National Bohemian, National, Detroit, MI, FT ............................................. 15.00
North Star, Associated, 3 cities, PT ............................................. 4.00
Old Crown Ale, Centilgre, Ft Wayne, IN, FT ............................................. 50.00
Pearl Draft, Pearl, 2 cities, PT ......... 1.00
Queens Brau, Queen City, Cumberland, MD, FT ............................................. 55.00
Red Top, Drewrys, South Bend, IN, PT ............................................. 10.00
Schiltz Light, Schlitz, 6 cities, PT .... 1.00
Stein Haus, Schell, New Ulm, MN, PT ............................................. 4.00
Tavern Pale, Atlantic, Chicago, IL, FT ............................................. 30.00
Topper, Eastern, Hammonton, NJ, PT ............................................. 4.00
Utica Club Pale Ale, West End, Utica, NY, FT ............................................. 50.00
Valley Forge, Valley Forge, Norristown, PA, FT ............................................. 20.00
Walter's Light, Walter, Pueblo, CO, PT ............................................. 4.00
West Virginia Pilsner, Little Switzerland, Huntington, WV, PT ...................... 5.00
Yuengling, Yuengling, Pottsville, PA, PT ............................................. 6.00

### 12 oz, Cone Top

Aero Club Pale Select, East Idaho, Pocatello, ID, CT ............................................. 125.00
Breuing's Lager, Rice Lake, Rice Lake, WI, CT ............................................. 65.00
Falstaff, Falstaff, 3 cities, CT ......... 30.00
Rahr's, Rahr's Green Bay, Green Bay, WI, CT ............................................. 55.00
Stag Premium Dry, Griesedieck-Western, 2 cities, CT ...................... 35.00
Ye Tavern, Lafayette, Lafayette, IN, CT ............................................. 95.00

### 15 and 16 oz

Altes, National, Detroit, MI, PT ........ 5.00
Burger, Burger, Cincinnati, OH, PT ............................................. 30.00
Champagne Velvet, Associated, 3 cities, PT ............................................. 12.00
Eastside Old Tap, Pabst, Los Angeles, CA, FT ............................................. 18.50
Hamm's Draft, Hamm, 3 cities, PT ............................................. 5.00
Mustang Malt Lager, Pittsburgh, Pittsburgh, PA, PT .................................. 25.00
Old German, Easter, Hammonton, NJ, PT ............................................. 5.00
Piels Light, Piels, Brooklyn, NY, FT ............................................. 25.00
Spur Stout M.L., Sick's Rainer, Seattle, WA, PT ............................................. 50.00
Whale's White Ale, National, 4 cities, PT ............................................. 35.00

# Beswick

**Collecting Hints:** Collectors have shortened the name of these interesting ceramics from House of Beswick to simply Beswick. There are five common marks that consist of "Beswick, England." Some include shape numbers and other information.

**History:** Beswick characters are well known to collectors and include figures from children's literature, as well as animals and other subjects. The firm was created by James Wright Beswick and his sons, John and Gilbert Beswick in 1894. Initial production was plain and decorated wares. By 1900, they were producing jugs, tea ware, dinner ware, flower pots, pedestals, figurines, vases, bread trays, and other household items. The factory was a family run organization for decades. Gilbert Beswick is credited with creating the company's shape numbering system and shape book in 1934 while he was sales manager and his nephew, John Ewart Beswick, was chairman and managing director.

The first full-time modeller, Arther Gredington, was hired in 1939. Many of the designs he created are still in production. James Hayward was an outstanding decorator and created many new patterns and shapes. He also is credited with experimenting and perfecting glazes used on Beswick wares.

By 1969, the family members were nearing their retirement years and had no successors, so the company was sold to Royal Doulton Tableware, Ltd. Many of the Beswick animals are still being continued by Royal Doulton, but several have been discontinued. In August of 1989, the animal line was renamed as "Doulton Animals" and numbering system instituted that includes DA numbers rather than the Beswick backstamp.

**References:** Diana Callow et al., *The Charlton Standard Catalogue of Beswick Animals*, 3rd ed., Charlton Press, 1998; Diana and John Callow, *The Charlton Standard Catalogue of Beswick Pottery*, Charlton Press, 1997; Jean Dale, *The Charlton Catalogue of Royal Doulton Beswick Figurines*, 6th ed., Charlton Press, 1998; Harvey May, *The Beswick Price Guide*, 3rd ed., Francis Joseph Publications, 1995, distributed by Krause Publications.

Character Mug
　Falstaff, inscribed, "Pistol with Wit or Steel, Merry Wives of Windsor," imp "Beswick, England, #1127," 1948-73, 4" h ...................................... 90.00
　Hamlet, inscribed "To Be or Not To Be," imp "Beswick, England, #1147," 1949-73, 4-1/4" h...................... 90.00
　Mr. Bumble, mkd "Beswick #2032, Parish Beadle," 4-3/4" h ........... 65.00
Child's Feeding Dish, Mickey and Donald on bicycle................ 140.00
Decanter, Loch Ness Monster, Beneagles Scotch Whiskey, modeled by A. Hallam, 1969 ........................... 75.00
Figure
　Amiable Guinea Pig, mkd "Beswick, England, #37, F. Warne & Co., Ltd., Copyright 1967," slight dent in hat, attributed as factory flaw, 3-1/2" h ............................................... 240.00
　Barnaby Rudge........................ 60.00
　Benjamin Ate A Lettuce Leaf, mkd "Beswick, Made in England, Beatrix Potter, F. Warne & Co.," 1992 Royal Doulton," 4-3/4" h .................... 40.00
　Benjamin Bunny, Royal Albert, mkd "Beswick, Made in England, Beatrix Pottery, F. Warne & Co., 1948, 1989 Royal Doulton" ....................... 36.00
　Black Bull, 4-1/2" h, 7-1/2" l .... 210.00
　Bulldog, white and tan, 2-1/4" h ............................................... 45.00
　Charalais Bull, wood stand, 6" h, 9" l ............................................. 225.00
　Charalais Cow and Calf, 4-1/4" h x 7-1/2" h cow, pr ......................... 235.00
　Chippy Hackee, Beatrix Potter, copyright 1979, 3-3/4" h.................... 55.00
　Foxy Whiskered Gentleman, mkd "Beswick, Made in England, Beatrix Potter, F. Warne & Co., 1954, 1989 Royal Doulton," 4-3/4" h ........... 36.00

Hereford Bull, 4-3/4" h, 7-1/2" l ............................................. 185.00
Hereford Bull, 6" h, 9" h .......... 225.00
Hereford Cow, 4-1/2" h, 6-3/4" l ............................................. 165.00
Jemima Puddleduck, mkd in gold "Beswick Ware, Made in England," Jemima
　Miss Muppet, Beatrix Potter gold mark .................................. 200.00
　Mr. Alderman Ptolemy, BP38 ............................................. 150.00
　Mrs. Floppay Bunney ........ 225.00
Owl, 4-1/2" h............................. 52.00
Palomino Horse, #1261, 6-3/4" h ............................................. 165.00
Peter Rabbit, mkd in gold "Beswick Ware, Made In England, 1997, Royal Doulton" .............................. 65.00
Puddleduck, Beatrix Potter, F. Warne & Co., 1997 Royal Doulton, #33, #15, #29," MIB .............................. 55.00
Samuel Whiskers, BP2 ........... 250.00
Scottie, white, ladybug on nose, #HN804, 1940-69 ................... 225.00
Siamese Cat Standing, #1896, 1963-80, oval mark, 6-1/2" h .......... 100.00
Swish Tail Horse, #1182, orig Beswick sticker, 8-1/2" h, 10" l ............................................. 225.00
Timmy Willie, from Johnny Town Mouse, mkd "Beswick, England, F. Warne & Co., Ltd., copyright 1949," 3" h .......................................... 45.00
Tom Kitten, mkd "Beswick Ware, Made in England, 1997 Royal Doulton," 3-1/2" h ........................ 65.00
Tom Kitten and Butterfly, BP3C ............................................. 275.00
Tony Weller............................... 85.00
Walking Horse and Jockey, #1037, mkd "Beswick England," #55, 8-1/2" h, 10-1/2" l................................. 475.00
Modelle Jug, shape #694, deep maroon leaves, stems, flowers, and bunny, stamped "Made in England, 694, Beswick Ware," 1939-62, 9-1/4" h, 6" w ........................................ 150.00
Plate, 7" d, Disney characters ...... 95.00
Teapot, Sairy Gump, #691, c1930, 5-1/4" h, slight minor crazing under glaze ..................................... 125.00
Vase
　#432, double handles, mkd "Beswick, Made in England, #432," 11-1/2" h, 9-1/4" w .................... 95.00
　#843, tulip, semi-gloss, white cornucopia type, base incised "Made in England, Beswick 843," 1940-54, 5-3/4" l, 3-1/2" w ......................... 50.00

# Bicycle Collectibles

**Collecting Hints:** Collectors divide bicycles into two groups—antique and classic. The antique category includes early high wheelers through safety bikes made into the 1920s and 1930s. Highly stylized bicycles

from the 1930s and 1940s represent the transitional step to the classic period, beginning in the late 1940s and running through the end of the balloon-tire era.

Unfortunately, there are no reliable guide books for the beginning collector. A good rule is that any older bike in good condition is worth collecting.

Restoration is an accepted practice, but never pay a high price for a bicycle that is rusted, incomplete, or repaired with non-original parts. Replacement of leather seats or rubber handle bars does not effect value since these have a short life.

Make certain to store an old bicycle high (hung by its frame to protect the tires) and dry (humidity should be no higher than 50%).

Do not forget all the secondary material that features bicycles, e.g., advertising premiums, brochures, catalogs, and posters. This material provides important historical data for research, especially for restoration.

Bicycle collectors and dealers gather each year on the last weekend in April at the Saline/Ann Arbor Swap Meet and Show in Michigan.

**History:** In 1818, Baron Karl von Drais, a German, invented the Draisienne, a push scooter, that is viewed as the "first" bicycle. In 1839, Patrick MacMillan, a Scot, added a treadle system; a few years later Pierre Michaux, a Frenchman, revolutionized the design by adding a pedal system. The bicycle was introduced in America at the 1876 Centennial.

Early bicycles were high wheelers with a heavy iron frame and two disproportionately sized wheels with wooden rims and tires. The exaggerated front wheel was for speed, the small rear wheel for balance.

James Starley, an Englishman, is responsible for developing a bicycle with two wheels of equal size. Pedals drove the rear wheels by means of a chain and sprocket. By 1892, wooden rim wheels were replaced by pneumatic air-filled tires, and these were followed by standard rubber tires with inner tubes.

The coaster brake was developed in 1898. This important milestone made cycling a true family sport. Bicycling became a cult among the urban middle class—as the new century dawned, over four million Americans owned bicycles.

The automobile challenged the popularity of bicycling in the 1920s. Since that time, interest in bicycling has been cyclical although technical advances continued. The 1970s was the decade of the ten speed.

The success of American Olympiads in cycling and the excitement of cycle racing, especially the Tour d'France, have kept the public's attention focused on the bicycle. However, the tremendous resurgence enjoyed by bicycling in the 1970s appears to have ended. The next craze is probably some distance in the future.

**References:** Jim Hurd, *Bicycle Blue Book,* Memory Lane Classics, 1997; Jay Pridmore and Jim Hurd, *The American Bicycle,* Motorbooks International, 1996; Neil S. Wood, *Evolution of the Bicycle,* Vol. 1 (1991, 1994 value update), Vol. 2 (1994), L-W Book Sales.

**Periodicals:** *Antique/Classic Bicycle News,* P.O. Box 1049, Ann Arbor, MI 48106; *Bicycle Trader,* P.O. Box 3324, Ashland, OR 97520; *Classic & Antique Bicycle Exchange,* 325 W. Hornbeam Drive, Longwood, FL 32779; *Classic Bike News,* 5046 E. Wilson Rd., Clio, MI, 48420; *National Antique & Classic Bicycle,* P.O. Box 5600, Pittsburgh, PA 15207.

**Collectors' Clubs:** Cascade Classic Cycle Club, 7935 SE Market St., Portland, OR 97215; Classic Bicycle and Whizzer Club, 35769 Simon, Clinton Township, MI 48035; International Veteran Cycle Association, 248 Highland Dr., Findlay, OH 45840; National Pedal Vehicle Association, 1720 Rupert, NE, Grand Rapids, MI 49505; The Wheelmen, 55 Bucknell Ave., Trenton, NJ 08619.

**Museum:** Schwinn History Center, Chicago.

Advertising Mirror, Bakersfield Cyclery and Novelty Works ................... 20.00
Badge
    L.A.W. 18th Annual Meet/Philadelphia/Aug. 4-7, 1897, diecut brass link, "Souvenir," pendant in shape of victory wreath around star symbol centered by logo of League of American Wheelman ......................... 65.00
    YMCA Bicycle Club/New Brunswick, NJ, 1896, gold luster metal link, inscribed "Mileage" hanger bar, pendant with victory wreath motif and YMCA inscription around triangle logo, back professionally engraved "Century-1896 YMCA Bicycle Club/ New Brunswick, NJ" ................. 75.00

Bicycle
Ace Cycle and Motor Works, metal label reading "George Tenby-Cycling champion of Wales- retired, 1879-1889," as-found orig condition ............................................. 150.00
Ames and Frost Co, Model #36 Imperial ................................. 500.00
AMF Roadmaster .................. 500.00
Bronco, boy's ...................... 5,500.00
Chilion, wood frame, 1898 ..... 100.00
Cleveland, lady's drive shaft model, 20" frame ............................... 290.00
Columbia
    Expert, 1887, 54" wheel, orig condition .............................. 2,500.00
    Fire Arrow ......................... 300.00
    5 Star Superb, 75th Anniversary edition ............................... 375.00
    Standard, 1883, 48" front wheel, restored condition .......... 2,700.00
    Twinbar .......................... 3,200.00
Dayton Champion .............. 4,620.00
Elgin
    Black Hawk, 1934 .......... 2,200.00
    Miss America, 1939, balloon tires ....................................... 1,320.00
Elliot, hickory safety, wooden spokes and fellows, c1898, as-found condition, needs retiring ................. 470.00
Excelsior, man's motor, orig olive drab, no tires ...................... 1,050.00
High Wheeler, Scottish, 42" h front wheel, primitive, excellent condition ........................................... 3,100.00
Huffy, Radiobike ................. 2,000.00
Lady's, hard tired safety type, 1891, good unrestored condition ........................................... 3,600.00
Monarch, Silver King, hex tube ............................................. 825.00
Overman Wheel Co., Victor Light, safety, man's, 25" frame, butterfly handlebars, c1894 ................. 395.00
Pope Mfg Co., Columbia Model #50, drive-shaft, orig condition ...... 400.00
Roadmaster, Luxury Liner ...... 600.00
Rollfast, Custom Built, Model V200 ........................................... 2,750.00
Schwinn
    Aerocycle Model 34 ....... 8,500.00
    Autocycle, B-107 ............ 1,750.00

**Bicycle, Veliopede, New York, referred to as "boneshaker," $7,670. Photo courtesy of Auction Team Breker.**

**Game of Bicycle Race, McLoughlin Bros., boxed board game, multicolored litho, wood box, 1895, $265.**

Corvette ........................... 300.00
Hornet .............................. 400.00
Mark II Jaguar .................. 750.00
Panther, Model D-77, girl's ........................................... 900.00
Phantom, Model D0-27 ..... 900.00
Starlet, Model D0-67 ........ 500.00
Seaman, wood frame .......... 3,630.00
Sears, Elgin
    Bluebird .......................... 7,000.00
    Robin .............................. 3,500.00
    Skylark ........................... 2,000.00
    Twin 30 ........................... 700.00
Shelby, Donald Duck ......... 2,000.00
Springfield Roadster, c1888, 50" to 100" ratchet drive, orig condition ........................................... 5,100.00
Sterling, tandem, lady's front three gear, c1897, orig condition ........................................... 1,200.00
TRB Alenax, ratchet drive, nice condition ............................. 110.00
Unknown Maker, hard-tired safety type ........................................ 700.00
Western Wheel Works, Chicago, IL, Otto, boy's, c1900, late high wheel, wooden spokes ................. 1,350.00
Whizzer, Model H, 1948 ..... 2,310.00
Bike Horn, Hopalong Cassidy, orig handlebar clamp ........................ 150.00
Book
    *Around the World on a Bicycle,* Fred A. Birchmore, autographed ..... 30.00
    Patterson, 150 line drawings ... 70.00
    *Bicycling World,* 4 volume set ........................................... 1,265.00
    *Riding High,* A. Judson Palmer, autographed .................................. 82.50
    *The Wheel and Cycle Trade Reviews,* 25 volume set ...... 4,100.00
Brochure, Schwinn-Built Bicycles, 3-1/4" x 6", illus of nine bicycles, c1948 ............................................. 55.00
Cabinet Card, man with high wheeler ............................................. 120.00
Catalog
    Eclipse, Elmira, NY ................. 46.00
    Flying Merkel, 1916 .............. 250.00
    G. W. Stevens Bike Suits, orig fabric swatches ............................. 100.00
    Imperial ................................. 25.00
    Indian Bicycle ........................ 90.00
    Iver Johnson, 1914 .............. 120.00
    Mead Cycle Co., Chicago, IL, c1923 ............................................. 14.00
    NSU Motorcycle .................... 110.00

Rollfast ...................................... 70.00
Springfield Roadster .............. 110.00
Victor Bicycle, 1898 .............. 200.00
White Flyer, 1890 .................. 880.00
Dance Card, 3-1/4" x 5-1/2", Nashua
Cycle Club, 1888, cardboard folder
.................................................... 25.00
Display, Dunlop Cycle, repair display
and repair outfit ......................... 70.00
Lamp
Argonaut ................................... 45.00
Evel Knievel Tail Light, Mego, 1974,
MOC ...........................................35.0
Lucas, Silver King, petroleum .. 95.00
Majestic Lamp .......................... 25.00
P & H Ltd., The Winner ............. 15.00
Solar Model S .......................... 55.00
Lapel Stud, 7/8" d, celluloid on metal,
c1896
America, red letter on white "Buy The
America and You Can't Go Wrong"
.................................................... 20.00
Bicycle Saddles, red, and white,
winged gargoyle trademark, Muller
Mfg Co., NY ............................... 25.00
Colonial Bicycles, red, white, and
blue, patriot shield symbol ....... 20.00
Columbia Bicycles, black and white,
nameplate inscribed "You See Them
Everywhere" ............................. 20.00
Conroy Bicycle, Willard & Conroy, CO,
NY, black, white, and red .......... 15.00
Crescent Bicycles, red lunar cres-
cent, white ground, black letters
.................................................... 20.00
Dey's Bike, red, white, and blue fig-
ural wheel ................................. 20.00
Falcon, olive green and pink logo,
tiny falcon image ...................... 20.00
Frontenac Bicycles, brown and white
.................................................... 15.00
Northampton Bicycles, olive green,
black, and white ....................... 15.00
Oquaga, white letters, rose pink
ground ...................................... 15.00
Phoenix Bike, black, white, and red,
trademark Phoenix bird rising from
ashes, slogan "It Stands The Racket"
.................................................... 20.00
Richmond Bicycle Company, black
and white .................................. 15.00
Spaulding, black, white, and red
.................................................... 10.00
Sylph Cycles Run Easy, black and
white .......................................... 15.00
The Fowler Bicycles, white letters,
plum ground .............................. 20.00
The Liberty, black letters, peach
ground, tiny slogan "American's
Representative Bicycle" ............ 25.00
The Winton, white letters, deep pur-
ple ground ................................. 15.00
Yellow Fellow, black letters, orange
ground, "Trans-Continental Relay
Souvenir," sponsored by NY Journal
Examiner ................................... 30.00
Lap Robe, cycling motif ............. 320.00
Magazine Tear Sheet
Murray Bicycles, Eliminator, Murray
Lightweights, and Murray Wildcats,
*Boys' Life, 1967* ........................ 3.00
Raleigh, Chopper, *Boys' Life,* 1970
.................................................... 3.00

Roadmaster, half sheet, *Saturday
Evening Post,* 1951 .................... 2.00
Schwinn Christmas, Krates, Orange
Krate, Lemon Peeler, Apple Krate,
and Pea Picker .......................... 3.00
Membership Cards, L.A.W., 1886 to
1907 ........................................ 130.00
Nameplate, early 1900s
2-1/2" h, aluminum, Bloomingdale's
Lexington, New York ................ 18.00
2-1/2" h, silvered sheet metal, Ward's
Hawthorne ............................... 15.00
3" h, curled brass, Roamer ...... 20.00
Photo Album, two cabinet cards, ten tin-
types of bicyclists ...................... 700.00
Photograph, William Witaschek, The
Great Calvert, 1937, 30th year on
road ........................................... 60.00
Pinback Button, 7/8" d, celluloid, c1896
Bellis Bicycles, multicolored .... 25.00
Ellsmore Bicycles, multicolored, red
and black lettering ................... 30.00
Mak-Nu, Expressly For Bicycle Use
.................................................... 15.00
Member Bicycle Riders Thrift
League ...................................... 23.00
Ride a Pope Bicycle, black, white,
and blue, green Tribune model .25.00
Stewart's Cycle Brake, blue image,
red letters, white ground .......... 15.00
Superb Ajax Cycles, white letters,
blue ground .............................. 15.00
Playing Cards, Monark, King Cooper,
1895 ........................................ 300.00
Quadracycle, leather seat and fenders,
tiller steering, handles for pumping
................................................ 1,000.00
Ribbon, Clerk of the Course, 1896
.................................................... 45.00
Seat
DeLuxe Messenger, leather, balloon
tire type bicycle ....................... 20.00
Monarch, twin .......................... 30.00
Sheet Music, *Velocipedia* ........... 110.00
Stickpin, 7/8" d celluloid, Lovell Dia-
mond Cycles, black and white, dia-
mond logo, c1896 ..................... 30.00
Tandem, Victor ....................... 1,760.00
Tire Setter, Improved Peerless .... 150.00
Trade Card, Clark Bicycle Co., Christ-
mas, Santa on high wheeler, 1880s
.................................................... 25.00
Tricycle
Boy's, butterfly handlebar, leather
padded seat ........................... 190.00
Gendron, c1900, tiller steering, 20"
wheel, restored ...................... 370.00
Girl's, tiller steering, 28" rear wheels,
front treadle drive ................... 270.00
Homer Benedict, invalid type .. 325.00
Hopalong Cassidy ................. 660.00
Victor, 25" wheels, c1890 .... 1,000.00

# Big Little Books

**Collecting Hints:** Ongoing research
on Big Little Books is a factor in shifting values. Condition always has
been a key. Few examples are in
mint condition since the books were
used heavily by the children who

owned them. Each collector strives
to obtain copies free from as many
defects (bent edges on cover, missing spine, torn pages, mutilation with
crayon or pencil, missing pages,
etc.) as possible.

The main character in a book will
also determine price since collectors
from other fields vie with Big Little
Book collectors for the same work.
Cowboy heroes (currently experienc-
ing renewed popularity), Dick Tracy,
Disney characters, Buck Rogers,
Flash Gordon, Charlie Chan, and The
Green Hornet are a few examples of
this crossover influence.

Until recently little attention was
given to the artists who produced
the books. Now, however, books by
Alex Raymond and Henry Vallely
command top dollar. Other desirable
artists are Al Capp, Allen Dean,
Alfred Andriola, and Will Gould. Personal taste still is a critical factor.

Little is known about production
runs for each book title. Scarcity
charts have been prepared but constantly are being revised. Books
tend to hit the market in hoards, with
prices fluctuating accordingly. However, the last decade has witnessed
price stabilization.

The introduction to Larry Lowery's
book includes an excellent section
on the care and storage of Big Little
Books. He also deserves credit for
the detailed research evident in
each listing.

**History:** Big Little Books, although a
trademark of the Whitman Publishing
Co., is a term used to describe a
wealth of children's books published from the 1930s to the present
day. Whitman and Saalfied Publishing Company dominated the field.
However, other publishers did enter
the market. Among them were
Engel-Van Wiseman, Lynn Publishing Co., Goldsmith Publishing Co.,
and Dell Publishing Co.

The origins of Big Little Books can
be traced to several series published by Whitman in the 1920s.
These included Fairy Tales, Forest
Friends, and Boy Adventure. The
first actual Big Little Book appeared
in 1933. Ten different page lengths
and eight different sizes were tried
by Whitman prior to the 1940s.

Whitman also deserves attention
for the various remarketing efforts it
undertook with many of its titles. It
contracted to provide Big Little Book
premiums for Cocomalt, Kool Aid,
Pan-Am Gas, Macy's, Lily-Tulip's Tar-

zan Ice Cream, and others. Among its series are Wee Little Books, Big Big Books, Nickel Books, Penny Books, and Famous Comics.

In the 1950s, television characters were introduced into Big Little Book format. Whitman Publishing became part of Western Publishing, owned by Mattel. Waldman and Son Publishing Co. under its subsidiary, Moby Books, issued its first book in the Big-Little-Book style in 1977.

**References:** Bill Borden, The Big Book of Big Little Books, Chronicle Books, 1997; Larry Jacobs, Big Little Books: A Collector's Reference & Value Guide, Collector Books, 1996; Lawrence Lowery, Lowery's Collector's Guide to Big Little Books and Similar Books, privately printed, 1981; Price Guide to Big Little Books & Better Little, Jumbo, Tiny Tales, A Fast-Action Story, etc., L-W Book Sales, 1995.

**Collectors' Club:** Big Little Book Collector Club of America, P.O. Box 1242, Danville, CA 94526.

**Notes:** Prices are for books in very fine condition: cover and spine intact, only slight bending at the corners, all pages present, only slightest discoloration of pages, a crisp book from cover color to inside pages, unless otherwise noted.

**Additional Listings:** Cartoon Characters, Cowboy Heroes, Disneyana, Space Adventurers.

**Big Little Books**

*Buck Rogers & The Super Dwarf of Space* .................................... 145.00
*Buffalo Bill and the Pony Express*. 35.00
*Daktari, Night of Terror,* 1968, bent cover ........................................ 15.00
*Danger Trails* ................................. 30.00
*Ella Cinders And The Mysterious House,* Whitman #1106, 1934 copyright .......................................... 50.00
*Fantastic Four In The House of Horrors,* Whitman, #575, 1968 ............... 22.00
*G-Man In Action* ............................ 75.00
*G-Man On Lightning Island* ........ 115.00
*Gunsmoke,* #1647 .......................... 22.50
*Mickey Mouse And Bobo The Elephant,* Whitman #1160, 1935 copyright .................................................. 75.00
*Pink Panther,* flip-it cartoons, 1976 .................................................... 6.00
*Pluto The Pup,* Whitman #1467, 1938 copyright ................................. 65.00
*Popeye, Ghost Ship to Treasure Island,* 1976, corner creased ................. 6.00
*Powder Smoke Range,* Harry Carey and Hoot Gibson ............................ 45.00
*Red Ryder Circus Luck,* #1466, 1949, worn, small tears, marks .......... 30.00
*Shooting Sheriffs* ........................... 25.00

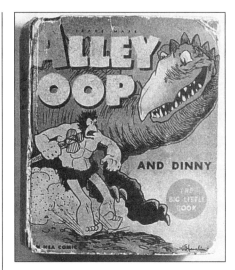

*Alley Oop and Dinny,* **Whitman, #763, worn, $20.**

*Skeezix At The Military Academy,* Whitman #1408, 1938 copyright ..... 30.00
*Smilin Jack And The Stratosphere Ascent,* Whitman #1152, 1937 copyright ........................................... 30.00
*Snow White and The Seven Dwarfs,* Whitman #1460, 1938 copyright .................................................. 60.00
*Terry & The War in the Jungle,* 1946, 4-1/2" x 3-1/2", name written on inside cover ........................................ 25.00
*Tom and Jerry Meet Mr. Fingers,* 1967 .................................................. 18.00
*Tom Beatty,* slight wear ................. 25.00
*Treasure Island,* Whitman #1141, 4-3/4" x 5-1/4", 1934 copyright, movie edition, Jackie Cooper, Wallace Berry .................................................. 100.00
*Tweety and Sylvester, The Magic Voice,* 1976 ............................................ 7.50
*Walt Disney's Mickey Mouse, Adventures in Outer Space,* 1968, creases in cover ....................................... 6.00

**Better Little Books**

*Brer Rabbit from Song of the South,* Whitman #1426, 1947 copyright .................................................. 75.00
*Bugs Bunny And The Pirate Loot,* Whitman #1403, 1947 copyright ..... 40.00
*Disney's Cinderella and the Magic Wand,* #711-10 ......................... 40.00
*Disney's Donald Duck, Ghost Morgan's Treasure,* #1411 ........................ 50.00
*Disney's Donald Duck, Up In The Air,* 1945, wear on cover and spine, light soiling ...................................... 25.00
*Disney's Mickey Mouse on Haunted Island,* #708-10 ...................... 50.00
*Disney's Silly Symphony Presents Donald Duck,* #1169 ................ 25.00
*Disney's Thumper and the 7 Dwarfs,* #1409 .......................................... 40.00
*Ghost Avenger,* Whitman #1462, 1943 copyright ................................. 30.00
*G-Men Breaking the Gambling Ring,* Whitman #1493, 1938 copyright .................................................. 40.00

*Inspector Charlie Chan,* Whitman #1424, 1942 copyright ............. 60.00
*Mickey Mouse In The Treasure Hunt,* 1941, wear and soiling ........... 45.00
*Mr. District Attorney,* Whitman #1408, 1941 copyright ........................ 50.00
*Radio Patrol,* Whitman #1496, 1939 copyright ................................. 30.00
*Tailspin Tommy All-Pictures Comics,* Whitman #1410, 1941 copyright .................................................. 25.00
*Uncle Sam's Sky Defenders,* Whitman #14612, 1941 copyright .......... 30.00

# Black Memorabilia

**Collecting Hints:** Black memorabilia was produced in vast quantities and variations. As a result, collectors have a large field from which to choose and should concentrate on one type of item or a limited combination of types.

Outstanding examples or extremely derogatory designs command higher prices. Certain categories, e.g., cookie jars, draw more collectors, resulting in higher prices. Regional pricing also is a factor.

New collectors frequently overpay for common items because they mistakenly assume all Black collectibles are rare or of great value. As in any other collecting field, misinformation and a lack of knowledge leads to these exaggerated values. The Black memorabilia collector is particularly vulnerable to this practice since so little documentation exists.

New collectors should familiarize themselves with the field by first studying the market, price trends, and existing reference material. Seeking out other collectors is especially valuable for the novice.

Black memorabilia has developed into an established collecting field and continues to experience increasing public attention and interest.

**History:** The term "Black memorabilia" refers to a broad range of collectibles that often overlap other collecting fields, e.g., toys and postcards. It also encompasses African artifacts, items created by slaves or related to the slavery era, modern Black cultural contributions to literature, art, etc., and material associated with the Civil Rights Movement and the Black experience throughout history.

The earliest known examples of Black memorabilia include primitive African designs and tribal artifacts. Black Americana dates back to the arrival of African natives upon American shores.

The advent of the 1900s saw an incredible amount and variety of material depicting Blacks, most often in a derogatory and dehumanizing manner that clearly reflected the stereotypical attitude held toward the Black race during this period. The popularity of Black portrayals in this unflattering fashion flourished as the century wore on.

As the growth of the Civil Rights Movement escalated and aroused public awareness of the Black plight, attitudes changed. Public outrage and pressure during the early 1950s eventually put a halt to these offensive stereotypes.

Black representations are still being produced in many forms, but no longer in the demoralizing designs of the past. These modern objects, while not as historically significant as earlier examples, will become the Black memorabilia of tomorrow.

**References:** Kyle Husfloen (ed.), *Black Americana Price Guide*, Antique Trader Books, 1997; J. L. Mashburn, *Black Americana Postcard Price Guide*, Colonial House (Box 609, Enka, NC 28728), 1996; J. P. Thompson, *Collecting Black Memorabilia, A Picture Price Guide*, L-W Book Sales, 1996.

**Periodicals:** *Black Ethnic Collectibles*, 1401 Asbury Court, Hyattsville, MD 20782; *Blackin'*, 559 22nd Ave., Rock Island, IL 61201; *Fabric of Life*, P.O. Box 1212, Bellevue, WA 98009.

**Collectors' Club:** Black Memorabilia Collector's Assoc., 2482 Devoe Ter, Bronx, NY 10468.

**Museums:** Black American West Museum, Denver, CO; Black Archives Research Center and Museum, Florida A&M University, Tallahassee, FL; Center for African Art, New York, NY; Great Plains Black Museum, Omaha, NE; Jazz Hall of Fame, New York, NY; John Brown Wax Museum, Harper's Ferry, WV; Museum of African American History, Detroit, MI; Museum of African Art, Smithsonian Institution, Washington, DC; National Baseball Hall of Fame, Cooperstown, NY; Robeson Archives, Howard University, Washington, DC; Schomburg Center for Research in Black Culture, New York, NY; Studio Museum, Harlem, NY.

Book, *The Golliwogg at the Sea,* Florence K. Upton, © 1898, Longmans, Green & Co., 11" x 8-3/4", $115.

**Reproduction Alert:** The number of Black memorabilia reproductions has increased during the 1980s. Many are made of easily reproducible materials and generally appear new. Collectors should beware of any item offered in large or unlimited quantities.

**Note:** The following price listing is based on items in excellent to mint condition. Major paint loss, chips, cracks, fading, tears, or other extreme signs of deterioration warrant a considerable reduction in value, except for very rare or limited production items. Collectors should expect a certain amount of wear on susceptible surfaces.

Ashtray, 3" d, bisque, boy in outhouse while other boy waits, marked "Japan" ................................. 35.00
Badge, Aunt Jemima Breakfast Club, 4" d, litho tin, sepia face, pink lips, yellow and red checkered bandanna, red ground, white letters "Eat A Better Breakfast," bar pin fastener, c1960 .................................. 50.00
Bank, still, cast iron
  4-1/4" x 4", Save and Smile, England ............................................. 395.00
  4-1/2" h, Mammy ..................... 95.00
  5-1/8" x 4-7/16", Pickanny, painted red shirt, blue bow tie, England ........................................ 440.00
  5-1/4" h, Darkey Sharecropper, painted, AC Williams, c1901 ...... 150
Bell, Mammy ............................... 45.00
Book
  *Little Black Sambo*, 1932 ......... 75.00
  *Minstrel Joke Book*, 1898 ......... 25.00
  *Night Fire*, Edward Kimbrough, Rinehart & Co., 1946, 1st edition .... 20.00
  *Turkey Trot and the Black Santa*, 1940s ........................................ 75.00
Bottle Opener, 7" h, figural, minstrel, painted wood ............................ 40.00
Carry Out Box, Coon Chicken Inn ............................................. 200.00
Cigar Box
  6-1/4" l, Sir Jonathon Brand ..... 45.00

  11" l, Old Plantation Brand, emb .............................................. 60.00
Cigarette Holder, 5-1/2" l, ceramic, boy with melon, melon bowl for ashes ............................................. 35.00
Clock, luncheon type, black women dec, 1950s ............................. 45.00
Comics Page, Kemple Duke of Dahomey, 1911 .............................. 45.00
Cookbook, Dixie Southern Cookbook .............................................. 50.00
Cookie Jar, Mammy
  Mosaic tile, yellow ................. 495.00
  Pearl China ........................... 650.00
Creamer and Sugar, Black Clown, stacking type .......................... 75.00
Cut-Out Sheet, 8" x 10-1/2", stiff paper, full color printed caricatures of jazz band members, intended to be used as table place cards, band members have brown faces, matching red, blue, and yellow marching band uniforms, each playing different instrument, Mayfair Novelty Co., c1930, unused ..................................... 60.00
Dart Board, 23" h, 14" w, tin over cardboard, Sambo, name on straw hat, Wyandotte Toy Mfg., some denting and scratching ......................... 80.00
Decanter, butler holding up bottle ............................................. 340.00
Doll, Cream of Wheat, 18" h, stuffed, chef, 1960s ............................. 60.00
Doorstop, 13-1/2" h, cast iron, Mammy, painted, Littco label .............. 265.00
Fan, cardboard, Jamup and Honey, black and white illus ................ 40.00
Figure
  2" h, diecut painted metal, porter, carrying suitcase, bird cage, golf clubs, and bat, 1930s .............. 65.00

**Advertising Trade Card, Dixon's Stove Polish, Mammy washing little girl, $15.**

**Doll, cloth, felt body, purple skirt, pink bow tie, 13-1/2" h, $80.**

4-1/2" h, bisque, woman, native clothing, marked "Occupied Japan" ....................................... 20.00
Game
7" x 10" x 1-1/2", Chocolate Splash, cardboard box, paper label, target game, Willis G Young Mfg, Chicago, 1916 copyright ........................ 150.00
13" x 13" x 1-1/2", The Game of Hitch Hiker, Whitman, 1937 copyright ................................................. 75.00
24" l, Three Black Crows, bean bag, painted wooden standing frame, swing out targets.................... 195.00
Humidor, 10-1/2" h, majolica, boy sitting on large melon, pipe in hand, small chip on foot and top............... 875.00
Letter Opener, 5-1/2" l, celluloid, alligator eating black boy, mkd "Made in Japan," 1930s.......................... 98.00
Magazine, *Life,* Dec. 8, 1972, featuring Diana Ross on cover................ 18.00
Menu, 12-1/2" h, Coon Chicken Inn, 1949, price insert ................... 300.00
Nodder
Girl, hp, porcelain, mkd "Japan" ................................................. 300.00
Mammy ................................... 125.00
Palm Puzzle, tin rim holding glass over emb glossy paper image
Caricature black face, blue shirt, green ground, dark red mouth slot, five tiny balls serve as teeth, German, c1920 ............................. 150.00
Caricature black youngster eating slice of watermelon, two tiny balls serve as eyes, 1930s ............... 85.00

Pencil Holder, 5-1/2" l, celluloid, alligator with black boy's head in mouth, c1930 ...................................... 40.00
Pinback Button
7/8" d, full color, Ten Days-Smoke Up, caricature of black man standing before Judge, art by Tep, c1912 ................................................. 25.00
1-1/8" d, full color, litho, inscribed "Factory No. 30, 2nd District, New York" on reverse
Don't You Love Me No Mo? black girl in pigtails wearing skimmer hat, daisy flower, art by Tad .......... 25.00
I Raise You, black man in uniform holding cable with word "elevator" net to him, art by Goldberg ...30.00
1-3/4" d, Decatur Corn Carnival and Exposition, yellow and black, Negro youngsters enjoying ears of corn, October 1899, Decatur, IL ..... 225.00
Pin Cushion, sitting black baby, movable arms and legs, tape measure .... 85.00
Pipe Rack, 12" l, figural, male head with large hat, brass...................... 225.00
Poster, paper mounted on linen cloth, titled "Girl Chicken Melon Dice Horse Oh What a Dream!," illus good things of life, only bottle of Ripple missing, Quigley litho, poor condition..... 175.00
Puzzle, Amos and Andy, Peposdent, 1932.................................... 90.00
Recipe Booklet, Knox Gelatin, black child on cov, 1915.................... 10.00
Recipe Holder, Mammy, wood...... 45.00
Reserve Card, Coon Chicken Inn ................................................. 100.00
Salt and Pepper Shakers, pr
Jemima & Uncle Mose, F & F, damaged........................................ 35.00
Jonah and Whale..................... 85.00
Kids in Basket ......................... 80.00
Leapfrog Boys ........................ 90.00
Mammy & Chef, 5" h ............... 55.00
Mammy & Chef, 8" h, ceramic, Japan, 1940s ........................ 115.00
Native and alligator, standing .. 70.00
Native riding alligator............... 70.00
Salty and Peppy, Pearl China ................................................. 225.00
Trainer and Seal ....................... 90.00
Valentine Couple, gray hair.... 195.00
Sign, diecut cardboard
7" d, Hambone Sweets, diecut cardboard, color graphics on both sides, black caricature aviator smiling and puffing on cigar while seated in aircraft, titled "Going Over," orig string loop handle, late 1920s ........... 38.00
24" h, 12" w, Golliwogg, porcelain ................................................. 275.00
24" h, 33" w, Red Cross Cotton, framed cardboard, illus of blacks' picking season on cotton plantation, copyright 1894, ..................... 200.00
Stove Pipe Vent Cover, 9-1/2" d, multicolored, black youngster with straw hat, holding banjo, looking at two others driving car made out of corn ear, watermelon wheels, passenger with pink plumed hat, brass frame and hanging chain, asbestos backing, c1900 ............................. 125.00

Tea Towel, boy and girl eating watermelon, pr................................... 25.00
Tea Towel Transfers, Pickannies, orig envelope ................................. 30.00
Tin
3-3/4" h, Delites Cocoa, paper label ................................................. 50.00
7-1/4" h, Sunny South Peanuts ................................................. 75.00
11" h, CD Kenney, Mammy's Favorite Brand Coffee, Mammy carrying coffeepot and cup ..................... 165.00
Tip Tray, 4" d, Cottolene Shortening, litho tin ................................... 60.00
Toy
Dancing Dan, in front of lamp post on stage, microphone remote attached to stage, 13" h, MIB...................... 375.00
Strutting Sam, tap dancer on pedestal, tin, battery operated, 11" h, MIB ................................................. 475.00
Tray, 12" d, Green River Whiskey, black man and horse......................... 95.00
Wall Plaque, head, chalk, pr....... 125.00

# Blue Ridge Pottery

**Collecting Hints:** Blue Ridge patterns are among the most established of the collectible American dinnerwares. Collectors pay a premium for artist-signed pieces. The Talisman Wallpaper dinnerware pattern, because of its original failure to attract buyers, is the most difficult dinnerware pattern to find. Among the harder to find shapes are the China demi-pot and the character jugs.

Patterns and forms made in the 1940s are the most popular. As in most dinnerware patterns, hollowware pieces command higher prices than flat pieces. Demi-sets that include the matching tray are considered a real find. Blue Ridge collectors must compete with children's dish collectors for miniature pieces.

Because the wares were hand decorated, identical pieces often contain minor variations. Develop a practiced eye to identify those that are most aesthetically pleasing. Minor color variations can change a pleasing pattern into one that is ordinary.

**History:** In 1917, the Carolina Clinchfield and Ohio Railroad, in an effort to promote industry along its line, purchased land along its right-of-way and established a pottery in Erwin, Tennessee. Erwin was an ideal location because of the availability of local white kaolin and feldspar, two of the chief ingredients in pottery. Workers for the new plant were recruited from East Liverpool and Sebring, Ohio, and Chester, Virginia.

In 1920, J. E. Owens purchased the pottery and received a charter for Southern Potteries, Incorporated. Within a few years, the pottery was sold to Charles W. Foreman. Foreman introduced hand painting under glaze and trained girls and women from the nearby hills to do the painting. By 1938, Southern Potteries, Incorporated, was producing Blue Ridge "Hand Painted under the Glaze" dinnerware. The principal sales thrust contrasted the Blue Ridge hand-painted ware with the decal ware produced by most other manufacturers.

Blue Ridge maintained a large national sales organization with eleven showrooms scattered nationwide. Few catalogs were issued and trade advertising was limited. As a result, researching Blue Ridge is difficult.

Most of the patterns used on Blue Ridge originated at the plant. Lena Watts, an Erwin native, was chief designer. Eventually, Watts left Blue Ridge and went to Stetson China Company.

Blue Ridge also made limited-production patterns for a number of leading department stores.

As the 1930s came to a close, Southern Potteries was experiencing strong competition from inexpensive Far Eastern imports, but World War II intervened and changed the company's fortune. Southern Potteries' work force increased tenfold, production averaged more than 300,000 pieces per week, and the company experienced a period of prosperity that lasted from the mid-1940s into the early 1950s.

By the mid-1950s, however, imports and the arrival of plastic dinnerware once again threatened Southern Potteries' market position. The company tried half-time production, but the end came on Jan. 31, 1957, when the stockholders voted to close the plant.

**References:** Betty and Bill Newbound, *Collector's Encyclopedia of Blue Ridge Dinnerware*, Collector Books, 1994, 1997 value update; —, *Southern Potteries, Inc.*, 3rd ed., Collector Books, 1989, 1995 value update; Frances and John Ruffin, *Blue Ridge China Today,* Schiffer Publishing, 1997.

**Periodicals:** *Blue Ridge Beacon Magazine,* P.O. Box 629, Mountain City, GA 30562; *National Blue Ridge Newsletter,* 144 Highland Drive, Blountville, TN 37617.

**Collectors' Club:** Blue Ridge Collectors Club, 208 Harris St., Erwin, TN 37650.

**Museum:** Unicoi Heritage Museum, Erwin, TN.

Annette's Wild Rose, pitcher, antique shape, 5" h ............................ 75.00
Apple, spoon rest ......................... 45.00
Applejack, Skyline-shape
    Coffeepot, Ovide ................... 235.00
    Plate
        6" d ...................................... 6.50
        9" d .................................... 16.00
    Platter ..................................... 28.00
    Vegetable Bowl, divided .......... 36.00
Appleyard, teapot, cov .............. 95.00
Artist Sgd, plate
    Flower Cabin, sgd "Mildred T. Broyles" ............................... 650.00
    Quail scene, sgd "Mildred T. Broyles" ............................... 900.00
Becky
    Egg Cup ................................. 30.00
    Plate
        8" d ...................................... 8.00
        10" d .................................... 12.00
Big Apple, cereal bowl, 6" d .......... 5.00
Big Blossom, pitcher, Grace shape, 5-3/4" h .................................... 95.00
Black Edge
    Bonbon Tray ........................... 82.50
    Chicken Shakers ..................... 85.00
    Chocolate Pot ....................... 190.00
    Powder Box ........................... 135.00
Blossom Top, salt and pepper shakers, pr. ......................................... 35.00
Bluebell Bouquet
Bowl, 9" d, some crazing ........... 20.00
    Gravy Boat .............................. 25.00
    Plate, 9" d ................................ 7.50
Calico
    Candy Box ............................. 175.00
    Teapot, colonial shape ........ 170.00 C
Carnival
    Creamer and Sugar ................. 30.00
    Mixing Bowl, 9-1/2" d .............. 20.00
    Platter, 13" l, oval .................... 18.00
Carol, 62 pc set ......................... 300.00
Carol's Roses, vegetable bowl, open, oval ......................................... 12.00
Cassandra, pie plate, maroon border ................................................ 25.00
Champagne Pinks, teapot, cov .... 95.00
Character Jug
    Daniel Boone ........................ 700.00
    Pioneer Woman ..................... 650.00
Cherry Bounce
    Platter, 11" l, oval .................... 18.00
    Vegetable Bowl, open, round ................................................ 20.00
Cherry, Cherry, platter, 12" l ......... 18.00
Chevron, teapot ........................ 145.00
Chick, pitcher, figural, 6" h, all white, vitreous china .............................. 75.00
Chickory, teapot, colonial shape, crazed inside ......................... 45.00
Chintz
    Bonbon ................................. 82.50
    Cake Plate, maple leaf shape, loop handle, molded grape cluster, 10" l ................................................ 50.00

**Plate, pink and blue flowers, green leaves, 9-1/4" d, $8.50.**

Candy Dish ............................. 90.00
Chocolate Pot ....................... 295.00
Christmas Doorway, plate .......... 115.00
Christmas Mistletoe, plate ........... 85.00
Christmas Packages
    Cup and Saucer ..................... 87.50
    Plate ..................................... 87.50
Christmas Tree, plate ................... 80.00
Chrysanthemum, platter .............. 18.50
Clara, pitcher, Galore ................. 70.00
Cock O' the Morn
    Cup and Saucer ..................... 20.00
    Fruit Bowl ................................. 9.00
    Plate, 10" d ............................. 20.00
    Snack set, plate and cup ......... 30.00
Cocky Locky, platter ................. 140.00
Colonial Rose, 61 pc set ........... 480.00
Crab Apple
    Dinner Service, six place settings, dinner plates, bread and butter plates, cups and saucers, berry bowls, creamer and sugar, platter and round vegetable bowl, price for 40 pc set ............................. 395.00
    Plate, 6" d ................................ 2.50
    Platter, 11" l, oval .................... 25.00
Cumberland, platter, 13" l, oval .... 25.00
Daffodil
    Cereal Bowl, 6" d .................... 12.00
    Creamer ................................. 12.00
    Cup and Saucer ..................... 12.50
    Plate, 6" d ................................ 9.50
    Plate, 10-1/2" d, dinner ........... 15.00
Dahlia, creamer ......................... 12.00
Darcy, plate, 8" sq .................... 10.00
Dazzle, bowl, tab handle ............. 12.50
Delphine
    Cigarette Box .......................... 75.00
    Vase ..................................... 95.00
Dorothy, bon bon ....................... 55.00
Duck in Hat
    Children's Feeding Dish ........... 55.00
    Teapot, child size .................. 125.00
Dutch Bouquet, colonial-shape
    Cereal Bowl, 6" d .................... 11.00
    Cup and Saucer ..................... 12.00
    Plate
        6" d, bread and butter .......... 9.00
        9-3/8" d, dinner .................. 16.00
Easter Parade
    Bonbon ................................. 65.00

Celery Tray, leaf shape............. 75.00
Chocolate Pot.......................... 175.00
Creamer and Sugar, open........ 85.00
Relish Dish, round.................... 75.00
Faimede Fruit, pitcher, Alice shape,
6-1/4" h ................................. 90.00
Festive, creamer ............................. 6.00
Flower Bowl, plate, 8-1/2" d .......... 25.00
French Peasant
Bonbon.................................. 165.00
Butter Pat ............................... 75.00
Candy Box, cov...................... 250.00
Chocolate Pot......................... 480.00
Creamer .................................. 75.00
Demitasse Cup and Saucer..... 75.00
Plate, 10" d ............................ 100.00
Server, center handle............... 95.00
Soup Bowl, two handles......... 135.00
Fruit Fantasy, cake plate, maple leaf-
shape, loop handle, molded grape
cluster, 10" l............................. 50.00
Fruit Punch, plate, 10-1/2" d, dinner,
colonial-shape......................... 16.00
Gladys, boot, backstamped in script,
"Boot 310/1"............................. 85.00
Grace, pitcher, green/blue............ 95.00
Grapes, salad set, bowl, four plates
.............................................. 135.00
Grape Wine, teapot, snub nose
.............................................. 225.00
Hampton pattern, vase, hibiscus shape,
5-1/2" h................................... 80.00
Helen, pitcher ............................... 90.00
Hibiscus, Milady pitcher ............. 175.00
Hilda, 55 pc set........................... 430.00
Irresistible, Martha snack tray..... 100.00
Jane, pitcher ............................. 110.00
Jigsaw, child's feeding dish.......... 90.00
King's Ransom, vegetable bowl, cov
................................................ 85.00
Lyonnaise, demitasse cup ........... 75.00
Mallard
Box, cov ................................. 975.00
Salt and pepper shakers, pr .. 395.00
Mardi Gras
Creamer .................................. 10.00
Pie Baker, candlewick-shape... 25.00
Plate, 9" d, colonial-shape ........ 8.00
Teapot ................................... 175.00
Millie's Pride, chocolate pot ........ 175.00
Language of Flowers, plate from salad
set ........................................... 85.00
Maple Leaf, cake tray ................... 50.00
Mexican, bowl............................. 150.00
Mountain Cherry, 20 pc set......... 175.00
Nocturne
Cup and Saucer, colonial-shape, red
edge......................................... 12.00
Plate, sq ................................. 12.50
Nove Rose
Bonbon, flat shell-shape .......... 55.00
Teapot, as is ........................... 135.00
Orinda
Cereal Bowl, 6" d, colonial-shape
................................................ 10.00
Cup and Saucer, colonial-shape
................................................ 12.00
Pansy Trio, pitcher, 7" h, spiral-shape
................................................ 65.00
Petit Point
Child's, tea set........................ 300.00
Coffeepot, cov......................... 145.00
Petunia Party
Cup ......................................... 20.00

Plate ....................................... 20.00
Pixie, bonbon tray ....................... 165.00
Poinsettia
Creamer ................................... 8.00
Cup and Saucer, colonial-shape
................................................ 10.00
Fruit Bowl, 5" d ......................... 5.00
Plate
6" d, bread and butter........... 3.00
8-1/2" d, luncheon, colonial-
shape ................................. 4.50
Provincal Farm Series, 6" sq plate
................................................ 85.00
Queen's Lace, plate, 10-1/2" d, used
................................................ 10.00
Ridge Daisy
Sugar, cov ............................. 16.50
Vegetable, round .................... 18.50
Ridge Rose Martha, snack tray .. 110.00
Rooster, cigarette set, cigarette box and
4 ashtrays ............................. 175.00
Roseanna, demitasse cup and saucer
................................................ 30.00
Rose Marie, chocolate pot.......... 175.00
Rustic Plaid, snack set, plate and cup,
price for set of six ................... 30.00
Rutledge, dinner service, Candlewick
shape, service for four plus serving
pieces, price for 22 pc set..... 230.00
Sculptured Fruit
Pie Server............................... 32.00
Pitcher, 7" h, 40 oz ................. 98.00
Seaside, box, cov, 3-1/2" x 4-1/2"
................................................ 98.00
Sherman Lily, cov, box, raised figural lily
on cov ................................... 995.00
Spiderweb, pink and charcoal gray
Cereal Bowl............................... 8.00
Cup and Saucer....................... 12.00
Fruit Bowl ................................. 6.00
Plate
Bread and Butter.................. 9.00
Dinner.................................. 9.00
Vegetable Bowl
Oval..................................... 18.00
Round.................................. 18.00
Spindrift, pie baker ...................... 28.00
Spring Blossom, creamer, piecrust
................................................ 20.00
Spring Hill Tulip, teapot, cov....... 110.00
Square Danish, snack set, plate and
cup........................................ 125.00
Stanhome Ivy, plate, 9-1/2" d, dinner,
Skyline-shape ........................... 6.00
Strawberry, fruit bowl, 5" d.............. 3.00
Strawberry Patch
Creamer ................................... 6.00
Cup and Saucer...................... 10.00
Plate
6" d, bread and butter........... 5.00
8" d, luncheon ...................... 5.00
10" d, dinner........................ 7.00
Soup Plate, flanged rim ............ 9.00
Sugar Bowl, cov...................... 10.00
Strawberry Sundae, vegetable bowl,
open, round ........................... 25.00
Summertime, celery tray, leaf-shape
................................................ 42.00
Sunfire, creamer, colonial-shape, teal
edge......................................... 20.00
Sunflower, colonial-shape
Creamer ................................... 20.00
Soup Plate, 8" d, flat................ 15.00

Sweet Clover, plate, dinner............. 8.00
Thanksgiving Turkey, plate, 10-1/4" d,
dinner..................................... 65.00
Tic-Tac
Set, 22 pc set........................ 275.00
Teapot ................................... 150.00
Vegetable, round ..................... 20.00
Tropical, plate, 9" d, Skyline-shape
................................................ 12.00
Tuffie Muffie, celery tray, leaf shape
edge repaired ......................... 40.00
Turkey with Acorns, platter, oval, Sky-
line-Clinchfield-shape............. 135.00
Verna, cake tray, maple leaf shape
................................................ 70.00
Vintage, plate, 11-1/2" d, colonial-shape
................................................ 28.00
Virginia, pitcher........................... 85.00
Weathervane
Fruit Bowl ............................... 18.00
Plate
6" sq, cock .......................... 60.00
9" d..................................... 48.00
10-1/2" d.............................. 40.00
Saucer ................................... 14.00
Wild Rose, pitcher, 7" h, spiral-shape
................................................ 75.00
Wild Strawberry, sugar .............. 135.00
Wrinkled Rose, teapot ................. 95.00

# Bookends

**Collecting Hints:** Since bookends were originally designed to be used in pairs, make sure you've got the proper set. Check for matching or sequential numbers, as well as damage or loss of decoration. Single bookends are sometimes marketed as doorstops or shelf sitters, and a careful eye is needed to find one-of-a-kind items.

**History:** No formal history of bookends is available, but it is not too difficult to imagine those eager for knowledge who began to accumulate books searching for something to hold them in an orderly fashion. Soon decorators and manufacturers saw the need and began production of bookends. Today bookends can be found in almost every type of material, especially metal and heavy ceramics, which lend their physical density to keep those books standing straight.

Bookends range from artistic copies of famous statuary to simple wooden blocks, offering collectors an endless adventure.

**Reference:** Robert Seecof, Donna Seecof, and Louis Kuritzky, *Bookend Revue*, Schiffer Publishing, 1996.

Anchors, 8" h
Brass, mounted to faux stone ....48.00
Brass, mounted on green marble
................................................ 90.00

B.P.O.E., bronzed cast iron, elk in high relief .......................................... 75.00

Cathedrals, 5-1/4" h, 4" w, 3 Gothic doorways, cast metal, copper-colored plating ............................. 32.00

Cheshire Cats, brass, c1930 ...... 135.00

Cocker Spaniels, 5-1/2" h, chalkware, few chips .................................. 30.00

Dice, figural white, black, and red dice mounted to marble squares ..... 35.00

Dolphins, 7-1/2" h, jumping, bronze, verdigris finish ............................ 80.00

Eagles, Frankart, bronzed metal finish .................................................... 50.00

Elephants, ivory, teakwood base .................................................. 165.00

End of the Trail, cast iron ........... 115.00

Falstaff and Henry V, 7-3/4" h, 5-3/4" w, Royal Doulton, D7089 and D7088, green backstamp "Hand Made and Hand Painted, Modelled by David B. Biggs," and company logo .... 410.00

Fleur-de-Lis, 10" x 5", copper, Roycroft orb mark ................................... 115.00

Flowers in Basket, cast iron, multicolored painted flowers, blue basket .................................................. 60.00

Garfield and Odie, 5" h, 4" w, paper label, glazed inkstamp mark "Enesco," 1983 ...................... 245.00

Globes, 7" h, brass, hardwood base .................................................. 105.00

Greek Ruins, figural, white alabaster, hand carved, c1920 .............. 495.00

Indians, painted cast metal, K & O Co., 1935 ...................................... 150.00

Kissing Children, Hubley, cast iron .................................................. 165.00

Laurel and Hardy, Royal Doulton .................................................. 340.00

Liberty Bell, 5" h, bronze .............. 35.00

Lincoln Memorial, plaster, bronze finish .................................................. 40.00

Lyres, 7" h, enameled brass, green shading to black at edges, stamped "Made in Israel" ...................... 48.00

Mandolin Players, 7-1/2" h, bronzed, cold painted spelter, celluloid faces, two tier marble bases ............ 475.00

Monks, reading books, cathedral shape, "Solitude" written on base, Art Pottery ............................. 150.00

Peonies Roseville, yellow floral dec .................................................. 135.00

Peterborough Cathedral, bronzed cast iron, inscribed "C" inside triangle inside circle, copyright 1928, 5" h .................................................. 120.00

Puppies, bronzed pot metal, three puppies resting their heads together, felt base ........................................ 70.00

Race Horse and Jockey, bronzed white metal, Art Deco ........................ 90.00

Ronson, 5-1/2" h, 4-1/4" w, metal, felt base, orig tag, slight damage to one .................................................. 130.00

Sailboats, 7" h, solid polished brass .................................................. 45.00

Sailing Ships, *Constitution*, chalkware, 5-1/2" ........................................ 15.00

Scotties, brass-tone, detailed casting .................................................. 245.00

Shells, 5" h, solid polished brass .................................................. 37.50

St. Francis, 7-1/2" h, kneeling with fox on one side, dove on other, Rookwood, shape #6883, designed by C. Zanetta, 1945 ........................ 525.00

Tom and Jerry, 8" h, Gorham, 1980 .................................................. 45.00

Wagon Train, painted cast iron, American Hardware Co., dated 1931, some loss to paint ...................... 90.00

Whales Heads, 5-1/2" h, bronze, verdigris finish ................................ 55.00

**Quimper, seated male and female, black, blue, and brown clothes, gold trim, brown bases, sgd "C. Millard, Henroit Quimper," 8-5/8" h, $600.**

# Books, Science Fiction

**Collecting Hints:** Science fiction can be collected in several areas: children or adult books, magazines, pulp magazines, etc., as well as by subject and author.

**History:** Collecting science fiction books has been a popular niche of the book collecting market for many years. Some collectors prefer modern editions, while others seek out those which were written in past centuries. Whatever the collecting criteria might be, collectors of this kind of book enjoy reading their treasures and gazing on the fanciful illustrations.

**References:** Allen Ahearn, *Book Collecting: A Comprehensive Guide*, G. P. Putnam's Sons, 1995; Allen and Patricia Ahearn, *Collected Books: The Guide to Values,* F. P. Putnam's Sons, 1997; *American Book Prices Current*, Bancroft Parkman, published annually; Michael L. Ciancone, *The Literary Legacy of the Space Age,* Amorea Press, 1999; Geoffrey Ashall Glaister, *Encyclopedia of the Book*, 2nd ed., available from Spoon River Press, 1996; John R. Gretton, *Baedeker's Guidebooks: A Checklist of English-Language Editions 1861-1939*, available from Spoon River Press, 1994; Sharon and Bob Huxford, *Huxford's Old Book Value Guide*, 10th ed., Collector Books, 1998; Norma Levarie, *Art & History of Books*, available from Spoon River Press, 1995; Gary Lovisi, *Collecting Science Fiction and Fantasy*, Alliance Publishing, 1997; Catherine Porter, *Collecting Books*, available from Spoon River Press, 1995; Caroline Seebohm, Estelle Ellis, and Christopher Simon Sykes, *At Home with Books: How Book Lovers Live with and Care for Their Libraries*, available from Spoon River Press, 1996.

**Periodicals:** *AB Bookman's Weekly,* P.O. Box AB, Clifton, NJ 07015; *Biblio Magazine,* 845 Wilamette St., P.O. Box 10603, Eugene, OR 97401; *Book Source Monthly,* 2007 Syosett Dr., P.O. Box 567, Cazenovia, NY 13035; *Rare Book Bulletin,* P.O. Box 201, Peoria, IL 61650; *The Book Collector's Magazine,* P.O. Box 65166, Tucson, AZ 85728.

*Across the Zodiac: The Story of a Wrecked Record,* Greg Percy, Trübner & Co., 1880, 2 volumes, contemporary half green calf gilt, red morocco lettering pieces, tops of spines worn .......................... 1,035.00

*A Columbus of Space,* Garrett Putnam Serviss, Appleton and Co., 1911, 4 color plates by Howard Heath, orig light green cloth, pictorial blockin on front cover, slightly rubbed .... 145.00

*A Journey in Other Worlds, A Romance of the Future,* John Jacob Astor, Appleton & Co., 1894, 10 plates, orig navy cloth cover, discolored, worn ................................................ 100.00

*A Pilgrims Progress in Other Worlds, Recounting the Wonderful Adventures of Ulysum Storries and His Discovery of the Lost Star "Eden,"* Nettie Parrish Martin, Mayhew Publishing Co., 1908, orig gray cloth, spine ends worn .............................. 230.00

*A Plunge Into Space,* Robert Cromie, 2nd edition, preface by Jules Verne, Frederick Warne & Co., London, 1891, orig brown cloth, spine rubbed ................................................ 635.00

*A Voyage to Cacklogallinia,* Samuel Brunt, J. Watson, London, 1727, engraved frontispiece, 167 pgs, spine and extremities rubbed, scattered foxing .......................... 3,910.00

*Between Planets,* Robert Heinlein, Charles Schribner's Sons, 1952, wear on edges ......................... 45.00

*Checok's Enterprise,* Walter Koenig ................................................. 6.00

*Danny Dunn & the Weather Machine,* Jay Williams and Raymond Abraskin, London, 1975, inscribed by authors ................................................. 10.00

*From the Earth to the Moon Direct in 97 Hours 20 Minutes, and a Trip Round It,* Jules Verne, Sampson Low, Marston, Low, and Searle, London, 1873, orig cloth, recased, spine ends chipped, corners worn, 80 plates, first English edition ..... 375.00

*In the Days of the Comet,* H. G. Wells, Macmillian and Co., 1906, orig green cloth gilt joints, spine ends slightly rubbed, 3 integral ad leaves at end, 4 leaves of inserted ads ......... 200.00

*Lieut. Gulliver Jones, His Vacation,* Edwin Lester Arnold, George Bell and Sons, London, 1905, orig red cloth, darkened spine, ends worn ................................................. 150.00

*Loma, A Citizen of Venus,* William Windsor, Windsor & Lewis Publishing Co., 1897, frontispiece portrait, phrenological text illus, orig dark red cloth gilt, faded spine ..................... 110.00

*Lost Worlds,* Leonard Cottrell, Horizon Book .......................................... 6.00

*Melbourne and Mars, My Mysterious Life on Two Planets, Extracts from the Diary of a Melbourne Merchant,* Joseph Fraser, Pater & Knapton, Melbourne, 1889 .................... 320.00

*Off on a Comet! A Journey Through Planetary Space,* Jules Verne, David McKay, Philadelphia, 1880s, orig cloth, 36 plates, worn ............. 125.00

*Starlog #30, Great Moments in Science Fiction,* Robert Wise .................. 6.00

*Star Guide,* Andre Norton, Harcourt, Brace & Co., 1955, 1st edition, dust jacket ....................................... 75.00

*Star Rangers,* Andre Norton, Harcourt, Brace & Co., 1953, 1st edition, worn dust jacket .............................. 50.00

*The Ant Men,* Eric North, John C. Winston Co. Publishers, 1955, 1st edition, dust jacket ..................... 125.00

*The Conquest of Space,* David Lasser, Penguin Press, 1931, orig cloth, gilt spine lettering rubbed off, rear hinged cracked..................... 375.00

*The Emperor of the Moon: A Face,* Aphra Behn, R. Holt, London, 1687, disbound, cloth folding case, first edition ................................... 980.00

*The First Men in the Moon,* H. G. Wells, George Newnes, London, 1901, 12 plates, orig blue-green cloth, stamped in black, spine bumped, first English edition, fourth binding .285.00

*The Goddess of Atvatabar, Being the History of the Discovery of the Interior World and Conquest of Atvatabar,* William R. Bradshaw, J. F. Douthitt, London, 1892, illus, orig light green cloth gilt cover, darkened spine, ends frayed, worn ....... 140.00

*The Life and Astonishing Adventures of John Daniel,* Ralph Morris, Robert Holden & Co., London, 1926, intro by N. M. Penzer, orig cloth, dj, front panel loose, one of 750 numbered copies ................................... 150.00

*The Moon Hoax: Or, a Discovery That the Moon Has a Vast Population of Human Beings,* Richard Adams Locke, William Gowans, 1859, wood engraved frontispiece, modern cloth cover ..................................... 815.00

*The Moon Metal,* Garrett Putnam Serviss, Harper & Brothers, 1900, orig cloth, accession stamp..................... 435.00

*The Moon Voyage,* Jules Verne, Ward, Lock & Co., London, 2 pages, orig cloth, half titled browned ...... 100.00

*The People of the Moon,* Tremlett Carter, London, 1895, 8 plates, 22 text illus by D'Aguilcourt, orig blue cloth cover stamped in red and silver, spine faded........................... 490.00

*The Sunless City,* Joyce Emmerson Preston Muddock, F. V. White & Co., London, 1905, orig green cloth, scattered foxing, worn .................. 260.00

*The Time Machine,* H. G. Wells, William Heinemann, London, 1895, orig gray cloth stamped in purple, soiled, darkened spine, first English version ................................................. 320.00

*The War of the Worlds,* H. G. Wells, Harper & Brothers, 1898, 16 plates, orig cloth, worn and discolored, recased, first American illus edition ................................................. 550.00

*Through Space to Mars,* Roy Rockwood, Cupples & Leon, 1910, orig brown cloth cover, 1st edition ............... 95.00

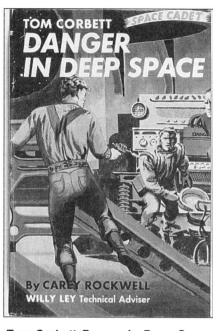

***Tom Corbett Danger In Deep Space,* Carey Rockwell, Willey Ley Technical Advisor, illus by Louis Glanzman, Grosset & Dunlap, 1953, $20.**

*To Mars Via the Moon,* Roy Rockwood, J. B. Lippincott Co., Philadelphia, 1911, orig navy cloth cover, 1st American edition, wear to cover ................................................. 75.00

*Tom Corbett, Space Cadet, Series #5, The Revolt on Venus,* Cary Rockwell, Grossett & Dunlap, dust jacket, some wear to book edges ....... 20.00

*Tom Swift and His Flying Lab, The New Tom Swift Jr. Adventures, #1,* Victor Appleton II, Grossett & Dunlap, damaged dust jacket..................... 20.00

*Tom Swift and His Jetmarine, The New Tom Swift Jr. Adventures, #2,* Victor Appleton II, Grossett & Dunlap, minor wear to dust jacket and book ..... 25.00

*Tom Swift and His Rocket Ship, The New Tom Swift Jr. Adventures, #3,* Victor Appleton II, Grossett & Dunlap, very good condition dust jacket and book.................................. 30.00

*Urania, A Romance,* Camille Flammarion, Chatto & Windus, illus by De Bieler, Gambar, Myrbach, orig tan cloth, darkened spine, ends worn ................................................. 290.00

# Bottle Openers, Figural

**Collecting Hints:** Condition is most important. Worn or missing paint, repainted surfaces, damage, or rust result in lower value.

**History:** Figural bottle openers were produced expressly to remove a bottle cap from a bottle. They were made in a variety of metals, including cast iron, brass, bronze, and white metal. Cast iron, brass, and bronze openers are generally solid castings; white metal openers are usually cast in hollow blown molds.

The vast majority of figural bottle openers date from the 1950s and 1960s. Paint variations on any particular figure are very common.

**References:** Donald Bull, *Price Guide to Beer Advertising, Openers and Corkscrews*, published by author, 1981; *Figural Bottle Openers*, Figural Bottle Opener Collectors Club, 1992.

**Collectors' Clubs:** Figural Bottle Opener Collectors Club, 3 Ave. A, Latrobe, PA 15650; Just For Openers, 3712 Sunningdale Way, Durham, NC 27707.

**Reproduction Alert.**

Advertising, Orange Crush, bright sliver luster, character and bottle, back "Compliments Orange-Crush Bottling Co.," c1930s......................35.00
Bear, 3-7/8" x 3-1/16", brass, wall mount, head, black highlights, John Wright Co. ................................70.00
Black Boy with alligator, 2-5/8" h, hands down, green alligator, Wilton Products .........................................150.00
Black Man, 4-3/8" x 3-3/4", wall mount, smiling, red, bow tie, Wilton Products ..................................................95.00
Cathy Coed, 4-1/8" h, cast iron, preppy girl holding stack of books, green base, white front, sgd "L & L Favors" ..............................................350.00
Cockatoo, 3-1/4" h, cast iron, orange and yellow chest ...................175.00
Cowboy with Guitar, 4-7/8" h, cast iron, yellow, brown, and gray guitar, green cactus, black shoes, red bandanna, John Wright Co. .....................110.00
Dinky Dan, 3-1/4" h, cast iron, preppy boy, hands in pockets, green base, sgd "Gadzik, Phila" on back..245.00
Do Do Bird, 2-3/4" h, cast iron, cream, black highlights, red beak .....175.00
Drunk leaning on lamp post, sign reads "Atlantic City, NJ," cast iron, 3-5/8" h ................................................45.00
Elephant, 3-1/16" h, sitting, trunk in circle, gray, pink nostrils, white toe nails, Wilton Products..............40.00
Four Eyes, 4" x 3-7/8", man with two sets of eyes, black hair and mustache, John Wright Co. ......................35.00
GOP Elephant, sitting, pink, 3-1/4" h ................................................55.00
Grass Skirt Dancer, 5" h, cast iron, black native girl, white sign and post, green base, sgd "Gadzik, Phila" on back .........................................275.00
Parrot, Avillar, corkscrew on base, beak as bottle opener, Art Deco style, 1929 .......................................35.00

**Harvard Brewing Co., Lowell, MA, red, white letters, 3-1/2" l, $17.50.**

Pelican, 3-3/4" h, cast iron, head up, cream, orange beak and feet, green base, John Wright Co. ...........150.00
Rooster
3-3/16" h, bronze, yellow, orange, black, and white body, orange-yellow feet, green base, tail opener, Wilton Products............................40.00
3-7/8" h, metal, black body, red comb, orange-yellow beak and feet, green base, opener under tail, John Wright Co. ...............................55.00
Sailor, 3-3/4" h, hitchhiking, white uniform, blue tie and shoes, white sign with black trim, John Wright Co. ................................................45.00
Seahorse, 4-1/4" h, brass, green, white highlights, green base with blue and black highlights........................75.00
Skunk, cast iron .........................148.00
Steamer, *Alexander Hamilton*, 3" l, used ................................................22.00

# Boxing Collectibles

**Collecting Hints:** Collectors of boxing memorabilia might wish to limit their collections to specific fighters. Today's fighters often retire and re-enter the ring, and new collectibles are being generated at a rapid rate.

**History:** Boxing, also known as prize fighting, is an old sport. The Romans enjoyed boxing competitions, and the sport was revived in the early part of the 18th century in England. The marquess of Queensberry introduced rules for the sport in 1865 and required the used of boxing gloves. Boxing became an Olympic sport in 1904.

Boxing was illegal in America until 1896, when New York became the first state to legalize it. Every state has a boxing commission or athletic organization to regulate the sport. Competition, limited to timed three-minute "rounds," takes place in a ring, which is usually 20 feet square. Professional boxers are divided into eight weight classes, ranging from flyweight to heavyweight.

**References:** David Bushing, *Sports Equipment Price Guide*, Krause Publications, 1995; Michael McKeever, *Collecting Sports Memorabilia*, Alliance Publishing, 1966.

**Periodicals:** *Boxing Collectors Newsletter*, 59 Bosson St., Revere, MA 02151; *Sports Collectors Digest*, 700 E. State St., Iola, WI 54990.

**Collectors' Clubs** Boxiana & Pugilistica Collectors International, P.O. Box 83135, Portland, OR 97203.

**Museum:** International Boxing Hall of Fame, Canastota, NY.

Autograph
Glove, Muhammad Ali, red Everlast glove sgd "Muhammad Ali aka Cassius Clay" ..............................150.00
Menu, Jack Dempsey's Restaurant, 7-3/4" x 12-1/4" cardboard folder menu from Dempsey's Corner restaurant, 50th St. and 8th Ave., New York, sgd twice in black ink on cov, plus autograph by "Al," c1940.........100.00
Photograph, Rock Marciano, 4" x 6", black and white, bold blue ink signature, matted and framed........995.00
Badge, 3" d black and white cello, "Tommie Smith-Ali Charity Fight," picturing Mayor Smith of Jersey City, NJ, as "The Urban Fighter" in preparation for exhibition charity bout with Muhammad Ali, also pictured, June 29, 1979..................................55.00
Book
*Boxing Record Reference*, 5" x 7-1/4", paperback published by Everlast Sports Publishing Co., 1929, 392 pgs, fighter profiles and portraits, green, black, and white cov..................35.00
*Jack Dempsey/The Idol of Histiana*, 1936 revised edition, Nat Fleischer, 158 pgs, inked autograph .......35.00
*Ruby Roberts Alias Bob Fitzsimmons*, Robert Davis, George H. Doran Company publishers, 1926, hard cover, orig dust jacket, several Fitzsimmons photos..............100.00

Muhammad Ali, belt buckle .......... 20.00

Bottle Cap, Joe Louis Punch, red and white tin cap, c1940 ................. 30.00

Boxing Gloves, Rocky Graziano, orig box .......................................... 145.00

Bust, John Sullivan, Red Top Beer .............................................. 250.00

Charm, Jack Dempsey, bright gold luster plastic, boxing glove, inscribed name on top, early 1950s ........ 35.00

Game, Muhammad Ali's Boxing Ring, mechanical, Mego Corp, 1976 copyright, Herbert Muhammad Enterprise Inc., orig box ............................ 65.00

Magazine, Sports Illustrated, June 18, 1973, George Foreman on cov .............................................. 20.00

Photograph

Ali-Ellis, 8" x 10" glossy black and white, ten different Muhammad Ali facial expressions and contortions explained by photo release caption "Actor, Fighter, Or Both-A Study in Many Faces of Muhammad Ali," lists live closed circuit telecast, July 26, 1971, Houston Astrodome ....... 40.00

Dempsey-Loughran, 7" x 9" glossy black and white, press release caption by Associated Press attached to rear, March 23, 1938 release date, Jack Dempsey in left, Tommy Loughran at right, attending Philadelphia dinner honoring State Boxing Commissioner Julies Aronson pictured in center ........................................ 25.00

Dempsey, US Army Signal Corps, 8-1/4" x 10" glossy black and white, Dempsey in military dress uniform, other military personnel and civilians, Signal Corps stamp dated Jan. 19, 1944 on back .................... 30.00

Pinback Button

Cerdan, Marcel, black and white photo, European middleweight who held US championship, c1948 .................................................. 35.00

Frazier-Ali, black and white, March 8, 1971, Madison Square Garden .................................................. 35.00

LaMotta, Jake, black and white photo, c1949 ........................... 30.00

Moore, Archie, gray and black photo, c1956 ........................... 15.00

Poster, Koncert King Promotions presents Farewell To A Legend Muhammad Ali in His Last Ring Appearance, March 12, Providence Civic Center, Providence, RI, also features bout with Marvelous Marvin Hagler in 10-bout round ......... 180.00

Press Badge, diecut octagon cardboard, inked authorization for "H & E Photog" for "Loughran vs. Walker" bout March 29, 1929, Chicago Stadium, pink silhouettes of boxers under inked name, printed "24" serial number, grommet for hanging .................................................. 85.00

Record Book, Blue Book, 1922 ..... 60.00

Trade Card, T9, Turkey Red, Abe Attell .............................................. 125.00

# Brastoff, Sascha

**Collecting Hints:** When collecting items made by Brastoff, take special note of the signature. Pieces made exclusively by Brastoff are marked with his full name. A "Sascha B" signature indicates he only supervised the production.

**History:** Internationally known designer, artist, sculptor, and ceramist Sascha Brastoff began producing ceramic artware in 1953. His hand-painted china originally commanded prices ranging from $25 to thousands of dollars for a single item. He also designed a full line of dinnerware.

**References:** Jack Chipman, *Collector's Encyclopedia of California Pottery*, 2nd ed., Collector Books, 1998; Lois Lehner, *Lehner's Encyclopedia of U.S. Marks on Pottery, Porcelain & Clay*, Collector Books, 1988.

Ashtray

5-1/4" d, round, domed ............ 20.00

5-1/2" l, leaf-shape, enamelware, brown bones, sgd .................... 25.00

7" d, Eskimo ............................. 60.00

8" l, kidney-shaped, house ...... 37.50

Basket, 17" h ............................... 150.00

Candleholders, pr, 8" h, walrus ..... 75.00

Charger, 17" d ........................... 150.00

Cigarette Box, cov, 5-3/8" l, 3-7/8" w, 1-3/4" h, grapes, gold ext., black int., sgd "Sascha B" ........................ 35.00

Coffeepot, 10" h, 11" w, gold and black ext., white, pink, and gold int., sgd "Sascha B" ................................. 45.00

Compote, 12" h, striped white ...... 85.00

Conch, 9-1/2" l, 6-1/2" w, 4-1/2" l, white, gold, blue, and brown, sgd "Sascha B" ............................................ 55.00

Figure

Horse, stylized, 12" x 11" ....... 185.00

Seal, amber ............................ 300.00

Whale, red, chipped tail ......... 275.00

Fruit Bowl, Surf Ballet, gold dec, emerald green ground, ftd .............. 40.00

Mug, 6" h, Eskimo and walrus ..... 75.00

Pitcher, abstract ballet scene, black ground, first factory ............... 300.00

Place Setting, 4 pc, marbleized, turquoise and silver top, white bottom, full signature, gold rooster trademark .................................................. 65.00

Plate

8-3/4" d, Surf Ballet, gold dec, emerald green ground .................... 35.00

12" d, pagoda design, curled lip .................................................. 85.00

Platter, 17-3/4" l, 14" w, rect, wavy rim, one large green and white leaf, shaded deep green ground, glossy finish .................................... 250.00

Sculpture, metal, fish, full signature engraved in gold colored plaque attached to marble base, 4-3/4" h .................................................. 395.00

Smoker Set, 13-1/2" l, 5-1/8" w #08 ashtray, houses dec, 9" x 8-3/4" #F40 bicycle seat shaped candy dish, 2-3/4" h, #61 lighter, 2-3/4" h #61 match holder, multicolored, gold trim, rooster trademark, price for set ...................... 50.00

Vase

9-1/2" h, rearing stallion ........... 95.00

12" h, Alaskan ...................... 250.00

# Brayton Laguna Pottery

**Collecting Hints:** Three marks were used by Brayton Laguna Pottery. The first mark reads "Brayton Laguna" and was registered in February of 1935. The second one was an arched semi-circle with the letters "Weston-Ware" above a 5-leaf decoration and was used about 1945. The third mark was "Brayton Laguna Pottery" in a hand-printed type script.

**History:** Durlin E. Brayton, a graduate of the Chicago Art Institute, began making pottery in his home in South Laguna Beach, California, in 1928. Brayton's bright hand-crafted matte glazed dinnerware as an instant hit and the business began to flourish. The line was expanded to include cookie jars, lamps, figurines, and other decorative objects. Durlin's wife, Webb, joined the firm and continued until her death in 1948. After Durlin died in 1951, employees operated the business. By 1963, competition proved to be too strong and the company ceased operation.

Chess Piece, King, 14" h ............ 155.00

Cookie Jar

Disney's Ringmaster from Pinocchio .......................................... 3,500.00

Partridges, teal background, golden brown partridges, black branches, #V-11, incised mark .............. 260.00

Creamer and Sugar, Calico Cat and Gingham Dog .......................... 90.00

Figure

Blackamoor, 8" h, with bowl ..... 75.00

Bull and cow, purple, minor glaze rob on top of bull's horn ......... 475.00

Car, 17" l, wood tone, stylized .................................................. 135.00

Chicken, blue, stylized .......... 135.00

Chicken, 7", yellow and wood tones .................................................. 65.00

Figaro, crouching, 1940s, 3-1/2" l, repaired chip to ear ................ 45.00

Fighting Pirates ..................... 455.00

Horses, pr, sgd "Betsy 1942," 5", black ink stamp "B.R.," one with damage to ears ...................... 40.00

Jon, flake ................................ 95.00

Miranda, flake ......................... 65.00

Owl, 8" l ................................ 70.00

Panther, black ...................... 200.00

Pelican, 7-1/2" h ....................... 32.00
Pheasant with baskets, 8" h, 1930s
............................................. 55.00
Quails, male and female, wood tone
............................................. 155.00
Sally ........................................... 35.00
Snow White's Deer, 6-1/2" h
............................................. 125.00
Flower Ring ................................. 35.00
Oak Bucket, glazed dec .............. 45.00
Planter, black and white, mkd "M18
Brayton Laguna Calif" ............. 55.00
Salt and Pepper Shakers, pr, Mammy
and Chef, c1940 ............. ...... 150.00

# Breweriana

**Collecting Hints:** Many collectors concentrate on items from one specific brewery or region. An item will bring slightly more when it is sold in its original locality. Regional collectors' clubs and shows abound.

**History:** Collecting material associated with the brewing industry developed in the 1960s when many local breweries ceased production. Three areas occupy the collectors' interest—pre-Prohibition material, advertising items for use in taverns, and premiums designed for an individual's use.

**References:** Herb and Helen Haydock, *World of Beer Memorabilia*, Collector Books, 1997; Jack McDougall and Steve Pawlowski, *United States Micro/Brew Pub Coaster Guide*, published by authors, 1995; Steve Pawlowski and Jack McDougall, *New Jersey Brewery Coasters*, published by authors, 1995; Dale P. Van Wieren (ed.), *American Breweries II*, East Coast Breweriana Association, 1995.

**Periodicals:** *All About Beer*, 1627 Marion Ave., Durham, NC 27705; *Barley Corn News*, P.O. Box 2328, Falls Church, VA 22042; *Suds 'n' Stuff*, 4765 Galacia Way, Oceanside, CA 92056.

**Collectors' Clubs:** American Breweriana Association Inc., P.O. Box 11157, Pueblo, CO 81001; East Coast Breweriana Association, P.O. Box 64, Chapel Hill, NC 27514; National Association of Breweriana Advertising, 2343 Met-To-Wee Lane, Wauwatosa, WI 53226.

**Museum:** The Museum of Beverage Containers & Advertising, Goodlettsville, TN.

**Reproduction Alert:** Advertising trays.

**Ashtray, Neuweiler's, white ground, blue bands on barrel, mkd "Germany," $27.50.**

Badge, American Brewers Assoc. Convention, 1899, "ABA" inscription, enamel and brass plated ......... 18.50
Bell, Sterling Beer, girl ................. 72.50
Blotter, 3" x 7-1/2", Bergdoll Brewing Co. 60th Anniversary, black and yellow Louis Bergdoll portrait, Christmas holly design, 1909, unused ...... 48.00
Bottle Opener
Fritz's Corner, Coeur D'Alene, Idaho
.............................................. 8.00
Miller Beer, 1955 ..................... 35.00
Calendar, 1907, Yuengling & Son Brewers & Bottlers, Pottsville, PA, four puppies at the bar, 34" x 26" frame
.......................................... 1,700.00
Charm
Burger Beer, transparent brown plastic, white letters, c1940 ............. 5.00
Pabst Blue Ribbon, blue plastic, paper wrapper label, c1950 .... 10.00
Rheingold Lager Beer, yellow plastic, black, white, and red paper wrapper, c1950 ........................ 12.00
Schlitz Beer, yellow plastic, paper wrapper, c1950 ......................... 8.00
Coaster, 4" d
Acme Beer, Cereal & Fruit Ltd., Honolulu, HI, red and black letters
.............................................. 7.00
Brugh Brau Beer, McDermott, Chicago, IL, black and gold letters
............................................. 18.00
Champagne Velvet Beer, Terre Haute Brewing, IN, man holding up glass of beer, red, blue, and black
............................................. 12.00
Golden Age Beer, Fernwood Brewing, PA, center glass of beer, red, blue, and yellow ...................... 50.00
Gunther's Beer, Gunther Brewing, Baltimore, MD, bear holding beer bottle, red, black, and yellow .......... 15.00
Cribbage Board, Drink Rhinelander Beer .......................................... 25.00
Decanter, Old Crow ..................... 30.00
Door Stop, Hanley's Ale, cast iron, bulldog .......................................... 565.00
Figure, Pfeiffer Brewing Co., chalkware
............................................. 45.00
Fishing Lure, Schlitz, bottle shape
............................................. 10.00
Foam Scraper, celluloid
Goetz Brewery ........................ 18.00

Meister Brau ............................ 20.00
Glass, clear ground
2-1/4" h, Grand Rapids Brewing Co. Silver Foam, Grand Rapids, Michigan, white letters, flake on inside rim
............................................. 25.00
2-1/4" h, Magnolia Old Bourbon, Portland, Oregon, insignia, flaring form shot glass ...................... 25.00
2-3/4" h, Compliments of Los Angles Brewing Co., white enamel dec of "Old Mission San Louis Reyy Founded 1796, gold band at top
............................................. 15.00
3-1/2" h, Milwaukee Brewing Co., Milwaukee, WI, acid etched name and factory scene ................... 50.00
4" h, The PH Zang Brewing Co., Denver, CO, acid etched name, gold band dec at top ........................ 25.00
Light, 8" l, 8" w, 5" h, Schiltz Bottled Beer, chain hung, electric, metal frame, painted screen advertisement, fringed bottom, colored glass jewels on sides, rewired ........ 675.00
Miniature Whiskey Jug, 4-3/4" h, Meredith's Diamond Club Rye Whiskey, blue-green lettering, company emblem, barley sprigs, serpent handle, gold trim at top ................ 50.00
Pinback Button
Miller High Life Beer, multicolored, lady seated on crescent moon, back paper "Member NRA," 1930s .. 20.00
P.B. Ale Dog, multicolored, dog image, back paper "P. B. Van Nostrand's Ale, Bunker Hill Breweries," early 1900s ............................. 80.00
Pitcher, 12-1/2" h, stoneware, German, large, pewter lid and thumbrest, print under glaze of musicians and couple frolicking in meadow .............. 250.00
Shot Glass
Henry Schnelten's Whiskeys, Quincy, IL, etched .............................. 20.00
Penn State, blue enamel logo .... 2.00
Peoria Co Club Whiskey, Peoria, IL, etched ..................................... 25.00
Shawhan Whiskey, Weston, MI, etched ..................................... 25.00
Sign
11" d, tin, White Rock, semi-clad fairy kneeling on white rock looking at reflection in water .............. 400.00
13-1/2" h, 9" l, Olympia Brew, tin over cardboard, trademark Tumwater scene, Chas. W. Shonk Co. litho
............................................. 450.00
21" h, 16" w, Imported Pilsener, tin curved corner type, Dutch maiden carrying six mugs of imported Pilsener, black background ...... 120.00
25-1/2" h, 16" w, Shmidt Beer, "Hello! Hello! Where's my Shmidt?" buxom beauty at college game, artist sgd "Earl Christy," framed ............. 210.00
28-1/2" h, 22-1/4" w, Budweiser, pre-prohibition, self framed tin, Gibson Girl holding glass and bottle of beer, wearing Anheuser Busch necklace, Mayer & Lavenson Co. litho, some light overall rust spots, denting, and scratching on frame ........... 1,500.00

**Sign, Burger Beer, Cincinnati's Famous Beer, 8" x 14-1/8", $70.**

43" h, 33" w, tin, Meadville Rye Whiskey, trademark logo of archangel sitting ton top of heart, orig frame with plaque "Meadville, PA, Distilling Co., Inc." ........................................ 250.00

Stein, Budweiser
    Hamburg, Germany, lidded, CS16
    .................................... 550.00
    Label Logo, CS18 ................. 455.00
    Pilque, German, CS5 ............. 310.00

Tab, litho tin, Ballantine slogan, white litho, red letters, three ring symbol, 1970s ...................................... 10.00

Tip Tray, tin litho
    4-1/8" d, Buffalo's Best Bets Bottled Beer, colorful spread-winged eagle, red, white, and blue shield, bolder border, red letters ..................... 60.00
    4-1/8" d, E. Robinson and Sons Pilsener Beer, emblem on deep burgundy horizontal ground, gold border with white letters ............... 75.00
    4-1/4" d, Angeles Brewing & Malting Co., bottle of beer with flag in background ...................................... 150.00
    4-1/4" d, Bartholomay Beers, Ales Importers, Rochester, NY, company emblem of winged wheel, beautiful maiden seated above ............ 100.00
    4-1/4" d, Beverwyck Lager, titled "Where the best beer is brewed," factory scene, horse drawn vehicles, Kaufmann & Strass Co. Litho, some rim chipping, small rust spot .... 250.00
    4-1/4" d, Detroit Brewing Co., trademark eagle among letter "D," Chas W. Shonk Co. Litho, overall light crazing and soiling, glass mark ................................................ 80.00
    4-1/4" d, Goebel Beer, Bavarian gentleman enjoying his mug of beer, Meek Co. litho, light overall crazing ................................................ 190.00
    4-1/4" d, Lehnert's Beer, stock stag, rack of antlers, overall light crazing and soiling ............................. 100.00
    4-1/4" d, National Beer, thoroughbred horse's head image, © 1908, Meek Co. Litho, light denting . 100.00
    4-1/4" d, Peter Doelger Beer, titled "Expressly for the Home," American eagle atop first prize award, Haeusermann M. M. Co. litho, overall crazing ..................................... 85.00
    4-1/4" d, Rainier Beer, trademark Mt. Rainier, Chas. W. Shonk Co. litho, some light fading .................. 155.00

4-1/4" d, Rushstaller's Lager, titled "Best Beer Brewed," Dutch waitress holding six steins, Kaufmann & Strauss Co. Litho.................... 160.00
4-1/4" d, Pennsy Select Beer, titled "Quick!! A Glass please for our mutual friend," vintage lady holding bottle while reaching for glass, Ivan B. Norhem Co. Litho ............. 300.00
4-1/4" d, West End Brewing Co., Lady Liberty draped in American flag standing next to American eagle and keg of Pilsener beer, rim chips ................................................ 150.00
4-1/4" d, Wunder Beer, three white stallions, H. D. Beach Co. litho, rim wear ......................................... 60.00
4-1/4" d, Yuengling's Beer, trademark eagle atop keg, Chas W. Shonk Co. Litho, some overall crazing, light scratching and soiling .......... 100.00
4-1/4" h, 6" l, Stegmaier Beer, factory scene, Chas W. Shonk Co Litho, hole in top rim .................................. 70.00
5" d, Indianapolis Brewing Co., titled "The World's Standard of Perfection," bottle of Gold Medal Beer, Kaufmann & Strauss Co. litho, some light crazing ........................................... 50.00
5" d, Los Angeles Brewing Co., "Home of East Side Beer," factory scene, Kaufmann & Strauss Co. Litho, some overall soiling, spotting, and rubbing ............................. 75.00
6" h, 4-1/4" w, King's Puremalt, vintage nurse carrying tray of King's Puremalt, light scratching and soiling ................................................ 70.00

Tray
    10" l, 13" w, Dick & Bros. Beer, factory scene, horse drawn vehicles, one red automobile, Chas. W. Shonk Co. litho, rim chips, dent in sky ................................................ 300.00
    12" d, Battleship *Maine* encircled by border of cannons, stars, and stripes, Chas. W. Shonk Co. litho, some inpainting to sky, light crazing and soiling ............................. 85.00
    12" d, Ebling Brewing Co., titled "The Teddys have found it at Last," family of bears guzzling case of beer, Chas. W. Shonk Co. litho ..... 450.00
    12" d, Red Raven Splits, trademark Red Raven with foot on vintage bottle, Chas. W. Shonk Co. litho ................................................ 200.00
    12-1/2" l, 16" w, Abe Freeman, pre-prohibition, policeman directing traffic in front of large Abe Freeman Liquor Store, Great Cliquot Club Ginger Ale and Penn Beer trucks in front of store, some rim chips, coated ................................................ 500.00
    13" d, C. A. Lammers Bottling Co, top of tray with bottles of products, center factory scene, floral garland with cherubs holding bottle of beer on either side, bottom mkd "Sole Bottlers for The Lang Brewing Co.," PH Zang Brewing Co. trademark, H. D. Beach & Co. litho ............. 375.00
    13" d, Dobler Brewing Co., girl with

long flowing hear, artist sgd "A. Asti," some denting, overall scratching ................................................ 55.00
13" d, Jno. T. Barbee & Co. Whisky, elderly man pouring glass of whiskey for 30 field hands, Standard Advertising Co. litho, chips and rim scratches .............................. 225.00
13" d, Virginia Dare Wine, print of Paul and Virginia next to over side bottles of wine, American Art Works litho, some minor inpainting to rim ................................................ 200.00
13-1/2" l, 16-1/2" w, Menominee River Brewing Co., factory scene, early river boats, railroad, and horse drawn wagons, Standard Advertising Co. litho, overall scratching, soiling, minor inpainting to sky.... 275.00
13-1/2" l, 16-1/2" w, Ruhstaller Lager, factory scene, early horse drawn vehicles, H. D. Beach Co. litho, some inpainting in sky .......... 275.00
13-3/4" l, 10-1/4" w, Americus Club Whiskey, San Francisco, pony sized bottle, minor crazing............. 220.00
16" d, Fehr's Beer, King Fehr handing Lady Liberty a glass of beer ................................................ 50.00
Whiskey Dispenser, 12-1/2" h, pedestal glass dispenser, engraved "Robertson's Dundee Whiskey, wooden spigot, missing top, some chipping to rims ................................ 50.00
Window Display, 39" h, 31-1/2" w, stained glass, scene of dancing jolly Bavarian holding beer mug, keg mkd "Bavarian Brewing Company," large wooden frame........... 1,100.00

# Bubblegum Cards, Nonsport

**Collecting Hints:** Don't buy individual cards; buy full sets. The price of a set is less than the sum of its individual cards. Any set should contain a sample of the wrapper plus any stickers that belong to the set.

Because these cards are readily available, make certain the sets you buy are in mint condition. You can buy boxes of gum packages and be 100% certain you will get at least one full set from a Topp's box. Donruss and Fleer average 85%.

Collectors should store cards in plastic sleeves. First place the wrapper, then the cards in numerical order.

**History:** The predecessors of the modern bubble gum (trading) cards are the tobacco insert cards of the late 19th century. From 1885 to 1894, there were more than 500 sets issued, with only about 25 devoted to sports. Trading cards lost their popularity in the decade following

World War I. However, in 1933, "Indian Gum" came out with a product containing a stick of bubble gum and a card in a waxed-paper package. A revolution had begun.

Goudey Gum and National Chicle controlled the market until the arrival of Gum, Inc. in 1936. Gum, Inc. issued The Lone Ranger and Superman sets in 1940. From 1943 to 1947, the market in cards was again quiet. In 1948, Bowman entered the picture, and a year later Topps Chewing Gum produced some nonsports cards. The ensuing war between Bowman and Topps ended in 1956, when Topps bought Bowman.

Although Topps enjoyed a dominant position in the baseball card market, it had continuous rivals in the non-sports field. Frank Fleer Company, Leaf Brands, and Philadelphia Chewing Gum provided competition in the 1960s; Fleer and Donruss Chewing Gum provide the modern-day assault.

**References:** John Neuner, *Checklist & Prices of U.S. Non-Sport Wrappers*, Wrapper King Inc., 1992.

**Periodicals:** *Non-Sport Report* (catalog from The Card Coach, but loaded with articles), P.O. Box 128, Plover, WI 54467; *Non-Sport Update*, 4019 Green St., P.O. Box 5858, Harrisburg, PA 17110; *Non-Sports Illustrated*, P.O. Box 126, Lincoln, MA 01773; *Wrapper*, P.O. Box 227, Geneva, IL 60134.

**Collectors' Club:** United States Cartophilic Society, P.O. Box 4020, St. Augustine, FL 32085.

Addams Family, set of 50 ............. 60.00
Alf, Topps, 1987, 69 cards, 18 stickers ................................................. 15.00
Antique Autos, Bowman, 953, 2-1/2" x 3-1/4", 48 cards, set ................. 50.00
Astronauts, Topps, 1963, 55 cards ................................................. 50.00
A-Team, Topps, 1983, 66 cards, 12 stickers ................................... 15.00
Battlestar Galactica, Topps, 1978, 132 cards, 22 stickers .................... 15.00
Bay City Rollers, Topps, 1975, 66 cards ................................ 20.00

**Davy Crockett, R712-I, King of the Wild Frontier, #1, Topps, 80 cards in set, $.75.**

Beatles, Topps, 1964 black and white ................................................. 2.00
Bionic Woman, Donruss, 1976, 44 cards ........................................ 40.00
Bird Series, Mecca, T43, 1910 ....... 3.00
Blackstone's Magic Tricks, Philadelphia Chewing Gum Co., 1953, 24 folders ................................................. 60.00
Brady Bunch, Topps, 1970, 88 cards ............................................. 150.00
Buck Rogers, Topps, 1979, cards and stickers ................................... 24.00
Casey & Kildare, Topps, 1962, 110 cards ........................................ 95.00
Charlie's Angels, Topps, 1977, Series 1, 55 cards ................................. 16.00
Close Encounters of the Third Kind, photo cards, ©Columbia 1977, full display box ............................... 45.00
Combat, Donruss, 1964, series 1, 66 cards ........................................ 55.00
Dark Shadows, Philadelphia Chewing Gum Co., 1969, Series 11, 66 cards, green ........................................... 80.00
Disneyland, Donruss, 1965, 66 cards, puzzle back ............................. 45.00
Drag Nationals, Fleer, 1972, 70 cards ................................................ 20.00
Dragon's Lair, Fleer, 1984, 63 stickers, 30 rub-off games .................... 18.00

**Stars of N. B. C., Bowman, 36 card series, 1952, left: #35, Williard Waterman; right: #33, John Cameron Swayze, each $1.25.**

Dukes of Hazzard, Topps, 1983, cards and stickers ........................... 24.00
Famous Americans, Topps, 1963, 80 cards ..................................... 260.00
Freedom's War, Topps, 1950-51 ..... 3.00
Good Guys & Bad Guys, Leaf, 1966, 72 cards ...................................... 50.00
Goofy Gags, Fleer, 1963, 55 cards ................................................. 15.00
Happy Days, Topps, unopened box with 36 packs, 1976 .............. 100.00
Happy Horoscopes, Philadelphia Chewing Gum Co., 1972, 72 cards ................................................. 20.00
James Bond, Thunderball .......... 100.00
Jets ................................................. 20.00
King Kong, Topps, 1965, 55 cards 20.00
Land of the Giants, English, orig wrapper ......................................... 500.00
Magnum PI, Donruss, 1973, 66 cards ................................................. 15.00
Man from U.N.C.L.E. .................... 75.00
Movie Stars, Bowman, 1948, 2-1/16" x 2-1/2", 36 cards, set ............... 85.00
Osmonds, Donruss, 1973, 66 cards ................................................. 35.00
Rockets ......................................... 20.00
Spaceman ..................................... 20.00
Stori-View Space Patrol, set, MIB ................................................. 75.00
Superman, #37, 38, 39, 44, 46, each ................................................. 18.00
Tarzan, Philadelphia Chewing Gum Co., 1966, 66 cards ........................ 40.00
Three Stooges, 1966 ................. 145.00
US Navy Victories, Bowman, 1954, 2-1/2" x 3-1/4", 48 cards, set with wrapper ...................................... 75.00
Voyage to the Bottom of the Sea ................................................. 400.00

# C

# Calculators

**Collecting Hints:** Mechanical calculators found at flea markets are often in very poor condition. Look for models in working order with no missing parts. Crank- or lever-operated machines are desirable, but 110-volt electro-mechanical machines have not attracted collector interest, perhaps because they are still so common.

Slide rules made of wood or metal are widely collected, but plastic models are not. Most slide rules are six to twelve inches in length. Longer rules and circular models are less common and more valuable.

Electronic calculators have no moving parts. Battery-operated or pocket models are desirable, while desktop printing machines generally are not. Like early transistor radios (1955-1965), the first pocket calculators (1970-1980) have become an exciting collectible. But unlike transistor radios, early pocket calculators are still easy to find at thrift stores and flea markets. Best of all, thrift stores often sell 1970s' models for less than $5. Models with display numbers that light up (LED type) were made only during the 1970s and are, thus, obsolete and collectible. Almost all pocket calculators made since 1980 have liquid crystal (black) display numbers. With the exception of novelty types, these newer models are not currently collectible. A very easy way to identify the early (1970s) models is to look for a socket (hole) for an adapter plug. Almost all early pocket calculators have an adapter socket, while newer pocket models do not. Collectors generally don't care if the adapter and cord are missing as long as the calculator has a socket. Fortunately for the collector, almost every pocket calculator has both the manufacturer's name and the model number printed clearly on the front or back of the case.

Although most collectors are only interested in small pocket calculators, some large desktop models are not being purchased by collectors. The collectable types do not print on paper tape but have Nixie Tube or CRT (TV screen) displays. Companies that made these desktop calculators include Anita, Canon, Casio, Commodore, Friden, IME, SCM, Sharp, Singer, Sony, Victor, Wang, and Wyle.

**History:** Although the abacus has been used for more than a thousand years, the first mechanical calculating devices were not invented until the 1600s. Few of these early machines survived, and those that did are now in museum collections. A very early handmade brass calculating device recently sold for several million dollars.

Calculators were not manufactured on a commercial scale until the early to mid-1800s. By the late 1800s, mechanical calculators were being produced by many companies, and some models, such as Felt's comptometer, are still found in flea markets today. Electric motors were added at the turn of this century, and these "electromechanical" calculators were still in common use in the 1960s. During the 1960s, transistorized desktop calculators began to appear but initially cost thousands of dollars.

In the early 1970s, thanks to the invention of the integrated circuit, which packed thousands of transistors onto a microchip, the first affordable electronic calculators began to appear. Pocket-sized electronic calculators came onto the market in 1971-1972 for $200 to $400. This was the end of the line for mechanical calculator and slide rule companies. Competition to produce cheaper electronic calculators soon reached a frenzy, and dozens of companies either went bankrupt or were quickly forced out of the calculator business—bad news for calculator manufacturers, but good news for collectors! By 1973, the price of a basic pocket calculator had fallen to the incredibly "low" price of $100 (about $300 in terms of today's adjusted currency). Today, a similar four-function calculator sells for about $5. Note that some manufacturers, like Texas Instruments and Unisonic, made dozens of different models. The first models made by a given company are generally the most sought after. Only two American companies—Texas Instruments and Hewlett-Packard—still produce pocket calculators.

**References:** William Aspray, *Computing Before Computers*, Iowa State University Press, 1990; Bruce Flamm and Guy Ball, *Collector's Guide to Pocket Calculators*, Wilson/ Barnett Publishing (14561 Livingston St., Tustin, CA 92680), 1997.

**Collectors' Clubs:** International Association of Calculator Collectors (IACC), 10455 Victoria Ave., Riverside, CA 92503; The Oughtred Society (slide rules), 2160 Middlefield Rd., Palo Alto, CA 94301.

**Museums:** Cambridge University Science Museum, Cambridge, England; National Museum of American History, Smithsonian Institution, Washington, DC.

**Advisor:** Bruce L. Flamm.

| | |
|---|---|
| Addometer | 25.00 |
| APF Mark 21 | 25.00 |
| Bohn Instant | 30.00 |
| Bonsei 3000 | 10.00 |
| Bomar 901B | 65.00 |
| Busicom Handy LE | 250.00 |
| Calcupen | 150.00 |
| Canon Pocketronic | 150.00 |
| Commodore | |
| 887D | 30.00 |
| MM1 | 70.00 |
| MM2 | 45.00 |
| MM3 | 25.00 |
| Corvus 411 | 30.00 |
| Craig | |
| 4501 | 50.00 |
| 4502 | 55.00 |
| 4509 | 35.00 |
| Crown CL 130 | 150.00 |
| Facit 1140 | 45.00 |
| Heathkit IC2006 | 50.00 |
| Hewlett Packard | |
| 35 | 100.00 |
| 55 | 80.00 |
| HP-01 Calculator wristwatch | 750.00 |
| Keystone, 390 | 50.00 |
| Kings Point | |
| 8412 | 40.00 |
| SC20 | 35.00 |
| Litronix 2220 | 25.00 |
| Lloyds 303 | 20.00 |
| National | 20.00 |
| Semiconductor 600 | 15.00 |
| Omron 606 | 35.00 |
| Radio Shake EC 425 | 45.00 |
| Rapid Data 800 | 35.00 |
| Rockwell 76 | 35.00 |
| Royal Digital 3 | 100.00 |
| Sanyo Icc 804D | 100.00 |
| Sharp EL 8 | 75.00 |
| Sinclair Sovereign | 110.00 |
| Summit K09V | 45.00 |

# Calendars

**Collecting Hints:** Value increases if all monthly pages are attached. Most calendars are bought by collectors who are interested in the subject illustrated on the calendar, rather than the calendar per se.

**History:** Calendars were a popular advertising giveaway in the late 19th century and during the first five decades of the 20th. Recently, a calendar craze has swept bookstores throughout America. These topic-oriented calendars contain little or no advertising.

**Reference:** Rick and Charlotte Martin, *Vintage Illustration: Discovering America's Calendar Artists*, Collectors Press (P.O. Box 230986, Portland, OR 97281).

**Collectors' Club:** Calendar Collector Society, 18222 Flower Hill Way #299, Gaithersburg, MD 20879.

**Additional Listings:** Pinup Art.

**Reproduction Alert.**

1893, Hood's Sarsaparilla, titled, "The Young Discoverers," little boy and girl looking at globe, 8-1/2" h, 6" w, some paper loss ...................... 75.00
1894, Hoyt's, lady's perfumed ...... 15.00
1889, Buckeye Fire Insurance, color illus of Victorian woman, 28" x 20" ................................................ 295.00
1890, Success Horse Collars, 14" x 24" ................................................ 360.00
1894, Hatfield and Kearney, children, folding, 12-1/2" x 7-1/2" ............ 85.00
1898, Fairbanks Fairy Floral Calendar, 6 pgs, orig string holder, 12" x 8-1/2" ................................................ 85.00
1901, Colgate, miniature, flower ... 20.00
1905, Rock Crystal Salt, Chicago, celluloid, memo pad ........................ 35.00
1907, Capewell Horse Nails, horse, buggy, horseless carriage, and horse shoer, J. Kerner and Shop, matted and framed, 13" ......... 150.00
1909, Bank of Waupun, emb lady ................................................ 35.00
1913, Gross Druggist, Harrisburg, PA, multicolored, celluloid .............. 35.00
1914, Youth's Companion, marching scene, easel back.................... 12.00
1916, Metropolitan Insurance ....... 20.00

**1898, Youth Companion, fold-out, 8" x 11" closed, $45.**

1918, American Glass Co., Cincinnati, celluloid, ruler and blotter, black and white illus .................................. 20.00
1921, DeLaval, little boy fishing.... 70.00
1922, Warren National Bank, Norman Rockwell illus ......................... 300.00
1926, Mary Pickford, Pompeian ... 50.00
1927, Wrigley's Double Mint Gum, 3-1/2" x 6"................................ 30.00
1928, Hartney Machine & Motor Works, titled "Discovered," two dogs pointing at prey in forest scene, 16-1/2" h, 10-1/2" w, full pad .................. 55.00
1929, Socony Products, 2-1/4" x 3-3/4", red, white, and blue celluloid pocket calendar, Standard Oil Co. of NY, Socony Motor Oils symbols and monthly calendar on one side, "Socony Special Gasoline" inscription and 1930 monthly calendar on other side ................................ 20.00
1930, Peter's Cartridges ............. 265.00
1931, DeLaval, illus by Norman Priss ................................................ 165.00
1934, Ramon's Brownies, six page flip-type, newsprint paper, 12-1/2" x 19", metal top edge........................ 35.00
1936, Oliver Tractors................... 75.00
1937, Traveller's, Currier and Ives illus ................................................ 40.00
1938, Mt. Airy Milling, Gold Medal Flour ................................................ 25.00
1939, Johnson Winged Gasoline.. 20.00
1940, American Book Co., school type, American Firsts ....................... 15.00
1941, When Winter Comes, Maxfield Parrish.................................... 195.00
1942, Tydol-Veedol, 8" x 8-1/2", wall type, opens to 8-1/2" x 13-1/2", color art of US military aircraft for each three months of year, closed cover has orange, sepia, and black and white design of Independence Hall ................................................ 40.00
1943, Esquire, illus by Vargas, orig envelope ................................ 50.00
1944, Stem Brothers, Skyesville AMOCO ................................... 18.50
1945, American Book Co., school type, Pacific scenes......................... 15.00
1946, Bathing Beauty, titled "I'll Say So," illus by Rolf Armstrong............. 75.00
1947, Hercules Powder .............. 175.00
1948, First Dates, 8" x 11"............. 25.00
1950, Welsh Florists, Reistertown, MD, flower pictures ........................ 12.00
1951, Four Seasons, illus by Norman Rockwell................................ 35.00
1954, Shell marine Lubricants, 2-1/4" x 3-1/2" thin plastic, yellow, Shell logo in center of saver ring, reverse side with red calendar .................... 25.00
1955, Farmer's Supply, 24 pgs, orig envelope .................................. 8.00
1956, Sealtest, 24 pgs, hanging type ................................................ 7.50
1963, Pasadena Tournament of Roses ................................................ 20.00
1969, Union Pacific RR Centennial ................................................ 20.00
1975, Arizona Highways................. 5.00
1976, Girl Scouts .......................... 6.00

# Cameras

**Collecting Hints:** Because of the sheer numbers of antique and classic cameras available, collectors often concentrate on specific eras, types, models, manufacturers, or country of origin.

Leica has been the top name in 35mm photography since the German company of Ernst Leitz introduced its landmark camera in 1925. Although prices are relatively stable, Leica cameras are generally expensive. Demand for them exists worldwide.

Kodak has been American's favorite camera since the introduction of the low-cost Brownie in 1900. As a result of the company's mass production and marketing, there is a surplus of many common models, both antique and modern.

The commercial success of Polaroid's instant-picture cameras has resulted in a surplus in the marketplace. Introduced in 1948, Polaroid cameras are not widely collected, and prices for most models remain low. The few exceptions are Polaroid cameras outfitted with superior optics.

Condition is of utmost importance unless the camera in question is particularly scarce. Shutters should function properly. Minimal wear is generally acceptable. Avoid cameras that have missing parts, damaged bellows, or major cosmetic problems.

In addition to precision instruments, camera collectors look for the odd and unusual models. Examples run the gamut from an inexpensive plastic camera that looks like a can of soda to a rare antique camera disguised to look like three books held together by a leather strap.

**History:** Of all the antique and classic cameras available, the most prized are those that took the earliest photographs known as daguerreotypes. The process was successfully developed by Louis-Jacques-Mandé Daguerre of Paris in 1839. These photographic images, made of thinly coated silver on copper plate, have a legion of collectors all their own. However, few of the cameras that photographed daguerreotypes have survived.

Edward Anthony became America's first maker of cameras and photographic equipment by founding E. Anthony in 1842. The company later became Ansco. Stereoscope photos were shown at London's Great Exhibition in 1851 and soon became the rage in Britain and Europe. Stereo cameras are recognized by their horizontally mounted twin lenses. Tintype photographs were introduce in 1856.

George Eastman's introduction of the Kodak camera in 1888 made photography accessible to the general public. Made by Frank Brownell for the Eastman Dry Plate & Film Co., it was the first commercially marketed roll-film camera. The original Kodak camera was factory loaded with 100 exposures. The finished pictures were round and 2-1/2 inches in diameter. Eastman Kodak's No. 2 Brownie, a box camera made of cardboard, became a best-seller shortly after it was introduced in 1902.

After manufacturing microscopes and optical equipment for 75 years, Ernst Leitz of Wetzlar, Germany, introduced the first Leica 35mm camera in 1925. Japanese companies entered the photography market with Minolta (Nifca) cameras circa 1928, Canon (Kwanon) in 1933, and Nippon Nogaku's Nikon range-finder cameras in 1948.

**References:** Michael McBroom, *McBroom's Camera Blue Book 1993-1994*, Amherst Media, 1993; Jim and Joan McKeown (eds.), *Price Guide to Antique and Classic Cameras 1997-1998*, Centennial Photo Service, 1996; Douglas St. Denny, *Hove International Blue Book Guide Prices for Classic and Collectable Cameras*, Hove Foto Books, 1992.

**Periodicals:** *Camera Shopper Magazine*, P.O. Box 1086, New Canaan, CT 06840; *Classic Camera*, P.O. Box 1270, New York, NY 10157; *Shutterbug*, 5211 S. Washington Ave., Titusville, FL 32780.

**Collectors' Clubs:** American Society of Camera Collectors, 4918 Alcove Ave., N. Hollywood, CA 91607; International Kodak Historical Society, P.O. Box 21, Flourtown, PA 19301; Leica Historical Society of America, 7611 Dornoch Lane, Dallas, TX 75248; National Stereoscopic Association, P.O. Box 14801, Columbus, OH 43214; Nikon Historical Society, P.O. Box 3213, Munster, IN 46321; Photographic Historical Society, P.O. Box 39563, Rochester, NY 14604; The Movie Machine Society, 50 Old Country Rd., Hudson, MA

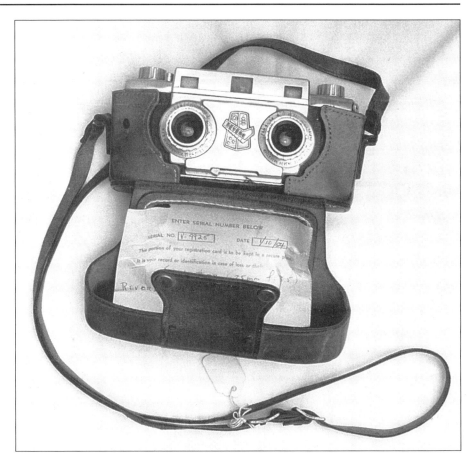

**Revere Stereo Camera, Model 33, 35mm, f35, $150.**

01749; Zeiss Historical Society, 300 Waxwing Drive, Cranbury, NJ 08512.

**Museum:** International Museum of Photography at George Eastman House, Rochester, NY.

**Advisor:** Tom Hoepf.

### Ansco (Birmingham, NY)

Automatic Reflex, quality twin lens reflex camera, 1947, f3.5 83mm Ansco Anastigmat lens, ground glass focusing screen............ 120.00

Karomat, 35mm strut-folding rangefinder camera, c1951, f2 50mm Schneider Xenon lens, Synchro-Compur shutter................ 60.00

Memo, half-frame 35mm camera, 1927, tubular view finder on top of box, black leatherette on wood body ................................................ 70.00

Royal 1A, folding roll film camera, c1925-1930, brown imitation skin covering, brown bellows.......... 35.00

Titan, c1949, horizontal folding roll film camera, f4.5 90mm Ansco Anastigmat lens, uses 120 film ........... 50.00

Vest Pocket No. 2, four-strut folding camera, c1915-1923, f7.5 Modico Anastigmat lens, folding lens cover, black leatherette finish, uses 120 film ................................................ 35.00

### Eastman Kodak (Rochester, NY)

Beau Brownie No. 2A box camera, 1930, two-tone Art Deco design on front of camera, Doublet lens, (various colors; rose color worth double to three times more)............... 100.00

Boy Scout Brownie box camera, Boy Scout emblem on Art Deco faceplate, 620 film (double the price for rare 120 film version) .............. 150.00

Girl Guide Vest Pocket folding camera, (English Girl Scouts), 1930, dark blue and black body.............. 240.00

Kodak Stereo Camera, c1955, 35mm camera, f3.5 35mm Anaston lenses ................................................ 125.00

Kodak Vest-Pocket Autographic folding camera, c1917, black, with case ................................................ 50.00

Kodak Vest Pocket Petite folding camera, 1929-1933, autographic model in lavender body and bellows, matching case ...................... 180.00

Kodak World's Fair Flash Camera, 1964, 127 film, with original pentagonal box shaped like the Kodak pavilion ................................................ 45.00

Motormatic 35, 35mm camera, c1960, spring-wind motor drive, built-in meter....................................... 40.00

No. 2 Stereo Kodak, c1900, stereo box camera, 8-1/4" x 6" x 5".......... 650.00

No. 3 Cartridge Kodak, 1900-1907, early roll film camera, 4-1/4" x 3-1/4" exposures, No. 119 size film, Bausch & Lomb lens in brass, maroon leather bellows ........................ 210.00

Rainbow Hawk-Eye Model C No. 2 box camera, 1929, red version, uses 120 film, has single viewfinder ........ 33.00

Retina I (postwar type) German-made 35mm camera, c1946, f3.5 50mm Kodak Ektar lens, 1/500 Compur Rapid shutter ............................. 85.00

Retina III Automatic German-made 35mm camera, c1962, f2.8 45mm Xenar lens, coupled rangefinder .................................................. 60.00

**Sears** (Chicago), Tower Reflex, inexpensive twin lens reflex camera, c1955, front-element focusing f9 85mm Roeschien Kreuznach lens, uses 120 film ............................ 40.00

**Voigtlander** (Braunschweig), Perkeo I folding camera, c1952, uses 120 roll film, f4.5 75mm Vaskar lens, Prontor shutter ...................................... 75.00

**Universal Camera Corp. (New York)**

Mercury Model CX 35mm camera, c1945, f3.5 35mm Universal Tricor lens, rotary shutter ................... 45.00

Univex AF, inexpensive vest-pocket camera, c1938, uses No. 00 film, various colors, cast metal body .................................................. 35.00

**Zeiss (Jena, Germany)**

Bob 510/2 folding camera, c1935, f7.7 0.5cm Nettar-Anastigmat lens, 2-1/4" x 3-1/4" exposures ......... 45.00

Box Tengor 56/2, box camera with chrome trim, 1948-1956, Frontar f9 lens.......................................... 35.00

# Candlewick Pattern

**Collecting Hints:** Select pieces without chips, cracks, or scratches. Learn the characteristics, shapes, and types of pieces Imperial made. Many items that are similar to Candlewick have been made by other companies and are often mixed with or labeled "Candlewick" at shops and shows. Learn to identify look-alikes and reproductions.

**History:** Candlewick, Imperial Glass Corporation's No. 400 pattern introduced in 1936, was made continuously until October 1982 when Imperial declared bankruptcy. In 1984, Imperial was sold to Lancaster-Colony Corporation and Consolidated Stores International, Inc. Imperial's assets, including inventory, molds, buildings, and equipment, were liquidated in 1985. Imperial's Candlewick molds were

bought by various groups, companies, and individuals.

At the liquidation sale, the buildings and site were purchased by Anna Maroon of Maroon Enterprises, Bridgeport, Ohio, with the intent of developing the site into a tourist attraction, Imperial Plaza. The Imperial glass outlet, The Hay Shed, the Bellaire Museum, and a few small businesses moved into the building, but the project failed, and the Imperial building deteriorated and was demolished in July 1995.

The Hay Shed outlet relocated to a building near the Imperial site and operates as a consignment shop for Imperial and other glass. At its 1996 convention, the National Imperial Glass Collector's Society started a drive to establish an Imperial museum and preserve the heritage of glassmaking that took place at Imperial for more than 80 years.

Candlewick is characterized by the crystal-drop beading used around the edges of many pieces; around the bases of tumblers, shakers, and other items; in the stems of glasses, compotes, and cake and cheese stands; on the handles of cups, pitchers, bowls, and serving pieces; on stoppers and finials; and on the handles of ladles, forks, and spoons. The beading is small on some pieces, larger and heavier on others.

A large variety of pieces were produced in the Candlewick pattern. More than 650 items and sets are known. Shapes include round, oval, oblong, heart, and square. Imperial added or discontinued items as popularity and demand warranted. The largest assortment of pieces and sets were made during the late 1940s and early 1950s.

Candlewick was produced mostly in crystal. Viennese Blue (pale blue, 1937-1938), Ritz Blue (cobalt, 1938-1941), and Ruby Red (red, 1937-1941) were made. Amber, black, emerald green, lavender, pink, and light yellow pieces also have been found. From 1977 to 1980, four items of 3400 Candlewick stemware were made in solid-color Ultra Blue, Nut Brown, Verde Green, and Sunshine Yellow. Solid-black stemware was made on an experimental basis at the same time.

Other decorations on Candlewick include silver overlay, gold encrustations, cuttings, etchings, and hand-painted designs. Pieces have been found with fired-on gold, red, blue, and green beading.

Blanks, i.e., plain pieces, were sold to many companies which decorated them with cuttings, hand paintings, and silver overlay, or fitted them with silver, chrome, or brass bases, pedestals, or lids. Shakers sold to DeVilbiss were made into atomizers. Irving W. Rice & Co. purchased Candlewick tray handles and trays and assembled boudoir sets consisting of a puff jar, two perfume bottled Candlewick tray. They also sold hand mirrors with large bead handles and Candlewick clocks made from ashtrays. Imperial made and sold Candlewick lamp parts, globes, and shades to several companies, including Lightolier Co., Midwest Chandelier Co., and H. A. Framburg & Co. Ceiling and wall fixtures, table, and floor lamps have been found with Candlewick parts.

**References:** Myrna and Bob Garrison, *Imperial's Boudoir, Etcetera,* 1996; National Imperial Glass Collector's Society, *Imperial Glass Encyclopedia, Vol. I: A–Cane,* The Glass Press, 1995; Virginia R. Scott, *Collector's Guide to Imperial Candlewick,* 1997 edition, available from author (275 Milledge Terrance, Athens, GA 30606); Mary M. Wetzel-Tomalka, *Candlewick: The Jewel of Imperial,* Books I and II, available from author (P.O. Box 594, Notre Dame, IN 46556-0594); —, *Candlewick, The Jewel of Imperial, Personal Inventory & Record Book,* available from author, 1998; —, *Candlewick, The Jewel of Imperial, Price Guide '99 and More,* available from author, 1998.

**Periodicals:** *Glasszette,* National Imperial Glass Collector's Society, P.O. Box 534, Bellaire, OH 43528; *Spyglass Newsletter,* Michiana Association of Candlewick Collectors, 17370 Battles Rd., South Bend, IN 46614; *The Candlewick Collector Newsletter,* National Candlewick Collector's Club, 6534 South Avenue, Holland, OH 43528; *TRIGC Quarterly Newsletter,* Texas Regional Imperial Glass Collectors, 2113 F. M. 367 East, Iowa Park, TX 76367.

**Videotapes:** National Imperial Glass Collectors Society, *Candlewick, at Home, in Any Home,* Vol. I, *Imperial Beauty* (Candlewick display), Vol. II, Seminar by Mary Wetzel and Virginia Scott, 1993 National Imperial Glass Collectors Society Convention (P.O. Box 534, Bellaire, OH 43528).

**Collectors' Clubs:** Candlewick Crystals of Arizona, 1122 W. Palo

Verde Drive, Phoenix, AZ 85013; Fox Valley Northern Illinois Imperial Enthusiasts, 38 W. 406 Gingerwood, Elgin, IL 60123; Maryland Imperial Candlewick Club, 23 Ashcroft Court, Arnold, MD 21012; Michiana Association of Candlewick Collectors, 17370 Battles Rd., South Bend, IN 46614; National Candlewick Collector's Club, 6534 South Avenue, Holland, OH 43528; National Imperial Glass Collector's Society, P.O. Box 534, Bellaire, OH 43528; Ohio Candlewick Collector's Club, 613 S. Patterson, Gibsonburg, OH 43431; Texas Regional Imperial Glass Collectors, 2113 F. M. 367 East, Iowa Park, TX 76367.

**Museum:** Bellaire Museum, Bellaire, OH 43906.

**Reproduction Alert:** When Imperial Glass Corp. was liquidated in 1985, all the molds were sold, but no accurate records were kept of all the buyers. It is known that Mirror Images, Lansing, Michigan, purchased more than 200 of the molds, and Boyd Crystal Art Glass, Cambridge, Ohio, purchased 18 small ones. Other molds went to private individuals and groups.

Since the late 1980s, Boyd Crystal Art Glass has used Candlewick molds to make items in various slag and clear colors. Boyd has marked its reproductions with its trademark, a "B" inside a diamond, which is pressed on the bottom of each article.

In 1985, Mirror Images had Viking Glass Co., New Martinsville, West Virginia, make the six-inch Candlewick basket, 400/40/0, in Alexandrite, and a four-piece child's set (consisting of a demitasse cup and saucer, six-inch plate, and five-inch nappy) in pink. In 1987, Viking produced clear plates, bowls, saucers, flat-based sugars and creamers (400/30 and 400/122), and the 400/29 tray for Mirror Images in crystal. These pieces have ground bottoms, are somewhat heavier than original Candlewick pieces, and are not marked. Shapes of items may differ from original Candlewick.

In late 1990, Dalzell-Viking Corporation, successor to Viking, began making Candlewick in Mirror Image's molds. They made five-piece place settings in crystal, black, cobalt, evergreen, and red. Most of these are marked, either "DALZELL" for the first-quality pieces, or "DX" for seconds. In January 1991, Dalzell added handled plates, bowls, and a five-section 400/112 center-well relish in crystal. A new pastel shade, Cranberry Mist, was added in 1992.

Since late 1995, Dalzell Viking has offered Candlewick Gold, clear with gold beads; Candlewick Pastels, also called Satins, in azure, crystal, green, yellow, and cranberry; eight-, ten, and twelve-inch plates, cups, and saucers, and 6-inch bowls were made, all marked only with a paper label.

In 1996, Dalzell added a punch bowl set with gold beads and also began to make Candlewick with silver beads. The Pastel Satin production has been extended to include the following: 400/231 three-piece square bowl set; 400/161 butter dish; 400/154 deviled-egg tray; 400/68D pastry tray with a heart center handle; 400/87C and /87F vases; a six-inch bowl on an eight-inch oval tray; and a four-ounce sherbet, similar to 400/63B compote. Dalzell also added Candlewick Frosts, dark amber, plum, blue, and sage green with frosted finish. All of the above are marked only with a Dalzell Viking paper label. Dalzell Viking Corp. went out of business in May 1998. All glass on hand, including Candlewick, was sold. Dalzell Candlewick is now being sold by many dealers, often mixed with Imperial Candlewick, sometimes marked "Rare Candlewick." Great care must be taken by collectors to learn the characteristics, many colors and decorations of the glass made by Dalzell Viking. The future use of Candlewick molds has not been announced by the owner, Mirror Images.

Glass with beaded edges closely resembling Candlewick is being made and imported to the United States by companies in Germany and Taiwan. The look-likes are being sold by many stores and through mail-order catalogs. Clear bowls, plates, and cake stands, some with gold beads, have been widely offered in catalogs and stores. Frosted candle tumblers and small plates with gold beads and a "Taiwan" label also are being sold in stores and by catalogs.

**Advisor:** Virginia R. Scott.

## Ashtray

400/150, 6" d, round, large beads
 Caramel slag........................... 120.00
 Cobalt blue ............................. 50.00
 Crystal...................................... 8.00
 Pink ........................................ 15.00

400/176, 3-1/4" square, large beads
 .............................................. 12.00
400/450, nested set, 4", 5", and 6"
 Colored, 4" blue, 5" yellow, 6" pink
 .............................................. 50.00
 Crystal..................................... 25.00
400/450, nested set, 4", 5", and 6", patriotic dec
 Colored, blue, yellow, pink....... 75.00
 Red, white, and blue.............. 175.00

## Atomizer

400/96 shaker, atomizer top, made by DeVilbiss............................... 125.00
400/167 shaker, atomizer top, amethyst
 .............................................. 175.00
400/167 shaker, atomizer top, aqua
 .............................................. 175.00
400/247 shaker, atomizer top, amethyst
 .............................................. 150.00
400/247 shaker, atomizer top, aqua
 .............................................. 150.00

**Banana Stand,** 400/103E, 11" d, 2 turned-up sides, 4-bead stem, crystal....................................... 1,500.00

**Basket**, crystal
400/37/0, 11", applied handle .... 150.00
400/40/0, 6-1/2", turned-up sides, applied handle........................ 50.00
400/273, 5", beaded top, beads on top of handle.............................. 225.00

**Bell**, 400/108, 4", 4-bead handle
 .............................................. 60.00

**Bonbon**, 400/51T, 6", heart shape, curved-over center handle, beaded edge
 Crystal..................................... 30.00
 Light Blue................................. 90.00
 Ruby red, crystal handle ....... 250.00

## Bowl

400/3F, 6", nappy, crystal.............. 10.00
400/52, 6" d, divided, crystal........ 20.00
400/74SC, 9" d, 4 ball toes, crimped
 Black, painted flowers ........... 250.00
 Crystal..................................... 60.00
 Light blue................................ 100.00
 Ruby red................................. 275.00
400/75B, 10-1/2" d, crystal ........... 40.00
400/84, 6-1/2" d, divided ............. 20.00
400/92B, 11" d, float bowl, cupped edge, crystal............................. 35.00
400/104B, 14" d, belled, large beads on sides ...................................... 75.00
400/427B, 4-3/4" d, 6" d, 7" d and 8-1/2" d, crystal, price for nested set
 .............................................. 75.00

## Bud Vase, crystal

400/25, 3-3/4" h, beaded foot, ball shape, crimped top ................. 35.00
400/28C, 8-1/2", trumpet shaped top, crimped, beaded ball bottom ... 75.00
400/107, 5-1/4" h, beaded foot, large beads, crimped top ................. 45.00
400/227, 8-1/2" h, beaded ball bottom, narrowed top slants, applied handle
 .............................................. 95.00

**Buffet Set,** 400/9266, 14" d 400/92D plate, 5-1/2" d 400/66E cheese compote, plain stem, 2 pcs ............ 70.00

**Butter, cov**, crystal
400/161, quarter pound, graduated beads on cov........................... 25.00

**Candy Box, 400/245, $300. Imperial Catalog cut provided by Virginia Scott.**

400/276, 6-3/4" x 4", California
    Beaded top, c1960 ............... 100.00
    Plain top, c1951 ..................... 125.00

**Cake Stand, crystal**
400/67D, 10" d, wedge marks on plate,
    1-bead stem
    Dome foot, c1939 ..................... 75.00
    Flat foot, c1943 ......................... 60.00
400/103D, 11" h, tall, 3-bead stem
    .................................................... 75.00
400/160, 14" d, 72 candle holes . 400.00

**Candleholder, crystal**
400/40CV, 5" h, round bowl, beaded or
    fluted vase insert ..................... 75.00
400/79R, 3-1/2" h, rolled saucer, small
    beads ......................................... 15.00
400/81, 3-1/2" h, dome ftd, small beads,
    round handle ............................. 60.00
400/115, 9" h, oval, beaded base, 3
    candle cups ............................. 125.00
400/115/2, 9" h, 2 eagle adapters
    .................................................. 350.00
400/175, 6-1/2" h, 3-bead stem .... 95.00
400/224, 5-1/2" h, ftd, 3 sections of
    arched beads on stem ........... 175.00
400/1752, 9" h, 3-bead stem, adapter,
    prisms ..................................... 250.00

**Candy Dish, cov, crystal**
400/59, 5-1/2" d, 2-bead finial ....... 40.00
400/110, 7" d, 3-part, 2-bead finial
    .................................................... 85.00

**Candy or jelly dish, 400/59, early style, $40. Imperial Catalog cut provided by Virginia Scott.**

400/140, 8" d, 1-bead stem
    Domed beaded foot, c1942
    .................................................. 500.00
    Flat foot, c1944 ..................... 200.00
400/245, 6-1/2" d, round bowl, sq cov,
    2-bead finial .......................... 300.00

**Celery Tray, crystal**
400/46, 11" l, oval, scalloped edge
    .................................................... 75.00
400/105, 13" l, oval, 2 curved
    beaded handles ....................... 35.00
**Champagne**, 3400, flared belled top,
    5 oz, 4 graduated beads in stem,
    crystal ....................................... 15.00
**Cheese and Cracker Set**, 400/88,
    5-1/2" ftd 400/88 cheese compote,
    10-1/2" d 400/72D handled plate,
    crystal ....................................... 45.00
**Cheese, Toast or Butter Dish**, 400/
    123, 7-3/4" d plate with cupped
    edge, domed cov with bubble knob,
    crystal ..................................... 275.00
**Cigarette Set,** 400/29/64/44 or 400/29/
    6, dome ftd 3" 400/44 cigarette
    holder, small beads, 4 nested 400/64
    2-3/4" d ashtrays, 400/29 kidney-
    shaped tray ............................. 85.00
**Clock,** 4", large beads, New Haven
    works, crystal ......................... 400.00
**Cocktail,** 4000/190, bell-shaped bowl,
    beads around foot, 4 oz, 3 bead
    stem, crystal ............................. 18.00
**Cocktail Set,** crystal, 400/97, 6" d 400/
    39 plate with 2-1/2" off-center indent,
    #111 1-bead cocktail glass ..... 35.00

**Compote, crystal**
400/48F, 8" d, beaded edge, 4-bead
    stem ......................................... 75.00
400/48F, 8" d, beaded edge, 5-bead
    .................................................. 200.00
400/67B, 9" d, flat, large bead stem,
    c1943 ..................................... 100.00
400/67B, 9" d, ribbed bowl, dome ftd,
    large bead stem, c1937 ......... 150.00
400/220, 5" d, 3-part, beaded edge,
    arched ....................................... 90.00
**Console Set,** crystal, bowl, pr candle-
    holders
400/100, 12" 400/92F flat bowl, cupped
    edge, pr 400/100 2-lite candlehold-
    ers, center circle of large beads
    .................................................... 90.00
400/8692L, 13" 400/92L mushroom
    bowl on 400/127B 7-1/2" d base, pr
    400/86 mushroom candleholders
    .................................................. 125.00
**Condiment Set,** crystal
400/1589, jam set, two cov 400/89 mar-
    malade jars, 3-bead ladles, oval 400/
    159 tray ..................................... 95.00
400/2946, oil and vinegar, pr, 400/164
    and 400/166 beaded foot cruets,
    kidney-shaped 400/29 tray ...... 90.00
**Cordial,** 3400, flared belled top, 4 grad-
    uated beads in stem, crystal ... 30.00
**Cordial Bottle,** 15 oz, beaded foot,
    3-bead stopper, handle
400/82, crystal, handle, c1938 .....225.00
400/82, crystal, handle, red stopper
    and base, c1938 .................... 275.00
400/82/2, crystal, no handle, c1941
    .................................................. 200.00

**Creamer and Sugar Set**
400/18, domed foot, large beads,
    creamer with plain handle attached
    at bottom, no handle on sugar, 1954-
    55 ........................................... 125.00
400/29/30, flat base, beaded question
    mark handles, 400/30, 7" l 400/29
    tray, crystal ............................... 30.00
400/31, beaded foot, plain handles,
    c1937
    Crystal ..................................... 40.00
    Blue .......................................... 60.00
400/31, plain foot, question mark han-
    dles, c1941, crystal ................. 25.00

**Cup and Saucer, beaded question
mark handles**
400/35, tea, round 400/35 cup, 400/35
    saucer ...................................... 12.00
400/35/252, no beads on cup handle
    Crystal ..................................... 25.00
    Light blue .................................. 40.00
400/37, coffee, slender 40/37 cup, 400/
    35 saucer ................................. 15.00
400/77, after dinner, small, slender
    5-1/2" d beaded saucer .......... 20.00
**Decanter,** 400/163, beaded foot, round
    stopper
    Crystal ................................... 195.00
    Crystal with red foot and stopper,
    c1938 ..................................... 250.00

**Dessert Tumbler, crystal**
400/18, domed beaded foot, rounded
    top, 6 oz .................................. 40.00
400/19, beaded base, straight sides,
    5 oz ......................................... 14.00
**Deviled Egg Tray,** 400/154, 11-1/2" d,
    twelve indents for eggs, heart-
    shaped center handle, crystal
    .................................................. 110.00
**Dresser Set,** I. Rice Co., 400/151 round
    mirrored tray; powder jar, beaded
    base, 3-bead cover; 2 round per-
    fume bottles, beaded base, 4-bead
    stoppers, 1942, 4 pc set ........ 250.00
**Epergne Set,** 400/196, 9" ftd 400/
    196FC flower candle holder, 1-bead
    stem, 7-3/4" h 2-bead peg vase,
    beaded top, peg to fit into candle
    cut, crystal ............................. 175.00

**Goblet, water, crystal**
400/190 Line, bell shaped bowl, hollow
    trumpet shaped stem with beads
    around foot, 10 oz ................... 17.50
3400 Line, flared bell bowl, 4 graduated
    beads in stem, 9 oz
    Crystal ..................................... 15.00
    Solid Colors, Verde Green, Ultra
    Blue, Sunshine Yellow, Nut Brown,
    c1977-80 ................................. 40.00
**Iced Tea Tumbler,** crystal, 12 oz, ftd
400/18, domed beaded foot, rounded
    top ........................................... 50.00
400/19, beaded base, straight sides
    .................................................. 15.00
3400 Line, solid Colors, Verde Green,
    Ultra Blue, Sunshine Yellow, Nut
    Brown, c1977-80 ..................... 40.00

**Jelly Server, crystal**
400/52, 6" d, divided dish, beaded
    edge, handles .......................... 20.00

**Mayonnaise Set, 400/84, 4 pc set, $75. Imperial Catalog cut provided by Virginia Scott.**

400/157, 4-3/4" d, ftd, 1-bead stem, no cover ........................................ 35.00
400/157, 4-3/4" d, ftd, 1-bead stem, 2-bead cov ............................. 65.00
**Juice Tumbler,** 400/18, domed beaded foot, straight sides, 5 oz .......... 12.00
**Lamp, Hurricane**
400/79R, 3-1/2" saucer candleholder, 9" chimney, 2 pc set
    Bohemian, cranberry flashed chimney, gold bird and leaves dec
    ........................................ 125.00
    Crystal ....................................... 100.00
400/152R, candleholder, chimney, and 100/152 adapter, crystal, 3 pc
    ........................................ 200.00
**Lemon Tray,** 400/221, 5-1/2" l, arched handle, crystal .......................... 35.00
**Marmalade Jar**
400/130, round 400/89 base, beaded cover with notch, 2-bead finial, 400/130 3-bead ladle ...................... 35.00
400/8918, 400/18 old-fashion tumbler, beaded notched cover with 2-bead finial, 400/130 3-bead ladle ..... 75.00
**Mayonnaise Set,** bowl, plate with indent, and ladle, crystal
400/23, 5-1/4" d 400/32D bowl, 7-1/2" d 400/23B plate, 400/135 3-bead ladle
    ........................................ 35.00
400/52/3, 400/23D 7-1/2" d handled plate with indent, 400/52B 5-1/2" d handled bowl, 400/135 ladle ..... 40.00
**Mint Dish,** 400/51F, 5" d, round, applied handle ...................................... 20.00
**Mirror,** domed beaded base, crystal, brass holder and frame, 2-sided mirror flips on hinges, made for I. Rice Co., 1940s ........................... 250.00
**Mustard Jar,** 400/156, beaded foot, notched beaded cov with 2-bead finial, 3-1/2" glass spoon, fleur-de-lis handle, crystal .......................... 40.00
**Old Fashion Tumbler,** 400/19, beaded base, straight sides, 7 oz ......... 20.00
**Parfait,** crystal, 3400, flared bell top, 1-bead stem, 6 oz ................... 50.00
**Pastry Tray,** crystal, 400/68D, 11-1/2" d beaded plate, center heart-shaped handle ...................................... 35.00
**Pitcher, crystal**
400/16, 16 oz, beaded question mark handle, plain base ................. 175.00

400/18, 16 oz, plain handle, beaded base ...................................... 225.00
400/18, 80 oz, plain handle, beaded base ...................................... 200.00
400/24, 80 oz, beaded question mark handle, plain base ................. 165.00
**Plate,** crystal
400/1D, 6" d, bread and butter ....... 8.00
400/3D, 7" d, salad ......................... 7.00
400/5D, 8-1/2" d, salad/dessert .... 10.00
400/7D, 9" d, luncheon ................ 15.00
400/10D, 10-1/4" d, dinner ............ 35.00
400/72C, 10" d, w handles, crimped
    ........................................ 25.00
400/145D, 12" d, 2 open handles
    ........................................ 30.00
**Punch Bowl Set,** crystal
400/20, 13" d six quart 400/20 bowl, 17" d 400/20V plate, twelve 400/37 punch cups, 400/91 ladle, 15 pc set
    ........................................ 225.00
400/128, 13" d 400/20 bowl, 10" 400/128 belled base, twelve 400/37 punch cups, 400/91 ladle ...... 300.00
400/210, 14-1/2" d ten quart 400/210 bowl, 9" belled 400/210 base, twelve 400/211 punch cups with round beaded handles, 400/91 ladle, 15 pc set ........................................ 800.00
**Relish,** beaded edge, crystal
400/54, 2-part, 6-1/2" l, 2 tab handles
    ........................................ 15.00
400/57, 8-1/2" l, oval, pickle/celery
    ........................................ 30.00
400/214, 10" l, oblong, cover with beaded top handle ............... 250.00
400/215, 3-part on one side, 1 section on other, 5-1/2" l, 2 tab handles
    ........................................ 50.00
400/256, 2-part, 10-1/2" l, oval, 2 tab handles ...................................... 25.00
400/262, 3-part, 10-1/2" l, 2 tab handles
    ........................................ 100.00
**Relish and Dressing Set,** crystal
400/1112, 10-1/2" 5-part 400/112 relish, 400/89 jar fits center well; long ladle, c1941 ............................. 85.00
400/1112, 10-1/2" 5-part 400/112 relish, 400/289 jar fits center well; 3-bead ladle, c1945 ........................... 70.00
**Salad Set,** crystal
400/735, 9" d handled heart-shaped 400/73H bowl, 700/75 fork and spoon set ............................. 150.00
400/75B, 10-1/2" d beaded 400/75B bowl, 13" d cupped 400/75V plate, 5-bead handles 400/75 fork and spoon set ................................. 75.00
**Salt and Pepper Shakers, pr,** beaded foot, crystal
400/96, bulbous, 8 beads, chrome tops
    ........................................ 20.00
400/96, 9 beads, flat bottom, plastic tops, c1941 ............................. 30.00
400/109, individual chrome tops
    ........................................ 12.00
400/116, 1-bead stem, no beads on foot, plastic or metal tops ........ 75.00
400/190, trumpet foot, chrome tops
    ........................................ 65.00
**Sauce Boat Set,** 400/169, oval gravy boat with handle, 9" oval plate with indent ................................... 125.00

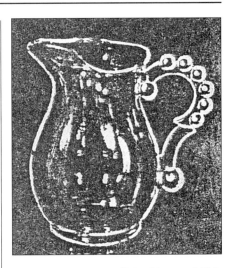

**Water Pitcher, 400/24, 80 oz, $200. Imperial Catalog cut provided by Virginia Scott.**

**Seafood Icer,** 400/190, 1 pc coupette
    ........................................ 60.00
**Sherbet,** 3400 line, flared bell top
    Low, 5 oz ................................. 12.00
    Tall, 5 oz .................................. 15.00
**Tidbit Server,** 400/2701, two tiers, 7-1/2" d and 10-1/2" d plates joined by metal rod, round handle at top
    Crystal ..................................... 60.00
    Emerald green ....................... 750.00
**Tidbit Set,** 400/750, 3 pc nested hearts, 4-1/2", 5-1/2", 6-1/2", beaded edges
    Crystal ..................................... 40.00
    Milk glass, 1950 ...................... 50.00
**Torte Plate**
400/20D, 17" d, flat, crystal ......... 40.00
400/20V, 17" d, cupped, crystal ... 60.00
**Tumbler,** water, ftd, crystal
400/18, domed beaded foot, rounded top, 9 oz ................................. 45.00
400/19, beaded base, straight sides, 10 oz, 4-3/4" h ............................ 12.00
**Vase,** crystal
400/87C, 8" h, crimped beaded top
    ........................................ 35.00
400/87F, 8" h, fan shaped ............. 30.00
400/87R, 7" h, rolled over beaded top
    ........................................ 40.00
**Wine**
400/190 Line, belled bowl, hollow trumpet stem with beads, 5 oz, crystal
    ........................................ 25.00
3400 Line, flared belled bowl, four graduated stems in base, 9 oz.
    Crystal ..................................... 25.00
    Ruby red bowl ....................... 125.00
    Solid Colors, Verde Green, Ultra Blue, Sunshine Yellow, Nut Brown, c1977-80 ................................. 40.00

# Candy Containers

**Collecting Hints:** Candy containers with original paint, candy, and closures command a high premium, but beware of reproduced parts and repainting. The closure is a critical part of each container; its absence detracts significantly from the value.

Small figural perfumes and other miniatures often are sold as candy containers. Study all reference books available and talk with other collectors before entering the market. Watch out for reproductions.

**History:** One of the first candy containers was manufactured in 1876 by Croft, Wilbur and Co., confectioneries. They filled a small glass Liberty Bell with candy and sold it at the 1876 Centennial Exposition in Philadelphia.

Jeannette, Pennsylvania, was a center for the packaging of candy in containers. Principal firms included Victory Glass, J. H. Millstein, T. H. Stough, and J. C. Crosetti. Earlier manufacturers were West Bros. (Grapeville, Pennsylvania), L. E. Smith (Mt. Pleasant, Pennsylvania), and Cambridge Glass (Cambridge, Ohio).

Candy containers, which usually sold for 10¢, were produced in shapes that would appeal to children. The containers remained popular until the 1960s when they became too expensive to mass produce.

**References:** *Candy Containers*, L-W Book Sales, 1996; George Eikelberner and Serge Agadjanian, *American Glass Candy Containers*, revised and published by Adele L. Bowden, 1986; Jennie Long, *Album of Candy Containers*, published by author, 1978; Robert Matthews, *Antiquers of Glass Candy Containers*, published by author, 1970.

**Collectors' Club:** Candy Container Collectors of America, P.O. Box 8707, Canton, OH 44711.

**Museums:** Cambridge Glass Museum, Cambridge, OH; L. E. Smith Glass, Mt. Pleasant, PA.

**Reproduction Alert.**

Bisque
  Pumpkin, 3" h, man .................. 40.00
  Witch, 5-1/2" h, holding vegetables
  .......................................... 40.00
Cardboard, duck, nodding head
  .......................................... 15.00
Chalk, turkey, metal feet, Germany
  .......................................... 30.00
Composition
  Black Cat, 5" h......................... 25.00
  Easter Chick, egg-shaped body,
  6-1/2" h.................................. 45.00

**Battleship, clear, 5-1/2" l, no closure, $9.**

Snowman, 4-1/2" h .................. 15.00
Glass
  Airplane, passenger, painted wheels and wings, screw on cap with tin propeller................................. 225.00
  Ambulance, Red Cross, paper label printed with Red Cross symbol, gold screw cap, printed "T. H. Stough"
  .......................................... 95.00
  Automobile
    Model T ............................. 20.00
    Sedan................................ 37.50
  Barney Google, with ball, repainted, orig closure ........................... 200.00
  Bath Tub, emb "Dolly's Bath Tub," open top, painted white ........ 315.00
  Battleship, four guns, cardboard closure, printed "Victory Glass Inc."
  .......................................... 45.00
  Bear ...................................... 30.00
  Bulldog, sitting, orig paint........ 85.00
  Carpet Sweeper, all orig ........ 210.00
  Chick, standing, painted yellow, tin closure .................................. 95.00
  Dog, blue ............................... 12.50
  Duck on nest, milk glass.......... 60.00
  Fire Engine, Little Boiler No. 1
  .......................................... 65.00
  Flapper, round base, paper mask
  .......................................... 25.00
  Girl, two geese, closure missing
  .......................................... 22.00
  Gun
    Pistol.................................. 35.00
    Revolver, emb "Indian Chief" on one side of grip, running horse emb on other side, screw cap closure ................................. 95.00
  Hanging Basket, attached chain, emb grape and vine dec, gold paint
  .......................................... 35.00
  Hen on Nest, Millstein ............. 15.00
  Horn ...................................... 25.00
  Jeep...................................... 27.50
  Lantern, beveled panel square, orig closure .................................. 72.00
  Locomotive, blown, cardboard tube, tin whistle, emb "E3," Stough..... 40.00
  Mantel Clock, orig dial, back mkd "Contents 3 oz. Av." ............. 235.009
  Owl, 4-3/8" h, stylized feathers, gold tin screw cap .......................... 90.00
  Pipe, blue ............................. 160.00
  Rabbit, holding carrot, 1947, Stough
  .......................................... 35.00
  Racer, #4 on grill, orig closure
  .......................................... 90.00

Rooster, crowing, gold screw cap closure ................................. 125.00
Scottie Dog ............................... 9.00
Ship......................................... 30.00
Telephone ............................... 50.00
Trunk, round top, milk glass, orig paint and closure................... 125.00
Papier-Mâché
  Apple, singing ....................... 200.00
  Black Cat, sitting on pumpkin, marked "Germany"................. 75.00
  Boot, red and white................. 24.00
  Chick, red comb, Germany ..... 65.00
  Irishman, top hat and pipe ...... 10.00
  Rabbit, standing, glass eyes ... 40.00
  Reindeer, metal antlers, glass eyes, marked "Germany".............. 200.00
  Skull, marked "Germany" ........ 75.00
Tin
  Building, 4 pcs, West Bros., c1913, 2-3/4" x 2"............................. 50.00
  Football, Germany .................. 15.00

# Candy Molds

**Collecting Hints:** Insist on molds in very good or mint condition. The candy shop had to carefully clean molds to insure good impressions each time. Molds with rust or signs of wear rapidly lose value.

**History:** The chocolate or candy shops of Europe and America used molds to make elaborate chocolate candy items for holiday and other festive occasions. The heyday for these items was 1880 to 1940. Mass production, competition, and the high cost of labor and supplies brought an end to local candy shops.

Chocolate mold makers are often difficult to determine. Unlike pewter ice cream molds, makers' marks were not always on the mold or were covered by frames. Eppelsheimer & Co. of New York marked many of their molds, either with their name or a design resembling a child's toy shop and "Trade Mark" and "NY."

Many chocolate molds were imported from Germany and Holland and are marked with the country of origin and, in some cases, the mold-maker's name.

**References:** Ray Broekel, *Chocolate Chronicles*, Wallace-Homestead, out of print; Eleanore Bunn, *Metal Molds*, Collector Books, out of print; Judene Divone, *Anton Reiche Chocolate Mould Reprint Catalog*, Oakton Hills Publications, 1983.

**Museum:** Wilbur's Americana Candy Museum, Lititz, PA.

**Reproduction Alert.**

## Chocolate Mold

Clamp type, no hinge, two pieces
   Copper, Indian, 7-1/2" h, marked "Germany" ................................ 45.00
   Pewter, dancer, 6-3/4" h, marked "Anton/Richet/Dresden" ........... 35.00
   Plastic, heavy gauge, baby carriage, 5-1/4" h, 6" l ................................ 12.00
Tin
      Basket, 1-1/2" x 4" .......... 40.00
      Bulldog, seated, 3" h ....... 45.00
      Chick on Egg, 4" w, 6" h, sgd "Anton Reiche A. G. Dresden Agents Bramigk & Co., London," also numbered ...... 50.00
      Cigar, 9-3/4" l ................... 25.00
      Knife, 7-3/4" l, 3-3/8" w, mkd "Wien #1236" ................. 35.00
      Rabbit, 6-1/4" h, standing, marked "Made in Germany" .............................. 25.00
      Rooster, 6-1/4" h ............. 45.00
      Teddy Bear, 11" h, marked "2644" .......................... 165.00
      Witch ............................. 40.00
Frame or Block Type, hinged, tin
   Chicks, 5" h, wearing bonnets, two cavities, marked "Made in Germany" ............................ 40.00
   Cowboy, holding lasso ........ 45.00
   Heart, emb cupid, double hinges .............................................. 65.00
   Jenny Lind, 3 parts ............. 95.00
   Lamb, small ........................ 50.00
   Lion .................................... 50.00
   Rabbit, eyeglasses, paint brushes, and pail, 3 part ................... 115.00
   Rooster, 10" h .................... 100.00
Tray Type
   Car, four door sedan, 3" x 5 .............................................. 15.00
   Cherries, 3 rows with 6 indentations, 7-7/8" x 4-1/8" ............. 24.00
   Egg, nine cavities, 15" l ....... 20.00
   Leaf, thirty rect bars, 2-1/2" x 10-1/2" ................................ 45.00
   Santa, four cavities, 4-1/2" h, 9-1/4" l, marked "Dresden/US Distributor/T C Weyland, NY" ... 95.00

## Hard Candy

Chicken on Nest, clamp type, two pcs, pewter ...................................... 65.00

**Rabbit playing drum, 3 cavities, Anton Riche, Dresden, #26024, tin, hinged, 10-5/8" w, 6" h, $48.**

Rose Lollipops, six cavities, clamp type, tin ............................................ 55.00

**Maple Sugar**

Dog's head, tin, clamp type, 2 pcs .............................................. 65.00
Elephant, clamp type, 2 pcs ......... 45.00
Fish, 8-1/2" l, 3-3/8" w, hand carved wood ...................................... 55.00
Girl and dog, buff clay, 4-1/4" w, 4-1/2" h .............................................. 35.00
Rabbit, wood, 1-3/4" w, 2" h, marked "Germany" .............................. 40.00

# Cap Guns

**Collecting Hints:** Condition is crucial to pricing. A broken spring that can be replaced is far less critical than a crack that cannot be repaired. Many older cast-iron cap pistols rusted and suffered other ravages of time. While restoration is acceptable, an unrestored gun in fine condition is more valuable than a restored example.

Beware of restrikes, reproductions, and new issues. Recasts often have a sandy or pebbled finish and lack the details found on the original pieces. Several of the molds for cast-iron cap pistols have survived. Owners have authorized restrikes as a means of raising money. New issues are frequently made with the intention of deceiving, and the restrikes are sold to the unknowing as period examples. Two prime examples are the Liberty Bell cap bomb and the Deadshot powder keg cap bomb.

It is important to know the full history of any post–World War II cap pistol, especially if it is one of a pair. Toy guns associated with a character or personality sell better than their generic counterparts. Some of the price difference is negated for products from leading manufacturers, e.g., Hubley. The presence of the original box, holster, and/or other accessories can add as much as 100% to the value of the gun.

**History:** Although the first toy gun patents date from the 1850s, toy guns did not play an important part in the American toy market until after the Civil War. In the 1870s, the toy cap gun was introduced.

Cast-iron cap pistols reached their pinnacle between 1870 and 1900, with J. & E. Stevens and Ives among the leading manufacturers. Realism took second place to artistic imagination. Designs ranged from leaf and scroll to animal and human

heads. The use of cast iron persisted until the advent of World War II, although guns made of glass, lead, paper, rubber, steel, tin, wood, and zinc are known from the 1920 to 1940 period.

In the 1950s, die-cast metal and plastic became the principal material from which cap guns were manufactured. Leading manufacturers of die-cast guns were Hubley, Kilgore, Mattel, and Nichols. Many of the guns were associated with television cowboys and detective heroes. Often the guns were part of larger sets that consisted of a holster and numerous other accessories.

Collecting cap and other toy guns began in the 1930s with the principal emphasis on cast-iron examples made between 1875 to 1915. In the mid-1980s, the collecting emphasis shifted to the cap pistols of the post-World War II period.

**References:** Rudy D'Angelo, *Cowboy Hero Cap Pistols,* Antique Trader Books, 1997; James L. Dundas, *Cap Guns with Values,* Schiffer Publishing, 1996; Jerrell Little, *Price Guide to Cowboy Cap Guns and Guitars,* L-W Book Sales, 1996; Jim Schlever, *Backyard Buckaroos: Collecting Western Toy Guns,* Books Americana/Krause Publications, 1996.

**Periodical:** Toy Gun Collectors of America Newsletter, 312 Sterling Way, Anaheim, CA 92807.

**Collectors' Club:** Toy Gun Collectors of America, 3009 Oleander Ave., San Marcos, CA 92069.

Dynamite, MIB ............................. 85.00
Hamilton, Cheyenne Shooter ........ 70.00
Hubley
   Cowboy, gold plated, black grips .............................................. 200.00
   Disintigrator, diecast, space gun .............................................. 600.00
   Early American Flintlock Jr., MIB .............................................. 95.00
   Flintlock Jr. ........................... 35.00
   Rodeo Patrol, cowboy on bucking hose, red, white, and blue, orig box .............................................. 150.00
   Texan, revolving cylinder, lever on side ...................................... 165.00
   Western Cap Pistol, white grips, black steer .............................. 50.00
Kilgore
   Border Patrol, cast iron ............ 70.00
   Buck, No. 407, red, navy, and white, black grips, orig box .............. 125.00
   Deputy, single holster, 2-1/4" wide fancy felt ................................ 200.00
   Derringer, sealed, MOC .......... 70.00
   Eagle ...................................... 40.00
   Mountie, orig box ..................... 45.00

Roy Rogers, illus .................... 185.00
Leslie-Henry
    Gene Autry, gold tone, MIB ..... 550.00
    Wild Bill Hickok, gold tone ..... 250.00
Lone Ranger, cast iron, unfired... 750.00
Lone Star/Wicke
    Dueling Pistol, 1970s, all metal, 8" l
    ............................................... 35.00
    Golden Eye 007 PPR, silencer, MOC
    ............................................... 65.00
    Tomorrow Never Dies 700 Glock,
    silencer, MOC .......................... 55.00
    Mattel
    Fanner 50, orig holster ............. 75.00
    Shootin Shell, double, holster
    ............................................. 250.00
    Red Ranger, cavalry style belt holder
    ............................................. 175.00
    Winchester Saddle Gun, orig box
    ............................................. 500.00
Nichols
    Derringer ................................. 48.00
    Spit Fire Rifle, 8-1/2" l ............... 75.00
    Stallion .45 Mark II, black grips,
    unfired ................................... 225.00
Roy Rogers
    Classy Guns & Holster, set .... 900.00
    Double holster and gun set, Roy's
    image on belt buckle, jeweled hol-
    ster ...................................... 1,250.00
    Mini-cap gun, holster, belt ..... 175.00
Schmidt
    Buck n' Bronc Deputy, unfired
    ............................................. 225.00
    Roy Rogers, guns in holster
    .......................................... 1,250.00
Stevens, J & E
    Buffalo Bill, repeating, 1920s, orig
    box ........................................ 320.00
    Lint Tom, cast iron, pistol ....... 400.00
Unidentified Maker
    Big Scout, cast iron, white grips
    ............................................. 100.00
    Captain Cutlass Pirate, diecast
    metal, 1970s, 10" l.................... 75.00
    Hero, cast iron, cowboy on grips
    ............................................... 45.00
    Western .................................. 50.00
Wyandotte, Red Ranger, dragoon style
    ............................................. 175.00
XTLD, pressed steel, colt .45, 1940s
    ............................................... 35.00

# Carnival Chalkware

**Collecting Hints:** Figures popular with many collectors today are the cartoon characters or movie stars. Hula girls, the fan dancer/nude type are also very sought after. Military and patriotic figures are up there as well. Some collectors key in on animals such as dogs, horses, elephants, etc., and others will look for the "bank" figures such as the "Fat Kewpie." It is possible, but not probable, that chalk string holders, and wall plaques, were given as prizes.

Also Parson Plaques and Pee Dee people have been mentioned, but no positive proof that they were carnival prizes. Some collectors will also collect items related to the carnival, such as "singing" birds on a stick, celluloid kewpies, fur monkeys on a stick, or the colorful canes.

**History:** *Step right up and win that little girl a 'Kewpie Doll'!* In 1906, the Rose O'Neill Kewpie doll was born and a few years down the road, look-alikes were coming out of the wood-work. Some of the early carnival prizes looked somewhat like the Rose O'Neill kewpie. Some were marked "Cupid" or "Rosie," some were made of composition, but most were made of plaster. The carny began referring to this prize as the "kewpie doll" and from that, all carnival plaster prizes were termed "kew-pie" dolls and this term was often heard well into the 1950s.

The era of chalkware carnival prices began around 1915, with the popularity at its greatest in the late 1930s and early 1940s, then began tapering off in the late 1940s and into the early 1950s. In the 1950s, you could still find a few plaster prizes, on the board walks and county fairs, in the warmer climate areas such as southern California. This era is not to be confused with another period, and that is the Pennsylvania chalk-ware of the early to mid-1800s.

Chalkware and plaster of paris is one and the same thing. There are various types of plaster of paris and the process in which it is mixed and poured, will cause you to find a varied degree of hardness in the figure. By its nature, plaster of paris is soft and porous, so consequently most figures found today are in less-than-mint condition. Mint condition means just that and deserves the higher value. Scratches, small chips, and a small amount of flaking would tend to lower the value. A large amount of paint loss, a poor paint job, repairs, repainting, or touch-up will tend to lower the value, and most collectors will certainly pass on these pieces.

Many figures are hollow, and this is done in the pouring of the plaster. After a short period of time, plaster will harden from the outside in. Most of the liquid is poured back out, leaving the outer wall to harden. Once the plaster was set, newspaper was wadded up and stuffed into the base, then more liquid plaster was poured to make the base solid.

Sometimes you will find the same figure completely solid. Flat back figures, of course, were solid, and it's possible that they were produced from the liquid poured out of the larger molds.

Beginning in the 1930s, studios and statuary companies began applying glitter to the figures. The sparkle caused that "Snow White" or "Mae West" to really come alive. Glue was first applied to certain areas and then the metallic glitter was sprinkled over. Since the glitter was probably produced from metal grindings or fine shavings, the metal, after a period of years, began tarnishing. Today, if you find one that shines like new, it means that someone has added that sparkle recently! The glitter today is made from plastic, will never tarnish, and tends to cheapen the figure.

The years of World War II found the carnival and the concession business at an all-time high. The hula girls and fan dancers, or any of the "girlie" figures, were very popular with the service men. Carnivals today are not nearly as lively and colorful as in those war years. The side shows, girlie shows, motordromes, etc. are no longer around. The popular "plaster" prize gave way to the easier to pack and unpacked "stuffed" animals. Not too many people know that prior to the "plaster" prize, "Teddie Bears" were given as prizes. Hamburgers, ice cream cones, carnival glass, and Sally Rand all got their start with the carnival.

Most producers, studios, statuary companies, etc., were located in the areas of New York, Chicago, Philadelphia, St. Louis, and Los Angeles. Some of the finest quality and popular pieces were produced in the Los Angeles area. Some chalkware was produced in eastern Canada.

**References:** Thomas G. Morris, *The Carnival Chalk Prize*, Prize Publishers, 1985, (P.O. Box 8307, Medford, OR 97504); —, *The Carnival Chalk Prize II*, Prize Publishers, 1993, (P.O. Box 8307, Medford, OR 97504).

**Advisor:** Thomas G. Morris.

Air Raid Warden, standing, holding American flag, 14" h, c1940 .... 95.00
Apache Babe, cap on side of her head, sweater, slacks, 15" h, some mkd "BG," 1936 ............................... 75.00
Army Air Force Pilot, standing at ease, picture frame, 7-1/2" x 5-1/2", c1940
    ............................................... 55.00

Bear Bank, dancing, wearing skirt and large bow, 12" h, c1940-50 ...... 45.00

Bird, American Eagle, mkd "God Bless America," 12" h, c1935-45 ....... 75.00

Bulldog, sitting, some with glass eyes, 5-1/4" h, c1930-45.................... 30.00

Cat and Fish Bowl, sitting looking into goldfish bowl, 9-1/2" h, c1940-50 ............................................. 75.00

Clown, two faces, one frowning, one smiling, 8" h, c1940-50............. 45.00

Dog, sitting, big smile, resembling cartoon characters Bimbo-Bonzo, 7" h, c1930-45 .................................. 45.00

Donald Duck, nephew, standing on drum, holding coin, 10-1/2" h, c1940-50 ............................................. 65.00

Elephant
    Circus or Parade, standing, no base, 10" h, c1930-40 ........................ 85.00
    Flat back, small first prize, 4" h, c1930-45 .................................... 8.00

Eugene the Jeep, standing, rare Popeye comic character, 13" to 14" h, c1930-40 ................................ 350.00

Fan Dancer, hands on hips, with feathers, mkd "Portland Statuary," 16" h, c1935-45 ................................. 185.00

Fat Kewpie, some are banks, some with finger in mouth, some with finger on tummy, 12" h, c1935-45 ........... 45.00

Gorilla, said to represent King Kong, standing 13-1/4" h, c1930-40 ... 50.00

Horse, circus, standing, some with feather plume, 11" h, c1935-45 ............................................. 45.00

Hula Girl, clam shell base, mkd "Hula Hula," flat back, 11-1/2" h, c1935-45 ................................................. 95.00

Lamp
    Nude Bust, Art Deco style, orig back glass, 8-1/2" h, c1930-40 ....... 135.00
    Rin Tin Tin, flat glass back, orig, 12-1/2" h, c1930-40 ..................... 145.00

Mae West, standing, mkd "Venice Dolls," 14" h, c1935-45........... 165.00

Majorette, marching, holding a baton, 15-1/4" h, c1940 ...................... 65.00

**Elephant, parade or circus, not marked, 10" h, $85. Photo courtesy of Thomas Morris.**

**Maggie and Jiggs, cartoon characters, mkd "Armistice," 11-1/4" h, $285.    Photo courtesy of Thomas Morris.**

Navy Wave, standing, mkd "Remember Pearl Harbor, Jenkins Studio, 1944," 9-1/2" h ................................. 110.00

Nude, reclining, some mkd "Rosemead Statuary," 5-1/2" h, c1940-50 ... 45.00

Olive Oyl, hands at sides, 8-1/2" h, c1935-45 ................................. 95.00

Penguin, resembles Kool adv character, no marks, glass eyes, 7-1/4" h, c1930-40 ................................. 50.00

Pig, bank, sitting, wearing a derby and smile, 10-3/4" h, c1940-50 ....... 55.00

Pinocchio, standing, hands in pockets, mkd "Jenkins, Venice, Ca," 9-1/2" h, c1947 ...................................... 55.00

Pluto, sitting, not marked Disney, 6" h, c1930-40 ................................. 55.00

Popeye, standing, arms crossed, some have pipes, 9-1/2" h, c1935-45 ............................................. 60.00

Sailor Girl, standing, hands behind back, billed cap, 8-3/4" h, c1935-45 ................................................. 30.00

Scottish Piper Girl, playing bagpipes, 15" h, c1935-45 ....................... 70.00

**Left:  Army WWII Soldier, mkd "Jenkins Studio, 1944," 8-3/4" h, $45; right: Navy WWII Sailor, mkd "Jenkins Studio, 1934," 9" h, $35.  Photo courtesy of Thomas Morris.**

Sheba Girl, pink or white plaster, several variations, hair tuffs, 13-1/2" h, c1920-30................................. 95.00

Ship, schooner, three dimensional, 10-1/2" h, c1930-40 ................. 45.00

Skunk, resembles Disney's Flower skunk, 4-1/2" h, c1945-55 ........ 45.00

Snake, coiled rattlesnake ashtray, 5-1/2" d, c1935-45 ................... 25.00

Snow Man, bank, top hat, scarf and cigar, mkd "Brooks Co.," 12" h, c1950...................................... 65.00

Tom and Jerry, Walt Kelly characters, 8-1/2" h, c1940-50 ...................... 55.00

Uncle Sam, rolling up his sleeve, three-dimensional, c1935-45 .......... 125.00

Vase, flowers on outside, some variations, 11-3/4" h, c1935-40 ........ 40.00

Wimpy, standing, hands behind his back, 9" h, c1930-45................ 65.00

Windmill, three-dimensional, 10-3/4" h, c1935-40................................. 25.00

# Cartoon Characters

**Collecting Hints:** Many collectible categories include objects related to cartoon characters. Cartoon characters appeared in advertising, books, comics, movies, television, and as a theme in thousands of products designed for children.

Concentrate on one character or the characters from a single comic or cartoon. Most collectors tend to focus on a character that was part of their childhood. Another collecting concentrates on the work of a single artist. Several artists produced more than one cartoon character.

The most popular cartoon characters of the early period are Barney Google, Betty Boop, Dick Tracy, Gasoline Alley, Li'l Abner, Little Orphan Annie, and Popeye. The movie cartoons produced Bugs Bunny, Felix the Cat, Mighty Mouse, Porky Pig, and a wealth of Disney characters. The popular modern cartoon characters include Garfield, Peanuts, and Snoopy.

**History:** The first daily comic strip was Bud Fisher's Mutt and Jeff which appeared in 1907. By the 1920s, the Sunday comics became an American institution. One of the leading syndicators was Captain Joseph Patterson of the News-Tribune. Patterson, who partially conceived and named Moon Mullins and Little Orphan Annie, worked with Chester Gould to develop Dick Tracy in the early 1930s.

Walt Disney and others pioneered the movie cartoon, both as shorts and full-length versions. Disney and Warner Brothers characters dominated from 1940-1960. With the advent of television, the cartoon characters of Hanna-Barbera, e.g., the Flintstones, added a third major force. Independent studios produced cartoon characters for television, and characters multiplied rapidly. By the 1970s, the trend was to produce strips with human characters, rather than the animated animals of the earlier period.

Successful cartoon characters create many spin-offs, including comic books, paperback books, Big Little Books games, dolls, room furnishings, and other materials which appeal to children. The secondary market products may produce more income for the cartoonist than the drawings themselves.

**References:** Bill Blackbeard (ed.), *R. F. Outcault's Yellow Kid*, Kitchen Sink Press, 1995; —, *Comic Strip Century*, Kitchen Sink Press, 1995; Bill Bruegman, *Cartoon Friends of the Baby Book Era*, Cap'n Penny Productions, 1993; *Cartoon & Character Toys of the 50s, 60s, & 70s*, L-W Book Sales, 1995; James D. Davis, *Collectible Novelty Phones*, Schiffer, 1998; Jeffrey M. Ellinport, *Collecting Original Comic Strip Art*, Antique Trader Books, 1999; Ted Hake, *Hake's Price Guide To Character Toys*, Gemstone Publishing, 1998; Jim Harmon, *Radio & TV Premiums*, Krause Publications, 1997; Maurice Horn and Richard Marshall (eds.), *World Encyclopedia of Comics*, Chelsea House Publications, out of print; David Longest, *Character Toys and Collectibles*, 1st Series (1984, 1992 value update), 2nd Series (1987, 1990 value update), Collector Books; —, *Cartoon Toys & Collectibles*, Collector Books, 1998; Rex Miller, *The Investor's Guide to Vintage Character Collectibles*, Krause Publications, 1999.

**Periodical:** *Frostbite Falls Far-Flung Flier* (Rocky & Bullwinkle), P.O. Box 39, Macedonia, OH 44056.

**Collectors' Clubs:** Betty Boop Fan Club, 6025 Fullerton Ave., Apt 2, Buena Park, CA 90621; Peanuts Collector Club, 539 Sudden Valley, Bellingham, WA 98226; Pogo Fan Club, 6908 Wentworth Ave. S., Richfield, MN 55423; Popeye Fan Club, Ste. 151, 5995 Stage Rd., Barlette, TN 38184; R. F. Outcault Society, 103 Doubloon Drive, Slidell, LA 70461.

**Museum:** The Museum of Cartoon Art, Port Chester, NY.

**Additional Listings:** Disneyana; also see the index for specific characters.

Autograph Album, Woody Woodpecker, 1981, sealed ............................ 24.00
Autograph Hound, Snoopy, pen in collar, Sutton, 1960s, orig tag, MIB
.................................................. 125.00
Baby Rattle, figural, Tom & Jerry
.................................................. 40.00
Bank
   Bugs Bunny, carrot barrel, Homecraft, vinyl, 1979, no stopper ... 25.00
   Fred Flintstone, plastic, gumball, working condition ..................... 55.00
   Popeye, plastic, gumball, working condition ......................... 55.00
Big Little Book, Whitman
   *Andy Panda and the Mad Dog Mystery*, #1431 .............................. 45.00
   *Porky Pig and His Gang*, #1404
.................................................. 50.00
   *Tweety and Sylvester*, 1976 ....... 6.00
Book
   *Mutt & Jeff*, Ball Publications, 1910, 15" x 6", 68 pages, hardcover
.................................................. 185.00
   *Prince Valiant, The New World Book*, #6, Hastings House, 1950s, hardcover .................................... 150.00

It's Fun To Read As You Hear

**Book and Record Set, child's, *Beep Beep The Road Runner, A Very Scary Lesson,* Peter Pan Records, Looney Tunes, Warner Bros., 45 rpm, $12.**

*Skippy and Other Humor*, Percy Crosby, Greenburg, 1929, 8-1/2" x 11-1/2", 64 pgs ...................... 95.00
*Uncle Wiggily and His Flying Rug*, Howard Garis, Whitman,1940, 6" x 7"
.................................................. 75.00
Bubble Pipe, Yogi Bear .............. 15.00
Cake Candle, Scooby, Grape Ape, Yogi, Hong Kong Phooey, MIP, each
.................................................. 10.00
Charm, figural
   Betty Boop, 1" h, celluloid, tinted, Japan, 1930s ....................... 45.00
   Rocky and Bullwinkle.............. 15.00
Child's Book, Felix The Cat Wonderbook, 1853 .............................. 25.00
Club Kit, Archie, pinback, club membership card, mailing envelope, 1950s ...................................... 85.00
Coloring Book
   *Bullwinkle*, General Mills, 1963
.................................................. 35.00
   *Flintstones Color By Number*, Whitman........................................ 22.00
   *Freckles*, Saalfield, 11" x 14", 1952, unused................................... 35.00
   *Just Kids*, King Features, 8" x 11", 1928, 16 pgs, unused ........... 75.00
   *Tennessee Tuxedo*, 1975 ......... 35.00
Cookbook, Blondie, 1947, hardcover, 142 pgs................................... 75.00
Cookie Jar
   Garfield ................................... 65.00
   Stan Laurel, Cumberland Ware
.................................................. 550.00
   Yogi Bear**,** head, authorized by Hanna Barbera ..................... 550.00
Doll
   Elmer Fudd, Dankin ................. 25.00
   Heckle and Jeckle, plush, pair 40.00
   Magilla Gorilla, plush, orig tag
.................................................. 30.00
   Popeye, Dankin, unused ......... 65.00
   Quick Draw McGraw, Knickerbocker, stuffed, 1962 ........................... 55.00

Drawing Desk, light-up, Scooby Doo and Friends, Lakeside, 1979, one page colored, orig box ............ 50.00
Eraser Head, Looney Toones, c1975
   Daffy ......................................... 10.00
   Sylvester ................................... 10.00
   Tweety ...................................... 10.00
Figure
   Charlie Brown, Peanuts, Hungerford, vinyl, small size ........................ 75.00
   Dudley Do-Right, Dakin, poseable, MIB .......................................... 200.00
   Felix, Sullivan, cast lead, c1920 ................................................ 385.00
   Froggie Gremlin ...................... 65.00
   Happy Hooligan, hand painted German bisque, 8" h .................... 245.00
   Jessica Rabbit, small ............... 20.00
   Lucy, Peanuts, Hungerford, vinyl, small size ................................. 75.00
   Pixie and Dixie, Goebel, vinyl, 1965, 4" h ............................................ 90.00
   Popeye, spinach can in hand, Dakin, poseable ................................. 75.00
   Sally, Peanuts, Hungerford, vinyl ................................................... 95.00
   Underdog, rubber cape, Jesco, 1985 .......................................... 55.00
Flashlight, Popeye, figural, King Features ............................................ 30.00
Game
   Barney Google an' Snuffy Smith, Milton Bradley, 1963, orig box ...... 40.00
   Bringing Up Father, Embee, 1920 ................................................ 600.00
   Little Lulu Adventure Game, Milton Bradley, 1945 ...................... 400.00
   Moon Mullins, 1930s ................ 75.00
   Popeye, 3-D, figural, boxed ..... 50.00
   Popeye vs. Brutus, boxing, Harmony, 1981, boxed ........................... 115.00
Greeting Card, Foxy Grandpa, mechanical, emb, diecut, 1906 ............ 65.00
Halloween Costume
   Casper, 1960s .......................... 45.00
   Fred Flintstone, 1973 ............... 85.00

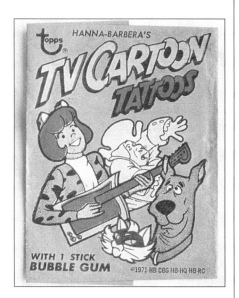

**Gum Card Wrapper, Topps, Hanna-Barbera, 1971, $5.**

**Hot Water Bottle, Sylvester and Tweety Bird, Warner Bros., Inc., Duarry, Spain, 12-1/4", $65.**

   Lil' Abner, 1950s ...................... 85.00
   Yogi Bear, 1974 ........................ 45.00
Handkerchief, Popeye, 9" x 9" .... 100.00
Hot Water Bottle, Tom & Jerry, figural, 12" h, pair .............................. 125.00
Kazoo, Woody Woodpecker, 7" l, red plastic, orig instructions, 1950s, MIB ................................................ 17.50
Lamp, Bugs Bunny, 13" h, figural, ©1970, Warner Bros., Holiday Fair Mfg., paper label ..................... 85.00
Lunch Box and Thermos, Road Runner ................................................ 65.00
Mechanical Book, *The Katzenjammer Kids,* Knerr, John Martin's House, 1945, 8" x 8", spiral bound, four mechanical pages ................... 45.00
Night Light
   Huckleberry Hound, image projects on ceiling, 1980, Hoyle, MIB .... 55.00
   Yogi Bear, ceramic ................... 55.00
Paint Book
   Brownies, Walt Kelly, Whitman, 1949, 11" x 15", unused ..................... 90.00
   Popeye, Whitman, 1937, 11" x 14", some pages used ................. 125.00
   Reg'lar Fellers, by Gene Byrnes, 1932, unused ........................... 45.00
Pencil Case
   Huckleberry Hound, 1960 ........ 40.00
   Popeye, large, 1930s ............... 95.00
Pencil Sharpener, Looney Tunes, WB, figural, vinyl ............................. 32.00
Periscope, Bullwinkle, MOC ......... 25.00
Pinback Button
   Archie Club, 1-1/2" d, 1950s .... 25.00
   Barney Google, Kellogg's Pep cereal, 3/4" d, late 1940s ......... 20.00

Daddy Warbucks, Kellogg's Pep cereal, 3/4" d, late 1940s ......... 45.00
New Funnies, Andy Panda, 1-1/4" d, black, white, red, bright yellow ground ...................................... 25.00
Popeye, Kellogg's Pep cereal, 3/4" d, late 1940s .................................. 60.00
Snuffy Smith, Kellogg's Pep cereal, 3/4" d, late 1940s .................... 45.00
Uncle Willie, Kellogg's Pep cereal, 3/4" d, late 1940s, some wear . 10.00
Yellow Kid, High Admiral Cigarettes, No. 3, Kid sitting in barrel, Mrs. Murphy mends clothes ................ 35.00
Pinball Game, Popeye, Lido, MOC ................................................ 38.00
Planter, Lil Abner's Mammy Yocum, white face, black eyes, glossy black cap, mfg. by Pearce, ©1952 Al Capp ......................................... 60.00
Playset, Dick Tracy, Ideal, orig box ................................................ 150.00
Pop-Up Book, *Popeye & The Magic Flute,* 1981, 6" x 5" ................... 13.00
Postcard
   Jiggs, dated 1920 .................... 50.00
   Katzenjammer Kids, c1910 ..... 45.00
   King Comics Contest Announcement, 1938 postmark ............. 125.00
Puppet, hand, Gumby and Pokey, pr ................................................ 45.00
Push Puppet
   Atom Ant ................................... 75.00
   Casper ..................................... 100.00
   Olive Oyl .................................. 35.00
Puzzle, frame tray
   Beetle Bailey, 1960s ................ 30.00
   Flintstones, Whitman, 1962 ...... 25.00
   Popeye .................................... 20.00
   Tom & Jerry, 1954 ................... 30.00
   Woody Woodpecker ................ 20.00
Puzzle, jigsaw
   Blondie, 1943, 9" x 14", missing 3 pieces ...................................... 22.00
   Popeye, 1942, 9" x 14", full color ................................................ 75.00
Radio, figural
   Casper, MIB .......................... 130.00
   Huckleberry Hound, Marksons, c1970, MIB ............................. 75.00
   Tom & Jerry .............................. 85.00
Record
   Felix the Cat, Peter Pan Record, 45 rpm, ©1959 King Features Syndicate, Inc. ................................... 30.00
   Quick Draw McGraw, Little Golden Record ..................................... 25.00
Salt and Pepper Shakers, pr, figural, Maggie and Jiggs, orange china holder, mkd "Made in Japan," 1930s ................................................ 75.00
Sign
   Joe Palooka, "Equal Job Opportunity," cardboard, red and black, 22" x 28", 1956 ............................... 120.00
   Snuffy Smith, patchwork tie, card stock, red, blue, and green, 6-1/2" x 11", 1940s ............................... 25.00
   Street & Smith Aviation, Bill Barnes, promoting magazine, card stock, red and black, 11" x 14", 1930s ... 450.00
Soap, Sparkle Plenty, figural, c1950, 4" h, diecut decorated box ...... 95.00

Squirt Pen and Ink, Archies, Ja-Ru, 1991 .......................................... 6.00
Statue
  Dick Tracy, full color ............... 275.00
  Lil Abner, full color, plaster .... 175.00
  Lulu and Tubby, painted, plaster, pr ........................................ 125.00
  Tom and Jerry, full color, ceramic, large, pr.................................. 125.00
  Yogi Bear, ceramic, Ideal, 7" h. 70.00
Stencil Set, Archies, Ja-Ru, 1986 . 10.00
Sticker Book, Scooby Doo ........... 25.00
Store Display
  Archies, silk-screened heavy card-board, easel back, 1948, 12" x 18" ............................................. 1,500.00
  Flintstone Stickers, 36 3-D stickers, 1977 ........................................ 65.00
  Magnetic Memo Holder, 8" h Porky, 4" h Magilla, Pixie and Betty Rubble, 8" x 10" card, 1970s ................. 55.00
  Malto-D-Meal, Andy Gump, ventrilo-quist dummy, 1930s, 12" x 12" ................................................. 45.00
Sword and Scabbard, Prince Valiant, Mattel ...................................... 35.00
Telephone, figural, Beetle Bailey, 10" h ................................................ 50.00
Television Tray, tin litho
  Quick Draw McGraw ................ 60.00
  Yogi Bear and Friends ............. 50.00
Tie Rack, Bugs Bunny, plastic, 4 figural heads .................................. 80.00
Toothbrush Holder, Gasoline Alley, fig-ural bisque, Walt, yellow shirt, red tie, blue pants, gray shoes, brown hair, holding Skeezix's hands, names incised on reverse, © F.A.S. 1930s, 80% orig paint ......................... 80.00
Toothpaste Dispenser, Bugs Bunny, Sears, 1973, MIB..................... 50.00
Toy
  Airplane, Olive Oyl, Corgi Jr., MIP ................................................. 20.00
  Car, Jerry, Corgi Jr., MIP .......... 20.00
  Car, Tom, Corgi Jr., MIP ........... 20.00
  Car, Woody Woodpecker, Sun Rub-ber.......................................... 75.00
  Circus, Flintstones, Kohner, 1965, MIB........................................ 175.00
  Motorcycle, Pink Panther, Corgi Jr., MIP ........................................ 25.00
  Set, Penelope Pitstop Flower Power Set, Larami, 1971, MOC........... 15.00
  Set, Yogi Bear Cast and Color, Stan-dard Toycraft, 1961, MIB.......... 65.00
  Telephone, Snoopy/Romper Room, Snoopy spins on top ................ 55.00
Valentine, Betty Boop, 3-1/2" x 4-1/2", mechanical, diecut round eyes, 1940 ................................................. 40.00
Vase, bud, Bugs Bunny, ceramic, 7" h ................................................. 70.00
Viewmaster Reels, Quick Draw McGraw, 1961, MIP................. 35.00
Walker, wind-up
  Garfield ..................................... 17.50
  Tom and Jerry, Masudaya, Japan, pr, MIB ....................................... 125.00
Waste Can, metal, Garfield........... 25.00
Writing Set, Whitman, 1932, 32 sheets with color illus of various comic char-acters, orig stickers................ 400.00
Wrist Watch, Smitty ..................... 200.00

# Catalina Pottery

**Collecting Hints:** Many dinnerware patterns, in addition to a wide variety of decorative pieces, were pro-duced under the Catalina name. From 1937 to 1947, many of the art-ware lines were made by Gladding, McBean and Company. Although the island plant was closed, many pieces made during this period were still marked "Catalina Island." In order to distinguish between pieces made before and after the Gladding, McBean takeover, collectors must learn the subtle differences in the various marks used.

**History:** The Catalina Pottery began producing clay building products in 1927 at its original location on Santa Catalina Island. In 1930, the pottery expanded its inventory to include decorative and utilitarian pieces. Dinnerware was added in 1931. Gladding, McBean and Company bought the firm in 1937 and closed the island plant, limiting production to the mainland. Ownership of the trademark reverted to the Catalina Island Company in 1947.

**References:** Susan and Al Bagdade, *Warman's American Pot-tery and Porcelain*, Wallace-Home-stead, 1994; Jack Chipman, *Collector's Encyclopedia of Califor-nia Pottery*, 2nd ed., Collector Books, 1998; Steve and Aisha Hoefs, *Catalina Island Pottery*, pub-lished by authors, 1993.

**Periodical:** Pottery Collectors Express, P.O. Box 221, Mayview, MO 64071.

Ashtray
  Fish, small, blue ........................ 60.00
  Sleeping Mexican, matte green, cold paint ....................................... 285.00
Bowl
  7" sq, Matrix, blue .................... 60.00
  8" l, oval, Matrix, yellow and maroon ................................................. 40.00
  10" sq, Matrix, blue .................. 70.00
  12" d, round, low, Matrix, blue ................................................. 45.00
  15" d, Angeleno ...................... 90.00
  17" d, oval, fluted, Matrix, yellow and green..................................... 90.00
Bud Vase, Angeleno, C105 ..... 45.00
Candlesticks, pr, Matrix, blue ....... 40.00
Cigarette Box, cov, horse's head, ivory ................................................. 475.00
Console Set, Art Deco style, light butter-scotch, 4" x 9" pr 3-lite candlehold-ers, 13" x 13-1/4" bowl with raised dec base, 3-1/2" x 9" 3-tier flower frog, brown ink mark "Catalina Made in USA"................................. 400.00

Egg Plate, 10" d, Matrix, blue ....... 24.00
Flower Bowl, low, flat, Capistrano
  C406, buff, satin green ........... 40.00
  C412, rect ............................... 35.00
  C419, oval............................... 48.00
Pipe Rest, Ivory Siesta, repaired ................................................. 250.00
Tray, Catalina Blue, 13-1/2" d...... 150.00
Vase
  4" x 10", white ext., white int., fluted, blue ink mark ......................... 225.00
  5-1/2" h, Matrix, yellow and maroon ................................................. 42.00
  8" h, Reseda Verde ................. 48.00
  8" x 12", white ext., blue int., incised mark ...................................... 260.00
  10" h, Capistrano, white, turquoise ................................................. 75.00
  12" h, Matrix, blue ................... 85.00

# Catalogs

**Collecting Hints:** The price of an old catalog is affected by the condi-tion, data, type of material adver-tised, and location of advertiser.

**History:** Catalogs are excellent research sources. The complete manufacturing line of a given item is often described, along with prices, styles, colors, etc. Old catalogs pro-vide a good way to date objects.

Sometimes old catalogs are reprinted so that collectors can iden-tify the companies' specialties. Such is the case with Imperial and The Cambridge Glass Co.

**References:** Ron Barlow and Ray Reynolds, *Insider's Guide to Old Books, Magazines, Newspapers, and Trade Catalogs*, Windmill Pub-lishing (2147 Windmill View Rd., El Cajon, CA 92020), 1996.

**Advisor:** Kenneth Schneringer.

American Concrete-Steel, Newark, NJ, 1912, 6 pgs, 7" x 10"................ 30.00
American Reedcraft Corp., New York, NY, c1929, 32 pgs, 7" x 10", creative handicrafts............................... 24.00
American Rug & Carpet Co., New York, NY, c1929, 24 pgs, 7" x 9" ....... 27.00
American Silver Truss Corp., Couder-sport, PA, 1933, 58 pgs, 6" x 9", *Black Diamond Line, Catalog No. 33* ............................................. 30.00
Atlas Portland Cement Co., New York, NY, 1916, 20 pgs, 8-1/2" x 11" ................................................. 27.00
Bear Brand & Bucilla Mfg., New York, NY, 1922, 32 pgs, 6" x 9", *Blue Book* ................................................. 15.00
Bellas Hess & Co., New York, NY, 1922, 280 pgs, 8" x 11", *New York Styles, Fall & Winter*, wraps chipped... 30.00
Boomer & Boschert Press, Syracuse, NY, 1882, 36 pgs, 5-3/4" x 9", wine and cider presses................... 32.00

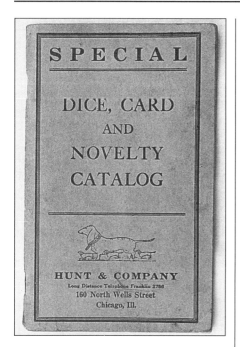

**Hunt & Co., Dice, Card and Novelty Catalog, c1920, $20.**

Brokaw Brothers, New York, NY, 1906, 16 pgs, 4-1/2" x 8-1/4", gentlemen's clothier .................................... 24.00

Browne-Morse Co., Muskegon, MI, 1922, 32 pgs, 8-1/2" x 11", steel filing cabinets ................................. 23.00

Butterick & Co., New York, 1878, 32 pgs, 7-1/2" x 10", fall women's clothing pattern catalog.................. 38.00

Century Furniture Co., Grand Rapids, MI, 1926, 154 pgs, 5-1/2" x 8", *Catalog No. 705*............................... 68.00

Chain Link Fence Co., Chicago, IL, c1929, 48 pgs, 8-1/4" x 11", *Catalog No. 6*........................................ 24.00

Chas. C. Hart Seed Co., Wethersfield, CT, 1924, 48 pgs, 7" x 10"........ 12.00

Dr. Jaeger's Sanitary Woolen System Co., New York, NY, 1915, 60 pgs, 6" x 7-3/4"..................................... 30.00

Eastern Townships Lighting, Walkerville, OH, c1929, 30 pgs, 6" x 9"....... 41.00

Eimer & Amend, New York, NY, early 1900s, 32 pgs, 3-3/8" x 6", *Bulletin 157, Electrical Laboratory Equipment*........................................ 22.00

F. E. Myers & Brother, Ashland, OH, 1894, 20 pgs, 6" x 8-3/4", Myers Spray Pumps........................... 18.00

Fenton Label Co., Inc., Philadelphia, PA, 1939, 32 pgs, 5-1/2" x 8-1/4", gummed labels ....................... 35.00

George W. Braunsdorf, Long Island, NY, 1939, 112 pgs, 3-1/2" x 5-3/4", pianos and organs.................... 16.00

Glen Rock Woolen Co., Somerville, NJ, 1914, 34 pgs, 7" x 10-1/4", fall-winter men's clothes .......................... 44.00

Hale, Cushman & Flint, Boston, MA, 1929, 18 pgs, 6" x 9-1/4", Christmas cards....................................... 26.00

Henry Hesse, New York, NY, 1902, 64 pgs, 5" x 7", *Catalogue No. 47*, woolen, worsted, and cotton knitting yarns, etc. ................................ 16.00

Jacobs Bird-House Mfg. Co., Waynesburg, PA, 1923, 44 pgs, 4-3/4" x 7-1/4", bird houses.................. 44.00

Kellogg, Mccay, Cameron, Chicago, IL, 1903, 28 pgs, 6-3/4" x 9-3/4", heating supplies ................................. 24.00

Knapp Brothers Mfg., Co., Chicago, IL, 1934, 18 pgs, 8-1/2" x 11", gifts ............................................ 12.00

Lincoln Watch & Jewelry, Chicago, IL, 1909, 74 pgs, 8-1/2" x 11"........ 45.00

Little Tree Farms, Framington Center, MA, 1927, 48 pgs, 8-1/2" x 11-1/2" ............................................ 13.00

Graves & Son, Rochester, NY, 1883, 34 pgs, 4" x 5-3/4", elevators ....... 14.00

Starrett Co., Athol, MA, 1938, 282 pgs, 5" x 7", *Catalog No. 26, Precision Tools*..................................... 15.00

Macandrews & Forbes Co., Camden, NJ, c1952, 12 pgs, 8-1/2" x 11", *The Story of Licorice,* highlighting product, uses, cuts of manufacturing process ........................................ 12.00

Montgomery Ward, Chicago, IL, 1972, 1,412 pgs, 8" x 11", fall-winter ............................................ 26.00

Marcus Furriers, Worchester, MA, c1930, 31 pgs, 8-1/2" x 11", *The Romance of Furs*..................... 14.00

National Lead Co., New York, NY, 1924, 15 pgs, 6" x 8-1/2"................... 21.00

Nonotuck Silk Co., Florence, MA, 1894, 98 pgs, 5" x 7-1/4", *Florence Home Needle Work* ........................... 12.00

Plymouth Cordage Co., N. Plymouth, MA, 1931, 31 pgs, 6" x 9", boating ropes...................................... 24.00

Prang Co., Chicago, IL, 1927, 48 pgs, 6" x 9", *Prang School Buyers Guide* ............................................ 24.00

Ridgey Trimmer Co., Springfield, OH, c1927, 48 pgs, 3-1/4" x 6"........ 15.00

Sam Laidacker, Scranton, PA, 1938, 80 pgs, 6" x 9", *The Standard Catalog of Anglo-American China, 1810-1850, Printed & Decorative Ware Made in England by the Staffordshire Potters for the Americans with Prices* ............................................ 32.00

Shakespeare Co., Kalamazoo, MI, 1951, 44 pgs, 8-1/4" x 11", *Catalog of Fine Wonderod Fishing Tackles*32.00

Sheldon Axle Co., Wilkes-Barre, PA, 1912, 104 pgs, 6" x 9", leaf springs ............................................ 30.00

Sherwin-Williams Co., Cleveland, OH, 1935, 16 pgs, 3-3/4" x 8".......... 16.00

Sohmer & Co., New York, NY, c1930, 20 pgs, 6" x 7-3/4", pianos ............ 33.00

Stephenson & Co., New York, NY, c1910, 32 pgs, 7-1/2" x 10-3/4", ladies fall styles........................ 32.00

Tumwater Lumber Mills Co., Tumwater, WA, 1925, 68 pgs, 7-3/4" x 10-1/2", *Catalog No. 25, Manufacturers of Ready Cut Homes*................... 34.00

United Shoe Machinery Corp., Boston, MA, 1920, 30 pgs, 6" x 9"......... 17.00

Verney Pipe Organ Co., Mason City, IA, early 1900s, 12 pgs, 3-1/2" x 6-1/4" ............................................ 23.00

W. Atlee Burpee Co., Philadelphia, PA, 1938, 144 pgs, 6" x 9"............. 10.00

Widow Jones, Boston, MA, 1905, 8 pgs, 4" x 10", young men's fall and winter clothing ................................. 26.00

Winthrop Furniture Co., Boston, MA, 1927, 72 pgs, 5-3/4" x 8-3/4" ... 45.00

# Cat Collectibles

**Collecting Hints:** Cat-related material can be found in almost all collecting categories—advertising items, dolls, figurines, folk art, fine art, jewelry, needlework, linens, plates, postcards, and stamps, to name just a few. Antique cats are scarce but modern objects d'feline are plentiful. The better ones, the limited editions and pieces created by established artists, such as Lowell Davis the now-deceased Thaddeus Krumeich, are future collectibles.

The cat collector competes with collectors from other areas. Chessie, the C & O Railroad cat, is collected by railroad and advertising buffs; Felix, Garfield, and other cartoon characters, plus cat-shaped toys and cat-related games, are loved by toy collectors. And cat postcards are collected by postcard collectors in general.

Because cat collectors are attracted to all cat items, all breeds, and realistic or abstract depictions, they tend to buy many items. It is best to specialize. Popular categories are fine art, antique porcelain cats, stamps, advertising, postcards and unique or unusual pieces. Up-and-coming collecting categories include first day covers, phone cards, and dolls. Kliban's cats, especially the ceramic examples, art by Louis Wain, good Victorian paintings, and cartoon cats are best-sellers in the secondary market.

**History:** The popular view of cats has been a roller coaster of opinion, from peaks of favoritism to valleys of superstition. Cats were deified in ancient Egypt and feared by Europeans in the Middle Ages. Customs and rituals resulted in brutal treatment of felines. Cats became associated with witchcraft, resulting in tales and superstitions which linger to the present. This lack of popularity adds to the scarcity of antique cat items.

**References:** Pauline Flick, *Cat Collectibles*, Wallace-Homestead, 1992; Marbena Jean Fyke, *Collectible Cats*, Collector Books, 1993.

**Collectors' Club:** Cat Collectors, 33161 Wendy Drive, Sterling Heights, MI 48310.

**Museums:** British Museum, London, England; The Cat Museum, Basel, Switzerland; Metropolitan Museum of Art, New York, NY.

**Reproduction Alert.**

**Advisor:** Marilyn Dipboye.

Book, *Old Possum's Book of Practical Cats,* T. S. Eliot, Faber & Faber, Ltd., London, 1957 ........................... 42.00
Bookends, pr, ceramic, one with black and white cat stretching his paw through to other bookend, second bookend has gray mouse with mallet, ready to strike extended cat's paw, incised "©1983" and ceramist's initials ............................... 35.00
Chalkware Figure, 7-1/2" h, Persian Cat, sitting up, pale yellow head, darkens to black chin and tail ................ 55.00
Child's Play Dishes, cup and saucer, cat on twig of pussy willows, mkd "Made in Japan" ...................... 15.00
Clock, 9" h, Sessions Clock Co., white ceramic cat holding clock, plastic cat as second hand, 1950s ..... 50.00
Comic Book, *Felix The Cat,* All Pictures Comics, 1945 ........................... 50.00
Figural
    4" h, pottery, pair, white with yellow nd black spots, blue bases, stamped in blue "Staffordshire, England" .................................. 35.00
    4" h, 2-3/4" l, three pink kittens, attached and seated on blue Victorian-style sofa with gold trim, stamped "© 1959 Bradley Onimco" ................................. 25.00
    8" h, Siamese, ceramic, model #4693, paper label "Lefton Japan" ................................. 28.00

8-1/4" h, porcelain, repro of Dresden cat, long haired, white, marked in blue "Museo First Edition," Mann Japan paper label, c1975...... 145.00
    10-1/2" h, Egyptian cat, museum repro, incised mark "©Austin production ©1965" ........................ 75.00
Handkerchief, embroidered........... 5.00
Letter Opener, 9" l, solid brass, arched back cat atop, incised "England" ................................................ 55.00
Mug, 3-1/4" h, ceramic, cat face, white, dark blue floral collar and handle, incised "Avon" ........................ 18.00
Nodder, 4-1/4" h, yellow, black stripes, fuzzy, blue rhinestone eyes, paper label "Made in Hong Kong" ....... 8.50
Pitcher, 8-1/4" h, glass, cat shape, tail forms handle, incised "WMF Germany" ....................................... 25.00
Planter
    6" l, composition, laying down cat holds balls of yard from sewing basket, incised "Pompadour 1984" ................................................ 6.50
    6" l, 5" h, pottery, stylized laughing cat, aqua, script "Weller Pottery" mark ......................................... 75.00
Plaque, bisque, applied full figure cat dancers, c1850-60 ................... 75.00
Plate
    6" d, china, cream colored, gold pattern around border, long-haired golden tabby cat fore transfer, Mount Clemens Pottery hallmark, c1935 ................................................ 25.00
    8" d, 1985 series, titled "Minou-ettes" by Vista Allegra, C. Pradalie, series includes various breeds, all with lacy curtain backgrounds................ 20.00
Postcard Album, 90 Christmas cat postcards, many foreign, c1958 to date ................................................ 150.00
Puzzle, 10-1/2" x 14", cardboard, yellow cat in blue pants and white sailor hat, playing concertino ........... 10.00
Salt and Pepper Shaker Sets, ceramic Cat shaped, Holt Howard, ©1958, meowers not working .............. 20.00

**Salt and Pepper Shakers, pr, ceramic, Mr. and Mrs. Black Cats, stamped "Japan," $15. Photo courtesy of Don Dipboye.**

**TV Lamp, ceramic, 2 Siamese cats, incised "©1958 Lane & Co., Van Nuys, CA, U.S.A.," $85. Photo courtesy of Don Dipboye.**

Garfield with Fishburger sandwich ................................................ 60.00
Hello Kitty, 3 pc set ................. 60.00
Mr. and Mrs. Black Cats, stamped "Japan" ...................................... 15.00
Sylvester and Tweety Bird with mallet ................................................ 60.00
Scrapbook, greeting and note cards, some with envelopes, approx 125 cards, c1940 to present........ 200.00
Serving Tray, 15" x 21", metal, painted gold, aqua border, two Siamese cats in center, sgd "Alexander" ....... 65.00
String Holder, 6-1/2" h, cat face shape, black and cream, blue ball of string, stamped with partial name of company, "James____ Chicago, Il" ................................................ 65.00
Tape Measure, celluloid case, pictures of playing cats, tape mkd "Made in U.S.A." ..................................... 35.00
Toby Mug, 9" h, porcelain, Puss n' Boots, Kevin Francis, modeled by Andrew Moss, limited edition ................................................ 295.00
Toy, 6" l, tin yellow and red cat, red ball and wheels, leather ears, push tail down and cat moves forward, mkd "MAR Toys Made in USA" ........ 95.00
TV Lamp, ceramic, shape of 2 Siamese cats, incised "©1958 Lane & Co., Van Nys, CA, U.S.A." ............. 85.00
Wall Plaque, 6-1/2" h, chalkware, Tabby cat face, red ears and big bow, green eyes .............................. 45.00

# Ceramic Arts Studio

**Collecting Hints:** Collectors should seek pieces which are free of damage and defects. Since this collecting area is relatively new, it

**Figural, pottery, white, yellow and black spots, blue bases, stamped in blue "Staffordshire, England," 4" h, pr, $35. Photo courtesy of Don Dipboye.**

behooves collectors to buy the best quality they can while prices are low. A careful eye should be used to find those unique pieces by designers such as Harrington.

A single firing process was used to make Ceramic Arts Studio wares. The pieces were fired after decorations were applied to the soft greenware. The firm's specially developed glazes have remained stable with little discoloration or crazing.

**History:** The Ceramic Arts Studio, Madison, Wisconsin, was originally formed by Lawrence Rabbit in 1940, while he was a student at the University of Wisconsin. He researched Wisconsin clay for a class project, and later produced hand-thrown pottery. By January of 1941, he went into partnership with fellow University of Wisconsin Student Reuben Sand. Sand became responsible for the administration, distribution, marketing, and management of the Studio.

Betty Harrington, who began her career in 1942, designed more than 600 figures and other items for the Studio through her 14-year career. She was influence by Martha Graham's modern dancers. In addition to her theater series, she created storybook character and nursery rhyme series. These series included figures, head vases, salt and pepper shaker sets, shelf sitters, and wall plaques. Harrington trained other designers but was responsible for most of the designs until the Studio closed in 1956.

During peak production years in the late 1940s, more than 100 people produced 500,000 pieces a year. The molds were sent to Japan after the studio closed. Japanese pieces are sometimes found in the marketplace, but the depth of the color and clarity does not equal that of the originals.

Ceramic Arts Studio wares were inexpensive—in the $2 to $3 range—and were marketed through department stores and by catalog sellers such as Montgomery Ward.

**Collectors' Club:** Ceramic Arts Studio Collectors Association, P.O. Box 46, Madison, WI 53701.

Figure
| | |
|---|---|
| Billy Goat | 68.50 |
| Blue Boy | 20.00 |
| Bright Eyes Cat | 27.00 |
| Chipmunk | 30.00 |
| Elise Elephant | 125.00 |
| Farm Boy and Girl, blue | 90.00 |
| Little Bo Peep | 24.00 |
| Love Birds | 22.00 |
| Skunk Family, 4 pcs | 150.00 |
| Winter Willie | 55.00 |

Head Vase
| | |
|---|---|
| Becky | 80.00 |
| Mci Ling | 85.00 |
| Pitcher, Adam and Eve | 60.00 |
| Razor Bank | 80.00 |

Salt and Pepper Shakers, pr
| | |
|---|---|
| Clown and Dog | 165.00 |
| Elephant and Boy | 170.00 |
| Fighting Chickens | 50.00 |
| Kangaroos, yellow and gray | 75.00 |
| Scottie dogs | 70.00 |
| Thai and Thai Thai | 70.00 |
| Wee Eskimos | 80.00 |
| Wee Pigs | 70.00 |

Shelf Sitter
| | |
|---|---|
| Banjo Girl | 60.00 |
| Collie, large | 80.00 |
| Elf on Mushroom | 40.00 |
| Wall Plaque, Cockatoo | 50.00 |

# Cereal Boxes

**Collecting Hints:** There are two keys to collecting cereal boxes. The first is graphics, i.e., the box features the picture of a major character or personality or a design that is extremely characteristic of its period. The second hinges on the premium advertised on the box.

Cereal boxes are divided into vintage boxes (those dating before 1970s) and modern boxes. Hoarding of modern cereal boxes began in the mid-1980s. Beware of paying premium prices for any boxes made after this date.

More desirable than cereal boxes themselves are large countertop and other cereal box display pieces. Cereal box collectors actively compete against advertising collectors for these items, thus driving up prices.

Many cereal box themes also cross over into other collecting categories. In many cases, these secondary collectors are responsible for maintaining high prices for some boxes. Once the outside demand is met, prices drop. Carefully study which market component is the principal price determinant.

**History:** Oatmeal and wheat cereals achieved popularity in the 19th century. They could be purchased in bulk from any general store. The first packaged, ready-to-eat breakfast cereals appeared around 1900. Initially, the packaging pitch contained an appeal directed to mothers.

Everything changed in the late 1930s and early 1940s. Companies such as General Mills, Quaker, Post, and Ralston redirected the packaging appeal to children, using as a hook the lure of premiums sent in exchange for one or more box lids or coupons. Many of these promotions were geared to the popular radio shows of the period. However, television advertising was most responsible for establishing a firm link between cereal manufacturers and children.

In the 1940s, General Mills successfully used the premium approach to introduce Cheerios and Kix. In the 1950s, sugar-coated cereals were the rage. By the 1960s and 1970s, cereal manufacturers linked the sale of their brands to licensed characters. As the popularity of characters faded, boxes—but not the cereal contents—were changed. Today an endless variety of cereal brands parade across supermarket shelves, some brands lasting less than a year.

**References:** Scott Bruce, *Cereal Box Bonanza*, Collector Books, 1995; Scott Bruce, *Cereal Boxes & Prizes, 1960s,* Flake World Publishing; Scott Bruce and Bill Crawford, *Cerealizing America,* Faber and Faber, 1995; Jim Harmon, *Radio & TV Premiums,* Krause Publications, 1997.

**Periodical:** *Flake,* P.O. Box 481, Cambridge, MA 02140.

**Collectors' Club:** Sugar-Charged Cereal Collectors, 92B N Bedford St., Arlington, VA 22201.

| | |
|---|---|
| Batman, Ralston, hologram T-shirt offer, 1989 | 9.00 |
| Boo Berry, hockey poster offer, 1980s | 150.00 |
| Cap'n Crunch, Treasure Hunt game board on back | 75.00 |
| Cheerios, aircraft carrier premium, 1960s | 120.00 |
| Corn Kix, Rocket Space O-Gauge, 1950s | 90.00 |
| Count Chocula, Car Bears offer, 1980s | 150.00 |
| Donkey Kong Junior, Ralston, baseball card pack, 1984 | 32.00 |
| Frankenberry, doll offer, 1980s | 150.00 |
| Froot Loops, Kellogg's, Mattel Fun on Wheels contest, 1970 | 30.00 |
| Highland Oats | 32.00 |

Kellogg's Corn Flakes
| | |
|---|---|
| Flicker ring offer, 1960s | 400.00 |
| Huckleberry Hound Fan Club offer, 1960s, Canada | 295.00 |
| Kix, General Mills, Rocket Trooper | 150.00 |

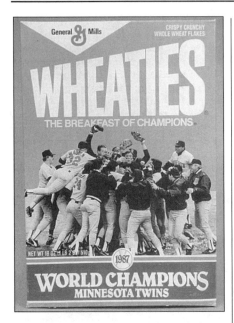

**Wheaties, General Mills, 1987 World Champions Minnesota Twins, 18 oz, $7.50.**

Nabisco Shredded Wheat, insert of Rin Tin Tin on front and back, 1950s .............................................. 100.00
Post Toasties, 7-1/2" x 10-1/2" cardboard panel on back of box, three black, yellow, red cut-outs of Snow White and Prince, Bashful and Dopey, 1937 copyright ............. 45.00
Quaker Puffed Rice, 5 oz, 1919 .... 22.00
Quick Quaker Oats, Roy Rogers branding iron ring offer ..................... 85.00
Rice Chex, red check design, 1950s .................................................. 65.00
Sugar Jets ...................................... 80.00
Superman Corn Flakes, 1950s ... 125.00
Wheaties, 1988 Redskin NFL Champions ............................................ 25.00

# Cereal Premiums

**Collecting Hints:** The rising collectibility of cereal premiums reflects the shift of emphasis from collectibles of the 1920-1940 period to those of the post-1945 era. The radio premium generation is getting older. They have watched the price of scarcer examples of their childhood treasures rise beyond the point of affordability. Further, these collectors are reaching an age when selling, rather than buying, dominates their mindset. It is time for a new generation to enter the picture—herald the arrival of the cereal premium.

At the moment, collectors do not differentiate between premiums that were found in the box and those that were obtained by sending in the requisite number of box tops. As collectors become more sophisticated, look for this distinction to occur.

The cereal premiums of most interest in the current market are those associated with a fictional advertising, cartoon, or television character. As a result, much of the pricing in this category is being driven by the non-cereal premium collector. This does not appear likely to change in the decade ahead.

Collectors of cereal premiums narrow their collecting by focusing on the premiums found in a single brand or those of one particular manufacturer—variables dependent on whether the concentration is on the 1945-1962 or post-1962 period. The lack of a comprehensive list of manufacturers, brands, and premiums often makes attribution a problem. When buying a cereal premium with which you are unfamiliar, insist that the seller indicate the manufacturer, brand name, and date on the sales receipt.

The importance of original packaging—much of which was nondescript—is unclear at the moment. Current collectors tend to leave sealed any unopened packages. Most examples on the market have not retained their original packaging.

At the moment, there is little enthusiasm for generic pieces. However, anyone who compares the history of Cracker Jack premium collecting with that of cereal premiums will quickly see the long-term potential for generic material.

**History:** Cereal premiums were introduced in the 1930s when manufacturers such as General Mills, Post, Quaker, and Ralston offered premiums to individuals who sent in the requisite number of box tops or coupons. Many of these premiums had a radio show tie-in.

Although the use of in-the-box premiums and on-pack promotions dates from the 1930s, this approach achieved its greatest popularity in the post-1945 period. Buildings, dolls, games, masks, and puzzles were just a few of the many items that a child could cut out by carefully following the directions on the back of a cereal box. Many in-box and on-pack promotional premiums related to a popular television program or movie.

When sugar-coated brands were introduced in the mid-1950s, advertising characters were developed to assist in the merchandising effort. Characters such as Captain Crunch, Sugar Bear, Tony the Tiger, and Toucan Sam achieved widespread recognition. Often in-box and on-pack promotions tied in directly with these characters.

In the 1970s, tie-ins were often more short-lived. Cereal manufacturers responded almost immediately to the latest movie or television craze, and local and regional promotions became prominent. One result of this trend is the shift in emphasis from the premium to the box itself as the important collectible unit. Cereal box collecting is now a separate category. The value of most boxes now exceeds any value for the premium associated with it.

**References:** Scott Bruce, *Cereal Box Bonanza*, Collector Books, 1995; Scott Bruce and Bill Crawford, *Cerealizing America*, Faber and Faber, 1995; Jim Harmon, *Radio & TV Premiums*, Krause Publications, 1997.

**Periodical:** *Flake*, P.O. Box 481, Cambridge, MA 02140.

Air Racers, Freakies, 1970s, complete set of 7, orig instructions and mailer .................................................. 45.00
Bank, Batman, Ralston Cereal, plastic, sealed in orig package, 1989 .................................................. 25.00
Beach Ball, Kellogg's, giant, inflatable .................................................. 25.00
Bike Plates, Kellogg's, mini
    Snap-Crackle-Pop ................... 15.00
    Tony the Tiger ......................... 15.00
Bowl Hanger
    Jungle Book, Baloo.................. 20.00
    Winnie the Pooh, Eeyore, blue and yellow..................................... 25.00
Canteen, Rice Krispies Pop, 1973 .................................................. 24.00
Cartoon Cut-Out, Quick Draw McGraw, Sugar Smacks box back ......... 35.00
Cereal Bowl, Tom Mix, Hot Ralston Cereal for Straight Shooters, white china, illus, copyright 1982, Ralston Purina...................................... 35.00
Charm, metal, gold finish
    Caveman Ogg ......................... 25.00
    Snap-Crackle-Pop .................. 20.00
Coin Purse, Barney, Flintstones, 1975 .................................................. 24.00
Coloring Kit, Post Corn Crackos, color-by-number pictures, box of colored pencils, instruction sheet, 1967, unused .................................... 125.00
Comics, *The Adventures of Little Orphan Annie*, 1941, Quaker Puffed Wheat & Rice Sparkles ............ 65.00
Decoder, Toucan Sam ................. 10.00
Doll
    Captain Crunch, plush, 14" l.... 75.00
    Scarecrow, Chex, cloth, 20"..... 40.00

Snap, Rice Krispies, orig box ..50.00
Tony the Tiger, Canada, orig tab,
1980 ..........................................60.00
Toucan Sam, Fruit Loops, orig box
...................................................50.00
Figure, plastic or vinyl
Boo Berry .............................175.00
Count Chocula .......................165.00
Frankenberry, flat ....................25.00
Freakies, green ........................35.00
Fruito Bruite............................165.00
Frogman, Kellogg's, orig stopper
...................................................35.00
Game
Bugs Bunny Space Race Game,
Post box back ..........................30.00
Trix Rabbit Tiddley Winks Kit ... 20.00
Gun, Quisp Smoke Gun, plastic, 1950s
.................................................120.00
Imprint Set, Cap'n Crunch ............45.00
Ink Blotter, Rice Krispies, Snap, Crackle
and Pop, 1930s, unused..........10.00
Mail Away, Post Cereal, 3 ring circus,
1990s, complete, orig mailer .. 45.00
Manual, Tom Mix, *Life of Tom Mix,* Ral-
ston, 1933, orig envelope ........75.00
Mask
Bugs Bunny, back of Post box,
1960s .......................................35.00
Count Chocula .........................20.00
Frankenberry............................20.00
Pinback
Betty Hutton, Quaker Puffed Wheat &
Rice...........................................12.00
Billy DeWolfe, Quaker Puffed Wheat
& Rice........................................12.00
Guy Madison, Quaker Puffed Wheat
& Rice........................................12.00
Joan Crawford, Quaker Puffed
Wheat & Rice ...........................12.00
Squadron, Pep Cereal, 1930s
...................................................25.00
Tony Tiger, Astronaut breakfast
game........................................24.00

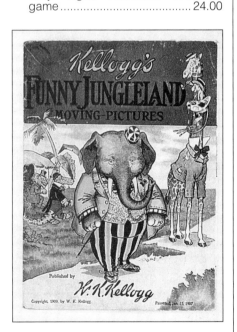

**Book, *Kellogg's Funny Jungleland,
Moving Pictures,* fold-out, ©1909, $24.**

Playset, Roy Rogers, ranch, Post,
1950s, orig packaging.............50.00
Push Puppet
Crackle, Rice Krispies, MOC ... 60.00
Pop, Rice Krispies ...................45.00
Snap, Rice Krispies, MOC .......60.00
Record, 45 RPM, Count Chocula
...................................................35.00
Ring
Captain Crunch, figural..........300.00
Count Chocula, secret compartment
.................................................275.00
Frankenberry, secret compartment
.................................................275.00
Krackle...................................150.00
Springees, flat rubber figures
Bullwinkle, yellow ....................15.00
Underdog, blue.........................15.00
Stickpin, Washington Crisps, Toasted
Corn Flakes, diecut thin celluloid, full
color US flag ............................30.00
Submarine, baking soda, 1970s, MIP
...................................................15.00
Watch Fob, Kellogg's Toasted Corn
Flakes, brass, box shape, red and
black lettering, blank reverse ....40.00
Whistle
Capt'n Crunch, balloon..............8.00
Trix, whistle and magnifier, red
...................................................25.00
Wrist Viewer, Capt'n Crunch, red, MIP
...................................................25.00

# Character & Promotional Glasses

**Collecting Hints:** Contemporary character and promotional glasses are usually produced in series. It is important to collect the full series, including any color variations. This is not as easy as it sounds. Sports team glasses are frequently issued regionally, i.e., Philadelphia Eagles glasses may appear just in the Philadelphia market while San Diego Charger glasses may be available only in the area around San Diego. Before paying a great deal of money for a recent glass, ask yourself if what may be rare in your area is common somewhere else. Any serious collectors needs this sense of perspective.

Some early examples were decorated with lead-based paint. They should not be used for drinking purposes.

Collectors place a premium on glasses with out-of-the-box luster. The mere act of washing a glass, in a dishwasher or even by hand, can lessen its value. Avoid examples with any evidence of fading.

Because of their wide availability, character and promotional drinking glasses should be collected only if they are in excellent to mint condition. Pay premium prices only for glasses that pre-date 1980. After that, glasses were hoarded in quantity by distributors, dealers, and collectors.

**History:** Character and promotional drinking glasses date to the movie premier of "Snow White and the Seven Dwarfs" in December of 1937. Libbey Glass and Walt Disney designed tumblers with a safety edge and sold them through variety stores and local dairies. The glasses proved extremely popular. Today collector glasses can be found for almost every Disney character, cartoon, and movie theme.

In 1953, Welch's began to package its jelly in decorated tumblers that featured Howdy Doody and his friends. Once again, the public's response was overwhelming. Welch's soon introduced tumblers with other cartoon characters, such as Mr. Magoo.

In the late 1960s, fast food restaurants and gasoline stations started to use drinking glasses as advertising premiums. Soft drink manufacturers like Coke and Pepsi saw the advertising potential and developed marketing plans focused on licensed characters and movies. Sport's team licensing also entered the picture. By the early 1980s, hundreds of new glasses were being issued each year.

As the 1980s drew to a close, plastic drinking cups replaced glasses, although the use of licensed images continued. While most collectors still prefer to collect glass, a few far-sighted individuals are stashing away pristine plastic examples.

**References:** Mark Chase and Michael Kelly, *Collectible Drinking Glasses: Identification and Values,* Collector Books, 1996; John Hervey, *Collector's Guide to Cartoon & Promotional Drinking Glasses,* L-W Book Sales, 1990, 1995 value update; Carol and Gene Markowski, *Tomart's Price Guide to Character & Promotional Glasses,* 2nd ed., Tomart Publications, 1993.

**Periodical:** *Collector Glass News,* P.O. Box 308, Slippery Rock, PA 16057.

**Collectors' Club:** Promotional Glass Collectors Association, 3001 Bethel Road, New Wilmington, PA 16142.

Animal Crackers, 1978
Dodo .......................................... 8.50
Lyle ............................................. 9.00
Annie and Sandy, Swenson's, 1982
................................................... 7.50
Arby's
BC Ice Age, riding on wheel, 1981
................................................... 9.00
Bullwinkle, Crossing the Delaware, 11 oz, 1976 ...................... 9.00
Charlie Chaplin, Movie Star series
................................................... 7.50
Daffy Duck, Head in Star ........... 6.00
Little Rascals ............................. 8.00
Monopoly, Just Visiting ............. 18.00
Rocky, In The Dawn's Early Light, 11 oz, 1976 ..................... 9.00
W. C. Fields ............................... 3.00
Wizard of Id, 1983 ................... 12.00
Zodiac, Scorpio ....................... 10.00
Archies, 1971, 8 oz
Archie Takes The Gang For A Ride
................................................... 4.50
Betty and Veronica Fashion Show
................................................... 4.00
Hot Dog Goes To School ........... 4.00
Aquaman, Chipper-Up Soda, Galena, IL ............................................. 46.00
Battlestar Galactica, 16 oz, Universal Studios, Inc., 1979
Commander Adama ................ 15.00
Cylon Warriors ......................... 15.00
Starbuck .................................. 15.00
Brockway, Al Capp, 1975
Daisy Mae ............................... 65.00
Lil Abner ................................. 55.00
Mammy .................................... 55.00
Sadie Hawkins ......................... 55.00
Burger Chef
Endangered Species, Bengal Tiger, 1978 ............................. 6.50
Jefferson, President Series ........ 6.00
Washington, Bicentennial Series
................................................... 7.00
Burger King
Burger King, 1989 ................... 10.00
Denver Broncos, Riley Odomos
................................................... 5.00
Have It Your Way, two drummers, piper, 1976 ......................... 10.00
Mark Twain Summer Festival, 1985, set of 4 in orig box ................... 35.00
Shake A Lot, 1979 .................... 9.00
Burger King and Coca-Cola, Star Wars
Empire Strikes Back, 16 oz, copyright Lucasfilm, 1980
Darth Vadar ........................ 15.00
Lando Calrissian ................. 18.00
Luke Skywalker .................... 15.00
R2-D2 and C-3PO .............. 15.00
Return of the Jedi, 16 oz, copyright Lucasfilm, 1983
C-3PO at the Ewok Village
................................................... 15.00
Jabba, Leia, and the Rebo Band, slightly faded ................... 12.00
Luke & Han, Fighting on Tatooine
................................................... 15.00
Luke Fighting Darth in the Throne Room ................................ 20.00
Coca Cola
Bag of French Fries, 1992, 6" ..... 8.00
Betty, tray girl .......................... 12.00

Collegiate Crest, University of Wisconsin, Milwaukee ................... 18.00
Disney on Parade ..................... 5.00
Happy Chef, stained glass design
................................................... 5.00
Heritage Collector Series, Patrick Henry ...................................... 6.00
Holly Hobbie, Good Friends Are Like Sunshine ................................. 6.50
Mothers Pizza, collector series
#2 of 6 .................................... 8.00
Outdoor Scene, buttered corn ... 5.00
Santa and Elves ...................... 7.50
Winter Wonderland, Sundblom image inside wreath, Coke logo on reverse, 5-3/4" h ...................... 5.00
DC Comics, Pepsi
Aquaman, 16 oz, 1978 ............ 15.00
Batman, 1966 ........................... 7.50
Green Lantern ............................ 8.50
Superman, 1975 ...................... 7.50
Domino's Pizza, 1988, Avoid the Noids, complete set of 4 .................... 25.00
Dr. Pepper
Happy Days, Pizza Hut, The Fonz
................................................... 10.00
Hot Air Balloon ........................ 9.00
Star Trek, Mr. Spock, 1976 ........ 8.00
Hanna Barbera Productions, Inc.
Hair Bear mug, blue plastic, 1971
................................................... 10.00
Larosa Pizzaria Parlor, 16 oz, Fred and Wilma, Yogi and Mr. Ranger, Scooby, Luigi, 1973 ................ 30.00
Square Bear mug, yellow plastic, 1971 ...................................... 10.00
Hardee's, Flintstones, The First 30 Years -1964, 16 oz, 1991
Going to the Drive-In ............... 5.00
Little Bamm-Bamm ................... 5.00
The Blessed Event .................... 6.50
The Snorkasaurus Story ............ 6.00
Marvel Comics
Amazing Spiderman, 1977 ........ 5.00
Howard the Duck, 1977 ............ 4.00
Hulk, 1978 ................................ 3.50
McDonalds
Big Mac, McVote, 1986 ............. 5.00
Disneyland, Adventureland ....... 3.00
Disney World 25th Anniversary, set of 4 ........................................ 30.00
Mayor McCheese Taking Pictures
................................................... 5.00
McDonald Action Series, 16 oz, 1977
Captain Crook ...................... 5.00
Hamburglar, slightly faded .... 4.00
Mayor McCheese ...................... 5.00
Ronald McDonald Saves The Falling Star, 1977 ............................. 6.00
Seattle Seahawks, Beeson Eller/Beamon ...................................... 10.00
Mobil, football, ten different logos, price for set ...................................... 20.00
National Periodical Publications
Batman .................................... 15.00
Robin, 6 oz, 1960s ................... 25.00
Superman, Fighting the Dragon, 5-1/4" h, 1965 ...................... 12.00
Wonder Woman ....................... 10.00
Paramount Pictures
Gulliver's Travels, 1939 ........... 40.00
Happy Days - Fonz, "Hey!" 16 oz, 1977 ...................................... 15.00

Pepsi
Batman, 16 oz, 1978, minor paint loss ........................................ 15.00
Bugs Bunny, 1973, Warner Bros. Inc. copyright ................................. 8.00
Bullwinkle ............................... 30.00
Chilly Willy, 16 oz ................... 38.00
Cool Cat/Hunter ...................... 28.00
Daffy Duck and Tasmanian Devil, 1976 ...................................... 15.00
Dudley Do-Right, black lettering, 16 oz .......................................... 30.00
Flash, 16 oz, 1976, minor mispaint
................................................... 15.00
Foghorn Leghorn, 16 oz, 1973, slightly faded ......................... 10.00
Leonardo TTV, Underdog, 16 oz
................................................... 14.00
Natasha, 12 oz, copyright P.A.T. Ward, slight fading ................. 35.00
Rescuers, Orville ...................... 5.00
Robin, 16 oz, 1978 .................. 18.00
Simon Bar Sinister, 12 oz ........ 40.00
Superman, 1975, slightly faded
................................................... 15.00
Tweety, 16 oz, thin glass, white lettering, 1973 .............................. 15.00
United Oil Baseball, Babe Ruth
................................................... 15.00
Pizza Hut
Bullwinkle, blue truck ............... 8.00
Care Bears, Friend Bear ......... 18.00

**McDonald's, Snoopy, Civilization is Over Rated!, $3.**

Denver Broncos, 25th Anniversary, #3 of 4 .........................................3.00
Dudley Do-right, helicopter........8.00
7-Up, Indiana Jones and the Temple of Dome, 16 oz, 1984
Down the River Rapids ..............8.00
High Priest Mola Ram ..............10.00
Indy Fighting ............................12.00
The Spiked Boom.....................10.00
Sunday Funnies
Gasoline Alley, 16 oz, copyright Chicago Tribune, Uncle Walt, Nina, Judy, Skeezix, 1976, slight paint loss .............................................15.00
Little Orphan Annie, 16 oz, copyright New York News, Orphan Annie, Sandy, Daddy Warbucks, ASP, Punjab, 1976 ...................................15.00
Moon Mullins, 16 oz, copyright New York News, Lord Plushbottom, Kayo, Willie, Lady Plushbottom, and Moon Mullins, 1976............................18.00
Smilin' Jack, 16 oz, copyright New York News, Rev Bob, Jack, Sizzle, Cindy, Sable, The Head, Fat Stuff, and Jim S ...............................15.00
Taco Bell, Star Trek III, 16 oz, copyright Paramount Pictures Corp., 1984
Lord Kruge ...............................12.00
The Search for Spock Enterprise Destroyed.................................15.00
Tommy Tucker Kola, Omaha, NE ....................................................40.00
Walt Disney
Goofy, 1937............................140.00
Goofy, Goofy and Pluto on back, 16 oz, Pepsi, copyright Walt Disney Productions, 1978 ...................12.00
Minnie Mouse...........................30.00
Warner Bros., Pepsi
Beaky Buzzard, 16 oz, thin glass, 1973 ........................................15.00
Cool Cat and Beaky Buzzard, 16 oz, 1976 ........................................15.00
Daffy Duck, 4 oz, 1976.............15.00
Elmer Fudd, 6 oz, 1976............15.00
Speedy/Slo Poke, hammer, orig Brockway sticker on base, 1976 ..................................................175.00
Taz and Bugs, #4 of 8 ..............10.00
Welch's, 8 oz
Archies .....................................4.50
Davy Crockett, Fought the War, orange and white .....................17.50
Flintstones .................................6.00
Kagran, Howdy Doody, Doodyville Circus, Clarabell, green...........20.00

# Children's Books

**Collecting Hints:** Most collectors look for books by a certain author or illustrator. Others are interested in books from a certain time period, such as the 19th century. Accumulating the complete run of a series, such as Tom Swift, Nancy Drew, or the Hardy Boys, is of interest to some collectors. Subject categories are popular, too, and include ethnic books, mechanical books, first editions, award-winning books, certain kinds of animals, rag books, Big Little Books, and those with photographic illustrations.

A good way to learn about children's books is to go to libraries and museums where special children's collections have been developed. Books on various aspects of children's literature are a necessity. You also should read a general reference on book collecting to provide you with background information. Eventually, you will want to own a few reference books most closely associated with your collection.

Although children's books can be found at all the usual places where antiques and collectibles are for sale, also seek out book and paper shows. Get to know dealers who specialize in children's books; ask to receive their lists or catalogs. Some dealers will try to locate books for your collection. Most stores specializing in used and out-of-print books have a section with children's books. Regular bookstores may carry the most recent works of authors or illustrators who are still working.

When purchasing books, consider the following: presence of a dust jacket or box, condition of the book, the edition, quality of illustrations and binding, and prominence of the author or illustrator. Books should be examined very carefully to make sure that all pages and illustrations are present. Missing pages will reduce the value of the book. Significant bits of information, particularly details of the book's edition, can be found on the title page and verso of the title page.

Try to buy books in the best condition you can afford. Even if your budget is limited, you can still find very nice inexpensive children's books if you keep looking.

**History:** William Caxton, a printer in England, is considered the first publisher of children's books. *Aesop's Fables*, printed in 1484, was one of his early publications. Other very early books include John Cotton's *Spiritual Milk for Boston Babes* in 1646, *Orbis Pictis* translated from the Latin about 1657, and *New England Primer* in 1691.

Early children's classics were *Robinson Crusoe* (1719), *Gulliver's Travels* (1726), and Perrault's *Tales of Mother Goose* (translated into English in 1729). The well-known "A Visit from St. Nicholas" by Clement C. Moore appeared in 1823. Some of the best-known children's works were published between 1840 and 1900, including Lear's *Book of Nonsense*, Andersen's and Grimm's *Fairy Tales*, *Alice in Wonderland*, *Hans Brinker*, *Little Women*, *Tom Sawyer*, *Treasure Island*, *Heidi*, *A Child's Garden of Verses*, and *Little Black Sambo*.

During the late 1800s, novelty children's books appeared. Lothar Meggendorfer, Ernest Nister, and Raphael Tuck were the best-known publishers of these fascinating pop-up and mechanical, or movable, books. The popularity of this type of book has continued to the present, and some of the early movable books are being reproduced, especially by Intervisual Communication, Inc., of California.

Series books for boys and girls were introduced around the turn of the century. The Stratemeyer Syndicate, established about 1906, became especially well known for series such as Tom Swift, the Bobbsey Twins, Nancy Drew, and the Hardy Boys.

After the turn of the century, biographies, poetry, and educational books became popular. Van Loon's *Story of Mankind* received the first Newberry Medal in 1922. This award, given for the year's most distinguished literature for children, was established to honor John Newberry, an English publisher of children's books.

Picture books became a major part of the children's book field, as photography and new technologies for reproducing illustrations developed. The Caldecott Medal, given for the most distinguished picture book published in the United States, was established in 1938. Dorothy Lathrop's *Animals of the Bible* was the first recipient of this award, which honors Randolph Caldecott, an English illustrator from the 1800s.

Books that tie in with children's television programs, e.g., "Sesame Street," and toys, e.g., Cabbage Patch dolls, have become prominent. Modern merchandising methods include multimedia packaging of various combinations of books, toys, puzzles, cassette tapes, videos, etc. There are even books which unfold and become a costume to be worn by children.

**References:** E. Lee Baumgarten, *Price Guide and Bibliographic*

*Check List for Children's & Illustrated Books 1880-1960*, published by author (Note: all the Baumgarten books are available from 718-1/2 W. John St., Martinsburg, WV 25401), 1996; —, *Price List for Children's and Illustrated Books for the Years 1880-1940, Sorted by Artist*, published by author, 1993; —, *Price List for Children's and Illustrated Books for the Years 1880-1940, Sorted by Author*, published by author, 1993; David & Virginia Brown, *Whitman Juvenile Books*, Collector Books, 1996; Alan Horne, *Dictionary of 20th Century British Book Illustrators*, available from Spoon River Press, 1994; Simon Houfe, *Dictionary of 19th Century British Book Illustrators*, revised ed., available from Spoon River Press, 1996; E. Christian Mattson and Thomas B. Davis, *A Collector's Guide to Hardcover Boys' Series Books*, published by authors, 1996; Diane McClure Jones and Rosemary Jones, *Collector's Guide to Children's Books*, Collector Books, 1997; Edward S. Postal, *Price Guide & Bibliography to Children's & Illustrated Books*, M & P Press (available from Spoon River Press, 2319C W. Rohmann, Peoria, IL 61604), 1995; *Price Guide to Big Little Books & Better Little, Jumbo, Tiny Tales, A Fast-Action Story, etc.*, L-W Book Sales, 1995; Albert Tillman, *Pop Up! Pop Up!*, Whalestooth Farm Publications (HC 1, Box 82, Olga, WA 98279).

**Periodicals:** *Book Source Monthly*, 2007 Syossett Drive, P.O. Box 567, Cazenovia, NY 13035; *Martha's KidLit Newsletter*, P.O. Box 1488, Ames, IA 50010; *Mystery & Adventure Series Review*, P.O. Box 3488, Tucson, AZ 85722; *The Authorized Edition Newsletter*, RR1, Box 73, Machias, ME 04654; *Yellowback Library*, P.O. Box 36172, Des Moines, IA 50315.

**Collectors' Clubs:** Louisa May Alcott Memorial Association, P.O. Box 343, Concord, MA 01742; Horatio Alger Society, 4907 Allison Drive, Lansing, MI 48910; International Wizard of Oz Club (L. Frank Baum), 220 N. 11th St., Escanaba, MI 49829; Thorton W. Burgess Society, Inc., P.O. Box 45, East Sandwich, MA 02537; Burroughs Bibliophiles (Edgar Rice Burroughs), Burroughs Memorial Collection, University of Louisville Library, Louisville, KY 40292; Randolph Caldecott Society, 112 Crooked Tree Trail, Moultrie

Trails, RR #4, Saint Augustine, FL 32086; Lewis Carroll Society of North America, 617 Rockford Rd., Silver Spring, MD 20902; Dickens Society, 100 Institute Rd., Worcester Polytech, Dept. of Humanities, Worcester, MA 01609; Kate Greenaway Society, P.O. Box 8, Norwood, PA 19074; Happyhours Brotherhood, 87 School St., Fall River, MA 02770; Kipling Society (Rudyard Kipling), c/o Dr. E. Karim, Dept. of English, Rockford College, Rockford, IL 61107; New York C. S. Lewis Society, c/o J. L. Daniel, 419 Springfield Ave., Westfield NJ 07092; Melville Society (Herman Melville), c/o D. Yannella, Dept. of English, Glassboro State College, Glassboro, NJ 08028; Mystery and Detective Series Review, P.O. Box 3488, Tucson, AZ 85722; Movable Book Society, P.O. Box 11645, New Brunswick, NJ 08906; Mythopoetic Society, P.O. Box 6707, Altadena, CA 91003; National Fantasy Fan Federation, 1920 Division St., Murphysboro, IL 62966; Series Book Collector Society, c/o J. Brahce, 5270 Moceri Lane, Grand Blanc, MI 48439; Society of Phantom Friends, P.O. Box 1437 North Highlands, CA 95660; Stowe-Day Foundation (Harriet Beecher Stowe), 77 Forest St., Hartford, CT 06105; American Hobbit Association (J. R. R. Tolkien), Rivendell-EA, 730-F Northland Rd, Forest Park, OH 45240; American Tolkien Society, P.O. Box 373, Highland, MI 48031; Tolkien Fellowships, c/o Bill Spicer, 329 N. Ave. 66, Los Angeles, CA 90042; Mark Twain Boyhood Home Association, 208 Hill St., Hannibal, MO 63401; Mark Twain Memorial, 351 Farmington Ave., Hartford, CT 06105; Mark Twain Research Foundation, Perry, MO 63462.

**Libraries:** American Antiquarian Society, Worcester, MA; Free Library of Philadelphia, Philadelphia, PA; Library of Congress, Washington, DC; Lucile Clark Memorial Children's Library, Central Michigan University, Mount Pleasant, MI; Pierpont Morgan Library, New York, NY; Toronto Public Library, Toronto, Ontario, Canada.

**Libraries and Museums:** Many of the clubs maintain museums. *Subject Collections* edited by Lee Ash contains a list of public and academic libraries which have children's book collections. Large collections can be found at Florida State University, Tallahassee, FL; Free Library of

Philadelphia, Philadelphia, PA; Library of Congress, Washington, DC; Pierpont Morgan Library, New York, NY; Toronto Public Library, Toronto, Ontario, Canada; Uncle Remus Museum (Joel Chandler Harris), Eatonton, GA; University of Minnesota, Walter Library, Minneapolis, MN; University of South Florida, Tampa, FL.

**Notes:** Prices are based on good-condition first editions with a dust jacket (dj). The absence of a dust jacket, later printings, and less-than-good condition are all factors that lower the value of a book.

Other factors which increase value are autographs, presence of a special box for books issued with one, and award-winning titles.

**Reprints:** A number of replicas are now appearing on the market, most having been published by Evergreen Press and Merrimack. A new Children's Classics series offers reprints of books illustrated by Jessie Willcox Smith, Edmund Dulac, Frederick Richardson, and others.

*A Child's Garden of Verses*, Saalfield, color front illus by Clara Burd ............................................... 10.00

*Alice's Adventures*, Altemus Co., 1897, orig dust jacket ...................... 45.00

*Big Bad Wolf*, David McCay, story and illus by Walt Disney Studios, 1933, 8-1/2" x 6-1/4" ........................... 60.00

*Billy Whiskers Treasure Hunt*, color frontis, black and white illus by Frances Brundage, Saalfield Publishing, 1928 ......................................... 20.00

*Boy Scouts in the Rockies*, Burt Co., 1913 ........................................... 30.00

*Calico Pup*, McLoughlin, 1939 ..... 20.00

*Child Life Mystery-Adventure Book*, M. Barrows, F. Cavanah, Rand McNally, 1936, 96 pgs, color illus .......... 12.50

*Child's Book of Country Stories*, A. E. Skinner, 1935, some color illus ............................................... 12.00

*Cowboys Quiz Me*, Whitman ........ 10.00

*Dennis the Menace Storybook*, 1960 ............................................... 25.00

*Dick and Jane, Think and Do*, teacher's edition, soft blue cover, 1940 ............................................... 75.00

*Dick & Jane, 1952, We Three*, Scott Foresman ................................. 35.00

*Five Little Peppers Grow Up*, Margaret Sidney, Lothrop, Boston, 1892, 527 pgs ........................................... 24.00

*Frances and the Irrepressibles At Buena Vista Farm*, Frances Trego Montgomery, black and white photo-like illus, Saalfield Publishing, 1905, inscription date 1910 .............. 65.00

**Dinny and Danny, Louis Slobodkin, $15.**

*Friendly Fairies,* Johnny Gruelle, color illus, P. F. Volland & Co. 1919, some damage.................................... 25.00
*Fun in Bed for Children,* Virginia Kirkus and Frank Scully, Simon & Schuster, 1935, 137 pgs.......................... 40.00
*Goldie the Goose That Laid the Golden Egg,* pop-up.............................. 18.00
*Hardy Boys,* Franklin Dixon, red cloth, glossy front illus by Walter Rogers
*Hunting for Hidden Gold,* Grosset & Dunlap, 1928, 1st edition......... 36.00
*The Shore Road Mystery,* Grosset & Dunlap, 1928, 1st edition......... 36.00
*Hiawatha & De Night in De Front From Chressmas,* Milt Gross, Doubleday, 1950, dj...................................... 25.00
*James and the Giant Peach,* Ronald Dahl, Nancy Ekholm Burkert illus, Knopf, 1961............................... 25.00
*Knit One, Purl One, A Little Girl's Knitting & Crochot Book,* Shield's & Wemple, Stokes Co., 1938, 93 pgs, photos, dj................................... 6.00
*Little Bear's Visit,* Else Minarik, Maurice Sendak illus, Harper & Row, 1961 .................................................. 32.00
*Little Big Book of Lassie,* The Shabby Sheik, Whitman, 1968 .............. 16.00
*Little Black Sambo,* hardcover, 24 colored illus................................. 190.00
*Little Red Riding Hood,* pop-up.... 35.00
*Little Sunny Stories,* Johnny Gruelle, color illus, M. A. Donohue & Co., 1930s ........................................ 35.00
*Lucky Landlady, Little Lulu,* Tell-A-Tale .................................................. 15.00
*Lullaby Land,* Eugene Field, drawings by Charles Robinson, Schribner, 1897........................................ 50.00
*Mary Poppins in the Park,* Harcourt, 1952, 1st ed., dj...................... 20.00

*Mother Goose Pop-Up Book,* Joan Walsh Anglund, 1st ed............ 10.00
*Nancy Drew Mystery,* Carolyn Keene, orig dust jacket ....................... 25.00
*Nipper, the Little Bull Pup,* D. L'Hommedieu, Lippencott, 1943, 1st ed., dj ................................................... 45.00
*Now We Are Six,* A. A. Milne, E. P. Dutton, 1961, emb cover................ 7.00
*One Hundred Best Poems for Boys and Girls,* Marjorie Barrows, Whitman, 1930...................................... 12.00
*Peter Pan in Kensington Gardens,* Sir James M. Barrie, Arthur Rackam illus, Scribner, 1919................ 30.00
*Rabbit Hill,* Robert Lawson, Viking, 1944, 1st edition ..................... 16.50
*Richard Scarry's Best Mother Goose Ever,* Richard Scarry, Golden Press, 1964, 94 pgs.......................... 15.00
*Sing Little Birdie,* Gertrude Heath, front and back cover illus by Fern Bisel Peat, color and black illus........ 22.50
*Stories of the Diamond,* Charles Coombs, illus by Charles H. Geer, Grosset & Dunlap, copyright 1951, hard cover, 194 pgs, well read .................................................. 5.00
*Surly Time & Other Stories,* Frances Hodgson Burnett, Scribs, 1914, 298 pgs, ex-library copy................. 5.00
*Tarzan & The Golden Lion,* E. R. Burroughs, black and white illus, Grosset & Dunlap, 1929, orange cover .................................................. 16.00
*Tarzan the Terrible,* E.R. Burroughs, black and white illus, Grosset & Dunlap, 1940s, orig dust jacket, worn .................................................. 35.00
*The Adventures of a Brownie,* Miss Murlock, Harper, 1872, 1st edition, black and white illus ........................ 22.50

**The Pop-up Book of Trucks, Random House, ©1974, $12.**

*The Bobbsey Twins, In A Great City,* 1917, green cover, dj.............. 25.00
*The New More Friends & Neighbors,* Gage........................................ 25.00
*The Night Before Christmas,* Clement C. Moore, color illus by Tasha Tudor, Rand McNally & Co., 1975, 1st printing........................................ 50.00
*The Platt & Munk Treasury of Stories for Children,* color illus by Tasha Tudor .................................................. 55.00
*The Pooh Perplex (In Which it is Discovered the Trye Meaning of the Pooh Stories),* Frederick Crews, Dutton, 1963, 150 pgs, red cloth, slight worn dg ......................................... 10.00
*The Real Diary of a Real Boy,* Henry Shute, black and white illus by Tasha Tudor, Richard Smith Co., 1967, dj .................................................. 45.00
*The Tale of the Land of Green Ginger,* Noel Langley, Wm. Morrow, 1938, 143 pgs................................... 40.00
*The Ugly Duck & Other Tales,* Hans Christian Anderson, John Alden, 1866, black and white dec ........ 5.00
*Three Little Pigs Pop-Up Book,* V. Kulbsta illus, Arita, 1977 .............. 25.00
*Tim Tyler in the Jungle,* pop-up, copyright 1935............................. 25.00
*Told Under The Magic Umbrella, Modern Fanciful Stories For Young Children,* Literature Comm. Assoc., Childhood Education, Elizabeth Orton Jones, MacMillan, 1940, set .................................................. 12.00
*Tom Swift, In the City of Gold,* 1912 .................................................. 30.00
*Tom Thumb's Picture Alphabet,* miniature, 19th C ........................... 40.00
*Uncle Wiggly's Holidays,* Howard Garis, Charles Graham, 1929 ........... 30.00
*Walt Disney's Bambi,* Idella Purnell, D. C. Heath Co., 1944 ................. 45.00

# Children's Dishes

**Collecting Hints:** Children's dishes were played with, so a bit of wear is to be expected. Avoid rusty metal dishes and broken glass dishes.

**History:** Dishes for children to play with have been popular from Victorian times to the present and have been made in aluminum, tin, china, and glass.

Many glass companies made small child-size sets in the same patterns as large table sets. This was especially true during the period when Depression glass was popular, and manufacturers made child-size pieces to complement the full-size lines.

**References:** Maureen Batkin, *Gifts for Good Children, Part II, 1890-1990,* Antique Collectors' Club, 1996; Doris Anderson Lechler, *Children's Glass Dishes, China and Fur-*

niture, Book I (1983, 1991 value update), Book II (1986, 1993 value update), Collector Books; Lorraine Punchard, *Playtime Kitchen Items and Table Accessories*, published by author, 1993; —, *Playtime Pottery & Porcelain from Europe and Asia*, Schiffer Publishing, 1996; —, *Playtime Pottery and Porcelain from the United Kingdom and the United States*, Schiffer Publishing, 1996; Noel Riley, *Gifts for Good Children*, Richard Dennis Publications (available from Antique Collectors' Club), 1991; Margaret and Kenn Whitmyer, *Collector's Encyclopedia of Children's Dishes*, Collector Books, 1993, 1995 value update.

**Collectors' Club:** Toy Dish Collectors, Box 159, Bethlehem, CT 06751.

**Additional Listings:** Akro Agate.

### Aluminum

Coffeepot, black wooden handle and knob ........................................ 25.00
Measuring Cup, graduated, handle ...................................................... 10.00
Silverware Set, four spoons, two forks, knife, pie server ...................... 10.00
Teapot, black wooden knob, swing handle ........................................ 20.00
**Cast Iron,** skillet, 5" from handle to edge, mkd "8" ......................... 15.00

### China

Blue Willow
    Creamer
        2" x 1-3/4" h ........................ 18.00
        2-1/4" x 1-3/4" h ................. 19.00
        2-3/4" x 2" h ....................... 18.00
        3-1/4" x 2-3/4" h ................. 18.00
    Cup
        1-3/4", Occupied Japan ...... 15.00
        2" ...................................... 12.00
        2-3/4" .............................. 10.00
    Cup and Saucer
        2-1/4" cup, 2-3/4" saucer ..... 15.00
        2-3/4" cup, 3-3/4" saucer ..... 15.00
    Plate
        3-3/4" d .............................. 9.00
        4-1/2" d .............................. 8.75
    Platter, 6-1/4" x 3-3/4", oval ...... 25.00
    Saucer, 3-1/4" d, Occupied Japan ........................................ 8.00
    Set, 26 pc .............................. 485.00
    Sugar, cov
        2-3/4" x 2-1/4" ..................... 24.50
        4-1/4" x 3-1/2" ..................... 24.75
    Teapot, cov, 4" ......................... 50.00
Geisha Girl, tea set, 4 place setting, creamer, sugar, teapot, chips ........................................ 125.00
Moss Rose
    Cup and Saucer ....................... 7.50
    Platter, oval ........................... 10.00
    Tea Set .................................. 125.00
Occupied Japan, teapot, cov ....... 85.00

### Depression-Era Glass

Bowl, Little Deb, ribbed .............. 15.00

Toy China Tea Set, white ground, boy and girl dec, mkd "Made in Japan," 17 pcs, orig box, $42.

Creamer
    Cherry Blossom, pink .............. 45.00
    Laurel, jadeite ........................ 45.00
Creamer and Sugar, Moderntone, pink ........................................ 30.00
Cup and Saucer
    Cherry Blossom ...................... 45.00
    Diana, pink ........................... 45.00
    Doric & Pansy, pink ................ 43.00
    Moderntone, beige ................. 20.00
Cup
    Homespun, crystal .................. 30.00
    Moderntone
        Blue .................................. 14.25
        Pink .................................. 14.25
        Yellow ............................... 14.25
Mixer, Glassbake, 3 ftd .............. 40.00
Plate
    Cherry Blossom, Delfite Blue ... 14.75
    Doric & Pansy, pink ................ 15.00
    Homespun, pink ..................... 15.00
    Laurel, red trim ...................... 15.00
    Moderntone
        Blue .................................. 12.00
        Green ................................ 12.00
        Pink .................................. 12.00
        Yellow ............................... 12.00
Saucer
    Doric & Pansy, teal ................. 15.00
    Moderntone
        Blue .................................. 9.75
        Green ................................ 9.75
        Pink .................................. 9.75
Set
    Cherry Blossom, 14 pc, blue delphite ................................... 250.00
    Diana, crystal, gold trim, rack, price for 12-pc set ........................ 125.00

### Pattern Glass

Berry Bowl, Fine Cut X ................ 20.00
Butter, cov, Doyle's 500, amber ... 100.00
Creamer
    Fernland ............................... 18.00
    Hawaiian Lei .......................... 15.00
Cup and Saucer, Lion .................. 45.00
Mug, Fighting Cats ..................... 35.00
Pitcher, Nursery Rhyme .............. 100.00
Punch Bowl Set, punch bowl and six cups
    Flattened Diamond and Sunburst ...................................... 75.00
    Tulip and Honeycomb ............ 90.00
Spooner, Menagerie Fish, amber 150.00
Sugar, cov
    Hawaiian Lei .......................... 35.00
    Nursery Rhyme ...................... 48.00
Table Set, 4 pcs
    Arrowhead in Oval ................. 95.00
    Beaded Swirl ......................... 125.00
Tumbler
    Nursery Rhyme ...................... 20.00
    Sandwich Ten Panel, sapphire blue ...................................... 145.00

### Plastic

Chocolate Set, Banner, service for four, napkin holder, silverware ........ 95.00
Dinnerware Set
    9 pcs, Tinkerbelle, Walt Disney, service for two .............................. 25.00
    11 pcs, Plasco, Queen of Hearts with rabbit, 2 plates, cups, creamer, forks, spoons, wear to decal, Plasco ...................................................... 8.00
    17 pcs
        Alice in Wonderland, Plasco, service for four, beige ............. 45.00

Tupperware, service for four, multicolored ................................ 65.00

Silverware Set
6 pcs, two knives, forks, and spoons, Plasco, pink, orig cardboard ..... 9.00
8 pcs, serving set, two knives, forks, and spoons, Bestmade, red, orig cardboard ................................... 7.50

# Christmas Collectibles

**Collecting Hints:** Beware of reproduction ornaments. They are usually brighter in color and have shinier paint than the originals. Older ornaments should show some signs of handling. It is common to find tops replaced on ornaments.

**History:** Early Christmas decorations and ornaments were handmade. In 1865, the Pennsylvania Dutch brought the first glass ornaments to America. By 1870, glass ornaments were being sold in major cities. By the turn of the century, the demand created a cottage industry in European countries. Several towns in Germany and Czechoslovakia produced lovely ornaments, which were imported by companies such as F. W. Woolworth and Sears Roebuck and Company, who found a ready market.

**References:** Robert Brenner, *Christmas through the Decades*, Schiffer Publishing, 1993; Beth Dees, *Santa's Guide to Contemporary Christmas Collectibles*, Krause Publications, 1997; Clara Johnson Scroggins, *Silver Christmas Ornaments*, Krause Publications, 1997; Lissa Bryan-Smith and Richard Smith, *Holiday Collectibles, Vintage Flea Market Treasures Price Guide*, Krause Publications, 1998.

**Periodicals:** *Golden Glow of Christmas Past*, 6401 Winsdale St., Golden Valley, MN 55427; *I Love Christmas*, P.O. Box 5708, Coralville, IA 52241; *Ornament Collector*, RR #1, Canton, IL 61520.

**Collectors' Club:** Golden Glow of Christmas Past, 6401 Winsdale St., Golden Valley, MN 55427.

**Museums:** Many museums prepare special Christmas exhibits.

**Reproduction Alert.**

**Additional Listings:** Santa Claus.

**Advisor:** Lissa Bryan-Smith and Richard Smith.

## Christmas Village/Garden

Animals
Camel, 6" h, composition, flocked, wood legs, mkd "Germany" ..... 45.00
Chicken, 1-1/2" h, composition, metal feet ................................. 10.00
Cow, 3-1/2" h, celluloid ............ 12.00
Duck, 1-1/2" h, celluloid, metal feet ............................................... 10.00
Elephant, 5" h, composition, bone tusks, mkd "Germany" ............. 75.00
Goat, 4" h, composition, wool covering, wood legs, metal horns ..... 30.00
Horse, 5" h, composition, wood legs, mkd "Germany" ...................... 35.00
Lamb, 1-1/2" h, plaster, standing, grassy base, mkd "Germany" .... 7.50
Ram, 3-1/2" h, celluloid ............. 8.00
Reindeer, 3" h, celluloid, brown . 8.00
Reindeer, 5" h, composition, brown, glass eyes, wood legs, mkd "Germany" ....................................... 60.00
Sheep, 5" h, composition, wool covering, wood legs, paper collar with bell, mkd "Germany" ................ 45.00
Stork, 3" h, celluloid body and legs ............................................... 12.00

Buildings
Bank Office, 4" h, plastic, multicolored ........................................... 15.00
Barn, 6" h, litho cardboard, "Built-Rite" .......................................... 30.00
Church, 4" h, cardboard, white, mica, mkd "Japan" .................. 10.00
House, 4" h, cardboard, cellophane windows, mkd "Japan" .............. 8.00

Fence
Plastic, 2" h, white, "Plasticville," 6 sections ................................... 24.00
Wood, 5" h, picket, white, wired for Christmas lights on each post, 4 sections, 24" l ...................... 55.00

People
Couple, 2" h, sitting on park bench, metal, USA ............................... 20.00
Skater, 2-1/2" h, metal, USA ..... 15.00
Sled Rider, 2" h, removable figure, mkd "France" ........................... 18.00

## Non-Tree Related Items

Bank, 5" h, snowman, white, black bowler hat, red scarf, orig box ............................................... 15.00
Book
The Littlest Snowman, Wonder Books, Grosset & Dunlap, 1958 ............................................... 7.50
The Night Before Christmas, Clement C. Moore, J. B. Lippencott, c1930, Arthur Rackham illus.... 85.00
Calling Card, 3-1/4" l, Season's Greetings, emb holly .......................... 5.00
Candleholders, 2-1/2" w, 6" l, 1-1/8" h, brass, poinsettias, price for pr ............................................... 125.00
Candy Box
4-1/2" l, cardboard, string handle, Merry Christmas, Happy New Year, carolers in village, 1920s .......... 8.00
10-1/2" l, cardboard, paper label, "Charms," red background, coach driving through village scene ............................................... 18.00

**Light Bulb, Kristal Star, painted and mica coated tin, plastic points, Mazda bulb, c1935, 4-1/4" h, $8.**

Candy Container, 7-1/2" h, snowman, pressed cardboard, black hat, opening in base, USA ..................... 40.00
Figure, Choir Boy, 3-1/2" h, hard plastic, red and white ........................... 4.50
Nativity
Boxed set, 14" h, 20" l, cardboard, fold-out, USA, 1950s ................ 24.00
Redware, Foltz, 1977 ............. 145.00
Pinback Button
7/8" d, metal, "Health to All," National Tuberculosis Assoc.................... 7.50
1-1/4" d, celluloid, "Shop in Danville," Santa head ............................ 15.00
Postcard, 3" x 5"
A Hearty Christmas Greeting, sledding Victorian children.............. 4.00
Wishing You A Very Happy Christmas, dog with riding crop in mouth, toy horse .................................. 5.00
Stocking
10" d, red cellophane, silver foil trim, electric candle inside ............. 18.00
12" l, red flannel, stenciled Santa and sleigh ...................................... 15.00
Tag, 2-3/4" l, Christmas Greetings, dog in wrapped box, made in USA ....... 2.00
Toy, 16-1/2" l, pull toy, St Nicholas, cast iron, gilt, blue, and black sleigh, two white horses....................... 1,400.00

**Tree-Related Items**

Beads, 48" l, glass, blue, paper tag, German................................... 20.00
Candy Cane, 6" l, chenille, red and white ....................................... 4.00
Icicles, 4" h, metal, twisted, color or silver, each .................................. 1.00
Light Bulb
Bubble, Noma........................... 3.50
Japanese Lantern, 4" h, milk glass ............................................... 14.00
Santa head, 2" h, milk glass .... 24.00
Snowman, 3" h, milk glass ....... 20.00
Ornament, beaded, 3" h, cross, double-sided, Czechoslovakian .......... 24.00

**Ornament, Christmas Tree, orange highlights, red capped mushrooms and Santa's face, 3-1/4" h, $80.**

Ornament, chromolithograph, tinsel trim, German
Angel, 7" h.................................20.00
Bell, 4" h, girl's face.................17.50
Ornament, glass
Clown bust, 2" h.......................35.00
Grape Bunch, gold, 5-1/2" l, 19th C
......................................................210.00
Heart, 3-1/2" h, red...................15.00
Pinecone, 3-1/2" d, unsilvered, tinsel inside......................................15.00
Round, 2-1/2" d, plain, red, pink, green, gold, or silver, each........3.00
Round, 3" d, striped, unsilvered, paper cap..................................6.00
Santa, 3" h................................35.00
Reflector, 3" d
Foil, set of 6..............................6.00
Metal, pierced tin.......................5.00
Tinsel, lead strips, orig box...........12.00
Tree
1-1/2" h, brush, green, red wood base..............................................4.00
3" h, brush, green, mica trim, red wood base.................................5.00
3" h, feather, green, red wood base
......................................................18.00
5" h, brush, green dec, glass beads, red wood base.........................12.00
12" h, feather, white sq red base, mkd "West Germany"...............72.00
36" h, feather, green, candle clips, round wood base, mkd "Germany"
......................................................300.00
Tree Stand, tin litho, lighted..........48.00

Tree Topper
6" h, angel, cardboard and spun glass.........................................25.00
9" h, silvered glass, multicolored
................................................20.00

# Cigar Collectibles

**Collecting Hints:** Concentrate on one geographical region or company. Cigar box labels usually are found in large concentrations. Check on availability before paying high prices.

**History:** Tobacco was one of the first export products of the American colonies. By 1750, smoking began to become socially acceptable for males. Cigar smoking was most popular from 1880 to 1930 when it was the custom for men to withdraw from the boardroom or dining table and participate in male-only conversation or activities.

Cigar companies were quick to recognize national political, sports and popular heroes. They encouraged them to use cigars and placed their faces on promotional material.

The lithograph printing press brought color and popularity to labels, seals, and bands. Many people have memories of cigar-band rings given by a grandfather or family friend. Cigars took second place to cigarettes in the 1940s. Today, there is less cigar- than cigarette-related material because fewer companies made cigars.

**References:** Edwin Barnes and Wayne Dunn, *Cigar-Label Art Visual Encyclopedia with Index and Price Guide*, published by authors (P.O. Box 3, Lake Forest, CA 92630), 1995; Jero L. Gardner, *The Art of the Smoke,* Schiffer Publishing, 1998; Gerald S. Petrone, *Tobacco Advertising*, Schiffer Publishing, 1996; Jerry Terranova and Douglas Congdon-Martin, *Antique Cigar Cutters & Lighters*, Schiffer Publishing, 1996; Nancy Wanvig, *Collector's Guide to Ashtrays*, Collector Books, 1997; Neil Wood, *Smoking Collectibles*, L-W Book Sales, 1994.

**Periodical:** *Tobacco Antiques and Collectibles Market*, Box 11652, Houston, TX 77293.

**Collectors' Clubs:** Cigar Label Collectors International, P.O. Box 66, Sharon Center, OH 44274; International Lighter Collectors, P.O. Box 536, Quitman, TX 75783; International Seal, Label and Cigar Band Society, 8915 E. Bellevue St., Tucson, AZ 85715; Pocket Lighter Preservation Guild, P.O. Box 1054, Addison, IL 60101.

**Museum:** Arnet Collection, New York Public Library, New York, NY.

Artwork, 5-1/2" w, 17" l, orig hand painted artwork designed for Black Fox Cigar can, orig Heekin Can Co. Art Dept. order form, also orig 10-1/2" x 10" velux photo type proof sheet.......................................200.00
Banner, 12" h, 9-1/2" w, Seminola 5¢ Cigar, painted velvet, Indian princess in center........................350.00
Box, oak, zinc liner.......................35.00
Cigar Cutter, figural
Boar's tusk.............................245.00
Pelican, cast iron.....................75.00
Cigar Holder
Amber, solid gold band...........65.00
Tortoiseshell.............................10.00
Cigar Piercer, 3" l, silvered brass, celluloid wrapper band inscribed "Westchester County Bar Association, Annual Dinner, 1995," sharp metal point.............................60.00
Display Cigar Box, 2-1/2" x 5-1/2" x 8-1/2", Certified Primo Cigar Box, wood, full color litho paper designs, c1930.......................................50.00

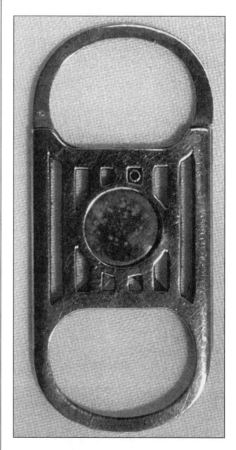

**Cutter, pocket style, scissors-type, sterling silver, 2-1/8" l, $42.**

**Label, Franklin D. Roosevelt, red, blue, and gold design, 6-1/4" x 9", $12.**

Dish, 7-1/8" d, all over multicolored cigar bands, diecut beautiful woman in center, green felt back ......... 35.00

Humidor, silverplated, bottle shaped, holds matches, cigars, cutter ............................................... 400.00

Label
    American Citizen......................... 7.00
    Canadian Club ............................ 7.00
    Tampa Girl ................................ 20.00

Lighter, 4-1/2" h, counter type, cast iron, bulldog-shape .......................... 90.00

Matchbook Holder, blued metal, c1920
    1-1/8" x 1-5/8", Muriel Cigars, celluloid insert, woman in multicolored portrait, small gold frame, dark red ground....................................... 65.00
    1-1/2" x 2-1/4", 1-1/2" oval celluloid, multicolored insert inscribed "For Gentlemen of Good Taste," well dressed gentleman seated in wicker chair, smoking cigar ................. 75.00

Match Safe, Union Made Cigars, bright silvered brass, celluloid cover with light blue Union Cigar label, black inscriptions and artwork, issued by Cigar Makers Union #97, Boston ............................................... 95.00

Pinback Button
    Bachelor Cigars, 100% Havana Filler, green and white, red serial number, c1930 .......................... 20.00
    Enjoy A Cigar, brown on yellow, slogan "Join The Cigar Enjoyment Parade," c1930 ........................ 30.00
    Recruit Little Cigars, 1" d, military cadet, red ground, white letters "Join The Army of Recruit Little Cigar Smokers," short product slogan on back paper, early 1900s .......... 40.00

Pocket Mirror, 2-1/8" d, Union Made Cigars, celluloid, detailed union label, light blue, black lettering, c1900 ....................................... 65.00

Notepad, 2" x 3", Hemmeter Cigar Co., floral and cigar design on cover, calendar, unused ........................... 25.00

Sign
    10" h, 13-1/2" w, Imperial Club Cigars, emb self-framed tin, full box of cigars, Sentenne & Green litho ............................................... 150.00

1-2/3" h, 17-1/2" l, Charles The Great Cigars, tin, shows full box of cigars, ashtray, fancy match safe, c1910, framed.................................... 275.00

12" h, 10" w, Roi-Tan Cigars, self framed tin over cardboard, oval, raised frame, couple looking at each other as lady lights his fire, c1910 ............................................... 650.00

14-1/2" d, Bill Dugan, cardboard, image of Dugan, framed........ 175.00

17-1/2" h, 13-1/2" w, three-dimensional emb paper and cardboard, Seminola Cigars, cameo of Indian princess, framed.................... 700.00

Tin
    Even Steven Cigars, 5-3/8" h, 3" w, 3" d, C. E. Blair, Harrisburg, PA, tin litho, adv for 5¢ cigars.................... 650.00
    Old Abe Cigars, round, paper label ............................................... 65.00
    Possum Cigars, full ................ 175.00
    Reichard's Cadet Cigar............ 85.00

Watch Fob, 1-3/4" d, United Cigar Makers League, black and white, mirror back, metal strap loop, c1900 ............................................... 65.00

# Cigarette Items

**Collecting Hints:** Don't overlook the advertising which appeared in the national magazines from the 1940s to 1960s. Many star and public heroes endorsed cigarettes. Modern promotional material for brands such as Marlboro and Salem has been issued in large quantities, and much has been put aside by collectors. Most collectors tend to concentrate on the pre-1950 period.

**History:** Although the cigarette industry dates back to the late 19th century, it was during the decades of the 1930s and 1940s that cigarettes became the primary tobacco product. The cigarette industry launched massive radio advertising and promotional campaigns. In the 1950s, television became the dominant advertising medium.

The Surgeon General's Report, which warned of the danger of cigarette smoking, led to restrictions on advertising and limited the places where cigarettes could be smoked. The industry reacted with a new advertising approach aimed at 20- to 40-year olds and at females. Recent government regulations and changes in public opinion towards smoking in general have altered the style and quantity of cigarette-related collectibles.

**References:** Art Anderson, *Casinos and Their Ashtrays*, published by author, 1994; *Cigarette Card Values*, Murray Cards International Ltd.,

1992; Urban K. and Christine Cummings, *The World's Greatest Lighter*, Bird Dog Books (P.O. Box 1482, Palo Alto, CA 94302), 1996; Urban K. Cummings, *Ronson, World's Greatest Lighter*, Bird Dog Books, 1993; Nancy Wanvig, *Collector's Guide to Ashtrays*, Collector Books, 1997; A. M. W. van Weert, *Legend of the Lighter*, Electa, 1995; Neil Wood, *Collecting Cigarette Lighters* (1994), Vol. II (1995), L-W Book Sales; —, *Smoking Collectibles*, L-W Book Sales, 1994.

**Periodical:** *Tobacco Antiques and Collectibles Market*, Box 11652, Houston, TX 77283.

**Collectors' Clubs:** Ashtray Collectors Club, P.O. Box 11652, Houston, TX 77293; Cigarette Pack Collectors Association, 61 Searle St., Georgetown, MA 01833; International Lighter Collectors, P.O. Box 536, Quitman, TX 75783; International Seal, Label & Cigar Band Society, 8915 E. Bellevue St., Tucson, AZ 85715; Pocket Lighter Preservation Guild, P.O. Box 1054, Addison, IL 60101.

Advertising Poster, Turkish Cross-Cut Cigarettes, paper roll-up poster, metal strips at top and bottom, shows insert cards for Leading Actors and Actresses, 29" l, 14" w ............................................... 1,550.00

Ashtray, unused, orig box
    Chesterfield ............................ 20.00
    Lucky Strike ............................ 20.00

Banner
    Chesterfield, Jerry Lewis and Dean Martin.................................... 195.00
    Old Gold Cigarettes, Not A Cough In The Car Load, 42" x 120"......... 95.00

Carton, Chesterfield, Christmas ... 12.00

Cigarette Card, American
    Allen & Ginter, Pirates of the Spanish Main, 1888 ............................... 15.00
    Kinney Tobacco Co., military and naval uniforms, 1887 ................ 5.00
    Wing Cigarettes, first series of fifty ............................................... 50.00

Cigarette Card Album
    Allen & Ginter, Napoleon ......... 60.00
    W. Duck & Sons, Terrors of America ............................................... 65.00

Cigarette Case
    2-1/2" x 3", tan leather and cardboard, Fatima, veiled lady in gold, "Ninth Annual Convention/A.A.C. of A./Baltimore, June 1913" on reverse ............................................... 35.00
    3" x 4", enameled, woman's, black, envelope style, red stone dec ............................................... 35.00

Clock, Vantage Cigarettes, battery operated ................................. 40.00

Counter Display, Raleigh, 16" h, 10" w, 8" d, figural papier-mâché, orig "Old King Cole" label.................... 325.00

Dexterity Puzzle, Camel Lights, clear styrene plastic keychain case, miniature replica of cigarette pack, small

square opening in top to capture nine miniature filter tip cigarettes in filter ends up, c1980 ............... 25.00
Game, Camel, The Game, MIB, 1992 ............................................. 10.00
Lighter
ASR, Ascot hidden watch, swivels ............................................. 82.00
Beatti Jet, pipe lighter, chrome 35.00
Beny, England, lift arm, lift top, c1930, worn silver plating over brass ................................................. 65.00
Corona, gun shape, chrome, black ................................................. 33.00
Crestline, musical, Colonel Reb & Confederate flag ...................... 50.00
Dunhill, with ruler .................... 70.00
Dupont
1950s, silver plated, slight wear ............................................. 50.00
1960s, gold plated butane ........................................... 175.00
Flaminaire, Limoges, cobalt blue and gold, table model, 3-1/2" h ....... 30.00
Jet 200, torpedo shape, black plastic and aluminum, MIB ............. 15.00
MEB, Austrian, pull part, patent April 2, 1912 .................................... 22.00
Playboy, brass, engraved bunny, MIB ......................................... 30.00
Rexxy, chrome, 1930s, 4 hinge mechanism, Swiss ................... 37.00
Rite Point, pocket clip, pen shape ................................................. 9.50
Ronson, Standard, England, hallmarked sterling silver, picture of Queen ...................................... 85.00
Stankyo, musical, brass, large ................................................. 45.00
Zippo
1959, Boston, ME RR, MIB ............................................. 42.50
1966, pin-up girl in collector's tin ............................................. 30.00
1968, slim submarine, Tullibee, SSN ...................................... 35.00
Matchbook Holder, hanging, Kool Cigarettes ........................................ 10.00
Matches, Jokers for Smokers, Bang Matches, risqué covers, price for set of twelve ................................... 20.00

**Pinback Button, Hassan Cigarette premium, white ground, black letters, red coat, 7/8" d, $12.**

**Thermometer, Salem, painted tin, 9-1/4" h, $20.**

Pack, Picayune .............................. 6.00
Pinback Button
High Admiral Cigarettes, red, white, and blue flag, white ground, blue letters "A National Favorite/High Admiral," c1896 ............................... 35.00
Perfection Cigarettes, multicolored image of lady, back paper with list of tobacco products .................... 20.00
Philip Morris Cigarettes, black, white, and fleshtones, c1930 ............. 50.00
Playing Cards, Camel Cigarettes ................................................. 25.00
Radio
Chester Cheetah, MIB ............. 35.00
Marlboro Pack, MIB ................. 65.00
Server, chrome, smokestack shape, Chase Chrome ........................ 66.00
Silk
1" l, Wm. Randolph Hearst for Governor ...................................... 10.00
3-3/4" l, Wm. McKinley ............. 25.00
Sign
19-1/2" h, 11" w, Mecca Cigarettes, paper, Art Deco lady with hat, Earl Christy artist, orig frame stenciled "Mecca Cigarettes" ................ 275.00
30-1/2" h, 20-1/2" w, Egyptienne Straights, paper, titled "Absolutely Pure," Mormon-type lady in bonnet over full pack, framed ........... 200.00
38" h, 24-1/2" w, El Principal Cigars, diecut cardboard, two full boxes of cigars, titled "The taste pleases - it really does" .............................. 60.00
Thermometer
Marlboro, Marlboro Man .......... 40.00
Winston Taste Good...Like a Cigarette Should, 9" d, round, metal ................................................. 60.00
Tin
Black Cat Cigarettes ................ 15.00
Cavalier, 100, oval .................... 12.00
Lucky Strike 100, round .......... 20.00
Murad, 5-1/2" x 3" x 1-1/4", Canadian, 1897 stamp ..................... 40.00
Pall Mall, 7" x 8", Christmas dec ................................................. 15.00
Phillip Morris, 50, round .......... 12.00

# Circus Items

**Collecting Hints:** Circus programs are one of the most popular items in this category. Individuals have collected them since the 1920s. Programs prior to the 1930s are hard to find; post-1930 material is readily available.

Model building plays an active part in collecting. Some kits are available; however, most collectors like to build models from scratch. Great attention is placed on accurate details.

There are many books published about the circus. These are sought by collectors for intrinsic, as well as research, value.

**History:** The 18th-century circus was a small traveling company of acrobats and jugglers, and the first record of an American troupe is from that time. Washington is known to have attended a circus performance.

By the mid-19th century, the tent circus with accompanying side shows and menagerie became popular throughout America. P. T. Barnum was one of the early circus promoters. His American Museum in New York featured live animal acts in 1841. Other successful Barnum promotions included Jenny Lind in 1850, Tom Thumb from 1843 to 1883, and Jumbo, who was purchased from the London Zoo in 1883.

The Ringlings and Barnum and Bailey brought a magical quality to the circus. The golden age of the tent circus was the 1920s to the 1940s, when a large circus consisted of over 100 railroad cars.

As television challenged live entertainment, the tent circus fell on hard times. Expenses for travel, food, staff, etc., mounted. A number of mergers took place, and many smaller companies simply went out of business. There are a few tent circuses remaining. However, most modern circuses now perform inside large convention centers.

**Periodical:** *Circus Report*, 525 Oak St., El Cerrito, CA 94530.

**Collectors' Clubs:** Circus Fans Association of America, P.O. Box 59710, Potomac, MD 20859; Circus Historical Society, 743 Beverly Park Place, Jackson, MI 49203; Circus Model Builders International, 347 Lonsdale Ave., Dayton, OH 45419.

**Museums:** Circus World Museum Library-Research Center, Baraboo, WI; P. T. Barnum Museum, Bridgeport, CT; Ringling Circus Museum, Sarasota, FL.

Broadside and Ephemera, 30-1/2" h, 22" w, litho, bright multi color image, various acrobats and jugglers balancing balls, tables, American shield in upper right hand corner surmounted by full spread winged eagle and bust of Edward Earle, sign reads "Edward Earle the Great American Equilibrist," Halbert Litho, Plymouth, England, sold with 7 cabinet photos and other photos of Mr. Earle, 3 cabinet views of other acrobats, one titled "Fredericks Gloss Lavan, celebrated American trio from Barnums Great American Circus USA," letter on Earle's personal stationery ............................ 1,200.00

Calendar, Circus World Museum, 1974 ........................................................ 5.00

Child's Book
*The Jolly Jump-Ups Book, See the Circus, Ringling Bros., The Greatest Show*, McLaughlin Bros., 1944, six pop-up scenes ......................... 95.00
*Toby Tyler or Ten Weeks With a Circus*, James Otis, G & D, 1923, dj, some wear ................................. 9.00

Circus Pass
Circus Hall of Fame, Sarasota, FL ................................................... 3.50
Covina, California Jr. Chamber of Commerce ................................... 3.50
Garden Grove Breakfast Lions Club ................................................... 3.50
King Bros., sponsored by fire company ............................................ 3.50
United Nations Circus, Bridgeport ................................................... 3.50
Von Bros. Three Ring Circus ...... 3.50
Wallace & Clark Trained Animal Circus ................................................... 3.50

Letterhead, Ringling Bros., multicolored, five brothers with crest, 1909 ................................................. 18.00

Menu, Greatest Show on Earth, Nov. 12, 1898, full color ......................... 100.00

Model, 1" scale
Bareback riders, man and woman, two horses ............................... 800.00
Clarke Bros. Circus, two wheel hitch ................................................. 50.00
Hay wagon and harness, blue and red ............................................ 300.00
Railroad flat car ...................... 200.00
Side show paraphernalia, fourteen set-ups ............................. 1,120.00

Pinback Button
Barnum '76 Festival, red, white, and blue ......................................... 10.00
Cole Bros., Clyde Beatty, 1930s ................................................. 25.00
King Reid Shows, black and white clown, red, yellow, and green accents, light blue ground, c1950 ................................................. 30.00
Little Hip And His Owner Prof. Andre, trained elephant, c1910 ........... 45.00

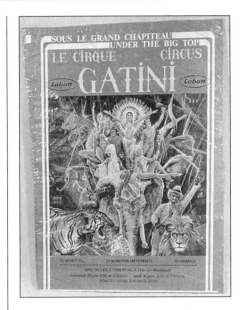

**Poster, Le Cirque, Gatini, Quebec, Canada, 1970s, 17" x 24", $25.**

Setlin & Wilson Shows, 1-3/4" d, black and white clown, red, yellow, and green accents, light blue ground, dark blue rim border, c1940 ................ 50.00
Playing Cards, Ringling Bros. and Barnum & Bailey Circus, miniature size ............................................... 12.00
Poster
Arthur Bros.
1940, Big Railroad Show, arrival parade with showgirls on horses and elephants ................... 90.00
1943, Amusing Wire Display, navy, orange, and red, tightrope walker in top hat ............... 170.00
Barnum & Bailey
1894, The Grand Equestrian Tournament, rough riders, inset Civil and Military horsemanship illus, Strobridge Litho ............... 725.00
1913, Lion and Tiger, reclining jungle cats, circus logo, Strobridge Litho ...................... 275.00
Clyde Beatty Circus, holds reign over field of wild jungle cats, date tag "July 4, Glendale Speedway" ................................................. 50.00
Cole Bros., All the Marvels, animal sin cages, Erie Litho ............. 210.00
Hagenbeck-Wallace, 1925, Capt. Clyde Beatty, World's Most Daring Trainer, posing with lions, tigers, and leopards pyramid .................. 270.00
King Bros., 1946, clown face, red and yellow, advertising arrival ................................................ 210.00
Ringling Bros. and Barnum & Bailey
1935, jolly clown portrait, blue ground, Erie Litho ............. 270.00
1938, The Greatest Wild Animal Display, presents Terrell Jacobs, World's Foremost Trainer, Strobridge Litho ...................... 625.00
1940, The Great Alzanax, high wire act, red ground .......... 150.00

Program
Barnum & Bailey, 1953 ............ 10.00
Cole Bros. Clyde Beatty, 1969, 24 pgs, 40 photos ......................... 5.00
Gentry Bros. & James Patterson, 1924 ...................................... 15.00
Hamid-Morgan, 1948 ............... 7.00
Ringling Bros. Barnum & Bailey, 1962, 53 pgs, 10 articles, 90 photos ................................................. 6.00
Record, Old Time Circus Calliola, Wurlitzer, Calliola, Paul Eakin's Gay 90's Village ...................................... 5.00
Routebook
Barnum & Bailey, 1906 .......... 225.00
Cristiani Bros. Circus, 1958 ..... 25.00
Forepaugh, Adam, shows, 1891 ................................................. 225.00
Sign, 43" x 65", Aqua Circus, wood, painted, scallop border, woman in 1890s garb with parachute.... 140.00
Souvenir Book, Ringling Bros. and Barnum & Bailey Circus, 1939 ...... 15.00
Ticket Stub Book, Hagenbeck-Wallace Circus, 1935 ......................... 10.00
Tour Route Schedule
Hubert Castle International 3 Ring Circus, 1973, #4, British Columbia ................................................. 5.00
Kelly Miller Circus, 1966, #22, NY, NJ, DE, MD ............................... 5.00
King Bros. Circus, 1967, #6, NY, PA, OH ...................................... 5.00
Polack Bros. Circus, 1969
#1, MI, VA, NC, KY, IN, PA .... 5.00
#4, AZ, CO, MO, UT, NV, CA ................................................. 5.00
#6, WA, NV, OR ................... 5.00
#8, TN, WV, VA, MD, MI, IL, IN ................................................. 5.00
Toy
Paper, Clyde Beatty, Hingee, unpunched, 1945 ................... 85.00
Playset, Marx, played-with condition, few broken pieces ................. 475.00
Set, Bergen Toy & Novelty Co., plastic figures, orig box
#250, 8 pcs ...................... 100.00
#251, 7 pcs ........................ 90.00
Wagon Wheel, wood, metal rim, red, white, and blue painted spokes ................................................. 250.00

# Cleminson Clay

**Collecting Hints:** Each piece produced by this firm was hand decorated with colored slip, which accounts for the slight variations from piece to piece. The Distlefink dinnerware line is currently finding favor with many collectors.

**History:** In 1941, Betty Cleminson established Cleminson Clay in the garage of her home in El Monte, California, with her husband, George, handling the business affairs. In 1943, the company expanded to a new plant constructed in El Monte, and its name was changed to The

California Cleminsons. In addition to a popular line of tableware called Distlefink, the pottery produced hand-decorated artware and kitchen accessories including pie birds, lazy Susans, spoon holders, and pitchers.

**Reference:** Jack Chipman, *Collector's Encyclopedia of California Pottery*, 2nd ed., Collector Books, 1998.

**Periodical:** *Pottery Collectors Express*, P.O. Box 221, Mayview, MO 64071.

Cookie Jar, cov
    Candy House ...........................95.00
    Card King, gold trim on hearts
    .......................................... 400.00
    Christmas House.....................150.00
Creamer and Sugar, Pop ..............20.00
Egg Separator..............................20.00
Hair Receiver, girl, 2 pcs .............35.00
Lazy Susan, Distlefink...................85.00
Pie Bird, rooster ..........................30.00
Pitcher, Distlefink .........................40.00
Plate, hillbilly ...............................24.00
Razor Bank, dome .......................20.00
Ring Holder, bulldog.....................20.00
Salt and Pepper Shakers, pr, male sailor "Old Salt," and female sailor "Hot Stuff," 5-1/4" h .........................75.00
String Holder, "You'll always have a 'pull' with me!," 5" h...............100.00
Timer, Timothy Timer, orig instructions ...................................................45.00
Wall Plaque, spray of flowers........60.00

# Clickers

**Collecting Hints:** Clickers with pictures are more desirable than clickers that display only printed words. Value is reduced by scratches in the paint and rust. Some companies issued several variations of a single design—be alert for them when collecting.

**History:** Clickers were a popular medium for advertising products, services, and people; and subjects ranged from plumbing supplies, political aspirants, soft drinks, and hotels, to beer and whiskey. The most commonly found clickers are those which were given to children in shoe stores to advertise brands such as Buster Brown, Poll Parrot, and Red Goose. Many shoe-store clickers have advertising-whistle mates.

Clickers were not confined to advertising. They were a popular holiday item, especially at Halloween. Impressed animal forms also provided a style for clickers.

The vast majority of clickers were made of tin. The older and rarer clickers were made of celluloid.

**Tastykake, blue ground, white letters, $9.**

### Advertising

Barton's Store, green on white, "New Hampshire's Biggest Store/Established 1850," tin flange snaps loudly ............................................... 35.00
Flavor-Kist Saltines, 1-3/4" l ......... 40.00
Gunther's Beer, white litho tin, red letters "The Beer That Clicks," Kirchof Co., 1930s ..................................... 25.00
Hughes Crescent Cottage Paints, multicolored image of can, white background, not working ................. 30.00
Lyon & Sons Brewing, Newark, NJ, Lyon's Beer ............................. 60.00
Oshkosh................................... 65.00
Quaker State, 1-7/8"................... 65.00
Reach for Old Style Beer............. 25.00
Red Goose Shoes, tin, 2" l........... 40.00
Tip Top Bread, Cisco Kid, six shooter gun, cardboard, 9-1/2" x 4-1/4" ................................................ 95.00
Twinkie Shoes, 1-7/8" l................. 80.00
Weatherbird Shoes, 1-3/4" l .......... 27.50
Weston's..................................... 38.00

### Mechanical

Beetle, diecut metal..................... 15.00
Boxer ........................................ 210.00
Cricket, yellow and black litho tin, 2" l ................................................ 10.00
Cowboy..................................... 245.00
Gun, figural
    Red, 1950s........................... 35.00
    Tommy Gun, plastic, yellow and green, 1950s........................... 8.00
Halloween, cat, plastic, 2-1/4" l .... 20.00
Ladybug, red and black litho tin, 1946 ................................................ 10.00

**Political**, "For Governor Lewis Emery Jr.," black, white, and red, silver horseshoe symbol, small green shamrocks, portrait framed by slogan "Let's Polish Off The Gang," Lincoln Party candidate, early 1900s, metal clicker............................. 65.00

# Clocks

**Collecting Hints:** Many clocks of the 20th century were reproductions of earlier styles. Therefore, dates should be verified by checking patent dates on the mechanism, makers' labels, and construction techniques.

The principal buyers for the advertising and figural clocks are not the clock collectors, but the specialists with whose area of interest the clock overlaps. For example, the Pluto alarm clock is of far greater importance to a Disneyana collector than to most clock collectors.

Condition is critical. Rust and non-working parts have a major affect on prices.

**History:** The clock always has served a dual function: decorative and utilitarian. Beginning in the late 19th century the clock became an important advertising vehicle, a tradition which continues today. As character and personality recognition became part of the American scene, clocks, whether alarm or wall models, were a logical extension. Novelty clocks, especially figural ones, were common from 1930 to the 1960s.

Since digital wristwatches and clocks became popular in the 1970s, clocks have been less commonly used as promotional items.

**Reference:** Robert and Harriet Swedberg, *Price Guide to Antique Clocks,* Krause Publications, 1998.

**Periodical:** *Clocks*, 4314 W. 238th St., Torrance, CA 90505; *Watch & Clock Review*, 2403 Champa St, Denver, CO 80205.

**Collectors' Club:** National Association of Watch and Clock Collectors, Inc., 514 Poplar St., Columbia, PA 17512.

**Museums:** American Clock & Watch Museum, Bristol, CT; Greensboro Clock Museum, Greensboro, NC; Museum of National Association of Watch and Clock Collectors, Columbia, PA; Old Clock Museum, Pharr, TX; Time Museum, Rockford, IL.

**Additional Listings:** See *Warman's Antiques and Collectibles Price Guide.*

Advertising
Bosch Super, spark plug illus, quartz ................................................ 35.00
Busch Beer, electrical, horse and rider scene, crossing valley near mountains of Busch ................. 35.00
Cincinnati Reds, logo, wood frame, electric, 1940s ......................... 60.00
Coca-Cola, "Drink Coca-Cola in Bottles," sq. wood case, electric, Selected Devices Co. NY ...... 215.00
Four Roses Whiskey, 14" sq, lights up, orig wiring, metal, glass front, 1950s .................................... 250.00
Frostie Root Beer, metal, fluorescent bulb........................................ 150.00

General Electric, peach, mirror, electric .............................................. 55.00
Jefferson "Golden Hour," electric ................................................... 85.00
John Deere, 14"d, round, electric ................................................... 65.00
Kodak, "Pictures Are Priceless-Use Kodak Film," 15-1/2", sq, lights up ................................................... 35.00
Lord Calvert, "Custom Distilled for Men of Distinction," black wood case, 11" x 12", 1940s.............. 70.00
Piels Beer, 15" x 11" .................. 85.00
Schlitz, lights, 1959 .................. 60.00
St. Joseph's Aspirin, neon...... 300.00
Tetley, Tea Time, 13", blue and gray, tin, Art Deco ............................. 85.00
Warren Telephone Co., Ashland, MA, oak .......................................... 80.00
Wise Potato Chip, owl, electric ................................................. 75.00

Alarm
Bradley, brass, double bells, Germany ........................................ 35.00
Hello Kitty, MIB........................ 65.00
Mickey Mouse, metal, Phinney-Walker, West Germany............. 40.00
Peter's Shoes, New Haven Clock Co., 4" x 4", Art Deco, c1930 ................................................. 50.00
Purina Poultry Chows, electric, three dials, red, white, and blue checkerboard bag ............................. 40.00
Tweety, Looney Tunes, talking, Janex, battery operated, 1978 ................................................. 65.00

Animated
Fish swimming around dial, Art Deco style, Sessions ...................... 250.00
Haddon, rocking grandmother ...................................... 175.00
Mastercrafter's, fireplace........ 115.00

**Chef, Sessions, electric, white case, 10-1/2" h, 7" w, $30.**

United
Ballerina, music box.......... 150.00
Boy, gold fishing, 1950s.... 175.00
Character
Davy Crockett, wall, pendulum ................................................. 75.00
Donald Duck, 9" h, wall, glazed china, 2-1/4" d case inscribed "Blessings," blue outfit, green glazed ground, orig gold sticker marked "Waechtersbach," inscribed "Walt Disney Productions, J.A. Sural Hanua/Main-Made in Germany," c1950 ................................... 175.00
Howdy Doody, talking.............. 65.00
Mickey Mouse, Bradley animated hands........................................ 45.00
Pluto, 4" x 5" x 9", electric, black, white, and red plastic, bone hands, moving eyes and tongue, c1940 ............................................... 100.00
Sesame Street, schoolhouse shape ................................................. 25.00
Trix The Rabbit, alarm, c1960 ................................................. 15.00
Figural
Artist's Palette, bakelite............ 35.00
Chef, 10-1/2" h, electric, wall, white, Sessions Clock Co., Forestville ................................................. 24.00
Doghouse, 11" h, iron, dog looking out, flowers............................. 80.00
Donut, 8-3/4" h, dark herbal green glaze, Clifton Art Pottery .......... 85.00
Refrigerator, 8-1/2" h, metal, painted white, GE label, Warren Telechron Co., Ashland, MA.................. 185.00
Spinning Wheel, Lux, animated ................................................. 80.00

# Clothing and Clothing Accessories

**Collecting Hints:** Vintage clothing should be clean and in good repair. Designer labels and original boxes can add to the value.

**History:** Clothing is collected and studied as a reference for learning about fashion, construction, and types of materials used. New collectors to this segment of the market are being attracted by designer label accessories, such as compacts and handbags. Other buyers of collectible clothing are looking for costumes for theater or other events, such as re-enactors.

**References:** Blanche Cirker (ed.), *1920s Fashions From B. Altman & Company*, Dover, 1999; Roseann Ettinger, *Fifties Forever! Popular Fashions for Men, Women, Boys, and Girls*, Schiffer, 1998; Roselyn Gerson, *Ladies' Compacts of the 19th and 20th Centuries*, Wallace-Homestead, 1989; —, *Vintage Vanity Bags and Purses*, Collector Books, 1994; Frances Johnson, *Compacts, Powder, and Paint*, Schiffer Publishing, 1996; Laura M. Mueller, *Collector's Encyclopedia of Compacts, Carryalls & Face Boxes*, Vol. I (1994, 1996 value update), Vol. II (1997), Collector Books; Richard Holiner, *Antique Purses*, Collector Books, 1996 value update; Susan Langley, *Vintage Hats & Bonnets, 1770-1970*, Collector Books, 1997; Mary Brooks Picken, *A Dictionary of Costume and Fashion: Historic and Modern*, Dover, 1999; Debra Wisniewski, *Antique and Collectible Buttons*, Collector Books, 1997; plus many out of print references.

**Periodicals:** *Glass Slipper*, 653 S. Orange Ave., Sarasota, FL 34236; *Lady's Gallery*, P.O. Box 1761, Independence, MO 64055; *Lill's Vintage Clothing Newsletter*, 19 Jamestown Drive, Cincinnati, OH 45241; *Vintage Clothing Newsletter*, P.O. Box 1422, Corvallis, OR 97339; *Vintage Gazette*, 194 Amity St., Amherst, MA 01002.

**Collectors' Clubs:** Compact Collectors Club, P.O. Box 40, Lynbrook, NY 11563; Costume Society of America, 55 Edgewater Drive, P.O. Box 73, Earleville, MD 21919; Federation of Vintage Fashion, P.O. Box 412, Alamo, CA 94507; Living History Association, P.O. Box 578, Wilmington, VT 05363; Textile & Costume Guild, 301 N. Pomona Ave., Fullerton, CA 92632; Vintage Fashion and Costume Jewelry Club, P.O. Box 265, Glen Oaks, NY 11004.

**Museums:** The Arizona Costume Institute, Phoenix Art Museum, Phoenix, AZ; Boston Museum of Fine Arts, Boston, MA; Chicago Historical Society, Chicago, IL; Detroit Historical Museum, Detroit, MI; Fashion Institute of Technology, New York, NY; Indianapolis Museum of Art, Indianapolis, IN; Los Angeles County Museum of Art, Costume and Textile Dept., Los Angeles, CA; Metropolitan Museum of Art, New York, NY; Missouri Historical Society, Saint Louis, MO; Museum at Stony Brook, Stony Brook, NY; Museum of Art, Rhode Island School of Design, Providence, RI; Museum of Vintage Fashion, Lafayette, CA; National Museum of American History, Washington, DC; Philadelphia College of Textiles & Science, Philadelphia, PA; Philadelphia Museum of Art, Philadelphia, PA; Valentine Museum, Richmond, VA; Wadsworth Atheneum, Hartford, CT; Western Reserve Historical Society, Cleveland, OH.

Apron, calico, red and white ......... 25.00
Baby Bonnet, cotton, tatted, ribbon rosettes ................................... 15.00
Bed Jacket, satin, pink, lavish ecru lace, labeled "B Altman & Co., NY," 1930s ........................................ 30.00
Bloomers
    Crepe Satin, peach, silk embroidery, lace trim, 1920s ...................... 18.00
    Wool, cream ............................ 25.00
Blouse
    Beaded taffeta, black, black glass beads at yoke, hand sewn ...... 85.00
    Chiffon, green, child's multiple rows of ruffles .................................. 15.00
    Cotton, white, cutwork, Victorian ..................................................... 20.00
    Lace, ecru, evening style, gathered waist, 1950s ........................... 18.00
    Poplin, white, middy style, c1910 ..................................................... 15.00
    Silk, cream, embroidered, 1900s ..................................................... 65.00
Bonnet
    Silk, hand crocheted lace ........ 36.00
    Straw, finely woven, worn silk lining ................................................... 135.00
Boudoir Cap, crocheted, pink rosettes ...................................................... 12.00
Bustle. canvas and woven wire .... 30.00
Cape
    Girl's, flannel wool, ivory, silk cord embroidery................................. 45.00
    Lady's, mohair, black, ankle length, c1930 ..................................... 75.00
Change Purse, cut steel beads, ecru crochet, push bottom clasp, fringe, leaf dec, 2-1/2" x 3-1/2", inscribed "B Cottle, 1847" ............................... 65.00
Christening Gown, white
    Cotton, matching bonnet, 47" l ..................................................... 100.00
    Cutwork embroidery bodice, tuck pleats around ruffled skirt ........ 65.00
    Machine sewn, lace, hand embroidery, 42" l ................................. 50.00
    Net, embroidered, silk slip, 44" l ..................................................... 150.00
Coat
    Baby's
        Cotton, gathered yoke and capelet, embroidery, flannel lining ..................................................... 25.00
        Silk, pink, label "Paris Best" 45.00
    Boy's, linen, hand stitched, dec cuffs ..................................................... 35.00
    Lady's
        Evening, black velour, brown highlights, satin lining, large cuffs and stand-up collar, frog closure at neck............................... 275.00
        Muskrat, bell shaped sleeves, c1940 ................................. 90.00
        Persian Lamb, black, matching hat ....................................... 75.00

Velvet, navy blue, beaded dec, black fox collar and cuffs, red satin lining, 1920s ............. 250.00
Wool, blue, beaver collar and cuffs, blouson, drop waist style, c1920 ............................... 100.00
Collar
    Beaded, white, 1930s ............. 12.00
    Cotton, white, embroidered, wide, scalloped ................................ 20.00
Compact
    Avon, oval, lid dec with blue and green checkerboard pattern.... 35.00
    Evans, goldtone and mother -of-pearl, compact and lipstick combination ...................................... 45.00
    Hudnut, Richard, Deauville, blue, cloisonné tango-chain vanity, metal mirror, compartments for power and rouge, lipstick attached to finger ring chain ................................... 200.00
    K & K, brass, colored engine tooled dec basket compact, multicolored silk flowers enclosed in plastic dome lid, emb swinging handle....... 125.00
    Rowanta, brown enamel, oval petit point compact.......................... 65.00
    Unknown Maker
        Enamel, ebony, eight-ball style ................................................ 115.00
        Enamel and goldtone, roll top style, Germany .................. 135.00
        Goldtone, heart shape, brocade lid ......................................... 50.00
        Lucite, blue, sterling silver repousse medallion of two doves ................................................ 135.00
        Plastic, red, white, and blue, Naval Officer's cap shape ................................................ 85.00
        Silver Plated, antique, triangular, hand mirror-shape, lipstick concealed in handle, int. and ext. mirrors, turquoise cabochon thumbpiece .......................... 155.00
    Volupt, USA, Adam and Eve, under apple tree............................... 50.00
    Whiting and Davis, CO, Piccadilly, gilded mesh, vanity bag, compact incorporated in front lid, carrying chain ................................... 250.00
    Woolworth, Karess, polished goldtone, corset shaped, vanity case, powder and rouge compartments ..................................................... 45.00
    Yardley, goldtone, vanity case, red, white, and blue emb design no lid, powder and rouge compartments ..................................................... 75.00
Dress
    Child's
        Cotton, day type, gold, net trim, c1900 ................................. 20.00
        Crepe, red, red beaded edge trim at collar and sleeves, minor holes and wear ........................... 25.00
        Georgette, pink, many layers of georgette and chiffon, c1920 ................................................ 75.00
        Gingham, blue and white, hand and machine sewn, white embroidery trim, 25" h ................... 50.00
        Knit, 2 pc, 1930 ................ 25.00

Lawn, white, lace, drop waist, c1910 .................................. 60.00
Linen, embroidered wisteria inserts, Irish lace trim........ 150.00
Net, silk lining, ruffles at neck, sleeves, pink rosette trim ..................................................... 120.00
Rayon, raspberry, accordion pleats, c1930 .................... 15.00
Silk, blue, floral print, lace trim, Victorian ........................... 150.00
Velvet, red, white nylon, Shirley Temple style, Cinderella tag ..................................................... 15.00
Wool, pink, lace trim, c1890 ..................................................... 125.00
    Lady's
        Batiste, white, lace, high neck, full skirt, long sleeves, c1900 ..................................................... 150.00
        Calico, blue, 2 pc, matching bonnet, c1900 ...................... 165.00
        Chiffon, blue, edges trimmed with braided fabric, 1925 .......... 40.00
        Lawn, drop waist .............. 60.00
        Satin, black, 1920s ............ 85.00
        Taffeta, blue, embossed dec, 1950s, dinner-type ............. 10.00
Dressing Gown, satin, ruby red, fagoted ruffled edges, 1930................. 28.00
Evening Gown
    Crepe, brown, matching velvet capelet with feather trim, c1930 ..................................................... 40.00
    Net and Taffeta, black, lace flowers, c1940................................... 48.00
    Organza, white, shirred, rhinestones, c1940 ................................... 45.00
Evening Jacket, crepe, pink, floral patterned sequins, lined, 1940 ..... 58.00
Gloves
    Lady's, kid, white, long ........... 20.00
    Men's, driving, leather, black, c1910 ..................................................... 25.00
Handbag
    Alligator, suede lining ............. 18.00
    Beaded, Abstract design, white and gray, milk glass beads, beaded handle, zipper, 5", marked "Czechoslovakia"................................... 20.00

**Handbag, Lucite, mkd "Florida Handbags," $35.**

Florals, pink and blue, shiny beads, gold frame ............................... 45.00
Lucite, pearlized, round lid, lunch box clasp, twisted handle, seashell dec .......................................... 17.50
Mesh, enameled, white ground, black leaf spray, Mandalian ..... 55.00
Patchwork, Seminole, drawstring, grass bottom, blue, c1960 ....... 25.00
Pearl, envelope, Hong Kong label ............................................. 15.00
Plastic, child's, red, imitation leather, three Scotties dec, silver frame and chain, int. mirror ....................... 20.00
Sequins, irid multicolored, silver and seed pearl dec, rhinestone clasp, fancy frame, Belgium ............... 30.00
Silk, clutch, black, cut steel beads, marked "France," c1930 .......... 42.00
Wool, hand-woven, New Mexico, Navajo rug design, white ground, Fred Harvey, c1940 ................. 35.00

Handkerchief
Children, 11" sq, printed, white cotton, red and black design, scene of children in goat coat, minor stains and small hole ........................... 30.00
Old Mother Hubbard, 10-3/4" x 18", printed, white cotton, red design, framed ...................................... 50.00
Snow White and the Seven Dwarfs, 1938, price for set .................. 225.00

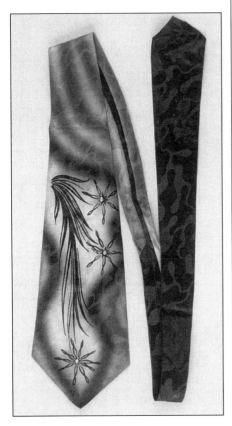

**Necktie, hand painted silk, Van Heusen, multicolored ground, dark red flowers with rhinestone centers, 4-1/4" w, $30.**

Hat, Lady's
Felt, beanie type, picture of Underdog, Bullwinkle, or Rocky, each ............................................. 20.00
Felt, cloche, black ................... 15.00
Satin, pillbox, black, netting ..... 18.00
Straw, red, orig label "Adolfo 11 NY and Paris," tag reads "Higbee Co., Cleveland," orig box, orig sales slip reads "Purchased 4-4-66, paid $18.54," signed by clerk that purchaser was going to wear it ..... 48.00
Hat and Purse Set, leopard skin pillbox, matching purse ...................... 100.00
Hosiery, color photo of Happy Days, The Fonz, Paramount, 1976 ..... 20.00
Muff
Marabou, white ........................ 45.00
Rabbit fur, white, child's ........... 25.00
Sable, brown, tails ................. 100.00
Necktie, men's, striped, rayon, 1930s ................................................. 3.00
Pajama's, girl's, baby doll style, cotton, pink hearts, 1960s ..................... 7.00
Petticoat, cotton, white
Crocheted insert, wide crocheted hem ......................................... 45.00
Three rows crochet trim ........... 40.00
Prom Gown
Georgette, yellow, embroidered bodice, strapless, c1960 ............... 25.00
Net and Taffeta, pink, layered skirt, bow trim, c1950 ...................... 35.00
Purse, Mexican, tooled leather, brown, white inserts ............................. 45.00
Sash, purple, beaded, c1850 ..... 100.00
Scarf
Cotton, dog print, marked "Occupied Japan" ............................ 18.00
Silk, man's, fringed .................. 15.00
Shawl
Cotton, mint green, fully embroidered, fringed edges, 1925 ..... 35.00
Paisley, Printed design, 66" x 128", minor wear and stains .............. 60.00
Woven Design, 68" x 69", minor damage ......................................... 165.00
Shoes
Boy's, leather, Oxford style, two tone brown ...................................... 35.00
Children's
Faux crocodile and suede, side buckle, rust, 1930s .............. 36.00
Leather
Mary Jane, two strap style, camel kid, side buttons, Buster Brown brand, 1930s ....... 42.00
Oxford, black kid, Buster Brown brand, 1930s ....... 40.00
Saddle, black and white, late 1950s ............................ 35.00
T-strap style, brown leather, black, rust, and tan suede, Red Goose brand, 1930s ......................................... 40.00
Lady's
Leather, boots, brown or black, lace up, pointed toes ........ 125.00
Leather, brown, high button top ........................................... 40.00
Low heels, black kid, black patent toes, Buster Brown brand ......................................... 145.00

Men's
Boots. work type, leather, early, 11" h, pr .............................. 25.00
Tennis, high top, c1920 ....... 20.00
Skirt
Linen, gore style, Edwardian type ............................................. 40.00
Polished Cotton, floral print, full, c1950 ...................................... 24.00
Wool, black, Victorian ............. 40.00
Socks, men's, rayon and silk, cotton toe an heal, black, colored arrow, 1950s ................................................. 5.00
Suit
Boy's, wool
Blazer, short pants, navy, 26" chest, Tom Sawyer brand .... 42.00
Herringbone, lined, Amish, c1920 ............................................. 40.00
Lady's, wool, navy pintucks, silk lining, 1921 ................................. 55.00
Teddy, yellow, pink emb trim on bodice, 1920s ...................................... 25.00
Travel Kit, gentleman's, alligator, seven accessories, c1940 ................. 18.00
Wedding Gown, satin, ivory, beading and embroidery, sheer sleeves, self train, matching long veil with blusher, c1970 ...................................... 75.00

# Coca-Cola Collectibles

**Collecting Hints:** Most Coca-Cola items were produced in large quantity; the company was a leader in sales and promotional materials. Don't ignore the large amount of Coca-Cola material printed in languages other than English. Remember, Coke has a worldwide market.

**History:** The originator of Coca-Cola was John Pemberton, a pharmacist from Atlanta, Georgia. In 1886, Dr. Pemberton introduced a patent medicine to relieve headaches, stomach disorders, and other minor maladies. Unfortunately, his failing health and meager finances forced him to sell his interest.

In 1888, Asa G. Candler became the sole owner of Coca-Cola. Candler improved the formula, increased the advertising budget, and widened the distribution. Accidentally, a patient was given a dose of the syrup mixed with carbonated water instead of the usual still water. The result was a tastier, more refreshing drink.

As sales increased in the 1890s, Candler recognized that the product was more suitable for the soft drink market and began advertising it as such. From these beginnings, a myriad of advertising items have been issued to invite all to "Drink Coca-Cola."

Dates of interest: "Coke" was first used in advertising in 1941. The distinctively shaped bottle was registered as a trademark on April 12, 1960.

**References:** Deborah Goldstein Hill, *Price Guide to Vintage Coca-Cola® Collectibles: 1896-1965,* Krause Publications, 1999; Allan Petretti, *Petretti's Coca-Cola Collectibles Price Guide,* 10th ed., Antique Trader Books, 1997.

**Collectors' Clubs:** Coca-Cola Collectors Club, 400 Monemar Ave., Baltimore, MD 21228; Coca-Cola Collectors Club International, P.O. Box 49166, Atlanta, GA 30359; Florida West Coast Chapter of the Coca-Cola Collectors Club International, 1007 Emerald Drive, Brandon, FL 33511.

**Museums:** Coca-Cola Memorabilia Museum of Elizabethtown, Inc., Elizabethtown, KY; The World of Coca-Cola Pavilion, Atlanta, GA.

**Reproduction Alert:** Coca-Cola trays.

Advertisement, picture of Eddie Fisher ..................................................... 8.00
Ashtray, 4" d, bright red, white logo, 1980s ........................................ 12.00
Bank
    Battery operated, red Coke machine shape ...................................... 175.00
    Coke Year of the Tiger, cute tiger beside large bottle, MIB ........... 40.00
Banner, 11" x 22", printed paper, c1951 .................................................... 15.00
Billfold, pigskin, 1950s ................. 25.00
Blotter, 3-1/2" x 7-1/2" stiff paper, colorful graphics of smiling Coca-Cola Sprite elf digging bottle of Coke out of snow bank, copyright 1953 Coca-Cola Co. .................................. 10.00
Book, *Portrait of a Business,* 1961, autographed by W. G. Kurtz .......... 75.00
Book Cover, 10" x 14", dark green stiff paper, advertising "Safety A.B.C.'s" motif in brown and red, copyright 1940, unfolded .......................... 5.00
Booklet, "Classic Cooking with Coca-Cola" .................................. 5.00
Bottle, commemorative
    Cincinnati Reds, World Champs, 1994 .............................................. 4.00
    Colorado Rockies, 1993 MLB Record Season ........................... 4.00
    Dallas Cowboy Superbowl, commemorative six bottle set ......... 30.00
    Denver Broncos 1st Team logo .. 4.00
    Detroit Red Wings, 70th anniversary .................................................. 4.00
    Eskimo Joe's ............................. 3.00
    Florida Aquarium ....................... 4.00
    Ft. Worth Stock Show ............... 4.00

    Graceland, 1995 ...................... 10.00
    Houston Rockets, Back to Back Champs, 1995 ........................ 3.00
    Kentucky Derby 122 ................. 4.00
    NBA All Star Weekend 1995, desert scene, NBA logo, Feb date, made and issued in Phoenix, AZ, limited to 300,000, six pack with orig bottles and contents ........................ 35.00
    Oriole Park at Camden Yards .... 4.00
    Selena, Five Years With You..... 35.00
    Texas Tech Lady Red Raiders ... 3.00
Bottle Carrier, shopping cart ........ 50.00
Box, wooden ................................ 65.00
Bridge Score Pad ........................ 12.00
Calendar, 1955 ........................... 52.50
Chalkboard, diner menu .............. 45.00
Check, used
    1946, May 3, bottle logo .......... 14.00
    1960, July 28, bottle logo, small hole ........................................... 8.00
    1961, April 14, bottle logo....... 12.00
Cigarette Lighter, miniature ......... 10.00
Clock, 15" sq, electric, metal ...... 115.00
Coaster, Santa Claus, set ........... 15.00
Cookie Jar, jug shaped, red label with Coca-Cola logo, McCoy ......... 80.00
Cuff Links, pr, bottle shape........... 45.00
Dart Board, 1950s ....................... 40.00
Door Push, 11" x 4", porcelain, 1930s ........................................... 85.00
Folder, 8-1/2" x 11", black, white, and red, 4 pgs plus overleaf, "More Profit Per Patron," Coca-Cola refreshment counter in movie house lobbies or vending machines, back text describes average weekly gross profits from lobby sales, late 1930s ........................................... 65.00
Glass
    Set, 8 glasses
        10 oz size, sealed in orig carton, Libbey, c1960 .................... 125.00
        16 oz size
            Georgia Green, Indiana Glass, 1992, bell shaped........... 14.00
            Polar Bear, "Always Cool, Always Coca-Cola," Indiana Glass, 1992 ................... 12.00
Ice Chest, airline cooler.............. 410.00
Ice Pick, with opener ................. 122.00
Kite, High Flyer, six ounce bottle illus, 1930s ........................................ 45.00
Magazine Ad
    *Life,* March 15, 1963 ................ 7.50
    *The Housewife,* 1910, matted and framed...................................... 70.00
Mail Away, model kit, Kit Carson, MIB ........................................... 85.00
Marbles, "Free with every carton" 35.00
Menu Board, 1950s .................... 175.00
Necktie, c1950........................... 35.00
Pencil Box, orig contents............. 35.00
Pencil Sharpener, figural bottle, cast metal ...................................... 45.00
Pinback Button
    Hi Fi Club, red, green, and yellow litho tin, brown bottle in center of red 45 rpm record, 1950s sponsorship of teen music TV show................ 30.00
    Insignia Series, 15-1/6" d, celluloid, Parisian Novelty Co., insert back paper with "Drink Coca-Cola" trade-

**Paperweight, clear, red ground, white letters, $55.**

mark along with designation of insignia, and series number, 1940s
    No. 7, 26th Bombardment Squadron, orange and gray .......... 75.00
    No. 8, Third Pursuit Squadron, black, white, red on gray triangle ........................................... 75.00
Ping Pong Paddle, set of four....... 35.00
Playing Cards, "It's The Real Thing," 1971 ........................................... 8.00
Pocket Knife, black, smooth handle, case in shape of Coca-Cola bottle, "Coke" engraved on each side ........................................... 200.00
Pocket Mirror, 2-3/4" oval, World War I Girl, 1917 ............................... 210.00
Post Card, 5-1/2" x 6-1/2" perforated cardboard sheets, lower half of back side for "Occupant," rest of address unused, red and dark green carton with white and fleshtone hand, upper half of card front with full color "Take home a carton" with young lady, lower half pictures full color six bottle carton, coupon for six free bottles and deposit of 12 cents, local sponsor Coca-Cola Bottling Works, Fort Wayne, IN, late 1930s, price for pr ........................................... 40.00
Poster, girl preparing to ice skate, copyright 1940, well worn ............ 105.00
Pretzel Dish, aluminum, c1938..... 45.00
Punchboard, 7" x 8", 1940s, unused ........................................... 8.00
Radio, bottle shape, MIB ............ 45.00
Salt and Pepper Shakers, pr, red, white logo, tin can-shape, unpunched holes, 1970s, MIB .................. 25.00
Sheet Music, *The Coca-Cola Girl,* 1927 ......................................... 145.00
Sign
    1-1/2" h, 28" l, porcelain, "Drink Coca Cola Fountain Service," some chipping and scratching ............. 225.00
    16-1/4" h, 5" w, diecut porcelain, bottle shape .............................. 160.00
Six Pack, full, 1993 Maine Black Bears, National Hockey Champs, Ltd., only sold in Maine ......................... 20.00
Thimble, aluminum ..................... 25.00
Tip Tray, Exposition Girl ............. 325.00
Toy
    Delivery Truck, Matchbox No. 38, 1958 ...................................... 60.00

**Tie Bar, All Star Dealer Campaign Award, 1950s, $32.**

Soda fountain dispenser, plastic, four miniature glasses............ 135.00
Tray
   Glass, square, International, 1967
   .................................................. 95.00
   Metal
      Boy eating sandwich, Rockwell
      .............................................. 220.00
      Girl preparing to ice skate, 1940
      .............................................. 130.00
      Hand pouring Coke into glass, "Coke Refreshes You Best," 1961
      ................................................ 10.00
      Menu Girl, 1950.................. 55.00
Uniform Patch, "Enjoy Coke" ......... 3.00
Whistle, litho tin, red, yellow, and black, "The Pause That Refreshes," 1930s
............................................. 100.00

# Cocktail Memorabilia

Collecting Hints: Concentrate on cocktail shakers that are style statements of their era. Make aesthetics, line, form, and materials principal focus points. A collection numbering in the hundreds can be built around examples of the streamlined-modern style.

Run your fingers around the edge of glass objects to check for chipping. A small chip reduces the price by a minimum of 30%. Shakers with brilliant sharp colors are more desirable than those made of clear glass.

Figural shakers are in a class of their own. Among the more common forms are bowling pins, dumbbells, golf bags, and penguins. Shakers based on the designs of Norman Bel

Geddes often command in excess of $500.

**History:** The cocktail shaker traces its origins as far back as 7000 B.C. and the South American jar gourd, a closed container used to mix liquids. The ancient Egyptians of 3500 B.C. added spices to fermented grain—perhaps history's first cocktails. Alcoholic drinks have been a part of recorded history into the modern era.

By the late 1800s, bartenders used a shaker as a standard tool. Passing the liquid back and forth between two containers created a much appreciated show.

The modern cocktail shaker arrived on the scene in the 1920s, when martinis were in vogue. Shapes tended to be stylish, and materials ranged from glass to sterling silver. Perhaps nothing symbolizes the Jazz Age more than the flapper dress and cocktail shaker. When Prohibition ended in 1933, the cocktail shaker enjoyed another surge of popularity.

Movies helped popularize the cocktail shaker. William Powell showed a bartender how to mix a proper martini in "The Thin Man," a tradition continued by James Bond in the 007 movies. Tom Cruise's portrayal of a bartender in "Cocktail" helped solidify the collecting interest in cocktail shakers during the 1980s.

Following World War II, a bar became a common fixture in many homes. Every home bar featured one or more cocktail shakers and/or cocktail shaker sets. Chrome-plated stainless-steel shakers replaced the sterling-silver shakers of the 1920s and 1930s. Major glass companies, such as Cambridge, Heisey, and Imperial, offered cocktail shakers.

Life in the fabulous '50s was filled with novelties; cocktail shakers were no exception. Figural and other forms of novelty shakers appeared.

The electric blender and ready-mix cocktail packets ended the reign of the cocktail shaker, and showmanship was replaced by button pushing.

**Reference:** Stephen Visakay, *Vintage Bar Ware*, Collector Books, 1997.

Bottle Stopper, figural
   Kissing Couple ....................... 25.00
   Man, tips hat ........................... 25.00
   Man, pop-up head .................. 40.00
Cocktail Shaker Figure, Go-Go Girl, MIB
............................................... 75.00
Cocktail Set
   Art Deco style, glass shaker, six tall glasses, five shorter glasses, stippled frosted surface, gold and colored mid bands, 1950s............ 65.00
   Farber Brother, 2 amber, 2 green, and 2 smoke cocktail glasses
   .............................................. 60.00
Cocktail Shaker
   Aluminum, hand wrought, straight sides, grooved Modernistic top, clear plastic knob lid, Buenilum
   .............................................. 25.00

Glass
Cambridge, Diane pattern, clear, matching glass top........... 145.00
Crackle Glass, MacBeth Evans, crystal................................24.00
New Martinsville, Moondrops, green, handle, top missing
............................................20.00
Sportsman Series, cobalt blue, white image, ship dec.........80.00
Cordial Set
Central Glass Co., Balda Orchid pattern, decanter, six matching cordial glasses....................................375.00
Farber Brothers, chrome plate, 7 pc set
........................................................55.00
Cup, Chase Chrome, Blue Moon
........................................................99.00
Decanter, orig stopper, glass
Bohemian, octagonal, clear with greenish tint, engraved forest and deer scene...........................100.00
Duncan Miller, First Love, 32 oz
............................................295.00
Farber Ware, Mandarin gold, 32 oz, 3400/92......................................60.00
Fostoria, American pattern, 24 oz, 9-1/2" h......................................100.00
Imperial, Cape Cod, etched "Rye"
........................................................70.00
Decanter Set, Czechoslovakian, figural owl decanter, four matching cups, blue ground, painted eyes.....200.00
Hors d'oeuvre Pick
Fruit, set of twelve ....................20.00
Man, top hat...............................3.50
Ice Bucket
Aluminum, hand wrought
Buenilum, ridged band handles, ring finial.............................20.00
Lehman, double twisted handles, plastic knob.........................18.00
Glass
Cambridge, Apple Blossom, amber..................................30.00
Duncan Miller, Canterbury, clear
............................................35.00
Fostoria, Baroque, yellow
............................................125.00
Imperial Glass, Cape Cod, clear
............................................125.00
Jewelry, pin and earrings set, large martini glass with olive, silvertone earrings with open-work, 1960s
........................................................35.00
Liquor Set
7" h golf club, shot glass on each end, one holds 1 oz, other 2 oz, golf ball cork screw, 6-1/4" bottle and can opener iron, 9" stirrer iron, orig box with red felt lining, unused.......20.00
14" h, marbleized plastic bowling ball container, chrome dispenser, shot glasses trimmed with red, green, or blue glass rings, gilded metal figural finial....................75.00
Martini Pitcher, Duncan Miller, First Love
........................................................165.00
Martini Set
James Bond, 32 oz stainless steel martini shaker, James Bond silhouette logo, two 8 oz martini glasses with satin etched 007 gun logo,

**Magazine Tear Sheet, Crockery and Glass Journal, April, 1933, "Here's Lookin' Atcha!," adv for Lewis and Conger, NY, black and white, $4.**

United Artist exclusive set, MIB
............................................................70.00
Rooster dec, martini pitcher, four matching tumblers, clear, red and black rooster dec....................35.00
Old Fashioned Tumbler, Fostoria, Coin, crystal ......................................35.00
Pilsner, Old Sandwich, Heisey, 10 oz, Moongleam green....................45.00
Shot Glass, Russel Wright, Theme Formal, ....................................................300.00
Stemware, glass
Champagne, Fostoria, Romance, crystal ......................................22.50
Cocktail, Fostoria, June, rose pink
............................................................65.00
Cordial, Cambridge, Caprice, crystal
............................................................10.00
Cordial, Heisey, Banded Flute, crystal ......................................................100.00
Goblet, Dancing Nymph, French Crystal......................................90.00
Wine, Heisey, Lariat, Moonglow cutting ......................................................35.00
Wine, Tiffin, Flanders, mandarin
............................................................40.00
Swizzle Stick, glass
Advertising, colored..................3.50
Amber .........................................1.50
Black ...........................................2.00
Christmas, set of six.................25.00
Man, top hat...............................3.50
Souvenir, Hotel Lexington, amethyst, 1939 World's Fair ....................20.00
Spatter knob, clear stirrer .........1.00
Toddy Mixer, crystal, green, 12 oz
............................................................24.00
Tom and Jerry Set
Fostoria, American pattern, bowl and eight mugs ................................340.00

Hall China, black, ftd bowl, eighteen 5 oz cups .............................240.00
Tray, 11" d, tin, red, black, and white, martini center, card border......55.00
Tumbler
Cambridge, Chantilly, crystal... 30.00
Crackle Glass, 5-1/4" h, orange
............................................................20.00
Duncan Miller, Terrace, red......37.50
Fostoria, June, yellow, ftd ........32.50
Heisey, New Era, ftd, 12 oz......25.00
Sportsman Series, cobalt blue, white windmill dec, 12 oz..................27.50
Whiskey
Duncan and Miller, amethyst, 1 oz
............................................................15.00
Farber Ware, 3400/92, amethyst, 2 oz, price for 6 pc set ............55.00
Fostoria, June, ftd, yellow ........75.00
Heisey, Yeoman, Sahara yellow
............................................................15.00
New Martinsville, Moondrops, cobalt blue...............................................20.0
Tiffin, Classic, 2 oz..................75.00

# Coloring Books

**Collecting Hints:** Look for coloring books in very good condition. Some collectors will pay a premium for unused coloring books.

**History:** Coloring books have made for decades, dating back to the early 1900s. These simple books offered children many happy hours of fun and could be purchased for a few pennies. Today the art of the coloring book is capturing the eye of many collectors, some for the illustrations, others because it connects with another collecting area, like cartoon or television characters.

Alvin and the Chipmunks, 1960s... 18.00
Astro Boy, unused ........................75.00
Banana Splits ...............................48.00
Battlestar Galactic, set ................75.00
Beetle Bailey.................................25.00
Ben Casey ....................................20.00
Ben Hur .........................................20.00
Black Hole, Whitman, Walt Disney Productions, 1979, unused ............6.00
Bob Hope, oversized....................25.00
Brenda Starr .................................25.00
Car 54 Where Are You, unused ....60.00
Catianooga Cats...........................25.00
Chilly Willy, unused ......................40.00
Choo Choo, Top Cat, unused.......45.00
Dick Van Dyke Show, unused.......75.00
Family Affair, Whitman, 1969 ........48.00
Frankenstein Jr. ...........................38.00
Gilligan's Island ...........................65.00
Hanna Barbera Sampson and Goliath
............................................................30.00
Happy Hooper...............................25.00
Julia ..............................................20.00
Kong ..............................................30.00
Krazy Kat ......................................25.00
Laugh-In ........................................20.00

**Walt Disney Productions' The Black Hole**, Whitman, ©1979, used, $3.

Leave It To Beaver ........................ 40.00
Muskie, Deputy Dwag .................. 25.00
My Mother The Car ....................... 30.00
Raggedy Ann, 1945 ...................... 28.00
Range Rider, Lowe, 1956, Jack
    Mahoney .................................. 40.00
Roger Ramjet ............................... 30.00
Sgt. Bilko, unused ........................ 60.00
Sigmund and the Sea Monsters ..... 42.00
Space 1999, Saalfield, 1975, unused
    .............................................. 20.00
Superboy, 1960s .......................... 25.00
Terry and the Pirates, Saalfield, 1940s
    .............................................. 75.00
Thunderbirds ............................... 30.00
Top Cat ....................................... 25.00
Wizard of Oz, Whitman, 1975, some
    pages colored .......................... 15.00
Woodsy Owl ................................. 15.00

# Comic Books

**Collecting Hints:** Remember, age does *not* determine value! Prices fluctuate according to supply and demand. Collectors should always buy comic books in the best possible condition. While archival restoration is available, it's frequently costly and may involve a certain amount of risk.

Comic books should be stored in an upright position away from sunlight, dampness, and insect infestations. Avoid stacking comic books because the weight of the uppermost books may cause acid and oils to migrate. As a result, covers on books near the bottom of the stack may become stained with material that is difficult or impossible to remove.

Golden Age (1939-1950s) Marvel and D.C. first issues and key later issues continue to gain in popularity, as do current favorites such as Marvel's X-Men and D.C.'s New Teen Titans.

**History:** Who would ever believe that an inexpensive, disposable product sold in the 1890s would be responsible for a current multimillion dollar industry? That 2¢ item—none other than the Sunday newspaper—has its modern counterpart in flashy comic books and related spin-offs.

Improved printing techniques helped 1890s newspaper publishers change from a weekly format to a daily one that included a full page of comics. The rotary printing press allowed the use of color in the "funnies," and comics soon became the newest form of advertising.

It wasn't long before these promotional giveaways were reprinted into books and sold in candy and stationery stores for 10¢ each. They appeared in various formats and sizes, many with odd shapes and cardboard covers. Others were printed on newsprint and resembled the comic books sold today. Comics printed prior to 1938 have value today only as historical artifacts or intellectual curiosities.

From 1939 to 1950, comic book publishers regaled readers with humor, adventure, Western, and mystery tales. Super heroes such as Batman, Superman, and Captain America first appeared in books during this era. This was the "Golden Age" of comics—a time for expansion and growth.

Unfortunately, the bubble burst in the spring of 1954 when Fredric Wertham published his book *Seduction of the Innocent*, which pointed a guilt-laden finger at the comic industry for corrupting youth, causing juvenile delinquency, and undermining American values. This book forced many publishers out of business, while others fought to establish a "comics code" to assure parents that comics complied with morality and decency mores. Thus, the "Silver Age" of comics is marked by a decline in the number of publishers, caused by the public uproar surrounding Wertham's book and the increased production costs of an inflationary economy.

The period starting with 1960 and continuing to the present has been marked by a resurgence of interest in comic books. Starting with Marvel's introduction of "The Fantastic Four" and "The Amazing Spiderman," the market has grown to the extent that many new publishers are now rubbing elbows with the giants and the competition is keen!

Part of the reason for this upswing must be credited to that same inflationary economy that spelled disaster for publishers in the 1950s. This time, however, people are buying valuable comics as a hedge against inflation. Even young people are aware of the market potential. Today's piggy-bank investors may well be tomorrow's Wall Street tycoons.

**References:** Mike Benton, *Comic Book in America*, Taylor Publishing, 1993; —, *Crime Comics*, Taylor Publishing, 1993; —, *Horror Comics*, Taylor Publishing, 1991; —, *Science Fiction Comics*, Taylor Publishing, 1992; —, *Superhero Comics of the Golden Age*, Taylor Publishing, 1992; —, *Superhero Comics of the Silver Age*, Taylor Publishing, 1992; *Comic Buyer's Guide*, Krause Publications, 1996; Maurice Horn (ed.), *World Encyclopedia of Comics*, Chelsea House, out of print; Dick Lupoff and Don Thompson (eds.), *All in Color for a Dime,* Krause Publications, 1997; Robert M. Overstreet, *Overstreet Comic Book Price Guide*, 29th ed., Avon Books, 1999; Maggie Thompson and Brent Frankenhoff, *1997 Comic Book Checklist & Price Guide*, 3rd ed., Krause Publications, 1996; Stuart W. Wells, III, *Science Fiction Collectibles: Identification & Price Guide*, Krause Publications, 1999.

**Periodicals:** *Comic Book Market Place*, P.O. Box 180900, Coronado, CA 92178; *Comic Buyers Guide*, 700 E. State St., Iola, WI 54990; *Comic Scene*, 475 Park Ave., New York, NY 10016; *Duckburg Times*, 3010 Wilshire Blvd. #362, Los Angeles, CA 90010; *Overstreet Comic Book Marketplace*, 801 20th St. NW, Ste. 3, Cleveland, TN 37311; *Overstreet's Advanced Collector*, 801 20th St. NW, Ste. 3, Cleveland, TN 37311; *Western Comics Journal*, 143 Milton St., Brooklyn, NY 11222.

**Collectors' Club:** Fawcett Collectors of America & Magazine Enterprise, Too!, 301 E. Buena Vista Ave., North Augusta, SC 29841.

**Videotape:** *Overstreet World of Comic Books,* Overstreet Productions and Tom Barker Video, 1994.

**Museum:** Museum of Cartoon Art, Rye, NY.

**Reproduction Alert:** Publishers frequently reprint popular stories, even complete books, so the buyer must pay strict attention to the title, not just the portion printed in outsized letters on the front cover. If there's ever any doubt, look inside at the fine print on the bottom of the inside cover or first page. The correct title will be printed there in capital letters.

Buyers also should pay attention to the size of the comic they purchase. Many customers recently have been misled by unscrupulous dealers. The comics offered are exact replicas of Golden Age D.C. titles which normally sell for thousands of dollars. The seller offers the large, 10-by-13-inch copy of Superman #1 in mint condition for $10 to $100. The naive collector jumps at the chance since he knows this book sells for thousands on the open market. When the buyer gets his "find" home and checks further, he discovers that he's paid way too much for the treasury-sized "Famous First Edition" comic printed in the mid-1970s by D.C. These comics originally sold for $1 each and are exact reprints except for the size. Several came with outer covers which announced the fact that they were reprints, but it didn't take long for dishonest dealers to remove these and sell the comic at greatly inflated prices.

**Notes:** Just like advertising, comic books affect and reflect the culture which nurtures them. Large letters, bright colors, and pulse-pounding action hype this product. Since good almost always triumphs over evil, many would say comics are as American as mom's apple pie. Yet there's truly something for every taste in the vast array of comics available today. There are underground (adult situation) comics, foreign comics, educational comics, and comics intended to promote the sale of products or services.

The following listing concentrates on mainstream American comics published between 1938 and 1985. Prices may vary from region to region due to excessive demand in some areas. Prices given are for

comic books in fine condition; that is, comics that are like-new in most respects, but may show a little wear. Comics should be complete; no pages or chunks missing.

| | |
|---|---|
| Action, #12, golden age, first Batman | 500.00 |
| Adventures Into The Unknown, #37 | 25.00 |
| Adventures Into Weird Worlds, #28 | 175.00 |
| After Dark, #8 | 30.00 |
| Airboy Comics, Vol. 8, #2 | 80.00 |
| Alice in Wonderland, #49 | 95.00 |
| All American Comics, #100, first Johnny Thunder | 125.00 |
| All American Men of War, DC, #19 | 65.00 |
| Amazing Adventures, Ziff Oavis, #4 | 30.00 |
| Annette's Life Story, Annette Funicello, #1100, Dell, 1960 | 80.00 |
| Astonishing, #33 | 25.00 |
| A-Team, Marvel, #2 | 25.00 |
| Baby Huey, Harvey, #14 | 8.00 |
| Beetle Bailey, Dell, #552 | 15.00 |
| Bewitched, #51 | 18.00 |
| Black Arrow, Classics Illustrated, 1946 | 28.00 |
| Black Beauty, #60 | 80.00 |
| Black Cat Mystery, #38 | 155.00 |
| Black Magic, Vol. 2, #5 | 160.00 |
| Blue Beetle, #49 | 75.00 |
| Blue Bolt Weird Tales, #114 | 70.00 |
| Bold Stories, #1 | 76.00 |
| Bugs Bunny Christmas Funnies, Dell, #3 | 20.00 |
| Bugs Bunny Vacation Funnies, Dell Giant, #4, glossy | 40.00 |
| Candy, #60 | 15.00 |
| Captain America, #30 | 200.00 |
| Captain Flight, #5 | 75.00 |
| Casper the Friendly Ghost, Harvey, #30 | 20.00 |
| Chamber of Chills, #15 | 135.00 |
| Cheyenne, #734 | 35.00 |
| Cisco Kid, Dell, #10 | 8.00 |
| Crime & Punishment, #89 | 20.00 |
| Crime Does Not Pay, #102 | 14.00 |
| Crime Reporter, #2 | 100.00 |
| Crimes by Women, #54 | 150.00 |
| Colt 45 | 20.00 |
| David Copperfield, #48 | 50.00 |
| Detective Comics, #140 | 150.00 |
| Dick Tracy, Harvey, #86 | 18.00 |
| Doctor Solar, Dell, #9 | 25.00 |
| Donald Duck, Dell, #31 | 12.00 |
| Eerie, #15 | 50.00 |
| Elmer Fudd, Dell, #558 | 8.00 |
| Fantastic Fears, #7 | 370.00 |
| Felix the Cat, #4 | 18.00 |
| Fighting America, #3, glossy | 220.00 |
| Fighting Fronts, Harvey, #5 | 8.00 |
| Forbidden Worlds, #29 | 20.00 |
| Gene Autry, Dell, #85 | 8.00 |
| Goofy, Dell, #562 | 19.00 |
| Green Mansions, #90 | 20.00 |
| Gypsy Colt, Dell, #568 | 12.00 |
| Hector Heathcote, #1 | 25.00 |
| Hopalong Cassidy, DC, #88 | 30.00 |
| Ivanhoe, Classics Illustrated | 20.00 |

| | |
|---|---|
| Jace Pearson of the Texas Rangers, Dell, #6 | 12.00 |
| Jet Fighters, #5 | 15.00 |
| Jetsons, #1 | 40.00 |
| Johnny Mack Brown, Dell, #618 | 35.00 |
| Journey Into Fear, #4 | 190.00 |
| Jungle #78 | 50.00 |
| Konga, #16 | 30.00 |
| Law Breakers Suspense, #11 | 100.00 |
| Lawman, #1035 | 20.00 |
| Little Iodine, Dell, #15 | 5.00 |
| Little Lulu, French | 15.00 |
| Lone Ranger, French | 35.00 |
| Lone Ranger's Famous Horse, Hi Yo Silver, Dell, #10 | 12.00 |
| Looney Tunes/Merry Melodies, Dell, #139 | 6.00 |
| Love Confessions, #47 | 10.00 |
| Love Secrets, #48 | 10.00 |
| Magnus Robot Fighter, Dell, #5 | 55.00 |
| Man From U.N.C.L.E., Dell, #9 | 35.00 |
| Manhunt, #14 | 100.00 |
| Man in Iron Mask, Classics Illustrated, #54 | 10.00 |
| Mannix, French | 25.00 |
| Marvel Tales, #112 | 230.00 |
| Maverick, #945 | 20.00 |
| Mickey Mouse Birthday Party, Dell, #1 | 25.00 |
| Mighty Samson, Dell, #8 | 10.00 |
| Moby Dick, Classics Illustrated, #5 | 45.00 |
| Murder Inc., #1 | 75.00 |
| Mysteries Weird & Strange, #6 | 18.00 |
| Mystery Comics, #2G | 40.00 |
| Mystery in Space, DC, #3 | 130.00 |
| Mystic Tales, #7 | 80.00 |
| Navy Combat, #14 | 30.00 |
| Oregon Trail, Classics Illustrated, #72 | 16.00 |
| Our Army At War, DC, #4 | 90.00 |
| Perfect Crime, #30 | 50.00 |
| Peter Panda, DC, #5 | 25.00 |
| Phantom Lady, #22 | 125.00 |
| Popeye, Dell, #29 | 22.00 |
| Porky Pig, Dell, #285 | 10.00 |
| Prairie, #58 | 70.00 |
| Punch, #12 | 100.00 |
| Quest of Zorro, Dell, #617 | 60.00 |
| Rangers, #14 | 75.00 |
| Real Heroes, #2 | 75.00 |
| Rex Allen, Dell, #2 | 80.00 |
| Rifleman | 15.00 |
| Rin Tin Tin, Dell, #12 | 15.00 |
| Rootie Kazootie, Dell, #4 | 12.00 |
| Rusty Riley, Dell, #554 | 8.00 |
| Scoop, #2 | 125.00 |
| Sea Wolf, Classics Illustrated, #85 | 10.00 |
| Sharp Comics, #2 | 75.00 |
| Silver Streak, #7 | 250.00 |
| Song of Hiawatha, #57 | 70.00 |
| Starling, #40 | 75.00 |
| Strange Adventures, DC, #13 | 45.00 |
| Strange Fantasy, #11 | 25.00 |
| Strange Stories of Suspense, #6 | 135.00 |
| Summer Love, #47 | 45.00 |
| Superman, #61 | 125.00 |
| Swiss Family Robinson, #42 | 10.00 |
| Tarzan, Dell, #113 | 10.00 |
| Tell It To The Marines, #7 | 5.00 |
| Terrific, #4 | 450.00 |
| The Texan, #12 | 100.00 |

**Tarzan #137, August 1963, Edgar Rice Burrough, K. K. Publications, $8.**

The Thing, #10 ............................. 315.00
Thrilling Crime, #49 ....................... 50.00
Tom & Jerry Summer Fun, Dell, #1
.................................................... 20.00
Tom Brown's School Days, #45 ..... 85.00
Tonto, Dell, #15 ............................... 6.00
Top Cat, #27 .................................. 20.00
Torchy, #1 .................................... 150.00
Thunder Agents, Dell, #17 ............ 27.00
Uncle Scrooge, Dell, #495 ............ 60.00
Underworld Crime, #7 .................... 75.00
Walt Disney Comics and Stories, Dell,
    #148 .......................................... 10.00
Wanted, #52 ................................... 50.00
War Birds, #2 ................................. 16.00
War Front, Harvey, #20 ................... 5.00
War Fury, #1 .................................. 50.00
War Stories, #3 ................................ 6.00
Western Stories, Classics Illustrated,
    #62 ............................................. 12.00
Weird Mysteries, #2 ....................... 75.00
Weird Tales of the Future, #7 ...... 125.00
Whack, #3 ...................................... 75.00
Wings, #85 ..................................... 90.00
Witches Tales, #24 ......................... 15.00
Wizard of Oz, Marvel, large format
.................................................... 35.00
Woody Woodpecker, Dell, #16 ....... 5.00
Worlds of Fear, #10 ...................... 100.00
Zane Grey's To The Last Man, Dell,
    #616 ............................................. 8.00

# Cookbooks

**Collecting Hints:** Look for books in good, clean condition. Watch for special interesting notes in margins.

**History:** Among the earliest American cookbooks are *Frugal Housewife or Complete Woman Cook* by Susanna Carter, published in Philadelphia in 1796, and *American Cookery* by Amelia Simmons, published in Hartford, Connecticut, in 1796. Cookbooks of this era were crudely written, for most cooks could not read well and measuring devices were not yet refined.

Collectible cookbooks include those used as premiums or advertisements. This type is much less expensive than the rare 18th-century books.

**References:** Bob Allen, *Guide to Collecting Cookbooks and Advertising Cookbooks*, Collector Books, 1990, 1995 value update; Linda J. Dickinson, *Price Guide to Cookbooks and Recipe Leaflets*, Collector Books, 1990, 1995 value update.

**Periodical:** *Cookbook Collectors' Exchange*, P.O. Box 32369, San Jose, CA 95152.

**Collectors' Club:** Cook Book Collectors Club of America, 231 E. James Blvd., P.O. Box 85, St. James, MO 65559.

*American Woman's Cook Book,* Ella Blackstone, Chicago, 1910, 384 pgs ............................................... 35.00
*Amy Vanderbilt's Complete Cookbook*, 1961, 811 pgs .......................... 15.00
*A Place Called Sweet Apple-Country Living & Southern Recipes*, Clestine Sibley, 1967, dj ........................ 10.00
*Blueberry Hill Menu Cookbook*, Elsie Masterson, Crowell, 1966, 1st printing, 373 pgs .............................. 7.50
*Cook's Tour of San Francisco*, Doris Muscatine, Scribners, 1963, lower back edge bumped ................... 9.50
*Forty Delightful Ways to Serve*, Green & Green Co., Dayton, OH, 1928, 16 pgs, 5" x 7" .............................. 9.00
*Gebhardt's Mexican Cookery for American Homes,* San Antonio, TX, 1932, 35 pgs, 4-5/8" x 7-1/4" .............. 11.00
*Lorain Cooking*, American Stove Company, 1930, 180 pgs .................. 9.00
*Luchow's German Festival Cookbook*, Gene & Fran Schoor, Doubleday, 1976, 1st edition, some edge wear, rubbed, light soil ........................ 9.50
*Magic in Herbs*, Leonie de Sounin, Gramercy, 1941 ......................... 9.50
*Mastering the Art of French Cooking*, Julia Child, 1961, 14th printing ................................................... 15.00
*Maxwell House, How to Make Good Coffee*, 1931, black and white illus ................................................... 12.00
*Midwestern Home Cookery, Suggested Recipes by L. Szathmary*, Promontory Press, 1974 ...................... 11.50
*Mrs. Miller's Amish Cook Book, Favorite Recipes From the Family of Miller's Home Cooking*, Berlin, OH, Dutch Home Products, 1973, 111 pgs
.................................................... 7.50

**Hershey's Recipes, Hershey Chocolate Corp., Hershey, PA, 32 pgs, 1949, 4-5/8" x 6-1/2", $7.50.**

*Mrs. Rorer's Philadelphia Cook Book, Mrs. S T Rover*, Arnold & Co., 1885, 1st edition, 8vo, 581 pgs, 16 pgs of ads ............................................. 20.00
*My Better Homes & Gardens Cook Book*, Meredith Publishing, 1935, 10th printing, tabs ...................... 7.00
*The Art of Creole Cookery*, Wm. Kaufman & Sister Mary Ursula Cooper, illus by Margot Tomes, Double Day, 1962, 1st edition, sgd by Sister Mary ................................................... 10.00
*The Blender Cookbook*, Seranne & Gaden, Doubleday, 1961, 288 pgs, dj ............................................... 5.00
*The California Heritage Cookbook*, Jr. League of Pasadena, Double Day, 1976 ............................................. 8.50
*The Chef's New Secret Cookbook*, Louis Szathmary, Hen Regmery, 1975, dg, some wear ................. 9.00
*The Cookie Cookbook*, Deloris K. Clem, Castle Books, 1966, slight edge wear ........................................... 11.50
*The Cookie Jar*, Josephine Perry, Gramercy, 1951, some edge wear ..................................................... 9.50
*The Home Book of French Cookery*, Mme Germaine Carter, Doubleday, 1950, some edge wear ............ 11.50
*The Poultry Cookbook*, Southern Living Cookbook Library, 1977, 192 pgs ..................................................... 9.50
*The Rocky Mountain Cookbook*, Menus & Recipes for a Hearty Country Cuisine, Connie Chesnel, Clarkson Potter, 1989, 1st edition, dg .......... 10.00
*The Soup and Sandwich Handbook*, Campbell Soups, thermal mug on cover, 1971 ............................. 12.00
*The White House Chef Cookbook*, Rene Verdon, 1968 ............................ 7.50
*The Wide, Wide World of Texas Cooking*, Morton G. Clark, Bonzana, 1970 ................................................... 11.50

# Cookie Cutters, Plastic

**Collecting Hints:** Plastic cookie cutters have become quite popular with collectors in recent years, as have other kitchen plastics. Plastic cookie cutters were mass produced in the thousands, and older examples are still available at reasonable prices. Popularity of certain cutters has driven up prices, but wise collectors should be patient in their search for Peanuts, Walt Disney, and other popular themes.

Many companies produced cookie cutter sets with anywhere from four to 12 pieces. Complete sets demand higher prices, but collectors can usually piece together the set at a reasonable cost. Collectors often specialize in various categories such as Hallmark or other manufacturers.

Cutters made by Educational Products, better known as HRM because of their mark, are quite prevalent and popular. The company continues to produce clear red plastic cutters in 150 different shapes. Some shapes have been discontinued, and older cutters cannot be distinguished from newer ones in the same shape. HRM also bought molds from other companies. The original cutters do not have the "HRM" mark and the handles differ. Current catalogs are available to help collectors identify objects (see **References**).

Collectors should concentrate on cutters with a manufacturer or copyright mark, and beware of those marked only "China," as they are hard to identify.

**History:** Plastic cookie cutters are predominantly made from Polystyrene, Styron, Acrylic, or Polypropylene, all of which were developed during the years between the late 1920s and early 1930s but were not used for kitchen items until the 1930s. The majority of cutters found today were made after 1950, and collectors are scooping up those dated as late as the 1970s. Older cutters were molded from hard plastic and are thus prone to cracks or chipping on the cutting edge. Also, most types of plastic scratch easily.

**References:** Cookie Craft, Educational Products annual catalogs (P.O. Box 295, Hope, NJ 07844);

Lee Stephenson and Byrna Fancher, *Guide to Hallmark Cookie Cutters*, published by authors (5909 Montebello, Haslett, MI 48840), n.d.; Phyllis S. Wetherill, *Cookie Cutters and Cookie Molds*, Schiffer Publishing, 1985 (out of print); Phyllis Whidden, *The HRM Book*, published by author (4286 Bond Ave., Holt, MI, 48842), n.d.

**Periodical:** *Cookies*, 9610 Greenview Lane, Manassas, VA 20109.

**Collectors' Club:** Cookie Cutter Collectors Club, 1167 Teal Rd. S.W., Dellroy, OH 44620.

**Reproduction Alert:** Discount and dollar stores sell cookie cutter sets marked "China" or "made in China" which may copy Hallmark or Wilton designs. One clue: the inside designs may not be as detailed. Some reproductions of HRM cutters have been made but the quality is not the same and colors may differ.

**Advisor:** Tina M. Carter.

| | |
|---|---|
| Avon, boy and girl, price for set | 10.00 |
| Bonny Ware, biscuit cutter, 2 sizes | 6.00 |
| Cabbage Patch Kids, Easy Bake, 3 pc set | 6.00 |
| Card Party Set, red-outlined cutters, boxed set | 10.00 |
| Donut and Cookie Cutter, 2 pc, red plastic | 4.50 |
| Gingerbread Boy | |
|   Betty Crocker, red | 3.50 |
|   Miller Co., 2 handles, MOC | 8.00 |
| Hallmark | |
|   Donald Duck, 1977 | 6.00 |
|   Football Player, 1983 | 5.00 |
|   Holly Hobbie, mid 1970s | 4.00 |
|   Mickey Mouse, 1977 | 6.00 |
|   Peanuts, mkd "United Features Syndicate," 1950s | 10.00 |
|   Raggedy Ann and Andy, mkd "Bobbs-Merrill" | 10.00 |
|   Snoopy, mkd "United Features Syndicate," 4 poses | 28.00 |
| HRM, Educational Products | |
|   Easter, set of 8, orig box | 15.00 |
|   Snowman, orig card | 3.00 |
|   Transparent red, crown mark | 1.00 |
| Hutzler | |
|   Circus Animals, c1960, orig package | 12.00 |
|   Set, 14 pcs, primary colors | 25.00 |
| Jell-O Jigglers, alphabet set, 1980s | 4.50 |
| KO, biscuit and cookie cutter, San Franciso, spring action, 2 pc cutter, green, white, or red | 10.00 |
| Loma, Ft. Worth, bell, transparent red, 1961 | 3.50 |
| McDonald's | |
|   Grimace, 1980 | 5.00 |
|   Ronald McDonald, 1980 | 5.00 |
| Pillsbury, Doughboy, white, dated 1989, still in production | 1.00 |
| Planters, Mr. Peanut, red or blue, 2 pc set | 18.00 |
| Stanley Products, various shapes, turquoise or wheat | 1.50 |
| Sun Giant, set of 3 sun cutters | 15.00 |
| Tupperware | |
|   Holiday set, 8 pcs, opaque red, mkd on handle | 5.00 |
|   Nested set, heart, flowers, biscuit | 3.00 |
| Wilton | |
|   Kittens, pink, 1990, 4 pc set | 6.00 |
|   Ninja Turtles, 1990, 4 pc set, orig package | 6.00 |
|   Twelve Days of Christmas, 12 pcs | 18.00 |

# Cookie Jars

**Collecting Hints:** It is not unusual to find two cookie jars made by the same company which have been decorated differently. These variations add some interest to cookie jar collections.

**History:** The date the first cookie was made is unknown. However, early forms of cookie jars can be found in several mediums, including glass and pottery. Perhaps it was the Depression that caused people to bake more cookies at home, coupled with the pretty Depression-era glass jars that created the first real interest in cookie jars. A canister, complete with matching lid, was made in the popular Kolorkraft line by Brush Pottery Company in Roseville, Ohio, in the 1920s. By embossing the word "Cookies" on it, the piece became one of the first such documented cookie jars. By 1931, McKee Glass Company, Jeannette, Pennsylvania, was advertising a cookie jar that consisted of a 5-1/2 inch with a lid, and by 1932, Hocking Glass was advertising a large glass jar with a wide screw-on metal lid. These products were additions to canister sets.

The clever figural jars so often associated with cookie jars were introduced by several companies during the early 1940s. Soon apples, animals, and comic characters were added to more colorful kitchens. Production of American cookie jars flourished until the mid- or late 1970s, when foreign competition became too great for several companies. However, a resurgence in the cookie jar collecting market has helped spur new companies to develop interesting jars, and production is starting to increase. As Americans fall in love with new characters, from "Sesame Street" to *Star Wars*, cookie jar manufacturers eagerly fill orders.

**References:** Fred and Joyce Herndon Roerig, *Collector's Encyclopedia of Cookie Jars*, Book I (1990, 1995 value update), Book II (1994), Book III (1998), Collector Books; Mike Schneider, *Complete Cookie Jar Book*, Schiffer Publishing, 1991; Mark and Ellen Supnick, *Wonderful World of Cookie Jars*, revised ed., L-W Book Sales, 1995; Ermagene Westfall, *Illustrated Value Guide to Cookie Jars* (1983, 1995 value update), Book II (1993, 1995 value update), Collector Books.

**Periodicals:** *Cookie Jar Express*, P.O. Box 221, Mayview, MO 64071; *Cookie Jarrin'*, RR #2, Box 504, Walterboro, SC 29488; *Crazed over Cookie Jars*, P.O. Box 254, Savanna, IL 61074.

**Collectors' Club:** Cookie Jar Collector's Club, 595 Cross River Rd., Katonah, NY 10536.

**Reproduction Alert:** Reproduction cookie jars are starting to plague the market. Oddly enough, it's not only the old cookie jars being reproduced. The cute blue Cookie Monster made by California Originals in 1970 has been copied. California Originals are clearly marked "©Muppets, Inc. 1970" along the base. Brayton Pottery's Mammy has been reproduced. Unmarked copies have been found in addition to well-made copies with a date on the bottom and new-looking decals on the apron. Other reproductions include American Bisque: Casper; Brush: elephant with an ice cream cone and Peter Pumpkin Eater; California Originals: Count and Cookie Monster; McCoy: Davy Crockett; Regal China: Davy Crockett; Robinson-Ransbottom: World War II soldier and Oscar.

### Abingdon Pottery

Jack-In-Box, ABC on front, incised mark "611" ...................................... 125.00
Money Sack ................................. 95.00

### Advertising

Cookie Bandit, Hallmark ............. 190.00
Keebler Tree House, Brush-McCoy ................................................. 100.00
Regency Insurance, Buick sedan, royal blue, Glenn Appleman ........... 800.00
Sid's Taxi, Glenn Appleman ........ 800.00

### American Bisque

Cat in a Basket, 12-1/2" h, chips inside rim ...................................... 40.00
Cowboy Boots ........................... 235.00

Churn Boy ................................. 225.00
Ernie ......................................... 95.00
Ice Cream Freezer ..................... 460.00
Milk and Cookies ....................... 225.00
Mr. Rabbit .................................. 185.00
Poodle, gold trim ....................... 275.00

### Avon

African Village ............................ 35.00
Spatter Bear .............................. 30.00
Townhouse, small, MIB ............... 15.00

### Brush

Bobby Baker .............................. 75.00
Clock ........................................ 185.00
Clown Bust, crazing ................... 375.00
Elephant, ice cream cone, gray body, purple jacket .......................... 610.00
Happy Bunny, heavy crazing ...... 250.00
Night Owl ................................... 75.00
Humpty Dumpty, cowboy hat ..... 350.00
Panda, black and white .............. 325.00

### California Originals

Koala on Stump ......................... 275.00
Seated Turtle .............................. 45.00
Tigger ....................................... 170.00
Winnie-the-Pooh ......................... 95.00
Woody Woodpecker ................. 1,200.00
**Cardinal**, French Chef .............. 225.00

### Certified International

Barney Rubble ............................ 65.00
Bugs Bunny ............................... 85.00
Christmas Bugs .......................... 95.00
Christmas Tweety, in stocking .... 125.00
Dino and Pebbles ....................... 65.00
Fred Flintstone ........................... 65.00
Talking Taz ................................. 95.00

### Clay Art

Humpty Dumpty .......................... 125.00
Toaster ...................................... 60.00
Wizard of Oz ............................... 90.00
**Cleminsons**, Card King, gold trim on hearts ................................. 400.00

### Doranne

Coca-Cola Bottle ....................... 150.00
Dragon ...................................... 275.00
Hound Dog, yellow ...................... 30.00
Mailbox ...................................... 90.00

### Enesco

Garfield ..................................... 90.00
Sugar Town General Store ........... 60.00

### Fitz and Floyd

Autumn Woods Rabbit ................. 70.00
Busy Bunnies Tree ..................... 145.00
Christmas Wreath Santa ............. 150.00
Cotton Tailors Hat Box ................ 95.00
English Garden Wheelbarrow ..... 145.00
Father Christmas ....................... 270.00
Herb Garden Rabbit .................... 95.00
Hydrangea Bears ...................... 150.00
Rocking Horse ........................... 265.00
Rose Terrace Rabbit .................... 80.00
Santa in airplane ....................... 195.00
Santa's Magic Workshop ........... 165.00
Sock Hoppers ........................... 290.00
Unicorn ...................................... 85.00
**Hall**, Gold Lace, Flareware, 9" h, gold trim, some rim chips ............... 50.00

### McCoy

Clyde Dog .................................. 165.00

**Morton Pottery Co., poodle, white, red and black dec, $30.**

Coffee Grinder, 10" h, some chips and age cracks .............................. 40.00
Football Boy ............................... 225.00
Friendship Space Ship ............... 165.00
Harley-Davidson Hog ................. 650.00
Hamm's Bear ............................. 300.00
Keebler Tree House .................... 750.00
Mammy ...................................... 90.00
Pepper, yellow ........................... 95.00
Raggedy Ann, mkd "USA 741" .. 150.00
Traffic Light ................................. 75.00
Woodsy Owl ............................... 325.00

### Metlox

Apple Barrel ............................... 75.00
Ballerina Bear ........................... 120.00
Chef Pierre ................................. 65.00
Cookie Bandit ............................ 215.00
Fido .......................................... 245.00
Francine ..................................... 95.00
Frosty ........................................ 65.00
Hen .......................................... 325.00
Hippo, gray ................................ 550.00
Mammy, polka dot dress ........... 450.00
Miss Cutie Pie ........................... 250.00
Mona-Monocionius Rose ........... 150.00
Panda Bear ................................. 95.00
Puddles, yellow coat ................... 35.00
Raggody Andy ........................... 165.00
Santa, head ............................... 600.00
Squirrel, pine cone ..................... 95.00
Tulip ......................................... 425.00
**Puriton**, intaglio ........................ 75.00

### Redwing Pottery

Dutch Girl, two shades of blue, cracked brown base, faded Redwing symbol and "Redwing Pottery, Hand Painted," 10-1/2" h, 6-3/4" w .................... 190.00
Friar Tuck, old nicks ................... 95.00

### Regal

Humpty Dumpty .......................... 300.00
Quaker Oats ............................... 150.00
Jim Beam, cylinder ...................... 90.00
Quaker Oats ............................... 145.00
**RRP CO**, Roseville, OH, Peter, Peter Pumpkin Eager, 9" w, 8" w, small flake on base in lid opening ........... 230.00

### Shawnee

Dutch Girl, mkd "USA," 11-1/2" h,
    7-1/2" w ................................... 200.00
Jill, 12" h, some age crazing, cracks, 2
    chips ....................................... 65.00
Mugsey ........................................ 475.00
Puss N Boots ............................... 275.00
Smiley, blue collar and black hooves
    ................................................. 270.00

### Treasure Craft

Bart Simpson, holding cookie ....... 75.00
Baseball ....................................... 75.00
Bird House .................................... 45.00
Cactus .......................................... 45.00
Dinosaur, large purple spots, gray
    body, blue spines, 11-1/2" h .... 65.00
Dorothy and Toto, Wizard of Oz, 1994
    ................................................. 350.00
Flop Ear Rabbit ............................ 50.00
Mickey Mouse ............................... 75.00
Noah's Ark .................................... 65.00
Peter Pumpkin Eater .................... 45.00
Pink Panther ................................. 175.00
Slot machine ................................. 125.00

### Twin Winton

Elf, Collector Series ..................... 175.00
Friar Tuck ..................................... 85.00
Gunfighter Rabbit, Collector Series
    ................................................. 250.00
Mother Goose, gray ..................... 165.00
Ranger Bear .................................. 45.00
**Vandor,** Popeye ......................... 410.00

### Warner Brothers

Bugs Bunny .................................. 40.00
Superman ...................................... 95.00
Sylvester & Tweety Bird ................ 40.00
Tweety on Flour Sack .................... 85.00
Yosemite Sam ............................... 35.00

# Coors Pottery

**Collecting Hints:** Coors Pottery collectors concentrate on cookie jars and the bright, solid-colored dinnerware lines made by the company in the tradition of Bauer and Homer Laughlin's Fiesta. Kitchen collectors focus on the company's utilitarian products.

Coors products were meant to be used; and, they were. Look for those pieces which still have bright and complete decorations. Add 10% if a period paper sales label is still attached.

**History:** J. J. Herold, a former designer and manager for companies such as J. B. Owens, Roseville Pottery, and Weller Pottery, moved to Golden, Colorado, late in the first decade of the 20th century. His experiments in making pottery from local clay attracted the attention of Adolph Coors, a brewery owner in the area. In 1910, Coors offered Herold the use of his abandoned Colorado Glass Works plant. Shortly thereafter, Herold founded the Herold China and Pottery Company for the purpose of making ovenproof china cooking utensils.

Herold left in January 1912 to work for Western Pottery Company in Denver. Coors and other stockholders kept the plant open and expanded its product line to include spark plugs and scientific wares. Herold Pottery also was known as the Golden Pottery. By 1914, a line of chemical porcelain products was available. Herold returned for a one-year stint as manager in 1915 and then left again to work for Guernsey Earthenware Company (Cambridge Art Pottery). An injunction prevented Guernsey from using formulas Herold had learned about while at Golden.

In 1920, the company's name legally became Coors Porcelain Company. The firm continued to concentrate on chemical, industrial, and scientific porcelain products. The household cooking line was trademarked "Thermo-Porcelain." A Thermo-Porcelain white hotel-ware line was developed, one result of which was Coors involvement in the manufacturer of dinnerware and other kitchen accessories.

In the 1930s, Coors introduced six colored, decorated dinnerware lines: Coorado, Golden Ivory, Golden Rainbow, Mello-Tone, Rock-Mount, and Rosebud Cook-N-Serve. The dinnerware had a high-gloss, colored glaze; vases tended to be matte glazed. When Prohibition ended in 1933, Coors also began making accessories for the tavern trade.

Dinnerware production stopped when the company switched to war-time production in 1941. When the war was over, the company did manufacture some ovenware, teapots, coffeemakers, beer mugs, ashtrays, and novelty items, but no dinnerware. Coffeemakers, ovenware, teapots, and vases were discontinued in the 1950s, mugs in the early 1960s, and ashtrays by the late 1970s.

Herman Coors, third son of Adolph Coors, founded the H. F. Coors Company at Englewood, California, in 1925. It was an entirely separate company from Coors Porcelain Company. H. F. Coors Company made hotel and institutional commercial pottery, dolls' heads, plumbing fixtures, and wall tiles.

**References:** Carol and Jim Carlton, *Colorado Pottery*, Collector Books, 1994; Robert H. Schneider, *Coors Rosebud Pottery*, published by author, 1984.

**Periodical:** *Coors Pottery Newsletter*, 3808 Carr Pl N., Seattle, WA 98103.

**Empire,** vase, green ................. 150.00

### Mello-Tone

Cereal Bowl, 6-1/2" d, coral pink .... 12.00
Cup and Saucer, spring green ..... 20.00
Gravy, attached underplate, azure blue
    ................................................. 25.00
Pitcher, 2 quart, coral pink ........... 30.00
Plate
    4" d, bread and butter, canary yellow
    ................................................. 9.00
    7" d, dinner, azure blue ........... 15.00
Platter, 15" l, oval, canary yellow .. 20.00
Vegetable Bowl, 9" d, spring green
    ................................................. 24.00

### Ram's Head

Bud Vase, white and green .......... 50.00
Vase, tan and green ..................... 60.00

### Rosebud

Baking Pan, green, large ............ 100.00
Bean Pot, D & F ............................ 40.00
Cake Plate, yellow ........................ 50.00
Casserole, 7" d, straight sided, rose
    ................................................. 70.00
Casserole, 7" d, straight sided, yellow,
    orig rack ................................... 85.00
Cookie Jar, banded ..................... 100.00
Cookie Jar, green ........................ 100.00
Custard, green .............................. 20.00
French Casserole, green ............... 80.00
Mixing Bowl
    5" d, green .............................. 60.00
    6" d, green .............................. 60.00
Pie Plate, green ............................ 80.00
Pitcher, cov, orange ................... 150.00
Plate
    6" d, bread and butter ............. 12.00
    7" d, salad .............................. 15.00
    9" d, dinner ............................. 20.00
Platter, green ................................ 60.00
Pudding Bowl, light rose .............. 75.00
Salt and Pepper Shakers, pr, table size,
    red ........................................... 50.00
Sugar Shaker, off-white .............. 250.00
Teapot, large, no lid, green ......... 100.00
Water Server, white, commemorative
    ................................................. 250.00
Water Server, with cap, green .... 200.00

# Cow Collectibles

**Collecting Hints:** Image is everything. It makes no difference if the object was made yesterday or 100 years ago, just so long as it pictures the collector's favorite bovine.

Cow collectors collect in quantity. Advertising and folk art collectors also vie for pieces displaying cow images.

Cow creamers, some dating as early as the 18th century, are a favorite specialized collecting category. Antiques devotees focus on early examples; most cow collectors are perfectly willing to settle for 20th-century examples.

In order for an object to be considered a true cow collectible, it must either be in the shape of a cow or have a picture of a cow on its surface. Milk- and dairy-related items without a cow image are not cow collectibles. T-shirts with cow sayings fall into a gray area.

**History:** The domesticated cow has been around for more than 8,000 years: cows are part of Greek mythology, the Egyptians worshipped Hathor the cow-goddess, and the Hindus still venerate the cow as a sacred being. Cows have long been a focal point for artists and sculptors.

Some of the more famous nursery rhymes feature a cow, e.g. "Hey, Diddle, Diddle" and "The House That Jack Built." Poetry and literature are rich with cow references.

It is impossible to divorce the cow from the dairy industry. Cow motifs appear throughout a wide range of dairy-product advertising, the three most popular images being the Guernsey, Holstein, and Jersey.

There are a number of famous 20th-century cows: early Disney cartoons featured Clarabelle; the dairy industry created Brooksie, Bossie, and *La Vache Qui Ri*; and, of course, there is Elsie. When she was at her peak of popularity, only the president of the United States had more public recognition than Elsie the Borden Cow. In the late 1930s, Elsie made her initial appearances in a series of medical journal advertisements for Borden's Eagle Brand condensed milk. Her popularity grew as a result of Borden's 1939-1940 World's Fair exhibition. A 1940 Hollywood appearance further enhanced her national reputation. In 1957, a name-Elsie's-calf contest produced three million entries. Borden briefly retired Elsie in the late 1960s, but the public demanded her return. Today she is once again found on labels, in animated commercials, and at live appearances across the country.

Alas, in this age of equality, the fabled bull receives short shrift. With the exception of Walt Disney's Ferdinand, the male of the species is relegated to a conspicuous second place.

**Reference:** Emily Margolin Gwathmey, *Wholly Cow!*, Abbeville Press, 1988.

**Periodical:** *Moosletter*, 240 Wahl Ave., Evans City, PA 16033.

Advertising Figure, Milka, hard plastic ................................................. 10.00
Bank, Nestle Nespray, figural, vinyl ................................................. 40.00
Blotter, 4" x 9-1/4", Cow Brand Baking Soda, cow illus, c1920 ............. 12.00
Booklet, Milk, An All-Round Food, Metropolitan Life Insurance, silhouettes on cov, c1930, 8 pgs ................. 3.00
Butter Print, wood, round
    4-1/2" d, standing cow, one piece turned handle, dark finish ...... 350.00
    5-1/4" d, cow with tree and flower, scrubbed white, one piece turned handle ................................... 175.00
Charm, 1" d, Swift's Brookfield, brass, emb cow on award base, inscribed "June Dairy Month Award," early 1900s ........................................ 17.50
Child's Book, *Bossy the Calf Who Lost Her Tinkle Bell*, G. A. Coke, McLoughlin, 1939 ................... 20.00
Cookie Jar, cov
    Cow Jumped Over The Moon, Doranne ................................. 250.00
    Elsie the Cow, Pottery Guild, late 1940s ..................................... 250.00
    Purple Cow, Metlox ................ 550.00
Figure, 3" x 5-1/2" x 4", Ferdinand, rubber, Seiberling, Walt Disney Enterprises copyright, c1930 ........... 85.00
Membership Pin, Guernsey 4-H Club, full color, plastic, c1940 ........... 15.00
Mug, 2-1/2" h, china, white, full color illus of Elsie, blue accent stripe, Juvenile Ware and Borden copyright, c1940 ...................................... 75.00
Pinback Button
    Guernsey's, yellow, brown, and white, c1930s .......................... 25.00
    Jerseys For Mine, A.J.C.C., multicolored scene, red rim, white lettering, c1920 ...................................... 55.00

**Pinback Button, Sharples Co., The Tubular Cream Separator, white ground, blue dress, 1-1/4" d, $24.**

Livestock Steer, blue and white, blue illus, 1901-12 .......................... 15.00
Sharples Cream Separators, multicolored, two young farm girls using product in pasture .................. 50.00
Whitings Milk, red, white, blue, gold circle accents around logo, 1930s ................................................. 20.00
Pitcher
    Black, glazed, orig sticker reads "Ellsworth" .............................. 35.00
    Stoneware, 8" h ..................... 240.00
Poster
    Bull Durham, 19-1/2" x 13-1/2", includes cow figure ............... 375.00
    Evaporated Milk-Pure Cow's Milk, black and white illus of cows, green ground, c1940 ...................... 25.00
    Swift's Annual Fertilizers, linen, dark blue steer illus and print, 1920s ................................................. 75.00
Ramp Walker, 3-1/2" l, plastic, brown and white, orig sealed cellophane bag, marked "Made in Hong Kong," 1950s ..................................... 15.00
Salt and Pepper shakers, pr, Elsie the Cow, head and shoulders ........ 85.00
Sugar, cov, figural, Elmer, c1940 ................................................. 40.00
Toy, Mozzy Moo-Moo, #190, MIB ................................................. 270.00

# Cowboy Heroes

**Collecting Hints:** Cowboy hero material was collected and saved in great numbers. Don't get fooled into thinking an object is rare—check carefully. Tom Mix material remains the most desirable, followed closely by Hopalong Cassidy, Roy Rogers, and Gene Autry memorabilia. Material associated with the Western stars of the silent era and early talking films still has not achieved its full potential as a collectible.

**History:** The era when the cowboy and longhorn cattle dominated the Great Western Plains was short, lasting only from the end of the Civil War to the late 1880s. Dime novelists romanticized this period and created a love affair in America's heart for the Golden West.

The cowboy was a prime entertainment subject in motion pictures. William S. Hart developed the character of the cowboy hero—often in love with his horse more than the girl. He was followed by Tom Mix, Ken Maynard, Tim McCoy, and Buck Jones. The "B" movie, the second feature of a double bill, was often of the cowboy genre.

In 1935, William Boyd starred in the first of the Hopalong Cassidy films. Gene Autry, "a singing cowboy," gained popularity over the airwaves, and by the late 1930s, Autry's Melody Ranch was a national institution on the air as well as on the screen. Roy Rogers replaced Autry as the featured cowboy at Republic Pictures in the mid-1940s. Although the Lone Ranger first starred in radio shows in 1933, he did not appear in movies until 1938.

The early years of television enhanced the careers of the big three—Autry, Boyd, and Rogers. The appearance of the Lone Ranger in shows made specifically for television strengthened the popularity of the cowboy hero. "Gunsmoke," "Wagon Train," "Rawhide," "The Rifleman," "Paladin," and "Bonanza" were just a few of the shows that followed.

By the early 1970s, the cowboy hero had fallen from grace, relegated to reruns or specials. In early 1983, the Library of Congress in Washington, D.C., conducted a major show on the cowboy heroes, perhaps a true indication that they are now a part of history.

**References:** Dana Cain, *Film & TV Animal Star Collectibles,* Antique Trader Books, 1998; Lee Felbinger, *Collector's Reference and Value Guide to the Long Ranger,* Collector Books, 1998; David R. Greenland, *Bonanza, A Viewer's Guide to the TV Legend,* R & G Publications (P.O. Box 605, Hillside, IL 60162); Ted Hake, *Hake's Guide to Cowboy Character Collectibles,* Wallace-Homestead, 1994; Jim Harmon, *Radio & TV Premiums,* Krause Publications, 1997; Jerrell Little, *Cowboy Cap Guns and Guitars,* L-W Book Sales, 1996; William Manns and Elizabeth Clair Flood, *Cowboys & The Trappings of the Old West,* Zon International Publishing Co., 1997; Rex Miller, *The Investor's Guide to Vintage Character Collectibles,* Krause Publications, 1999; Jim Schleyer, *Collecting Toy Western Guns,* Krause Publications, 1996; Neil Summers, *Official TV Western Book,* Vol. 1 (1987), Vol. 2 (1989), Vol. 3 (1991), Vol. 4 (1992), The Old West Shop Publishing.

**Periodicals:** *Collecting Hollywood,* American Collectors Exchange, 2401 Broad St., Chattanooga, TN 37408; *Cowboy Collector Newsletter,* P.O. Box 7486, Long Beach, CA 90807; *Favorite Westerns & Serial World,* Rte. 1, Box 103, Vernon Center, MN 56090; *Westerner,* Box 5232-32, Vienna, WV 26105.

**Collectors' Club:** Friends of Hopalong Cassidy Fan Club, 6310 Friendship Drive, New Concord, OH 43762.

**Museums:** Gene Autry Western Heritage Museum, Los Angeles, CA; National Cowboy Hall of Fame and Western Heroes, Oklahoma City, OK; Roy Rogers Museum, Victorville, CA.

**Additional Listings:** Western Americana.

### Annie Oakley

Comic Book, #1 ............................ 25.00
Dixie Cup Picture, Barbara Stanwyck ................................................ 50.00
Game, board, Milton Bradley ....... 45.00
Record, 45 rpm, mint in sleeve ..... 20.00

### Bonanza

Charm Bracelet, c1970s, six charms, gold colored metal, MIB .......... 35.00
Coloring Book, unused ................ 30.00
Gun Set, Marx ........................... 660.00
Magazine
    Parade .................................. 25.00
    Police Gazette ....................... 30.00
Playing Cards, shows orig cast, sealed deck of 54 cards, orig plastic box, 1970s ..................................... 18.00
Poster, Ponderosa, 22-1/2" x 17", c1967, facsimile autographs of cast.... 18.00
Sheet Music, pictures of 4 stars ... 42.00

### Buck Jones

BB Gun, 36", wood stock with printed sundial, metal side with name, metal compass insert, Daisy ............. 90.00
Better Little Book, *Buck Jones and The Two-Gun Kid,* Whitman, #1404, 1937 ................................................ 30.00
Big Little Book, *The Fighting Code,* #1104, Columbia Pictures, artists, Pat Patterson, author, 1934, 160 pgs, hard cover, soft spine ............. 35.00
Book
    *Rocky Rhodes,* Five Star Library Series, #15, Engel-Van Wiseman, Universal Pictures, artist, adapted by Harry Ormiston, 1935, 160 pgs, hard cover ....................................... 35.00

**Bonanza, game, Michigan Rummy, Parker Bros., $25.**

*Songs of the Western Trails,* 60 pgs, words and music, 9" x 12", 1940 copyright ................................. 40.00
Magazine, *Remember When Magazine,* 8-1/2" x 11", Jones on cov, story and black and white photos inside, 1974 ......................................... 7.50
Pinback Button, Bucks Jones Club, enamel on brass, horseshoe, picture in center, 1930s ................ 15.00

### Buffalo Bill

Cabinet Photo, 4-1/4" x 6-1/2", black and white close-up portrait, c1890 ................................................ 75.00
Figurine, 2-1/8", metal, Blenheim ................................................ 20.00
Show poster .............................. 700.00

### Cisco Kid

Album, bread label, Freihofer's, 16 labels, 1952 ........................... 320.00
Bowl ........................................... 40.00
Gun, premium, red, white, and blue cardboard, Cisco's picture on handle, clicker mounted inside, advertises TV show and Tip-Top Bread ................................................ 45.00
Ring, saddle .............................. 500.00
Snack Set, plate and mug ........... 50.00

### Davy Crockett

Bath Mat, chenille ....................... 50.00
Bib, paper, large .......................... 6.00
Doll, 22-1/2" h, plush, vinyl clothing, belt, and tag, "Official Frontierland Doll inspired by Walt Disney's Davy Crockett," c1950, Gund, hat missing ................................................ 45.00
Frontier Suitcase ......................... 60.00
Game, Davy Crockett Rescue Game, compass, 1955 ......................... 45.00
Lamp Shade, orig factory cello wrap ................................................ 150.00
Potato Chip Bag, Canadian .......... 75.00
Puzzle, frame tray, Fess Parker .... 35.00
Record, Crockett Meets Woody Woodpecker, 78 rpm. ....................... 125.00
Ring, compass, expansion band ................................................ 175.00
Sheet Music, Fess Parker, for accordion ................................................ 25.00
Shirt, boy's, unused, orig tags ...... 40.00
Tru-Vue Cards, MIP ..................... 60.00
Wrist Watch, arrows as hands, orig band ......................................... 85.00

### Gabby Hayes

Child's Book, *Jack In Box,* hardcover ................................................ 125.00
Coloring Book, 8" x 10-1/2", Magic Dial Funny coloring Book, diecut television screen opening in front with disk wheel, Samuel Lowe Co., c1950 ................................................ 50.00
Comic Book, Quaker Oats giveaway ................................................ 25.00
Dixie Cup Picture, color, Bill Elliott and Gabby ..................................... 50.00
Ring, cannon ............................ 185.00
Rocking horse ........................... 200.00

### Gene Autry

Gun and Holster set, cast iron.... 500.00
Lobby Card, Spanish ................... 30.00

**Davy Crockett, pocket knife, Fess Parker, Walt Disney, $25.**

Pennant, Gene Autry & Champ, from rodeo show, 1949.....................60.00
Souvenir Program, 20 pgs, c1950, five full page ads for Autry merchandise .................................................25.00
Sweater, child's .............................65.00

**Gene Autry, sheet music, *That Silver Haired Daddy of Mine,* MM Cole Publishing Co., 1932, $18.50.**

Writing Tablet ...............................55.00
**Gunsmoke**
Annual, 1975.................................45.00
Board Game, photo cover with James Arness, British.........................70.00
Comic Book, #720, 4-color ...........20.00
Doll, Matt Dillon, limited edition, MIB ................................................30.00
Hartland Figure, with horse, no accessories ......................................65.00
Little Golden Book, 1958 .............20.00
Magazine, TV Guide.....................25.00
Notepad, Amanda Blake, unused ................................................45.00
Pencil box, Hasbro, 1961 .............18.00

**Gunsmoke, book, authorized edition featuring Matt Dillion, written by Robert Turner, illus by Robert L. Jenney, Whitman, 1958, $20.**

**Hopalong Cassidy**
Bag, Jo Mar Ice Cream ...............50.00
Bedspread, chenille ...................100.00
Book
*Hopalong Cassidy Television Book,* 1950, glossy hardcover, mechanical dial moves images around small TV screen on cover, 30 page story, *Hoppy and Lucky at Copper Gulch,* full color photo on front and back ..............................................100.00
*Trail Dust,* A. L. Burt edition, dust jacket .......................................75.00
Chow Set, small, dish, plate, and glass ..............................................280.00
Comic Book, Bond Bread
The Mad Barber.......................80.00
The Strange Legacy ...............80.00

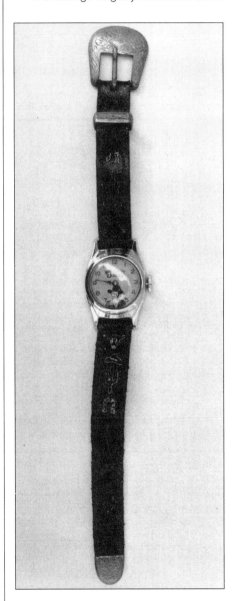

**Hopalong Cassidy, watch, black band with faded white designs, back inscribed "Good Luck from Hoppy, US Time," 8-1/2" l, worn, $125.**

Drinking Glass, black image, breakfast, lunch, dinner, each .................. 65.00
Ear Muffs, red ............................. 175.00
Game, board ................................... 75.00
    Hair Bow, girl's, hairpin, orig card
    ............................................. 100.00
Laundry Bag, plastic, orig container and product card ................. 850.00
Little Golden Book, *Hopalong Cassidy & Bar 20* ............................ 25.00
Lobby Card, *Mystery Man,* set of 8, mint in envelope ............................ 400.00
Lunch Box, red, cloud decal, no thermos .......................................... 150.00
Magazine
    Time ..................................... 120.00
    TV Guide, 1949 ..................... 250.00
Manual, Film Exploration .............. 50.00
Neckerchief Slide, steer head, red eyes
    ............................................... 55.00
Paperback Book, *Hopalong Cassidy Returns* ................................ 30.00
    Pencil Box, some orig contents
    ............................................. 100.00
Puzzle, frame tray ........................ 45.00
Record, double set
    *Hopalong Cassidy and the Singing Bandit* ............................... 55.00
    *Hopalong Cassidy and the Square Dance Hold Up* ..................... 55.00
Shooting Gallery, tin litho, 1950s, some wear ................................. 495.00
Sign, Hopalong Cassidy Rides Again, The Knickerbocker News, cardboard, 11" x 21" ..................... 225.00
Soap, Topper, Castile ................. 125.00
Spurs, Olympia ........................... 200.00
Thermos, yellow, no lid ................ 75.00
Wallet, child's, special agent pass
    ............................................... 45.00
Wallpaper Section, 3-1/2" x 18"
    ............................................. 175.00
Wrist Cuffs, small, black, pr ........ 220.00

### John Wayne

Arcade Card, c1950 ...................... 4.00
Clock Plaque, wooden ................. 45.00
Coin, metal, gold, c1979 ............... 7.50
Coloring Book, 11" x 15", 32 pgs, ten colored pages, Saalfield, #2354-15, 1951 copyright ..................... 50.00
Doll, Horse Soldier, Effanbee, MIB
    ............................................. 185.00
Holster Set, leather belt, two holsters with name on side, orig box, early 1950s ........................................ 45.00
Knife, memorial, metal and plastic, "The Duke--John Wayne (1907-1979)"
    ............................................... 10.00
Movie Still, 8" x 10", black and white
    ................................................. 4.00
Paper Dolls, 1980, unused .......... 30.00
Pinback Button, 2-1/2" d, In Memory of a Great American ..................... 5.00
Record Album, Horse Soldiers, soundtrack, 1959 ................... 50.00
Sheet Music, *Put Your Arms Around Me, Honey,* 9" x 12", 4 pgs, black and white photo, of Wayne, Martha Scott and Dale Evans, 1937 copyright
    ............................................... 15.00
Standee, cardboard .................... 35.00

### Ken Maynard

Autograph, 8" x 10" black and white glossy photo, black inked signature "Ken Maynard 1941" ............. 125.00
Big Little Book
    *Ken Maynard in Western Justice,* Whitman, #1430, Irwin Myers, artist, Rex Loomis, author, 1938, standard size, 432 pgs, hard cover ........ 22.00
    *Strawberry Roan,* Saalfield, Universal Pictures, artist, Grace Mack, author, 1934, 4-3/4" x 5-1/4", 160 pgs, hard cover ..................... 22.00
Premium, photo, 9" x 11", color, black and white "In Old Santa Fe" scenes on back, Dixie ......................... 30.00

**Kit Carson,** gun and holder set
    ............................................. 500.00

### Lone Ranger

Badge, deputy, secret compartment, secret folder ......................... 150.00
Belt, glow-in-the-dark ................. 85.00
Caps, repeating roll, 1940s, orig box of 20 rolls, MIB ......................... 35.00
Child's Outfit, red shirt, 1940s .... 100.00
Flashlight, pistol gun ................... 45.00
Game, horseshoes ...................... 75.00
Gun, pressed steel ...................... 60.00
Holster, double, no guns ............ 250.00
Insert, Bond Bread, 10¢ insert, uncut sheet, 1938 ............................ 85.00
Keychain, solid silver bullet ......... 65.00
Membership Kit, letter, certificate, card, orig mailer, Merita Bread, 1939
    ............................................. 125.00
Model, comic scenes, Aurora, MIB
    Lone Ranger ........................... 45.00
    Tonto, orig sealed box ............ 75.00
Ped-O-Meter ............................... 30.00
Pencil Sharpener, bullet shape, Merita Bread ...................................... 40.00
Photo, 8" x 10", color, Lone Range and Tonto, facsimile autograph of Clayton Moore ................................ 25.00
Ring
    Atomic Bomb ......................... 155.00
    Filmstrip Ring, orig papers and mailer ................................... 350.00
    Flashlight ring ....................... 110.00
    Gold Ore/Meteorite ............ 3,000.00
    Marine Corps, secret compartment
    ............................................. 500.00
    Weather, orig litmus paper ..... 350.00
Soap, Tonto, figural, Castile, c1940, MIB
    ............................................. 120.00
Star, tin, Merita Bread .................. 50.00
Toothbrush Holder, figural, 1930s
    ............................................. 115.00
Toy, litho tin, Marx, Lone Ranger riding Silver, MIB ............................ 725.00
Water Pistol, hard plastic, Durham, 1974, figural, MOC ................. 75.00

### Maverick

Eras-O Picture Book, 1960, unused, sealed, MIB ......................... 100.00
Magazine, TV Guide, James Garner cover ...................................... 30.00
**Rawhide,** television storybook, 1962
    ............................................... 60.00

### Red Ryder

BB Gun, Daisy, 50th Anniversary
    ............................................... 90.00
Pocket Knife ............................. 450.00

### Restless Gun

Book, Whitman, 1959 ................... 15.00
Comic, Dell, #1146 ...................... 20.00
Game, board ............................... 60.00

### Rin Tin Tin

Big Little Book, Rin Tin Tin & The Hidden Treasure ......................... 18.00
Comic Book, Dell, #12 ................. 15.00
Paint By Number, large ................ 60.00
Ring, magic, instructions ............ 450.00
Stuffed Toy, large ....................... 45.00
Wonda-Scope ............................. 85.00

### Roy Rogers

Autograph, 8" x 10" color photo
    Roy Rogers ............................ 55.00
    Roy Rogers and Dale Evans .... 65.00
Book, *Trigger to the Rescue* ......... 25.00
Camera, Herbert George Co., orig instructions, some damage to orig box ...................................... 250.00
Canteen Holder, gold lettering on suede
    ............................................... 95.00
Cereal Bowl, ceramic, 6-1/4" d ..... 85.00
Dixie Ice Cream Picture
    Dale Evans ............................. 50.00
    Roy Rogers, 1938 ................... 60.00
Gloves, pr ................................. 150.00
Lunch Box, thermos, metal, used
    ............................................... 75.00
Magazine Cover, Roy, Dale and Trigger, New York News, 1958 ............. 48.00
Membership Card, photo, Del Comics, orig mailer .......................... 210.00
Mug, Quaker Oats, head shape
    ............................................... 50.00
Pinback Button
    Bullet ..................................... 25.00
    Pat Brady ............................... 15.00
    Roy's Brands ......................... 20.00
    Roy's Guns ............................ 20.00
    Sheriff .................................... 20.00
    Trigger .................................... 25.00
Pocket Knife ............................. 100.00
Ring
    Branding Iron ........................ 225.00
    Hat, sterling .......................... 675.00
    Magnifying ............................ 120.00
    Microscope ........................... 125.00
    Saddle, silver ........................ 450.00
Tie Slide, metal, 2" l, 1950s ......... 30.00

### Straight Arrow

Ring
    Arrow ..................................... 65.00
    Face ....................................... 90.00
    Nugget Cave ......................... 200.00
**The Rebel,** postcard, Johnny Yuma, fan club ........................................ 40.00

### The Rifleman

Game, board ............................... 85.00
Magazine, Guns, Chuck Connors on cover, article ........................... 55.00
Notepad, cover photo of Connors and Crawford ................................ 45.00

## Tim McCoy

Autograph, 8" x 10" glossy black and white photo, purple inked signature "Best Wishes Tim McCoy," c 1940 ................................................ 75.00
Better Little Book, *Tim McCoy And The Sandy Gulch Stampedc*, Whitman, #1490, 1939 ............................. 40.00
Big Little book, *The Prescott Kid*, Whitman, #1152, Columbia Pictures, artist, adapted by Eleanor Packer, 1935, 4-5/8" x 5-1/4", 160 pgs, hard cover, soft spine ...................... 25.00
Lobby Poster, 11" x 14", set of 8, 1930s Fighting Renegade ............... 100.00
Straight Shooter ..................... 125.00
Premium, photo, 9" x 11", color, black and white movie scenes on back, Dixie ......................................... 15.00

## Tom Mix

Arrowhead, Lucite.......................... 85.00
Badge
  Straight Shooters, orig mailer
  ............................................... 150.00
  Wrangler's ............................. 150.00
Decoder Badge, Six Shooter, 1930s radio show premium .............. 150.00
Fob, gold ore ................................ 65.00
Manual, secret writing................. 100.00
Pocket Knife, Straight Shooters, slight use .......................................... 40.00
Ring
  Look Around, instructions, orig mailer ...................................... 225.00
  Magnet, 1930s Ralston Radio show premium ................................... 95.00
  Mystery Picture, photo missing
  ............................................... 75.00
  Siren, red TV film, instructions, orig mailer ..................................... 500.00
  Sliding whistle, 1930s Ralston Radio show premium....................... 135.00
  Straight Shooter ................... 100.00
Telescope and Bird Call, Golden Bullet
  ............................................... 75.00
Television Set, film, orig mailer.... 100.00

## Wagon Train

Magazine, Look, cast on cover..... 20.00
Target Game, English, illus box
  ............................................... 195.00

## Wild Bill Hickok

Game, Built-Rite............................ 45.00
Gun and holster, double ............. 500.00

## Wyatt Earp

Badge, Marshall's, illus of Hugh O'Brien on card, 1957 ............................ 40.00
Book, *Wyatt Earp, U. S. Marshall,* Stewart Holbrook, E. Richardson illus, Hale Landmark Books, Random House, 1956, 180 pgs................ 7.00
Hartland figure, 1958, played with condition ...................................... 100.00
Magazine, TV Guide .................... 18.00
Paint Box........................................ 35.00
Record, Wyatt Earp Sings, Hugh O'Brien........................................ 35.00
Shirt, child's.................................. 40.00

## Miscellaneous

Book, *Lone Cowboy, My Life Story,* Will James, Schribner, 1930, 1st edition, dj............................................. 100.00
Child's Outfit, Bat Masterson, size 4, unused, MIB.......................... 225.00
Cowboy Boot Box, child size, J. C. Penneys, 1950s............................ 48.00
Dixie Cup Picture, color, Smiley Burnett
  ............................................... 65.00
Pencil, pistol, card only, 1950....... 25.00
Holster and Belt, thigh tie, single
  ............................................... 200.00
Store Display, Mattel's Shootin Shells Bullets ................................... 85.00
Straight Razor, nickel inlay, cowboy on horse ...................................... 125.00
T-shirt Transfer, The Virginian........ 20.00
Whistle, 6" l, Fess Parker as Daniel Boone, Autolite, instructions on one side of box, late 1950s............. 15.00

# Cracker Jack

**Collecting Hints:** Most collectors concentrate on the pre-plastic era. Toys in the original packaging are very rare. One possibility for specializing is collecting toys from a given decade, for example World War II soldiers, tanks, artillery pieces, and other war-related items.

Many prizes are marked "Cracker Jack" or carry a picture of the Sailor Boy and Bingo, his dog. Unmarked prizes can be confused with gumball machine novelties or prizes from Checkers, a rival firm.

**History:** F. W. Rueckheim, a popcorn store owner in Chicago, introduced a mixture of popcorn, peanuts, and molasses at the World's Columbian Exposition in 1893. Three years later the name Cracker Jack was applied to it. It gained popularity quickly and by 1908 appeared in the lyrics of "Take Me out to the Ball Game."

In 1910, Rueckheim included on each box coupons which could be redeemed for prizes. In 1912, prizes were packaged directly in the boxes. The early prizes were made of paper, tin, lead, wood, and porcelain. Plastic prizes were introduced in 1948.

The Borden Company's Cracker Jack prize collection includes more than 10,000 examples; but this is not all of them. More examples are still to be found in drawer bottoms, old jewelry boxes, and attics.

Items currently included in the product boxes are largely paper, the plastic magnifying glass being one exception. The company buys toys in lots of 25 million and keeps hundreds of prizes in circulation at one time. Borden's annual production is about 400 million boxes.

**Reference:** Alex Jaramillo, *Cracker Jack Prizes*, Abbeville Press, 1989.

**Collectors' Club:** Cracker Jack Collectors Association, 108 Central St., Rowley, MA 01969.

**Museum:** Columbus Science Museum, Columbus, OH.

Baseball Score Counter, 3-1/2"... 150.00
Bendee Figure, MOC..................... 6.00
Book, *Cracker Jack Painting & Drawing Book,* Saalfield, 1917, 24 pgs
  ............................................... 40.00
Booklet
  Cracker Jack In Switzerland, 4 pgs, 1926 copyright........................ 50.00
  Cracker Jack Riddles, red, white, and blue, cov, 42 pgs, 1920s
  ............................................... 60.00
Bookmark, Spaniel, brown and white diecut litho tin, marked "Cracker Jack".................................... 35.00
Box, 7" h, rd, white, and blue cardboard, 1930s............................ 40.00
Cereal Cup, Ralston ....................... 5.00
Clicker, aluminum, pear-shaped, 1949
  ............................................... 35.00
Coin, 1" d, Mystery Club, emb aluminum, presidential profile, back emb "Join Cracker Jack Mystery Club/ Save This Coin," 1930s............. 20.00
Doll, 12" h, vinyl, Vogue Dolls, orig unopened display card, 1980 copyright........................................ 35.00
Game, Cracker Jack Toy Surprise Game, Milton Bradley, orig box, 1976
  ............................................... 35.00
Lapel Stud
  Cracker Jack Air Corps, very dark luster, metal wings, 1930s ....... 45.00
  Cracker Jack Police, dark finish, metal, star badge shape, 1930s
  ............................................... 30.00
Lunch Box, metal, Aladdin Industries, c1979....................................... 30.00
Pencil, 3-1/2" l, red name.............. 15.00
Pinback Button, 1-1/4" d, multicolored portrait illus of young lady, back inscribed "Cracker Jack 5 cents Candied Popcorn and Roasted Peanuts," early 1900s.................... 60.00
Pinball Game, MOC........................ 6.00

**Caboose, gray plastic, $7.50.**

Post Card, 3" x 5-1/2" d, Cracker Jack Bears #7, bears greeting President Roosevelt, 1907 postmark ....... 25.00

Prize

Battleship, red enameled white metal, portholes on both sides ................................................. 17.50

Binoculars, dark finish white metal ................................................. 12.00

Carnival Barker, black, white, and red litho, stand-up turning chance wheel ......................................... 50.00

Gun, Smith & Wesson .38 replica, black finish white metal ........... 20.00

Magnet, silvered wire horseshoe magnet, orig red and white marked "Made in Japan" paper wrapper ................................................. 15.00

Man's Shoe, dark finish white metal, hobnail sole design ................. 30.00

Model T Touring Car, dark finish white metal .............................. 35.00

Owl, red, blue, and yellow emb stiff paper stand-up, marked "Cracker Jack" ......................................... 40.00

Pocket Watch, dark silver luster white metal

Ornate back, 9:27 time ....... 30.00

Plain back, 4:00 time ........... 35.00

Rocking Chair, yellow enameled litho tin doll furniture chair, curved slat back ......................................... 20.00

Rocking Horse, dark blue wash tint ................................................. 20.00

Scottie, bright silver luster white metal ......................................... 25.00

Spinner Top, red, white, and blue litho, Cracker Jack mystery toy box 35.00

Train Engine, dark white metal, engine and joined coal car ...... 20.00

Train Passenger Car, litho tin, black and yellow, 1930s, some rust ................................................. 25.00

Watch, litho tin, pocket watch, gold flashing, black and white dial, 1930s ................................................. 50.00

Whistle, green enameled tin, top side inscribed "Close End with Fingers" ......................................... 35.00

Stand-Up, litho tin

Lion, green and black, unmarked, 1930s ......................................... 70.00

Sailboat Prize, red, white, and blue, mkd "DM 38," and "Dowst Mfg, Chicago, U.S.A.," unmarked, lightly rubbed, 1930s ......................... 40.00

Smitty, full color, white background, dark green rim, 1930s .............. 80.00

Tilt Card, sq cardboard, flicker image of sailor passing ball from one hand to the other, back mkd "Tilt Card To And Fro" and Cracker Jack marking, Borden, Inc., Columbus, 1950s ................................................. 12.00

Watch, litho, 1940s, near mint ...... 75.00

# D

# Degenhart Glass

**Collecting Hints:** Degenhart pressed glass novelties are collected by mold (Forget-Me-Not toothpick holders or all Degenhart toothpick holders), by individual colors (Rubina or Bloody Mary), or by group colors (opaque, iridescent, crystal, or slag).

Correct color identification is a key factor when collecting Degenhart glass. Because of the slight variations in the hundreds of colors produced at the Degenhart Crystal Art Glass factory from 1947-1978, it is important for beginning collectors to learn to distinguish Degenhart colors, particularly the green and blue variations. Seek guidance from knowledgeable collectors or dealers. Side-by-side color comparison is extremely helpful.

Later glass produced by the factory can be distinguished by the "D" in a heart trademark or a "D" by itself on molds where there was insufficient space for the full mark. Use of the "D" mark began around 1972, and by late 1977 most of the molds had been marked. From c1947-1972, pieces were not marked except for owls and the occasional piece hand stamped with a block letter "D" as it came out of the mold. This hand stamping was used from 1967-1972.

Collecting unmarked Degenhart glass made from 1947-c1970 poses no problem once a collector becomes familiar with the molds and colors which were used during that period. Some of the most desirable colors, such as Amethyst & White Slag, Amethyst Carnival, and Custard Slag, are unmarked. Keep in mind that some colors, e.g., Custard (opaque yellow), Heliotrope (opaque purple), and Tomato (opaque orange red), were used repeatedly, and both marked and unmarked pieces can be found, depending on production date.

**History:** John (1884-1964) and Elizabeth (1889-1978) Degenhart operated the Crystal Art Glass factory of Cambridge, Ohio, from 1947-1978. The factory specialized in reproduction pressed glass novelties and paperweights. More than 50 molds were worked by this factory including ten toothpick holders, five salts, and six animal-covered dishes of various sizes.

When the factory ceased operation, many of the molds were purchased by Boyd Crystal Art Glass, Cambridge, Ohio. Boyd has issued pieces in many new colors and has marked them all with a "B" in a diamond.

**References:** Gene Florence, *Degenhart Glass and Paperweights*, Degenhart Paperweight and Glass Museum, 1982.

**Collectors' Club:** Friends of Degenhart, Degenhart Paperweight and Glass Museum, Inc., 65323 Highland Hills Rd., P.O. Box 186, Cambridge, OH 43725.

**Museum:** The Degenhart Paperweight and Glass Museum, Inc., Cambridge, OH. The museum displays all types of Ohio valley glass.

**Reproduction Alert:** Although most of the Degenhart molds were reproductions themselves, there are contemporary pieces that can be confusing such as Kanawha's bird salt and bow slipper; L. G. Wright's mini-slipper, Daisy & Button salt, and 5-inch robin-covered dish; and many other contemporary American pieces. The 3-inch-bird salt and mini-pitcher also are made by an unknown glassmaker in Taiwan.

| | |
|---|---|
| Bell, 1976, lavender | 12.00 |
| Candy Jar, cov, amberina | 24.00 |
| Child's Mug, Stork and Peacock | 25.00 |
| Coaster, intro 1974, mkd 1975, crystal | 9.00 |
| Creamer and Sugar, Daisy and Button, carnival | 45.00 |
| Cup Plate | |
|   Heart and Lyre, mulberry | 18.00 |
|   Seal of Ohio, sunset | 15.00 |
| Hand, mkd, Crown Tuscan | 22.00 |
| Hen, covered dish, ebony, 3-1/2" | 24.00 |
| Jewel Box, heart shape, blue | 38.00 |
| Owl, intro 1967, mkd 1967 | |
|   Bloody Mary | 55.00 |
|   Clear | 30.00 |
|   Custard Opaque | 22.00 |
|   Ebony | 22.00 |
|   Jade | 32.00 |
|   Lime ice | 24.00 |
|   Milk Glass, blue | 18.00 |
|   Milk Glass, white | 20.00 |
|   Opalescent white | 15.00 |
|   Peach | 12.00 |
|   Pigeon Blood | 24.00 |
|   Vaseline | 30.00 |
| Plate, Elizabeth | 20.00 |
| Pooch | |
|   Amethyst | 40.00 |

**Salt, bird, purple slag, 3" l, $27.50.**

| | |
|---|---|
| Baby Green | 22.00 |
| Bittersweet | 15.50 |
| Brown | 15.00 |
| Canary | 17.50 |
| Charcoal | 20.25 |
| Cobalt Blue | 28.00 |
| Fawn | 17.50 |
| Henri Blue | 15.50 |
| Heather Bloom | 27.50 |
| Milk Glass, blue | 15.50 |
| Periwinkle | 31.00 |
| Rosemary Pink | 18.00 |
| Royal Violet | 24.00 |
| Priscilla, Rose Marie, June, 1976 | 65.00 |
| Robin, covered dish, Taffeta, mkd | 55.00 |
| Salt and Pepper Shakers, pr, bird, sapphire | 18.00 |
| Tomahawk, vaseline | 17.50 |
| Toothpick Holder | |
|   Basket, milk glass, white | 18.00 |
|   Beaded Heart, lemon custard | 20.00 |
|   Colonial Drape and Heart, custard | 20.00 |
|   Elephant's Head | |
|     Jade | 24.00 |
|     Sapphire | 15.00 |
|   Forget-Me-Not | |
|     Bloody Mark | 24.00 |
|     Lavender Blue | 15.00 |
|   Hat, Daisy and Button | |
|     Amber | 12.00 |
|     Amberina | 20.00 |
| Wine Glass, Buzz Saw | |
|   Cobalt Blue | 20.00 |
|   Milk Glass, blue | 22.00 |
|   Vaseline | 20.00 |

# Depression Glass

**Collecting Hint:** Many collectors specialize in one pattern; others collect by a particular color.

**History:** Depression glass was made from 1920-1940. It was an inexpensive machine-made glass and was produced by several companies in various patterns and colors. The number of forms made in different patterns also varied.

The colors varied from company to company. The number of items made in each pattern also varied. Knowing the proper name of a pattern is the key to collecting. Collectors should be prepared to do research.

**References:** Tom and Neila Bredehoft, *Fifty Years of Collectible Glass, 1920-1970*, Antique Trader Books, 1997; Gene Florence, *Collectible Glassware from the 40's, 50's, 60's*, 4th ed., Collector Books, 1997; ——, *Collector's Encyclopedia of Depression Glass*, 14th ed., Collector Books, 1998; ——, *Elegant Glassware of the Depression Era*, 8th ed., Collector Books, 1998; ——, *Kitchen Glassware of the Depression Era*, 5th Edition, Collector Books, (1995, 1999 value update); ——, *Pocket Guide to Depression Glass & More, 1920-1960s*, 11th ed., Collector Books, 1998; ——, *Stemware Identification Featuring Cordials with Values, 1920s-1960s*, Collector Books, 1997; ——, *Very Rare Glassware of the Depression Era*, 1st Series (1988, 1991 value update), 2nd Series (1991), 3rd Series (1993), 4th Series (1996), 5th Series (1996), Collector Books; Jim and Barbara Mauzy, *Mauzy's Comprehensive Handbook of Depression Glass Prices*, Schiffer, 1999; Ellen T. Schroy, *Warman's Depression Glass*, Krause Publications, 1997; Kent G. Washburn, *Price Survey*, 4th ed., published by author, 1994; Hazel Marie Weatherman, *Colored Glassware of the Depression Era*, Book 2, published by author 1974, available in reprint; ——, *1984 Supplement & Price Trends for Colored Glassware of the Depression Era*, Book 1, published by author, 1984.

**Periodicals:** *Fire-King News*, P.O. Box 473, Addison, AL 35540; *Kitchen Antiques & Collectible News*, 4645 Laurel Ridge Dr., Harrisburg, PA 17110; *The Daze, Inc.*, P.O. Box 57, Otisville, MI 48463.

**Collectors' Clubs:** Big "D" Pression Glass Club, 10 Windling Creek Trail, Garland, TX 75043; Buckeye Dee Geer's, 2501 Campbell St., Sandusky, OH 44870; Canadian Depression Glass Club, P.O. Box 104, Mississaugua, Ontario L53 2K1 Canada; Clearwater Depression Glass Club, 10038 62nd Terrace North, St. Petersburg, FL 33708; Crescent City Depression Glass Club, 140 Commerce St., Gretna, LA 70056; Depression Era Glass Society of Wisconsin, 1534 S. Wisconsin Ave., Racine, WI 53403; Depression Glass Club of Greater Rochester, P.O. Box 10362, Rochester, NY 14610; Depression Glass Club of North East Florida, 2604 Jolly Rd., Jacksonville, FL 33207; Fostoria Glass collectors, Inc., P.O. Box 1625, Orange, CA 92668; Greater Tulsa Depression Era Glass Club, P.O. Box 470763, Tulsa, OK 74147-0763; Heart of America Glass Collectors, 14404 E. 36th Ter., Independence, MO, 64055; Illinois Valley Depression Glass Club, RR 1, Box 52, Rushville, IL 62681; Iowa Depression Glass Association, 5871 Vista Drive, Apt. 725, West Des Moines, IA 50266; Land of Sunshine Depression Glass Club, P.O. Box 560275, Orlando, FL 32856-0275; Lincoln Land Depression Glass Club, 1625 Dial Court, Springfield, IL 62704; National Depression Glass Association, Inc., P.O. Box 8264, Wichita, KS 67209; Northeast Florida Depression Glass Club, P.O. Box 338, Whitehouse, FL 32220; North Jersey Dee Geer's, 82 High Street, Butler, NJ 07405; Peach State Depression Glass Club, 4174 Reef Rd., Marietta, GA 30066; Phoenix and Consolidated Glass Collectors' Club, P.O. Box 182082, Arlington, TX 76096-2082; Southern Illinois Diamond H Seekers, 1203 N. Yale, O'Fallon, IL 62269; 20-30-40 Society, Inc., P.O. Box 856, LaGrange, IL 60525; Western Reserve Depression Glass Club, 8669 Courtland Drive, Strongsville, OH 44136.

**Websites:** *DG Shopper Online,* The WWW Depression Era Glass Magazine, http://www.dgshopper.com.

**Reproduction Alert:** Reproductions of Depression Glass patterns can be a real problem. Some are easy to detect, but others are very good. Now that there are reproductions of the reproductions, the only hope for collectors is to know what they are buying and to buy from reputable dealers and/or other collectors. Most of the current Depression Glass reference books have excellent sections on reproductions. The following items with an † have been reproduced, but beware that there are more reproductions being brought into the marketplace.

**BOWKNOT**

Unknown maker, late 1920s. Made in green.

| | Green |
|---|---|
| Berry Bowl, 4-1/2" d | 16.00 |
| Cereal Bowl, 5-1/2" d | 20.00 |
| Cup | 14.00 |

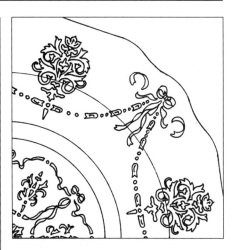

**BOWKNOT**

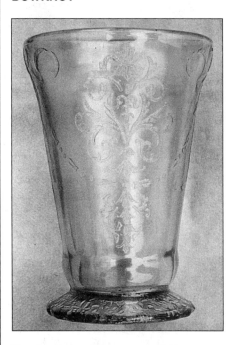

Bowknot, tumbler, green, $15.

| | |
|---|---|
| Plate, 7" d, salad | 12.50 |
| Sherbet, low, ftd | 24.00 |
| Tumbler, 10 oz, 5" h, flat | 15.00 |
| Tumbler, 10 oz, 5" h, ftd | 15.00 |

**DEWDROP**

Manufactured by Jeannette Glass Company, Jeannette, PA, from 1953 to 1956. Made in crystal.

| | Crystal |
|---|---|
| Bowl, 4-3/4" d | 7.00 |
| Bowl, 8-1/2" d | 20.00 |
| Bowl, 10-3/8" d | 20.00 |
| Butter, cov | 30.00 |
| Candy Dish, cov, 7" d | 24.00 |
| Casserole, cov | 24.00 |
| Creamer | 8.50 |
| Iced Tea Tumbler, 15 oz | 17.50 |
| Lazy Susan, 13" d tray | 29.00 |
| Pitcher, 1/2 gallon, ftd | 48.00 |

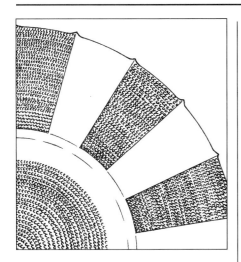

## DEWDROP

Plate, 11-1/2" d............................20.00
Punch Cup ..................................... 4.00
Punch Bowl Set, bowl,12 cups ..... 65.00
Snack Cup ..................................... 4.00
Snack Plate, indent for cup............. 5.00
Relish, leaf-shape, handle .............. 9.00
Sugar, cov ...................................14.00
Tumbler, 9 oz...............................15.00

## FLORAGOLD, Louisa

Manufactured by Jeannette Glass Company, Jeannette, PA, 1950s. Made in iridescent. Some large comports were later made in ice blue, crystal, red-yellow, and shell pink.

| Item | Iridescent |
| --- | --- |
| Ashtray, 4" d | 10.00 |
| Bowl, 4-1/2" sq | 6.50 |
| Bowl, 5-1/4" d, ruffled | 16.00 |
| Bowl, 8-1/2" d, sq | 8.00 |
| Bowl, 8-1/2" d, ruffled | 12.00 |
| Butter Dish, cov, 1/4 pound, oblong | 24.00 |
| Butter Dish, cov, round, 5-1/2" sq base | 675.00 |
| Candlesticks, pr, double branch | 50.00 |
| Candy Dish, 1 handle | 15.00 |
| Candy or Cheese Dish, cov, 6-3/4" d | 110.00 |
| Candy, 5-3/4" l, 4 feet | 7.50 |
| Celery Vase | 395.00 |
| Cereal Bowl, 5-1/2" d, round | 35.00 |
| Coaster, 4" d | 10.00 |
| Comport, 5-1/4", plain top | 595.00 |
| Comport, 5-1/4", ruffled top | 695.00 |
| Creamer | 10.00 |
| Cup | 5.00 |
| Fruit Bowl, 5-1/2" d, ruffled | 8.50 |
| Fruits Bowl, 12" d, ruffled, large | 8.00 |
| Nappy, 5" d, one handle | 11.00 |
| Pitcher, 64 oz | 40.00 |
| Plate, 5-1/4" d, sherbet | 15.00 |
| Plate, 8-1/2" d, dinner | 35.00 |
| Platter, 11-1/4" d | 22.00 |
| Salad Bowl, 9-1/2" d, deep | 42.50 |
| Salt and Pepper Shakers, pr, plastic tops | 35.00 |
| Saucer, 5-1/4" d | 12.00 |
| Sherbet, low, ftd | 16.00 |

Sugar ............................................. 15.00
Sugar Lid ...................................... 15.00
Tidbit, wooden post ...................... 35.00
Tray, 13-1/2" d .............................. 22.50
Tray, 13-1/2" d, with indent............ 45.00
Tumbler, 11 oz, ftd ....................... 18.00
Tumbler, 10 oz, ftd ....................... 18.00
Tumbler, 15 oz, ftd ...................... 110.00
Vase............................................ 395.00

## FLORAL and DIAMOND BAND

### FLORAL and DIAMOND BAND

Manufactured by U.S. Glass Company, Pittsburgh, PA, late 1920s. Made in pink and green with limited production in black, crystal, and iridescent.

| Item | Green | Pink |
| --- | --- | --- |
| Berry Bowl, 4-1/2" d | 8.00 | 7.00 |
| Berry Bowl, 8" d | 12.00 | 13.00 |
| Butter Dish, cov | 120.00 | 125.00 |
| Compote, 5-1/2" h | 16.50 | 15.00 |
| Creamer, 4-3/4" | 20.00 | 17.50 |
| Iced Tea Tumbler, 5" h | 38.00 | 32.50 |
| Nappy, 5-3/4" d, handle | 12.00 | 11.00 |
| Pitcher, 42 oz, 8" h | 95.00 | 90.00 |
| Plate, 8" d, luncheon | 40.00 | 40.00 |
| Sherbet | 7.00 | 6.50 |
| Sugar, 5-1/4" | 15.00 | 14.00 |
| Tumbler, 4" h, water | 24.00 | 22.00 |

### FOREST GREEN

Manufactured by Anchor Hocking Glass Company, Lancaster, OH, and Long Island City, NY, from 1950-1957. Made only in forest green.

| Item | Forest Green |
| --- | --- |
| Ashtray, 3-1/2" sq | 3.50 |
| Ashtray, 4-5/8" sq | 5.50 |
| Ashtray, 5-3/4" hexagon | 8.00 |
| Ashtray, 5-3/4" sq | 7.50 |
| Batter Bowl, spout | 25.00 |

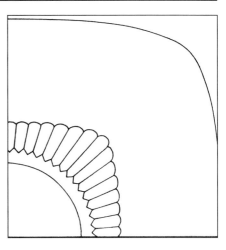

## FOREST GREEN

| Berry Bowl, large | 15.00 |
| --- | --- |
| Berry Bowl, small | 5.50 |
| Bowl, 4-1/2" w, sq | 5.50 |
| Bowl, 5-1/4" deep | 8.00 |
| Bowl, 6" w, sq | 18.00 |
| Bowl, 6-1/2" d, scalloped | 9.00 |
| Bowl, 7-3/8" w, sq | 30.00 |
| Bowl, 7-1/2" d, crimped | 10.00 |
| Cocktail, 3-1/2 oz | 12.00 |
| Cocktail, 4-1/2 oz | 14.00 |
| Creamer, flat | 17.50 |
| Cup, sq | 7.00 |
| Dessert Bowl, 4-3/4" d | 5.00 |
| Goblet, 9 oz | 10.00 |
| Goblet, 9-1/2 oz | 14.00 |
| Iced Tea Tumbler, 13 oz | 8.00 |
| Iced Tea Tumbler, 14 oz, Boopie | 8.00 |
| Iced Tea Tumbler, 15 oz, tall | 10.00 |
| Iced Tea Tumbler, 32 oz, giant | 18.00 |
| Ivy Ball, 4" h | 5.00 |
| Juice Tumbler, 4 oz | 10.00 |
| Juice Tumbler, 5-1/2 oz | 12.50 |
| Juice Roly Poly Tumbler, 3-3/8" h | 5.00 |
| Ladle, all green glass | 80.00 |
| Mixing Bowl, 6" d | 8.00 |
| Pitcher, 22 oz | 22.50 |
| Pitcher, 36 oz | 25.00 |
| Pitcher, 86 oz, round | 45.00 |
| Plate, 6-3/4" d, salad | 7.50 |
| Plate, 7" w, sq | 6.75 |
| Plate, 8-3/8" d, luncheon | 7.00 |
| Plate, 9-1/4" d, dinner | 30.00 |
| Platter, 11" l, rect | 22.00 |
| Popcorn Bowl, 5-1/4" d | 10.00 |
| Punch Bowl | 25.00 |
| Punch Bowl and Stand | 45.00 |
| Punch Cup | 2.25 |
| Roly Poly Tumbler, 5-1/8" h | 6.50 |
| Salad Bowl, 7-3/8" d | 12.00 |
| Saucer, 5-3/8" w | 3.00 |
| Sherbet, 6 oz | 9.00 |
| Sherbet, 6 oz, Boopie | 7.00 |
| Sherbet, flat | 7.50 |
| Soup Bowl, 6" d | 17.00 |
| Sugar, flat | 7.00 |
| Tray, 6" x 10", 2 handles | 30.00 |
| Tumbler, 5 oz, 3-1/2" h | 4.00 |
| Tumbler, 7 oz | 4.50 |
| Tumbler, 5-1/4" h | 4.00 |
| Tumbler, 9-1/2" oz, tall | 8.00 |

Tumbler, 9 oz, fancy .......................... 7.00
Tumbler, 9 oz, table ......................... 5.00
Tumbler, 10 oz, 4-1/2" h, ftd ............ 7.50
Tumbler, 11 oz .............................. 7.00
Tumbler, 14 oz, 5" h ....................... 8.00
Tumbler, 15 oz, long boy ............... 10.00
Vase, 6-3/8" h .............................. 4.00
Vase, 9" h .................................. 8.00
Vegetable Bowl, 8-1/2" l, oval ....... 24.00

## GEORGIAN, Lovebirds

Manufactured by Federal Glass Company, Columbus, OH, from 1931-1936. Made in green.

| Item | Green |
|---|---|
| Berry Bowl, 4-1/2" d | 7.00 |
| Berry Bowl, 7-1/2" d, large | 62.00 |
| Bowl, 6-1/2" d, deep | 65.00 |
| Butter Dish, cov | 80.00 |
| Cereal Bowl, 5-3/4" d | 26.00 |
| Cold Cuts Server, 18-1/2" d, wood, seven openings for 5" d Coasters | 825.00 |
| Creamer, 3" d, ftd | 15.00 |
| Creamer, 4" d, ftd | 15.00 |
| Cup | 6.50 |
| Cup and Saucer | 12.75 |
| Hot Plate, 5" d, center design | 48.00 |

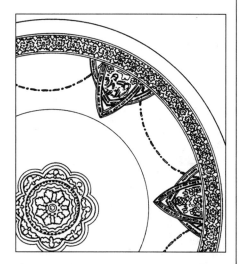

**GEORGIAN**

**Georgian, cup and saucer, green, $12.75.**

Plate, 6" d, sherbet ......................... 6.50
Plate, 8" d, luncheon .................... 10.00
Plate, 9-1/4" d, center design only
.......................................... 25.00
Plate, 9-1/4" d, dinner .................. 30.00
Platter, 11-1/2" l, closed handle .... 70.00
Saucer ...................................... 3.50
Sherbet, ftd ............................... 16.00
Sugar Cover, 3" d ........................ 35.00
Sugar Cover, 4" d ........................ 35.00
Sugar, 3" d, ftd ........................... 15.00
Sugar, 4" d, ftd ........................... 15.00
Tumbler, 9 oz, 4" h, flat ................ 60.00
Tumbler 12 oz, 5-1/4" h, flat ........ 135.00
Vegetable Bowl, 9" l, oval ............ 65.00

## JUBILEE

Manufactured by Lancaster Glass Company, Lancaster, OH, early 1930s. Made in pink and yellow.

| Item | Pink | Yellow |
|---|---|---|
| Bowl, 8" d, 5-1/8" h, 3 legs | 265.00 | 215.00 |
| Bowl, 11-1/2" d, 3 legs | 250.00 | 250.00 |
| Bowl, 11-1/2" d, 3 legs, curved in | — | 250.00 |
| Bowl, 13" d, 3 legs | 250.00 | 235.00 |
| Cake Tray, 11" d, 2 handles | 75.00 | 85.00 |
| Candlesticks, pr | 190.00 | 190.00 |
| Candy Jar, cov, 3 legs | 325.00 | 325.00 |
| Cheese and Cracker Set | 265.00 | 255.00 |
| Cordial, 1 oz, 4" h | — | 245.00 |
| Creame | 45.00 | 30.00 |
| Cup | 40.00 | 15.00 |
| Fruit Bowl, 9" d, handle | — | 125.00 |
| Fruit Bowl, 11-1/2" h, flat | 200.00 | 165.00 |
| Goblet, 3 oz, 4-7/8" h | — | 150.00 |
| Goblet, 11 oz, 7-1/2" h | — | 75.00 |

**JUBILEE**

Iced Tea Tumbler, 12-1/2 oz,
6-1/8" h ................—...... 135.00
Juice Tumbler, 6 oz, 5" h,
ftd ........................—...... 100.00
Mayonnaise, plate, orig ladle
................ 315.00..... 285.00
Mayonnaise Underplate
................ 125.00..... 110.00
Plate, 7" d, salad ........ 25.00........ 14.00
Plate, 8-3/4" d, luncheon
................ 30.00........ 16.50
Plate, 14" d, 3 legs ..........—...... 210.00
Sandwich Plate,
13-1/2" d ............. 95.00........ 65.00
Sandwich Tray, 11" d,
center handle...... 200.00...... 250.00
Saucer ................. 15.00......... 8.00
Sherbet, 8 oz, 3" h ..........—...... 75.00
Sherbet/Champagne, 7 oz,
5-1/2" h ...................—...... 75.00
Sugar ....................... 40.00........ 24.00
Tumbler, 10 oz, 6" h, ftd
................ 75.00........ 50.00
Vase, 12" h ....................—...... 365.00

## MOONSTONE

Manufactured by Anchor Hocking Glass Company, Lancaster, OH, from 1941-1946. Made in crystal with opalescent hobnails and Ocean Green with opalescent hobnails.

| Item | Crystal | Ocean Green |
|---|---|---|
| Berry Bowl, 5-1/2" d | 18.00 | — |
| Bonbon, heart shape, handle | 13.00 | — |
| Bowl, 6-1/2" d, crimped, handle | 20.00 | — |
| Bowl, 7-1/4" d, flat | 14.00 | — |
| Bowl, 9-1/2" d, crimped | 20.00 | — |
| Candleholder, pr | 25.00 | — |
| Candy Jar, cov, 6" h | 30.00 | — |
| Cigarette Box, cov | 25.00 | — |
| Creamer | 9.50 | 9.50 |
| Cup | 8.00 | 10.00 |
| Dessert Bowl, 5-1/2" d, crimped | 9.50 | — |
| Goblet, 10 oz | 24.00 | 24.00 |

**MOONSTONE**

Plate, 6-1/4" d, sherbet
.................................. 6.00 ........... 7.00
Plate, 8-3/8" d,
    luncheon .............. 15.00 ......... 15.00
Puff Box, cov, 4-3/4" d,
    round ..................... 25.00 ............. —
Relish, 7 1/4" d,
    divided ................. 12.50 ............. —
Relish, cloverleaf........ 12.50 ............. —
Sandwich Plate,
    10-3/4" d................ 28.00 ............. —
Saucer ...................... 6.00 ......... 6.00
Sherbet, ftd ................ 7.00 ......... 7.00
Sugar, ftd ................... 9.50 ......... 9.50
Vase, 5-1/2" h, bud..... 10.00 ............. —
Vase, 6-1/2" h, ruffled... 8.00 ............. —

## PATRICK

Manufactured by Lancaster Glass Company, Lancaster, OH, early 1930s. Made in pink and yellow.

| Item | Pink | Yellow |
| --- | --- | --- |
| Candlesticks, pr....... | 150.00 | 160.00 |
| Candy Dish, 3 ftd..... | 155.00 | 165.00 |
| Cheese and Cracker Set...................... | 150.00 | 130.00 |
| Cocktail, 4" h............... | 85.00 | 85.00 |
| Console Bowl, 11" d.. | 150.00 | 150.00 |
| Creamer..................... | 75.00 | 40.00 |
| Cup........................... | 70.00 | 40.00 |
| Fruit Bowl, 9" d, handle ................ | 172.00 | 120.00 |
| Goblet, 10 oz, 6" h.... | 100.00 | 75.00 |
| Juice Goblet, 6 oz, 4-3/4" h.............. | 95.00 | 75.00 |
| Mayonnaise, 3 piece ........................ | 185.00 | 80.00 |
| Plate, 7" d, sherbet..... | 20.00 | 15.00 |
| Plate, 7-1/2" d, salad.. | 25.00 | 20.00 |
| Plate, 8" d, luncheon.. | 45.00 | 30.00 |
| Saucer ...................... | 20.00 | 12.00 |
| Sherbet, 4-3/4" d........ | 65.00 | 40.00 |
| Sugar ........................ | 75.00 | 38.00 |
| Tray, 11" d, center handle........ | 85.00 | 95.00 |
| Tray, 11" d, two handles......... | 145.00 | 65.00 |

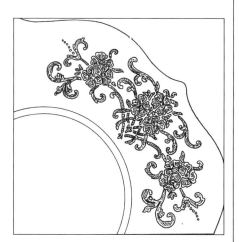

**PATRICK**

**SUNBURST**

**SUNBURST, Herringbone**
Manufactured by Jeannette Glass Company, Jeannette, PA, late 1930s. Made in crystal.

| Item | Crystal |
| --- | --- |
| Berry Bowl, 4-3/4" d...................... | 6.50 |
| Berry Bowl, 8-1/2" d...................... | 15.00 |
| Bowl, 10-1/2" d............................. | 20.00 |
| Candlesticks, pr, double.............. | 35.00 |
| Creamer, ftd................................ | 16.00 |
| Cup ........................................... | 7.50 |
| Cup and Saucer ........................... | 8.00 |
| Plate, 5-1/2" d.............................. | 11.00 |
| Plate, 9-1/4" d, dinner .................. | 15.00 |
| Relish, 2 part.............................. | 14.00 |
| Sandwich Plate, 11-3/4" d............. | 15.00 |
| Saucer ....................................... | 3.00 |
| Sherbet ...................................... | 12.00 |
| Sugar ......................................... | 16.00 |
| Tumbler, 4" h, 9 oz, flat................. | 18.00 |

**THISTLE**
Manufactured by MacBeth-Evans, Charleroi, PA, about 1929-1930. Made in crystal, green, pink, and yellow. Production was limited in crystal and yel-

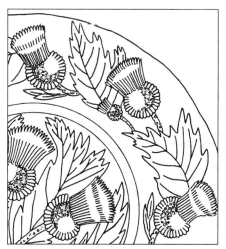

**THISTLE**

low. Reproductions: † Recent reproductions have been found in pink, a darker emerald green, and wisteria. Several of the reproductions have a scalloped edge. Reproductions include the cake plate, fruit bowl, pitcher, salt and pepper shakers, and a small tumbler.

| Item | Green | Pink |
| --- | --- | --- |
| Cake Plate, 13" d, heavy †.............. | 150.00 | 125.00 |
| Cereal Bowl, 5-1/2" d ................ | 27.50 | 80.00 |
| Cup, thin .................... | 32.00 | 24.00 |
| Fruit Bowl, 10-1/4" d † ......... | 295.00 | 195.00 |
| Plate, 8" d, luncheon.. | 22.00 | 18.00 |
| Plate, 10-1/4" d, grill .. | 32.00 | 28.00 |
| Saucer ...................... | 12.00 | 12.00 |

# Dirigibles

**Collecting Hints:** All types of dirigible material remain stable. Specialize in one specific topic, e.g., material about one airship, models and toys, or postcards. The field is very broad, and a collector might exhaust his funds trying to be comprehensive. The most common collecting trend focuses on material relating to specific flights.

**History:** The terms "airship" and "dirigible" are synonymous. Dirigible (from Latin) means steerable and the term originally applied to bicycles although it evolved into a synonym for airship.

There are three types of dirigibles: 1) Rigid—a zeppelin, e.g., *Hindenburg*, *Graf*, *Shenandoah*; 2) Non-Rigid—a blimp, e.g., those flown by the Navy or bearing Goodyear advertising; and 3) Semi-Rigid—non-rigid with a keel, e.g., *Norge* and *Italia*. Only non-rigid and semi-rigid dirigibles were made prior to 1900. Hot-air balloons, barrage balloons, hydrogen balloons, and similar types are not dirigibles because they are not directable. They go where the wind takes them.

Zeppelins were made from 1900-1940, the last being the *LZ130*, sister ship to the *Hindenburg*. The *Graf* zeppelin was the most successful one, flying between 1928-1940. The *Hindenburg*, which flew in 1936 and 1937, was the most famous due to the spectacular fire that destroyed it in 1937.

America never used its four zeppelins for passenger travel; they were strictly for military use. The Naval Air Station at Lakehurst, New

Jersey, where the well-known zeppelins docked, is still open, although its name has been changed to the Naval Air Engineering Center. The last Navy blimp flew from Lakehurst in 1962.

**References:** Walter Curley, *Graf Zeppelin's Flights to South America*, Spellman Museum, 1970; Arthur Falk, *Hindenburg Crash Mail*, Clear Color Litho, 1976; Sieger, *Zeppelin Post Katalog* (in German), Wurttemberg, 1981.

**Collectors' Club:** Zeppelin Collectors Club, c/o Aerophilatelic Federation, P.O. Box 1239, Elgin, IL 60121.

**Museum:** Navy Lakehurst Historical Society, Cinnaminson, NJ.

**Reproduction Alert.**

Bank, 6-1/2" l, *Graf Zeppelin,* silver painted cast iron, c1920 .......... 55.00
Book, *The Story of the Airship Goodyear,* Hugh Allen, Goodyear Tire and Rubber Co., 1932, hardcover, 96 pgs .................................... 24.00
Brochure, 5-1/2" x 8", "Al-Cariod, The Ideal Antacid," *Los Angeles* illus
................................................. 25.00
Candy Mold, 10" l, 3-1/2" h, *Los Angeles,* tin ..................................... 135.00
Child's Book
*Tom Swift, His Airship*, Grosset & Dunlap ....................................... 50.00
*Tom Swift*, Big Dirigible, Grosset & Dunlap, 1930 ............................ 42.00
Employee Badge, 2-1/8", black and white, Lakehurst, NJ, 1939 ....... 35.00
Game, *Graf Zeppelin* World Flight Game, 14" x 21-1/2" box, 11" x 15" orig box, German instructions, 1928 flight ...................................... 250.00
Magazine
*Literary Digest,* 1933, article on crash of the *Akron* ...................... 6.00
*Popular Science,* 1923, dirigible on cover .......................................... 8.75
Needlebook, China Clipper brand
................................................. 12.00
Patch, Zeppelin *Eckener Spende,* cloth, brass rim, Germany, 1930s ...... 60.00

**Booklet, Flying A Gasoline, figural, c1935, 9-3/8" l, $25.**

Pennant, 29" l, *Graf Zeppelin*, brown felt, white airship and inscription
................................................. 125.00
Photo, black and white, identified on back
Aero Squadron and Dirigible, World War I ...................................... 200.00
French Dirigible, World War I ... 20.00
*Graf Zeppelin,* Goodyear ......... 28.00
*Hindenburg in Flames* ............. 15.00
*USS Los Angeles* ..................... 15.00
*USS Macon*, Goodyear ............ 15.00
*USS Shenandoah* ..................... 60.00
Pin, 1-7/8", diecut aluminum, detailed airship inset, black and white glossy photo of Count Ferdinand Von Zeppelin, c1920 ........................... 195.00
Pinback Button, 1-1/4" d, red, white, and blue, zeppelin in hanger at Lakehurst Naval Air Station, 1930s
................................................. 75.00
Post Card
Advertising, Poole Pianos, Boston, view of dirigible floating over Public Gardens, unused ...................... 8.50
Dirigible in flight approaching Empire State building, used .................... 4.00
Dirigible *France* in flight, unused
................................................. 7.50
Zeppelin flying over Rio de Janeiro, Brazil, black and white ............. 24.00
Zeppelin IV, c1910, used ......... 15.00
Poster, Pernot Biscuits, shows dirigible and men eating, c1915, 16" x 22"
................................................. 125.00
Schedule, 4" x 9" folded glossy paper, *Hindenburg, Graf Zeppelin,* interior black and white photos, plans, menus, text on flights, published March 1937 by German Zeppelin Transport Co. and American Zeppelin Transport, Inc. .................... 75.00
Stereo View, *Dirigible R-24,* Minneola
................................................. 10.00
Tie, silk, hand painted dirigible, 1930s
................................................. 25.00
Token, *Macon* and *Akron*, silver, 1931-33, uncirculated, Longines Symphonette Series ........................... 20.00
Toy
*Graf Zeppelin*, 2-1/2" x 4-1/2", red, white, and blue diecut paper mounted to wood, rubber bands, toy whizzes when swung, Japanese, c1930 ...................................... 25.00
Sky Rangers, tin ...................... 50.00
*USS Los Angeles,* Tootsie Toy, 1937 ....................................... 72.00
Trading Card, Chinese dirigible, E-40, 1912 ....................................... 12.00
Wings, sterling ........................... 175.00

# Disneyana

**Collecting Hints:** The products from the 1930s command the most attention. Disneyana is a popular subject, and items tend to be priced on the high side.

Condition should be a prime consideration before purchasing any item. An incomplete toy or game should sell for 40-50% less than one in mint condition.

**History:** Walt Disney and the creations of the famous Disney Studios hold a place of fondness and enchantment in the hearts of people throughout the world. The 1928 release of "Steamboat Willie," featuring Mickey Mouse, heralded an entertainment empire.

Walt and his brother, Roy, were shrewd businessmen. From the beginning, they licensed the reproduction of Disney characters on products ranging from wristwatches to clothing.

The market in Disneyana has been established by a few determined dealers and auction houses. Hake's Americana and Collectibles has specialized in Disney material for more than three decades. Sotheby's Collector Carousel auctions and Christie's auctions have continued the trend.

Walt Disney characters are popular throughout the world. Belgium is a leading producer of Disneyana, along with England, France, and Japan. The Disney characters often take on the regional characteristics of the host country; don't be surprised to find a strange-looking Mickey Mouse or Donald Duck. Disney has opened theme parks in Japan and France, Disney retail stores in America, and holds company sponsored collector conventions, all resulting in ever increasing Disney collectibles.

**References:** Ted Hake, *Hake's Guide to Character Toy Premiums*, Gemstone Publishing (1966 Greenspring, Ste. 405, Timonium, MD 21093), 1996; Robert Heide and John Gilman, *Disneyana: Classic Collectibles 1928-1958*, Hyperion, 1994; Rex Miller, *The Investor's Guide to Vintage Character Collectibles,* Krause Publications, 1999; Maxine A. Pinksy, *Marx Toys: Robots, Space, Comic, Disney & TV Characters*, Schiffer Publishing, 1996; Walton Rawls, *Disney Dons Dogtags*, Abbeville Press, 1992; Tom Tumbusch, *Tomart's Illustrated Disneyana Catalog and Price Guide*, Vols. 1, 2, 3, and 4, Tomart Publications, 1985;.

**Collectors' Clubs:** Imagination Guild, P.O. Box 907, Boulder Creek, CA 95006; Mouse Club East, P.O. Box 3195, Wakefield, MA 01880;

National Fantasy Club for Disneyana Collector & Enthusiasts, P.O. Box 19212, Irvine, CA 92713.

**Archives:** Walt Disney Archives, Burbank, CA.

**Additional Listings:** Animation Art.

**Advisor:** Ted Hake.

## Bambi

Bud Vase, 5-1/2" h, Goebel, Bambi figure standing in front of tree stump vase, incised "DJS 428," full bee mark, 1950s ............................. 180.00

Comic Book, *Walt Disney's Bambi,* 7-3/4" x 10-1/4", KK Publications, Inc., 1941 copyright, 32 pgs, glossy cover, large story art and text, used as premium by various stores, room for advertising on back ............ 75.00

Figure, Thumper, 1-1/4" painted and glazed ceramic, tan, brown, and pink, Hagen-Renaker, 1940s ... 50.00

Poster, 14-1/4" x 20", Prevent Forest Fires, issued by U.S. Dept. of Agricultural Forest Service, 1943, reads "Please Mister, Don't Be Careless. Prevent Forest Fires/Greater Danger Than Ever!" ............................. 200.00

Studio Fan Card, 7-1/8" x 9-1/4", stiff tan paper, brown design, facsimile Walt Disney signature, 1942 ............ 35.00

## Cinderella

Figure, 5-1/4", painted and glazed ceramic, blue and white dress, 1970s ........................................ 25.00

Magazine, 8-1/4" x 11", *Newsweek,* Feb. 13, 1950, three-page article, color cover ........................................ 25.00

Watch, Bradley, 2-3/4" x 6-1/2" deep blue hard plastic case, hinged lid, 1" dia. goldtone case, white vinyl straps, 1973, full color case insert ........................................ 45.00

## Disneyland

Coloring Book, *The Dutch Boy Disneyland Coloring Book,* copyright 1957, 8-1/2" x 11", premium from Dutch Boy paints ................................. 15.00

Guide Book, 6" x 8-3/4", 20 pgs, stiff glossy covers, artwork, two photos of Walt Disney, c1955 ................. 125.00

Magazine, Disneyland Magazine, No. 1, 10-1/4" x 12-1/2", Fawcett Publication, 1972 copyright, 16 pgs, color art ........................................... 30.00

Pamphlet, *Your Guide To Disneyland,* 3-1/2" x 8", issued by Bank of America, 1955 copyright, opens to 13-1/2" x 16" with map on one side, other side with text and Bank of America CA locations .................................... 30.00

Pinback Button, 4" d, Main Street Commemorative, blue text, 3000th Performance Sept. 4, 1991, color photo of Main Street Electrical Parade, castle in background ........................... 35.00

Plate, 9-1/2" d, white china, gold trim, six large color illus, pierced for hanging, c1950 ............................... 60.00

Punch-Out Book, *Disneyland Punch-Out Book,* Gold Press Inc., copyright 1963, 7-1/2" x 13", unpunched ............................................ 150.00

## Donald Duck

Bank, dime register, 2-1/2" x 2-1/2" x 3/4", tin litho, late 1930s ......... 250.00

Blotter, 4" x 7", Sunoco, color illus of Donald pinning "Quick Starting" medal on gas pump, early 1940s ............................................ 60.00

Book, *Donald Duck Sees South America,* D. C. Heath & Co., Walt Disney Storybooks, hardcover, 6-1/4" x 5-1/2" ..................................... 40.00

Comic Book, *Donald and Mickey,* Firestone Christmas premium, copyright 1947, 7" x 10-1/4", excellent condition ............................................ 90.00

Figure, bisque
3-1/4" h, Donald with head turned to side, hands straight down at sides, mkd "Japan," 1930s, some paint wear ..................................... 45.00
4" h, with violin, mkd "Japan," number incised on back ............... 200.00

Matchbox Holder, 1" x 1-1/2" x 1/2", black, hard plastic, high relief images of Donald and nephew, blue and white outfits, pink shirt and hat on nephew, mkd "Potter & Moore/England," c1940 ...................... 50.00

Nodder, wind-up, 5-1/4" h, celluloid figure attached to domed painted tin base, mkd "TT, Made in Japan," 1930s, fine condition .............. 500.00

Pencil, 5-1/2" l, red, white, and blue, Donald Duck Bread, loaf of bread, imprint of Ungles Baking Co., 1950s ............................................ 25.00

Pencil Sharpener, 1" d dark green plastic, octagonal, full color decal of Donald waving, c1940 ............. 60.00

Sprinkling Can, 3" h, Ohio Art, tin litho, copyright 1938, Donald walking and tripping over brick, some surface damage ................................. 145.00

Thermometer, 6" x 6" ceramic Sportsman plaque, Donald as bowler, black text, Kemper-Thomas Co., 1940s ...................................... 35.00

Viewmaster Set, 4-1/2" x 4-1/2" envelope, color photo, 3 reels, single inner sleeve, orig story booklet, Donald, Chip n' Dale and Uncle Scrooge, 1960s ....................... 25.00

## Dumbo

Card Game, 2-1/2" x 3-1/2" x 3/4" deep blue and white box, 45 cards and instructions, English, marked "Pepy Series," c1941 ...................... 125.00

Cookie Jar, 7" x 9" x 13" h, glazed white china, over glaze green, orange, blue, and dark brown paint, turnabout type, Leeds China, late 1940s ............................................ 100.00

Puzzle, Jaymar, 1950s, orig 7" x 10" box ................................................. 15.00

## Lady and the Tramp

Book, *Lady,* Whitman Tell-a-Tale, 1954 copyright, 5-1/2" x 6-1/2", 28 pgs, color art ................................... 20.00

Jock, 2-1/2" x 3-1/2" stiff plastic sheet, punch-out figure of Jock, issued by Scotch Brand tape, c1955 ....... 25.00

Sheet Music, Hanson Publications, copyright 1955 Walt Disney Music Co., 9" x 12" folio ..................... 40.00

## Mickey Mouse

Better Little Book, *Mickey Mouse and the Lazy Daisy Mystery,* Whitman, #1433, copyright 1947 ............. 55.00

Big Little Book, *Mickey Mouse The Mail Pilot,* Whitman, copyright 1933, softcover, 3-1/2" x 4-3/4", some wear ................................................. 60.00

Book
*Mickey Mouse Waddle Book,* Blue ribbon Books, copyright 1934, hardcover, 7-3/4" x 10-1/4", 27 pg story, missing waddle figures, fine .... 85.00
*The Adventures of Mickey Mouse Book!,* David McKay Co., copyright

**Donald Duck Acrobat Gym Toys, Linemar, 9" x 7" orig box, $400.**

1931, hardcover, 5-1/2" x 7-1/2", 32 pgs, shows wear, good condition ....................................................55.00

Coloring Book, *Another Mickey Mouse Coloring Book,* Saalfield Publishing, copyright 1935, 10-3/4" x 15", 28 pgs, used, some signs of aging ....................................................40.00

Doll, 4-1/2" x 7-1/2" x 12" h, Knickerbocker, stuffed cloth and composition, oilcloth eyes and thick felt ears, 1930s, some fading, played-with condition ...............................250.00

Figure
1-1/2" h, bisque, 1930s, red pants, green shoes, one hand raised, Japan ........................................40.00
4" h, glazed bisque, playing violin, mkd "Made in Japan," distributed in Canada ...............................150.00

Get Well Card, 4" x 5", diecut, Hallmark, 1930s ....................................35.00

Mug, 2-1/2" h, china, Mickey riding Henry Horse, 1930s, mkd "Made in Japan" ......................................195.00

Pencil Box, 3-1/2" x 5" x 3/4", paper covered cardboard, snap closure, Dixon, 1930s ...............................90.00

Plate, 7" d, Mickey and Pluto, white, orange rim, large color center image, Salem China Co., mkd "Patriot China" and Disney name, 1930s ...................................150.00

Sand Pail, 8" h, 8-1/4" d, tin litho, Ohio Art Co., copyright 1938, Mickey, Minnie, and Goofy, Donald carrying groceries in wagon pulled by Pluto, very fine condition............................350.00

Tin, 5-1/2" x 6" x 2", hexagonal, hinged lid, six illus on sides, Australian, 1930s ....................................185.00

Toothbrush Holder, 2" x 2-3/4" x 4" h, china, Disney copyright, Maw & Sons, 1930s ...........................400.00

Watch, Bradley, 2" x 3" x 2" clear and black plastic case, 1" d silvered metal case, 1970s...................35.00

Wee Little Book, Whitman, copyright 1934, 3" x 3-1/4", from boxed set, very fine condition
*Mickey Mouse At The Carnival*
....................................................45.00

**Walt Disney's Ferdinand the Bull, ©1936 by Monro Leaf and Robert Lawson, 10-1/8" x 9-1/4", 12 pgs, $40.**

*Mickey Mouse Wins The Race*
....................................................45.00

## Mickey Mouse Club

Lunch Box, 7" x 8" x 4", emb metal, Aladdin, c1963.........................75.00

Membership Certificate, 8-1/2" x 11", tan parchment-like paper, black text, repeated gold Mickey portrait, facsimile Mickey signature and seal design, unused........................30.00

Record, Mickey Mouse Club March, 7" x 7" colorful stiff paper sleeve, 45 rpm record, Disneyland label, 1962 copyright....................................20.00

Stick-Ons Set, 8-1/2" x 13" x 1" deep colorful box, Standard Toykraft, 1961 copyright, colorful fabric pieces, 8 x 9" stiff cardboard section with felt covering...................................30.00

Thermos, 6-1/2" h, metal, color illus, white cup, Mickey as band leader, other characters playing instruments, Aladdin Industries, 1960s ....................................................50.00

Wallet, 3-1/4" x 4", vinyl, snap closure, image of Mickey, flocked ears, 1950s, autographed b Annette Funicello .....................................150.00

## Minnie Mouse

Ashtray, green dress, white polka dots, red hat, yellow flower .............150.00

Cigarette Holder, 1-1/2" x 3-1/4" x 2-1/2" h, white china, gold trim, Minnie images on both sides, one side brushing hair, other side with finger point in the air ........................225.00

Figure, bisque
3-1/4" h, nurse, yellow dress, dark orange polka dots, gold hat, orange shoes, silver case with orange cross, 1930s..................................80.00
3-1/2" h, light blue dress, green hat, yellow shoes, holding tan and gold mandolin, 1930s, incised "C69" on back ...................................75.00

## Pinocchio

Book, *Pinocchio,* Whitman, copyright 1939, Cocomalt premium, 8-1/2" x 11", excellent condition............35.00

Figure, 3" h, bisque, blue, red, yellow, brown shoes, c1940 ................30.00

Magazine, *The American Girl,* January 1940, 8-1/2" x 11-1/2" l............20.00

Sheet Music, Pinocchio Song Hit Folio, 9" x 12", 16 pgs of words and music, 1940 copyright, Allan & Co., Pty Ltd. Australian issue........................20.00

Toy, Pinocchio Pop Pal, 3" h, hard plastic push button, Kohner, c1970, dark brown, tree stump opens to review three-dimensional Pinocchio, squeaks ...................................15.00

Whistle, 1-1/2" h, Jiminy Cricket, aluminum, name, image, and Disney copyright stamped on stem, c1960 ....................................................10.00

## Pluto

Candle, 1-1/2" x 2" x 3-1/2", figural, green base, red and brown dog dish, black and white eye stickers, 1960s, unused ..........................12.00

Card Game, 5" x 6-1/2" box, 35 playing cards, Whitman, 1939 copyright, black, white, and red illus........50.00

Figure, 1-3/4" h, painted and glazed ceramic, brown, black, and white accents, red collar, Shaw sticker missing, 1950s......................125.00

Picture, framed, 4-1/4" x 5-3/4", Reliance Art Co., black, and gold wood frame, image printed on back of glass, orig cardboard backing ....................................................60.00

Salt and Pepper Shakers, pr, 3-1/4" h, glazed white china, over glaze black and red paint dec, Leeds China, unmarked, 1947......................30.00

Toy, Marx Wiz Walker, 5" x 9" diecut card, 1-1/2" long hard plastic ramp walker, metal legs, yellow, black, and red, small Disney copyright, c1960 ....................................................25.00

## Snow White

Book, *Snow White and the Seven Dwarfs Storybook,* Whitman, copyright 1938, soft cover, 8-1/2" x 11-1/4", very fine .....................35.00

Cake Decoration Figure, 1-5/8" h, Dopey, bisque, deep pink hat, yellow coat, green pants, tan shoes, c1938 ....................................................35.00

Figure
3-1/2" h, Happy, hard celluloid head, pipe cleaner beard, arms, and legs, red fabric hat, red felt jacket, black belt, brown pants, green shoes, 1938......................................40.00
6-1/2" h, Snow White, painted and glazed china, blue and yellow dress, deep pink bow and facial features, black hair, Leeds China, c1949 ....................................................65.00

Mask, diecut stiff paper, premium from Stroehmann's Bread, ad for Snow White Cake, marked "Part-T-Mask/Eison-Freeman Co, Inc., poem on back, 1937 copyright
Doc, 9-1/4" x 11" ......................25.00
Grumpy, 9-1/4" x 13" ...............25.00
Snow White, 7-3/4" x 8-1/4" ......30.00
Witch, 8" x 10-1/4" ...................45.00

**Snow White dime register bank, $150.**

Paint Book, 10-3/4" x 15", Whitman #696, 1938 copyright, 40 pgs, one pg crayoned, four painted ....... 75.00

Paper Dolls, 10" x 12-3/4", Whitman, 1972 copyright, stiff paper full color covers, six glossy pages of outfits, unused ....................................... 30.00

### Winnie The Pooh

Game, 9" x 17" x 1-1/2" deep colorful box, Parker Brothers, 1964 copyright, 16-1/2" x 16-1/2" board, fabric "grab-bag," plastic disks, four figural playing pieces.......................... 30.00

Glass, 4-3/4" h, black design, Canadian, text on back reads "Inspired by Walt Disney's Winnie The Pooh and The Honey Tree," 1965 copyright ................................................ 40.00

Viewmaster Set, 4-1/2" x 4-1/2" envelope, color photo, 3 reels, color booklet and catalog, copyright 1964 ................................................ 20.00

### Zorro

Book, *Zorro Golden Book,* Golden Press, 1958 copyright, 9-1/4" x 12-1/4", stuff cover, 32 pgs, color and black, white, and red story art, very fine ................................... 20.00

Gloves, 4-1/2" x 7-1/2", vinyl cuff section, black fabric fingers, black, white, and red, Zorro image and name, orig staple, red and blue Disneyland Gloves tag, late 1950s, unused ................................... 25.00

Hat, 12" x 12-1/2" x 3", black starched straw, thin felt trim, orig black and white fabric chin strap, black and white patch, c1940.................. 60.00

Punch-Out Book, *Giant Funtime Book,* Pocket Books, copyright 1958, 7-1/4" x 13", thin cardboard, 4 inside pages with punch-outs, unpunched ................................................ 125.00

Viewmaster Set, 4-1/2" x 4-1/2" envelope, color photos, 3 reels, black and white booklet, copyright 1958 ................................................ 30.00

Wind-Up, 4-1/4" h hard plastic, built-in key, Zorro and horse Toronado, Durham Industries, copyright 1975 ................................................ 40.00

# Dog Collectibles

**Collecting Hints:** A collection of dog-related items may be based on one particular breed or may be composed of items picturing a dog or even dog-shaped objects. With millions of dog owners in the United States, dog collectibles are very popular.

**History:** Dogs, long recognized as "Man's Best Friend," have been associated with humans since the early cavemen. The first dogs probably were used for hunting and protection against the wilder animals.

After man learned that dogs could be taught to provide useful services, many types of dogs were bred and trained for specific purposes. More than 100 breeds of dogs have evolved from the first dog which roamed the earth over 15 million years ago. Today, dogs are still hunters, protectors, and herders, and are trained to see, hear, and perform routine tasks for handicapped people.

Man has continued to domesticate the dog, developing today's popular breeds. The American Kennel Club has divided the breeds into seven classifications: herding, hounds, sporting, non-sporting, terriers, toy breeds, and working dogs.

The first modern dog show was in Newcastle, England, in 1859. Its success spawned many other shows. The breeding of prize dogs became popular, and the bloodlines of important dogs were established and recorded. Today, the dogs with the most impressive pedigrees command the highest prices.

As dogs' popularity grew, so did the frequency of their appearance on objects. They became popular in literature, paintings, and other art forms.

**References:** Elaine Butler, *Poodle Collectibles of the 50s & 60s,* L-W Book Sales, 1996; Dana Cain, *Film & TV Animal Star Collectibles,* Antique Trader Books, 1998; Candace Sten Davis and Patricia Baugh, *A Treasury of Scottie Dog Collectibles,* Collector Books, 1998; Alice L. Muncaster and Ellen Sawyer, *The Dog Made Me Buy It!,* Crown Publishers, 1990; William Secord, *Dog Painting,* Antique Collectors' Club, 1992.

**Collectors' Clubs:** Canine Collectibles Club of America, 736 N. Western Ave., Suite 314, Lake Forest, IL 60045; Collectively Speaking, 428 Philadelphia Rd., Joppa, MD 21085; Wee Scots, Inc., P.O. Box 1512, Columbus, IN 47202.

**Museum:** The Dog Museum of America, Jarville House, St. Louis, MO.

**Advisor:** Jocelyn C. Mousley.

Ashtray, Scottie, Stangl................. 72.00

Bank
RCA Nipper, foot reglued......... 90.00
Scottie, Hubley...................... 115.00
St. Bernard, cast iron, painted black and gold................................ 130.00

Advertising Mirror, Nipper, His Master's Voice written on table, multicolored, 2-3/4" x 1-3/4" oval, $95.

Bookends, pr
3-3/4" h, 2-1/2" w, 3-1/4" l, yellow dog, mkd "Made in Japan"...... 35.00
6-1/4" h, Scottie, black satin glass ................................................ 215.00

Book
*Secrets of Show Dog Handling,* M. Miglorina, Arco, 1982, 127 pgs ................................................ 7.00
*The Complete Lap Retriever, It's History, Development & Function As A Sporting Dog,* H. Warwick, Howell, 1969, 304 pgs......................... 7.00
*The Dog of the South,* Charles Portis, Alfred Knopf, 1979, 1st edition ................................................ 7.50

Bowl, 10" d, "DOG" written on side, yellow ware.................................. 55.00

Brush, figural, ceramic, Marutomoware, Made in Japan, c1950, 6-3/4" l ................................................ 22.00

Calendar, Texaco, Scottie and girl on telephone, 1959...................... 20.00

Calendar Plate, 1910, black and white Bulldog, white china, gold trim ................................................ 45.00

Candy Dish, cov, glass, Bulldog .. 75.00

Cigarette Box, large emb Borzoi heads ................................................ 35.00

Cigarette Lighter, English Setter, Zippo, painted, 1950......................... 125.00

Cocktail Glasses, Scottie dec, set of 6 ................................................ 55.00

Color and Activity Book, 1979, unused ................................................ 50.00

Cookie Jar, 9" h, mkd "Made in Japan," small nick in lid ......................... 25.00

Creamer, large, dog and child, mkd "Teplitz, Stellmacher"............... 65.00

Dinnerware, Lassie, Melmac, 3 pc snack set .............................. 75.00

Doorstop, painted cast iron
Setter, on point, side view, black and white, Hubley ......................... 300.00
Terrier..................................... 175.00

Dresser Jar, cov, satin glass, dog on top ................................................ 45.00

Dresser Tray, four French Poodles doing can-can, sgd "Clement" ........ 125.00

Figure
Basset Hound, Napco ............. 40.00
Beagle, #1072, Llardo ........... 140.00

**Figure, Bulldog, tan and brown, red collar, incised "Germany, 2777," 5" h, $48.**

Bloodhound, bronze, David, The Bloodhound of Prince Napoleon, by Jules-Bertrand Gelibert, c1847 ................................. 7,625.00
Bonzo Dog, 3" h, bisque, mkd "Germany," c1920 ......................... 45.00
Borzoi, Mortens Studios, #749 ................................. 125.00
Collie, bisque, black and brown ................................. 40.00
Dachshund, Beswick, #1469 ... 50.00
German Shepherd, Royal Dux, porcelain ......................... 65.00
Jack Russell Terrier, bisque, puppy ................................. 25.00
Newfoundland, reclining, bronze, Emanuel Fremiert ............... 1,525.00
Poodle, sitting, Goebel, matte finish ................................. 90.00
Pug, Mortens Studios, #738 ... 125.00
Schnauzer, bronze, dark brown patina, Maximillien-Louis Fiot ................................. 2,850.00
Spaniel, 4-1/2" h, china, gold trimmed collar with locket, Staffordshire ......................... 135.00
Jewelry, pin
    Bedlingham Terrier ................... 40.00
    Cocker spaniel, sterling silver, emb detail, mkd "Cini" ..................... 90.00

**License, Dog Tax, Ashland, 1891, diecut metal, $12.**

Magazine, Dog, 1941 ................... 24.00
Model Kit, My Lassie, Gabriel, 1976, MIB ......................... 115.00
Nodder
    Dalmatian ................................. 80.00
    German Shepherd ................... 75.00
Patch, Rin Tin Tin insignia, set of 7 ................................. 25.00
Pen Tray, Labrador, bronze ........... 45.00
Pipe Rack, Terrier and Bulldog peeking over fence ................................. 35.00
Planter, ceramic
    Cocker Spaniel, white, Royal Copley ................................. 40.00
    Spotted Dog, McCoy ............. 145.00
Salt and Pepper Shakers, pr
    Poodle, heads, Rosemeade .. 165.00
    RCA Nipper, Lenox ................... 75.00
String Holder, Scottie, figural ...... 125.00
Stuffed Dog, Lassie, vinyl collar ... 75.00
Toy
    Fisher-Price, #240, boy with dog on tractor, gong bell ...................... 70.00
    Snoopy, pull toy, ears move ..... 40.00
Vase, Poodle, Sascha Brastoff ..... 75.00
Wallet, Lassie, orig mailer ........... 100.00
Wall Plaque, Collie, Mortens Studio ................................. 24.00

# Dollhouse Furnishings

**Collecting Hints:** Dollhouse furnishings are children's toys, so some wear is to be expected. It is possible to find entire room sets in original boxes, and these sets command high prices.

**History:** Dollhouse furnishings are the tiny articles used to furnish and accessorize a dollhouse. Materials and methods of production range from fine handmade wooden pieces to molded plastic items. Several toy manufacturers, such as Tootsietoy, Petite Princess, and Renwal, made dollhouse furnishings.

There is renewed interest in collecting dollhouses and dollhouse furnishings. Many artists and craftsmen devote hours to making furniture and accessories to scale. These types of handmade dollhouse furnishings are not included in this listing. They do, however, affect the market by offering buyers a choice between old pieces and modern handcrafted ones.

**References:** Flora Gill Jacobs, *Dolls Houses in America*, Charles Scribner's Sons, 1974; Constance Eileen King, *Dolls and Dolls Houses*, Hamlyn, 1989; Jean Mahan, *Doll Furniture, 1950s-1980s, Identification and Price Guide,* Hobby House Press, 1997; Dian Zillner, *Antique Dollhouses and Their Furnishings*, Schiffer Publishing, 1998.

**Periodicals:** *Doll Castle News*, P.O. Box 247, Washington, NJ 07882; *Miniature Collector*, 30595 Eight Mile, Livonia, MI 48152; *Nutshell News*, P.O. Box 1612, Waukesha, WI 53187.

**Collectors' Clubs:** Dollhouse & Miniature Collectors, P.O. Box 16, Bellaire, MI 49615; National Association of Miniature Enthusiasts, P.O. Box 69, Carmel, IN 46032.

**Museums:** Margaret Woodbury Strong Museum, Rochester, NY; Mildred Mahoney Jubilee Doll House Museum, Fort Erie, Canada; Toy and Miniature Museum of Kansas City, Kansas City, MO; Toy Museum of Atlanta, Atlanta, GA; Washington Dolls' House and Toy Museum, Washington, DC.

Baker's Rack, metal, wood cutting board, 3-1/2" w, 6-1/2" h ........... 10.00
Bar Stool, oak, 2-1/4" h ................... 5.00
Bathroom Set, Tootiestoy, 10 pcs, orig box ............................... 80.00
Bath Tub, metal, Tootsietoy ........... 15.00
Bed
    Four poster, patterned cloth spread, matching dust ruffle and canopy ................................. 20.00
    Twin, Renwal ........................... 10.00
Bedroom Suite, bed, 5 drawer highboy, 4 drawer dresser, mirror, 2 side tables, mahogany finish ........... 45.00
Buffet, Petite Princess, MIB ......... 20.00
Canister Set, yellow plastic, 4 canisters, lids ............................... 5.00

**Boxed Set, Nancy Forbes, No. 4502, 18 pcs, $35.**

Corner Cabinet, oak, 3-1/2" w, 6-1/2" h ................................................. 20.00
Curio Cabinet, wood ...................... 22.00
Dining Room Suite, blond finish, red patterned fabric seats, 7 pc .... 30.00
Dressing Mirror ............................. 10.00
Fireplace, Renwal, brown ............. 35.00
Grand Piano and Bench ............... 12.50
Grandfather's Clock, wood, working ................................................. 45.00
High Chair, cast iron ..................... 25.00
Ironing Board, Kilgore, folding, cast iron, c1930 .............................. 24.00
Kitchen Appliances, refrigerator, sink in cabinet, stove, plastic .............. 30.00
Kitchen Chair, woven wood seat .... 4.00
Kitchen Suite, plastic, Ideal, c1940, MIB, 7 pcs ............................... 35.00
Living Room Suite
  Contemporary, floral print, wood and fabric, 5 pcs ............................ 30.00
  Victorian, deep burgundy upholstery, parlor sofa, Queen Anne style side arm and side chairs, coffee table, 1" to 1' scale, 4 pc set ................... 40.00
Nursery Set, pink and yellow plastic, 5 pcs ............................................ 25.00
Radio, Renwal ............................... 30.00
Rocking Chair, wood, colonial style 9.00
Rolltop Desk, wood ....................... 10.00
Settee, Arcade, cast iron ............. 80.00
Sewing Machine, moveable treadle, wood case, 3-1/8" w, 3" h ........... 5.00
Sofa, Tootsietoy, metal ................. 35.00
Study Suite, mahogany finished wood, red velvet, 8 pcs ...................... 22.50

Table, drop leaf, wood .................... 7.50
Tea Cart, wood ............................... 8.00
Tea Set, porcelain, 1-1/2" h teapot, 3-1/2" w tray, white ground, blue florals, 10 pcs ................................ 9.00
Wing Chair, matching footstool, floral pattern ...................................... 12.00

# Dolls

**Collecting Hints:** The most important criteria in buying dolls are sentiment and condition. The value of a particular doll increases if it is a childhood favorite or family heirloom.

When pricing a doll, condition is the most important aspect. Excellent condition means that the doll has all original parts, a wig that is not soiled or restyled, skin surface free of marks and blemishes, the original free-moving sleep eyes, and mechanical parts that are all operational. Original clothing means original dress, underclothes, shoes, and socks—all in excellent and clean condition, and preferably with original tags and labels.

A doll that is mint in the original box is listed as "MIB." Many modern collectible doll prices depend on the inclusion of the original box. Mattel's original Barbie doll, for example, is valued at more than $1,000 MIB. However, without the original box, the doll is worth much less. Another pricing consideration is appeal. How important and valuable a particular doll is depends on the individual's collection.

Modern and 20th-century dolls are highly collectible. They offer many appealing features to collectors, one of which is an affordable price tag. Modern dolls are readily available at flea markets, garage sales, swap meets, etc.

Other determinants for collectors is whether the size of a doll is such that it can be artfully displayed and whether it is made of materials that can be easily cleaned and maintained.

**History:** The history of modern doll manufacturers is long and varied. Competition between companies often resulted in similar doll-making procedures, molds, and ideas. When Effanbee was successful with the Patsy dolls, Horsman soon followed with a Patsy look-alike named Dorothy. Vogue's Ginny doll was imitated by Cosmopolitan's Ginger. Some manufacturers reused molds and changed sizes and names to produce similar dolls for many years.

Dolls have always been popular with Americans. The early Patsy dolls with their own wardrobes were a success in the 1930s and 1940s. During the 1950s the popularity of Vogue's Ginny Doll generated the sales of dolls, clothes, and accessories. The next decade of children enjoyed Mattel's Barbie. Doll collecting has become a major hobby, and collectors will determine what the next hot collectible will be.

**References:** J. Michael Augustyniak, *Thirty Years of Mattel Fashion Dolls, 1967 Through 1997: Identification and Value Guide*, Collector Books, 1998; Kim Avery, *The World of Raggedy Ann Collectibles*, Collector Books, 1997; Carla Marie Cross, *Modern Doll Rarities, Antique Trader Books*, 1997; Linda Crowsey, *Madame Alexander Collector's Dolls Price Guide*, #22, Collector Books, 1997; Maryanne Dolan, *The World of Dolls, A Collector's Identification and Value Guide*, Krause Publications, 1999; Jan Foulke, *12th Blue Book Dolls & Values*, Hobby House Press, 1995; Beth Gunther, *Crissy Doll and Her Friends: Guide for Collectors*, Antique Trader Books, 1998; Patricia Hall, *Johnny Gruelle: Creator of Rag-*

gedy Ann and Andy, Pelican Publishing (1101 Monroe St., Gretna, LA 70053), 1993; Dawn Herlocher, 200 Years of Dolls, Antique Trader Books, 1996; R. Lane Herron, Warman's Dolls, Krause Publications, 1998; Judith Izen and Carol Stover, Collector's Guide to Vogue Dolls, Collector Books, 1997; Polly Judd, Cloth Dolls of the 1920s and 1930s, Hobby House Press, 1990; Polly and Pam Judd, Composition Dolls, Vol. I (1991), Vol. II (1994), Hobby House Press; ―, European Costumed Dolls, Hobby House Press, 1994; ――, Glamour Dolls of the 1950s & 1960s, revised ed., Hobby House Press, 1993; ―, Hard Plastic Dolls, Book I (3rd ed., 1993), Book II (Revised, 1994), Hobby House Press; Kathy and Don Lewis, Chatty Cathy Dolls, Collector Books, 1994; Michele Karl, Composition & Wood Dolls and Toys: A Collector's Reference Guide, Antique Trader Books, 1998; Ursula R. Mertz, Collector's Encyclopedia of American Composition Dolls, 1900 to 1950, Collector Books, 1999; Patsy Moyer, Doll Values, Antique to Modern, Collector Books, 1997; ―, Modern Collectible Dolls, Collector Books, 1997; Joleen Ashman Robison and Kay Sellers, Advertising Dolls, Collector Books, 1980, 1994 value update; Cindy Sabulis and Susan Weglewski, Collector's Guide to Tammy, Collector Books, 1997; Patricia N. Schoonmaker, Patsy Doll Family, Hobby House Press, 1992; Patricia R. Smith, Collector's Encyclopedia of Madame Alexander Dolls, Collector Books, 1991, 1994 value update; ―, Modern Collector's Dolls, Series 1–7 (1973-1995), 1995 value update, Collector Books; ―, Patricia Smith's Doll Values, 11th ed., Collector Books, 1995; Robert Reed, Bears and Dolls in Advertising, Antique Trader Books, 1998; Evelyn Robson Stahlendorf, Charlton Standard Catalogue of Canadian Dolls, 3rd ed., Charlton Press, 1996; Andrew Tabbat, Collector's World of Raggedy Ann and Andy, Dollmasters, 1996.

**Periodicals:** Celebrity Doll Journal, 5 Court Pl., Puyallup, WA 98372; Cloth Doll Magazine, P.O. Box 1089, Mt. Shasta, CA 96067; Costume Quarterly for Doll Collectors, 118-01 Sutter Ave., Jamaica, NY 11420; Doll Collector's Price Guide, 306 E. Parr Rd., Berne IN 46711; Doll Life, 243 Newton-Sparta Rd., Newton, NJ 07860; Doll Reader, 6405 Flank Dr., Harrisburg, PA 17112; Doll Times, 218 West Woodin Blvd., Dallas, TX 75224; Doll World, P.O. Box 9001, Big Sandy, TX 75755; Dolls–The Collector's Magazine, P.O. Box 1972, Marion, OH 43305; Rags, P.O. Box 823, Atlanta, GA 30301.

**Collectors' Clubs:** Cabbage Patch Kids Collectors Club, P.O. Box 714, Cleveland, GA 30528; Chatty Cathy Collectors Club, 2610 Dover St., Piscataway, NJ 08854; Ginny Doll Club, 9628 Hidden Oaks Circle, Tampa, FL 33612; Ideal Doll Collector's Club, P.O. Box 623, Lexington, MA 02173; Madame Alexander Fan Club, P.O. Box 330, Mundeline, IL 60060; United Federation of Doll Clubs, 8B East St., P.O. Box 14146, Parkville, MO 64152.

**Museums:** Doll Museum, Newport, RI; Margaret Woodbury Strong Museum, Rochester, NY; Museum of Collectible Dolls, Lakeland, FL; Yesteryears Museum, Sandwich, MA.

**Additional Listings:** Barbie.

**Note:** All dolls listed here are in excellent condition and have their original clothes, unless otherwise noted.

**Advertising.** Advertising dolls come in many shape and sizes. They range from composition, vinyl, and plastic to stuffed cloth. Value is enhanced when the original mailing envelope, packaging, or box is included.

Allied Van Lines, 18" h, 7" w, soiled
................................................. 10.00
Blue Bonnet, 12" h, 5" w, 1986 mail-in premium.................................... 25.00
Buddy Lee, 12" h, hard plastic head, large painted eyes, hard plastic body, jointed at shoulders, molded and painted black boots, orig Lee denim shirt, bib overalls, hat, and red bandanna, mkd Buddy Lee on back, Lee on Hat, Union Made on label on back of paints ......... 350.00
Chlorox, Lots of Legs, 12" l, 4" w, 1985 ................................................. 25.00
Coco Wheat, Gretchen, 1949, 12-1/2" h, cloth, stuffed ........................... 25.00
Johnson Wax, Minnie Mouse, 11-1/2" h, 6" w, Applause, 1988 mail-in premium, mint in orig envelope..... 20.00
Jolly Green Giant, 16" l, 6" w, 1969 mail-in premium, mint in orig envelope
................................................. 50.00
Little Debbie, 12" h, 4" w, 1985 mail-in premium, mint in orig envelope ..50.00
Lysol, 1988 mail-in premium, mint in orig envelope
  Fancy Fresh, 7" h, 5" w............. 20.00
  Squeaky Clean, 7" h, 5" w........ 20.00
Northern Tissue, 16" h, 6-1/2" w, 1987 mail-in premium, mint in orig envelope.......................................... 60.00
Planters Peanut, Mr. Peanut, 17" h, 6" w, monocle on left eye, 1960s, slightly soiled ...................................... 20.00
Scrubbing Bubbles, Mr. Bubble, 10" h, 7" w, plush.............................. 20.00
Twinkie the Kid, 36" h, store contest premium ...................................... 125.00

**American Character.** The American Character Doll Company was founded in 1918 and made high quality dolls. When the company was liquidated in 1968, many molds were purchased by the Ideal Toy Company. American Character Dolls are marked with the full company name, "Amer. Char." or "Amer. Char" in a circle. Early composition dolls were marked "Petite."

Baby, 16" h, composition head, stuffed cloth body and limbs, molded painted brown hair, brown sleep eyes, c1925 .......................... 125.00
Betsy McCall, 8" h, hard plastic, jointed knees, brunette rooted hair, sleep eyes, orig red and white striped skirt, white organdy top, red shoes, c1960 .................................................. 45.00
Bottle Tot, 13" h, composition head, body mark, orig tagged clothes
.................................................. 175.00
Carol Ann Beery, 16" h, composition head, 5 pc composition child body, green sleep eyes, closed mouth, orig mohair wig with braid across forehead, orig white pique dress, matching sun suit and bonnet, orig socks and snap shoes, mkd "Petite, Sally" on back of head, "Petite" on body, right foot broken and reglued, tips of right thumb and little finger broken.................................... 440.00
Sweet Sue, 15" h, blond wig, blue sleep eyes, rose dec white taffeta dress, pearl pin, silver dance shoes, all orig
.................................................. 200.00
Tiny Tears, 12" h, hard plastic head, 5 pc rubber body, blue sleep eyes, open nurser mouth, rooted hair, orig pink and white dress, unplayed with condition, orig clothing and accessories appear to never have been removed from box.................. 550.00
Toni, 10" h, collegiate outfit, orig booklet
.................................................. 70.00

**Arranbee.** This company was founded in 1922. Arranbee's finest dolls were made in hard plastic. Two of Arranbee's most popular dolls were Nancy, and later, Nanette. The company was sold to Vogue Dolls, Inc., in 1959. Marks used by this company include "Arranbee," "R&B," and "Made in USA."

Angel Skin, 13" h, stuffed soft vinyl head, stuffed magic skin body and limbs, molded, painted hair, inset stationary blue eyes, closed mouth, mkd R & B on head, orig tag: The R & B Family/Rock Me/Nanette/Little Angel, Dream Baby/Baby Bunting, Angel Skin/Taffy, c1954, MIB....80.00

Baby Bunting, 15" h, vinylite plastic head, stuffed magic skin body, molded, painted hair, pink fleece bunting, mkd 17BBS/R & B/D6 on head, orig tag reads: Head is of Vinylite Plastic by Bakelite Company ....................................... 60.00

Dream Baby, 20" h, composition shoulder-head, cloth body, painted hair, redressed, c1925 ................... 110.00

Little Dear, 8" h, stuffed vinyl body, rooted hair, blue sleep eyes, c1956 ............................................... 80.00

Littlest Angel, 11" h, vinyl head, hard plastic body, jointed, rooted dark brown hair, mkd R & B on head, 1959 ......................................... 40.00

Nancy, 21" h, composition, blue glass eyes, orig dress and cut-out shoes ............................................ 395.00

Nancy Lee, 14" h, composition head, 5 pc composition child body, brown sleep eyes, closed mouth, orig mohair wig in orig set, orig long yellow dress with gold polka dots, matching bonnet, orig yellow taffeta underclothing, socks and shoes, mkd "R & B" faintly on back of head ............................................ 250.00

Nanette, 15" h, all hard plastic, glued on wig, sleep eyes, walker, cotton pinafore, straw hat, 1952, MIB.... 250.00

Rosie, 19" h, composition, swivel head, cloth body, molded hair, 1935 .................................................. 85.00

## Character and Personality. 

Many doll companies made dolls to resemble popular characters found in the funnies, the movies, radio, and later television.

Alf the Alien................................... 30.00
Beany, Mattel ................................. 95.00
Bert, Sesame Street, Knickerbocker, 1981, MIB.................................. 25.00
Brooke Shields, MIB ..................... 30.00
Captain Caveman, stuffed, 30" h .............................................. 65.00
Carrie, Little House on the Prairie, ©1975, Knickerbocker, MIB..... 50.00
Charlie McCarthy, composition, movable mouth, 1930s ................. 185.00
Cher, 12" h, ©1975 Mego, MIB..... 50.00
Clown, Lee Middleton, 15" h, pink and white lacy outfit, lace umbrella, pink hair, green and pink feather in hair, all vinyl ................................... 135.00
ET, fuzzy, brown, marble eyes ...... 30.00
Farrah Fawcett, 12" h, Mego, MIB ............................................ 125.00
General Douglas MacArthur, composition .......................................... 225.00
Gizmo, squeaker............................ 30.00
Grinch Who Stole Christmas, Santa hat .............................................. 95.00
John Boy Walton, Mego, MIB ....... 75.00
Kristy McNichol, 8" h, MIB ............ 45.00

**Cosmopolitan, Ginger, hard plastic, walker, braided auburn wig, sleep eyes, 7-1/2" h, $25.**

Little Lulu, MIB............................ 125.00
Mary Ellen Walton, Mego, MIB ..... 75.00
Mary Poppin, c1964, MIB ............. 30.00
Smokey the Bear, Ideal, talking, MIB .............................................. 355.00
Sunbonnet Baby, Molly, Mandy or May, ©1975, Knickerbocker, MIB, each ............................................... 25.00
Tony Tennille, 12-1/4" h, ©1977 Mego, Moonlight & Magnolias, MIB.... 45.00
Wizard of Oz, Cowardly Lion, ©1974 Mego, MIB .............................. 35.00

## Cosmopolitan Doll Company. 

Little recorded history is available about this company. Dolls dating from the late 1940s through the 1960s are found with the mark of CDC. It is believed that the company made many unmarked dolls. One of their most popular dolls was Ginger, made in 1955-1956, which was a take-off of Vogue Doll's Ginny. Many of these Ginger dolls are found with original clothes made by the Terri Lee Doll Company.

Ginger, 7-1/2" h
    Hard plastic, glued on wig, walker, head turns, 1955, ice skating outfit ................................................ 45.00
    Vinyl head, hard plastic body, arms, and legs, rooted medium blond hair, closed mouth, mkd Ginger on head, 1956 ........................................ 35.00
Little Miss Ginger, 8-1/2" h, vinyl head, hard plastic body, rooted ash blond hair, closed mouth, high heel feet, mkd Little Miss Ginger, 1956 ... 20.00

Merri, 14" h, plastic, rooted blond hair, high heel feet, red gown, white fur trim, mkd AE1406/41, backward AE on lower back, 1960 ............... 20.00

## Deluxe Reading, Deluxe Topper, Topper Corporation, Topper Toys. 

Deluxe Reading, Deluxe Topper, Topper Corporation, Topper Toys, and Deluxe Toy Creations are all names used by Deluxe Toys. This company specialized in dolls that can do things. The company went out of business in 1972.

Baby Party, 10" h, vinyl head and arms, hard plastic body and legs, rooted blond hair, painted eyes, blows whistle and balloon, redressed....... 35.00
Dawn and Friends, 6" h, vinyl, jointed at neck, shoulders, waist, hips, poseable legs, rooted hair, mkd "©1970/Topper Corp/Hong Kong" on lower back, additional mark on head
    Angie, black hair, brown eyes, mkd 51/D10 ..................................... 10.00
    Dale, negro, black hair, brown eyes, mkd 4/H86 ............................... 12.00
    Dawn, blond hair, blue eyes, mkd 343/S11A ............................... 15.00
Sweet Amy School Girl, 23" h, vinyl head, one pc latex body, mkd "A-!" on head, MIB .......................... 50.00

## Eegee Doll Mfg. Company. 

The owner and founder of this company was E. G. Goldberger. He began his company in 1917, marking his dolls "E.G." Other marks used by the company include "E. Goldberger" and "Eegee." This American doll company is one of the longest lasting doll manufacturers.

Dimples, 11" h, vinyl head, cloth bean bag type body, rooted blond hair, painted eyes, dimples, music box, key wind on back, mkd "148D/Eegee Co."........................................ 24.00
Granny, 14" h, vinyl head, plastic body, long white hair in bun, hair grows, mature face, mkd "Eegee/3".... 65.00
Karne Ballerina, 21" h, hard plastic and vinyl, rooted hair, sleep eyes, jointed at knees, ankles, neck, shoulders, and hips, ballet shoes, satin and net ballet dress, c1958, MIB.......... 45.00
Layette Baby, 14" h, hard plastic head, latex body, molded, painted hair, glassine sleep eyes, orig layette, c1948, MIB ............................. 65.00
My Fair Lady, 19" h, vinyl head and body, blond hair, black net, orig costume, c1958............................ 55.00

## Effanbee Doll Corp. 

The Effanbee Doll Corporation was founded in 1912 by Bernard E. Fleischaker and Hugo Baum. Its most successful line was the Patsy Doll and its many variations. Patsy was such a success that a whole wardrobe was designed and it also sold well. This was the first successful marketing of a doll and her wardrobe.

Effanbee experimented with materials as well as molds. Rubber was first used in 1930; the use of hard plastic began in 1949. Today vinyl has replaced composition. Effanbee is still making dolls and has become one of the major manufacturers of limited edition collector dolls.

Anne Shirley, 15" h, composition head, 5 pc composition body, blue sleep eyes, closed mouth, orig mohair wig, orig black velvet dress with gold and red stars, mkd on back, Effanbee Durable dolls on metal heart bracelet ............................................. 200.00

Baby Dainty, 14" h, composition shoulder head, painted blue eyes, closed mouth, painted teeth, molded and painted hair, cloth body, composition arms and legs, orig blue print dress, matching bonnet and underclothing, orig socks and shoes ............. 150.00

Barbara Lou, 21" h, composition head, 5 pc composition body, brown sleep eyes, open mouth, 4 upper teeth, orig human hair wig, orig blue jumper dress, white blouse, matching romper, white apron, socks, black leatherette flange tie shoes, mkd "Effanbee, Ann-Shirley" on back, clothing pale, lips repainted ............................................. 350.00

Bobbsey Twins, ©1982 Stratemeyer Syndicates, MIB
   Flossie ...................................... 45.00
   Freddie ...................................... 45.00

Dy-Dee Baby, 12" h, hard plastic head, 5 pc rubber baby body, blue sleep eyes, open nurser mouth, orig skin wig, orig pink dotted Swiss dress, matching bonnet, orig Effanbee Dy-Dee Baby case with orig clothing, accessories, Mennon products, mkd "Effanbee Dy-Dee Baby (patent numbers)" on back, "Dy-Dee Baby, The Almost Human Doll, An Effanbee Play Product" on inside of case, lightly played with condition ... 525.00

Faith Wick Originals, Wicked Witch, MIB ............................................. 60.00

Madame Butterfly Collection, Madame Butterfly, ©1983, MIB ............... 45.00

Marilee, 30", composition shoulder head, composition arms and legs, blue tin sleep eyes, open mouth with 4 upper teeth, orig blond mohair wig, cloth body, orig pale green organdy ruffled dress, matching underclothes and bonnet, mkd "Effanbee, Marilee, Copyr. Doll" on back of shoulder plate, fine crazing .................. 350.00

Patsy-Ann, 19" h, composition head and child body, bent right arm, green sleep eyes, closed rosebud mouth, orig mohair wig over molded hair, orig white dress with green dots and trim, matching romper and hat, orig socks, black straps shoes, mkd

"Effanbee, Patsy-Ann," with copyright and patent numbers, some play wear ......................................... 325.00

Patsy-Lou, 22" h, composition head, 5 pc composition body, bent right arm, green sleep eyes, closed mouth, molded and painted hair, well-made copy of Patsy style dress, orig socks and snap shoes, orig blue-green felt coat with gold appliqué and trim, matching tam hat, mkd "Effanbee Patsy-Lou" on back ................ 375.00

Patsy-Mae, 30" h, composition head, cloth body, composition arms and legs, composition shoulder plate, brown sleep eyes, closed mouth, orig human hair wig, tagged orig white organdy dress with red trim and print, metal heart bracelet, mkd "Effanbee, Patsy-Mae" on back of head, "Effanbee Lovums, ©, Pat. No. 1,383,558" on shoulder plate. 800.00

Storybook Doll, Little Bo Peep, MIB ................................................. 40.00

**Hasbro.** Hasbro is primarily a toy manufacturer founded by Henry and Hillel Hassenfeld in Pawtucket, RI, in 1923. One of its most popular dolls was GI Joe and his friends. Hasbro is also noted for its advertising and personality dolls.

Amanda, Sweet Dreams, 17" h, stuffed gingham head and body, yarn hair, black felt eyes, button nose, embroidered smile, eyelet lace trimmed night cap, orchid print dress, 1974 ................................................. 12.00

Choo Choo Charlie, 9" h, soft vinyl head, stuffed cotton bean bag body, rooted hair, painted eyes, mkd "©1973 Quaker City Chocolate & Conf'y Co, Inc." ........................ 20.00

Lookin' Smart Maxine, ©1987, MIB ................................................. 25.00

Maxine's Friend, Ashley, ©1987, MIB ................................................. 35.00

Maxine's Friend, Kristen, ©1987, MIB ................................................. 35.00

**Horsman Dolls Company, Inc**. The Horsman Dolls Company, Inc. was founded in 1865 by E. I. Horsman, who began importing dolls. Soon after the founding, Horsman produced bisque dolls. It was the first company to produce the Campbell Kids. Horsman invented "Fairy Skin" in 1946, "Miracle Hair" in 1952, and "Super Flex" in 1954. The Horsman process for synthetic rubber and early vinyl has always been of high quality.

Alice In Wonderland, MIB ............. 95.00

Baby Bumps, 12" h, Negro, cloth body, arms, legs, painted hair, eyes, large well molded ears, orig romper, c1912 ...................................... 250.00

Baby Dimples, 14" h, composition flange head, child torso, composition arms and lower legs, blue tin

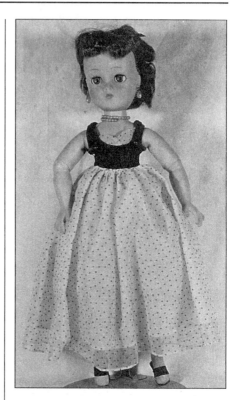

Horsman, Cindy, #82, orig clothes, 1959, 18" h, $115.

sleep eyes, open mouth with two teeth, molded and painted hair, orig tagged dress, leatherette baby shoes, mkd "©E.I.H. Co. Inc." ................................................. 200.00

Bye-Lo, 14" h, vinyl head, arms, and legs, cloth body, molded straight hair, painted eyes, christening outfit, mkd "Horsman Doll/1972" on head, MIB ....................................... 50.00

Joyce, 18" h, composition shoulder, head, arms, and legs, cloth body, glued on bright red mohair hair ................................................. 50.00

Peterkin, 11" h, composition, character face, molded hair, painted side glancing eyes, watermelon smile, c1915 ...................................... 215.00

Pram Baby, 19" h, vinyl, jointed head, glass sleep eyes, closed mouth, coos ......................................... 65.00

Ruthie, 12-1/2" h, all vinyl rooted black hair, Oriental hair style, long straight legs, dimpled knees, mkd 12-6aa on upper legs, B-1 on upper arms ................................................. 30.00

Rosebud, 20" h, composition head, arms and legs, cloth body, painted eyes, human hair wig ............. 100.00

**Ideal Toy Corp.** The Ideal Toy Company was formed in 1902 by Morris Michtom to produce his teddy bear. By 1915, the company had become a leader in the industry by introducing the first sleep eyes. In 1939, Ideal developed "Magic Skin." It was the first company to use plastic. Some of its most popular lines include Shirley Temple, Betsy Wetsy, and Toni dolls.

Clapping, 15" h, composition flange head, cloth body with clapping mechanism in torso, composition hands, blue sleep eyes, closed mouth, molded and painted blond hair, white baby dress, mkd "Ideal" in diamond, rub on nose, some flaking and soil............................ 115.00
Dennis the Menace, cloth, MIB..... 55.00
Harriet Hubbard, 21" h, vinyl head, blue sleep eyes, closed mouth, saran wig, hard plastic body, vinyl arms, orig flowered pique dress, white organdy pinafore, orig socks and shoes, orig cardboard tag with 3 plastic curlers, orig Stern Brothers price tag, mkd "MK 21, Ideal Doll" on back of head.......................... 225.00
Jody the Country Girl, ©1976, MIB
................................................ 45.00
Miss Ideal, 25" h, Photographer's Model, vinyl head, rigid vinyl body, jointed at shoulders, waist, hips, and ankles, blue sleep eyes, rooted nylon hair, orig clothes, mkd ©Ideal

**Ideal, walker, hard plastic, mkd "Ideal Doll, W16" on head, 17-1/2" h, $30.**

Toy Corp. SP-25-S: on head, ©Ideal Toy Corp P-25" on back orig box with promotional paper, Playwave Kit in orig hatbox, Styling Hints wrist tag, some water stains to orig box
................................................ 350.00
Shirley Temple
15" h, vinyl head, 5 pc vinyl body, hazel sleep eyes, open-closed mouth, six upper teeth, dimples, rooted hair in orig set, orig dress with red velvet bodice, white taffeta skirt with nylon overlay, lace trim, orig underclothes, pearl crown, mkd "Ideal Doll ST-15-N" on back of head, c1941.......... 325.00
18" h, composition head, 5 pc composition child body, hazel sleep eyes, open mouth with 6 upper teeth, orig mohair wig, orig tagged flower print dress, orig underclothing, socks and shoes, mkd "Shirley Temple" on head and body ... 600.00
Suntan Dodi and her Suntan Doodles, ©1977, MIB.............................. 75.00
Taylor Jones, 12" h fashion doll, hair changes color, ©1976, MIB..... 75.00
Thumbelina, 18", vinyl flange head, cloth body with vinyl arms and legs, painted blue eyes, open-closed mouth, rooted synthetic hair, large wooden knob on back for winding to operate baby wiggling mechanism, orig blue and white knit outfit, mkd "Ideal Toy Corp. 77-16" on back of head, orig box........................ 225.00
Tony, 14" h, hard plastic head, 5 pc hard plastic walker body, blue sleep eyes, closed mouth, orig brunette wig, orig blue dress, white organdy bodice, orig underclothes and shoes, mkd "P-90 Ideal Doll" on head and "Ideal Doll 90 W" on back, orig Play Wave set with some orig contents, partial orig box....... 450.00

**Madame Alexander.** The Madame Alexander Doll Company was started in 1923 by Bertha Alexander. The dolls made by this company are beautifully designed with exquisite costumes. They have made hundreds of dolls, including several series, such as the International Dolls and the Americana Dolls.

Marks used by this company include "Madame Alexander," "Alexander," "Alex," and many are unmarked on the body but can be identified by clothing tags. Today Madame Alexander continues to make dolls which are very collectible. Many dolls are made for a limited time period of one year. Others are offered for several years before being discontinued.

Americana Series, 8" h
Amish Boy, orig clothes, c1965
................................................ 450.00
Colonial Girl, orig clothes, c1962
................................................ 350.00

**Madame Alexander, Princess Elizabeth, 22" h, $600. Photo courtesy of McMasters Doll Auctions.**

Binnie Walker, 17" h, hard plastic, blond hair, black striped dress, yellow pinafore, and straw hat, MIB, c1950
................................................ 500.00
Bride, 20" h, composition head, blue sleep eyes, closed mouth, orig mohair wig in orig set, 5 pc composition body, tagged bride dress, orig underclothes and veil, flowers in hand, factory paint and finish flaws, mkd "Madame Alexander, New York, U.S.A." on dress tag ............. 525.00
Bridesmaid, 17" h, composition, composition head, brown sleep eyes, closed mouth, orig mohair wig in orig set, 5 pc composition body, tagged pink taffeta dress, orig underclothes, flowers in hair, mkd "Mme Alexander" on head "Madame Alexander, New York, U.S.A." on dress tag, unplayed with condition
................................................ 675.00
Emelie, 7" h, composition head, painted brow eyes, closed mouth, molded and painted brow hair, 5 pc composition toddler body, orig tagged lavender dress, matching bonnet, socks, center snap leatherette shoes, mkd "Alexander" on back of head, "Dionne Quintuplets, Madame Alexander, New York" on dress tag, name on pin.......................... 200.00
International Series, 8" h
Germany, ©1975, MIB ............. 50.00
Greek Boy, jointed knees, 1968
................................................ 275.00
Morocco................................. 225.00

Norway, #584, ©1975, MIB ...... 50.00
Thailand, ©1970 ................... 135.00
Little Women Series
#412, Beth, ©1975, MIB ......... 50.00
#416, Laurie, © 975, MIB ........ 50.00
#1320, Amy, MIB ..................... 65.00
Princess Elizabeth, 17" h, composition head, hazel sleep eyes, open mouth with 2 upper teeth, human hair wig, 5 pc composition child body, orig pink taffeta dress, pink flowers in hair ..................... 245.00
Scarlett, 17" h, composition head, green sleep eyes, closed mouth, orig black human hair wig in orig set, 5 pc composition body, orig tagged blue, orange, and green flowered dress, orig underclothes, green velvet coat, matching bonnet, mkd "Mme Alexander" on back of head, "Scarlett O'Hara, Madame Alexander, N.Y. U.S.A. All Rights Reserved" on dress tag, near mint ...................... 1,450.00
Sonja Henie, 20" h, composition head, brown sleep eyes, open mouth with 6 teeth, orig blond human hair wig in orig set, 5 pc composition body, orig pink taffeta skating dress, pink marabou trim, gold skates ..... 900.00
Wendy-Ann, 9" h, composition, jointed at neck, shoulders, and hips, human hair, wig, painted eyes, orig clothes, mkd "Wendy-Ann Mme Alexander" ................................ 265.00

**Mary Hoyer.** The Mary Hoyer Doll Manufacturing Company was named for its founder, in 1925. Mary Hoyer operated a yarn shop and soon began designing doll clothes. She then wanted a perfect doll and approached well-known sculptor Bernard Lipfert, who designed the popular doll. The Fiberoid Doll Company, New York, produced composition Mary Hoyer dolls until 1946, when hard plastic production began. Mary Hoyer continued until the 1970s, when all production of these popular dolls ceased. Mary Hoyer's family has recently released a vinyl version of the vintage Mary Hoyer doll.

Cowgirl, 14" h, hard plastic, 5 pc hard plastic body, blue sleep eyes, orig set brunette wig, cowgirl outfit, one orig felt boot, mark: Original Mary Hoyer Doll ............................. 360.00
Girl, 14" h, composition head, 5 pc composition body, blue sleep eyes, closed mouth, mohair wig, 3 pc navy blue knit outfit, orig socks and black center snap leatherette shoes, mkd "The Mary Hoyer Doll" on back ................................. 325.00
Walker, 14" h, hard plastic, 5 pc hard plastic body, blue sleep eyes, closed mouth, orig saran wig in braids, peach knit two pc outfit, matching cap and panties, gold sandals, trunk with 5 complete Mary Hoyer outfits,

mkd "Made in U.S.A., Mary Hoyer" in black ink on back, circular mark ................................. 240.00

**Mattel, Inc.** Mattel, Inc. was started in 1945. First production of this toy company was in the doll house furniture line. The toy line was expanded to include music boxes, guns, and several character-type dolls. The most celebrated doll they make is Barbie, which was designed by one of the company's founders, Ruth Handler, in 1958.

Bozo The Clown, 16" h, vinyl head, cloth body, pull talk string, c1962 ..... 65.00
Cheerful Tearful, 12" h, vinyl head and body, orig clothes, 1966 .......... 35.00
Charmin Cathy, 25" h, vinyl head and arms, plastic body and legs, rooted blond hair, blue side glancing sleep eyes, closed mouth, original clothes and metal trunk, 1961 .......... 100.00
Chatty Cathy, 18" h, soft vinyl head, hard plastic body, rooted blond dynel hair, blue sleep eyes, open mouth, two teeth, voice box, MIB, c1965 ...................................... 65.00
Chicken of the Sea Mermaid, 14" h, long blond yarn hair, diamond patterned green body, yellow tail fin with green polka dots, orig box, 1974 ...... 45.00
Truly Scrumptious, Chitty Chitty Bang Bang, 11-1/2" h, vinyl, straight legs, blond hair, pink and white gown, matching hat, mkd Mattel, #1108, c1969 ...................................... 90.00

**Sun Rubber Co.** The Sun Rubber Company produced all rubber or lasloid vinyl dolls. Many have molded features and clothes.

Betty Bows, 11" h, rubber, fully jointed, molded hair, blue sleep eyes, drinks and wets, mkd Betty Bows/copyright The Sun Rubber Co./Barberton, OH USA/34A, c1953 ...................... 35.00
Gerber Baby, 11" h, all rubber, molded, painted hair, open nurser mouth, dimples, crossed baby legs, mkd Gerber Baby/Gerber Products Co. on head .................................. 45.00
Happy Kappy, 7" h, one piece rubber body, molded painted hair, painted blue eyes, open/closed mouth, yellow hat, mkd The Sun Rubber Co./Barberton, OH/Made in USA/Ruth E. Newton/New York/NY .............. 25.00
Tod-L-Dee, 10-1/2" h, one piece rubber body, molded painted hair, open nurser mouth, molded diaper, shoes, and socks ............................... 25.00

**Terri Lee Dolls.** The founder and designer of the Terri Lee family was Mrs. Violet Lee Gradwohl of Lincoln, Nebraska. She made the first Terri Lee doll in 1948. Jerri Lee, a brother, was trademarked in 1948. Connie Lee joined the family in 1955. Mrs. Gradwohl issued lifetime guarantees

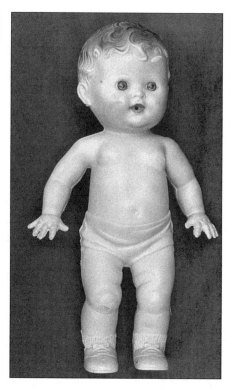

Sun Rubber, Tod-L-Dee, one pc head and body, molded hair, mkd, 10-1/2" h, $20.

for each doll, which were honored until the demise of the company in 1958.

Baby Linda, 9" h, all vinyl, molded painted hair, black eyes, c1951 ................................. 95.00
Jerri Lee, 16" h, hard plastic, jointed at neck, shoulders, and hips, orig curly wig, painted eyes, orig clothing and accessories, mkd Jerri Lee ... 225.00
Patty Jo, 17" h, hard plastic, swivel head, jointed hard plastic body, black styled wig, painted brown eyes, closed mouth, orig dress, c1946 ................................. 450.00
Terri Lee, 10" h, hard plastic head, 5 pc hard plastic body, walking mechanism, brown inset eyes, closed mouth, tagged long blue taffeta dress, mkd "©" on head and back, "Terri Lee" on dress, "Tiny Terri Lee, Manufactured by Terri Lee, ® Apple Valley, Calif" on red box ........ 225.00
Tiny Jerri Lee, 10" h, hard plastic, fully jointed, blond curly wig, brown sleep eyes, closed mouth .............. 175.00

**Vogue.** Vogue Dolls, Inc. was founded by Mrs. Jennie H. Graves. She began a small doll shop which specialized in well-made costumes. The original business of doll clothing led to a cottage industry which employed more than 500 home sewers in 1950. This branch of the industry peaked in the late 1950s, with more than 800 home workers plus several hundred more at the factory.

During World War II, the shortages created a market for an American doll source. Mrs. Graves created the Ginny doll and promoted her heavily. The Ginny Doll was the first doll created with a separate wardrobe and accessories. For many years, Vogue issued one hundred new outfits for Ginny alone. It continued to produce its own dolls and clothing for other doll manufacturers. Ginny Dolls reached their heyday in the 1950s and are still being made today.

Alpine Lady, 13" h, blond, ethnic costume, 1930s, mkd .................. 200.00
Baby Dear, 12" h, all composition, bent baby limbs, 1961 ..................... 40.00
Betty Jane, 12" h, all composition, bent right arm, braided pigtails, red plaid woven cotton dress, white eyelet trim; orig tag Vogue Dolls Inc., 1947 ................................................. 85.00
Crib Crow Baby, 7-1/2" h, all hard plastic, curved baby legs, painted eyes, blond synthetic ringlets wig, orig tagged dress, rubber pants, c1949 ................................................. 425.00
Ginny, 8" h, all hard plastic, painted eyes, molded hair, mohair wig, mkd "Vogue" on head, "Vogue Doll" on back, Springtime, c1948 ........ 115.00
Hug a Bye Baby, 22" h, pink pajamas, MIB............................................ 40.00
Toodles, Bride, 8" h, composition head, 5 pc composition child body, painted blue eyes to side, closed mouth, orig blond mohair wig, orig organdy bride dress with flocked design, orig underclothes, lace trimmed veil, orig white flowers, mkd "Vogue" on back of head, "Doll Co." on back ... 185.00
Toodles, Julie, #8-10B, 8" h, composition head, 5 pc composition body, painted blue eyes to side, closed mouth, orig mohair wig, orig tagged dark green knit bib pants, red felt squirrel trim, multicolored striped knit shirt and matching hat, orig socks and leatherette shoes, silver hoe with wooden handle, mkd "Vogue" on back, "Vogue Dolls, Inc., Medford, Mass" on pants tag................ 155.00
Walking Ginny, 8" h, ballerina, poodle cut wig, 1954, walking mechanism, mkd "Ginny Vogue Dolls, Inc., Pat. Pend., Made in USA" ............. 110.00

# Drugstore Collectibles

**Collecting Hints:** There are several considerations when starting a drugstore collection: 1) Buy the best that you can afford. (It is wise to pay a bit more for mint/near-mint items if available.) 2) Look for excellent graphics on the packaging of items. 3) Do not buy anything that is rusty or damp. 4) Before purchasing an item, ask the dealer to remove price tags or prices written on the piece. (If this isn't possible, determine how badly you want the item.) 5) Buy a variety of items. (Consider placing several similar items together on a shelf for increased visual effect.) 6) Purchase examples from a variety of time periods.

**History:** The increasing diversity of health-related occupations has also encouraged an awareness of pharmaceutical materials, items that appeared in drugstores from the turn of the century through the 1950s. Products manufactured before the Pure Food and Drug Act of 1906 are eagerly sought by collectors. Patent medicines, medicinal tins, items from a specific pharmaceutical company, dental items, and shaving supplies are a key collecting specialties.

The copyright date on a package, graphics, style of lettering, or the popularity of a specific item at a particular period in history are clues to dating a product. Pharmacists who have been in the business for a number of years are good sources for information, as are old manufacturing directories which are available at regional libraries.

**References:** Al Bergevin, *Drugstore Tins & Their Prices*, Wallace-Homestead, 1990; A. Walker Bingham, *Snake-Oil Syndrome*, Christopher Publishing House, 1994; Douglas Congdon-Martin, *Drugstore & Soda Fountain Antiques*, Schiffer Publishing, 1991; Martin R Lipp, *Medical Museums USA*, McGraw Hill Publishing, 1991; Patricia McDaniel, *Drugstore Collectibles*, Wallace-Homestead, 1994.

**Periodical:** *Siren Soundings*, 1439 Main St., Brewster, MA 02631.

**Museums:** National Museum of Health & Medicine, Walter Reed Medical Center, Washington, DC; New England Fire & History Museum, Brewster, MA.

**Advisor:** Patricia McDaniel.

**Beauty Products**

Alco-Mist Body Spray, Rexall Drug Company, Los Angeles, St. Louis, Boston, and Toronto, "contains skin softener to prevent dryness, plus hexachlorophene alcohol," 7 oz, 6-1/2" x 4-1/8" round metal can, white with blue stripes in front, broken lid, full ............................................. 8.00
Breck Hair Spray, John Breck, Inc., Springfield, MA, "Super Hold, Beautiful Hair," 3/4 oz, 4" x 7/8" round, light blue metal bottle with black printing, full ............................... 3.00
Matey Easy-Rinse Shampoo, J. Nelson Prewitt, Inc., Rochester, NY, "kind to eyes," 7 fl oz, 7-1/4" x 2-1/4" round green bottle with white label, drawing of children dressed as pirates on boat on the ocean, full .............. 7.50
Nivea Skin Oil, Duke Laboratories, Inc., USA, "Liquid Cream for Dry Skin for Chapping for The Bath," 1 pint, 7" x 2-3/4" x 2-3/4" clear bottle with white and blue label, 1/4 full ............. 12.00

**Chemical Companies**

Cream Neohetramine, Wyeth Incorporated, Philadelphia, PA, 1 oz, tan metal tube, white and blue label, 5-3/4" x 1-1/4" x 1" box of same colors, 3/4 full ............................... 10.00

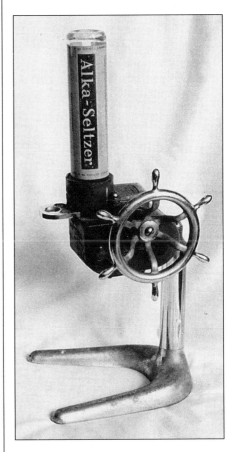

**Alka-Seltzer Dispenser, cast iron, chrome plated, 13-1/4" h, $85.**

Mallinckrodt Ammonium Carbonate, Mallinckrodt Chemical Works, St. Louis, New York, and Montreal, 1 lb, 6-1/4" x 2-3/4" x 4" brown bottle, white and light blue label, 3/4 full bottle .......................................... 8.00

Myrrh, Eli Lilly & Co., Indianapolis, IN, 1/4 pint, 5-1/4" x 2" round brown bottle, light green label with black writing, Lilly written in red, 1/8 full .......................................... 35.00

Puretest Cascara Sagrada Aromatic No. 54, The Rexall Store, United Drug Company, Boston & St. Louis, "A valuable tonic Laxative for the relief of habitual constipation," 4 fl oz, 5-1/4" x 2-1/4" x 1-1/2" brown bottle, white and blue label, 3/4 full bottle ....................................... 20.00

Sodium Salicylate, Burroughs Wellcome & Co., London, Montreal, Sydney, Cape Town, Milan, Bombay, Shanghai, Buenos Aires, 100 tabs, 3-1/2" x 2" x 1-1/2" clear bottle, beige label, half full bottle ......................... 32.00

Sopronol Powder, Wyeth Laboratories, Philadelphia, PA, "for Dermatophytosis ("Athlete's Foot")," 4" x 1-7/8" round white can with blue printing, screw-on plastic lid, full .......... 13.00

Spirit Ammonia Aromatic U.S.P., Rexall Drug Company, Los Angeles, Boston, St. Louis, "Reflex stimulant, useful as a first aid in fainting," 1 fl oz, 3-1/4" x 1-3/4" x 1" brown bottle, blue and white label, 1/4 full .............. 7.00

Thyroid, U. S. P., Eli Lilly & Company, Indianapolis, IN, 100 tabs, 3" x 1" x 3/4" brown bottle, white label, black and red printing, full bottle ............ 25.00

UD Fluidextract Grindelia, United Drug Company, Boston & St. Louis, "Contains 60 per cent alcohol," 4 fl oz, 5" x 2" round brown bottle, cream and brown label, 3/4 full bottle ........ 18.00

### Cold and Cough

Bronchola Special, Bronchola Company, Peoria, IL, "for coughs due to colds," 4 fl oz, 4-1/2" x 1-3/4" round clear bottle, white printing, full bottle .................................................. 8.00

Coldene, Pharma-Craft Cl., Batavia, IL, "for symptomatic relief of colds, headache, neuralgia and other muscular pains and aches," 20 tabs, 2-1/2" x 1-1/2" x 1-1/2" red box with white lettering, full bottle inside .................................................. 8.50

Dr. Jayne's Expectorant, Dr. D. Jayne & Son, Inc., Philadelphia, PA, "for coughs due to colds, soothes quickly without opium," 2 fl oz, 5-1/2" x 1-3/4" x 1" brown bottle, white label with red and black printing, picture of frontier man with bulls and covered wagon, full bottle ............ 15.00

Grove's Cold Tablets, Grove Laboratories Incorporated, St. Louis, MO, analgesic, antipyretic, laxative, 20 tabs, 1/2" x 2" x 1-1/2" white box, red and black lettering, enclosed in cellophane .................................... 3.75

Mycinaire Antibacterial Nasal Spray, The Pfeiffer Co., St. Louis, MO, decongestant, antihistaminic, "relieves stuffy nose accompanying colds hay fever sinus congestion," 20 cc., 3-3/4" x 2" x 1" white box with burgundy printing, full bottle inside .................................................. 9.00

### Dental

Chloresium Dental Ointment, Rystan Company, Inc., Mount Vernon, NY, "A therapeutic chlorophyll preparation," 1/2 oz, white metal tube with dark green, 4-1/8" x 7/8" x 3/4" light green box with white stripes and dark green printing, full tube ..... 5.00

Dr. West's Insta-Clean Denture Cleanser, Weco Products Co., Chicago, IL, "Cleanses 2-5 minutes, dentures, bridges," 4 fl oz, 4-1/4" x 1-7/8" round, clear bottle with white printing, full of red liquid ........... 8.00

Rexall Denturex, Rexall Drug Company, Los Angeles, St. Louis, and Toronto, false teeth cleaner, "No brushing, cleans all by itself," 7-1/2 oz, 6" x 3" x 1-3/8" oval tin, white, red, and light blue, full ..................................... 8.00

Super-White Kolyno's Toothpaste, Whitehall Laboratories, Inc., New York, NY, "All-new Super-White Kolyno's combines three modern cleansing ingredients in a delightfully refreshing toothpaste. Super-White Kolyno's helps restore natural brightness of teeth, destroy mouth odors and sweeten breath. Brushing teeth after meals with Super-White Kolyno's is as effective in preventing decay as is the use of any dentifrice," 2.8 oz, 6" x 1" x 1" white metal tube with red writing, full ........... 4.00

### First Aid

Bell's Camphor Ice, Bell Chemical Cl., Chicago, IL, "for chapped skin, burns, sunburn," 1 oz, 3/4" x 3" x 1-3/4" yellow and brown tin, full ................. 12.00

Itch-Me-Not, Sorbol Company, Mechanicsburg, OH, "A palliative aid in relieving the itching and burning of eczema, non-poisonous insect bites, athlete's foot, ivy poisoning and other externally caused skin irritations," 4 fl oz, 4-1/2" x 2" round brown bottle, white, yellow, green and red label, full.............................. 12.00

Medi-Quik Medicated Cream, Lehn & Fink Products Corporation, Bloomfield, NJ, "for chapped, cracked skin, detergent hands, minor burns, simple diaper rash," 1-1/2 oz, 5-3/4" x 1-1/2" x 1-1/4" white box with red and turquoise, full tube inside ... 8.25

Red Cross Adhesive Tape, Johnson & Johnson, New Brunswick, NJ, Chicago, IL, adhesive tape, waterproof, 1 inch, 10 yards, 1-1/2" x 3" round tin, white with red and blue printing, unopened .................................. 9.00

Sanifit Vaccination Shield, Eagle Druggists Supply Co., Inc., New York, NY, "Celluloid Protector (ventilated) 'curved to fit'," 3-1/4" x 2-1/2" x 5/8" white box with red printing, name in red cross .................................. 6.00

### Herbs

Acacia Gum U. S. P., S. B. Penick & Company, New York and Chicago, 1/4 lb., 3" x 2-1/2" x 2-1/2" square tin, yellow with brown print, full........ 9.00

Orris Root, S. B. Penick & Company, New York and Chicago, 1/4 lb., 3" x 2-1/2" x 2-1/2" square tin, white with black and blue, full ................... 7.50

Sunflower Seed, S. B. Penick & Company, New York and Chicago, 1 lb., 6" x 4-1/4" x 4-1/4" square tin, yellow with brown print, full................ 13.00

### Infants and Children

Baby Care Shampoo, Rexall Drug Company, Los Angeles and Toronto, "As gentle as a shampoo can be," 5 fl oz, clear bottle with yellow printing, 6-1/2" x 2-1/2" x 1-1/2" yellow box with white and blue, full bottle ................... 15.00

Deca-Vi-Sol Chewable Vitamins with Iron, Mead Johnson Laboratories, Evansville, IN, 50 tabs, 3" x 1-3/8" x 1-3/8" brown bottle with white and pink label, boy and girl silhouettes, full bottle ................................. 7.00

Feostat Hematinic, Westerfield Laboratories Inc., Cincinnati, OH, "For prevention and treatment of iron deficiency anemia," 6" x 2-1/4" x 1-1/2" brown bottle, white label with red and black printing, large lid with measures marked around outside ............. 18.00

Playtex Baby Powder, International Latex Corporation, Playtex Park, Dover, DE, "Soothes new bon skin (from head to toe). Antiseptic, contains a scientific antiseptic that checks many skin germs," 6 oz, 5-3/8" x 2-1/8" round shaker, shiny pink with flat pink and blue printing, 3/4 full .................. 10.00

### Laxatives

Innerclean Herbal Laxative, Innerclean Company, Beaumont, CA, "An Aromatic Herb Compound For Occasional Constipation," 1-1/8 oz, 3-3/4" x 2-1/4" x 1" yellow box with blue and red printing, full........................ 12.00

Kemp's Laxative Tablets, Orator F. Woodward, Le Roy, NY, "for stomach, liver, & bowels, dose as a Laxative, 1, as a Cathartic, 2, as a Physic, 3," 30 tabs, 2-1/2" x 1-1/2" x 1/2" gray box with black printing, full........ 7.00

Lane's Tea, Kemp & Lane, Inc., Le Roy, NY, "The family medicine, for occasional constipation and faulty intestinal elimination," 1-3/4 oz, 3-3/4" x 2-3/8" x 1-1/4" yellow box with red printing, full .............................. 8.50

Saxon Compound Senna Powder, Royal Pharmacal Corporation, New York, NY, laxative, 2 oz, 2-5/8" x 2-1/2" x 1-3/4" tin with blue and white label, full... 6.00

**Deer Skin Prophylactics, silver and black box, 2-1/4" x 2" x 3/4", $9.**

### Miscellaneous

Cellasin, The Cellasin Co., Buffalo, NY, "Cellasin is derived from fungi, and acts in an alkaline medium and at body temperature. Indestructible, in the system, by acids or by other ferments," 200 tabs, 4-1/2" x 2" x 1-1/2" brown bottle with white label, black writing, edged in red, half full ................................................. 18.00

Chap-ans Medicated Hand Cream, Miller-Morton Company, Richmond, Virginia, 4 oz, 2-1/2" x 2-1/2" round white jar with red and blue writing, blue picture of hand, full ............ 8.50

Smith-Junior's Certified Liquid Color Red Shade, Smith-Junior Co., Rochester, NY, 1 pint, 7-1/2" x 3" round clear bottle, white, orange, and black label, 1/3 full of red liquid ............................ 15.00

### Stomach

Allimin, Van Patten Pharmaceutical Co., Chicago, IL, "Active Ingredient: Dehydrated Garlic," 25 tabs, 3-3/4" x 1-7/8" x 5/8" white box with blue and red, full ...................................... 5.00

Ca•ma•sil Antacid Powder, Ca•ma•sil Company, Baltimore, MD, "for the temporary relief of gastric hyperacidity, sour stomach, heartburn and flatulence," 6 oz., 5-1/4" x 4" x 2-1/2" oval tin with light blue background and dark blue stripe, full .......... 14.00

Hofmann's Diarol for Upset Stomach, Hofmann's Drugs, Massillon, OH, 4 fl oz, 4-3/4" x 2" round brown bottle, white label with light blue printing, full .............................................. 7.50

GMD, Dr. Pierce's Golden Medical Discovery, Pierce's Proprietaries, Inc., New York, NY, 100 tabs, "In cases of gas pains, heartburn and other symptoms of common indigestion when the cause is not organic," clear bottle, blue label in 3-3/4" x 2-1/2" x 1-1/2" blue box, black printing, full bottle ......................................... 8.50

Tums, "for the tummy in hyperacidity," 2-1/4" x-3/4" round yellow metal tin, Tums impressed on top, black stripes down the sides, mottled metal ......................................... 8.00

# E

# Electrical Appliances

**Collecting Hints:** Small electric appliances are still readily available and can be found at estate and garage sales, flea markets, auctions, antiques malls, and best of all, in the back of your mom's upper cabinets or even in Grandma's attic! Most can still be found at antique malls, etc. for a reasonable price. However, in recent years, due to collectors, decorators, and the foreign market, some appliances, mostly toasters that are "high style" art deco, have been commanding an almost unbelievable and dramatic rise in value. Porcelain and porcelain insert appliances have risen sharply as well as some electric irons.

Most old toasters, waffle irons, and other appliances still work. When buying an old appliance ask if it works and ask the *seller* to plug it in to see if it heats.

**Note:** use extreme caution, there could be a short due to many factors (dirt, bare wires, etc.). On "flip flop" type toasters (the most numerous kind) check to see if the elements are intact around the mica and not broken.

Most appliances used a standard-size cord which are still available at hardware stores. Some of the early companies had appliances that would only accept cords peculiar to that company. In such an instance, buy the appliance only if the cord accompanies it.

Unless you plan to use an appliance for display only or for parts, don't buy it if it doesn't work or is in rusted or poor condition.

Dirt does not count! With a little care, time, and diligence, most old appliances will clean up to a sparkling appearance. Aluminum magwheel polish, available at auto parts stores, can be used with a soft rag for wonderful results. *No steel wool!* Also, a non-abrasive kitchen cleanser can be a great help.

As with most collectibles, the original box or instructions can add 25%-50% to the value of the piece. Also, beware of brass or copper appliances (usually coffee pots) because these were originally chrome or nickel. Devalue these by 50%.

**History:** The first all electric-kitchen appeared at the 1893 Chicago World's Fair and included a dishwasher that looked like a torture device and a range. Electric appliances for the home began gaining popularity just after 1900 in the major eastern and western cities. Appliances were sold door-to-door by their inventors. Small appliances did not gain favor in the rural areas until the late 1910s and early 1920s. However, most people did not trust electricity.

By the 1920s, competition among electrical companies was keen and there were many innovations. Changes occurred frequently, but the electric servants were here to stay. Most small appliance companies were bought by bigger firms. These, in turn, have been swallowed up by the huge conglomerates of today.

By the 1930s, it was evident that our new electric servants were making life a lot easier and were here to stay. The American housewife, even in rural areas, was beginning to depend on the electric age, enthusiastically accepting each new invention.

Some firsts in electrical appliances are:

| | |
|---|---|
| 1882 | Patent for electric iron (H. W. Seeley [Hotpoint]) |
| 1903 | Detachable cord (G.E. Iron) |
| 1905 | G.E. Toaster (Model X-2) |
| 1905 | Westinghouse toaster (Toaster Stove) |
| 1909 | Travel iron (G.E.) |
| 1911 | Electric frying pan (Westinghouse) |
| 1912 | Electric waffle iron (Westinghouse) |
| 1917 | Table Stove (Armstrong) |
| 1918 | Toaster/Percolator (Armstrong "Perc-O-Toaster") |
| 1920 | Heat indicator on waffle iron (Armstrong) |
| 1920 | Flip-flop toasters (many companies) |
| 1920 | Mixer on permanent base (Hobart Kitchen Aid) |
| 1923 | Portable mixer (Air-O-Mix "Whip-All") |
| 1924 | Automatic iron (Westinghouse) |
| 1924 | Home malt mixer (Hamilton Beach #1) |
| 1926 | Automatic pop-up toaster (Toastmaster Model 1-A-1) |
| 1926 | Steam iron (Eldec) |
| 1937 | Home coffee mill (Hobart Kitchen Aid) |
| 1937 | Automatic coffee maker (Farberware "Coffee Robot") |
| 1937 | Conveyance toaster ("Toast-O-Lator") |

**References:** E. Townsend Artman, *Toasters*, Schiffer Publishing, 1996; Jane H. Clehar, *Kitchens and Kitchenware*, Wallace-Homestead, 1986; Linda Campbell Franklin, *300 Years of Kitchen Collectibles*, 4th ed., Krause Publications, 1998; Don Fredgant, *Electrical Collectibles, Relics of the Electrical Age*, Padre Publications, 1981; Helen Greguire, *Collector's Guide to Toasters & Accessories*, Collector Books, 1997; Earl Lifshey, (ed.), *The Housewares Story*, National Housewares Manufacturers Association, 1973; Gary Miller and K. M. Scotty Mitchell, *Price Guide to Collectible Kitchen Appliances*, Wallace-Homestead, 1991.

**Collectors' Club:** Electric Breakfast Club, P.O. Box 306, White Mills, PA 18473.

**Advisors:** Gary L. Miller and K. M. (Scotty) Mitchell.

## Blenders

Berstead Drink Mixer, 1930s, Eskimo Kitchen Mechanic, Berstead Mfg. Co., domed chrome motor, single shaft, lift-off metal base with receptacle for tapered ribbed glass, 12" ................................................. 35.00

Chronmaster Mixall, 1930s, Chronmaster Electric Corp., NY & Chicago, chrome and black motor, single shaft on hinged black base, orig silver-striped glass ............................ 40.00

Dorby Whipper, 1940s, Model E, chrome motor with black Bakelite handle, off/on toggle, clear, measured Vidrio glass ................... 35.00

Electromix Whipper, 1930s, Chicago, ivory colored, offset metal motor housing with push-down break, filler hole in lid, measured glass base, 7-1/2" ........................................ 30.00

Gilbert Mixer, Polar Cub, 1929, A.C. Gilbert Co., New Haven, CT, 10" h, lift-off gray painted metal, rear switch, blue wood handle, premium for Wesson-Snowdrift, orig box .......... 125.00

Hamilton Beach Malt Machine, forerunner to home malt maker
  Mid-1920s, Cyclone #1, 19" h, heavy nickel housing, sq stand on marble base, int push-down switch... 350.00
  1930s, 18-1/2" h, chrome motor, green cast base, push-up switch, nickel cup ............................. 180.00

**Coleman, c1930s, clear, spherical glass body, applied glass handle, high Art Deco design, $225. Photo courtesy of Gary Miller and Scotty Mitchell.**

Kenmore Hand Mixer, 1940s, Sears, Roebuck & Co., Chicago, small, cream-colored plastic, single 4-1/2" beater, orig box, booklet, warranty and hanger plate...................... 35.00

Kenmore Whipper, 1940s, Sears, Roebuck & Co., Chicago
4-1/2" h, cream colored plastic, single beater, orig box, booklet, warranty, and hanger plate............ 25.00
8-1/2" h, cream-colored metal domed top, large blue Bakelite knob, clear glass bottom .................. 25.00

Knapp Monarch Whipper, mid-1930s, St. Louis, 9-1/2" h, white metal motor, red plastic top handle, round mild glass base with reeded, fin feet, white plastic beater.................. 65.00

Kwick Way, St. Louis, 7-1/2" h, white metal motor top over angular clear glass base, no switch, decal label ................................................. 35.00

Made-Rite Drink Mixer, 1930s, Weinig Made Rite Co., Cleveland, lightweight metal, cream and green motor, single shaft, no switch, stamped, permanent support, no glass ......... 30.00

Silex Blender, 1940s, NY, sq, white cast base, push-button switch, silver foil, Art Deco label, clear glass 4-cup top with vertical "Silex" on black stripe, plastic lid.................................... 35.00

Unmarked Whipper, late 1920s-early 1930s, 7-1/2" h, green metal motor housing, green Depression glass "Vidrio" cup, unusual serpentine shaft ........................................ 25.00

### Chafing dishes

American Beauty, c1910, American Electrical Heater Co., Detroit, MI, 3-part, nickel on cooper, base serves as hot-water container and has sealed element, separate plugs mkd "fast" and "slow," black painted wood handles and knob .......... 50.00

Manning Bowman, 1930s, Meriden, CT, bright chrome Art Deco design, reeded edges, 2-part top on hotplate base, black Bakelite knob and handles .................................. 75.00

Universal, c1910, Landers, Frary & Clark, New Britain, CT, nickel on copper faceted 3-part body, sealed element in base hot-water pan, 3-prong heat adjuster in base, large black wood handle and knob ......................... 50.00

### Coffee Makers and Sets

Coleman, 1930s, clear, spherical glass body, applied glass handle, high Art Deco design stands on 4 chrome fins surrounding black Bakelite column, toggle switch, chrome lid with black knob ............................ 225.00

Farberware Coffee Robot, coffee set, 1937, S.W. Farber, Brooklyn, NY, coffee maker #500, set #501, 2-part coffee dripolator, creamer, open sugar and tray, nickel chrome, walnut handles, orig booklet, price for set ............................................... 125.00

Manning Bowman, Meriden, CT, Percolator Urn, late 1920s, article #250, 3-part aluminum body, unique design prevents re-perking, front spigot, out-turned handles, clear glass insert in domed lid, 12-1/2" h ............................................... 50.00

Percolator, 1930s, high Art Deco, chrome, vertical reeding around top edges, coffee makers have black wood handles, others have black Bakelite, tab feet
Chafing Dish/Hotplate, 3 part, 11" round, lid ............................ 65.00

Coffee Percolator, 9" h......... 45.00
Coffee Percolator, 12" h, glass insert .................................. 65.00
Food Warmer, large 23" oval, 2 white Hall China inserts, chrome lids, black Bakelite knobs, detached cord .................. 250.00
Waffle Iron, round on flat 10" sq base, Bakelite feet ............. 35.00

Meriden Homelectrics Percolator Set, 1920s, Manning Bowman Co., Meriden, CT, catalog #32, ser. #4-30, 15" h percolator/urn, creamer, open sugar, nickel chrome vertically faceted bodies, urn on short cabriole legs, upturned black wood handles, glass knob insert on top, set ............... 95.00

Porcelier, Breakfast Set, 1930s, Greensburg, PA, all-porcelain bodies accented by basketweave design, floral transfers, silver line dec, many different designs were manufactured
Coffee Urn ............................ 125.00
Cream and Sugar, cov............. 50.00
Percolator #5007................... 125.00
Sandwich Grill #5004............. 250.00
Set....................................... 1,425.00
Toaster #5002 ....................... 800.00

Rome Electric Percolator, 1910-20s, Rome Mfg. Co., Rome, NY, coffee urn #CEU 47, 14" w, chrome, flared black wooden handles, turned feet...... 25.00

Royal Rochester Percolator, 1930s, Robeson Rochester Corp., Rochester, NY #D-30, almost-white porcelain, slight greenish luster around shoulder and spout, spring bouquet floral transfer, chrome lid and base, clear glass insert ...................................... 125.00

**Manning Bowman, 1930s, high Art Deco chrome, vertical reeding around top edges, coffee makers have black wood handles, others have black Bakelite, tab feet, set $460. Photo courtesy of Gary Miller and Scotty Mitchell.**

#D-33, chrome cylinder, Art Deco design, painted wide black band, round clear glass stepped lid, large black knob, black side handle attached by curved chrome piece at top ............................................. 75.00

Model E610, 3 pc set, lusterware bodies, mkd "Fraunfelter China, OH," tall vertically faceted alternating stripes of orange luster and white with floral transfers, set .......... 190.00

Sunbeam, Chicago Flexible Shaft Co., Model 14, 1930s, 3 part, stands 15" h overall, slender chrome cylinder of high Art Deco design, painted black bands, stands atop small round hotplate with handle control that registers from 100 to 700 degrees, larger chrome top is dripolater type, chrome lid, matching lidded creamer and sugar, set ....................... 250.00

Universal, Landers, Frary & Clark, New Britain, CT

Breakfast Set, 1930s, cream-colored porcelain, blue and orange floral transfers, waffle iron on pierced chrome base has porcelain insert, front drop handle

Creamer and sugar, cov...... 45.00
Percolator #E6927 ............. 150.00
Syrup, chrome cov ............. 60.00
Waffle Iron E6324 .............. 125.00

Coffee Set

c1915, coffee urn #E9219, 14" h, squat cabriole legs, large wood ear-shaped handles; nickel bodies, oval tray, price for 4-pc set .............................................. 85.00

1920s, coffee urn #E9119-1, 16-1/2" h, chrome, chrome handles, swirl glass insert, octagonal body, handled tray, price for 4-pc set .................................... 150.00

## Egg cookers

Hankscraft Co., 1920s, Madison, WI
Model #599, yellow china base, large dish on top of domed chrome serves as knob and filler with hole in bottom, instructions on metal plate on bottom .............................. 35.00
Model #730, Art Deco design, ivory china, silver trim, cooker, 4 egg cups and nickel tray ......................... 50.00

Rochester Stamping Co., c1910, Rochester, NY, egg-shaped, 4-part chrome on small base, interior fitted with skillet with turned black wood handle, 6-egg holder with lift-out handle, enclosed heating element .................................................. 65.00

## Food Cookers

Eureka Portable Oven, 1930s, Eureka Vacuum Cleaner Co., Detroit, MI, 15" x 13" x 19", Art Deco style, cream-colored painted body, black edges, sides fold down and contain hot plates on chrome surfaces, int fitted with wire racks, controls across bottom front .......................... 200.00

Everhot, 1920s, Swartz Baugh Mfg. Co., Toledo, OH, EC Junior 10, 13" h, large chrome and black cylindrical

body, aluminum cov, Art Deco design, "Everhot" embossed on front, int fitted with rack, 2 open semicircular pans, 1 round cov pan, 3-prong heat control .............. 50.00

Hankscraft, 1920s, Madison, WI, green enamel pan, detachable hinge-pin chrome cov, green ceramic lusterware knob, chrome base, black wood handles flare from sides of body ...................................... 85.00

Nesco Electric Casserole, early 1930s, National Enamel & Stamping Co., Inc., Milwaukee, WI, 9" d, forerunner of crock pot, cream-colored body with green enamel cov, high/low control, 3-prong plug .................... 50.00

Quality Brand, 1920s, Great Northern Mfg. Co., Chicago, IL, model #950, 14" h, cylindrical body, insulated sides and cov, fitted int with cov aluminum pans, brown with red stripe body, lift-out rods ..................... 40.00

Westinghouse, roaster oven, 1940s, white metal painted body, aluminum top with window on top, gray plastic handle, includes lift-out gray graniteware pan, 3 clear glass dishes with lids, matching stand with clock timer and storage door ........... 50.00

## Hot Plates

Edison-Hotpoint, c1910, Edison Electric, NY, Chicago and Ontario, CA, solid iron surface, clay-filled int, very heavy pierced legs, ceramic feet, copper control with ceramic knob .................................................. 35.00

El Stovo, c1910, Pacific Electric Heating Co., sometimes mkd "G.E. Hotpoint," solid iron surface, clay-filled int, very heavy pierced legs, pad feet, no control ...................................... 25.00

Landers, Frary & Clark (Universal), Thermax, 1920s, iron top with pierced swirl design on nickel tripod base, 4 prongs to heat outer ring, inner ring or both, requires special two head cord .......................... 25.00

Unmarked, 1920s, square nickel chrome 9" body, no control, stands on slightly angled legs................. 8.00

Volcano, 1930s, Hilco Engineering Co., Chicago, IL, slightly conical nickel body, black wood handle, slide lever as control on side that lifts grate .................................................. 40.00

Westinghouse, 1920s, Mansfield, OH, 7-1/2" d top with green porcelain-metal top surrounding element, hollow legs, no control ................. 25.00

## Miscellaneous

Angelus-Campfire Bar-B-Q Marshmallow Toaster, 1920s, Milwaukee, WI, 3" sq, flat top, pierced pyramid top piece, base on loop, wire legs with rubber-encased feet, flat wire forks
Used ....................................... 75.00
With orig box .......................... 125.00

Clock/Timer, late 1930s, made for Montgomery Ward & Co., cream body, silver and red face, curved glass, body swivels on weighted base, clock

mechanism winds up manually, cord at back with appliance receptacle .................................................. 40.00

Coffee Grinder, Kitchen Aid, Hobart, Troy, OH, model #A-9, heavy cream-colored cast base with motor, course/fine adjustment on neck, clear glass jar container with screw-off top serves as storage for beans .................................................. 75.00

Food Warmer, Chase Chrome, 1930s, Art Deco design, 22-1/2" x 11", rect chrome body, reeded,chamfered corners, wide cylindrical Bakelite handles, two large unmarked white porcelain inserts, two small inserts have chrome lids, black cylinder knobs, hollow body, attached cord, off/on switch.......................... 450.00

Miracle Flour Sifter, c1934, Chicago, IL, electric, cream body, blue wood hold-down button handle at base, vibrates flour through wire strainer .................................................. 35.00

Sunkist Juicer, 1930s, 9" h, opaque green Depression glass top, int. metal strainer, chrome body/motor housing with dark green painted center, metal "Sunkist" plate on front .................................................. 85.00

Universal Tea Kettle, c1910, Landers, Frary & Clark, New Britain, CT, model #E973, bright nickel 1-pc squat body and base, long spout, black painted wood high curved handle on pierced vertically curved mounts.......... 45.00

Vita-Juicer, 1930s, Kold King Distributing Corp., Los Angeles, Hoek Rotor Mfg. Co., Reseda, CA, 10" h, heavy, cream-painted cast metal, base motor, container and lid fitted with lock groove and lock-down wire handle, aluminum pusher fits in top holder...................................... 35.00

## Mixers

Dominion Modern Mode, 1923-33, Dominion Electrical Mfg. Co., Minneapolis, MN, faceted, angular Art Deco body and base, 3-speed rear lever control, runs on A.C. or D.C., 2 custard glass bowls and juicer, mechanism to control beater height .................................................. 75.00

General Electric, 1938, G.E. Corp., upright housed motor, no speed control, 3 synchronized beaters in a row, work light shines in handle, 2 white glass bowls, black Bakelite handle, ser. #10-A................................. 50.00

Hamilton Beach, 1930s, Racine, WI, model G, cream-colored metal, black Bakelite handle, on/off lever control, "Mix Guide" in window below handle, mixer lifts off base to become portable, 2 white glass bowls ........................................ 45.00

Hobart Kitchen Aid, 1939, Model K 4-B, looks like the ones of today but quite a bit heavier, cream body trimmed in heavy aluminum, heavy cast aluminum bowl screws to base, dough hook, beater, whisk, can opener, metal grinder

Attachment, each.....................25.00
Mixer only................................125.00

Sunbeam Mixmaster
Attachments, fit most models
    Bean slicer ..........................20.00
    Can opener ........................15.00
    Churn .................................50.00
    Coffee grinder ....................25.00
    Drink mixer ........................15.00
    Grater, slicer, shredder, 3 blades
    ..................................................35.00
    Grinder/chopper..................25.00
    Juicer, mayonnaise maker ..20.00
    Knife sharpener..................15.00
    Pea sheller.........................10.00
    Potato peeler......................35.00
    Power unit..........................10.00
    Ricer ..................................20.00
    Silver polisher and buffer ....10.00
Cabinet, 60-1/2" x 24".............295.00
.Mixmaster, early 1930s, Chicago Flexible Shaft Co., model K, cream-colored body, fold-over black wood handle, rear speed control, light green opaque Depression glass bowls, juicer and strainer, orig booklet ..............................................65.00

## Popcorn Poppers

Berstead, 1930s, model #302, sq, chrome, body with circular int, Fry Glass lid, large black knob on top, rod through lid for stirring ........45.00
Dominion Popper, 1920s, Minneapolis, MN, Style #75, one pc cylindrical nickel body, pierced band, cabriole lets, red painted wood side handles and turned knob, hand crank
..................................................25.00
Excel, 1920s, Excel Electric Co., Muncie, IN, 1-pc cylindrical nickel body, metal handles form legs, lock-down levers, hand crank, black wood knob, top vent holes.................25.00
Manning Bowman, early 1940s, Meriden, CT, model #500, detachable large aluminum container, fits chrome hot plate, glass lid emb with floral motif, black Bakelite knob, never used ..............................15.00
Rapaport, 1920s, Rapaport Bros., Inc., Chicago, 5-1/2" sq black base, metal legs, round aluminum upper part with attached lid and red knob, chrome handle squeezes through slot in side to agitate corn........25.00
U.S. Mfg. Corp., 1930s, Decatur, IL
#1, all one unit, cylindrical, round body, painted aluminum, top crank, 3 painted red vertical wood dowels legs ..........................................20.00
#10, body and lid separate from hot plate base, top crank handle ...15.00
White Cross, c1918, National Stamping & Electrical Co., Chicago, IL, tin can base with heater and cord, wire basket fits onto can, metal top with stirrer mounted through handle, woo handle to side, primitive...........30.00

## Toasters

Dominion Mfg. Co., mid 1920s, Minneapolis, MN, flip-flop type, bright chrome pierced body, green wooden handles, Bakelite tab door openers, never used ...............................60.00
Edison Appliance Co., c1918, NY, cat. #214-T-5, open nickel body with free-swinging tab closures at top, single side knob, removable toast warming rack .........................................125.00
General Electric, 1908, model E-12, white porcelain base, wire body, removable wire toast rack, porcelain plug with screw-in socket cord
Complete, rack and cord....... 600.00
Decorated with rose garlands, complete, rack and cord ..............800.00
General Mills, early 1940s, Minneapolis, MN, cat. #GM5A, 2-slice pop-up chrome body, wheat dec on side, black Bakelite base, A.C. or D.C., red knob, light/dark control.....45.00
Heat Master, 1923-35, sq chrome body, rounded corners, end opening, 2-slice, manual operation, black Bakelite handle and feet..........60.00
Kenmore, early 1940s, Sears, Roebuck & Co., Chicago, mechanical, 2-slice pop-up, chrome body, rounded edges and sides, black Bakelite handles, mechanical clock mechanism, light/dark control ...........30.00
Knapp Monarch Reverso, 1930, cat. #505, light-weight rect nickel body, rounded corners, black painted base, flip-flop doors with tab handles, no mica, wires stretched across ......................................70.00
Manning Bowman, early 1920s, cat. #1225, open nickel body, black Bakelite knobs that open toast cages that completely turn over .......125.00

**Toast-O-Later, 1938, Model "G," Mechanical Wonder, chrome body, high Art Deco style, unique design, $450. Photo courtesy of Gary Miller and Scotty Mitchell.**

Miracle Toaster, Miracle Electric Co., Chicago, IL, late 1930s, cat. #210, slightly rounded gray enamel body, black Bakelite handles, flip-flop type, never used...............................30.00
Montgomery Ward & Co., mid-1930s, Chicago, IL, model #94-KW2298-B, flip-flop type, solid nickel-chrome body, Bakelite handle on end opens both doors simultaneously.......50.00
Steel Craft, late 1920s, open, painted green wire construction, flip-flop type, red painted wood knobs and feet...........................................65.00
Sunbeam
Chicago Flexible Shaft Co., early 1920s, model B, 5" x 9", flat, rect dec chrome body, round, reeded legs, hexagonal Bakelite feet, double wire cages flip over horizontally, small drop bail handles for carrying ...........125.00
Sunbeam Corp., Chicago, IL, 1936, good Art Deco design, rect chrome with rounded corners, black Bakelite base, heat indicator light on front, sits into fitted clear glass "Hostess" tray.........................................225.00
Toastmaster, 1927, Waters-Genter Co., Minneapolis, MN
Model 1-A-1, recognized as first automatic pop-up, chrome Art Deco body, louvered sides, rounded end, manual clock timer mechanism, light/dark control from A to G, panic button....................................250.00
Model 1-A-3, third model, chrome Art Deco body, vertically scalloped sides, mechanical clock mechanism, light/dark knob.......................150.00
Toastolater, Model "G" Mechanical Wonder, 1938, chrome body, high Art deco style, ovoid shape, toast walks through on little tooth-like conveyers, falls out opposite end, Bakelite base and knobs, adjustable light/dark control, off/on switch, attached cord, unique design
..................................................450.00
Universal, Landers, Frary & Clark
1913-15, nickel body, flat base, tab feet, pierced concave spring-loaded doors, permanent warming rack
..................................................60.00
Late 1910s-20s, open chrome body, rect base, vertical center hinged door cages, manually allows toast to swing out and around, out turned wood handles, mint condition..................125.00
Model #3 7542, mechanical toaster with clock mechanism, single slice, circular design on side of nickel chrome body, end pops open and out
Double .............................125.00
Single ...............................90.00
Unmarked, 1920s, nickel, pierced body, tab handles, flat warming rack top
..................................................25.00
Westinghouse
Toaster Stove, 1909, Mansfield, OH, flat rect body, 4 flat strip plates, removable cabriole legs, tray and wire rack, orig box and paper guarantee, never used.................175.00

Turnover Toaster, 1920s, Mansfield, OH, cat. #TT3, nickel body, pierced doors and top, flat tab handles, pierced, flat warming rack top
............................................................. 45.00

## Waffle Irons and Sandwich Grills

Armstrong Waffle Iron, 1920, model W, first example with heat read/thermometer light on top, 7" round nickel body, black wood handles, distinctive prongs, with cord ............. 45.00

Berstead Mfg. Co., Fostoria, OH and Oaksville, Ontario, Canada
Low profile, 1930s, rounded chrome body, little curved Bakelite feet, front drop handles, top heat indicator and wheat shaft dec........................30.00
Victorian, 1920s, 10" l rect nickel body, permanent plates, flared legs on curved mounts, black turned handles ........................................... 20.00

Coleman Waffle Iron, early 1930s, Coleman Lamp & Stove Co., Wichita, KS, high Art Deco style, chrome, low profile, small b&w porcelain top impala insert, black Bakelite handles
................................................................. 85.00

Dominion Electric Co., double waffle iron, 1940s, Mansfield, OH, chrome rect stepped body, 2 round waffle grills, separate temperature controls, red light heat indicator, walnut handles, top circular dec, special 2-headed cord ......................... 35.00

Electrahot Double Waffle Iron, 1940s, Mansfield, OH, two 6" sets of plates mounted on oval base, heat indicators with surrounding dec on top
................................................................. 30.00

Excelsior Waffle Iron, 1930s, Perfection Electric Co., New Washington, OH, 6" round white porcelainized iron body, 4 little stamped legs, plug in front, turned painted wood handle
................................................................. 25.00

Fitzgerald Star Waffle Iron, 1920s, Torrington, CT, 7", solid flared base, unique handle design locks in position for raising or carrying ........ 35.00

General Electric Waffle Iron, early 1940s, 8" round chrome body, ivory Bakelite handles and heat control/off front lever, top dec of circle of stars surrounding stripes and leaves ....... 35.00

Hostess Sandwich Grill, 1930s, All Rite Co., Rushville, IN, 5" sq cast-aluminum body, angled at bottom to form feet, screw-off wood handle, orig box and booklet of suggestions...... 65.00

Hotpoint Waffle Iron, 1920s, Edison, General Electric, Chicago, IL and Ontario, CA
"Automatic" below front handle, rotating cold/hot in small front window, round chrome body, top dec, ivory Bakelite handles, scalloped base dec................................... 35.00
"Edison" on bottom but "Hotpoint" emb on front, nickel body, pierced, flared base, top edge faceted as is base edge, large faceted black painted wood upturned side handles, large front knob ............... 30.00

Lady Hibbard Sandwich Grill, 1930s, Hibbard, Spencer, Bartlet & Co., Chicago, IL, nickel rect body, cast cabriole legs, black wood side handles, front handle swivels to form foot for top plate enabling use of both plates as grills, drip spout ................................... 25.00

Majestic Waffle Iron/Hot Cake Griddle, 1920s, Majestic Electric Appliance Corp., San Francisco, CA, innovative 8" round reversible plates, little pierced "tower" on top with Bakelite cap that serves as foot for use as double grill when opened out, nickel body, brown Bakelite front swing handle ...................................... 45.00

Manning Bowman, Meriden, CT
Sandwich Grill/Waffle Iron/Frying Pan, early 1920s, rect nickel 10-1/2" x 6-1/2" body, drip tube, indented grill plates serve as frying pan, black wood handles, 2 sets of plates 35.00
Twin-O-Matic Waffle Iron, late 1930s, Art Deco design, top heat indicator with rotating knob, chrome body flips over in brown Bakelite stand mounted on chrome base...... 125.00

Sampson Waffle Iron, 1930s, Sampson United Corp., Rochester, NY, Art Deco design, chrome boy with wing-like flared Bakelite side handles set asymmetrically, stationary front handle ............................................. 40.00

Torrid Waffle Iron, 1920s, Beardsley & Wolcott Mfg. Co., Waterbury, CT, flared base, 7-1/2" round plated-chrome body, green up-turned handles and front knob, front window indicates "too cold," "too hot," and "bake" ........35.00

Universal Waffle iron, 1930s, Landers, Frary & Clark, part of larger breakfast set, large floral dec porcelain inset into chrome body, pierced, round, flared pedestal base, up-turned handles, fancy mounted front drop handle, light/dark adjustment ............... 100.00

Unmarked
Sandwich Grill, 6" x 14-1/2", nickel body, short angled legs, will accommodate 3 sandwiches............... 20.00
Waffle Iron, 1930s, 5" sq body, light weight aluminum plates set into nickel, stamped, angled legs, little pad feet, red or green front wood knob, rounded humps on plates
................................................... 18.00

Westinghouse Waffle Iron, 1905-21 patent date, rect chrome body, mechanical front handle with wood hand-hold, removable cabriole legs slip into body slots, off/on switch
................................................... 90.00

# Elephant Collectibles

**Collecting Hints:** There are vast quantities of elephant-shaped and elephant-related items. Concentrate on one type of object (toys, vases, bookends, etc.), one substance (china, wood, paper), one chronological period, or one type of elephant (African or Indian). The elephants of Africa and India do differ, a fact not widely recognized.

Perhaps the most popular elephant collectibles are those related to Jumbo and Dumbo, the Disney character who was a circus outcast and the first flying elephant. GOP material associated with the Republican party is usually left to the political collector.

Because of the large number of items available, stress quality. Study the market carefully before buying. Interest in elephant collecting is subject to phases, is and is currently at a modest level.

**History:** Elephants were unique and fascinating when they first reached America. Early specimens were shown in barns and moved at night to avoid anyone getting a free look. The arrival of Jumbo in England, his subsequent purchase by P. T. Barnum, and his removal to America brought elephant mania to new heights.

Elephant have always been a main attraction at American zoological parks. The popularity of the circus in the early 20th century kept attention focused on elephants.

Hunting elephants was considered "big game" sport, and President Theodore Roosevelt was one well-known participant. The hunt always focused on finding the largest known example. It is not a surprise that an elephant dominates the entrance to the Museum of Natural History of the Smithsonian Institution in Washington, D.C.

Television, through shows such as "Wild Kingdom," has contributed to

**Figure, ivory, 1-3/8" x 1-3/4", $40.**

knowledge about all wild animals, including the now quite-commonplace elephant.

**Periodical:** *Jumbo Jargon*, 1002 W. 25th St., Erie, PA 16502.

**Collectors' Club:** The National Elephant Collector's Society, 380 Medford St., Somerville, MA 02145.

Advertising Trade Card, 4-7/8" x 3", Clark's Spool Cotton, Jumbo's Arrival, sepia, white, adv on back ........................................... 7.50

Bank, metal, red elephant, green base, mkd "Vasio," c1936, 5" h.......... 65.00

Battery Operated, 3-1/4" x 4" x 6", playing cymbal and drum, made by M & M, Japan, c1960 ...................... 45.00

Book, Edward Allen, *Fun By The Ton* ........................................... 20.00

Bottle opener, figural, cast iron, sitting, trunk raised
Brown, pink eyes and tongue, 3-1/2" h...................................55.00
Pink, "GOP" on base, 3-1/4" h ........................................... 55.00

Child's Book, *Kellogg's Funny Jungleland Moving Pictures,* ©1909, published by W. K. Kellogg, patented Jan. 15, 1907, fold-out sections ........................................... 24.00

Christmas Ornament
3" h, silver emb cardboard, Dresden, Germany ............................... 140.00
3-1/2" l, blown glass, gray body, red blanket ...................................95.00

**Ink Blotter, Hummel Warehouse, Allentown, PA, July 1941 calendar, 6-1/8" x 3-3/8", $7.50.**

Doll, advertising, Toppie the Elephant ............................................... 225.00

Figure
1-1/2" h, 2" l, ceramic, shaded gray glaze .......................................... 8.00
3" h, 2-1/2" l, glass, trunk raised ............................................... 12.00
4-1/4" h, porcelain, acrobat, pastel blue, white, beige, triangular gold "Royal Dux" sticker, oval "Made in Czech Republic" sticker .......... 55.00
23-1/2" h, teak, carved adult and baby, 20th C, one tusk missing ............................................... 140.00

Lamp, elephant with girl, hand painted, Japan, 14" h.............................. 45.00

Letter Opener, 7-1/2" l, celluloid, marked "Depose-Germany," c1900 ............................................... 40.00

Mug, Frankoma, 1970s................ 20.00

Napkin Ring, Bakelite, navy blue, c1940 ............................................... 65.00

Nodder, 3-1/2" l, 1-3/4" h, celluloid, gray back and head, pink ears, white belly, silver painted tusks......... 35.00

Pin, gold tone, figural ................... 25.00

Pinback Button, Rub-No-More, gray and black image of elephant in household attire, using trunk as shower for baby elephant standing in washing pan ...................... 25.00

Planter, 8" x 5-1/2", figural, pottery, unmarked................................. 20.00

Postcard, Elephant Hotel, Margate City, NJ, 1953 .................................. 7.50

Poster, 47" x 58", Lil Nil Cigarette Papers, litho, trumpeting elephant, linen backing ........................ 250.00

Salt and Pepper Shakers, pr, figural, mkd "Japan" ............................. 24.00

Sign, 15" x 13", Brown's Jumbo Bread, diecut tin, elephant with trunk curled down, blanket on back, c1930 ............................................... 150.00

Tobacco Tag, tin, diecut, Red Elephant Tobacco ..................................... 7.50

Toy
3-1/2" h, 4-1/4" l, Jumbo, litho tin wind, mkd "U. S. Zone Germany" ............................................... 85.00
5" h, Elmer Elephant, gray, bow tie and hat, rubber, Sieberling .... 165.00

Vase, figural handle, ivory matte finish ............................................... 125.00

# F

# Farm Collectibles

**Collecting Hints:** The country look makes farm implements and other items very popular with interior decorators. Often items are varnished or refinished to make them more appealing but, in fact, this lowers their value as far as the serious collector is concerned.

Farm items were used heavily; collectors should look for signs of use to add individuality and authenticity to the pieces.

When collecting farm toys, it is best to specialize in a single type, e.g., cast iron, models by one specific company, models of one type of farm machinery, or models in one size (1/16 scale being the most popular). Farm collectibles made after 1940 have not yet achieved great popularity.

**History:** Initially, farm products were made by local craftsmen—the blacksmith, wheelwright, or the farmer himself. Product designs varied greatly.

The industrial age and the golden age of American agriculture go hand in hand. The farm market was important to manufacturers between 1880 and 1900. Farmers demanded quality products, capable of withstanding hard use. In the 1940s, urban growth began to draw attention away from the rural areas, and the consolidation of farms began. Larger machinery was developed.

The vast majority of farm models date between the early 1920s and the present. Manufacturers of farm equipment, such as John Deere, International Harvester, Massey-Ferguson, Ford, and White Motors, issued models to correspond to their full-sized products. These firms contracted with America's leading toy manufacturers, such as Arcade Company, Dent, Ertl, Hubley, Killgore, and Vindex, to make the models.

**References:** Nick Baldwin and Andrew Morland, *Classic Tractors of the World: A to Z Coverage of the World's Most Fascinating Tractors*, Voyageur Press; C. Lee Criswell and Clarence L. Criswell Sr., *Criswel"s Pedal Tractor Guide*, Criswell Press, 1999; David Erb and Eldon Brumbaugh, *Full Steam Ahead: J. I. Case Tractors & Equipment*, American Society of Agricultural Engineers, 1993; Jim Moffet, *American Corn Huskers*, Off Beat Books, 1994; Robert Rauhauser, *Hog Oilers Plus*, published by author (Box 766, RR #2, Thomasville, PA 17364), 1996; C. H. Wendel, *Encyclopedia of American Farm Implements & Antiques*, Krause Publications, 1997; —, *Unusual Vintage Tractors*, Krause Publications, 1996.

**Periodicals:** *Antique Power*, P.O. Box 1000, Westerville, OH 43081; *Belt Pulley*, P.O. Box 83, Nokomis, IL 62075; *Country Wagon Journal*, P.O. Box 331, W. Milford, NJ 07480; *Farm & Horticultural Equipment Collector*, Kelsey House, 77 High St., Beckenham Kent BR3 1AN England; *Farm Antiques News*, 812 N. Third St., Tarkio, MO 64491; *Farm Collector*, 1503 SW 42nd St., Topeka, KS 66609, *Iron-Men Album*, P.O. Box 328, Lancaster, PA 17603; *Rusty Iron Monthly*, P.O. Box 342, Sandwich, IL 60548; *Spec-Tuclar News*, P.O. Box 324, Dyersville, IA 52040; *Toy Farmer*, H C 2, Box 5, LaMoure, ND 58458; *Toy Tractor Times*, P.O. Box 156, Osage, IA 50461; *Tractor Classics*, P.O. Box 191, Listowel, Ontario N4H 3HE Canada; *Turtle River Toy News & Oliver Collector's News*, RR1, Box 44, Manvel, ND 58256.

**Collectors' Clubs:** Antique Engine, Tractor & Toy Club, 5731 Paradise Rd., Slatington, PA 18080; Cast Iron Seat Collectors Association, P.O. Box 14, Ionia, MO 65335; CTM Farm Toy & Collectors Club, P.O. Box 489, Rocanville, Saskatchewan S0A 3L0 Canada; Early American Steam Engine & Old Equipment Society, P.O. Box 652, Red Lion, PA 17356; Ertl Replicas Collectors' Club, Hwys 136 and 20, Dyersville, IA 52040; Farm Toy Collectors Club, P.O. Box 38, Boxholm, IA 50040; International Harvester Collectors, RR2, Box 286, Winamac, IN 46996.

**Museums:** Billings Farm & Museum, Woodstock, VT; Bucks County Historical Society, Doylestown, PA; Carroll County Farm Museum, Westminster, MD; Living History Farms, Urbandale, IA; Makoti Threshers Museum, Makoti, ND; National Agricultural Center & Hall of Fame, Bonner Springs, KS; Never Rest Museum, Mason, MI; New York State Historical Association and The Farmers' Museum, Cooperstown, NY; Pennsylvania Farm Museum, Landis Valley, PA.

Barn Hinge, 27" l, wrought iron, strap type ........................................... 75.00
Book
    *Come Back to the Farm,* Jesse Stuart, McGraw Hill, 1971, 1st edition ................................................. 25.00
    *Market Milk,* Ernest Kelly & Clarence Clement, Wiley & Sons, 1923, 445 pgs .......................................... 20.00
    *Starting Right with Turkeys,* G. T. Klein, MacMillan, 1947, 129 pgs ................................................. 15.00
Branding Iron, Lazy B, wrought iron ................................................ 40.00
Card, Olds Patent Wheel Wagon, celluloid, multicolored, white ground, black letters, reverse with detailed aerial factory scene of Fort Wayne, IN .............................................. 80.00
Catalog
    Adriance Platt & Co., Poughkeepsie, NY, 1905, 48 pgs, 7-1/4" x 9-1/2", farm machinery ...................... 48.00
    American Steel & Wire Co., New York, NY, 1913, 22 pgs, 6" x 6-3/4", fencing ................................... 17.00
    Buckeye Incubator Co., Springfield, OH, 1900s, 64 pgs, 6" x 9" ....... 24.00
    D. Hill Nursery Co., Dundee, IL, 1930, 40 pgs, 9" x 11-1/2", 75th anniversary evergreen catalog ....... 22.00
    E. A. Strout Farm Agency, New York, NY, 1925, 190 pgs, 7-3/4" x 10-3/4" ................................................. 36.00
    IHC of America, Inc., Chicago, IL, disk harrow, 1909, 32 pgs, 6-1/2" x 8" ............................................... 44.00
    Kemp & Burpee Mfg. Co., Syracuse, NY, 1895, 8 pgs, 5-3/4" x 8-3/4", 4 pictures of Kemp Manure Spreader ............................................... 18.00
    Keystone Farm Machine Co., York, PA, 8 pgs, 6" x 9-3/4" .............. 24.00
    Moline Plow Co., Moline, IL, 1908, 32 pgs, 6" x 8-3/4" ......................... 32.00
    Pioneer Thresher Co., Shortsville, NY, 1939, 12 pgs, 7-1/2" x 10" ......... 28.00
Chick Feeder, tin .......................... 20.00
Clip, Moline Wagon Co., red wagon wheel, orange background, silver lettered inscriptions "Light Running and Durable," insert brass pencil clip .......................................... 75.00
Corn Dryer, hanging, wrought iron ..27.50
Egg Candler, 8" h, tin, kerosene burner, mica window .......................... 30.00
Egg Crate, tin .............................. 12.00
Feed Bag, cotton
    Black illus of sheet .................. 12.00
    Floral print, washed .................. 5.00
    Geometric print, yellow and green ................................................. 7.00
Flax Comb, 17-1/2" l, wrought iron, ram's horn finials .................... 135.00
Flicker Tag, Dairylea Milk, cardboard keychain tag, full color image of Miss Dairylea, flicker image "Look Both Ways Before Crossing," c1960 ................................................. 12.00
Flipper Pin, diecut thin celluloid
    Dain Hay Machinery, multicolored image of Great Dane dog, red and white sponsor name on back ..... 50.00

**Label, Cousin Elmer Brand Quality Vegetables, multicolored, $4.**

Globe Scranton Feed, diecut, egg-shaped pin, black and white text, Albert Dickinson Co., early 1900s ................................................. 80.00
Swift's Chicken Feed, black and white farm bird, inscribed "Swift's Premium Milk Fed Chickens" ... 25.00
Grain Shovel, wood, carved dec ................................................. 300.00
Hay Rake, 48-1/2" l, varnished ..... 65.00
Implement Seat, Hoover & Co., cast iron ................................................. 115.00
Memo Booklet, Superior Drill Co., Springfield, OH, celluloid cover, full color illus, tan leather piping, 1907 calendar, 4 pgs describing farm products, other illus ................. 45.00
Name Tag, Grain Dealers Convention, diecut celluloid, full color illus of train at grain elevator, corn husk background ..................................... 35.00
Pinback Button
  Case Farm Machinery Eagle, multi-colored, adult eagle, world globe ................................................. 40.00
  Daybreak Fertilizer, red rooster, white ground, black letters ................ 20.00
  Fulton & Walker Co., Best Wagons for Business, Philadelphia, multicolored image of delivery wagon ................................................. 85.00
  Huber Steam Tractor, multicolored image of "The New Huber," blue rim, white letters ............................... 75.00
  New Idea Manure Spreader, multicolored scene of horse-drawn spreader "At Work In The Field" ................................................. 85.00
  Page Wire Fence, Adrian, MI, rect aluminum, early 1900s ............. 10.00
  Racine-Sattley Line, red and white logo, black background ........... 10.00
  Russell & Company, The Boss, Massillon, OH, multicolored image of brown bull symbol .................... 60.00

Sharples Cream Separator, multicolored image, blue background, white letters ......................................... 40.00
St. Joseph Pump and Mfg. Co., The Only Perfection Water Elevator Purifier, c1896 ................................ 55.00
Pocket Mirror, Empire Cream Separator, multicolored celluloid, blond milkmaid, ethnic outfit, soft dark green background, slogan "Nothing Else Will Do," early 1900s ...... 150.00
Seed Dryer, chestnut frame, pine spindles, 21" x 43" .......................... 85.00
Shove, cast iron, wood handle ..... 30.00
Stickpin
  J. I. Case Co., figural, brass logo, eagle poised on world globe, early 1900s ..................................... 20.00
  Racine-Sattley Line, brass pin, red enameled, early 1900s ............ 25.00
Stud
  IHC, brass, late 1890s ............. 10.00
  Sharples "The Russian," white porcelain, blue and black letters, slogan "The Bowl Alone Revolves" of cream separator, c1898 ...................... 60.00
Tape Measure, McCormick Harvesting Machine, celluloid canister, finely detailed black and white aerial illus of Chicago factory, titled "Largest Works in the World," early 1900s harvester machine ........................ 80.00
Testimonial Circular, Eureka Mower Co., Towanda, PA, 1883, for new model, testimonials from customers, 44 pgs, 5-3/4" x 8-3/4" .......................... 24.00
Toy
  Combine, Case, diecast, 1/16 scale, plastic reel, Ertl, 1974 .............. 90.00
  Corn Picker, pressed steel, 1/16 scale, John Deere, Carter, 1952 ................................................. 135.00
  Disc, diecast, 1/16 scale, International Harvester, Ertl, 1965 ....... 65.00
  Grain Drill, pressed steel, 1/16 scale, John Deere, Carter, 1965 ....... 150.00
  Plow, McCormick-Deering, cast iron, red, yellow wheels, Arcade, 1932 ................................................. 95.00
  Tractor, Ford, Tootsie Toy, rubber wheels ................................... 45.00
  Tractor, International Harvester, nickel-plated man, rubber wheels, c1940 ................................... 325.00
  Tractor, Tru-Scale, Carter, diecast, 1/16 scale, 1975 ...................... 75.00
Wagon Seat, 42" l, wood, wrought iron trim, hinged compartment ..... 250.00

# Fast Food Memorabilia

**Collecting Hints:** Premiums, made primarily of cardboard or plastic and of recent vintage, are the mainstay of today's fast food collector. Other collectible items are advertising signs and posters, character dolls, promotional glasses, and tray liners. In fact, anything associated with a restaurant chain is collectible, although McDonald's items are the most popular.

Collectors should concentrate only on items in mint condition. Premiums should be unassembled or sealed in an unopened plastic bag.

Collecting fast food memorabilia has grown rapidly, and, more than ever before, the fast food chains continue to churn out an amazing array of collectibles.

**History:** During the period just after World War II, the only convenience restaurants were the coffee shops and diners located along America's highways or in the towns and cities. As suburbia grew, young families created a demand for a faster and less-expensive type of food service.

Ray A. Kroc responded by opening his first McDonald's drive-in restaurant in Des Plaines, Illinois, in 1955. By offering a limited menu of hamburgers, french fries, and drinks, Kroc kept his costs and prices down. This successful concept of assembly-line food preparation soon was imitated, but never surpassed, by a myriad of competitors.

By the mid-1960s the race was on, and franchising was seen as the new economic frontier. As the competition increased, the need to develop advertising promotions became imperative. A plethora of promotional give-aways entered the scene.

**References:** Gary Henriques and Audre DuVall, *McDonald's Collectibles*, Collector Books, 1997.

**Periodicals:** *Collecting Tips Newsletter*, P.O. Box 633, Joplin, MO 64802; *Fast Food Collectors Express*, P.O. Box 221, Mayview, MO 64071; *World of Fast Food Collectibles Newsletter*, P.O. Box 64, Powder Springs, GA 30073.

**Collectors' Clubs:** McD International Pin Club, 3587 Oak Ridge, Slatington, PA 18080; McDonald's Collectors Club, 424 White Rd., Fremont, OH 43420; McDonald's Collectors Club, 255 New Lenox Road, Lenox, MA 01240.

**Note:** Prices are for mint condition items sealed in their original wrappers or packages and unassembled.

**Reference:** Gail Pope and Keith Hammond, *Fast Food Toys,* 2nd ed., Schiffer Publishing, 1998.

**Periodicals:** *Collecting Fast Food & Advertising Premiums,* 9 Ellacombe

Rd., Longwell Green, Bristol, BS15 6BQ UK; *Collecting Tips Newsletter*, P.O. Box 633, Joplin, MO 64802; *The Fast Food Collectors Express,* P.O. Box 221, Mayview, MO 64071-0221.

## A&W

Doll, Root Beer Bear, plush........... 32.00
Mug, glass ....................................... 5.00
Pitcher and Glasses, Root Beer Bear and A & W logo, 1970s, 7 pc set ................................................ 60.00
Puppet, hand, Root Beer Bear, cloth .............................................. 12.00

## Big Boy

Ashtray, glass, red and white logo.... 4.00
Bank, 9-1/4" g, figural, vinyl, smiling full figure boy, blue letters, red and white checkered overalls, incised trademark on bottom, c1960........... 85.00
Menu, punch-out puppet, kiddie menu ............................................ 45.00
Nodder, papier-mâché head, 5" h .............................................. 10.00
Pinback Button, Big Boy Club, red, white, blue, and brown hair, c1950 .............................................. 65.00
Salt and Pepper Shakers, pr, china, 1960s ..................................... 125.00
Tee Shirt, white ground, red, white, and black trademark ...................... 10.00

## Burger King

Bicycle Clip, colorful wheel spokes, 1981 .......................................... 6.00
Calendar, Olympic games theme, 1980 ........................................... 4.00
Card game, Burger King Rummy, orig box, 1978 ................................. 12.00
Doll, 16" h, King, cloth, printed red, yellow, flesh, black, and white........ 7.50
Frisbee, 9-1/2" d, R2-D2, C3PO, and Darth Vader, Empire Strikes Back, 1981 ........................................ 17.50
Glider, King Glider, Styrofoam, 1978 ................................................ 2.50
Pinback Button, 3/4" d, Happy face, Burger King logo eyes ............... 6.00
Trading Cards, The Empire Strikes Back, complete set of 36 ........ 37.50
Yo-Yo, Yum Yum, Duncan Yo-Yo, 1979 ................................................ 5.00

## Dairy Queen

Meal Box, Hot Doggity, Dennis the Menace .............................................. 3.50
Salt Shaker, chocolate dip ice cream cone, 4-1/4" h........................... 22.00

**Burger King, guest card, good for one Whopper, c1990, $1.**

Spoon, red plastic, long handle, ice cream cone top........................ 1.00
Sundae Dish, 3-1/2" x 8-1/4" x 1-1/4" deep, green molded plastic, designed ,like boat, curlicue of simulated ice cream scoop for handle, diecut Dairy Queen name, Lynn-Sign Molded Plastic Co., Boston, early 1960s ...................................... 12.00

## Denny's

Menu, plastic coated, c1960 .......... 2.50
Puppet, hand, Deputy Dan, 1976......3.00
Ring, brass, expansion bands, trace of orig yellow paint, center brown "D," 1970s ...................................... 60.00

## Howard Johnson

Ashtray............................................. 30.00
Bank.................................................. 35.00
Drinking Glass, multicolored logo, 4-1/4" h, 2-1/2" d ..................... 32.00
Ice Cream Cup, sample size, paper, 1-1/2" h, 1-1/2" d ..................... 12.00
Menu, ice cream cover .................... 2.00
Post Card, Howard Johnson's Motor Lodge, Middletown, NJ, unused ................................................ 3.50

## Kentucky Fried Chicken

Bank, Colonel Sanders, vinyl, turns, Japan, 1960s ......................... 275.00
Box, 1969.......................................... 35.00
Pinback Button, Vote for Col. Sanders, KFC, blue and white, c1972, 1-1/2" d...................................... 24.00
Salt and Pepper Shakers, pr, Col. Harland Sanders, figural, 4-1/4" h, smiling full figures, one on white base, one on black base, incised name, Starting Plastics Ltd., London, Canadian premium, c1970 ............... 34.00

## McDonalds

Bank, 6" vinyl figure, made for Canton store opening ........................... 20.00
Coloring Book, Ronald McDonald Goes to the Moon, 9" x 12-1/4", 1967, 12 pgs, black and white story, unused ............................................ 125.00
Cup Holder, dark blue, orig packaging ................................................ 3.50
Doll
  Hamburglar, played with condition ............................................ 15.00
  Ronald McDonald, stuffed, 1978 ............................................ 35.00
Employee Cap, 12-1/2" x 11-1/2", flattened unused service cap, blue cardboard headband with yellow arch symbol on each side, white mesh open crown, mid-1960s ...............15.00
Happy Meal Box Proof Sheet, 18-1/4" x 23-3/4" white stiff paper printer's proof, full color image in center, four sided box design American Tail, Mouse in the Moon puzzle, finger puppets, characters flying away on pigeon Henri, ©1988 McDonald's Corp, unfolded ......................... 15.00
Muppet Babies characters, Egyptian theme, ©1986 McDonald's Corp, unfolded....................................... 15.00
Happy Meal Display, Marvel Super Heroes ...................................... 75.00

Happy Meal Prize, Genie and Building 5, from Aladdin and the King of Thieves, MIB ............................. 4.00
Lunch Box, orig thermos, 1982 .... 22.00
Map, Ronald McDonald Map of the Moon, 1969.............................. 7.50
Patch, cloth, red, white, blue, and yellow stitching, Ronald McDonald ................................................ 2.00
Plate, Snowman, Melmac, 1977 ... 25.00
Puppet, hand, plastic, Ronald McDonald, c1977 ...................... 2.00
Ruler, Ronald McDonald, cardboard, early 1970s .............................. 12.00
Space Packet, MIP ......................... 16.00
Teenie Beanie Babies, 1997, set of 10, MIP, complete set ................... 48.00
Valentines, strip of 6 different valentines, 1978....................... 3.00

## Pizza Hut

Paper Napkin, logo.......................... .50
Puppet, hand, Pizza Pete .............. 2.00

## Taco Bell

Banner, full color, Batman & Robin, 1997, full cast, 2' x 25', unused ................................................ 150.00
Store Display, Godzilla, 18" h, 18" w, holds 6 premiums, 1 missing... 75.00
Straw, monster eye, MISB, 1997, set of 6........................................... 20.00
Toy, Godzilla, sealed, 1977, set of 7 ................................................ 20.00

## Wendy's

Flying Ring, Fun Flyer, plastic, 3-1/2" d ................................................ 3.50
Meal Box, The Good Stuff Gang, 1988 ................................................ 3.00
Mug, Wendy's Old Fashioned Hamburgers, ceramic, red, white, and black trademark, 1970s............. 6.50

# Fiesta Ware

**Collecting Hints:** Whenever possible, buy pieces without any cracks, chips, or scratches. Fiesta ware can be identified by bands of concentric circles.

**History:** The Homer Laughlin China Company introduced Fiesta dinnerware in January 1936 at the Pottery and Glass Show in Pittsburgh, Pennsylvania. Frederick Rhead designed the pattern; Arthur Kraft and Bill Bensford molded it. Dr. A. V. Bleininger and H. W. Thiemecke developed the glazes. A vigorous marketing campaign took place between 1939 and 1943.

The original five colors were red, dark blue, light green (with a trace of blue), brilliant yellow, and ivory. In mid-1937, turquoise was added. Red was removed in 1943 because some of the chemicals used to produce it were essential to the war effort; it did not reappear until 1959.

In 1951, light green, dark blue, and ivory were retired and forest green, rose, chartreuse, and gray were added to the line. Other color changes took place in the late 1950s, including the addition of a medium green.

Fiesta ware was redesigned in 1969 and discontinued about 1972. In 1986, Fiesta was reintroduced by Homer Laughlin China Company. The new china body shrinks more than the old semi-vitreous and ironstone pieces, thus making the new pieces slightly smaller than the earlier pieces. The modern colors are also different in tone or hue, e.g., the cobalt blue is darker than the old blue. Other modern colors are black, white, apricot, and rose.

**References:** Susan and Al Bagdade, *Warman's American Pottery and Porcelain*, Wallace-Homestead, 1994; Sharon and Bob Huxford, *Collectors Encyclopedia of Fiesta with Harlequin and Riviera*, 7th ed., Collector Books, 1992 value update.

**Periodical:** *Fiesta Collectors Quarterly*, 19238 Dorchester Circle, Strongsville, OH 44136.

**Collectors' Clubs:** Fiesta Club of America, P.O. Box 15383, Loves Park, IL 61115; Fiesta Collectors Club, 19238 Dorchester Circle, Strongsville, OH 44136.

Ashtray, 5-1/2" d
  Cobalt blue ............................... 45.00
  Red ........................................... 55.00
  Yellow ....................................... 30.00
Bud Vase, 6-1/2" h
  Ivory, chip ................................ 60.00
  Red .......................................... 175.00
Calendar Plate, ivory, 1954, 10" d
  ................................................. 55.00
Candleholders, pr, bulb
  Ivory ........................................ 115.00
  Light Green ............................... 90.00
  Turquoise ................................. 115.00
Candleholders, pr, tripod
  Ivory ........................................ 800.00
  Turquoise .................................. 800.00
  Yellow ....................................... 700.00
Carafe, cov, light green ............. 185.00
Casserole, cov
  Cobalt Blue .............................. 200.00
  Gray ......................................... 375.00
  Yellow, large ............................. 85.00
Chop Plate, 14-1/4" d
  Chartreuse ................................ 65.00
  Gray .......................................... 70.00
  Ivory ......................................... 60.00
  Yellow ....................................... 30.00
Coffeepot, cov
  Cobalt Blue .............................. 300.00
  Green ....................................... 225.00
  Ivory ......................................... 195.00

Rose .......................................... 850.00
Yellow ........................................ 135.00
Comport, low
  Turquoise, 12" d ...................... 100.00
  Yellow ...................................... 125.00
Creamer
  Chartreuse ................................ 40.00
  Cobalt Blue, stick handle ......... 50.00
  Medium Green ........................... 80.00
  Rose .......................................... 35.00
  Turquoise, stick handle ........... 115.00
  Yellow, stick handle ................. 50.00
Cream Soup
  Cobalt blue ............................... 90.00
  Light green ................................ 50.00
  Red ........................................... 50.00
  Rose .......................................... 95.00
  Turquoise .................................. 30.00
  Yellow ....................................... 30.00
Cup and Saucer
  Chartreuse ................................ 28.00
  Gray .......................................... 26.00
  Ivory ......................................... 24.00
  Light Green ............................... 20.00
  Medium Green ........................... 60.00
  Red ........................................... 30.00
  Rose .......................................... 30.00
  Turquoise .................................. 24.00
  Yellow ....................................... 24.00
Deep Plate
  Chartreuse ................................ 50.00
  Gray .......................................... 50.00
  Ivory ......................................... 40.00
  Red ........................................... 50.00
Demitasse Cup and Saucer
  Cobalt blue ............................. 100.00
  Ivory ......................................... 60.00
  Turquoise .................................. 70.00
  Yellow ...................................... 115.00
Dessert Bowl, 6" d
  Gray .......................................... 40.00
  Medium Green ........................... 65.00
  Rose .......................................... 65.00
  Turquoise .................................. 30.00
  Yellow ....................................... 25.00
Egg Cup
  Gray ......................................... 175.00
  Light Green ............................... 65.00
  Yellow ....................................... 45.00
Fruit Bowl
  4-3/4" d
    Cobalt blue ............................. 25.00
    Gray ........................................ 25.00
    Ivory ....................................... 20.00
    Red ......................................... 30.00
    Yellow ..................................... 15.00
  5-1/2" d
    Ivory ....................................... 20.00
    Yellow ..................................... 15.00
Fruit Bowl, 11-3/4" d
  Cobalt Blue .............................. 350.00
  Red .......................................... 420.00
Gravy, turquoise ......................... 40.00
Grill Plate, 10-1/2" d
  Cobalt blue ............................... 17.50
  Yellow ....................................... 20.00
Juice Pitcher, disc, 5-1/2" h
  Cobalt blue .............................. 135.00
  Yellow ....................................... 60.00
Juice Tumbler, 4-1/2" h
  Cobalt blue ............................... 45.00
  Light green ................................ 55.00
  Rose .......................................... 60.00

Turquoise .................................. 45.00
Yellow ........................................ 40.00
Marmalade, red .......................... 400.00
Mixing Bowl
  #1, red .................................... 180.00
  #2, cobalt blue ......................... 200.00
  #3, ivory .................................... 80.00
  #4, light green .......................... 85.00
  #5, turquoise ............................ 85.00
  #6, light green ........................ 110.00
  #7, cobalt blue ........................ 200.00
Mixing Bowl Lid, red, medium size
  ............................................... 750.00
Mug
  Gray .......................................... 85.00
  Light green ................................ 50.00
  Rose .......................................... 75.00
  Turquoise .................................. 50.00
Mustard, cov
  Cobalt blue .............................. 245.00
  Turquoise ................................. 185.00
  Yellow ...................................... 175.00
Nappy Bowl, 9-1/2" d
  Cobalt blue ............................... 45.00
  Ivory ......................................... 50.00
  Turquoise .................................. 35.00
Onion Soup, cov, ivory .............. 375.00
Plate, 6" d
  Forest green ............................... 5.00
  Ivory ........................................... 7.50
  Medium green ........................... 20.00
  Turquoise .................................... 5.00
Plate, 7" d
  Green .......................................... 6.50
  Ivory ........................................... 8.50
  Turquoise .................................... 7.50
Plate, 9" d
  Light green ................................ 10.00
  Medium green ........................... 40.00
  Turquoise .................................. 10.00
  Yellow ....................................... 10.00
Platter, 12-1/2" l
  Cobalt blue ............................... 30.00
  Gray .......................................... 50.00
  Turquoise .................................. 30.00
  Yellow ....................................... 25.00
Relish
  Cobalt base, red center, light green, ivory, yellow, and cobalt blue side inserts, slight chips ............... 300.00

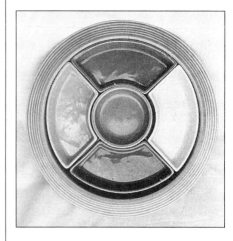

**Relish Tray, 4 part, cobalt blue, yellow, white, and orange, $200.**

Yellow base, cobalt blue center, four yellow inserts, gold trim ......... 135.00
Yellow base, light green center, red, ivory, yellow, and light green side inserts ..................................... 175.00

Salad Bowl, individual size
Medium green......................... 135.00
Red.......................................... 110.00
Salad Bowl, 9-3/8" d, yellow........ 100.00

Salt and Pepper Shakers, pr
Cobalt blue.............................. 24.00
Yellow...................................... 40.00

Sauce Boat
Ivory ....................................... 40.00
Rose......................................... 60.00
Yellow ...................................... 45.00
Soup Plate, turquoise.................... 35.00

Sugar Bowl, cov
Chartreuse .............................. 70.00
Gray......................................... 80.00
Rose......................................... 70.00

Sweets Compote
Light green ............................... 75.00
Yellow ...................................... 80.00
Syrup, turquoise, green top ........ 150.00

Teapot, cov, medium size
Red.......................................... 175.00
Yellow ...................................... 100.00
Tray, figure 8, turquoise............... 300.00

Utility Tray
Cobalt blue.............................. 17.50
Light green............................... 25.00
Red.......................................... 70.00
Turquoise................................. 20.00

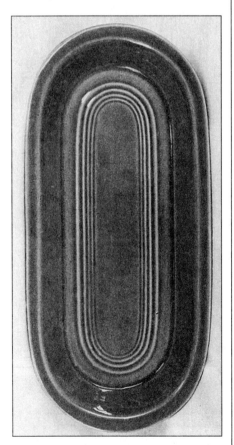

**Utility Tray, turquoise, $15.**

Water Pitcher, disc
Ivory ....................................... 140.00
Light green............................... 165.00
Turquoise ................................. 90.00
Water Tumbler, cobalt blue........... 80.00

# Firehouse Collectibles

**Collecting Hints:** For a period of time, it was fashionable to put a date on the back of firemen's helmets. This date is usually the date the fire company was organized, not the date the helmet was made.

Firehouse collectibles cover a very broad area. The older, scarcer collectibles, such as helmets and fire marks, command high prices. The newer collectibles, e.g., cards and badges, are more reasonably priced.

**History:** The volunteer fire company has played a vital role in the protection and social growth of many towns and rural areas. Paid professional firemen are usually found in large metropolitan areas. Each fire company prided itself on its equipment and uniforms. Annual conventions and parades, which gave the individual fire companies a chance to show off their equipment, produced a wealth of firehouse-related collectibles.

**References:** Andrew G. Gurka, *Hot Stuff!: Firefighting Collectibles*, L-W Book Sales, 1994, 1996 value update; Charles V. Hansen, *History of American Firefighting Toys*, Greenberg Publishing, 1990; James Piatti, *Firehouse Memorabilia*, Avon Books, 1994; Donald F. Wood and Wayne Sorenson, *American Volunteer Fire Trucks*, Krause Publications, 1993; ——, *Big City Fire Trucks, 1900-1950*, Krause Publications, 1996.

**Periodical:** *Fire Apparatus Journal*, P.O. Box 121205, Staten Island, NY 10314.

**Collectors' Clubs:** Antique Fire Apparatus Club of America, 5420 S. Kedvale Ave., Chicago, IL 60632; Fire Collectors Club, P.O. Box 992, Milwaukee, WI 53201; Fire Mark Circle of the Americas, 2859 Marlin Dr., Chamblee, GA 30341; Great Lakes International Antique Fire Apparatus Association, 4457 285th St., Toledo, OH 43611; International Fire Buff Associates, Inc., 7509 Chesapeake Ave., Baltimore, MD 21219; Interna-

tional Fire Photographers Association, P.O. Box 8337, Rolling Meadows, IL 60008; Society for the Preservation & Appreciation of Motor Fire Apparatus in America, P.O. Box 2005, Syracuse, NY 13320.

**Museums:** There are many museums devoted to firehouse collectibles. Large collections are housed at the following: American Museum of Fire Fighting, Corton Falls, NY; Fire Museum of Maryland, Lutherville, MD; Hall of Flame, Scottsdale,

**Bookmark, Smokey the Bear, yellow and brown, $1.**

AZ; Insurance Company of North America (I.N.A.) Museum, Philadelphia, PA; New England Fire & History Museum, Brewster, MA; New York City Fire Museum, New York, NY; Oklahoma State Fireman's Association Museum, Inc., Oklahoma City, OK; San Francisco Fire Dept. Pioneer Memorial Museum, San Francisco, CA.

Alarm Box, cast iron, pedestal, emb "City of Chicago," restored .... 285.00

Badge
  1-3/4" x 1-3/4", relief image of fire hydrant on one side, hook and ladder on other, Mineola Fire Dept., c1950 ...................................... 10.00
  2" x 2", relief image of fire hydrant on one side, hook and ladder on other, Mineola Fire Dept., c1950 ........ 10.00

Bell, brass, 12" .............................. 85.00

Belt, black lather, white lettering ... 75.00

Booklet, Constitution of the International Brotherhood of Firemen and Oilers, last revision 1971 ..................... 10.00

Bucket, galvanized tin, red lettering, "Fire Only" ............................... 35.00

Daguerreotype, fireman, hat, horn, and uniform, tinted ........................ 500.00

Extinguisher, Harden, hand grenade type, blue glass, patent Aug. 8, 1871 .................................................. 90.00

Fire Engine Name Plate
  Ahrens-Fox .............................. 15.00
  LaFrance .................................. 17.50
  Mack Trucks, bulldog .............. 25.00

First Day Cover, 300th Anniversary of Volunteer Firemen's Association, unaddressed ............................. 10.00

Hose Nozzle, brass ....................... 50.00

Liquor Decanter, Fireman's Thirst Extinguisher .................................... 20.00

Little Golden Book, *Five Little Firemen,* 1949 ........................................ 7.50

Magazine
  Fire Lines, Dec 1935 ................ 35.00
  NFPA Fireman, 1966 .................. 7.50

Negative, glass, Chicago Fire Dept. #6 pumper .............................. 45.00

Patch, 3-7/8" d, Texas State Fireman's Association ............................... 7.50

Photograph, 4-3/4" x 6-3/4", silver print of c1900 parade, firemen marching down gaily decorated street .... 20.00

Pinback Button, convention, 1-3/4" d, Pennsylvania State Firemen's Convention Dark blue cello button, colorful image of Irishman smoking pipe, shaking hands with fireman, light blue ribbon, 1-1/4" green and white "guest" cello button, Harrisburg, PA, October, 1914 ....................... 20.00
  White button, colorful image of firehouse and hat, black text around border "Lebanon Co. Fireman's Convention, Myerstown, PA, June 15, 1929," red, white, and blue ribbon .................................................. 15.00

Post Card, real photo, unused
  Firemen searching for victims of 1906 fire ................................ 10.00

Main Fire Station, Water Street, Piqua, OH ................................. 5.00

Ribbon
  Aug. 18, 1901, Veteran Firemen's Association League Muster, Lawrence, blue ribbon, white celluloid button with fire implements ......... 45.00
  1958, Firemen's Celebration, multicolored pinback, some wear to 3-3/4" l ribbon ........................... 18.00

Ring, Jr. Fire Marshall, Hartford Insurance, 1950s ............................. 20.00

Salesman Sample, boots, 5" h, rubber, scale model, pull loops, mkd "Candee," c1890 ............................ 70.00

Tankard, 5-1/2" h, Smokey Bear 40th Anniversary, 1944-1984 New Jersey Forest Fire Service, pottery, mkd "Official Licensee to the NJ State Firemen's Convention," and "Made by Let Us Mug You, Spring Lake, NJ" .................................................. 60.00

Tie Tac, 1/2" d, "Member, County Firemen's Ass'n," 10K gold mounting, keystone shape, blue and rust colored enamel, center white enamel "6" .................................................. 30.00

Tintype, unidentified fireman wearing dress uniform, holding speaking trumpet ................................. 110.00

**Whiskey Bottle, Volunteer Firefighter #3, 1979, Valiant Volunteer, Old Commonwealth, $50.**

Toy
  Chief Car, litho tin, friction powered, 1960s, 16" l ........................... 75.00
  Mickey Mouse Fire Truck, Sun Rubber ..................................... 80.00

Watch Fob, 1-1/4" d, aluminum, accepted by small red fire helmet, New Kensington, PA, firehouse, inscription "1928 Wet Penna. Volunteer Fireman's Assn," back reads "33rd Annual Convention/The Aluminum City/Aug 1926," black leather strap .......... 15.00

# Fire King

**Collecting Hints:** Anchor Hocking's Fire-King is a contemporary of Pyrex and other "oven-proof" glassware of the 1940s and 1950s. It is only within the past decade that collectors have begun to focus on this material. As a result, prices fluctuate and a stable market is several years in the future.

In 1938, Anchor Hocking introduced a line of children's dishes which became part of the Fire-King line. A popular pattern is Little Bo Peep. Like all children's dishes, these objects command strong prices.

Some Fire-King collectors focus on a single color. Jane Ray, a jade-ite-colored pattern, was introduced in 1945. In 1948, the color was first used in a series of restaurant wares and it was discontinued in 1963. This color saw a dramatic increase in prices and collector interest in the late 1990s.

Fire-King was sold in sets. Add an additional 25-35% to the price of the individual pieces for an intact set in its original box.

Fire-King pieces are found with two types of marks. The first is a mold mark directly on the piece; the second, an oval foil paper label.

**History:** Fire-King was a product of the Anchor Hocking Glass Company. In 1905, Isaac J. Collins founded the Hocking Glass Company along the banks of the Hocking River near Lancaster, Ohio. On March 6, 1924, fire completely destroyed the plant, but it was rebuilt in six months. Hocking produced pressed glass dinnerware, many patterns of which are considered Depression glass.

In 1937, Hocking Glass Company merged with the Anchor Cap Company and became Anchor Hocking Glass Corporation. Shortly thereafter, the new company began to manufacture glass ovenware that could withstand high temperatures in a kitchen oven.

Production of oven-proof glass marked "FIRE-KING" began in 1942 and lasted until 1976. Dinnerware patterns include Alice, Charm, Fleurette, Game Bird, Honeysuckle, Jane Ray, Laurel, Primrose, Turquoise Blue, Swirl, and Wheat. Utilitarian kitchen items and ovenware patterns also were produced.

Housewives eagerly purchased Fire-King sets and could also assemble sets of matching dinnerware and ovenware patterns. Advertising encouraged consumers to purchase prepackaged starter, luncheon, baking, and snack sets, as well as casseroles. Oven glassware items included almost everything needed to completely stock the kitchen.

Fire-King patterns are found in azurite, forest green, gray, ivory, jade-ite, peach luster, pink, plain white, ruby red, sapphire blue, opaque turquoise, and white with an assortment of rim colors. To increase sales, decals were applied.

**References:** Gene Florence, *Anchor Hocking's Fire King & More,* Collector Books, 1998; —, *Collectible Glassware from the 40s, 50s, 60s,* 4th ed., Collector Books, 1998; —, *Kitchen Glassware of the Depression Years,* 5th ed., Collector Books, 1995, 1997 value update; Gary and Dale Kilgo and Jerry and Gail Wilkins, *Collectors Guide to Anchor Hocking's Fire-King Glassware,* K & W Collectibles Publisher, 1991; —, *Collectors Guide to Anchor Hocking's Fire-King Glassware, Volume II,* K & W Collectibles Publisher, 1998; April M. Tvorak, *Fire-King,* 5th ed., published by author (P.O. Box 126, Canon City, CO 81215), 1997.

**Periodicals:** *Fire-King Monthly,* P.O. Box 70594, Tuscaloosa, AL 35407; *Fire-King News,* K & W Collectibles, Inc., P.O. Box 374, Addison, AL 35540.

**Collectors' Club:** Fire-King Collectors Club, 1161 Woodrow St, #3, Redwood City, CA 94061.

**References:** Gene Florence, *Anchor Hocking's Fire-King & More,* Collector Books, 1998; —, *Collectible Glassware from the 40s, 50s, 60s,* 4th ed., Collector Books, 1998; Gary Kilgo et. al., *A Collectors Guide to Anchor Hocking's Fire-King Glassware,* 2nd ed., published by authors, 1997.

**Periodical:** *The Fire-King News,* P.O. Box 473, Addison, AL 35540.

**Collectors' Club:** The Fire-King Collectors Club, 1406 E. 14th St., Des Moines, IA 50316.

### Dinnerware

Berry Bowl
    Charm, Azurite, 4-3/4" d ............ 5.00
    Jane Ray, ivory ........................ 55.00
    Laurel Gray, 4-1/2" d ................. 6.00
    Restaurant Ware, jade-ite, heavy, 4-3/4" d .................................. 15.00
Bowl
    Bubble, Peach Luster, 8-3/8" d ................................................ 9.00
    Turquoise, Splashproof, 3 qt .... 25.00
Cake Plate, Country Kitchens, 9" d ................................................ 6.50
Cereal Bowl
    Charm, Azurite, 6" d ............... 18.00
    Restaurant Ware, jade-ite, heavy, 5" d .................................. 35.00
Child's Plate, divided, Turquoise, 7-1/2" d .................................. 40.00
Chili Bowl
    Peach Luster, copper tint .......... 7.00
    Restaurant Ware, jade-ite, heavy ................................................ 15.00
Creamer and Sugar
    Laurel Gray ............................. 7.00
    Restaurant Ware, jade-ite, heavy ................................................ 35.00
Cup and Saucer
    Alice, jade-ite ........................ 12.00
    Crystal Wheat ........................... 8.00
    Honeysuckle ............................. 6.00
    Jane Ray ............................... 15.00
    Laurel Gray ............................. 5.00
    Primrose, base reads "Oven Fireking Ware #14 (cup), #35 (saucer), Made in USA" .............................. 9.00
    Restaurant Ware, jade-ite, heavy ................................................ 18.00
    St. Denis, jade-ite ................... 15.00
    Swirl, Azurite .......................... 8.00
    Swirl, Ivory ............................. 7.00
Custard Cup, Candleglow ............. 2.50
Demitasse Cup and Saucer
    Fishscale Luster ..................... 35.00
    Jane Ray, jade-ite ................... 85.00
    Luster Shell .......................... 10.00
Dessert Bowl
    Game Bird pattern, Canadian Goose dec ..................................... 5.00
    Laurel Leaf, peach luster, 4-7/8" d, base reads "Oven Fireking Ware, Made in USA," some scratches from use ..................................... 2.50
    Royal Ruby .............................. 6.50
    Vienna Lace ............................. 2.50
Dinner Plate
    Alice, jade-ite ........................ 70.00
    Blue Mosaic ............................. 8.00
    Game Bird, pheasant dec ......... 9.00
    Jane Ray, 9" d, ivory ............... 55.00
    Laurel Gray ............................. 8.00
    Leaf and Blossom, green and pink ................................................ 8.50
    Restaurant Ware, jade-ite, heavy, 9" d .................................. 32.00
    Swirl, Azurite .......................... 8.50
    Swirl, Ivory, orig label ............. 11.00
    Vienna Lace ............................. 3.50

Grill Plate, Restaurant Ware, jade-ite, heavy ................................... 35.00
Luncheon Plate
    Charm, Azurite, 8-3/8" d .......... 5.50
    Restaurant Ware, jade-ite, heavy ................................................ 85.00
Mug
    Bubble, Peach Luster .............. 3.50
    Game Bird Pattern, Mallard Duck dec .................................... 10.00
    Red Rose ................................ 4.00
    Restaurant Ware, jade-ite, heavy ................................................ 15.00
    Sapphire Blue ......................... 25.00
    White, mkd "Anchor Hocking Fireking, Made in USA" ............. 4.00
Pie Pan, Swirl, Ivory, orig label ..... 15.00
Platter
    Restaurant Ware, jade-ite, heavy, 9-1/4" l .............................. 60.00
    Swirl, Azurite, oval ................... 20.00
    Wheat, 9" x 12" base reads "Oven Fireking Ware," some scratches from use ..................................... 12.00
Range Shaker, Swirl, Ivory, orig tulip top ................................................ 24.00
Relish, Turquoise Blue, 3 part, gold trim ................................................ 12.00
Salad Plate
    Alice, jade-ite ........................ 14.00
    Restaurant Ware, jade-ite, heavy ................................................ 15.00
    Swirl, Azurite ........................... 7.00
Serving Plate, Laurel Gray, 11" l ... 40.00
Snack Set
    Colonial Lady, ruby and crystal ................................................ 12.00
    Swirl, Ivory, gold trim ............... 7.50
Soup Bowl
    Jane Ray, 7-5/8" d ................... 30.00
    Meadow Green ......................... 6.50
    Swirl, Ivory, flat, orig label ........ 12.00
    Wheat, 5-1/2" d, base reads "Oven Fireking Ware, Made in USA, #11" ................................................ 5.00
Starter Set
    Swirl, Ivory, orig pictorial box, 4 dinner plates, 4 cups and saucers, set ................................................ 60.00
    Turquoise, orig box .................. 75.00
Tumbler, Game Bird dec, mallard duck, pheasant, or ruffled grouse dec ................................................ 12.00
Vase, Deco, jade-ite ................... 18.00
Vegetable Bowl, Luster Shell .......... 6.50

### Kitchenware

Batter Bowl, jade-ite ................... 45.00
Bowl, Tulip, 9-1/2" d ................... 35.00
Coffee Maker, Silex, 2 cup, 2 pc .. 25.00
Eggcup, jade-ite ........................ 40.00
Grease Jar
    Red Dots, white ...................... 35.00
    Stripes ................................. 35.00
    Tulip, ivory or white ................. 35.00
Hot Plate, Sapphire Blue ............. 18.00
Lid, Philbe, 5" x 9" .................... 35.00
Measuring Cup, Sapphire Blue .... 18.50
Mixing Bowl
    Beaded Rim, white, 4-7/8" d ...... 8.00
    Jade-ite, 2 handles, spout ....... 35.00
Mixing Bowl Set, Red Dots, 7", 8", 9", white ..................................... 70.00

**Hot Plate, light blue, 10-3/8" w handle to handle, $15.**

Nurser, Sapphire Blue, 4 oz .......... 10.00
Refrigerator Jar, Philbe, large, jade-ite,
    lid missing ................................ 40.00
Salt and Pepper Shakers, pr
    Red Dots, white ........................ 45.00
    Stripes ..................................... 37.50
Utility Bowl, Sapphire Blue, 8-1/4" d
    ............................................... 20.00

**Ovenware**
Au Gratin Covered Casserole, Blue
    Applique, 11" l, mkd "#433 Anchor
    Hocking Fireking Oven Proof, #9,
    Made in USA, 1-1/2 Qt, USA" ... 14.00
Baking Dish
    Blue Appliqué, 9-1/4" l, deep, quart,
    mkd "#436 Anchor Hocking Fireking
    Oven Proof, #18, Made in USA, 1 Qt,
    USA" .......................................... 9.00
    Sapphire Blue, individual serving
    size ............................................. 4.50
Cake Pan, Wheat, 8" d, bottom stamp
    reads #450, Anchor Hocking, Firek-
    ing Ovenware, Made in USA, 8,"
    some scratches from use ......... 15.00
Casserole, cov
    Peach Luster, copper tint, tab lids,
    orig label .................................... 7.50
    Sapphire Blue, 1 pint ............... 15.00
Custard Cup, crystal, orig label ...... 3.00
Loaf Pan
    Blue Applique, 10-3/4" l, mkd "Anchor
    Hocking Fireking Oven Proof, #9,
    Made in USA, 1 qt, USA ............ 12.00
    Sapphire Blue .......................... 17.50
Pie Plate, crystal, 10 oz .................. 4.00
Roaster, Sapphire Blue, 2 pcs ...... 90.00
Utility Bowl, Sapphire Blue, 7" d ..... 14.00

# Fishing Collectibles

**Collecting Hints:** The types of fishing items collected are rapidly expanding as the rare specimens become more expensive and harder to locate. New categories include landing nets, minnow traps, bait boxes, advertising signs, catalogs, and fish decoys used in ice spearing.

Items in original containers and in mint condition command top prices. There is little collector value if paint has been spread over the original decoration or if rods have been refinished or are broken.

Early wooden plugs (before 1920), split bamboo fly rods made by the master craftsmen of that era, and reels constructed of German silver with special detail or unique mechanical features are the items most sought by advanced collectors.

The number of serious collectors is steadily increasing as indicated by the membership in the National Fishing Lure Collectors Club which has approximately 2,000 active members.

**History:** Early man caught fish with crude spears and hooks made of bone, horn, or flint. By the mid-1800s, metal lures with attached hooks were produced in New York State. Later, the metal was curved and glass beads added to make them more attractive. Spinners with painted-wood bodies and glass eyes appeared around 1890. Soon after, wood plugs with glass eyes were being produced by many different makers. Patents, which were issued in large numbers around this time, covered the development of hook hangers, body styles, and devices to add movement to the plug as it was drawn through the water. The wood plug era lasted up to the mid-1930s when plugs constructed of plastic were introduced.

With the development of casting plugs, it became necessary to produce fishing reels capable of accomplishing the task with ease. Reels first appeared as a simple device to hold a fishing line. Improvements included multiplying gears, retrieving line levelers, drags, clicks, and a variety of construction materials. The range of quality in reel manufacture varied considerably. Collectors are mainly interested in reels made with high-quality materials and workmanship, or those exhibiting unusual features.

Early fishing rods, which were made of solid wood, were heavy and prone to breakage. By gluing together tapered strips of split bamboo, a rod was fashioned which was light in weight and had greatly improved strength. The early split-bamboo rods were round and were wrapped with silk to hold them together. As glue improved, fewer wrappings were needed, and rods became slim and lightweight. Rods were built in various lengths and thicknesses, depending upon the type of fishing and bait used. Rodmakers' names and models can usually be found on the metal parts of the handle or on the rod near the handle.

**References:** Jim Bourdon, *South Bend: Their Artificial Bates and Reels*, John Shoffner (P.O. Box 250, Fife Lake, MI 49633), 1996; Ralf Coykendall, Jr., *Coykendall's Complete Guide to Sporting Collectibles*, Wallace-Homestead, 1996; D. B. Homel, *Antique & Collectible Fishing Rods*, Forrest Park Publishers, 1997; Art, Brad, and Scott Kimball, *The Fish Decoy*, Vol. II (1987), Vol. III (1993), Aardvark; George S. Lawson, *Fishing Tackle Collectibles*, 1998, Monterey Bay Publishing; Chris Sanford, *The Best of British Baits*, 1997, published by author (P.O. Box 256, Esher, Surrey, KT10 9WA England); Harold E. Smith, *Collector's Guide to Creek Chub Lures & Collectibles*, Collector Books, 1997.

**Periodicals:** *American Fly Fisher*, P.O. Box 42, Manchester, VT 05254; *Antique Angler Newsletter*, P.O. Box K, Stockton, NJ 08559; *Fishing Collectibles*, P.O. Box 2797, Kennebunkport, ME 04046; *Fishing Collectibles Magazine*, 2005 Tree House Lane, Plano, TX 75023; *The Fisherman's Trader*, P.O. Box 203, Gillette, NJ 07933; *Sporting Classics*, 3031 Scotsman Road, Columbia, SC 29223.

**Collectors' Clubs:** American Fish Decoy Association, P.O. Box 252, Boulder Junction, WI 54512; Carolina Antique Tackle Collectors, 619 Elm Ave., Columbia, SC 29205; Florida Antique Tackle Collectors, P.O. Box 420703, Kissimmee, Fl 34742-00703; National Fishing Lure Collectors Club, P.O. Box 0184, Chicago, IL 60690; Old Reel Collectors Association, Inc., 3501 Riverview Dr., P.O. Box 2540, Weirton, WV 26062.

**Museums:** American Fishing Tackle Mfg. Association Museum, Arlington Heights, IL; American Museum of Fly Fishing, Manchester, VT; Sayner Museum, Sayner, WI; Museum of Fishing, Winter Haven, FL; National Freshwater Hall of Fame, Hayward, WI; National Heddon Museum, Dowagiac, MI.

**Reproduction Alert:** Lures and fish decoys.

Badge, 1-3/4" d, Fishing, Trapping,
    Hunting License, NY, 1930 ...... 55.00

**Creel, Form-Fit, crushed willow, leather bindings, 14" l, 9" h, 7" w, $35.**

Bobber, hand painted
 5" l, panfish float, black, red, and white stripes .............................. 12.00
 12" l, pike float, yellow, green, and red stripes ............................... 24.00
Book, US Commission of Fish & Fisheries In United States, Report of the Commissioner for 1886, Government Printing Office ......................... 35.00
Cartoon, 8-1/2" x 6-1/2" drawing, 2 black children fishing with 2 white children, captioned ................. 20.00
Cigarette Card, King of England deep sea fishing, New Zealand, 1937 ................................................. 8.00
Clock, mechanical, fish punching hole in side of boat with moving hammer, Hero Clock Co., wind-up, mkd "Made in China" ...................... 40.00
Creel, wicker, used, good condition
 Large ...................................... 110.00
 Small ......................................... 30.00
Cup, 4-5/8" x 2-5/8", cream ground, brown scene of man fishing on river, slogan "Reserved For a Wonderful Guy," gold Lenox mark ............ 22.00
Decoy, fish, wood
 6-1/2" l, Leroy Howell, gray body, black metal fins ...................... 115.00
 7" l, Ice King, perch, painted, Bear Creek Co. ................................. 75.00
Figure
 4" h, Jimmy Chuck, fishing hole, Jan Hagara's Make Believe Series ................................................. 50.00
 5" h, porcelain, Snoopy fishing 20.00
Fly, salmon, Paul Jorgensen ....... 450.00

**Decoy, perch, c1940, Michigan, 5-1/2" l, $48.**

License Holder, paper envelope, Florida Game and Fresh Water Commission, stamped with County Judge's name ...................................... 22.00
Lure, used, good condition
 Al Foss Dixie Wiggler, #13, 1928, metal box, extra hook, pocket catalog, 3-1/2" l ........................... 100.00
 Carters Bestever, red and white, pressed eyes, 3" l .................... 10.00
 Creek Chub Co., jointed pike, perch finish, glass eyes, orig box ...... 24.00
 Heddon, Dowagiac Minnow, series 100, wood, red and yellow stripes, olive green strip down back, glass eyes, 2-3/4" l ......................... 300.00
 Musky Minnow ...................... 900.00
 Paw-Paw, sucker, perch finish, tack eyes ........................................ 30.00
 Pfleuger, Never Fail Minnow, 3 hook, early perch finish, hand painted gill marks, large glass eyes, unmarked props, never-fail take hangers ................................................. 300.00
 Shakespeare, mouse white and red, thin body, glass eyes, 3-5/8" l ................................................. 30.00
 South Bend, Panatellia, green crackle-back finish, glass eyes, boxed ...................................... 50.00
 Strike-It-Lure, green, yellow, and red spots, glass eyes ................... 40.00
 Virgin Fishing Lucky Lure, orig card "Fishing Supplies Reco's Sporting Goods Store, Springfield, Ohio," 3-1/2" h .................................. 95.00
Magazine
 Hunting and Fishing, November 1938 ........................................ 12.00
 Outdoors Magazine, March 1937, Lloyd Bodi-Action lures back cover ad ............................................ 12.00
Magazine Tear Sheet
 Literary Digest, 1919, illus by Gerrit A. Beneker ............................. 10.00
 Outdoor Life, 1956, ABU reflex spinning lures, Garcia Platyl, and Garcia Mitchell spinning reel ................. 4.00
Minnow Trap, 12" x 10" x 10", hand made, metal and mesh, hinged door ................................................. 35.00
Music Box, 11-1/4" x 3-3/4" x 12-1/4" h, fishing trawler, moving crane brings full net aboard, plays "Somewhere Beyond The Sea" .................... 25.00
Patch, 3-3/4" x 5"
 Atlantic City Tuna Tournament .. 12.00
 Atlantic City Surf Fishing Tournament ................................................. 12.00
Post Card
 Fishing Pier, Asbury Park, NJ, date 1932 in pencil, unused ............. 3.00
 Indian fishing scene, white border, used ......................................... 8.00
Print
 Fishing lures, c1945, matted, 11" x 14" .................................. 20.00
 Michigan River by John Scott from the Garcia Collection, mkd with title and "Lithographed in USA," slight border discoloration, 20" x 12" ................................................. 10.00

Puzzle, 6-3/4" x 9-3/4", Fishing Village, advertising Campfire Marshmallows ................................................. 24.00
Reel
 A. F. Meissel Mfg., Takapart No. 480, Pat. 1904-98 .......................... 50.00
 B. F. Meek & Sons, Louisville, KY, No. 3 ..................................... 350.00
 Hardy, Perfect Fly Reel, English, 3-3/8" x 1-1/4" ...................... 165.00
 Hendryx Safety Reel, trout ..... 995.00
 H. L. Leonard, Pat. #191813, 4" d, salmon, German silver and hard rubber, mkd ............................... 475.00
 Penn-Jic Master No. 500, 3" d ................................................. 65.00
 South Bend, #1131A, casting, shiny finish, orig box ....................... 18.00
 Union Hardware Co., raised pillar type, nickel and brass ............. 25.00
 Unmarked, wood, brass fittings, c1880-1920, 6" d .................... 85.00
 Winchester, Model #1135, fly, black finish ....................................... 65.00
Rod
 Hardy, 7' 2", 1 tip, split bamboo fly, English .................................. 200.00
 H. L. Leonard, 6-1/2' ........... 1,450.00
 Horrocks & Illotson, 9' 3", 2 tips, split-bamboo fly, maroon wraps ...... 50.00
 Montaque, bamboo, 2 tips, orig case ................................................. 135.00
 Orvis Impregnated Battenkill, 8-1/2', 2 tips, splint-bamboo fly, cloth bag, aluminum tube ....................... 250.00
 Shakespeare, 9', Premier Model, 3 pcs, 2 tips, split-bamboo fly, red silk wrappings, cloth bag, metal tube ................................................. 75.00
 Union Hardware Co., 7-1/2', Kingfisher, saltwater boat rod, split-bamboo fly, dark brown wraps ....... 35.00
 Unmarked, fly fishing, heavy signs of use ........................................... 20.00
Scale, brass, "Chamllons Improved, New York, Pat. Dec. 10, 1967" ................................................. 30.00
Tackle Box, leather .................... 450.00
Tie Clip, articulated fish, 1-3/4" l .... 18.00
Tile, 6" d, Currier and Ives type print, Winter Sports--Pickerel Fishing, hanger on back ........................ 3.00
Tray, aluminum, lady fishing, catches skirt with hook and lifts it up in the back, red and black dec, scalloped edge ...................................... 165.00
Trout Net, 22-3/4", nice wood, orig net ................................................. 100.00

# Flag Collectibles

**Collecting Hints:** Public Law 829, 77th Congress, approved Dec. 22, 1942, outlines a detailed set of rules for flag etiquette. Collectors should become familiar with this law.

The amount of material on which the American flag is portrayed is limitless. Collectors tend to focus on those items on which the flag enjoys a prominent position.

**History:** The Continental or Grand Union flag, consisting of 13 alternate red and white stripes with a British Union Jack in the upper left corner, was first used on Jan. 1, 1776, on Prospect Hill near Boston. On June 14, 1777, the Continental Congress adopted a flag design similar to the Continental flag, but with the Union Jack replaced by a blue field with thirteen stars. The stars could be arranged in any fashion. The claim that Betsy Ross made the first Stars and Stripes lacks historical documentation.

On Jan. 13, 1794, Congress voted to add two stars and two stripes to the flag in recognition of Vermont and Kentucky joining the Union. On April 18, 1818, when there were 20 states, Congress adopted a law returning to the original 13 stripes and adding a new star for each state admitted. The stars were to be added on the July 4th following admission. The 49th star, for Alaska, was added July 4, 1959; the 50th star, for Hawaii, was added July 4, 1960.

**Reference:** Boleslow and Marie-Louis D'Otrange Mastai, *Stars and Stripes*, Alfred Knopf, 1973.

**Collectors' Club:** North American Vexillological Association, Ste. 225, 1977 N. Olden Ave., Trenton, NJ 08618.

**Museums:** State capitals in northern states; Hardisty Flag Museum, Hardisty, Alberta, Canada; Prattaugan Museum, Prattville, AL.

Advertising
  Ribbon, Leonards Spool Silk, Northampton, MA, silk ............. 20.00
  Trade Card
    Hub Gore, 3-1/2" x 6-1/4", Uncle Same holding shoe, saying "Hub Gore Makers of Elastic For Shoes, It Was Honored at the World's Fair of 1893," ............................... 9.00
    Major's Cement, 3" x 4-1/4", two American flags decorating display of 125 lb weights holding suspended object, full color, adv "Major's Leather Cement-For-Sale By Druggists and Crockery Dealers" ......................................... 9.00
    Merrick's Thread, 2-3/4" x 4-1/2", two infant children, one beating Civil War type drum, other waving flag, titled "Young America" ................................................. 4.00
Armband, World War II, 48 star flag, worn by paratrooper on D-Day invasion, two safety pins ................ 45.00
Badge, with ribbon, gold colored pin "Tower of Jewels, 1915-San Francisco," red white, and blue ribbon,

button reads "Admission day - PPIE Sept. 9, 1915, Admit One," US and CA flags and building dec ....... 60.00
Bandanna, 22" x 25", silk, flag inside wreath of 36 stars ................. 140.00
Book, *Proud New Flags,* F. Van Wyck Mason, 1951, orig dj ............... 20.00
Booklet
  *Flags and Emblems of Texas,* Dept of Publicity for Texas Centennial Celebration ...................................... 5.00
  *Our Flag, Display and Respect,* Marine Corps, 28 pgs, 1942 ...... 5.00
Button
  1/2" d, glass dome, flag printed inside, 6 mounted on card ....... 20.00
  1-3/4" d, horse button, glass dome with eagle and flag ................. 24.00
Catalog, Chicago Flag & Decorating, Chicago, IL, c1928, 32 pgs, 6" x 9", Catalog No. 30 ...................... 27.00
Certificate, Betsy Ross Flag Association, 1917, serial #38181, Series N, 12" x 16", C. H. Weisgerber painting ................................................... 55.00
Clock, God Bless America, mantel, World War II vintage, small American flag waves back and forth as second hand, Howard Miller Mfg. ...... 150.00
Envelope
  Civil War, angry eagle with shield hanging from his mouth and ribbon that reads "Liberty of Death," 34 large stars going around all four edges; each state has its name within its own star .................... 48.00
  Printed semblance's of Stars and Stripes with 45 stars covering address side ......................... 220.00
Flag
  29 star, 7" x 10", parade flag, coarse cotton material, Great Star pattern, used during Mexican-American War, discolored ............................. 135.00
  36 star, 21-1/2" x 36", parade flag, mounted on stick, five point star design, star pattern of 6,6,6,6,6,6 .................................................. 95.00
  36 star, 25" x 22", parade flag, printed muslin ......................... 95.00
  37 star, 16" x 24", parade flag, 1867-1877, muslin, all printed ........... 50.00
  38 star, 12-1/2" x 22", coarse muslin, mounted on stick, star pattern of 6,7,6,6,7,6 ............................. 12.00

**Flag, 36 stars, parade type, printed muslin, 35" x 22", $75.**

45 star, 3-1/2" x 2-1/4", child's parade type, pattern of 8,7,7,7,7,8 and five point star ................................. 25.00
45 star, 32" x 47", 1896-1908, printed on silk, bright colors, black heading and no grommets ..................... 95.00
46 star, 4" x 5", 1908-1912, stars sewn on, Oklahoma ................. 65.00
48 star, 5-3/4" x 4-1/2", 1912-1959, printed on heavy canvas-type material, used on D-Day in Infantry invasion, men wore them under the camouflage net on their helmets ......................................................... 75.00
49 star, 4" x 5-1/4", 1959-1960, child's parade flag, silk, wood stick, Alaska ...................................... 45.00
Handkerchief, World War I, flags of US and France, embroidered
  A Kiss from France .................. 15.00
  Souvenir France 1919 ............. 15.00
  To My Dear Sweetheart ........... 15.00
Lapel Stud, red, white, and blue enamel flag, white ground, Harrison/Morton 1888, enameled brass ............. 35.00
Letterhead, 11" x 8-1/2", Independence Hall, Liberty Bell, two crossed American flags, Sesquicentennial International Exposition ....................... 25.00
Magic Lantern Slide, 42 star flag, c1889, hand tinted, mounted in wood ...................................... 30.00
Magnifying Glass, pocket, 3/4" x 1-1/4", oval, Voorhees Rubber Co. adv, American flag artwork ............. 37.00
Match Box, 1-1/2" x 2-3/4", Civil War period, emb, picture of Stars and Stripes on one side, Miss Columbia on reverse ............................... 65.00
Plate
  St. Louis World's Fair, Washington, Jefferson, Lafayette and Napoleon's faces, very colorful, 1904 ...... 120.00
  Washington's Headquarters, Newburg, NY, 1783-1883, crossed flags under house, 10" d .................. 95.00
Playing Cards, Hall of Science and Avenue of Flags ............................. 65.00

**Plate, St. Louis Fair, portraits of Washington, Jefferson, Lafayette and Napoleon, 1904, $60.**

Post Card
    Printed semblances of Stars and Stripes covering address side, picture of Wm. H. Taft for President .............................................. 15.00
    Printed semblances of Stars and Stripes covering address side, picture of Wm. H. Taft for president, July 4, 1908, 46 stars, used ........... 18.00
Poster, 14" x 29", lithograph, "History of Old Glory," Babbitt soap giveaway .............................................. 145.00
Print, 11-1/4" x 15-1/2", Currier and Ives, "The Star Spangled Banner," #481 .............................................. 175.00
Scarf, numerous multicolored flags and expos name and dates in center, sailing ships border, white ground .............................................. 95.00
Sheet Music
    *Miss America*, two step by J Edmund Barnum, lady with stars, red and white striped dress, large flowing flag ..................................... 20.00
    *Stars and Stripes Forever March*, John Phillip Sousa portrait in upper left hand corner, Old Glory in center, published by John Church Co . ................................................. 20.00
Song Sheet, published by Chas Magnus, NY, 5" x 8" *The Female Auctioneer*, lady dressed in costume, waving flag .............................. 30.00
    *The Flag with The 34 Stars*, six verses and chorus, illus of soldiers marching with hand colored flag ................................................. 35.00
Spoon, 4-1/2" l, Jefferson, eagle, 2 flags, globe, "1904, St. Louis" on handle, Electric Building in bowl, Louisiana Monument and Cascade Gardens on back, US Silver Co . ................................................. 55.00
Stevensgraph, post card, "Hands Across the Sea, embroidered English and American flags, hands shaking, mkd "Woven in Silk, R. M. S. Aquitana," used ................... 35.00
Stickpin
    Celluloid, American flag, 48 stars, advertising, S A Cook for US Senator ................................................. 20.00
    Metal, 1-3/4" h, red, white, and blue painted furling flag at half staff, sign at left "Vietnam 1961-," orig cardboard box with clear plastic window inscribed "Wear This Pin For Peace," Pace Emblem Company, New York, NY, c1970 ................................. 35.00
Teapot, 9" h, cream ground, State of Texas, United States, France, Spain, Republic of Texas and Confederacy Mexico flags, titled below, red and blue line on spout cap ........... 475.00
Token, 3-3/4" d, "The Dix Token Coin," Civil War, commemorates the order of General John Adams Dix, Jan. 29, 1861, "If anyone attempts to haul down the American flag, shoot him on the spot," copper-colored coin, picture of "The Flag of Our Union" on one side and quote on the other ................................................. 10.00

Tray, 13" d, West End Brewing Co., American flag draped over Lady Liberty, standing next to keg of West End Brewing Co. Beer, Kaufmann & Strauss Co. litho ..................... 250.00
Watch Fob, Sesqui-Centennial, Liberty Bell and American flags, dates 1776-1926, crossed rifles at bottom .............................................. 40.00

# Flashlights

**Collecting Hints:** Flashlight collecting is like many other categories: name brands count, and if the manufacturer is not known, the value is much lower. Check for brand name and/or trademark, patent date, or patent number, and any other information that will help identify the manufacturer and the date the Item was made. Also check the overall outside appearance, and look for signs of wear, dents, splits, scratches, discoloration, rust, corrosion, deformities, etc. Carefully look for any cracks in the metal on both ends of tubular flashlights, and determine if both ends can be unscrewed easily.

End caps and switches are the most reliable way to identify the date and make since these parts cannot be easily changed. The finish, as well as the design, should be the same on both ends. Check all rivets and make sure they are intact. Brass becomes brittle with age, and it is not uncommon to find splits on both the lens ring and end caps.

The lens cap should be checked for any visible chips and paint chips. The reflector may be silvered and should be checked for tarnish and scratches. A rusty spring or corrosion damage is a clear sign that the batteries have leaked, which may affect the switch mechanism. Make sure the bulb is original, threaded, flanged, or an unusual shape. The entire flashlight should be checked for completeness, making sure the lens caps and rings all match and all switches work.

Flashlight collectors rely on old catalogs and magazine advertisements to help date and identify their flashlights. They are especially drawn to material with detailed illustrations of switches, finishes, and proper end caps.

Many collectors specialize in one type of flashlight, such as pocket watch, vest pocket, pistol, or character flashlights.

**History:** The flashlight evolved from early bicycle lights. The first bicycle light was invented by Acme Electric Lamp Company of New York City in 1896. A year later, the Ohio Electric Works Company advertised bicycle lights. In 1898, Conrad Hubert, who had been selling electric scarf pins, bought a wood bicycle-light patent and began manufacturing them under the name American Electrical Novelty and Mfg. Co. This company later became the American Eveready Company. Owen T. Bugg patented a tubular bicycle light in 1898. The next year, Conrad Hubert worked with an inventor who patented the first tubular handheld flashlight, which became the basis for the flashlight industry.

Conrad Hubert moved swiftly to take advantage of this unique tubular electrical "novelty." He displayed his products at the first electrical show at Madison Square Garden and again at the Paris Exposition in 1900. He won the only award at the exposition for "Portable Electric Lamps." He had opened offices in London, Berlin, Paris, Chicago, Montreal, and Sydney by 1901.

After the death of Hubert, Joshua Lionel Cowan, founder of Lionel trains, began taking credit for inventing the flashlight. He often gave detailed accounts of his invention, changing specifics from one account to another. However, his timetable, which coincided with that of Conrad Hubert, clouds the facts of flashlight history.

American Eveready has dominated the flashlight and battery industry since the beginning. In 1906, National Carbon bought one-half interest in American Eveready for $200,000. It purchased the remaining interest in 1914 for an additional $2,000,000. Companies such as Rayovac, Yale, Franco, Bond, Beacon, Delta, Uneedit, Saunders, Winchester, Sharpleigh, and Underwood also made many interesting flashlights.

**References:** *Collector's Digest Flashlights*, L-W Book Sales, 1995; Stuart Schneider, *Collecting Flashlights*, Schiffer Publishing, 1996.

**Collectors' Club:** Flashlight Collectors of America, P.O. Box 4095, Tustin, CA 92681.

Character
    CP30, keychain, 1996 ............... 4.00
    Elmo, Sesame Street ................. 3.50

**Pennsylvania Railroad, Bright Star, domed glass, 7-1/2" l, $55.**

Frankenstein, Halloween type, 9-1/2" l, green and black plastic, 1960s .......................................... 55.00
Hanna Barbera, 3", interchangeable faces, Flintstone, Huckleberry Hound, and Yogi Bear, 1975, MOC .................................................. 15.00
Hulk Hogan, WWF, 1991 .......... 12.00
Lion King, Scar, MIP................... 9.00
Mighty Mouse, four color, 1981, MIP .............................................. 7.50
Peter Pan, McDonald's .............. 5.00
Pluto, hard plastic .................... 12.00
Precious Moments, 4-1/2" h, Heavenly Light, angel, 1980............. 35.00
Roy Rogers, orig box ............. 175.00
Ultimate Warrior, WWF, 1991 .... 11.00
X-Files ...................................... 50.00
Ever Ready
   Hexagon/dome lens, metal ribbed body, black enamel end cap, on-off thumb switch, 1900s ................. 55.00
   Masterlight ................................ 80.00
   Octagon, 3 cell, brass.............. 25.00
   Union Carbide........................... 6.00
Girl Scout, military style, clip ........ 12.00
Irwin, raygun ................................. 65.00
Pocket Type, 1931, orig batteries
   .............................................. 20.00
Ray O Vac .................................... 14.00
Rose Brand, MIB.......................... 15.00
Surlite, 1950s ................................ 5.00
Victorinox, Fieldmaster, combination knife and flashlight................... 24.00
Winchester, 22-K, copper case, #1818 ........................................ 35.00
Yale, chrome, heavy glass lens .... 48.00

# Florence Ceramics

**Collecting Hints:** Pieces of Florence Ceramics are well marked. Most figures have their names marked on the bottom. Six different backstamps were used, all containing a variation of the name of the company, location, and/or ©.

Florence Ceramics is a relatively new collectible. As a result, stable national pricing has not yet been achieved. It pays to shop around.

Several figures have articulated fingers; some figures were issued with both articulated and closed fingers. The former type command a slight premium.

Look for figures with especially rich colors, elaborate decorations— such as bows, flowers, lace, ringlets, and tresses—and gold trim. Aqua, beige, maroon, and gray, occasionally highlighted with green or maroon, are most commonly found on economy-line figures. Yellow is hard to find.

**History:** In 1939, following the death of a young son, Florence Ward began working with clay as a way of dealing with her grief. Her first pieces were figures of children, individually shaped, decorated, and fired in a workshop in her Pasadena, California, garage. Untrained at first, she attended a ceramics class in 1942.

She continued to sell her pottery as a means of supplementing her income during World War II. Her business grew, and in 1946 the Florence Ceramics Company moved to a plant located on the east side of Pasadena. Clifford, Ward's husband, and Clifford, Jr., another son, joined the firm.

With the acquisition of increased production facilities, Florence Ceramics began exhibiting its wares at major Los Angeles gift shows. A worldwide business quickly developed. In 1949, a modern factory featuring a continuous tunnel kiln was opened at 74 South San Gabriel Boulevard in Pasadena. More than 100 employees worked at the new plant.

Florence Ceramics produced semi-porcelain figurines that featured historic couples in period costumes and ladies and gentlemen outfitted in costumes copied from late 19th-century Godey fashions. Fictional characters, including movie-related ones such as Rhett and Scarlet from "Gone with the Wind," were made. Inexpensive small figurines of children and figural vases also were manufactured.

Florence Ceramics offered a full line of period decorative accessories that included birds, busts, candleholders, clock frames, smoking sets, wall plaques, and wall pockets. Lamp bases, which were made using some of the figural pieces, were offered for sale with custom shades.

In 1956, the company employed Betty Davenport Ford, a modeler, to develop a line of bisque-finished animal figures. The series included cats, dogs, doves, rabbits, and squirrels. A minimal airbrush deco-

ration was added. Production lasted only two years.

Florence Ceramics was sold to Scripto Corporation following the death of Clifford Ward in 1964. Scripto retained the Florence Ceramics name but produced primarily advertising specialty wares. The plant closed in 1977.

**References:** Susan and Al Bagdade, *Warman's American Pottery and Porcelain*, Wallace-Homestead, 1994; Jack Chipman, *Collector's Encyclopedia of California Pottery*, Collector Books, 1992, 1995 value update; Harvey Duke, *Official Identification and Price Guide to Pottery and Porcelain*, 8th ed., House of Collectibles, 1995; Lois Lehner, *Lehner's Encyclopedia of U.S. Marks on Pottery, Porcelain & Clay*, Collector Books, 1988.

**Periodical:** Florence Collector's Club Newsletter, P.O. Box 122, Richland, WA 99352.

Bust, white, 9-1/2" h
   Choir Boy ................................. 75.00
   Pamela and David ................. 300.00
Cigarette Box, cov
   Lady's head, green, cameo ... 125.00
   Winter...................................... 245.00
Dealer Sign ................................. 350.00
Figure
   Abigail..................................... 160.00
   Ava, yellow.............................. 300.00
   Bea, teal and rose, 7-1/4" h ... 150.00
   Blue Boy .................................. 295.00
   Camile...................................... 245.00
   Charmaine, green ................... 460.00
   Choir Boy ................................. 45.00
   Claudia, 8-1/2" h, gray over pink ............................................. 200.00
   Della, green and sand, 7-1/4" h ............................................. 175.00
   Douglas ................................... 240.00
   Edward..................................... 430.00
   Elaine, white and gold, 6" h ..... 85.00
   Elizabeth ................................. 600.00
   Grace, 7-1/2" h, light green.... 185.00
   Irene, 6" h, beige and green .... 55.00
   Jeanette, 7-1/2" h, olive green ............................................. 140.00
   Jim, white and gold ................. 75.00
   Lady Diana, 9-1/2" h, separated fingers, lace collar and bodice, applied flowers .................................. 195.00
   Melanie, 7-1/2" h, beige with green ............................................. 110.00
   Mermaid................................... 125.00
   Pinkie and Blue Boy, 12" h, pr ............................................. 325.00
   Priscillia, 7-1/2" h, gray ......... 155.00
   Rebecca, gray and maroon... 250.00
   Rhett ....................................... 350.00
   Sarah ...................................... 115.00
   Scarlett.................................... 175.00
   Sue Ellen, 8", gray with maroon ............................................. 150.00
   Tess, light green.................... 430.00

Victoria, pink, hat ................... 530.00
Vivian, pink ............................ 360.00
Flower Holder
Lea, green and rose, 6" h ......... 60.00
Peg, beige and green, 7-1/2" h
.............................................. 60.00
Lamp, David and Betsy, price for pr
............................................ 500.00
Wall Plaque, full figured ladies, maroon
and green, price for pr ........... 200.00

# Flow Blue China, American

**Collecting Hints:** As with any Flow Blue china, value for American-made pieces depends upon condition, quality, pattern, and type. Avoid those pieces with flaws which cannot be repaired unless you plan to use them only for decorative purposes.

**History:** When imported Flow Blue china, i.e., English, German, etc., became popular, American manufacturers soon followed suit. There is great variation in quality. Compared to European makers, the number of U.S. manufacturers is small. The most well-known are the French China Co., Homer Laughlin China Co., Mercer Pottery Co., Sebring Pottery Co., Warwick China, and Wheeling Pottery Co.

**References:** Mary Frank Gaston, *Collectors Encyclopedia of Flow Blue*, Collector Books, Paducah, KY, 1983; Norma Jean Hoener, *Flow Blue China: Additional Patterns and New Information*, Flow Blue International Collectors Club (11560 W. 95th #297, Overland Park, KS 66214); Jeffrey B. Snyder, *Historic Flow Blue*, Schiffer Publications, 1994; ——, *Pocket Guide to Flow Blue*, Schiffer Publications, 1995; Petra Williams, *Flow Blue China—An Aid to Identification*, Vols. I, II, and III, Fountain House East (P.O. Box 99298, Jeffersontown, KY 40299), 1971-1991.

**Collectors' Club:** Flow Blue International Collectors Club, 11560 W. 95th #297, Overland Park, KS 66214.

**Museum:** Margaret Woodbury Strong Museum, Rochester, NY.

**Additional Listings:** See *Warman's Antiques and Collectibles Price Guide.*

**Advisor:** Ellen G. King

Advertising Ashtray, Sebring China Co.,
cherub decal in center, 4-1/2" d
.............................................. 95.00
Argyle, J & E Mayer
Bone Dish ................................ 50.00

**Advertising Ashtray, Sebring China Co., cherub decal center, 4-1/2" d, $95. Photo courtesy of Ellen King.**

Butter Pat ................................ 35.00
Milk Pitcher, 7" h .................... 145.00
Autumn Leaves, Warwick
Jardiniere, 8" x 7-1/2" ............ 550.00
Plate, 10-1/2" d ..................... 125.00
Relish, 8" l .............................. 90.00
Cato, J & E Mayer, small platter,
8" x 10" ................................. 95.00
Calico, Warwick
Creamer ................................ 235.00
Tray, 6-1/2" x 9" ..................... 110.00
Colonial, Homer Laughlin Co.
Plate, 10" d ............................ 65.00
Teacup and Saucer .................. 85.00
Vegetable Tureen, cov .......... 225.00
Cracked Ice, International Pottery
Bowl, open, round, 10" d ....... 150.00
Cake Plate, open handle, 10-1/4" d
............................................ 135.00
Chocolate Pot, cov ................ 375.00
Demitasse Cup and Saucer ..... 65.00

**La Belle/Blue Diamond, Wheeling Pottery, biscuit jar, 8-1/2", $450. Photo courtesy of Ellen King.**

Delph, Sebring Pottery
Butter Pat, 3" d ....................... 35.00
Plate, 9" d ............................... 60.00
Soup Bowl, 8" d ....................... 55.00
Wash Bowl, 17" d .................. 300.00
Fernery, Knowles, Taylor, Knowles, soap
dish, covered, no insert ........ 125.00
Hawthorne, Mercer Pottery
Plate, 8" d ............................... 50.00
Platter, 13" l .......................... 165.00
Vegetable Tureen, cov .......... 250.00
La Belle/Blue Diamond, Wheeling Pottery
Biscuit Jar, 8-1/2" .................. 450.00
Bone Dish, individual .............. 65.00
Butter Dish, cover, base, insert
............................................ 750.00
Butter Pat ................................ 45.00
Cake Plate, closed handles ... 240.00
Charger, round
11-1/2" d ........................... 350.00
14" d ................................. 450.00
Creamer and Sugar, cov ........ 375.00
Dessert/Vegetable Bowl, individual,
5-1/2" d .................................. 45.00
Fruit Bowl, ftd, 12" d .............. 275.00
Ice Cream Tray, 13-5/8" ......... 375.00
Plate
7-1/2" d .............................. 45.00
10" d ................................... 75.00
Platter, 15" l .......................... 250.00
Punch Cup, ftd ....................... 450.00
Relish, long, oval, 8" l ............ 275.00
Serving Bowl
Oval, 10-1/4" x 9" .............. 250.00
Round, 9-1/2" d ................. 295.00
Soup Bowl, 9" d ..................... 100.00
Syrup Pitcher, pewter lid ........ 315.00
Teacup and Saucer ............... 125.00
Vegetable Tureen, cov .......... 295.00
Wash Pitcher, small, 2 quart
............................................ 550.00
La Francaise, The French China Co.
Butter Dish, cover, insert ........ 175.00
Butter Pat ................................ 32.00
Creamer, 5" h .......................... 85.00
Dessert/Vegetable Bowl, individual,
floral decal .............................. 30.00
Plate
9" d, floral decal ................. 50.00
9-1/2" d, gold tracery .......... 55.00
Platter
13-1/2" l ............................. 95.00
15" l ................................... 175.00
Salt and Pepper Shakers, pr, round,
squat ..................................... 125.00

**La Francaise, The French China Co., left, dessert bowl, $30; right, plate, 9" d, $50. Photo courtesy of Ellen King.**

**Unknown Pattern, Warwick, tea set, teapot, creamer, sugar, tray, $1,100. Photo courtesy of Ellen King.**

Soup Bowl, 8" d .......................... 45.00
Teacup and Saucer, floral decal
............................................... 70.00
Vegetable Tureen, cov, ivy pattern
............................................. 325.00
Luzerene, Mercer Pottery
   Plate
      8" d ....................................... 65.00
      10" d ................................... 100.00
   Platter, 19" d ........................... 400.00
   Soup Bowl, rimmed, 9-1/2" d ... 75.00
   Teapot with lid ......................... 425.00
Paisley, Mercer Pottery
   Plate, 8" d ................................. 75.00
   Platter
      14" l ..................................... 250.00
      16" l ..................................... 300.00
   Soup Bowl
      7-1/4" d ................................. 50.00
      8-7/8" d, rimmed .................. 75.00
   Soup Tureen, covered, no lid or tray
   ............................................. 495.00
Pansy, Warwick
   Cake Plate, handles, 10" d ..... 180.00
   Charger, 14" d, round ............. 350.00
   Creamer, 6" h .......................... 325.00
   Relish/Celery Dish, 12-1/2" l,
      5-1/2" w .............................. 110.00
Poppy, Warwick
   Dessert/Vegetable Bowl, individual,
      6" d ...................................... 35.00
   Syrup Pitcher, pewter lid ........ 250.00
   Vegetable, round, open, 10" d
   ............................................. 150.00
Royal Blue, Burgess & Campbell
   Butter Pat ................................. 35.00
   Plate, 9-7/8" d .......................... 80.00
   Soup Bowl, rimmed, 9" d .......... 55.00
Snowflake, Knowles, Taylor, Knowles,
   plate, 9" d ................................. 65.00

Unknown Pattern, Warwick, tea set, teapot, creamer, sugar, tray ..... 1,100.00
Wild Rose, Warwick
   Berry Set, 10" d master bowl, 6 individual bowls ........................... 375.00
   Chocolate Set, covered chocolate pot, 5 cups and saucers ..... 1,500.00
Windmill, The French China Co.
   Butter Pat, 3" d ........................ 38.00
   Platter, 13" l ........................... 125.00
   Relish, long oval, 10" l ............. 45.00
Winona, The French China Co.
   Pitcher, 5" h ........................... 125.00
   Plate, 6" d ............................... 40.00
   Platter, 14" l ............................ 95.00
   Teacup and Saucer ................. 65.00
   Toothbrush Holder, upright .... 110.00

# Football Cards

**Collecting Hints:** Condition is critical—buy cards that are in very good condition, i.e., free from any creases and damaged corners. When possible, strive to acquire cards in excellent to mint condition. The introduction to Rob Erbe's *American Premium Guide to Baseball Cards* (Books Americana, 1982) includes photographs which illustrate how to determine the condition of a card. What applies to baseball cards is equally true for football cards.

Devise a collecting strategy, such as cards related to one year, one player, Heisman trophy winners, or one team. A large quantity of cards is available; a novice collector can be easily overwhelmed.

**History:** Football cards have been printed since the 1890s. However, it was not until 1933 that the first bubble gum football card appeared in the Goudey Sport Kings set. In 1935, National Chickle of Cambridge, Massachusetts, produced the first full set of gum cards devoted exclusively to football.

Both Leaf Gum of Chicago and Bowman Gum of Philadelphia produced sets of football cards in 1948. Leaf discontinued production after its 1949 issue; Bowman continued until 1955.

Topps Chewing Gum entered the market in 1950 with its college-stars set. Topps became a fixture in the football card market with its 1955 All-American set. From 1956 thorough 1963, Topps printed card sets of National Football League players, combining them with the American Football League players in 1961.

Topps produced sets with only American Football League players from 1964 to 1967. The Philadelphia Gum Company made National Football League card sets during this period. Beginning in 1968 and continuing to the present, Topps has produced sets of National Football League cards, the name adopted after the merger of the two leagues.

**References:** *All Sport Alphabetical Price Guide*, Krause Publications, 1995; *Football, Basketball & Hockey Price Guide*, Krause Publications, 1991; *1999 Sports Collectors Almanac*, Krause Publications, 1999; *Standard Catalog of Football, Basketball & Hockey Cards*, 2nd ed., Krause Publications, 1996.

**Periodicals:** *Beckett Football Card Magazine*, 4887 Alpha Rd., Ste. 200, Dallas, TX 75244; *Card Trade*, 700 E. State St., Iola, WI 54990; *Sports Cards*, 700 E. State St., Iola, WI 54990; *Sports Collectors Digest*, 700 E. State St., Iola, WI 54990.

**Bowman Card Company**
1948
   Complete Set (108) ............ 6,200.00
   Common Player (1-108) ........... 15.00
1951
   Complete Set (144) ............. 1,500.00
   Common Player (1-144) ........... 18.00
1952, Large
   Complete Set (144) .......... 12,000.00
   Common Player (1-72) ............. 25.00
   Common Player (73-144) ........ 35.50
1952, Small
   Complete Set (144) ............. 5,500.00

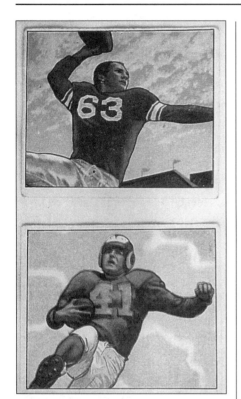

**Bowman, 1950, top: #5, Y. A. Tittle, Jr., bottom, #16, Glen Davis, each $20.**

Common Player (1-72) ............. 18.50
Common Player (73-144) ......... 24.00
1954
    Complete Set (128) ............. 1,600.00
    Common Player (1-64) .............. 6.50
    Common Player (65-96) ........... 15.00
    Common Player (97-128) .......... 5.50
1995
    Complete Set (357) ................ 125.00
    Common Player ............................ 10
    Expansion Foil .............................. 25
    Minor Star ................................... 20
    Wax Box ................................... 80.00
1998 Bowman Best, complete set
    .................................................. 100.00
1998, Chrome
    Complete Set (220) ................ 550.00
    Common Player .......................... 30
    Common Rookie ......................... 3.50
    Minor Star ................................... 80

**Fleer**
1960
    Complete Set (132) ................ 750.00
    Common Player (1-32) ............... 3.25
1961
    Complete Set (220) ............. 1,625.00
    Common Player (1-132) .............. 4.25
    Common Player (133-220) ......... 4.75
    Uncut, 132 cards ................... 650.00
1963
    Complete Set (89) ............... 1,800.00
    Common Player (1-88) .............. 7.50
1990, hand collated set ............... 10.00

**Leaf**
1948
    Complete Set (98) ............... 6,000.00

Common Player (1-49) ............. 22.00
Common Player (1-98) ........... 100.00
1949
    Complete Set (49) .............. 2,000.00
    Common Player (1-49) ............. 25.00
1998
    Complete Set (300) ................ 450.00
    Common Player ............................ 15
    Common Rookie ........................ 2.00
    Minor Stars .................................. 30

**Philadelphia**
1964
    Complete Set (198) ................ 950.00
    Common Player (1-198) ............. 2.00
1966
    Complete Set (198) ................ 950.00
    Common Player (1-198) ............. 2.75

**Pro Set, 1990**
    Factory sealed set ..................... 5.00
    Hand collated set .................... 17.00

**Score**
1989
    Complete Set (330) ................ 220.00
    Common Player (1-330) ............... 10
    Minor Star ................................... 20
    Wax Box ................................. 500.00
1990, factory sealed set ............... 10.00

**Stadium Club**
1991
    Complete Set (500) ................. 90.00
    Common Player ........................... 20
    Hand Collated Set .................... 90.00
    Minor Star ................................... 40
    Wax Box ................................... 90.00
1992
    Complete Set (700) ................ 150.00
    Common Series 1 (300) ........... 15.00
    Common Series 2 (300) ........... 15.00
    Common Player ........................... 10

**Topps**
1956
    Complete Set (121) ............. 1,100.00
    Common Player (1-120) ............. 3.75
1958
    Complete Set (132) ............. 1,350.00
    Common Player (1-132) ............. 3.75
1960
    Complete Set (132) ................ 650.00
    Common Player (1-132) ............. 2.25
1962
    Complete Set (176) ............. 1,825.00
    Common Player (1-176) ............. 3.65
1964
    Complete Set (176) ............. 1,450.00
    Common Player (1-176) ............. 3.50
    Common Player SP ................... 3.00
1966
    Complete Set (132) ............. 1,250.00
    Common Player (1-132) ............. 4.20
1968
    Complete Set (219) ................ 725.00
    Common Player (1-131) ............... 50
    Common Player (132-219) ........... 75
1970
    Complete Set (263) ............. 2,500.00
    Common Player (1-132) ............... 75
    Common Player (133-263) ........... 85
1972
    Complete Set (351) ............. 2,300.00
    Common Player (1-132) ............... 50

Common Player (133-263) ........... 75
Common Player (264-351) ....... 20.00
1975
    Complete Set (528) ................ 355.00
    Common Player (1-528) ............... 25
1977
    Complete Set (528) ................ 225.00
    Common Player (1-528) ............... 15
1979
    Complete Set (528) ................ 125.00
    Common Player (1-528) ............... 15
1981
    Complete Set (528) ................ 250.00
    Common Player (1-528) ............... 20
1983
    Complete Set (396) .................. 50.00
    Common Player (1-396) ............... 10
    Common Player DP ..................... 05
1985
    Complete Set (396) .................. 80.00
    Common Player (1-396) ............... 05
    Wax Pack, unopened .............. 90.00
1987
    Complete Set (396) .................. 40.00
    Common Player (1-396) ............... 05
1990
    Complete Set (528) .................. 15.00
    Common Player (1-528) ............... 03
1996, Chrome
    Complete Set (165) ................ 160.00
    Common Player ........................... 25
    Common Rookies ...................... 1.00
    Minor Stars ................................. 50
    Wax Box ................................. 180.00
1997, Chrome
    Complete Set (165) ................ 180.00
    Common Player ........................... 40
    Minor Star ................................... 75
    Wax Box ................................. 220.00

**Upper Deck**
1991
    Factory sealed set ................... 17.00
    Hand collated set .................... 15.00
1996, Game Jersey
    Complete Set (10) ............... 4,000.00
    Common Player ...................... 150.00
1997, Game Jersey
    Complete Set (10) ............... 3,000.00
    Common Player ...................... 150.00
1998, Super Powers
    Complete Set (30) .................. 45.00
    Common Player ........................... 50
    Minor Stars ............................... 1.00

# Football Collectibles

**Collecting Hints:** Collectors of football items may decide to specialize in one team, one conference, or one type of collectible, i.e., helmets or pennants. Collectors should not overlook the wealth of items generated by colleges, high schools, and even younger participants.

**History:** The first American college football match was between Princeton and Rutgers in New Brunswick, New Jersey, in 1869. Harvard documents a more rugby-type game in the 1870s. A professional football association was founded in 1920 and renamed the National Football League (NFL) in 1922. Football really took off after World War II and grew to 28 teams in two conferences by the 1980s. Expansion continued until 30 teams were playing by 1995.

The Super Bowl was created in 1967 and has become the exciting termination of the season for many fans. The Canadian Football League (CFL) was created in 1959 and oversees a professional circuit.

**References:** Mark Allen Baker, *All Sport Autograph Guide*, Krause Publications, 1994; David Bushing, *Sports Equipment Price Guide*, Krause Publications, 1995; Roderick A. Malloy, *Malloy's Sports Collectibles Value Guide*, Wallace-Homestead, 1994; Michael McKeever, *Collecting Sports Memorabilia*, Alliance Publishing, 1966.

**Periodical:** *Sports Collectors Digest*, 700 E. State St., Iola, WI 54990.

Bobbing Head, 3-1/2" x 3-1/2" x 7-1/2" box, 7" h painted composition figure, spring-mounted head, gold round base, gold helmet striped in green, green jersey and stockings, gold trousers, foil sticker reads "Sports Specialities, Japan, 67," box label with 1968 copyright................. 50.00
Candy Container, tin litho, football shape, 2" l, 1" w........................ 18.00
Doll, 7-1/2" h, celluloid head, hands, and feet, straw body, celluloid pinback button with "Yale" with attached ribbon and tin litho football, emb "Japan" on back of head ......... 40.00
Drinking Glass, Seagram V.O. Golden Quarterback Challenge 1990, football player on one side with facsimile signature, VO decal on other, 8 oz, set of 8 ..................................... 24.00
Football, leather, Wilson, NFL ....... 25.00
Game, Tom Hamilton's Pigskin Football Game, 1935 .......................... 265.00
Hartland Figurine
Arnett ..................................... 300.00
Browns, orig box ....................... 95.00
Giants, orig box...................... 150.00
Jersey, game used
Collins, J, LA Rams, white mesh, 1980s .................................... 225.00
Johnson, Tim, Redskins, 1990s, red mesh, autographed............... 250.00
Marino, Dan, Dolphins, aqua, autographed ................................ 350.00
Reeves, Eagles, white mesh, 1990s ........................................ 110.00
Selman, D, Tampa Bay, white mesh, 1970s .................................... 325.00
Warren, Univ. of Miami, white mesh, Fiesta Bowl, 1990s ................. 245.00

Williams, T, Dallas Cowboys, white mesh, name plate restored, 1980s ............................................. 145.00
Lunchbox, NFL/AFC, 1978 Broncos Bengals, helmets on side, NFL logo on back, some wear, orig thermos ............................................. 30.00
Magazine Tear Sheet, Wilson football, ball with "grip-ability," Paul Hornung, Boy's Life, 1967 .............. 4.00
Nodder, Cleveland Browns, sq brown wood base ............................. 75.00
Patch, Super Bowl V, 1970, Baltimore and Dallas................................ 60.00
Pennant
Chicago Bears, 11-1/2" x 28-1/2" black felt, "Bears" in orange, orange, green, and red football art, orange felt trim strip, late 1940s........... 25.00
Cincinnati Bengal's Super Bowl 16 AFC Champions, orange ......... 65.00
Denver Broncos World Championship, 1977 .............................. 45.00
Notre Dame, 1957 Conference Champions, gold filled, football shaped, chain ......................... 75.00
Photograph, autographed
B. Blades, R. Crockett, K. Scott, and W. White ................................ 45.00
Ray Crockett, Detroit, 8" x 10".... 5.00
Luther Eliss, Detroit, 8" x 10" ...... 5.00
Desmond Howard, Washington, 8" x 10" ................................... 10.00
Pete Mitchell, Jaguars, 8" x 10" .... 4.00
Herman Moore, NFL Official .... 80.00
Ed Murray, Detroit, 8" x 10" ........ 5.00
Kevin Scott, Detroit, 8" x 10" ....... 5.00
Bo Schembechler, Univ. of Michigan, 8" x 10" ................................. 19.00
William White, Detroit, 8" x 10" ..................................................... 4.00
Pinback Button
NFL Teams Official Booster Series, mail premium from H. J. Heinz, c1967, 1-5/8" d, litho
Atlanta Falcons, red and black helmet, white ground, black letters ......... 18.00
Baltimore Colts, blue and white, light surface wear ........................... 15.00
Detroit Lions, blue and silver, white letters ..................................... 20.00
New York Giants, black and white helmet, orange ground, white letters ..................................................... 20.00
Philadelphia Eagles, green and silver........................................ 18.00
Super Bowl XV/ABC Sports, 1981, black and white, gray rim, black letters, Superdome, New Orleans, Oakland Raiders and Philadelphia eagles ..................................... 30.00
Playset, Bob Griese, Gale Sayers, orig box............................................ 245.00
Post Card, young boy with football and turkey, postmarked Nov. 23, 1909 ..................................................... 5.00
Press Badge, U.S.C., blue lettering, taupe gray cello, "Camera" operator at Nov. 1, 1924 game, Los Angeles Coliseum, freshmen teams from Univ. of Southern CA and Univ. of CA ..................................................... 80.00

**Tobacco Silk, West Point, US Military Academy, football cheers, Richmond Straight Cut Cigarettes, $15.**

Program
New York Giants-Chicago Bears Playoff, 7-3/4" x 10-1/2", official program for Dec. 30, 1956 National Football league championship game, Yankee Stadium, red, white, and blue art on cov, 20 pages, black and white photos and profiles of players......... 30.00
Penn State-Navy Homecoming Game, 8" x 10-1/2", official program for Oct. 15, 1955 game, Beaver Field, Penn State Centennial celebration, 64 pgs, player photos, blue, white, and gold cov design ..... 35.00
Soda Bottle, Dr. Pepper, 1972 Commemorative, Miami Dolphins, unopened ............................... 95.00
Radio, NFL 50th Anniversary, Chiquita ................................................. 45.00
Telephone, figural, NFL, NRMIB ... 30.00
Ticket Stub
American Football League Championship, 1967, Oakland and Houston ..................................................... 25.00
NFC Division, 1977, Minnesota and LA Rams ................................ 12.00
Super Bowl I, 1966, Green Bay and Kansas City............................ 125.00
Wire Service Photo, Dallas Cowboys owner Jerry Jones and Jimmy Johnson, 1989 ....................... 3.50
Yearbook, Green Bay Packers, 1974, autographed by coaches and players ................................... 35.00

# Franciscan Dinnerware

**Collecting Hints:** The emphasis on Franciscan art pottery and dinnerware has overshadowed the many other collectible lines from Gladding, McBean and Company. Keep your eye open for Tropico Art Ware, made between 1934 and 1937. This company also made some high-style birdbaths, florists' vases, flowerpots, garden urns, and hotel cigarette snuffers. Catalina Art Ware (1937-1941) also is attracting collector attention.

Most buyers of Franciscan's big three patterns (Apple, Desert Rose, and Ivy) are seeking replacement pieces for sets currently in use. As a result, prices tend to be somewhat inflated, especially for hollow pieces. Keep in mind that these patterns were popular throughout the country.

Early Franciscan lines, which are similar to Bauer designs and Homer Laughlin's Fiesta, can be distinguished from their more popular counterparts by differences in shape and color. These pieces are more commonly found on the West Coast than the East.

**History:** Gladding, McBean and Company, Los Angeles, California, produced the Franciscan dinnerware patterns at their Glendale, California, pottery. The company began in 1875 as a manufacturer of sewer pipe and terra-cotta tile. In 1922, Gladding, McBean and Company acquired Tropico Pottery in Glendale, and in 1933 the West Coast properties of American Encaustic Tile.

In 1934, the company began producing and marketing dinnerware and art pottery under the name Franciscan Ware. Franciscan dinnerware had talc (magnesium silicate) rather than clay as a base. Early lines, which used bright primary colors on plain shapes, include Coronado, El Patio, Metropolitan, Montecito, Padua, and Rancho. As the line developed, more graceful shapes and pastel colors were introduced.

Three patterns are considered Franciscan classics. The Apple pattern with its embossed body, hand decoration, and underglaze staining was introduced in 1940. The Desert Rose pattern (1941) is the most popular dinnerware pattern ever manufactured in the United States. Ivy, the last of the big three, was first made in 1948.

There are three distinct types of Franciscan products: 1) masterpiece china, a high-quality translucent ceramic; 2) earthenware, a cream-colored ware found in a variety of decal- and hand-decorated

patterns; and 3) whitestone or white earthenware.

Gladding, McBean and Company became Interpace Corporation in 1963. In 1979, Josiah Wedgwood and Sons, Ltd., acquired the company. In 1986, the Glendale plant was closed, marking the end of American production.

**References:** Susan and Al Bagdade, *Warman's American Pottery and Porcelain*, Wallace-Homestead, 1994; Jack Chipman, *Collector's Encyclopedia of California Pottery*, Collector Books, 1992, 1995 value update.

**Collectors' Club:** Franciscan Collectors Club USA, 8412 5th Ave. NE, Seattle, WA 98115.

## Apple

| | |
|---|---|
| Ashtray | 25.00 |
| Beer Mug, 17 oz | 85.00 |
| Bowl, ftd | 22.00 |
| Bread and Butter Plate | 14.00 |
| Casserole, cov, individual | 55.00 |
| Chop Plate, 12" d | 75.00 |
| Coaster | 65.00 |
| Cocoa Mug | 125.00 |
| Compote, large | 125.00 |
| Creamer and Sugar | 60.00 |
| Cup and Saucer | |
|     Coffee | 9.50 |
|     Jumbo | 70.00 |
| Dinner Plate | 20.00 |
| Grill Plate | 140.00 |
| Gravy and Underplate | 42.00 |
| Jam Jar | 135.00 |
| Juice Tumbler | 37.50 |
| Mixing Bowl, 9" d | 90.00 |
| Platter, 12-3/4" d | 50.00 |
| Salad Plate | 18.00 |
| Salt and Pepper Shakers, pr, small | |
| | 36.00 |
| Syrup Pitcher | 80.00 |
| Teapot, cov | 65.00 |
| Tumbler | 20.00 |
| Turkey Platter | 320.00 |
| Tureen, ftd | 435.00 |
| Vegetable Bowl, 7-1/2" l | 65.00 |

## Coronado

| | |
|---|---|
| Bowl, turquoise, 7-1/2" d | 17.50 |
| Bread and Butter Plate, turquoise | |
| | 4.25 |
| Butter Dish, cov, turquoise | 32.00 |
| Candlesticks, pr, ivory satin | 48.00 |
| Chop Plate, 12" d, yellow | 20.00 |
| Creamer, yellow | 12.00 |
| Cup and Saucer, coral, matte | 9.50 |
| Demitasse Cup and Saucer, white | |
| | 37.50 |
| Dinner Plate | |
|     Coral, glossy | 9.50 |
|     Turquoise | 12.00 |
| Nut Cup | |
|     Maroon | 70.00 |
|     Turquoise, glossy | 70.00 |
|     Turquoise, glossy, orig box | 120.00 |
| Platter, 15" l, oval, yellow | 17.50 |
| Sugar, cov, coral, glossy | 13.00 |

| | |
|---|---|
| Vegetable Bowl, yellow | 35.00 |

### Daisy

| | |
|---|---|
| Milk Pitcher | 80.00 |
| Vegetable Bowl | 40.00 |

### Desert Rose

| | |
|---|---|
| After Dinner Cup and Saucer | 50.00 |
| Ashtray, individual size | 18.00 |
| Baking Dish | |
|     Oblong | 275.00 |
|     Square | 175.00 |
| Bell, Danbury Mint | 100.00 |
| Bowl, 9" d | 45.00 |
| Bread and Butter Plate, 6-1/2" d | 5.00 |
| Butter Dish | 30.00 |
| Candlesticks, pr | 75.00 |
| Casserole | |
|     1-1/2 quart | 75.00 |
|     2-1/2 quart | 700.00 |
| Celery Tray, 4-1/2" x 10-1/2" | 35.00 |
| Cereal Bowl, 6" d | 10.00 |
| Child's Plate | 165.00 |
| Chop Plate | |
|     12" d | 75.00 |
|     14" d | 95.00 |
| Cigarette Box | 140.00 |
| Coffeepot, cov | 115.00 |
| Compote | 75.00 |
| Creamer and Sugar | 40.00 |
| Cup and Saucer | 15.00 |
| Dessert Plate, coupe | 75.00 |
| Dinner Plate 10-1/2" d | 18.00 |
| Eggcup | 35.00 |
| Fruit Bowl | 6.00 |
| Gravy, underplate | 65.00 |
| Grill Plate | 95.00 |
| Luncheon Plate, 8-1/2" d | 12.00 |
| Milk Pitcher | 75.00 |
| Mug, 16 oz | 40.00 |
| Party Plate, coupe | 200.00 |
| Pickle Dish | 45.00 |
| Platter, 19" l | 225.00 |

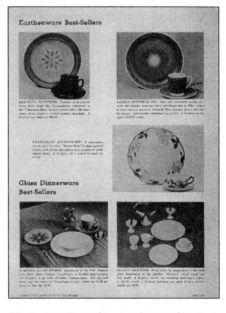

**Magazine Tear Sheet, China Glass & Tablewares, August 1967, featuring Desert Rose, noting it's a pace-setter for the past 26 years, $2.**

Relish, 3-part .................................. 90.00
Salad Bowl ..................................... 95.00
Side Salad ..................................... 32.00
Sherbet ......................................... 20.00
Snack Plate ................................. 195.00
Soup Bowl ..................................... 18.00
Tea Cup and Saucer .................... 10.00
Tea Jar, cov ................................ 150.00
Tea Tile, square ............................ 50.00
Toast Cover ................................. 155.00
Vegetable Bowl, 9" l ..................... 32.00
Water Pitcher, 2-1/2" quart ........... 95.00

**Fresh Fruit**, tile, 6" ........................ 50.00

### Ivy
Bowl, 7-1/4" d ................................ 40.00
Bread and Butter Plate, 6-1/2" d ... 12.00
Cereal Bowl ................................... 22.00
Creamer ........................................ 30.00
Cup and Saucer ............................ 20.00
Fruit Bowl, 5-1/4" d ....................... 14.00
Gravy, underplate ......................... 80.00
Platter, 12" l ................................. 70.00
Relish, 11" l .................................. 58.00
Salad Bowl, 11" d, ftd ................. 150.00
Salt and Pepper Shakers, pr, small
.......................................................... 35.00
Sugar, lid ...................................... 50.00
Tumbler, 10 oz .............................. 48.00
Turkey Platter, 19" l ..................... 325.00
Vegetable Bowl, divided ............... 40.00

**Magnolia**, creamer and sugar ...... 75.00

### Meadow Rose
Bowl, 6" d ....................................... 9.00
Butter Dish, cov ............................ 65.00
Cereal Bowl ................................... 20.00
Goblet .......................................... 175.00
Luncheon Plate, 8" d .................... 14.00
Side Salad ..................................... 45.00
Snack Plate ................................. 170.00
Teapot .......................................... 200.00

### Poppy
Cup and Saucer ............................ 32.00
Dinner Plate .................................. 37.50
Fruit Bowl ...................................... 30.00
Gravy, underplate ....................... 175.00
Platter, oval ................................. 170.00
Salad Plate, 8" d ........................... 35.00
Salt and Pepper Shakers, pr ......... 60.00
Tumbler ....................................... 148.00
Vegetable Bowl ........................... 130.00

**Rosemore**, demitasse cup and saucer
.......................................................... 45.00

### Starburst
Ashtray .......................................... 60.00
Bon Bon Dish ................................ 45.00
Butter Dish, cov ............................ 45.00
Casserole, cov, large .................. 265.00
Chop Plate ..................................... 62.00
Cup and Saucer ............................ 25.00
Dinner Plate .................................. 18.00
Fruit Bowl ...................................... 12.00
Jelly Dish ...................................... 45.00
Nappy ............................................ 35.00
Side Salad Plate, crescent shape
.......................................................... 27.50
Soup Bowl ..................................... 20.00
TV Plate ......................................... 75.00

**Wildflower**, plate, 9-1/2" d ............ 80.00

**Willow,** chop plate, 14" d .......... 275.00

# Fraternal Organizations and Service Clubs

**Collecting Hints:** Fraternal items are broken down into three groups. The first focuses on the literature, pins, badges, and costume paraphernalia which belonged to individual members of each organization. This material can be found easily. The second group consists of the ornaments and furniture used in lodge halls for ceremonial purposes. Many of these items were made locally and are highly symbolic. Folk art collectors have latched on to them and have driven prices artificially high.

The third group relates to the regional and national conventions of the fraternal organizations and service clubs. Each meeting generally produces a number of specialized souvenir items. During conventions public visibility is heightened; hence, convention souvenirs are the most commonly found items.

**History:** Benevolent and secret societies played an important part in American life from the late 18th century to the mid-20th century. Groups ranged from Eagles, Elks, Moose, and Orioles to Odd Fellows, Redmen, and Woodmen. These societies had their own lodges or meeting halls, held secret ceremonies, practiced clearly defined rituals, and held conventions and regional meetings. All these factors led to the availability of collectible material.

Initially, the societies were organized to aid members or their families in times of distress. By the late 19th century, they evolved into important social clubs, and women's auxiliaries were organized. In the 1950s, increased interest in civil rights led to attacks on the covert and often discriminatory practices of these societies. Americans had more outlets for leisure and social life, and less need for the benevolent aspects of the groups. Membership in fraternal organizations, with the exception of the Masons, dropped significantly. Many local chapters closed and sold their lodge halls, resulting in the appearance of many fraternal items in the antiques market. As collecting interest in these fraternal organizations wanes, some collectors are turning towards collecting service clubs, such as Lions, Rotary, where they are more familiar with the names and ideals or the organization.

**Museums:** Iowa Masonic Library & Museum, Cedar Rapids, IA; Knights of Columbus Headquarters Museum, New Haven, CT; Masonic Grand Lodge Library & Museum of Texas, Waco, TX; Museum of Our National Heritage, Lexington, MA; Odd Fellows Historical Society, Payepte, ID.

### American Legion
Medal, 1-1/4" d .............................. 8.00
Pin
    Auxiliary 3/8" d .......................... 6.00
    Sons of American Legion 1/2" h
    ...................................................... 8.00
    VFW 60 Years 1899-1959, Makan's
    Vigilanties ............................... 10.00
Pinback Button
    12th Grand Promenade, Camden, NJ, 1932, American Legion, shows train and boat, attached ribbon .......... 12.00
    19th Annual Grande Promenade. Sept. 7-9, 1939, Cape May, NJ, attached ribbon and medallion
    .................................................... 12.00
Presentation Key, mkd "VFW 10 64"
.......................................................... 10.00
Shoulder Patch .............................. 6.00

### Benevolent & Protective Order of Elks, B.P.O.E.
Ashtray, bronze ............................ 30.00
Book, Ellis, Charles, Elk's Authentic History of Elk's, 1910, purple cov, 700 pgs ............................................. 35.00
Bookends, pr, bronzed, high relief of BPOE elk ................................... 80.00
Calendar Plate, 1907, 9-1/2", Order of Elks center ............................... 50.00
Collar Box, leather, drawer, Elk emblem
.......................................................... 40.00
Container, 2" x 1-1/2", brass, presented to Bert Cook, Norwalk, Ohio .... 25.00

**BPOE, shaving mug, elk, gold trim, mkd "T & V Limoges, France," $195.**

Fountain Pen, 10K gold ............... 20.00
Paperweight, round, glass, elk ..... 20.00
Pinback Button, BPOE, 1910 ........ 22.00
Plate, Grand Lodge Reunion, Philadel-
phia, July 15-20, 1907, tin ........ 50.00
Shaving Mug, BPOE, pink and white,
gold elk's head and name, crossed
American flags and floral dec .... 95.00
Tie Tac, elk's head ....................... 12.00
Tie Rack, 7" x 8", wall type, plated brass
............................................... 15.00
Watch Fob, elk's head, two teeth
............................................. 150.00

**Fraternal Order of Eagles, F.O.E.**

Ashtray ........................................ 17.50
Pinback Button
1-1/4" d, attached 1-1/2" l ribbon,
"Visiting Brother, East Orange, NJ,
Lodge 630" ............................. 30.00
1-1/2" d, 2-1/2" l ribbon, "Dedication,
New Home, Dunellen Lodge, No.
1488, Oct. 27, 1927" ............... 45.00
2" d, attached 4" l red, white, and blue
ribbon, "Guest, Plainfield Aerie F.O.E.
Instituted Oct. 11, 1904" ........... 30.00
2" d, braided copper rim, white cello
button, colorful image of eagle flying
with American flag, sunburst background, red lettering "Pottsville Aerie
No. 134, F.O.E.," red, white, and blue
ribbon .................................... 10.00
Name Tag, pinback
Attached ribbon and belt buckle,
"Plainfield 885" ......................... 38.00
Attached ribbon and key tag, "Plainfield 885, Asbury Park, June 22,
1933" ...................................... 42.00
Watch Fob, bronze, F.O.E., Liberty, Truth,
Justice, Equality, 1918 ............... 20.00

**Improved Order of Red Man**

Badge Ribbon
2-1/2" x 7-3/4", red, blue, orange,
and green ribbon, brass accent
bade at top, color cello image of
eagle, black text, name, embroidered flag design, brass hanger at
bottom, 3/4" black and white cello
with image of Stourbridge Lion locomotive, gold accent ribbon, imprint
"Great Council Pennsylvania, Mauch
Chunk Flower Moon G.S.D. 406,"
early 1900s .............................. 25.00
2-1/2" x 8-3/4", green, blue, and red
ribbon, gold braids at bottom,
attached three part brass accent
hanger badge with 1" d black and
white cello of male Indian, yellow
and red accents, silver text on ribbon "Menton Tribe, No. 511, Imp'd
O-R-M Spring Glen, PA," early 1920s
............................................... 15.00
Grave Marker, brass, Indian on top
............................................... 50.00
Post Card, 3-1/2" x 5-1/2", red Indian
and bow, Pequod Tribe, No. 47,
Improved Order of Red Man, Instituted April 17, 1874, Atlantic City,
New Jersey, The Sunshine Tribe,
membership election info. on reverse
................................................. 5.00

**IOOF, pinback button, Philadelphia, 7/8" d, $7.50**

**Independent Order of Odd Fellows, I.O.O.F**

Badge, hanging, 1893 World's Colom-
bian Exposition, Chicago souvenir,
brass, inlaid black enamel ....... 60.00
Coin, nickel silver, detailed graphics
............................................... 40.00
Goblet, etched ............................. 48.00
Letterhead, 7-1/2" x 9-3/4", Canal Lodge
No 48, Searsmont, ME, 1840s
............................................... 20.00
Plate, 8", Royal Copenhagen, Frigate,
1905 ...................................... 100.00
Shaving Mug, multi-shaded, green
transfer, F.L.T. in chain link, marked
"C T Atlwasser Silesia" ............. 65.00
Teaspoon, SS, 1915 .................... 25.00
Trivet, 8-1/4" l, insignia and heart in
hand in laurel wreath ............... 30.00
Watch Fob, 94th Anniversary, April 12,
1913 ...................................... 32.00

**Knights of Columbus**

Fez .............................................. 20.00
Paperweight, glass, clear, milk glass
insert, black logo, floral border
............................................... 30.00
Plate, Vienna Art, 1905 .............. 320.00
Shaving Mug, name and emblem
............................................. 100.00
Sword and Scabbard, brass hilt, black
grips, raised eagle dec, metal scab-
bard ........................................ 55.00

**Knights of Pythias**

Goblet, green, 1900 .................... 220.00
Medal, bar pin: "Conn Lodge 37,"
medallion: "Knights of Pythias,"
name on back .......................... 38.00
Pinback Button, 7/8" d .................. 9.00
Shaving Mug, armor center, gold lettering and trim, marked "T & V France"
and artist initials ..................... 125.00
Sword ........................................ 650.00

**Knights Templar**

Letter Opener, bronze ................. 15.00
Mug, blue, symbols, 1910 ........... 35.00

Plate, 10", Grand Knights Templar Com-
mandery, 54 Annual Conclave, Harrisburg, PA, 1909 ..................... 90.00

**Lions Club**

Ashtray, smoke colored glass, gold
emblem and lettering, New York City
convention commemorative, orig
box, 1960s .............................. 12.00
Parade Ribbon, 2" x 5", 1982 ......... 5.00
Patch, Montreal Convention, 1979 .... 2.25
Pin, Illinois State Convention, 1981
................................................. 2.50
Salt and Pepper Shakers, pr, 1-3/4" h,
white, blue trim, "IOWA" printed on
back, mkd "Milford Pottery by
KlayKraft," stoppers missing ...... 12.00
Spoon, Florida, sterling silver ....... 15.00
Tie Bar, Anson ............................... 4.00

**Loyal Order of Moose**

Ashtray, brass, emb ...................... 8.50
Bolo Tie, emblem ........................... 7.50
Membership Certificate, 15" x 20",
Lodge 22, 1930s, framed ........ 15.00
Plate, 9-3/4" l, oval, P.A.P., Loyal Order
of Moose, back mkd "Grindley Hotel
Ware, England, 1930" .............. 15.00
Post Card, Williamsport, PA ........... 4.00
Ring, man's, 10K gold ................. 35.00
Shaving Mug, black, gold trim, brown
moose, "Vic Chamar," marked T & V
Limoges ................................. 620.00
Watch Fob, double tooth ............. 75.00

**Masonic**

Apron .......................................... 40.00
Bar Pin, celluloid Masonic emblem,
"Junior Order of United American
Mechanics," Pat. Whitehead & Hoag
Co., Newark, NJ ....................... 15.00
Belt Buckle, SP ............................ 24.00
Catalog, Henderson-Ames Co., Masonic
Lodge Supplies, 1924, 104 pgs
............................................... 50.00
Cuff Links and Money Clip, Masonic
emblem, gold plate, MOP accents,
mkd "Anson," orig box ............. 65.00
Cup Plate, Beth Horon Lodge,
Brookline, MA, September 1870,
light blue transfer, gilt trim ....... 85.00
Hat, York Rite, light blue, gold and
green trim, "50" inside wreath on
front, size 7-1/8 ....................... 50.00
Letter Opener, white plastic case, mkd
"Jordan Lodge No. 247, F & AM,
Robert Rogove, WN, 1967," Masonic
emblem .................................. 20.00
Medal, 1882 ................................ 40.00
Money Clip, Masonic emblem, Swank
............................................... 12.00
Name Tag, Jester, Albuquerque Court
No. 24, goldtone Jester, rhinestone
edge, magnetic pocket attachment
............................................... 10.00
Plate, Shenango China ................. 85.00
Shot Glass, emblem on front .......... 6.00
Stick Pin, Masonic emblem .......... 18.00
Tie Bar, sterling
Masonic emblem hanging on chain,
rusted clip ............................... 28.00
Shovel shape, Swank ............... 15.00
Tie Tac, 5/8" d, "New Jersey F & A.M.,
25 years" ................................ 10.00

## Order of Eastern Star

Acceptance Letter, to Mrs. D. Barrington, West Hallock, IL, from I. J. Case, Secretary, Alta, IL, 1895 ................... 12.00

Button, 11/16" d, metal shank, marcasite and gilt.............................. 10.00

Charm Bracelet, 19 charms, sterling silver, some damage and missing rhinestones............................... 35.00

Cup Plate, Pairpoint ........................ 7.50

Divided Dish, 6-7/8" l, 4-1/16" w, divided into 3 compartments, white ground, decals, gold edge, "Made in Japan" foil sticker ................................ 25.00

Pendant, silvertone setting, rhinestones and rubies ................................ 48.00

Pin, 50 Years ................................... 5.00

## Rotary International

Anniversary Plate, Bing and Grondahl, 75th anniversary ...................... 15.00

Badge, white, light blue and yellow lettering, US flag and Rotary flag in center, ship wheel, Cincinnati Rotary Club, Convention I. A. of R. C., San Francisco, 1915, bottom reads "Cincinnati Wants You In 1916" ...... 40.00

Banner, International Understanding Week, rosewood cylinder with engraved plaque, Budge-Budge Rotary Club International, West Bengel, India ................................. 25.00

Book, Kingspoint, TN, directory, 1937 ...................................... 20.00

Brick, 1924, Kansas, some wear .. 15.00

Compact ....................................... 30.00

Gavel, hardwood, Memphis.......... 12.50

Lapel Pin ...................................... 10.00

Money Clip, sterling silver............. 10.00

Pamphlet, No. 24, 1919 .................. 5.00

Pinback, Plainfield Inter-City Tract & Field Meet, 1925, Rotary International," attached ribbon and medallion.......................................... 16.00

Trivet, cast iron, Boyertown, PA ...... 6.25

## Salvation Army

Book, Salvation Army Miniature Biography, No. 4, Elizabeth Swift Brengle, 56 pgs...................................... 12.00

Coke Bottle, 10 oz........................ 30.00

Figure, caroler, Salvation Army lady, Byers Choice, 1994................... 75.00

Medallion, 1-1/4" d, "The Salvation Army," emb "With Heart to God and Hand to Man 1880-1955" on reverse ......................................... 18.00

Pin, 3/4" h, 1-1/4" l, "The Salvation Army" with a red "S" over a bar ......................................... 28.00

Ring, sterling, enamel emblem..... 30.00

Soldier's Ticket, 3-1/8" x 4", lavender, for KS and MO district, text on back ......................................... 15.00

## Shrine

Belt Buckle, silvertone, emblem ... 20.00

Candle, 4-1/2" d, 4" h, Ballut Abyad, fez, yarn tassel, glitter and paper sabre holder ..................................... 35.00

Candlesticks, pr, cut glass, 1900 ......................................... 100.00

Fez, 7-3/4" size, Khiva, goldtone sabre tassel clip, worn leather liner ......................................... 65.00

Goblet, ruby stained, St. Paul, 1907 ......................................... 70.00

Lapel Pin, 32nd emblem, SS ........ 20.00

Loving Cup, 3 handles, Niagara falls, 1905 ...................................... 45.00

Mug, Shriners, Syria Temple, Pittsburgh, 1895 ........................... 125.00

Nodder, papier-mâché, Mystic Shrine decal on fez, string tassel, orig paint ......................................... 35.00

Tumbler, 4-1/2" h, milk glass, gold embalms, c1910 ..................... 60.00

## Woodmen of the World

Bar Pin, celluloid picture of pair of hands shaking, ribbon reads "Carlisle, Camp No. 5472, Modern Woodmen of America Carlisle, Penna," brass beaded bottom tassels ......................................... 18.00

Camp Book, 1937......................... 10.00

Costume Catalog, 1914................. 25.00

Ink Blotter...................................... 9.00

Medallion, Woodmen of the World Golden Anniversary 1890-1940, three portraits on reverse......... 12.00

Tobacco Silk ................................. 7.50

Wallet, ID card, 1918 ................... 25.00

Watch Fob.................................... 20.00

# Frog Collectibles

**Collecting Hints:** The frog is a popular theme in art work, often in a secondary position. As with other animals, the frog collector competes with those from other subject areas.

The frog has lent its name to several items from flower frog to railroad frog switches to the device which attaches a scabbard to a belt. True frog collectors usually include examples of these in their collections.

**History:** A frog is small, with bulging eyes, long back legs, and no tail. The first frogs appeared about 180 million years ago; today there are more than 2,000 species.

Throughout history, frogs have been a source of superstition. According to one myth, frogs fall from the sky during rain.

Frog characters have appeared in cartoons, on television, and in movies. Flip the Frog is one example. The Buster Brown show featured Froggy the Gremlin. Kermit the Frog is a Muppet star, both on television and in the movies.

**Collectors' Club:** Frog Pond, P.O. Box 193, Beech Grove, IN 46107.

**Museum:** Frog Fantasies Museum, Eureka Springs, AR.

Ashtray, 3" h, 3-1/2" d, frog sitting on leaf ashtray, smoking pipe, polka dot shirt, base stamped in red "Handpainted Japan" ........................ 24.00

Bank, 6" h, pottery, seated, green glaze ......................................... 30.00

Beanie Baby, Legs the Frog, retired ......................................... 15.00

Candy Mold, 5", tin, chocolate ..... 45.00

Canister Set, three covered jars and 11" h cookie jar, Sears, 1979 ......................................... 125.00

Christmas Ornament, blown glass, crouching position, c1930 ....... 25.00

Clicker, 3" l, Life of Party Products, Kirchhof, Newark, NJ............... 15.00

Condiment Set, figural salt and pepper shakers on tray, mkd "Hand decorated Shafford, Japan"............. 48.00

Doll, 17" x 13", Freckles the Frog, cloth, Kellogg's, 1935 ..................... 135.00

Door Stop, 3-1/2" l, metal, figural, paint chipped, rust spots.................. 15.00

Fast Food Premium, 12" h, McDonald's, Kermit the Frog, NHL, hockey uniform, 1995.............................. 10.00

Figure
2-3/4" x 3-1/4", bisque, two frogs sitting in front of two eggs ........... 75.00
6-1/4" h, green Eosin glaze, designed in 1971, Judith Nádor ......................................... 250.00

Garden Ornament, 5" x 6", bronze ......................................... 45.00

Jewelry, pin
1-1/2" x 1", green Austrian crystal body, clear crystal legs............ 12.00
1-1/2" x 1-1/4", goldtone, green Austrian crystal eyes..................... 12.00
2" l, green enamel, goldtone legs ......................................... 15.00

Limited Edition Figure, The Frog Prince, Franklin Mint, 1986, bisque ..... 30.00

Planter, Flip the Frog, ceramic.... 100.00

Salt and Pepper Set, figural on tray, 3 pcs, Occupied Japan........... 12.50

Sparkler, frog with tie, Roselane .... 25.00

Stuffed Toy, Avon Birthstone Full O' Beans, March, Tad the Frog, simulated aquamarine stone on molded hand tag, MISB........................ 8.00

Toothpick Holder, frog pulling snail shell, SP ................................. 55.00

**Figure, stuffed frog, wooden horn, $30.**

Toy
    3" h, Flip the Frog, wood, jointed, green, beige hands and feet, raised eyeballs, c1930.........................75.00
    10-1/2" h, Croaker the Frog, rubber, Rempel Man, boxed.................45.00

# Fruit Jars

**Collecting Hints:** Old canning jars can be found at flea markets, household sales, and antiques shows. Interest in fruit jars is stable.

Some collectors base their collections on a specific geographical area, others on one manufacturer or one color. Another possible way to collect fruit jars is by patent date. More than 50 different types bear a patent date of 1858. It is important to remember that the patent date does not necessarily indicate the year in which the jar was made.

**History:** An innovative Philadelphia glassmaker, Thomas W. Dyott, began promoting his glass canning jars in 1829. John Landis Mason patented the screw-type canning jar on Nov. 30, 1858. The progress of the American glass industry and manufacturing processes can be studied through the development of fruit jars. Early handmade jars record bits of local history.

Many devices were developed to close the jars securely. Closures can be as simple as cork or wax seal. Other closures include zinc lids, glass, wire bails, metal screw bands, and today's rubber-sealed metal lids. Lids of fruit jars can be a separate collectible, but most collectors want a complete fruit jar.

**References:** Douglas M. Leybourne, Jr., *Red Book No. 7*, published by author (P.O. Box 5417, N. Muskegon, MI 49445), 1993; Dick Roller (comp.), *Indiana Glass Factories Notes*, Acorn Press, 1994; Bill Schroeder, *1000 Fruit Jars*, 5th ed., Collector Books, 1987, 1995 value update.

**Periodical:** *Fruit Jar Newsletter*, 364 Gregory Ave., West Orange, NJ 07052.

**Collectors' Clubs:** Ball Collectors Club, 22203 Doncaster, Riverview, MI 48192; Federation of Historical Bottle Collectors, Inc., 88 Sweetbriar Branch, Longwood, FL 32750; Midwest Antique Fruit Jar & Bottle Club, P.O. Box 38, Flat Rock, IN 47234.

**Note:** Fruit Jars listed below are

**Ball Special, qt, clear, $45.**

machine made unless otherwise noted.

Advance, Pat. App'd For, qt, aqua, ground lip.................................95.00
Atlas, qt, #109, cornflower............35.00
Automatic, qt, aqua, #177.........225.00
Ball, letter "B" reversed, qt, green, #221.....................................15.00
Beaver, circular, qt, aqua, #424-1....................................30.00
BBGM Co, qt, aqua, #197............35.00
Brighton, circular, qt, aqua, #512.....................................85.00
Columbia, qt, pale green, #641....30.00
Crown, qt, apple green, #697.......20.00
Crystal Jar, Patd Dec. 17, 1878, qt, clear, ground lip......................70.00
Dandy, #751, half gallon, aqua.....70.00
Everlasting, #952, qt, aqua...........35.00
Flaccus, circular, qt, aqua, #1014 .....................................................75.00
Fruit Keeper, qt, aqua, #1042.......65.00
Globe, #1123, qt, aqua.................25.00
Griffen's, qt, aqua, #1154 ...........225.00
Holmes, qt, amber, #1235 ............35.00
High Grade, qt, aqua, ground lip, zinc lid ..........................................150.00
Imp, half gallon, aqua.................150.00
Independent, qt, light purple, #1308.....................................50.00
Kerr, qt, aqua, #1371....................65.00
Mason, #1664-1, qt, aqua ............25.00
Mason 1872, #1749, half gallon, aqua ..........................................50.00
Pet, qt, aqua, applied mouth........55.00
Safety, qt, amber, #2534.............175.00

Star, qt, aqua, ground lip, zinc insert and screw band.....................275.00
Sun, qt, aqua, #2761..................125.00
The Pearl, qt, aqua, ground lip, screw band .........................................40.00
Wilcox, qt, aqua, #3000..............100.00

# Funeral Memorabilia

**Collecting Hints:** Funeral memorabilia should be collected because of love of the items not strong financial incentives. Advertising hand fans and calendars were produced in abundance and, therefore, are easy to find. Items which predate the decline of the in-home wake will be much rarer and worth a great deal more than later items.

**History:** Funeral rites are as old as humanity, and as diverse as the many religions and cultures. Being a funeral director became an acceptable career in the late 19th century. Today's funeral directors' responsibilities encompass everything from the removal of the body through burial. The undertaker of the 1860s was probably a carpenter who also made caskets and was sometimes involved in preserving the body but not in planning the funeral. During this era, in-home embalming and wakes predominated. This tradition was carried on into the early 20th century in most cities but more extensively in rural areas. Most of the *momento mori* (which translates to "remember, you must die") items to be found are from this period. These include casket plates, mourning cards, post-mortem photographs, and mourning jewelry.

Casket plates were mounted to the casket until the procession to the cemetery commenced, at which time they were given to the family. Plates had engraved sayings such as "At Rest," "Mother," "Father," "Rest in Peace," and "Our Darling" or "Our Babe," and sometimes also contained pertinent information about the deceased. Mourning cards were given to friends and relatives and were typically black with gold-leaf lettering and designs. They would name the deceased, give birth and death dates, and often had poems or reverent sayings. Post-mortem photographs were popular and many variations can be found. Most of these show a person laid in a coffin, although earlier photographs and tintypes can be found with parents holding their deceased child or members of the family posing around a seated corpse. Postmortem photographs can be found from as late as the 1950s.

Mourning jewelry is widely collected. Examples may be woven from the hair of the deceased or include locks of hair. Hair jewelry can be found in many forms, often with the name of the deceased or date of death memorialized. Mourning jewelry was made of celluloid, jet, and other black materials.

Funeral parlors began to appear more frequently at the beginning of the 20th century. The undertaker of yesterday became the funeral director of today—the person solely responsible for the care of the deceased. The custom of *momento mori* fell into decline and, for the most part, disappeared by the beginning of the 1920s.

**Museum:** The American Funeral Home Museum, Houston, TX.

Altar Stand, fold-up, orig black case, c1910 ........................................ 70.00
Bible, fitted pine box, "presented by" plaque blank ............................ 10.00
Brooch, 2" x 2-1/2", celluloid, black, emb "In Memoriam," 1870s ... 100.00

**Memorial, gilt dec on black ground, framed, ©1892 by t. W. Campbell, Elgin, IL, 26" h, 14-1/2" w, $50.**

Brush, wood, Wunderlich & Harris, Funeral Directors, 1930s.......... 25.00
Bumper Flag, blue, white cross, 1940s ...................................................... 35.00

Calendar, 1947, Crowell Funeral Home ................................................. 25.00
Casket Plate, silver finish, "Our Darling" ................................................. 18.00
Casket Stand, Windsor, mahogany, late 18th C, pr .............................. 495.00
Clock, wall, lights up, Barre Guild Monuments, 1950s ....................... 150.00
Cooling Board, portable, wood, brass hardware, B. F. Gleason, Rochester, NY, late 19th C ....................... 200.00
Embalming Equipment, box full, 1920s .................................... 600.00
Embalming Fluid Bottle, 7-1/2" h, Frigid Fluid, paper label, screw top, 1940s ...................................... 12.00
Head Elevator, stainless steel, 1930s ...................................... 48.00
Memorial Sacred Heart, The Crane and Breed Casket Co., brass, box, 1930s ...................................... 45.00
Photograph
    Memorial type, President and Mrs. William McKinley, framed, pr ... 22.50
    Snapshot, deceased black woman, viewing in private home, 1920s ................................................. 30.00
Sign
    Reserved Funeral Parking, on stand ................................................. 215.00
    Reserved Pallbearer, to be placed over back of chair ................... 30.00
Torchere, Aladdin, orig shade .... 160.00
Transport Case, child size, black, two top handles, adjustable sides ................................................. 120.00

# G

## Gambling Collectibles

**Collecting Hints:** All the equipment used in the various banking games, such as Chuck-A-Luck, Faro, Hazard, Keno, and Roulette, are collected today. Cheating devices used by professional sharpers are highly sought.

Almost all the different types of casino "money" are collected. In the gaming industry, "checks" refers to chips with a stated value; "chips" do not have a stated value. Their value is determined at the time of play.

The methods used by coin collectors are also the best way to store chips, checks, and tokens.

A well-rounded gambling-collectibles display also includes old books, prints, postcards, photographs, and articles relating to the field.

**History:** History reveals that gambling in America always has been a popular pastime for the general public, as well as a sure way for sharpers to make a "quick buck."

Government agencies and other entities use lotteries to supplement taxes and raise funds for schools, libraries, and other civic projects. Many of the state and city lotteries of the late 18th and early 19th centuries proved to be dishonest, a fact which adds to the collecting appeal. Lottery tickets, broadsides, ads, and brochures are very ornate and make excellent displays when mounted and framed.

Most of the gambling paraphernalia was manufactured by gambling supply houses that were located throughout the country. They sold their equipment through catalogs. As the majority of the equipment offered was "gaffed," the catalogs never were meant to be viewed by the general public. These catalogs, which provide excellent information for collectors, are difficult to find.

**References:** Art Anderson, *Casinos and Their Ashtrays*, published by author (P.O. Box 1403, Flint, MI 48504), 1994.

**Collectors' Club:** Casino Chips & Gaming Tokens Collector Club, 5410 Banbury Drive, Worthington, OH 43235.

**Machine, Bajazzo, c1904, $2,877. Photo courtesy of Auction Team Breker.**

Advertising Game, Tydol, spinner ................................................ 37.50
Ashtray, You Pay, 1950s, spinner.... 8.50
Book
  *Blackjack, Winner's Handbook*, Patterson................................. 12.00
  *Card Tricks, Magic, Gambling Guidebook*, 1st ed., ................. 18.00
  *Darwin Ortiz on Casino Gambling* ................................................ 3.50
  *The Gambling Man*, C. Cookson, 1975, 1st ed. ........................... 5.00
  *Tricks with Cards, Complete Manual of Card Conjuring*, Professor Hoffman, 250 pgs, hardcover, gold lettering, 1st ed., 1889 ..................... 20.00
Card Counter, plated, imitation ivory face, black lettering ............... 20.00
Card press, 9-1/2" x 4-1/2" x 3", dovetailed, holds 10 decks, handle ................................................ 140.00
Catalog, H. C. Evans & Co., Secret Blue Book, Gambling Supply, 1936, 72 pgs................................................ 55.00
Cigarette Lighter, lucite, dice........ 24.00
Cuff Links, dice ............................. 17.50
Dice
  Bakelite, golf sayings............... 32.00
  Weighted, black and white, always total 12, set of three ................. 40.00
Faro Cards, sq corners, Samuel Hart & Co., NY, complete ................. 125.00
Faro Chip Rack, 18" l, 10" w, blue-green billiard cloth lining.................... 80.00
Faro Layout, felt, walnut trim, George Mason & Co., Denver............. 575.00
Gambling Sheet, 1935 World Series, unused ..................................... 28.00

Game
  Bing, Beat Dealer's Shake, House Takes All Ties, potable dice game, 1890s, numbered felt board, leather bumper and cup with pair of dice, 23" w, 17-1/2" deep................ 300.00
  Rollem Dice Games, late 1950s, British Crown Colony Hong Kong, miniature dice roll on spinning table ................................................ 2.00
Keno Cards, 136, wood, paper and material covering, H. C. Evans & Co., Chicago.......................... 250.00
Keno Hopper, walnut, blue-green billiard cloth lining bowl, plated metal mouth, acorn finial, 3 carved feet ................................................ 450.00
Label, New Deal, gambling, cards, apple crate size ........................ 6.50
Matchbook, Golden Nugget, gambling hall on cover ............................. 1.50
Photo, scene of gambling in old western saloon ............................... 37.50
Poker Chip
  Horseshoe Club...................... 14.50
  Mother of Pearl, set of 4.......... 24.00

**Whiskey Bottle, Michters, Atlantic City, china, $30.**

Post Card, Pioneer Gambling Club, Downtown Las Vegas................. 9.00
Print, Nautical Dog, 1866.............. 25.00
Roulette Chip Rack, walnut, holds 1,500 chips ...................................... 120.00
Roulette Wheel, 8" d, wood and metal, single and double zero decals, 4 prong spinner, cloth layout.... 45.00
Shot Glass, ribbed dec, porcelain dice in bottom .................................. 25.00
Token
    French, 5 Franc......................... 6.50
    Majestic Casino, $1................... 2.00
    Trump Casino, $1 ...................... 2.25
Watch Fob, Golden Nugget Gambling Hall.......................................... 12.00
Wheel of Fortune, 20" d, 30 numbers, hand decorated yellow and white, cut-out paneled center, red ground ............................................... 150.00

# Games

**Collecting Hints:** Make certain a game has all its parts. The box lid or instruction booklet usually contains a list of all pieces. Collectors tend to specialize by theme, e.g., Western, science fiction, Disney, etc. The price of most television games falls into the $10 to $25 range, offering the beginning collector a chance to acquire a large number of games without spending huge sums.

Don't stack game boxes more than five deep or mix sizes. Place a piece of acid-free paper between each game to prevent bleeding from inks and to minimize wear. Keep the games stored in a dry location; but remember, extremes of dryness or moisture are both undesirable.

**History:** A board game dating from 4000 B.C. was discovered in ruins in upper Egypt. Board games were used throughout recorded history but reached their greatest popularity during the Victorian era. Most board games combine skill (e.g., chess), luck and ability (e.g., cards), and pure chance (dice). By 1900, Milton Bradley, Parker Brothers, C. H. Joslin, and McLoughlin were the leading manufacturers.

Monopoly was invented in 1933 and first issued by Parker Brothers in 1935. Before the advent of television, the board game was a staple of evening entertainment. Many board games from the 1930s and 1940s focused on radio personalities, e.g., Fibber McGee or The Quiz Kids.

In the late 1940s the game industry responded to the popularity of television, and TV board games were at their zenith from 1955 to 1968. Movies, e.g., James Bond fea-

tures, also led to the creation of games but never to the extent of television programs.

**References:** *Board Games of the 50s, 60s, and 70s with Prices*, L-W Book Sales, 1994; Lee Dennis, *Warman's Antique American Games, 1840-1940*, 2nd ed., Wallace-Homestead, 1991; *Caroline Goodfellow, Collector's Guide to Games and Puzzles*, The Apple Press, 1991; Rex Miller, *The Investor's Guide to Vintage Character Collectibles*, Krause Publications, 1999.

**Periodicals:** Toy Shop, 700 E. State St., Iola, WI 54990; Toy Trader, P.O. Box 1050, Dubuque, IA 52004.

**Collectors' Clubs:** American Game Collectors Association, P.O. Box 44, Dresher, PA 19025; American Play Money Society, 2044 Pine Lake Trail NW, Arab, AL 35016; Gamers Alliance, P.O. Box 197, East Meadow, NY 11554.

**Board**

Acquire, Avalon ........................... 25.00
Action Man, English..................... 45.00
Addams Family Reunion, Pressman, 1991, sealed, MIB................... 20.00
Alien............................................. 25.00
Apple's Way, Milton Bradley, 1974 ............................................... 25.00
Are You Being Served, English..... 30.00
Around the World in 80 Days, large ............................................... 35.00
Arrest and Trial, Chuck Connors ............................................... 35.00
Barney Miller, Parker Bros, 1977 ............................................... 24.00
Batman Returns, Parker Bros, 3-D, 1992, MISB ........................... 25.00
Beat the Clock, Lowell, 1954, 1st ed ............................................... 65.00
Beetle Bailey................................. 25.00
Ben Hur, C. Heston photo box, British ............................................... 110.00
Blondie.......................................... 25.00
Boots and Saddles, Gardner, 1958 ............................................... 48.00
Bozo the Clown Circus Game, Transogram...................................... 15.00
Branded, Milton Bradley, 1956 ..... 65.00
Camelot, Parker Bros., 1940s....... 24.00
Candid Camera ............................ 30.00
Candy Land, Milton Bradley, 1949, 1st ed.................................... 45.00
Captain Caveman, sealed............. 40.00
Captain Gallant Adventure Board Game, Transogram, 1950s ...... 48.00
Captain Video, Milton Bradley, 1950 ............................................... 125.00
Carrier Strike, Milton Bradley, 1977 ............................................... 35.00
Casey Jones ................................ 30.00
Casper the Ghost ......................... 75.00
Charge Account, Lowell, 1961 ..... 12.00
Cheyenne, photo box, British ............................................... 100.00

Chutes and Ladders, 1956, 1st ed ............................................... 20.00
Circus Boy .................................... 70.00
Clash of the Titans...................... 50.00
Clue, Parker Bros., 1949, 1st ed ............................................... 35.00
Contack, Parker Bros, 1939.......... 45.00
Dark Towers, Milton Bradley, 1981 ............................................... 150.00
Dick Tracy Crime Stopper, MIB ............................................... 100.00
Doc Holiday.................................. 40.00
Doctor Dolittle, 3-D action game, Mattel, sealed ................................. 125.00
Donn Prairie Race ....................... 30.00
Dracula, figural ........................... 50.00
Dragnet, Transogram, 1955.......... 60.00
Dream House................................. 25.00
Dynamite Shack, Milton Bradley, 1968............................................ 35.00
Easy Money, Milton Bradley .......... 7.50
Escape from New York ................. 40.00
Ewoks ......................................... 25.00
Family Ties.................................... 20.00
Fantastic Voyage......................... 25.00
Fess Parker's Trail Blazers Game ............................................... 60.00
Flintstone Kids, 1967 ................... 25.00
Fox Hunt, E. S. Lowe Co., 1940s.. 20.00
Frankenstein, Jr. ......................... 50.00
Fugitive, Ideal, 1964 ................. 280.00
Funky Phantom............................. 25.00
Gas Crisis, 1979, factory seal, MIB ............................................... 12.00
General Hospital, Cardinal, 1982 ............................................. 18.00
Gentle Ben, Mattel, 1968........... 250.00
Get Smart, time bomb, Ideal, 1965 ............................................... 75.00
G-Men, Melvin Purvis, Parker Bros, 1930s ................................... 200.00
Gilligan's Island, 2 small pieces missing ............................................. 195.00
Goodbye Mr. Chips ..................... 25.00
Gray Ghost .................................. 95.00
Green Hornet, Milton Bradley, 1966 ............................................... 90.00
Hair Bear Bunch .......................... 25.00
Happy Days, Italian ..................... 35.00
Hardy Boys, 1959........................ 35.00
Have Gun Will Travel ................... 70.00
Howdy Doody, TV show, 1950s ............................................... 125.00
Huckleberry Hound Bumps, Transogram, 1961.......................... 50.00

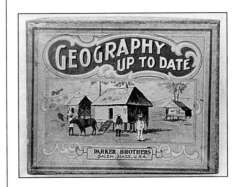

**Board game, Geography Up To Date, Parker Bros., early 1900, $25.**

I Spy.................................................50.00
It's About Time ...........................200.00
Jackie Gleason, Away We Go, 1956
........................................................165.00
King Oil, Milton Bradley, 1974 ......45.00
Knight Rider..................................25.00
Land of the Lost, 1975 ..................40.00
Lassie, Whiting, 1955....................25.00
Leave It To Beaver Ambush Game,
    Hasbro, 1969 ..........................120.00
Let's Face It, Hassenfield Bros., 4 plas-
    tic Mr. Potato Heads, 15" sq box,
    1950s ......................................140.00
Little House on the Prairie.............25.00
Little Lulu.....................................180.00
Looney Tunes, 1968......................45.00
Lost in Space ..............................135.00
MAD, Parker Bros, 1979, MIB.......20.00
Magic Robot Quiz, England, 1950s
........................................................65.00
M*A*S*H, Milton Bradley, 1981.....20.00
Matchbox Traffic Game, 1967.......50.00
Mighty Comics, Super Heroes, Tran-
    sogram, 1966 .............................60.00
Mighty Mouse Rescue, 1950s ......45.00
Mod Squad ..................................165.00
Monopoly, Parker Bros., modern ....5.00
Mostly Ghostly .............................30.00
Mystery Date................................125.00
Name That Tune, Milton Bradley,
    1959 ..........................................20.00
Nancy Drew Mystery Game, Parker
    Bros, 1959 ...............................100.00
New Avengers ..............................60.00
No Time for Sergeants .................25.00
Nurses, Ideal, 1963......................25.00
Perry Mason, Transogram, 1959.....45.00
Pinky Lee, Who Am I, 1950s.........60.00
Pit, Parker Bros. ............................7.50
Prisoner of Zenda, Milton Bradley,
    1930s .........................................25.00
Quick Draw McGraw Private Eye Game,
    Milton Bradley, 1960 .................45.00
Raggedy Ann, 1954......................25.00
Raiders of the Lost Ark, Kenner,
    1981 ..........................................48.00
Return A Putt, Bing Crosby, 1950s,
    MIB.............................................50.00
Road Runner, ©Warner Bros., Milton
    Bradley, 1968 ............................70.00
Ruff and Ready, Transogram, 1962
........................................................35.00
Sea Hunt, Lowell, 1961 ................35.00
Sgt. Preston, Milton Bradley,
    1956 ..........................................32.00
Shotgun Slade .............................40.00
Sigmund and the Sea Monsters,
    sealed ........................................40.00
Silly Sidney, Transogram, 1963.....55.00
Six Million Dollar Man, Bionic Crisis,
    Parker Bros, 1976 .....................24.00
Snagglepuss.................................35.00
Space Angel, Transogram,
    ©1965 ........................................75.00
Spot A Car Bingo .........................10.00
Spoutsie Hot Potato, Ohio Art, MIB
........................................................25.00
Star Trek, Ideal.............................60.00
Stock Market Deluxe, Whitman,
    1963 ..........................................30.00
Sub Search, Milton Bradley,
    1973 ..........................................35.00
Superboy, Hasbro, 1950s .............50.00

Surfside Six, Lowell, 1959.............65.00
S.W.A.T. ........................................20.00
Swoop Space Game, 1969...........30.00
Tank Command, Ideal....................48.00
Terry Toons, Ideal.........................45.00
The Rebel, Ideal, 1961 .................66.00
Three Stooges, Lowell, 1959 ......230.00
Thunderbirds, Parker Bros.,
    1968............................................55.00
Tic Tac Dough, Transogram, 1957,
    1st ed. ........................................25.00
Titanic, Ideal .................................45.00
Tom Hamilton's Pigskin Football Game,
    Parker Bros., 1946 ..................175.00
Treasure Hunt, Milton Bradley ........7.50
Twiggy ..........................................40.00
Twilight Zone................................195.00
Uncle Wiggily, 1930s ...................45.00
Untouchables, Transogram ..........55.00
Virginian, Transogram, 1962.........40.00
Watergate Scandal, American Sym-
    bolic, 1973 .................................18.00
Wolfman, 1960s...........................195.00
Woody Woodpecker ......................25.00
You're Out, Corey Game Co.,
    1941 ..........................................40.00
Zorro, Whitman, 1958 ..................30.00

**Card**

Bewitched.....................................195.00
Carol Burnette..............................25.00
Dallas ...........................................20.00
Dick Tracy.....................................45.00
Doctor Dolittle, Whitman...............40.00
Dukes of Hazzard .........................15.00
E. T. ..............................................25.00
F-Troop.........................................70.00
Howdy Doody ...............................48.00
I-Spy.............................................75.00
Llya Kurykakin ..............................35.00
Mork & Mindy................................18.00
Munsters .......................................50.00
Shazam .........................................15.00
Twelve O'Clock High ....................40.00
Voyage to the Bottom of the Sea, Milton
    Bradley, 1964............................20.00

# Gasoline Collectibles

**Collecting Hints:** There still is plenty of material stored in old garages; try to find cooperative owners. If your budget is modest, concentrate on paper ephemera, such as maps. Regional items will bring slightly more in their area of origin.

**History:** The selling of gasoline has come full circle. The general store, livery stable, and blacksmith were the first to sell gasoline. Gas stations, so prevalent from the 1930s to the 1960s, have almost disappeared, partially due to the 1973 gas crises. The loss of independently owned stations is doubly felt because they also were centers for automobile repair. Today gas sales at mini-markets are common.

The abolition of credit cards by ARCO marked another shift, as did price reduction for cash sales by other brands. The growing numbers of "pay-at-the-pump" stations will also influence the marketplace. Elimination of free maps, promotional trinkets, and other advertising material already is a factor. As more and more stores in shopping centers sell oil, parts, and other related automobile products, it is doubtful if the gasoline station will ever recover its past position.

**References:** Mark Anderton, *Encyclopedia of Petroliana, Identification and Price Guide,* Krause Publications, 1999; Scott Benjamin and Wayne Henderson, *Gas Pump Globes,* Motorbooks International (P.O. Box 1, Osceola, WI 54020), 1993; Jim and Nancy Schaut, *American Automobilia,* Wallace-Homestead, 1994.

**Periodicals:** *Hemmings Motor News,* Box 100, Bennington, VT 05201; *Mobilia,* P.O. Box 575, Middlebury, VT 05753; *Petroleum Collectibles Monthly,* 411 Forest St., La Grange, OH 44050.

**Collectors' Clubs:** American Petroleum Collectors/Iowa Gas, 6555 Colby Ave., Des Moines, IA 50311; International Petroliana Collectors Association, P.O. Box 937, Powell, OH 43065-0937; Spark Plug Collectors of America, 14018 NE 85th St., Elk River, MN 55330; World Oil Can Collector's Organization, 20 Worley Rd., Marshall, NC 28753.

**Reproduction Alert:** Small advertising signs and pump globes have been extensively reproduced.

Banner
    8" l, Texaco Havoline, plastic ......65.00
    36-1/2" h, 60" h, Sunoco Winter Oil
        and Grease, heavy cloth, Mickey
        Mouse illus, ©Walt Disney 1939
    ........................................................650.00
Car Attachment, Shell Oil, 3-3/4" x 5-1/2"
    metal domed image of Shell symbol,
    three colorful International Code
    Flags, late 1930s .....................190.00
Charm Bracelet, Tidewater Oil Co., gold
    plated metal, detailed Flying A logos,
    Veedol Oil can charms .............150.00
Coloring Book, Esso Happy Motoring,
    unused .......................................25.00
Decal Sheet, Esso, 3-1/2" x 3-1/2",
    white, red letters, beige ground,
    Palm Brothers, Decalomania Co.,
    NY, c1950 ....................................3.00
Employee Badge, Texaco, enameled
    ........................................................350.00
Fan, 10-1/2" l, 7-5/8" w, Sinclair Opaline
    Motor Oil, adv on back ............75.00

**Clip Board, Sinclair, aluminum, 6-1/8" x 7-1/8", $27.50.**

Kit, Amoco Word Building Contest, 4-1/4" x 8-3/4", black and white envelope, instruction and blank folder, perforated card spelling "American Oil Company," contest dated Jan. 31, 1934, unused ..................... 20.00
License Plate Attachment, Sunoco, 1940 ...................................... 100.00
Pin, Mobil Oil, 1932 ..................... 35.00
Radio, Texaco .............................. 65.00
Shirt, Texaco .............................. 45.00
Sign
   Esso Elephant Keroscene, porcelain .................................................... 875.00
   Good Gulf Gasoline, porcelain, flange ...................................... 550.00
   Sinclair Gas, porcelain .......... 100.00
   Socony Motor Oil, 15" d, curved heavy porcelain, Standard Oil Co., NY, some damage .................. 325.00
Thermometer
   Shell Anti-Freeze ..................... 85.00
   Sunoco, 6-3/4" h, 3-3/4" w, tin, raised finish, diecut, emb airplane in flight, adv below, blue and white, black lettering .................................... 275.00

**Oil Can, Penn-Glenn Oil works, red and yellow, blue lettering, 2 gallon, $20.**

# G. I. Joe Collectibles

**Collecting Hints:** It is extremely important to determine the manufacturing date of any G.I. Joe doll or related figure. The ideal method takes discipline—do a point-by-point comparison with the dolls described and dated in the existing reference books. Be alert to subtle variations; you do not have a match unless all details are exactly the same. It also is helpful to learn the proper period costume for each doll variation.

Accessory pieces can be every bit as valuable as the dolls themselves. Whenever possible, accessory pieces should be accompanied by their original packaging and paper inserts.

G.I. Joe dolls and accessories were produced in the millions. Rarity is not a factor; condition is. When buying dolls or accessories as collectibles, as opposed to acquiring them for play, do not purchase any items in less than fine condition.

**History:** Hasbro Manufacturing Company produced the first G.I. Joe twelve-inch posable action figures in 1964. The original line consisted of one male action figure for each branch of the military service. Their outfits were styled after uniforms from World War II, the Korean Conflict, and the Vietnam Conflict.

In 1965, the first Black figure was introduced. The year 1967 saw two additions to the line—a female nurse and Talking G.I. Joe. To keep abreast of changing times, Joe received flocked hair and a beard in 1970.

The creation of the G.I. Joe Adventure Team made Joe a prodigious explorer, hunter, deep sea diver, and astronaut, rather than just an American serviceman. Due to the Arab oil embargo in 1976, and its impact on the plastics industry, the figure was renamed Super Joe and reduced in height to eight inches. Production was halted in 1977.

In 1982, G.I. Joe staged his comeback. A few changes were made to the character line and to the way in which the figures were presented. The Great American Hero line now consists of three-and-three-quarter-inch posable plastic figures with code names that correspond to the various costumes. The new Joes deal with contemporary and science fiction villains and issues.

**References:** John Marshall, *Action Figures of the 1980s,* Schiffer Publishing, 1998; John Michling, *GI Joe: The Complete Story of America's Favorite Man of Action,* Chronicle Books, 1998; Vincent Santelmo, *Complete Encyclopedia to GI Joe,* 2nd ed., Krause Publications, 1996, and *GI Joe Identification & Price Guide: 1964-1998,* Krause Publications, 1999; ——, *Official 30th Anniversary Salute to G.I. Joe,* Krause Publications, 1994.

**Periodicals:** *GI Joe Patrol,* P.O. Box 2362, Hot Springs, AR 71913. *The Barracks: The GI Joe Collectors Magazine,* 14 Bostwick Pl, New Milford, CT 06776,

**Collectors' Club:** GI Joe Collectors Club, 12513 Birchfalls Drive, Raleigh, NC 27614; GI Joe: Steel Brigade Club, 8362 Lomay Ave, Westminster, CA 92683.

**Accessories Pack**, made for sale in Spain, Hasbro, c1975
#1 ................................................ 18.00
#2 ................................................ 19.00
#3 ................................................ 15.00
#4 ................................................ 12.00

**Action Figure**
Action Man Soldier, 30th Anniversary ............................................... 150.00
Action Marine Medic, equipment ........................................... 300.00
Action Marine, parade dress uniform ........................................... 150.00
Action Navy Attack, orange vest ............................................... 195.00
Action MP, incomplete uniform ............................................... 195.00
Action Navy, deep sea diver ...... 295.00
Action Navy, shore patrol........... 295.00
Action Soldier, combat field jacket and gear ...................................... 225.00
Action Soldier of the World, British Commando, no medal or clip ........ 400.00
Action Soldier of the World, Japanese Imperial Soldier, no medal, no bayonet ........................... 550.00
Action Soldier, orig box, some paperwork ...................................... 300.00
Action Soldier, talking, red head ............................................... 175.00
Action Soldier, West Point Cadet ............................................... 275.00
Airborne Military Police, Kay-Bee Exclusive ........................................... 50.00
Arctic Joe Colton, mail order, 12" h ............................................... 200.00
A.T.A.A. Adventurer, Kung Fu grip, orig box ...................................... 225.00
A. T. Sea Adventurer, life-like hair and beard, MIB .......................... 1125.00
Classic, Historical Commanders Edition, #4, General Colin Powell, MIB ............................................... 50.00
Francis Curry, Medal of Honor ...... 75.00

**Various G.I. Joe action figures.**

G. I. Joe, 50th Anniversary, WWII limited commemorative, Target exclusive, MIB............................................ 40.00
Marine, black, Masterpiece .......... 75.00
Navy Seal, FAO, 12" h................. 200.00
Pilot, blond, Masterpiece............ 100.00
Sailor, black, Masterpiece ............ 75.00
Set, 1994, pilot, Marine, Navy, Soldier, 3-1/4" h, MIB........................... 100.00
Soldier, 30th Anniversary, 12" h .... 75.00
**Coloring Book**, 48 pgs, Spanish text, 1989.......................................... 15.00
**Foot Locker**, 20th Anniversary ..... 200.00
**Gear,** Classic Collection
Mission gear, M-60 gunner's pit, MOC ................................................. 15.00
US Coast Guard, MIB ................... 30.00

**Outfit**

Action Soldier, scuba bottom, orig card, some tape .............................. 175.00
A. T. Dangerous Mission, action outfit, MOC .......................................... 50.00
A. T. Jungle Ordeal, MOC............. 50.00
Marine Dress Parade Set, #7710, 1964 ..................................... 565.00
Pilot Scramble Set, #7807l 1965 ................................................ 450.00
**Playset,** Atomic Man Secret Outpost, good box.................................. 85.00
**Ring**, 30th Anniversary, reddish-pink stone ........................................ 400.00
**Set,** Home for the Holidays, Wal-Mart ................................................. 50.00

**Vehicle**

Adventure Team Vehicle Set, #7005, 1970, NRFB.............................. 350.00
Desert Patrol Attack Jeep Set, #8030, 1967 ................................... 3,350.00
Fight for Survival Set, Polar Explorer, #7982, 1969 ......................... 650.00
Official Sea Sled and Frogman Set, #8050, 1966 .......................... 600.00

Space Capsule, Convention Exclusive ................................................ 200.00

**Weapon**

Bayonet....................................... 15.00
Flare pistol ................................... 2.00
M-16............................................ 30.00
Night stick................................... 20.00

# Golf Collectibles

**Collecting Hints:** Condition is becoming more important as collectors' sophistication and knowledge grow. The newer the item, the better the condition should be.

It is extremely rare to find a club or ball made before 1800; in fact, any equipment made before 1850 is scarce. Few books on the subject were published before 1857.

Most equipment made after 1895 is quite readily available. Common items, such as scorecards, ball markers, golf pencils, and bag tags, have negligible value. Some modern equipment, p-3 articularly from the years between 1950 and 1965, is in demand, but primarily to use for actual play rather than to collect or display.

The very old material is generally found in Scotland and England, unless items were brought to America early in this century. Christie's, Sotheby's, and Phillips' each hold several major auctions of golf collectibles every year in London, Edinburgh, and Chester. Golf collectible sales often coincide with the British Open Cham-

pionship each July. Although the English market is more established, the American market is growing rapidly, and auctions of golf items and memorabilia now are held in the United States as well as overseas.

The price of golf clubs escalated tremendously in the 1970s but stabilized in more recent years. For many years, golf book prices remained static, but they rose dramatically in the 1980s. Art prints, drawings, etchings, etc., have not seen dramatic changes in value, but pottery, china, glass, and other secondary items, especially those by Royal Doulton, have attracted premium prices.

**History:** Golf has been played in Scotland since the 15th century, and existing documents indicate golf was played in America before the Revolution. However, it was played primarily by "gentry" until the less expensive and more durable "guttie" ball was introduced in 1848. This development led to increased participation and play spread to England and other countries, especially where Scottish immigrants settled. The great popularity of golf began about 1890 in both England and the United States.

**References:** Sarah Fabian Baddiel, *World of Golf Collectables*, Wellfleet Press, 1992; Chuck Furjanic, *Antique Golf Collectibles, A Price and Reference Guide,* Krause Publications, 1997; John F. Hotchkiss, *Collectible Golf Balls*, Antique Trader Books, 1997; John M. Olman and Morton W. Olman, *Golf Antiques & Other Treasures of the Game*, expanded ed., Market Street Press, 1993; Beverly Robb, *Collectible Golfing Novelties*, Schiffer Publishing, 1992; Shirley and Jerry Sprung, *Decorative Golf Collectibles: Collector's Information, Current Prices*, Glentiques, 1991; Mark Wilson (ed.), *Golf Club Identification & Price Guide III*, Ralph Maltby Enterprises, 1993.

**Periodicals:** *Golfiana Magazine*, P.O. Box 688, Edwardsville, IL 62025; *US Golf Classics & Heritage Hickories*, 5407 Pennock Point Rd., Jupiter, FL 33458.

**Collectors' Clubs:** Golf Club Collectors Association, 640 E. Liberty St., Girard, OH 44420; Golf Collectors' Society, P.O. Box 20546, Dayton, OH 45420; Logo Golf Ball Collector's Association, 4552 Barclay Fairway, Lake Worth, Fl 33467.

**Tee, Manhattan Tee, The Reddy Tee Co., patented 1915, rubber, $65.**

**Museums:** PGA/World Golf Hall of Fame, Pinehurst, NC; Ralph Miller Memorial Library, City of Industry, CA; United States Golf Association, "Golf House," Far Hills, NJ.

Ball
   Haskell, bramble, patent 1899 ................................................ 50.00
   Lynx, rubber core ..................... 18.00
   Mitchell, Manchester, gutty ...... 60.00
   Spring Vale Hawk, bramble ..... 35.00
Book
   *Golf-A New Approach,* Lloyd Mangrum, Whittlesey House, 1949, 127 pgs, illus of golf swings ............ 10.00
   *Golf In The Sun All Year Round,* Robert H. K. Browning, 1931.......... 38.00
   *How To Play Your Best Golf All The Time,* Tommy Armor, Simon & Schuster, 1953, 151 pgs .......... 10.00
   *Understanding Golf,* John Gordon, 1926 ......................................... 40.00
Club
   Burke, juvenile, mashie, wood shaft ................................................ 30.00
   C. S. Butchart, scare-head driver, stamped shaft .......................... 48.00
   Hagen, iron-man sand wedge, wood shaft ............................................ 170.00
   McGregor, Tourney 693W driver, c1953, steel shaft................... 150.00
   Spaulding, Cash-in Putter, steel shaft............................... 65.00
   Wilson, wedge, staff model, c1959, steel shaft............................... 60.00
Golf Bag, Osmond Patent Caddy, ashwood, leather handles, straps, canvas club tube, ball pocket...... 270.00
Mug, hickory shaft, pewter ........... 45.00
Paperweight, US Open, 1980 ....... 32.00

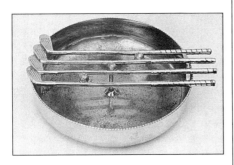

**Ashtray, Chase Chrome, four golf clubs, 5" w, 4-1/8" d, $32.**

Pin Tray, figural, lady golfer, Schafer & Vater ....................................... 235.00
Program, Bob Hope Desert Classic, 1967 ....................................... 20.00

# Gonder Pottery

**Collecting Hints:** Learn the Gonder glazes and forms. Once you do, you will have no trouble identifying the pieces. Since production occurred recently, many examples still can be found stored in basements and sold at garage sales. Anticipating higher prices, dealers have been buying Gonder pieces and saving them for future sale.

**History:** Lawton Gonder purchased the Zane Pottery of Zanesville, Ohio, in 1941. Previously, Gonder had worked for the Ohio Pottery, American Encaustic Tiling, Cherry Art Tile, and Florence Pottery. He was a consultant for Fraunfelter China and Standard Tile. Gonder renamed Zane Pottery "Gonder Ceramic Arts, Inc."

Gonder's pottery was high-priced for its time. Besides a glaze of mingled colors, the pottery made flambé, gold crackle, and reproduction Chinese crackle glazes. Many shapes followed the Rum Rill patterns from the Florence Pottery.

Almost all Gonder Pottery is marked. Some had paper labels, but the majority had one of the following impressed marks: "GONDER CERAMIC ART," "Gonder/Original" in script, "Gonder" in script, "GONDER/U.S.A.," "Gonder [script]/U.S.A.," or "GONDER" in a semicircle.

The company expanded in 1946, opening the Elgee pottery, which made lamp bases, but that plant was destroyed by fire in 1954. A brief expansion occurred at the main plant, but production ceased in 1957.

**References:** Susan and Al Bagdade, *Warman's American Pottery and Porcelain,* Wallace-Homestead, 1994; Ron Hoopes,

*Collector's Guide and History of Gonder Pottery,* L-W Books, 1992.

**Collectors' Clubs:** American Art Pottery Association, 125 E. Rose Ave., St. Louis, MO 63119; Gonder Collectors, P.O. Box 21, Crooksville, OH 43731.

Bookends, pr, 10-1/2" h, horses, yellow, brown glaze .......................... 135.00
Console Set, #561, fish, 12" l bowl, pr 5" l candleholders, rose glaze ... 115.00
Cornucopia, 7-1/4" l, blue and gray ................................................ 15.00
Ewer, 13-1/2" h, 11-1/2" w, Shell and Starfish................................... 85.00
Figure
   Asian Woman, carrying basket, light green ....................................... 12.00
   Chinese Water Bearers, man and woman, tan, copyright 1949, one suspended vessel repaired ..... 25.00
Lamp
   12" h, 10" w, Flying Ducks, chartreuse and dark green ............. 75.00
   17-1/2" h, Swan, blue............... 65.00
   30" h, Polynesian Girl, tan figure of girl, molded flowers, arms extended to strings that end in vessels, lime green finial, orig red shade.... 130.00
Panther, 12" l................................ 55.00
Pedestal Stand, 5-3/4" x 4-1/2", mirror black, mkd "Gonder USA 35," pr ................................................ 50.00
Planter, H-82, turquoise and brown ................................................ 20.00
Salt and Pepper Shakers, pr, 2-3/4" h, 1-3/4" sq, white ground, yellow speckled trim, orig stickers ............... 30.00
Vase
   6-1/2" h, H401, shell, yellow, mkd ................................................ 27.50
   7" h, red Flambe, mkd "Gonder Original 360".................................. 40.00
   8" h, H80, tan, gold and pink highlights ........................................... 24.00
   8-1/2" h, 4-1/4" w, stork, rich brown ................................................ 35.00
   8-1/2" h, 5" w, H-52, Art Deco, soft blue over pink ....................... 40.00
   8-1/2" h, 6-1/2" d, off-white, light gray and pink highlights, pink int..... 30.00
   8-3/4" h, H-68, yellow, pink, and green ......................................... 20.00
   9-1/4" h, 7-3/4" w, maroon drip glaze ................................................ 20.00
   10" h, #593, feather, brown agate ................................................ 30.00

**Candleholders, turquoise ext., pink coral int., mkd "E-14 Gonder," 4-3/4" d, $15.**

# Graniteware

**Collecting Hints:** Old graniteware is heavier than new graniteware. Pieces with cast iron handles date from 1870 to 1890; wood handles date from 1900 to 1910. Other dating clues are seams, wood knobs, and tin lids.

**History:** Graniteware is the name commonly given to enamel-coated iron or steel kitchenware.

The first graniteware was made in Germany in the 1830s. Graniteware was not produced in the United States until the 1860s. At the start of World War I, when European companies turned to manufacturing war weapons, American producers took over the market.

Gray and white were the most common graniteware colors, although each company made their own special shades of blue, green, brown, violet, cream, or red.

**References:** Helen Greguire, *Collector's Encyclopedia of Graniteware*, Book 1 (1990, 1994 value update), Book 2 (1993, 1997), Collector Books.

**Collectors' Club:** National Graniteware Society, P.O. Box 10013, Cedar Rapids, IA 52410.

Baking Pan, 9" x 13" x 2-1/2" h, white, black trim, some wear.............. 15.00
Berry Pail, cov, Stransky Steelware, gray and blue......................... 225.00
Bowl
  6-1/8" d, blue and white, medium swirl, black trim, c1960 ............ 35.00
  8" w, 3-1/4" h, red and white stripes ................................... 32.00
  8" w, 10-1/2" l, gray, oval .......... 35.00
  11-1/2" w, 5-1/2" h, cobalt blue and white, heavy use ...................... 25.00
Candleholder, white, round base
  .................................................. 65.00
Coffee Boiler, 12-1/2" h, 10" d, gray mottled, side handle, top handle with wood hand-hold, tin lid, some slight discoloration and light rust..... 135.00
Coffeepot
  11-1/4" h, 6-1/4" d, cobalt blue, gray graniteware 1 pc insert, glass lid mkd "Break-No-More Cardella Mfg. Co., Cleveland, Ohio," some dark spots ......................................... 75.00
  11-1/2" h, 10-1/2" w, white, black trim, mkd "Vollrath Co., 7 Cups, Kook King," patent date of 1934, some enamel loss........................... 125.00
  12" h, 6-1/2" d, cream and green, green depression-era glass insert, attributed to Lisk Mfg., clear insert ................................................ 100.00
Corner Strainer, 8-3/4" w, cream and green, use, some light rust ...... 15.00

Cup, cream and green, rolled rim, one ding on edge, wear to edge of handle ...................................... 45.00
Cup and Plate, 4" h x 2-1/4" cup, 9-1/4" d plate, white, black trim, wear, some dings, set of plates.....................40.00
Dipper, 14-1/4" l, 5-1/2" x 3" dipper, white, fine speckled black and blue trim, heavy use......................... 30.00
Frying Pan, 7-1/4" w, blue and white speckled, some wear and rust ................................................ 45.00
Funnel
  4" w, 4" l, white, cobalt blue trim, wear, scuff marks on handle and tip of spout.................................. 25.00
  6-1/2" w, 6" l, gray, handle........ 28.00
  7-3/4" w, 9" l, gray mottled, some wear ................................................ 85.00
Grill Plate, 11-1/4" d, green and white, large swirl, black trim, c1960... 42.50
Hospital Tray, 10" l, 4-1/2" w, kidney shaped, white, cobalt blue trim ................................................ 12.00
Ladle, 14" l, white, heavy wear, dings, rust........................................... 10.00
Lid, some wear
  8-1/2" d, blue and white swirl, wood knob.......................................... 10.00
  9-1/2" d, brown and white swirl ................................................ 28.00
  10" d, mottled gray................... 15.00
Mending Kit, Mendets, directions on back, 2 missing........................... 9.50
Mixing Bowl
  10" d, 4" h, blue and white speckle, darker blue rim trim, some wear, few dings ..................................... 45.00
  11" d, 5-1/4" h, green, black trim, dull int., some wear................... 30.00
  12-1/4" d, 5-1/4" h, green, black trim, flat rim, some wear.................. 35.00
Mold, 9" d, 3" d, gray, some wear and chipping.................................. 35.00
Mug, 4" d, 2-1/4" h, white, black trim, some wear .............................. 12.50
Onion Bin ................................... 125.00
Oven Thermometer, 3" h, 2-1/2" w, Cooper Cookbook Thermometer, green base, chrome over glass thermometer, graphics of cookbook, dishes with suggested temperatures, thermometer cracked, some rust...............50.00
Pan
  6" w, 3" h, cobalt blue and white, some wear .............................. 30.00
  8" w, 4" d, cobalt blue and white, light rust .................................. 35.00
Pan Lid Rack, 7-1/4" w tapers to 2-1/4" w, 24" l, red shades to mustard yellow, 3 hooks....................... 300.00
Pie Plate
  9-1/4" d, 1" h, blue swirls.......... 40.00
  9-3/4" d, gray mottled, some wear ................................................ 9.00
  10" d, cream and green, some wear ................................................ 10.00
Plate
  9" d, cream and green, flat rim, some wear ...................................... 35.00
  9" d, gray and white ................. 20.00
  10-1/4" d, orange and white, large swirl, black trim, c1960 ........... 35.00

**Pie Plate, gray mottled, 9-3/4" d, some wear, $9.**

Platter, 14" l, medium blue and white swirl....................................... 195.00
Pot, cov
  5-1/2" h, 10" d, black and white speckled base and lid, some wear ................................................ 35.00
  6-1/2" h, 7-3/4" d, white, black trim, matching lid, some wear ......... 27.50
  6-1/2" h, 11" d, solid black base, bright red lid, int. dull from use ................................................ 48.00
  7-1/2" h, 11" d, white, black trim, some use marks, bottom darkened from use................................... 35.00
Roaster, cov
  12-3/4" l, 8" w, 4-1/4" h, cream and green, white int., vents along edge of lid, indented handle, some wear ................................................ 65.00
  17" l, 13" w, 7-1/2" h, gray mottled, metal rack, indented handle, some wear....................................... 35.00
  17-1/2" l, 11-1/2" w, 8" h, oval, solid cobalt blue, emb "Savory," some wear....................................... 60.00
  18-1/2" l, 12" w, 9-1/2" h, black base, white lid, some wear................ 75.00
  19" l, 13" w, 8-1/2" h, cream and green, heavy wear ................... 35.00
Sauce Pan, 3-1/2" h, 8-1/4" d, gray mottled........................................... 20.00
Soup Plate, 10-1/2" d, dark blue, black trim, some wear, rust, set of 3.....35.00
Stew Pot
  7-1/2" d, 9-1/2" h, light blue speckled, closed rolled handles, some wear....................................... 35.00
  8" d, 4" h, white, black trim and lid, dull from use, wear.................. 35.00
Strainer
  Blue and white, double handles ................................................ 50.00
  Blue and white, single handle, c1940.................................... 30.00
  Cobalt blue and white speckled, 10-1/4" d, some wear.............. 35.00
  Dark brown and white spatter, 11" d, 3" h, few chips ......................... 85.00
Teapot
  5" h, 9-1/2" w, yellow, red, orange, blue, and green swirls, black handle, spout, and rim, several chips ................................................ 525.00

10" h, solid blue, chrome lid with clear glass insert knob, slight wear and rust ................................... 150.00
Tea Steeper, 4-1/4" h, 4-1/4" d, mottled gray, wear .............................. 145.00
Tray, 14-1/2" l, mottled gray, some wear ................................................ 35.00
Urinal, 10-1/2" l, white, black trim, some wear and rust ......................... 25.00
Utensil Holder, wall, large, small dippers, skimmer, side dipper, 14-1/2" x 19", deep blue/green ............. 250.00
Utility Pan, 9" l, 2-3/4" h, cream, black trim, some wear........................ 12.00
Wall Pan, 10" w, white, blue trim, spout, mkd "Made in Germany" ......... 35.00
Wash Pan

8" d, 2-1/2" h, gray, some wear ................................................ 15.00

12" d, 3-1/2" h, gray mottled, flat rim with hole for hanging, dull int., some rust ......................................... 18.00

# Griswold

**Collecting Hints**: Griswold offers varied challenges to all collectors, and made thousands of different products: cast aluminum, chrome plated, nickel plated, and porcelain items in addition to cast iron. Griswold items range from a few dollars to several thousand dollars. Griswold also made advertising items, products for companies such as Sears, as well as items only marked with their pattern number. There are still many items made by Griswold that are unknown to the collector community. Condition is very important. Items that are pitted, cracked, warped, rusted or chipped have very little value to collectors.

**History:** The predecessor company of The Griswold Manufacturing Company, The Selden and Griswold Manufacturing Company, was started as a family enterprise in 1865. In 1884, the Griswolds bought the Seldons' portion of the business and changed the name to The Griswold Manufacturing Company. The business remained in operation in Erie, PA until it was sold to Wagner in 1957. Items with the Griswold and Wagner markings or those with the Griswold logo without Erie, PA were made after 1957 and are not very collectible.

**References**: Jon B. Haussler, *Griswold Muffin Pans,* Schiffer Publishing, 1997; David G. Smith and Chuck Wafford, *The Book of Griswold & Wagner,* Schiffer Publishing, 1995.

**Periodical**: Kettles 'n Cookware, P.O. Box 247, Perrysburg, NY 14129.

**Collectors' Club**: Griswold & Cast Iron Cookware Association, (G & CICA), 3007 Plum St., Erie, PA 16508.

**Advisor:** Jon B. Haussler, 1806 Brownstone Ave., SW, Decatur, AL 35603.

**Reproduction Alert**: There are reproductions of a few Griswold items. For the most part, the reproductions have a grainy finish and the lettering is uneven and not a sharp as the genuine items. Reproductions do not present a significant problem for the advanced collector. However, new collectors and general line antique dealers are often fooled. The No. 262 small corn stick pan, the No. 0 skillet, and the Santa Claus mold are the most commonly encountered reproduced items. The real Griswold Santa has a tongue and the reproductions do not. There are some fake Griswold items such as a toy Heart and Star waffle iron (Griswold never made one).

**Note:** Prices are for items that are in excellent as made condition with NO damage.

**Abbreviations:** EPU is Erie, Pa. USA; HR is Heat Ring;

### Skillet
No. 0 Block Logo .......................... 85.00
No. 2 Slant Logo ......................... 500.00
No. 2 Block Logo Smooth Bottom ................................................ 350.00
No. 2 Block Logo HR ............... 1,000.00
No. 3 Small Logo .......................... 10.00
No. 4 Block HR ........................... 450.00
No. 4 Block Smooth Bottom.......... 50.00
No. 5 Block HR ........................... 450.00
No. 5 Block Smooth Bottom.......... 30.00
No. 5 Victor ................................ 500.00
No. 6 Block HR ............................ 60.00
No. 6 Victor ................................ 150.00
No. 7 Block Smooth Bottom.......... 25.00
No. 7 Victor, fully marked............. 40.00

**No. 50, hearts/star pan, $2,000.**

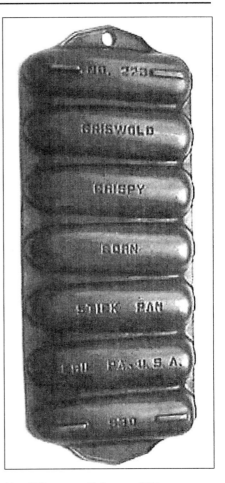

**No. 273, corn stick pan, $25.**

No. 8 Block Smooth Bottom ......... 25.00
No. 8 Erie Outside HR .................. 30.00
No. 8 Erie Spider ..................... 2,000.00
No. 8 Small Logo ........................ 15.00
No. 8 Victor ............................... 30.00
No. 9 Small Logo ........................ 20.00
No. 10 Block Logo HR .................. 60.00
No. 11 Block Logo HR ................ 150.00
No. 12 Block Logo HR .................. 75.00
No. 12 Erie Outside HR .............. 170.00
No. 12 Small Logo HR .................. 50.00
No. 13 Block Logo HR ............. 1,200.00
No. 13 Slant Logo EPU ............ 1,000.00
No. 14 Block Logo HR ................ 175.00
No. 15 Oval Fish Skillet.............. 250.00
No. 20 Block Logo EPU ............. 700.00
Colonial Breakfast Skillet ............. 45.00
5 in 1 Breakfast Skillet ............... 175.00
Square Egg Skillet ....................... 45.00
Square Skillet w/Glass Lid ........... 90.00

### Muffin Pan
No. 1 Gem Pan Slant Logo ......... 250.00
No 2 Gem Pan w/Pattern Number (941) ...................................... 400.00
No. 3 Gem Pan Slant Logo EPU ................................................ 600.00
No. 9 Brownie Cake Pan............. 150.00
No. 10 Popover Pan .................... 35.00
No. 11 French Roll Pan................ 40.00
No. 12 Gem Pan Slant Logo ....... 500.00

No. 17 French Roll ...................... 125.00
No. 18 Popover Pan, fully marked
.................................................. 60.00
No. 19 Golfball Pan..................... 450.00
No. 20 Turk Head, mkd "Griswold"
.................................................. 550.00
No. 21 Bread Stick Pan............... 125.00
No. 22 Bread Stick Pan................. 35.00
No. 23 Bread Stick Pan.............. 100.00
No. 27 Wheat Stick Pan ............. 225.00
No. 28 Wheat Stick Pan ............. 225.00
No. 32 Danish Cake Pan............... 35.00
No. 34 Plett Pan, Slant Logo........ 60.00
No. 34 Plett Pan, Small Logo ........ 15.00
No. 50 Hearts/Star Pan ........... 2,000.00
No. 100 Hearts/Star Pan ............. 900.00
No. 140 Turk Head Pan............... 125.00
No. 262 Corn Stick Pan ................ 60.00
No. 272 Corn or Wheat Stick Pan
.................................................. 125.00
No. 273 Corn Stick Pan ................ 25.00
No. 283 Corn Stick Pan ............. 100.00

**Other**

Ashtray with Matchholder
    Round ..................................... 25.00
    Square .................................... 35.00
Double Broiler............................. 250.00
Fluter, Fixed Handle, Erie........... 500.00
Griddle, Block Logo, handled
    No. 6 ................................... 100.00
    No. 7 ..................................... 40.00
    No. 8 ..................................... 30.00
    No. 9 ..................................... 30.00
    No. 10 ................................... 40.00
Ice Shave
    No. 1 ................................... 100.00
    No. 2 ................................... 150.00
Mold
    Lamb.................................... 100.00
    Rabbit .................................. 200.00
    Santa.................................... 600.00
Patty Mold Set, with box
    No. 1 ..................................... 35.00
    No. 2 ..................................... 45.00

Pup, marked "Griswold Pup 30"
.................................................. 275.00
Roaster and Trivet, oval, fully marked
    No. 3 ................................... 600.00
    No. 7 ................................... 500.00
Skillet Lid, Raised Letter
    No. 8 ..................................... 40.00
    No. 10 ................................. 125.00
    No. 12 ................................. 250.00
Tite-Top Dutch Oven with Trivet
    No. 6 ................................... 400.00
    No. 7 ................................... 125.00
    No. 8 ..................................... 80.00
    No. 9 ..................................... 95.00
    No. 10 ................................. 150.00
Tobacco Cutter, Star, No. 3........... 95.00
Waffle Iron, American, low base
    No. 6 ................................... 400.00
    No. 7 ..................................... 90.00
    No. 8 ..................................... 40.00
    No. 9 ..................................... 75.00
Waffle Iron, Hearts/Star,
    No. 18 ................................. 150.00
Wax Ladle, Erie.......................... 150.00

# H

## Haeger Potteries

**Collecting Hints:** One of the interesting facets of this company's past is that it successfully built and operated a working pottery facility at the Chicago World's Fair in 1933 and 1934. Several different marks were used through the long history of this popular china.

**History:** Haeger Pottery has an interesting history. Starting as a brick yard in Dundee, IL, in 1871, David H. Haeger formed a company which would develop into an art pottery and commercial pottery. After David was succeeded by son Edmund H. Haeger in 1900, he began to produce an art pottery line in 1914. Because of their high quality luster glazes and soft pastels, the dinnerware line was a success.

A line named "Royal Haeger" was introduced in 1938, with the Royal Haeger Lamp Company forming in 1939. This expansion was enhanced by the purchase of a pottery building in Macomb, IL, where it soon began to make it's florist trade art pottery line.

Today members of the Haeger family are still involved in the pottery.

**Reference:** Joe Paradis and Joyce Paradis, The House of Haeger 1914-1944: The Revitalization of American Art Pottery, Schiffer, 1999.

**Collectors' Club:** Haeger Pottery Collectors of America, 5021 Toyon Way, Antioch, CA 94509.

Ashtray
  #2043, slight bottom chip ........ 10.00
  #2094 ............................. 25.00
Bookends, pr, rams, 9" h............... 30.00
Candleholders, pr
  Agate, pink mauve, light blue swirled feathers, 4-1/2" h ....................... 45.00
  Cornucopia ............................ 45.00
Candy Dish, cov, textured white, sgd "Royal Haeger" ........................ 12.00
Cigarette Holder and Ashtray, textured white, sgd "Royal Haeger," 10" x 6-1/4" ................................. 10.00
Compote, 11", #3130 .................... 60.00
Ewer, 15" ............................. 75.00
Figure
  Bird of Paradise ...................... 65.00
  Bull, gold weave glaze........... 200.00
  Cat, seated, 6" h..................... 24.00
  Polar Bear ............................ 55.00
  Pouter Pigeon, 7" h................... 24.00
  Rooster, 20" h ....................... 175.00
  Seal ................................. 35.00

Squirrel..................................... 35.00
Flower Frog
  Bird in flight, #R-125 ................ 70.00
  Deer, standing, #R-104 ............ 20.00
  Nude bather, #77, mkd "Royal Haeger," c1927, 5" d, 7" h ............ 165.00
Flower Pot, 4-1/4" h, 5-1/2" d ........ 20.00
Hanging Basket, owl, matte white, mkd "Royal Haeger Owl, #5015" ..... 55.00
Lamp, table
  Cabbage Rose, pink and white 35.00
  Mermaid, multicolored ............. 60.00
Pitcher
  9" h, brown, Earthgraphic, match head, ding on base.................. 50.00
  10" h, rig paper label, stamp mark, 10" h ................................ 85.00
Planter
  Bull, gold weave, glazed ....... 275.00
  Cat, #507, 8-1/2" ................... 45.00
  Donkey Cart, #R-754 .............. 15.00
  Duck, stone lace, glazed ........ 30.00
  Pot House, 5-1/2", wear ............ 6.00
  Square, 5" w, 5" h, blue, antiqued gold trim, water marks, pr........ 30.00
Serving Dish, Gold Tweed, 16" ..... 32.00
Swan, raised wings, light gray and brown, 9" l, mkd "Royal Haeger" 45.00
Tea Set, acorn finials................... 100.00
Vase
  7-1/2" h, Colonial girl, pink ....... 30.00
  8-1/2" x 12", fan shaped, silver overlay, turquoise ground, some crazing ........................................ 400.00
  10" h, agate, pink mauve, light blue swirled feathers....................... 95.00
  11" h, Delft style, cylindrical..... 36.00
  11-3/4" h, 7" w, creamy green, blue stamp "Haeger, U.S.A.," and worn silver stamp............................. 25.00
  12" h, brown wrap, #4182 ...... 100.00
  12" h, Earthgraphic, marigold 100.00

## Hall China

**Collecting Hints:** Hall China Company identified many of its patterns by name, but some of these are being gradually changed by dealers. A good example is the Silhouette pattern, which is also known as Taverne. Many shapes are also referred to by more than one name, i.e., Radiance is also known as Sunshine, Terrace as Stepdown, and Pert as Sani-Grid.

Because of their high quality, most Hall China pieces are still in wonderful condition. There is no reason to pay full price for imperfect pieces.

**History:** Hall China Company was formed as a result of the dissolution of the East Liverpool Potteries Company. Robert Hall, a partner in the merger, died within months of establishing the new company. Robert T. Hall, his son, took over.

At first the company produced the same semi-porcelain dinnerware and toiletware that was being made at the other potteries in East Liverpool, Ohio. Robert T. Hall began experiments to duplicate an ancient Chinese one-fire process that would produce a non-crazing vitrified china, with body and glaze fired at the same time. He succeeded in 1911 and Hall products have been made that way ever since.

Hall's basic products—hotel and restaurant institutional ware—are sold to the trade only. However, the firm also has produced many retail and premium lines, e.g. Autumn Leaf for Jewel Tea and Blue Bouquet for the Standard Coffee Co. of New Orleans. A popular line is the gold-decorated teapots that were introduced for retail sale in 1920. In 1931, kitchenware was introduced, soon followed by dinnerware. These lines were made in both solid colors and with decals for retail and premium sales.

Hall is still producing china at its plant in East Liverpool, Ohio.

**References:** Susan and Al Bagdade, Warman's American Pottery and Porcelain, Wallace-Homestead, 1994; Harvey Duke, Hall: Price Guide Update, ELO Books, 1992; C. L. Miller, Jewel Tea Grocery Products with Values, Schiffer Publishing, 1996; —, Jewel Tea: Sales and Housewares Collectibles, Schiffer Publishing, 1995; Jim and Lynn Salko, Halls Autumn Leaf China and Jewel Tea Collectibles, published by authors (143 Topeg Dr., Severna Park, MD 21146), 1996; Margaret and Kenn Whitmyer, Collector's Encyclopedia of Hall China, 2nd ed., Collector Books, 1994, 1997 value update.

**Periodical:** Hall China Encore, 317 N. Pleasant St., Oberlin, OH 44074.

**Collectors' Clubs:** Autumn Leaf Reissues Association, 19238 Dorchester Cr, Strongsville, OH 44136; Hall Collector's Club, P.O. Box 360488, Cleveland, OH 44136; National Autumn Leaf Collectors Club, 7346 Shamrock Dr., Indianapolis, IN 46217.

**Notes:** For several years, Hall has been reissuing many of its products as part of its new solid-color Americana retail line. If you are a new collector and are unsure if an item is new or old, you may want to buy only the items with decals or gold decorations, as these pieces have not been reissued and there is, apparently, no intention of doing so. Prices have dropped slightly on some of the original solid-colored items because of the reissues.

### Dinnerware Patterns

#### Autumn Leaf

| | |
|---|---|
| Baking Dish, individual | 65.00 |
| Bean Pot, two handles | 180.00 |
| Berry Bowl, 5-1/2" d | 5.00 |
| Butter Dish, cov, 1 lb | 255.00 |
| Coffeepot, cov, rayed, 8 cup, gold double circle mark "Tested and approved by Mary Dunbar, Jewell Homemaker's Institute" | 60.00 |
| Cookie Jar, cov | 175.00 |
| Creamer and Sugar, cov, ruffled-D | 35.00 |
| Cream Soup | 35.00 |
| Cup and Saucer, St Denis | 50.00 |
| Custard Cup | 24.50 |
| Dinner Plate, 9" d | 6.50 |
| French Baker, 4-1/2" l | 70.00 |
| Gravy Boat | 20.00 |
| Hot Pad, tin back, 7-1/4" | 35.00 |
| Jug, ball | 60.00 |

Mixing Bowl
| | |
|---|---|
| 7-1/2" x 4" | 35.00 |
| 8-3/4" x 4-1/2" | 45.00 |
| Platter, 9" x 5-1/2" | 25.00 |
| Range Salt and Pepper Shakers, pr | 35.00 |
| Salt and Pepper Shakers, pr | 15.00 |
| Serving Tray, metal | 55.00 |
| Stack Set | 75.00 |
| Teapot, cov, marked "Jewel" | 90.00 |

Tumbler, glass, frosted
| | |
|---|---|
| 3-3/4" h | 40.00 |
| 5-1/2" h | 22.00 |
| Vase | 200.00 |
| Vegetable Bowl, oval, divided | 175.00 |

#### Crocus

Bowl, Radiance
| | |
|---|---|
| 6-1/8" d, 3" h | 45.00 |
| 7" d | 30.00 |
| 9" d | 45.00 |
| Bread and Butter Plate, 7-1/4" d | 10.00 |

**Autumn Leaf, plate, 9-1/4" d, $12.**

| | |
|---|---|
| Butter Dish, cov, 1 lb | 550.00 |
| Cake Plate | 25.00 |
| Casserole, cov | 60.00 |
| Cereal Bowl, 6" d | 15.00 |
| Coffeepot, Terrace | 100.00 |
| Dinner Plate | 36.00 |
| Gravy Boat | 32.00 |
| Jug, ball | 195.00 |
| Luncheon Plate, 9" d | 15.00 |
| Salad Plate, 8-1/4" d | 12.00 |
| Platter, 13-1/4" l | 35.00 |
| Salt and Pepper Shakers, pr, teardrop shape | 45.00 |
| Soup Tureen | 395.00 |
| Teapot, banded | 175.00 |
| Tidbit, 3 tier | 50.00 |
| **Golden Glo,** casserole, 3 qt | 30.00 |

#### Orange Poppy

| | |
|---|---|
| Bean Pot | 105.00 |
| Cake Plate | 18.00 |
| Casserole, 8" l, oval | 65.00 |
| Coffee Canister | 325.00 |
| Coffeepot | 80.00 |
| Custard | 6.00 |
| Hot Plate, 9-1/2" d | 36.00 |
| Platter, 13" l | 18.00 |
| Salad Bowl | 12.00 |
| Salt and Pepper Shakers, pr, handled | 35.00 |
| Sugar, Great American mark | 30.00 |
| Teapot, Boston | 350.00 |
| Vegetable Bowl, round | 25.00 |

#### Red Dot (a.k.a. Eggshell Polka Dot)

| | |
|---|---|
| Baker, 13-1/2" l, fish-shape | 45.00 |
| Bean Pot, small, #1 | 95.00 |
| Bowl, 8-1/2" d | 25.00 |
| Casserole, cov, oval or round | 40.00 |
| Coquette, 4" d, handle | 25.00 |
| Drip Jar, tab handle, #1188 | 45.00 |
| Jug, cov, #2 or #4 | 125.00 |
| Mustard, cov, slotted lid | 95.00 |
| Onion Soup, cov | 45.00 |
| Pitcher, Baron | 95.00 |
| Range Shakers, salt, pepper, flour, sugar | 150.00 |
| Shirred Egg Dish, 6-1/2" d | 25.00 |
| Tom and Jerry Punch Bowl Set, bowl and 12 mugs | 250.00 |

#### Red Poppy

| | |
|---|---|
| Bowl | 10.00 |
| Cereal Bowl, 6" d | 18.50 |
| Coffeepot, Daniel, metal dropper | 40.00 |
| Cup and Saucer | 15.00 |
| Custard Cup, Radiance | 17.50 |
| Dinner Plate, 10" d | 17.50 |
| Drip Jar | 30.00 |
| Salt and Pepper Shakers, pr, egg shape | 45.00 |
| Soup Plate, flat | 20.00 |
| Stack Set | 75.00 |

#### Taverne

Bowl, Medallion
| | |
|---|---|
| 6" d | 20.00 |
| 7" d | 25.00 |
| Casserole, medallion | 75.00 |
| Coffeepot, 5-band | 125.00 |
| Coffee Server, medallion | 150.00 |
| Drip Jar, cov | 40.00 |
| French Baker, 8" d | 30.00 |
| Iced Tea Glass | 50.00 |
| Jug, #3 | 45.00 |

**Magazine Tear Sheet, Crockery and Glass Journal, November 1932, black and white, $5.**

Leftover, cov
| | |
|---|---|
| 4" x 8" | 70.00 |
| 8" x 8" | 85.00 |
| Pretzel Jar, cov | 165.00 |
| Salad Bowl, 9" d | 25.00 |
| Salt and Pepper Shakers, pr, 5-band | 75.00 |
| Saucer | 10.00 |

Teapot
| | |
|---|---|
| Medallion | 125.00 |
| Streamline, no lid | 100.00 |

### Kitchenware Patterns

#### Blue Garden/Blue Blossom

| | |
|---|---|
| Batter Jar | 250.00 |
| Butter, cov, Radiance | 475.00 |
| Casserole, #4, Sundial | 75.00 |
| Cookie Jar, cov | 375.00 |
| Jug, loop handle | 245.00 |
| Left Over, loop handle | 195.00 |
| Mixing Bowl, 6" d | 85.00 |
| Range Shakers, handle | 90.00 |
| Refrigerator Bowl, cov, loop handle | 155.00 |
| Syrup Pitcher, banded | 395.00 |

#### Chinese Red

| | |
|---|---|
| Ashtray, triangular | 30.00 |
| Batter Bowl, Five Band | 75.00 |
| Bean Pot, #5 | 155.00 |
| Casserole, tab handle | 28.00 |
| Creamer and Sugar, cov, Morning | 95.00 |
| Drip Jar, open, #1188 | 35.00 |
| Jug, ball, #3 | 45.00 |
| Leftover, Zephyr | 165.00 |
| Pretzel Jar, cov | 125.00 |
| Ramekin | 50.00 |
| Water Bottle, Zephyr | 90.00 |

### Refrigerator Ware and Commercial Ware

| | |
|---|---|
| Barnaby's Beer, mug | 15.00 |
| Dealer Sign, cobalt blue | 35.00 |

General Electric Adonis, water server
    Blue and yellow..........................55.00
    Gray and yellow .........................55.00
Hotpoint, leftover, rect....................60.00
Jolly Green Giant, mug .................15.00
Lipton Tea, creamer....................135.00
Phoenix, water server, delphinium 45.00
Westinghouse
    Bowl, blue .................................45.00
    Butter Dish, cov, yellow, Hercules
    .................................................30.00
    Left Over
        Delphite..............................16.00
        Yellow, Hercules .................30.00
    Water Server, green, General...95.00

**Rose White**

Bean Pot, cov..............................115.00
Bowl ...............................................10.00
Casserole, cov, tab handles .........27.50
Jug, 7-1/2" h, Perk.........................40.00
Pitcher, small.................................30.00
Salt and Pepper Shakers, pr.........35.00

**Wild Poppy (a.k.a. Poppy and Wheat)**

Bean Pot ......................................225.00
Casserole, cov, Sundial, #1 ........125.00
Cookie Jar, cov, Five Band .........300.00
Custard, Radiance.........................20.00
Salt and Pepper Shakers, pr, handles
    ...............................................100.00
Shirred Egg Dish
    5-1/4" d....................................40.00
    6" d ..........................................40.00
Stack Set, Radiance ...................175.00
Sugar, handle.................................75.00
Teapot, cov, 6 cup, Manhattan ...400.00
Tea Tile, 6" sq...............................85.00

**Teapots**

Airflow, orange, 6 cup ................100.00
Aladdin, yellow, gold trim, infusor. 45.00
Albany, brown, gold trim...............70.00
Baltimore, yellow...........................50.00
Basket, canary yellow, gold trim. 110.00
Cube, 1 cup, turquoise...............125.00
Doughnut, cobalt blue ................165.00
Flareware .......................................60.00
Globe
    Canary Yellow .........................80.00
    Cobalt Blue, gold trim ............225.00
    Emerald Green, gold trim.........95.00
    Light Green, gold trim ..............80.00
Manhattan, blue .............................65.00
McCormick, turquoise, 2 cup, emb
    ...............................................110.00
Newport, pink, floral decal, 5 cup 50.00
Philadelphia, green, gold trim, c1920
    .................................................75.00
Royal, ivory .................................150.00
Sundial, yellow, safety handle.......75.00
Teamster, double spout, yellow and
    gold........................................110.00
Twin Spout, emerald green...........80.00
Windshield, gold dot dec, gold label
    .................................................65.00

# Harker Pottery

**Collecting Hints:** In 1965, Harker China had the capacity to annually produce 25 million pieces of dinnerware. Hence, there is a great deal of Harker material available at garage sales and flea markets.

Shapes and forms changed through the decades of production. Many patterns were kept in production for decades, and the same pattern was often made using different colors for the background. Patterns designed to have mass appeals include those like Colonial Lady, which was popular at "dish nites" at the movies or other businesses.

Between 1935 and 1955, Columbia Chinaware, which was organized to market Harker products in small towns across the country, promoted enamel ware, glass, and aluminum products. One of Columbia Chinaware's patterns was Autumn Leaf, which is eagerly sought by collectors.

The Harker Company used a large variety of backstamps and names. Hotoven cookware featured a scroll, draped over pots, with a kiln design at top. Columbia Chinaware had a circular stamp showing the Statue of Liberty.

Collectors should consider buying Harker patterns by famous designers. Among these are Russel Wright's White Clover and George Bauer's Cameoware. Or an interesting collection could focus on one object, e.g., a sugar or creamer, collected in a variety of patterns from different historical periods. Watch for unusual pieces. The Countryside pattern features a rolling pin, scoop, and cake server.

**History:** The Harker Company began in 1840 when Benjamin Harker, an English slater turned farmer in East Liverpool, Ohio, built a kiln and began making yellowware products from clay deposits on his land. The business was managed by members of the Harker family until the Civil War, at which time David Boyce, a brother-in-law, took over the operation. Although a Harker resumed management after the war, members of the Boyce family also assumed key roles within the firm; David G. Boyce, a grandson of David, served as president.

In 1879, the first whiteware products were introduced. The company was able to overcome severe financial problems which were caused by a disastrous flood in 1884. In 1931, the company moved to Chester, West Virginia, to escape repeated flooding. In 1945, Harker introduced Cameoware made by the engobe process in which a layered effect was achieved by placing a copper mask over the bisque and then sand blasting to leave the design imprint. The white rose pattern on blue ground was marketed as White Rose Carv Kraft in Montgomery Ward stores.

In the 1960s, Harker made a Rockingham ware line which included the hound-handled pitcher and mugs. The Jeannette Glass Company purchased the Harker Company and the plant was closed in March 1972. Ohio Stoneware, Inc., utilized the plant building until it was destroyed by fire in 1975.

**References:** Susan and Al Bagdade, *Warman's American Pottery and Porcelain*, Wallace-Homestead, 1994; Neva W. Colbert, *Collector's Guide to Harker Pottery, U.S.A.*, Collector Books, 1993; Jo Cunningham, *Collector's Encyclopedia of American Dinnerware*, Collector Books, 1982, 1995 value update.

**Additional Listings:** Russel Wright.

**Cameo**

Bowl, 8" d, Zephyr, blue...............15.00
Casserole, cov, square, blue........50.00
Cheese Box, cov, Zephyr, blue ....42.00
Creamer, Gem, blue ....................35.00
Cup and Saucer, Shell Ware, blue .. 15.00
Dish, lug handle, Shell Ware, blue 10.00
Pie Baker, Dainty Flower, blue, 10" d
    .................................................75.00
Plate
    7-1/2" d, Shell Ware, blue ........10.00
    9-3/4" d, Virginia, pink..............12.00
Platter, Shell Ware, blue................20.00
Range Shaker, Dainty Flower, blue.. 20.00
Rolling Pin, blue............................85.00
Salad Bowl, 6-1/2" w, square, blue .. 15.00
Sugar, Virginia, blue ....................20.00

**Petit Point Rose**

Batter Bowl ...................................60.00
Bowl, 8-1/2" d ...............................15.00

**Berry Dish, gray border, floral centers $3.**

Cake Plate.................................20.00
Cake Server ...............................15.00
Casserole, cov, 8-1/2" d...............15.00
Coffeepot...................................42.00
Cup and Saucer...........................18.00
Dinner Plate, 8-1/2" d..................12.00
Pie Baker,..................................15.00
Spoon........................................20.00
Sugar, cov.................................15.00

**Red Apple**
Cheese Plate, 10" d .....................22.00
Custard........................................7.50
Dinner Plate, 10" d......................12.00
Fork...........................................25.00
Mixing Bowl, 9" d........................30.00
Pie Baker, 9" d............................27.50
Rolling Pin, #2...........................150.00
Salad Bowl, 9" d, swirl................24.00
Spoon........................................25.00
Utility Tray, 11" l.........................22.00
Vegetable Bowl, 9" d...................30.00

# Hockey Collectibles

**Collecting Hints:** Hockey collectibles lend themselves to two types of collecting—by team or by item. Collectors should buy what appeals to them, as this is a relatively new collecting area and secondary market prices are not yet well established. Hockey collectibles are generally quite regional, with more collectibles found in colder climates, like Canada, where junior leagues abound. As college teams and players become more recognized, expect to find more related collectibles appearing in the marketplace.

**History:** The sport of ice hockey dates back to 1855, when the first game was played in Kingston, Ontario, behind the barracks of the Royal Canadian Rifles. By 1885, a formal league of four teams in Kingston was formed, including a college team from McGill University. The sport was introduced to the United States in the early 1890s. The National Hockey League was organized in 1917 in Montreal and consisted of Canadian and US teams. It wasn't until 1927 that hockey became an Olympic sport, with the more experienced Canadian teams winning the first four Olympics.

The prestigious Stanley Cup was created in 1893, when the Governor General of Canada, Frederick Arthur, Lord Stanley of Preston, offered a cup valued at less than $50. This cup remained a Canadian treasure until the early 1900s, when the rules changed and it became the prize for professional world teams.

The increasing popularity of pro-hockey is causing a new collecting area for fans and non-fans alike.

Another area of hockey collecting are trading cards. Parkhurst issued sets from 1951 to 1964, except for the 1956-57 season, including Canadian teams. Topps entered the scene in 1954 with a series, based on the American teams. A company by the name of O-Pee-Chee was a producer of hockey cards in the 1930s and re-entered the marketplace with a series starting in 1968. By the 1990s, Bowman, O-Pee-Chee, Pro Set, Score, and Upper Deck were issuing sets, many with special cards.

**Periodical:** *Sports Collectors Digest,* 700 E. State St., Iola, WI 54990; *Sports Cards Magazine & Price Guide,* 700 E. State St., Iola, WI 54990.

Game, Phil & Tony Esposito's Action
    Hockey, Parker Bros., 1973 ..... 80.00
Hockey Puck, autographed
Ed Belfour, Chicago......................12.00
Shawn Burr ...................................3.00
Kris Draper .................................12.60
Grant Fuhr, St. Louis ...................15.00
Bill Gadsby .................................10.00
Tomas Holstrom ...........................10.00
Gordie Howe................................40.00
Jaromir Jagr ................................18.00
Larry Jeffrey .................................5.00
Mike Keenan, 1994 Stanley Cup cham-
    pions, NY Rangers..................35.00
Craig Mactavish, 1994 Stanley Cup
    champions, NY Rangers..........30.00
Rocket Richard ............................30.00
Bryan Watson ...............................5.00
Jersey, used
    Belfour, Dallas.......................115.00
    Clifford, #14, Michigan State.. 150.00
    Draper, #35, Sabres, 1992-93 ..225.00
    Guay, #29, Canucks, 1990s... 160.00
    Gusanov, #5, Nordiques, 1990s
    ...............................................225.00
    Jagr, Starter ..........................165.00
    Shields, #4, Univ. of Denver, 1980s
    ...............................................150.00
    Stumpef, #16, Bruins, 1996-97
    ...............................................400.00
    Vergeen, CCM ......................115.00
Photograph, 8" x 10", autographed
    Bobby Baun ..............................5.00
    Jean Beilveau ..........................12.00
    John Bucyk ...............................8.00
    Alex DelVecchio.........................7.00
    Reggie Flemming......................8.00
    Bill Gadsby .............................10.00
    Kevin Hodson ...........................5.00
    Sheldon Kennedy .....................8.00
    Igor Lanionov ..........................12.00
    Lanny McDonald......................12.00
    Bob Rouse ................................8.00
    Henri Richard ..........................10.00
    Maurice Richard ......................25.00
    Norm Ulman ..............................7.00
    Gary Unger ...............................6.00
    Lefty Wilson, as coach...............5.00

Benny Wolf.................................. 6.00
Trading Card
    Classic Image, 1995/96........... 35.00
    Finest 1, 1998/99 .................... 95.00
    Leaf II, 1993/94......................... 2.00
    OPC, 1989/90 .......................... 24.00
    OPC Premier, 1994/95 ............. 24.00
    Parkhurst, 1994/95................... 25.00
    Score, American foil, 1990/91.... 7.00
    Stadium Card, 1991/92............. 12.00
    Topps, Super Skills, 1995/96 ... 20.00
    Ultra II, 1992/93....................... 25.00
    Ultra II Jumbo, 1994/95 ........... 30.00
    Upper Deck, Set I, 1993/94 ..... 14.00

# Holiday Collectibles

**Collecting Hints:** Collectors often start with one holiday and eventually branch out and collect all the holidays. Reasonably priced items can still be found—especially items from the 1950s and 1960s.

**History:** Holidays are an important part of American life. Many have both secular and religious overtones such as Christmas, St. Patrick's Day, Easter, Valentine's Day, and Halloween. National holidays such as the Fourth of July and Thanksgiving are part of one's yearly planning. Collectors usually consider President's Day, Memorial Day, Flag Day, and the Fourth of July as part of the general category of patriotic collectibles.

Each holiday has its own origins and background and owes its current face to a variety of legends, lore, and customs. Holiday decorations were popularized by German cottage industries at the turn of the century. Germany dominated the holiday market until the 1920s, when Japan began producing holiday items. Both countries lost their place during World War II and U.S. manufacturers filled the American appetite for holiday decorations.

**Reference:** Lissa Bryan-Smith and Richard Smith, *Holiday Collectibles, Vintage Flea Market Treasures Price Guide,* Krause Publications, 1998.

**Periodicals:** *BooNews,* P.O. Box 143, Brookfield, IL 60513; *Pyrofax Magazine,* P.O. Box 2010, Saratoga, CA 95070; *St. Patrick Notes,* 10802, Greenscreek Drive, Suite 703, Houston, TX 77070; *Trick or Treat Trader,* P.O. Box 499, Winchester, NH 03470.

**Reproduction Alert.**

**Easter, post card, Art Nouveau woman, Germany, unused, $45.**

**Additional Listings:** Christmas Items, Flag Collectibles, Patriotic Collectibles, Santa Claus, Valentines.

**Advisors:** Lissa Bryan-Smith and Richard Smith.

### Easter

Basket, reed, carrying handle
    6" h, pink, Germany ................. 20.00
    12" h, red, green, and natural, Mexican .......................................... 15.00
Candy Container
    4" h, rabbit, yellow hard plastic, holding egg with lollipops, USA ........ 6.00
    6-1/2" l, egg, multicolored tin litho, USA ......................................... 18.00
    7" h, chicken, yellow flocked cardboard, head on spring, West Germany, 1960s .............................. 35.00
    9" h, rabbit, brown flocked papier-mâché, glass eyes ................... 80.00
Egg
    3" l, cardboard, violets dec, gold Dresden trim, Germany ............ 25.00
    4-1/2" l, milk glass, hp flowers .. 25.00
Eggcup, rabbit and chick, price for pr
    .............................................. 20.00
Figure
    1-3/4" h, yellow and orange celluloid chick, Japan ............................. 15.00
    2-1/2" h, cotton batting rabbit, cardboard ears, holding carrot, Germany
    .............................................. 15.00
    3-1/2" h mother rabbit with three 1-1/2" h baby rabbits, pot metal, painted white, German .......... 65.00
    4-1/2" h, celluloid, pastel rabbits, male holding basket of eggs, female holding chicken, VCO trademark, Viscoloid Co ............................. 95.00
    4-1/2" h, yellow cotton batting chick, glass eyes, wire feet, Germany . 30.00

6" h, yellow hard plastic mother rabbit, blue apron, pink hat ........... 10.00
Postcard
    A Happy Easter To You, hen and chicks, clutch of rose eggs in violets, Raphael Tuck ............................ 6.50
    A Peaceful Easter, girl and rabbit looking at Easter eggs, 1911 ..... 5.00
    Easter Greetings, 4 chicks looking at eggs hanging on apple tree, Germany ........................................ 5.00
Roly Poly, celluloid, egg, teal blue, mother hen and chicks, VCO trademark ....................................... 85.00
Squeak Toy, 8" h, rabbit ................. 9.00

**Halloween, celluloid oil on pumpkin, black, green and red, 3-1/2" h, $50.**

Toy, figural, celluloid, rabbit pushing egg buggy with chick, VCO trademark ........................................ 70.00

### Halloween

Candy Box, cov, 5" x7", yellow and black ........................................... 8.00
Candy Box Label ........................... 3.00
Candy Container
    3" h, pressed cardboard black cat head, cutout eyes and mouth, wire handle, Germany .................... 60.00
    3" h, 7" l, papier-mâché witch's black shoe, opens on bottom .......... 200.00
    4" h, painted glass pumpkin, scary face, wire handle, metal screw-on lid
    ............................................ 125.00
    7" h, papier-mâché pumpkin, cutout eyes and mouth with tissue paper, wire handle, candleholder in base, Germany ................................. 85.00
Clicker, litho tin, orange and black, frog shape, mkd "T. Cohn, USA" ....... 7.50
Favor, 4" h, horn, orange celluloid, black stenciled witch, VCO .............. 45.00
Figure
    2-3/4" h, cat ................................ 15.00
    4" h, celluloid witch sitting on moon
    ............................................ 345.00
    5" h, hard plastic scarecrow with pumpkin head ................................... 12.00
    9" h, cardboard black cat, flat, moveable legs and tail, Beistle Co., USA ...20.00
Hat, cardboard and crepe paper, Germany
    4" h, black and orange ............ 17.50
    10" h, black and orange, gold and black cardboard band ............. 25.00
Horn
    8" h, paper, orange and black, wood mouthpiece, Germany ............. 12.00
    9" h, cardboard, orange and black, cat, witch, and moon litho figures, USA ......................................... 15.00
Mask
    Boy, papier-mâché, painted face, cloth ties, stamped "Germany" ........... 35.00
    Devil, rubber, red, black, and white, rubber ties ............................... 18.00
    Duck, buckram, molded bill, cloth ties ........................................... 30.00
Noisemaker, tin ............................. 10.00
Postcard
    Girl scared by pumpkin in mirror, Raphael Tuck ........................... 20.00
    Witch riding broom ................. 10.00
Pumpkin, 6" d, metal .................... 35.00
Roly Poly, 3" h, celluloid, black cat, VCO trademark .................................. 85.00
Scrap Picture, 6" x 9", cats .......... 35.00
Spoon, child's, bowl depicts witch and cat on broom, handle engraved "Victoria Louise," sterling silver, Mechanics Sterling Co. ...................... 200.00
String Holder, winking witch, pumpkin
    ............................................ 125.00
Tambourine, 6" d, metal ............... 35.00
Toy, 2-3/4" h, witch driving pumpkin vehicle, celluloid, VCO ........... 90.00

### St. Patrick's Day

Candy Box, 8-1/2" h, green cardboard shamrock ................................. 18.00

Candy Container
   3" h, green and gold cardboard hat, base label "Loft Candy Corp." . 25.00
   4" l, brown pressed cardboard potato, velvet green and gold shamrock, Germany ...................................... 45.00
   4-1/2" h, composition Irish Girl, holding harp, standing on box, Germany ............................................................ 75.00
Figure
   4" l, green flocked composition pig, Germany ................................ 50.00
   6" h, composition man, green felt coat, spring legs, beer stein .... 65.00
   7" h, celluloid leprechaun, holding pig, Japan ............................... 32.00
Magazine Cover, *Life,* March 15, 1923, cherub wearing Irish hat, playing harp .............................................. 15.00
Nodder, 3" h, bisque Irish boy, Germany ............................................................ 45.00
Postcard
   Ireland Forever, scenes of Ireland, shamrock, green, and gold ........ 4.00
   On March 17 May You Be Seen a Wearing of the Green, Irish man standing on "17," Quality Cards, The A. M. Davis Co., Boston, 1912 ... 4.50
Shamrock, 2-1/2" l, green silk floss-wrapped wire, small bisque hat attached to center ...................... 5.00

## Thanksgiving

Candle, figural, wax
   3" h, pilgrim couple .................... 5.00
   4" h, gobbler, USA ...................... 5.00
Candy Container, turkey, composition, metal legs, removable head
   5" h, horsehair beard ............... 60.00
   7-1/2" .................................... 250.00
Greeting Card, The Mayflower, With Joyful Thanksgiving Wishes ....... 8.00
Place Card Holder, 2-1/2" h, standing celluloid turkey, holder at base of metal spring legs ...................... 20.00
Postcard, A Joyous Thanksgiving, boy carving pumpkin, 1913 .............. 5.00
Turkey, paper .................................. 5.00

# Holt-Howard Collectibles

**Collecting Hints:** Here is a collecting area that's so hot with collectors, the prices are changing even as the ink is drying on this page. Remember that *Warman's* is a price guide, intended to help you determine a fair price. In the instance of Holt Howard collectibles, we've tried to present accurate prices. So, if you find a great piece at a slightly higher price, that's terrific and if you find one for less than what we've got listed, even better. The whole field of 1950s-60s ceramics is quite hot right now with collectors enjoying novelty pieces.

Holt-Howard pieces were marked with an ink-stamp. Many were also copyright dated. Some pieces were marked only with a foil sticker, especially the small pieces, where a stamp mark was too difficult. Four types of foil stickers have been identified.

**History:** Three young entrepreneurs, A. Grant Holt and brothers John and Robert Howard, started Holt-Howard from their apartment in Manhattan in 1949. All three of the partners were great salesmen, but product development was handled by Robert, while John managed sales. Grant was in charge of financial affairs and office management. By 1955, operations were large enough to move the company to Connecticut, but they still maintained their New York showroom and later added a showroom in Los Angeles. Production facilities eventually expanded to Holt-Howard Canada; Holt-Howard West, Holt-Howard International.

The company's first successful line was Angel-Abra, followed closely by its Christmas line. This early success spurred the partners to expand their wares. Their line of Christmas and kitchen-related giftware was popular with 1950s consumers. Probably the most famous line was Pixieware, which began production in 1958. Production of these whimsical pieces continued until 1962. Other lines, such as Cozy Kittens and Merry Mouse, brought even more smiles as they invaded homes in many forms. One thing that remained constant with all Holt-Howard products was a high quality of materials and workmanship, innovation, and good design.

The founders of this unique company sold their interests to General Housewares Corp. in 1968, where it became part of the giftware group. By 1974, the three original partners had left the firm. By 1990, what remained of Holt-Howard was sold to Kay Dee Designs of Rhode Island.

**Reference:** Walter Dworkin, *Price Guide to Holt-Howard Collectibles and Related Ceramicwares of the '50s and '60s,* Krause Publications, 1998.

**Advisor:** Walter Dworkin.

## Christmas

Ashtray/Cigarette Holder, Starry-eyed Santa ...................................... 45.00
Candle Climbers, Ole Snowy, snowman, set ............................................ 45.00
Candle Holders
   Ermine Angels, with snowflake rings, set ....................................... 45.00
   Santa King ............................... 85.00
   Wee Three Kings, set of 3 ........ 60.00
Cookie Jar, pop-up, Santa .......... 150.00
Cookie Jar/Candy Jar Combination, Santa ..................................... 155.00
Creamer and Sugar, Winking Santa ............................................................ 55.00
Head Vase, My Fair Lady ............. 65.00
Napkin Holder, Santa, 4" ............. 25.00
Pitcher and Mug Set, Winking Santa ............................................................ 70.00
Planter, Ermine Angel ................. 35.00
Punch Bowl Set, punch bowl and eight mugs, Santa ........................ 145.00
Salt and Pepper Shakers, pr
   Holly Girls ............................. 20.00
   Rock 'n' Roll Santas, on springs ............................................... 65.00
   Snow Babies ........................... 35.00
   Winking Santa ......................... 38.00
Server, divided tray, Santa King .. 50.00
Wall Pocket, Santa ornament........ 45.00

### Cozy Kittens

Cookie Jar, pop-up ..................... 250.00
Memo Minder .............................. 90.00
Mustard Condiment Jar ............. 180.00
Salt and Pepper Shakers, pr ........ 20.00
String Holder .............................. 45.00
Sugar Pour .................................. 85.00

### Jeeves, butler

Ashtray ....................................... 70.00
Chip Dish .................................... 80.00
Liquor Decanter ........................ 165.00
Martini Shaker Set .................... 195.00
Olives Condiment Jar ................ 135.00

### Merry Mouse

Crock, "Stinky Cheese" .............. 50.00
Match Mouse ............................... 70.00
Salt and Pepper Shakers, pr ........ 40.00

### Miscellaneous

Ashtray
   Golfer Image ......................... 110.00
   Li'l Old Lace .......................... 50.00
Bank, bobbing
   Coin Clown ............................ 135.00
   Dandy Lion ............................ 135.00
Bud Vase, Daisy Dorables........... 70.00
Candelabra, Li'l Old Lace, spiral.. 50.00
Candle Climbers, Honey Bunnies, with bases, set .............................. 85.00
Candle Rings, Ballerina, set ......... 48.00
Cookie Jar, pop-up, Clown ......... 225.00
Salt and Pepper Shakers with Napkin Holder, Winking Wabbits.......... 60.00
Salt and Pepper Shakers, pr
   Bell Bottom Gobs (sailors)....... 50.00
   Bunnies in baskets ................. 32.00
   Chattercoons, Peppy and Salty . 38.00
   Daisy Doodles, ponytail girls ... 40.00
   Goose 'n' Golden Egg ............. 35.00
   Lovebirds, yellow.................... 35.00
   Pink cat, white poodle ............ 35.00
   Rock 'n' Doll Kids, on springs.. 75.00

### Red Rooster, "Coq Rouge"

Butter Dish, cov ......................... 55.00
Candle Holders, pr ..................... 30.00
Cereal Bowl ................................ 15.00
Cookie Jar .................................. 90.00

Creamer and Sugar ..................... 45.00
Dinner Plate .................................. 18.00
Egg Cup ........................................ 15.00
Mustard Condiment Jar ............... 45.00
Salt and Pepper Shakers, pr, 4-1/2"
................................................. 25.00

# Homer Laughlin

**Collecting Hints:** The original 1871-1890 trademark used the term "Laughlin Brothers." The next trademark featured the American eagle astride the prostrate British lion. The third mark, which featured the "HLC" monogram, has appeared, with slight variations, on all dinnerware since about 1900. The 1900 version included a number that identified month, year, and plant at which the product was made. Letter codes were used in later periods.

So much attention has been given to Fiesta that other interesting Homer Laughlin patterns have not achieved the popularity which they deserve, and prices for these less-recognized patterns are still moderate. Some of the patterns made during the 1930s and 1940s have highly artistic contemporary designs.

Virginia Rose is not a pattern name but a shape on which several different decals were used. Delicate pink flowers are the most common.

**History:** Homer Laughlin and his brother, Shakespeare, built two pottery kilns in East Liverpool, Ohio, in 1871. Shakespeare resigned in 1879, leaving Homer to operate the business alone. Laughlin became one of the first firms to produce American-made whiteware. In 1896, William Wills and a Pittsburgh group led by Marcus Aaron bought the Laughlin firm.

Expansion followed. Two new plants were built in Laughlin Station, Ohio. In 1906, the first Newall, West Virginia, plant (#4) was built in. Plant #6, which was built at Newall in 1923, featured a continuous-tunnel kiln. Similar kilns were added at the other plants. Other advances instituted by the company include spray glazing and mechanical jiggering.

Between 1930 and 1960, several new dinnerware lines were added, including the Wells Art Glaze line. Ovenserve and Kitchen Kraft were cookware products. The colored-glaze lines of Fiesta, Harlequin, and Rhythm captured major market shares. In 1959, a translucent table china line was introduced. Today, the annual manufacturing capacity is more than 45 million pieces.

**References:** Susan and Al Bagdade, *Warman's American Pottery and Porcelain*, Wallace-Homestead, 1994; Jo Cunningham, *Collector's Encyclopedia of American Dinnerware*, Collector Books, 1982, 1995 value update; —, Homer Laughlin, *A Giant Among Dishes, 1973-1939*, Schiffer, 1998; Bob and Sharon Huxford, *Collector's Encyclopedia of Fiesta with Harlequin and Riviera*, 7th ed., Collector Books, 1992; Joanne Jasper, *Collector's Encyclopedia of Homer Laughlin China*, Collector Books, 1993, 1995 value update; Richard G. Racheter, *Collector's Guide to Homer Laughlin's Virginia Rose*, Collector Books, 1997.

**Periodicals:** *Fiesta Collectors Quarterly*, 19238 Dorchester Circle, Strongsville, OH 44136; *Laughlin Eagle*, 1270 63rd Terrace S., St. Petersburg, FL 33705.

**Reproduction Alert:** Harlequin and Fiesta lines were reissued in 1978 and marked accordingly.

**Additional Listings:** Fiesta.

### Harlequin

Baker, oval, spruce ....................... 22.00
Berry Bowl
    Maroon ...................................... 6.50
    Spruce ...................................... 6.00
    Turquoise .................................. 6.00
    Yellow ....................................... 6.50
Candlestick, red ......................... 195.00
Creamer, individual size
    Mauve ..................................... 23.00
    Orange ..................................... 20.00
    Spruce ..................................... 25.00
Cream Soup
    Mauve ..................................... 22.00
    Orange ..................................... 22.00
Cup, rose ..................................... 6.50
Cup and Saucer
    Spruce ..................................... 10.00
    Yellow ...................................... 10.00
Deep Plate
    Gray ........................................ 45.00
    Mauve ..................................... 28.00
    Medium Green ......................... 95.00
    Turquoise ................................ 22.00
Dinner Plate, 10" d, mauve .......... 15.00
Eggcup, double
    Chartreuse .............................. 20.00
    Gray ........................................ 24.50
    Maroon .................................... 22.00
    Rose ........................................ 24.50
Eggcup, single
    Maroon .................................... 30.00
    Mauve ..................................... 25.00
    Orange ..................................... 25.00
Nappy, 9" d
    Turquoise ................................ 18.50
    Yellow ...................................... 18.50
Nut Dish
    Mauve ..................................... 15.00

**Magazine Tear Sheet, Pottery Glass & Brass Salesman, July 1937, Kitchen Kraft OvenServe, black and white, $4.50**

    Orange ..................................... 15.00
    Rose ........................................ 20.00
    Spruce ..................................... 15.00
Platter
    11" l, maroon .......................... 18.00
    13" l, oval, rose ...................... 13.00
Relish Insert
    Maroon .................................... 50.00
    Mauve ..................................... 75.00
    Red .......................................... 35.00
    Rose ........................................ 90.00
    Yellow ...................................... 75.00
Relish Tray, turquoise base, yellow, red, mauve, and turquoise inserts ... 495.00
Salad Bowl, individual
    Chartreuse .............................. 45.00
    Light Green .............................. 45.00
    Mauve ..................................... 45.00
    Medium Green ....................... 175.00
    Yellow ...................................... 25.00
Salt and Pepper Shakers, pr
    Gray ........................................ 10.00
    Maroon .................................... 10.00
    Mauve ....................................... 8.00
    Yellow ...................................... 12.00
Sauceboat, rose .......................... 15.00

### Kitchen Kraft

Cake Server, cobalt blue ............ 145.00
Casserole, cov, individual
    Cobalt Blue ........................... 200.00
    Light Green ............................ 150.00
    Red ........................................ 255.00
    Yellow .................................... 110.00
Casserole, cov, 7-1/2" d, cobalt blue
................................................. 70.00
Casserole, cov, 8-1/2" h, yellow .... 65.00
Cream Soup Bowl, double handle, pink
................................................... 6.00
Fork
    Cobalt Blue ........................... 150.00
    Light Green .............................. 82.50

Mixing Bowl
   6" d, red.................................... 99.00
   8" d, green................................. 99.00
Pie Plate, cobalt blue, 10" d........ 30.25
Platter, green............................... 38.00
Refrigerator Unit, yellow and light green,
   stacking...........................44.00 each
Salt and Pepper Shakers, pr, red.. 93.50
Spoon, red.................................... 93.50

**Mexicana**
Baker, oval................................... 25.00
Batter Jug, cov............................. 80.00
Bowl, 5" d.................................... 20.00
Cake Server................................. 30.00
Creamer....................................... 20.00
Cup and Saucer............................ 15.00
Dinner Plate, 9" d........................ 15.00
Jar, cov, orig paper label.............. 90.00
Nappy........................................... 25.00
Pie Baker..................................... 35.00
Soup, flat..................................... 24.00
**Nautilus,** plate, 9-1/4" d, eggshell.. 8.00

**Priscilla**
Cup and Saucer.............................. 8.00
Dinner Plate................................. 10.00
Gravy Boat................................... 12.00
Vegetable Bowl
   Divided................................... 18.00
   Oval........................................ 15.00

**Riviera**
Baker, oval, ivory......................... 15.00
Bowl, 5-1/2" d, ivory...................... 7.00
Butter Dish, cov, 1/4 lb, Century
   Green or red......................... 195.00
   Turquoise.............................. 295.00
Casserole, cov
   Green.................................... 125.00
   Ivory..................................... 125.00
   Mauve................................... 110.00
   Red....................................... 125.00
Creamer, blue or ivory.................... 9.00
Cup
   Blue......................................... 7.00
   Green....................................... 7.00
   Ivory........................................ 7.00
   Light Green............................ 11.00
   Red.......................................... 7.00
   Yellow...................................... 7.00
Demitasse Cup and Saucer, Century,
   ivory...................................... 95.00
Juice Pitcher, yellow.................... 185.00
Juice Tumbler
   Green..................................... 85.00
   Ivory...................................... 95.00
   Mauve.................................... 95.00
   Red........................................ 95.00
   Turquoise............................... 95.00
   Yellow.................................... 85.00
Nappy
   Green..................................... 20.00
   Mauve.................................... 25.00
   Red........................................ 25.00
   Yellow.................................... 20.00
Oatmeal Bowl, Century
   Green..................................... 65.00
   Ivory...................................... 65.00
   Yellow.................................... 65.00
Plate, 6" d
   Ivory........................................ 5.00
   Light green.............................. 9.50
   Red.......................................... 9.50

Plate, 9" d
   Blue....................................... 12.00
   Green..................................... 12.00
   Ivory...................................... 12.00
   Red........................................ 12.00
   Yellow.................................... 12.00
Platter
   Ivory...................................... 12.00
   Yellow.................................... 22.00
Soup Plate, flat, red..................... 32.00
Saucer
   Green....................................... 3.00
   Ivory........................................ 3.00
Sugar, cov
   Green..................................... 10.00
   Ivory...................................... 10.00
Tumbler, handle, Century
   Green..................................... 55.00
   Mauve.................................... 75.00
   Red........................................ 95.00

**Virginia Rose**
Baker, oval, 8" l........................... 20.00
Butter, cov, jade.......................... 75.00
Creamer and Sugar, cov............... 35.00
Cup and Saucer.............................. 4.00
Dinner Plate, 9" d.......................... 7.50
Fruit Bowl, 5-1/2" d....................... 5.00
Mixing Bowl, large....................... 47.00
Nappy, 10" d................................ 20.00
Pie Plate...................................... 24.00
Platter, 11-1/2" l, platinum edge.... 21.00
Set.............................................. 150.00
Soup............................................. 7.50
Tray, handles............................... 25.00
Vegetable, cov............................. 42.00
**Wells Art Glaze,** batter jug.......... 30.00

# Horse Collectibles

**Collecting Hints:** The hottest area in equine memorabilia continues to be figures. Early Breyer plastic horse figures are especially sought after. You can tell the early models by their glossy finish, although those with faux woodgrain finish or the unrealistic Wedgewood blue or Florentine gold "decorator" finish are harder to find. Breyers are designed by artists familiar with equine anatomy and are as close as possible as the "real thing." Hartland horses remain popular especially those representing Western movie and television characters, like Roy Rogers and Trigger or Dale Evans and Buttermilk. Historical characters, especially General Robert E. Lee on his horse, Traveler, are in demand as well. The ears of plastic figures are especially vulnerable, so check the ear tips. Paint rubs greatly reduce the value of plastic model horses.

Ceramic figurines, whether of English origin like Wades and Beswick, German like Goebel or American manufacture like Hagen-Renaker of California, remain a strong part of the market. Well-detailed ceramic Japanese horse figures made in the 1950s and 1960s have risen in popularity and price. Check ceramic figures carefully for chips, cracks and repairs, especially on legs and tails.

There are few categories of collecting that do not feature some sort of equine image. Advertising featuring the horse has always been popular, especially early memorabilia featuring the famous trotter Dan Patch. Saddle and tack catalogs, Wild West show posters, movie posters, and even Anheuser-Busch advertising featuring its beloved Clydesdale team are all avidly collected by horse lovers.

Kentucky Derby glass prices have leveled off somewhat, except for examples from the '50s and before. The 1941-44 beetleware (an early plastic) continue to bring thousands of dollars. Carousel horses remain a high-ticket item but beware of imported hand-carved imitations. These are well done and nice as a decorator item, but don't be fooled into paying the price demanded of a Mueller, Loof or Denzel figure. It is best to find these figures at auctions where you can obtain a written guarantee of their origin.

Horse-drawn toys, whether cast iron or lithographed tin, seem to be a real bargain these days, especially when compared with automobile toys of the same era. Their performance at auctions and sales is just starting to improve, and they still provide a nice, affordable find for the horse enthusiast. The most popular horse-drawn toys remain the circus vehicles, an attraction for circus collectors along with horse lovers. Do be careful buying cast iron as many of the vehicles have been reproduced. Gaudy paint, ill-fitting parts, and a surface that feels rough to the touch should cause the warning lights to flash. Reproductions are worth maybe $25 as a decorative item, but have no value as a collectible. If you are not sure, it is best to do all your buying from a dealer that you trust.

Collectors are also drawn to equine relatives, especially mules and burros. With the current popularity of Winnie the Pooh memorabilia, everyone from toddlers to grannies want anything featuring Pooh's self-deprecating donkey friend, Eeyore.

**History:** Horses are not indigenous to the United States, but were brought here by various means. The wild horses of the American Southwest are descended from Spanish Mustangs brought here by the Conquistadors. Later, English stock would arrive with the settlers on the East Coast, where they were used for farming and transportation and even as foods source. In those days, a person's social status was determined by the quantity and quality of the horses he owned. Remember the condescending phrase, "one-horse town?"

Daily life in the early days of the United States would have been much harder on humans were it not for the horse. They were used for transportation of products, pulling plows on farms, rushing a country doctor to his patients and later, for recreational sports like racing and rodeo. Even in the early days of the automobile, horse-drawn tankers normally transported gasoline to the local service station from the distributor.

As our means of transportation gradually shifted from the horse to automobiles, trains and airplanes, the horse was no longer a necessity to folks, especially those living in cities and suburbs. Today, horses still earn their keep by rounding up stray cattle, looking for lost people in remote areas, and in competition. For the most part, today's horses are pampered family pets living a sheltered life that the hard-working draft animal of the 1800s could only dream about.

**References:** Felicia Browell, *Breyer Animal Collectors Guide,* Collector Books, 1998; Jan Lindenberger, *501 Collectible Horses,* Schiffer, 1995; Gayle Roller, *The Charlton Standard Catalogue of Hagen-Renaker,* Charlton Press, 1999; Gayle Roller, Kathleen Rose and Joan Berkwitz, *The Hagen-Renaker Handbook*, published by authors, 1989; Jim and Nancy Schaut, *Collecting the Old West,* Krause Publications, 1999; —, *Horsin' Around,* L-W Books, 1990.

**Periodicals:** *Carousel News and Trader,* 87 Park Avenue W., Suite 206, Mansfield OH 44902; *The Equine Image,* P.O. Box 916, Ft. Dodge, IA 50501; *The Glass Menagerie,* 5440 El Arbol, Carlsbad CA 92008

**Museums:** American Quarter Horse Heritage Center and Museum, Kerrville, TX; American Work Horse Museum, Peaonian Springs, VA; Appaloosa Museum and Heritage Center, Moscow, ID; International Museum of the Horse, Lexington, KY; Kentucky Derby Museum, Louisville KY; Pony Express National Memorial, St. Joseph MO; Trotting Horse Museum, Goshen, NY.

**Advisors:** Jim and Nancy Schaut.

### Horse Equipment and Related Items

Bells
  8" I metal strap, 4 graduated cast bells affixed, attaches to wagon or sleigh shaft .............................. 125.00
  84" I leather strap, 40 identical nickel bells, strap shows wear, tug hook ................................................. 200.00
Bit
  Calvary, Civil War era, "US" spots at cheeks ................................... 200.00
  Eagle figure, mkd "G.S. Garcia" ............................................... 950.00
  Silver overlay, floral design, mkd "Crockett" .............................. 125.00
Blanket
  Canvas with straps, 1930s ....... 75.00
  Carriage robe, buffalo ............ 875.00
  Saddle, Navajo weaving, early 1900s, some wear .................. 750.00
Bridle
  Calvary, mule bridle, brass "US" spots ...................................... 225.00
  Horsehair, woven, prison made ................................................. 2,500.00
Bridle Rosette
  Brass, military, eagle motif ....... 50.00
  Glass with rose motif inside, mkd "Chapman" .............................. 40.00
Brush, Calvary, stamped "US," patent date 1850, Herbert Brush Mfg. Co., never used .............................. 95.00
Catalog
  Chicago, 1929, polo saddles and equipment .............................. 75.00

**Bridle Rosette, mkd "Chapman," rose motif, $40. Photo courtesy and Jim and Nancy Schaut.**

Kelly Brothers, 1960s, bits, spurs, etc. ........................................... 60.00
Collar, draft horse, leather-covered wood, brass trim .................... 150.00
Curry Comb, tin back, leather handle, early 1900s ........................... 45.00
Harness Decorations (Horse Brasses)
  Lion, rampant in center, England ................................................. 40.00
  Rearing horse in center, backstamped "England" ................. 55.00
Hobbles, chain and leather, sideline type ...................................... 150.00
Hoof Pick, bone handle, Wastenholm, Germany, patent date 1885 ..... 55.00
Horse Drawn Vehicle
  Creators Popcorn Wagon, unrestored ................................... 7,500.00
  Stagecoach, Half-scale detailed, excellent condition ............. 3,500.00
  Watkins Products Delivery Wagon, restored ............................... 2,500.00
Horsehide rug, 48" by 72", black & white ........................................ 250.00
Lasso
  Braided rawhide, Mexican reata ................................................. 250.00
  Horsehair ............................... 175.00
Mane and Tail Comb, Oliver Slant Tooth, 1940s ........................................ 40.00
Newspaper, Horse & Stable Weekly, Boston, Jan. 2, 1891 ................ 35.00
Saddle, McClelland military type, large fenders, early 1890s .............. 950.00
Spurs, Buermann, star mark and "Hercules Bronze," old leathers .... 450.00
Stud Book
  American Quarter Horse Stud Book and Registry, 1959 ................... 50.00
  Palomino Progress, Stud Book & Registry, 1966 ......................... 75.00
Wagon Seat, springs, padded seat, replaced leather upholstery ... 250.00
Watering Trough, hollowed-out log, tin liner, 2' by 72" ........................ 225.00

### Horse Theme Items

Bank
  Arcade, still bank, cast iron horse, Buster Brown and Tige adv, 4-1/2" tall ........................................ 450.00
  Ertl, horse and tank wagon, Texaco adv ......................................... 50.00
Blanket, brown and tan wool, Roy Rogers and Trigger,1950s, twin size ................................................. 250.00
Book
  *American Trotting and Pacing Horses*, Henry V. Coats, 1st ed., 1902, 8 volumes ................... 400.00
  *The Black Stallion*, Walter Farley, 1st ed., dust jacket ....................... 25.00
  *The Horse in Art*, John Baskett, NY Graphic Society, Boston, 1980 50.00
Calendar, 1907, cardboard, Dousman Milling, cowgirl and horse ........ 75.00
Carousel Horse, jumper, flag on side, C. W. Parker, American, 1918 . 6,500.00
Catalog, D. F. Mangels Carousel Works, Coney Island, NY, 28 pages, 1918 ............................................. 300.00
Clock, United, brass horse, Western saddle, wood base ................ 125.00

**Breyer, Proud Arabian Mare, glossy alabaster, 1956-60, $55. Photo courtesy and Jim and Nancy Schaut.**

Cookie Cutter, prancing horse, bobtail, flat back, 6-1/2" by 7-1/2" ......... 75.00
Cookie Jar, McCoy, Circus Horse . 50.00
Decanter, Man O'War, Ezra Brooks ................................................ 25.00
Decanter, Avon, brown glass thoroughbred ................................. 10.00
Doorstop, racehorse, stamped "Virginia Metalcrafters," 1949 ...... 195.00
Fan, Moxie advertising, rocking horse, 1920s ..................................... 55.00
Figure
　Beswick, reclining foal, 3", brown, white blaze on forehead .......... 75.00
　Breyer, glossy black rearing horse ............................................... 125.00
　Hagen-Renaker Pegasus, 1985, mini ................................................ 35.00
　Hartland, Roy Rogers and Trigger, near mint .............................. 225.00
　Heisey Clydesdale, amber glass ................................................. 95.00
　Rookwood, #6140, 1939 ........ 400.00
　Summit Art Glass, blue, short legs ................................................. 25.00
　Vernon Kilns, Disney, unicorn, black "Fantasia" ............................ 600.00
　Wade, Tom Smith pony ........... 45.00
Fruit Crate label, Bronco, bucking horse ................................................. 25.00
Game
　Pony Express, cast metal horses, 1948 ......................................... 75.00
　Horse Race, mechanical, 1890s, France ................................... 1,500.00
Hobby Horse, Tom Mix's Tony, wood horse on platform ................... 950.00
Jewelry, pin, figural
　Donkey with baskets, Mexican sterling .......................................... 25.00
　Horse, celluloid ...................... 35.00
Magazine, Western Horseman, Volume 1 #1, 1935 ............................. 50.00
Mug
　Clydesdales, 1st in Series, Certamarte Brazil for Anheuser-Busch .. 45.00
　Donkey, figural, Democratic Convention souvenir, Frankoma ........ 50.00

**Mug, Famous Clydesdales, first in series, $45. Photo courtesy and Jim and Nancy Schaut.**

Nodder
　Donkey in suit, carrying US flag 5.00
　Horse, celluloid, mkd "Occupied Japan" ..................................... 75.00
Plate
　10" d, 1964 Palomino Horse Show, First Place, silverplated ............ 50.00
　13" d, Wallace, Rodeo pattern ................................................. 175.00
Puppet, hand, Mr. Ed, plush ......... 75.00
Post Card
　Bucking Bronco, Prescott AZ Rodeo, 1920s ....................................... 20.00
　Three draft horses, German, pre-1920, used ............................... 15.00
Poster
　Berry Exhibitions, Dayton, OH, Saddle Horse Contest, 1913 ........ 350.00
　Studebaker Wagons, multiple tears and tape, 1909 ..................... 175.00
Program, Kentucky Derby, 1964, signed by artist "Shoofly" ..................... 75.00
Rocking Horse, white, black spots, horsehair mane and tail, 75% original paint, handmade, one rocker split ........................................ 450.00
Salt and Pepper Shakers, pr, figural mules, very detailed ................. 25.00
Sheet Music, *Dan Patch March*, famous trotter on cover, fair condition .. 65.00
Sign
　Hunter Cigars, tin, 19" by 27", fox hunter with horse .................. 300.00
　Mobil Oil, porcelain on steel, 6' long, red Pegasus...................... 1,500.00
Snowdome, Budweiser Clydesdales, 1988 limited edition................. 75.00
Toy
　Circus Wagon, 14" long, cast iron, mkd "Kenton"...................... 1,200.00
　Fire pumper, 3 horses, cast iron, Hubley.............................. 1,750.00
　Hay cart, Gibbs, paper lithographed ................................................. 495.00

Tray, Genessee Twelve Horse Ale, 12" d ............................................. 125.00
Valentine, cowboy on horse, 1910, unused.................................... 30.00
Weather Vane, running horse, with base ................................................. 50.00
Windmill Weight, Dempster, bobtail horse, 17" l ........................... 950.00

# Hull Pottery

**Collecting Hints:** Distinctive markings on the bottom of Hull Pottery vases help the collector to identify them immediately. Early stoneware pottery has an "H." The famous matte pieces, a favorite of most collectors, contain pattern numbers. For example, Camelia pieces are marked with numbers in the 100's, Iris pieces have 400 numbers, and Wildflower a "W" preceding their number. Most of Hull's vases are also marked with their height in inches, making it easy to determine their value. Items made after 1950 are usually glossy and are marked "hull" or "Hull" in large script letters.

Hull collectors are beginning to seriously collect the glossy ware and kitchen items.

**History:** In 1905, Addis E. Hull purchased the Acme Pottery Co. in Crooksville, Ohio. In 1917, A. E. Hull Pottery Co. began to make a line of art pottery for florists and gift shops. The company also made novelties, kitchenware, and stoneware. During the Depression, the company primarily produced tiles.

Hull's Little Red Riding Hood kitchenware was manufactured between 1943 and 1957 and is a favorite of collectors, including many who do not collect other Hull items.

In 1950, the factory was destroyed by a flood and fire, but by 1952 it was back in production, operating under the Hull Pottery Company name. At this time, Hull added its newer glossy finish pottery, plus the firm developed pieces sold in flower shops under the Regal and Floraline trade names. Hull's brown House 'n' Garden line of kitchen and dinnerware achieved great popularity and was the main line being produced prior to the plant's closing in 1986.

**References:** Joan Gray Hull, *Hull: The Heavenly Pottery*, 6th ed., published by author, 1998; —, *Hull: The Heavenly Pottery Shirt Pocket Price Guide*, published by author, 1999;

**Open Rose (Rose), 109-10-1/2", $150. Photo courtesy of Joan Hull.**

Brenda Roberts, *Roberts Ultimate Encyclopedia of Hull Pottery*, Walsworth Publishing, 1992; —, *Collectors Encyclopedia of Hull Pottery*, Collector Books, 1980, 1995 value update; —, *Companion Guide to Roberts' Ultimate Encyclopedia of Hull Pottery*, Walsworth Publishing Co, 1992; Mark E. Supnick, *Collecting Hull Pottery's Little Red Riding Hood*, L-W Book Sales, 1989, 1992 value update.

**Periodical:** *Hull Pottery News*, 7768 Meadow Drive, Hillsboro, MO 63050.

**Collectors' Club:** The Hull Pottery Association, 11023 Tunnel Hill NE, New Lexington, OH 43764.

**Advisor:** Joan Hull.

### Pre-1950 Patterns

Bow Knot
    B3, 6" vase ............................. 250.00
    B7, 8-1/2" vase ....................... 300.00
    B13, double cornucopia ........ 295.00
    B28, 10" d plate ................... 1,200.00
Dogwood (Wildflower)
    504, 8-1/2" vase ..................... 150.00
    507, 5-1/2" teapot ................... 350.00
    514, 4" jardiniere ................... 110.00
Iris
    405, 4-3/4" vase ....................... 80.00
    406, 7" vase ............................. 125.00
    412, 7" hanging planter .......... 175.00
Jack-In-The-Pulpit/Calla Lily
    500/32, 10" bowl ..................... 185.00
    505, 6" vase ............................. 125.00

**Waterlily teapot, L-18, 6", $225. Photo courtesy of Joan Hull.**

    550, 7" vase ............................ 140.00
Magnolia
    4, 6-1/4" vase .......................... 55.00
    8, 10-1/2" vase ....................... 175.00
    14, 4-3/4" pitcher ..................... 55.00
    22, 12-1/2" vase ..................... 300.00
Magnolia (Pink Gloss)
    H5, 6-1/2" vase ........................ 35.00
    H17, 12-1/2" vase ................... 225.00
Open Rose (Camelia)
    105, 7" pitcher ........................ 225.00
    114, 8-1/2" jardiniere ............. 375.00
    120, 6-1/2" vase ..................... 135.00
    140, 10-1/2" basket ............. 1,300.00
Orchid
    301, 10" vase .......................... 325.00
    306, 6-3/4" bud vase .............. 145.00
    311, 13" pitcher ...................... 675.00
Pinecone, 55, 6" vase ................ 150.00
Poppy
    606, 6-1/2" vase ..................... 200.00
    607, 8-1/2" vase ..................... 250.00
    609, 9" wall planter ................ 450.00
Rosella
    R1, 5" vase ............................... 35.00
    R8, 6-1/2" vase ........................ 75.00
    R15, 8-1/2" vase ...................... 85.00
Stoneware
26H, vase .................................... 85.00
536H, 9" jardiniere ..................... 120.00
Thistle, #53, 6" ........................... 150.00
Tulip
    101-33, 9" vase ...................... 245.00
    109-33, 8" pitcher ................... 235.00
    110-33, 6" vase ...................... 150.00
Waterlily
    L-8, 8-1/4" vase ...................... 165.00
    L-18, 6" teapot ....................... 225.00
    L-19, 5" creamer ..................... 75.00
    L-20, 5" sugar ......................... 75.00
Wildflower
    54, 6-1/2" vase ...................... 175.00
    66, 100-1/2" basket ............. 2,000.00
    76, 8-1/2" vase ...................... 350.00
    W-3, 5-1/2" vase ...................... 55.00
    W-8, 7-1/2" vase ...................... 90.00
    W-18, 12-1/2" vase ................ 300.00
Woodland (matte)
    W1, 5-1/2" vase ....................... 95.00
    W10, 11" cornucopia ............. 195.00
    W25, 12-1/2" vase ................. 425.00

### Post-1950 Patterns (Glossy)

Blossom Flite
    T8, basket .............................. 125.00
    T10, 16-1/2" console bowl ...... 125.00

    T11, candleholders, pr ............ 75.00
Butterfly
    B4, 6" bonbon dish ................. 50.00
    B13, 8" basket ....................... 150.00
    B15, 13-1/2" pitcher .............. 300.00
Ebbtide
    E3, 7-1/2" mermaid cornucopia
    ........................................... 225.00
    E7, 11" fish vase ................... 175.00
    E12, 15-3/4" console ............. 200.00
Figural Planters
    27, Madonna, standing ........... 30.00
    82, clown ................................ 50.00
    95, twin geese ........................ 50.00
Parchment & Pine
    S-5, 10-1/2" scroll planter ......... 85.00
    S-15, 8" coffeepot ................. 150.00
Serenade (Birds)
    S7, 8-1/2" vase ....................... 65.00
    S15, 11-1/2" ftd fruit bowl ...... 110.00
Sunglow
    51, 7-1/2" cov casserole .......... 50.00
    80, wall pocket, cup and saucer
    ............................................. 75.00
    95, 8-1/4" vase ....................... 45.00
Tokay (Grapes)
    4, 8-1/4" vase ......................... 95.00
    12, 12" vase .......................... 125.00
    19, large leaf dish ................... 95.00
Tropicana, T53, 8-1/2" vase ........ 550.00
Woodland
    W-6, 6-1/2" pitcher .................. 65.00
    W-9, 8-3/4" basket ................. 110.00
    W-13, 7-1/2" shell wall pocket.. 95.00

# Hummel Items

**Collecting Hints:** A key to pricing Hummel figures is the mark. All authentic Hummel pieces bear both the signature "M. I. Hummel" and a Goebel trademark. Various trademarks were used to identify the year of production:

Crown Mark (trademark 1) 1935-1949
    Full Bee (trademark 2)1950-1959
    Stylized Bee (trademark 3)1957-1972
    Three Line Mark (trademark 4) 1964-1972
    Last Bee Mark (trademark 5) 1972-1979
    Missing Bee Mark (trademark 6) 1979-1990

Current Mark or New Crown Mark (trademark 7)1991 to the present.

    Collectors are advised to buy pieces with the early marks whenever possible. Since production runs were large, almost all figurines, no matter what the mark, exist in large numbers.

    Prices fluctuate a great deal. Antiques newspapers, such as *The Antique Trader*, often carry ads by dealers offering discounts on the modern pieces. The slightest damage to a piece lowers the value significantly.

Before World War II and for a few years after, the Goebel Company made objects, such as vases, for export. These often had the early mark. Prices are modest for these items because few collectors are interested in them; the Hummel books do not even list them. This aspect of Goebel Company production would be an excellent subject for a research project.

**History:** Hummel items are the original creations of Berta Hummel, who was born in 1909 in Massing, Bavaria, Germany. At age 18 she was enrolled in the Academy of Fine Arts in Munich to further her mastery of drawing and the palette. Berta entered the Convent of Siessen and became Sister Maria Innocentia in 1934. While in this Franciscan cloister, she continued drawing and painting images of her childhood friends.

In 1935, W. Goebel Co. in Rodental, Germany, began producing Sister Maria Innocentia's sketches as three-dimensional bisque figurines. The Schmid Brothers of Randolph, Massachusetts, introduced the figurines to America and became Goebel's U.S. distributor.

In 1967, Goebel began distributing Hummel items in the United States. A controversy developed between the two companies, the Hummel family, and the convent. Law suits and counter-suits ensued. The German courts finally effected a compromise: the convent held legal rights to all works produced by Sister Maria Innocentia from 1934 until her death in 1946 and licensed Goebel to reproduce these works; Schmid was to deal directly with the Hummel family for permission to reproduce any pre-convent art.

**References:** Carl F. Luckey, *Luckey's Hummel Figurines & Plates*, 11th ed., Krause Publications, 1997; Robert L. Miller, *No. 1 Price Guide to M. I. Hummel: Figurines, Plates, More...*, 6th ed., Portfolio Press, 1995; ---, *Hummels 1978-1998: 20 Years of "Miller on Hummel" Columns*, Collector News, 1998.

**Collectors' Clubs:** Hummel Collector's Club, 1261 University Dr., Yardley, PA 19067; M. I. Hummel Club,

Goebel Plaza, Rte 31, P.O. Box 11, Pennington, NJ 08534.

**Museum:** Hummel Museum, New Braunfels, TX.

Anniversary Plate
   1975, Stormy Weather, #280, FE
   ........................................... 165.00
   1979, Singing Lesson ............. 50.00
Ashtray
   Boy With Bird, #166 ................ 80.00
   Joyful, #33................................ 75.00
   Let's Sing, #114 ...................... 75.00
Bank, Little Thrifty, c1972............. 50.00
Bell
   1975, orig box......................... 65.00
   1980, bas relief, MIB............... 70.00
Calendar, 1955, 12 illus ............... 15.00
Candlestick, Girl With Fir Tree, 1956
   ................................................ 35.00
Christmas Plate
   1971, Heavenly Angel, #264.. 725.00
   1972, Hear Ye, Hear Ye, #265 125.00
   1973, Globe Trotter, #266......... 70.00
   1974, Goose Girl, #267.......... 100.00
   1975, Ride Into Christmas, #268
   ................................................ 90.00
   1976, Apple Tee Girl, #269 .... 880.00
   1977, Apple Tree Boy, #270..... 95.00
   1978, Happy Pastime, #271 .... 75.00
   1979, Singing Lesson, #272 .... 85.00
   1980, School Girl, #273 ......... 100.00
   1981, Umbrella Boy, #274...... 100.00
   1983, Postman, #276............. 110.00

**Doll, Christyl, red scarf, red, white, blue, and white dress, brown felt slippers, orig wrist tag, blue paper label on slipper, 12" h, $95.**

**Figure, Wayside Harmony, #III-1, full bee mark, 5-1/2" h, $215.**

   1984, A Gift From Heaven, #277
   .............................................. 105.00
   1985, Chick Girl, #278 ........... 110.00
   1986, Playmates, #279 .......... 135.00
   1987, Feeding Time, #283..... 135.00
   1988, Little Goat Herder, #284
   .............................................. 135.00
   1989, Farm Boy ..................... 115.00
Doll
   Carnival, porcelain................ 190.00
   Chimney Sweep........................ 80.00
   Easter Greetings, porcelain... 200.00
   Gretel ...................................... 60.00
   Hansel...................................... 60.00
   Little Knitter............................. 65.00
   Postman, porcelain................ 200.00
   Rose, pink................................ 50.00
Figure
   Adoration, #23/111, 7-1/8", trademark 5 ................................... 375.00
   Apple Tree Boy, #142/I, 6"...... 290.00
   Apple Tree Girl, #141/I , 6"..... 290.00
   Artist, #304, trademark 6 ......... 90.00
   Barnyard Hero, #195/2/0, trademark 2 ....................................... 115.00
   Be Patient, 6", Trademark 3 ... 145.00
   Book Worm, #3/I ................... 490.00
   Brother, #95 ......................... 230.00
   Builder, #305, trademark 4 ...... 82.00
   Carnival, #328, trademark 6 .... 80.00
   Chicken Licken ..................... 240.00
   Coquettes, #179 ................... 280.00
   Crossroads, #331, 6-3/4" ....... 360.00
   Doll Bath, #319, trademark 5... 75.00
   Doll Mother, stylized bee mark
   .............................................. 135.00
   Duet, #130, trademark 1........ 300.00
   Eventide, Trademark 3........... 135.00
   Farewell ................................ 325.00
   Feather Friends, #344 .......... 365.00
   Friend or Foe, #434 ............. 285.00
   Gay Adventure, #356, trademark 6
   ................................................ 75.00

Gil with Doll, #239, trademark 6
............................................... 25.00
Good Hunting, #307, trademark 4
............................................... 130.00
Goose Girl, #47/0, trademark 2, 4-1/4"
............................................... 200.00
Happy Birthday, #176/0, 6" ... 245.00
Happy Pastime, #69 ............. 190.00
Hear Ye, #15/0, trademark 1 .. 300.00
Herald Angels, #37, trademark 2
............................................... 80.00
Just Resting, #112/l, trademark 1
............................................... 300.00
Kiss Me, #311, trademark 4 ... 145.00
Little Fiddler, #4, trademark 1 250.00
Little Gardener, #72, trademark 2
............................................... 60.00
Little Scholar, #80, Trademark 3
............................................... 55.00
Lot Sheep, #68/0, Trademark 3 .. 72.00
Merry Wanderer, #7/ll, trademark 1
............................................... 500.00
Mischief Maker ..................... 290.00
Out Of Danger, #56B ........... 290.00
Photographer, trademark .... 2225.00
Puppy Love, #1, Trademark 3 .. 75.00
Retreat to Safety, #201/2/0, trademark 4 ................................... 90.00
School Girl, #81/2/0, Trademark 3
............................................... 60.00
Sensitive Hunter ................... 240.00
She Loves Me, She Loves Me Not
............................................... 225.00
Stormy Weather, #71/l ........... 370.00
Sweet Music, #186, trademark 1
............................................... 125.00
Telling Her Secret, #196/0, trademark 2 ................................... 235.00
Tuneful Angel, #359, trademark 6
............................................... 45.00
Village Boy, #51/2/0, trademark 1
............................................... 115.00
Waiter, #154/0, trademark 2 . 1309.00
Wash Day, #321, trademark 4 .. 80.00
Weary Wanderer, #204, trademark 6
............................................... 80.00
Worship, #84/0, trademark 1 .. 250.00
Font
Angel Cloud, #206, trademark 4
............................................... 25.00
Angel Sitting, #167, trademark 4
............................................... 40.00
Angel with Birds, #22/0, trademark 6
............................................... 18.00
Angels At Prayer, #91B, Trademark 3
............................................... 70.00
Child With Flowers, #36/0, trademark 2 ................................... 48.00
Good Shepherd, #35/0, trademark 6
............................................... 25.00
Madonna and Child, #243, trademark 6 ................................... 25.00
Worship, #164, trademark 2 ... 120.00
Inkwell, With Loving Greetings, blue
............................................... 135.00
Lamp
Apple Tree Boy, #M/230, trademark 5
............................................... 165.00
Birthday Serenade, #M/231/1, trademark 2, reverse mold ............ 900.00
Culprits, #44, crown mark, c1930, orig wiring, 9-1/2" h ............... 475.00

Good Friends, #M/228, trademark 5
............................................... 165.00
Just Resting, #M/225/11, trademark 5 ............................................. 175.00
Loves Me, Loves Me Not, #M/227, trademark 2, c1970 ............... 180.00
Out of Danger, trademark 2 ... 275.00
Music Box
Chick Girl ............................. 235.00
Ride Into Christmas .............. 240.00
Nativity Figures
Angel Serenade, #214/D/11 .... 40.00
Donkey, #214/J/11 .................. 35.00
Infant Jesus, #260 ................. 80.00
King, kneeling on one knee, #214/M/11 ...................................... 100.00
Lamb, #214/0/11 .................... 15.00
Little Tooter, #214/H/11 ........... 65.00
Madonna, #214/A/M/11 ........ 110.00
Stable, 3 pc, #214/S11 ........... 35.00
Print, Moonlight Return, litho, FE 500.00

# Hunting Collectibles

**Collecting Hints:** Sporting-minded collectors can easily find more and more items to add to their collections. Most flea markets yield everything from big-game trophy heads to canoes to hunting licenses.

**History:** Hunting became a necessity as soon as man discovered it could end hunger pains. Hunting collectibles, also known as sporting collectibles, encompass those items used for hunting, whether fox or big game. Today's hunters often choose to use binoculars and cameras in lieu of rifles, arrows, or caveman's clubs.

**Reference:** Ralf Coykendall, Jr., *Coykendall's Complete Guide to Sporting Collectibles*, Wallace-Homestead, 1996; Donna Toneilli, *Top f the Line Hunting Collectibles,* Schiffer, 1998.

**Periodical:** *Sporting Classics,* 3031 Scotsman Road, Columbia, SC 29223; *Sporting Collector's Monthly,* P.O. Box 305, Camden Wyoming, DE 19934; *Sports Collectors Digest,* 700 E. State St., Iola, WI 54990.

Award Badge, NRA
Marksman, dark silver luster, hanger bar, First Class on center bar... 12.00
Marksman, First Class, NRA 50 Ft Award, 2" l ............................... 18.00
Pro-Marksman, Junior Division, 1-3/4" l
............................................... 16.00
Sharpshooter, brass link badge on hanger bar, Junior Division ...... 10.00
Book
*Night Hunting,* J. E. Williams, Southern Farm Cook Hound Kennels, 1911, 98 pgs, black and white photos ......................................... 35.00

*30 Years A Hunter, 15 Years Interpreter for Cornstalk & Blacksnake, Indian Chiefs On The Allegany River,* Philip Tome, 1854, 200 pgs ..... 35.00
Broadside, litho
14-1/2" h, 12" w, DuPont Powders, two anxious duck hunters pecking out of camp, "Just look at 'em," image by Edmund Osthaus, c1910 ......... 50.00
42" h, 28" w, Western-Winchester, hunter preparing to shoot red squirrel, autumn foliage, Weimer Pursell litho, © 1955 ........................... 70.00
Call
Crow, Charles Perdew, Henry, IL, fair condition .............................. 175.00
Duck, Herter's, orig box ........... 35.00
Turkey Hooter Owl, Olt, orig box
............................................... 35.00
Catalog
Dave Cook Sporting Goods, 48 pgs, 1968 ....................................... 5.00
Edw Tryon Sporting Goods, 72 pgs, 1923 ..................................... 27.50
Kirtland Bros. Sporting Goods, 16 pgs, 1924 ................................ 15.00
Winchester Rifle, John Wayne cover, 16 pgs, 1982 .......................... 8.50
Counter Felt
Dead Shot Powder, "Kill Your Bird Not Your Shoulder," multicolored on black, trimmed ........................ 90.00
Winchester, "Shoot Where You Aim"
............................................... 175.00
Decoy Basket, clam-style .......... 200.00
Handbook, Winchester Ammunition, 112 pgs, 1951 ..................... 13.50
Head, mounted, fine condition
Alaskan Wolf ......................... 350.00
Deer ....................................... 75.00
Elk .......................................... 400.00
Elk Horns .............................. 275.00
Moose ................................... 450.00
License
New Jersey, 1933, blue and white, black serial number, minor rust on back ...................................... 50.00
North Carolina, 1929-30, pale blue and white, black serial number .. 80.00

**Pinback Button, DuPont Powders, The Record Breakers, white letters, red border, partridge in center, 1" d, $60.**

Ontario Guide, 1935, black and white, red numerals, worn........ 20.00
West Virginia, 1934, blue and black, non-resident, black serial number on white band .............................. 80.00
Wisconsin, 1932, black and white, some wear................................ 25.00
Magazine
*American Rifleman*, Aug. 15, 1924 (cover detached) .................... 12.00
*Hunting and Fishing*, Feb., 1938, Myrna Loy and Lucky Strike back cover color ad ......................... 12.00
Magazine Tear Sheet, half page size, 1949
Western World Champion Ammunition, "Even bull strength is no match for the New Silver Tip"............... 3.50

Winchester, "Bag A Buck," model 94, 70, and 12.................................. 3.50
Pinback Button
Peters Ammunition, multicolored duck hunting scene, center red letter "P".............................................. 55.00
Shoot Peters Shells, multicolored red and brass shotgun shell, white background, black letters................ 20.00
Winchester, Topperweins, sepia portrait of husband wife sharpshooters, pale yellow ground, white rim, black letters, "The Wonderful Topperweins Who Always Shoot, Winchester Guns and Cartridges," blue lettering, red "W" for Winchester.................. 80.00
Shooter's Box, fired brass shells, 24 ................................................. 280.00

Skiff, gunning, canvas covered, Harve de Grace, MD, tidewaters, c1910 ............................................... 500.00
Stickpin, Smith Guns, celluloid, multicolored, oval, brass insert back, inscribed "The Hunter Arms Co, Fulton, NY"................................. 120.00
Target Ball, glass
Amber, Bogardus.................. 255.00
Green, basketweave, shooting figure ............................................... 185.00

# Ice Cream Collectibles

**Collecting Hints:** The ice cream collector has many competitors. Those who do not have a specialty collection are sometimes hampered by the regional collector, i.e., an individual who exclusively collects ice cream memorabilia related to a specific manufacturer or area. Many ice cream collectibles are associated with a specific dairy, thus adding dairy collectors to the equation. Since most ice cream was made of milk, milk and milk bottle collectors also hover around the edge of the ice cream collecting scene, and do not forget to factor in the cow collector (ice cream advertising often features cows). Advertising, food mold, kitchen, and premium collectors are secondary considerations. The result is fierce competition for ice cream material, often resulting in higher prices.

When buying an ice cream tray, the scene is the most important element. Most trays were stock items with the store or firm's name added later. Condition is critical.

Beware of reproductions. They became part of the ice cream collectibles world in the 1980s. Many reproductions are introduced into the market as "warehouse" finds. Although these items look old, many are poor copies or fantasy pieces.

**History:** During the 1st century A.D. in ancient Rome, nearby mountains provided the Emperor Nero with snow and ice which he flavored with fruit pulp and honey. This fruit ice was the forerunner of ice cream. The next development occurred in the 13th century. Among the many treasures that Marco Polo brought back from the Orient was a recipe for a frozen milk dessert resembling sherbet.

In the 1530s, Catherine de Medici, bride of King Henry II of France, introduced Italian ices to the French court. By the end of the 16th century, ices had evolved into a product similar to today's modern ice cream. By the middle of the 17th century, ice cream became fashionable at the English court.

Ice cream changed from being a luxury food for kings and their courts to a popular commodity in 1670 when the Cafe Procope (rue de l'Ancienne) in Paris introduced ice cream to the general populace, and by 1700 the first ice cream recipe book appeared. Ice cream was the rage of 18th-century Europe.

Ice cream appeared in America by the early 18th century. In 1777, an advertisement by Philip Lenzi, confectioner, appeared in the New York *Gazette* noting that ice cream was available on a daily basis. George Washington was an ice cream enthusiast, spending more than $200 with a New York ice cream merchant in 1790. Thomas Jefferson developed an eighteen-step process to make ice cream and is credited with the invention of baked Alaska.

By the mid-19th century, ice cream "gardens" sprang up in major urban areas, and by the late 1820s the ice cream street vendor arrived on the scene. However, because ice cream was still difficult to prepare, production remained largely in commercial hands.

In 1846, Nancy Johnson invented the hand-cranked ice cream freezer, allowing ice cream to enter the average American household. As the century progressed, the ice cream parlor arrived on the scene and homemade ice cream competed with commercial products from local, regional, and national dairies.

The arrival of the home refrigerator/freezer and large commercial freezers in grocery stores marked the beginning of the end for the ice cream parlor. A few survived into the post-World War II era. The drugstore soda fountain, which replaced many of them, became, in turn, a thing of the past in the 1970s when drugstore chains arrived on the scene.

Americans consume more ice cream than any other nation in the world. But Americans do not hold a monopoly. Ice cream reigns worldwide as one of the most popular foods known. In France it is called *glace*; in Germany, *eis*; and in Russia, *marozhnye*. No matter what it is called, ice cream is eaten and enjoyed around the globe.

**References:** Paul Dickson, *Great American Ice Cream Book*, Galahad Books, out of print; Ralph Pomeroy, *Ice Cream Connection*, Paddington Press, out of print; Wayne Smith, *Ice Cream Dippers*, published by author, 1986.

Also check general price guides to advertising and advertising character collectibles for ice cream-related material.

**Collector's Club:** Ice Screamers, P.O. Box 5387, Lancaster, PA 17601.

**Museums:** Greenfield Village, Dearborn, MI; Museum of Science and Industry, Finigran's Ice Cream Parlor, Chicago, IL; Smithsonian Institution, Washington, D.C.

Advertisement, McVey Ice Cream ............................................. 265.00
Advertising Trade Card, Lightning Blizzard Freezers, diecut, girl giving dish of ice cream out window, mother hand cranking ice cream freezer on reverse ...................................... 15.00
Book, *Snow Ice Cream Makers Guide*, B Heller & Co., 1911 ............... 15.00
Carton, Hershey's Ice Cream, one pint, orange and blue ..................... 18.00
Catalog, Ice Cream maker's Formulary & Price List, Frank A. Beeler, 1910-15 ............................................ 30.00
Christmas Decoration, 6-1/2" x 10" diecut stuff paper string hanger, front illus of Santa making deliveries on foot, holding Christmas wreath under one arm, Merry Christmas placard in other hand, Bartholomay Ice Cream inscription in black on white snow, 1930s .................................... 125.00
Clock, Breyer's Ice Cream, wood, sailboat, chrome sails ................... 50.00
Cone Dispenser, glass, copper insert ............................................ 350.00
Doll, Eskimo Pie .......................... 12.00
Film, "Ice Cream Face," Our Gang Comedy, 1930s, 16 mm, 2-1/4" orig sq box ...................................... 25.00
Ice Cream Fork, sterling silver, set of 12
    Debussy, Towle ...................... 480.00
    Rose Point, Wallace .............. 325.00
Ice Cream Knife, sterling silver, repousse dec, Kirk ................... 85.00
Ice Cream Maker
    Alaska, 4 qt ............................ 40.00
    Unknown maker, tin, hand crank, used ...................................... 80.00
    White Mountain, triple motion .. 45.00
Ice Cream Scoop Rest, Hendler's Ice Cream, molded brass, inscription "Friendship of Hendler's The Velvet Kind," 1930-40 ......................... 45.00
Ice Cream Spoon, sterling, set of six
    Chantilly pattern, Gorham ........ 95.00
    Etruscan, Gorham .................. 365.00
    Naturalistic, Gorham .............. 260.00
Menu Clip, Fairmont Ice Cream, 1930-40 ................................................. 18.50
Mold, pewter
    Cherub ................................... 90.00
    Cupid on Heart ....................... 40.00
    Grape Cluster ......................... 30.00
    Heart, Eppelsmeier ................. 40.00
    Indian .................................... 45.00
    Lady's Shoe ............................ 25.00
    Potato .................................... 45.00
    Question Mark ........................ 50.00
    Star in Circle .......................... 40.00
    Turkey .................................... 45.00
Pennant, Tellings Ice Cream, felt, children making ice cream ............ 90.00

**Tray, Imperial Ice Cream, black and yellow, 17-1/4" x 12-1/4", $90.**

Pinback Button
  3/4" d, Good Humor Deerslayer Scout, orange, blue, and white litho, c1930 ..................................... 25.00
  7/8" d, Artic Rainbow Ice Cream Cones, multicolored, celluloid, c1912 ....................................... 25.00
  1" d, National Ice Cream Week, blue and white, Ice Cream Review, rim copyright, 1930s ..................... 20.00
  1-1/4" d, Frosty Treat, red, white, and blue, female ice skater, red outfit, c1930 ....................................... 25.00
Print, girl with puppy and ice cream, Bessie Pease Gutmann .......... 110.00
Pocket Mirror, Better Made Ice Cream ................................................ 35.00
Record Brush, Abbotts Ice Cream, celluloid, soft bristles, mkd "Sixth Anniversary," pale red brick left and right, pale blue sky, lettering, pale blue rim, 3-1/2" d ............................. 40.00
Scoop
  Gilchrest #31 ........................... 95.00
  Gilchrest #33 ......................... 125.00

No-Pak, #31, hole in scoop ...... 85.00
Williamson, wear ...................... 15.00
Sign
  Jack & Jill Ice Cream Cake Roll, 8-1/2" x 19-1/2", full color, paper, image of housewife holding slice of ice cream cake, ©Newly Weds Baking Co., c1940 ........................................ 24.00
  Williams Ice Cream, The Cream of Perfection, 13-1/2" h, 17-1/2" w, two sided, flanged tin, one side fair condition, other poor ..................... 85.00
Song Brochure, Hendler's Ice Cream, 1950s ......................................... 2.00
Tape Measure, Abbotts Ice Cream, black, white, and red illus ........ 20.00
Thermometer, Abbottmaid Ice Cream, 2" x 6-1/4", 1920s ..................... 45.00
Toy
  2" x 4-1/4" x 2", litho tin, Mister Softee Truck, red, white, and blue, silver and black accents, Mister Softee image on three sides, friction, marked "Made in Japan," 1960s
  .................................................. 40.00

2-1/2" l, diecast metal truck, Commer Ice Cream Canteen, Lyons Maid decals in black, white, red, and yellow, white 3-D figure, Matchbox, c1963 ...................................... 35.00
4" h, ice cream vendor, litho tin wind-up, Depose France, 1930s .... 795.00
Tray
  13" d, Furnas Ice Cream, titled "In Old Kentucky," young girl caressing horse, ©1912, American Art Works litho, some inpainting, bottom rim repainted and relettered ........ 175.00
  13" l, 10-1/2" w, Pangburns Pear Food Ice Cream, animated scene of Palmer Cox Brownies and huge dish of ice cream ........................... 350.00
Truck Driver's Manual, Jack & Jill, 4-1/2" x 6", black and white, 20 pgs, red accent cover, some scattered spots on cover, late 1930s ................. 18.00
Whistle, Puritan Dairy Ice Cream, yellow tin litho, black letters, c1930 .... 35.00

# Insulators

**Collecting Hints:** Learn the shapes of the insulators and the abbreviations which appear on them. Some commonly found abbreviations are: "B" (Brookfield), "B & O" (Baltimore and Ohio), "EC&M Co SF" (Electrical Construction and Maintenance Company of San Francisco), "ER" (Erie Railroad), "WGM Co" (Western Glass Manufacturing Company), and "WUT Co" (Western Union Telegraph Company).

The majority of the insulators are priced below $50. However, there are examples of threaded and threadless insulators which have exceeded $2,000. There has been little movement in the price of glass insulators for the past several years. The top insulators in each category are:

Threaded

  CD 139, Combination Safety/Pat. Applied for, aqua ............ 2,500.00

  CD 180, Liquid Insulator/blank, ice aqua ......................... 2,500.00

  CD 138-9, Patent Applied for/blank, aqua ................... 2,400.00

  CD 176, Lower wire ridge, Whitall Tatum Co. No. 12 made in U.S.A./lower wire ridge, Patent No. 1708038, straw ............... 2,300.00

  CD 181, no name and no embossing ..................... 2,200.00

Threadless

  CD 731, no name and no embossing, white milk glass
  ...................................... 3,000.00

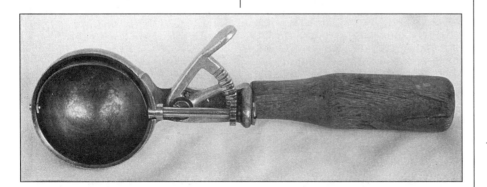

**Scoop, Peerless, mechanical, wood handle, aluminum, 8-3/8" l, $20.**

CD 739, no name and no embossing, similar to jade green milk glass .........................3,000.00

CD 737, Leffert's/blank, green ..........................................2,500.00

CD 790, no name and no embossing, known as Tea Pot, aqua ...............................2,200.00

CD 788, no name and no embossing, known as slash top ..........................................2,200.00

The six Fry Glass insulators are not counted in this survey. They are not common threadless insulators because they were made only between 1844 and 1865.

**History:** The invention of the telegraph in 1832 created the need for a glass or ceramic insulator. The first patent was given to Ezra Cornell in 1844. The principal manufacturing era lasted from 1850 to the mid-1900s. Leading companies included Armstrong (1938-1969), Brookfield (1865-1922), California (1912-1916), Gayner (1920-1922), Hemingray (1871-1919), Lynchburg (1923-1925), Maydwell (1935-1940), McLaughlin (1923-1925), and Whitall Tatum (1920-1938).

Initially, insulators were threadless. Shortly after the Civil War, L. A. Cauvet received a patent for a threaded insulator. Drip points prevented water from laying on the insulator and causing a short. The double skirt kept moisture from the peg or pin.

There are about 500 different styles of glass insulators, each of which has been given a "CD" (consolidated design) number as found in N. R. Woodward's *Glass Insulator in America*. The style of the insulator is the only key to the numbering. Colors and names of the makers and all lettering found on the same style insulator have nothing to do with the CD number.

**References:** Marilyn Albers and N.R. Woodward, *Glass Insulators from Outside North America*, 2nd Revision, and companion price guide, available from authors (14715 Oak Bend Drive, Houston, TX 77079), 1993; Michael G. *Guthrie, Fake, Altered and Repaired Insulators*, by Michael G. Guthrie, available from author (1209 W. Menlo, Fresno, CA 93711), 1988; Mark Lauckner, *Canadian Railway Communications Insulators 1880-1920*, available from author (Mayne Island,

B.C. Canada V0N-2J0), 1995; *Rarity and Price Guide*, available from author, 1998; John and Carol McDougald, *Insulators*, 2 Vols., available from authors (P.O. Box 1003, St. Charles, IL 60174) 1990; —, *1998 Price Guide for Insulators*, available from authors, 1998; N. R. Woodward, *Glass Insulator in America*, published by author, 1973; Fred Padgett, *Dreams of Glass: The Story of William McLaughlin and His Glass Company*, available from author (P.O. Box 1122, Livermore, CA 94551), 1996

**Periodicals:** *Crown Jewels of the Wire*, P.O. Box 1003, St. Charles, IL 60174; *Rainbow Riders' Trading Post*, P.O. Box 1423, Port Heuneme, CA 93044.

**Collectors' Clubs:** Capital District Insulator Club, 41 Crestwood Dr., Schenectady, NY 12306; Central Florida Insulator Collectors Club, 707 NE 113th St, North Miami, FL 33161; Chesapeake Bay Insulator Club, 10 Ridge Rd., Catonsville, MD 21228; Lone Star Insulator Club, P.O. Box 1317, Buna, TX 77612; National Insulator Association, 1315 Old Mill Path, Broadview Heights, OH 44147; Yankee Polecat Insulator Club, 79 New Boltom Rd., Manchester, CT 06040.

**Museums:** Big Thicket Museum, Saratoga, TX; Edison Plaza Museum, Beaumont, TX.

**Website:** http://www.insulators.com

CD 102, Brookfield, aqua ...............5.00
CD 102, C. G. I. Co., smoky amethyst .................................................10.00
CD 102, Diamond
Ice blue.....................................5.00
Light aqua, wrinkles and bubbles ..................................................2.00
Light aqua, milk swirls, skirt chip ................................................20.00
CD 121, Diamond, light aqua, chips ..................................................2.00
CD 121, McLaughlin
Dark emerald ..........................12.00
Dark yellow-green...................30.00
CD 134, C. E. L. Co., jade-ite-type, flat base chip, embossing ............90.00
CD 134, G. E. Co., aqua...............10.00
CD 143, Canadian Pacific Railway Co., light yellow-green.......................5.00
CD 143, Standard, aqua, 2 small chips .................................................10.00
CD 145, E. D. R., light blue, bruise, chips ......................................10.00
CD 145, McLaughlin, light cornflower, fracture in front.........................25.00
CD 145, no embossing, Canadian, peach, rub ................................7.00

Hemingray, #9, aqua, 3-3/4" h, $7.50.

CD 152, Diamond
Blue........................................ 15.00
Ice green ............................... 10.00
Light green.............................. 10.00
CD 154, Diamond
Dark straw............................... 5.00
Ice green, emb ........................ 5.00
Peach...................................... 5.00
Straw, threaded skirt, chip......... 5.00
CD 154, Dominion
Light aqua, large #, chip ......... 12.50
Light green, emb ...................... 5.00
Straw....................................... 5.00
Yellow-green tint ..................... 30.00
CD 154, Hemingray, blue ......... 24.00
CD 155, Armstrong, dark olive ..... 12.00
CD 155, Dominion, ice aqua ......... 5.00
CD 162, Hemingray, medium blue....6.00
CD 162, McLaughlin
Dark aqua sage ........................ 5.00
Dark blue sage ....................... 10.00
CD 162, N. E. G. M. Co., green, seed bubbles, chip........................... 25.00
CD 164, Hemingray, ice blue, milk streak .................................... 5.00
CD 164, Maydwell, pink, mold #3 10.00
CD 164, McLaughlin
Dark emerald .......................... 10.00
Light blue ............................... 10.00
Light yellow-green ................... 10.00
CD 168, Hemingray, ice green ..... 10.00
CD 233, Pyrex, clear..................... 5.00
CD 238, Hemingray, green tint ....... 5.00
CD 257, Hemingray
Blue-aqua ............................... 20.00
Ice green, wide groove............ 20.00

# Irons

**Collecting Hints:** Heavy rusting, pitting, and missing parts detract from an iron's value. More advanced collectors may accept some of these defects on a rare or unusual iron. However, the beginning collector is urged to concentrate on irons in very good to excellent condition.

Many unusual types of irons came from Europe and the Orient. These foreign examples are desirable, especially since some models were prototypes for later American-made irons.

Irons made between 1850 to 1910 are plentiful and varied. Many models and novelty irons still have not been documented by collectors.

Electric irons are just beginning to find favor among collectors but are not being added to older collections. Those with special features (temperature indicators, self-contained stands, sets) and those with Deco styling are the most desirable.

**History:** Ironing devices have been used for many centuries, with the earliest references dating from 1100. Irons from medieval times, the Renaissance, and the early industrial eras can be found in Europe but are rare. Fine engraved brass irons and hand-wrought irons predominated prior to 1850. After 1850, the iron underwent a series of rapid evolutionary changes.

Between 1850 and 1910, irons were heated in four ways: 1) a hot metal slug was inserted into the body, 2) a burning solid, e.g., coal or charcoal, was placed in the body, 3) a liquid or gas, e.g., alcohol, gasoline, or natural gas, was fed from an external tank and burned in the body, or 4) conduction heat was used, usually by drawing heat from a stove top.

**References:** Dave Irons, *Irons by Irons*, published by author, 1994; —, *More Irons by Irons*, published by author, 1996; —, *Pressing Iron Patents*, published by author, 1994. Note: The books by Dave Irons are available from the author at 223 Covered Bridge Rd, Northampton, PA 18067.

**Periodical:** *Iron Talk*, P.O. Box 68, Waelder, TX 78959.

**Collectors' Clubs:** Club of the Friends of Ancient Smoothing Irons, P.O. Box 215, Carlsbad, CA 92008; Midwest Sad Iron Collectors Club, 24 Nob Hill Dr., St. Louis, MO 63138.

**Museums:** Henry Ford Museum, Dearborn, MI; Shelburne Museum, Shelburne, VT; Sturbridge Village, Sturbridge, MA.

**Reproduction Alert:** The most frequently reproduced irons are the miniatures, especially the swan's neck and flat irons. Reproductions of some large European varieties have been made, but poor construction, use of thin metals, and the unusually fine condition easily identifies them as new. More and more European styles are being reproduced each year. Construction techniques are better than before and aging processes can fool many knowledgeable collectors. Look for heavy pitting on the reproductions and two or more irons that are exactly alike. Few American irons have been reproduced at this time, other than the miniatures.

**Advisors:** David and Sue Irons.

### Charcoal

Box
    Double chimney, Ne Plus Ultra, 1902 ........................................ 200.00
    Moveable chimney, Chinese, 1930s ........................................... 80.00
    Tall chimney, E. Bless, R. Drake, 1852 ....................................... 100.00
Pan, Japanese, rounded top surface, no designs, long handle .......... 75.00

### Children's

Block Grip
    ACW, 3-3/8" ............................. 75.00
    Geneva, IL, #2-1/2 .................. 110.00
    Sleeve, Walker, Boston, 4-3/4" ............................................... 160.00
    Wapak #2, 4" ............................ 60.00
Cast Swan, mold mark under beak, 2" ............................................... 110.00
Charcoal, black, figural latch head ............................................... 140.00
Dover Sadiron, No. 812, 4" ........... 50.00
Enterprise, #115, 3-7/8" ................ 90.00
French
    PG, thing base, 4" .................... 50.00
    Rooster design, 4" .................. 180.00
Glass, candy container, 3-7/8" ...... 40.00
Goffer, wire "S" standard, brass barrel ............................................... 150.00
Hollow Grip, handle folded under, Kenrick, 3" ....................................... 80.00
Ober, Chagrin Falls, O.
    No. 1, sleeve .......................... 150.00
    No. 15, 4-3/8" ........................ 160.00
Slug, brass, English, 3-1/4" ......... 130.00
Wire Handle
    Cast, no marks, 2-1/2" ............. 40.00
    Mexican, Amozoc, engraved with leaves, 2-3/4" ......................... 150.00
Wood Grip
    Dover, USA, 3-1/2" ................... 50.00

Liberty Head, 3-3/4" ................ 85.00
Victor #10 ............................. 150.00

### Flat Irons

All cast iron
    English, Cannon, 5-1/4" .......... 40.00
    French, Le Caiffa, #5, 6-1/2" .... 75.00
    Ober #6 .................................. 50.00
    Wapak #4 ................................ 20.00
Boxed set of Enterprise, 5 irons, 3 handles, 2 trivets ......................... 350.00
Cold Handle
    Enterprise, Star Iron, 6-7/8" ...... 60.00
    Slant handle, 7-3/8" ............... 150.00
    Universal Thermo Co., 6-3/8" ... 100.00
    Weida's Pat 1876, 7" ............. 150.00

### Fluters

Combination Type
    Charcoal, M.S.. Pease, rocker in handle ................................... 190.00
    Hewitt 1873 Revolving .......... 250.00
    Knapp Aug. 2, '70, flutes inside ............................................... 160.00
Machine Type
    Crown, Am Machine, Phila, PA ............................................... 150.00
    Dudley, fluter, 1876 ............... 300.00
    Orig Knox, North Bros., Phila, PA ............................................... 160.00
Rocker Type
    Geneva, IL, "Heat This" on base ............................................... 70.00
    The Best .................................. 75.00
    The Erie, clip on top rocker.... 200.00
Roller
    Am. Machine, wood handle ..... 80.00
    Clarks, curved handle .......... 175.00

### Goffering

All brass, English, tripod Queen Anne feet ........................................... 275.00
Double Barrel, cast iron, openwork, cast base ........................................ 450.00
"S" wire standard, round base, common ............................................... 100.00

### Liquid Fuel

Gasoline
    Coleman, Model 5, green enamel ............................................... 170.00
    Jubilee Iron, 1904 ................. 150.00
    Sun Mfg. Co., 1904 ............... 125.00
    The Monitor, tank in front ........ 80.00

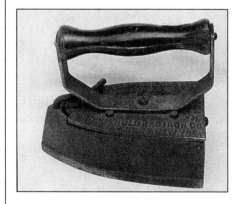

**Natural Gas, Household Gas Iron Co., Phila. & NY, $25.**

**Speciality, polishing, mkd "P. J. O.," $25.**

Natural Gas
    Acetylene Stove Mfg. Co. ........ 75.00
    Fletcher Laurel, gray, white agate
    .............................................. 185.00
    Iwantu Comfort gas iron........... 70.00
    Wright 1911............................. 90.00

**Special Purpose**

Hat
    Ball on wood handle ................ 85.00
    Egg on a stand ...................... 150.00
    Slug, Mahony, 8 slide gate.... 120.00
    Wood handle, 2 curved grooves in
    bottom.................................... 110.00

Miscellaneous
    Flower/leaf, two brass pcs ..... 100.00
    Glove form, all brass, 4 fingers
    .............................................. 150.00
    Sleeve, cast, rope handle ........ 45.00
    Sleeve, long handle ............... 150.00
    Sleeve, 2 pc cold handle, Sensible

#5............................................. 50.00

Polishers
    Carron #2, round bottom ......... 80.00
    Enterprise, No. 101................. 90.00
    French, grid bottom .............. 120.00
    Mahony, grid bottom............... 50.00
    Sweeney Iron, 1896 .............. 150.00

**Slug**

Box
    Danish, all brass, small size, open-
    work handle, 5" ...................... 160.00
    European, drop-in back, leather
    wrapped handle ................... 200.00
    Oxtongue
        Brass, saw grip wood handle,
        hinged gate...................... 190.00
        Brown Foster, top lifts off... 250.00
        Handmade, "L" handle, wrought
        iron, 1800s ........................ 200.00

# J

# Jewelry, Costume

**Collecting Hints**: Scarcity and demand drive the market for costume jewelry. Demand is greatest for pieces marked with a recognizable and sought-after designer's or manufacturer's name. Name alone, however, does not guarantee high value. Collectors should also consider quality of design and manufacture, size, and color. Condition is of primary importance because costume jewelry is easily damaged and difficult to repair well. Certain types of unsigned pieces, particularly those made of Bakelite and other plastics, generate collector interest. Because costume jewelry is wearable, pieces should be chosen with personal style and wardrobe in mind.

**History**: The term "costume jewelry" was not used until the 1920s, when Coco Chanel made the wearing of frankly faux jewels an acceptable part of haute couture. Prior to the Jazz Age, manufacturers mass-produced imitation jewelry—exact copies of the real thing. Fine jewelry continued to exert its influence on costume jewelry in the 20th-century but, because they were liberated from the costly constraints of valuable gemstones and metals, designers could be more extravagant in producing pieces made of non-precious materials.

By the 1930s, when more cost-effective methods were developed, casting superseded die-stamping in mass-production. The Great Depression instigated the use of the first entirely synthesized plastic, trade named "Bakelite," for colorful and inexpensive jewelry. During World War II, restrictions and shortages forced manufacturers to turn to sterling silver as a replacement for base white metals, and to experiment with new materials such as Lucite (DuPont's trade name for acrylic). Today, Lucite and sterling vermeil (gold-plated) animals and other figurals of the period, known as jelly bellies, are highly collectible. Other World War II novelty items were made of make-do materials such as wood, ceramic, textiles, and natural pods and seeds.

In the prosperous 1950s, high-fashion rhinestone, faux pearl, and colored-glass jewelry signed with the names of well-known couturiers and other designers was sold in elegant department stores. A matching suite—necklace, bracelet, earrings, brooch—was the proper complement to the ensemble of a well-groomed 1950s' woman.

**References**: Lillian Baker, *Fifty Years of Collectible Fashion Jewelry*, Collector Books, 1986, 1992 value update; —, *100 Years of Collectible Jewelry*, Collector Books, 1978, 1993 value update; —, *Twentieth Century Fashionable Plastic Jewelry*, Collector Books, 1992; Joanne Dubbs Ball, *Costume Jewelers*, Schiffer, 1990; Dee Battle and Alayne Lesser, *Best of Bakelite and Other Plastic Jewelry*, Schiffer, 1995; Vivienne Becker, *Fabulous Costume Jewelry*, Schiffer, 1993; Howard L. Bell, Jr., *Cuff Jewelry*, published by author, 1994; Jeanenne Bell, *Answers to Questions about Old Jewelry*, 4th Edition, Krause Publications, 1995; Matthew L. Burkholz and Linda Lictenberg Kaplan, *Copper Art Jewelry*, Schiffer, 1992; Deanna Farneti Cera (ed.), *Jewels of Fantasy*, Harry N. Abrams, 1992; Maryanne Dolan, *Collecting Rhinestone Jewelry*, 4th Edition, Krause Publications, 1998; Roseann Ettinger, *Forties & Fifties Popular Jewelry*, Schiffer, 1994; —, *Popular Jewelry*, Schiffer, 1990; —, *Popular Jewelry of the 60s, 70s, and 80s*, Schiffer, 1997; Tony Grasso, *Bakelite Jewelry*, Chartwell, 1996; Gabrielle Greindl, *Gems of Costume Jewelry*, Abbeville Press, 1990; S. Sylvia Henzel, *Collectible Costume Jewelry*, revised ed., Wallace-Homestead, 1987, 1990 value update; Mary Jo Izard, *Wooden Jewelry and Novelties*, Schiffer, 1998; Sibylle Jargstorf, *Baubles, Buttons and Beads*, Schiffer, 1991; —, *Glass in Jewelry*, Schiffer, 1991; Lyngerde Kelley and Nancy Schiffer, *Plastic Jewelry*, Schiffer, 1987, 1995 value update; J. J. Kellner, *First Complete Reference Guide Siam Sterling Nielloware*, published by author, 1993; Jack and Elynore "Pet" Kerins, *Collecting Antique Stickpins*, Collector Books, 1995; Jan Lindenberger, *Collecting Plastic Jewelry*, Schiffer, 1996; J. L. Lynnlee, *All That Glitters*, Schiffer, Ltd., 1986, 1993 value update; Harrice Simons Miller, *Costume Jewelry*, 2nd Edition, Avon Books, 1994; Fred Rezazadeh, *Costume Jewelry, a Practical Handbook & Value Guide*, Collector Books, 1998; Christie Romero, *Warman's Jewelry*, 2nd edi-

tion, Krause Publications, 1998; Nancy N. Schiffer, *Costume Jewelry*, Schiffer, 1988, 1992 value update; —, *Fun Jewelry*, Revised and Updated, Schiffer, 1996; —, *Rhinestones!*, Schiffer, 1993; —, *Silver Jewelry Designs*, Schiffer, 1997; Sheryl Gross Shatz, *What's It Made of?*, 3rd Edition, published by author (10931 Hunting Horn Dr., Santa Ana, CA 92705), 1996; Cherri Simonds, *Collectible Costume Jewelry*, Collector Books, 1997; Nicholas D. Snider, *Antique Sweetheart Jewelry*, Schiffer, 1996.

**Periodical:** *Auction Market Resource for Gems & Jewelry*, P.O. Box 7683, Rego Park, NY 11374

**Videotapes:** C. Jeanenne Bell, "Antique and Collectible Jewelry Video Series," Vol. I (1994), Vol. II (1994), Antique Images; Christie Romero, "Hidden Treasures," Venture Entertainment Group (P.O. Box 55113, Sherman Oaks, CA 91413), 1992, 1995 value update.

**Collectors' Clubs**: Leaping Frog Antique Jewelry and Collectable Club, 4841 Martin Luther Blvd., Sacramento, CA 95820; National Cuff Link Society, P.O. Box 346, Prospect Heights, IL 60070; Vintage Fashion & Costume Jewelry Club, P.O. Box 265, Glen Oaks, NY 11004.

**Reproduction Alert**: Recasts and knockoffs are widespread. Copies of high-end signed pieces—e.g., Trifari jelly bellies, Eisenberg Originals, and Boucher—are common. New Bakelite (sometimes called "fakelite") and marriages of old Bakelite parts are also cropping up in many areas.

### Bracelet

Ciner, hinged bangle, zebra motif, black and white painted enamel, green cabochon glass eyes, colorless rhinestone accents, sgd, c1960 ....... 140.00

Eisenberg

Linked clusters of marquise-cut colorless rhinestones, v-spring and box clasp sgd "Eisenberg" (block letters), safety chain, c1950, 7-1/2" l ....... 60.00

Original, links of lg cushion-cut aqua-colored rhinestones alternating with rows of three sm circ colorless rhinestones, wm, v-spring and box clasp, sgd "Eisenberg Original," c1935-40, 7" l ..................... 210.00

Haskell, Miriam, strand of lg textured faux pearls flanked by two strands of smaller textured faux pearls, ornate multi-loop bow motif front clasp of faux seed pearls and colorless rhinestones, sgd "Miriam Haskell" on oval plate, c1950, 7-1/2" l ............. 135.00

**Bracelet, link, glass, gold-plated brass, enamel, c. 1930-35, three links of prong-set floral/foliate pattern molded green glass rectangular cabochons alternating with four domed square gold-plated brass with geometric design enameled in red, white and black, marked "GERMANY" and marked M in triangle, spring ring closure, 3/4" w x 7-1/2", $300. (Charles Pinkham Collection).**

Hollycraft
Link, lg multi-colored emerald-cut rhinestones flanked by white metal S-scrolls set with multi-colored circ-cut rhinestones, foldover clasp, safety chain, sgd, "Hollycraft COPR 1957," 7" l ................................ 82.00
Sq links set throughout with multi-colored rhinestones, variety of shapes, goldtone metal, foldover clasp, safety chain, sgd "Hollycraft," 7-1/2" l x 1-1/4" w .................... 135.00
Jomaz, hinged bangle, domed oval hinged at the sides, with irregularly-shaped cells of translucent blue and green painted enamel within gp raised edges, central crossover design pavé-set with sm colorless rhinestones, rhinestone-set thumbpiece on V-spring, sgd "JOMAZ," c1965, 2-1/4" inside dia ......... 165.00
Rebajes, copper link, seven appl die-struck leaves, mkd "Rebajes," v-spring and box clasp, c1950, 1" w x 6-1/2" ........................................ 65.00
Renoir, copper cuff, openwork block design, sgd "Renoir," c1950, 2" w ................................................. 35.00
Tortolani, hinged bangle, goldtone, three-dimensional zodiac figures interspersed with stars, sgd "© Tortolani" in script, snap clasp at center opening, c1960, 2-1/2" w at center ................................................. 200.00

Unknown Maker
Bangle, Bakelite, apple juice color, carved ropetwist design, c1935, 1-1/2" w ............................... 357.50
Bangle, Bakelite, laminated, striped red, yellow, and dk blue Bakelite (oxidized, was red, white, and blue), c1940, 3/4" w .......................... 200.00

Bangle, hinged, carved wood horse's head with painted eye and leather bridle surmounting a leather-topped circ wood disk, leather laced through punched holes and wrapped around outside edge, mounted on a hinged, shaped wood bangle with leather lacing through holes around center, c1940-45, top 1-3/4" dia, 2-1/8" inside dia ...........................................200.00
Bangle, hinged, sterling with black Bakelite inlaid dots, Taxco (Mexico) maker's mark, 1-1/4" w........... 825.00
Charm, sterling, c1950-55, six ster charms of Cub Scout emblems, labeled "CUB SCOUTS BSA" (one also reading "DEN MOTHER," another "BOBCAT") in circ, sq, and rect shapes on a ster chain, spring ring closure, all pieces mkd "STERLING," chain 7-3/4" tl ................................................75.00

**Brooch/Pin**

Artisan, floral spray with ribbon, nine faux pearl flower buds, three with colorless baguette rhinestone stems, sm colorless rhinestones. throughout, all stones replaced, mkd "ARTISAN N.Y.," safety catch, c1945, 3-7/8" w x 2-3/4" ............................... 100.00
Boucher
Bunch of three radishes with leaves, red and green enamel, pavé colorless rhinestones around bottom of each, rhodium-plated wm roots and stems, sgd "MB" with symbol for Marcel Boucher, c1940, 2-1/2" w x 3" ................................................. 740.50

**Brooch/pin, rhinestones, rhodium-plated white metal, painted enamel, 1. 1935, depicting a peacock with scrolled tail feathers, two rows of large marquise-cut colorless rhinestones and white-metal wire terminating in large pink, blue, yellow and green rhinestones, body in small colorless pavé rhinestones, blue rhinestone eye, traces of enamel on feet and crest, safety catch, 2-1/8" w x 3-3/4", $225. (Leigh Leshner collection).**

Flower head, six petals pavé-set with sm yellow rhinestones, each bisected by a line of colorless baguette rhinestones, cluster of sm blue rhinestones in center, turned edges of petals pavé-set with colorless rhinestones, textured gold-toned finish on rev, mkd "© Boucher" (block letters) # 7713, c1950-60, 2-3/8" ..................... 230.00
Cini, sterling, foliate spray with five articulated drops, each set with an oval moonstone, appl plaque on rev mkd "Sterling by Cini," c1940, 2-1/4" w x 4-3/8" .............................. 175.00
Coro
Coffee pot shape, pierced gp white metal with floral decoration in red, green, blue and colorless r.s., colorless rhinestone-set handle, red rhinestone-set base, sgd "Coro," c1940, 1-1/2" w x 2-1/8" ......... 235.00
Sterling vermeil, lg fancy key shape, top center prong-set with a lg blue glass cabochon flanked by two smaller red glass cabochons, sm colorless rhinestone-set heart-shaped frame entwined with gp sterling snakes, red r.s. eyes, surmounted by a blue glass cabochon, key terminal prong-set with red glass cabochon (missing two others), sm colorless rhinestones, rev mkd "STERLING Coro-Craft" with Pegasus trademark, c1945, 4-3/8" w x 1-1/2" ............350.00
Sterling vermeil, stylized floral spray with two lg prong-set faceted lozenge-shaped pink glass blossoms and sm colorless rhinestones pavé-set in gp stems and leaves, rev sgd "CoroCraft STERLING," c1940-45, 2-1/4" w x 4" ........................................250.00
Stylized rooster with lg faceted rect red glass center, painted enamel tail and features in red, green, black and white, mkd "Coro," c1940, 2-1/4" w x 2-1/8"..................................... 185.00
Eisenberg
Lg leaf motif, lg oval colorless rhinestones outlined in smaller circ colorless rhinestones, with "veins" of very sm rhinestones, sgd "Eisenberg Ice©," c1955-60, 3" w x 2-1/2" ................................................. 70.00
Original, opposed C-scrolls tapering down to a point forming a fancy shield shape, set throughout with lg and med oval, emerald-cut and marquise-shaped pink rhinestones, outlined with sm colorless rhinestones, prong-set in gp white metal, appl plate on rev mkd "Eisenberg Original," c1935-40, 3-1/4" w x 3-1/2" ...................... 250.00
Overlapping open circles of colorless circ rhinestones and opaque white circ cabochons, outlined with a row of marquise-shaped opaque white cabochons along one side, sgd "Eisenberg" (block letters), c1950, 2" x 2" .......................... 50.00
Tiger motif, top view, textured gold-tone metal set throughout with sm colorless rhinestones, sgd "Eisenberg Ice©," c1970, 3-1/4" x 1-1/2 .......85.00

Haskell, Miriam, gp brass wreath of ivy leaves and vines intertwined with opaque green glass seed beads around lg central opaque green glass circ cabochon, appl oval plate on rev sgd "Miriam Haskell," c1950, 2" dia ................................. 105.00

Hollycraft
Floral wreath design, lg center circ red rhinestone encircled by goldtone floral and foliate motifs set with sm red rhinestones, sgd "Hollycraft, Copr 1954," 1-1/2" w x 3/8" ...... 40.00
Pinwheel design of pale to dk green circ and marquise-shaped rhinestones, sgd "Hollycraft, Copr 1952," 2" dia ...................................... 100.00

Kenneth J. Lane
Butterfly motif, prong-set throughout with multicolored marquise-shaped and circ rhinestones, sgd "KJL," c1970, 3" x 3" ........................... 57.00
Maltese cross of lg green oval cabochons and circ green rhinestones around center circ blue rhinestone, outlined in marquise and sq-cut colorless rhinestones, sgd "KJL," c1965, 3" x 3" ........................... 35.00

Schreiner
Circ cluster of mottled orange and dark green cabochons interspersed with aurora borealis rhinestones and faux pearls, sgd "Schreiner New York," c1955-60, 2-1/4" dia ...... 100.00
Domed triangular cluster, center circ dk blue rose-cut rhinestone encircled by sm circ pale blue rhinestones, three sm opaque turquoise cabochons prong-set around circle, lg oval and circ lt and dk blue rose-cut rhinestones prong-set around outer edges, sgd "Schreiner New York," c1960, 2-1/4" x 2-1/4" ................. 85.00

Trifari
Faux pearl spray, green enamel leaves with colorless rhinestone accents, sgd "Trifari©," c1950, 2-1/8" w x 1-1/4" ................................... 55.00
Vendome, abstract floral spray, shades of pink and fuchsia lg and sm marquise-shaped rhinestones mounted on goldtone wires, suspending articulated lg pink pear-shaped rhinestones, two at top, one at bottom, sgd "Vendome," c1960, 1-3/4" w x 3-1/2" tl .................... 70.00

Weiss
Star-shaped cluster of lg pear-shaped and smaller marquise-shaped colorless rhinestones prong-set in rhodium-plated wm, sgd "Albert Weiss New York," c1950, 1-1/2" dia ..... 40.00

Unknown maker
Bakelite, red bar suspending three red cutout anchor motifs from brass jump rings, c1940, 1-3/4" w x 2-1/2" ............................................. 50.00
Bakelite and wood, tinted wood log cross-section suspending six carved green Bakelite cherries from vinyl-coated string (coating partially flaked off), c1935, 3-1/4" tl ..... 130.00
Bakelite, baseball bat-shaped bar,

mottled green and yellow, suspending a carved yellow baseball glove with ball from vinyl-coated lacing, c1935-40, 2-1/2" w x 2" ......... 675.00
Bakelite, carved orange carrot with green coated vinyl string top, c1935, 4" l ..................................... 585.00
Bakelite, carved disk with moon face, butterscotch color, c1935, 2" dia, missing pinstem .............. 105.00
Celluloid, oval laminated gray and black plaque with appl gray pharaoh's head, c1925, 1-3/4" w x 2-1/4" ............................................. 65.00
Lucite, rev-carved and tinted red, bird in flight, ptd eye, 4-1/4" wing span ...................................... 52.00
Lucite, tinted yellow pear, carved dk wood leaves, 2" w x 3" ............ 58.00
Molded plastic, white, partly ptd red and blue, depicting two Scottie dogs riding a motorcycle, c1940, 1-1/2" w x 1-1/8" ................................. 68.00
Wood, carved lt brown elephant's head with ears spread, ptd glass eyes, colorless Lucite tusks, riveted pin back assembly, c1935-40, 5" w x 3-1/2" .................................. 100.00

## Clip

Eisenberg Original
Retro Modern, goldtone floral spray with lg emerald-cut green rhinestone at base, smaller emerald-cut green rhinestone encircled by circ-cut green rhinestones forming flowerhead, marquise-cut green rhinestones in center of second flowerhead, sgd "Eisenberg Original," c1940-45, 3-1/4" w x 2-1/2" ............................................. 155.00
Sterling, lg foliate spray, multiple "branches," each with a line of sm colorless rhinestones terminating in a lg oval rhinestone, sgd "Eisenberg Original," mkd "sterling," c1940, 2-1/4" w x 4" ......................... 250.00
Penguin in a tux with blue "moonstone" glass cab belly, pavé colorless rhinestone accents, black and red ptd details, double-pronged hinged clip on rev, c1935, 3/4" w x 1-1/2" ............................................. 30.00
Staret, openwork shield shape set throughout with lg oval and sm circ colorless rhinestones (3 sm stones missing), c1935-40, sgd "Staret," 2-1/8" w x 2-1/2" .................... 115.00
Trifari, ptd enamel floral spray, red flowers, colorless rhinestone centers and accents, green leaves, brown stems on rhodium-plated white metal, c1935-40, sgd "Trifari," 1-1/2" w x 2-1/2" ......................................... 90.00

## Cuff Links, pr

Christian Dior, gold filled, textured ovals, orig box, c1960, sgd "Christian Dior," ................................. 36.00
Georg Jensen, sterling, rect checkerboard pattern, c1950, sgd "Georg Jensen" in dotted oval, "sterling Denmark," #113 .................... 162.00

Duette, Coro, sgd
"Jelly belly" fish, sterling vermeil, Lucite centers, colorless rhinestone accents, red glass cab eyes, blue glass cab mouths, c1940, sgd "Coro Duette," mkd "sterling," 1931 pat no., 2-1/2" w x 1-3/4" ............. 300.00
Retro, opposed goldtone swirls set with colorless rhinestones, sgd "Coro Duette," 1931 patent no., 2-1/2" w x 1-1/2" ................................ 75.00

## Earrings, pr

Chanel, faux pearl "puffy" heart suspended from circ faux pearl surmount, in textured goldtone setting, orig box, c1965-70, sgd "© Chanel," clip backs, 2" l ...................... 75.00
Ciner, textured goldtone circ domes, sm faux pearls in star-cut settings, c1960, clip backs sgd "Ciner," 1" dia ............................................. 32.50
Eisenberg, clusters of prong-set cobalt blue marquise and circ rhinestones, sm colorless rhinestone accents, c1950, sgd "Eisenberg" in block letters, clip backs, 3/4" w x 1-1/4 .............................................. 53.00
Hollycraft, lg multicolored clusters of circ, oval, marquise and baguette rhinestones prong-set in goldtone metal, sgd "Hollycraft Copr 1955," screwbacks, 1-1/2" l ............... 138.00
KJL, "shrimp," split ribbed shell shape, half in faux coral plastic, other half polished gp wm, clip backs, c1970, mkd "KJL" on appl oval for Kenneth J. Lane, 1/2" w x 1" ................................................ 75.00
Matisse, circ domed red-enameled disk with appl copper dome at bottom and appl copper wires at top forming an abstract eye, c1952, one clipback earring mkd "Matisse" in script, 3/4" dia ....................... 20.00
Rebajes, copper, oval swirls around central domes, c1950, clip backs sgd "Rebajes," 1" x 1-1/4" ........ 55.00
Robert, flowerhead clusters of green rhinestones, faux pearl centers, c1950, clip backs mkd "Robert," 7/8" dia ............................................. 34.00
Sarah Coventry, textured silvertone apples with leaves, c1955-60, clip backs sgd "Sarah Cov," 1" w x 1-1/4" ............................................. 44.00
Sascha Brastoff, enamel on copper concave disks with yellow rooster motif on white ground, c1950, 1" dia ................................................ 38.00
Weiss, flowerhead clips, lg dk blue circ rhinestone encircled by marquise-cut lt blue rhinestones, c1950, sgd "Weiss" on clipback, 1" dia ................................................ 36.50

## Necklace

Bonaz, Auguste, Galalith (casein plastic), central oval plaque, half red, half black, overlapping two smaller oval plaques flanked by grad rounded rect links, one side red, the other side black, Fr, sgd "Auguste Bonaz," metal barrel clasp; provenance:

worn by Barbra Streisand in the movie "The Main Event," c1930, approx 16" tl ........................ 3,450.00

Eisenberg, double row torsade of emerald-cut colorless rhinestones, surmounted by two short rows of circ colorless r.s. at center, continuing to a sm r.s.-set chain and keyhole clasp mkd "EISENBERG," c1950, 1" w (at center), 17-1/4" tl ................... 250.00

Haskell, Miriam, clusters of three molded red glass and brass bead flowerheads with red rhinestone centers, suspended from red molded flowerhead beads, brass and colorless faceted glass rondels, alternating with red faceted glass beads, continuing to a hook clasp, c1960, mkd "MIRIAM HASKELL" on attached oval hang tag, 20" tl .............. 420.00

Unknown Maker

Brown cellulose acetate chain suspending five Bakelite oranges, 3/4" dia, and six green cellulose acetate leaves, c1935-40, 17" tl .......... 400.00

Western motifs, seven charms: gun, two whiskey jugs, two cowboy boots, accordion, and hat, suspended from brown celluloid chain, brass spring ring closure, c1940, 16-1/4" tl, boot charm 3/4" w x 1-3/8" ............... 70.00

Vendome, a row of paired circ-cut aurora borealis alternating with single circ-cut amber-colored rhinestones, suspending clusters of sm and lg circ-cut and emerald-cut green, orange, aurora borealis and amber-colored rhinestones, fancy pronged wm settings, terminating in a rhinestone-set chain and hook clasp mkd "© VENDOME," appl plaque rev center mkd "Vendôme," c1960, 1-7/8" w x 18" tl ........... 115.00

**Pendant**

Eisenberg, owl on a branch in dk, medium, and lt green, and black ptd enamel, suspended from a gp wm snake chain, pendant rev mkd "EISENBERG," c1970, pendant 1-1/4" w x 2-1/2" (with bail), chain 20-1/22" tl ................................................. 50.00

Joseff of Hollywood, stamped gp brass in a design of three overlapping circ disks with open scroll and geometric motif, suspending by two outside and two inside crossing chains a lg circ disk with geo design, c1950, appl plate on rev mkd "Joseff," hook and ring clasp on gp brass foxtail chain, pendant 3" w x 5", chain 16" tl ................................................. 200.00

Unknown maker

Lucite "ice cube" held by rhodium-plated wm tongs on a matching lg curb link chain, pendant 1-3/4" w x 4", chain 30" tl .......................... 75.00

Red Lucite heart pendant surmounted by appl sterling silver Air Force emblem, suspended from red celluloid chain, c1945, pendant 1-3/4" w x 1-3/4", chain 19" tl ............. 145.00

**Ring,** Vogue, triangular cluster, one lg half-round faux pearl, two flowerheads, each center set with five colorless rhinestones encircled by glass cabs, one streaked turq-colored and the other mottled green, c1960, mkd "VOGUE," adjustable shank, 1-7/8" w x 1-5/8" ............ 50.00

**Suite**

Coro, necklace and earrings, necklace of ten linked foliate motifs, each with lg central oval blue alternating with green faux moonstone cab framed by smaller circ blue faux moonstones and blue rhinestones set in silvertone metal branches, matching clip earrings, c1950, all pcs mkd "©Coro," necklace with adjustable hook closure, 17-1/2" tl, earrings 1/2" w x 3/4" ..................................... 85.00

Eisenberg, brooch and earrings, foliate clusters of circ and marquise lg and med rhinestones, shades of green with sm colorless accents, c1950, sgd "Eisenberg" (block letters), brooch 2-1/4" w x 2-3/4", clip earrings 1" w x 1-1/4" .................. 225.00

Haskell, Miriam, bracelet, brooch, and earrings, floral clusters of pastel pink and blue glass beads, pale blue seed beads, and pale blue enameled petals on brooch and earrings, bracelet a floral cluster at the top of a double-hinged gp bangle, clip-back earrings a single flowerhead, c1960-65, all pieces mkd "MIRIAM HASKELL" on appl oval plate, bracelet 1-1/3" w x 2" (at top), 2-1/2" inside dia, brooch 2-3/4" w x 1-1/2", earrings 3/4" dia .......................... 335.00

Hobé, necklace and earrings, lariat-style necklace of goldtone metal mesh with circ central ornament and terminals set with marquise-cut citrine- and topaz-colored rhinestones, hook closure, matching clip earrings of clustered marquise rhinestones, c1950, sgd "Hobé," necklace 26-1/2" tl, center 1-3/4" w, earrings 1" w x 1-1/2" ...................................................... 108.00

Hollycraft, brooch and earrings, triangular openwork Christmas tree of intersecting ropetwist textured lines forming lozenge pattern, set with red, blue, yellow and green circ rhinestones in centers, surmounted by a rhinestone-set star, matching clip-back earrings, c1955-60, mkd "©HOLLYCRAFT," brooch 1-1/4" w x 2-3/8", earrings 3/4" w x 1-1/8" ............ 150.00

Kramer of New York, collar and bracelet, flexible openwork rows of lg and sm circ gray and aurora borealis rhinestones, c1950, sgd "Kramer of New York," collar with adjustable hook closure, 16" l, bracelet 7" l, both 1" w .............................................. 100.00

Mazer Bros., necklace and bracelet, Retro Modern, necklace of open gp links alternating with colorless rhinestone-set links suspending a central gp and rhinestone-set scrolled rib-

bon bow with two lg molded clear glass cherries and three grad clear glass cabs, mkd "Z" on rev, matching bracelet of linked molded glass cherries alternating with clear glass cab and rhinestone-set scrolls, mkd "K" on rev, both pcs mkd "Mazer," c1940, fold over clasps, necklace 16" tl, center 2-1/4" w x 2-1/2, bracelet 1" w x 7-1/2" ...................... 175.00

Rebajes, necklace and bracelet, linked pairs of copper leaves, c1950, sgd "Rebajes," 7/8" w, necklace 15" l, bracelet 7-1/2" l, can be joined to form longer necklace ............... 80.00

Regency, bracelet, brooch and earrings, clusters of champagne-colored, aurora borealis and colorless marquise and circ rhinestones, c1955, mkd "Regency," bracelet 7-1/4" l, brooch 2" dia, clip earrings 1-1/2" l .................................................. 80.00

Trifari, necklace and earrings, necklace three strands of round faux jade glass beads, knotted between each, terminating in an ornamental front clasp, 1-1/2" w x 1", goldtone foliate motif set with two lg and three sm oval green glass cabs, 20" tl, matching button-style clip earrings with central circ green glass cab, 1" dia, c1950, sgd "Trifari" (crown mk) ..................... 95.00

Weiss, necklace, bracelet, and brooch, lt blue circ, pear-shaped and marquise glass cabochons and circ rhinestones, necklace of lg pear-shaped cab flanked by four smaller pear-shaped cabs alternating with marquise cabs and circ rhinestones, continuing to a chain of circ rhinestones, hook closure, sgd "Weiss," flexible bracelet of alternating circ and marquise cabs between two rows of sm circ rhinestones sgd "Weiss," brooch a lg star shape of five pear-shaped cabs encircling circ cabs and rhinestones, unmkd, c1950, necklace 18" tl, bracelet 7" tl, brooch 2-3/8" dia ..................... 55.00

# Jukeboxes

**Collecting Hints:** Jukebox chronology falls into four distinct periods:

In the pre-1938 period, jukeboxes were constructed mainly of wood and resembled a radio or phonograph cabinet. Wurlitzer jukeboxes from this era are the most collectible, but their value usually is under $600.

From 1938 to 1948, the addition of plastics and animation units gave the jukebox a gaudier appearance. These jukeboxes played 78-RPM records. Wurlitzer jukeboxes are king, with Rock-Ola the second most popular. This era contains the most valuable models, e.g., Wurlitzer models 750, 850, 950, 1015, and 1080.

The 1940 to 1960 period is referred to as the Seeburg era. Jukeboxes of this vintage are collected for the "Happy Days" feeling (named for the TV show): drive-in food, long skirts, sweater girls, and good times. The jukeboxes, which play 45-RPM records, rate second in value to those of the 1938-1948 period, with prices usually are under $1,500.

The 1961 and newer jukeboxes often are not considered collectible because the record mechanism is not visible, thus removing an alluring quality.

There are exceptions to these generalizations. Collectors should have a price and identification guide to help make choices. Many original and reproduction parts are available for Seeburg and Wurlitzer jukeboxes. In many cases, incomplete jukeboxes can be restored. Jukeboxes that are in working order and can be maintained in that condition are the best machines to own.

Do not buy any jukebox without taking time to thoroughly educate yourself, making sure you know how collectible the particular machine is and how missing components will affect its value.

**History:** First came the phonograph. When electrical amplification became possible, the coin-operated phonograph, known as the jukebox, evolved.

The heyday of the jukebox was the 1940s. Between 1946 and 1947, Wurlitzer produced 56,000 model-1015 jukeboxes, the largest production run of all time. The jukebox was the center of every teenage hangout, from drugstores and restaurants to pool halls and dance parlors. They even invaded some private homes. Jukeboxes were cheaper than a live band, and, unlike radio, allowed listeners to hear their favorite songs whenever and as often as wished.

Styles changed in the 1960s. Portable radios coupled with "Top 40" radio stations fulfilled the desire for daily repetition of songs. Television changed evening entertainment patterns, and the jukebox vanished.

**References:** Michael Adams, Jürgen Lukas, and Thomas Maschke, *Jukeboxes*, Schiffer Publishing, 1995; Jerry Ayliffe, *American Premium Guide to Jukeboxes and Slot Machines*, 3rd Edition, Books Americana, 1991; Rick Botts, *Complete Identification Guide to the Wurlitzer Jukebox*, published by author, 1984; —, *Jukebox Restoration Guide*, published by author, 1985; Stephan K. Loots, *Official Victory Glass Price Guide to Antique Jukeboxes*, published by author, 1997; Vincent Lynch, *American Jukebox*, Chronicle Books, 1990; Scott Wood (ed.), *Blast from the Past, Jukeboxes*, L-W Book Sales, 1992.

**Periodicals:** *Always Jukin'*, 221 Yesler Way, Seattle, WA 98104; *Antique Amusements, Slot Machine & Jukebox Gazette*, 909 26th St. NW, Washington, DC 20037; *Chicagoland Program*, 414 N. Prospect Manor Ave., Mt. Prospect, IL 60056; *Coin-Op Classics*, 17844 Toiyabe St., Fountain Valley, CA 92708; *Gameroom*, P.O. Box 41, Keyport, NJ 07735; *Jukebox Collector*, 2534 SE 60th Ct. #216, Des Moines, IA 50317; *Loose Change*, 1515 South Commerce St., Las Vegas, NV 89102-2703.

**Museums:** Jukeboxes have not reached the status of museum pieces. The best way to see 100 or more jukeboxes in one place is to visit a coin-op show.

**Advisor:** Rick Botts.

AMI
    Model A .............................. 1,250.00
    Model B ................................. 800.00
    Model C ................................. 500.00
    Model D ................................. 400.00
    Model E................................. 500.00
Mills
    Model Empress................... 1,500.00
    Throne of Music .................... 850.00
Packard, Manhattan ............... 2,750.00
Rock-Ola
    Model 1422...................... 2,400.00
    Model 1426...................... 2,400.00
    Model 1428...................... 2,400.00
    Model 1432........................ 900.00
    Model 1434........................ 950.00
    Model 1436........................ 900.00
    Model 1438........................ 950.00
Seeburg
    Model 147........................ 675.00
    Model HF100G .................... 950.00
    Model HF100R .................... 950.00
    Model M100B .................... 850.00
    Model M100C .................... 950.00
    Model V-200...................... 1,400.00
Wurlitzer
    Model 412........................ 850.00
    Model 600...................... 1,200.00
    Model 700...................... 3,000.00
    Model 750...................... 5,000.00
    Model 800...................... 4,500.00
    Model 1015.................... 4,750.00

# K

## Kewpies

**Collecting Hints:** Study the dolls carefully before purchasing. Remember that composition dolls were made until the 1950s; hence, every example is not an early one.

Many collectors concentrate only on Kewpie items. A specialized collection might include other O'Neill designs, such as Scootles, Ragsy, Kewpie-Gal, Kewpie-Kins, and Ho-Ho.

The vast majority of Kewpie material is sold in the doll market where prices are relatively stable. Pricing at collectibles shows and malls fluctuates because sellers may not be familiar with the overall Kewpie market.

**History:** Rose Cecil O'Neill (1876-1944) was a famous artist, novelist, illustrator, poet, and sculptor, as well as being the creator of the Kewpie doll. O'Neill's drawing *Temptation* won her a children's art prize at the age of 14 and launched her career as an illustrator.

The Kewpie first appeared in art form in the December 1909 issue of *Ladies Home Journal* in a piece titled, "Kewpies' Christmas Frolic." The first Kewpie doll appeared in 1913. Although Geo. Borgfeldt Co. controlled the production and distribution rights to Kewpie material, Joseph L. Kallus assisted in design and manufacture through his firm, the Cameo Doll Company.

Kewpie dolls and china-decorated items rapidly appeared on the market. Many were manufactured in Germany, where 28 different factories made Kewpie-related products during the peak production years.

O'Neill eventually moved to southwest Missouri, settling at Bonniebrook near Bear Creek. She died there in 1944, and in 1947 Bonniebrook burned to the ground.

Production of Kewpie items did not stop at O'Neill's death. Kewpie material still appears as limited edition collectibles.

**References:** Janet A. Banneck, *Antique Postcards of Rose O'Neill*, Greater Chicago Productions, 1992; *Kewpie Kompanion*, Theriault's, 1994.

**Periodical:** *Traveler*, P.O. Box 4032, Portland, OR 97208.

**Collectors' Club:** International Rose O'Neill Club, P.O. Box 668, Branson, MO 65616.

**Museum:** Shepherd of the Hills Farm and Memorial Museum, near Branson, MO.

Reproduction Alert.

Blanket, 5" x 6", felt fabric, 1914 Rose O'Neill copyright fleshtone images, blue sky, tan buildings, red stitched border ....................................... 8.00
Candy Container, Kewpie standing by barrel, sun turned purple tint ... 30.00
Clip, 5/8" l, sterling, imp trademark ................................................. 30.00
Cookbook, *Jell-O Girl Entertains* .. 25.00
Dealer Sign, "The Rose O'Neill Kewpie Collection by Enesco," sgd "O'Neill," 1991, 3-3/4" h ........................... 45.00
Doll
  1-3/4" h, celluloid ..................... 40.00
  2-1/2" h, celluloid, some paint missing ............................................. 20.00
  3" h, cloth, wings, not signed .. 100.00
  8" h, chalk, black skin tone ...... 65.00
  9" h, vinyl, jointed at neck, shoulders, and hips, mkd "Cameo," two small discoloration marks, orig pantaloons ................................................. 45.00
  10" h, vinyl, head turns, mkd "Cameo" ................................... 55.00
  12" h, vinyl, orig tab, mkd "Cameo" ............................................... 125.00
Figure, Lefton
  Bewildered ............................... 12.00
  Content, 5" h ........................... 27.50
  Holding foot, 3" h ..................... 12.00
  On belly, 3-3/4" l ...................... 12.00
  Playing golf, 4" h ..................... 32.00
  Puzzled, 5" h ........................... 27.50
  Winking, 5" h ........................... 30.00
Night Light, figural, orig foil sticker "Lefton Trade Mark Exclusives Japan," #5718 stamped on bottom, 6-1/2" h .................................... 75.00
Pendant, small ............................. 10.00

**Plate, 7 Kewpies, mkd "Royal Rudolstadt, Rose O'Neill, Kewpie, Germany," 8-5/8" d, $175.**

Perfume Bottle, 2-1/2" h, porcelain, painted, glazed, stamped "Germany" in red on base, stopper missing, small chip ...................... 135.00
Pin, 2" h, A & M, mkd "Truart Sterling" ................................................. 40.00
Planter, bisque Kewpie pushing garden cart, mkd "Occupied Japan" ... 25.00
Post Card, "Can't think of an earthly thing to say, Cept I hope you are happy Valentine's Day," Kewpie writing valentines, ©Rosie O'Neill, postmarked Feb. 12, 1925, published by Gibson Art Co. ......................... 20.00
Tray, Purity Ice Cream, 17-1/2" x 12", large Kewpie holding tray with strawberry sundae on it .................. 575.00
Vase, 5-1/2" h, rim chip repaired.... 95.00

# Kitchen Collectibles

**Collecting Hints:** Bargains still can be found, especially at flea markets and garage sales. An appliance's design can help determine its age, e.g., an Art Deco toaster or coffeepot was made around 1910 to 1920.

The country decorating craze has caused most collectors to concentrate on the 1860 to 1900 period. Kitchen products of the 1900 to 1940s, with their enamel glazes and dependability, are just coming into vogue.

**History:** The kitchen was a focal point in a family's environment until frozen food, TV dinners, and microwaves changed both meal preparation and dining habits.

Many early kitchen utensils were handmade and prized by their owners. Next came a period of utilitarian products made of tin and other metals. When the housewife no longer wished to work in a sterile environment, enamel and plastic products added color, and their unique design served both aesthetic and functional purposes.

The advent of home electricity changed the type and style of kitchen products. Fads affected many items. High technology already has made inroads into the kitchen, and another revolution seems at hand.

**References:** Ellen Bercovici, Bobbie Zucker Bryson and Deborah Gillham, *Collectibles for the Kitchen, Bath and Beyond,* Antique Trader Books, 1998; Walter Dworkin, *Price Guide to Holt Howard Collectibles,* Krause Publications, 1998; Linda Fields, *Four & Twenty Blackbirds: A*

*Pictorial Identification and Value Guide for Pie Birds,* published by author, (158 Bagsby Hill Lane, Dover, TN 37058); Linda Campbell Franklin, *300 Years of Housekeeping Collectibles,* Books Americana, 1992; ——, *300 Years of Kitchen Collectibles,* 4th ed., Krause Publications, 1997; *Griswold Cast Iron,* Vol. 1 (1993), Vol. 2 (1995), L-W Book Sales; *Griswold Manufacturing Co. 1918 Catalog Reprint,* L-W Book Sales, 1996; Barbara Mauzy, *Bakelite in the Kitchen,* Schiffer, 1998; ---, *The Complete Book of Kitchen Collecting,* Schiffer, 1997; Diane W. Stoneback, *Kitchen Collectibles: The Essential Buyer's Guide,* Wallace-Homestead, 1994; Don Thornton, *Beat This: The Eggbeater Chronicles,* Off Beat Books (1345 Poplar Ave., Sunnyvale, CA 94087), 1994.

**Periodicals:** *Cast Iron Cookware News,* 28 Angela Ave., San Anselmo, CA 94960; *Cookies,* 9610 Greenview Lane, Manassas, VA 20109; *Griswold Cast Iron Collectors' News & Marketplace,* P.O. Box 521, North East, PA 16428; *Kettles 'n Cookware,* P.O. Box B, Perrysville, NY 14129; *Kitchen Antiques & Collectibles News,* 4645 Laurel Ridge Dr., Harrisburg, PA 17110; *Piebirds Unlimited,* 14 Harmony School Rd., Flemington, NJ 08822.

**Collectors' Clubs:** Association of Coffee Mill Enthusiasts, 5941 Wilkerson Rd., Rex, GA 30273; Cookie Cutter Collectors Club, 1167 Teal Rd., SW, Dellroy, OH 44620; Corn Items Collectors Association, Inc., 613 North Long St., Shelbyville, IL 62565; Eggcup Collectors' Corner, 67 Stevens Ave., Old Bridge, NJ 08857; Griswold & Cast Iron Cookware Association, 54 Macon Ave., Asheville, NC 28801; International Society for Apple Parer Enthusiasts, 3911 Morgan Center Rd, Utica, OH 43080; Jelly Jammers Club, 110 White Oak Dr., Butler, PA 16001; Kollectors of Old Kitchen Stuff, 501 Market St., Mifflinburg, PA 17844; National Reamer Collectors Association, 47 Midlinc Court, Gaithersburg, MD 20878-1996; Pie Bird Collectors Club, 158 Bagsby Hill Lane, Dover, TN 37058.

**Museums and Libraries:** Culinary Archives and Museum, Johnson & Wales University, Providence, RI; Culinary Institute of America; H. B. Meek Library, Cornell University;

**Advertising Trade Card, New Hub Range, Smith & Anthony Stove Co., Boston, Mass, scene of people sledding, adv on back, $10.**

Judith Basin Museum, Stanford, MT; Kern County Museum, Bakersfield, CA; Mandeville Library, University of CA, San Diego, CA; Schlesinger Library, Radcliff College; Strong Museum, Rochester, NY; Wilbur Chocolate Co, Lititz, PA.

**Additional Listings:** Advertising, Cookbooks, Griswold, Kitchen Glassware, Reamers.

Angel Food Pan, 10" d .................. 28.00
Apple Corer, White Mountain, orig box
................................................. 30.00
Apple Peeler, Turntable No. 98 ..... 85.00
Basket, 4-1/2" d, 5-1/2" h, wire, folding, tulip form ................................. 45.00
Basting Spoon, granite, cobalt blue handle ..................................... 15.00
Biscuit Cutter, 1-12" d, tin, bail ...... 10.00
Bowl
    Treasure Craft, green, large, fruit edged handles ......................... 10.00
    Walnut, 10" w, 11" l, 3" h .......... 65.00
Box, Campfire Marshmallows, 1-1/2" x 3-1/2" x 6-3/4", red, white, and blue lid, Campfire Co., Milwaukee, c1920, lid with Boy Scouts toasting marshmallows over campfire, other panel with housewife frosting cake with marshmallow topping, recipes on side panel, offer for Campfire Recipe Book .......................................... 60.00
Bread Board, 12" d, 7-1/2" l, pine handle
................................................. 90.00
Bread Box, tin, 12" l, white, red top
................................................. 20.00

Breadstick Pan, nickeled cast iron, Wagner Ware .......................... 35.00
Bundt Pan, iron, scalloped, 4-1/2" x 10-1/2" ........................................ 45.00
Butter Churn, Dazy, No. 40, wood paddles ...................................... 125.00
Butter Fork, 7" x 2-1/2", hand carved maple ..................................... 25.00
Butter Mold, 1-3/4" x 3-1/2", turned maple, carved floral design ..... 45.00
Butter Paddle, 10" x 5", hand carved maple ..................................... 75.00
Butter Hook, 7/8", Miller's Cocoa, multicolored celluloid oval, meal hook, c1896 .................................... 40.00
Cake Pan, tin
    8" d, Swans Down Cake Flour ... 15.00
    12", black, wire loop handle, Fries
    .............................................. 12.00
Can Opener
    Cast Iron, fish figure, c1865 ... 140.00
    Metal, red wood handle .......... 15.00
Catalog
    A. J. Lindemann & Hoverson, Milwaukee, WI, c1932, 34 pgs, 8" x 11"
    .............................................. 21.00
    Calumet Baking Powder Co., Chicago, IL, 1923, 24 pgs, 5" x 8"
    .............................................. 12.00
    International Harvester, Chicago, IL, 1952, 8 pgs, 8-1/4" x 10-3/4", refrigerators ................................. 13.00
    Revere Copper & Brass Co., Rome, NY, 1936, 8 pgs, 3" x 6", cooking utensils ................................ 13.00
    Rochester Stamping Co., Rochester, NY, 64 pgs, 4-1/2" x 7", chafing dishes ................................... 26.00
    Standard Electric Stove, Toledo, OH, 1927, 32 pgs, 8-1/2" x 11" ..... 30.00
Cheese Grater, hanging, white china, gold trim, enameled blue forget-me-not dec ..................................... 70.00
Cheese Slicer, enameled wood handle, marked "Unsco-Germany" ...... 10.00
Cherry Seeder, Dandy 50A, orig damaged box .............................. 12.50
Chopping Knife, 6-1/2" l, Henry Disston & Sons, curved steel blade, wood handle .................................... 20.00
Cleanser, Guardian Service, unopened, black and silver Art Deco design
................................................. 35.00

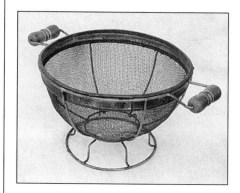

**Colander, wire frame, green painted wood handles, 8-1/2" d top, $35.**

Clothes Sprinkler, ceramic, figural Chinese Man, Shawnee Pottery .............................................. 110.00
Elephant ..................................... 75.00

Coffee Grinder
Lap type, drawer with porcelain knob, crank handle, brass cup, sgd "D. D. Post, Lahasaka, PA, Maker" ........................................ 225.00
Table-top type, Enterprise Model 10, clamp-on, orig stenciling ........ 65.00
Wall, Arcade, crystal ............... 65.00

Cornstick Pan, Junior Krusty Korn Kobs, italic "Wagner Ware" trademark ....................................... 85.00

Dipper, 7" l, copper, tin lined, forged brass handle, imp "M M" on side .............................................. 75.00

Dish Pan, enamel, gray ................ 15.00

Dough Bowl, 12-1/2" d, wood ....... 55.00

Dough Maker, 11" h, 11" d, chartreuse aluminum, wood handle, mkd "Mirro, The Finest Aluminum Made in the USA" ......................................... 75.00

Dust Pan and Broom, Kitchen Prayer Lady ........................................ 265.00

Dutch Oven, cov, cast iron, unmarked .............................................. 25.00

Eggcup
Baby Bird ................................. 45.00
Bonzo, figural, Germany, 1920s .............................................. 125.00
Charlie McCarthy, lusterware, Canadian, 1930s ............................. 60.00
Pluto, 1930s .......................... 125.00
Popeye, 1930s, multicolored .............................................. 110.00

Egg Poacher, red enamel, gray enamel insert, 3-3/4" x 8" ..................... 24.00

Egg Separator, aluminum, 9" l ........ 7.00

Egg Timer
Chef .......................................... 50.00
Girl on phone .......................... 50.00
Winking Chef, timer on back .... 195.00

Egg Whip, spring-type, enameled wood handle ...................................... 10.00

Fan, Ward's Bread, 7" x 7" diecut cardboard, 4-1/2" l wood handle, full-color fairy-tale flour mill scene, inspirational verse and name of Ward Bread, reverse with two elf-like youngsters advertising "Dainty Maid" and "Tip-Top" bread, 1930s ...................... 50.00

Flour Sifter, Bromweld's, side crank, red wood knob .............................. 15.00

Folder
2-1/2" x 3", opens to 2-1/2" x 8-3/4", Jell-O recipes, full color strawberry Jell-O dessert, 1920s ............... 20.00
3-1/2" x 6", opens to 7" x 12" sheet, full color, Jell-O, America's Most Famous Dessert/Of What And How Made, 1920s ............................ 20.00

Food Chopper, Universal ................. 8.00

Food Mill, Foley, 2 pcs ................. 20.00

Funnel, Elliptical, gray graniteware .............................................. 30.00

Hot Pad Holder, black boy, chalkware, 1940s, 8" h, chips .................... 55.00

Iced Tea Dispenser, Lord Calvert Hotel, Baltimore, MD, black base and cov, 1940s .................................... 375.00

Jelly Mold, 3-1/2" d, 3-1/2" h, tin, Madeline, stamped "Of 539" ............. 25.00

Lemon Squeezer
6-1/2" l, tin plated iron .............. 20.00
11" l, hinged maple .................. 65.00

Meat Grinder, Sargent & Co., Patent March 8, 1892 ......................... 40.00

Meat Tenderizer, 2" x 2-1/2" x 3", rect, iron, heavy handle ................... 40.00

Meat Thermometer, 6" l, hanging, Taylor .............................................. 10.00

Mixing Spoon, wood handle, slotted bowl, Androck, Made in USA ... 18.50

Mouli-Julienne, rotary cutter, 3 interchangeable cutting and shredding discs, orig box, c1950 ............. 30.00

Napkin Holder, figural, lady, ceramic, Kreiss ..................................... 60.00

Oven Broom, 10-1/2" l, birch, splint, hewn handle, New York State, c1830 .............................................. 45.00

Oyster Ladle, tin .......................... 30.00

Pantry Box, 6-1/2" x 12-1/2" d, red paint, four overlapping fingers ......... 365.00

Pea Sheller, 12" h, screw clamp, black wood handle, Vaughans .......... 40.00

Pie Bird
Blue and gray, long neck ......... 90.00
Yellow and brown, long neck ... 90.00

Pitcher, 8" h, pink and yellow, marked "Royal Copley" ........................ 35.00

Potato Masher, 9" h, zig zag wire end, red catalin handle ................... 10.00

Rolling Pin
Stainless steel .......................... 9.00
Wooden, 17" l, red handles ...... 35.00

Salt and Pepper shakers, pr, Kitchen Prayer Lady, pink ...................... 8.00

Salt Box, 8" x 17-1/2", rect, pine, hinged lid .......................................... 120.00

Sifter, three screens, colorful litho tin .............................................. 20.00

Skillet, cast iron, Wagner Ware No. 3, italic trademark "Wagner Ware, Sidney-O" ..................................... 15.00

Strainer, wire mesh bowl, twisted wire and wood handle .................... 10.00

Strawberry Huller, Nip-It, 1906 ....... 4.00

Tea Caddy, 8-1/2" h, tin, painted, red fruit, yellow leaves, orig cap ... 265.00

Tea Kettle, copper, gooseneck, dovetailed, sgd "JMWE" and hallmark .............................................. 175.00

Teapot and Salt and Pepper Shakers, aluminum, four cup teapot, cov with red finial, orig strainer with red handle, orig box, mkd "Highly Polished Aluminum, Made in Japan" ..... 25.00

Tin, rect, Krispy Crackers ............. 35.00

Tomato Slicer, enameled wood handle, orig litho sleeve ...................... 18.00

Toothpick Holder, Kitchen Prayer Lady, white ....................................... 15.00

Vegetable Basket, 7" d, 5" h, wire, tapered, bale handle, 1870 ..... 55.00

Vegetable Grater, Schroeter, tin, iron back, wood handle, old blue paint .............................................. 40.00

Wall Plaque
Fruit, paint scuffed, 1950s ......... 8.00
Parrot, chalkware, 10" x 6", chips .............................................. 12.00

Whisk, 10" l, snow shoe-shape, twisted wire handle .............................. 15.00

# Kitchen Glassware

**Collecting Hints:** Glassware for the kitchen was made in quantity. Although collectors do tolerate signs of use, they will not accept pieces with heavy damage. Many of the products contain applied decals; these should be in good condition. A collection can be built inexpensively by concentrating on one form, such as canister sets, measuring cups, or reamers.

**History:** The Depression era brought inexpensive kitchen and table products to center stage. The companies in the forefront of production included Hocking, Hazel Atlas, McKee, U.S. Glass, and Westmoreland.

Kitchen glassware complemented Depression glass. Many items were produced in the same color and style. Because the glass was molded, added decorative elements included ribs, fluting, arches and thumbprint patterns. In order to be durable, the glassware had to be thick. This resulted in forms which were difficult to handle at times and often awkward aesthetically. After World War II, aluminum products began to replace kitchen glassware.

**Raisin Seeder, Ezy Raisin Seeder, patent May 21, 1895, clamp grip, 5" h, $245.**

**References:** Gene Florence, *Kitchen Glassware of the Depression Years*, 5th ed., Collector Books, 1995, 1997 value update; Garry Kilgo and Dale, Jerry, and Gail Wilkins, *Collectors Guide to Anchor Hocking's Fire-King Glassware*, K & W Collectibles Publisher, 1991; ----, *Collectors Guide to Anchor Hocking's Fire-King Glassware, Volume II*, K & W Collectibles Publisher, 1998; Susan Tobier Rogove and Marcia Buan Steinhauer, *Pyrex by Corning*, The Glass Press, 1993; April M. Tvorak, *Fire-King '95*, published by author, 1995; ----, *Fire-King II*, published by author, 1993; ----, *History And Price Guide to Fire-King*, VAL Enterprises, 1992; ----, *Pyrex Price Guide*, published by author, 1992.

**Periodical:** Kitchen Antiques & Collectibles News, 4645 Laurel Ridge Dr., Harrisburg, PA 17110.

**Collectors' Club:** Glass Knife Collectors Club, P.O. Box 342, Los Alamitos, CA 90720.

Batter Bowl
    Anchor Hocking, set of 7", 8", 9", and 10" d, rimmed, transparent green ........................................................95.00
    Black ships dec ........................ 25.00
    Tufglass, two handles, two spouts ........................................................45.00
Batter Jug, McKee, red.............. 175.00
Beer Mug, yellow ......................... 40.00
Bowl
    5-1/2" d, red, platonite, Criss-Cross ........................................................12.50
    6" d, jade-ite, Jeannette .......... 16.00
    7-1/2" d, cobalt blue, Hazel Atlas ........................................................45.00
    8" d, green, Hocking ............... 15.00
    8" d, Orange Dot, custard ........ 32.00
    8-1/2" l, oval, Pyrex, beige, two handles, blue dec, 1-1/2 quart ...... 15.00
    10" d, emerald glo ................... 50.00
Butter Box, cov, 2 pound size, green ........................................................145.00
Butter Dish, cov, 1 pound size
    Criss Cross
        Cobalt Blue........................ 150.00
        Crystal ................................ 20.00

**Butter Dish, light blue opaque, $35.**

Federal, amber, 1 lb................ 35.00
Hocking, crystal ...................... 25.00
Jade-ite ................................... 95.00
Canister
    3" h, jade-ite, Jeannette
        Allspice ............................. 65.00
        Ginger ............................... 65.00
        Nutmeg ............................. 65.00
        Pepper ............................... 65.00
        Plain .................................. 90.00
    5-1/2" h, sq, coffee, jade-ite, Jeannette ................................................. 55.00
    6" h, green, screw-on lid, smooth ................................................. 38.00
    16 oz, tea, jade-ite, round ...... 175.00
    20 oz, tea, Delphite, round .... 275.00
    28 oz, sugar, jade-ite ............. 300.00
    40 oz, coffee, Delphite, round ................................................. 450.00
    40 oz, coffee, jade-ite, round ................................................. 300.00
    52 oz, jade-ite, lid .................. 80.00
Casserole, cov, white, Pyrex........ 25.00
Cheese Dish, cov, slicer, opaque white ................................................. 90.00
Coffeepot, 4 cup, Pyrex .............. 15.00
Creamer, Criss-Cross, crystal....... 40.00
Cruet, stopper, Crystolite, amber ....30.00
Curtain Tiebacks, pr
    2-1/2" d, knob-type, pink.......... 35.00
    3-1/2" d, flat, floral, green and pink ................................................. 20.00
    4-1/2" d, flat, floral, amber....... 25.00
Custard, green, Tufglas ................. 6.00
Drawer Pull, crystal
    Double type ........................... 10.00
    Knob ...................................... 3.00
Drippings Jar, cov, jade-ite, Jeannette ................................................. 32.00
Egg Cup, double, black .............. 12.00
Flour Shaker
    Deco, ivory, black lettering ...... 45.00
    Roman Arch, ivory .................. 45.00
Fork and Spoon, amber handle.... 45.00
Fruit Bowl, Sunkist, pink.............. 335.00
Funnel, green ............................. 35.00
Furniture Caster, 3" d, transparent green, Hazel-Atlas ................... 40.00
Grease Jar
    Red Dots, white....................... 30.00
    Seville Yellow, black trim .......... 35.00
    Tulips, cov, Hocking ................ 15.00
Hand Beater, 32 oz measuring cup base
    Green ..................................... 45.00
    Green, stippled texture ........... 45.00
Iced Tea Spoons, colored handles, set of 12 ..................................... 60.00
Knife
    Block, 8-1/4" l
        Crystal, orig box................. 28.00
        Green ............................... 45.00
    Flower, pink, 9-1/4" l............... 50.00
    Plain, 9-1/8" l, green............... 40.00
    Stonex
        Dark amber, MIB .............. 375.00
        Light amber, MIB .............. 360.00
        Milk glass ......................... 500.00
    Three Leaf
        Crystal............................... 15.00
        Green ............................... 35.00
    Three Star
        Blue .................................. 38.00

Crystal, orig box................. 38.00
Pink ................................... 25.00
Lemon Reamer
    Delphite, Jeannette................. 80.00
    Jade-ite, Jeannette ................. 35.00
    Pink, Hazel-Atlas .................... 35.00
Loaf Pan, cov, 5" x 8", Glassbake, clear, knob finial ............................. 35.00
Mayonnaise Ladle
    Amber, flat.............................. 9.75
    Pink, transparent.................... 20.00
Measuring Cup
    2 oz, 1/4 cup, jade-ite, Jeannette ................................................. 40.00
    8 oz
        Delphite, 1 spout.............. 110.00
        Fire-King, 1 spout............... 18.50
        Green, transparent............. 18.00
    16 oz
        Cobalt Blue, Hazel-Atlas... 175.00
        Fired-on Green................. 20.00
        Green ............................... 22.00
        Green, stick handle, US Glass ............................................. 28.50
        Milk glass, white................ 22.00
        Set, jade-ite, 4 pcs........... 125.00
Mixing Bowl
    5-3/4" d, yellow banded dot, Pyrex ................................................. 8.00
    6-1/2" d, amber, Federal .......... 10.00
    6-1/2" d, green, Restwell.......... 10.00
    7-1/4" d, yellow banded dot, Pyrex ................................................. 10.00
    7-1/2" d, cobalt blue, Hazel-Atlas ................................................. 42.00
    7-1/2" d, Criss-Cross, blue....... 85.00
    8-1/2" d, cobalt blue, Hazel-Atlas ................................................. 50.00
    8-1/2" d, Criss-Cross, blue..... 100.00
    9-1/2" d, amber, Federal ......... 18.00
    11" d, Vitrock, white ............... 15.00
    Nested Set, white, ivy dec, Hazel Atlas...................................... 50.00
Mug, Ranger Joe, Hazel-Atlas
    Blue......................................... 9.50
    Red ......................................... 9.50
Napkin Holder, Paramount, pink ................................................. 550.00
Pitcher
    Delphite, 2 cup ..................... 150.00
    Jade-ite, sunflower in base...... 40.00
Range Shaker, sq, flour, jade-ite, Jeannette .................................... 30.00
Refrigerator Bowl, cov, Jennyware, pink, 16 oz, round..................... 48.00
Refrigerator Dish, cov
    4" x 4", Criss-Cross, blue ......... 35.00
    4" x 5", jade-ite ....................... 80.00
    4" x 8", Criss-Cross, blue ....... 100.00
    4" x 8", floral carved, transparent green, US Glass..................... 30.00
    4-1/2" x 4-1/2" sq
        Jade-ite, Jeannette ............ 15.00
        Pink, Jennyware ................. 35.00
    5" x 8", jade-ite ....................... 80.00
    5" x 10", jade-ite ................... 150.00
    6" x 3", transparent green, Tufglass ................................................. 45.00
    6-1/2" sq, Poppy Cocklebur, transparent green, US Glass .......... 55.00
    8" x 8", sq, amber, Federal....... 25.00
    8-1/2" x 4-1/2", jade-ite, Jeannette ................................................. 32.00

32 oz, round, jade-ite, Jeannette
............................................... 35.00
Relish, 8-1/2" x 13" oval, delfite, divided,
Pyrex ......................................... 20.00
Rolling Pin, clambroth, metal handles
............................................... 125.00
Salad Fork and Spoon, blue ......... 55.00
Salt and Pepper Shakers, pr
Cobalt Blue, red lids, Hazel-Atlas
............................................... 30.00
Jade-ite, 150.00
Jennyware, ftd, pink ................. 55.00
Ribbed, jade-ite, Jeannette ...... 22.00
Roman Arches, black, minor dam-
age to lids ............................... 45.00
Ships, red trim, red lids ............ 55.00
Salt Box, 4-1/2" x 3-3/4", crystal .... 25.00
Skillet, jade-ite, 1 spout .............. 150.00
Spice Set, green lids, Scotty Dog dec,
green tier holder, cinnamon, ginger,
red, pepper, paprika, mustard,
cloves, allspice, set ................ 325.00
Spoon, clear, Higbee ................... 25.00
Straw Holder, green transparent
............................................... 500.00
Sugar, cov
Criss-Cross design, transparent
green, Hazel-Atlas ................... 35.00
Roman Arch, custard, red dot
............................................... 60.00
Sugar Shaker
Green .................................... 145.00
Jade-ite ................................. 175.00
Syrup Pitcher
Crystal, gold catalin handle ..... 12.00
Crystal, flower etch ................. 35.00
Green, Hazel-Atlas ................. 45.00
Tom & Jerry Set, custard, bowl and 12
mugs ...................................... 135.00
Towel Bar, 24" l, crystal, orig hardware
............................................... 15.00
Tumbler, Hazel Atlas, white
3-1/2" h, 9 oz ............................ 5.00
4-1/2" h, 16 oz .......................... 7.00
Vase, bud, jade-ite, Jeannette ...... 14.00
Water Bottle, clear, glass lid, Hocking
............................................... 24.00

# Knowles, Edwin M.

**Collecting Hints:** Do not confuse
Edwin M. Knowles China Company
with Knowles, Taylor, and Knowles,
also a manufacturer of fine dinnerware. They are two separate companies. The only Edwin M. Knowles
China Company mark that might be
confusing is "Knowles" spelled with
a large "K."

Knowles dinnerware lines
enjoyed modest sales success. No
one line dominated, but the following
are among the more popular lines
with collectors: Deanna, a solid-
color line found occasionally with
decals and introduced in 1938;
Esquire, designed by Russel Wright
and manufactured between 1956

and 1962; and Yorktown, a modernistic design introduced in 1936 and
found in a variety of decal patterns
such as Bar Harbor, Golden Wheat,
Penthouse, and Water Lily.

When collecting pieces with
decals, buy only those with transfers
that are complete and still retain their
vivid colors. Edwin M. Knowles
China Company did make Utility
Ware that has found some favor with
collectors of kitchenware. Utility
Ware sells for between one-half and
two-thirds of the price of similar
pieces in the dinnerware patterns.

**History:** In 1900, Edwin M. Knowles
established the Edwin M. Knowles
China Company in Chester, West
Virginia. Company offices were
located in East Liverpool, Ohio. The
company made semiporcelain dinnerware, kitchenware, specialties,
and toilet wares and was known for
its commitment to having the most
modern and best equipped plants in
the industry.

In 1913, a second plant in Newell,
West Virginia, was opened. The
company operated its Chester, West
Virginia, pottery until 1931, at which
time the plant was sold to the Harker
Pottery Company. Production continued at the Newell pottery. Edwin M.
Knowles China Company ceased
operations in 1963.

The Edwin M. Knowles Company
name resurfaced in the 1970s when
the Bradford Exchange acquired
rights to use it. You will see the
Knowles name on some of The
Bradford Exchange's collector plate
series, e.g., Gone with the Wind and
the Wizard of Oz. The name also has
been attached to Rockwell items.
Bradford pieces marked "Knowles"
are made by off-shore manufacturers and are not produced in the
United States at either of the old
Knowles' locations.

**References:** Susan and Al
Bagdade, *Warman's American Pottery and Porcelain*, Wallace-Homestead, 1994; Jo Cunningham,
*Collector's Encyclopedia of Ameri-
can Dinnerware*, Collector Books,
1982, 1995 value update; Lois Lehner, *Lehner's Encyclopedia of U.S.
Marks on Pottery, Porcelain & Clay*,
Collector Books, 1988.

**Beverly,** bread and butter plate ..... 4.00

**Deanna**

Butter Dish, open, dark blue ......... 15.00
Coffeepot, cov, red and blue stripes
............................................... 42.00

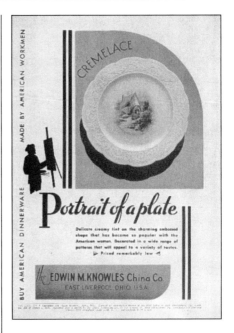

**Magazine Tear Sheet, Crockery and
Glass Journal, April 1933, Cremelace,
$4.**

Creamer and Sugar, cov, light blue
............................................... 25.00
Dinner, Plate, dark blue, 10" d ...... 12.00
Platter, 12" d, green ..................... 17.50
Vegetable Bowl, 8" d, orange-red
............................................... 20.00

**Esquire**

Bread and Butter Plate, Botanica, 6-1/4"
d ............................................ 7.50
Cereal Bowl, 6-1/4" d, Queen Anne's
Lace ...................................... 10.00
Cup and Saucer, Grass ............... 15.00
Dinner Plate, Seeds, 10-3/4" d ..... 17.50
Fruit Bowl, 5-1/2" d, Snowflower ... 10.00
Platter, 16" l, oval, Solar ............... 35.00
Teapot, Botanica ......................... 95.00
Vegetable Bowl, divided, Grass ... 60.00

**Mexican**

Bowl ....................................... 35.00
Platter ..................................... 47.50

**Souvenir Plate,** San Francisco Day,
Alcatraz, Treasure Island, 10" d
............................................... 75.00

**Yorktown**

Berry Bowl, wheat dec .................. 8.00
Bread and Butter Plate, cadet blue, 6" d
............................................... 6.00
Cake Plate, white ground, blue daisies
............................................... 7.50
Casserole, cadet blue ................. 35.00
Cereal Bowl, 6" d, russet ............... 7.50
Chop Plate, 10-3/4" d, yellow ....... 18.00
Cup and Saucer, floral dec ........... 15.00
Dinner Plate, sailboats ................. 12.50
Gravy Boat, pink ......................... 20.00
Platter, sailboats ........................ 10.00
Soup Bowl, floral dec .................... 8.50
Teapot, green ............................. 50.00

# L

# Labels

**Collecting Hints:** Damaged, trimmed, or torn labels are less valuable than labels in mint condition. Collectors prefer labels that can be removed from the product and stored flat in drawers or albums.

**History:** The first fruit-crate art was created by California fruit growers about 1880. The labels became very colorful and covered many subjects. Most depict the type of fruit held in the box. Cardboard boxes replaced fruit crates in the 1940s, making the labels collectible.

Over the last decade, label collectors have begun to widen their collecting range. Today, can, luggage, and wine labels are sought as well as cigar, fruit crate, and other household-type labels.

**References:** Joe Davidson, *Fruit Crate Art*, Wellfleet Press, 1990; Lynn Johnson and Michael O'Leary, *En Route: Label Art from the Golden Age of Air Travel*, Chronicle Books, 1993; Gorden T. McClelland and Jay T. Last, *Fruit Box Labels*, Hillcrest Press (3412-G MacArthur Blvd., Santa Ana, CA 92704), 1995; Gerard S. Petrone, *Cigar Box Labels: Portraits of Life, Mirrors of History*, Schiffer, 1998.

**Collectors' Clubs:** Citrus Label Society, 131 Miramonte Dr., Fullerton, CA 92365; Florida Citrus Labels Collectors Assoc., P.O. Box 547636, Orlando, FL 32854; International Seal, Label & Cigar Band Society, 8915 E. Bellevue St., Tucson, AZ 85715; Society of Antique Label Collectors, P.O. Box 24811, Tampa FL 33623.

**Advisor:** Lorie Cairns.

## Fruit Crate

Apple, 10-1/2" x 9"
Appleton, Art Nouveau lady sniffing pink roses, apples, ranch scene ........................................ 5.00
Bird Valley, big blue crow perched on shield, orange ground .......... 2.00
Buddy, grinning baby, 2 apples, dated 1920, blue ground .......... 6.00
Cliff, gorge and river scene, old car approaching bridge .................. 4.00
Dainty Maid, little girl holding apple, blue ground .............................. 2.00
Family Choice, cartoon family standing behind small house, red ground, Topeka, KS .................. 2.00

Apple, Wilko Brand, yellow apple, red, blue, and green border, 11" x 9", $2.

Heart of Washington, arrow points to Malaga ...................................... 1.00
Land O'Lakes, bird's eye view of town and river, big red apple, WI ........................................ 3.00
Mountain Goat, white goat standing on cliff, snow capped mountains and forest, turquoise sky ................... 2.00
Red Winner, Indian lady riding white horse ...................................... 4.00
Silver Spur, rope script words encircle spur, red ground .................. 2.00
Skookum, smiling Indian looking at lettering, blue ground ............... 3.00
Grape, 13" x 4"
American Pride, eagle, shield, orange, blue, and white .............. .25
Bear Mountain, 2 bears, scenic farm, mountains, house ...................... 1.50
Black Joe, smiling elderly black man, blue ground ...................... 1.50
Buck Rock, buck standing near big rock .......................................... 1.50
King's Ruby, red ruby gemstone, aqua ground ........................... .25
Mont Elisa, girl holding big bunch of purple grapes, yellow ground .. 50.00
Paul Dobson, bunch of red grapes, scenic vineyard, river, mountains ........................................ .25
Rosa De Maggio, 3 red roses, bunch of purple grapes ........................... .50
Try One, bunches of red and yellow grapes, blue ground ................... .25
White Horse, galloping white horse, black ground ........................... .50
Lemon, 12-1/2" x 8-3/4"
All Year, orchard scene, mountains, cacti, desert vegetation, black border, Fillmore ............................ 2.00
Cambria, brown eagle, 2 torches, blue ground, brown border, Placentia ............................................ 1.00
Estero, estuary scene, clipper ships near sheer rocky coastline, palm trees, dark green ground, Goleta ........................................ 2.00
Gateway, 2 horseback riders in redwood forest, sprig of lemon blossoms, dark blue ground, Lemon Cove ........................................ 2.00

Lemon, Splendid, country scene, 12-1/2" x 8-3/4", $2.25.

Keeper, pair of fancy keys, Santa Paula ........................................ 2.00
Montalvo, pink mountains in oval, blue ground, Saticoy ................. 3.00
Oxnard, man tilling soil, ox team, mission in background ............. 2.00
Panama, map of USA and Mexico showing trade routes from Santa Barbara thru Panama Canal, Santa Barbara ........................................ 2.00
Santa, carrying bag of goodies, dated 1928, Santa Paula .......... 5.00
Sea Gull, large white flying bird, black tipped wings, ocean and sky, Upland ........................................ 8.50
Sunside, 2 lemons and leaves, orange and brown ground, Santa Paula ........................................ 1.00
Orange, 10" x 11"
Airship, old 4 propeller commercial plane, royal blue ground, Fillmore ........................................ 15.00
Annie Laurie, Scottish lassie, bright plaid, Strathmore ...................... 4.00
Athlete, 3 runners reaching finish line, stadium setting, Claremont ........................................ 5.00
Blue Goose, blue fowl, orange ground, Los Angeles ................. 2.00
Brownies, several Brownies preparing orange juice, yellow sun, blue ground, Lemon Cove ................. 5.00
Coed, smiling graduate, purple ground, Claremont ...................... 2.00
Daisy, large white flower, green leaves, black ground, Covina .... 3.00
Fancia, matador smoking, seaside, Rialto ........................................ 5.00
Gold Buckle, gilt outline of buckle, orchard scene, 2 large oranges, royal blue ground, East Highlands ........................................ 3.00
Green Mill, mill, yellow sky, Placentia ........................................ 4.00
Have One, hand holding partially peeled orange, royal blue, Lemon Cove ........................................ 2.00
Hi Tone, green musical notes, black ground, Upland ...................... 1.00
Irvale, big orange, red bordered blue diamond, green ground, Irvine ... 2.00
Lily, 2 large white calla lilies, green leaves, black ground, Exeter ..... 2.50
Miracle, genie holding tray with 3 oranges, orchard and mountain scene, dated 1928, Placentia .... 4.00

**Orange, Sunkist, Rocky Hill, Indian chief on horseback, Exeter, CA, $4.**

Orbit, meteor in shape of an orange, streaking thru starry evening skies, royal blue ground, Exeter........... 5.00
Pala Brave, large Indian Chief, wearing headdress, maroon ground, Placentia ......................................... 4.00
Royal Knight, knight in armor on horseback, castle, yellow ground, Redlands.................................... 2.00
Sierra Vista, scenic groves, snowy mountains, Porterville............... 10.00
Strength, large gray elephant with tusks, yellow ground, Santa Paula ................................................. 30.00
Tesoro Rancho, ranch home and palms, Placentia........................ 3.00
Unicorn, galloping pinto unicorn, E. Highlands................................. 25.00
Velvet, draped velvet, Sunkist orange, dated 1929, Irvine......... 3.00
Pear, 10-3/4" x 7-1/4"
   Big City, skyscrapers, orange ground.........................................50
   Boy Blue, little boy blowing horn ................................................. 3.00
   Don't Worry, cute little buy, black ground....................................... 2.00
   High Hand, hand holding 4 aces, blue ground............................. 1.200
   Keystone Fruit Co., big red Keystone, navy ground ................... 1.00
   Old Gold, fancy yellow letters, red and bluc ground ........................ 1.00
   Quail, CA quail walking thru grass ................................................. 5.00
   Snow-Gem, snow laden lettering, blue ground................................. 2.00
   Tulip, bunch of 3 colorful tulips, black ground............................. 6.00

**Miscellaneous**

Betty Ann Baking Powder, little redhead girl, pink dress, skipping rope, white ground, gilt border, Hastings, NE ................................................. 3.00
Boyer's Oil Polish, boots and shoes, 3-1/8" x 1-1/8" ................................... .25
Campfire Coffee, bubbling granite ware coffee pot on campfire, 3-3/8" x 17" ................................................. 4.00
Cap'n John Clam Nectar Bouillon, captain, whole clams, stylized dolphins, Canada ...................................... 1.00

Clabber Girl Baking Powder, girl carrying plate of biscuits, family scene ................................................. 1.00
Farmer's Pride, catsup, 2" x 2-3/4".....25
Happy Day Soda, rising sun and rays, sailboat on lake, PA .....................25
Hi Plane, pancake flour, aqua plane flying over stack of pancakes on plate, recipe, 9" x 12-3/4" ..................... 2.00
Imperial Tooth Wash, oval, Art Nouveau florals ...........................................75
New England, map of 6 New England states, ginger ale .........................25
Pearson's Red Top Snuff, Victorian lady, deep red and black, 2-3/8" x 5-1/2" ........................................................50
Royal Blue Stores Coffee, steaming cup of coffee, emb, gilt, 5" x 14" ....... 6.00
Wisk Shaving Cream, man's face, black, blue, and silver, 3" x 5" ..................25

**Tin Can**

Alpine, mountain climber figure, bowl with white kidney beans................50
Blueberry Hill, blueberry cluster and blueberry pie, emb, gilt.............. 2.50
Bob White, bird surveying farm scene, big tomato................................. 2.50
Butterfly, Telephone Peas, emb, gilt ................................................. 2.00
Country Maid, blue and white milk maid standing beside cow, carrying milk pail, blue and red "skimmed milk" ................................................. 3.00
Crossroads, scenes of old cabin and man making syrup in big kettle.. 2.00
Fairfax Hall, big white mansion and grounds................................. 1.00
Little Joe, whistling black youngster going fishing, peas .................... 2.00
Oceana County, bright red cherries, gilt, 11" x 6-1/2" ................................. 1.00
Penrod, 3 children in costumes, little dog, red tomato ......................... 2.00
Rowley's, white corn, red ground, gilt, c1920 ................................. 1.00
Sinatra's, picture of Frank singing, black ground, dated 1990, 4" x 11" ..... 5.00
Teacup, teacup and saucer, evaporated milk............................................... 2.00
Woodlake, images of big lake and grove scene ................................25

**Vegetables**

Bear, big brown bear with map of CA between paws, 5" x " ................. 1.00
Blue Mink, blue mink, colorful background, 6-1/2" x 5-1/2" ............... 1.00
Conestoga, covered red wagon and ox team, desert ground, 7" x 9" ...... 2.00
Deer Valley, russet buck, ranch scene, 4-1/4" x 6-1/2"................................75
Don't Cry, black youth shooting dice, yams, 9" sq ............................... 5.00
Hillview, farm scene, yams, 4-1/2" x 7" ........................................................50
Nob Hill, San Francisco skyscrapers, navy ..............................................75
Sky Path, small plane sky writing name, blue ground .............................. 1.00
White House, vegetables in splint basket, white mansion, 7" x 9" ......... 1.00

# Lamps

**Collecting Hints:** Be aware that every lamp has two values—a collectible value and a decorative value. Often the decorative value exceeds the collectible value, in part because most lamps are purchased as decorative accessories, often as accent pieces in a period room setting.

In the 1990s, the hot lamp collectibles were the odd-shaped examples from the 1950s. Some of these were abstract; some, figural. While 1950s lamps continue to sell well as part of the 1950s/1960s revival, prices have stabilized primarily because of the market saturation resulting from the large quantity of lamps of this era that survived in attics and basements, due, in large part, to the promotional efforts of J. W. Courter. One man can make a market.

Within the past five years, collector interest is spreading to other manufacturers and into electric lamps, although Aladdin is still one of the most sought after names in lamps.

Just as post-World War II collectors discovered figural transistor and character radios, so also are they discovering motion lamps, many of which are character related. Look for a growing interest in character lamps and a corresponding rise in prices.

**History:** The kerosene lamp was the predominant lighting device during the 19th century and the first quarter of the 20th century. However, its death knell was sounded in 1879 when Thomas A. Edison developed a viable electric light bulb.

The success of the electric lamp depended on the availability of electricity. However, what we take for granted today did not arrive in many rural areas until the 1930s.

Most electric lamps were designed to serve as silent compliments to period design styles. They were meant to blend, rather than stand out. Pairs were quite common.

Famous industrial designers did lend their talents to lamp design, and their products are eagerly sought by collectors. Bradley and Hubbard and Handel are two companies whose products have attracted strong collector interest.

**References:** *Better Electric Lamps of the 20s and 30s*, L-W Book Sales,

1997; *Quality Electric Lamps*, L-W Book Sales, 1992, 1996 value update; J. W. Courter, Aladdin Collectors Manual & Price Guide #18, *Kerosene Mantle Lamps*, published by author (note: all the Courter books are available from the author, 3935 Kelley Rd., Kevil, KY 42053), 1998; —, *Aladdin Electric Lamps Price Guide #2*, published by author, 1993; —, *Angle Lamps: Collectors Manual & Price Guide*, published by author, 1992, *Electric Lighting of the 20s & 30s*, Vol. 1 (1988, 1998 value update), Vol. 2 (1994, 1998 value update), L-W Book Sales; Bill and Linda Montgomery, *Animation Motion Lamps*, L-W Book Sales, 1991; Leland and Crystal Payton, *Turned On: Decorative Lamps of the 'Fifties*, Abbeville Press, 1989; Sam and Anna Samuelian, *Collector's Guide to Motion Lamps*, Collector Books, 1998; Calvin Shepherd, *50s T.V. Lamps*, Schiffer, 1998.

**Periodical:** Light Revival, 35 W. Elm Ave., Quincy, MA 02170.

**Collectors' Clubs:** Aladdin Knights of the Mystic Light, 3935 Kelley Rd., Kevil, KY 42053; Coleman Collector Network, 1822 E Fernwood, Wichita, KS 67216; Historical Lighting Society of Canada, 9013 Oxbox Rd., North East, PA 16428.

Akro Agate, lavender and blue marbled
   shade ........................................ 350.00
Aladdin, Alacite, electric
   #25 ........................................... 48.00
   #185A ....................................... 25.00
   #236 ......................................... 55.00

**Owl, spread wings, Kron mark, Midwest Potteries, Inc., 12" h, $75. Photo courtesy of Doris & Burdell Hall.**

#266 ............................................ 50.00
#351, round wall ...................... 65.00
#354, rect wall ......................... 65.00
Bedroom
   Art Deco, Chase Chrome, round base, conical shade, c1930 .... 90.00
   Southern Belle, blue, orig shade
   .................................................. 80.00
Character
   Fred Flintstone, 13-1/4" h, painted vinyl, black metal base, missing shade ...................................... 45.00
   Hula Girl, Dodge Inc., 1938, bronzed metal, shimming grass skirt
   .............................................. 1,600.00
   Mickey Mouse, 4" d, 6-1/2" h, globular metal base, beige ground, three Mickey decals around sides, Soreng-Manegold Co. ............. 85.00
Children's
   ABC Blocks, wood and plastic, linen over cardboard shade ............. 20.00
   Bambi, plastic, 1950s .............. 30.00
   Cookie Monster, figural, Sesame Street characters on shade ..... 45.00
   Elephant, figural, ceramic, carousel beaded shade ....................... 195.00
   Football Player, 14-1/2" h, hollow plaster, football player standing next to figural football standard, linen over cardboard shade, WK, Japan, Sears, Roebuck, 1978 ............. 25.00
Headboard, pink, chrome ............ 65.00
Lava, Lava Simplex Corp., c1968
   .................................................. 80.00
Motion
   Antique Cars, Econolite, 1957, 11" h
   ................................................ 110.00
   Cheers Bar, sexy girls, MIB .... 125.00
   Fireside Peanut Vendor, dancing devil graphics, 1930s ............. 400.00
   Forest Fire, Econolite, 1955 ..... 95.00
   Fountain of Youth ................... 150.00
   Goldfish, green satin glass, 1931
   ................................................ 325.00
   Niagara Falls, Goodman, extra wide style ...................................... 140.00
   Snow Scene, bridge, Econolite
   ................................................ 165.00
Organ Grinder, monkey, pink ........ 95.00
Radio, Michael Lumitone ............ 200.00
Stenographer's, Emeralite, clamps onto desk ........................................ 395.00
Television
   Gondola, ceramic, brown with gold trim, marked "Copyright Premco Mfg. Co., Chicago, IL, 1954," 16" w, 7" h ........................................ 45.00
   Horse Head, ceramic, 12" x 10-3/4"
   .................................................. 25.00
   Panther, black, 8-1/2" x 6-1/2"
   .................................................. 35.00
   Ship, 11" x 10-1/2", gold trim... 35..00

# Limited Edition Collectibles

**Collecting Hints:** The first item issued in a series usually commands a higher price. When buying a limited-edition collectible, be aware that

the original box and/or certificates increase the value of the piece. Be alert to special discounts and sales.

**History:** Limited-edition plate collecting began with the advent of Christmas plates issued by Bing and Grondahl in 1895. Royal Copenhagen soon followed. During the late 1960s and early 1970s, several potteries, glass factories, and mints began to issue plates, bells, eggs, mugs, etc., which commemorated special events, people, places, or holidays. For a period of time, these items increased in popularity and value, but in the late 1970s, the market became flooded with many collectibles and prices declined.

There are many new issues of collector items annually. Some of these collectibles can be found listed under specific headings, such as Hummel, Norman Rockwell, etc.

**References:** Jay Brown, *The Complete Guide To Limited Edition Art Prints*, Krause Publications, 1999; *Collectors' Information Bureau Collectibles Market Guide & Price Index*, 15th ed., Collectors' Information Bureau (5065 Shoreline Rd., Ste. 200, Barrington, IL 60010), 1997; Pat Owen, *Bing & Grondahl Christmas Plates*, Landfall Press, 1995; Mary Sieber (ed.), *1997 Price Guide to Limited Edition Collectibles*, Krause Publications, 1997; Rosie Wells (ed.), *Official 1993 Secondary Market Price Guide for Precious Moments Collectibles*, 11th ed., Rosie Wells Enterprises, 1993.

**Periodicals:** *Collector Editions*, 170 Fifth Ave., 12th Floor, New York, NY 10010; *Collector's Bulletin*, 22341 E. Wells Rd., Canton IL 61520; *Collectors Mart Magazine*, 700 E. State St., Iola, WI 54990; *Collector News & Antique Reporter*, P.O. Box 156, Grundy Center, IA 50638; *Contemporary Doll Magazine*, 30595 Eight Mile, Livonia, MI 48152; *Hallmarkers Holiday Happening Collectors Club*, 6151 Main St., Springfield, OR 97478; *Insight on Collectibles*, 103 Lakeshore Rd., Ste. 202, St Catharines, Ontario L2N 2T6 Canada; *International Collectible Showcase*, One Westminster Pl, Lake Forest, IL 60045; *Ornament Trader Magazine*, P.O. Box 7908, Clearwater, FL 34618; *Plate World*, 9200 N. Maryland Ave., Niles, IL 60648.

**Collectors' Clubs:** Annalee Doll Society, P.O. Box 1137, Meredith, NH 03253; Anri Collector's Society,

P.O. Box 380760, Duncanville, TX 75183-0760; Club Anri, 55 Parcella Park Dr., Randolph, MA 02368; Del-Mar-Pa Ornament Kollector's Club, 131 S. Tartan Dr., Elkton, MD 21921; Disney Once Up A Classic Collectors Club, 11443, Dulcet Ave., Northridge, CA 91326; Donald Zolan Collectors Society, 133 E. Carillo St., Santa Barbara, CA 93101; Dreamsicles Club, 1120 California Ave., Corona, CA 91719-3324; Franklin Heirloom Doll Club, US Route 1, Franklin Center, PA 19091; Franklin Mint Collectors Society, US Rte. 1, Franklin Center, PA 19091; Gorham Collectors Club, P.O. Box 6472, Providence, RI 02940; Hallmark Keepsake Ornament Collectors' Club, P.O. Box 419034, Kansas City, MO 61441-6034; International Plate Collectors Guild, P.O. Box 487, Artesia, CA 90702; Jan Hagara Collectors' Club, 40114 Industrial Park North, Georgetown, TX 78626; Lladro Collectors Society, 43 W. 57th St., New York, NY 10019; Lowell Davis Farm Club, 55 Pacella Park Dr., Randolph, MA 02368; Modern Doll Club, 9628 Hidden Oaks Cr., Tampa, FL 33612; Precious Moments Collectors' Club, One Enesco Plaza, P.O. Box 1466, Elk Grove Village, IL 60009; Royal Doulton International Collectors' Club, 701 Cottontail Lane, Somerset, NJ 08873; Sarah's Attic Forever Friends Collectors Club, http://www.sarahasttic.com; Wedgwood Society of Boston, 28 Birchwood Drive, Hampstead, NH 03841.

**Museum:** Bradford Museum, Niles, IL.

**Abbreviation:** FE = First Edition.

**Bells**

Anri, J. Ferrandiz, artist, wooden
1976, Christmas, FE ................ 52.00
1977, Christmas ....................... 45.00
1978, Christmas ....................... 40.00
1979, Christmas ....................... 30.00
1980, The Christmas King ....... 15.00
1981, Lighting the Way ........... 15.00
1982, Caring ........................... 15.00
1983, Behold ........................... 15.00
1985, Nature's Dream ............. 15.00
1987, The Wedding Bell, silver
................................................ 25.00
1988, Bride Belles, Caroline .... 27.50
1989, Christmas Pow-Pow ....... 25.00
1990, Indian Brave .................. 25.00
Bing & Grondahl, Christmas, annual
1980, Christmas in the Woods . 45.00
1981, Christmas Peace ............ 40.00
1982, Christmas Tree .............. 40.00
1983, Christmas in Old Town ... 40.00
1984, Christmas Letter ............. 40.00

1985, Christmas Eve at the Farmhouse ....................................... 40.00
1986, Silent Night, Holy Night .... 40.00
1987, Snowman's Christmas Eve
................................................ 40.00
1988, Old Poet's Christmas ..... 40.00
1989, Christmas Anchorage .... 45.00
1990, Changing of the Guards
................................................ 45.00
1991, Copenhagen Stock Exchange
................................................ 50.00
1992, Christmas at the Rectory
................................................ 55.00
1993, Father Christmas in Copenhagen ..................................... 66.00
Danbury Mint, Norman Rockwell artist
1975, Doctor and Doll ............... 50.00
1976, Saying Grace ................. 40.00
1977, Santa's Mail ................... 40.00
1979, Friend in Need ............... 30.00
Enesco Corp., Precious Moments
1981, Jesus Loves Me ............. 40.00
1982, Mother Sew Dear ........... 35.00
1983, Surrounded with Joy ...... 60.00
1984, Wishing You a Merry Christmas ....................................... 45.00
1989, Your Love Is Special to Me
................................................ 20.00
1990, Here Comes the Bride ... 25.00
1991, May Your Christmas Be Merry
................................................ 30.00
1992, But the Greatest of These Is Love ........................................ 25.00
Franklin Mint, 1979, Unicorn, porcelain
................................................ 35.00
Gorham
Currier & Ives, mini
1976, Christmas Sleigh Ride
................................................ 30.00
1977, American Homestead
................................................ 25.00
1979, Sleigh Ride ................ 20.00
1980, Christmas in the Country
................................................ 20.00
1982, Christmas Visitation ... 18.00
1984, Hitching Up .............. 15.00
1987, Early Winter .............. 18.00
Norman Rockwell, artist
1975, Sweet Song So Young
................................................ 50.00
1976, Snow Sculpture ......... 45.00
1977, Chilling Chore, Christmas
................................................ 35.00
1978, Gay Blades .............. 23.00
1979, Beguiling Buttercup .... 30.00
1980, Flying High .............. 25.00
1981, Ski Skills, Christmas .. 27.00
1982, Young Man's Fancy .... 30.00
1983, Christmas Medley ..... 30.00
1984, Young Love .............. 28.00
1985, Yuletide Reflections .... 32.50
1986, Home for the Holidays
................................................ 32.50
1987, Merry Christmas Grandma
................................................ 30.00
1988, The Homecoming ...... 37.50
(Hummel, see HUMMEL)
Hutschenreuther, 1978, Christmas
................................................ 8.00
Lenox, Songs of Christmas
1991, We Wish You a Merry Christmas ....................................... 45.00
1993, Jingle Bells .................... 55.00

**Reco, Mother Goose series, 1980, Little Boy Blue, John McClelland, artist, 8-1/2" d, $100.**

1995, Hark the Herald Angels Sing
................................................ 60.00
Lladro, Christmas
1987 ..................................... 90.00
1988 ..................................... 80.00
1989 ..................................... 90.00
1990 ..................................... 45.00
1991 ..................................... 40.00
1992 ..................................... 35.00
Pickard
1977, The First Noel, FE .......... 75.00
1978, O Little Town of Bethlehem
................................................ 70.00
1979, Silent Night ................... 80.00
1980, Hark! The Herald Angels Sing
................................................ 80.00
Reco International
1980, I Love You, FE ............... 20.00
1981, Sea Echoes ................... 20.00
1982, Talk to Me ..................... 20.00
1988, Charity .......................... 15.00
1989, The Wedding ................. 15.00
Reed and Barton
Noel, Musical Bells
1980 ................................... 65.00
1983 ................................... 45.00
1984 ................................... 45.00
1986 ................................... 55.00
1989 ................................... 50.00
1992 ................................... 40.00
Yuletide
1981, Yuletide Holiday ........ 20.00
1982, Little Shepherd .......... 20.00
1985, Caroler ..................... 25.00
1987, Jolly St. Nick ............. 25.00
1988, Christmas Morning .... 20.00
1990, The Wreath Bearer .... 15.00
1992, My Special Friend ..... 20.00
1995, Christmas Puppy ...... 18.00
River Shore, Rockwell children Series
1977
First Day of School ............. 70.00
School Play ........................ 70.00
1978
Five Cents a Glass ............. 35.00
Garden Girl ........................ 37.00
Schmid
Peanuts
1976, Woodstock ............... 25.00

1977, Woodstock's Christmas
................................................ 18.00
1978, Mother's Day ............ 15.00
1979, A Special Letter......... 25.00
1980, Waiting for Santa ....... 25.00
1981, Mission for Mom ....... 20.00
1982, Perfect Performance.... 18.00
1983, Peanuts in Concert..... 12.00
1984, Snoopy and the Beagle Scouts ..................................12.00

Walt Disney, Christmas
1985, Snow Big ................... 15.00
1986, Tree for Two .............. 15.00
1987, Merry Mouse Medley .. 17.50
1988, Warm Winter Ride ..... 18.00
1989, Merry Mickey Claus .. 24.00
1990, Holly Jolly Christmas... 25.00
1991, Mickey & Minnie's Rockin' Christmas ............................25.00

Zemsky
1978, Christmas ................. 20.00
1979, Christmas, pewter ..... 25.00

Towle Silversmiths, SP
1980, ball .......................... 17.50
1982, musical...................... 27.50
1984, musical...................... 25.00
1986, ball .......................... 30.00
1988, musical...................... 35.00

Wedgwood
1979, Penguins, FE................... 40.00
1981, Polar Bears..................... 45.00
1982, Moose ........................... 40.00
1983, Fur Seals ....................... 50.00
1984, Ibex .............................. 60.00
1985, Puffin ............................ 60.00
1986, Ermine........................... 60.00

## Christmas Ornaments

Anri
Disney Four Star Collection, Disney Studios
1989, Maestro Mickey ......... 75.00
1990, Minnie Mouse............ 50.00
Ferrandiz Woodcarvings, J. Ferrandiz, artist
1988, Heavenly Drummer ... 250.00
1989, Heavenly Strings ..... 175.00

Bing & Grondahl, Santa Claus
1989, Santa's Workshop .......... 55.00
1990, Santa's Sleigh................ 55.00
1991, The Journey ................... 40.00
1994, Christmas Stories .......... 25.00

Danbury Mint, angel, 4" ............... 45.00

Dave Grossman Creations
Gone with the Wind
1987, Ashley....................... 40.00
1989, Mammy...................... 15.00
1990, Scarlett, red dress ..... 18.00
Rockwell Collection, annual figurine ornament
1978, Caroler...................... 44.00
1979, Drum for Tommy ........ 28.00
1983, Fiddler ...................... 27.00
1987, Skating Lesson.......... 30.00
1992, On the Ice................. 30.00

Enesco, Precious Moments, S. Butcher, artist
1982, Dropping in for Christmas
................................................ 40.00
1983, O Come All Ye Faithful ... 55.00
1985, God Sent His Love ......... 35.00
1986, Rocking Horse .............. 25.00
1988, Cheers to the Leader ..... 35.00

1992, I'm Nuts About You ........ 15.00
1994, You Are Always in My Heart
................................................ 20.00

Gorham, Annual Snowflake, SS
1972 .............................. 100.00
1973 ................................ 90.00
1976 ................................ 60.00
1981 .............................. 300.00
1987 ................................ 80.00
1990 ................................ 65.00
1994 ................................ 45.00

Hallmark
1974, Mary Hamilton, orig, Charmer Design............................... 7.50
1975, Betsy Clark.................... 7.50
1979, Special Teacher, satin...... 4.50
1980, Baby's First Christmas ... 15.00
1981
Candyville Express ............ 25.00
Friendly Fiddler ................. 15.00
St. Nicholas, tin ................. 10.00
1982
Cookie Mouse .................. 17.50
Cowboy Snowman ............. 10.00
Jingling Teddy................... 12.00
Peeking Elf ......................... 6.50
Soldier, clothespin, FE......... 25.00

Haviland
1972 .................................. 8.00
1973 .................................. 8.00
1974 ................................ 12.00
1975 .................................. 6.00
1976 .................................. 6.00
1977 .................................. 8.00
1978 .................................. 7.50
1979 .................................. 7.50
1980 ................................ 18.00
1981 ................................ 20.00
1982 ................................ 22.00

International Silver, Twelve Days of Christmas, SS, each ................ 25.00

Lenox, 1982, FE, snowflake emb porcelain, 24K gold finials, date, 6" h
................................................ 40.00

Lladro, Christmas Ball
1989 ................................ 60.00
1990 ................................ 70.00
1993 ................................ 50.00
1994 ................................ 50.00
1995 ................................ 50.00

Lunt
1974, Trefoil......................... 20.00
1980, Medallion .................... 18.00

Reed & Barton
Carousel Horse, SP
1988 ................................ 20.00
1990 ................................ 15.00
1994 ................................ 15.00

Christmas Cross
SS
1971 .............................. 350.00
1973 ................................ 87.00
1976 ................................ 80.00
1982 .............................. 140.00
1985 ................................ 80.00
1991 ................................ 75.00
1994 ................................ 35.00
24K gold over SS
1971 .............................. 300.00
1974 ................................ 55.00
1978 ................................ 50.00
1982 ................................ 43.00
1989 ................................ 38.00

1992 ................................ 40.00
1994 ................................ 45.00
1995 ................................ 45.00

Schmid
Paddington Bear, 1982
Ball....................................... 5.00
Figural ................................ 10.00
Raggedy Ann
1976, FE ............................. 6.00
1977 .................................. 3.50
1978 .................................. 3.00
1979 .................................. 3.25
1980 .................................. 3.00
1982, figural ...................... 10.00
Walt Disney
1974, FE ........................... 15.00
1975 .................................. 5.00
1976 ................................ 10.00
1977 .................................. 4.50
1978 .................................. 4.00
1979 .................................. 4.00
1980 .................................. 3.50
1981 .................................. 3.00
1982, figural ...................... 10.00

Towle
Twelve Days of Christmas medallion, SS
1971, Partridge in a Pear Tree
................................................ 550.00
1972, Two Turtle Doves..... 275.00
1973, Three French Hens
................................................ 100.00
1974, Four Calling Birds ... 150.00
1975, Five Golden Rings .. 100.00
1976, Six Geese a Laying
................................................ 125.00
1977, Seven Swans a Swimming
................................................ 200.00
1978, Eight Maids a Milking
................................................ 100.00
1979, Nine Ladies Dancing
................................................ 100.00
1980, Ten Lords a Leaping
................................................ 100.00
1981, Eleven Pipers Piping
................................................ 100.00
1982, Twelve Drummers Drumming ............................... 100.00
Songs of Christmas Medallions
1978, Silent Night................ 70.00
1979, Deck the Halls........... 70.00
1980, Jingle Bells................ 80.00
1981, Hark the Herald Angels Sing ................................. 130.00
1983, Silver Bells ............... 75.00
1984, Let It Snow ............... 75.00
1987, White Christmas........ 70.00

Wallace Silversmiths
Sleigh Bells, SP
1971 .............................. 900.00
1972 .............................. 450.00
1977 .............................. 200.00
1978 .............................. 100.00
1983 ................................ 90.00
1988 ................................ 50.00
1990 ................................ 50.00
1994 ................................ 30.00
Candy Canes
1981, Peppermint ............. 200.00
1982, Wintergreen............. 100.00
1983, Cinnamon................. 60.00
1986, Christmas Candle ..... 40.00
1991, Christmas Goose ...... 30.00
1994, Canes....................... 20.00

## Dolls

Annalee Mobilitee Dolls, Inc.
Doll Society, Folk Heroes, A. Thorndike, artist, 10" h
1984, Johnny Appleseed ............950.00
1985, Annie Oakley ..........700.00
1988, Sherlock Holmes .....450.00
1991, Christopher Columbus ............300.00
1995, Pocahontas ..............80.00
Doll Society, Logo Kids, A. Thorndike, artist
1985, Christmas Logo with Cookie ..........................650.00
1987, Naughty Logo..........400.00
1989, Christmas Morning Logo ............150.00
1992, Back to School Logo ............80.00

Ashton Drake
Brandon ...............................75.00
Hans ....................................85.00
Little Florence..........................85.00
Little Squirt ...............................47.00
Mary ...................................75.00
Michelle..............................85.00
Miki .....................................83.00
Ricky ...................................40.00
Ship & I................................80.00
Sweetie................................55.00
Where's Jamie.........................65.00
Yummy ................................47.00

Enesco Imports, Precious Moments
1981, Mikey, 18" h ..................225.00
1982, Tammy, 18" h .............650.00
1983, Katie Lynne, 16" h ........185.00
1984, Kristy, 12" h ................160.00
1985, Bethany, 12" h ..............145.00
1986, Bong Bong, 13" h.........165.00
1987, Angie, The Angel of Mercy ............160.00
1989, Wishing You Cloudless Skies ............115.00
1990, The Voice of Spring......150.00
1991, You Have Touched So Many Hearts ...............................90.00

Gorham
Gorham Dolls, S. Stone Aiken, artist
1981
Cecile, 16" .....................750.00
Christopher, 19".............500.00
1982
Baby in apricot dress, 16" ............350.00
Baby in blue dress, 12" ............300.00
1983, Jennifer, bride, 19" ............700.00
1985
Alexander, 19" ...............400.00
Odette, 19" ....................450.00
1986
Alissa .............................300.00
Emily, 14".......................375.00
1987, Juliet.......................375.00

Holly Hobbie, 1983
Blue girl
14"...................................225.00
18"...................................280.00
Little Amy, 14"....................235.00
Yesterday's Memories, 18" ............360.00

Limited Edition, S. Stone Aiken, artist
1982, Allison, 19"............ 4,300.00
1983, Ashley, 19"...............950.00
1984, Nicole,19"...............850.00
1985, Lydia, 19"............... 1,650.00
1986, Noel, Christmas, 19" ............750.00
1988, Andrew, 19" .............720.00
Valentine Ladies, P. Valentine, artist
1987
Elizabeth ......................450.00
Marianna......................400.00
1988, Felicia.......................300.00
1989
Julianna........................275.00
Rose.............................275.00

Hamilton Collection
1981, Hakata, Peony Maiden ............150.00
1985, Heather ........................125.00
1986, Nicole..........................50.00
1987, Priscilla........................50.00
1988, Mr. Spock ......................75.00
1989, Scotty .........................75.00

Lawton
Crystal Winter.......................325.00
Emperor's Nightingale............400.00
Marigold Garden ...................425.00

Royal Doulton by Nisbet
Little Model .........................185.00
Pink Sash ...........................145.00
Royal Baby...........................350.00
The Muffs ............................175.00
Winter ..................................180.00

Seymour Mann, Connoisseur Collection
1984, Miss Debutante............180.00
1985, Wendy ........................150.00
1986, Camelot Fairy...............225.00
1987, Dawn..........................175.00
1988, Jolie............................150.00
1989, Elizabeth .....................200.00
1990, Baby Sunshine..............90.00
1991, Dephine ......................125.00

## Eggs

Anri, 1979, Beatrix Potter...............5.00
Cybis Studios, 1983, FE .............300.00
Ferrandiz
1978, FE..................................15.00
1979......................................12.00
1980......................................9.50
1981......................................9.00
1982......................................8.00
1983......................................18.00
Franklin Mint, 1979, porcelain ......35.00
Goebel
1978, Easter............................10.00
1979, Easter..............................8.00
1980
Crystal .............................6.00
Easter..............................12.00
1981, Easter............................10.00
1982, Easter..............................8.00
1983, Easter............................28.00
Gorham, bone china, pink rose, 4-1/4" ............18.00
Noritake, Easter
1971, FE..................................75.00
1972......................................35.00
1973......................................18.00
1974......................................8.00
1975......................................10.00
1976......................................10.00

1977......................................12.50
1978......................................14.00
1979......................................14.00
1980......................................14.00
1981......................................15.00
1982......................................15.00
1983......................................28.00
1984......................................20.00
Royal Bayreuth
1975......................................8.50
1976......................................6.50
1977......................................5.50
1979......................................16.00
1980......................................15.00
Wedgwood
1977......................................35.00
1978......................................25.00
1979......................................18.00
1983......................................40.00

## Figurines

Anri, Sarah Kay, artist
1983, Morning Chores, 6", FE ............475.00
1984, Flowers for You, 6" .......400.00
1985, Afternoon Tea, 6"..........325.00
1986, Our Puppy, 1-1/2"..........90.00
1987, Little Nanny, 4" ............180.00
1988, Purrfect Day, 6"............400.00
1989, Garden Party, 4"..........195.00
1990, Season's Greetings, 4" ............225.00
1991, Season's Joy, 4" ..........250.00

Cybis
1963, Magnolia ....................400.00
1964, Rebecca .....................345.00
1965, Christmas Rose ..........750.00
1967, Kitten, blue ribbon .......500.00
1968, Narcissus ...................500.00
1969, Clematis with house wren ............315.00
1970, Dutch Crocus..............750.00
1971, Appaloosa Colt ............285.00
1972, Pansies ......................350.00
1973, Goldilocks ..................325.00
1974, Mary, Mary ..................750.00
1975, George Washington Bust ............300.00
1976, Bunny..........................125.00
1977, Tiffin ............................400.00
1978, Edith............................300.00
1982, Spring Bouquet............750.00
1985, Nativity Lamb................125.00
1986, Dapple Gray Foal ........185.00

Dave Grossman Designs, Norman Rockwell Collection
1973
Back to School...................40.00
Redhead ..........................200.00
1975, Discovery ...................160.00
1978, At the Doctor...............175.00
1980, Handkerchief ...............95.00
1981, Spirit of Education .......100.00
1982, American Mother .........110.00
1987, Young Love .................100.00

Department 56, Snowbabies
1986, Hold on Tight ...............12.00
1987, Down the Hill We Go......20.00
1988, Tiny Trio......................60.00
1989, Icy Igloo ......................35.00
1990, A Special Delivery .........12.00
1991, Just for You ..................20.00

Enesco Corp., Precious Moments
  1979, Jesus Loves Me ............... 30.00
  1980, Come Let Us Adore Him
    ...................................................... 90.00
  1981, But Love Goes on Forever
    .................................................... 165.00
  1982, I Believe in Miracles ....... 90.00
  1983, Sharing Our Season ..... 110.00
  1984, Joy to the World ............. 40.00
  1985, Baby's First Christmas ... 35.00
  1986, God Bless America ......... 50.00
  1987, This Is the Day the Lord Hath
  Made ...................................................... 35.00
  1988, Faith Takes the Plunge
    ...................................................... 30.00
  1989, Wishing You Roads of Happi-
  ness .......................................................... 50.00
  1990, To My Favorite Fan ......... 15.00
(Hummel, see HUMMEL)
Lladro
  1970, Girl with Guitar .......... 1,800.00
  1971
    Hamlet ...................... 3,000.00
    Oriental Man .................... 1,800.00
  1972, Turkey Group ............. 1,500.00
  1973
    Buck Hunters ................. 2,700.00
    Passionate Dance .......... 4250.00
    Turtle Doves ................... 2,375.00
  1974
    Ducks at Pond ............... 5,500.00
    Partridge ....................... 1,800.00
  1978
    Car in Trouble ..................... 6,000
    Flight of Gazelles ........... 3,000.00
    Henry VII ....................... 1,100.00
  1981
    Nest of Eagles, with base
      ........................................ 10,000.00
    Philippine Folklore .......... 2,000.00
    The Rescue ................... 5,000.00
  1983
    Bather .............................. 950.00
    In the Distance .............. 1,100.00
    Reclining Nude ................. 650.00
    Tranquillity .................... 1,300.00
    Youth .............................. 1,000.00
  1985, Thoroughbred Horse, with
  base .................................................... 600.00
  1986, Oriental Music, with base
    ...................................................... 2,400.00
  1989
    Southern Tea ................. 2,200.00
  1991, Champion ................. 1,900.00
  1992, Tea in the Garden ...... 9,500.00
  1993
    Autumn Glow, with base.... 770.00
    Indian Brave ................... 2,200.00
River Shore
  1978, Akiku, Baby Seal, FE.... 145.00
  1979, Rosecoe, red fox kit ....... 50.00
  1980, Lamb ............................. 48.00
  1981, Zuela, elephant ............. 60.00
  1982, Kay's Doll ..................... 90.00
(Rockwell, Norman, see NORMAN
  ROCKWELL)
Royal Doulton
  Beatrix Potter
    Benjamin Bunny .................. 25.00
    Lady Mouse........................ 20.00
    Mrs. Rabbit & Bunnies ........ 25.00
    Old Mr. Brown ..................... 20.00
    Peter Rabbit ....................... 25.00

    Rebecca Puddle-Duck........ 20.00
  Bunnykins
    Autumn Days..................... 17.00
    Clean Sweep ..................... 14.00
    Family Photograph ............. 24.00
    Grandpa's Story ................. 17.00
    Sleepy Time ...................... 12.00
    Springtime ........................ 18.00
    Tally Ho............................ 15.00
  Dickens
    Mrs. Bardell....................... 24.00
    Scrooge ........................... 25.00
  Lord of Rings, Tolkien
    Aragorn ............................ 45.00
    Bilbo ................................ 35.00
    Gandalf ............................ 50.00
    Gimli ................................ 45.00
    Gollum ............................. 35.00
    Legolas ............................ 45.00
  Myths and Maidens
    1982, Lady and the Unicorn,
    HN2825 ......................... 2,400.00
    1983, Leda and the Swan,
    HN2826 ......................... 2,800.00
    1984, Juno and the Peacock,
    HN2827 ......................... 3,000.00
    1985, Europa and the Bull,
    HN2828 ......................... 3,000.00
    1986, Diana the Huntress,
    HN2829 ......................... 3,000.00
  Prestige Figure, 1964, Indian Brave,
  HN2376 ............................. 5,250.00
  Royalty
    1973, Queen Elizabeth II,
    HN2502 ......................... 1,775.00
    1981
      Duke of Edinburgh, HN2386
        .................................. 440.00
      Prince of Wales, HN2884
        ............................... 1,000.00
    1982
      Princess of Wales, HN2887
        ............................... 1,450.00
      Lady Diana Spencer, HN2885
        .................................. 500.00
    1986, Duchess of York, HN3086
      .................................... 600.00
    1990, Queen Elizabeth, the
    Queen Mother, HN3189 .... 450.00
  Royal Orleans Porcelain, Marilyn Mon-
    roe ..................................... 80.00
  Schmid
    1979, Country Road ............... 275.00
    1980, Two's Company............. 45.00
    1981, Plum Tuckered Out ...... 225.00
    1982, Right Church, Wrong Pew
      ...................................... 80.00
    1983, Stirring Up Trouble ....... 165.00
    1984, Catnapping Too ............ 72.00
    1985, Out of Step..................... 45.00

**Mugs**
Bing & Grondahl, 1978, FE.......... 50.00
Franklin Mint, 1979, Father's Day
  ...................................................... 40.00
Gorham 1981, Bugs Bunny ............. 8.00
Lynell Studios, 1983, FE, Gnome Series
  Gnome Sweet Gnome................ 6.50
  Mama Gnome .......................... 7.00
Royal Copenhagen
  1967, large........................... 200.00
  1968, large........................... 24.00
  1972, large........................... 24.00

  1976, large........................... 25.00
  1979, small .......................... 28.00
  1980
    Large ............................. 65.00
    Small ............................. 25.00
  1981
    Large ............................. 70.00
    Small ............................. 35.00
  1983, small .......................... 30.00
Schmid, Zemsky, musical, 1981, Paddington Bear ......................... 25.00
Wedgwood
  1971, Christmas ..................... 35.00
  1972, Christmas ..................... 30.00
  1973, Christmas ..................... 40.00
  1974, Christmas ..................... 30.00
  1975, Christmas ..................... 30.00
  1976, Christmas ..................... 30.00
  1977, Father's Day ................. 25.00
  1978, Father's Day ................. 25.00
  1979, Christmas ..................... 25.00
  1980, Christmas ..................... 25.00
  1981, Christmas ..................... 35.00
  1982, Christmas ..................... 40.00

**Music Boxes**
Anri
  Jemima ................................. 100.00
  Peter Rabbit.......................... 100.00
  Pigling ................................. 100.00
Ferrandiz
  Chorale ................................ 125.00
  Drummer............................... 185.00
  Flower Girl............................ 150.00
  Going Home .......................... 275.00
  The Letter ............................ 150.00
  Proud Mother ........................ 140.00
  Spring Arrivals ...................... 120.00
  Wanderlust............................ 110.00
Gorham
  Cardinal, double, 6" h, hp, sculp-
  tured, porcelain...................... 30.00
  Happy Birthday, animals.......... 35.00
  Santa & Sleigh, 6" h ............... 20.00
  Sesame Street, Big Bird & Snowman,
  7" h...................................... 24.00
Schmid
  Peanuts
    30th Anniversary ................. 18.00
    1981
      Christmas...................... 28.00
      Mother's Day .................. 18.00
    1982
      Christmas...................... 30.00
      Mother's Day .................. 20.00
  Raggedy Ann
    1980 ................................. 15.00
    1981 ................................. 15.00
    1982, Flying High ............... 20.00
  Walt Disney
    1980, Christmas, FE........... 42.00
    1981, Christmas ................. 30.00
    1982, Christmas ................. 25.00

**Plates**
Anri (Italy)
  Christmas, J. Ferrandiz, 12" d
    1972, Christ in the Manger
      .................................. 230.00
    1973, Christmas ................. 220.00
    1974, Holy Night ................. 90.00
    1975, Flight into Egypt ........ 80.00
    1976, Tree of Life ............... 60.00
    1977, Girl with Flowers ...... 175.00

1978, Leading the Way ..... 165.00
1979, The Drummer .......... 170.00
1980, Rejoice .................... 150.00
1981, Spreading the Word
.................................... 150.00
1982, The Shepherd Family
.................................... 150.00
1983, Peace Attend Thee
.................................... 150.00
Mother's Day, J. Ferrandiz
1972, Mother Sewing ........ 200.00
1973, Alpine Mother & Child
.................................... 150.00
1974, Mother Holding Child
.................................... 150.00
1975, Dove Girl ................. 150.00
1976, Mother Knitting ........ 200.00
1977, Alpine Stroll ............. 125.00
1978, The Beginning ......... 150.00
1979, All Hearts ................ 165.00
1980, Spring Arrivals ......... 160.00
1981, Harmony.................. 150.00
1982, With Love................. 150.00
Bareuther (Germany), Christmas, Hans
Mueller artist, 8" d
1967, Stiftskirche, FE ............... 90.00
1968, Kapplkirche ..................... 25.00
1969, Christkindlmarkt ........... 20.00
1970, Chapel in Oberndorf ...... 18.00
1971, Toys for Sale.................. 20.00
1972, Christmas in Munich ...... 35.00
1973, Christmas Sleigh Ride.... 20.00
1974, Church in the Black Forest
.................................... 20.00
1975, Snowman ...................... 25.00
1 976, Chapel in the Hills ........ 25.00
1977, Story Time ..................... 30.00
1978, Mittenwald..................... 30.00
1979, Winter Day..................... 40.00
1980, Miltenberg..................... 38.00
1981, Walk in the Forest........... 40.00
1982, Bad Wimpfen ................. 40.00
1983, The Night Before Christmas
.................................... 45.00
1984, Zeil on the River Main ... 42.50
1985, Winter Wonderland ........ 42.50
1986, Christmas in Forchhe ..... 42.50
1987, Decorating the Tree........ 46.50
1988, St. Coloman Church....... 80.00
1989, Sleigh Ride.................... 50.00
1990, The Old Forge in Rothenburg
.................................... 50.00
1991, Christmas Joy ................ 55.00
1992, Marketplace in Heppenheim
.................................... 55.00
Berlin (Germany), Christmas, various
artists, 7-3/4" d
1970, Christmas in Bernkastel
.................................... 130.00
1971, Christmas in Rothenburg on
Tauber ................................ 30.00
1972, Christmas in Michelstadt
.................................... 50.00
1973, Christmas in Wendelstein
.................................... 42.00
1974, Christmas in Bremen...... 25.00
1975, Christmas in Dortland .... 60.00
1976, Christmas Eve in Augsburg
.................................... 30.00
1977, Christmas Eve in Hamburg
.................................... 32.00
1978, Christmas Market at the Berlin
Cathedral ............................. 55.00

1979, Christmas Eve in Greetsiel
.................................... 55.00
1980, Christmas Eve in Miltenberg
.................................... 55.00
1981, Christmas Eve in Hahnenklee
.................................... 50.00
1982, Christmas Eve in Wasserburg
.................................... 55.00
1983, Chapel in Oberndorf...... 55.00
1984, Christmas in Ramsau..... 50.00
1985, Christmas Eve in Bad
Wimpfen................................ 55.00
1986, Christmas Eve in Gelnhaus
.................................... 65.00
1987, Christmas Eve in Goslar
.................................... 70.00
1988, Christmas Eve in Ruhpolding
.................................... 100.00
1989, Christmas Eve in Freidechs-
dadt..................................... 100.00
1990, Christmas Eve in Parten-
kirchen ................................ 80.00
1991, Christmas Eve in Allendorf
.................................... 80.00
Bing and Grondahl (Denmark)
Christmas, various artists, 7" d
1895, Behind the Frozen Window
.................................... 3,400.00
1896, New Moon Over Snow-Cov-
ered Trees ..................... 1,975.00
1897, Christmas Meal of the Spar-
rows................................... 725.00
1898, Christmas Roses and
Christmas Star................... 700.00
1899, The Crows Enjoying Christ-
mas ................................. 900.00
1900, Church Bells Chiming in
Christmas .......................... 800.00
1901, The Three Wise Men from
the East ............................ 450.00
1902, Interior of a Gothic Church
.................................... 285.00
1903, Happy Expectation of Chil-
dren................................... 150.00
1904, View of Copenhagen from
Frederiksberg Hill.............. 125.00
1905, Anxiety of the Coming
Christmas Night ................ 130.00
1906, Sleighing to Church on
Christmas Eve .................. 135.00
1907, The Little Match Girl
.................................... 175.00
1908, St. Petri Church of Copen-
hagen................................... 85.00
1909, Happiness Over the Yule
Tree ................................... 100.00
1910, The Old Organist....... 90.00
1911, First It Was Sung by Angels
to Shepherds in the Fields .. 80.00
1912, Going to Church on Christ-
mas Eve ............................. 80.00
1913, Bringing Home the Yule
Tree ................................... 90.00
1914, Royal Castle of Amalien-
borg, Copenhagen.............. 75.00
1915, Chained Dog Getting Double Meal on Christmas Eve
.................................... 120.00
1916, Christmas Prayer of the
Sparrows............................. 85.00
1917, Arrival of the Christmas
Boat..................................... 75.00
1918, Fishing Boat Returning

Home for Christmas ............ 85.00
1919, Outside the Lighted Win-
dow ...................................... 80.00
1920, Hare in the Snow....... 70.00
1921, Pigeons in the Castle Court
.................................... 55.00
1922, Star of Bethlehem ..... 75.00
1923, Royal Hunting Castle, The
Hermitage ........................... 55.00
1924, Lighthouse in Danish
Waters ................................. 65.00
1925, The Child's Christmas
.................................... 70.00
1926, Churchgoers on Christmas
Day....................................... 65.00
1927, Skating Couple ......... 80.00
1928, Eskimo Looking at Village
Church in Greenland........... 60.00
1929, Fox Outside Farm ...... 80.00
1930, Yule Tree in Town Hall
Square of Copenhagen....... 85.00
1931, Arrival of the Christmas
Train ..................................... 75.00
1932, Lifeboat at Work ........ 90.00
1933, The Korsor-Nyborg Ferry
.................................... 70.00
1934, Church Bell in Tower
.................................... 70.00
1935, Lillebelt Bridge Connect-
ing Funen with Jutland........ 65.00
1936, Royal Guard ............. 70.00
1937, Arrival of Christmas Guests
.................................... 75.00
1938, Lighting the Candles
.................................... 110.00
1939, Ole Lock-Eye, The Sand-
man ..................................... 150.00
1940, Delivering Christmas Let-
ters ...................................... 170.00
1941, Horses Enjoying Christmas
Meal in Stable .................... 345.00
1942, Danish Farm on Christmas
Night ................................... 150.00
1943, The Ribe Cathedral
.................................... 155.00
1944, Sorgenfri Castle ...... 120.00
1945, The Old Water Mill... 135.00
1946, Commemoration Cross in
Honor of Danish Sailors Who Lost
Their Lives in World War II .. 85.00
1947, Dybbol Mill ............... 70.00
1948, Watchman, Sculpture of
Town Hall, Copenhagen...... 80.00
1949, Landsoldaten, 19th Century
Danish Soldier.................... 70.00
1950, Kronborg Castle at Elsinore
.................................... 150.00
1951, Jens Bang, New Passenger
Boat Running Between Copenhagen and Aalborg........... 115.00
1952, Old Copenhagen Canals at
Wintertime with Thorvaldsen
Museum in Background....... 85.00
1953, Royal Boat in Greenland
Waters ............................... 125.00
1954, Birthplace of Hans Chris-
tian Andersen, with Snowman
.................................... 100.00
1955, Kalundborg Church
.................................... 115.00
1956, Christmas in Copenhagen
.................................... 140.00
1957, Christmas Candles.... 155.00

1958, Santa Claus ............. 100.00
1959, Christmas Eve ........ 120.00
1960, Danish Village Church
................................................ 180.00
1961, Winter Harmony ...... 115.00
1962, Winter Night............. 80.00
1963, The Christmas Elf .... 120.00
1964, The Fir Tree and Hare
................................................. 50.00
1965, Bringing Home the Christmas Tree ............................ 65.00
1966, Home for Christmas .. 50.00
1967, Sharing the Joy of Christmas................................... 48.00
1968, Christmas in Church ... 45.00
1969, Arrival of Christmas Guests
................................................ 30.00
1970, Pheasants in the Snow at Christmas ...................... 20.00
1971, Christmas at Home.... 20.00
1972, Christmas in Greenland
................................................ 20.00
1973, Country Christmas .... 25.00
1974, Christmas in the Village
................................................ 20.00
1975, The Old Water Mill..... 24.00
1976, Christmas Welcome .. 25.00
1977, Copenhagen Christmas
................................................ 25.00
1978, A Christmas Tale ....... 30.00
1979, White Christmas ....... 30.00
1980, Christmas in the Woods
................................................ 42.50
1981, Christmas Peace ....... 50.00
1982, The Christmas Tree ... 55.00
1983, Christmas in Old Town
................................................ 55.00
1984, Christmas Letter........ 55.00
1985, Christmas Eve at the Farmhouse.................................. 55.00
1986, Silent Night, Holy Night
................................................ 55.00
1987, The Snowman's Christmas Eve .................................. 60.00
1988, In the Kings Garden .. 72.00
1989, Christmas Anchorage
................................................ 65.00
1990, Changing of the Guards
................................................ 60.00
1991, Copenhagen Stock Exchange ............................ 70.00
1992, Christmas at the Rectory
................................................ 65.00
1993, Father Christmas in Copenhagen ................................. 65.00
1994, A Day at the Deer Park
................................................ 80.00
1995, The Towers of Copenhagen
................................................ 85.00
1996, Winter at the Old Mill
................................................ 70.00
1997, Country Christmas .... 65.00
1998, Santa the Storyteller
................................................ 65.00
1999, Dancing on Christmas Eve
................................................ 65.00

Christmas in America
1986, Williamsburg............ 150.00
1987, Christmas at the White House................................... 25.00
1988, Christmas at Rockefeller Center................................. 45.00
1989, Christmas in New England
................................................ 45.00

1990, Christmas Eve At The Capitol ...................................... 42.00
1991, Christmas at Independence Hall ....................... 45.00
1991, Williamsburg, Jubilee
................................................ 45.00
1992, Christmas in San Francisco
................................................ 45.00
1993, Coming Home for Christmas ................................... 36.00
1994, Christmas Eve in Alaska
................................................ 47.00
1995, Christmas Eve at the Mississippi.............................. 36.00
Mother's Day, Henry Thelander, artist, 6" d
1969, Dog and Puppies .... 325.00
1970, Bird and Chicks ........ 25.00
1971, Cat and Kitten .......... 24.00
1972, Mare and Foal .......... 20.00
1973, Duck and Ducklings ....20.00
1974, Bear and Cubs.......... 24.00
1975, Doe and Fawns ........ 20.00
1976, Swan Family ............. 22.00
1977, Squirrel and Young.... 25.00
1978, Heron ....................... 20.00
1979, Fox and Cubs........... 20.00
1980, Woodpecker and Young
................................................ 30.00
1981, Hare and Young ........ 30.00
1982, Lioness and Cubs ..... 45.00
1983, Raccoon and Young
................................................ 25.00
1984, Stork and Nestlings... 30.00
1985, Bear and Cubs.......... 30.00
1986, Elephant with Calf ..... 40.00
1987, Sheep with Lambs .... 50.00
1988, Lapwing Mother with Chicks ............................... 75.00
1989, Cow with Calf ........... 48.00
1990, Hen with Chicks ........ 50.00
1991, The Nanny Goat and Her Two Frisky Kids ................... 75.00
1992, Panda with Cubs....... 80.00
1993, St. Bernard Dog and Puppies ................................. 55.00
1994, Cat with Kittens ........ 80.00
1995, Hedgehog with Young
................................................ 55.00
1996, Koala with Young....... 60.00
Franklin Mint (United States)
Audubon Society Birds
1972, Goldfinch................ 115.00
1972, Wood Duck ............. 110.00
1973, Cardinal................. 110.00
1973, Ruffled Grouse ........ 120.00
Christmas, Norman Rockwell, artist, etched SS, 8" d
1970, Bringing Home the Tree
................................................ 275.00
1971, Under the Mistletoe
................................................ 125.00
1972, The Carolers............ 125.00
1973, Trimming the Tree.... 100.00
1974, Hanging the Wreath
................................................ 100.00
1975, Home for Christmas
................................................ 125.00
(Goebel, Germany, see Hummel)
Haviland & Parlon (France)
Christmas Series, various artists, 10" d
1972, Madonna and Child, Raphael, FE........................ 80.00

1973, Madonna, Feruzzi ..... 95.00
1974, Cowper Madonna and Child, Raphael .................... 40.00
1975, Madonna and Child, Murillo
................................................ 45.00
1976, Madonna and Child, Botticelli................................... 50.00
1977, Madonna and Child, Bellini
................................................ 40.00
1978, Madonna and Child, Fra Filippo, Lippi .......................... 65.00
1979, Madonna of the Eucharist, Botticelli ........................... 150.00
Lady and the Unicorn Series, artist unknown, 10" d
1977, To My Only Desire, FE
................................................ 60.00
1978, Sight......................... 40.00
1979, Sound........................ 50.00
1980, Touch ...................... 110.00
1981, Scent........................ 60.00
1982, Taste......................... 80.00
Tapestry Series, artists unknown, 10" d
1971, The Unicorn in Captivity
................................................ 145.00
1972, Start of the Hunt........ 70.00
1973, Chase of the Unicorn
................................................ 120.00
1974, End of the Hunt ......... 120.00
1975, The Unicorn Surrounded
................................................ 75.00
1976, The Unicorn is Brought to the Castle .......................... 55.00
Edwin M. Knowles (United States)
American Holidays Series, Don Spaulding, artist, 8-1/2" d
1978, Fourth of July, FE ...... 35.00
1979, Thanksgiving............. 35.00
1980, Easter....................... 30.00
1981, Valentine's Day.......... 25.00
1982, Father's Day ............. 35.00
1983, Christmas.................. 35.00
1984, Mother's Day ............ 20.00
Annie Series
1983
    Annie and Sandy, FE ...... 25.00
    Daddy Warbucks............ 20.00
    Annie & Grace ............... 19.00
1984, Annie and the Orphans
................................................ 20.00
1985, Tomorrow.................. 21.00
1986
    Annie, Lily and Rooster... 24.00
    Grand Finale ................... 24.00
Gone with the Wind Series, Raymond Kursar, artist, 8-1/2" d
1978, Scarlett, FE.............. 300.00
1979, Ashley ..................... 225.00
1980, Melanie .................... 75.00
1981, Rhett........................ 50.00
1982, Mammy Lacing Scarlett
................................................ 60.00
1983, Melanie Gives Birth ... 85.00
1984, Scarlett's Green Dress
................................................ 50.00
1985
    Rhett and Bonnie ........... 35.00
    Scarlett and Rhett: The Finale
................................................ 30.00
Wizard of Oz Series, James Auckland, artist, 8-1/2" d
1977, Over the Rainbow, FE
................................................ 65.00

1978
    If I Only Had a Brain ....... 30.00
    If I Only Had a Heart ....... 30.00
    If I Were King of the Forest
    .................................. 30.00
1979
    Wicked Witch of the West
    .................................. 35.00
    Follow the Yellow Brick Road
    .................................. 35.00
    Wonderful Wizard of Oz .. 50.00
    1980, The Grand Finale (We're Off
    to See The Wizard) ............. 60.00
Lalique (France), Annual Series, lead
crystal, Marie-Claude Lalique, artist,
8-1/2" d
    1965, Deux Oiseaux (Two Birds), FE
    .................................. 800.00
    1966, Rose de Songerie (Dream
    Rose)............................ 215.00
    1967, Ballet de Poisson (Fish Ballet)
    .................................. 200.00
    1968, Gazelle Fantaisie (Gazelle
    Fantasy) ......................... 70.00
    1969, Papillon (Butterfly).......... 80.00
    1970, Paon (Peacock).............. 50.00
    1971, Hibou (Owl)................. 60.00
    1972, Coquillage (Shell).......... 55.00
    1973, Petit Geai (Jayling)........ 60.00
    1974, Sous d'Argent (Silver Pennies)
    .................................. 65.00
    1975, Due de Poisson (Fish Duet)
    .................................. 75.00
    1976, Aigle (Eagle) ............... 100.00
Lenox (United States)
    Boehm Bird Series, Edward Marshall
    Boehm, artist, 10-1/2" d
    1970, Wood Thrush, FE..... 135.00
    1971, Goldfinch.................. 60.00
    1972, Mountain Bluebird ..... 40.00
    1973, Meadowlark............... 50.00
    1974, Rufous Hummingbird
    .................................. 45.00
    1975, American Redstart .... 50.00
    1976, Cardinal.................... 58.00
    1977, Robins ...................... 55.00
    1978, Mockingbirds ............ 60.00
    1979, Golden-Crowned Kinglets
    .................................. 65.00
    1980, Black-Throated Blue War-
    blers ............................... 75.00
    1981, Eastern Phoebes....... 90.00
    Boehm Woodland Wildlife Series,
    Edward Marshall Boehm, artist,
    10-1/2"
    1973, Raccoons, FE............ 80.00
    1974, Red Foxes ................. 50.00
    1975, Cottontail Rabbits..... 60.00
    1976, Eastern Chipmunks... 60.00
    1977, Beaver...................... 60.00
    1978, Whitetail Deer............ 60.00
    1979, Squirrels ................... 75.00
    1980, Bobcats .................... 90.00
    1981, Martens .................... 100.00
    1982, River Otters ............. 100.00
Lladro (Spain)
    Christmas, 8" d, undisclosed artists
    1971, Caroling.................... 30.00
    1972, Icarolers.................... 35.00
    1973, Boy & Girl ................. 50.00
    1974, Carolers.................... 75.00
    1975, Cherubs.................... 60.00
    1976, Christ Child............... 50.00

    1977, Nativity ...................... 70.00
    1978, Caroling Child ........... 50.00
    1979, Snow Dance.............. 80.00
Mother's Day, undisclosed artists
    1971, Kiss of the Child ........ 75.00
    1972, Birds & Chicks .......... 30.00
    1973, Mother & Children ..... 35.00
    1974, Nursing Mother ....... 135.00
    1975, Mother & Child .......... 55.00
    1976, Virgil ........................ 50.00
    1977, Mother & Daughter.... 60.00
    1978, New Arrival................ 55.00
    1979, Off to School ............. 90.00
Reco International Corp. (United States)
Days Gone By, Sandra Kuck, artist
    1983
        Sunday Best.................... 55.00
        Amy's Magic Horse......... 30.00
    1984
        Little Anglers .................. 30.00
        Little Tutor ...................... 30.00
        Easter at Grandma's ....... 30.00
McClelland's Children's Circus
Series, John McClelland, artist, 9" d
    1981, Tommy the Clown, FE
    .................................. 45.00
    1982, Katie the Tightrope Walker
    .................................. 35.00
    1983, Johnny the Strongman
    .................................. 35.00
    1984, Maggie the Animal Trainer
    .................................. 30.00
McClelland's Mother Goose Series,
John McClelland, artist, 8-1/2" d
    1979, Mary, Mary, FE......... 250.00
    1980, Little Boy Blue ......... 100.00
    1981, Little Miss Muffet ....... 30.00
    1982, Little Jack Horner ...... 30.00
    1983, Little Bo Peep............ 40.00
    1984, Diddle, Diddle Dumpling
    .................................. 30.00
    1985, Mary Had a Little Lamb
    .................................. 42.00
    1986, Jack and Jill .............. 25.00
Reed & Barton (United States)
    Christmas Series, Damascene sil-
    ver, 11" d through 1978, 8" d 1979-
    1981
    1970, A Partridge in a Pear Tree,
    FE .................................. 200.00
    1971, We Three Kings of Orient
    Are.................................. 65.00
    1972, Hark! The Herald Angels
    Sing.................................. 60.00
    1973, Adoration of the Kings
    .................................. 75.00
    1974, The Adoration of the Magi
    .................................. 60.00
    1975, Adoration of the Kings
    .................................. 65.00
    1976, Morning Train ........... 60.00
    1977, Decorating the Church
    .................................. 60.00
    1978, The General Store at Christ-
    mas Time.......................... 67.00
    1979, Merry Old Santa Claus
    .................................. 65.00
    1980, Gathering Christmas
    Greens ............................. 75.00
    1981, The Shopkeeper at Christ-
    mas .................................. 75.00

(Rockwell, see Norman Rockwell)
Rosenthal (Germany)
    Christmas, Bjorn Wiinblad, artist
    1971, Maria & Child .......... 700.00
    1972, Caspar ................... 550.00
    1973, Melchior ................. 375.00
    1974, Balthazar................. 500.00
    1975, The Annunciation.... 190.00
    1976, Angel with Trumpet
    .................................. 200.00
    1977, Adoration of Shepherds
    .................................. 225.00
    1978, Angel with Harp ...... 275.00
    1979, Exodus From Egypt
    .................................. 310.00
    1980, Angel with a Glockenspiel
    .................................. 360.00
    1981, Christ Child Visits Temple
    .................................. 365.00
    1982, Christening of Christ
    .................................. 375.00
    Christmas, various artists, 8-1/2" d
    1910, Winter Peace........... 550.00
    1911, The Three Wise Men
    .................................. 325.00
    1912, Shooting Stars......... 250.00
    1913, Christmas Lights ..... 235.00
    1914, Christmas Song ...... 350.00
    1915, Walking to Church... 180.00
    1916, Christmas During War
    .................................. 235.00
    1917, Angel of Peace ....... 210.00
    1918, Peace on Earth ....... 210.00
    1919, St. Christopher with the
    Christ Child ...................... 225.00
    1920, The Manger in Bethlehem
    .................................. 325.00
    1921, Christmas in the Mountains
    .................................. 200.00
    1922, Advent Branch ........ 200.00
    1923, Children in the Winter Wood
    .................................. 200.00
    1924, Deer in the Woods.....200.00
    1925, The Three Wise Men
    .................................. 200.00
    1926, Christmas in the Mountains
    .................................. 175.00
    1927, Station on the Way.....200.00
    1928, Chalet Christmas ..... 175.00
    1929, Christmas in the Alps
    .................................. 225.00
    1930, Group of Deer Under the
    Pines ............................... 225.00
    1931, Path of the Magi...... 225.00
    1932, Christ Child ............ 195.00
    1933, Through the Night to Light
    .................................. 190.00
    1934, Christmas Peace..... 200.00
    1935, Christmas By the Sea
    .................................. 185.00
    1936, Nürnberg Angel ...... 185.00
    1937, Berchtesgaden ....... 195.00
    1938, Christmas in the Alps
    .................................. 190.00
    1939, Schneekoppe Mountain
    .................................. 195.00
    1940, Marien Church in Danzig
    .................................. 250.00
    1941, Strassburg Cathedral
    .................................. 250.00
    1942, Marianburg Castle .. 300.00
    1943, Winter Idyll ............. 300.00
    1944, Wood Scape .......... 275.00

1945, Christmas Peace ..... 370.00
1946, Christmas in an Alpine Valley ...................... 250.00
1947, The Dillingen Madonna ...................... 975.00
1948, Message to the Shepherds ...................... 850.00
1949, The Holy Family ....... 185.00
1950, Christmas in the Forest ...................... 175.00
1951, Star of Bethlehem .... 450.00
1952, Christmas in the Alps ...................... 190.00
1953, The Holy Light ...... 185.00
1954, Christmas Eve ........ 180.00
1955, Christmas in a Village ...................... 190.00
1956, Christmas in the Alps ...................... 185.00
1957, Christmas by the Sea ...................... 195.00
1958, Christmas Eve ........ 185.00
1959, Midnight Mass ........ 195.00
1960, Christmas Eve in a Small Village ...................... 190.00
1961, Solitary Christmas ... 225.00
1962, Christmas Eve ........ 185.00
1963, Silent Night ............ 185.00
1964, Christmas Market in Nürnberg ...................... 225.00
1965, Christmas in Munich ...................... 185.00
1966, Christmas in Ulm ..... 250.00
1967, Christmas in Regensburg ...................... 185.00
1968, Christmas in Bremen ...................... 190.00
1969, Christmas in Rothenburg ...................... 220.00
1970, Christmas in Cologne ...................... 165.00
1971, Christmas in Garmisch ...................... 100.00
1972, Christmas in Franconia ...................... 90.00
1973, Christmas in Lubeck-Holstein ...................... 110.00
1974, Christmas in Wurzburg ...................... 95.00

Royal Copenhagen (Denmark)
  Christmas, various artists, 6" d 1908, 1909, 1910; 7" d 1911 to present
    1909, Danish Landscape ... 150.00
    1910, The Magi ................ 120.00
    1911, Danish Landscape ...................... 135.00
    1912, Elderly Couple by Christmas Tree ...................... 120.00
    1913, Spire of Frederik's Church, Copenhagen ...................... 125.00
    1914, Sparrows in Tree at Church of the Holy Spirit, Copenhagen ...................... 100.00
    1915, Danish Landscape .. 150.00
    1916, Shepherd in the Field on Christmas Night ............... 85.00
    1917, Tower of Our Savior's Church, Copenhagen .......... 90.00
    1918, Sheep and Shepherds ...................... 80.00
    1919, In the Park ............... 80.00
    1920, Mary with the Child Jesus ...................... 75.00

1921, Aabenraa Marketplace ...................... 75.00
1922, Three Singing Angels ...................... 70.00
1923, Danish Landscape .... 70.00
1924, Christmas Star Over the Sea and Sailing Ship ........ 100.00
1925, Street Scene from Christianshavn, Copenhagen ...... 85.00
1926, View of Christmas Canal, Copenhagen ...................... 75.00
1927, Ship's Boy at the Tiller on Christmas Night ............... 140.00
1928, Vicar's Family on Way to Church ...................... 75.00
1929, Grundtvig Church, Copenhagen ...................... 100.00
1930, Fishing Boats on the Way to the Harbor ...................... 80.00
1931, Mother and Child ...... 90.00
1932, Frederiksberg Gardens with Statue of Frederik VI .... 90.00
1933, The Great Belt Ferry ...................... 110.00
1934, The Hermitage Castle ...................... 115.00
1935, Fishing Boat off Kronborg Castle ...................... 145.00
1936, Roskilde Cathedral ... 130.00
1937, Christmas Scene in Main Street, Copenhagen .......... 135.00
1938, Round Church in Osterlars on Bornholm ...................... 200.00
1939, Expeditionary Ship in Pack-Ice of Greenland ............... 180.00
1940, The Good Shepherd ...................... 300.00
1941, Danish Village Church ...................... 250.00
1942, Bell Tower of Old Church in Jutland ...................... 300.00
1943, Flight of Holy Family to Egypt ...................... 425.00
1944, Typical Danish Winter Scene ...................... 160.00
1945, A Peaceful Motif ...... 325.00
1946, Zealand Village Church ...................... 150.00
1947, The Good Shepherd ...................... 210.00

**Royal Copenhagen, 1970, Christmas Rose and Cat, 7-1/4" d, $40.**

1948, Nodebo Church at Christmastime ...................... 150.00
1949, Our Lady's Cathedral, Copenhagen ...................... 165.00
1950, Boeslunde Church, Zealand ...................... 175.00
1951, Christmas Angel ..... 300.00
1952, Christmas in the Forest ...................... 120.00
1953, Frederiksborg Castle ...................... 120.00
1954, Amalienborg Palace, Copenhagen ...................... 150.00
1955, Fano Girl ................. 185.00
1956, Rosenborg Castle, Copenhagen ...................... 160.00
1957, The Good Shepherd ...................... 115.00
1958, Sunshine over Greenland ...................... 140.00
1959, Christmas Night ...... 120.00
1960, The Stag................. 125.00
1961, Training Ship Danmark ...................... 155.00
1962, The Little Mermaid at Wintertime ...................... 200.00
1963, Hojsager Mill ........... 80.00
1964, Fetching the Tree ...... 75.00
1965, Little Skaters ............ 60.00
1966, Blackbird................. 55.00
1967, The Royal Oak ......... 45.00
1968, The Last Umiak ........ 40.00
1969, The Old Farmyard ..... 35.00
1970, Christmas Rose and Cat ...................... 40.00
1971, Hare in Winter .......... 80.00
1972, In the Desert ............ 30.00
1973, Train Homeward Bound for Christmas ...................... 22.00
1974, Winter Twilight .......... 30.00
1975, Queen's Palace ........ 20.00
1976, Danish Watermill ....... 35.00
1977, Immervad Bridge ...... 25.00
1978, Greenland Scenery ... 33.00
1979, Choosing the Christmas Tree ...................... 50.00
1980, Bringing Home the Tree ...................... 45.00
1981, Admiring the Christmas Tree ...................... 55.00
1982, Waiting for Christmas ...................... 60.00
1983, Merry Christmas........ 50.00
1984, Jingle Bells............... 55.00
1985, Snowman ................. 65.00
1986, Christmas Vacation ... 55.00
1987, Winter Birds.............. 58.00
1988, Christmas Eve in Copenhagen ...................... 65.00
1989, The Old Skating Pond ...................... 70.00
1990, Christmas at Tivoli... 130.00
1991, The Festival of Santa Lucia ...................... 100.00
1992, The Queen's Carriage ...................... 85.00
1993, Christmas Guests ..... 95.00
1994, Christmas Shopping ...................... 75.00
1996, Lighting the Street Lamp ...................... 70.00
1997, Roskilde Cathedral ... 80.00
1998, Coming Home for Christmas ...................... 55.00

1999, The Sleigh Ride ......... 60.00
Christmas In Denmark
 1991, Bringing Home the Tree
 ............................................ 48.00
 1992, Christmas Shopping ... 45.00
 1993, The Skating Party ...... 45.00
 1994, The Sleigh Ride ......... 45.00
 1995, Christmas Tales ......... 45.00
 1996, Christmas Eve .......... 45.00
Mother's Day, various artists, 6-1/4" d
 1971, American Mother ..... 125.00
 1972, Oriental Mother .......... 60.00
 1973, Danish Mother ........... 60.00
 1974, Greenland Mother ..... 55.00
 1975, Bird in Nest ............... 50.00
 1976, Mermaids .................. 50.00
 1977, The Twins ................. 50.00
 1978, Mother and Child ....... 25.00
 1979, A Loving Mother ........ 30.00
 1980, An Outing with Mother
 ............................................ 35.00
 1981, Reunion .................... 40.00
 1982, The Children's Hour ... 45.00
Royal Doulton (Great Britain)
 Beswick Christmas Series, various
 artists, earthenware in hand-cast
 bas-relief, 8" sq
 1972, Christmas in England, FE
 ............................................ 40.00
 1973, Christmas in Mexico .... 25.00
 1974, Christmas in Bulgaria... 40.00
 1975, Christmas in Norway .... 54.00
 1976, Christmas in Holland.... 45.00
 1977, Christmas in Poland.... 100.00
 1978, Christmas in America ... 45.00
 Mother and Child Series, Edna Hibel,
 artist, 8" d
 1973, Colette and Child, FE
 .......................................... 450.00
 1974, Sayuri and Child ...... 150.00
 1975, Kristina and Child .... 125.00
 1976, Marilyn and Child ..... 100.00
 1977, Lucia and Child ....... 100.00
 1978, Kathleen and Child.... 95.00
 Valentine's Day Series, artists
 unknown, 8-1/4" d
 1976, Victorian Boy and Girl
 ............................................ 60.00
 1977, My Sweetest Friend... 40.00
 1978, If I Love You .............. 40.00
 1979, My Valentine ............. 40.00
 1980, On a Swing ............... 40.00
 1981, Sweet Music ............. 35.00
 1982, From My Heart .......... 40.00
 1983, Cherub's Song .......... 45.00
 1984, Love in Bloom ........... 40.00
 1985, Accept These Flowers
 ............................................ 40.00
Schmid (Japan)
 Christmas, J. Malfertheiner, artist
 1971, St. Jakob in Groden, FE
 .......................................... 125.00
 1972, Pipers at Alberobello
 .......................................... 120.00
 1973, Alpine Horn ............. 375.00
 1974, Young Man and Girl
 .......................................... 100.00
 1975, Christmas in Ireland
 ............................................ 90.00
 1976, Alpine Christmas ..... 200.00
 1977, Legend of Heligenblut
 .......................................... 125.00
 1978, Klockler Singers ...... 175.00

**Schmid, Peanuts, 1973, $120.**

1979, Moss Gatherers ....... 130.00
1980, Wintry Churchgoing
 .......................................... 165.00
1981, Santa Claus in Tyrol
 .......................................... 160.00
1982, The Star Singers ...... 160.00
1983, Unto Us a Child Is Born
 .......................................... 150.00
1984, Yuletide in the Valley
 .......................................... 150.00
1985, Good Morning, Good Year
 .......................................... 160.00
1986, A Goreden Christmas
 ............................................ 75.00
1987, Down from the Alps
 .......................................... 175.00
Disney Christmas Series, undis-
closed artists, 7-1/2" d
 1973, Sleigh Ride, FE ........ 400.00
 1974, Decorating the Tree
 .......................................... 175.00
 1975, Caroling .................... 20.00
 1976, Building a Snowman
 ............................................ 35.00
 1977, Down the Chimney.... 25.00
 1978, Night Before Christmas
 ............................................ 20.00
 1979, Santa's Surprise ........ 20.00
 1980, Sleigh Ride ............... 30.00
 1981, Happy Holidays ........ 18.00
 1982, Winter Games ........... 20.00
 1987, Snow White Golden Anniversary ............................... 48.00
 1988, Mickey Mouse & Minnie
 Mouse 60th ......................... 50.00
 1989, Sleeping Beauty 30th Anniversary ............................... 75.00
 1990, Fantasia Relief .......... 25.00
Disney Mother's Day Series
 1974, Flowers for Mother, FE
 ............................................ 80.00
 1975, Snow White and the Seven
 Dwarfs ................................ 45.00
 1976, Minnie Mouse and Friends
 ............................................ 20.00
 1977, Pluto's Pals ............... 25.00
 1978, Flowers for Bambi ..... 20.00
 1979, Happy Feet .............. 25.00
 1980, Minnie's Surprise ....... 20.00
 1981, Playmates.................. 25.00
 1982, A Dream Come True
 ............................................ 20.00

Peanuts Christmas Series, Charles
Schulz, artist, 7-1/2" d
 1972, Snoopy Guides the Sleigh,
 FE ........................................ 90.00
 1973, Christmas Eve at the Dog-
 house ................................ 120.00
 1974, Christmas Eve at the Fireplace .................................. 65.00
 1975, Woodstock, Santa Claus
 ............................................ 15.00
 1976, Woodstock's Christmas
 ............................................ 30.00
 1977, Deck the Doghouse .... 15.00
 1978, Filling the Stocking.... 20.00
 1979, Christmas at Hand .... 20.00
 1980, Waiting for Santa ....... 48.00
 1981, A Christmas Wish ...... 20.00
 1982, Perfect Performance . 35.00
Peanuts Mother's Day Series,
Charles Schulz, artist, 7-1/2" d
 1972, Linus, FE .................. 50.00
 1973, Mom? ....................... 45.00
 1974, Snoopy and Woodstock on
 Parade ................................ 40.00
 1975, A Kiss for Lucy .......... 38.00
 1976, Linus and Snoopy ..... 35.00
 1977, Dear Mom ................. 30.00
 1978, Thoughts That Count
 ............................................ 25.00
 1979, A Special Letter ........ 20.00
 1980, A Tribute to Mom ....... 20.00
 1981, Mission for Mom ........ 20.00
 1982, Which Way to Mother?
 ............................................ 20.00
Peanuts Valentine's Day Series,
Charles Schulz, artist, 7-1/2" d
 1977, Home Is Where the Heart
 Is, FE .................................. 25.00
 1978, Heavenly Bliss .......... 28.00
 1979, Love Match ............... 20.00
 1980, From Snoopy, With Love
 ............................................ 24.00
 1981, Hearts-a-Flutter ......... 20.00
 1982, Love Patch ............... 18.00

**Stein, Rockwell Museum, River Pilot,
5-1/8" h, $15.**

Raggedy Ann Annual Series, undisclosed artist, 7-1/2" d
　1980, The Sunshine Wagon
　...................................... 65.00
　1981, The Raggedy Shuffle
　...................................... 25.00
　1982, Flying High ................ 20.00
　1983, Winning Streak .......... 20.00
　1984, Rocking Rodeo.......... 22.50
　1987, O Come, Little Children
　...................................... 160.00
Wedgwood (Great Britain)
Calendar Series
　1971, Victorian Almanac, FE
　...................................... 20.00
　1972, The Carousel ............. 15.00
　1973, Bountiful Butterfly ...... 14.00
　1974, Camelot..................... 65.00
　1975, Children's Games...... 18.00
　1976, Robin ........................ 25.00
　1977, Tonatiuh .................... 28.00
　1978, Samurai ..................... 32.00
　1979, Sacred Scarab .......... 32.00
　1980, Safari ........................ 40.00
　1981, Horses...................... 42.50
　1982, Wild West ................. 50.00
　1983, The Age of the Reptiles
　...................................... 50.00
　1984, Dogs......................... 55.00
　1985, Cats.......................... 55.00
　1986, British Birds .............. 50.00
　1987, Water Birds................ 50.00
　1988, Sea Birds.................. 50.00
Christmas Series, jasper stoneware, 8" d
　1969, Windsor Castle, FE
　...................................... 225.00
　1970, Christmas in Trafalgar Square................................. 30.00
　1971, Piccadilly Circus, London
　...................................... 40.00
　1972, St. Paul's Cathedral ... 40.00
　1973, The Tower of London
　...................................... 45.00
　1974, The Houses of Parliament
　...................................... 40.00
　1975, Tower Bridge ............. 40.00
　1976, Hampton Court.......... 46.00
　1977, Westminster Abbey ... 48.00
　1978, The Horse Guards..... 55.00
　1979, Buckingham Palace .. 55.00
　1980, St. James Palace....... 70.00
　1981, Marble Arch............... 75.00
　1982, Lambeth Palace ........ 80.00
　1983, All Souls, Langham Palace
　...................................... 80.00
　1984, Constitution Hill ......... 80.00
　1985, The Tate Gallery ........ 80.00
　1986, The Albert Memorial ... 80.00
　1987, Guildhall ................... 80.00
Mothers Series, jasper stoneware, 6-1/2" d
　1971, Sportive Love, FE ...... 25.00
　1972, The Sewing Lesson ... 20.00
　1973, The Baptism of Achilles
　...................................... 20.00
　1974, Domestic Employment
　...................................... 30.00
　1975, Mother and Child....... 35.00
　1976, The Spinner ............... 35.00
　1977, Leisure Time.............. 30.00
　1978, Swan and Cygnets.... 35.00
　1979, Deer and Fawn.......... 35.00

1980, Birds........................... 48.00
1981, Mare and Foal ........... 50.00
1982, Cherubs with Swing .. 55.00
1983, Cupid and Butterfly ... 55.00
1984, Musical Cupids ......... 55.00
1985, Cupids and Doves .... 55.00
1986, Anemones................. 55.00
1987, Tiger Lily.................... 55.00

# Little Golden Books

**Collecting Hints:** Little Golden Books offer something for everybody. Collectors can pursue titles according to favorite author, illustrator, television show, film, or comic strip character. Disney titles enjoy a special place with nostalgia buffs. An increasingly popular goal is to own one copy of each title and number.

Books published in the '40s, '50s and '60s are in the most demand at this time. Books from this period were assigned individual numbers which are usually found on the front cover of the book except for the earliest titles, for which the title must be checked against the numbered list at the back of the book.

Although the publisher tried to adhere to a policy of one number for each title during the first 30 years, numbers were reassigned to new titles as old titles were eliminated. Also, when an earlier book was re-edited and/or re-illustrated, it was given a new number.

Most of the first 36 books had blue paper spines and a dust jacket. Subsequent books were issued with a golden-brown mottled spine, which was replaced in 1950 by a shiny gold spine.

Early books had 42 pages. In the late 1940s, the format was gradually changed to 28 pages, then to 24 pages in the mid-1950s. Early 42- and 28-page books had no price on the cover. Later the 25¢ price appeared on the front cover, then 29¢, followed by 39¢. In the early 1950s, books were produced with two lines that formed a bar across the top of the front cover. This bar was eliminated in the early '60s.

Little Golden Books can still be found at yard sales and flea markets. Other sources include friends, relatives, and charity book sales, especially if they have a separate children's table. Also attend doll and book shows—good places to find books with paper dolls, puzzles, or

cutouts. Toy dealers are also a good source for Disney, television, and cowboy titles.

Look for books in good or better condition. Covers should be bright, with the spine paper intact. Rubbing, ink and crayon markings, or torn pages lessen the value of the book. Unless extensive, pencil marks are fairly easy to remove by gently stroking in one direction with an art-gum eraser. Do not rub back and forth.

Within the past two years, collecting interest has increased dramatically, thus driving up prices for the most unusual and hard-to-find titles. Prices for the majority of titles are still at a reasonable level.

**History:** Simon & Schuster published the first Little Golden Books in September 1942. They were conceived and created by the Artists & Writers Guild Inc., which was an arm of the Western Printing and Lithographing Company. More than 1.5 million copies of the initial twelve titles (each 42 pages long and priced at 25¢) were sold within the first five months of publication. By the end of World War II, 39 million Little Golden Books had been sold.

A Disney series was begun in 1944, and Big and Giant Golden Books followed that same year. In 1949, the first Goldencraft editions were introduced. Instead of side-stapled cardboard, these books had cloth covers and were sewn so that they could withstand school and library use. In 1958, Giant Little Golden Books were introduced, most combining three previously published titles into one book. In that same year, Simon & Schuster sold Little Golden Books to Western Printing and Lithographing Company and Pocket Books. The titles then appeared under the Golden Press imprint. Eventually, Western, now known as Western Publishing Company, Inc., bought out Pocket Books' interest in Little Golden Books.

In 1986, Western celebrated the one-billionth Little Golden Book by issuing special commemorative editions of some of its most popular titles, such as *Poky Little Puppy* and *Cinderella*.

**Notes:** Prices are based on a mint-condition book from the first printing. The printing edition is determined by looking at the lower right-hand corner of the back page. The letter found there indicates the printing of that particular title and edition. "A" is the first printing, "B" the next, and so forth. Occasionally the letter is hidden under the spine or was placed in the upper right-hand corner, so look closely. Early titles will have their edition indicated in the front of the book.

Any dust jacket, puzzles, stencils, cutouts, stamps, tissues, tape, or pages should be intact as issued. If not, the book's value suffers a drastic reduction of up to 80% off the listed price. Books that are badly worn, incomplete, or badly torn are worth little. Sometimes they are useful as temporary fillers for gaps in a collection.

**Reference:** Steve Santi, *Collecting Little Golden Books*, 3rd ed., Krause Publications, 1998.

**Collectors' Club:** Golden Book Club, 19626 Ricardo Ave., Hayward, CA 94541.

*Annie Oakley*, #221-25, 1955, name inside front cover, some corners damaged .................................. 10.00
*Bozo the Clown*, 2nd ed. ................ 8.00
*Bugs Bunny's Birthday*, 1st ed., 1950, fair condition ............................ 7.00
*Captain Kangaroo*, #261, 1956, penciled name on front page .......... 5.00
*Cars and Trucks*, 5th printing, 1971, wear to cover ......................... 12.00
*Chitty Chitty Bang Bang* ............... 20.00
*Colors Are Nice*, 2nd ed. ............... 5.00
*Counting Rhymes*, 1946, fair condition .................................................. 8.00
*Daniel Boone*, #256, 1956, penciled name on front page ................... 6.00
*Davy Crockett's Keelboat Race*, 1955, fair condition ............................ 9.00
*Dick Tracy*, 1962, slight wear to cover .................................................. 18.00
*Ding Dong School, The Magic Wagon*, 1st ed., 1955 ........................... 15.00
*Doctor Dan At The Circus*, 1st edition, 1960, does not include band-aid, fair condition ............................... 40.00
*Dumbo's Book of Colors*, #1015-23, name written on front page ........ 2.00
*Exploring Space*, 1958 ................. 20.00
*Four Little Kittens*, #322, 1973, 6th printing, slight wear ..................... 4.00
*Frosty the Snow Man*, 1951 ......... 18.00
*Gene Autry and Champion*, 1956, slight use ............................................ 25.00
*Gordon's Jet Flight*, #A48, 1961, activity book, insert missing ................. 65.00
*Gunsmoke*, 1958 .......................... 20.00
*Hokey Wolf and Ding-A-Ling*, Hanna-Barbera, 1st ed., 1961 ............. 12.00
*Hop, Little Kangaroo*, #558 ............ 5.00
*Heidi*, 1st ed., 1954 ........................ 6.00
*Hopalong Cassidy and the Bar 20 Cowboy*, 1952, unused ................... 40.00
*Howdy Doody Magic Hats* ............ 20.00
*Howdy Doody's Circus*, 1st ed., 1950 .................................................. 16.00

***Three Little Kittens,*** #381, ©1942, well read, $5.

*Lady and the Tramp* ........................ 3.00
*Little Golden Book of Dinosaurs*, #355, penciled name on front page, some rubs ............................................ 4.00
*Little Golden Book of Dogs*, #532, some cover damage ............................ 4.00
*Little Golden Book of Horses*, #459, birthday greetings written inside .................................................. 4.00
*Little Golden Dictionary*, 18th printing, 1969 .............................................. 4.00
*Mickey's Christmas Carol*, #459-09, 1983, good condition ................. 2.00
*My First Book*, 1942, name written in front .......................................... 12.00
*1-2-3 Juggle with Me*, 1st ed. ........ 6.00
*Peter Rabbit*, #505, 1970, good condition .................................................. 2.00
*Prayers for Children*, 1942, 9th printing, some writing on cover, last page missing ..................................... 10.00
*Rudolph the Red Nosed Reindeer*, 1958 .................................................. 18.00
*Scuffy the Tugboat*, #310-41, 1974, some crayon marks ..................... 1.00
*Seven Dwarfs Found A House*, 6-1/2" x 8", Simon & Schuster, 1952 copyright, fourth printing, 1957, 25 pgs, color illus .............................. 20.00
*The Christmas Donkey*, 1984 ......... 3.00
*The Christmas Story*, 1952 ............ 6.00
*The Cold Blooded Penguin*, 6-3/4" x 8", Simon & Schuster, 1946 second printing, 24 pgs, full color ........ 60.00
*The Friendly Book*, 2nd ed. ............ 6.00
*The Fuzzy Duckling*, 1949 ............ 10.00
*The Gingerbread Man*, 6th ed. ........ 5.00
*The Golden Egg*, #486, illus by Lillian Obligado, name scribbled in front, 1973, slight wear ...................... 4.00
*The Happy Little Whale*, 3rd ed. ...... 5.00
*The Little Red Caboose*, 13th ed. .................................................. 5.00
*The Monster at the end of this Book, Starring Lovable, Furry Old Grover*, Sesame St., 2nd ed. ................. 4.00

*The Tiny Tawny Kitten*, 1st ed., 1969 .................................................. 13.00
*The Wonderful School*, 1st ed. ....... 8.00
*Tottle*, 1945 ................................. 12.00
*Twelve Days of Christmas, A Christmas Carol*, 1983 ............................. 8.00
*Underdog* ..................................... 20.00
*Walt Disney's Goofy—Movie Star*, 1956, red spine ................................. 27.50
*Walt Disney's Old Yeller*, 3rd ed., 1950s .................................................. 12.00
*Walt Disney's Uncle Remus*, #D85, 1945 .................................................. 45.00
*Walt Disney's Winne-the-Pooh and Tigger*, 4th ed. ................................ 5.00
*Wheels*, 1st ed., 1952 .................... 8.00
*Where is the Bear?* 2nd ed. ............ 6.00
*Wizard of Oz*, 1st edition ............. 22.00
*Woody Woodpecker*, 1961 ........... 24.00
*Woodsy Owl*, 1974 ....................... 24.00
*Zorro*, 1958 ................................. 15.00

# Little Red Riding Hood

**Collecting Hints:** Little Red Riding Hood was a hot collectible in the 1990s. Prices for many pieces are in the hundreds of dollars; those for advertising plaques and baby dishes are in the thousands. As collectors complete their collections, the numbers of active buyers are decreasing.

A great unanswered question at this time is how many Little Red Riding Hood pieces were actually made. Attempts at determining production levels have been unsuccessful. The market could well be eventually flooded with these items, especially the most commonly found pieces. New collectors are advised to proceed with caution.

Undecorated blanks are commonly found. Their value is between 25% and 50% less than decorated examples.

**History:** On June 29, 1943, the United States Patent Office issued design patent #135,889 to Louise Elizabeth Bauer, Zanesville, Ohio, assignor to the A. E. Hull Pottery Company, Incorporated, Crooksville, Ohio, for a "Design for a Cookie Jar." Thus was born Hull's Little Red Riding Hood line, produced and distributed between 1943 and 1957.

The traditional story is that A. E. Hull only made the blanks. Decoration of the pieces was done by the Royal China and Novelty Company of Chicago, Illinois. When decoration was complete, the pieces were returned to Hull for distribution.

**Tea Set, $800. Photo courtesy of Joan Hull.**

Recent scholarship suggests a somewhat different approach.

Mark Supnick, author of *Hull Pottery's "Little Red Riding Hood": A Pictorial Reference and Price Guide* believes that A. E. Hull only made the blanks for early cookie jars and the dresser jar with a large bow in the front. These can be identified by the creamy off-white color of the pottery. The majority of pieces were made from a very white pottery, a body Supnick attributes to The Royal China and Novelty Company, a division of Regal China. Given the similarity in form to items in Royal China and Novelty Company's Old McDonald's Farm line, Supnick concludes that Hull contracted with Royal China and Novelty for production as well as decoration.

Many hand-painted and decal variations are encountered, e.g., the wolf jar is found with a black, brown, red, or yellow base.

**Reference:** Mark E. Supnick, *Collecting Hull Pottery's "Little Red Riding Hood,"* L-W Book Sales, 1989, 1992 value update.

**Reproduction Alert:** Be alert for a Mexican-produced cookie jar that closely resembles Hull's Little Red Riding Hood piece. The Mexican example is slightly shorter than Hull's 13-inch height.

| | |
|---|---:|
| Allspice Jar | 375.00 |
| Bank, standing | 575.00 |
| Cereal Canister | 950.00 |
| Coffee Canister | 750.00 |
| Cookie Jar | |
|    Gold stars, red shoes | 300.00 |
|    Poinsettia trim | 300.00 |
| Creamer | |
|    Pour through type | 300.00 |
|    Side pour | 145.00 |
|    Tab handle | 275.00 |
| Flour Canister | 375.00 |
| Lamp | 2,000.00 |
| Match Holder, Little Red Riding Hood and Wolf, striker, Staffordshire | 75.00 |
| Milk Pitcher | 400.00 |
| Mustard, orig spoon | 250.00 |
| Range Shakers, pr | 150.00 |
| Salt and Pepper Shakers, pr | |
|    3-1/4" h, incised "135889," gold trim | 140.00 |
|    5-1/2" h | 150.00 |
| Sugar Bowl, cov, crawling | 275.00 |
| Sugar Canister | 600.00 |
| Tea Canister | 750.00 |
| Teapot, cov | 325.00 |

# Lottery Tickets

**Collecting Hints:** Most people throw away their losing lottery tickets but there is something else you can do with them. You can collect them and even trade them just like you did with baseball cards when you were younger.

The Lottery Collector's Society was formed in 1988 when a group of friends, who lived in different states, decided to collect and trade their state's losing instant scratch-off tickets with each other. These are the tickets that contain latex, which can be rubbed off with the edge of a coin to determine whether they are a winner or a loser. Word soon spread about this club and as others joined, the ranks swelled to more than 800 members and is now international in scope.

The goal of the club has always been to promote the hobby of lottery ticket collecting. Recently club members fought to get two new words into the English language. The first word was "lotology," which is the name they have given their hobby, and the second word was "lotologist," which is what they call themselves. These words are now listed in Miriam Webster's Collegiate Dictionary.

Keeping up to date on current tickets is a challenge, but how does one know about the instant ticket releases from a year ago, or two years ago or even 20 years ago? Simple. The Lottery Collector's Society has a ticket catalog that lists every instant ticket ever released. The list is in order by release date and each ticket is given a number. This acts as a checklist for the tickets from all the US and Canadian lottery jurisdictions, dating back to the very first instant ticket released more than 25 years ago.

**History:** The modern lottery started in New Hampshire in 1964 with the formation of the New Hampshire Sweepstakes Commission; it was Massachusetts which released the first instant ticket in 1974. The game, called "The Instant Game," was innovative for its time. No longer would people have to wait a few days to determine whether they were a winner or a loser. They could now find out right away. The player could win if any of his four numbers matched 'the instant number,' a type of game still being played today.

That first game cost $1 and while the majority of the games today still cost this amount, tickets have sold for as much as $25 each. In this case, the game was put out by the Connecticut lottery in 1993 and was called, "Gift Horse." You still had to match your number to the 'gift horse number,' but it just cost you more. Because of the cost of this ticket, it was one of the most difficult tickets to find. But it is not the rarest.

The most difficult ticket to find is contained within a set of tickets put out by the Illinois lottery in 1976. The set, called "Presidents," was a 35-ticket set with each ticket picturing one of the 35 presidents up until that time. People who purchased those tickets were encouraged to save their losers since they were told one president would be selected and then holders of that particular ticket could send it in as part of a second-chance drawing. The ticket picturing Herbert Hoover was the one selected and is now considered the most difficult ticket to find. Despite these tough tickets, there are thousands of tickets easily available and many are being traded everyday.

Tickets from those early days of the lottery were very small, with some measuring one inch by one inch. Today's tickets come in all sizes. While the majority of them can still fit in the palm of your hand, several have been as large as the Pennsylvania issue "Super Bingo" from 1996, which measured 8 inches by 6 inches. Some tickets have even taken a less traditional shape than the square or rectangular shapes commonly used. The New Jersey lottery had a ticket in the shape of a Christmas tree for the holiday season. The Oregon lottery had a ticket in the shape of a snowman for a winter-theme ticket. The Pennsylvania lottery released a round ticket for a game called "Silver Dollars." Many states have also released a ticket in the shape of a sock during the holiday season called, "Stocking Stuffer." These odd-shaped tickets are called die-cuts.

Many famous celebrities have also appeared on instant scratch-off tickets. Marilyn Monroe, Michael J. Fox, John Goodman, Sylvester Stallone, Lucille Ball, the Three Stooges and Laurel and Hardy are just a few of them. Recent tickets have also featured the casts of such television shows as Baywatch, Gilligan's Island, and The Munsters. Even baseball legends, football hall of famers and professional wrestlers have been immortalized on instant scratch-off tickets.

There are three different types of instant scratch-off tickets collected and traded. The most popular are the tickets that have already been scratched and determined to be losers. These are the most readily available since the majority of the tickets are losers and can be found thrown in the trash can of your local retailer. Mint tickets are also collected and traded. These are tickets which have not been scratched but must be purchased. Then there are the sample-voids, which are promotional tickets given to retailers from the lottery to display for those who hide their tickets behind the counter.

While instant scratch-off tickets are the most widely collected, a lotologist can collect just about anything pertaining to the lottery. There are the paper tickets, which are the machine-generated tickets used in either a Powerball game or a daily three-digit number game. Then there are the placards, which are over-sized cardboard reproductions of tickets currently offered for sale. Other items include pull tabs, which is another form of lottery gaming, lapel pins, buttons, magnets, pens, pencils, bet slips, keychains, mugs, bumperstickers and everything else a lottery might use to promote itself.

**Periodical:** *The Lotologist Monthly,* 2 Sherwood Terrace, Yonkers, NY 10704-3343.

**Collectors' Club:** Lottery Collector's Society, 2 Sherwood Terrace, Yonkers, NY 10704-3343, e-mail Lotteryfan@aol.com.

**Advisor:** Arthur Rein.

Canadian, Halloween, unscratched 1.25
Colorado, 1983, #6, Tic Tac Toe
.................................................. 50.00
Colorado, 1987, #2, Colorado Millionaire ........................................... 50.00
Connecticut, 1993, $30, Gift Horse
.................................................. 30.00
Cuba, Julio Antonio Mella, 1966, used
.................................................. 3.00
Florida
Run for the Money, 1992, unused
.................................................. 3.00
Illinois, 1975, #2EE, Herbert Hoover
.................................................. 300.00
Illinois, 1977, #3B Constitution ... 250.00
Indiana, Cash Madness, 1993, unused
.................................................. 9.50
Iowa, 1989, #37 Christmas Card
.................................................. 150.00
New Hampshire, Harley Davidson Motorcycle, shows Harley Davidson Sportser 1200 Custom Motorcycle, used ........................................... 2.00
New York, Cold Cash, 1992, unused
.................................................. 18.50
Oregon, Treasure Island, 1992, unused
.................................................. 13.50
Pennsylvania, Cash Excelsior, 1993, unused example of ticket that was recalled because it too closely duplicated one offered by Ohio ....... 20.00

**Drumstick Doubler, 1999, trading value only.**

**PA 500, 1999, trading value only.**

Rhode Island
Baseball, 1977, #2 ................... 75.00
Double Bingo, 1977, #2 .......... 75.00
Holiday, green, 1990, unused
.............................................. 16.25
Power Play, 1991, expired ....... 18.00
Vermont, I Love Lucy, used ............ 6.50
Vietnam, multicolored, 1965, used
.............................................. 5.00
West Virginia, 5 Card Draw, 1991, used
.............................................. 3.00
Wisconsin
Star Trek, sample ticket, marked "Void", shows USS Voyager ....... 4.00
Tic Tac 8's, 1992, unused .......... 3.00

# Lunch Kits

**Collecting Hints:** The thermos is an integral part of the lunch kit. The two must be present for full value. There has been a tendency in recent years to remove the thermos from the lunch box and price the two separately. The wise collector will resist this trend.

Scratches and rust detract from a metal kit's value and lower value by more than 50%.

**History:** Lunch kits date back to the 19th century when tin boxes were used by factory workers and field hands. The modern children's lunch kit, the form most sought by today's collector, was first sold in the 1930s. Gender, Paeschke & Frey Co. of Milwaukee, Wisconsin, issued a No. 9100 Mickey Mouse lunch kit for the 1935 Christmas trade. An oval lunch kit of a streamlined train, mkd "Decoware," dates from the same period.

Television brought the decorated lunch box into the forefront. The following are some of the leading manufacturers: Aladdin Company; Landers, Frary and Clark; Ohio Art (successor to Hibbard, Spencer, Bartlett & Co.) of Bryan, Ohio; Thermos/King Seeley; and Universal.

**References:** Larry Aikins, *Pictorial Price Guide to Metal Lunch Boxes &*

*Thermoses*, L-W Book Sales, 1992, 1996 value update; ——, *Pictorial Price Guide to Vinyl & Plastic Lunch Boxes & Thermoses*, L-W Book Sales, 1992, 1995 value update; Philip R. Norman, *1993 Lunch Box & Thermos Price Guide*, published by author, 1992; Allen Woodall and Sean Brickell, *Illustrated Encyclopedia of Metal Lunch Boxes*, Schiffer Publishing, 1992.

**Periodical:** *Paileontologist's Report*, P.O. Box 3255, Burbank, CA 91508.

**Collectors' Club:** Step into the Ring, 829 Jackson St Ext., Sandusky, OH 44870.

Annie, Aladdin, metal, 1981......... 20.00
Archies, 1969................................ 85.00
Astronauts, dome type, 1960...... 250.00
Battle Kit, 1965............................ 135.00
Bionic Woman, Aladdin, plastic, Canadian flags on lunch box and thermos, 1970s.......................... 60.00
Bobby Orr, Aladdin, all plastic, metal snaps,1970s.......................... 125.00
Campus Queen, orig thermos, 1967
............................................. 35.00
Care Bear Cousins, 1985............. 18.00
Clash of the Titans, King Seeley, metal, 1980 ............................. 20.00
Corsage, 1964 ............................. 20.00
Cracker Jack, 1969...................... 75.00
Dark Crystal, orig thermos, 1982, unused ................................... 35.00
Denim Diner, dome top, 1975....... 25.00
Dick Tracy, no thermos .............. 150.00
Disney Snow White, orig thermos, 1975
............................................. 30.00
Donnie & Marie, vinyl, 1977........ 135.00
Dragon's Lair, orig thermos, 1983
............................................. 25.00
Dukes of Hazzard, Aladdin, 1980, plastic, orig thermos ....................... 30.00
Engine Co. #1, puffy vinyl, 1974 ... 30.00
E. T., 1982 ................................... 20.00
Fall Guy........................................ 35.00
Fat Albert, 1973 ........................... 55.00
Flag, 1970.................................... 20.00
Flowers, Ohio Art, metal, 1960s.... 25.00
Fritos, generic thermos, 1979....... 90.00

Ghostland, no thermos ................. 35.00
G. I. Joe, orig thermos, 1980........ 20.00
Green Horner, 1967 ..................... 525.00
Gremlins, 1984 ............................. 20.00
Hair Bear Bunch, 1971 ................. 28.00
Happy Days, 1977......................... 65.00
Harlem Globetrotters, 1971 .......... 20.00
Holly Hobbie, vinyl, white, 1972 ... 30.00
Hot Wheels, red plastic, 1984 ...... 25.00
How The West Was Won, orig thermos, 1976 ........................................ 25.00
Inch High Pirate Eye .................... 40.00
It's About Time, dome top........... 185.00
James Bond, metal...................... 155.00
Jetsons, dome top ...................... 650.00
Jiminey Cricket, 2 handles, Canadian, 1950s ....................................... 145.00
Jr. Miss, 1978.............................. 15.00
Kewtie Pie, vinyl.......................... 180.00
Knight Rider, 1983 ....................... 22.00
Knitting, Ohio Art, metal, 1960s.... 30.00
Kung Fu ...................................... 55.00
Land of the Giants ...................... 125.00
Lawman, 1961
    Metal lunch box .................... 100.00
    Thermos................................. 35.00
Legend of the Lone Ranger, Aladdin, 1980, metal, some wear........... 24.00
Little Ballerina, vinyl, red, 1975..... 25.00
Masters of the Universe, orig thermos, 1984........................................ 20.00

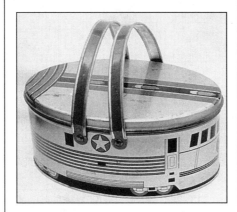

**Train, oval, silver and red, 8-1/2" l, $25.**

Mickey Mouse Club, red rim, 1977
............................................. 48.00
Miss America, 1972...................... 85.00
Mod Tulips, dome top, 1975........ 450.00
Mork and Mindy, 1979 .................. 35.00
Muppet Babies, orig thermos, 1985
............................................. 20.00
New Mickey Mouse Club, orig thermos, 1977 ........................................ 25.00
NFL, 1962.................................... 30.00
Paramedics, 1978, no thermos .... 65.00
Patriotic, 1974.............................. 20.00
Peanuts Gang, playing baseball, orig tags........................................ 60.00
Perk's Dragon, thermos, 1978...... 30.00
Peter Pan, 1969 ........................... 20.00
Pink Panther and Sons, 1984 ....... 60.00
Plaid, vinyl, steel thermos, 1960s
............................................. 28.00
Pro Sports, Ohio Art, 1974, metal
............................................. 30.00
Queen Elizabeth, metal, basket style, 1953 ........................................ 40.00
Raggedy Ann and Andy, orig thermos, 1973 ........................................ 22.00
Return of the Jedi, 1983 ............... 25.00
Roy Rogers and Dale Evans, American, metal, orig thermos in poor condition, 1953, wear to lunch box
............................................. 20.00
Satellite, used ............................. 60.00
Secret of Nimh, orig thermos, 1982, unused ................................... 25.00
Smokey the Bear, vinyl, some wear to bottom................................... 145.00
Snow White, Ohio Art, 1980......... 22.00
Speed Buggy ............................... 35.00
Sport Goofy, 1984........................ 15.00
Sports Afield ............................... 50.00
Star Trek, plastic, orig thermos, Canadian...................................... 100.00
Strawberry Shortcake, vinyl, orig thermos, 1980 ............................... 20.00
Tapestry, 1963 ............................. 20.00
Teenager Square, used ................. 5.00
US Space Corps, orig thermos, 1984
............................................. 420.00
Wags n' Whiskers, 1978 ............... 15.00
Wee Pals Kid Power, 1974........... 40.00
Wild Frontier, magnetic pieces, no thermos ...................................... 40.00
Young Western, metal, basket style, 1950s ...................................... 50.00

# M

# Magazine Covers and Tear Sheets

**Collecting Hints:** A good cover should show the artist's signature, have the mailing label nonexistent or in a place that does not detract from the design element, and have edges which are crisp but not trimmed.

When framing vintage paper, use acid-free mat board and tape with a water-soluble glue base, such as brown-paper gum tape or linen tape. The tape should only be affixed to the back side of the illustration. The rule of thumb is do not do anything that cannot be easily undone.

Do not hang framed vintage paper in direct sunlight (causes fading) or in a high-humidity area such as a bathroom or above a kitchen sink (causes wrinkles in both the mat and artwork).

**History:** Magazine cover design attracted some of America's leading illustrators. Maxfield Parrish, Erte, Leyendecker, and Norman Rockwell were dominate in the 20th century. In the mid-1930s, photographic covers gradually replaced the illustrated covers. One of the leaders in the industry was *Life*, which emphasized photojournalism.

Magazine covers are frequently collected according to artist-signed covers, subject matter, or historical events. Artist-signed covers feature a commercially printed artist's signature on the cover, or the artist is identified inside as "Cover by...." The majority of collected covers are in full color and show significant design elements. Black memorabilia is often reflected in magazine covers and tear sheets, and it is frequently collected for the positive affect it has on African-Americans. However, sometimes it is a reflection of the times in which it was printed and may represent subjects in an unfavorable light.

Many of America's leading artists also created the illustrations for magazine advertisements. The ads made characters such as the Campbell Kids, the Dutch Girl, and Snap, Crackle and Pop world famous.

**References:** Check local libraries for books about specific illustrators such as Parrish, Rockwell, and Jessie Wilcox Smith.

**Periodicals:** *Illustrator Collector's News*, P.O. Box 1958, Sequim, WA 98392; *Paper Collectors' Marketplace* (*PCM*), P.O. Box 128, Scandinavia, WI 54977.

**Notes:** As more and more magazines are destroyed for the tear sheets, complete magazines rise in value proportionate to the decrease in supply. If a magazine is in mint condition, it should be left intact. We do NOT encourage removing illustrations from complete magazines. The complete magazine is the best tool for interpreting a specific historical time period. Editorial and advertising together define the spirit of the era.

Artist Signed
Armstrong, Rolf ........................ 27.50
Christy, Howard Chandler ........ 15.00
Drayton, Grace .......................... 7.50
Eastman, Ruth .......................... 10.00
Fisher, Harrison ....................... 30.00
Flagg, James Montgomery ...... 10.00
Gutmann, Bessie Pease .......... 30.00
King, Hamilton ........................ 15.00
Leyendecker ........................... 17.50
Mucha, Alphonse ..................... 50.00
O'Neill, Rose ........................... 15.00
Parrish, Maxfield ..................... 50.00
Smith, Jessie Wilcox ............... 25.00
Twelvetrees, Charles ............... 18.00

Automobile
Pre-1918, black and white ......... 8.50
Pre-1918, color ....................... 10.00
1919-1937, black and white ...... 5.00
1919-1937, color ..................... 10.00
1938-1941, black and white ...... 8.00
1938-1941, color ..................... 10.00
1942-1955, black and white ...... 5.00
1942-1955, color ..................... 10.00

Aviation
Pre-1935, black and white ......... 5.00
Pre-1935, color .......................... 7.50
Post-1935, black and white ....... 3.50
Post-1935, color ........................ 5.00

Beverage
Beer, identified brand, color ...... 8.00
Coca-Cola, pre-1925, color ..... 10.00
Wines and Liquors .................... 5.00

Black Memorabilia
Cover with personality ............. 20.00
Tear sheet with adv ................. 15.00

Fashion
Pre-1930, color .......................... 7.50
Post-1930, color ........................ 9.00

Firearms
Christmas Time is Crosman Time, illus of rifles, Boys' Life, 1969 .... 3.00
Winchester, Boys' Life, 1968, shows models 250, 270, and 290 ......... 2.00
Winchester, Outdoor Life, 1953, shows model 70, 43, 94, and 12 .............................................. 3.50
Winchester, Outdoor Life, 1956 .................................................. 3.00

Food
Campbell Kids, large format .... 12.00
Clark's Teaberry Gum, 13-1/2" x 5-1/2", 1942, matted and shrink wrapped .................................................. 15.00
Cream of Wheat, 13-1/2" x 5-1/2", Lil' Abner graphic, matted and shrink wrapped ................................. 15.00
Junket Powder, 13-1/2" x 5-1/2", 1943 ad, matted and shrink wrapped .................................................. 15.00
Kara Syrup, 13-1/2" x 5-1/2", features Dionne Quints, matted and shrink wrapped ................................. 15.00
Jewelry, color ............................. 5.00

Miscellaneous
Corby's, 1956 ............................. 8.00

**Chrysler '63,** *Saturday Evening Post*, **Oct. 27, 1962, $7.50.**

**Waterford,** *China and Glass Tablewares*, **Ebel-Doctorow Publications, Inc., October 1973, full color, $4.50.**

Every Ready Flashlight, 1915, Halloween theme.............................. 7.50
Magic Chef, 1946....................... 5.00
Hiram Walker with Alfred Glassell, Jr., 1955...................... 8.00
Sunny Brook, 1954..................... 6.00
Watkins Vitamins, 1956 ............. 8.00
Tobacco, Philip Morris, 13-1/2" x 5-1/2", matted and shrink wrapped..... 15.00
Toy
Erector Set ................................ 5.00
Trains, Lionel or Ives ................. 8.00
Viewmaster, 13-1/2" x 5-1/2", matted and shrink wrapped................ 15.00

# Magazines

**Collecting Hints:** A rule of thumb for pricing general magazines with covers designed by popular artists is the more you would enjoy displaying a copy on your coffee table, the more elite the publication, or the more the advertising or editorial content relates to today's collectibles, the higher the price. *Life* magazine went into millions of homes each week, *Harper's Bazaar* and *Vogue* did not. Upper-class families tended to discard last month's publication, while middle-class families found the art on the *Saturday Evening Post* and *Collier's* irresistible and saved them. The greater the supply, the lower the price.

**History:** In the early 1700s, general magazines were a major source of information for the reader. Literary magazines, such as *Harper's*, became popular in the 19th century. By 1900, the first photo-journal magazines appeared. *Life*, the most famous example, was started by Henry Luce in 1932.

Magazines created for women featured "how to" articles about cooking, sewing, decorating, and child care. Many of the publications were entirely devoted to fashion and living a fashionable life, such as *Harper's Bazaar* and *Vogue*. Men's magazines were directed at masculine interests of the time, such as hunting, fishing, and woodworking, supplemented with appropriate "girlie" titles.

**References:** Ron Barlow and Ray Reynolds, *Insider's Guide to Old Books, Magazines, Newspapers, and Trade Catalogs*, Windmill Publishing (2147 Windmill View Rd., El Cajon, CA 92020), 1996; Denis C. Jackson, *Men's "Girlie" Magazines*, 3rd ed., published by author (P.O. Box 1958, Sequim, WA 98392), 1991; —, *Master's Price & Identifica-tion Guide to Old Magazines*, published by author (P.O. Box 1958, Sequim, WA 98392), 1992; Steven Lomazow, *American Periodicals*, published by author (414 Smith Manor Blvd., W. Orange, NJ 07052), 1996; *Old Magazine Price Guide*, L-W Book Sales, 1994, 1996 value update; Frank M. Robinson and Lawrence Davidson, *Pulp Culture: The Art of Fiction Magazines,* Collectors Press, Inc., 1998; Lee Server, *Danger Is My Business: An Illustrated History of the Fabulous Pulp Magazines*, Chronicle Books, 1993; Gene Utz, *Collecting Paper*, Books Americana, 1993.

**Periodicals:** *Collecting Cult Magazines*, 449 12th St., #2-R, Brooklyn, NY 11215; *Illustrator Collector's News*, P.O. Box 1958, Sequim, WA 98392; *Paper Collectors' Marketplace (PCM)*, P.O. Box 128, Scandinavia, WI 54977; *Pulp & Paperback Market Newsletter,* 5813 York Ave., Edina, MN 55410.

**Notes:** General magazine prices listed below are retail prices. They may be considerably higher than what would be offered for an entire collection filling your basement or garage. Bulk prices for common magazines such as *Life*, *Collier's*, and *Saturday Evening Post* generally range between 50¢ and $1 per issue. Magazine dealers have to sort through many issues to find those which may be saleable, some protect individual issues, covers, or tear sheets with plastic covering, etc. before they can realize a profit for more common magazines.

*Airman*, Official Air Force Journal, 1961, March.......................... 3.00
*Alfred Hitchcock Mystery* ............... 5.00
*American Childhood*, 1941, April ... 5.00
*American Golfer*, December, 1932
.................................................. 10.00
*American Heritage*, 1958, October, Pocahontas cover...................... 6.00
*American Motorist*, 1916................ 10.00
*Antiques*, 1966, June..................... 5.00
*Argosy*, 1952................................. 2.50
*Arizona Highway*
1959, December, Prickly Pear in Bloom...................................... 5.00
1960, July, Navajo portrait.......... 7.00
*Atlantic*, 1954, July, Churchill cover
.................................................... 6.00
*Aviation*, 1928 ............................. 15.00
*Beckett*
Charles Barkley on cov.............. 8.50
Michael Jordan on cover .......... 7.50
*Better Homes and Gardens*, 1942, Dec
.................................................... 6.00
*Better Photo*, 1913......................... 4.00
*Billiard's Digest* ............................. 1.00

*Boy's Life*
1955, June, Boy Scout Statue cover, Coca-Cola ad ........................... 5.00
1970, Oct, Bill Bradley cover..... 6.00
*Chatterbox*, bound year, 1917, 10" x 7-1/2", 412 pgs............................ 25.00
*Child's Life*, 1930 ......................... 4.00
*Collier's*, Maxfield Parrish cov, rows of soldiers, Nov. 16, 1912 ............ 50.00
*Confidential*, 1966, Aug, Sammy Davis cover.......................................... 8.00
*Confidential Confessions*, 1959, August
.................................................... 3.00
*Cosmopolitan*, 1910 ..................... 6.00
*Crime Detective*, Steve McQueen on cover, 1950s............................ 65.00
*Delineator*, 1904........................... 20.00
*Ellery Queen Mystery Magazine*, 1950s
.................................................... 5.00
*Esquire*, 1937, April ..................... 15.50
*Etude*, 1942, November, West Point choir article ............................... 5.00
*Family Circle*, 1954 ....................... 5.00
*Farm & Fireside*, 1923, March, boy and dog cover ................................. 6.00
*Farm Journal*
1923, February, boy on cover.... 9.00
1927, December, Santa and Elves on cover...................................... 8.50
1940, March, sheep and lion cover
.................................................... 5.00
*Farm Life,* 1923, September, cows in pasture cover............................. 6.00
*Fate,* 1953, Atlantis....................... 7.50
*Film in Review*, 1971, Lucille Ball
.................................................. 25.00
*Friends,* 1965, May, NY World's Fair cover, Errol Flynn article ........... 9.00
*Front Page Detective*, 1952, August
.................................................... 3.00
*Golden Book Magazine*, 1929, six months bound........................ 35.00
*Good Housekeeping*, 1965 ........... 4.00
*Hit Parade*, 1947, September, Jane Greer cover.............................. 7.00
*Horticulture*, 1959, December, poinsettia cover.................................... 3.50
*Jack & Jill*, 1961 .......................... 10.00
*Jewelers' Weekly*, 1889, New York, 88 pgs, 7" x 10"........................... 18.00
*Junior Natural History*, 1954, April, goat cover......................................... 4.00
*Junior Scholastic*, April 21, 1954, large black and white cover photo of 13-year-old student and robot ...... 30.00
*Ladies Home Journal*, 1960, June
.................................................... 5.00
*Life*
1940, December 30, Britain's Desert Fighters on cover....................... 7.00
1953, July 13, Hillary Climb, Mt. Everest, adv with stars............. 12.00
1961, July 7, Ike Down on the Farm cover..................................... 10.00
1962, October 12, Pope John XXIII cover...................................... 9.00
1964, March 20, Lodge in Saigon cover, Malcolm X story.............. 6.00
1970, July 17, Rose Kennedy at 80 cover..................................... 11.00
1971, October 15, Disney World Opens cover, Joan Crawford article
.................................................... 9.00

***Life,*** **Hopalong Cassidy, June 12, 1950, $10.**

1972, July 7, George McGovern cover, Pandas in DC article ....... 5.00
*Literary Digest*, 1937, May 1, Princess Elizabeth cover ......................... 7.00
*Look*
　Davy Crockett, Walt Disney cover ............................................ 38.00
　Gary Cooper as Lou Gehrig cover ............................................ 45.00
*McCall's*, 1961, Christmas Make-It Ideas ........................................ 4.00
*Mechanix Illustrated*, May, 1954, Creature from the Black Lagoon color cover ....................................... 65.00
*Modern Screen*, 1946, August, Gregory Peck cover, Lucy Ball cover photo ............................................ 15.00
*Motion Picture*, 1959, October, Sandra Dee cover, Fabian article ......... 10.00
*National Geographic*, 1965, August, tribute to Sir Winston Churchill, 137 pgs ......................................... 45.00
*Newsweek*, 1974, Aug. 19, Proc. Ford cov, special issue ....................... 6.00
*Photo Screen*, 1973, July, Waltons cover ............................................ 8.00
*Playthings*, 1959 ......................... 35.00
*Popular Aviation*, 1933 ................. 10.00
*Popular Science*, Steve McQueen on cover, 1966 ............................ 40.00
*Quick*, 1950, July 24, Princess Elizabeth cover ......................... 8.00
*Quilter's Newsletter* ...................... 2.50
*Radio and TV Mirror*, Lucille Ball, 1950 ............................................ 50.00
*Redbook*, June, 1925 ..................... 5.00
*Rexall*, 1939, June, Nan Gray cover, Judy Garland article ................. 5.00
*Saturday Evening Post*
　1955, Nov. 5, Nehru, Rockwell cover ...................................... 12.00
　1963, Jan. 19, Beverly Hillbillies cover ...................................... 30.00

1964, May 2, Fischer Quints cover ............................................ 12.00
*Scouting*, 1973, Sept., Soap Box Derby cover ...................................... 3.00
*Secrets*, 1959, January ................... 3.00
*Silk*, spoof, Monkees .................... 25.00
*Silver Screen*, 1973, June, Bunkers cover, Brady Bunch article ........ 8.00
*Song Hits*, 1953, March, Janet Leigh cover, Johnnie Ray article .......... 6.00
*Story Parade*, 1952, June ............... 4.00
*Successful Farming*, 1941, May ..... 5.00
*Time*
　1942, Nov. 30, Halsey cover ...... 6.00
　1944, June 19, Eisenhower cover ............................................ 8.00
　1973, Jan. 29, Nixon Caricature cover ...................................... 5.00
　1987, Dec. 7, Shirley Maclaine ............................................ 3.00
*Today's Health*, 1960, June, Kate Smith cover ...................................... 4.00
*Teen Magazine*, Annette kissing Sgt. Garcia (Zorro) ........................ 40.00
*TV Dial*, Roy Rogers, Hopalong Cassidy, Gene Autry on cover ............................................ 140.00
*TV Digest*, Lucille Ball and Ricky in motorboat, Philadelphia, 1952 ............................................ 135.00
*TV Guide*
　Beverly Hillbillies ...................... 60.00
　Branded ................................... 25.00
　Lawman ................................... 25.00
　Lil'Abner ................................. 50.00
　Lost in Space ........................... 75.00
　Maverick, James Garner .......... 30.00
　Paladin ................................... 25.00
　Rebel ...................................... 25.00
　That Girl .................................. 18.00
　Wild Wild West ........................ 30.00
　Zorro, Guy Williams ................. 45.00
*TV People*, Bonzana cover .......... 40.00
*TV Radio Mirror*, photo of Honeymooner's Art Carney and others on cover, article on Honeymooners, April, 1960 ............................. 20.00
*TV Week*, Dick Tracy, 1960s ......... 35.00
*Vogue*, April, 1936 ....................... 10.00
*Wee Wisdom*, 1939, July ............... 7.50
*Western Horseman*, complete run, 1951 thru 1963 ................................ 75.00
*Women's Day*, 1943, October, cover price 2 cents ........................... 7.00
*Woman's World*, March, 1936 ........ 2.00
*Workbasket*, whole year, 1962 ....... 5.00

# Marbles

**Collecting Hints:** Handmade glass marbles usually command higher prices than machine-made glass, clay, or mineral marbles. There are a few notable exceptions, e.g., machine-made comic strip marbles were made for a limited time only and are highly prized by collectors. Care must be taken in purchasing this particular type since the comic figure was stenciled on the marble. A layer of glass was to be overlaid

on the stencil, but sometimes this process was not completed. In such cases, the stencils rub or wear off.

Some of the rarer examples of handmade marbles are Clambroth, Lutz, Indian Swirls, Peppermint Swirls, and Sulphides. Marble values are normally determined by their type, size, and condition. Usually, the larger the marble, the more valuable it is within its category.

A marble in mint condition is unmarred and has the best possible condition with a clear surface. It may have surface abrasions caused by rubbing while in its original package. A marble in good condition may have a few small surface dings, scratches, and slight surface cloudiness. However, the core must be easily seen, and the marble must be free of large chips or fractures.

**History:** Marbles date back to ancient Greece, Rome, Egypt, and other early civilizations. In England, Good Friday is known as "Marbles Day" because the game was considered a respectable and quiet pastime for the hallowed day.

During the American Civil War, soldiers carried marbles and a small board to play solitaire, a game whose object was to jump the marbles until only one was left in the center of the board.

In the last few generations, school children have identified marbles as "peewees," "shooters," "commies," and "cat's eyes." A National Marbles Tournament has been held each year in June since 1922.

**References:** Paul Baumann, *Collecting Antique Marbles, Identification and Price Guide*, 3rd ed., Krause Publications, 1999; Robert Block, *Marbles Identification and Price Guide*, 2nd ed., Schiffor Publishing, 1998; Stanley A. Block, *Marble Mania,* Schiffer Publishing, 1998; Everett Grist, *Antique and Collectible Marbles*, 3rd ed., Collector Books, 1992, 1996 value update; —, *Everett Grist's Big Book of Marbles*, Collector Books, 1993, 1997 value update; —, *Everett Grist's Machine Made and Contemporary Marbles*, 2nd ed., Collector Books, 1995, 1997 value update; Dennis Webb, *Greenberg's Guide to Marbles*, Greenberg Publishing, 1994.

**Collectors' Clubs:** Buckeye Marble Collectors Club, 437 Meadowbrook Dr., Newark, OH 43055; Marble Collectors Unlimited, P.O. Box 206,

Northboro, MA 01532; Marble Collectors Society of America, P.O. Box 222, Trumbull, CT 06611; National Marble Club of America, 440 Eaton Rd., Drexel Hill, PA 19026; Sea-Tac Marble Collectors Club, P.O. Box 793, Monroe, WA 98272; Southern California Marble Club, 18361-1 Strathern St, Reseda, CA 91335.

**Museums:** Corning Museum of Glass, Corning, NY; Sandwich Glass Museum, Sandwich, MA; Smithsonian Institution, Museum of Natural History, Washington, DC; Wheaton Village Museum, Millville, NJ.

**Reproduction Alert:** Comic marbles and some machine-made marbles are being reproduced, as are some polyvinyl packages, mesh packages, and original boxes.

**Notes:** Handmade marbles listed below are common examples in mint condition. Unusual examples command prices that are 2 to 20 times higher. Mint condition machine-made marbles priced here have a diameter between 9/16 and 11/16 inch, unless otherwise noted.

## Handmade Marbles

### End of Day
Onionskin
    Confetti onionskin, 2-3/8" .... 1,575.00
    Onionskin with mica, 3/4" d.... 975.00
    Suspended mica ................ 1,100.00

### Lutz
Amber glass ribbon ..................... 475.00
Banded, 1" ................................. 265.00
Black glass ................................. 525.00
Blue and orange ribbon core ..... 280.00
Cranberry ribbon, 1-1/16" d ........ 325.00
End of day, 2-1/4" d ................ 1,882.00
Pink onionskin ............................ 200.00

### Mica
3/4" d, peppermint ...................... 300.00
1" d ........................................... 100.00
1-1/2" ........................................ 200.00

### Other
Clambroth, red on black ............. 240.00
Opaque, red on pink banded ..... 240.00
Translucent, Butterfly ............... 3,650.00
Sulphide
    Duck, tri-color paint............. 1,100.00
    Girl petting dog ...................... 450.00
    Pair of kissing love birds ........ 750.00
    Wild Boar, 2-3/8" d ................ 670.00

### Swirl
Banded, 1" ................................... 75.00
Divided Core, 1-3/4" .................... 150.00
End of cane double ribbon ......... 353.00
Indian Swirl, 1-1/6" d, blue bands, translucent ................................. 3,550.00
Joseph, multicolored .................. 290.00
Latticino Core
    Bright red swirl ....................... 325.00
    Cyan blue ................................ 490.00

Green Mist, 1" d, with mica ......... 650.00
Ribbon Core
    3/4" ........................................ 80.00
    1-1/2" ................................... 200.00
Solid Core
    1-7/8", red ......................... 2,350.00
    2-5/16", lobed ................... 1,150.00

## Machine-Made Marbles

### Akro Agate
Boxed Set
    1 red slag, orig box ............. 1,350.00
    100 sparklers ..................... 5,300.00
Corkscrew, 1-13/16" d, Royal Blue
    .............................................. 165.00
Helmet Patch ................................. 3.00
Lemonade corkscrew ................... 17.50
Moonstone .................................... 12.00
Popeye corkscrew, green/yellow .. 20.00
Swirl oxblood ................................ 20.00

### Christensen Agate Co.
American Agate ........................... 48.00
Cobra/Cyclone ........................... 750.00
Electric Swirl ............................... 75.00
Flame Swirl, 3 color ................... 300.00
Guinea ....................................... 350.00
Slag ............................................. 30.00

### Marble King Co.
Color Matrix, multicolor opaque
    Bumblebee ............................... 2.00
    Girl Scout/John Deere, yellow/green
    .................................................. 8.50
    Spiderman, blue/red .............. 250.00
    Tiger, orange/black ................. 25.00
    Wasp, red/black ........................ 5.00
    Two-Color, white matrix ............... .20
    White Matrix ............................... .25

### Master Marble Co.
Patch ............................................ 1.10
Sunburst
    Clear ...................................... 22.00
    Opaque ..................................... 5.00

### M. F. Christensen & Son
Brick, 9/16" to 11/16" .................. 65.00
Opaque, set of 8, orig box ....... 1,600.00
Slag, 1-7/8" d ............................. 375.00

### Peltier Glass Co.
Boxed Set, five comics .............. 525.00
Christmas Tree, shooter size ...... 220.00
Liberty, 3/4" d ............................ 200.00
Moon comic ............................... 310.00
Peerless Patch ............................. 5.50
Slag ............................................. 20.00
Sunset, Muddy, Acme Reefer, Tri-Color, 7-Up ........................................... 1.00
Superman, mint, wet ................. 175.00
Two-color Rainbo, old type .......... 20.00

### Transitional
Chocolate-brown Navarre transition, resembles a banded agate
    .......................................... 1,000.00
Ground pontil oxblood with complete white and yellow design ........ 725.00
Ground pontil hand gathered, green, white, red, and pink ................ 325.00
Horizontal swirl Navarre, 1-1/8"
    .......................................... 1,350.00

### Vitro Agate/Gladding Vitro Co.
All red ............................................. .25
Blackie ........................................... .50
Conqueror ..................................... 1.10
Hybrid Cat's Eye ........................... 2.00
Oxblood Patch ............................... 8.00
Patch and Ribbon Transparent ......... .25
Victory ........................................... 3.00

# Matchcovers

**Collecting Hints:** Matchcovers generally had large production runs; very few are considered rare. Most collectors try to obtain unused covers. They remove the matches, flatten the covers, and mount them in albums which are arranged by category.

Trading is the principal means of exchange among collectors, usually on a one-for-one basis. At flea markets and shows, beer or pinup art ("girlie") matchcovers frequently are priced at $1 to $5. Actually those interested in such covers would be best advised to join one of the collector clubs and get involved in swapping.

**History:** The book match was invented by Joshua Pusey, a Philadelphia lawyer, who also was a chemist in his spare time. In 1892, Pusey put ten cardboard matches into a cover of plain white board and sold 200 of them to the Mendelson Opera Company which, in turn, hand-printed messages on the front.

The first machine-made matchbook was made by the Binghamton Match Company, Binghamton, New York, for the Piso Company of Warren, Pennsylvania.

Few covers survive from the late 1890s to the 1930s. The modern craze for collecting matchcovers was started when a set of ten covers was issued for the Century of Progress exhibit at the 1933 Chicago World's Fair.

The golden age of matchcovers was the mid-1940s through the early 1960s when the covers were a popular advertising medium. Principal manufacturers included Atlas Match, Brown and Bigelow, Crown Match, Diamond Match, Lion Match, Ohio Match, and Universal Match.

The arrival of throwaway lighters, such as BIC, brought an end to the matchcover era. Today, manufacturing costs for a matchbook can range from less than 1¢ to 8¢ for a special die-cut cover. As a result, matchcovers no longer are an attractive free giveaway, and, therefore, many of the older, more desirable covers are experiencing a marked increase in value. Collectors have also turned to the small pocket-type boxes as a way of enhancing and building their collections.

**References:** Bill Retskin, *Match-cover Collector's Price Guide*, 2nd ed., Antique Trader Books, 1997; H. Thomas Steele, Jim Heimann, Rod Dyer, *Close Cover before Striking*, Abbeville Press, 1987.

**Periodicals:** *Match Hunter*, 740 Poplar, Boulder, CO, 80304; *Match-cover Classified*, 16425 Dam Rd #3, Clearlake, CA 95422.

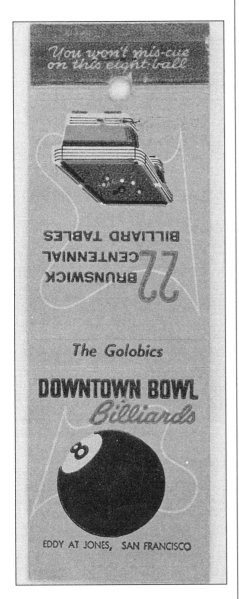

**Downtown Bowl Billiards, San Francisco, Lion Match Co., $.20.**

**Collectors' Clubs:** American Matchcover Collecting Club, P.O. Box 18481, Asheville, NC 28814, http://www.matchcovers.com; Liberty Bell Matchcover Club, 5001 Albridge Way, Mount Laurel, NJ 08054; Long Beach Matchcover Club, 2501 W Sunflower H-5, Santa Ana, CA 92704; Newmoon Matchbox & Label Club, 425 E. 51st St., New York, NY 10022; Rathkamp Matchcover Society, 2920 E. 77th St., Tulsa, OK 74136; Trans-Canada Matchcover Club, P.O. Box 219, Caledonia, Ontario, Canada N0A-1A0; Windy City Matchcover Club, 3104 Fargo Ave., Chicago, IL 60645; there are also many regional clubs throughout the United States and Canada.

**Special Covers**

| | |
|---|---|
| Apollo Flights, 8-18, Cameo | 5.00 |
| Basketball Schedule, U.S.C., 1953-54 season | 20.00 |
| Chicago Cubs, Diamond Match Co., complete first set, 1934 | 175.00 |
| Dwight D Eisenhower, 5 Star General | 17.50 |
| Economy Blue Print, girlies, set of 6, 1950s | 48.00 |
| Hawaiian Mermaid | 2.25 |
| Hillbilly, set of 5 | |
| 1950 | 5.00 |
| 1953 | 5.00 |
| 1954 | 7.50 |
| 1556 | 40.00 |
| Hog's Breath Inn, San Carlos, CA | 1.00 |
| KFC, Colonel Sanders, Tampa, FL | 2.00 |
| Las Vegas Casino, Jewelite | 2.50 |
| Presidential Helicopter, Marine One | 12.00 |
| Presidential Yacht, Patricia | 12.00 |
| Pull for Wilkie, Pullquick Match | 30.00 |
| Stoeckle Select Beer, Giant, Stoeckle Brewery | 7.50 |
| Thomas Dewey, For President, 1948 | 1.25 |
| US Royal Tire, Olathe, KS | 2.00 |
| *USS Rockbridge* Attack Transporter | 3.00 |
| Washington Redskins, set of 20 | 40.00 |

**Topics**

| | |
|---|---|
| Airlines | .45 |
| Americana | .15 |
| Atlas, four color | .15 |
| Banks | .15 |
| Barber Shop | .75 |
| Beer and Brewery | .75 |
| Best Western, stock design | .15 |
| Bowling Alleys | .15 |
| Cameo's, Universal trademark | .15 |
| Canadian, four color | .20 |
| Chinese Restaurants | .10 |
| Christmas | .25 |
| Classiques | .50 |
| Colleges | .10 |
| Contours, diecut | .20 |
| Conventions | .15 |
| Country Clubs | .15 |

| | |
|---|---|
| Dated | .15 |
| Diamond Quality | .50 |
| Fairs | .25 |
| Features | .20 |
| Folities, Universal trademark | .10 |
| Foreign | .05 |
| Fraternal | .15 |
| Full Length | .20 |
| Giants | .50 |
| Girlies, stock design | .50 |
| Group One, non-advertising, old | .50 |
| Holiday Inns, stock design | .20 |
| Jewelites | .15 |
| Jewels | .15 |
| Knot Holes | .25 |
| Matchorama's, Universal trademark | .15 |
| Matchtones, Universal trademark | .15 |
| Midgets | .25 |
| Navy Ships | .35 |
| Odd Strikers | .45 |
| Patriotic | .25 |
| Pearltone | .20 |
| Personalities | 1.00 |
| Political | 1.00 |
| Pull Quick | 1.00 |
| Radio and Television | .45 |
| Railroads | .55 |
| Rainbows, Universal trademark | .25 |
| Restaurants | .20 |
| Savings & Loans | .25 |
| Service, old | .25 |
| Ship Lines | .25 |
| Signets, Universal trademark | .10 |
| Small towns | .20 |
| Soft Drinks | .85 |
| Souvenir | .25 |
| Sports, old | 1.00 |
| Ten Strikes | .15 |
| Transportation | .25 |
| Truck Lines | .20 |
| U. S. Air Force, 1940s | 1.50 |
| U. S. Army, 1940s | 1.00 |
| VA Hospitals | .20 |
| Whiskey | .35 |
| World War II | 1.00 |

# McCoy Pottery

**Collecting Hint:** Several marks were used by the McCoy Pottery Co. Take the time to learn the marks and the variations. Pieces can often be dated by according to the mark.

Most of the pottery marked "McCoy" was made by the Nelson McCoy Co.

**History:** The J. W. McCoy Pottery Co. was established in Roseville, Ohio, in September 1899. The early McCoy company produced both stoneware and some art pottery lines, including Rosewood. In October 1911, three potteries merged creating the Brush-McCoy Pottery Co. This firm continued to produce the original McCoy lines and added several new art lines. Much of the early pottery is not marked.

In 1910, Nelson McCoy and his father, J. W. McCoy, founded the Nelson McCoy Sanitary Stoneware Co. In 1925, the McCoy family sold their interest in the Brush-McCoy Pottery Co. and started to expand and improve the Nelson McCoy Co. The new company produced stoneware, earthenware specialties, and artware.

**References:** Susan and Al Bagdade, *Warman's American Pottery and Porcelain*, Wallace-Homestead, 1994; Bob Hanson, Craig Nissen and Margaret Hanson, *McCoy Pottery*, Collector Books, 1996; Sharon and Bob Huxford, *Collector's Encyclopedia of Brush-McCoy Pottery*, Collector Books, 1996; —, *Collectors Encyclopedia of McCoy Pottery*, Collector Books, 1980, 1997 value update.

**Periodicals:** *NM Express*, 3081 Rock Creek Dr., Broomfield, CO 80020.

**Reproduction Alert:** Unfortunately, Nelson McCoy never registered his McCoy trademark, a fact discovered by Roger Jensen of Tennessee. As a result, Jensen began using the McCoy mark on a series of ceramic reproductions made in the early 1990s. While the marks on these recently made pieces copy the original, Jensen made objects which were never produced by the Nelson McCoy Co. The best known example is the Red Riding Hood cookie jar which was originally designed by Hull and also made by Regal China.

The McCoy fakes are a perfect example of how a mark on a piece can be deceptive. A mark alone is not proof that a piece is period or old. Knowing the proper marks and what was and was not made in respect to forms, shapes, and decorative motifs is critical in authenticating a pattern.

Ashtray, Seagram's VO, Imported Canadian Whiskey, black, gold letters .......................................... 15.00
Baker, oval, Brown Drip, 9-1/4" l ... 12.00
Bank, Centennial Bear, sgd, numbered .......................................... 110.00
Basket, black and white, emb weave ext., double handle ................. 25.00
Bean Pot, brown
  #2 .......................................... 35.00
  #22 .......................................... 60.00
Bird Bath .......................................... 28.00
Bowl, 8-1/2" x 3", green ................. 50.00
Canister, vegetable dec, white ground, mkd "McCoy #216M," 10" h, lid cracked .......................................... 15.00

**Magazine Tear Sheet, China Glass & Tablewares, July 1971, $3.**

Casserole, open, Brown Drip .......... 4.00
Center Bowl, 5-1/2" h, Classic Line, pedestal, turquoise, brushed gold .......................................... 35.00
Clock, Jug Time, 7" h, c1924, small chip, not running ................... 200.00
Cookie Jar, cov
  Coffee Grinder ......................... 50.00
  Colonial Fireplace ................. 150.00
  Cottage .......................................... 120.00
  Covered Wagon ..................... 155.00
  Kookie Kettle, black ............... 55.00
  Mr. and Mrs. Owl ................... 155.00
  Oaken Bucket .......................... 40.00
  Pontiac Indian ........................ 400.00
  Potbelly stove, black .............. 50.00
  Puppy, with sign .................... 135.00
  Sad Clown ............................... 125.00
  Schoolhouse .......................... 225.00
  Strawberry, white ................... 35.00
  Tea Kettle, black .................... 40.00
  Tourist Car .......................................... 150.00
  Train, black .......................................... 150.00

W C Fields .......................... 400.00
  Woodsey Owl ........................ 345.00
Cornucopia, yellow .................... 20.00
Creamer
  Brown Drip, 3-1/2" h .................. 6.00
  Elsie the Cow ......................... 20.00
Custard Cup, vertical ridges, green
  .......................................... 5.00
Decanter, Apollo Mission ............. 45.00
Dog Food Dish, emb Scottie ........ 15.00
Figurine, lion .......................................... 65.00
Flower Bowl, Grecian, 12" d, 3" h, 24k gold marbling .......................... 24.00
Hanging Basket, stoneware, marked "Nelson McCoy," 1926 ............ 20.00
Jardiniere, 8" h, Springwood, white, lilac colored flowers, minor hairline
  .......................................... 65.00
Mug
  Surburbia, yellow ................... 10.00
  Willow Ware, brown, c1926 ...... 15.00
Pitcher
  Brown, Drip, 5" h, 16 oz ............ 9.00
  Elephant, figural, tan glaze, c1940
  .......................................... 32.00
  Water Lily, c1935 ................... 20.00
Planter
  Duck and egg, yellow .............. 30.00
  Old car .......................................... 20.00
  Wishing Well .......................... 20.00
Salt and Pepper Shakers, pr, figural, cucumber and mango, 1954 ... 20.00
Spoon Rest
  Butterfly, dark green, 1953 ...... 15.00
  Penguin, black, white, and red, 1953
  .......................................... 20.00
Sugar, cov, emb face and scrolls, red glazed cover .......................... 10.00
Teapot
  Brown Drip, short spout ........... 20.00
  Grecian, 1958 ........................ 30.00
  Sunburst Gold, 1957 ............... 25.00
Vase
  Brocade, green ....................... 25.00
  Cylindrical, applied pink flower, 6-1/2" h .......................................... 38.00
  Double Handles, green, 8" h, 1948
  .......................................... 50.00
  Lily, single flower, three leaves, 7-1/2" h .......................................... 42.00
Wall Pocket
  Basketweave .......................... 80.00
  Butterfly, white ..................... 150.00
  Iron Trivet ............................. 40.00
  Lily .......................................... 70.00
Wren House .......................... 145.00

**Watering Pitcher, turtle, green, yellow eyes, mouth, and floral trim, 9-1/2" l, $25.**

# McKee Glass

**Collecting Hint:** McKee Glass was mass produced in most colors. Therefore, a collector should avoid chipped or damaged pieces.

**History:** The McKee Glass Company was established in 1843 in Pittsburgh, Pennsylvania, and in 1852 it opened a factory to produce pressed glass. In 1888, the company relocated to Jeannette, Pennsylvania, an area that contained several firms that made Depression-era wares. McKee produced many types of glass, including glass window panes, tumblers, tablewares, Depression glass, milk glass, and bar and utility objects, and continued working at the Jeannette location until 1951 when it was sold to the Thatcher Manufacturing Co.

McKee named its colors Chalaine Blue, Custard, Seville Yellow, and Skokie Green. They preferred Skokie Green to jade-ite which was popular with other manufacturers at the time. McKee also used these opaque colors as the background for several patterns, including dots of red, green, and black, and red ships. A few items were decorated with decals. Most of the canisters and shakers were lettered in black indicating the purpose for which they were intended.

**Reference:** Gene Florence, *Kitchen Glassware of the Depression Years*, 5th ed., Collector Books, 1995, 1999 value update.

Batter Bowl, Skokie green............. 45.00
Bottoms Up Tumbler, orig coaster, Patent #77725, light emerald
............................................... 175.00
Bowl, 4-1/2" d, Skokie green......... 12.00
Butter Dish, red ships on white..... 30.00
Candlesticks, pr, custard, Laurel pattern............................................. 35.00
Canister
  3-1/2" h, 24 oz, open, red ships on white ................................................ 14.00
  4" h, ivory, round
    Covered............................. 18.00
    Open .................................. 10.00
  4-1/2" h, red ships on white, open
    ................................................ 35.00
  5-1/2" h, 6" w, cov
    Ivory .................................. 37.00
    Skokie green, coffee ........... 55.00
  6" h, cereal, Seville yellow, open
    ................................................ 47.00
Cordial, Rock Crystal................... 12.00
Creamer, custard ......................... 24.00
Dish, cov, 4" x 5", red ships, white ground................................................ 20.00
Dresser Tray, milk glass ............... 35.00

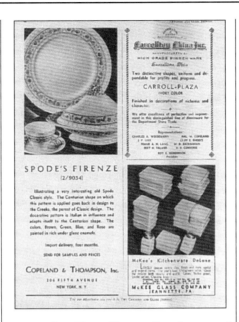

**Magazine Tear Sheet, *Crockery and Glass Journal*, November 1932, showing McKee's Kitchenware DeLuxe, black and white, $3.**

Dripping Dish, 4" x 5", cov, Skokie green
............................................... 30.00
Egg Beater Bowl, ivory, one spout
............................................... 30.00
Egg Cup, custard ......................... 8.50
Flour Shaker, Chalaine Blue, square
............................................... 125.00
Lemon Reamer, Skokie green....... 30.00
Measuring Cup
  Red ships, white ground.......... 28.00
  Seville Yellow, four cup, ftd .... 120.00
Pitcher
  Dark Skokie green, 16 oz......... 75.00
  Skokie green, 16 oz ................. 37.00
  Wild Rose and Bowknot, frosted, gilt dec.......................................... 75.00
  Yutec, Eclipse, marked "Prescut"
    ................................................ 45.00
Range Shaker
  Lady, salt, pepper, flour, and sugar
    ................................................ 135.00
  Roman Arch, custard, blue dots, salt, pepper, flour, and sugar ........ 135.00
Refrigerator Dish
  4" x 5", open, red ships, white ground
    ................................................ 7.00
  5" x 4-1/2", cov, ivory ............... 23.00
  5" x 8"
    Covered
      Ivory .............................. 32.00
      Seville Yellow ................. 47.00
      Skokie Green ................. 40.00
    Open, red ships, white ground
      ................................................ 9.00
Salt and Pepper Shakers, pr
  Amethyst, orig tops, some wear
    ................................................ 24.00
  Custard, Laurel pattern............ 42.00
  Red ships, white ground.......... 30.00
Sandwich Server, center handle, Rock Crystal, red ............................. 165.00

Shaker, Seville Yellow, sq
  Flour ........................................ 50.00
  Plain ........................................ 25.00
  Sugar ....................................... 50.00
Tom and Jerry Mug, white ............. 5.00
Tumbler
  4" h, flat
    Ivory .................................. 12.00
    Sextec, crystal ................... 20.00
  4-1/2" h, ftd
    Ivory .................................. 12.00
    Seville Yellow...................... 14.00
Water Cooler Set, vaseline, orig carton
............................................... 350.00

# Metlox Pottery

**Collecting Hints:** The choices of patterns and backstamps is overwhelming. Collectors should, therefore, concentrate on one specific line and pattern. Among the most popular Poppytrail patterns are California Ivy, Homestead Provincial, and Red Rooster.

The recent cookie jar craze has attracted a number of collectors to Metlox's cookie jar line. Most examples sell within a narrow price range. The Little Red Riding Hood jar is an exception, often selling at two to three times the price of other cookie jars.

**History:** In 1921, T. C. Prouty and Willis, his son, founded Proutyline Products, a company designed to develop Prouty's various inventions. In 1922, Prouty built a tile plant in Hermosa Beach to manufacture decorative and standard wall and floor tiles.

Metlox (a contraction of metallic oxide) was established in 1927. Prouty built a modern all-steel factory in Manhattan Beach to manufacture outdoor ceramic signs, but the Depression impacted strongly on this type of business. When T. C. Prouty died in 1931, Willis reorganized the company and began to produce a line of solid-color dinnerware similar to that produced by Bauer. In 1934, the line was fully developed and sold under the Poppytrail trademark, chosen because the poppy is California's official state flower. Fifteen different colors were produced over an eight-year period.

Other dinnerware lines produced in the 1930s include Mission Bell, sold exclusively by Sears Roebuck and Company, Pintoria, based on an English Staffordshire line, and Yorkshire, patterned after Gladding-McBean's Coronado line. Most of these lines did not survive World War II.

In the late 1930s, Metlox employed the services of Carl Romanelli, a designer of figurines, miniatures, and Zodiac vases. He created a line for Metlox called Modern Masterpieces, which featured bookends, busts, figural vases, figures, and wall pockets.

During World War II, Metlox devoted its manufacturing efforts to the production of machine parts and parts for the B-25 bombers. When the war ended, Metlox returned to dinnerware production.

In 1947, Evan K. Shaw, whose American Pottery in Los Angeles had been destroyed by fire, purchased Metlox. Production of hand-painted dinnerware patterns accelerated: California Ivy was introduced in 1946, California Provincial and Homestead Provincial in 1950, Red Rooster in 1955, California Strawberry in 1961, Sculptured Grape in 1963, and Della Robbia in 1965. In the 1950s, Bob Allen and Mel Shaw, art directors, introduced a number of new shapes and lines, including Aztec, California Contempora, California Free Form, California Mobile, and Navajo.

When Vernon Kilns ceased operation in 1958, Metlox bought the trade name and select dinnerware molds and established a separate Vernon Ware branch. Under the direction of Doug Bothwell, the line soon rivaled the Poppytrail patterns.

Artware continued to flourish in the 1950s and 1960s. Harrison McIntosh was one of the key designers. Two popular lines were American Royal Horses and Nostalgia, scale-model antique carriages. Between 1946 and 1956 Metlox made a series of ceramic cartoon characters under license from Walt Disney.

A line of planters designed by Helen Slater and Poppets, doll-like stoneware flower holders, were marketed in the 1960s and 1970s. Recent production included novelty cookie jars and Colorstax, a revival solid-color dinnerware.

Management remained in the Shaw family. Evan K. was joined by his two children, Ken and Melinda. Kenneth Avery, Melinda's husband, eventually became plant manager. When Evan K. died in 1980, Kenneth Avery became president. In 1988 Melinda Avery became the guiding force. The company ceased operations in 1989.

**References:** Susan and Al Bagdade, *Warman's American Pottery and Porcelain*, Wallace-Homestead, 1994; Jack Chipman, *Collector's Encyclopedia of California Pottery*, 2nd ed., Collector Books, 1998; Carl Gibbs Jr., *Collector's Encyclopedia of Metlox Potteries*, Collector Books, 1995; Lois Lehner, *Lehner's Encyclopedia of U.S. Marks on Pottery, Porcelain & Clay*, Collector Books, 1988.

**Antique Grape**

Casserole
  One quart ................................. 55.00
  Two quart ................................ 75.00
Creamer ....................................... 18.00
Cup and Saucer ........................... 12.00
Gravy, one pint ........................... 32.00
Pitcher, water ............................ 125.00
Platter
  9" l ......................................... 32.00
  14" l ....................................... 40.00
Salad Plate, 7" d ......................... 10.00
Salt and Pepper Shakers, pr ........ 20.00
Soup Bowl, 7" d ........................... 12.00
Sugar, cov .................................. 20.00
Teapot, cov .............................. 115.00
Vegetable Bowl
  8-1/2" d, divided ..................... 35.00
  9-1/2" d
    Divided ................................. 37.00
    Undivided ............................. 35.00

**Blue Provincial**

Bowl, 11" d ................................. 44.00
Bread and Butter Plate, 6" d .......... 8.00
Bread Server ............................... 65.00
Clock, steeple ........................... 145.00
Coffeepot .................................... 95.00
Cookie Jar ................................. 225.00
Creamer ...................................... 24.00
Cup and Saucer ........................... 14.00
Dinner Plate, 10" d ....................... 14.00
Eggcup ........................................ 50.00
Gravy ......................................... 36.00
Salad Bowl ................................. 175.00
Salad Plate ................................. 14.00
Salt and Pepper Shakers, pr ........ 55.00
Soup, lug handle .......................... 20.00
Sugar, cov .................................. 28.00
Tid-Bit, 3 tier ............................ 185.00

**California Ivy**

Bowl, 9" d ................................... 36.00
Bread and Butter Plate, 6" d .......... 2.00
Butter, cov .................................. 40.00
Coaster ....................................... 16.00
Creamer ...................................... 14.00
Cup ............................................... 9.00
Dinner Plate, 10-1/4" d .................. 9.00
Gravy Boat, California Ivy ............. 10.00
Hors d'oeuvres ............................ 25.00
Platter, 13" l, oval ....................... 36.00
Saucer .......................................... 1.00
Sugar, cov .................................. 17.00
Vegetable, 9-3/4" l, oval, divided ..... 32.00

**California Provincial**

Bread Server ............................... 65.00

Chop Plate ................................... 75.00
Coaster ....................................... 20.00
Cocoa Mug ................................... 40.00
Coffee Canister ........................... 55.00
Coffeepot, cov ............................. 85.00
Condiment Set, jam and mustard, lids
  ................................................ 65.00
Creamer ...................................... 22.00
Cup and Saucer ........................... 16.00
Dinner Plate, 10" d ....................... 17.50
Gravy, handle, 1 pint .................... 40.00
Luncheon Plate, 8" d .................... 32.00
Mug, 8 oz .................................... 65.00
Platter, 13-1/2" l .......................... 45.00
Salad Plate, 7-1/2" d .................... 10.00
Salt and Pepper Shakers, pr ........ 27.00
Soup Bowl, 5" d, lug handle ......... 22.00
Sugar Bowl, cov .......................... 28.00
Sugar Canister ............................ 70.00
Tea Canister ................................ 70.00
Vegetable
  Covered .................................. 85.00
  Open, 8 1/2" d, round, basket dec
  ................................................ 50.00

**California Strawberry**

Bowl, 9" d, divided ....................... 40.00
Bread and Butter Plate, 6" d .......... 6.00
Butter, cov .................................. 45.00
Creamer ...................................... 20.00
Cup and Saucer ........................... 35.00
Dinner Plate, 10" d ....................... 15.00
Fruit Bowl, 5-1/2" d ..................... 10.00
Platter, 13" l, oval ....................... 30.00
Salad Bowl .................................. 50.00
Salad Plate, 8" d ......................... 10.00
Soup Bowl, 6-3/4" d ..................... 15.00
Sugar, cov .................................. 20.00
Vegetable Bowl
  Covered .................................. 35.00
  Round ..................................... 25.00

**Camelia California**

Bowl, 6-1/2" d ............................... 7.00
Bread and Butter Plate .................. 6.00
Dinner Plate ................................ 10.00
Salad Plate ................................... 8.00
Soup Bowl .................................... 15.00
Vegetable Bowl, 10" l, oval ........... 35.00

**Colonial Homestead**

Coffee Service, cov coffeepot, creamer, cov sugar ................. 48.00
Cookie Jar, cov ............................ 42.00
Cup and Saucer ............................. 6.50
Flour Canister ............................. 35.00

**Contempora**, Water Pitcher ....... 200.00

**Della Robia**

Bowl, 10-3/4" d ............................ 32.00
Platter, 14" d ............................... 32.00

**Homestead Provincial**

Bowl, 6" d ................................... 10.00
Butter Dish, cov ........................... 60.00
Canister Set, 4 pc ...................... 295.00
Casserole, cov ............................ 75.00
Coffeepot, cov, blue .................... 125.00
Cookie Jar, cov ............................ 90.00
Creamer and Sugar ...................... 30.00
Cup and Saucer ........................... 12.00
Fruit Bowl, 6" d ........................... 12.00
Gravy Boat, one handle ................ 45.00
Matchbox Holder .......................... 65.00
Platter, 14" l ............................... 50.00

**Magazine Tear Sheet, *China Glass & Tablewares*, August 1967, including Metlox Vernon Delia Robbia pattern, $3.**

Salad Plate, 7" d............................ 7.00
Salt and Pepper Shakers, pr......... 30.00
Tea Kettle, cov ............................ 115.00

**Provincial Rose**

Bowl, tab handle .......................... 20.00
Butter, cov................................... 55.00
Coffee Server.............................. 75.00
Cookies Canister......................... 90.00
Creamer...................................... 28.00
Cruet Set, 5 pcs ........................ 180.00
Gravy, two spouts ....................... 28.00
Milk Pitcher ................................ 38.00
Mug............................................ 35.00
Pitcher, large.............................. 68.00
Platter, 9-3/8" l or 14-3/4" l.......... 45.00
Soup, flat.................................... 18.00
Vegetable, cov............................ 70.00

**Red Rooster**

Ashtray, large.............................. 30.00
Bowl, 6" d..................................... 5.00
Bread Server............................... 50.00
Butter Dish, cov .......................... 50.00
Canister Set, 8 pcs ................... 150.00
Casserole, cov, Kettle ................. 55.00
Cereal Bowl, deep ...................... 15.00
Chop Plate .................................. 40.00
Coaster ...................................... 20.00
Coffeepot, cov, 6 cup .................. 85.00
Creamer, green ........................... 15.00
Cruet Set, 8 pcs........................ 150.00
Cup and Saucer........................... 10.00
Dinner Plate, 10" d........................ 7.50
Fruit Bowl ..................................... 8.00
Gravy, handle.............................. 30.00
Luncheon Plate............................. 5.00
Mug............................................ 15.00
Mustard Jar, cov ......................... 45.00
Pitcher, figural, 14" h................. 695.00
Platter, 13" l ............................... 25.00
Salt and Pepper Shakers, pr......... 15.00

Server, five part, divided............. 100.00
Soup Bowl, Provincial ................... 11.00
Teapot, cov, 6 cup ....................... 80.00
Tumbler, 11 oz ............................ 15.00
Turkey Platter ............................ 200.00
Vegetable Bowl
　　Divided, stick handle ............... 24.00
　　Round ...................................... 28.00

**Sculptured Daisy**

Apothecary Jar ............................ 95.00
Bowl, handle
　　7" d........................................ 28.00
　　8" d........................................ 35.00
Cereal Bowl, 7" d ........................ 12.00
Coffeepot.................................... 95.00
Creamer...................................... 18.00
Cup and Saucer ........................... 12.00
Dinner Plate, 10" d....................... 15.00
Gravy, handle, 1 pint.................... 32.00
Luncheon Plate, 7-1/2" d ............... 8.00
Mug, 7 oz ................................... 35.00
Salad Bowl................................... 95.00
Salad Fork and Spoon ............... 125.00
Server, twin, 10" l......................... 55.00
Soap Dish ................................... 38.00
Sugar, cov................................... 24.00
Tumbler....................................... 38.00
Vegetable, cov, 1 quart................ 45.00

**Sculptured Grape**

Bowl
　　8-1/2" d................................... 27.00
　　9-1/2" d................................... 30.00
Canister Set, 4 pc ...................... 240.00
Cereal Bowl ................................ 15.00
Creamer and Sugar ..................... 45.00
Cup and Saucer ........................... 16.00
Dinner Plate ............................... 17.50
Fruit Bowl ................................... 12.00
Platter
　　10" l, oval............................... 30.00
　　12" l, oval............................... 40.00
Salad Plate, 7-1/2" d ................... 10.00
Vegetable.................................... 24.00

**Sculptured Zinnia**

Bread and Butter Plate, 6" d .......... 7.25
Butter Dish, cov .......................... 50.00
Cereal Bowl ................................ 14.00
Chop Plate, 12" d........................ 15.00
Creamer...................................... 16.00
Cup and Saucer ........................... 14.00
Dinner Plate, 10" d........................ 9.50
Fruit Bowl ................................... 12.00
Luncheon Plate, 8" d..................... 9.00
Platter, oval
　　11" l ...................................... 28.00
　　12" l ...................................... 38.00
Salad Bowl, 12" d......................... 48.00
Salt and Pepper Shakers, pr ........ 16.00
Sugar, cov.................................. 17.50
Vegetable Bowl
　　8" d........................................ 30.00
　　8-1/2" d, divided...................... 28.00
　　9-1/2" d, divided...................... 32.00

# Model Kits

**Collecting Hints:** Model kits, assembled or unassembled, are one of the hot collectibles of the 1990s. Even assembled examples, pro-

vided they are done well, have value.

In many cases, a kit's value is centered more on the character or object it represents than on the kit itself. The high prices paid for monster-related kits is tied directly to the current monster collecting craze, which means a portion of the value is speculative.

Box art can influence a kit's value. When individual boxes sell in the $40 to $100 range, it becomes clear that they are treated as *objets d'art*, a dangerous pricing trend. The value of the box is easily understood when you place an assembled model beside the lid. All too often, it is the box that is more exciting.

**History:** The plastic scale-model kit originated in England in the mid-1930s with the manufacture of 1/72 Frog Penguin kits. The concept caught on during World War II when scale models were used in identification training. After the war companies such as Empire Plastics, Hawk, Lindberg, Renwal, and Varney introduced plastic model kits to American hobbyists. The 1950s witnessed the arrival of Aurora and Monogram in the United States, Airfix in the United Kingdom, Heller in France, and Hasegawa and Marusan in Japan.

The 1960s was the golden age of the plastic kit model. Kits featured greater detail and accuracy than the early examples, and three scale sizes dominated: 1/48, 1/72, and 1/144. The oil crisis in the 1970s caused a temporary set back to the industry.

A revival of interest in plastic scale-model kits occurred in the late 1980s. At the same time, collector interest began to develop. The initial collecting focus was on automobile model kits from the 1950s and early 1960s. By the end of the 1980s interest had shifted to character and monster kits.

**References:** Bill Bruegman, *Aurora*, Cap'n Penny Productions, 1992; Gordy Dutt, *Aurora: A Collection of Classic Instruction Sheets, Vol. 1, Figures*, published by author (P.O. Box 201, Sharon Center, OH 44274), 1992; —, *Collectible Figure Kits of the 50s, 60s & 70s*, Gordy's Kitbuilders Magazine (P.O. Box 201, Sharon Center, OH 44274), 1995; *Fantasies in Plastic: Directory of Old and New Model Car Kits, Promotionals, and Resin Cast Bodies*, C & C Collectibles, 1991; Thomas Graham, *Green-*

berg's *Guide to Aurora Model Kits*, Kalbach Books, 1998; Rick Polizzi, *Classic Plastic Model Kits: Identification & Value Guide*, Collector Books, 1996.

**Periodicals:** *Kit Builders and Glue Sniffers*, P.O. Box 201, Sharon Center, OH 44274; *Model and Toy Collector*, P.O. Box 347240, Cleveland, OH 44134.

**Videotape:** *Aurora Figure Kit*, Time Machine (P.O. Box 1022, Southport, CT 06490-2022).

**Collectors' Clubs:** International Figure Kit Club, P.O. Box 201, Sharon Center, OH 44274; Kit Collectors International, P.O. Box 38, Stanton, CA 90680; Society for the Preservation and Encouragement of Scale Model Kit Collecting, 3213 Hardy Dr., Edmond, OK 73013.

Allison, engine parts package, AMT, unused ...................................... 25.00
American Astronaut, Aurora, 1967, MIB ............................................. 115.00
Apollo Saturn Rocket, Monogram, 1968, MIB........................................ 35.00
Anzio Beach, Aurora, built ............. 70.00
Batman, Aurora, MIB ................... 270.00
Bell AH-1G Assault Copter, Aurora, MIB ................................................. 60.00
Billiken Creature.......................... 250.00
Black Night, series 2, Aurora, MIB ............................................... 35.00
Boeing 707 Astrop Jet, Aurora, 1965 ............................................... 55.00
Bonzana, Revell, MIB................. 150.00
Buck Rogers Marauder, Monogram, sealed, MIB................................. 30.00
Camaro, t-top, AMT ...................... 20.00
Cannonball Run Ambulance, MPC, sealed, MIB................................. 30.00
Captain Kidd Bloodthirsty Pirate, Aurora ............................................... 150.00
Cherokee Sports roadster, Hawk, 1964, MIB................................................. 25.00
Chevy, 51, Fleetline, AMT ............. 45.00
Cobra Tee Way-Out Rod, Pyro, 1/16 scale, MIB ................................. 90.00
Corvette, 57, MPC, 1/16 scale, sealed, MIB.............................................. 65.00
Custom T-Bird, Aurora, 1963........ 40.00

**Revell, VW Pickup with ATV, 1:32 scale, partially put together, $5.**

Dick Tracy Space Coupe, Aurora, sealed ...................................... 235.00
Don the Snake Prudhomme, 1/24 rear engine dragster, Revell, sealed ............................................... 90.00
Double Whammy, Henri Studebaker, 1953, AMT, sealed ................... 85.00
Dracula
    Aurora ...................................... 350.00
    Monogram................................. 40.00
Drag Strip, accessory pack, AMT, MIB ............................................... 40.00
Drop Out Bus, Aurora, box only.... 20.00
Flying Saucer, Aurora ................. 150.00
Ford, Fairlane, 1956, customizing kit, Revell, 1958, MIB..................... 80.00
Ford, Model T pick-up, Monogram, 1975, MIB................................. 35.00
Forgotten Prisoner ...................... 150.00
Frankenstein, glow, Aurora, MIB ............................................... 200.00
George Washington, Aurora, 1965, MIB ............................................... 125.00
Ghostrider Vette, MPC, sealed, MIB ............................................... 30.00
Godzilla, glow, Monogram, 1978 ............................................... 250.00
Hunchback of Notre Dame, Aurora, Anthony Quinn box, MIB........ 275.00
Invaders UFO, Aurora................. 250.00
Jaguar CC120 Roadster, Aurora, 1961 ............................................... 35.00
Japanese Submarine, Aurora, Young Models Builder's Club box, MIB ............................................... 38.00
Knight Rider................................. 25.00
Land of the Giants, snake scene, Aurora, box and instructions only ............................................... 180.00
Lockhead U-2 Spy Plane, Hawk, sealed, MIB................................. 55.00
Lost In Space Robot, Aurora, MIB ............................................... 680.00
Mail Truck, show road, George Barris design, MPC ............................ 50.00
Mark II Ford GT, AMT.................. 40.00
Masarati Auto, Aurora, 1966, MIB ............................................... 40.00
MASH Camp Swampy, MIB, sealed ............................................... 20.00
Mercedes Roadster, Lindberg, motorized, 1/32 scale, MIB .............. 25.00
Mister Mulligan Plane, Hawk, BIG ............................................... 15.00
Monogram Relic Kothuga, Revell, sealed, MIB................................. 25.00
Munsters, Koach, AMT, 1964 ............................................... 1,330.00
Mustang, 1/16 scale, AMT, sealed ............................................... 45.00
Old Ironsides, *USS Constitution,* "S" kit, Revell, 1956, MIB.................... 48.00
Old Timers Stanley Steamer, Aurora, 1961, MIB................................. 100.00
Paul McCartney, Revell, 1964..... 300.00
Phantom of the Opera, Aurora, #428, ©1963 Universal Pictures, MIB ............................................... 300.00
Pilgrim Observer, MPC Space Station, sealed, MIB................................. 25.00
Polaris Nuclear Sub Ethan Allan, Renwal.......................................... 40.00

Predicta Futuristic Car, Monogram, 1964, MIB ................................. 75.00
Prehistoric Scenes, Cro-Magnum Woman, Aurora, sealed, MIB... 85.00
Ranch Wagon Western, Revell, horse drawn, 1950s ............................ 35.00
Rat Fink, Revell, MIB ................. 115.00
Return of the Saint, Jaguar CJ, Revell, 1/25 scale .............................. 25.00
Seaview, Aurora, sealed, MIB..... 330.00
Scottish Lad, Aurora, MIB............ 55.00
Scottish Lass, Aurora, MIB .......... 65.00
Sikorsky HH-3 Jolly Green Giant, Aurora, some damage to orig box ............................................... 40.00
Smokey and the Bandit, Ertl, unbuilt in box.......................................... 45.00
Sopwith Camel, Aurora, unused... 45.00
Spider-Man, Aurora, orig box ..... 200.00
Star Trek, Klingon Battle Cruiser, AMT, MIB .......................................... 120.00
Street Fever Vette, MPC, 1978, sealed ............................................... 30.00
Supecharged 56 Chevy, Monogram ............................................... 40.00
Superman, Aurora, 1963, MIB.... 375.00
Talos anti-aircraft missile, Revell, 1957, MIB ........................................... 45.00
Tarzan, Aurora, 1967, box only..... 75.00
The Invisible Pigeon, Renwal ....... 75.00
The White House, Empire............. 75.00
Time Tunnel, Lunar, 1989 .......... 250.00
TransAm, 10th, MPC, MIB ........... 25.00
US Army MB Munitions Carrier, Aurora, 1/4 scale, plastic, sealed, MIB ............................................... 75.00
Wacky Back Wacker Machine, Aurora, 1965, MIB ............................... 350.00
Warlord TransAm, MPC, MIB ........ 30.00
Welcome Back Kotter, Sweathogs Dream Machine, MPC, 1986, sealed ............................................... 55.00

# Monsters

**Collecting Hints:** This is a category rampant with speculative fever. Prices rise and fall rapidly, depending on the momentary popularity of a figure or family group. Study the market carefully before becoming a participant.

Stress condition and completeness. Do not buy any item in less than fine condition. Check carefully to make certain that all parts or elements are present.

Since the material in this category is of recent origin, no one is certain how much has survived. Hoards are not uncommon, and it is possible to find examples at garage sales. It pays to shop around before paying a high price.

While an excellent collection of two-dimensional material, e.g., comic books, magazines, and posters, can be assembled, concentrate on three-dimensional material. Several other crazes, e.g., model kit collecting, cross over into monster collecting, thus adding to price confusion.

**History:** The release of Famous Monsters of Filmland in 1958 helped initiate an avalanche of monster related merchandise in the 60s.The popularity of the classic monsters such Frankenstein, Dracula, The Mummy and the Creature From the Black Lagoon, plus the addition humorous television spoofs like "The Munsters" and "The Addams Family" set the foundation for a substantial and enthusiastic group of collectors in today's market.

"Star Trek" helped bring about a shift in the 70s away from monsters and toward science fiction. There were still monster toys and games being made, but they were not nearly as well received as they had been in the 60s. Subsequently, companies such as AHI, Mego and Lincoln, which manufactured monster items during that period, have become very popular collecting pieces.

The 80s belonged to a new generation of monsters like Jason, Freddy Krueger, and Michael Myers. Even though their movies were amazingly popular, their ruthless exploits made it difficult to produce merchandise that could be sold to all ages. Already a proven success, products promoting classic monsters were manufactured and even gained momentum during that time.

The 90s has seen an explosion in monster collectibles. Beginning in 1991, with the release of numerous different monster items by several different companies such as Hasbro, Exclusive Premier, Trendmaster. Monster merchandise flooded toy racks everywhere. The availability and affordable pricing of these new items have created an excitement in monster collecting that will last well beyond the year 2000.

**References:** Dana Cain, *Collecting Japanese Movie Monsters*, Antique Trader Books, 1998; Ted Hake, *Hake's Guide to TV Collectibles*, Wallace-Homestead, 1990; Carol Markowski and Bill Sikora, *Tomart's Price Guide to Action Figure Collectibles*, revised ed., Tomart Publications, 1992; Stuart W. Wells, III, *Science Fiction Collectibles: Identification & Price Guide,* Krause Publications, 1999.

**Periodicals:** *Future News*, 5619 Pilgrim Rd., Baltimore, MD 21214; *G-Fan*, Box 3468, Steinbach, Manitoba, Canada ROA 2AO; *Japanese Giants*, 5727 N. Oketo, Chicago, IL 60631; *Kaiju Review—The Journal of Japanese Monster Culture*, Suite 5F, 301 E. 64th St., New York, NY 10021; *Monster Attack Team—The Japanese Monster Superhero & Fantasy Fanzine*, P.O. Box 800875, Houston, TX 77280; *Questnews*, 12440 Moorpark St., Suite 150, Studio City, CA 91604.

**Collectors' Club:** Club 13, P.O. Box 733, Bellefonte, PA 16823.

**Advisor:** Patrick M. Leer.

### Dracula

Figure
   Imperial, 7-1/2" h, 1986, MOC ................................................ 20.00
   Limited Edition, Exclusive Premiere Bela Lugosi Count Dracula...... 20.00
Model, Aurora, 1962, in box, excellent condition ............................... 275.00
Motionette, Telco Dracula, arms and head move, eyes flash, laughing sound, 17" h, MIB..................... 30.00
Photograph, Bela Lugosi as Count Dracula, black and white, 8" x 10" ................................................ 6.00
Pinback Button, black and white picture, color background, 1960s. 15.00
Puzzle, Jaymar, 1965, MIB ........... 65.00

### Elvira

Autographed Photograph, color 8" x 10", sexy pose, sgd ................. 40.00

**Dracula, action figure, Imperial, 7-1/2" h, 1986, MOC, $20. Photo Courtesy of Patrick Leer.**

Beer Bottle, Night Brew, 1996 ........ 5.00
Poster, Elvira Moonbathing, One Stop Posters, 1987 ........................... 20.00
Standee, Coors, life-size
   Halloween, mint ...................... 35.00
   Inflatable, 1994, mint .............. 85.00
Video, "Dead of the Night," Hosted by Elvira, VHS Thriller Video ........ 15.00

### Frankenstein

Comic Book, *Frankenstein*, Dell Movie Classic, mint ............................ 20.00
Figure, Imperial, 7-1/2" h, 1986, MOC ................................................ 20.00
Film
   "Abbott and Costello Meet Frankenstein," 8mm, mint .................... 20.00
   "Frankenstein," Super 8mm film, Castle, mint........................... 25.00
Magazine, *Life*, September 1964 Boris Karloff cover, mint ................... 10.00
Model, Aurora, 1961, MIB........... 275.00
Paddle Ball Game, Frankenstein Classic Movie Monster Masher....... 10.00
Pez, 1960s, mint ........................ 250.00

### Godzilla

Action Play Set, 4" h Godzilla combat men and vehicles, Trendmasters ................................................ 15.00
Figure
   Bendable Godzilla, Trendmaster, 1994, 4" h, MOC ..................... 8.00
   Shogun Warrior, Toho, Mattel, 1977, 19" h, with box, mint.............. 120.00
Game, Godzilla Game, Mattel, 1977 ................................................ 85.00
Inflatable, Giant Godzilla Toho, Imperial, 6', with orig box, mint............... 35.00
Poster, Godzilla King of the Monsters, one sheet, United States Release, 1956, mint .......................... 3,000.00

### Hammer

Autographed photograph, color
   Christopher Lee, sgd "Dracula" ................................................ 35.00
   Peter Cushing, sgd "Dr. Frankenstein" ............................... 45.00
Lobby Card, *Horror of Dracula*, 1958, mint ...................................... 100.00
Magazine
   *Famous Monsters of Filmland*, #131 Christopher Lee As Dracula cover, mint .......................................... 12.00
   *Hammer Horror*, #1 Christopher Lee as Frankenstein cover, mint .... 20.00
Poster, Curse of Frankenstein, theatrical one sheet, 1957, mint ........... 225.00
Pressbook, Horror of Dracula, 1958, near mint ............................... 95.00
Trading Card, Hammer Horror, series #1 to 81 cards, each..................... 20.00
Munsters
Coloring Book, The Munsters Coloring Book, Whitman, 1965, mint...... 50.00
Figure
   Grandpa, Exclusive Premier Limited Edition of 12,000, 1998, 9" h, MIB ................................................ 30.00
   Herman, Presents, 1991, 8-1/2" h, excellent ................................. 20.00
Lunch Box and Thermos, King Seely, 1965, near mint..................... 275.00

Model Kit, Munster Koach, AMT, 1964, good condition ........................ 100.00
Puppet, Herman, Ideal, 1965 Ideal, in box, excellent ........................ 350.00
Puzzle, Munster's Puzzle, Dragula, Whitman, 1964, MIB ................ 48.00

### The Creature From The Black Lagoon

Film, *The Creature Walks Among Us*, Castle Films, 8mm ..................... 35.00
Game, Creature From The Black Lagoon Mystery Game, Hasbro, 1963, MIB ............................. 300.00
Puzzle, Western, 200 pieces, 1990, MIB ................................................... 8.00
Snow Globe, 4-1/2" h, Hamilton, 1991, MIB ............................................ 25.00
Soakie, 10" h, Colgate-Palmolive, 1960s, mint .............................. 140.00
Toy, wind-up, Robot House, 1991, MIB ................................................ 110.00

### The Exorcist

Autographed Photograph, Linda Blair, 8" x 10", Exorcist, Reagan Possessed ...................................... 40.00
Lobby Card, Reagan Possessed ................................................. 12.00
Magazine, *Mad*, #170; Oct. 1974; Exorcist cover, mint .......................... 5.00

### The Nightmare Before Christmas

Figure, Jack as Santa, Hasbro, 1993, MOC .................... 45.00
Jack in Silver Coffin, Junn Planning Japan, 1993, 16" l ..................... 80.00
Mug, Jack's head with box, Applause, 1993 ............................................ 35.00
Neck Tie, Jack in Coffin, Disney, 1993 ................................................ 30.00
Walk, Schock and Barrel in Rolling Tub, Applause, 1993, 4" x 5" ............ 18.00
Watch, Burger King, four different styles, each ............................... 20.00

### The Nightmare on Elm Street/Freddy Krueger

Blades, Freddy Krueger Plastic Blades, Marty Toys, 1984, MOC ........... 25.00
Doll, RIP Horror Collection Series, Limited Edition, Freddy Krueger, 1998 ................................................. 48.00
Figure, Freddy Krueger, LJN, 8-1/2" h, MOC ............................................ 20.00
Spitball, Freddy Krueger or victim. LJN, 1989, MOC, each ..................... 10.00
Toy
    Maxx FX, Matchbox, 1989, boxed set, MIB ...................................... 40.00
    Talking Freddy Krueger, Matchbox, 18" h, MIB ............................... 35.00

# Morton Potteries

**Collecting Hints:** The potteries of Morton, Illinois, used local clay until 1940. The clay fired out to a golden ecru color which is quite easy to recognize. After 1940, southern and eastern clays were shipped to Morton, but these clays fired out white. Thus, later wares are easily distinguishable from the earlier ones.

Few pieces were marked by the potteries. Incised and raised marks for the Morton Pottery Works, the Cliftwood Art Potteries, Inc., and the Morton Pottery Company do surface at times. Occasionally, the Cliftwood, Midwest, Morton Pottery Company, and American Art Pottery affixed paper labels, and some pieces have survived with these intact.

Glazes from the early period, 1877 to 1920, usually were Rockingham types, both mottled and solid. Yellowware also was standard during the early period. Occasionally, a dark cobalt blue was produced, but this color is rare. Colorful drip glazes and solid colors came into use after 1920.

**History:** Pottery was produced in Morton, Illinois, for 99 years. In 1877, six Rapp brothers, who emigrated from Germany, began the first pottery, Morton Pottery Works. Over the years, sons, cousins, and nephews became involved, and the other Morton pottery operations were spin-offs from this original Rapp brothers' firm. When it was taken over in 1915 by second-generation Rapps, Morton Pottery Works became the Morton Earthenware Company. Work at that pottery was terminated by World War I.

The Cliftwood Art Potteries, Inc., which operated from 1920 to 1940, was organized by one of the original founders of the Morton Pottery Works and his four sons. They sold out in 1940, and the production of figurines, lamps, novelties, and vases was continued by the Midwest Potteries, Inc., until a disastrous fire in March 1944 brought an end to that operation. By 1947, the brothers, who had operated the Cliftwood Art Potteries, Inc., came back into the pottery business. They established the short-lived American Art Potteries. The American Art Potteries made flower bowls, lamps, planters, some unusual flower frogs and vases. Their wares were marketed by florists and gift shops. Production at American Art Potteries was halted in 1961. Of all the wares of the Morton potteries, the products of the American Art Potteries are the most elusive.

Morton Pottery Company, which had the longest existence of all of the potteries in Morton, was organized in 1922 by the same brothers who had operated the Morton Earthenware Company. The Morton Pottery Company specialized in beer steins, kitchenwares, and novelty items for chain stores and gift shops. They also produced some of the Vincent Price National Treasures reproductions for Sears Roebuck and Company in the mid-1960s. The Morton Pottery closed in 1976, thus ending almost 100 years of pottery production in Morton.

**Reference:** Doris and Burdell Hall, *Morton's Potteries*, Vol. 2, L-W Book Sales, 1995.

**Museums:** Illinois State Museum, Springfield, IL; Morton Public Library (permanent exhibit), Morton, IL.

**Advisor:** Doris and Burdell Hall.

### Morton Pottery Works, Morton Earthenware Co., 1877-1917

Bank, acorn, green, Acorn Stove Co. adv, 3-1/2" h ............................ 60.00
Bean Pot, individual, yellow ware
Half pint ................................................. 30.00
Quarter pint ......................................... 20.00
Butter Churn, brown Rockingham, 4 gallon ...................................... 250.00
Coffeepot, individual, brown Rockingham, three-quarters pint .......... 40.00
Coffeepot, brown Rockingham, 5 pints ................................................. 130.00
Jardiniere, leaf dec, 7" d
Brown ................................................... 40.00
Cobalt blue ......................................... 60.00
Green ................................................... 50.00
Miniature
    Coffeepot, brown Rockingham, 3-1/2" h ........................................ 75.00
    Milk pitcher, cobalt blue, 3-3/4" h ................................................ 60.00
Mug, 1 pint, brown Rockingham .. 60.00
Pie Baker, yellow ware, 10" d ...... 125.00
Teapot
    Pear shape, yellow ware, 1 cup ................................................ 50.00

**Morton Pottery Works, acorn bank, green, adv Acorn Stove Co., 3-1/2" h, $60. Photo courtesy of Doris & Burdell Hall.**

Rebecca at the Well, brown Rockingham, 8-1/2 pints ..................... 150.00
Restaurant, nesting, with cover, brown, 3 pcs ............................ 60.00
Urinal, shovel shape
Brown Rockingham................. 50.00
Yellow ware .............................. 65.00

## Cliftwood Art Potteries, Inc., 1920-1940

Bookends, pr, tree trunk with woodpeckers, chocolate brown drip glaze, 6" x 5" x 3-1/2".............. 100.00
Compote, 4-dolphin base, Old Rose high gloss, 6" h, 8-1/2" d .......... 90.00
Console, 4-dolphin base, matte ivory ext., Old Rose high gloss int., 6" h, 12" l ........................................ 100.00
Figure
Billiken, brown, 11" h.............. 100.00
Bulldog, Nero, gray grip, 11" h
.................................................... 95.00
Elephant trumpeting, Blue Mulberry
.................................................... 55.00
German Shepherd, reclining, brown drip, 11"................................. 150.00
Lamp
Ball shape jug, single handle, pink/orchid drip, 7" h........................ 70.00
Desk, elephant figure, natural colors, 8" h ............................................ 80.00
Donut shape, clock insert, brown drip, 11" h.............................. 150.00
Egyptian design, snake/fish handles, cobalt, 30" h ........................... 125.00

Egyptian design, 2 handles, blue/gray drip, 8-1/4" h ................... 60.00
Pretzel Jar, barrel shape, brown drip, 7-1/2" h ......................................... 75.00
Vase
Bud, brown drip, 7" h .............. 25.00
Fan shape, brass knuckle handles, cobalt blue, 9" h ...................... 40.00
Heron figural, matte turquoise, 6" h
.................................................... 20.00
Tree trunk, herbage, green, 8-1/4" h
.................................................... 60.00

## Midwest Potteries, Inc., 1940-1944

Figure
Baseball player, batter, gray uniform, 7-1/4" h.................................. 300.00
Baseball player, catcher, white uniform, 6-3/4" h......................... 275.00
Baseball player, umpire, black suit and cap, 6-1/4" h ................... 250.00
Cockatoo, green, yellow, and brown spray 8-1/2" h........................ 25.00
Crane, green and yellow spray, 11" h
.................................................... 35.00
Ducks, 3 in a row, 6-1/2" l, 2-1/2" h, white, yellow dec .................... 24.00
Flying fish, blue and yellow spray, 9" h.............................................. 35.00
Flying seagull, white and gold dec, 12" h ........................................ 40.00
Heron, blue-yellow spray glaze, gold dec............................................ 40.00
Miniature
Frog, green drip, 1" h.............. 12.00

**Midwest Potteries, Inc., TV lamp, pug and poodle, Kron mark, 14" h, $90. Photo courtesy of Doris & Burdell Hall.**

Rabbit, white and pink, 1-1/2" h
.................................................... 14.00
Squirrel, brown drip, 2" h ......... 14.00
Swan, matte white, 2" h............ 14.00
Turtle, green drip, 1" h ............. 12.00
TV Lamp
Owl with spread wings, Kron mark, 12" h......................................... 75.00
Pug and poodle, Kron mark, 14" h
.................................................... 90.00
Siamese cats, pr, Kron mark, 13" h
.................................................... 65.00
Teddy bear, Kron mark, 10" h
.................................................... 80.00
Vase, bud, hand, 6-1/2" h
Flesh color .............................. 24.00
14k gold.................................... 30.00

## Morton Pottery Company, 1922-1976

Bank, hen, hand painted dec, 4" h
.................................................... 50.00
Bookends, pr
Four closed books, Atlas attached
.................................................... 20.00
Four closed books, baby shoes attached.................................. 18.00
Two open books....................... 14.00
Christmas Item, Santa
Cigarette box, ashtray hat ....... 25.00
Figure, gold bell, stands by black cauldron................................... 22.00
Mug.......................................... 18.00
Plate, face, 12" d..................... 50.00
Cookie Jar
Basket of fruit, green, naturally colored fruit.................................. 50.00
Hen, chick finial, white, black wash
.................................................. 130.00
Panda, black and white .......... 75.00
Turkey, chick finial
Brown.............................. 150.00
White .............................. 220.00

**Clifton Art Potteries, figure, Billiken, brown, 11" h, $100. Photo courtesy of Doris & Burdell Hall.**

**Midwest Potteries, Inc., figure, flying fish, blue and yellow spray, 9" h, $35. Photo courtesy of Doris & Burdell Hall.**

**Morton Pottery Company, Christmas cigarette box, ashtray hat, $25. Photo courtesy of Doris & Burdell Hall.**

Flowerpot Soaker
    Bird, blue and yellow .............. 20.00
    Calla lily, yellow and green....... 18.00
    Hound dog, brown and white .. 24.00
Head Vase
    Betty Grable type .................... 35.00
    1920s hairstyle, wide floppy brim hat
    .................................................. 60.00
    1940s hairstyle, pillbox hat ...... 50.00
Night Light
    Old women in shoe, yellow house, red roof.................................... 40.00
    Praying child, prayer in wall hanging shadow box........................... 40.00
    Teddy bear, brown spray glaze, hand painted dec, heart-shaped nose ......................................... 50.00
Planter
    Davy Crockett as boy, bear beside open stump............................. 50.00
    Dog figure on pair of rockers ... 18.00
    Elephant figure on pair of rockers
    .................................................. 20.00
    Hen figure on pair of rockers ... 16.00

**Morton Pottery Company, head vases, left: 1940s hairstyle, pillbox hat, $50; right: 1920s hairstyle, wide floppy brim hat, $60. Photo courtesy of Doris & Burdell Hall.**

    Horse figure on pair of rockers
    .................................................. 16.00
    Pig figure on pair of rockers..... 18.00
    Rabbit, female, with umbrella, beside blue egg .....................................24.00
    Rooster figure on pair of rockers
    .................................................. 16.00
Salt and Pepper Shakers, chick, white, black wash, 1-3/4" h, each....... 75.00
Toothpick Holder, chick, white, black wash, 1-3/4" h ......................... 75.00

### American Art Potteries, 1947-1963

Console Set, petal design, 10" l x 6-1/2" h bowl, pr 1-3/4" h candleholders, pink and gray spray glaze ....... 30.00
Creamer, bird, tail as handle, black and green spray glaze .................... 18.00
Figure
    Leaping deer, antlers, #502, white/ gold dec.................................. 40.00
    Leaping fawn, #503, green/brown spray........................................ 30.00
    Leaping horse, #504, brown/tan spray........................................ 35.00
    Squirrel sitting erect, #311, brown/ gray spray................................ 20.00
    Tiger, roaring, #456, natural spray colors ...................................... 40.00
Planter
    Elephant, curved trunk, #94E ..... 18.00
    Lamb, pink bow, #456D........... 25.00
    Pheasant, natural colors, spray glaze, 8-1/2" h, 18" l ................ 45.00
    Swan, pink/mauve/gold decor, #319G ..................................... 27.00
TV Lamp
    Afgan hounds, black, 15" h...... 70.00
    Doe with fawn, green/yellow spray, #322J ...................................... 40.00
    Fish with extended dorsal fin, blue/ white spray, #328U .................. 30.00
Vase
    Feather shape, gray and yellow spray glaze, 10-1/2" h .............. 35.00
    Ruffled tulip, ivory, pink, and blue spray glaze, 9" h ...................... 35.00
Wall Pocket
    Apple, red and green, 3 leaves, 5" h
    .................................................. 24.00
    Chrysanthemum blossom, mauve and green spray glaze, 7-1/2" h
    .................................................. 28.00

# Movie Memorabilia

**Collecting Hints:** Collectors tend to focus on the blockbuster hits, with "Gone with the Wind" and "Casablanca" among the market leaders. Cartoon images, especially Disney material, are also very popular.

Much of the material is two-dimensional, and collectors have just begun to look for three-dimensional objects, although the majority of these are related to stars and personalities rather than movies.

The market went crazy with speculation in the mid-1970s. Prices fell in the 1980s as a result of self-discipline compounded by the large number of reproductions, many of European origin, which flooded the market.

**History:** By the 1930s and into the 1940s, the star system had reached its zenith, and studios spent elaborate sums promoting their major stars. Initially, movie studios and their public relations firms tightly controlled the distribution of material such as press books, scripts, preview flyers, costumes, and props. Copyrights have expired on many of these items, and reproductions abound.

The current interest in Hollywood memorabilia can be traced to the pop-art craze of the 1960s. Film festivals increased the desire for decorative film-related materials, and movie posters became a hot collectible.

Piracy, which has always plagued Hollywood, is responsible for the release of many items into the market. Today the home video presents new challenges to the industry.

**References:** Pauline Bartel, *Complete Gone with the Wind Sourcebook*, Taylor Publishing, 1993; Dana Cain, *Collecting Japanese Movie Monsters*, Antique Trader Books, 1998; —, *Film & TV Animal Star Collectibles*, Antique Trader Books, 1998; *Big Reel Annual*, Antique Trader Books, 1996; Anthony Curtis, *Lyle Film & Rock 'n' Roll Collectibles*, Berkley Publishing, 1996; Tony Fusco, *Posters*, 2nd ed., Avon Books, 1994; Rex Miller, *The Investor's Guide to Vintage Character Collectibles*, Krause Publications, 1999; Robert Osborne, *65 Years of the Oscar*, Abbeville, 1994; Christopher Sausville, *Planet of the Apes Collectibles*, Schiffer, 1998; Marion Short, *Hollywood Movie Songs: Collectible Sheet Music*, Schiffer, 1999; Frank Thompson, *AMC's Great Christmas Movies*, Taylor Publishing Co., 1998; Jon R. Warren, *Collecting Hollywood: The Movie Poster Price Guide*, 4th ed., American Collectors Exchange, 1997; Stuart W. Wells, III, *Science Fiction Collectibles: Identification & Price Guide*, Krause Publications, 1999.

**Periodicals:** *Autograph Times*, 2303 N. 44th St., #225, Phoenix, AZ 85008; *Big Reel*, P.O. Box 83, Madison, NC 27025; *Celebrity Collector,* P.O. Box 1115, Boston, MA 02117; *Classic Images,* P.O. Box 809, Muscatine, IA 52761; *Collecting Hollywood,* 2401 Broad St., Chattanooga, TN 37408; *Gone with the Wind Collector's Newsletter,* 1347 Greenmoss Dr., Richmond, VA 23225; *Hollywood & Vine,* P.O Box 717, Madison, NC 27025; *Hollywood Collectibles,* 4099 McEwen Dr., Ste. 350, Dallas, TX 75244; *Movie Advertising Collector,* P.O. Box 28587, Philadelphia, PA 19149; *Movie Collectors' World,* P.O. Box 309, Fraser, MI 48026; *Movie Poster Update,* 2401 Broad St., Chattanooga, TN 37408; *Poorman's VHS Movie Collectors Newsletter,* 902 E. Country Cables, Phoenix, AZ 85022; *Silent Film Newsletter,* 140 7th Ave., New York, NY 10011; *Spielberg Film Society Newsletter,* P.O. Box 13712, Tucson, AZ 85732; *Under Western Skies,* Route 3, Box 263H, Waynesville, NC 28786.

**Collectors' Clubs:** Emerald City Club, 153 E. Main St., New Albany, IN 47150; Hollywood Studio Collectors Club, 3960 Laurel Canyon Blvd., Ste. 450, Studio City, CA 91604; Manuscript Society, 350 N. Niagara St., Burbank, CA 91505; Old Time Western Film Club, P.O. Box 142, Silver City, NC 27344; Western Film Appreciation Society, 1914 112 St., Edmonton, Alberta T6J 5P8 Canada; Western Film Preservation Society, Inc., Raleigh Chapter, 1012 Vance St., Raleigh, NC 27608.

**Additional Listings:** Animation Art, Cartoon Characters, Cowboy Heroes, Disneyana, Movie Personalities.

Advertisement
   Harvey Girls, Judy Garland...... 15.00
   Heat's On, Mae West ............... 15.00
Almanac, Motion Picture Magazine, 1945 ........................................ 42.00
Book
   *Clockwork Orange,* Anthony Burgess, first edition, hardback ....80.00
   *Gone with the Wind,* Margaret Mitchell, 1938.................................... 10.00
Booklet, *Down to the Sea in Ships,* 1920s preview, produced by Elmer Clifton, released by Hodkinson Pictures, 18 pgs............................. 20.00
Catalog, McGull's Camera & Film Exchange Inc., New York, NY, c1942, 84 pgs, 4" x 9", catalog of 16mm silent motion picture film library, Victory edition .............................. 25.00
Chair, War of the Worlds, director's chair, Gene Barry ................... 150.00
Christmas Stocking, *ET,* cotton ..... 15.00

Cookbook, Gone With The Wind, 5-1/2" x 7-1/4", soft cover, 48 pgs, Pebeco Toothpaste premium, c1939 .... 45.00
Dish, 10-1/4" d, white china, blue dec with facsimile signatures of over 25 movie stars around rim, images of Hollywood Bowl, Ciro's Sunset Strip, Grauman's Chinese Theatre, Earl Carroll's Theatre Restaurant, Brown Derby Restaurant, NBC Studios, mkd "Vernon Kilns," 1940s .... 120.00
Doll
   Bond, James, 007, Gilbert, 1964, MIB.......................................... 400.00
   Oddjob, Gilbert, 1965, 11" h, orig first issue box......................... 485.00
Film
   "Have Badge, Will Chase," Abbott and Costello, Castle Films No. 850, 50', 8MM, orig box................... 22.50
   "Oh Doctor," Three Stooges, 16 mm, 4" sq box................................... 35.00
   "The Fast Getaway," Charlie Chaplin, 16 mm, 2.5" box....................... 25.00
Game, Sons of Hercules, 9-1/2" x 19" box, ©1965 Milton Bradley and ©1968 Embassy Pictures Corp.
   ................................................... 65.00
Gasoline Premium, Wings, Herald, sponsored by General Violet Ray Anti-Knock Gasoline, 1927 Paramount Picture, starring Clara Bow, Charles Rogers, Gary Cooper, green tone photos, 4 pgs, 10" x 15-1/2"
   ................................................... 40.00
Gum Card Box, Planet of the Apes, Topps, 1967, 24 bubble gum card packs ..................................... 100.00
Gum Card Set, James Bond, Philadelphia Gum Co, 1965, complete set of 66 photo cards...................... 100.00
Handbill
   Men Are Not Gods, Miriam Hopkins, 6" x 9", 1930s ......................... 20.00
   Spellbound, Gregory Peck and I Bergmann, 8" x 11", 4 pgs ....... 25.00
Handkerchief, Gone With The Wind, 13" sq, early 1940s
   Bonnie Blue, sheer white fabric, purple, orange, turquoise, and yellow floral design, 2 corners with image of Rhett and Bonnie Blue, other 2 corners with Bonnie on horseback
   ................................................... 75.00
   Scarlet O'Hara, floral design, yellow, rose, green, black, white, and gold, black diecut foil sticker ........... 60.00
License Plate
   Batman, used by Michael Keaton, Gotham City .......................... 165.00
   Fargo........................................ 15.00
Lobby Card
   Gone with the Wind, set of 6, first Italian release, 1948............... 130.00
   Lost Horizon, Mexican release, 12-1/2" x 16-1/2" .............................. 35.00
   Miss Tatlock's Millions, Robert Stack, Dorothy Wood, 1948, framed... 45.00
   Rawhide Rangers, Johnny Mack Brown, Universal..................... 20.00
   Target, Tim Holt, RKO, 1952 .... 24.00

**Poster, Apache Rifles, Admiral Pictures, Audie Murphy, 1964, $20.**

The Runaway, Paramount, produced by Famous Players-Lasky Corp., starring Clara Bow, Warner Baxler, George Bancroft, William Powell, large inscription "A. William de Mile," in pale yellow lettering, gray movie title, 1926, 11" x 14".................. 40.00
The Sad Sack, Jerry Lewis ..... 30.00
Who's Minding the Store, Jerry Lewis
   ................................................... 30.00
Magazine
   *The Hollywood Way To A Beautiful Body,* 9" x 12", Fawcett, ©1937
   ................................................... 20.00
   3-D Screen/Hollywood Pin-Ups, 8-1/2" x 11", issue #1, ©1963, 32 pgs, starlet photos................... 55.00
Movie Folder, Son of the Sheik, Valentino ......................................... 25.00
Newspaper Clippings, Gone with the Wind, group of 20, c1948 ........ 30.00
Paint Set, Tom Sawyer, Paramount, 1931........................................ 32.00
Pistol, used by Bruce Willis for Die Hard
   ................................................... 500.00
Playbill, Laffing Room Only, Olsen and Johnson, 1945 ......................... 10.00
Playing Cards, Gone with the Wind, tin container................................... 12.00
Poster
   Angel In My Pocket, Andy Griffith, full sheet ...................................... 100.00
   Arson, Inc., three-sheet, 41" x 81", 1949 Lippert Productions, starring Robert Lowery and Anne Gwynne, folded to 10-1/2" x 15"............. 95.00
   Background to Danger, George Raft and Sidney Greenstreet, 1943 movie
   ................................................... 85.00
   Bomba and the Jungle Girl, six-sheet, 80" x 80", 1953 Monogram Pictures, folded to 11" x 14" ..... 90.00

Cinderella, full color, 1920s, 20" x 30"
.............................................. 150.00
Mrs. Bridget O'Brien, John Sheridan, stone litho, 1905, 20" x 30" ..... 350.00
Press Book
Circus World, John Wayne, 14 pgs ................................................ 25.00
Girl Happy, Elvis Presley, 1964 ................................................ 25.00
Mary Poppins, Julie Andrews .. 15.00
The Caine Mutiny, Humphrey Bogart, 18 pcs ..................................... 35.00
Pulp
Doc Savage ............................. 35.00
Tell It To The Marines, ©1927, Jacobsen-Hodgkinson Corp., MGM, 128 pgs, 5-1/4" x 8", soft cover ....... 48.00
Puzzle
Babes in Toyland, Annette and Tommy Sands, WD Jaymar, frame tray, 1961, 9" x 12" ................... 30.00
No Other Woman, RKO Radio Picture, starring Irene Dunne, Eric Linden, and Charles Bickford, jigsaw, full color, 10" x 15-1/2" orig box
.............................................. 40.00
Record, The Wild One, orig motion picture soundtrack, Decca, 1954
.............................................. 135.00
Sheet Music, As Time Goes By, Casablanca, photographs of Humphrey Bogart, Ingrid Bergmann, and Paul Henreid on cov ...................... 148.00
Souvenir Book
Gone With The Wind, 1939 .... 115.00
Lawrence of Arabia, Peter O'Toole, colored photos, two fold-out double page maps ............................. 18.00
Since You Went Away, Selznick, 1944, 9" x 12", 20 pgs ............... 25.00
The Song of Bernadette, 9" x 11-1/2", 20 pgs, 1944 religious movie, full color cov Norman Rockwell illus of Jennifer Jones ......................... 40.00
White Shadows In The South Seas, MGM, 1928 ............................. 40.00
Textile, James Bond, pillow case, illus of Bond and other characters ...... 70.00
Toy, James Bond Shooting Attaché Case, MPC, 1965, orig box
.............................................. 1,165.00
Viewer Glasses, 3-D, Bwana Devil, folded 2" x 6" cardboard eyeglasses, Polaroid lenses, 1954 jungle adventure .......................................... 15.00
Window Card, High Noon, Gary Cooper, 14" x 22", 1952 ......................... 75.00

# Movie Personalities

**Collecting Hints:** Focus on one star. Today, the four most popular stars are Humphrey Bogart, Clark Gable, Jean Harlow, and Marilyn Monroe. Many of the stars of the silent era are being overlooked by the modern collector.

Remember that stars have big support staffs. Not all autographed items were or are signed by the star directly. Signatures should be checked carefully against a known original.

Many stars had fan clubs and the fans tended to hold on to the materials they assembled. The collector should be prepared to hunt and do research. A great deal of material rests in private hands.

**History:** The star system and Hollywood are synonymous. The studios spent elaborate sums of money promoting their stars. Chaplin, Valentino, and Pickford gave way to Garbo and Gable.

The movie magazine was a key vehicle in the promotion. *Motion Picture, Movie Weekly, Motion Picture World,* and *Photoplay* are just a few examples of this genre, although *Photoplay* was the most sensational.

The film star had no private life and cults grew up around many of them. By the 1970s the star system of the 1930s and 1940s had lost its luster. The popularity of stars is much shorter lived today.

**References:** *Big Reel Annual,* Antique Trader Books, 1996; Kevin Martin, *Signatures of the Stars,* Antique Trader Books, 1998; Rex Miller, *The Investor's Guide to Vintage Character Collectibles,* Krause Publications, 1999; Robert Osborne, *65 Years of the Oscar,* Abbeville, 1994; Jon R. Warren, *Collecting Hollywood: The Movie Poster Price Guide,* 4th ed., American Collectors Exchange, 1994; Stuart W. Wells, III, *Science Fiction Collectibles: Identification & Price Guide,* Krause Publications, 1999.

**Periodicals:** *Autograph Times,* 2303 N. 44th St., #225, Phoenix, AZ 85008; *Big Reel,* P.O. Box 83, Madison, NC 27025; *Celebrity Collector,* P.O. Box 1115, Boston, MA 02117; *Classic Images,* P.O. Box 809, Muscatine, IA 52761; *Collecting Hollywood,* 2401 Broad St., Chattanooga, TN 37408; *Gone with the Wind Collector's Newsletter,* 1347 Greenmoss Dr., Richmond, VA 23225; *Hollywood & Vine,* P.O. Box 717, Madison, NC 27025; *Hollywood Collectibles,* 4099 McEwen Dr., Ste 350, Dallas, TX 75244; *Movie Advertising Collector,* P.O. Box 28587, Philadelphia, PA 19149; *Movie Collectors' World,* P.O. Box 309, Fraser, MI 48026; *Movie Poster Update,* 2401 Broad St., Chattanooga, TN 37408; *Silent Film Newsletter,* 140 7th Ave.,

New York, NY 10011; *Under Western Skies,* Rte. 3, Box 263H, Waynesville, NC 28786.

**Collectors' Clubs:** All About Marilyn, P.O. Box 291176, Los Angeles, CA 90029; Emerald City Club, 153 E. Main St., New Albany, IN 47150; Hollywood Studio Collectors Club, 3960 Laurel Canyon Blvd., Ste 450, Studio City, CA 91604; Manuscript Society, 350 N. Niagara St,. Burbank, CA 91505; Old Time Western Film Club, P.O. Box 142, Silver City, NC 27344; Western Film Appreciation Society, 1914 112 St, Edmonton, Alberta T6J 5P8 Canada; Western Film Preservation Society, Inc., Raleigh Chapter, 1012 Vance St., Raleigh, NC 27608.

**Additional Listings:** Autographs, Cowboy Heroes, Magazines, Movie Memorabilia.

Abbott & Costello, game, Who's On First, 9-1/2" x 19", Selchow & Righter Co., ©ZIV International ........... 50.00
Allen, Woody, magazine, *Life,* March 21, 1969 ................................... 9.00
Astaire, Fred
Magazine, *Life,* Dec. 30, 1940 ..... 7.00
Sheet Music, *My Shining Hour* .. 7.50
Bacall, Lauren, magazine, *Life,* April 3, 1970 ......................................... 7.00
Bardot, Brigitte
Book, *Brigitte Bardot,* Francoise Sagan, 1976, 100 pgs, 12-1/2" x 9-1/2"
.............................................. 10.00
Magazine, *Life,* July 28, 1961 ..... 15.00
Bergmann, Ingrid, magazine
*Life,* Oct. 13, 1967 ..................... 8.00
*Look,* Nov. 11, 1958 ............... 12.00
Bow, Clara, arcade card, black and white portrait, tan background .. 2.50
Brando, Marlon
Book, *Brando,* Charles Highman, hard back .................................. 10.00
Magazine, *Life,* Dec. 14, 1962
.............................................. 12.00
Bushman, Francis X., silent star, pennant, Metro .............................. 25.00
Cantor, Eddie
Big Little Book, *Eddie Cantor In An Hour With You,* Whitman, #774, ©1934, 4-3/4" x 5-1/4" ............. 40.00
Pin, Eddie Cantor Magic Club, 1-1/2" d, brass, black facial features, red, background, tall hat, Pebeco Toothpaste, 1935 ........................... 50.00
Chaplin, Charlie
Cartoon Book, Charlie Chaplin In The Movies, 1917 ................... 65.00
Figure, 2-1/2" x 8", stuffed leather, full length portrait image, inked in black on natural tan leather, black felt back, 1920s ........................... 72.00
Pencil Box, 2" x 8", full figure illus
.............................................. 60.00
Sheet Music, Charlie Chaplin Walk, ©1915 Rossiter Music Co., Chicago
.............................................. 20.00

Coogan, Jackie
    Arcade Card, black and white portrait, tan background................. 2.00
    Clicker, metal, adv for peanut butter ............................................... 24.00
    Pencil Box, minor rust ............. 12.00
Cooper, Jackie, book, *Jackie Cooper in Peck's Bad Boy,* Saalfield, #1084, ©1934, 4-/4" x 5-1/4", some wear ................................................. 35.00
Crawford, Joan, pocket mirror, black and white photo, mid-1920s, tiny facsimile signature ........................ 65.00
Crosby, Bing
    Box, ice cream ........................... 8.00
    Game, Call Me Lucky, Parker Bros., 1954, black and white portrait on box lid, 19-1/2" sq playing board ............................................... 30.00
    Magazine, *Look,* June 7, 1960, Bing and family cover...................... 13.00
Davis, Bette
    Coloring Book, 10" x 13", Merrill, 1942......................................... 24.00
    Movie Poster, *Hush Hush Sweet Charlotte,* 27" x 41"................. 35.00
    Press Book, *The Catered Affair,* 20 pgs........................................... 30.00
Dean, James, scrap book of press cuttings and photographs, anniversary book, and 1955 magazine ....... 82.00
Etting, Ruth, autographed photo, 8-1/2" x 11-1/2", black and white glossy, soft focus glamour pose .......... 40.00
Farnum, William, silent star, pennant, Fox ............................................ 25.00

**Cigarette Card, Marlene Dietrich, Wills Cigarettes, 1930s, 1-1/4" x 2-5/8", $14.50**

Fields, W. C., record album, 10-1/2" x 12", Variety Records, United Artist label, ©1946 ............................ 60.00
Funicello, Annette, magazine, *Teen Screen*................................. 20.00
Gabor, Zsa Zsa, magazine, *Life,* Oct. 15, 1951 ................................. 22.50
Gleason, Jackie, magazine
    *Life,* Nov. 2, 1959 ......................... 15.00
    *Look,* Nov. 15, 1966, with Art Carney on cover ...................................... 12.50
Harlow, Jean, post card, 3-1/2" x 45-1/2", glossy, small facsimile signature, fan card, 1930s, unused................... 30.00
Hope, Bob, magazine
    *Life,* Jan. 29, 1971 ................... 10.00
    *Post,* Nov. 9, 1963.................... 16.00
    *Time,* Sept. 20, 1943 .............. 15.00
Kelly, Grace, coloring book, Whitman, 1956, few pages colored ........ 45.00
Lake, Arthur, arcade card, Educational Pictures, black and white, tan background ..................................... 2.50
Laurel & Hardy
    Arcade Card, Stan Laurel, Paramount Pictures, black and white, tan background ............................... 2.25
    Doll, Stan, 9-1/2" h, Bend'em Doll, Knickerbocker Toys, Harry Harmon Pictures Corp., vinyl, flexible legs, orig tags.................................. 40.00
    Movie Poster, *Four Clowns,* 27" x 41" ................................................. 45.00
    Salt and Pepper Shakers, pr, 1/2" x 2-1/2" x 4" white china tray, 4" h Laurel with black derby, 3" h Hardy with brown derby, Beswick, England, 3 pcs ....................................... 115.00
Leigh, Janet, magazine, *Motion Picture,* August 1959 ................... 10.00
Loren, Sophia, magazine, *Life,* Nov. 14, 1960........................................ 15.00
Marx, Zippo, arcade card, black and white portrait, tan background ..... 2.50
McQueen, Steve, magazine, *Life,* July 12, 1963 ................................. 15.00
Midler, Bette, magazine, *Time,* March 2, 1987 .......................................... 3.00
Monroe, Marilyn
    Cologne Spray, 1983, MIB ....... 45.00
    Doll, Tristar, 11-1/2" h .............. 45.00
    Newspaper Supplement, New York, Sunday, 1982 ........................... 20.00
    Novak, Kim, fan club kit, wallet, photos, and Christmas card, 1966 ............................................... 25.00
Our Gang
    Premium Card, Yuengling's Ice Cream, black and white or color tinted image, set of ten, 1-1/4" x 3", c1930................................... 125.00
    Puzzle, 11" x 14" brown envelope, 80 pcs, sponsored by McKesson's Milk of Magnesia, scene of Our Gang characters in a soda fountain ............................................. 135.00
Pickford, Mary
    Magazine, *Photoplay,* September, 1914, full color cover, article with photos................................... 45.00
    Pennant, Famous Players Film Co. ............................................... 35.00
    Photograph Signed, 1930........ 55.00

Powell, Eleanor, arcade card, black and white portrait, tan background .. 2.00
Redford, Robert, magazine, *Argosy,* cover story, August, 1974 ......... 5.00
Rogers, Ginger
    Magazine, *Life,* Nov. 5, 1951 ... 15.00
    Photograph Signed, 5" x 7", color, Alhambra Theatre 1940 roster on back...................................... 15.00
Shore, Dinah, Emmy ............... 2,460.00
Sinatra, Frank, magazine
    *Life,* April 23, 1965.................... 15.00
    *TV Guide,* May 14, 1954, New England edition, full color cover photo...................................... 45.00
Sparks, Ned, arcade card, black and white portrait, tan background .. 2.00
Stanwyck, Barbara
    Box, Vita-Sert Chocolates 1940s, illus on lid.............................. 150.00
    Press Book, Gambling lady, 11" x 17", 1934, Warner Bros., some wear .............................................. 30.00
Streisand, Barbara, set of eight lobby cards for "Funny Girl," 27 black and white stills, "Funny Girl" program, two "Funny Girl" records........ 123.00
Temple, Shirley, cereal box, Quaker Puffed Wheat, c1939 ............. 110.00
Three Stooges
    Fan Photo, 5" x 6", full color, Three Stooges on flying carpet, steering wheel gripped by Larry, facsimile signatures, c1960 .................... 20.00
    Pinback Button, Carter is Doing the Work of 3 Men, black on yellow, cartoon images, c1980 .................. 8.00
    Punch-Out Book, 7-1/2" x 13", Golden Press, 1962 ................. 75.00
West, Mae, magazine, *Life,* April 18, 1969........................................... 7.00
White, Pearl, silent star, pennant, Pathe ............................................... 20.00

# Music Boxes

**Collecting Hints:** A music box can be inserted into any figurine or box-shaped object. The objects priced below are only those in which the music box is secondary to the piece. Antique music boxes are covered in *Warman's Antiques and Collectibles Price Guide.*

Some collectors tend to focus on one tune, trying to collect each of the various ways it has been used. Others concentrate on a musical toy form, such as dolls or teddy bears. A popular item is the musical jewel box, prevalent between 1880 and 1930.

**History:** The insertion of a small music box into toys and other products dates back to the 18th century. Initially, these were primarily given to children of the aristocracy; but the mass production of music boxes in the late 19th century made them available to everyone.

The music box toy enjoyed greater popularity in Europe than in America. Some of the finest examples are of European origin. After World War II there was an influx of inexpensive music box toys from the Far East. The popularity of the musical toy suffered as people reacted negatively to these inferior products.

**References:** Gilbert Bahl, *Music Boxes*, Courage Books, Running Press, 1993; Arthur W. J. G. Ord-Hume, *The Musical Box*, Schiffer Publishing, 1995.

**Collectors' Clubs:** Musical Box Society International, 12140 Anchor Lane, SW, Moore Haven, Fl 334/1; Musical Box Society of Great Britain, The Willows, 102 High St., Landbeach, Cambridge CB4 4DT England.

**Museums:** Bellms Car and Music of Yesterday, Sarasota, FL; Lockwood Matthews Mansion Museum, Norwalk, CT; Miles Musical Museum, Eureka Springs, AR; Musical Museum, Deansboro, NY; Musical Wonder House Museum, Iscasset, ME.

Ballerina, 9" h, bisque, glass eyes, cylinder base, French ................. 300.00
Bank, plastic, Gorham, 7-1/2" h
    Acrobat, green ......................... 18.00
    Cyclist, red ............................. 18.00
Barrel Organ, 5-1/2" h, Ohio Art...... 5.00
Bear, hand carved ........................ 65.00
Bird Cage, singing bird, German
    ............................................. 250.00
Bird, figural, ceramic
    Cardinal, 6-1/2" h .................... 18.00
    Dove, 6-1/4" h.......................... 15.00
    Owl, 6" h ................................. 20.00
Box
    1-1/4" x 4-1/4" x 3-1/2", Thorens cylinder, grained wood case plays Bicycle Built for Two ....................... 45.00

**Elvis Presley, ceramic, plays "Love Me Tender," Japan, 7-3/4" h, $75.**

2-1/2" h, Santa, white, plays Jingle Bells ........................................... 8.00
2-1/2" h, snowman and lady, red, plays Frosty the Snowman........ 8.00
2-1/2" x 3-1/2" x 6-1/2", leather, porcelain plaque painting of five mallards on cov ........................... 70.00
Children on Merry Go Round, 7-3/4" h, wood, figures move, plays Around the World in 80 Days............... 22.00
Children on See Saw, 7" h, wood, figures move in time to music ...... 20.00
Christmas Tree Stand, revolving, Germany ......................................... 65.00
Church, 4" x 6", tin, hand crank, Germany ..................................... 125.00

Cigar holder, 15" h, wood and brass
    ............................................... 75.00
Clown, 5-1/2" h, plastic, dome Gorham
    ............................................... 18.00
Coffee Grinder shape, 3" h........... 30.00
Dog, 12" h, Nipper, ceramic ......... 45.00
Doll
    Drum Major, 15" h, blue uniform, plays Cecile ......................... 100.00
    Sammy Kay, 11" h, composition, sways....................................... 65.00
Dove, figural, ceramic ................. 18.00
Easter Egg, tin ............................ 15.00
Evening in Paris, illus of different cosmetics, velvet and silver box .......... 125.00
Kitten with ball, 5-1/2" h, ceramic ....18.00
Man, leaning against lamp post, cast iron, plays How Dry I Am, New York City souvenir ........................... 18.00
Merry-Go-Round, three horses and riders, 1904................................. 45.00
Paddington Bear ......................... 45.00
Peanuts
    Schroeder at his piano, bust of Beethoven, plays "Beethoven's Emperor's Waltz," Anri, 1971 ....275.00
    Snoopy, Red Baron in airplane, orig box........................................ 225.00
Phonograph, 5-3/4" x 3-1/4" x 3-1/4", miniature, upright, wind-up, Swiss
    ............................................... 78.00
Powder Box, 3-1/2" x 4-1/4", metal, silver, litho cov, c1940 ................. 25.00
7-Up Can, Love Story theme........ 45.00
Stein, 5" h, porcelain, diamond dec
    ............................................... 35.00
Three Little Pigs, animated, wood, Disneyland key, Disneyland labels
    ............................................. 245.00
Toy
    Bear, hand carved, spin with hand
    ............................................... 65.00
    Chimp, jolly ............................. 35.00
    Clock, Hickory Dickory, Mattel, 1952
    ............................................... 25.00
    Ferris Wheel, moving, cardboard, c1940, MIB ............................ 15.00
    Santa Claus, 14" h, head moves
    ............................................... 35.00

# N

# Napkin Rings

**Collecting Hints:** Concentrate on napkin rings of unusual design or shape. This is one collectible that still can be used on a daily basis. However, determine the proper cleaning and care methods for each type of material. Many celluloid items have been ruined because they were stored in an area that was too dry or were washed in water that was too hot.

Napkin rings with an engraved initial or monogram are worth less than those without personalized markings. Many collectors and dealers have these marks removed professionally if it will not harm the ring.

**History:** Napkin rings enjoyed a prominent role on the American dinner table during most of the 19th and early 20th centuries. Figural napkin rings were used in upper-class households. The vast majority of people used a simple napkin ring, although these could be elegant as well. Engraving, relief designs, and carving turned simple rings into works of art. When cast metal and molded plastic became popular, shaped rings, especially for children, were introduced.

The arrival of inexpensive paper products and fast and frozen foods, along with a faster-paced lifestyle, reduced American's concern for elegant daily dining. The napkin ring has almost disappeared from the dining table.

**Reference:** Lillian Gottschalk and Sandra Whitson, *Figural Napkin Rings*, Collector Books, 1996.

Aluminum, engraved "World's Fair, St. Louis, 1904," engraved US flag ...................................................... 50.00
Bakelite, 1940s
  Angelfish, deep blue marbled ... 70.00
  Elephant, navy blue .................. 65.00
  Popeye, orange, some wear to orig decal ...................................... 140.00
  Rabbit, bright yellow ............... 75.00
  Rocking Horse, red, orig eye ............................................... 225.00
Brass, 2 elves, dog, dragon, and leaf dec, emb .................................. 20.00
Cloisonné, dragon, white ground ............................................... 25.00
Glass, twisted hollow tube forms ring, Dorofee Glass, set of 10 .......... 50.00
Ivory, carved openwork ............... 20.00
Metal, lady holding stick, c1942 ... 15.00

**Geisha Girl, River's Edge pattern, green border, $37.50.**

Porcelain
  Butterfly, porcelain, hand painted, red "Made in Japan" mark, 3" w 6.50
  Man, Art Deco design, mkd "Noritake" ...................................... 32.00
  Owl, seated on ring .................. 20.00
  Rose, cream ground, gold trim, mkd "Nippon" ................................. 50.00
Silver, plated
  Bulldog, Dingo Boy ................ 125.00
  Cat, arched back ................... 125.00
  Dog, pulling sled, emb greyhounds on sides, engraved "Sara," Meriden .............................................. 165.00
  Nude Man, holding torch, sq base .............................................. 150.00
  Parrot, rect base, Rogers Mfg Co. ................................................ 48.00
  Plain ring with cutout "A," unmarked .................................................. 6.00
Silver, sterling
  Cherubs, pair of seated figures, worn ...................................... 70.00
  Koala Bear, Australian, 2" x 3" .............................................. 70.00
  Lily, oval ring, engraved flowers, Rogers and Brothers, c1870, 1-1/2" h .............................................. 150.00
  Mickey Mouse ......................... 80.00
  Peacock, standing ................... 60.00
  Plain, monogrammed "A.D.A.," worn smooth in places, 1" w, 1-3/4" d .............................................. 45.00
  Plain, monogrammed "H. F.," 3-4/" w, 2-1/4" l .................................. 35.00
  Swan pulling wheeled napkin ring, Meriden Britannia, c1896, 2-3/4" h .............................................. 550.00

# New Martinsville-Viking Glass

**Collecting Hints:** Before 1935, New Martinsville glass was made in a wide variety of colors. Later glass was only made in crystal, blue, ruby, and pink.

Look for cocktail, beverage, liquor, vanity, smoking, and console sets. Amusing figures of barnyard animals, sea creatures, dogs, and bears were produced.

Both Rainbow Art Glass and Viking Glass handmade their products and affixed a paper label. Rainbow Art Glass pieces are beautifully colored, and the animal figures are more abstract in design than those of New Martinsville. Viking makes plain, colored, cut, and etched tableware, novelties, and gift items. Viking began making black glass in 1979.

**History:** The New Martinsville Glass Manufacturing Company, founded in 1901, took its name from its West Virginia location. Early products, made from opal glass, were decorative and utilitarian. Later, pressed crystal tableware with flashed-on ruby or gold decorations was made. In the 1920s, innovative color and designs made vanity, liquor, and smoking sets popular. Dinner sets in patterns such as Radiance, Moondrops, and Dancing Girl, as well as new colors, cuttings, and etchings were produced. In the 1940s, black glass was formed into perfume bottles, bowls with swan handles, and flower bowls. In 1944, the company was sold and reorganized as the Viking Glass Company.

The Rainbow Art Glass Company, Huntington, West Virginia, was established in 1942 by Henry Manus, a Dutch immigrant. This company produced small, hand-fashioned animals and decorative ware of opal, spatter, cased, and crackle glass. Rainbow Art Glass also decorated for other companies. In the early 1970s, Viking acquired Rainbow Art Glass Company and continued the production of the small animals.

The Viking Glass Company was acquired by Kenneth Dalzell in 1986. The company's name was changed to Dalzell-Viking Glass. Production included items made with Viking molds, some animal figures were reintroduced, and other items were made using new colors. In late 1998, Dalzell-Viking closed.

**References:** Lee Garmon and Dick Spencer, *Glass Animals of the Depression Era*, Collector Books, 1993; James Measell, *New Martinsville Glass*, The Glass Press, 1994; Naomi L. Over, *Ruby Glass of the 20th Century*, The Glass Press, 1990, 1993-94 value update; Hazel Marie Weatherman, *Colored Glassware of the Depression Era*, Book 2, Glassworks, 1982.

By special permission of the Sandwich Historical Society

**VIKING**
INTRODUCES
**"DIAMOND THUMBPRINT"**

Authentic Replicas
of Early American Pattern Glass

**Magazine Tear Sheet, Diamond Thumbprint pattern,** *China and Glass Tablewares,* **January 1972, $3.**

Ashtray, fish, 4" d ........................... 12.00
Basket, Janice .............................. 65.00
Beer Mug, pink ............................. 25.00
Bowl
    5" d, Peach Blow, scalloped rim
    ................................................ 60.00
    10" d, Meadow Wreath, crimped
    ................................................ 35.00
    12" d, Radiance, amber ........... 40.00
Cake Plate, 14" d, Hostmaster, amber
    ................................................ 25.00
Candlestick, clear
    Double, etched floral design, 5-1/4"
    h, 7-1/4" w ............................... 24.00
    Figural, squirrel, 4-3/4" l, 3-1/2" w, 6-
    3/4" h, pr ................................ 120.00
Celery Dish, swan, 8" l neck, 6" h
    ................................................ 25.00
Chip and Dip Set, 14" d, orange, Viking
    ................................................ 30.00
Cigarette Holder, cart shaped ...... 20.00
Compote, fired-on color, handpainted
    base trim, wear to gold trim, 4-1/4" h
    ................................................ 22.50
Cordial, Moondrops, 1 oz, amber, silver
    dec .......................................... 25.00
Creamer and Sugar, individual size,
    Moondrops, red ....................... 35.00
Cup and Saucer
    Fancy Square, jade ................. 15.00
    Hostmaster, ruby ..................... 10.00
    Moondrops, amber ................... 15.00
    Radiance, red .......................... 27.50
Decanter
    Nice Kitty, green ...................... 55.00
    Volkstead Pup, crystal ............. 75.00
Figure
    Bird, clear, 1960s ................... 15.00
    Chick, baby, clear ................... 45.00
    Dog, 8-1/2" l, orange, Viking, #1316
    ................................................ 37.50
    Duck, 15" l, orange, Viking ....... 50.00
    Eagle, clear ............................. 60.00

Elephant, clear ........................... 80.00
Giraffe, 7" h, clear .................... 20.00
Hen, clear ................................ 60.00
Horse, head up, clear .............. 90.00
Owl, 8-1/2" h, orange, Viking ... 100.00
Rooster, large, clear ................. 85.00
Seal, clear ............................... 80.00
Goblet
    Diamond Thumbprint .............. 12.00
    Hostmaster, cobalt blue .......... 24.00
    Mt. Vernon, cobalt blue ........... 20.00
Handkerchief Bowl, 5" x 5-1/2",
    crimped, deep orange, orig red and
    gold "Hand Made Viking" sticker
    ................................................ 20.00
Honey Jar, cov, Radiance, ruby .... 45.00
Iced Tea Tumbler, ftd, Prelude etching,
    crystal ..................................... 15.00
Marmalade, cov, Janice ............. 25.00
Mug, Georgian, ruby ................. 18.00
Nappy, Prelude, 5" d, heart shaped,
    handle ..................................... 20.00
Pitcher, orange, Viking .............. 24.00
Plate
    7-1/2" w, Fancy Square, jade ..... 8.00
    8" d, Radiance, red, slight wear
    ................................................ 13.00
    8-1/2" d, Moondrops, red ........ 20.00
    11" d, Meadow Wreath, clear ... 20.00
    14" d, Florentine ..................... 25.00
Relish Bowl, Radiance, 3 part, amber,
    9" d .......................................... 18.00
Relish Set, glass relish dish with 3 small
    feet and orig Viking sticker, Flair pat-
    tern silverplated relish spoon and
    pickle fork, mkd "1847 Rogers Broth-
    ers," MIB ................................. 25.00
Sherbet, #34, jade green ............. 12.00
Stopper, jade-ite, fan-shaped petals, 2-
    1/4" w, small crack ...................... 6.50
Swan, back forms bowl, 5" x 6" x 5-1/4"
    Amber ..................................... 35.00
    Clear ....................................... 25.00
Tumbler
    Georgian, ruby ........................ 25.00
    Hostmaster, cobalt blue ........... 10.00
    Oscar, amber .......................... 12.00
Vanity Set, Judy, 3 pcs, green and crys-
    tal, cologne bottle, stopper, tray
    ................................................ 95.00
Vase
    Epic, sapphire blue, Viking, 17-1/2" h
    ................................................ 25.00
    Shell, leaded crystal, 5" h, pr. 125.00
Whiskey, Moondrops, amethyst .... 20.00

# Newspapers, Headline Editions

**Collecting Hints:** All newspapers must be complete with a minimum of chipping and cracking. Post-1880 newsprint is made of wood pulp and deteriorates quickly without proper care. Pre-1880 newsprint was composed of cotton and rag fiber and has survived much better than its wood-pulp counterpart.

Front pages only of 20th-century newspapers command about 60% of the value for the entire issue, since the primary use for these papers is display. Pre-20th-century issues are collectible only if complete, as banner headlines were rarely used. These papers tend to run between four and eight pages in length.

Major city issues are preferable, although any newspaper providing a dramatic headline is collectible. Banner headlines, those extending completely across the paper, are most desirable. Those papers from the city in which an event happened command a substantial premium over the prices listed below. A premium is also paid for a complete series, such as all 20th-century election reports.

Twentieth-century newspapers should be stored away from high humidity and out of direct sunlight. Issues should be placed flat in polyethylene bags or in acid-free folders that are slightly larger than the paper.

Although not as commonly found, newspapers from the 17th through the 19th centuries are highly collectible, particularly those from the Revolutionary War, War of 1812, Civil War, and those reporting Indian and desperado events.

Two of the most commonly reprinted papers are the *Ulster County Gazette*, of Jan. 4, 1800, dealing with Washington's death and the *N.Y. Herald* of April 15, 1865, concerning Lincoln's death. If you have either of these papers, chances are you have a reprint.

**History:** America's first successful newspaper was *The Boston Newsletter*, founded in 1704. The newspaper industry grew rapidly and reached its pinnacle in the early 20th century. Within the last decade many great evening papers have ceased publication, and many local papers have been purchased by the large chains.

Collecting headline-edition newspapers has become popular during the last 20 years, largely because of the decorative value of the headlines. Also, individuals like to collect newspapers related to the great events which they have witnessed or which have been romanticized through the movies, television, and other media. Historical events, the Old West, and the gangster era are particularly popular subjects.

**References:** Ron Barlow and Ray Reynolds, *Insider's Guide to Old*

*Books, Magazines, Newspapers, and Trade Catalogs*, Windmill Publishing (2147 Windmill View Rd., El Cajon, CA 92020), 1996; Gene Utz, *Collecting Paper*, Books Americana, 1993.

**Periodical:** *Paper Collectors' Marketplace* (*PCM*), P.O. Box 128, Scandinavia, WI 54977.

**Advisor:** Tim Hughes.

**Notes:** The following listing includes prices of issues dating more than 200 years old, but concentrates on newspapers of the 20th century. The date given is the date of the event itself; the newspaper coverage usually appeared the following day.

1778, average Revolutionary War newspaper...................................... 250.00
1795, typical late 18th Century newspaper............................................. 25.00
1813, typical War of 1812 newspaper .............................................. 15.00
1816, March 6, Battle of the Alamo ............................................ 240.00
1861, April 12, Civil War begins.... 170.00
1862, March 9, Battle of the Monitor vs. Merrimac................................ 135.00
1863, typical Civil War newspaper ............................................ 14.00
1863, July 4, The Battle of Gettysburg ............................................ 185.00
1865, April 14, Lincoln is assassinated at Ford's Theater .................... 600.00
1876, June 25, Custer's Massacre, but not reported in newspapers until July 7 or later................................ 175.00
1882, April 3, Jesse James is killed ............................................ 180.00
1893, June 20, Lizzie Borden found not guilty......................................... 78.00
1901, Sept. 6, President McKinley is shot .......................................... 55.00
1903, Dec. 17, Wright Brothers first flight in their airplane............. 325.00
1908, Nov. 3, President Taft is elected ............................................ 25.00
1912, Jan. 6, New Mexico joins the Union......................................... 24.00
1912, April 15, The *Titanic* hits an iceberg and sinks ....................... 600.00
1915, May 7, The *Lusitania* is sunk ............................................ 375.00
1917, April 6, War is declared, the US enters WWI............................. 35.00
1918, typical World War I newspaper
1919, Jan. 6, Teddy Roosevelt dies ............................................ 30.00
1920, Jan. 5, Babe Ruth is sold to the Yankees.................................... 57.00
1921, March 4, Harding is inaugurated
1923, Feb. 16, opening of King Tut's tomb..................................... 37.00
1924, Nov. 4, Coolidge is elected. 29.00
1925, July 21, Scopes is convicted, the Monkey Trial............................ 35.00
1926, May 8, Byrd reaches the North Pole .......................................... 27.00

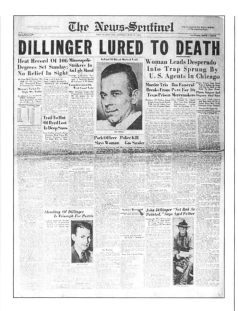

**The News Sentinel, July 22, Death of Dillinger, $170.**

1926, Oct. 6, Babe Ruth hits 3 home runs in World Series, shattering 6 records.................................... 63.00
1927, May 21, Lindbergh successfully lands in Paris.......................... 85.00
1927, Sept. 30, Babe Ruth hits his 60th homerun............................... 210.00
1928, June 18, Amelia Earhart crosses the Atlantic.............................. 78.00
1928, Nov. 6, Hoover elected ....... 21.00
1929, Feb. 14, St. Valentine's Day Massacre................................... 170.00
1929, Oct. 28, Stock Market Crash, report of Monday's closing .... 130.00
1931, June 5, Al Capone prosecuted for tax evasion.............................. 37.00
1932, March 1, Lindbergh baby is kidnapped ................................... 57.00
1932, May 12, Lindbergh baby is found dead.......................................... 59.00
1932, Aug. 24, Amelia Earhart's record flight across America............... 28.00
1933, Jan. 7, President Coolidge dies ................................................ 30.00
1933, Jan. 31, Hitler becomes Chancellor of Germany ........................ 25.00
1933, March 4, Franklin D. Roosevelt is inaugurated............................. 25.00
1933, April 7, End of Prohibition ... 38.00
1933, Sept. 22, Dillinger is captured in Dayton, Ohio .......................... 38.00
1933, Dec. 5, Prohibition is repealed ................................................ 35.00
1934, May 23, Bonnie & Clyde are killed in Louisiana.......................... 210.00
1934, July 22, Death of Dillinger ................................................ 170.00
1934, Aug. 2, Hitler proclaims himself Fuehrer and Reich Chancellor ................................................ 23.00
1935, June 3, Babe Ruth retires from baseball.................................. 40.00
1935, Aug. 16, Will Rogers and Wiley Post are killed .......................... 35.00

**The Detroit News, Truman's Proclamation, War Ends, $36.**

1936, April 4, Bruno Hauptmann is executed....................................... 28.00
1936, Aug. 3, Jesse Owens captures 100 meter gold at Berlin Olympics ................................................ 25.00
1937, May 6, the Hindenburg disaster at Lakehurst, New Jersey ...... 110.00
1937, July 3, Amelia Earhart disappears ................................................ 70.00
1938, March 12, Hitler takes Austria ................................................ 23.00
1939, May 2, Lou Gehrig's consecutive game streak ends.................... 68.00
1940, Nov. 6, Roosevelt is elected ................................................ 27.00
1941, June 2, Lou Gehrig dies ..... 58.00
1941, July 17, Joe DiMaggio's last game of hitting streak (56th).... 33.00
1941, Dec. 7, Pearl Harbor attack ................................................ 40.00
1942, May 8, Battle in Coral Sea ... 15.00
1943, typical World War II newspaper ................................................ 4.00
1943, Jan. 6, Death of George Washington Carver.......................... 20.00
1944, June 6, D-Day Invasion of France ................................................ 35.00
1944, Dec. 16, Battle of the Bulge begins, continuing through Dec. 26 ................................................ 15.00
1945, Feb. 19, Iwo Jima .............. 25.00
1945, April 12, President Franklin D. Roosevelt dies ......................... 25.00
1945, May 8, Germany surrenders, V-E Day ......................................... 36.00
1945, Aug. 9, the atomic bomb is dropped on Nagasaki, Japan.. 35.00
1945, Aug. 14, Japan quit, V-J Day ................................................ 36.00
1948, Aug. 14, Babe Ruth dies .... 70.00
1950, June 28, the Korean War begins ................................................ 22.00

**Dallas Morning News, Nov. 22, 1963, Kennedy Slain, $125.**

1952, Sept. 24, Marciano new boxing champion .................................. 22.00
1954, Jan. 14, Joe DiMaggio marries Marilyn Monroe ........................ 35.00
1955, Oct. 4, Brooklyn Dodgers win the World Series .......................... 30.00
1958, July 1, Alaska joins union .... 18.00
1960, Nov. 8, John F. Kennedy is elected ...................................... 35.00
1961, Oct. 1, Roger Maris hits his 61st home run, breaking Babe Ruth's record ................................... 110.00

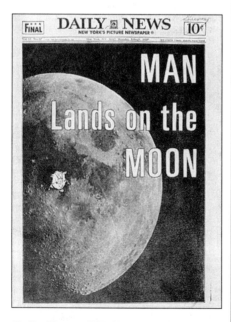

**Daily News, NY, Man Lands on the Moon, July 21, 1969, $35.**

1962, Feb. 21, John Glenn orbits the earth ......................................... 23.00
1962, Aug. 6, Marilyn Monroe dies ................................................ 72.00
1963, Aug. 28, Civil Rights march on Washington, "I have a dream..." speech by Martin Luther King, Jr. ................................................ 37.00
1963, Nov. 22, John F. Kennedy is assassinated ........................... 25.00
1965, Feb. 21, Malcolm X is assassinated in New York City ............. 70.00
1965, Sept. 9, Sandy Kofax pitches a perfect game .......................... 26.00
1967, Jan. 16, first Superbowl, Green Bay Packers defeat Kansas City Chiefs ..................................... 20.00
1968, April 15, Martin Luther King is assassinated ........................... 43.00
1969, July 21, Man walks on the moon ................................................ 26.00
1970, April 15, beginning of the Apollo 13 flight ................................. 13.00
1972, Nov. 5, Nixon is re-elected .. 14.00
1973, Jan. 26, Vietnam war ends . 20.00
1977, Aug. 1, Elvis Presley dies in Memphis ......................................... 23.00

# Niloak Pottery

**Collecting Hints:** Mission ware pottery is characterized by swirling layers of browns, blues, reds, and cream. Very few pieces are glazed on both the outside and inside; usually only the interior is glazed.

**History:** Niloak Pottery was made near Benton, Arkansas. Charles Dean Hyten, the founder of this pottery, experimented with the native clay and tried to preserve the natural colors. By 1911, he had perfected a method that produced the desired effect, resulting in the popular Mission ware. The pieces were marked "Niloak," which is Kaolin—the type of fine porcelain clay used—spelled backwards.

After a devastating fire, the pottery was rebuilt and named Eagle Pottery. This factory included enough space to add a novelty pottery line which was introduced in 1929. This line continued until 1934 and usually bears the name "Hywood-Niloak." After 1934, "Hywood" was dropped from the mark. Mr. Hyten left the pottery in 1941, and in 1946 the operation closed.

**References:** Susan and Al Bagdade, *Warman's American Pottery and Porcelain*, Wallace-Homestead, 1994; David Edwin Gifford, *Collector's Encyclopedia of Niloak*, Collector Books, 1993; Ralph and Terry Kovel, *Kovels' American Art Pottery*, Crown Publishers, 1993.

**Videotape:** Ralph and Terry Kovel, *Collecting with the Kovels: American Art Pottery*, available from producers (P.O. Box 22990, Beachwood, OH 44122).

**Collectors' Club:** Arkansas Pottery Collectors Society, 12 Normandy Rd., Little Rock, AR 72007.

Ashtray, blue glaze, hat shape ..... 12.00
Cornucopia Vase, 3-3/8" h, mkd, pr ................................................ 35.00
Creamer and Sugar, Hywood line, rose glaze ...................................... 37.50
Ewer
   7" h, yellow, small brown patch under glaze at base of handle ........... 50.00
   16-1/2" h, Ozark Dawn .......... 150.00
Figure
   Canoe, matte white ................. 35.00
   Frog, matte green ................... 30.00
   Polar Bear, matte white ............ 45.00
Planter
   Bear, tan ................................... 24.00
   Duck, pink and blue ................ 24.00
   Elephant, 6" h, matte maroon, standing on drum with "N" on side ... 72.00
   Fox, red .................................... 27.50
   Frog, yellow .............................. 50.00
   Kangaroo, white, brown accents ................................................ 20.00
   Rabbit, green ............................ 18.00
   Squirrel, 6" h, holding nut, pale pink, mkd ........................................... 65.00
   Swan, 8" h, matte pink, blue shading, mkd "Niloak" ............................ 75.00
Vase
   4" h, Mission Ware, second art mark ............................................... 110.00
   5-1/2" h, Mission Ware, orig foil sticker "Niloak Potteries at Benton Arkansas" ............................. 165.00
   6" h, Hywood line, blue glaze, leaf ................................................ 25.00
   7" h, Mission Ware, mkd ........ 165.00
   8" h, strawberry, pink, gray-green leaves, orig paper label on one, mkd, pr .................................. 150.00
   10" h, Mission Ware, orig paper label, small flake ................... 195.00
   10-1/2" h, Mission Ware, second art mark ...................................... 500.00

**Planter, camel, ochre, brown trim, mkd, 3-1/2" x 4-1/2", $32.50.**

# Nippon China

**Collecting Hints:** The Nippon market of the late 1990s was hurt by the flood of new reproductions, many of which are marked and appear quite like their vintage counterparts. Here are some tips to distinguish old marks from new:

A common old mark consisted of a central wreath open at the top with the letter M in the center. "Hand Painted" flowed around the top of the wreath; "NIPPO Box N" around the bottom. The modern fake mark reverses the wreath (it is open at the bottom) and places an hourglass form not an "M" in its middle.

An old leaf mark, approximately one-quarter inch wide, has "Hand" with "Painted" below to the left of the stem and "NIPPO Box N" beneath. The newer mark has the identical lettering but the size is now one-half, rather than one-quarter, inch.

An old mark consisted of "Hand Painted" arched above a solid rising sun logo with "NIPPO Box N" in a straight line beneath. The modern fake mark has the same lettering pattern but the central logo looks like a mound with a jagged line enclosing a blank space above it.

**History:** Nippon, Japanese handpainted porcelain, was made for export between 1891 and 1921. In 1891, when the McKinley tariff act proclaimed that all items of foreign manufacture be stamped with their country of origin, Japan chose to use "Nippon." In 1921, the United States decided the word "Nippon" no longer was acceptable and required all Japanese wares to be marked "Japan," ending the Nippon era.

**Marks:** There are more than 220 recorded Nippon backstamps or marks; the three most popular are the wreath, maple leaf, and rising sun. Wares with variations of all three marks are being reproduced today. A knowledgeable collector can easily spot the reproductions by the mark variances.

The majority of the marks are found in three different colors: green, blue, or magenta. Colors indicate the quality of the porcelain used: green for first-grade porcelain, blue for second-grade, and magenta for third-grade. Marks were applied by two methods: decal stickers under glaze and imprinting directly on the porcelain.

**References:** Joan Van Patten, *Collector's Encyclopedia of Nippon Porcelain*, 1st Series (1979, 1997 value update), 2nd Series (1982, 1997 value update), 3rd Series (1986, 1996 value update), 4th Series, (1997), Collector Books; 5th Series (1998); Kathy Wojciechowski, *Wonderful World of Nippon Porcelain*, Schiffer Publishing, 1992.

**Collectors' Clubs:** ARK-LA-TEX Nippon Club, 6800 Arapaho Rd., #1057, Dallas, TX 75248; Dixieland Nippon Club, P.O. Box 1712, Centerville, VA 22020; International Nippon Collectors Club, 1417 Steele St., Fort Myers, FL 33901; Lakes & Plains Nippon Collectors Society, P.O. Box 230, Peotone, IL 60468-0230; Long Island Nippon Collectors Club, 145 Andover Place, W. Hempstead, NY 11552; MD-PA Collectors' Club, 1016 Erwin Dr., Joppa, MD 21085; New England Nippon Collectors Club, 64 Burt Rd., Springfield, MA 01118; Sunshine State Nippon Collectors' Club, P.O. Box 425, Frostproof, FL 33843; Upstate New York Nippon Collectors' Club, 122 Laurel Ave, Herkimer, NY 13350.

Reproduction Alert.

**Additional Listings:** See Warman's Antiques & Collectibles Price Guide.

Bowl
  6-1/2" d, ftd, purple and white grapes, golden background.... 90.00
  8" d, white, handpainted peach trees, light blue and lavender highlights, gold trim, attached square open handles, blue mark "J. B. & Sons handpainted Nippon" ..... 85.00
Butter Dish, cov, florals, mkd "Hand Painted RC Nippon"................. 40.00
Calling Card Tray, 7-3/4" x 6", Dragonware, blue maple leaf mark ..... 48.00
Chocolate Set, chocolate pot, creamer, sugar, 5 sets of octagonal cups and saucers, 4 sets of round cups and saucers, white flying bird motif, gold trim, some damage and wear .................................................. 985.00
Compote, 8-1/2" d, 4-3/8" h, Wedgwood and rose nosegay dec, wreath mark ................................................ 200.00
Creamer and Sugar, handpainted florals, gold trim ........................... 80.00
Dresser Jar, handpainted floral dec, green wreath mark ................ 100.00
Ferner, 6" w, floral dec, gold beading, 4 handles, green "M" in wreath mark ................................................ 125.00
Hair Receiver and Powder Dish, pink flowers, light blue center band, gold trim, small brushed gold feet... 90.00
Hatpin Holder, 4-3/4" h, florals, wear to gold trim, mkd "Hand Painted Nippon" ......................................... 95.00

**Celery Set, handled serving dish, pink and white flowers, green leaves, tan band, purple stamp mark, "M" in wreath, 4" l matching salts, 12-1/2" l, $70.**

Jam Jar, cov, matching underplate, deep cobalt blue, heavily raised gold cartouches, allover gold dec, pink and pale apricot flowers, 2 handles, blue leaf mark .............. 145.00
Nut Bowl
  3-5/8" l, 2-3/8" w, handpainted flowers, blue mark "Noritake Nippon" .................................................. 8.50
  5" d, 3 ball feet, bright colors, purple and white grape clusters with leaves, mkd "Hand Painted Nippon" with wreath and "M" in green .......... 85.00
Open Salt, 3" w, hand painted, mauve flowers, gold trim, pr ............... 30.00
Pitcher, 7" h, slate gray ground, Moriage seal gulls, leaf mark.............. 250.00
Plate, 6-3/8" d, hand painted flowers, "M" in green wreath mark ........ 17.50
Serving Tray, 11" d, gold and burgundy medallions inside gold fluted rim, multicolored roses and leaves center, gold open pierced handles, Royal Kinran mark ................. 225.00
Sugar Shaker, white ground, pink and red roses, gold trim, cork bottom, single handle ........................... 45.00
Teapot, 6-1/2" h, Dragonware, some wear ......................................... 32.00
Tea Strainer, pink roses ............... 50.00
Trivet, 6" d, octagonal, mark #47, pink and blue flowers, brown basket type border, worn gold trim ............. 25.00
Vase
  8" h, handpainted florals, green wreath mark ............................ 95.00
  8-1/2" h, two handles, scenic design, blue pagoda mark ................. 165.00
  9-3/4" h, blue floral pattern, green "M" in wreath mark................ 100.00

# Noritake Azalea China

**Collecting Hints:** There are several backstamps on the Azalea pattern of Noritake China. The approximate dates are:

Prior to 1921: Blue rising sun, printed "Hand painted NIPPON"

1921-1923: Green wreath with M, printed "Noritake, Hand painted, Made in Japan"

1923-1930s: Green wreath with M, printed "Noritake, Hand painted, Made in Japan 19322"

1925-1930s: Red wreath with M, printed "Noritake, Hand painted, Made in Japan 19322"

1935-1940: Red azalea sprig, printed "Noritake Azalea Patt., Hand painted, Japan No. 19322/252622."

Most of the saucers and under-plates do not have a backstamp. Those that do are stamped "Azalea 19322/252622."

Most collectors assemble sets and are not concerned with specific marks. Those concentrating on specific marks, particularly the "NIPPON" one, may pay higher prices.

Pieces of Azalea pattern china are available through replacement services.

**History:** The Azalea pattern of Noritake China was first produced in the early 1900s. Each piece of fine china was hand painted. The individuality of the artists makes it almost impossible to find two pieces with identical painting.

In the early 1900s, the Larkin Company of Buffalo, New York, sold many household items to the American public through its catalog (similar to the Sears Roebuck and Company catalog). In the 1924 Larkin catalog, a basic Azalea pattern serving set was advertised. The set included the larger coffee cups with the blue rising sun backstamp.

Two forces came together in the 1920s to make the Azalea pattern of Noritake China one of the most popular household patterns in this century. First, the Larkin Company initiated its "Larkin Plan," encouraging housewives to sign up to become "Larkin Secretaries." Each Larkin Secretary formed a small neighborhood group of five or more women who would purchase Larkin products. The Larkin Secretary earned premiums based on the volume of orders she obtained and could then exchange these premiums for household items, including Azalea china.

Second, many households in the 1920s could not afford to spend all at one time the amount needed to purchase a complete set of fine china. The Larkin Club Plan enabled them to eventually complete sets of the Azalea pattern by buying items one or a few at a time.

Over the years, and to provide more enticements, additional pieces, such as the nut/fruit shell-shaped bowl, candy jar, and child's tea set were offered. Glassware, originally classified as "crystal," was introduced in the 1930s but was not well received.

It became somewhat of a status symbol to "own a set of Azalea." The Azalea pattern china advertisement in the 1931 Larkin catalog claimed, "Our Most Popular China."

Some Azalea pieces were advertised in the Larkin catalogs for 19 consecutive years, while others were advertised for only four or five years. These latter pieces are scarcer, resulting in a faster appreciation in value.

Most serious collectors would like to own the child's tea set, which we believe was advertised in only two Larkin Fall catalogs, and the so-called salesmen's samples, which were never advertised for sale.

The Larkin Company ceased distribution in 1945.

**References:** Larkin catalogs from 1916 through 1941.

**Notes:** The Larkin catalog numbers are given in parentheses behind each listing. If arranged numerically, you will notice gaps. For example, numbers 41 through 53 are missing. Noritake's Scenic pattern, presently called Tree in the Meadow, also was popular during this time period. Many of the missing Azalea numbers were assigned to Scenic pieces.

Basket (193) ............................... 125.00
Bonbon Dish, 6-1/4" d (184) ......... 45.00
Bouillon Cup and Saucer, 5-1/4" (124)
.................................................. 20.00
Bowl, shell shaped ..................... 325.00
Butter Pat (312) ............................ 65.00

Butter Tub, insert (54) ................... 45.00
Cake Plate (10) ............................. 35.00
Casserole, cov (16) ....................... 75.00
Celery Dish (444) ........................ 250.00
Cheese Dish, cov (315) .............. 125.00
Coffeepot (182) ........................... 500.00
Condiment Set (14) ....................... 75.00
Creamer (7) ................................... 25.00
Cruet, orig stopper (190) ............ 165.00
Cup and Saucer (2) ....................... 17.00
Demitasse Cup and Saucer (183)
.................................................. 125.00
Dinner Plate (13) .......................... 22.00
Egg Cup (120) ............................... 55.00
Grapefruit Bowl (185) ................. 115.00
Gravy Boat (40) ............................. 50.00
Jam Jar, cov (125) ....................... 110.00
Lemon Tray, handle (121) ............. 30.00
Luncheon Plate (4) ....................... 15.00
Mayonnaise Set (3) ....................... 50.00
Milk Pitcher, quart (100) ............. 165.00
Platter, 12" l (56) .......................... 50.00
Relish, 4 sections (119) .............. 110.00
Relish, undivided, oval ................. 65.00
Salad Bowl, 10" d (12) .................. 35.00
Salt and Pepper Shakers, pr ........ 25.00
Spooner (189) ............................... 90.00
Syrup, cov (97) ............................. 95.00
Teapot (15) .................................... 95.00
Toothpick Holder (192) ................. 95.00
Vegetable Bowl, oval (101) ........... 45.00

# Nutcrackers

**Collecting Hints:** The most popular modern nutcrackers are the military and civilian figures which are made in East Germany. These are collected primarily for show and not for practicality.

Nutcracker design responded to each decorating phase through the 1950s. The figural nutcrackers of the Art Deco and Art Nouveau periods are much in demand. Concentrating on 19th-century models results in a display of cast-iron ingenuity. These nutcrackers were meant to be used.

Several cast-iron animal models have been reproduced. Signs of heavy use is one indication of age.

**History:** Nuts keep well for long periods, up to two years, and have served as a dessert or additive to cakes, pies, bread, etc., since the colonial period. Americans' favorite nuts are walnuts, chestnuts, pecans, and almonds.

The first nutcrackers were crude hammers or club devices. The challenge was to find a cracker that would crack the shell but leave the nut intact. By the mid-19th century, cast-iron nutcrackers in animal shapes appeared. Usually the nut was placed in the jaw section of the animal and the tail pressed as the lever to crack the nut.

**Teapot, 5-1/2" h, $95.**

The 19th- and early 20th-century patent records abound with nutcracker inventions. In 1916, a lever-operated cracker which could be clamped to the table was patented as the Home Nut Cracker, St. Louis, Missouri. Perhaps one of the most durable designs was patented on Jan. 28, 1889, and sold as the Quakenbush plated model. This hand model is plain at the top where the grip teeth are located and has twist-style handles on the lower half of each arm. The arms end in an acorn finial.

**References:** Judith A. Rittenhouse, *Ornamental and Figural Nutcrackers*, Collector Books, 1993; James Rollband, *American Nutcrackers*, Off Beat Books (1345 Poplar Ave., Sunnyvale, CA 94087), 1996.

**Collectors' Club:** Nutcracker Collectors' Club, 12204 Fox Run Drive, Chesterland, OH 44026.

Cat, brass ..................................... 50.00
Dog
   6" h, brass ................................ 60.00
   6" h, 13" l, cast iron, SP ............ 75.00
Elephant, 5" h, 10" l, orig paint, c1920
   ................................................... 75.00
Fish, 5" l, brass ............................ 30.00
Gendarme, 3" x 6", wood, mkd "Paris"
   ................................................... 36.00
Jester, head, brass ....................... 80.00
Lady's Leg, wood ......................... 35.00
Monkey, head, brass ................... 37.50
Pheasant, bronze ...................... 115.00
Pliers Type
   Cast iron ................................. 15.00
   Steel, adjustable ..................... 15.00
   Sterling silver .......................... 40.00
Punch and Judy, figural, brass ..... 95.00
Rabbit, head, wood, glass eyes, hand carved, German .................... 110.00
Ram, wood, glass eyes ............... 75.00

**Dog, nickel on iron, L. A. Althoff Co., $75.**

Rooster, cast iron ......................... 35.00
Sailor and Woman, brass ............. 85.00
Skull and Cross Bones, cast iron
   ................................................... 90.00
Squirrel, cast iron ......................... 35.00
Twist and screw type, nickel-plated cast iron ......................................... 15.00

# O

# Occupied Japan

**Collecting Hints:** Buyers should be aware that a rubber stamp can be used to mark "Occupied Japan" on the base of objects. Fingernail polish remover can be used to test a mark. An original mark will remain intact since it is under the glaze; fake marks will disappear. This procedure should not be used on unglazed pieces. Visual examination is the best way to identify a fake mark on an unglazed item. Damaged pieces have little value unless the item is extremely rare. Focus on pieces which are well-made and nicely decorated. There are many inferior examples.

From the beginning of the American occupation of Japan until April 28, 1952, objects made in that country were marked "Japan," "Made in Japan," "Occupied Japan," or "Made in Occupied Japan." Only pieces marked with the last two designations are of major interest to Occupied Japan collectors. The first two marks also were used during other time periods.

**History:** The Japanese economy was devastated when World War II ended. To secure necessary hard currency, the Japanese pottery industry produced thousands of figurines and other knickknacks for export. The variety of products is endless—ashtrays, dinnerware, lamps, planters, souvenir items, toys, vases, etc. Initially, the figurines attracted the largest number of collectors; today many collectors focus on other types of pieces.

**References:** Gene Florence, *Price Guide to Collector's Encyclopedia of Occupied Japan*, Collector Books, 1996 (updated prices for 5-book series *Collector's Encyclopedia of Occupied Japan*); David C. Gould and Donna Crevar-Donaldson, *Occupied Japan Toys with Prices*, L-W Book Sales, 1993; Lynette Parmer, *Collecting Occupied Japan*, Schiffer Publishing, 1997; Carole Bess White, *Collector's Guide to Made in Japan Ceramics*, Book I (1994), Book II (1996) Collector Books.

**Collectors' Club:** Occupied Japan Club, 29 Freeborn St., Newport, RI 02840; Occupied Japan Collectors Club, 18309 Faysmith Ave., Torrance, CA 90504.

Ashtray
  Frog, ceramic, sitting on lily pad, 5" l, 3" w, 2-1/2" h ............................ 32.00
  Pikes Peak, metal, emb scene, oval ................................................... 3.00
  Young boy smoking cigar, bobbing head, metal, 4-3/4" h ................ 55.00
Basket, china, miniature, floral dec 5.00
Bell, chef holding wine bottle and glass, 3" h ............................................. 24.00
Bookends, pr, sailing ships, emb wood ................................................ 75.00
Box, cov, inlaid, dog motif ........... 15.00
Candleholder, 4" h, 4-1/2" w, 2-lite, seated angel holding bouquet ................................................ 24.00
Children's Play Dishes, Blue Willow, 18 pc set ..................................... 375.00
Cigarette Box, cov, china, rect, blue floral dec, gold trim ....................... 15.00
Cigarette Lighter, silver colored metal, mkd .................................................. 10.00
Cigarette Set, plated metal, cov box, Scottie dog dec, matching lighter ................................................ 20.00
Clicker, beetle, silver colored ......... 5.00
Clock, bisque, dancing couple in colonial garb, floral encrusted case, 10-1/2" h ................................... 250.00
Coaster Set, papier-mâché box, floral dec, price for 6 pc set ............. 18.00
Compass, pocket-watch shape.... 20.00
Cornucopia, china, white, pink roses, gold trim .................................... 35.00
Creamer and Sugar, 3-3/4" h, hand-painted flowers, mkd "Hand Painted Prudence 1954" ..................... 18.50
Crumb Tray, metal, emb New York scenes ..................................... 10.00
Cup and Saucer
  Checkered borders, black and white ................................................. 6.00
  Floral dec, blue ....................... 12.50
Demitasse Cup and Saucer, white, yellow and red flowers ................ 10.00
Dish, china, fish shape ................ 10.00
Doll, celluloid, baby wearing snowsuit, jointed ..................................... 40.00
Doll House Furnishings, china
  Couch, white, pink roses, 3" l... 15.00
  Lamp, white base, green shade, gold trim ................................... 10.00
Figure
  1-1/4" x 5", farm girl with scarf, egg basket beside her, red mark .... 15.00
  2-1/2" h, 3-1/4" w, three puppies in a basket, red mark .................... 10.00
  3" h, Colonial lady, red stamped mark ......................................... 12.00
  3" h, seated gentleman playing grand piano, 2 pcs ................. 15.00
  3-3/4" h, metal, cowboy on rearing horse ....................................... 15.00
  4-1/4" h, girl with milk pails ...... 17.50
  4-1/2" h, Hummel-type, Best Pal, American Children series, red mark ................................................ 160.00
  4-3/4" h, ballerina, bisque ........ 35.00
  5" h, jumping horses ................ 12.00

**Figure, beetle, black top hat, green body, white violin, mkd, 3" h, $15.**

  5-1/2" h, lady seated in chair, reading sheet music ....................... 15.00
  6" h, lady with netted skirt, mkd "Lenwille" and "Occupied Japan" .. 30.00
  6" h, 2" w, man ......................... 25.00
  6-1/2" h, French couple............. 35.00
  7" x 4-1/2", couple .................... 35.00
  8" h, woman, porcelain, lavender and yellow dress ...................... 20.00
  8" h, 3-1/2" w, man holding flower ................................................ 40.00
  8-1/2" h, lady, china, hp ......... 145.00
Flower Frog, bisque, girl with bird on shoulder, pastel highlights, gold trim ................................................ 48.00
Harmonica, Butterfly, orig box...... 17.50
Head Vase, Oriental girl, china..... 18.00
Honey Jar, bee hive, bee finial ..... 25.00
Incense Burner, woman................ 20.00
Lantern, 4-1/2" h, owl motif .......... 35.00
Match Holder, hanging type
  2-3/4" h, Hummel-type Goose Girl ................................................ 15.00
  4" h, Colonial lady, green and white background ............................ 12.00
Mat, hooked, 4-1/4" d, cream center, brown, teal, and green border with 3 daisy like flowers, orig label ... 20.00
Mug, china
  Boy Handle ............................. 14.00
  Indian Chief ............................ 35.00
  MacArthur ............................... 55.00
Napkins, damask, orig paper labels, price for set of six .................... 45.00
Necklace, pearls, double strand, orig paper label ................................ 12.00
Nodder, celluloid, figural, elephant, white body, green and gold trim, 3-1/2" l, 2-1/2" h ................................... 25.00
Noise Maker, horn, gold ............. 25.00
Perfume Bottle, glass, blue, 4" h .. 15.00
Piano Baby, hp ........................... 65.00

Pincushion, metal, grand piano shape, red velvet cushion .................... 15.00

Planter, figural

Baby booties, blue trim .............. 8.00
Cat, sitting up ........................... 10.00
Dog, with basket ...................... 20.00
Donkey Pulling Cart ................. 10.00
Rabbit .......................................12.50
Regal Carriage .......................... 7.50
Wheelbarrow, floral dec, red mark, 2-1/2" h, 3-1/2" l ......................... 5.00

Plate

Cabin Scene, chickens in yard 18.00
Cherries, lacy edge ................. 25.00
Wooded scene by water's edge, 8-1/8" d ...................................... 7.50

Platter, Courley pattern, heavy gold trim .................................................... 30.00

Powder Jar, cov, Wedgwood style, blue and white, 3" d ........................ 15.00

Salt and Pepper Shakers, pr

Arab Boys ............................... 17.50
Coolies, orig box ..................... 25.00
Hat, one brown, one black ....... 15.00
Pigs, large ears ....................... 12.00

Shelf Sitter, Little Boy Blue ............ 15.00

Silent Butler, metal ........................ 15.00

Stein, man and woman with dog, 8-1/2" h .................................................... 40.00

Tape Measure, pig, stamped "Occupied Japan" .................................. 45.00

Teapot, 6-3/4" h, individual size, chocolate brown mirror glaze ........... 12.00

Tea Set, miniature, china, floral dec .................................................... 25.00

Toby Pitcher, barkeeper, holding mugs, 5" h ......................................... 30.00

Toothpick holder, puppy in barrel ... 6.00

Toy

Baby Pontiac, litho tin windup, car, orig box .................................... 65.00
Boy on Sled, windup, litho tin, MIB .................................................. 150.00
Camel, walker, celluloid, MIB ... 120.00
Cherry Cook, windup ............... 90.00
Dancing Couple, celluloid, MIB .................................................. 95.00
Hopping Dog, windup .............. 22.50
Minstrel Monkey, celluloid, MIB .................................................. 175.00
Monkey, windup, plays banjo, orig box .................................................. 75.00
Trick Seal, windup .................. 880.00

Tray, rect, papier mâché, black ground, gold floral dec ........................... 8.00

Vase

3" h, white ground, painted flowers .................................................... 7.50
5-1/4" h, Hummel type boy reading book ......................................... 25.00

Wall Plaque, Victorian lady, flowers .................................................... 18.00

Wall Pocket, man with four arms seated on elephant, gold trim, green mark .................................................... 20.00

# Ocean Liner Collectibles

**Collecting Hints:** Don't concentrate only on ships of American registry, although many collectors try to gather material from only one liner or ship line. Objects associated with ships involved in disasters, such as the Titanic, often command higher prices.

**History:** Transoceanic travel falls into two distinct periods—the era of the great Clipper ships and the era of the diesel-powered ocean liners. The latter craft reached their golden age between 1900 and 1940. An ocean liner is a city unto itself. Most have their own printing rooms to produce a wealth of daily memorabilia. Companies, such as Cunard and Holland-America, encourage passengers to acquire souvenirs with the company logo and ship's name. Word-of-mouth is a principal form of advertising. Certain ships acquired a unique mystic. The Queen Elizabeth, Queen Mary, and United States became symbols of elegance and style. Today the cruise ship dominates the world of the ocean liner.

**References:** John Adams, Ocean Steamers, New Cavendish Books, 1992 Karl D. Spence, How to Identify and Price Ocean Liner Collectibles, published by author, 1991; James Steele, Queen Mary, Phaidon, 1995.

**Collectors' Clubs:** Oceanic Navigation Research Society, Inc., P.O. Box 8005, Studio City, CA 91608; Steamship Historical Society of America, Inc., 300 Ray Dr., Ste. 4, Providence, RI 02906; Titanic Historical Society, P.O. Box 51053, Indian Orchard, MA 01151.

**Periodical:** Voyage, P.O. Box 7007, Freehold, NJ 07728.

**Museums:** Mystic Seaport, Mystic, CT; South Street Seaport Museum, New York, NY; University of Baltimore, Steamship Historical Society Collection, Baltimore, MD.

Ashtray

Pacific Far East Steamship, ceramic .................................................... 25.00
Princess, glass ........................ 15.00
RMS Queen Elizabeth I, Cunard Line, wooden ship's wheel, glass insert over color center photo .................................................... 30.00

Baggage Tag, French Line, first class, unused ...................................... 7.50

Belt Buckle, RMS Queen Elizabeth II, Cunard Line, chrome plated solid brass, black outline of ship, name in red ............................................. 14.00

Booklet

Independence, American Export Lines, 1966 Gala Springtime Cruise, itinerary and deck plan inserts .................................................... 24.00

White Star Line, sailing list, 1933 .................................................... 40.00

Bottle Opener, RS Queen Mary, ship floats in handle ........................ 30.00

Brochure

Cunard and Anchor-Donaldson Line, Canadian Service. The Historic St. Lawrence River Route to Europe, late 1920s ......................................... 7.50
Cunard Line, Getting There is Half the Fun, 16 pgs, 1952 ................ 6.00
Empress of Japan, Transatlantic sailings, 1930-31 ....................... 10.00
Italian Line, Six Cruises to the Mediterranean and Egypt, 1934 ...... 12.00

Change Tray, American Line Ship .................................................. 100.00

Cigarette Lighter, RMS Queen Mary .................................................... 32.00

Coffee Cup, SS United States ...... 32.00

Compact, Empress of Canada, Canadian Pacific Line, Stratton, line flag logo, ship's name in enameled front medallion ................................. 40.00

Cruise Book, Scythia, 1929 ......... 40.00

Deck Card, Concordia Lines, Norway .................................................... 18.00

Deck Plan

MV Westerdamn 1950, multicolored .................................................... 15.00
RMSP Avon, The Royal Mail Steam Packet, December 1909 .......... 32.00
RMS Samaria, Cunard Line, Plan of Tourist Accommodation ........... 15.00
SS Hamburg, 1930, fold out .... 35.00

Dish, RMS Queen Mary, Cunard Line, ceramic, 5" l, oval, color portrait, gold edge, Staffordshire .......... 37.50

Display, Mediterranean Americhe, 1927, easel back, artwork by Riccobaldi ...................................... 165.00

Excursion Announcement, SS Cuba .................................................... 20.00

Goblet, RMS Queen Elizabeth II, Cunard Line, souvenir, etched image and name, manufactured by Stuart Crystal, #1305 ........................ 225.00

Key Chain, Carnival, Lucite, ship photo .................................................... 4.00

Landing Arrangements Card, RMS Caronia, July 28, 1950 ............... 5.00

Letter Opener, HMS Liverpool, silver, enamel dec, 1921 .................... 72.00

Menu

Grace Line, SS Santa Rose, dinner, June 18, 1964 ........................... 5.00
Ile de France, July 12, 1938, dinner .................................................... 5.00
RMS Caronia, breakfast, Aug. 2, 1950, 1 page card ..................... 6.00
SS Leonardo Da Vinci, January 1973 .................................................... 6.00
SS Lurline, Matson Lines, Commodore's Dinner, March 3, 1959, 12" x 9" .................................................. 20.50
SS Manhattan, United States Lines, 6" x 10", 4 pgs, 1933, dinner, cream-colored cover with Arch of Triumph, deckled edges ........................... 7.50

Newspaper

RMS Caronia, Ocean Times, Aug. 1, 1950, 4 pgs ........................... 10.00

RMS Queen Mary, May 10, 1950, 12 pgs ........................................... 15.00
Note Paper
　Cunard White Star, blue ............. 5.00
　M/S Osloofjord, 2 color views of ship
　.................................................... 6.00
　RMS Queen Mary, beige ............ 6.00
Passenger List
　RMS Aquitania, full color illus of ship
　.................................................. 50.00
　SS Leviathan, 1924 .................. 15.00
　St. Louis, American Line, eastbound trip, Feb. 10, 1906 ................... 35.00
Passport Cover, Red Star Line, fabric, ship illus ................................... 27.50
Pencil, mechanical, Cunard liner Mauretania, black and white, 5" l, "Right Point," gold metal accent tip, metal clip with black and white illus of passenger ship, name in black and red letters, c1930 ........................... 24.00
Pinback Button
　Carnival Cruises ........................ 3.00
　Lusitana, 1-1/4" d, multicolored
　.................................................. 50.00
　Mauertana, 1-1/4" d, multicolored, early 1900s ............................. 35.00
　RMS Queen Elizabeth I, Cunard Line, 1-3/4", photo, "World's Largest Liner" at bottom ......................... 8.00
Playing Cards
　Alaska Steamship .................... 15.00
　Eastern Steamship Corp., c1950
　.................................................. 15.00
　Holland American Line, double deck
　.................................................. 25.00
　SS Badger, double deck .......... 20.00
　SS Spartan, double deck ......... 20.00
　Swedish American Lines, orig slip case ......................................... 18.00
Pocket Mirror, Queen Mary, sepia photo, New York harbor scene, c1930 ...................................... 75.00
Post Card
　Andania, Cunard Line ............... 6.00
　Aurania, Cunard Line ................ 6.00
　RMS Olympia, unused ............. 75.00
Poster, Grace Line, Caribbean, 1949 C Evers, illus of tourists, ship, cars, and boats, 23" x 30" ............... 200.00
Print
　Moor-McCormack Lines ........... 85.00
　Titanic, 15 x 22-1/2", black and white, text of sinking, published by Tichnor Bros., Boston ............... 60.00
Program of Events
　Cunard, RMS Caronia, Aug. 1, 1950
　.................................................... 6.00
　Cunard, RMS Queen Mary, May 12, 1950 ......................................... 6.00
　Race Card, Cunard White Star RMS Caronia ................................... 7.00
　RMS Queen Mary, some ink marks
　.................................................... 7.00
Razor Towel, Cunard White Star, paper
　.................................................... 5.00
Souvenir Spoon
　Cunard White Star, demitasse, silver plated ...................................... 20.00
　Transylvania Anchor Line, silver plated, twisted handle, blue enameled ring, flag, and crest .......... 75.00

**Tin, Oceanic Cut Plug, Scotten, Dillon Co., Detroit, 6" x 3-7/8" x 3-1/8", $35.**

Stationery
　RMS Queen Mary, Cunard Line, note paper, matching envelope, color portrait, line, and ship name, 5" x 7"
　................................................. 10.00
　Royal Mail Steamer, two sheets of paper, matching envelope ....... 20.00
　Sylvania, Cunard Line, beige, color portrait, line, and ship name, 5-1/4" x 6-3/4" ...................................... 8.00
Steamer Directory, Clyde-Mallory Lines, c1920 ...................................... 12.00
Ticket Folio, Cunard Line, c1928
　.................................................. 50.00
Tie Clasp, Cunard Line RMS Queen Mary, gold tone, red, white, and blue enameled ship ......................... 18.00
Timetable, Monticello Steamship Co., "On the Bay of San Francisco," 1907
　.................................................. 65.00
Tin, US Bremen at sea on front panel, 1930s ..................................... 55.00

# Olympics Collectibles

**Collecting Hints:** Collectors of Olympic materials should remember that the Olympic Games have been a multi-language event. Collectors may not wish to limit their collections to English-only examples. The other important fact to remember is that the more recent the Olympiad, the greater the number of items that have survived. Items from the 1996 Olympics have not yet reached the secondary market, but things from 1988 are beginning to surface. More collectibles tend to enter the antiques and collectibles marketplace during the years the games are scheduled, creating more interest in this fast-growing field.

**History:** Organized amateur sports games originated in ancient Greece. The games were held every four years beginning about 776 B.C. At first running events were the only type held, but many different events

have been added over the years. The Olympics as we know them were revived in Athens about 1896. After that date, the games were held in a different city around the world every four years. The number of participants, competing nations, and events have increased steadily. Women were first allowed to participate in the games in 1912. The winter games began in 1924 and were held on a four-year schedule until 1992 when they were rescheduled so that they would alternate at a two year interval with the more traditional summer games.

**References:** Michael McKeever, Collecting Sports Memorabilia, Alliance Publishing, 1966.

**Periodicals:** Olympic Collectors Newsletter, P.O. Box 41630, Tucson, AZ 85717; Sports Collectors Digest, 700 E. State St., Iola, WI 54990.

**Collectors' Clubs:** Olympic Pin Collector's Club, 1386 Fifth St., Schenectady, NY 12303.

Badge, 1980 Winter Olympics, 2-1/2" d, celluloid, color image of mascot raccoon as hockey player, white ground, black letters ................ 20.00
Book, Sarajevo 1984 Winter Olympics
　.................................................. 12.00
Bowl, Campbell Kids, 1984 Sarajevo
　.................................................. 12.00
Calendar, 1992, Coca-Cola ........... 5.00
Cigarette Lighter, 1976, Montreal
　.................................................. 12.00
Doll, 1980 Winter Olympics raccoon mascot, Chiquita, 14" h, stuffed cloth, gray, black, and white face, blue body, orange gloves, skating boots, separate white vinyl racing bib pullover vest, orig stitched tag with licensing authorization, Chase Bag Co. ................................... 40.00
Fan, Tenth Olympic Games/1932/Los Angeles, folding paper type, balsa sticks, chapel building illus, Olympic symbol, Japan ........................ 40.00
Glass, 5-1/2" h, 1932 Olympics, clear, frosted white picture ................ 50.00
Keychain, 1984, Los Angeles ......... 6.50
License Plate Holder, 1932, aluminum, two athletes holding the world, "Los Angeles" in raised letters ....... 150.00
Magazine, *Sports Illustrated*, Sept. 5, 1960, Rome Olympics Ceremonies
　.................................................... 7.50
Map, 1960, Rome Olympics, 6" x 10" folder opens to 10" x 35", eight color maps on both sides, Automobile Club of Italy sponsor ............... 15.00
Pamphlet, 1936 Berlin ................. 80.00
Paperweight, 1992, Coca-Cola McDonald's ............................. 12.00
Pennant, 1968 Mexico, felt .......... 24.00

Pin
    1928, Olympic Fund, red, and white enameled brass, miniature shield, sold for 50¢ to help defray expenses of American team, orig card .... 25.00
    1964, Innsbruck Winter Olympics, Austrian made, black, white, and red accent enamels, gold finish ..... 65.00
    1980, Moscow Olympics Figural mascot bear as soccer player, blue, white, and brown enamels, gold luster ............................................. 20.00
    Official symbol flanked by deep red porcelain enamel under Russian inscription, gold luster ............. 15.00
    1984, Calgary Winter Olympics, official symbols in five colors, white ground, double needle post and clutch fasteners ......................... 8.00
    1984, Los Angeles Olympics, Fuji, domed acrylic on metal, symbolic cartoon US eagle holding Olympic torch, needle post and clutch fastener ........................................ 10.00
    1988, Seoul Summer Olympics, domed acrylic, three enamel colors, gold luster, needle post and clutch fastener ..................................... 5.00
    1992, Albertville Winter Olympics, CBS, domed acrylic, gold luster, white enamel, tiny Olympic rings in five colors .................................. 5.00
    1996, Atlanta Olympics pre-event promotion pin, cartoon baseball player, four colors, gold above bar inscription "Atlanta 1996/1000 Days/ October 23, 1993," needle post and clutch fastener .......................... 2.00
Pin Display, 1988 Olympics, 1-3/4" x 6" x 8" cover box, wooden display frame, high gloss finish, very dark mahogany enamel, frame holds recessed glass over gold luster metal title plate identifying Jeep as official sponsor of U. S. Olympic team, five different jeep pins comprising limited edition set .................................. 30.00
Plate, 7" d, 1968, gold leaf, Mexico and torch dec .................................. 60.00
Post Card
    1912 Stockholm Olympics, black and white photo ....................... 30.00
    1936, view of Berlin Olympics, Olympic cancel ............................... 15.50
    1988, Korea, Coca-Cola, set #1. 7.50
Stadium Cushion, 11" x 13-1/2", 1956 Summer Olympics, red vinyl, yellow, white, and blue Olympics logo ................................................. 48.00
Puzzle, Olympics, 1932 ................ 70.00
Stick Pin
    1940, sterling-like silvered metal, Helsinki, Finland, torch flame under Olympics rings symbol, above 1940 date .......................................... 80.00
    1964, silvered metal, Tokyo, rings above Olympic symbol ............ 35.00
    1972, gold luster, Sapporo, winter, red, white, and blue enamels... 30.00
    1978, gold luster, Innsbruck, winter, red and blue enamels, blue ground ................................................. 25.00

**Stickpin, XXII, Moscow, 1980, $15.**

    1980, Moscow Olympics, miniature Gold Olympics rings under miniature image of Soviet flag, dark red porcelain enamel accents ................. 18.00
Token
    1948, London ........................... 12.00
    1984, Los Angeles, orig case .. 17.50
Toy, 1992 Olympic Bobsled Run, wooden replica, 1-1/2" h x 2" w x 8-1/2" l, wire handgrip rail and bumper bar, two front skis swivel left and right, driver unit inscribed "U.S.A.," thumb tack steering wheel, Olympic symbols on riding surface ........................... 200.00
Tray, 1976 Olympics, Montreal, litho metal, Coca-Cola adv .............. 40.00
Venue Guide, staff, 1996 .............. 12.00

# Owl Collectibles

**Collecting Hints:** If you collect the "creature of the night" or the "wise old owl," any page of this book might conceivably contain a related object since the owl theme can be found in hundreds of collectible categories, including advertising trade cards, books, buttons, and postcards, to name a few. Don't confine yourself just to old or antique owls. Owl figurines, owl themes on limited edition collectors' plates, and handcrafted items from modern artisans are plentiful. There are many examples available in every price range.

**History:** Owls have existed on earth for more than 60 million years. They have been used as a decorative motif since before Christ. An owl and Athena appeared on an ancient Greek coin. Every culture has superstitions surrounding the owl. Some believe the owl represented good luck, others viewed it as an evil omen. The owl has remained a popular symbol in Halloween material. Of course, the owl's wisdom is often attached to scholarly pursuits. Expanding this theme, the National Park Service uses Woodsey to "Give A Hoot, Don't Pollute."

**Reproduction Alert:** Reproduction fruit crate labels with owl motifs are common. Westmoreland Glass molds have been sold to several different manufacturers. The owl sitting on two books is being reissued with the original "W" still on top of the books. The three-owl plate mold also was sold. Imperial Glass owl molds have also found new owners.

Advertising Trade Card, Colburn's Philadelphia Mustard, diecut ......... 10.00
Ashtray, ceramic, 3 cut owls, figural ................................................. 30.00
Bank, tin, owl illus on each side ... 50.00
Blotter, "Whoo? Oswald, I told you we couldn't get away with that bone!", 2 puppies under a tree, owl sitting on branch, Harry N. Johnson, Real Estate & Insurance, Highlands, NJ ................................................. 10.00
Book
    *An Owl Came To Stay*, Clair Rome, Crown Pub., NY, 1980 ............... 7.50
    *Owls in the Family*, Farley Mowat, Little, Brown & Co., 1961 ...................... 1.00
Bookends, pr
    Brass, Frankart ...................... 135.00
    Bronze, head, sgd "M Carr" .. 120.00
Book Rack, expanding ................. 55.00
Calendar Plate, 1912, owl on open book, Berlin, NE ....................... 25.00

**Door Knocker, brown, yellow eyes, green ribbon, $85.**

Calling Card Tray, 8-1/2" x 7", quadruple plate, emb music staff and "Should Owl's Acquaintance Be Forgot," two owls sitting on back of tray ...... 85.00
Candy Container, owl on branch
............................................ 50.00
Clock, 6-1/2" h, wood, hand carved
............................................ 100.00
Coal Hod, brass, figural ............. 300.00
Decoy, 13", papier-mâché, double faced, glass eyes, brown, small white area on chest ................. 65.00
Figure
Degenhart, custard ................. 37.50

Fenton, 3" h, carnival glass ...... 24.00
Mosser, 4" h, carnival glass ..... 20.00
Viking, 8-1/2" h, orange ............ 90.00
Inkwell, figural, Noritake ............. 125.00
Lamp, candle, 5-1/4", snow white china, owl shaped shade, stump shaped base, fitted candleholder, mkd "R S Germany" ............................... 225.00
Letter Opener, brass ..................... 25.00
Limited Edition Plate, Goebel, Wildlife Series, barn owl, 1976 ............. 35.00
Mask, papier-mâché, c1915 ........ 90.00
Match Holder
2-/12" h, dark green, Wetzel Glass Co.
................................................ 8.00
8" h, 3" w, metal, hanging type ..... 18.00
Medal
Leeds International Exhibition, 1890, 2-1/4", metal, white bust of Queen Victoria on one side ................. 25.00
Natural History Society of Montreal, 1-3/4", bronze, cast, owl with branch in beak ..................................... 20.00
Mustard Jar, cov, 5" h, milk glass, screw top, glass insert, Atterbury .... 165.00
Napkin Ring, standing owl, silver plated
................................................ 150.00
Owl Drug Co.
Bottle, 3-1/2" h, cork top, clear, Oil of Sweet Almond label, 1 oz .......... 5.00
Shot Glass, one wing ................... 17.50
Soda Bottle, 9-1/2" h, blob top, teal green, two wings, San Francisco
................................................ 50.00
Paperweight, cast iron, owl family, two babies, third baby in papa's arms
................................................ 45.00
Pin, blue, green, and gold enamel, amber eyes, faux pearl and rhinestone trim ............................... 20.00
Pitcher
8" h, 6" d top, pressed glass, owl shape ..................................... 110.00
9-1/2" h, cov, china, semi-vitreous, Edwin M Knowles China Co..... 37.50
Plate, milk glass
6" d, three owl heads, fluted open work edge, gold paint ............. 65.00
7-1/2" d, owl lovers, 7-1/2" d .... 40.00

**Salt and Pepper Shakers, metal, yellow eyes, 3" h, 2-1/4" 2, $70.**

Salt and Pepper Shakers, pr, 3-1/4"h, china, brown and white, mortarboard hats, scholarly expression, horn rim glasses ..................................... 10.00
Sheet Music
Beautiful Ohio, owl on cover ...... 3.50
The Pansy and the Owl ............. 4.50
Shot Glasses, head removes to show 4 shot glasses, stamped "Viking, Germany," each shot glass stamped "Germany," some use marks ... 42.00
Tape Measure, brass, glass eyes, mkd "Germany" ............................... 40.00
Thermometer, 6" h, plaster body .. 75.00
Tin, Owl Brand Shoe Polish .......... 37.50
Toothbrush Holder, figural, Syroco
................................................ 12.50
Valentine, 15" l, girl and boy riding balloon, owl sitting on moon above, "Nobody's looking but the owl and the moon!" ................................. 8.00
Vase, 7" h, gold owls, white ground, Phoenix Glass ........................ 175.00

# P

# Padlocks

**Collecting Hints:** There is a wide range of padlocks that can interest a collector, so many collectors specialize in just one category, such as *Railroad* or *Logo*. Collectors can also specialize in one manufacturer, or in miniatures. Just being old and scarce is not usually enough. They must have some special appeal, have an interesting design or have historical significance. The most competitive and expensive area is the embossed brass locks from the old defunct short line railroads and the very early locks from the larger railroads.

There is a new dimension in lock collecting—auctions on the Internet. You can see a great variety of locks, but watch out for pitfalls. The first is that you tend to bid more than you had intended. Many of the locks are sold at much more than they would sell for at a lock or railroad show. Another is the inadequate or misleading information on many of the locks offered. The sellers do not usually intend to mislead with their information; they just do not know enough about old locks to describe them properly. Sellers do not understand that a dent in an old lock is equivalent to a chip in a cut glass dish, and a lock that has been taken apart is equivalent to a Roseville teapot with a glued on handle. It is surprising how keys increase the bid prices of locks; most collectors do not place much value on keys unless they are original.

There are a number of words and phrases used in the Internet lock descriptions that must be completely disregarded. Some of them are "rare," "Civil War," "railroad," "old," "odd," "must have," "professional," "cool," "antique," "large," "huge," etc., also "Wells Fargo" & "Keenkutter" (see **Reproduction & Fake Alert**). Buyers must look at the photos to decide for themselves and not hesitate to e-mail sellers to eliminate any doubts about the condition, markings, size, etc.

A lock stamped with the name of a small company from the 1850s can be worth many times more than a similar lock made by a large manufacturer. There are always exceptions. For example, the *Wrought Iron*

*Lever* locks, called "Smokies," do not have much value no matter how old or scarce. Locks in some categories can be several times more valuable than similar appearing locks in other categories. For example, locks in the *Story* category are worth several times more than similar locks in the *Warded* category.

Identifying many old padlocks is possible with either markings on the lock or illustrations from old catalogs, but for some padlocks this is difficult or impossible. They are not marked, and the manufacturer evidently did not publish catalogs. Identical locks can be marked by different manufacturers as a result of one company acquiring another. Dating can also be a problem. Some of the manufacturers made the same locks for more than fifty years, and there are Yale models that were made for almost 100 years. A lock can be made the same year as the patent date, or the date can still be marked on the lock long after the patent expired. A definitive book on United States lock companies, their padlocks, and padlock construction has not been published.

Original keys can increase the value of locks, but other keys have little value to most collectors. Having a key made can cost more than the value of the lock, and locksmiths who are not familiar with the antique value of old locks can do irreparable damage. If you have repairs or a key made, make sure that the locksmith is an expert on old locks, and that you have complete agreement on the cost. Repairs, cracks, holes, internal damage, or appreciable dents drastically reduce the value of locks.

**History:** Padlocks of all shapes and sizes have been made in Europe and Asia since the 1600s; however, American collectors generally prefer American manufactured locks. In the 1830s Elijah Rickard was making screw key padlocks. He stamped some of them "B & O RR" for the Baltimore & Ohio Railroad. These were the first marked railroad locks. In the 1840s, safe lock manufacturers were adapting their lever tumbler designs to padlocks. Also in the 1840s, the first pin tumbler padlocks were made in the Yale Lock Shop. In the 1850s, a few companies were making lever tumbler padlocks simpler than the safe lock designs. Other companies started making low-qual-

ity padlocks based on cabinet and door lock designs. The United States Post Office was ordering locks with various postal markings, and Linus Yale, Junior, patented the pin tumbler lock. In 1860, Wilson Bohannan returned from the California gold fields, patented a simple, reliable brass lever padlock and started his manufacturing company. The brass lever and similar iron lever padlocks were subsequently manufactured in large quantities by many companies. Wilson Bohannan is still an independent company, and the pin tumbler lock is the worldwide standard medium security lock.

**Lock Companies:** About 250 United States lock manufacturers have been identified. Eight prolific companies were:

Adams & Westlake, 1857—, "Adlake" tradename started c1900, made railroad locks.

Eagle Lock Co., 1833-1976, a general line of padlocks from 1880, with padlock dates from 1867.

Mallory, Wheeler & Co., 1865-1910, partnership history started in 1834, predominant manufacturer of wrought iron lever (Smokies) padlocks.

Miller Lock Co. (D. K. Miller from 1870 to c1880) Miller Lock Co. to 1930, a general line of padlocks, and a pre-dominant manufacturer of railroad locks.

Slaymaker Lock Co. 1888-1985, dates include name changes, partnership changes, mergers. A general line of padlocks, and a predominate manufacturer of railroad switch locks.

Star Lock Works, 1836-1926, largest manufacturer of Scandinavian padlocks, also made many other types.

Yale & Towne Mfg. Co., 1884 —, Yale Lock Mfg. Co. from 1868 to 1884, started c1840 by Linus Yale, SR as the "Yale Lock Shop," started producing padlocks c1875.

Wilson Bohannan, 1860 —, made mostly brass lever padlocks to the early 1900s, then changed to the pin tumbler type. Made many railroad and logo locks.

**Padlock Types:** Padlocks are categorized primarily according to tradition or use: *Story, Railroad,* etc. The secondary classification is according to the type of construction. For example, if a brass lever lock is marked with a railroad name, it is called a *Railroad* lock. *Scandinavian* locks have always been called "Scandinavians." *Story* locks became a common term in the 1970s; in the catalogs of the late 1800s, they were listed in various ways.

*Railroad*, *Express* and *Logo* locks are identified with the names of the companies that bought and used them. Story locks are a series of odd- and heart-shaped cast-iron padlocks with decorative or figural embossments.

Governmental agencies and thousands of companies had locks custom made with their names to create *Logo* locks. *Logo* locks are not to be confused with locks that are embossed with the names of jobbers. This applies particularly to the six-lever push key locks. If "6-Lever" is included in the name, it is not a *Logo* lock. Since 1827, about 10,000 railroad companies have crisscrossed the United States. Most of these companies used at least two types of locks; some used dozens of types.

**References:** Franklin M. Arnall, *The Padlock Collector, Illustrations and Prices of 2,800 Padlocks of the Last 100 Years,* Sixth Edition, 1996, The Collector (P.O. Box 253, Claremont, CA 91711)

**Collectors' Club:** West Coast Lock Collectors, 1427 Lincoln Blvd., Santa Monica, CA 90401.

**Museum:** Lock Museum of America, P.O. Box 104, Terryville, CT 06786.

**Advisor:** Franklin M. Arnall.

**Reproduction & Fake Alert:** A reproduction is new but made as a copy of an old item. A fake is not necessarily a copy of an old item. The "Wells Fargo" locks with the plaques fastened to the back, old locks with "Wells Fargo," "W F Co." or "W F Co. Ex" stamped on the lock, and the "KeenKutter" locks with the barrel type keyholes are good examples of **FAKES.** The steel "Winchester" six-lever locks with the crude rivets are reproductions. Beware of bargains, especially locks on the Internet when bids seem too low. Beware of brass *Story* locks, locks from the Middle East and India, yellow brass switch locks, and switch lock keys. All *Story* locks are embossed cast iron, except the small "N H" and the small "Japanese Pattern" were made in both cast iron and brass; however, there are excellent cast iron reproductions of the

Skull & Crossbones lock. Some of the cast iron *Story* locks were brass plated and some were nickel plated.

Screw key, trick, iron lever, and brass lever padlocks are being imported from the Middle East. The crudely cast new switch lock keys are obvious. The high quality counterfeits are expertly stamped with various railroad initials on old blanks, tumbled to simulate wear, and aged with acid. They can be detected only by an expert.

Authentic *Railroad*, *Express* and *Logo* locks will have only one user name. The size and shape will be like other locks that were in common use at the time, except for a few modified locks made for the U.S. government. All components of an old lock must have exactly the same color and finish. The front, back, or drop of an old lock can be expertly replaced with a reproduced part embossed with the name or initials of a railroad, express company, or other user.

**Note:** The prices shown are for padlocks in original condition and without keys.

### Brass Lever

Chubb Detector, 5" h .................. 400.00
Fraim, emb raised letters, 2-7/8" h
.............................................. 20.00
Good Luck, both sides, 2-3/4" h ... 45.00
Good Luck, one side, 2-3/4" h ...... 35.00
Keenkutter, both sides, 3-3/4" h
.............................................. 100.00
New Champion 6 Lever ................. 4.00
Squire, 3" h .................................. 5.00
The U.L. Co. of N.Y., Pat May 7 and Oct. 7. 89, 3-3/8" h ........................ 375.00
T. Slaight, Patent Oct. 2-6, 3-1/4" h
.............................................. 30.00

**Browns Patent, July 4, 1971, 3" h, $25. Photo courtesy of Franklin Arnall.**

W. Bohannan, 3-1/8" h ................ 15.00
Winchester, emb raised letters ... 175.00
Yale, Y & T, rect, keyhole in bottom, emb.
1-1/2" to 2" w ............................. 3.00
3" w .......................................... 65.00

### Combination

5 brass lettered dials, 2-1/2" w ... 125.00
Iowa Lock & Mfg. Co. , zinc, 3-1/2" h
.............................................. 80.00
J.B. Miller Keyless Lock Co. ........... 5.00
Junkunc Bros, 2-5/8" h ................. 10.00
Quaint Mfg. Co. Aug. 24, 1917, 4" h
.............................................. 350.00
Rochester, Warranted, 2-1/2" h ... 150.00
Sesame
Brass or zinc case, 2-1/2" h ..... 30.00
Corbin, brass case .................... 2.00
Dudley Lock Corp. ..................... 5.00
Steel case & brass dial, 2-1/2" h .... 4.00
The Edwards Mfg Co, No-Key, 2-3/4" h
.............................................. 25.00

### Commemorative

AYPEX, 1909 Seattle emb, steel
.............................................. 250.00
Dan Patch emb on one side, a horseshoe emb on opposite side, cast iron
.............................................. 175.00
Worlds Fair, 1904, St. Louis, on brass emb on opposite side, brass case
.............................................. 150.00

### Express

AM. EX. Co., emb in vertical panel down the back, brass lever type
.............................................. 600.00
AM RY EX, stamped on shackle & back, steel, iron lever type ................ 30.00
Pacific Ex Co, emb on back, brass, lever push key type, 2-3/8" dia
.............................................. 900.00
W F & Co EX, emb in vertical panel down the back, brass lever type
.............................................. 800.00

### Iron Lever (includes steel locks)

Dragons embossed, steel ........... 15.00
E. Trempel, Patd. April 4, 71, 3" h
.............................................. 45.00
Hatchet lock (shaped like a hatchet), steel with brass shackle ........ 450.00
Kinglock, 8-1/2" h, wt 10 lbs ....... 350.00
Pyes Patent, Sept. 8, 1856, Oct. 16, 1860. ...................................... 30.00
Star Lock Works, 4-1/2" h ............. 90.00
Topaz embossed, steel ............... 10.00
Wilson Bohannan, 3-1/4" h ........... 15.00

### Lever Push Key

Aztec 6-Lever, emb, 2-1/4" dia ... 135.00
Baffler 6 Lever, 2-3/4" h ................ 5.00
California, emb, 2-1/4" dia .......... 450.00
Champion 6-Lever, emb, 2-1/4" dia
.............................................. 5.00
Crank, S B Co., emb, 2-7/8" h ...... 35.00
Keystone 6-Lever, emb, 2-1/4" dia
.............................................. 15.00
Miller, Six Secure Levers, iron case, brass panels, 3-7/8" h ............. 15.00
Union 6-Lever, emb, 2-1/4" dia ..... 20.00

### Logo

Canada Excise, emb, Yale, Canada, pin tumbler push key type .......... 200.00

Fisher Body, Flint, Best ................ 25.00
Hudson Motor Car Co., with Hudson logo, Yale, emb ...................... 120.00
Mid Continent Pipeline Co, W B.... 15.00
Nash, Best........................................ 50.00
Ordnance Dept., crossed rifles, emb, Yale .............................................. 10.00
Packard Electrical Division, Best.. 50.00
76, Best............................................ 25.00
S O Co., Best .................................. 20.00
Sun Pipeline Co., Yale, emb ........ 35.00
Texaco, T, Best................................ 45.00
U S Forest Service, emb pine tree, Yale ............................................ 140.00
U S N, Several manufacturers ...... 15.00
Western Union Tel Co., brass lever type ................................................ 30.00
Western Union Telegraph, lever push key type ...................................... 400.00

### Pin Tumbler

Corbin, brass case:
    1-1/4" to 2" w, keyhole in bottom .................................................... 2.00
    3" w, keyhole in bottom ............ 50.00
    3" w, keyhole in front ............... 15.00
Corbin, steel case.......................... 5.00
Hurd, brass case, 3-1/8" h.............. 5.00
O V B, Our Very Best, H.S.B. Co., brass .............................................. 150.00
S & CO, emb, intertwined, brass, 3" h ...................................................... 20.00
Segal
    Brass case, 4-1/4" h ................. 30.00
    keyhole in front, brass, 3-5/8" h .................................................... 45.00
Simmons, S H Co., emb, brass case .................................................... 35.00
Unit, brass case, 3" h.................... 60.00
Yale
    Brass case, emb both sides ...... 2.00
    Iron case, round brass panels ... 5.00
    Nickel plated, with dust cover ... 30.00

**Frisco, Keenkutter, $700. Photo courtesy of Franklin Arnall.**

### Railroad

General Purpose & Signal
    Ames Sword, brass lever type....20.00
    C & O, Yale, emb, pin tumbler type .................................................... 30.00
    D & RG, emb, brass lever type .................................................. 175.00
    Illinois Central Signal, emb, brass lever type ................................ 20.00
    K C S Ry, emb, lever push key type .................................................. 375.00
    L & N, emb, lever push key type .................................................... 80.00
    New Jersey Central, Corbin, pin tumbler type ................................ 30.00
    N Y C, emb, pin tumbler push key type .................................................... 50.00
    P & R, indented, brass lever type .................................................... 35.00
    Santa Fe, Keenkutter emb on opposite side ...................................... 350.00
    SO Pacific Co. CS 24, Roadway & Bridge .................................... 35.00
    Steel, iron lever type ............... 10.00
    Union Pacific, CS 21, Roadway & Bridge .................................... 35.00
Switch, brass
    A & V, emb in panel down back .................................................. 350.00
    C & A RR , emb in panel down back .................................................. 275.00
    C & A RR, stamped on shackle .................................................... 60.00
    C M & St. P RR, emb in panel down back .................................................. 150.00
    CR RR, stamped on shackle, H.C. Jones, Patented June 12, 1854 .................................................. 290.00
    L & NW RR, stamped on shackle .................................................... 35.00
    M C RR, stamped on lock, Detroit Brass Works, Patd April 2, 1867 .................................................. 150.00
    N P RR, emb in panel down back .................................................. 135.00
    PRR, emb across back, A & W or Fraim ...................................... 140.00
    SO PAC Co, emb on panel & on drop .................................................... 80.00
    Union Pacific, emb in panel down back ...................................... 70.00
    U S Y of O, stamped on back .. 15.00
Switch, steel:
    AT & SF Ry, other common railroads .................................................... 5.00
    D S S & A Ry ........................... 25.00
    FRISCO emb on brass drop .... 25.00

### Scandinavian

Brass, 2-1/2" h .............................. 30.00
Corbin, emb, brass, 2-1/2" h....... 125.00
Iron, 2-1/2" h ................................ 20.00
J.H.W. Climax, iron, 3-1/2" h ........ 40.00
R & E, No. 5, iron, 2-1/2" h ........... 35.00
Romer & Co., Patd Oct. 20.74, iron, 4" h .................................................. 85.00
Star emb on bottom, iron
    1-1/2" ...................................... 15.00
    3-1/2" h .................................... 40.00
    4-1/2" h .................................. 130.00

### Six Lever and Eight Lever

Armory Eight Lever, steel............. 25.00
Corbin Six Lever, steel .................. 5.00

**Phila County Prison, 3-5/8" h, $60. Photo courtesy of Franklin Arnall.**

Quality Six Lever, Simmons, steel... 5.00
Samson Eight Lever
    Brass....................................... 20.00
    Steel........................................ 10.00
Stilleto Six Lever, steel ................. 20.00
Super Lever, steel......................... 5.00

### Story, emb cast iron

Floral & Scroll, shield shape
    2-3/8" h................................... 125.00
    3-3/8" h................................... 175.00
Mail Pouch emb, shaped like a mail pouch, Russell & Irwin Mfg. Co. .................................................. 200.00
Skull & Crossbones emb, 3-1/4" h .................................................. 200.00
"The Evil Eye," an eye & eyebrow emb, with floral, 3-1/4" h ................. 800.00

### Warded

Floral & scroll, emb, rect. case, cast iron, 2-1/2" h............................ 20.00
Hawk, a hawk emb, brass, 2 5/8" h .................................................... 40.00
Horsehead emb on front, floral on back, brass, 2-1/8" h.......................... 45.00
Magic, emb, brass case, 2-3/4" h .....5.00
Old Glory, emb, brass case, 2-5/8" h .................................................... 10.00
S. E. Co., Patd March 31, 1887, iron, 3-3/4" h................................... 95.00
Shapleigh, brass case, 2" h.......... 15.00
Simmons, iron case, brass panels .................................................... 20.00
St. Louis, emb, brass, 2" h........... 20.00
Van Camp, emb, brass case, 2-3/4" h .................................................... 20.00
W emb in diamond, brass case, 2-1/2" h .................................................... 10.00
Winchester, both sides, brass case, 2-1/8" h................................... 125.00
1904, emb, brass case, 2-1/8" h .... 5.00

### Wrought Iron Lever, (Smokies, Shield), with brass drops

DM & Co., 4-1/2" h........................ 25.00
Floral emb on drop, 3-5/8" h......... 20.00

Head of dog emb on drop, 4-1/2" h
.............................................. 50.00
Improved tumbler lock, 5-3/4" h.... 45.00
R & E Co., 3-1/8" h ....................... 15.00
S & Co., intertwined, 3-5/8" h ........ 10.00
WW & Co., 3-1/2" h ....................... 15.00

# Paper Dolls

**Collecting Hints:** Most paper dolls that are collected are in uncut books, on intact sheets, or in boxed sets. Cut sets are priced at 50% of an uncut set, providing all dolls, clothing, and accessories are still present.

Many paper doll books have been reprinted. An identical reprint has just slightly less value than the original. If the dolls have been redrawn, the price is reduced significantly.

**History:** The origin of the paper doll can be traced back to the jumping jacks (pantins) of Europe. By the 19th century, boxed or die-cut sheets of paper dolls were available featuring famous dancers, opera stars, performers such as Jenny Lind, and many general subjects. Raphael Tuck began to produce ornate dolls in series form in the 1880s in England.

The advertising industry turned to paper dolls to sell products. Early magazines, such as *Ladies' Home Journal*, *Good Housekeeping*, and *McCall's*, used paper doll inserts. Children's publications, like *Jack and Jill*, picked up the practice.

Cardboard-covered paper doll books first appeared and were mass-marketed in the 1920s. Lowe, Merrill, Saalfield, and Whitman were the leading publishers. The 1940s saw the advent of paper doll books featuring celebrities drawn from screen and radio, and later from television. A few comic characters, such as Brenda Starr, also made it to paper doll fame.

By the 1950s, paper doll books were less popular and production decreased. Modern books are either politically or celebrity oriented.

**References:** Lorraine Mieszala, *Collector's Guide to Barbie Doll Paper Dolls, Identification & Values*, Collector Books, 1997; Mary Young, *Collector's Guide to Magazine Paper Dolls*, Collector Books, 1990; Mary Young, *Tomart's Price Guide to Lowe and Whitman Paper Dolls*, Tomart Publications, 1993.

**Periodicals:** Celebrity Doll Journal, 5 Court Pl, Puyallup, WA 98372; Loretta's Place Paper Doll Newsletter, 808 Lee Ave., Tifton, GA 31794; Midwest Paper Dolls & Toys Quarterly, P.O. Box 131, Galesburg, KS 66740; Northern Lights Paperdoll News, P.O. Box 871189, Wasilla, AK 99687; Paper Doll Gazette, Route #2, Box 52, Princeton, IN 47670; Paper Doll News, P.O. Box 807, Vivian, LA 71082; Paperdoll Review, P.O. Box 584, Princeton, IN 47670; PD Pal, 5341 Gawain #883, San Antonio, TX 78218.

**Collectors' Clubs:** Original Paper Doll Artist Guild, P.O. Box 176, Skandia, MI 49885; United Federation of Doll Clubs, 10920 N Ambassador, Kansas City, MO 64153.

**Museums:** Children's Museum, Indianapolis, IN; Detroit Children's Museum, Detroit, MI; Kent State University Library, Kent, OH; Margaret Woodbury Strong Museum, Rochester, NY; Museum of the City of New York, New York, NY; Newark Museum, Newark, NJ.

**Notes:** Prices are based on uncut, mint, original paper dolls in book or uncut-sheet form. It is not unusual for companies to have assigned the same number to different titles.

American Family of Confederacy .... 12.00
Ancient Egyptian Costumes ......... 12.00
Baby Sister and Baby Brother Dolls, Merrill, uncut book .................. 10.00
Baby Sparkle Plenty, Saalfield, 1948, uncut book .............................. 60.00
Ballerina Barbie, Whitman, uncut
.............................................. 12.00
Ballet, Nancie Swanberg ................ 8.00
Barbie, uncut book ...................... 15.00
Betsy McCall and Sandy McCall, 1958, uncut sheet ............................ 17.50
Children from Other Lands, Whitman, 1961, unused ........................ 20.00
Cinderella Steps Out, Lowe, 1948, uncut book .............................. 20.00
Dionne Quintuplets, cut ............... 75.00
Doris Day, Whitman, 1956, uncut book
.............................................. 60.00
Drayton Paper Doll, uncut
   Alice, 2 outfits ........................ 12.00
   Anna, 3 outfits ........................ 10.00
   Baby and Baby Doll, 3 outfits .. 15.00
   Betty, 2 outfits ........................ 12.00
   Fido, 5 outfits ......................... 10.00
   Fred, 2 outfits ......................... 15.00
   Harriet, 3 outfits ...................... 15.00
   Jane, 4 outfits ......................... 15.00
   Kitty, 6 outfits ......................... 12.00
   Phyllis, 4 outfits ...................... 10.00
Family Affair, 1968, orig box ......... 12.50
Girl Scouts, Brownies, c1950, MIB
.............................................. 40.00
Happy Bride, Whitman, 1967, uncut book ...................................... 20.00
Jane Powell, 1962, uncut book ..... 75.00

Janet Leigh, Abbott, 1958, uncut book
.............................................. 60.00
Jill and Joan, 1965 ...................... 15.00
Laugh-In, unused ........................ 35.00
Liberty Fair Dressing Doll, Miss Liberty cardboard doll, flags on wood stick, cut, c1900, 7" x 13" blue and white box .......................................... 65.00
Little Lulu, boxed ......................... 25.00
Little Miss America, Saalfield, unused
.............................................. 20.00
Little Women, 1981, uncut ........... 12.00
Loretta Young Paper Dolls and Coloring Book ...................................... 52.00
Majorette Paper Dolls, Saalfield, 1957, unused book .............................. 10.00
Malibu Francie, Whitman, uncut... 12.00
Malibu Skipper, Whitman, 1973.... 17.50
Millie the Model ......................... 10.00
Nancy, Whitman, 1971, unused.... 40.00
Nanny and the Professor, Saalfield, 1970, uncut book ..................... 15.00
Nursery Rhyme, Hallmark, uncut ....27.50
Nutcracker Ballet, Tom Tierney, full color, 1981, uncut ................... 15.00
Pat and Pru, 1958 ...................... 15.50
Patty Duke Paper Doll Book, punch-out type, 1964, partially used ......... 20.00
Playhouse Dolls, Stephens Co., 1949, uncut book .............................. 20.00
Princess Diana ........................... 15.00
Raggedy Ann & Andy Paper Dolls Book, Saalfield, 1944, Johnny Gruelle Co., 4 pgs of clothes .......................... 50.00
Rosemary Clooney, Bonnie Book, 1958, uncut ...................................... 70.00
Secret Garden ........................... 15.50
Shari Lewis, Saalfield, 1958, uncut book
.............................................. 20.00
Skipper, Whitman, boxed, uncut .. 12.00
Southern Belles .......................... 14.50
Sports Time, Whitman, 1952, uncut book ...................................... 20.00

**Walking Paper Doll Family, Ruth Upham, Saalfield, #1074, 1934, uncut, $25.**

Storybook Kiddle, Mattel, Whitman
................................................ 15.75
That Girl, MIB ................................ 55.00
The Ginghams Paper Dolls & Play Set,
    unused ...................................... 24.00
Tubsy, Whitman, 1968 ................... 35.00
Tuesday Weld, Saalfield, 1960, orig
    box, unused .............................. 60.00
Twins Around The World ................ 7.50
Vivien Leigh, uncut ....................... 15.00
Walt Disney's Snow White, 1972 ..... 15.50
Wedding Party, Saalfield, 1951, unused
    book ........................................ 20.00

# Paperback Books

**Collecting Hints:** For collecting or investment purposes, buy only items in fine or better condition because books of lower-quality are too numerous to be of value. Unique items, such as paperbacks in dust jackets or in boxes, often are worth more.

Most collections are assembled around one or more unifying themes, such as author (Edgar Rice Burroughs, Dashiell Hammett, Louis L'Amour, Raymond Chandler, Zane Grey, William Irish, Cornell Woolrich, etc.), fictional genre (mysteries, science fiction, westerns, etc.), publisher (early Avon, Dell, and Popular Library are best known), cover artist (Frank Frazetta, R. C. M. Heade, Rudolph Belarski, Roy Krenkel, Vaughn Bode, etc.), or books with uniquely appealing graphic design (Dell map backs and Ace double novels).

Because paperbacks still turn up in large lots, collectors need to be cautious. Books that are in fine or excellent condition are uncommon. Currently, many dealers charge upper-level prices for books that are not in correspondingly good condition. Dealers' argument that top-condition examples are just too scarce is not valid, just self-serving.

**History:** Paperback volumes have existed since the 15th century. Mass-market paperback books, most popular with collectors, were printed after 1938. These exist in a variety of formats, from the standard-size paperback and its smaller predecessor to odd sizes like 64-page short novels (which sold for 10¢) and 5-1/4- by 7-1/2-inch volumes known as "digests." Some books came in a dust jacket; some were boxed.

Today there are not as many companies publishing mass-market paperbacks as there were between 1938 and 1950. Books of this period are characterized by lurid and color-ful cover art and title lettering not unlike that of the pulp magazines. Many early paperback publishers were also involved in the production of pulps, and merely moved their graphic style and many of their authors to paperbacks.

**References:** *Collectible Vintage Paperbacks at Auction 1995*, available from Spoon River Press (2319C W. Rohmann, Peoria, IL 61604, 1995; Bob and Sharon Huxford, *Huxford's Paperback Value Guide*, Collector Books, 1994; Gary Lovisi, *Collecting Science Fiction and Fantasy*, Alliance Publishing, 1997; Kurt Peer, *TV Tie-Ins: A Bibliography of American TV Tie-In Paperbacks*, Neptune Publishing, 1997; Dawn E. Reno and Jacque Tiegs, *Collecting Romance Novels*, Alliance Publishers, 1995; Frank M. Robinson and Lawrence Davidson, *Pulp Culture: The Art of Fiction Magazines*, Collectors Press, Inc., 1998; Lee Server, *Over My Dead Body: The Sensational Age of the American Paperback*, Chronicle Books, 1994.

**Periodicals:** *Books Are Everything*, 302 Martin Dr., Richmond, KY 40475; *Paperback Parade*, P.O. Box 209, Brooklyn, NY 11228; *Pulp and Paperback Market Newsletter*, 5813 York Ave., Edina, MN 55410.

**Museum:** University of Minnesota's Hess Collection of Popular Literature, Minneapolis, MN.

**Notes:** Prices are given for books in fine condition. Divide by three to get the price for books in good condition; increase price by 50% for books in near mint condition.

Adams Family Strike Back ............ 60.00
Adventures of Creighton Holmes, Ned
    Hubbell, Popular ...................... 10.00
Baa Baa Black Sheep, Gregory Boyington, Dell ...................................... 3.00
Baby and Child Care, Dr. Benjamin
    Spock, 1956, 502 pgs ............... 5.00
Battle Cry, Leon Uris, Bantam ........ 3.00
Bedroom Tramp, Bill Adams, Playtime
    .................................................. 12.00
Beverly Hillbillies Book of Country
    Humor ...................................... 20.00
Bluebeard's Seventh Wife, William Irish,
    Popular Library ......................... 9.00
Bright Path to Adventure, Gordon Sinclair, Harlequin ........................... 5.00
Conquest of the Planet of the Apes,
    John Jakes, 5th printing, 1974, ink
    mark .......................................... 5.00
Cry Slaughter, Avon ....................... 3.00
Dr. Prescott's Secret, Peggy Gaddin,
    Beacon ...................................... 3.00
Fighting Coach, Jackson Scholz,
    Comet ........................................ 3.00

Future Science Fiction, 1950s ...... 20.00
Get Smart, complete set of 9 ........ 50.00
Girl from U.N.C.L.E., The Birds of a
    Feather Affair, #11 ................... 12.50
Grabhorn Bounty, Clifton Adams, Ace
    .................................................. 7.50
Guide Book for the Edison Institute
    Museum and Greenfield Village,
    ©1937 ...................................... 20.00
He Who Laughs Lasts...And
    Lasts...And Lasts, Roy H. Hicks, DD,
    1976, 63 pgs ............................. 5.00
I'll Be Glad When You're Dead, Dana
    Lynn, Quick Reader ................... 5.00
Jackie Robinson Story, Arthur Mann, J
    Low Co. ..................................... 45.00
Judy Garland, James Juneau, Pyramid,
    1974 .......................................... 18.00
Land of the Giants ........................ 15.00
Leave It To Beaver ........................ 15.00
Laverne and Shirley ........................ 5.00
Life and Loves of Lana Turner, W.
    Wright, Windom House .............. 3.50
Murder of the Circus Queen, Anthony
    Abbot, Popular ......................... 10.00
Open Heart Open Home, Karen Burton
    Mains, ©David C. Cook Publishing,
    1976, 199 pgs ........................... 5.00
Return of a Fighter, Ernest Haycox,
    Corgi, 1956 .............................. 15.00
Sgt. Bilco ..................................... 15.00
Spider, 2/43, 6/43, 12/43, each .... 75.00
Start Muzzleloading, An Introduction to
    the Black Powder Sport, Ian Phillips,
    3" x 5" ...................................... 10.00
Tales of Voodoo, Vol. 7 #1, Eerie Publications, January 1974. Pool of Evil,
    Midnight Hag, and The Blood Slave
    .................................................. 6.00
Tarzan and The Lost Empire, Edgar
    Rice Burroughs, Ace .................. 8.00
The Avengers, The Magnetic Man, #8,
    Berkley, 1968 ............................. 8.00
The Book of Revelation, Harry R. Boer,
    ©African Christian Press, 1979, USA
    edition by William B. Erdmans Publishing, 157 pgs ........................ 5.00
The Democratic Book, 1936, 14" x 11",
    394 pgs .................................... 55.00
The Real Life Story of Fess Parker, Dell
    Magazine ................................. 50.00
The Story of Walt Disney, Martin and
    Miller, Dell ................................. 5.00
The Wedding Journey, Walter
    Edmonds, Dell ........................... 5.00
We Are The Public Enemy, Alan Hynd,
    Gold Medal ................................ 5.00
Wuthering Heights, Emily Bronte, Quick
    Reader ....................................... 7.50

# Patriotic Collectibles

**Collecting Hints:** Concentrate on one symbol, e.g., the eagle, flag, Statue of Liberty, or Uncle Sam. Remember that the symbol is not always the principal attraction; don't miss items with the symbol in a secondary role.

Colored material is more desirable than black and white. Many items are two-dimensional, e.g., posters and signs. Seek three-dimensional objects to add balance and interest to a collection.

Much of the patriotic material focuses on our national holidays, especially the Fourth of July; but other holidays to consider are Flag Day, Labor Day, Memorial Day, and Veterans' Day.

Finally, look to the foreign market. Our symbols are used abroad, both positively and negatively. A novel collection would be one based on how Uncle Sam is portrayed on posters and other materials from Communist countries.

**History:** Patriotic symbols developed along with the American nation. The eagle, among the greatest of our nation's symbols, has appeared on countless objects since it was chosen to be part of the American seal.

Uncle Sam arrived on the American scene in the mid-19th century and was firmly established by the Civil War. Uncle Sam did have female counterparts—Columbia and the Goddess of Liberty. He often appeared together with one or both of them on advertising trade cards, buttons, posters, textiles, etc. His modern appearance came about largely as the result of drawings by Thomas Nast in *Harper's Weekly* and James Montgomery Flagg's famous World War I recruiting poster, "I Want You." Perhaps the leading promoter of the Uncle Sam image was the American toy industry, aided by the celebration of the American Centennial in 1876 and Bicentennial in 1976. A surge of Uncle Sam–related toys occurred in the 1930s led by American Flyer's inexpensive version of an earlier lithographed tin, flat-sided Uncle Sam bicycle string toy.

**Reference:** Gerald Czulewicz, *Foremost Guide to Uncle Sam Collectibles*, Collector Books, 1995; Nicholas Steward, *James Montgomery Flagg: Uncle Sam and Beyond*, Collector's Press, 1997.

**Periodical:** *Pyrofax Magazine*, P.O. Box 2010, Saratoga, CA 95070.

**Collectors' Club:** Statue of Liberty Collectors' Club, P.O. Box 535, Chautauqua, NY 14722.

**Museum:** 4th of July Americana & Fireworks Museum, New Castle, PA.

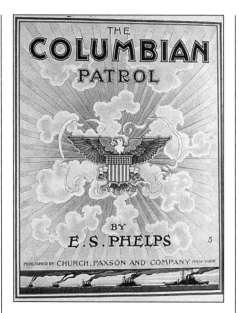

**Sheet Music,** *The Columbian Patrol,* **E. S. Phelps, $10.**

**Additional Listings:** Flag Collectibles.

### Eagle

Badge, U.S.N.R., dark copper luster, eagle and patriotic symbols, inscription for Naval reserve ............... 20.00
Bookends, 5-1/2" l, cast white metal, worn .......................................... 50.00
Change Tray, 4" d, Hebbrun House Coal, eagle in center, holding banner, wood grain ground ............ 50.00
Cookie Cutter, 6-1/2" l, tin ............. 90.00
Fan, 8" x 9" diecut cardboard, 4" wood handle, full color eagle front, black and white illus text on back for Ontario Drill Co, Baltimore, ©1908 ............................................... 85.00
Figure, 6" h, pot metal, gold paint ............................................. 35.00
Pinback Button, 7/8" d, 2nd Liberty Loan, Let The Eagle Scream Appeal, multicolored, blue letters ......... 20.00

**Tray, Francis Scott Key medallion, "Old Glory," border of flags, shields, and text, litho tin, 1814-1914, $65.**

Watch Fob, 1" d, silvered brass, shield shape, attached silvered brass horseshoe, raised eagle on front, red white, and blue enameled name "American Badge Co.," c1900 .................... 45.00

### Fans and Shields

Fan, diecut shield, red, white, and blue cardboard, "America First," sailor raising deck flag, warships in background, biplane flying overhead, back with sponsors names and song lyrics, 7" x 9" ............................ 45.00
Lapel Stud, Colonial Bicycles, red, white, and blue shield symbol .............. 20.00
Medal, Victory Liberty Loan, US Treasury Dept. ............................... 15.00
Note Pad Holder, kitten with red, white, and blue shield, wearing US Navy cap, 7-1/4" x 9", some wear ..... 25.00
Paperweight, 3" d, celluloid over weighted metal, mirror bottom, full color images of 12 Allied flags, local sponsor art center ................... 35.00
Pocket Mirror, Beautifers of Homes, red, white, and gold patriotic shield shape, black lettering .............. 40.00
Stickpin
Advertising, diecut celluloid red, white, and blue American flag on front, black and white adv. on back for Artistic Pianos, brass stickpin, early 1900s ............................. 30.00
G. A. R. Encampment, stiff paper red, white, and blue flag, mounted to metal stickpin, "Welcome Comrades" ...................................... 35.00
Watch Fob, silvered brass, shield shape, attached silvered brass horseshoe, raised eagle on front, red, white, and blue enameled name, American Badge Co., c1900 .................... 48.00

### Liberty Bell

Book, *The Centennial Liberty Bell,* Philadelphia, 1876, hard cover ........ 18.00
Button, Liberty Bell, plastic shelf shank, 3/4" d ........................................ 2.50
Paperweight 6" h, cast iron ........... 60.00
Pinback Button, National Relief Assurance Co, Philadelphia, multicolored eagle and Liberty Bell, dark blue ground, c1900 ........................ 20.00
Pocket Mirror, Bell's Coffee, green Liberty bell trademark, mocha and java specialties, J H Bell & Co, Chicago ................................................. 60.00
Post Card
Glorious 4th of July, minor wear ................................................. 6.00
Independence Hall, Philadelphia, sepia .......................................... 8.50
Liberty Bell Trolley, insignia on front ................................................. 10.00
Sheet Music, Liberty Bell Time To Ring Again, 1918 ............................. 10.00
Tape Measure, 1-3/4" d, celluloid case, blue and white design, logo and inscription for Missouri and Kansas telephone company, reverse "When You Telephone, Use The Bell," cloth tape, c1900 ............................. 40.00

### Statue of Liberty

Bell, hand painted, Fenton............ 35.00
Bookends, pr, leather, carved design, 1930s ....................................... 70.00
Brooch, silver-tone, red, white, and blue rhinestones, sgd "Wendy Gell," 4" h ................................................. 65.00
Cigarette Case, painted metal, 1940s ................................................. 30.00
Clock, Seth Thomas.................... 400.00
Hat, heavy paper, "Liberty," red, white and blue, picture of Statue, c1918 ................................................. 25.00
Lamp, 5-1/2" h, dark copper finished white metal, holds small electrical bulb, wooden base, sliding base opens to hold battery, c1920 ................................................. 40.00
Needle Book, World's Best, airplane, ship, world, 6 needle packets.... 20.00
Paperweight, glass and plaster, 1880 ................................................. 150.00
Playing Cards, "606," US Playing Card Co, Cincinnati, OH, picture of Statue of Liberty and flags of nations, gold edges, complete, orig box....... 20.00
Sheet Music, *Liberty Enlightening The World*, 1885 ........................... 100.00
Tin, Wiles Biscuit Company, Bakers of Sunshine Biscuits, NY, signing of Constitution, Gold Rush, Statue of Liberty, bail handle, some wear ................................................. 25.00

### Uncle Sam

Advertising Trade Card, 3-1/2" x 6-1/4", Hub Gore, Uncle Sam holding shoe, saying "Hub Gore Makers of Elastic For Shoes...It Was Honored At The World's Fair of 1893" ................ 15.00
Doll, eagle, striped top hat, Japan, 1984, 18" h, MIB..................... 200.00
Magazine Tear Sheet, 5-1/2" x 8-1/2", Uncle Sam Holding a "Health Bill" under his arm, looking at Cream of Wheat advertising billboard, ©1915 ................................................. 22.00
Pinback Button, 1-1/4" d, America Always, red, white, blue, and flesh-tone ........................................... 25.00
Pocket Mirror, Watertown Times Newspaper........................................ 75.00
Salt and Pepper Shakers, pr, 1-1/2" x 2-1/2" x 2", painted plaster, glossy white, black, and red accents, red, white, and blue top hat ........... 65.00
Stickpin, 1", diecut, white metal, tinted cherry red trousers and hat, blue coat, marching pose, c1898 .... 35.00
Tray, Cascade Beer, San Francisco, Uncle Sam and five ethnic people ................................................. 675.00
Watch Fob, brass, detailed Uncle Sam kicking large bullet into stomach of Kaiser, red, white, and blue flags ................................................. 75.00

### George Washington

Pinback Button
 Cherry Smash, multicolored portrait of George, background shades from burgundy to olive green, inscription "Cherry Smash," early 1900s..... 20.00
 Two flags on white background, orange and blue ribbon with token with emb Theme Building on one side, George Washington on other ................................................. 45.00
Sheet Music, *Father of the Land We Love*, lyrics and music by George M. Cohan, cover artist James Montgomery Flagg, illus of George Washington on cov, 1931 ...................... 12.00
Spoon, 4-1/2" l, George at top of handle, stars on handle, flags and staffs, shield with NY World's Fair in bowl, National Silver Co. ................... 35.00
Teapot, white ironstone, portrait of George Washington, excerpts from Declaration of Independence, mkd "Ellgreave Adin of Woods and Sons, England, Genuine Ironstone," 5-3/4" h ................................................. 40.00

# Pennsbury Pottery

**Collecting Hints:** Concentrate on one pattern or type. Since the wares were hand carved, aesthetic quality differs from piece to piece. Look for those with a strong design sense and a high quality of execution.

Buy only clearly marked pieces. Look for decorator and designer initials that can be easily identified.

Pennsbury collectors are concentrated in the Middle Atlantic states. Many of the company's commemorative and novelty pieces relate to businesses and events in that region, thus commanding the highest prices when sold within that area.

**History:** In 1950, Henry and Lee Below established Pennsbury Pottery, named for its close proximity to William Penn's estate "Pennsbury," three miles west of Morrisville, Pennsylvania. Henry, a ceramic engineer and mold maker, and Lee, a designer and modeler, had previously worked for Stangl Pottery in Trenton, New Jersey.

Many of Pennsbury's forms, motifs, and manufacturing techniques have Stangl roots. A line of birds similar to those produced by Stangl were among the earliest Pennsbury products. The carved-design technique is also of Stangl origin; high bas-relief molds are not.

Most Pennsbury products are easily identified by their brown-wash background. The company also made pieces featuring other background colors so do not make the mistake of assuming that a piece is not Pennsbury if it does not have a brown wash.

Pennsbury motifs are heavily nostalgic, often farm- or Pennsylvania German-related. Among the most popular lines were Amish, Black Rooster, Delft Toleware, Eagle, Family, Folkart, Gay Ninety, Harvest, Hex, Quartet, Red Barn, Red Rooster, Slick-Chick, and Christmas plates (1960-1970). The pottery made a large number of commemorative, novelty, and special-order pieces.

In the late 1950s, the company had 16 employees, mostly local housewives and young girls. By 1963, at the company's peak, there were 46 employees. Cheap foreign imports cut deeply into the pottery's profits, and by the late 1960s, just more than 20 employees remained.

Marks differ from piece to piece, depending on the person who signed it or the artist who sculpted the mold. Some initials still have not been identified.

Henry Below died on Dec. 21, 1959, leaving the pottery in trust for his wife and three children with instructions that it be sold upon the death of his wife. She died on Dec. 12, 1968, and in October 1970 the Pennsbury Pottery filed for bankruptcy. The contents were auctioned off on Dec. 18, 1970. On May 18, 1971, a fire destroyed the pottery and support buildings.

**References:** Susan and Al Bagdade, *Warman's American Pottery and Porcelain*, Wallace-Homestead, 1994; Lucile Henzke, *Pennsbury Pottery*, Schiffer Publishing, 1990; Mike Schneider, *Stangl and Pennsbury Birds*, Schiffer Publishing, 1994.

**Look-Alike Alert:** The Lewis Brothers Pottery, Trenton, New Jersey, purchased 50 of the Pennsbury molds. Although they were supposed to remove the Pennsbury name from the molds, this was not done in all instances. Further, two Pennsbury employees moved to Lewis Brothers when Pennsbury closed, helping to produce a number of pieces that are reminiscent of Pennsbury's products. Many of Pennsbury's major lines, including the Harvest and Rooster patterns, plaques, birds, and highly unusual molds, were not reproduced.

Glen View, Langhorne, Pennsylvania, continued marketing the 1970s Angel Christmas plate with Pennsbury markings. The company continued the Christmas plate line into the 1970s, utilizing the Pennsbury brown-wash background. In 1975, Lenape Products, a division of

Pennington, bought Glen View and continued making Pennsbury-like products.

Ashtray
    Don't Be So Doppish, 5" l ......... 20.00
    Doylestown Trust ..................... 30.00
    Hex Sign, earthtones .............. 27.50
    Outen the Light .......................... 20.00
    Such Schmootzers ................... 20.00
    What Giffs, Amish pattern ....... 20.00
Bank, jug, pig, "Stuff Me" ........... 100.00
Beer Mug, Red Rooster ............... 28.00
Bird
    Bird on Nest .......................... 300.00
    Goldfinch, #102 ..................... 200.00
Bread Tray, rect, wheat motif ....... 45.00
Cake Stand, Amish ...................... 75.00
Candleholders, pr, Red Roosters
    ................................................. 85.00
Canister set, cov, Black Rooster dec, 9" h flour and sugar, 8" tea and coffee
    ............................................... 425.00
Coaster, Shultz ........................... 17.50
Coffeepot, cov, 8" h, Rooster ...... 110.00
Cream Pitcher
    Large, Hex Sign ...................... 55.00
    Medium, Distilfink .................... 45.00
    Small, Hex Sign ...................... 25.00
Cruet, stopper, Amish .................. 40.00
Cup and Saucer
    Black Rooster .......................... 20.00
    Red Rooster ............................ 17.50
Desk Basket, Exchange Club ....... 40.00
Dinner Plate, Hex pattern ............ 17.50
Egg Cup, Red Rooster pattern ..... 25.00
Mug
    Eagle ....................................... 25.00
    Schiaraflia Filadelfia, owl and seal
    ................................................. 30.00
    Sweet Adeline .......................... 20.00
Pie Plate
    Apple Tree pattern ................... 37.50
    Mother serving pie ................... 75.00
Pitcher
    Amish man, 2-1/2" h ................ 12.00
    Amish woman, 5" h ................... 45.00
    Eagle pattern .......................... 65.00
    Hex Sign, 4" ............................ 20.00
    Red Rooster, 3-3/4" ................. 18.00
Plaque
    Amish Family, 8" d ................... 55.00
    It is whole empty, 4" ................ 20.00

**Pie Plate, PA German motif, double eagle, 9-1/2" d, $55.**

Pennsylvania RR 1888, Tiger Locomotive, 8" x 5-5/8" ................... 48.00
    Pops half et already, 4" ............ 20.00
Plate
    Black Rooster, 10" d ................ 15.00
    Hex Sign, 8" d ......................... 20.00
    Hex Sign, 10" d ....................... 20.00
Pretzel Bowl, large, Sweet Adeline
    ................................................. 60.00
Salt and Pepper Shakers, pr, Amish heads ...................................... 60.00
Snack Set, Red Rooster ............... 30.00
Snack Tray, matching cup, Red Rooster
    ................................................. 25.00
Teapot, Red Rooster pattern ........ 65.00
Tea Tile, 6" d, skunk "Why Be Disagreeable" .................................... 60.00
Vegetable Dish, divided, Red Rooster
    ................................................. 32.00
Wall Pocket, 10" h, bellows-shape, eagle motif .............................. 50.00

# Pens and Pencils

**Collecting Hints:** Price is lessened dramatically by any defects such as scratches, cracks, dents, warping, missing parts, bent levers, sprung clips, nib damage, or mechanical damage. Engraved initials or names do not seriously detract from the price.

**History:** The steel pen point, or "nib," was invented by Samuel Harrison in 1780. It was not commercially produced in quantity until the 1880s when Richard Esterbrook entered the field. The holders became increasingly elaborate. Mother-of-pearl, gold, sterling silver, and other fine materials were used to fashion holders of distinction. Many of these pens can be found along with their original velvet-lined presentation cases.

Lewis Waterman invented the fountain pen in the 1880s. Three other leading pioneers in the field were Parker, Sheaffer (first lever filling action, 1913), and Wahl-Eversharp.

The mechanical pencil was patented in 1822 by Sampson Mordan. The original slide-type action developed into the spiral mechanical pencil. Wahl-Eversharp was responsible for the automatic "clic," or repeater-type, mechanism which is used on ball-points today.

The flexible nib that enabled the writer to individualize his penmanship came to an end when Reynolds introduced the ball-point pen in October 1945.

**References:** Deborah Crosby, *Victorian Pencils: Tools to Jewels,* Schiffer Publishing, 1998; George Fischler and Stuart Schneider, *Fountain Pens*

*and Pencils,* Schiffer Publishing, 1990; —, *Illustrated Guide to Antique Writing Instruments,* 2nd ed., Schiffer, 1997; Henry Gostony and Stuard Schneider, *The Incredible Ball Point Pen,* Schiffer Publishing, 1998; Regina Martini, *Pens & Pencils: A Collector's Handbook,* 2nd ed., Schifer Publishing, 1998.

**Periodicals:** *Pen World Magazine,* P.O. Box, 6007, Kingwood, TX 77325; *Pens,* P.O. Box 64, Teaneck, NJ 07666.

**Collectors' Clubs:** American Pencil Collectors Society, 2222 S. Milwood, Wichita, KS 67213; Pen Collectors of American, P.O. Box 821449, Houston, TX 77282; Pen Fancier's Club, 1169 Overcash Dr., Dunedin, FL 34698.

### Desk Set
Conklin, Endura Model, black marble base, two pens, side lever fill, double narrow gold color bands, mkd "Patent Nov. 17, 1925," on pen barrel, black-brown overlay color ................. 125.00
Moore, gray and black marble base, black pen, 12 carat nib, side lever fill
    ................................................. 75.00
Sheaffer, Triumph Lifetime, green marble base, two black snorkel design pens, c1940 ............................ 95.00

### Pen
Advertising
    Coca-Cola, 1996, polar bear, Coca-Cola bottle clip .......................... 8.00
    Westinghouse, emblem in window, Garland, maroon and silver ....... 8.00
Character
    Playboy, red ink ........................ 7.50
    Taz, Looney Toons, Stylus Pen, Tax on clip ...................................... 8.00
    Tweety Bird, blue, Tweety on clip
    ................................................... 8.00
Conklin
    Model 20, 5-5/16" l, #2 Conklin pint-nib, black crescent filler #20, gold clip, narrow gold band on cap, patent date May 28, 1918 stamped on clip ..................................... 75.00
    Model 25P, ladies filigree cap ribbon, black, crescent filler, 1923 ....... 70.00
    Model 30, black hard rubber, 1903
    ................................................. 75.00
Cross, gold colored, seashells engraved on clip ..................................... 10.00
Dunn, black, red barrel, goldplated trim, c1920 ......................................... 40.00
Epenco, black case, goldplated trim
    ................................................. 25.00
Esterbrook, red case, black end cap, orig box .................................... 35.00
Eversharp
    CA Model, ball point pen, black, gold filled cap, 1946 ............... 42.00
Doric
    Desk pen, gold seal, green marble cov, lever fill, large adjustable nib, c1935 .......................... 55.00

**Fountain Pen, Morrison, black, chrome plated cap, 14 kt tip, mkd "USA, Lever Fill, Morrison Fountain Pen Co. NY, NY, USA," $20.**

Fountain pen, amber threading, restored .............................. 225.00
Hallmark, wood, dark colored ......... 9.00
Marvel, black chased hand rubber, eyedropper, 1906 ........................... 75.00
Moore
    Black, lady's ribbon pen, three narrow gold bands on cap, lever fill, patent nib #2 ........................... 70.00
    Rose color, fancy band around cap, warranted nib, side lever filler ...65.00
Parker
    Blue-Diamond-51, black, goldplated cap, button filled, 1942 ............ 70.00
    Duofold
        Deluxe, pen and pencil set, black and pearl, three narrow gold color bands on cap, push button fill, 1929 .................................. 575.00
        Senior, Flashing Black, 1923 ......................................... 185.00
        Streamline, burgundy and black, double narrow band on cap, 1932 ......................................... 125.00
    Lucky Curve, ring pen, black hard rubber, gold filled trim, 19212 .... 85.00
    Model 48, ring top, gold filled barrel and cap, button filled, 1915 ..... 150.00
    Parker 51, brown, jewel on cap, Vacumatic filler, mkd "Made in USA" ............................................. 75.00
    Vacumatic, gray-black, arrow clip, arrow design engraved on nib, silver color clip and band on cap, oversized model, 1932.................. 125.00
Political
    Bush-Quayle '92, bluetone bald eagle, red, white, and blue stars and strips design ............................. 7.50
    George Bush for President in '88, elephant emblem, red lettering, white ground ............................. 9.00
    Mike Dukakis for President in '88, donkey emblem, blue lettering, white ground........................................ 8.00
    Reynolds, Model 2, orig ball point, c1945 ....................................... 75.00

Security, check protector, red hard rubber, gold filled trim, 1923 ......... 85.00
Sheaffer
    Strato Writer, ball point pen, gold filled metal mountings, 1948.... 65.00
    White Dot, green jade, goldplated trim, lever filled, 1923............... 95.00
    White Dot Lifetime, classic torpedo design cap and body, lever filler on side, 1930 ............................. 115.00
Wahl
    Lady's, ribbon pen, double narrow band on cap, 14 carat #2 nib, lever fill, 1928.................................... 75.00
    Tempoint No. 305A, gold filled metal mounted, eyedropper, 1919 ................................................. 145.00
Wahl-Eversharp, gold seal, black, gold filled trim, lever filled, 1930 .... 125.00
Waterman
    Model #12, mottled brow, 14 carat gold bands, 1886................... 125.00
    Model 42-1/2V, Safety, gold filigree, retractable screw action nib, 1906 ................................................. 135.00
    Model #71, ripple red, hard rubber case, goldplated trim, white clip, lever filled, 1925.................... 150.00
    Taperite, black, gold filled metal mounted cap, gold filled trim, lever filled, c1949 ............................. 75.00

**Pencil**

Advertising
    A. J. Spaulding Brothers, NY, silver lettering "Put Importance to the History and Tradition," Reimei........ 8.00
    Broadman Supplies, red logo, 23rd Psalm printed in blue ................ 8.50
    Guy M. Grove Co. Plumbing & Heating. Funkstown, MD, 1968 monthly calendars, black on orange, Rite Graph brand ............................. 9.00
    RCA, gold-colored Cross, "RCA" on clip ......................................... 8.00
    Tom's 24 Hour Service, Electric Motor, Pick Up and Delivery, phone number and Bakersfield, CA address, "USA" on clip, mechanical type............................................ 8.00
Eversharp, lady's, silverplated, c1920 ................................................. 25.00
Souvenir
    "1898-1948 - Golden Anniversary, New York City" emb on side, blue and orange stripes, brass sq eraser head, 12" l ................................. 8.50
    "Souvenir of Saginaw" in silver writing on side, red, white, and blue, metal dome cap, thick, 1920s, 12-1/2" l .................................................8.50
Wahl-Eversharp, gold filled, metal mounted, 1919......................... 35.00
Zippo, black, gold trim ................. 10.00

# Pepsi-Cola Collectibles

**Collecting Hints:** Items advertising Pepsi, Hires, and a number of other soft drink companies became hot

collectibles in the 1980s, fueled in part by the pricey nature of Coca-Cola items. The Pepsi market is still young; and, some price fluctuations occur.

Pepsi-Cola enjoys a much stronger market position in many foreign countries than it does in the United States.

Reproductions, copycats, and fantasy items are part of the Pepsi collecting scene. Be on the alert for the Pepsi and Pete pillow issued in the 1970s, a 12-inch-high ceramic statue of a woman holding a glass of Pepsi, a Pepsi glass-front clock, a Pepsi double-bed quilt, and set of four Pepsi glasses. These are just a few of the suspect items, some of which were done under license from Pepsi-Cola.

**History:** Pepsi-Cola was developed by Caleb D. Bradham, a pharmacist and drugstore owner in New Bern, North Carolina. Like many drugstores of its time, Bradham provided "soda" mixes for his customers and friends. His favorite was "Brad's Drink," which he began to call "Pepsi-Cola" in 1898. Its popularity spread, and in 1902 Bradham turned the operation of his drugstore over to an assistant and devoted all his energy to perfecting and promoting Pepsi-Cola. He sold 2,008 gallons of Pepsi-Cola syrup his first three months and by 1904 was bottling Pepsi-Cola for mass consumption. He sold his first franchise within a short time.

By the end of the first decade of the 20th century, Bradham had organized a network of more than 250 bottlers in 24 states. The company's fortunes sank shortly after World War I when it suffered large losses in the sugar market. Bankruptcy and reorganization followed. Roy Megargel, whose Wall Street firm advised Bradham, helped keep the name alive. A second bankruptcy occurred in 1931, but the company survived.

In 1933, Pepsi-Cola doubled the size of its bottle but held the price at 5¢. Sales soared. Under the direction of Walter Mack, 1938-1951, Pepsi challenged Coca-Cola for market dominance. In the 1950s, Pepsi advertising featured slogans such as "Pepsi Cola Hits the Spot, Twelve Full Ounces That's a Lot."

PepsiCo. is currently a division of Beatrice. It has a worldwide reputation and actually is the number one soft drink in many foreign countries.

**References:** James C. Ayers, *Pepsi-Cola Bottles Collectors Guide*, published by author (P.O. Box 1377, Mt. Airy, NC 27030), 1995; Everette and Mary Lloyd, *Pepsi-Cola Collectibles*, Schiffer Publishing, 1993; Bill Vehling and Michael Hunt, *Pepsi-Cola Collectibles*, Vol. 1 (1990, 1993 value update), Vol. 2 (1990, 1992 value update), Vol. 3 (1993, 1995 value update), L-W Book Sales.

**Collectors' Clubs:** Ozark Mountain Pepsi Collectors Club, P.O. Box 575631, Modesto, CA 95357; Pepsi-Cola Collectors Club, P.O. Box 1275, Covina, CA 91722.

**Museum:** Pepsi-Cola Company Archives, Purchase, NY.

Bottle, long neck, painted label with Richard Petty.............................. 6.00
Bottle Carrier, six bottle-type, aluminum ........................................... 52.50
Bottle Opener, church-key type, some rust ......................................... 6.50
Calendar, 1955, card stock, 12" x 20" .............................................. 400.00
Character Drinking Glass
  Daffy Duck and Pepe, mkd "part of a collector series, Warner Brothers Inc., 1976" with Pepsi logo, 6-1/4" h ......................................... 8.00
  Uh-Huh Diet Pepsi ..................... 4.00
Cigarette Lighter, 4" l, metal, bottle cap illus on side, 1950s ................ 150.00
Clock, wall type............................ 40.00
Cooler, aluminum ......................... 200.00
Drinking Glass, Wonder Woman, yellow boots, 1978 ................................ 30.00
Door Push, wrought iron, 1960s ... 65.00
Fan, 10" sq, cardboard, wood handle, c1940 ......................................... 75.00
Figure, 5-1/2" h, 30 Anniversary, pewter, billboard center with bottle cap and "Cool" and cat figure leaning on it with one elbow, feet crossed, limited edition of 250 ......................... 60.00
Fountain Glass, 5" h, syrup line, double dot............................................. 45.00
Key Chain, Pepsi Beach Club, 1960s ........................................... 35.00
Letterhead, 8-1/2" x 11", Pepsi-Cola Bottling Works, Greensboro, NC, 1916 ........................................ 100.00
Mileage Chart, tin, framed ........... 45.00
Model Kit, Car in a Bottle, Monogram, ©1975, factory sealed ............. 50.00
Napkin, 19" sq, cloth, c1940........ 25.00
Notepad, 2-1/2" x 4-1/2", cardboard cov, red and black logo, 1914 calendar ........................................ 35.00
Pinback Button, 1" d, celluloid, double dot, Phila Badge Co............... 45.00
Pushbar, porcelain, Canadian, French, 1950s ....................................... 75.00
Radio, can shape......................... 40.00
Record, "Recorded message from your Man in Service," WWII, orig record, sleeve, and mailer, 1940s, unused ........................................ 45.00
Ruler, 12" l, tin, c1950 ................. 20.00

Salt and Pepper Shakers, pr, miniature bottles ...................................... 10.00
Santa, hard vinyl face, sponge body, red velvet suit, white vinyl belt and boots, orig box ........................ 65.00
Sign
  3-1/2" x 10", emb tin, dark green, white, and red, mkd "Crown Cork & Seal Co., Baltimore, USA" c1910 ........................................ 650.00
  9" d, celluloid and tin, "Ice Cold Pepsi-Cola Sold Here," 1930s 300.00
  12" x 8", plastic, "Take Home Pepsi," light-up type, bottle cap illus, 1950s ........................................ 160.00
  18" x 6", porcelain, red, white, and blue banner, double dotted logo, "America's Biggest Nickel's Worth" ........................................ 300.00
  22" x 7", paper, "Have A Pepsi," man, woman, and bottle cap illus, 1950s ........................................ 35.00
  24" x 28", tin, "Drink Pepsi-Cola," bottle cap illus, 1950s............. 55.00
Store Display
  Looney Tunes, 6 plastic Slurpee cups, 1978 ........................... 100.00
  Xena, standee, life size, unused ........................................ 38.00
Thermometer, 27-1/4" h, 7-1/8" w, double dot, some wear and stains ........................................ 365.00
Thimble, plastic, red and blue on yellow, "America's Choice," Pepsi logo ........................................ 7.50
Toy
  Car, diecast, #38, 1993, 1:64 scale, MOC............................ 6.50
  Delivery Truck, 2-1/2" x 7-1/2" x 2", white plastic body, black wood wheels, red, white, and blue ... Pepsi decal, three white plastic cases with 24 plastic bottles, Marx Toys, c1940 ........................................ 95.00
  Walkie Talkies, by NASTA, orig box mkd "FBI Jr." ....................... 75.00
Tray
  Bottle cap shape, round, 1940 ........................................ 325.00
  Coney Island, 1955................. 50.00
Uniform Patch, 7" ....................... 15.00
Walkie-Talkie, bottle shape .......... 25.00
Watch, bottle cap style, Pepsi logo, hot pink vinyl band...................... 25.00

# PEZ

**Collecting Hints:** PEZ became a hot collectible in the late 1980s. Its rise was due in part to the use of licensed cartoon characters as heads on PEZ dispensers. Initially, PEZ containers were an extremely affordable collectible. Generic subjects often sold for less than $5, character containers for less than $10.

Before investing large amounts of money in PEZ containers, it is important to recognize that: 1) they are produced in large quantities—millions, 2) PEZ containers are usually saved by their original buyers, not disposed of when emptied, and 3) no collecting category stays hot forever. PEZ prices fluctuate. Advertised price and field price for the same container can differ by as much as 50%, depending on who is selling.

Starting a PEZ collection is simple. Go to a local store that sells PEZ and purchase the current group of products. Then scour flea markets, garage sales, and antique shows for older examples.

**History:** Vienna, Austria, is the birthplace of PEZ. In 1927, Eduard Haas, an Austrian food mogul, invented PEZ and marketed it as a cigarette substitute, i.e., an adult mint. He added peppermint oil to a candy formula, compressed the product into small rectangular bricks, and named it PEZ, an abbreviation for the German word *Pfefferminz*. Production of PEZ was halted by World War II. When the product appeared again after the war, it was packaged in a dispenser that resembled a BIC lighter. These early 1950s dispensers had no heads.

PEZ arrived in the United States in 1952. PEZ-HAAS received United States Patent #2,620,061 for its "table dispensing receptacle," but the public response was less than overwhelming. Rather than withdraw from the market, Haas repositioned his product to appeal to children by adding fruit flavors. PEZ's success was assured when it became both a candy and a toy combined into one product. In some cases, the shape of the dispenser mimics an actual toy, e.g., a space gun. Most frequently, appealing heads were simply added to the tops of the standard rectangular containers.

PEZ carefully guards its design and production information. As a result, collectors differ on important questions such as dating and numbers of variations. Further complicating the issue is PEZ production outside the United States. A company in Linz, Austria, with PEZ rights to the rest of the world, including Canada, frequently issues PEZ containers with heads not issued by PEZ Candy, Inc., an independent privately owned company which by agreement manufactures and markets PEZ only in the United States.

PEZ Candy, Inc., is located in Connecticut.

The American and Austrian PEZ companies use a common agent to manage the production of dispensers. The result is that occasionally the same container is issued by both companies. However, when this occurs, the packaging may be entirely different.

PEZ Candy, Inc., issues generic, seasonal, and licensed-character containers. Container design is continually evaluated and upgraded. The Mickey Mouse container has been changed more than a dozen times.

Today PEZ candy is manufactured at plants in Austria, Hungary, Yugoslavia, and the United States. Previously, plants had been located in Czechoslovakia, Germany, and Mexico. Dispensers are produced at plants in Austria, China, Hong Kong, Hungary, and Slovenia.

**References:** Richard Geary, *PEZ Collectibles*, 2nd ed., Schiffer Publishing, 1998; David Welch, *Collecting Pez*, Bubba Scrubba Publications, 1994.

**Periodical:** *PEZ Collector's News,* P.O. Box 124, Sea Cliff, NY 11579; *Positively PEZ*, 3851 Gable Lane #513, Indianapolis, IN 46208.

## Dispenser

Angel, Christmas, 1960s ................ 5.00
Baloo, Jungle Book, no feet .......... 85.00
Barney Bear, MGM cartoon character, 1980s ..................................... 20.00
Baseball Glove, 1960s ................ 110.00
Batman, black, 1985 .................... 40.00
Bouncer Beagle Boy, MOC ............ 5.00
Boy with Hat, PEZ Pal, 1960 ........ 10.00
Bride, PEZ Pal, 1960 .................. 250.00
Bugs Bunny, 1979, with feet .......... 7.50
Bullwinkle, 1960s ....................... 150.00
Camel, Melody Maker ................... 40.00
Captain America, no feet, MIP ...... 65.00
Captain Hook, Walt Disney, red stem, no feet, patent # on base ........ 45.00
Casper, yellow diecut stem, orig shipping stock ............................. 300.00
Cat, red derby, no feet ................. 95.00
Charlie Brown, frown, MIP .............. 9.00
Clown, long face, no feet ............. 85.00
Cool Cat, Warner Brothers cartoon character, 1970s ..................... 35.00
Crocodile ..................................... 5.00
Clown, Melody Maker, MOC ......... 10.00
Dalmatian ................................... 20.00
Doctor, stethoscope, incomplete ................................................ 150.00
Dog, Melody Maker ..................... 25.00
Donald Duck, no feet, patent # on base ............................................. 20.00
Donald Duck's Nephew, blue hat ... 5.00
Donkey, Melody Maker, MOC ....... 10.00

Donkey Kong Jr., premium, 1980s ............................................... 200.00
Droopy Dog ................................. 5.00
Dumbo ....................................... 25.00
Elephant ...................................... 5.00
Fozzie Bear, Sesame Street, 1991 ................................................. 2.00
Frog, Melody Maker ..................... 30.00
Goofy, no feet, MIP ..................... 25.00
Gyro ............................................ 5.00
Happy Bear, circus, 1970s .......... 10.00
Hippo .......................................... 5.00
Hulk, no feet, MIP ...................... 35.00
Icee Bear, lavender stem ............. 10.00
Indian Chief ............................... 150.00
Jerry ............................................ 5.00
King Louie .................................. 15.00
Koala ........................................... 5.00
Koala, Melody Maker ................... 30.00
Lamb, Melody Maker .................... 40.00
Lil Wolf ...................................... 15.00
Little Lulu, hand painted .............. 85.00
Little Pig, Disney, no feet ............ 25.00
Lion .............................................. 7.50
Maharaja, no feet, patent # on base ................................................. 45.00
Mary Poppins, floppy hat ............ 800.00
Mexican, one earring .................. 140.00
Mickey, no feet, patent # on base ................................................. 20.00
Monkey, Melody Maker ................ 25.00
Moo Moo Cow, Kooky Zoo, 1960s ................................................. 25.00
Mopsy, Beatrix Potter, Eden, 1972 ................................................. 30.00
Mowgli ....................................... 18.00
Octopus, orange and black .......... 75.00
Orange, crazy fruit, 1970s ........... 40.00
Panda, Melody Maker, MOC ........ 10.00
Panther, Kooky Zoo, 1970s ......... 40.00
Papa ............................................ 5.00
Parrot, Melody Maker, MOC ........ 10.00
Penguin, Melody Maker, MOC ..... 10.00
Pineapple, crazy fruit, 1970s ...... 200.00
Pirate, Pez Pal, 1960 ................. 25.00
Pluto, moveable ears ................... 10.00
Policeman, Pez Pal, c1979 .......... 15.00
Popeye, removable pipe, no feet, MIP ................................................. 65.00
Practical Pig, no feet, patent # on base ............................................. 25.00
Raven, Kooky Zoo, 1970s ........... 12.00
Rhino, Melody Maker, MOC ......... 10.00
Roadrunner, Melody Maker, MOC ................................................. 15.00
Robot, blue, 3-1/2" h, c1950 ....... 75.00
Santa Claus, painted eyes ............ 5.00
Sheik, no feet, patent # on base ................................................. 45.00
Silly Clown, 1970s ..................... 25.00
Smurf ........................................... 5.00
Smurfette ..................................... 5.00
Space Gun ................................. 150.00
Spaceman, full body, 1950s ........ 90.00
Spider-Man, no feet .................... 15.00
Spike ........................................... 5.00
Stewardess, Pez Pal, 1960 ......... 40.00
The Flash, hand painted .............. 85.00
Thor, black stem ........................ 350.00
Tom, multiple piece head ............ 10.00
Tuffy, multiple piece head ........... 10.00
Webbly, MOC ............................... 5.00
Winnie the Pooh .......................... 20.00

Wounded Soldier, Bicentennial, 1976 ................................................. 75.00
Yappy Dog, Kooky Zoo, 1970s ..... 80.00
Yosemite Sam .............................. 5.00
Zorro, Disney, 1960s
**Other**
Brochure, fold-out poster, Bicentennial, Happy Birthday America ....... 195.00
Clicker, 1-1/2" l, tin litho, PEZ Girl, stamped "W. Germany," worn .... 60.00
Flag, paper, duck ......................... 18.00
Flyer
    Circus dispensers adv ............. 75.00
    Golden Pez ............................. 70.00
Lapel Pin, 1950 ......................... 100.00
Luggage Tag, laminated ............. 10.00
Mask
    Hulk, logo ................................ 22.00
    Spider-Man, logo .................... 20.00
Outfit
    Cowgirl, MOC ........................... 5.00
    Nurse, MOC .............................. 5.00
    Robin Hood, MOC ..................... 5.00
    Santa, MOC .............................. 5.00
Vehicle, German, 1970s
    Crane Truck ............................ 30.00
    Dump Bed, small ....................... 3.00
    Flatbed with cars .................... 45.00
    Ladder Truck ........................... 30.00
    Stakebed Truck, large, license plate ................................................. 45.00
    Tanker .................................... 30.00

# Phoenix Bird China

**Collecting Hints:** Within this particular design of primarily blue and white Japanese chinaware, there are more than 500 different shapes and sizes, and more than 100 different factory marks that have been cataloged. The pieces vary greatly, not only in the quality of chinaware itself—from very thick to eggshell thin—but also in design execution, even the shades of blue vary from powder blue to deep cobalt. All of these factors, as well as condition, should be considered when determining prices. Especially important is the border width of the design, "superior" widths are preferred over the more common, narrower border. Another important consideration is that pieces with "Japan" appearing below the cherry blossom mark generally have a better-quality print and also were made in some of the more unique shapes.

Note that the Phoenix Bird's body is facing *forward* while its head is facing *back over its wings*, that is, the head looks opposite the direction the body is facing. Occasionally, on one side of a rounded piece, such as a creamer, sugar, or teapot, the phoenix's stance is reversed, but this is not the norm. Note, too, the phoenix always has at least four and no more than seven spots on its chest, and its wings are spread out and upward.

Green and white pieces are *very rare*. Do not confuse the Phoenix Bird pattern with the Flying Dragon design that does, in fact, come in either green and white or blue and white. Multicolored Phoenix Bird pieces are also rare and these oddities are generally carelessly painted, not the usual high-quality of the blue and white examples. Another pattern that can be confused with Phoenix Bird is Flying Turkey. The latter design was more often hand-painted while Phoenix Bird was generally decorated by transfer printing. Furthermore, Flying Turkey has a heart-like border with a dot inside each heart. The few pieces of Phoenix Bird with this border, rather than the "cloud & mountain" (C/M) border are referred to as HO-O and rarely have a mark.

Because there are so many different shapes available, buying Phoenix Bird sight unseen can be risky. Insist on a sketch of the shape or a photocopy of the actual piece if at all possible—flat pieces copy well—but a photograph is best. Also ask for the dimensions as well as the mark on the bottom. The latter will sometimes give you a clue as to the quality of the piece.

**History:** The manufacture of the Phoenix Bird design began in the late 19th century, and pieces were marked "Nippon" from 1891-1921. Large quantities of this ware were imported into the United States from the 1920s through the 1940s. A smaller amount went into a few European countries and are so marked, each in their own way. The vast majority of Phoenix Bird was of the transfer-print variety; hand-painted pieces with Japanese characters underneath are rare.

The pattern was primarily sold, retail, through Woolworth's 5 & 10¢ stores. It could also be ordered, wholesale, from the catalogs of Butler Brothers and the Charles William Stores in New York. However, only the most basic shapes were offered through the catalogs. The pattern was also carried by A. A. Vantine Company, New York. The products, which were exported by Morimura Brothers, Japan, were known at that time as Blue Howo Bird China. Morimura used two different marks: "Japan" below a convex "M" under two crossed branches or "Made in Japan" beneath a concave "M" inside a wreath with an open bottom.

Phoenix Bird pieces could also be acquired as premiums. A simple breakfast set could be obtained by selling a particular number of subscriptions to *Needlecraft* magazine. During the early 1900s, two different brands of coffee and tea included a cup and saucer with purchase, and some pieces were available as premiums into the 1930s.

While no ads have yet been found, three-piece tea sets (teapot, creamer, and sugar) in children's play sets, were made at some point in time. To date, six different sets have been cataloged, along with small cups, saucers, and plates.

There are several other patterns which are considered to be in the phoenix family: Flying Turkey (an all-over pattern that was hand-painted or transfer-printed), Twin Phoenix (a Noritake border-only pattern), Howo (a Noritake all-over pattern), Flying Dragon (available in blue and white and green and white, and marked with six Japanese characters), and Firebird (the bird's tail flows downward; usually hand-painted and character-marked). Most Japanese potteries were destroyed during World War II making it difficult to trace production of these related patterns.

Two different styles of coffeepots and after-dinner cups and saucers, as well as child-size and adult size cups and saucers, have been found marked "Made in Occupied Japan" and/or "Maruta." Myott, Son & Company copied Phoenix Bird in England around 1936 and named the pattern Satsuma. These earthenware pieces do not have the same intense blue of the Japanese-made wares

**References:** Joan Collett Oates, *Phoenix Bird Chinaware*, Books I-IV, 1984-1989, published by author (685 S. Washington, Constantine, MI 49042).

**Periodical:** *Phoenix Bird Discoveries* (*PBDs*), 685 S. Washington, Constantine, MI 49042.

**Museums:** Alice Brayton House, Green Animals Topiary Gardens, Newport, RI; Charles A. Lindberg Home, Little Falls, MN; Historic Cherry Hill, Albany, NY; Huntingdon County Historical Society, Huntingdon, PA; Laura Ingalls-Wilder/Rose Lane Historic Home, Mansfield, MO; Majestic Castle (Casa Loma), Toronto, Canada; W. H. Stark House, Orange, TX; Val-Kill Cottage, Hyde Park, NY.

**Reproduction Alert:** Approximately 20 pieces of Phoenix Bird were produced in the late 1960s; these are now called Post-1970 Phoenix Bird. They are not reproductions, as such, because the pieces are not identical to nor of the same shape as earlier Phoenix Bird. Generally, these later pieces do not have a backstamp, although they did originally come with a "JAPAN" sticker that could be easily removed. Distinguishing characteristics of the newer wares are a milk-white rather than a grayish body, sparsity of design, especially near the bottom, and a more brilliant blue color in the designs.

Takahashia Imports, California, created a new style of "Phnx" (their term) that has been on the market since the late 1970s and was featured in gift catalogs in the 1980s. The phoenix itself is different on these blue and white porcelain pieces and the wares have no border design, making it easy to distinguish them from true Phoenix Bird. Phnx is a unique pattern in its own right and has been purchased by many Phoenix Bird collectors as conversation pieces. Some Takahashi pieces come with a blue backstamp, but most were originally marked with a round, gold sticker naming the firm. Collectors call it "T-Bird," for short.

**Advisor:** Joan Collett Oates.

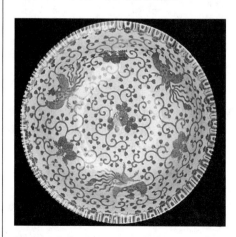

**Bowl, marked "Japan/T" in flower, 10" d, 2-5/8" h, $20.**

**Hot water pot #4, mark #17, 5-3/4" h, $48.**

**Note:** Since there are several different shapes within some categories of Phoenix Bird, the various shapes are given a style number in the listings below. This numbering system corresponds to that used in the books by Joan Collett Oates.

| | |
|---|---|
| Candy/Nut Tub | 25.00 |
| Cereal Bowl | 15.00 |
| Chocolate Pot (#1) | 145.00 |
| Coaster | 230.00 |
| Coffee Pot, "A," post-1970 | 45.00 |

Cup and Saucer
| | |
|---|---|
| Adult (#3) | 15.00 |
| After-dinner (#4) | 18.00 |
| Children's | 15.00 |

| | |
|---|---|
| Chocolate (#1) | 22.00 |
| Eggcup, double cup | 15.00 |
| Gravy Ladle, #1 | 65.00 |
| Gravy Tureen, cover, attached underplate (#2) | 130.00 |
| Jam/Jelly Jar | 55.00 |
| Marmalade Spoon | 15.00 |

Plate
| | |
|---|---|
| Dinner, 9-3/4" d | 48.00 |
| Grille, sectional | 52.00 |
| Luncheon, 8-1/2" d | 20.00 |
| Tea/toast, round, no cup | 30.00 |

Platter, oval, plain edge
| | |
|---|---|
| 14" l | 110.00 |
| 17" l | 185.00 |
| Soup Dish, 7-1/4" d | 35.00 |
| Sugar Basin, extra large | 85.00 |
| Syrup Pitcher (#5) | 28.00 |

Teapot
| | |
|---|---|
| #3, fat/squatty | 45.00 |
| #4, fat/round | 55.00 |
| Toothpick Holder (#3) | 45.00 |

# Pig Collectibles

**Collecting Hints:** Bisque and porcelain pig items from late 19th-century European potters are most widely sought by collectors. Souvenir items should have decals which are in good condition; occasionally the gilding wears off from rubbing or washing.

**History:** Historically, the pig has been important as a source of food and has also been an economic factor in rural areas of Europe and America. It was one of the first animals imported into the American colonies. A fatted sow was the standard gift to a rural preacher on his birthday or holiday.

As a decorative motif, the pig gained prominence with the figurines and planters made in the late 19th century by English, German, and Austrian potters. These "pink" porcelain pigs with green decoration were popular souvenir or prize items at fairs and carnivals or could be purchased at five-and-dime stores.

Many pig figurines were banks, and by the early 20th century "Piggy Bank" became a synonym for coin bank. When tourist attractions became popular along America's coasts and in the mountain areas, many of the pig designs showed up as souvenir items with gilt decals identifying the area.

The pig motif appeared on the advertising items associated with farm products and life. Movie cartoons introduced Porky Pig and Walt Disney's "Three Little Pigs."

In the late 1970s, pig collectibles caught fire again. Specialty shops selling nothing but pig-related items were found in the New England area. In a 1981 issue, *Time* magazine devoted a page and a half to the pig phenomena.

**Reproduction Alert:** Reproductions of three German-style painted bisque figurines have been spotted in the market. They are pig by outhouse, pig playing piano, and pig poking out of large purse. The porcelain is much rougher and the green is a darker shade.

**Additional Listings:** Cartoon Characters, Disneyana.

**Advisor:** Mary Hamburg.

Bank
| | |
|---|---|
| Pig poking out of drum | 110.00 |
| Small pig holding black binoculars | 105.00 |
| Barometer | 105.00 |
| Crock, 3" h, small pig, orange seal | 95.00 |
| Dice, with large pig | 110.00 |

Figure
| | |
|---|---|
| Canoe, single gold pig in yellow canoe, 1930s | 75.00 |
| Chef Pig, frying pan basket in back, 3-1/2" h | 115.00 |
| Engaged, pig looking in outhouse | 100.00 |
| Forty Winks, fat pig on pillow | 90.00 |
| Large pig in front of house | 85.00 |
| Large sleeping pig, holding black camera case | 105.00 |
| Mama pig and piglet looking over carrots, "Let Me Also Have Some Mother," 2" h, 3" w | 95.00 |
| Mama pig holding piglet in blue blanket, looking at small rabbit, 4-1/4" w | 95.00 |

**Sauceboat and shaped underplate, Kiku outside of sauce (6" x 2-1/2" h x 2-1/2" w), cutout on underplate (7" x 6"), neither piece is marked; superior quality, #1-A, book 1, $125. Photo courtesy of Joan C. Oates.**

Pig at water trough, along side tree, 3-1/2" h .................................. 95.00
Pig along side newspaper stand ........................................................ 95.00
Pig beside large basket ......... 100.00
Pig beside open coin bag, gold coins falling out ...................... 100.00
Pig driving old car ................. 105.00
Pig holding bags of money, "My System" ................................... 110.00
Pig in cradle ............................ 80.00
Pig in small open buggy .......... 85.00
Pig looking in mirror, trimmed in pink ...................................... 115.00
Pig on sled ............................... 95.00
Pig sitting on end of bellows .... 95.00
Pig swinging on tree, large white pig looking, "Mind How You Fall," 3-3/4" h ........................................... 100.00
Pig with bag, bisque ............... 80.00
Pig with red lobster pulling let ........................................... 110.00
Pig with wheel barrow, pipe, 5-1/2" w ........................................... 100.00
Small pig in tub ....................... 95.00
Small pig pulling cart ............. 105.00
This Little Pig Went To Market, pig holding basket, 3" h ............... 110.00
Two pigs playing cards, "Hearts are Trumps," 3-1/2" h, 3-3/4" w ..... 105.00
Inkwell, 3" h, pink pig sitting on top of inkwell ....................................... 95.00
Match Holder
  Large bisque pink pig with "Scratch My Back," small pig with "Me Too," 5" w ...................................... 110.00
  Pig holding flag, 2 black kids in boat, striker on match holder .......... 400.00
Match Safe
  Pig standing next to match safe, orange seal ........................... 100.00
  Pink pig poking head through fence, 4-1/2" w ................................... 95.00
Pin Dish
  4-3/4" w, 3-1/2" h, older couple pink pigs, top hat, green bow tie, umbrella, yellow bonnet and bow, "Grandma" on dish ................ 125.00
  5" w, large yellow and green horseshoe, pink pig, stamped "Made in Germany" ............................... 90.00
Salt Dish
  Casino Wash, fat pig, 2 dishes ........................................... 100.00
  Chef pig with shamrocks, salt cellars on each side, 4-1/4" h ........... 110.00
  Three little pigs around water trough, 2-1/2" h ................................. 75.00
  Two pigs along side bucket, stamped "Made in Germany," 3-1/2" h ..... 70.00
Shoe
  Child's, green, pig sitting inside ........................................... 85.00
  Lady's, green, single pink pig, 4-1/2" l ........................................... 90.00
Souvenir, stamped "Made in Germany"
  3" h, gold pig sitting along side well, orange top, Souvenir of Chicago, I.L., 1930s ................................ 75.00
  3" w, two pigs, Souvenir of Watertown, N.Y. ................................. 90.00
Toothpick Holder
  2-1/2" h, small and large pig in front of open mushroom ................... 95.00

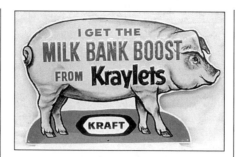

**Sign, Kraft, metal, 11-1/2" h, 18-1/2" l, $95.**

2-3/4" h, two little pigs in front of egg ........................................... 75.00
3" h, pig with mug in hand, leaning on fence ................................... 75.00
3-1/4" l, pink pig pushing wheel barrow, worn ................................... 65.00
3-3/4" h, pig with racquet, "Lawn Tennis" ................................... 85.00
4" h, 3 large pigs in front of water trough ...................................... 80.00
Vase, 7-1/4" l, red devil's arm around pink pig, sitting on log .......... 110.00

# Pinball Machines

**Collecting Hints:** Cosmetic condition is of paramount importance. Graphics are unique to specific models, especially backglass and playfield plastics, making replacements scarce. Because they are complex, graphics are difficult, if not impossible, to repair. Prices in this listing are for games in working condition that are considered cosmetically good and have 95% or more of backglass decoration present.

Some wear is expected in pinballs as a sign that the game was a good one, but bare wood detracts from overall condition. Watch for signs of loose ink on the rear of the glass. Unrestorable games with good cosmetics are valuable because they can be used to help restore other games. A non-working game is worth 30-40% less than a working one.

Add 10% if the paper items, such as score card, instruction card, and schematic, are present and in good condition. It is fair to suggest that regardless of mechanical condition, a game in good cosmetic condition is worth roughly twice that of the same game in poor cosmetic condition.

Pinball collecting is a new hobby which is still developing. It can be started inexpensively, but requires space to maintain. The tremendous diversity of models made has prevented the market from becoming well developed. There are relatively few people who restore antique pinball machines and then sell them. Expect to buy games in non-working condition and learn to repair them yourself.

**History:** Pinball machines can be traced back to the mid-1700s. However, it was not until Gottlieb introduced Baffle Ball in 1931, during the Depression, that pinball machines caught on and became a popular and commercial success because people were hungry for something novel and for the opportunity to make money. Pinball machines offered both. The first games were entirely mechanical, cost about $20, and were produced in large numbers—25,000 to 50,000 machines of the same model were not uncommon.

Pinball developments include:
1932-addition of legs
1933-electric, at first using batteries
1936-addition of bumpers
1947-advent of flippers
1950-kicking rubbers
1953-score totalers
1954-multiple players
1977-solid-state electronics

The size of the machines changed over the years. The early countertops were 16 by 32 inches. Later models were freestanding with the base measuring 21 by 52 inches and the back box, 24 by 30 inches.

Most pinballs were made in Chicago. Major manufacturers were Gottlieb, Williams, and Bally.

The total number of pinball models that have been manufactured has not been precisely determined. Some suggest more than 10,000 different models from 200-plus makers. After 1940 most models were produced in quantities of 500 to 2,000; occasionally, games had production figures as high as 10,000. Pinball machines have always enjoyed a high attrition rate. New models made the most money and were introduced by several of the major manufacturers at the rate of one entirely new model every three weeks during the mid-1940s and 1950s. Today new models are introduced at a slower rate, averaging four to six new games per year.

Most pinball owners used the older games for spare parts to repair newer models. Earning life was less than three years in most markets.

Many games were warehoused or destroyed to keep them from competing with the newest games. At the very least, the coin mechanisms were removed before the game was sold.

Pinball art is part of the popular culture and the kinetic art movement. The strength of their pinball playfield design made D. Gottlieb & Co. the premier maker through the 1950s and into the 1970s. During the 1960s, their fame grew because of their animated backglasses, which both amused and attracted players. The combination of animation and availability make the 1960s machines a target for collectors.

The advent of solid-state games in 1977, coupled with the video-game boom, dramatically changed the pinball-machine market. Solid-state game production increased as manufacturers attempted to replace all obsolete electromechanical games. Initially, Bally was the predominant maker, but Williams has since attained this position. Although solid-state games made electromechanical ones commercially obsolete, collectors who are rediscovering the silver ball are helping the pinball machine recover some of its popularity.

**References:** Richard Bueschel, *Collector's Guide to Vintage Coin Machines*, Schiffer Publishing, 1995; —, *Encyclopedia of Pinball: Contact to Bumper, 1934-1936, Vol. 2,* Silverball Amusements, 1997; Heribert Eiden and Jurgen Lukas, *Pinball Machines*, Schiffer Publishing, 1992, 1997 value update; Bill Kurtz, *Arcade Treasures*, Schiffer Publishing, 1994—, *Slot Machines and Coin-Op Games*, Chartwell Books, 1991; Donald Mueting and Robert Hawkins, *Pinball Reference Guide*, Mead Co., 1979.

**Periodicals:** *Coin Drop International*, 5815 W 52nd Ave., Denver, CO 80212; *Coin Slot*, 4401 Zephyr St., Wheat Ridge, CO 80033; *Coin-Op Classics*, 17844 Toiyabe St., Fountain Valley, CA 92708; *Gameroom*, 1014 Mt. Tabor Rd., New Albany, IN 47150; *PinGame Journal*, 31937 Olde Franklin Dr., Farmington Hills, MI 48334; *Pinhead Classified*, 1945 N. St., Suite 111, Newman, CA 95360; *Pinball Trader*, P.O. Box 1795, Campbell, CA 95009.

**Notes:** Pinballs are listed by machine name and fall into various classifications: novelty with no awards; replay, which awards free game; add-a-ball, which awards extra balls instead of games; and bingo, where players add additional coins to increase the odds of winning. Some payout games made in the mid- to late 1930s paid out coins for achieving scoring objectives. After the first add-a-ball games in 1960, many game designs were issued as both replay and add-a-ball, with different game names and slight modifications to the game rules, but similar art work.

**Advisor:** Bob Levy.

**Bally**

1933, Airway, first mechanical scoring ............................................. 350.00
1951, Coney Island, bingo ......... 400.00
1963, Moon Shot, replay ............. 300.00
1968
   Rock Makers, replay, unusual playfield ........................................ 300.00
   Safari, replay ......................... 275.00
1973, Nip-It, ball grabber ........... 225.00
1975, Bon Voyage, replay .......... 275.00
1978, Lost World, electronic ....... 350.00

**Chicago Coin**

1948, Spinball, spinner action .... 175.00
1974, Gin, replay ........................ 175.00
**Exhibit**, 1941, Big Parade, patriotic theme, classic art .................. 450.00

**Genco**

1937, Cargo .............................. 375.00
1949, Black Gold, replay ........... 325.00

**Gottlieb**

1936, Daily Races, 1-ball............ 375.00
1948, Buccaneer, replay, mirrored graphics................................. 350.00
1950, Just 21, tunnel shooter ..... 325.00
1958, Duette, replay, first 2-player ............................................. 325.00
1956, Auto Race, replay ............. 350.00
1965, Cow Poke, animation classic ............................................. 475.00
1967, King of Dinosaurs, replay, roto ............................................. 375.00
1968, Spin-a-Card, replay .......... 300.00
1971, Roller Coaster, replay, multi-level ............................................. 325.00
1977, Target Alpha, multi-player. 350.00
1981, Black Hole, electronic, multi-level ............................................. 475.00
**Mills Novelty Co.,** 1932, Official, push-button ball lift ........................ 350.00
**Pacific Amusement**, 1934, Lite-A-Line, first light-up backboard ......... 400.00

**Rock-Ola**

1932, Juggle Ball, countertop, road ball manipulator ........................... 300.00
1935, flash, early free play ......... 325.00

**United**

1948, Caribbean, replay............. 225.00
1951, ABC, first bingo ............... 400.00

**Williams**

1948, Yanks, baseball theme, animated ............................................. 400.00
1953, Army-Navy, replay, reel scoring ............................................. 300.00
1958, Gusher, disappearing bumper ............................................. 375.00
1961, Metro, replay.................... 225.00
1964, Palooka, add-a-ball ......... 400.00
1967, Touchdown, animated ...... 250.00
1972, Olympic Hockey, replay . 275.090
1973, Travel Time, timed play..... 225.00
1977, Grand Prix, replay............. 350.00
1980, Firepower, electronic ........ 450.00

# Pin-Up Art

**Collecting Hints:** Try to collect calendars that are intact. There is a growing practice among dealers to separate calendar pages, cut off the date information, and sell the individual sheets in hopes of making more money. Buyers are urged not to support this practice.

Concentrate on the work of one artist. Little research has been done on the pinup artists so it is a wide open field. The original art on which calendar sheets and magazine covers are based has begun to appear on the market. High prices are being asked for both the oil paintings and pastel examples, but the market is not yet stabilized—beware!

Pinup material can be found in many other collectible categories. Usually the items are referred to as "girlies." Many secondary pinup items are not signed, but a collector can easily identify an artist's style.

**History:** Charles Dana Gibson introduced the first true pinup girl when he created the Gibson Girl in the early 1900s. Other artists who followed his example included Howard Chandler Christy, Coles Phillips, and Charles Sheldon. The film magazines of the 1920s, such as *Film Fun* and *Real Screen Fun*, developed the concept further. Their front covers featuring minimally clad beauties were designed to attract a male readership.

During the 1930s popular cover artists included Charles Sheldon, Cardwell Higgins, and George Petty. Sheldon did calendar art as well as covers for Brown & Bigelow. *Esquire* began in 1933; its first Petty gatefold appeared in 1939.

The golden age of pinup art was 1935 to 1955. The 1940s brought Alberto Vargas (the final "s" was dropped at *Esquire's* request), Gillete Elvgren, Billy DeVorss, Joyce

Ballantyne, and Earl Moran into the picture. Pinup art appeared everywhere—magazine covers, blotters, souvenir items, posters, punchboards, etc. Many artists besides those mentioned here adopted the style.

Photographic advertising and changing American tastes ended the pinup reign by the early 1960s.

**References:** Max Allen Collins and Drake Elvgren, *Elvgren: His Life & Art,* Collectors Press, 1998; Denis C. Jackson, *Price and Identification Guide to Alberto Vargas and George Petty,* 2nd ed., published by author (P.O. Box 1958, Sequim, WA 98382), 1987; —, *Price and Identification Guide to Coles Philips,* published by author (P.O. Box 1958, Sequim, WA 98382), 1986; —, *The Price & ID Guide to Pin-Ups & Glamour Art,* TICN, 1996; Charles G. Martignette and Louis K. Meisel, *The Great American Pin-Up,* taschen, 1996; Leland and Crystal Payton, *Girlie Collectibles,* Martin's Griffin, 1996; *Pinup Poster Book,* Collectors Press, 1995; Norman I. Platnick, *Coles Phillips,* published by author (50 Brentwood Rd., Bayshore, NY 11706) 1996.

**Periodicals:** *Glamour Girls: Then and Now,* P.O. Box 34501, Washington, DC 20043; *The Illustrator Collector's News,* P.O. Box 1958, Sequim, WA 98382.

Blotter, 3-1/2" x 6", cardboard, full color sgd art by Rolf Armstrong, blond haired nude seated at edge of pond waters, 1935 Brown & Bigelow©, unused ................................... 45.00
Box, 4-1/4" x 4-1/4" x 1-3/4", red and white, color graphics of high heeled smiling girl, bow and arrow, large red heart background, logo "Hit For His Heart," Pioneer Belts, c1940 ..... 28.00
Calendar
  1942, Esquire, Varga Girl, plastic spiral binding, 12 pgs, horizontal format, verses by Phil Stack, 8-1/2" x 12" ........................................... 75.00
  1945, Starlight, Earl Moran, full color nude blond, dark green drape, black ground ..................................... 40.00
  1948, Esquire Glamour Gallery, paper wall type, full color pin-up art for each month, contributing artists include Ben-Hur Baz, Fritz Willis, Joe DeMers, Al Moore, J Frederick Smith, Ron Wicks, 8-1/2" x 12" ..................... 65.00
  1951, Esquire, desk type, Al Moore graphics, 12 pgs, 5-1/2" x 6" .... 38.00
  1952, Thompson Studio, sketches, orig envelope ........................... 50.00

**Calendar, Marilyn Monroe, 1954/55, $3,644. Photo courtesy of Auction Team Breker.**

Coaster, 3-1/4" d, litho tin, full color pin-up art, faint lettering "Ray Raedel," orange rim, from 1960 PA Fireman's Convention, price for 5 pc set .... 75.00
Date Book, 5" x 7", Esquire, color cover, spiral binding, full color pin-up photos, 1943 ©George Hurrell ....... 35.00
Greeting Card
  Christmas, illus of Bettie Page, by Olivia ........................................... 8.50
  Happy Birthday, illus of Bettie Page, by Olivia ................................... 7.50
  Wedding, Varga bride, 5-1/2" x 8", blank int. .................................... 9.00
Hair Pin, orig 4" x 5-1/2" yellow, red, black, and white card, Petty, artist sgd, 1948, MOC ..................... 25.00
Illusion Card, Polly Peel, 3-1/2" x 4-1/2" thin white cardboard, two plain white cardboard stripes to be separated and inserted between acetate layers of picture, model undresses as stripe cards are inserted or removed, 1940s ..................................... 35.00
Keychain, Elvgren insert, 1-1/2" x 2", slotted plastic case, full color insert, metal keychain, c1950
  A Hitch In Time, girl adjusting stocking as dog looks on ................. 35.00
  Belle Ringer, girl doing laundry, skirt caught in ringer ...................... 25.00
  Look What I've Got, leggy girl fishing ..................................................... 25.00
  See-Worthy, leggy girl boating ..................................................... 25.00
Magazine
  *Esquire,* June, 1942, Jane Russell centerfold by Petty, anti-Nazi theme ..................................................... 60.00
  *Prevue,* Jan 1953, Marilyn Monroe cov, article ................................. 35.00
Magazine Tear Sheet, Kentucky Club, 1956 ........................................... 6.00

**Match Book Cover, George Petty artist, Superior Match Co., Martin Tavern, Chicago, each $5.**

Notepad, Gil Elvgren cov, adv Deltronix, each titled and sgd, unused, 4" x 6-1/2"
  Budding Out ............................. 6.00
  Stepping Out ............................. 5.00
  Waiting Long? ........................... 5.00
  Wrong Nail ............................... 5.00
Novelty, Talking Wolf, mechanical head, 5-1/2" x 6" black, white, and red diecut display box, cover art of pretty girl holding full dimensioned 3" cream colored caricature of wolf head, panting tongue, bow tie, tuxedo jacket, small lapel flower, says "Hello Sweetheart" when activated, Noma Electric Corp., early 1950s ................................. 70.00
Pocket Knife, 4" l, silvered steel, single blade, black and white cello side panel insert photos, one with full figure nude, holding garment, similar photo on other side, knife blade mkd "U.S.A.," c1940s ..................... 35.00
Post Card, 3-1/2" x 5-1/2", hand tinted, Mexican, unused ........................ 8.00
Print
  Moran, Dreamin, 15-1/2" x 15-1/2", minor flaws, matted ............... 125.00
  Mozert, Zoe, calendar top, Sweet Dreams, framed, 16" x 20" ..... 300.00
  Munson, each titled and sgd, wood frame, 10" x 12"
    Doc Said All I Needed Was Glasses ........................... 110.00
    Don't You Just L-O-O-OVE These Cushions ........................... 95.00
    Oh You Do Remember My Voice ........................................... 95.00
    Shall I Turn Around? ......... 115.00
  Withers of Hollywood, artist and models, 1952 ......................... 225.00
Sample Calendar, wall type
  Armstrong, 11" x 23", full color art sgd by Rolf Armstrong, brunette model, red and white 2 pc swimsuit, titled "Tip Top," text for Brown & Bigelow, St. Paul, Minn., calendar for March, 1951 ........................... 75.00
  Frahm Art, 16" x 33", art print titled "Spare?" 1958 copyright of A. Fox,

credit line to artist Arthur E. Frahm, blond bowler, calendar for January 1960 .......................................... 85.00

Stand-Up Card, 4-3/4" x 10" diecut cardboard, perforations for folding to form model figure standing on triangular display, full color Moran art, titled "Not So Dusty" pretty brunette in sheer green cleaning outfit, high heels, c1950, unused .............. 15.00

Trade Card, comic images, synopsis of artist work on back of card

#13, I Never Get Things Straight, Joyce Ballantyne ........................ 4.50
#28, Tail Wind, Gil Elvgren ......... 4.50
#29, How'd You Like to Hold My Hand, Zoe Mozert ...................... 4.50
#31, Construction Sight, Scott Pike .................................................. 4.50

# Planters

**Collecting Hints:** Planters are available in a wide array of shapes and colors. Seek out the best examples available. Because many planters were made inexpensively and meant to be used with dirt, water, and growing plants, it is not unusual to find wear and minor interior scratches and damage.

Collectors of modern planters should carefully save any packaging or brochures which illustrate the planter. The brochures issued as sales promotions by florists will become the advertising collectibles of tomorrow. Collectors of specialty planters should check to make sure all decorations are included, e.g., ladies' heads should be complete with original necklaces and earrings.

Collectors should be careful to determine that the object is a true planter and not a mismatched canister or vase that has been home to a plant.

**History:** As soon as houseplants became an important part of interior decoration, planters were created. Some planters are simply vessels given a new lease on life, such as crock or chamber pot. Other items, such as jardinieres, window boxes, and hanging baskets were designed specially to hold growing materials. Many manufacturers created these interesting shapes and colors to compliment not only the plant but also the interior design of the room where it was placed.

Like cookie jars, wonderful figural planters were created in the 1940s and have continued to present times. Many major companies, such as McCoy and Roseville, created an inexpensive line of planters for use by florists. Some of these same planters are now eagerly sought by collectors. Florists have learned this valuable lesson, and today planters issued by organizations like FTD are dated.

Some planters, such as the popular ladies' heads, were made by small firms and were distributed regionally. These charming figural planters give a wonderful perspective on the fashion and colors that were popular at the time of their manufacture.

**References:** Kathleen Cole, *Encyclopedia of Head Vases*, Schiffer Publishing, 1996; Betty and Bill Newbound, *Collector's Encyclopedia of Figural Planters & Vases*, Collector Books, 1997; —, *Collector's Encyclopedia of Wall Pockets, Identification an Values*, Collector Books, 1996, 1998 value update; Mike Posgay and Ian Warner, *World of Head Vase Planters*, The Glass Press, 1992; Mary Zavada, *Lady Head Vases*, revised ed., Schiffer Publishing, 1994.

**Periodical:** *Head Hunter Newsletter*, Box 83H, Scarsdale, NY 10583.

**Collectors' Club:** Wall Pocket Collectors Club, 1356 Tahiti, St. Louis, MO 63128.

### Figural

Auto, 9" x 4-1/2", ceramic, Birchwood line, McCoy, some wear to yellow trim ............................................ 45.00
Bambi, mkd "Walt Disney Productions" ................................................. 65.00
Basket, yellow and brown, McCoy 35.00
Birds on a Perch, four white, yellow, and black birds, brown tree branch, glossy glaze, mkd "Shawnee 502" ................................................. 35.00
Blackamoor, heavy gold trim ........ 35.00
Butterfly on Log, brown and white, glossy glaze, mkd "Shawnee USA 524" ........................................... 10.00
Cactus and Cowboy, natural colors, Morton Pottery ........................ 15.00
Cart, blue exterior, yellow interior, glossy glaze, Shawnee, mkd "USA 775" ........................................... 10.00
Cat, coral glaze, green box, McCoy, c1950 ...................................... 12.00
Cat, white, mkd "Haeger" .............. 7.50
Conch Shell, yellow and green, glossy glaze, Hull ................................ 35.00
Cradle, pink, McCoy ..................... 10.00
Dachshund, brown, glossy glaze, Hull ................................................. 75.00
Deer, pale brown and greens, glazed, unmarked ................................ 55.00
Dog, light green, white accents, McCoy ................................................. 10.00

Donkey, standing, small Mexican figure sleeping in front of legs, baskets on back, high gloss, white, 6" h ...... 9.00
Elf, sitting on large shoe, multicolored, glossy glaze, mkd "Shawnee 765" ................................................. 10.00
Fawns, standing pair, 5" x 3-1/2", McCoy, 1957 ............................ 38.00
Giraffe, 9" h, green, glossy glaze, Hull ................................................. 35.00
Globe, blue and green, yellow stand, glossy glaze mkd "Shawnee USA" ................................................. 15.00
Goat, gray, red harness, McCoy .. 15.00
Gondola, yellow, McCoy .............. 18.00
Goose, Hull, #80 ......................... 30.00
Guitar, black, semi-gloss, mkd "Red Wing USA #M-1484" ............... 15.00
Lady, two wolfhounds, Brayton Laguna, 11" h, 7-1/2" w .......................... 175.00
Lamb, white, blue bow, McCoy .... 10.00
Lion, white, McCoy, c1940 .......... 12.00
Log, 7" l, white, Niloak ................. 18.00
Mallard, head down, Royal Copley ................................................. 20.00
Mouse, leaning on cheese wedge, multicolored, glossy glaze, Shawnee, mkd "USA 705" ....................... 15.00
Parrot, 5", white, orange accents.. 18.00
Pelican, turquoise, matte glaze, McCoy, mkd " NM USA" ...................... 12.00
Piano, upright, green, glossy glaze, Shawnee, mkd "USA 528" ....... 18.00
Policeman and Donkey, 5", blue, Niloak ................................................. 35.00
Quail, 9-1/2" h, natural color spray glaze, American Art Potteries .. 25.00
Raggedy Ann, holding baby bottle, 6" h, incised "Relpo 6565" ............... 45.00
Santa Claus, fleshtone, red, and white, Morton.................................... 25.00
Scottie Dog, Royal Copley ........... 15.00
Shoe, bronzed-type, McCoy........... 8.00
Skunk, 6-1/2" h, black and white, pastel pink and blue basket, airbrushed, Brush-McCoy, #249 ................. 35.00
Snoopy, 7" h, ceramic, "Snoopy" on round planter container, paint wear on figure.................................. 40.00
Stork, McCoy ............................... 10.00

**Lamb, white, pink bow, #456D, American Art Potteries, $25. Photo courtesy of Doris & Burdell Hall.**

Swan, turquoise, purple wing tips, unmarked ................................... 7.50
Turkey, brown, red wattle, Morton. 12.00
Wally Walrus, ceramic, 1950 ........ 50.00
Whale, 10" l, black, Freeman McFarlin, .......................................................... 50.00
Wishing Well, 7-1/4" h, dusty rose, Niloak .............................................. 20.00

**Head Types**

Baby, 5-3/4" h, blond hair, open eyes, pink cheeks, open mouth, pink ruffled bonnet tied under chin, pink dress, unmkd ............................ 18.50
Black Lady, 5" h, young, downcast eyes, yellow turban, red sarong, large gold hoop earrings, three-strand pearl necklace, Japan ........................ 45.00
Cowboy, 6" h, brown hair, blue eyes, yellow hat and neckerchief, white shirt, yellow star badge, unmkd .................................................... 35.00
Girl, 5-1/4" h, long blond hair, straight bangs, blue flowers at ponytail on top of head, eyes looking right, raised hand, slender neck, blue press, Parma by AAI, Japan, A-222 .................................................... 25.00
Howdy Doody ............................. 45.00
Jackie Onaiss ........................... 350.00
Lady, 7" h, brown hair, downcast eyes, raised right hand, black hat with white and gold ribbon, black dress, white glove with gold accents, pearl drop earrings and necklace, Inarco, C-2322 ................................... 35.00
Nurse, 5-3/4" h, short blond hair, downcast eyes, raised right hand, white cap with Red Cross insignia, white uniform with gold accents, painted fingernails, unmarked ............. 45.00

**Wall Pocket**

Acorn, light brown, mkd "Frankoma 190" ........................................ 25.00
Baby and Diaper, mkd "4921, Japan" .......................................................... 15.00
Broom, inverted, mkd "L & C Ceramics ©Hollywood Hand Made" .... 25.00
Cocker Spaniel, head, mkd "Royal Copley" ...................................... 20.00
Cowboy Boot, figural, blue and white, speckled, mkd "Frankoma 133" .......................................................... 30.00
Cup and Saucer, blue, B-24 ....... 265.00
Fish, yellow stripes, mkd "Gilner Calif. C .......................................................... 25.00
Geisha Girl ................................. 70.00
Grape Cluster, mkd "Royal Haeger R-745 USA" ................................... 25.00
Harlequin heads, boy and girl, Japan .......................................................... 65.00
Horseshoe, horse head center ..... 30.00
Lily, yellow, McCoy ...................... 25.00
Peacock, mkd "West Coast Pottery, California, USA-441" ................... 45.00
Sandy and Jean, head-type, boy and girl, blue plaid shirts, minor damage, price for pr ............................... 75.00
Straw Hat, mkd "Stewart G McCullock ©Calif" ................................... 15.00
Teapot, pink apple dec, Shawnee .......................................................... 30.00

Umbrella, black, white handle, mkd "McCoy USA" ........................... 40.00
Whisk Broom, blue, B-27 ........... 265.00

# Planters Peanuts

**Collecting Hints:** Planters Peanuts memorabilia is easily identified by the famous Mr. Peanut trademark. Items made between 1906 and 1916 have the "Planters Nut And Chocolate Company" logo.

Papier-mâché, die-cut, and ceramic pieces must be in very good condition. Cast-iron and tin pieces should be free of rust and dents and have good graphics and color.

**History:** Amedeo Obici and Mario Peruzzi organized the Planters Nut And Chocolate Company in Wilkes-Barre, Pennsylvania, in 1906. Obici had conducted a small peanut business for several years and was known locally as the "Peanut Specialist."

At first, Spanish salted red skins were sold for 10¢ per pound. Soon after, Obici developed the whole, white, blanched peanut, and this product became consumers' favorite.

In 1916, a young Italian boy submitted a rough version of the now-famous monocled and distinguished Mr. Peanut as an entry in a contest held by Planters to develop a trademark. A wide variety of premium and promotional items were soon based on this character.

Planters eventually was purchased by Standard Brands, which itself later became a division of Nabisco.

**Reference:** Jan Lindenberger, *Planters Peanut Collectibles Since 1961*, Schiffer Publishing, 1995.

**Collectors' Club:** Peanut Pals, P.O. Box 4465, Huntsville, AL 35815.

Reproduction Alert.

Ashtray, 6" x 5", emb, silvered metal, 1906-56 ................................... 50.00
Bank, plastic, Mr. Peanut ............. 18.00
Beach Ball, 13" d, 7" h Mr. Peanut image, mail premium, 1970s-80s .......................................................... 24.00
Belt, orig box, "Nabisco Dinah Shore Invitational Golf Tournament, Swing into profits with Planters," blue fabric, leather belt, brass buckle with Mr. Peanut, mkd "1984" on back, MIB ........................................ 40.00
Book, *The Complete World of Planter's Mr. Peanut,* info and recipes, back mkd "Litho U.S.A. 67," 8-1/2" x 11" .......................................................... 28.00

**Container, plastic, holds one pound of peanuts, $8.50.**

Booklet, Peanut Pals, 3-1/2" x 6", 24 pgs, peanut characters Percy and Peter meet Mr. Peanut at factory, 1927© ...................................... 65.00
Bookmark, diecut, cardboard, 1920 .......................................................... 25.00
Cigarette Lighter, plastic, yellow .. 20.00
Coloring Book, 8-1/4" x 11", 32 pgs, orig letter dated June 16, 1928, Planters Nut & Chocolate Co., Wikes-Barre, PA letterhead, 9" x 12" envelope, six pgs neatly water colored, rest unused ................................... 75.00
Doll, wooden, jointed, 1930s ...... 275.00
Figure, Mr. Peanut, 6" h, flexible, 1991, Planter's Lifesavers Co ........... 15.00
Jar
  Barrel-shaped ...................... 195.00
  Six-sided .............................. 75.00
Key Chain, figural, peanut shape, tan .......................................................... 20.00
Lamp, figural, glowing Mr. Peanut .......................................................... 325.00
Magazine Tear Sheet, family walking Dalmatian, 1960 ......................... 9.00
Mechanical Pencil, blue and yellow figural Mr. Peanut on top ............. 15.00
Mug, ceramic, large, gold trim ..... 40.00
Nut Spoon, blue, red, tan, and green, price for set ............................. 28.00
Paint Book, Mr. Peanut, orig mailer, unused, 1929 ............................ 80.00
Peanut Bag, 8-1/2" h, 3-1/2" w, glassine, unused ................................... 18.00
Peanut Butter Machine, MIB ........ 50.00
Peanut Butter Spreader, red .......... 6.00
Pin, Mr. Peanut
  75th Anniversary 1906-1981, enameled ................................... 28.00
  NY World's Fair, 1-3/4" h, wooden, Mr. Peanut resting against Trylon, inscribed "1940 World's Fair," red name on top hat, Perisphere behind crossed legs ......................... 110.00
Pinback Button
  Planters Golden Jubilee, brown letters, gold litho ground, c1956.. 80.00
  Vote for Mr. Peanut, black, white, and red litho, c1940 ...................... 50.00
Salt and Pepper Shakers, pr, Mr. Peanut .......................................................... 30.00
Serving Spoon, 5-1/4" l, SP, Carlton, c1930 ................................... 15.00
Straw, 8" h, plastic, figural Mr. Peanut .......................................................... 9.50
Swizzle Stick, figural ...................... 4.25

Tab, 1-1/2" d, diecut litho metal, yellow, black, and white Mr. Peanut, 1920 ............................................... 15.00
Tin, ten pound size ........................ 65.00
Toothbrush, Mr. Peanut, yellow, MIP ............................................... 15.00
Whistle, figural ........................ 25.00

# Plastics

**Collecting Hints:** Thermoplastic collectibles can be ruined when exposed to heat, flame, or a hot-pin test.

**History:** The term "plastic" is derived from the Greek word "Plasti-kos," which means pliable. Therefore, any material which can be made pliable, and formed into a desired shape, technically falls into the category of plastic. For the collector, two categories of plastics should be recognized: natural and synthetic.

Natural plastics are organic materials which are found in nature. The most common natural plastics are tortoiseshell and cattle horn. They have been used for hundreds of years to make both utilitarian and luxury items. Natural plastics were harvested and cleaned, then softened in hot liquid. Once pliable, they were manipulated into shape by a variety of methods including carving, sawing, and press molding.

Semi-synthetic and synthetic plastics are those which are man-made from combinations of organic and/or chemical substances. The most commonly collected plastics in this category include the earliest examples: 1870—Celluloid (pyroxylin plastic), 1890—Casine (milk protein and formaldehyde), and 1907—Bakelite (phenol formaldehyde).

The years between World Wars I and II gave birth to the modern plastics age. Beetleware, a urea formaldehyde plastic with properties similar to Bakelite, was introduced in 1928. Lumarith, a trade name for cellulose acetate plastic, was introduced in 1929 and served as a nonflammable replacement for celluloid.

During the Great Depression, the plastics industry developed at an astounding rate with the introduction of acrylic and polymer plastics: Polystyrene and Poly-vinyl-chloride—PVC (1930), Methylmethacrylic (1934), Melamine (1935), and Poly-ethylene (1939). Today all of these plastics are collected in hundreds of forms.

All plastics fall into one of two categories: thermoplastic or thermoset. Thermoplastics are those which are molded by the application of heat and pressure, then cooled. Additional applications of heat will resoften or melt the material. Tor toiseshell, horn, celluloid, cellulose acetate, polystyrene, polyethylene, and acrylic fall into this category.

Thermoset plastics are those which are molded by the application of heat and pressure, then upon cooing, permanently hardened. While they are resistant to high temperatures, they are subject to cracking over time. Thermoset plastics include Bakelite, Beetleware, and Melmac.

Acrylic Plastic, introduced in 1927 by Rohm & Haas as "Prespex" or "Plexiglas," is used instead of curved glass in airplane cockpits. In 1937, Dupont introduced Lucite, a thermoplastic acrylic resin that could be either crystal clear or opaque, tinted any color and cast, carved or molded.

Bakelite is the registered trade name for the first entirely synthetic plastic. It was developed by Leo H. Baekeland in 1907 using carbolic acid and formaldehyde. Commonly called phenolic resin, Bakelite is a tough, thermoset plastic that can be cast or molded by heat and pressure.

Celluloid was the first commercially successful semi-synthetic plastic. Introduced as a denture-base material in 1970, it reigned supreme as the most versatile man-made plastic for 40 years.

**References:** Corinne Davidov and Ginny Redington Dawes, *Bakelite Jewelry Book*, Abbeville Press, 1988; Bill Hanlon, *Plastic Toys*, Schiffer Publishing, 1993; Lyngerda Kelley and Nancy Schiffer, *Plastic Jewelry*, Schiffer Publishing, 1987, 1994 value update; Karina Parry, *Bakelite Bangle Price & Identification Guide*, Krause Publications, 1999; Joan Van Patten and Elmer and Peggy Williams, *Celluloid Treasures of the Victorian Era,* Collector Books, 1999; Gregory R. Zimmer and Alvin Daigle, Jr., *Melmac Dinnerware*, L-W Book Sales, 1997.

**Museum:** National Plastic Museum, Leominster, MA.

**Advisor:** Julie P. Robinson.

## Acrylic

Bedside Stand, 3 pc twisted acrylic rod base, round glass top............ 250.00
Beverage Pitcher, clear acrylic cylinder, designed by Neal Small, 1970 ............................................... 45.00
Bracelet, 3/4" bangle, green, opaque, orig tag "Genuine Lucite" ........ 10.00
Brush and Comb, translucent pink set, nylon bristles, mkd "Dupont Lucite," orig box.................................... 15.00
Business Card Holder, sea shells suspended in rect base, c1965 ...... 6.00
Buttons, pearlescent pink squares, metal loop, set of 8 on orig card ............................................... 4.00
Clock
  Alarm, keywind, Black Forest works, octagonal translucent green case ............................................... 25.00
  Electric, chrome and Lucite, cylinder shaped, rotating disc that changes color, pink, yellow, purple, and green reflect in fact, c1970s .............. 65.00
Compact, 4" sq translucent case, applied sunburst medallion gold glitter acrylic, Roger & Gallet, mfg. by Donmark Creations, Co, 1946........................150.00
Cufflinks, pr, Krementz, toggle findings, paperweight style, fishing fly suspended in lucite........................ 35.00
Drafting Tools, Rhom & Haas Plexiglass, set of two rulers, two triangles, and semi-circle, c1940 ................... 20.00
Dress Clips, green opaque lucite, triangular, chevron design, rim set with rhinestones .............................. 18.00
Etagere, 60" h, free standing triangular shape shelf, clear acrylic with four mirror shelves, pointed finial.....550.00
Hand Mirror, beveled acrylic handle and frame, U-shaped mirror, sterling floral ornament, c1946............. 55.00
Lamp, chrome cylinder base, 3" d solid lucite ball top, flickering red, white, and blue lights in base reflect through bubbles in acrylic globe, c1976...................................... 22.00
Napkin Ring, translucent lucite, square shape, rounded edges, circular center, c1960, price for 4 pc set ...... 10.00
Paperweight
  2" x 1", rect cube, suspended purple rose............................................. 5.00
  3" cube, translucent lucite, suspended JFK 50 cent piece, c1965 ................................................... 8.00
Pin
  Apple, pink lucite, gold plated stem and leaf, Sarah Coventry, c1970 ................................................... 20.00
  Dragonfly, pearlescent green lucite wings, enamel paint over pot metal, c1960........................................ 8.00
  Turtle, jelly belly, aqua lucite center, pot metal, red painted eyes, c1950 ................................................... 12.00
Purse
Basketweave chrome, 8" x 4", clear lucite bottom, black lucite hinged to and handle, c1955.................. 55.00

Clutch, smoky gray lucite, camera case shape, hinge opening, c1950 ............................................ 45.00

Vanity
4-1/2" x 4-1/2", envelope type front, white marbleized, Elgin American ........................... 100.00
7" x 4" oblong oval, compartmentalized lid, tortoise colored, Wilardy Original ................. 145.00

Ring, sterling, square emerald green lucite jewel, c1960 .............. 85.00

Tumbler, clear 8 oz octagonal shape, chevron design, Art Deco revival, Norse Products, price for 4 pc set ............................................ 25.00

Wall Shelf, 30" x 6", translucent neon pink, 1970s ............................ 25.00

**Bakelite**

Ashtray, 8" d, black and white ...... 45.00
Bar Pin, dangling heart, bright red catalin ............................................ 150.00
Bracelet, bangle
1/2" wide, carved leaf design, red catalin, ........................................ 45.00
3/4" wide, reverse carved floral design, translucent amber ..... 150.00
Buckle, 2-1/2" w, rect, carved flower on each end, dark blue ................. 20.00
Button, 1 large, 4 small, oval, two holes, translucent amber and brown swirl, price for 5 pc set ...................... 12.00
Cake Server, green handle .......... 12.00
Chess set, butterscotch and marbleized brown ............................. 400.00
Clock, 12" h, Western Electric, Gothic shape, dark brown .................. 65.00
Crib Toy, amber, green, and orange opaque catalin, shape of girl doll, 17 separate pieces strung together ............................................ 125.00
Corn Cob Holder, diamond shaped, two prongs, red or green, price for pr ............................................ 15.00
Dominoes ...................................... 65.00
Dress Clip, triangular, chevron grooves, green, price for pr .................. 65.00
Hors d'oeuvre Pick set, square base in shape of die, 6 dice topped picks ............................................ 110.00
Manicure Box, Cleopatra, mfg. by GE, black and red Art Deco .......... 165.00
Napkin Ring, figural
Animal shape, red, green, or butterscotch ...................................... 45.00
Trylon and Perisphere, orange, green, red, and yellow, price for pr ............................................ 75.00
Pie Crimper, marbleized butterscotch handle ........................................ 4.00
Pin, figural, cat, yellow catalin, chrome ............................................ 95.00
Poker Chips, black, maroon, butterscotch, maroon holder ........... 130.00
Rattle, barbell shape, five rings, red, green, and butterscotch .......... 90.00
Ring
Dome top, floral carving, butterscotch ...................................... 75.00
Square, starburst carving, brown ............................................ 65.00
Ring Box
Clam shell style, streamline modern

grooves, orange and butterscotch swirl ............................................ 85.00
Semi-circular, hinged lift top, square base, mottled green and yellow, ............................................ 75.00
Salt and Pepper Shakers, pr
Figural brown bird shaped holder, amber shakers ...................... 120.00
Gear shape, chrome lids, marbleized caramel, 2" h .................. 85.00
Washington Monument souvenir, obelisk shape, cream colored ............................................ 65.00
Serving Tray, oval dark blue with inlaid strips of chrome, Art Deco style ............................................ 350.00
Shaving Brush and Stand, deep red, Catalin, c1940 ....................... 35.00
Stationery Box, 7" x 8", molded brown, Art Deco winged horse design, American Stationery Co., 1937 ............................................ 75.00
Telephone, Stromberg Carlson, cradle-stylo, black ............................. 50.00
Toothpick Holder, dachshund, green ............................................ 95.00
Utensil set, knife, fork, spoon, marbleized red and yellow handles .... 16.00
Yo-Yo, mottled green, mkd "Regal PDC" ............................................ 30.00

**Celluloid**

Animal
Cow, 6", purple, red rhinestone eyes, mkd "Made in Occupied Japan" ............................................ 22.00
Dog, 3", black Scottie, mkd "Made in USA" .......................................... 20.00
Horse, 7" l, cream color, brown highlights, hp eyes, intertwined VCO mark ........................................ 45.00
Bar Pin, 2-3/4" l, ivory grained, orange and brown layered pearlessence, hp rose motif ................................. 12.00
Bookmark, 4-1/2" l, cream colored diecut celluloid, poinsettia motif, Psalm 22, printed by Meek Co ................ 15.00
Bracelet, bangle, translucent amber celluloid, double row of green rhinestones ...................................... 25.00
Collar and Cuff set, Champion brand ............................................ 25.00
Collar Box, 6" x 6", olive colored, emb celluloid with floral motif, picture of beautiful woman on top .......... 45.00
Doll, 5" h, Kewpie-type, movable arms, molded clothing and cap, mkd "Made in Japan" ...................... 22.00

**Pin, celluloid, basket of flowers, green leaves, pink basket, $42.**

Dresser Set, comb, brush, mirror, tray, powder, box, and hair receiver, marked "Ivory Pyralin," price for 6 pc set .............................................. 65.00
Dresser Tray, 8" oval, imitation tortoise shell rim, glass and lace center ............................................ 35.00
Fan, 6" w, ivory colored, hp floral motif, blue satin ribbon ..................... 18.00
Haircomb, 6" l, pale amber, blue rhinestones, painted blue bird motif ............................................ 55.00
Ink Blotter Booklet, 8-1/2" l, 1-1/2" w, wood grained celluloid, black lettering, "Jennison Co., Engineers & Contractors, Fitchburg, Mass," 1917 calendar, 8" ruler markings ...... 30.00
Kewpie, 2-1/4" h, #43660, hp features, blue wings ................................. 40.00
Letter Opener, 8-1/4" l, ivory grained cream celluloid, black lettering "Smith & Nichols, 141 Milk St., Boston, WAX" ................................. 25.00
Match Safe, 2-1/4" x 1-1/2", color photo scenes from Atlantic City, NJ ............................................ 18.00
Necktie Box, 12-1/2" x 3-3/4", reverse painted Art Nouveau design, cream, brown, and coral ..................... 48.00
Picture Frame, 8" x 10", oval, ivory grained celluloid, easel back ..... 18.00
Pinback Button, 1-1/4" d, dangling 1" celluloid camel, Shriner's logo ............................................ 55.00
Pocket Mirror, 2-1/2" oval, souvenir of Niagara Falls, printed colored drawing of Falls ............................. 18.00
Purse, 4-1/4" d, clam shell-type, amber colored celluloid, leather strap ............................................ 45.00
Rattle
4" l, blue and white egg shape, white handle ...................................... 18.00
4-3/4" l, figural, little girl playing lute, pink .......................................... 45.00
Toy
2-1/2" d, roly-poly, realistic chicken, weighted base ......................... 35.00
5" h, duck in police uniform, cream and teal blue, movable legs, VCO, USA .......................................... 75.00
Vase, 8" h, conical, weighted base, translucent amber and cream pearlessence ................................. 12.00

# Playboy Collectibles

**Collecting Hints:** Antique shows typically do not offer a Playboy collector a vast selection of items to choose from and searching for them can become frustrating. Currently, Playboy collectibles are very popular and most easily obtained on the Internet. Literally thousands of listings can be found on a daily basis by searching on-line auctions.

When buying a *Playboy* magazine, who is on the cover or in a pictorial of an issue is many times more important than how old the magazine is. For the most part, there is no reason to buy a magazine if the centerfold has been removed. Having the subscription cards in tact, especially if there is a popular centerfold model on the front, will slightly add to the issue's value. Because *Playboy* has been printing over a million copies since 1955, only purchase magazines that are in fine condition or preferably better.

**History:** The first *Playboy* magazine was released in December of 1953. Owner and publisher Hugh M. (Marston) Hefner did not put a date on the cover because he was not sure if there would be another copy. Fortunately for *Playboy*, and collectors, there was at least one more copy because that issue debuted the famous Rabbit Head logo. The popular Femlin was introduced into Party Jokes section of the August,1955 magazine. She was drawn by LeRoy Neiman.

The first Playboy club opened in 1960. In just over a year, it had become the most visited night club in the world. After yielding a seemingly endless supply of ashtrays, mugs, swizzle sticks and other collectibles, the last state side club closed in 1988. Currently, *Playboy* has over 4 million subscribers and still offers its own line of merchandise.

**Advisor:** Patrick M. Leer.

Ashtray
   Clear glass, rabbit head in center, mint ............................... 12.00
   Orange, 3-3/4" x 3-3/4", Femlin logo in center, mint........................... 10.00
   Smoked black glass, 3-3/4" x 3-3/4", Femlin logo in center, mint ....... 12.00
   White, 5-5/8" x 5-5/8", black rabbit head in center, mint ................. 15.00
   White and gold, 3-3/4" x 3-3/4", VIP in center........................................ I5.00
   Yellow, 3-3/4" x 3-3/4", Femlin logo in center, mint .............................. 18.00
Cigarette Lighter
   Playboy Bunny, George Petty, Zippo, orig collector's case, mint ........ 55.00
   Rabbit head logo on front, black case, Japan, mint..................... 18.00
   Rabbit head logo on front, cream/ yellow case, Japan, mint.......... 20.00
   White rabbit head logo on front, black case, 6-1/2" x 4-1/2", mint ................................................. 85.00
Magazine, *Playboy*
   First Issue, Marilyn Monroe on cover, good condition.................... 1,500.00
   First Issue, Marilyn Monroe on cover, near mint condition ............. 2,500.00
   1955, January, Bettie Page centerfold, good condition ............... 300.00

1955, January, Bettie Page centerfold, near mint condition ........ 475.00
1965, February, Beatles interview, mint ......................................... 15.00
1968, November, with centerfold, fine ............................................. 7.00
1985, September, Madonna on cover, last stapled issue .......... 13.00
1994, November, Pamela Anderson on cover, autographed, mint.... 50.00
1995, January, Drew Barrymore cover, mint............................... 20.00
Mug
   Black, Playboy Club, gold Femlin logo, mint ................................. 15.00
   Clear, black rabbit head logo, 9-3/4" h, mint ..................................... 12.00
   Green, black rabbit head logo, 9-3/4" h, mint ..................................... 18.00
   White, black rabbit head logo, 9-3/4" h, mint ..................................... 15.00
Puzzle, centerfold, box
   1967, Playmate Paige Young, opened, no centerfold picture, very good......................................... 25.00
   1970s, Playmate Life Size Puzzle, MIB.......................................... 200.00
Puzzle, centerfold, canister
   1968, Playmate Jean Bell, opened, fair.......................................... 12.00
   1970, unopened, with centerfold picture, excellent .......................... 45.00
   1973, Bonnie Large, unopened, excellent..................................... 50.00
Swizzle Stick, 8-1/4" l
   Black or white, Playboy on side, each.......................................... 1.00
   Blue, orange, red ,or green, Playboy on side, each ............................. 4.00
Tankard, aluminum, rabbit head logo engraved on side, mint............ 10.00
Video, 1990-98 Video Playmate Review ................................................. 17.50

**Mug, black, Playboy Club, gold Fremlin logo, $15. Photo Courtesy of Patrick Leer.**

Wall Calendar
   1958, first, fine, no sleeve........ 70.00
   1960-64, Playmate Calendar, orig envelope, mint, each .............. 55.00
   1970, 1971, 1972, 1973, 1974, 1975, 1976, no envelope, mint, each 10.00
   1976, orig envelope, mint ........ 18.00

# Playing Cards

**Collecting Hints:** Always purchase complete decks in very good condition. Know the exact number of cards needed for a full deck—an American straight deck has 52 cards and usually a joker; pinochle requires 48 cards; tarot decks use 78. In addition to decks, collectors seek very early uncut sheets and single cards.

Many collectors focus on topics; for instance, politics, trains, World's Fairs, animals, airlines, or advertising. Most collectors of travel-souvenir cards prefer a photographic scene on the face.

The most valuable playing card decks are unusual either in respect to publisher, size, shape, or subject. Prices remain modest for decks of cards from the late 19th and 20th centuries.

**History:** Playing cards were first used in China in the 12th century. By 1400, playing cards were in use throughout Europe.

French cards are known specifically for their ornate designs. The first American cards were published by Jazaniah Ford, Milton, Massachusetts, in the late 1700s. United States innovations include upper-corner indexes, classic joker, standard size, and slick finish for shuffling ease. Bicycle Brand was introduced in 1885 by the U.S. Playing Card Company of Cincinnati.

Card designs have been drawn or printed in every conceivable size and on a variety of surfaces. Miniature playing cards appealed to children. Novelty decks came in round, crooked, and die-cut shapes. Numerous card games, beside those using the standard four-suit deck, were created for adults and children.

**References:** Phil Bollhagen (comp.), *Great Book of Railroad Playing Cards*, published by author, 1991; Everett Grist, *Advertising Playing Cards*, Collector Books, 1992.

**Collectors' Clubs:** American Antique Deck Collectors Club, 204

Gorham Ave., Hamden, CT 06514; American Game Collectors Assoc., P.O. Box 44, Dresher, PA 19025; Chicago Playing Card Collectors, Inc., 1559 West Platt Blvd., Chicago, IL 60626; 52 Plus Joker, 204 Gorham Ave., Hamden, CT 06514; International Playing Card Society, 3570 Delaware Common, Indianapolis, IN 46220; Playing Card Collectors Assoc., 337 Avelon St #4, Roundlake, IL 60073.

**Museum:** Playing Card Museum, Cincinnati Art Museum, Cincinnati, OH.

**Notes:** The following list is organized by both topic and country. Although concentrating heavily on cards by American manufacturers, some foreign-made examples are included.

Advertising
    Blue Bonnet Margarine, Blue Bonnet Girl illus ..................................... 15.00
    Champion Spark Plugs, repeating logo ............................................ 12.00
    IGA Food Store, line drawing of store ............................................... 8.00
    Inclinator Company of America, Harrisburg, blue .............................. 10.00
    Jefferson Motor Company, Jefferson, GA, Mercury outboard motors, two decks, slip case ....................... 75.00
    Key to '53 - Salesmanship, double deck, one with robin, other with squirrel ..................................... 10.00
    Kool Cigarettes, cigarette pack image ............................................ 15.00
    Life Savers, multicolored .......... 10.00
    Monarch Better Outdoor Garments, clothing tag with lion logo ........ 12.00
    Robbins Potato Co., sailboat on ocean, rope and anchor border ............................................... 10.00
    Sinclair Oil, red oil well logo, white ground, gold and red borders ............................................... 12.00
    Superior Dairy, National Pro Football Hall of Fame building .............. 12.00
Aviation
    Delta Air Lines, New York, traffic cop ............................................... 15.00
    Northwest Orient, Oriental phrases ............................................... 8.00
    WWII, airplane spotter, orig box ............................................... 8.00
Brewery
    Arrow Beer, gold arrows, lettering, and border, red ground ............ 15.00
    Old Tavern Lager Beer, black and white factory scene ................. 18.00
Casino
    Caesars Palace, Las Vegas, Nevada, gold logos, dark blue ground ........................................ 8.50
    Golden Nugget Gambling Hall, mirror image of white lettering surrounded by gold scrollwork and nugget ...................................... 12.00

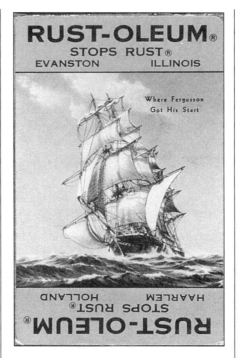

**Advertising, Rust-Oleum, Brown & Bigelow, $10.**

Cause, Prince of Wales National Relief Fund, WWI, 1914, MIB ............. 40.00
Railroad
    Chicago, Milwaukee & St. Paul, 53 scenic views, 1919, orig box ... 50.00
    New York, New Haven & Hartford RR, orig box and wrapper ....... 75.00
Souvenir
    Chicago, Sears Tower, skyline ............................................... 15.00
    Holland American Line, blue or red ............................................... 9.00
    Kennedy Space Center, FL, Space Shuttle, lift-off photo ................. 12.00
    Royal Caribbean, red, anchors, and ships ...................................... 10.00
World Fairs and Expositions
    Century of Progress, Belgian Village, plastic case ............................. 85.00
    Golden Gate Exposition, 2 sets, one with distant view of Tower of the Sun during day, other night view, orig box ............................................... 95.00
    New York, one deck with colored rendering of Theme building, other side with various buildings, orig black box ................................. 80.00
    Pan-American Exposition, Official Souvenir, different fair scenes ............................................... 95.00

# Pocket Knives

**Collecting Hints:** The pocket knife collector has to compete with those who collect in other categories.

The pocket knife with a celluloid handle and advertising underneath dates back to the 1880s. Celluloid-handled knives are considered much more desirable than the plastic-handled models. Collectors also tend to shy away from purely souvenir-related knives.

**History:** Pocket knife collectors fall into two main types: 1) those who concentrate on the utilitarian and functional knives from firms such as Alcas, Case, Colonial, Ka-Bar, Queen, Remington, Schrade, and Winchester; and 2) those interested in advertising, character, and other knives, which, while meant to be used, were sold with a secondary function in mind. These knives were made by companies such as Aerial Cutlery Co., Canton Cutlery Co., Golden Rule Cutlery Co., Imperial Knife Company, and Novelty Cutlery Co.

The larger manufacturing firms also made advertising, character, and figural knives. Some knives were giveaways or sold for a small premium, but most were sold in general stores and souvenir shops.

**References:** Jerry and Elaine Heuring, *Keen Kutter Collectibles*, 2nd ed., Collector Books, 1990, 1993 value update; Jacob N. Jarrett, *Price Guide to Pocket Knives*, L-W Book Sales, 1993, 1995 value update; Bernard Levine, *Levine's Guide to Knives and Their Values*, 4th ed., Krause Publications, 1997; Jim Sargent, *Sargent's American Premium Guide to Knives and Razors*, 5th ed., Krause Publications, 1999; J. Bruce Voyles, *American Blade Collectors Association Price Guide to Antique Knives*, Krause Publications, 1995; Ken Warner, ed., *Knives 2000*, 20th ed., Krause Publications, 1999.

**Periodicals:** *Blade*, 700 E. State St., Iola, WI 54990; *Edges*, P.O. Box 22007, Chattanooga, TN 37422; *Knife World*, P.O. Box 3395, Knoxville, TN 37927.

**Collectors' Clubs:** American Blade Collectors, P.O. Box 22007, Chattanooga, TN 37422; Canadian Knife Collectors Club, 3141 Jessuca Ct., Mississauga, ON L5C 1X7 Canada; Ka-Bar Knife Collectors Club, P.O. Box 406, Olean, NY 14760; National Knife Collectors Assoc., P.O. Box 21070, Chattanooga, TN 37421.

**Museum:** National Knife Museum, Chattanooga, TN.

**Reproduction Alert:** Advertising knives, especially those bearing

Coca-Cola advertising, have been heavily reproduced.

Advertising
Champion Spark Plugs ............ 35.00
Kaiers Beer ............................. 55.00
Phillips 66, knife and file, Zippo
................................................ 20.00
Platts Bros., 4 blades, Congress type
................................................ 55.00
Purina, checkerboard dec, 3-3/4" l
................................................ 30.00
Snap-On, Captain DL-2, Dura-Lens diamond nail file, precision scissors, 1-1/2" blade, Schrade Cutlery .... 12.00
Swift's Canned Foods, 5" l, ivory celluloid ..................................... 150.00

Baseball
Babe Ruth, 2-1/2" l, facsimile signature, Camillus Cutlery Co. ...... 125.00
Chicago Cubs, 3-3/8" l, 2 blades, plastic grips ............................ 18.00

Character
Dick Tracy, red and white, celluloid
................................................ 45.00
Jimmie Allen, silver wings ........ 70.00
Roy Rogers, 3-3/4" l, black and white
................................................ 55.00
The Little Colonel, orig display with 12 knives on board, late 1950s
.............................................. 250.00

Figural
Dachshund, key chain and knife
................................................ 12.00
Fish, 2-3/4" l, silver, Kero Co., Curby, Pat. 1885 ............................... 120.00
Shoe, 5-1/8" l, horn, steel blade, 19th C .......................................... 350.00

Hunter, Puma, folding
Game Warden .......................... 45.00
Plainsman ................................ 40.00
Prince ...................................... 60.00
Single blade ........................... 175.00

Political, Nixon Agnew, Re-elect President in 1972, blue lettering, white marbleized surface, portrait sketches, 2 blades, 2-3/4" l ........................ 30.00
Unmarked, gold filled, two tone, 2-1/2" x 11/16", blade mkd "stainless steel," some wear ............................... 30.00

World's Fair and Expositions
1836-1936, Texas Centennial, cream colored handle with bull, hay, state flag and emblem, 2 blades ...... 72.00

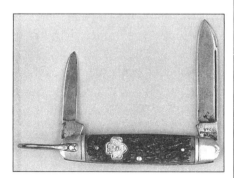

**Girl Scout, Utica, black plastic handles, aluminum liners, 2 blades, mkd "GSA #11-312," 3-3/8" l, $24.**

1935 ........................................ 40.00
1939, Golden Gate Bridge, 5-1/2" l, two blades, cream colored pearl-type handle, name of fair and city
................................................ 80.00

# Police Collectibles

**Collecting Hints:** Police-related items are primarily collected by people employed in law enforcement areas. Collectors often base their collection on badges or material from a specific locality. As a result, prices are regionalized, e.g., a California collector is more interested in California material than items from another state.

Condition is critical. Badges were worn everyday so some deterioration is to be expected.

The popularity of televised police shows has attracted many non-law enforcement people to the field of police collectibles.

**History:** The first American colonists appointed one of their own to maintain and enforce the laws of the land. The local sheriff held an important social and political position.

The mid-19th century witnessed the development of two important trends: the growth of the professional police force in cities and the romanticizing of the Western lawman. Arthur Conan Doyle's Sherlock Holmes novels popularized police methods. Magazines, such as the *Police Gazette*, kept the public's attention focused on the sensationalism of police work.

The Gangster era of the 1920s and 1930s and the arrival of the "G-Men," glamorized by Hollywood movies, kept police work in the limelight. Television capitalized on the public enthusiasm for police drama with shows such as "Dragnet," "The Untouchables," "Starsky and Hutch," "Hill Street Blues," and "NYPD Blue."

**References:** Monty McCord, *Police Cars*, Krause Publications, 1991; —, *Law Enforcement Memorabilia, Price and Identification Guide*, Krause Publications, 1998; Don Stewart, *Collectors Guide: Handcuffs & Restraints*, Key Collectors International, 1993; —, *Collectors Guide: The Yale & Towne Mfg Co.*, Key Collectors International, 1982.

**Periodical:** *Police Collectors News*, RR1 Box 14, Baldwin, WI 54002.

**Museums:** American Police Center & Museum, Chicago, IL; American Police Hall of Fame & Museum, Miami, FL; New York City Police Academy Museum, New York, NY; Suffolk County Police Dept. Museum, Yaphank, NY.

**Reproduction Alert:** Police badges.

Automobile Emblem, Safe Driver, San Diego Police, mkd "Entenmann Los Angeles," safety clasp ............... 8.00
Badge
Illinois State Police, Corporal ... 65.00
New Mexico Deputy Sheriff, 1967
.............................................. 175.00
Belt Buckle, NYC, brass .............. 75.00
Call Box, Chicago Police, cast aluminum, c1920 ........................... 125.00
Coffee Cup, white china, logo of NYCTPD ................................... 7.50
Ephemera
Letterhead, Arkansas State Penitentiary, letterhead dated Jan, 1949, discussing purchase of fishing equipment from PA company, sgd "Hugh Stockton," 2 pages ....... 10.00
License, for Ramona Hotel, Nevada, 1940s, signed by county treasurer, county auditor, and chief of police
................................................ 5.00
Summons for parking ticket, City of New York, 1943 ........................ 5.00
Figures, lead, Bahama Police marching band ...................................... 135.00
Magazine, *NOW*, London, Jan. 18, 1980, cover with police and pickets, "Showdown Over Steel" ............. 5.00
Magazine Tear Sheet
Beech Nut Gum, Norman Rockwell illus of policeman, 1937 .......... 12.00

**Badge, Railway Police, D. L. & W. R. R. Co., c1920, $85.**

Conoco Germ Processed Oil, illus of Police Motorcycle Stunt Team, Lieut. Gainer in Command, *Saturday Evening Post*, Aug. 3, 1940, 10-1/2" x 13-1/4" ............................................. 15.00

Newspaper, New York Times, July 2, 1861, "No more permits to pass the lines. Arrest of Police Commissioners" ........................................... 45.00

Nodder, policeman, mkd "Japan" ................................................. 20.00

Patch
   Alabama Marine Police .............. 6.00
   Federal Protection Service ......... 5.00
   Georgetown Police ..................... 4.50
   Illinois State Police, 2 colors ...... 7.50
   Massachusetts Capitol Building, 6 colors ...................................... 12.00
   St. Louis County Police .............. 4.00
   West Point, Mississippi, Police... 3.00

Photo
   Cabinet Card, Royal Canadian Police, pencil identification marks ............................................. 7.50
   Group, 31-1/2" x 11-1/2", Pres Dwight D. Eisenhower with White House Police, July 8, 1957, taken on South Lawn, group of 125 police in full uniform, 1950s, framed ................. 50.00

Plate, Texas Ranger Anniversary, 1973, sterling silver .......................... 135.00

Post Card, Texas Ranger on horseback ................................................. 7.50

Salt and Pepper Shakers, pr, figural, white, gold trim.......................... 5.00

Sheet Music, *Police Parade March*, c1917 ..................................... 25.00

Toy, car, battery operated, green, red light on top, some wear............ 90.00

Trophy, 19th Annual Police Pistol Tournament, Teaneck Pistol Range, NJ, metal ......................................... 60.00

Uniform Button, 3/4" d, brasstone
   Birmingham Police Dept. ........... 8.25
   Charleston Police ...................... 8.50
   Cincinnati Police, scales of justice center .................................... 9.00
   Philadelphia Police..................... 8.00
   Toledo Police, ........................... 8.00

# Political and Campaign Items

**Collecting Hints:** Items priced below $100 sell frequently enough to establish firm prices. Items above that price fluctuate according to supply and demand. Many individuals now recognize the value of acquiring political items and holding them for future sale. As a result, modern material has a relatively low market value, unless few examples were produced.

Knowledgeable collectors also keep in touch with Presidential libraries to find out what type of souvenir items they are offering for sale. This information is helpful in determining which items on the market originated at the time of actual campaigns, and these are the ones collectors should concentrate on acquiring.

The pioneering work on the identification of political buttons has been done by Theodore L. Hake, whose books are listed below. Two other books have greatly assisted in the identification and cataloging of pre-1896 campaign materials: Herbert R. Collins's *Threads of History* and Edmund B. Sullivan's *American Political Badges and Medalets 1789-1892*.

**History:** Since 1800, the American presidency always has been a contest between two or more candidates. Initially, souvenirs were issued to celebrate victories. Items issued during a campaign to show support for a candidate were widely distributed beginning with the William Henry Harrison campaign of 1840.

There is a wide variety of campaign items—buttons, bandannas, tokens, pins, etc. The only limiting factor has been the promoter's imagination. The advent of television campaigning has reduced the quantity of individual items, and modern campaigns do not seem to have the variety of materials that were issued earlier.

Modern collectors should be aware of Kennedy material. Much has been reproduced and many items were issued after his death.

**References:** Herbert Collins, *Threads of History*, Smithsonian Institution Press, 1979; Theodore L. Hake, *Encyclopedia of Political Buttons, United States, 1896-1972*, Americana & Collectibles Press, 1985, (P.O. Box 1444, York, PA 17405); —, *Political Buttons, Book II, 1920-1976*, Americana & Collectibles Press, 1977; —, *Political Buttons, Book III, 1789-1916*, Americana & Collectibles Press, 1978; Note: Theodore L. Hake issued a revised set of prices for his three books in 1998; —, *Hake's Guide to Presidential Campaign Collectibles*, Wallace-Homestead, 1992; Edward Krohn, *National Political Convention Tickets and Other Convention Ephemera*, David G. Phillips Publishing Co. Inc. (P.O. Box 611388, No. Miami, FL 33161), 1996; Keith Melder, *Hail to the Candidate*, Smithsonian Institution Press, 1992; James W. Milgram, *Presidential Campaign Illustrated Envelopes and Letter Paper 1840-1972*, David G. Phillips Publishing Co. Inc. (P.O. Box 611388, No. Miami, FL 33161), 1996; Edmund B. Sullivan, *American Political Badges and Medalets, 1789-1892*, Quarterman Publications, 1981; —, *Collecting Political Americana*, Christopher Publishing House, 1991; Mark Warda, *Political Campaign Stamps*, Krause Publications, 1998.

**Periodicals:** *Autograph Times*, 2303 N. 44th St., #225, Phoenix, AZ 85008; *Political Bandwagon*, P.O. Box 348, Leola, PA 17540; *Political Collector Newspaper*, P.O. Box 5171, York, PA 17405.

**Collectors' Clubs:** American Political Items Collectors, P.O. Box 340339, San Antonio, TX 78234; Button Pusher, P.O. Box 4, Coopersburg, PA 18036; Ford Political Items Collectors, 18222 Flower Hill Way #299, Gaithersburg, MD 20879; Indiana Political Collectors Club, P.O. Box 11141, Indianapolis, IN 46201; NIXCO, Nixon Collectors Organization, 975 Maunawili Cr., Kailua, HI 96734; *Rail Splitter* (Abraham Lincoln), Box 275, New York, NY 10044; Third Party Hopefuls, 503 Kings Canyon Blvd., Galesburg, IL 61401.

**Museums:** Museum of American Political Life, Hartford, CT; Smithsonian Institution, Washington, DC; Western Reserve Historical Society, Cleveland, OH.

**Advisor:** Ted Hake.

### Abraham Lincoln, 1860, 1864

Book, cartoon history, hard bound set, Albert Shaw, volume 1 signed by author, gold imprinted spines, political cartoons and photographs, 1929 ................................................. 80.00

Medalet, one side with spread wing eagle and slogan "Success To Republican Principles," other side emb "Millions for Freedom, Not One Cent For Slavery" .................. 100.00

### Benjamin Harrison, 1888, 1892

Pinback, 2" h, mechanical, "Presidential Chair, silvered brass, real sepia photo of Harrison, seat is on a spring and can be closed, seat reads "Who Shall Occupy It?" 1888 ......... 250.00

Print, sepia portraits of Pres. And Mrs. Harrison, 4-1/4" x 6-1/2", brown card mount, c1888 .......................... 20.00

Silk, 2-1/2" x 4", Harrison and Morton, red, white, and blue flag design, names in dark blue, 1888 ........ 40.00

### William McKinley, 1896

Jugate, black and white photos of McKinley and Teddy Roosevelt, red, white, and blue accent bow, backpaper reads "National Equipment Co.," Whitehead and Hoag, 1900..... 20.00

Lapel Stud, black and white photo in center, dark blue and bright red stars on cream rim ................... 20.00

Paperweight, 2-1/2" x 3", solid brass bust, c1896 .............................. 60.00

Paperweight, 2-1/2" x 4", glass, rect, center sepia portrait, c1896..... 40.00

Pinback Button, 7/8" d, black and white photo, gold trim, diamond design flanked by red, white, and blue star and stripe motif, bright gold outer motif ......................................... 30.00

Pinback Button, 1-1/4" d, rebus, black on cream, "Count Me For (picture of McKinley) And A Full (picture of dinner pail)" .................................. 225.00

Ribbon, 2-1/2" x 7", "Our Standard" platform, black and white, cream ground, brass eagle and flags bar pin hanger at top..................... 90.00

### Teddy Roosevelt, 1901, 1909

Pinback Button, rebus, "For President" large full color design of red rose, green stem, center above lettering "Velt," no back paper ............. 200.00

Pinback Button, "Vote For Roosevelt Use Maple City Soap," dark red, cream lettering, 1904 ............. 210.00

### Woodrow Wilson, 1912, 1916

Ashtray, 3" x 4", raised imp of young Wilson, inscription "Justice" on sword handle and "Humanity" on side of book, 1908-20 .............. 18.00

Campaign Ribbon, 3" x 6", red, white, and blue, "Democratic ticket, above and below crossed flags, Wilson/Marshall..................................... 35.00

Pinback Button, 1-7/8", red, white, and blue, blue name ....................... 20.00

Postcard, 3-1/4" x 5-1/2", "Our Next President," black on pale green, "Magic Moving Pictures Cared," push/pull black and white flicker of Teddy Roosevelt, Taft, or Wilson, 1912 ......................................... 40.00

### Warren G. Harding, 1920

Pinback Button, "For President Warren G. Harding," photo center, white rim, blue lettering ............................ 15.00

Stereoscopic Card, set of 5, showing Harding and wife at visits, speeches, and vacations, c1920.............. 20.00

### Herbert Hoover, 1928, 1932

Campaign Ring, Hoover 1928, nonadjustable silvered brass, ornate enameled designs ................... 30.00

Pinback Button, "Be Safe Be Hoover," emb brass, bright brass raised areas, dark blue painted background..................................... 15.00

Pinback Button, "Engineers For Hoover, 9/16" l diecut building, brass letter, dark blue enameled ground .... 35.00

### Franklin D. Roosevelt, 1932, 1936, 1940, 1944

Button, 3-1/2" d, red, white, and blue, large black and white center photo, c1936 ...................................... 35.00

Campaign Ribbon, 2" x 6-1/2", blue and white, imprinted "Roosevelt Reception/Los Angeles/September 24th 1932"........................................ 20.00

Jugate, 1-1/4", Roosevelt/Garner, red, white, and blue, star and stripe design, blue illus portraits........ 40.00

Mug, Happy Days Are Here Again, 3" d, 5" h, green glazed ceramic, c1933 ................................................ 24.00

Pillow Cover, 16" x 18", large black photo of FDR in wicker chair on front, navy border, blue piping, bright orange fabric back, c1932-36................ 60.00

Pinback Button, 1-3/4" d, black and white portrait, gray and white background, thin white rim edge, c1936 ........ 45.00

Ribbon, 1-1/2" x 5", white and blue striped fabric, gold type "We Want Roosevelt," 1938 ...................... 25.00

Sheet Music, 9" x 12", *On With Roosevelt,* red, white, and blue, 4 pgs, words and music by Louise Graeser, 1938 .......................... 10.00

Sign, 14" x 22", thin cardboard, bluetone photos, red and blue type, white ground, titled Insure Wisconsin For Roosevelt/General Election/Tuesday Nov. 3, 1936" .................. 250.00

### Alfred Landon, 1936

Campaign Card, 2-1/4" x 4" heavy paper card for election day, 1936 .................................................. 10.00

Napkin, 13-1/2" sq brown on white in paper, Landon's sunflower art in center as compass, folds to 7" sq, c1936 .................................................. 18.00

Pinback Button, brown and yellow sunflower, dark green rim .............. 10.00

### Wendell Willkie, 1940

Car Attachment, 3-1/2" h, black and white, 1940............................. 50.00

Pinback Button, "Democrats for Willkie," blue and cream litho, red rim......12.00

Pinback Button, "Willkie Contributor," white lettering, red and blue segments ......................................... 8.00

### Harry S. Truman, 1948

Booklet, "The Democratic Digest, June-July 1950," 7-1/2" x 10-3/4", 32 pgs, black and white, photos, text of Democratic stand ................... 20.00

**Pinback Buttons, left: Willkie, red, white, and blue, $8; right: The Constitutionalists, No Third Term, red, white, and blue, 7/8" d, $5.**

**Plate, Republican National Convention, San Francisco, 1956, mkd "Vernon Kilns," 12-3/4" d, $65.**

Inauguration Button, 3-1/2" d, red, white, and blue, black and white center photo ............................ 90.00

Pinback Button, "Our President Harry S. Truman," 1-1/2" d, black and white ................................................ 40.00

Pinback Button, Truman Memorial, graytone photo in center, black and white rim, 1972 ...................... 12.00

### Dwight Eisenhower, 1952, 1956

Inauguration Invitation, 9" x 12-1/2" stiff paper, printed in script, presidential emblem emb in gold at top, 1957 ................................................ 20.00

License Plate, 3" x 5", black on orange steel, Ike ................................. 35.00

Matchbook, "Citizens for Eisenhower, red, white and blue pack, Reading, PA, hotel sponsor, used ........... 12.00

Pinback Button, "I Like Ike," red, white, and blue rim, bluetone photo .... 7.50

Pinback Button, "Peace-Progress-Prosperity/I Like Ike," bluetone photo, white ground, blue and red slogan ................................................ 10.00

### Richard M. Nixon, 1960, 1968, 1972

Bendee, 4" h, painted rubber figure of Nixon, jointed swivel arms, hands giving victory sign, 1" d suction cup attached to top of head, c1972 ................................................ 20.00

Bubble Gum Cigars, 4-1/2" x 5", red, white, and blue box, 22 cigars, "Win with Dick" on labels, black and white photo of Nixon on box lid......... 35.00

Button, Inauguration, ribbon badge, 2" d blue on gold button, 2" x 7" blue fabric ribbon, gold type, "President Richard M. Nixon Inauguration, Jan. 20, 1973, Lancaster County, Pennsylvania" ................................... 25.00

Car Antenna Flag, 4" x 9-1/2", Pat for First Lady, plastic, 1960.......... 25.00

Handout, Victorygram, 5-1/2" x 8-1/2", handout designed as replica of paper telegram sent to Texas supporter in 1968, stamped with date "1968 Nov. 4 PM 2 29" ............. 15.00

Jugate, Nixon/Agnew, 1972, black and white photos, red, white, and blue eagle and shield design, white background ...................................... 15.00

Magazine, *Newsweek Election Preview '60,* illus of Nixon and Kennedy on cover, 126 pgs, Nov. 7, 1960 ... 15.00

Pinback Button, Inauguration Day, black and white photo, black, red, and blue lettering, white background, red, white, and blue stylized flag ............................... 18.00

Ticket, 3-1/2" x 6", Nixon/Lodge Campaign Breakfast, Oct. 5, 1960, Hotel Commodore, New York City, 7/8" d red, white, and blue "Nixon/Lodge" button attached ..................30.00

### John F. Kennedy, 1960

Ashtray, 4" x 4-1/2", smoked glass, black and white photos of JFK and RFK at center, gold trim, birth and death dates, gold stars, famous quotes, c1968 ......................... 25.00

Button, 4" d, litho tin, red and black, white background .................... 35.00

Coloring Book, 10" x 13", stiff paper, red, white, blue, and black cover, 24 pgs, satirical cartoons, 1962 ... 20.00

Magazine
  *Photoplay,* March 1964, full color cover of Pres and First Lady, special section entitled "Jack & Jackie - Their Courtship," 7 page article on "JFK, the Assassin Was Not Alone," black and white and color photos ................................................ 15.00
  *US News & World Report,* Nov. 21, 1960, full color photo of Kennedy on cover ...................................... 25.00

Souvenir Plate, 6-1/2" d, President and Mrs. John F. Kennedy, painted full color illus, c1961 ...................... 20.00

### Lyndon Johnson, 1964

Glass, 5-1/2" h, clear glass, Kosygin Summit, Glassboro State College, NJ, June 1967, black and white illus of meeting place ....................... 20.00

Hat, 4" x 11", plastic, campaign style, red, white, and blue stripes, black and white illus of Johnson on right, "LBJ for the USA" ..................... 10.00

Pen, give-away, gold presidential logo, facsimile signature on black plastic, gold metal top and clip, felt tipped pen frayed ............................... 15.00

### Barry Goldwater, 1964

Antenna Attachment, 4" x 6-1/2", red and blue lettering, white background, spring tension ............. 15.00

Pinback Button, "Goldwater In '64," light blue tone lettering and photo, white ground, red rim .......................... 7.50

Stickpin, elephant, diecut plastic, wearing Goldwater-style eyeglasses
  .................................................. 5.00

Tie Tack, diecut letters, brass luster, needlepost and clutch back ...... 5.00

### Jimmy Carter, 1976

Bandanna, 28" sq, Carter-Mondale, white and green, 1980 ............. 25.00

Inauguration Medal, 5" x 6" x 2" white cardboard box, blue presidential seal on top, solid bronze medal, antique finish, diecut repository lined in dark blue felt, parchment authenticity certificate, "Sculptured by Julian Harris/Minted by the Franklin Mint" .......................................... 30.00

Jugate, Carter/Mondale, rect badge, black and white photo in diamond shape, red, white, and blue flag designs, browntone photos of Thomas Jefferson, White House, Statue of Liberty, and eagle, 1980 ...... 15.00

Press Badge, ABC News, Democratic National Convention, black on pink ................................................. 5.00

Watch, 1-1/4" d dial with brown, rd, gray, and blue caricature figure, reads "Official Jimmy Cater from Peanuts to President," Goober Time Company, 1976, stainless steel back, gold colored metal bezel .......................... 50.00

### Ronald Reagan, 1980, 1984

Christmas Card, 1982, unused, 6" x 8", orig envelope ........................... 15.00

License Plate, Presidential Inauguration, red, white, and blue aluminum, 1981 ........................................ 17.50

Pinback Button, "Carry On For The Duke/Reagan in 80," 3" d, bluetone photo, blue lettering, white ground, center illus of John Wayne ....... 12.00

Pinback Button, "NJ/Reagan Youth Staff," dark blue on white .......... 5.00

### George Bush, 1980, 1984, 1988

Bumper Sticker, 3-1/2" x 9-1/2", "Bush/Quayle '88," red, white, and blue ................................................. 2.50

Pinback Button, "Bush Defeats Clinton," black and white photo of Truman holding copy of newspaper with Dewey headline," 1992 .............. 3.00

Pinback Button, "I Was There," Bush/Quayle Re-Nomination," bright red on white.................................. 5.00

### Bill Clinton, 1992, 1996

Inauguration Program, 8-1/2" x 11", 24 pgs, full color photos ............... 15.00

Jugate, black and white photos, bright red rim, "Clinton for President, Carol Moseley Braun for US Senate" .. 5.00

Pinback Button, "Blow Bill Blow," full color photo of Clinton playing sax, red, white, and blue vertical striped background, 1992 ........................ 2.00

Pinback Button, "Just Say No," back and white photo of Clinton over printed by bright red, black lettering, 1992 ........................................ 5.00

# Post Cards

**Collecting Hints:** Concentrate on one subject area, publisher, or illus-

trator. Collect cards in mint condition, when possible.

The more common the holiday, the larger the city, the more popular the tourist attraction, the easier it will be to find post cards on the subject because of the millions of cards that were originally available. The smaller runs of "real" photo postcards are the most desirable of the scenic cards. Photographic cards of families and individuals, unless they show occupations, unusual toys, dolls, or teddy bears, have little value.

Stamps and cancellation marks may sometimes affect the value of cards. Consult a philatelic guide.

Post cards fall into two main categories: view cards and topics. View cards are easiest to sell in their local geographic region. European view cards, while very interesting, are difficult to sell in America.

It must be stressed that age alone does not determine price. A birthday post card from 1918 may sell for only 10¢ while a political campaign card from the 1950s may bring $10. The price of every collectible is governed by supply and demand.

Although cards from 1898 to 1918 are the most popular with collectors, the increasing costs of postcards from this era have turned attention to postcards from the 1920s, 1930s, and 1940s. Art Deco cards from the 1920-1930 period are the most desirable. The 1940s "linens," so called because of their textured linenlike paper surface, are the most popular cards of that time period.

Cards from the 1950 to 1970 period are called "Chromes" because of their shiny surface.

**History:** The golden age of post cards dates from 1898 to 1918. Cards printed earlier are collected for their postal history. Post cards prior to 1898 are called "pioneer" cards.

European publishers, especially in England and Germany, produced the vast majority of cards during the golden age. The major postcard publishers are Raphael Tuck (England), Paul Finkenrath of Berlin (PFB-German), and Whitney, Detroit Publishing Co., and John Winsch (United States). However, many American publishers had their stock produced in Europe, hence, "Made in Bavaria" imprints. While some Tuck cards are high priced, many are still available in the "10¢" boxes.

Styles changed rapidly, and manufacturers responded to every need. The linen post card which gained popularity in the 1940s was quickly replaced by the chrome cards of the post-1950 period.

**References:** Janet A. Banneck, *Antique Postcards of Rose O'Neill*, Greater Chicago Productions, 1992; Jody Blake and Jeannette Lasansky, *Rural Delivery: Real Photo Postcards from Central Pennsylvania*, Union County Historical Society (Union County Courthouse, Lewisburg, PA 17837), 1996; Juli Kernall, *Postcard Collector 1999 Annual & Price Guide*, 8th ed., Antique Trader Books, 1998; J. L. Mashburn, *Artist-Signed Postcard Price Guide*, Colonial House, 1993 (Note: all Mashburn books are available from Box 609, Enka, NC 28728); —, *Black Americana Postcard Price Guide*, 2nd ed., Colonial House, 1999; —, *Fantasy Postcards with Price Guide*, Colonial House, 1996; —, *Postcard Price Guide*, 3rd ed., Colonial House, 1997; —, *Super Rare Postcards of Harrison Fisher*, Colonial House, 1992; Frederic and Mary Megson, *American Advertising Postcards*, published by authors, 1985; —, *American Exposition Postcards*, The Postcard Lovers, 1992; Susan Brown Nicholson, *Antique Postcard Sets and Series Price Guide*, Greater Chicago Productions, 1993; —, *Encyclopedia of Antique Postcards*, Wallace-Homestead, 1994; *Postcard Collector Annual*, 6th ed., Antique Trader Books, 1996; Cynthia Rubin and Morgan Williams, *Larger Than Life; The American Tall-Tale Postcard*, Abbeville Press, 1990; Nouhad A. Saleh, *Guide to Artist's Signatures and Monograms on Postcards*, Minerva Press, 1993; Robert Ward, *Investment Guide to North American Real Photo Postcards*, Antique Paper Guild, 1991; Jane Wood, *Collector's Guide to Postcards*, L-W Book Sales, 1984, 1997 value update.

**Periodicals:** *Barr's Postcard News*, 70 S. 6th St., Lansing, IA 52151; *Gloria's Corner*, P.O. Box 507, Denison, TX 75021; *Postcard Collector*, 121 N. Main St., Iola, WI 54945.

**Collectors' Clubs:** *Barr's Postcard News* and the *Postcard Collector* publish lists of more than 50 regional clubs in the United States and Canada.

**Notes:** The following prices are for cards in excellent to mint condition—no sign of edge wear, no creases, untrimmed, no writing on the picture side of the card, no tears, and no dirt. Each defect reduces the price given by 10%.

## Advertising

Adv on linens, large product image ........................................... 6.00
Adv on chromes, large product image ........................................... 2.50
Automobile adv
    American prior to 1920 ........... 20.00
    European prior to 1920 ........... 12.50
    Oldsmobile 88 Super, 4 door sedan, 1952 ........................................... 7.50
    Pontiac Chieftan, 2 door sedan, 1949 ........................................... 7.50
    Pontiac Streamliner, 4 door sedan, 1949 ........................................... 8.00
Campbell Soup adv
    Horizontal format ..................... 30.00
    Vertical format ........................ 100.00
Coca-Cola adv
    Duster girl in car ................... 450.00
    Hamilton King ........................ 250.00
Diner Adv, linen era ..................... 12.50
DuPont Gun
    Birds ....................................... 30.00
    Dogs ..................................... 100.00
    Zeppelin ................................ 150.00
Elgin Watch Co ............................... 6.00
Formica, chrome era ...................... 3.00
Heinz, Ocean Pier, Atlantic City, NY, 1910s ........................................ 5.00
Hotel-Motel
    Chrome ................................... 1.50
    Early ....................................... 3.50
    Linen era ................................. 7.50
McDonald's chrome era ................. 2.00
Michelin Tire Company, featuring Michelin man ................................. 30.00
R. J. Reynolds, chrome era ........... 9.00
Rockford Watch, calendar series ........................................ 17.50
Wells Fargo, colored sketch, Wells Fargo stage racing with Indians, history on back, postmarked 1915 ........................................ 10.00
Wood's Boston Coffees, black and white oval portraits of George and Martha Washington ................. 7.50
Zeno Gum, mechanical ................ 35.00

## Artist Signed

Atwell, Mabel Lucie
    Early by Tuck ........................... 17.50
    Regular, comic .......................... 9.00
Bertiglia, children ........................ 15.50
Boileau, Philip
    By Reinthal Neuman ............... 18.00
    By Raphael Tuck ................... 100.00
    By other ................................... 35.00
Boulanger, Maurice, cats
    Large images ........................... 25.00
    Many, in action ........................ 12.50
Browne, Tom
    American Baseball series, green background ............................. 10.00
    English comic series ................. 5.00
Brundage, Frances
    Children ................................... 3.00

**Artist Signed, E. Ebner, children, $9.**

    Early Tuck Chromolithograph .. 32.00
Caldecott
    Early ....................................... 12.00
    1974 reprints ............................ 1.00
Carmichael, comic ........................ 5.00
Carr, Gene, comic ........................ 15.50
Chiostri, Art Deco ........................ 20.00
Christy, Howard Chandler ........... 17.50
Clapsaddle, Ellen Hattie
    Children ................................. 20.00
    Floral, sleds, crosses ............... 9.00
    Unsigned, Wolf Publishing Co ........................................ 12.00
    Valentine, mechanical ............. 45.00
Corbella, Art Deco ....................... 12.50
Corbett, Bertha, sunbonnets ........ 15.00
Curtis, E., children ........................ 4.00
Daniell, Eva, Art Nouveau, Tuck ... 85.00
Drayton/Weiderseim, Grace (Campbell's Kids) ............................. 35.00
Dwig
    Comic ...................................... 5.00
    Halloween ............................... 15.00
Fidler, Alie Luella, women ............. 6.00
Fisher, Harrison ........................... 17.50
Gibson, Charles Dana, sepia ......... 9.00
Golay, Mary, flowers ..................... 4.50
Greenaway, Kate, sgd ............... 350.00
Greiner, M
    Blacks ..................................... 17.50
    Children ................................... 5.00
    Molly and Her Teddy ............... 12.50
Griggs, H. B. ................................ 10.00
Gutmann, Bessie Pease ............... 12.50
Hays, Margaret ............................ 10.00
Humphrey, Maud, sgd .................. 70.00
Innes, John, western ..................... 5.00
Johnson, J., children ..................... 7.50
Kirchner, Raphael
    First period ........................... 125.00
    Second period ........................ 65.00
    Third period ........................... 50.00
    Santa .................................... 200.00
Klein, Catherine
    Floral ....................................... 4.50
    Alphabet ................................ 12.00
    Alphabet, letters X, Y, Z ......... 25.00
Koehler, Mela, early ..................... 65.00
Mauzan, Art Deco ......................... 15.00
May, Phil, English comic series .... 12.00
McCay, Winsor, "Little Nemo" ....... 25.00
Mucha, Alphonse
    Art Nouveau, months of the year ........................................ 200.00
    Slavic period, murals .............. 75.00
    Women, full card design ........ 600.00
O'Neill, Rose
    Gross Publishing Company ... 125.00

**Linen, Wm. W. Doud Post No. 98, American Legion, Rochester, NY, unused, $12.**

Ice Cream adv ........................ 100.00
Kewpies .................................... 35.00
Pickings from Puck-Blacks .... 100.00
Suffrage
    Babies .............................. 200.00
    Kewpies............................ 125.00
Opper, Frederick, comic .............. 10.00
Outcault ...................................... 15.00
Parkinson, Ethel, children .............. 7.00
Patella, women............................ 15.00
Payne, Harry ............................... 15.00
Phillips, Cole, fade-away style ...... 25.00
Price, Mary Evans.......................... 5.00
Remington, Frederic .................... 35.00
Robinson, Robert......................... 15.00
Rockwell, Norman........................ 35.00
Russell, Charles............................. 9.00
Sager, Xavier............................... 15.00
Schmucker, Samuel
    Halloween greetings ................ 65.00
    New Years .............................. 25.00
    Silk, any greeting.................... 55.00
    St. Patrick's Day greetings ....... 15.00
    Valentine greetings ................. 15.00
Shinn, Cobb .................................. 4.00
Smith, Jessie Wilcox, seven different
    images ................................... 15.00
Studdy, Bonzo Dog ...................... 12.50
Tam, Jean, women ....................... 20.00
Thiele, Arthur
    Blacks
        Large faces ...................... 25.00
        On bikes........................... 45.00
    Cats
        In action.......................... 15.00
        Large heads ..................... 20.00
    Pigs, large heads .................... 25.00
Twelvetrees, Charles, comic, children
    ................................................ 7.50
Underwood, Clarence..................... 9.00
Upton, Florence, Golliwoggs, Tuck
    .............................................. 35.00
Wain, Louis
    Cat.......................................... 45.00
    Dog ........................................ 25.00
    Frog........................................ 35.00
    Paper doll, cat........................ 200.00
    Santa and cat........................ 100.00
Wall, Bernhardt, sunbonnets ........ 15.00
Wood, Lawson ............................. 10.00

**Folder**

Carlsbad Caverns, 10 cards, glossy
    black and white photos, 1930s .... 8.00
Corning Glass, 10 cards of glass pat-
    terns, 1950s ............................. 9.00

Hialeah Racing, 1940s .................. 7.50
PA Turnpike, 18 view, Minsky Bros
    .................................................. 9.00

**Greetings**

April Fools
    American comic........................ 4.00
    French litho with fish ............... 12.50
Birthday
    Floral ...................................... 1.00
    Children .................................. 1.50
Christmas, no Santa ...................... 1.25
Christmas, Santa
    Artists signed .......................... 15.00
    Black face, Coontown series
    ................................................ 100.00
    German, highly embossed ...... 15.00
    Hold to light type................... 100.00
    Installment, unused............... 100.00
    Kirchner ................................. 200.00
    P.F.B. Publishing Company ...... 20.00
    Red Suits............................... 15.00
    Silk Appliqué .......................... 40.00
    Suits other than red................. 17.50
Easter, printed in Germany
    Boy in sailor suit, holding chick, high
    top boots, hens and roosters, "Best
    Easter Wishes," postmarked Grand
    Rapids, MI, 1912...................... 8.00
    Boy on egg cart, wheels of forget-
    me-nots, pulled by 2 chicks, "Happy
    Easter-Tide," postmarked Kalama-
    zoo, MI, 1913 ........................... 8.00
    Boy with arm full of pussy willows
    and forget-me-nots, 3 lambs, "Easter
    Greetings," postmarked Columbus,
    Ohio, 1910 ............................... 9.00
    Children playing in open egg,
    "Happy Easter" ........................ 6.00
    Victorian boy and girl gathering Eas-
    ter eggs, "Easter Greeting," unused
    ................................................ 12.00
    Victorian boy pushing egg entwined
    with roses, "Easter Greeting,"
    unused .................................... 15.00
    Victorian child pushing egg buggy
    filled with forget-me-nots and back
    chick, "A Very Happy Easter To You,"
    postmarked 1903..................... 10.00
Fourth of July
    Children .................................. 8.00
    Uncle Sam ............................... 12.00
    Others .................................... 4.50
Ground Hog Day
    Early, i.e. Lounsbury Publishing
    ................................................ 250.00
    After 1930 ............................... 20.00

**Motel, typical, Fenway Motor Hotel, Boston, MA, postmarked 1963, used, $2.**

**Salt Lake City, tiny bag of salt glued to front, used, $5.**

Halloween
    Children .................................. 5.00
    Children, extremely colorful or artists
    sgd.......................................... 12.00
    Winsch Publishing ................... 45.00
Labor Day
    Lounsbury Publishing ............. 125.00
    Nash Publishing ...................... 95.00
Leap Year ................................... 5.00
Mother's Day, early ...................... 8.00
New Year
    Bells........................................ 1.25
    Children or Father Time ............ 9.50
    Winsch Publishing, beautiful women
    ................................................ 15.00
St. Patrick's Day
    Children .................................. 6.50
    No children .............................. 4.50
Thanksgiving
    Children .................................. 6.50
    No children .............................. 2.50
    Uncle Sam ............................... 7.50
Valentines
    Children, women....................... 8.50
    Hearts, comic .......................... 4.00
    Winsch Publishing, beautiful women
    ................................................ 18.00

**Humor**

It's the Same Old Moon - -But OH!
How It Has Changed!, Curt Teich &
Co., Chicago, unused ............ 12.00
"Will You Be My Teddy Bear?" Red
Cliffe, CO, leather, postmarked 1909
    ................................................ 7.50

**Patriotic**

Decoration Day............................. 7.00
Lincoln........................................ 7.50
Patriotic Songs ............................. 4.00
Uncle Sam .................................. 12.00
Washington.................................. 7.50
World War II, linen ........................ 4.50

**Photographic**

Atlantic City Boardwalk, postmarked
    1919...................................... 9.00
Children under Christmas trees.... 14.50
Children with animals or toys........ 12.00
Christmas trees............................. 8.50
Circus Performer, identified and close-
    up............................................ 15.00
Constitution Mall, government area,
    theme center, used ................... 9.00
Diamond Green Ramblers, Silver City
    ................................................ 7.00
Exaggerations
    Conrad Publishing, after 1935
    ................................................ 10.00

Martin Publishing ..................... 12.50
Martin Publishing, US Coin ...... 75.00
Indian chiefs, five chiefs in full regalia, emb, postmarked 1910 ........... 12.00
Lincoln Statue on Lincoln Memorial Bridge, Milwaukee, WI, used ..... 6.50
Main Streets
Large cities .............................. 12.50
Unidentified towns ..................... 7.50
With trains or trolleys ................ 19.50
Men peeling potatoes, Co. B, 311th Inf. Kitchen Mechanics, Camp Dix, unused .................................... 10.00
People
Military with flags ....................... 5.00
Occupation, American ............. 15.00
Portraits, instant relatives ........... 1.00
Unusual studio backdrops ......... 5.00
Railroad Depots .......................... 20.00
Railroad Depots, with trains ......... 22.50
Shop Exteriors, identified ............. 12.00
Shop Interiors, identified location
........................................ 25.00
The Belles of California, 3 elderly Indian women sitting in field, color, postmarked 1907 CA ..................... 12.00
The Old Indian Whale Hunter of Puget Sound, kneeling on the shore and leaning against dug-out ........... 10.00
Visit Backstage at Radio City, NBC Studio Tour, black and white, postmarked 1937 ............................. 7.50

**Political and Social History**

Blacks ........................................... 12.00
Campaign
1900 ...................................... 100.00
1904 ........................................ 65.00
1908 ........................................ 35.00
Col. Roosevelt's Home, Oyster Bay, Long Island, NY, postmarked 1922
........................................ 7.50
McKinley Monument, Buffalo, NY, needlework type emb, postmarked 1907
........................................ 15.00
McKinley Monument, Canton, OH, emb, muted gray and pink .................. 9.00
Muriel Humphrey, portrait and facsimile signature, reverse with Muriel Humphrey's Beef Soup recipe ........... 8.50
President Franklin Roosevelt
Posing with rangers in front of giant CA redwoods ................... 9.50
Speaking at dedication of Great Smoky Mountains National Park, linen finish .............................. 8.50
President and Mrs. Woodrow Wilson, tinted ...................................... 10.00
Prohibition ....................................... 8.00
Richard Nixon, Vote Republican, 1960, colored ....................................... 7.50
School Delinquency, fill-in the blank 1932 post card, mailed in Baltimore, MD ............................................. 7.50
Suffrage
Cargill publisher ....................... 15.00
Clapsaddle ............................... 50.00
General ................................... 12.50
Kewpie ................................... 125.00
Parades .................................. 12.50
Taft and Sherman, oval portraits with facsimile signatures, Capitol building in background .......................... 10.00

Washington DC, The New White House Sideboard designed by Mrs. Roosevelt, large marble top sideboard with two eagles ................ 7.50
William H. Taft, dark sepia tone photo
........................................ 7.50
William Jennings Bryan
Addressing his Sunday School Class, Miami, Florida, huge crowd in amphitheater, palm trees, color tinted, used .............................. 7.00
Home of F. R. Rogers, Dayton, Tenn. Where Wm. Jennings Bryan died July 26, 1925, unused ................ 9.00
Sepia tone photo ....................... 8.00
Willkie, "Think! Who Nominated Hitler? — Hitler. Who Nominated Mussolini? — Mussolini. Who Nominated Stalin? — Stalin. Who Nominated Roosevelt? — Roosevelt. Who Nominated Willkie? — The People Vote for Willkie" ........12.00

**World Fairs and Expositions**

Chicago, 1933-34
Electrical Building at night, postmarked 1934 ........................... 10.00
Federal Building at night, postmarked 1934 ........................... 10.00
Havoline Thermometer, postmarked 1933 ..................................... 10.00
Golden Gate, 1939, , black and white, unused
Court of Reflections ................. 12.00
Court of the Moon .................... 12.00
Court of the Pacifica ................ 12.00
Tower of the Sun ........................... 8.00
New York, 1939, Aeroplane view, full color, linen, unused ................. 8.50
New York, 1964-65, Coca-Cola Company Pavilion, unused ................ 7.50
St. Louis 1764-1964 Bicentennial, city flag, unused ............................ 6.50
St. Louis, 1904, Compliments of Rice & Hutchins, Shoemakers, Boston, Manufactures Building, souvenir inscription at upper right corner, unused .................................... 70.00

# Elvis Presley

**Collecting Hints:** Official Elvis Presley items are usually copyrighted and many are dated.

Learn to differentiate between items licensed during Elvis's lifetime and the wealth of "fantasy" items issued after his death. The latter are collectible but have nowhere near the value of the pre-1977 material.

Also accept the fact that many of the modern limited edition items are purely speculative investments. It is best to buy them because you like them and plan to live with them for an extended period of time, not because you might realize a profit.

**History:** As a rock 'n' roll star, Elvis Presley was one of the first singers to target teen-agers in his promotional efforts. The first Elvis merchandise appeared in 1956. During the following years, new merchandise was added both in America and foreign countries. After his death in 1977, a vast number of new Elvis collectibles appeared.

**References:** Pauline Bartel, *Everything Elvis*, Taylor Publishing, 1995; Jerry Osborne, *Official Price Guide to Elvis Presley Records and Memorabilia*, House of Collectibles, 1994.

**Collectors' Clubs:** Elvis Forever TCB Fan Club, P.O. Box 1066, Pinellas Park, FL 34665; Graceland News Fan Club, P.O. Box 452, Rutherford, NJ 07070.

**Museums:** Graceland, Memphis, TN; Jimmy Velvet's Elvis Presley Museum, Franklin, TN.

Beverage Tent Card, Sahara Tahoe concert, logo ................................. 15.00
Book
*Meet Elvis Presley,* Favius Friedman, ©1971, 1973, 1977, paperback, 128 pgs, includes epilogue written after Presley's death, 7-3/4" x 5-1/4"
........................................ 10.00
*Operation Elvis,* Alan Levy, Henry Holt and Co., ©1960, hardcover
........................................ 12.00
First Day Cover, pink Cadillac, issued January 1993, Memphis, TN, canceled Tupelo, MS ..................... 7.50
Calendar, 1977, Tribute to Elvis, Boxcar Enterprises, 12" x 13" .............. 50.00
Flicker Button, 2-1/4" d, black and white photos of Elvis playing guitar, titled "Love Me Tender," ©1958 Elvis Presley Enterprises ........................ 25.00
Game, King of Rock, unopened
........................................ 25.00
Magazine, *Saturday Evening Post,* July/August, 1985, "Legends that Won't Die" ........................................ 10.00
Poster Book ................................. 10.00

**Record, Elvis' Christmas Album, RCA Victor, $28.**

# Punchboards

**Collecting Hints:** Punchboards which are unpunched are collectible. A board which has been punched has little value unless it is an extremely rare design. Like most advertising items, price is determined by graphics and subject matter.

The majority of punchboards sell in the $8 to $30 range. At the high end of the range are boards such as Golden Gate Bridge ($85) and Baseball Classic ($100).

**History:** Punchboards are self-contained games of chance made of pressed paper that has holes and coded tickets inside each hole. For an agreed amount, the player uses a "punch" to extract the ticket of his or her choice. Prizes are awarded to the winning ticket. Punch prices can be 1¢, 2¢, 3¢, 5¢, 10¢, 20¢, 50¢, $1, or more.

Not all tickets were numbered. Fruit symbols were used extensively as well as animals. Some punchboards had no printing at all, just colored tickets. Other ticket themes included dice, cards, dominoes, and words. One early board featured Mack Sennet bathing beauties.

Punchboards come in an endless variety of styles. Names reflect the themes of the boards: Barrel of Winners, Break the Bank, Baseball, More Smokes, Lucky Lulu and Take It Off are just a few.

At first punchboards winners were awarded cash. As a response to attempts to outlaw gambling, prizes were switched to candy, cigars, cigarettes, jewelry, radios, clocks, cameras, sporting goods, toys, beer, chocolate, etc.

The golden age of punchboards was from the 1920s to the 1950s. Attention was focused on the keyed punchboard in the film "The Flim Flam Man." This negative publicity hurt the punchboard industry.

**Museum:** Amusement Sales, Midvale, UT.

**Advisor:** Clark Phelps.

Ace High, 13" x 17", deck of cards for jackpot ..................................... 90.00
Barrel of Cigarettes, 10" x 10", Lucky Strike Green ............................ 44.00
Bars & Bells, 13" x 8-1/2", deck of cards, fruit symbols ........................ 135.00
Baseball Push Card, 7" x 10", 1¢, candy prize ......................................... 10.00
Basketball Push Card, 6" x 9", thin, 1¢, candy prize ............................. 10.00

**Liquor Bottle, McCormick, Yours, Elvis, '55, $95.**

PEZ Container, stem gold outfit, hand-painted ...................................... 80.00
Poster, movie, 22" x 28", Elvis Presley Kid Galahad, half-sheet, ©1962 United Artists ........................... 40.00
Puzzle, The King, Springbok, 1992, 1000 pieces .............................. 50.00
Radio, figural, MIB ......................... 50.00
Record
Blue Suede Shoes/Tutti Fruiti, RCA Victor, 45 rpm, 1956 .................. 60.00
Fun in Acapulco, RCA Victor, orig soundtrack, 1963 ...................... 50.00
Our Memories of Elvis, black label, DNT ............................................ 75.00
Personally Elvis, blue label, double pocket, silhouette..................... 50.00
Roustabout, RCA Victor, orig soundtrack, 1964 ...................... 50.00
Spinout, black label, DOT, RCA, white top................................... 35.00
Welcome to My World, black label, DNT, LP .................................... 30.00
Sheet Music, Love Me, 1954 ........ 35.00
Tab, 2" d, litho tin, blue, gold lettering, "I Love Elvis," metallic gold background, 1970s......................... 15.00
Tumbler, early 1970s.................... 48.00
Waste Can, litho tin, c1977 .......... 55.00

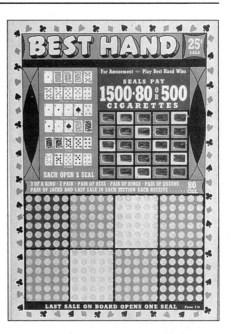

**Best Hand, poker hand tickets, 1-1/4" thick, $40. Photo courtesy of Clark J. Phelps.**

Beat the Seven, 10" x 10", card tickets determine winners .................. 35.00
Best Hand, poker hand tickets, 6-1/2" x 11", 1-1/4" thick, pays out in cigarettes ......................................... 40.00
Big Game, 8" x 10-1/2" ................. 30.00
Candy Special, 4-1/2" x 7-1/2", penny candy board ............................ 24.00
Cash In, 8-1/2" x 9", sack of money ............................................... 18.00
Double of Nothing, 9" x 10", trade stimulator......................................... 36.00
Fin Baby, 19" x 6", folding pull tab ............................................... 32.00

**Professor Charley, Superior Mfg., 1946, $16. Photo courtesy of Clark J. Phelps.**

**Win A Seal, wooden puncher, colored foil, 1920s, $70. Photo courtesy of Clark J. Phelps.**

Five on One, 11" x 11" ................... 18.00
Five Tens, 10" x 13" ....................... 18.00
Glades Chocolates, 7" x 9", set of three boards, factory wrapped ......... 75.00
Good Punching, 9-1/2" x 10", cowboy motif ........................................ 36.00
Home Run Derby, 10" x 12", baseball theme, green baseball park ..... 75.00
Jackpot Bingo, 10" x 8", thick card jackpot ............................................. 10.00
Joe's Special, 11" x 14" ................ 20.00
Johnson's Chocolates, 9" x 11", Elvgren girl ......................................... 35.00
Lu Lu Board, 10" x 11", colored tickets ................................................... 28.00
More Smokes, 10-1/2" x 10-1/2", red, white, and blue tickets ............. 24.00
Musical Money, 12" x 14" .............. 43.00
Nestle's Chocolate, 9" x 8-1/2", 2¢ board ........................................... 45.00
Nickel Fins, 12" x 15", cash board, colorful jackpot ........................... 40.00
Odd Pennies, 6-3/4" x 11", small change, 2¢ and 3¢ board ........ 45.00
Palm Chart, 20" x 11-1/2", 1936, orig envelope ................................... 8.00
Perry's Prizes, 9-1/2" x 13" ........... 60.00
Pocket Board, 2" x 2-3/4", great action cartoon graphic .......... ......... 8.00
Positive Prizes, 12" x 17", diecut field for prizes of your choice ............... 25.00
Pots A Plenty, 11" x 17-1/2" .......... 26.00
Premium Prizes, 10" x 12" ............. 20.00
Professor Charley, 1946, Superior Mfg. Typical 25¢ cash board .......... 16.00
Section Play, 8-1/2" x 10" ............. 18.00
So Sweet, 13-1/2" x 13" ................ 40.00
Speedy Tens, 10" x 13" ................. 18.00
Stars & Stripes, 9" x 14", red, white and blue, jackpot card ................... 26.00
Take It Or Leave It, 12" x 14" ......... 85.00
Tavern Maid, 9-1/2" x 13-1/2", cans of beer prize ............................... 55.00
Three Sure Hits, 10" x 13" ............. 24.00
Tu Pots, 12" x 18" ......................... 44.00
Win A Buck, 4-1/2" x 7-1/2" ........... 12.00
Win A Seal, 1920s, wooden puncher, 6 numbers on a ticket, colored foil ................................................... 70.00

# Purinton Pottery

**Collecting Hints:** The most popular patterns among collectors are Apple, Intaglio (brown), Normandy Plaid (red), Maywood, and Pennsylvania Dutch. Variations, e.g., Intaglio with a green ground, are known for many of these patterns.

Purinton also made a number of kitchenware and specialty pieces. These should not be overlooked. Among the harder-to-find items are animal figurines, tea tiles, and the Tom and Jerry bowl and mug set.

**History:** Bernard Purinton founded Purinton Pottery in 1936 in Wellsville, Ohio. This pilot plant produced decorative dinnerware, as well as some special-order pieces. In 1940, Roy Underwood, President of Knox Glass Company, approached Purinton about moving his operation to Knox's community, Shippenville.

In 1941, the pottery relocated to a newly built plant in Shippenville, Pennsylvania. The company's first product at the new plant, a two-cup premium teapot for McCormick Tea Company, rolled off the line on Dec. 7, 1941.

Dorothy Purinton and William H. Blair, her brother, were the chief designers for the company. Maywood, Plaid, and several Pennsylvania German designs were among the patterns attributed to Dorothy Purinton. William Blair, a graduate of the Cleveland School of Art, designed the Apple and Intaglio patterns.

Initially, slipware was cast. Later it was pressed using a Ram Press process. Clays came from Florida, Kentucky, North Carolina, and Tennessee.

Purinton Pottery did not use decals as did many of its competitors. Greenware was hand painted by locally trained decorators who then dipped the decorated pieces into glaze. This demanded a specially formulated body and a more expensive manufacturing process. Hand painting also allowed for some of the variations in technique and colors found on Purinton ware today.

Purinton made a complete dinnerware line for each pattern, plus a host of accessory pieces ranging from candleholders to vases. Dinnerware patterns were open stock. Purinton's ware received national distribution, and select lines were exported.

The plant ceased operations in 1958, reopened briefly, and finally closed for good in 1959. Cheap foreign imports were cited as the cause of the company's decline.

**References:** Jamie Bero-Johnson, *Purinton Pottery,* Schiffer Publishing, 1997; Pat Dole, *Purinton Pottery,* Denton Publishing, 1990; Susan Morris, *Purinton Pottery,* Collector Books, 1994.

**Periodical:** *Purinton Pastimes,* 20401 Ivybridge Ct., Gaithersburg, MD 20879.

**Collectors' Club:** Purinton Pottery Convention, P.O. Box 9394, Arlington, VA 22219.

Baker, Apple, 6" x 4" ................... 30.00
Bank, Raggedy Andy, 6-1/2" h ..... 80.00
Canister
  Flour, Brown Intaglio, square, wooden lid .............................. 95.00
  Set
    Apple, 4 pc, wire rack ....... 225.00
    Pennsylvania Dutch .......... 195.00
  Sugar
    Brown Intaglio, square, wooden lid ....................................... 95.00
    Fruit dec, cobalt blue trim ... 95.00
Casserole, cov
  Apple, oval .............................. 25.00
  Brown Intaglio, 9" d ................. 50.00
Cereal Bowl
  Apple ...................................... 18.00
  Brown Intaglio ......................... 12.00
  Pennsylvania Dutch ................. 15.00
Chop Plate
  Apple ...................................... 20.00
  Brown Intaglio, 12" d ............... 40.00
Coffee Mug, Plaid ......................... 1.00
Coffeepot, cov, Apple ................... 60.00
Cornucopia .................................. 20.00
Cookie Jar, cov
  Apple ...................................... 40.00
  Howdy Doody ....................... 250.00
  Pennsylvania Dutch ................. 55.00
Creamer
  Apple, double spout, 1-1/2" h ................................................ 12.00
  Fruits ...................................... 10.00
  Normandy Plaid ....................... 40.00
Cruet, Pennsylvania Dutch, jug-shape, price for pr ............................. 50.00
Cup and Saucer
  Apple ...................................... 24.00
  Brown Intaglio ......................... 10.00
  Normandy Plaid ....................... 17.50
Dessert Bowl, Brown Intaglio ....... 10.00
Drip Jar, cov
  Apple ...................................... 20.00
  Daisy ...................................... 80.00
  Plaid ....................................... 20.00
Honey Jug
  Red Intaglio ............................ 95.00
  Red Ivy ................................... 35.00
Jug
  Dutch, Fruits, 2 pint ................. 12.00
  Rebecca, Mountain Rose ........ 40.00

Juice Tumbler
    Fruits, apple and pear.............. 12.00
    Maywood................................. 15.00
Lazy Susan, Fruits, apple finial, painted
    pear, plum, pineapple, and cherries
    ............................................. 250.00
Marmalade, cov, Maywood.......... 32.00
Pitcher
    Apple, 6" h............................... 45.00
    Fruits ....................................... 32.00
Plate
    8" d, Apple .............................. 10.00
    8-1/2" d, Apple ....................... 22.00
    9" d, Normandy Plaid .............. 20.00
    9-1/2" d, Fruits........................ 15.00
    9-3/4" d, Plaid......................... 15.00
    10" d, Brown Intaglio ............... 14.00
    12" d, Apple, grill..................... 20.00

Platter
    Brown Intaglio, 11" l, oval......... 35.00
    Maywood, 12" l, oblong ........... 30.00
    Normandy Plaid, 12" l .............. 55.00
Relish Dish
    Fruits, divided, three parts, handle
    ............................................... 18.50
    Starflower, divided .................. 30.00
Roll Tray, Brown Intaglio, 11" l....... 35.00
Salt and Pepper Shakers, pr
    Apple ....................................... 18.00
    Palm Trees ............................ 100.00
    Plaid ........................................ 15.00
    Shake and Pour, 4-1/4" h.......... 65.00
Snack Set, Intaglio...................... 20.00
Soup and Sandwich Set, Rubel, bowl
    and plate.................................. 7.50

Sugar Bowl
    Apple, open ............................. 20.00
    Normandy Plaid, cov ............... 40.00
Tea and Toast Set, Apple, plate and cup
    ............................................... 30.00
Teapot, cov
    Apple ....................................... 35.00
    Fruits, 2 cup............................. 7.50
    Maywood, 6 cup ...................... 35.00
Tea Tile Trivet............................ 115.00
Vegetable
    Apple, oval............................... 20.00
    Brown Intaglio, 8-1/2" d........... 25.00
    Normandy Plaid
        8-1/2" d............................. 40.00
        10-1/2" l, divided ............... 50.00

# R

# Racing Collectibles

**Collecting Hints:** This is a field of heroes and also fans. Collectors love the winners; a household name counts. Losers are important only when major races are involved. Pre-1945 material is especially desirable because few individuals were into collecting prior to that time.

The field does have problems with reproductions and copycats. Check every item carefully. Beware of paying premium prices for items made within the last 20 years.

Auto racing items are one of the hot collectible markets of the 1990s. Although interest in Indy 500 collectibles remains strong, the market is dominated by NASCAR collectibles. In fact, the market is so strong that racing collectibles have their own separate show circuit and supporting literature.

There are so many horse racing collectibles that specialization is required from the beginning. Collector focuses include a particular horse racing type or a specific horse race, a breed or specific horse, or racing prints and images. Each year there are a number of specialized auctions devoted to horse racing. These range from sporting prints sales at the major New York auction houses to benefit auctions for the Thoroughbred Retirement Foundation.

**History:** Man's quest for speed is as old as time. Although this category focuses primarily on automobile and horse racing, other types of racing memorabilia are included. If it moves, it will and can be raced.

Automobile racing began before the turn of the century. Many of the earliest races took place in Europe. By the first decade of the 20th century, automobile racing was part of the American scene.

The Indianapolis 500 began in 1911 and was interrupted only by World War II. In addition to Formula 1 racing, the NASCAR circuit has achieved tremendous popularity with American racing fans. Cult heroes such as Richard Petty have become household names.

The history of horse racing dates back to the domestication of the horse itself. Prehistoric cave drawings illustrate horses racing. The Greeks engaged in chariot racing as early as 600 B.C. As civilization spread, so did the racing of horses. Each ethnic group and culture added its own unique slant.

The British developed the concept of the Thoroughbred, a group of horses that are descendants of three great Arabian stallions—Carley Arabian, Byerley Turk, and Goldolphin Arabian. Horse racing received royal sponsorship and became the Sport of Kings.

Horse racing reached America during the colonial period. By the 1800s, four-mile match races between regional champions were common. In 1863, Saratoga Race Track was built. The first Belmont Stakes was run at Jerome Park in 1867. As the 19th century ended, more than 300 race tracks operated seasonal cards. By 1908, the number of American race tracks had been reduced to 25 as a result of widespread opposition to gambling.

The premier American horse race is the Kentucky Derby. Programs date from 1924 and glasses, a favorite with collectors, from the late 1930s.

**References:** Mark Allen Baker, *Auto Racing Memorabilia*, Krause Publications, 1996; Bill Coulter, *Stock Car Model Kit Encyclopedia and Price Guide,* Krause Publications, 1999; Jack Mackenzie, *Indy 500 Buyers Guide*, published by author (6940 Wildridge Rd., Indianapolis, IN 46256), 1996.

**Periodicals:** *Collector's World*, P.O. Box 562029, Charlotte, NC 28256; *Racing Collectibles Price Guide*, P.O. Box 608114, Orlando, FL 32860.

**Collectors' Clubs:** National Indy 500 Collectors Club, 10505 N. Delaware St., Indianapolis, IN 46280; Sport of Kings Society, 1406 Annen Ln., Madison, WI 53711.

**Museums:** Aiken Thoroughbred Racing Hall of Fame & Museum, Aiken, SC; Harness Racing Hall of Fame, Goshen, NY; Indianapolis Motor Speedway Hall of Fame Museum, Speedway, IN; International Motor Sports Hall of Fame, Talladega, AL; Kentucky Derby Museum, Louisville, KY; National Museum of Racing & Hall of Fame, Saratoga Springs, NY.

**Additional Listings:** Horse Collectibles.

**Auto**

Ashtray, Smokin Joe Camel, pocket ................................................. 10.00
Bank, Robert Yates, diecast, 1994 ................................................. 7.50
Banner, Coors Light, slight wear .. 10.00
Book, *The Speed Merchants, The World of Road Racing, The Men, The Machines, The Tracks,* Michael Keyser, Prentice Hall, 1973, 1st edition, dj................................................ 15.00
Bubble Gum Cards, Grid, Formula I, factory set, 200 cards.............. 15.00
Calendar, 1995, NASCAR, Winston Cup Series...................................... 10.00
Display, Pepsi Racing, Jeff Gordon, life size ........................................ 325.00
Drinking Cup, 6-1/4" h, plastic, racing car theme, Pepsi 89 Car, "Pepsi Official Soft Drink of the Daytona 500," red plastic cap, reverse side with racing flags and their meanings 1.00
Helmet, 1950s, used ................... 17.50
Jacket, Rusty Wallace Miller NASCAR ................................................. 50.00
Magazine, *National Speed Sport News,* 65 issues, 1970s..................... 55.00
Magazine Tear Sheet, MGB, British Racing Green.......................... 12.00
Patch, Ford Racing, 1960s............. 7.50
Phone Card, NASCAR, Assetts Racing ................................................. 2.50
Photograph, 11" x 13", color, titled "One Last Lap, A Final Tribute to Davey & Alan, Nov. 14, 1993, Atlanta Motor Speedway" ............................. 15.00
Pinball Game, Mickey & Donald Speed Way, Ideal, tin and plastic........ 80.00
Playing Cards, Dale Earnhardt....... 4.50
Post Card
   Fairway Park, Casey, IL, postmarked 1908........................................ 10.00
   Miami Jockey Club, postmarked 1930.......................................... 7.50
   Palm Beach, FL, early view, postmarked 1907............................. 9.00
   Saratoga Race Track Grand Stand, postmarked 1911..................... 7.50

**Poster, "The Driving Force," text on back relating to sponsor, International Association of Machinists and Aerospace Workers, union logo and trademark, full color, 10" w, 8" h, $3.**

Press Kit
Kenny Schrader Kodiak, 1991
............................................. 15.00
Ricky Rudd Tide, 1994............. 12.00
Rusty Wallace Miller, 1994 ....... 12.00
Terry Labonte, Skoal, 1990 ..... 18.00
Press Pass, NASCAR.................... 45.00
Stein, Avon.................................. 17.50
Stock Certificate, Western Racing, Inc., 1958 ......................................... 5.00
Toy, car
1997 Hot Wheels Pro Racing, Bill Elliott stock car, #94, McDonald's, MIP............................................. 6.00
1997 Hot Wheels Pro Racing Car, Citgo, Michael Waltrip, MIP........ 8.00
1997 Hot Wheels Pro Racing Car, Spam, Mike Wallace, MIP .......... 8.00
1998 Winner's Circle Car, 40th annual Daytona 500, Dale Earnhardt, MIP............................................. 8.00
1998 Winner's Circle G M Goodwrench Car, Dale Earnhardt Lifetime Series, 1996 Olympic Chevrolet Monte Carlo, MIP ...................... 8.00
T-Shirt, Rusty Wallace, black, front "Midnight Hour Approaches #2 Rusty Wallace," back reads "#2 Rusty Wallace Miller Penske Racing," size XL
............................................. 8.00

**Dog**
Post Card
Dog Track, Tampa, FL.................... 7.00
Hialeah, Miami, FL, unused ............ 7.00
Hollywood Kennel Club, Hollywood, FL, unused ........................................ 6.00
Kenilworth Race Track, Buffalo, NY, early view, unused ...................... 9.00
Tray, tin litho, running greyhounds
............................................. 15.00

**Horse**
Badge, 3" d, Budweiser Million, Second Running, Aug. 29, 1982, full color illus ........................................... 10.00
Drinking Glass
Kentucky Derby, 1964, frosted, brown illus, gold lettering ......... 35.00
Saratoga Travers Stakes, 1995
............................................. 12.00
Figure, 5" x 2-1/2", mkd "Occupied Japan"...................................... 85.00
Lobby Card, Pride of the Blue Grass
............................................. 15.00
Mug, 5-1/2" h, Hollywood Gold Cup, Hollywood Park
Seabiscuit, 1938 ..................... 6.00
Slew of Damascus,1949 ........... 6.00
Needle Book, 4-1/2" x 4-3/4", Steep Chase, cardboard, full color art, 1930s ........................................ 30.00
Pinback Button, 1-3/4" d, Pimlico Preakness, multicolored, horse head illus, white ground, blue lettering, 1960s
............................................. 20.00
Plate, "Compliments of Peterson & Wallin, Orion, IL," 8-1/4" d, horse race dec ............................................. 65.00
Post Card
Going to the Post at Hialeah Park, Miami, FL, unused..................... 6.50
Man O' War, unused.................. 6.00

Sunshine Park, Oldsmar, FL, unused
............................................. 8.50
Stickpin, brass, jockey cap over entwined initials, green and white enamel accents, 1906 ............. 30.00
Ticket, Kentucky Derby, May 1936
............................................. 10.00

# Radio Characters and Personalities

**Collecting Hints:** Many items associated with radio characters and personalities were offered as premiums. This category focuses mostly on the non-premium items. Radio premiums are listed separately in this book.

Don't overlook the vast amount of material related to the radio shows themselves. This includes scripts, props, and a wealth of publicity material. Many autographed photographs appear on the market. Books, especially Big Little Books and similar types, featured many radio-related characters and stories.

Radio characters and personalities found their way into movies and television. Serious collectors exclude the products which spun off from these other two areas.

**History:** The radio show was a dominant force in American life from the 1920s to the early 1950s. "Amos 'n' Andy" began in 1929, "The Shadow" in 1930, and "Chandu the Magician" in 1932. Although many of the characters were fictional, the individuals who portrayed them became public idols. A number of figures achieved fame on their own—Eddie Cantor, Don McNeill of "The Breakfast Club," George Burns and Gracie Allen, Arthur Godfrey, and Jack Benny.

Sponsors and manufacturers were quick to capitalize on the fame of the radio characters and personalities. Premiums were offered as part of the shows' themes. However, merchandising did not stop with premiums. Many non-premium items, such as bubble gum cards, figurines, games, publicity photographs, and dolls, were issued. Magazine advertisements often featured radio personalities.

**References:** Jim Harmon, *Radio & TV Premiums,* Krause Publications, 1997; Rex Miller, *The Investor's Guide to Vintage Character Collectibles,* Krause Publications, 1999; Jon D. Swartz and Robert C. Reinehr, *Handbook of Old-Time Radio,*

Scarecrow Press, 1993.

**Periodicals:** *Friends of Old Time Radio,* P.O. Box 4321, Hamden, CT 06514; *Hello Again,* P.O. Box 4321, Hamden, CT 06514; *Nostalgia Digest and Radio Guide,* Box 421, Morton Grove, IL 60053; *Old Time Radio Digest,* 4114 Montgomery Rd., Cincinnati, OH 45212.

**Collectors' Clubs:** Friends of Vic & Sade, 7232 N. Keystone Ave., Lincolnwood, IL 60646; Golden Radio Buffs of Maryland, Inc., 301 Jeanwood Ct., Baltimore, MD 21222; Illinois Old Radio Shows Society, 10 S 540 County Line Rd, Hinsdale, IL 60521; Manuscript Society, 350 N Niagara St, Burbank, CA 91505; National Lum & Abner Society, #81 Sharon Blvd., Dora, IL 35062; North America Radio Archives, 134 Vincewood Dr., Nicholasville, KY 40356; Old Time Radio Club, 56 Christen Ct., Lancaster, NY 14086; Old Time Radio Collectors Traders Society, 725 Cardigan Ct., Naperville, IL 60565; Oldtime Radio Show Collectors Association, 45 Barry St., Sudbury, Ontario P3B 3H6 Canada; Pow-Wow, 301 E. Buena Vista Ave., N. Augusta, SC 29841; Radio Collectors of America, Ardsley Circle, Brockton, MA 02402; Society to Preserve & Encourage Radio Drama, Variety & Comedy, P.O. Box 7177, Van Nuys, CA 91409.

**Museum:** Museum of Broadcasting, New York, NY.

**Additional Listings:** Big Little Books, Comic Books, Radio Premiums, Super Heroes.

**Amos n' Andy**
Game, Card Party, M. Davis Co., 2 score pads, 8 tallies, orig box, 1938
............................................. 75.00
Get Well Card, 4-1/2" x 5-1/2", black and white photo, Hall Brothers, 1931
............................................. 32.00
Photo, 5" x 7", browntone, matte finish, Pepsodent Co., 1929 ............... 30.00
Record Set.................................. 50.00

**Captain Midnight**
Photo, Captain Midnight with Patsy and Chuck, Skelly Oil...................... 35.00
Token Medallion, Captain Midnight, Skelly Oil ................................. 35.00

**Don Winslow**
Bank, 2-1/4" h, Uncle Don's Earnest Saver Club, oval, paper label, photo and cartoon illus, Greenwich Savings Bank, New York City, 1930s
............................................. 40.00
Salt and Pepper Shakers, pr, full color, plaster..................................... 75.00

## Edgar Bergen and Charlie McCarthy

Bubble Gum Wrapper, Bergen's Better Bubble Gum .............................. 10.00
Costume, Charlie, Edgar Bergen Productions, 1950s ........................ 45.00
Game, Charlie McCarthy Radio Party Game, orig envelope .............. 65.00
Pencil Sharpener, figural, diecut plastic, color decal, 1930s .................. 72.00
Soap, 4" h, figural, orig box, Kerk Guild, 1930-40 ................................... 75.00

## Fibber McGee and Molly

Fan Card, 8" x 10", black and white glossy, 11 cast members, Kolynos Dental Cream, ©1933 .............. 60.00
Menu, 9-1/2" x 12-1/4", Brown Derby, autographed .......................... 120.00
Record, 10-1/4" x 12", four 78 RPM records, live broadcasts, colorful cover, 1947 ............................. 55.00
Flying Family, Cocomalt, puzzle, 1932, orig envelope ........................... 60.00

## Jack Armstrong

Ped-o-Meter ................................. 30.00
Reel, magnetic tape, The All American Boy Radio Shows, 15 minute episodes, 1940-41, 7 pcs ............. 75.00
Ring, baseball ............................. 500.00

## Jack Benny

Magazine, Jack Benny and Rochester, Look ....................................... 22.00
Program, 9" x 12", black and white photos, Phil Harris signature, 12 pgs, late 1930s ................................ 27.50

## Jimmie Allen

Model, 19" l airplane, Thunderbolt, orig box, 1930s ............................. 120.00
Photo, teen-age aviator ................. 40.00

## Joe Penner

Sheet Music, Don't Never Do-o-o That, black and yellow cover, ©1934 T. B. Harms Co. ............................... 25.00
Valentine, 4-1/2" x 7", mechanical, diecut, holding duck on shoulder, "I'll Gladly Buy A Duck," 1930-40 ................................................ 24.00

**Pinback Button, Uncle Don's Ice Cream Club, Borden's, cream and read, 1" d, $18.50.**

## Little Orphan Annie

Book
*Little Orphan Annie and the Circus*, Cupples & Leon, 1927, 7" x 9", hardcover ........................................ 60.00
*Secret Society Signs & Signals*, Little Orphan Annie, 1937 ............... 115.00
Coloring Book, Little Orphan Annie, McLaughlin, 19303, 10" x 13" ................................................ 120.00
Decoder, Little Orphan Annie, 1936 ................................................ 40.00
Manual, Secret Society, orig mailer ................................................ 125.00
Mug
　Aqua, orange top ................... 150.00
　Green, red top ....................... 100.00
　Light tan, orange top .............. 70.00
Puzzle, Famous Comics, #1, 1930s ................................................ 135.00
Ring, Secret Message ............... 335.00
Watch Box, 1938, white ............. 250.00

## Major Bowes,

clock, 5-1/2" h, Ingersol, metal, brass luster, raised numerals, 1930s ................................... 145.00

**Quiz Kids,** game, Rapaport Bros., electric, orig box and instructions .. 25.00

## The Shadow

Book, *The Living Shadow*, Maxwell Grant, c193 l ......................... 10.00
Figure, 7" h, china, glossy black cloak and hat, c1930 .................... 265.00
Ring, Secret Agent, MIB ............. 130.00
Rubber Stamp ............................ 40.00
Toy, super jet, plastic, orig package ................................................ 45.00

**Young Explorers Club,** badge .... 50.00

# Radio Premiums

**Collecting Hints:** Most collections are centered around one or two specific personalities or radio programs.

**History:** Radio premiums are nostalgic reminders of the radio shows of childhood. Sponsors of shows frequently used their products as a means of earning premiums, such as saving box tops to exchange for gifts related to a program or personality.

**References:** Ted Hake, *Hake's Price Guide to Character Toy Premiums*, Collector Books, 1996; Jim Harmon, *Radio & TV Premiums,* Krause Publications, 1997; Robert M. Overstreet, *Overstreet Premium Ring Price Guide*, Gemstone Publishing, 1995; —, *Overstreet Toy Ring Price Guide*, 2nd ed., Collector Books, 1996; Tom Tumbusch, *Tomart's Price Guide to Radio Premium and Cereal Box Collectibles*, Wallace-Homestead, 1991.

**Periodical:** *Box Top Bonanza*, 3403 46th Ave., Moline, IL 61265.

**Reproduction Alert.**

**Additional Listings:** Radio Characters and Personalities.

Book
　*Amos 'n' Andy,* Rand McNally & Co., ©1929, hardcover, autographed ................................................ 265.00
　*Buck Rogers Solar Scouts Handbook,* ©1936 ........................ 275.00
Booklet, Zenith Radios, Jack Benny, Burns & Allen, Boswells, 1930s ................................................ 45.00
Catalog, 8-1/4" x 10-1/4", Tom Mix premiums, orig folder .................... 35.00
Certificate, 6" x 8-1/2", Counter-Spy Junior Agents Club, Pepsi-Cola, c1950 ................................................ 28.50
Comic Book, Foldess, #36 .......... 15.00
Flashlight, Sgt. Preston, 3" l, plastic, black, red, and green color discs, facsimile signature, ©1949 ...... 25.00

**Game, Little Orphan Annie, Milton Bradley, 1927, $125.**

**Mug, Little Orphan Annie, Beetle War, Ovaltine, $30.**

Identification Bracelet, Tom Mix, silvered brass chain, disc, 2 six guns, Ralston address and serial number, 1947 .......................................... 55.00
Membership Card
  Green Hornet ........................... 15.00
  Superman, 1940 ...................... 24.00
Mug, Ovaltine, Captain Midnight, red plastic, colorful decal, c1953
  ................................................... 70.00
Newspaper Advertisement, Sky King, Name-A-Plane Contest, 1950s
  ................................................... 25.00
Patch
  Captain Midnight, iron-on ........ 30.00
  Jack Armstrong, Future Champions of America, 1943 ...................... 22.00
Photo
  Buck Rogers, Buck and Wilma, 7-1/2" x 10", black and white, facsimile signatures, Cocomalt, c1934 .......... 85.00
  Captain Midnight, Chuck Ramsey, 6" x 7-1/2", black and white, white facsimile signature, Skelly Oil, 1939
  ................................................... 70.00
  Jack Armstrong, Blackstar, 1933
  ................................................... 20.00
Pinback Button, Lone Ranger Safety Club, 1934............................... 22.00
Puzzle
  9" x 12", Just Plain Bill, Kolynos Dental Cream, 150 pcs, orig envelope
  ................................................... 32.00
  9" x 12-1/2", Tucker County Horse Race, Little Orphan Annie, orig instruction sheet and mailing box, Ovaltine, c1933 ........................ 75.00
Sheet Music, *Little Orphan Annie's Song,* Harold Gray illus cov, Ovaltine, 1931, 4 pgs ...................... 27.50
Whistle, Jimmy Allen, brass, c1936
  ................................................... 30.00

# Radios

**Collecting Hints:** Radio collectors divide into three groups: those who collect because of nostalgia, those interested in history and/or acquiring radios that represent specific periods, and collectors of personality and figural radios. Most collectors find broadcasting, and therefore broadcast receivers, of primary interest.

Broadcast receivers can be divided into these significant categories:

Crystal sets and battery powered receivers of the early 1920s

Rectangular electric table models of the late 1920s

Cathedrals, tombstones, and consoles of the '30s

Midget plastic portables and wood-cabinet table models built before and after World War II

Shaped radios with cases made of Bakelite or other plastic

Personality and figural radios made between the 1930s and the 1960s.

Because the prime nostalgic period seems to be the decade of the '30s, the cathedral style, socket-powered radios (e.g., the Philco series) have become sought after items. Recently young collectors have exhibited interest in the plastic-cabinet radios built between 1945 and 1960.

Newer radio collectors are influenced by novelty, with the outside appearance the most important feature. The radio must play; but shape, color, decoration, and condition of the case far outweigh the internal workings of the set in determining desirability and, consequently, price. Enclosures that resemble things or figures (e.g., Mickey Mouse) command premium prices. The square table models of the later '30s and the midget sets of the late 1930s and 1940s have recently attracted the attention of collectors.

The value of a radio is directly proportional to its appearance and its operating condition. Minor scratches are to be expected as is alligatoring of the surface finish, but gouges, cracks, and delaminated surfaces adversely affect prices, as will a crack, a broken place where plastic closures belong, or missing parts, tubes, or components. If major repairs are required to make the set work, the price must reflect this potential expense.

Many collectors specialize in radio-related memorabilia, brand names, or in a facet of radio paraphernalia such as loudspeakers, tubes, or microphones. As a result, auxiliary and radio-related items are becoming collectibles along with radios themselves.

Very rare radios usually go directly to major collectors, seldom appearing in the general market. Wireless equipment and radios used commercially before World War I are considered rare and are not listed here.

**History:** The radio was invented more than 100 years ago. Marconi was the first to assemble and employ the transmission and reception instruments that permitted electric messages to be sent without the use of direct connections. The early name for radio was "Wireless," and its first application was to control ships in 1898. Early wireless equipment is not generally considered collectible since its historic value makes it important for museum display.

Between 1905 and the end of World War I, many technical advances, including the invention of the vacuum tube by DeForest, increased communication technology and encouraged amateur interest. The receiving equipment from that period is desired by collectors and historians but is rarely available.

By 1920, radio technology allowed broadcasts to large numbers of people simultaneously and music could be brought directly from concert halls into living rooms. The result was the development of a new art that changed the American way of life during the 1920s. The world became familiar through the radio in an average listener's home.

Radio receivers changed substantially in the decade of the '20s, going from black boxes—with many knobs and dials—powered by expensive and messy batteries, to stylish furniture, simple to use, and operated from the house current that had become the standard source of home energy. During the '20s, radios grew more complicated and powerful, as well as more ornate. Consoles appeared, loudspeakers were incorporated into them, and sound fidelity became an important consideration.

In the early 1930s, demand changed. The large expensive console gave way to small but effective table models. The era of the "cathedral" and the "tombstone" began. By the end of the thirties, the midget radio had become popular. Quality of sound was replaced by a price reduction, and most homes had more than one radio.

Shortly after World War II, the miniature tubes developed for the military were utilized in domestic radios. The result was further reduction in size and a substantial improvement in quality. The advent of FM also speeded improvements. Plastic technology made possible the production of attractive cases in many styles and colors.

The other development that drastically changed the radio receiver was the invention of the transistor in 1927. A whole new family of radio sets that could be carried in the shirt pocket became popular. Their popularity grew as they became less and less expensive, but their low cost meant that they were frequently thrown away when they stopped working. Today they are not easy to find in good condition and are, therefore, quite collectible.

**References:** John H. Bryant and Harold N. Cones, *Zenith Trans-Oceanic*, Schiffer Publishing, 1995; Marty and Sue Bunis, *Collector's Guide to Antique Radios*, 4th ed., Collector Books, 1997; —, *Collector's Guide to Transistor Radios*, 2nd ed., Collector Books, 1996; Marty Bunis and Robert F. Breed, *Collector's Guide to Novelty Radios*, Collector Books, 1995; *Evolution of the Radio*, Vol I (1991, 1994 value update), Vol. II (1993), L-W Book Sales; Harold Cones and John Bryant, *Zenith Radio: The Early Years, 1919-1935*, Schiffer Publishing, 1997; Chuck Dachis, *Radios by Hallicrafters*, Schiffer Publishing, 1996; Roger Handy, Maureen Erbe, and Aileen Farnan Antonier, *Made in Japan: Transistor Radios of the 1950s and 1960s*, Chronicle Books, 1993; David Johnson, *Guide to Old Radios: Pointers, Pictures, and Prices*, 2nd ed., Wallace-Homestead, 1995; Ken Jupp and Leslie Piña, *Genuine Plastic Radios of the Mid-Century*, Schiffer Publishing, 1998; Harry Poster, *Poster's Radio & Television Price Guide*, 2nd ed., Wallace-Homestead, 1994; —, *Illustrated Price Guide to Vintage Televisions and Deco Radios*, published by author, 1991; Ron Ramirez, *Philco Radio*, Schiffer Publishing, 1993; B. Eric Rhoads, *Blast from the Past*, available from author (800-226-7857), 1996; Norman Smith, *Transistor Radios: 1954-1968*, Schiffer Publishing, 1998; Mark Stein, *Machine Age to Jet Age, Radiomania's Guide to Tabletop Radios—1933-1959*, published by author (2109 Carterdale Rd., Baltimore, MD 21209.

**Periodicals:** *Antique Radio Classified*, P.O. Box 2, Carlisle, MA 01746; *Antique Radio Topics*, Box 28572, Dallas, TX 75228; *Horn Speaker*, P.O. Box 1193, Mabank, TX 75147; *Radio Age*, 636 Cambridge Rd., Augusta, GA 30909; *Transistor Network*, RR1, Box 36, Bradford, NH 03221.

**Videotape:** Roger Handy and Eric Wrobbel, *Favorite Transistor Radios*, available from producers (20802 Exhibit Ct., Woodland Hills, CA 91367).

**Collectors' Clubs:** Antique Radio Club of America, 300 Washington Trails, Washington, PA 15301; Antique Wireless Association, 59 Main St., Bloomfield, NY 14469; New England Antique Radio Club, RR1 Box 36, Bradford, NH 03221; Vintage Radio & Phonograph Society, Inc., P.O. Box 165345, Irving, TX 75016.

**Museums:** Antique Radio Museum, St. Louis, MO; Antique Wireless Association's Electronic Communication Museum, Bloomfield, NY; Caperton's Radio Museum, Louisville, KY; Muchow's Historical Radio Museum, Elgin, IL; Museum of Broadcast Communications, Chicago, IL; Museum of Wonderful Wireless, Minneapolis, MN; New England Museum of Wireless and Steam, East Greenwich, RI; Voice of the Twenties, Orient, NY.

**Advisor:** Lewis S. Walters.

**Notes:** The prices listed are for sets in average to good condition and are based upon an electrically complete receiver that operates when powered.

## Admiral

Portable
    #33 ........................................... 30.00
    #35 ........................................... 30.00
    #37 ........................................... 30.00
    #217, leatherette ..................... 40.00

    #909, All World ........................ 85.00
Y-2127, Imperial 8, c1959 ............. 45.00
**Air King**, tombstone, Art Deco
    ......................................... 3,000.00

## Arvin

Hopalong Cassidy, larietenna .... 525.00
Rhythm Baby #417 ..................... 275.00
Table
    #444 ...................................... 100.00
    #522A ....................................... 65.00
Tombstone, #617, Rhythm Maid
    ........................................... 215.00

## Atwater Kent

Breadboard
    Model 9A ............................. 550.00
    Model 10, orig tags ............. 1,400.00
    Model 10C ............................ 930.00
Cathedral, 80, c1931 ................. 380.00
Table
    #55, Keil ................................ 225.00
    #318, dome ........................... 115.00
Tombstone, #854 ........................ 155.00
Type R Horn ............................... 200.00
**Bulova**, clock radio
#100 ............................................. 40.00
#120 ............................................. 40.00
**Colonial**, New World Radio ..... 1,000.00
**Columbia**, table radio, oak ........ 125.00

## Crosley

Ace V ........................................... 80.00
Bandbox, #600, 1927 ................. 425.00
Battery Operated, #4-28 ............. 130.00
Dashboard .................................. 120.00
Gemchest, #609 ......................... 175.00
Liffella, 1N cathedral ................... 175.00
Pup, with box .............................. 500.00
Sheraton, cathedral ..................... 290.00
Showbox, #706 ........................... 100.00
Super Buddy Boy ........................ 125.00
**Dumont**, RA346, table, scroll work, 1938 .......................................... 110.00

## Emerson

AU-190, Catalin, tombstone .... 1,500.00
BT-245 .................................... 1,200.00
#274, Bakelite, brown ................ 185.00
#409, Mickey ........................... 1,400.00
#411, Mickey ........................... 1,400.00
#570, Memento .......................... 110.00
#640, Portable ............................. 30.00
#888, Vanguard .......................... 60.00

## Fada

#43 ............................................. 240.00
#53X ........................................... 200.00
#60W ............................................ 75.00
#115, bullet shape ...................... 850.00
#136 ........................................ 1,000.00
#252 ........................................... 575.00
#625, rounded end, slide rule dial
    ........................................... 700.00

## Federal

#58DX ......................................... 500.00
#110 ........................................... 550.00

## General Electric

#81, c1934 ................................. 200.00
#400 ............................................. 30.00
#410 ............................................. 30.00
#411 ............................................. 30.00
#414 ............................................. 30.00
#515 ............................................. 25.00

**Transistor, Telefunken TR-1, 1955, first German transistor, $3,197. Photo courtesy of Auction Team Breker.**

#517, clock radio ............................ 25.00
K-126 ............................................ 150.00
Tombstone .................................... 250.00

**Grebe**
CR-9 ............................................. 500.00
CR-12 ........................................... 600.00
MU-1 ............................................ 200.00

**Halicrafters**
TW-200 ......................................... 125.00
TW-600 ......................................... 100.00

**Majestic**
Charlie McCarthy ..................... 1,000.00
#92 .............................................. 125.00
#381 ............................................. 225.00
**Metrodyne,** Super 7, 1925 ......... 265.00

**Motorola**
#68X11Q Art Deco ........................ 75.00
Jet Plane ....................................... 55.00
Jewel Box ...................................... 80.00
M logo ........................................... 25.00
Pixie .............................................. 45.00
Ranger, portable ........................... 40.00
Ranger #700 .................................. 45.00
Table, plastic ................................. 35.00
**Olympic,** radio with phonograph
...................................................... 40.00

**Paragon**
DA-2, table ................................... 475.00
RD-5, table ................................... 600.00

**Philco**
T-7 126, transistor ........................ 65.00
T1000, clock radio ........................ 80.00

#17, cathedral ............................. 250.00
#20, cathedral ............................. 250.00
#37, cathedral, 1937 ................... 175.00
#37, table, 2 tone .......................... 75.00
#38, cathedral ............................. 250.00
#40, console, wood ..................... 150.00
#46, table ...................................... 20.00
#49, Boomerang .......................... 475.00
#49, Transitone ............................. 35.00
#52, Transitone ............................. 40.00
#60, cathedral ............................. 175.00
#62, table, 2 tone .......................... 75.00
#84, cathedral, 1937 ................... 175.00
#132, table .................................... 20.00
#180, console, wood ................... 150.00
#501, Boomerang ........................ 475.00
#506, Transitone ........................... 40.00
#544, Transitone ........................... 40.00
#551, 1928 .................................. 145.00
**Radiobar,** glasses and decanters
.................................................. 1,500.00

**Radio Corporation of America, RCA**
La Siesta ...................................... 300.00
Radiola
#18, with speaker ................... 115.00
#20 ......................................... 165.00
#24 ......................................... 170.00
#28, console .......................... 200.00
#33 ........................................... 40.00
#6X7, table, plastic ................. 25.00
8BT-7LE, portable .................... 35.00
40X56, World's Fair ............. 1,000.00

**Silvertone, Sears**
#1, table ........................................ 75.00
#1582, cathedral, wood .............. 225.00
#1955, tombstone ....................... 135.00
#9205, plastic, transistor ............. 40.00
**Sony,** transistor
TFM-151, 1960 ....................... 50.00
TR-63, 1958 .......................... 145.00

**Sparton**
#506, Blue Bird, Art Deco ........ 3,300.00
#5218 ............................................ 95.00
Blue Bird Reproduction .............. 150.00
**Stewart Warner,** table, slant ...... 175.00
**Stromberg Carlson,** #636A, console
...................................................... 125.00
**Westinghouse,** Model WR-602 ... 50.00

**Zenith**
#6D2615, table, boomerang dial
........................................................ 95.00
Royal
#500, transistor, owl eye .......... 75.00
#500D, transistor ...................... 55.00
#750L, transistor, leather case
............................................... 40.00
Trans-Occanic ............................. 175.00
Zephyr, multiband ......................... 75.00

# Railroad Items

**Collecting Hints:** Most collectors concentrate on one railroad as opposed to one type of object. Railroad material always brings a higher price in the area in which it originated. Local collectors tend to concentrate on local railroads. The highest prices are paid for material

from railroads which operated for only a short time. Nostalgia also influences collectors.

There are many local railroad clubs. Railroad buffs tend to have their own specialized swap meets and exhibitions. A large one is held in Gaithersburg, Maryland, in the fall each year.

**History:** It was a canal company, the Delaware and Hudson, which used the first steam locomotive in America. The Stourbridge Lion moved coal from the mines to the canal wharves. Just as America was entering its great canal era in 1825, the railroad was gaining a foothold. The Commonwealth of Pennsylvania did not heed William Strickland's advice to concentrate on building railroads instead of canals.

By the 1840s, railroad transportation was well-established. Numerous private companies were organized, although many remained in business for only a short time.

During the Civil War, the effectiveness of the railroad was demonstrated. Immediately following the war, the transcontinental railroad was completed, and entrepreneurs such as Gould and Vanderbilt created financial empires. Mergers generated huge systems. The golden age of the railroad extended from the 1880s to the 1940s.

After 1950, the railroads suffered from poor management, a bloated labor force, lack of maintenance, and competition from other forms of transportation. Thousands of miles of track were abandoned. Many railroads failed or merged together. The 1970s saw the federal government enter the picture with Conrail and Amtrak. Today railroads still are fighting for survival.

**References:** Stanley L. Baker, *Railroad Collectibles*, 4th ed., Collector Books, 1990, 1996 value update; Richard C. Barrett, *Illustrated Encyclopedia of Railroad Lighting*, Railroad Research Publications, 1994; *Collectible Lanterns*, L-W Book Sales, 1996; Barbara J. Conroy, *Restaurant China: Restaurant, Airline, Ship & Railroad Dinnerware, Volume 1*, Collector Books, 1998; David Dreimiller, *Dressel Railway Lamp & Signal Company*, Hiram Press, 1995; Joseph F. Farrell, Jr., *Illustrated Guide to Peter Gray Railroad Hardware*, Hiram Press, 1994; Anthony Hobson, *Lanterns That Lit Our World*, Hiram Press, reprinted 1996;

Richard Luckin, *Dining on Rails, An Encyclopedia of Railroad China,* RK Publishing, 1998; —, *Mimbres to Mimbreno,* RK Publishing, 1992; Everett L. Maffett, *Silver Banquet II,* Silver Press, 1990; Larry R. Paul, *Sparkling Crystal: A Collector's Guide to Railroad Glassware,* Railroadiana Collectors Association, Inc., 1990; Don Stewart, *Railroad Switch Keys & Padlocks,* 2nd ed., Key Collectors International, 1993.

**Periodicals:** *Key, Lock and Lantern,* P.O. Box 65, Demarest, NJ 07627; *The Main Line Journal,* P.O. Box 121, Steamwood, IL 60107; *Railfan & Railroad,* P.O. Box 700, Newton, NJ 07860-0700; *Trains,* P.O. Box 1612, Waukesha, WI 53187; *U.S. Rail News,* P.O. Box 7007, Huntingdon Woods, MI 48070.

**Collectors' Clubs:** Canadian Railroad Historical Association, 120 Rue St. Pierre, St. Constant, Quebec J5A 2G9 Canada; Chesapeake & Ohio Historical Society, Inc., P.O. Box 79, Clifton Forge, VA 24422; Key, Lock and Lantern, P.O. Box 65, Demarest, NJ 07627; Illinois Central Railroad Historical Society, 14818 Cliron Park, Midlothian, IL 60445; New York Central System Historical Society, Inc., P.O. Box 58994, Philadelphia, PA 19102-8994; Railroad Enthusiasts, 102 Dean Rd., Brookline, MA 02146; Railroadiana Collectors Association, 795 Aspen Dr., Buffalo Grove, IL 60089; Railway and Locomotive Historical Society, P.O. Box 1418, Westford, MA 01886; Twentieth Century Railroad Club, 329 W. 18th St., Suite 902, Chicago, IL 60616.

**Museums:** Baltimore and Ohio Railroad, Baltimore, MD; California State Railroad Museum, Sacramento, CA; Museum of Transportation, Brookline, MA; New York Museum of Transportation, West Henrietta, NY.

Baggage Check, Texas Central RR, 1-5/8" x 2", brass, Poole Bros., Chicago ........................................ 38.50
Blanket, Canadian Pacific ............. 85.00
Blotter, Soo Line, 1920s, unused .... 5.00
Bond, New York Central, January 1948 ................................................ 4.00
Book
    *Electric Railways of Northeastern Ohio,* Central Electric Railfans Assoc., 1965 ............................ 37.50
    *Highball, A Pageant of Trains,* Lucius Beebe, Bonanza Books, 1945, 225 pgs ............................................ 22.50
    *Northern Ohio's Interurban's & Rapid Transit Railways, Trolleys, & Trains Too,* Harry Christiansen, 1965, 176 pgs ............................................ 37.50

*Oliphant's Earning Power of Railroads 1946,* James H. Oliphant & Co., 1946, 556 pgs .................. 10.00
Booklet
    By the Way of the Canyons, Soo Line, 1907 ............................... 20.00
    Union Pacific RR, 1926 ........... 15.00
Brochure
    Eastern Summer Trips, B & O .. 12.00
    Florida East Coast Railway & Steamship Co., January 1900, 39 pgs ............................................. 150.00
    Holiday Haunts, Adirondacks & 1,000 Islands, NYC, 1940, 63 pgs .............................................. 20.00
Caboose Marker, Atlantic Coast Line RR Co., 1900, 4-way lamp ........... 385.00
Calendar Card, 2-1/4" x 3-3/4", Gulf, Mobil & Northern, celluloid, red, white, and blue vest type, 1937, shows "The Rebel/The South's First Streamlined Air Conditioned Train," reverse with railway route from Illinois to Gulf of Mexico .............. 35.00
Calendar
    1943, Burlington Zephyr .......... 90.00
    1961, PA RR Transportation Center, Six Penn Center Plaza, Philadelphia, plastic, wallet size ...................... 5.00
Catalog, Hibbard Spencer Barlett & Co., Railway and Manufacturer's Supplies, 1907, 632 pgs .......... 55.00
Car Inspector's Record, D & RGW, Ridway, filled in, 1928 .................... 10.00
Cereal Premium, tin sign, set of ten ................................................ 35.00
China
    Bouillon Cup, WP, feather Friver, top logo, Shenango ........................ 75.00
    Butter Pat, Mimbreno, Syracuse China, full backstamp .............. 30.00
    Celery Dish, Union Pacific, 10" l, oval, blue and gold pattern, backstamped "Scannel China" ........ 40.00
    Coffee Cup, Illinois Central, Coral pattern ..................................... 20.00
    Creamer, B & O Centenary .... 65.00
    Cup and Saucer
        B & O, Capital ..................... 50.00
        NYC, Mercury, Syracuse, backstamped ............................. 55.00
        Southern Pacific ................... 65.00
    Demitasse Cup and Saucer, CMSTP & P, Traveler, Syracuse, backstamped ........................... 85.00
    Dish, Santa Fe Super Chief ...... 65.00
    Mustard Container, cov, small, white china, red PR RR keystone logo ................................................ 45.00
    Plate
        Missouri Pacific, state flowers .......................................... 275.00
        NP, dinner, Yellowstone Park Line logo, top mkd, Shenango ........................................... 145.00
        NYC, dinner, Mohawk, salmon pink and black, top mkd ..... 45.00
    Platter
        Southern, Peach Blossom, top mkd with logo and "Southern Serves The South," Buffalo China .......................................... 125.00

Union Pacific, 8" l, oval, Challenger pattern, top mkd "The Challenger," backstamped Union Pacific RR ........................... 45.00
Sauce Dish, NYNH & H, Indian Tree pattern, Buffalo China backstamp ................................................ 35.00
Sherbet, PRR, Keystone, Buffalo China ...................................... 65.00
Soup Plate
    B & O, Capitol, Shenango China ........................................... 85.00
    PRR, Purple Laurel, 6-1/2" d, broad lip, Sterling China ..... 40.00
Coaster, Central RR, New Jersey, Statue of Liberty logo, set of 6 ............ 15.00
Coloring Book, Union Pacific RR giveaway, 29 pgs, 1954, 8" x 10" ....... 20.00
Commemorative Plate, 10-1/2" d, B & O Railroad, blue transfer scene of Harper's Ferry, Lamberton China, 13-1/4" d turned wood frame ...... 165.00
Conductor's Report, Wiscasset, Waterville & Farmington Railway, CO, filled in, 1920s .................................. 5.00
Creamer, Canadian Pacific, SP, mkd "England" ................................ 25.00
Freight Receipt, NY, Lake Erie & Western RR, dated 1883 .................. 4.00
Hat Rack, overhead type, coach, wood and bras, 6 brass double-sided hooks ..................................... 200.00
Head Rest Cover, PRR, tan ground, brown logo, 15" x 18" .............. 15.00
Highball Glasses, clear, gold and white dec, PR RR, set of 4 ............. 150.00
Lamp
    Caboose, side, int., C & O Railroad, c1920, price for pr ................. 350.00
    Pullman, brass, early electric, white Bakelite shade, heavy wall brackets, 7-1/2" h, price for pr ............... 145.00
Lantern
    Adams & Westlake, conductor's, carbide, nickel over brass .......... 195.00
    D & H, clear globe ................. 250.00
    Missouri Pacific, hand, 4" clear globe ................................................ 75.00
    New York Central, bell bottom, red globe, 6" h, Deitz No. 6, raised letters ............................................. 100.00
    Southern Railway, red globe ............................................. 150.00
Magazine, *Railway Age,* 190, 64 pgs, 9" x 12" ......................................... 9.00

**Game, Twentieth Century Limited, Parker Bros., $150.**

**Level and grade indicator, patent and mfg. by Edward Helb, 24" l, $225.**

Map, Atlantic Coast Line, large route, c1950 ...................................... 150.00
Mechanical Pencil, Northwestern Transit, Michigan City, Benton Harbor, Valparaiso, South Bend, La Porte, Chicago, Detroit, celluloid, made by Ritepoint, St. Louis ................... 10.00
Membership Card, American Association Railroad Ticket Agents, issued, 1931 ........................................ 10.00
Menu, Amtrak, Good Morning, single card, 7" x 11" .............................. 3.50
Napkin, linen
　Burlington Route, 20" sq, white, woven logo .............................. 10.00
　C & O, blue monogram .............. 8.50
　Rio Grande, white, woven logo
　................................................ 12.00
Oil Can, Locomotive Oil .............. 100.00
Padlock, Rock Island, orig key ..... 35.00
Paperweight, 6" x 2" x 2-1/2", General American Car Co., Modern Milk Transportation, Refrigerated Glass lined Tank Car ........................ 120.00
Pass
　Ft. Wayne, Cincinnati & Louisville and White Water, 2-1/2" x 3-3/4" white card, green accents, purple ink stamp facsimile signature of president, 1889 ................................ 12.00
　Grand Trunk Railway Co. of Canada, 2-1/2" x 4", black and white, red year date, printed facsimile signature of general manager, 1889 ............ 15.00
　Hartford & Connecticut Western railroad, 2-1/4" x 3-5/8", black and white, red accent, number sgd in black ink by president, 1889.... 12.00
　Ohio, Indiana, and Western, 2-1/4" x 3-3/4", black and white, ornately printed, signed in ink by general manager, 1889 ........................ 12.00
Playing Cards
　Chessie .................................. 20.00
　Denver & Rio Grande Railways
　................................................ 35.00

EJ & ERR................................. 20.00
Pocket Mirror
　2-1/8" d, Frisco System, steam train in mountains........................... 165.00
　2-3/8" l, 1-5/8" w, Travelers Insurance Co., Hartford, CT, steam train
　.............................................. 220.00
Print, First Railway Train, E. L. Henry, 1894, published by *Illustrated America,* April 21, 1894, 16" x 37-1/2", orig frame...................................... 450.00
Ribbon, Brotherhood of Railroad Men, Grand Union Picnic, Harrisburg, PA, June 27, 1901, 1-7/8" x 5-1/2", dark red, gold accent lettering ....... 12.00
Sign, Seaboard RR, "Explosives," 1948
　.............................................. 19.00
Step, Pullman RR Station, wood, hand cut out on top, 21" w, 10" h ...... 25.00
Stock Certificate, B & O Railroad, 1920
　.............................................. 14.00
Sugar Tongs, Canadian Pacific, SP, mkd "England"........................ 20.00
Ticket, Pennsylvania Railroad Co., identification check, exchange ticket, and passenger's ticket............. 15.00
Timetable
　Erie Railroad, 1907 ................. 32.00
　L&N Kansas City Southern, 1955
　................................................ 8.50
　Southern Pacific RR, 1915 ....... 22.00
Voucher, Union Pacific, Denver and Gulf Railway, 1890s .......................... 5.00
Watchman's Station Box, iron ....... 25.00

# Reamers

**Collecting Hints**: Reamers are seldom found in mint condition. Cone and rim nicks are usually acceptable, but cracked pieces sell for considerably less. Ceramic figurals and American-made glass examples are collected more than any other types.

Reamer collecting, which can be an endless hobby, first became popular as a sideline to Depression glass collecting in the mid-1960s. It may be impossible to assemble a collection that includes one of every example made. One-of-a-kind items do exist, as some examples were never put into mass production.

**History**: Devices for getting the juice from citrus fruit have been around almost as long as the fruit itself. These devices were made from all types of material—from wood to glass and from nickel plate and sterling silver to fine china.

Many different kinds of mechanical reamers were devised before the first glass one was pressed around 1885. Very few new designs have appeared since 1940, when frozen juice first entered the market. Modern-day ceramists are making clown and teapot-shaped reamers.

**References:** Gene Florence, *Kitchen Glassware of the Depression Years*, 5th Edition, 1995, 1999 value update, Collector Books; Mary Walker, *And Even More Reamers*, BNMC, 1998 (14542 Ventura Blvd., Suite 206, Sherman Oaks, CA 91403).

**Collectors Club:** National Reamer Collectors Association, 47 Midline Court, Gaithersburg, MD 20878. Home Page URL - http://www.reamers.org.

**Reproduction Alert:** Many glass reamers are being reproduced at this time. Some are American reissues from original molds, while others are made from old reamers in Asia. The Asian reamers are usually easy to spot since they are made from poor quality glass that feels greasy and is generally thicker than that used in the originals. Many reproductions are being made in colors which were never used originally, but some of the reamers being made from the original molds are the same colors as the originals, making them harder to detect. There are also several new ceramic reamers being made. One series looks like an old piece of flow blue or English china, and is mkd with a crested "Victoria Ironstone" on the bottom.

An old 5-inch Imperial Glass Co. reamer, originally made in clear glass, was reproduced for Edna Barnes in dark amethyst; 1,500 were made. The reproduction is mkd "IG" and "81."

Mrs. Barnes has also reproduced several old 4-1/2-inch Jenkins Glass Co. reamers in limited editions. The reproductions are also made in a 2-1/4-inch size. All Jenkins' copies are mkd with a "B" in a circle. Collectors should consult Gene Florence's book for information about glass reproductions. Also, the National Reamer Collectors Association keeps its members up to date on the latest reproductions.

**Notes:** The first book on reamers, now out of print, was written by Ken and Linda Ricketts in 1974. Their numbering system was continued by Mary Walker in her first two books, *Reamers (200 Years)*, 1980, and *More Reamers (200 Years)*, 1983, both published by Muski Publishers, Sherman Oaks, CA, and both now out of print, and in her newest book, *And Many More Reamers*. The Ricketts-Walker numbers will be found in the china and metal sections. The numbers in parentheses in the glass section are from Gene Florence's Kitchen Glassware of the Depression Years, and indicate the page number, row number and item number to be referenced.

**Advisor:** Judy Smith.

### China and Ceramic

Austria, 3-3/4" h, white, pink flowers, green trim (D-106) ..................... 85.00
Bavaria, 3-1/2" h, white, red, yellow and green flowers, gold trim, 2 pc (E-119) ........................................... 90.00
Czechoslovakia, 6" h, orange shape, white, green leaves mkd, "Erphila," 2-pc, (L-17) ............................. 55.00
England
3-1/2" h, white, orange and yellow flowers, (D-107) ........................ 75.00
3-3/4" h, orange shape, orange body, green leaves, 2 pc, (L-20) ........................................... 15.00
Germany
3 -1/2" h, scrolling flow blue dec., white ground (E-60) ................. 75.00
5" d, Goebel, yellow (E-108) .... 85.00
Japan
3" h, saucer-type on pedestal, loop handle fruit dec, (D-59) ........... 55.00
3-1/4" h, hand painted, white, floral dec, mkd "Nippon," 2 pc ......... 65.00
3-3/4" h, strawberry shape, red, green leaves and handle, mkd "Occupied Japan," 2 pc, (L-38) ................................................. 85.00
4-3/4" h, lemon, yellow, white flowers, green leaves (L-40) ................. 55.00
5" h, orange, textured orange-peel exterior, yellow, green leaves, white interior (L-39) ........................... 50.00
8-1/2" h, pitcher and tumbler, blue and white windmill dec (P-87) ........... 65.00

United States
Jiffy Juicer, large bowl, cone center, elongated loop handle, 10 colors known, U.S. Pat. 2,130,755 Sept. 20, 1938, (A-5) ..................... 90.00
Red Wing (A-7) .................... 125.00
United States Ade-O-Matic Genuine, 8" h, green (A-11) ........... 125.00
Universal Cambridge, 9" h, Beige w/ pink flowers (A-28) ................ 185.00
Zippy, 3-1/4" h, 6-1/2" w, hand crank cone, Wolverine Products, Detroit, MI, several colors, (A-4) ........ 125.00

**Glass** (Measurements indicate width, not including spout and handle.)

Anchor Hocking Glass Co., 6-1/4" d, lime green, pouring spout (155-4-3) ................................................. 30.00
Federal, transparent green, pointed cone (151-3-4) ........................ 25.00
Fry, 6-5/16" d, opalescent, pouring spout (149-6-1) ........................ 45.00
Fluted ruffle, rose, (149-5-3) ....... 225.00
Hazel Atlas
Criss-Cross, orange size, pink (153-2-2) ................................... 300.00
Criss-Cross, crystal, tab handle, small (153-5-3) ........................ 20.00
Indiana Glass Co., green, horizontal handle (151-5-3) ..................... 25.00
Jeannette Glass Co.
Delphite Jennyware, small, (159-3-1) ................................................. 95.00
Pink Jennyware, small ((159-4-4) ................................................. 130.00
Light Jadite, 2 cup, 2 pc. (159-2-3) ................................................. 40.00
McKee
White, embossed Sunkist (163-1-4) ................................................. 12.00
Vaseline green embossed Sunkist (162-5-4) ................................. 50.00
Chalaine blue, embossed Sunkist (162-3-3) ............................... 225.00
U.S. Glass Co., light pink, 2-cup pitcher set (167-2-1) ........................... 45.00

**Metal**

Aluminum, Pat, 8" l, 161609, Minneapolis, MN ......................................... 5.00
Bernard Rice & Sons, Apollo EPNS, 3-3/4" h, 2 pc (PM-70) ......... 122.00
Cocktail Shaker set, Kinsway Plato, German, one pint (PM-49) ....... 76.00
Derby S.P. Co., International Co., 1923 EPNS W.M. Mounts (PM-74) .. 215.00
Dunlap's Improved, 9-1/2" l, iron hinge (M-17) ..................................... 32.00
Gem Squeezer, aluminum crank handle, table model 2 pc (M-100) ........11.00
Hong Kong, 2-1/2" h, stainless steel, flat, 2 pc (M-205) ...................... 9.00
Kwicky Juicer, aluminum, pan style, Quam Nichols Co. (M-97) .......... 9.00
Nasco-Royal, 6" l, scissors type (M-265) ................................................. 8.00
Presto Juicer, metal stand, porcelain juicer (M-112) ....................... 125.00
Wagner Ware, 6" d, cast aluminum, skillet shape, long rect. seed dams beneath cone, hole in handle, 2 spouts (M-96) ........................... 40.00

Williams, 9-3/4" l, iron , hinged, glass insert (M-60) ........................... 45.00
Yates, EPNS, 4-3/4" d, 2 pc (PM-73) ................................................. 185.00

# Records

**Collecting Hints:** Collectors tend to focus on one particular music field, e.g., jazz, the big bands, or rock 'n' roll, or on one artist. Purchase records with original dust jackets and covers whenever possible.

Also check the records carefully for scratches. If the sound quality has been affected, the record is worthless.

Proper storage of records is critical to maintaining their value. Keep stacks small. It is best to store them vertically. Place acid-free paper between the albums to prevent bleeding of ink from one cover to the next.

**History:** The first records, which were cylinders produced by Thomas Edison in 1877, were played on a phonograph of his design. Edison received a patent in 1878, but soon dropped the project in order to perfect the light bulb.

Alexander Graham Bell, Edison's friend, was excited about the phonograph and developed the graphaphone, which was marketed successfully by 1889. Early phonographs and graphaphones had hand cranks to wind the mechanism and keep the cylinders moving.

About 1900, Emile Berliner developed a phonograph which used a flat disc, similar to today's records. The United States Gramophone Company marketed his design in 1901. This company eventually became RCA Victor. By 1910, discs were more popular than cylinders.

The record industry continued to develop as new technology improved processes and sound quality. Initially, 78-RPM records were made. These were replaced by 45 RPMs, then by 33-1/3 RPMs, and, finally, by compact discs.

**References:** Steven C. Barr, *Almost Complete 78 RPM Record Dating Guide (II)*, Yesterday Once Again, 1992; Les R. Docks, *American Premium Record Guide, 1900-1965*, 5th ed., Krause Publications, 1997; Steve Gelfand, *Television Theme Recordings*, Popular Culture, 1993; *Goldmine Price Guide to 45 RPM Records*, Krause Publications, 1996;

*Goldmine's 1997 Annual,* Krause Publications, 1996; *Goldmine's Price Guide to Alternative Records,* Krause Publications, 1996; *Goldmine Roots of Rock Digest,* Krause Publications, 1999; Anthony J. Gribin and Matthew M. Schiff, *Doo-Wop,* Krause Publications, 1992; Joe Lindsay (comp.), *Picture Discs of the World Price Guide,* BIOdisc, 1990; Ron Lofman, *Goldmine's Celebrity Vocals,* Krause Publications, 1994; Tom Neely, *Goldmine's Price Guide to Alternative Records,* Krause Publications, 1996; —, *Goldmine Record Album Price Guide,* Krause Publications, 1999; R. Michael Murray, *The Golden Age of Walt Disney Records, 1933-1988,* Antique Trader Books, 1997; Tim Neely, *Goldmine Christmas Record Price Guide,* Krause Publications, 1997; —, *Goldmine Price Guide to Alternative Records,* Krause Publications, 1996; —, *Goldmine Price Guide to 45 RPM Records,* Krause Publications, 1996; Tim Neely and Dave Thompson, *Goldmine British Invasion Record Price Guide,* Krause Publications, 1997; Jerry Osborne, *Rockin' Records,* Antique Trader Books, 1998; Ronald L. Smith, *Goldmine's Comedy Record Price Guide,* Krause Publications, 1996; Charles Szabla, *Goldmine 45 RPM Picture Sleeve Price Guide,* Krause Publications, 1998; Neal Umphred, *Goldmine's Price Guide to Collectible Jazz Albums,* 2nd ed., Krause Publications, 1994; —, *Goldmine's Price Guide to Collectible Record Albums,* 5th ed., Krause Publications, 1996; —, *Goldmine's Rock 'n' Roll 45 RPM Record Price Guide,* 3rd ed., Krause Publications, 1994.

**Periodicals:** *Cadence,* Cadence Building, Redwood, NY 13679; *DIS-Coveries Magazine,* P.O. Box 309, Fraser, MI 48026; *Goldmine,* 700 E. State St., Iola, WI 54990; *Joslin's Jazz Journal,* P.O. Box 213, Parsons, KS 67357; *New Amberola Graphic,* 37 Caledonia St., St. Johnsbury, VT 05819; *Record Collectors Monthly,* P.O. Box 75, Mendham, NJ 07945; *Record Finder,* P.O. Box 1047, Glen Allen, VA 23060.

**Collectors' Clubs:** Collectors Record Club, 1206 Decatur St., New Orleans, LA 70116; International Assoc. of Jazz Record Collectors, P.O. Box 75155, Tampa, FL 33605.

**Note:** Prices are for first pressings in original dust jackets or albums.

**Additional Listings:** Elvis Presley, Rock 'n' Roll.

Andy Griffith, This is Andy Griffith, LP ................................................ 100.00
Annie Oakley, 45 rpm ................... 15.00
Bonic Woman ............................. 20.00
Bonanza
    Chevrolet promo ..................... 25.00
    High Chapparal ...................... 35.00
Bourbon Street Beat ..................... 25.00
Brady Bunch, membership application ................................................ 38.00
Clint Eastwood, Rawhide, Cameo #C-1056, autographed ................ 245.00
Dark Shadows, orig poster .......... 30.00
Drag Boats, 33-1/3 rpm, factory sealed ................................................ 25.00
Dragnet, 78 rpm, Jack Webb cover ................................................ 30.00
Evel Knieval .............................. 65.00
Farrah Fawcett, 45 rpm .............. 40.00
Godzilla, 1985, 45 rpm, "I Was Afraid to Love You," Jill Elliott ......... 30.00
Goober Sings, Andy Griffith .......... 35.00
Green Acres ................................ 25.00
Groovy Goolies ........................... 50.00
Hair Bear Bunch, 45 rpm, 1970s, illus sleeve ..................................... 10.00
Hot Rod Granny, Hanna-Barbera . 50.00
Howdy Doody
    Christmas .............................. 24.00
    Clowns with Jazz, Normal Paris Trio, Golden Crest, 1950s ............. 50.00
Jackie Robinson/Pee Wee Reese, double set ............................... 185.00
James Bond, Hanna-Barbera ....... 40.00
Joe DiMaggio, Little Johnny Strikeout, double, 78 rpm .................... 135.00
Johnny Quest, Hanna-Barbera, 45 rpm ................................................ 28.00
Josie & the Pussycats, Capitol, soundtrack, 1970 ................... 300.00
Kung Fu ..................................... 25.00
Les Adventures of Tin Tin, French, Decca, 33 rpm ........................ 65.00

**Walt Disney's Musical Highlights From The Mickey Mouse Club TV Show, Disneyland Records, DQ-1227, 33-1/3 rpm, 1962, $20.**

Little Black Jacobs and the Twins, double set ................................. 85.00
Lone Ranger, 3-1 ......................... 25.00
Mad Magazine .............................. 35.00
Mannix ....................................... 25.00
Mighty Hercules ........................... 95.00
Mr. Ed, TV series soundtrack, Colpix CP209 ................................... 125.00
Ozzie and Harriet ........................ 25.00
Petticoat Junction, 45 rpm .......... 24.00
Return of he Pink Panther, United Artists, 1970s, 45 rpm ................ 30.00
Ronald Reagan on GE Theatre ..... 25.00
Roy Rogers, Little Golden Record ................................................ 15.00
Secret Squirrel, Hanna-Barbera, 45 rpm ....................................... 30.00
Shotgun Slade ............................ 25.00
Spike Jones, Kiddies Nutcracker Suite, RCA, three 78 RPM records in orig portfolio .............................. 35.00
Squiddly Diddly, Hanna-Barbera, 45 rpm ....................................... 35.00
Zorro, by The Chardettes, promo . 38.00

# Red Wing Pottery

**Collecting Hints:** Red Wing Pottery can be found with various marks and paper labels. Some of the marks include a stamped red wing, a raised "Red Wing U.S.A. #___," or an impressed "Red Wing U.S.A. #___." Paper labels were used as early as 1930. Some pieces were identified only by a paper label that was easily lost.

Many manufacturers used the same mold patterns. Study the references to become familiar with the Red Wing forms.

**History:** The category of Red Wing Pottery covers several potteries which started in Red Wing, Minn. The first pottery, named Red Wing Stoneware Company, was started in 1868 by David Hallem. The primary product of this company was stoneware. The mark used by this company was a red wing stamped under the glaze. The Minnesota Stoneware Company was started in 1883. The North Star Stoneware Company opened a factory in the same area in 1892 and went out of business in 1896. The mark used by this company included a raised star and the words "Red Wing."

The Red Wing Stoneware Company and the Minnesota Stoneware Company merged in 1892. The new company was called the Red Wing Union Stoneware Company. The new company made stoneware until 1920, when it introduced a line of pottery.

In 1936, the name of the company was changed to Red Wing Potteries Incorporated. It continued to make pottery until the 1940s. During the 1930s, the company introduced several lines of dinnerware. These patterns, which were all hand painted, were very popular and sold through department stores, Sears Roebuck and Company, and gift stamp centers. The production of dinnerware declined in the 1950s. The company began producing hotel and restaurant china in the early 1960s. The plant was closed in 1967.

**References:** Dan and Gail DePasquale and Larry Peterson, *Red Wing Collectibles*, Collector Books, 1985, 1995 value update; —, *Red Wing Stoneware*, Collector Books, 1983, 1994 value update; B. L. Dollen, *Red Wing Art Pottery*, Collector Books, 1997; B. L. and R. L. Dollen, *Red Wing Art Pottery Book II,* Collector Books, 1998; Ray Reiss, *Red Wing Art Pottery Including Pottery Made for Rum Rill*, published by author (2144 N. Leavitt, Chicago, IL 60647), 1996; ---, *Red Wing Dinnerware: Price and Identification Guide,* Property Publishing, 1997; Gary and Bonnie Tefft, *Red Wing Potters and Their Wares*, 2nd ed., Locust Enterprises, 1987, 1995 value update.

**Collectors' Clubs:** Red Wing Collectors Society, 624 Jones St., Eveleth, MN 55734; RumRill Society, PO Box 2161, Hudson, OH 44236.

Ashtray, horse head, #M1472....... 80.00
Basket, white, semi gloss ............. 32.00
Bean Pot, cov, Tampico ............... 35.00
Beverage Server, cov, Tampico
................................................. 125.00
Bookends, pr, fan and scroll, green
......... ...................................... 20.00
Bowl
Cloverleaf, glossy, gray int., yellow ext. ......................................... 32.00
Lute Song, 5" ............................ 12.00
Spatterware, #4 ........................ 85.00
Bread and Butter Plate, 6-1/2" d
Bob White .................................. 7.50
Lute Song .................................. 9.00
Pepe .......................................... 4.00
Pompeii ...................................... 5.00
Random Harvest ........................ 6.00
Tampico...................................... 6.50
Butter Crock, "Hazel Creamery Butter," bail handle, 5 lb size, lid ........ 275.00
Butter Dish, rect, Bob White ......... 45.00
Candleholders, pr, Medieval......... 50.00
Candy Dish, three part, hexagon, gray, semi glass .............................. 15.00
Casserole, cov
Bob White................................. 45.00
Tampico.................................... 25.00

**Compote, mauve, shaped base and standard, scalloped rim, mkd "M5008," 6-1/4" h, $35.**

Celery Tray
Lute Song, 16" l ....................... 18.50
Random Harvest ...................... 12.00
Smart Set ................................. 25.00
Cereal Bowl
Damask...................................... 7.50
Pompeii ...................................... 9.00
Chop Plate, 12" d, Capistrano ...... 20.00
Compote
Blue and Brown ....................... 60.00
Blue Fleck ................................ 45.00
Orchid Cherub ......................... 60.00
Console Set, bowl and matching candlesticks, Renaissance Deer
................................................. 120.00
Cookie Jar
Drummer Boy......................... 600.00
Friar Tuck, blue ...................... 200.00
Katrina, beige ......................... 125.00
Round Up................................ 400.00
Cornucopia, Swirl, #736 ............... 32.00
Creamer and Sugar
Bob White ................................ 30.00
Lute Song ................................. 25.00
Smart Set ................................. 85.00
Crock, two gallons, birch leaf dec
................................................... 50.00
Cruet, Town and Country, chartreuse
............. ................................... 25.00
Cup and Saucer
Bob White ................................ 18.50
Capistrano ............................... 15.00
Magnolia .................................... 7.50
Tampico ................................... 10.00
Custard Cup, Fondos, green and pink
................................................... 18.50
Dinner Plate, 10" d
Bob White ................................ 14.00
Lotus .......................................... 8.50
Magnolia .................................. 12.00
Tampico ................................... 12.00
Town and Country, blue ............. 9.25
Flower Block, Dolphin................... 35.00
Fruit Bowl, Lute Song..................... 9.00
Gravy Boat, Driftwood, blue ......... 19.00
Hors d'oeuvre Bird, Bob White ..... 50.00
Leaf Dish, 11" x 11", green .......... 60.00
Mug
Bob White ............................ .... 75.00

Tampico ..................................... 65.00
Nappy
Country Garden ....................... 20.00
Lotus .......................................... 8.50
Pitcher
Bob White ................................ 35.00
Brushed Ware, 8-1/4" h.......... 225.00
Tampico . ...,,................... 30.00
Planter
Birch ........................................ 25.00
Loop shape, green and silver
................................................... 50.00
Platter
Bob White, 13" l ...................... 20.00
Lute Song, 13" l....................... 18.00
Tampico, 1" l ........................... 20.00
Town and Country, chartreuse
................................................... 18.50
Refrigerator Jar, 5 lb, blue, diffused, no lid, hairlines.............................. 85.00
Relish
Bob White, 3 part..................... 30.00
Smart Set ................................. 32.00
Town and Country, blue, 7" x 5"
................................................... 12.00
Salad Bowl, Pheasant, blue and green
................................................... 45.00
Salt and Pepper Shakers, pr
Bob White ................................ 30.00
Brittany, Provincial .................. 15.00
Shell, ftd, 11" x 9" ......................... 80.00
Teapot
Mediterranean ......................... 65.00
Smart Set ............................... 295.00
Trivet, Minnesota Centennial ........ 75.00
Vase
Boot, #651 ............................... 70.00
Brushed Ware, #144 crane motif
................................................... 55.00
Calla, blue and yellow ............. 80.00
Classic-shape, 9" h, swan handles, cream, high glaze, marked "Rumrill"
................................................... 75.00
Fan-shape, 7-1/2" h, #892, blue, pink int................................................ 48.00
Gray and rose, B1426.............. 30.00
Vegetable Bowl
Bob White, divided .................. 35.00
Lute Song, divided .................. 24.00
Smart Set, 9" d ........................ 35.00
Town and Country, chartreuse . 15.00
Wall Pocket, Gardenia, matte ivory
................................................... 35.00
Warmer, two step......................... 35.00

# Robots

**Collecting Hints:** Robots are identified by the markings on the robot or box and from names assigned by the trade. Hence, some robots have more than one name. Research is required to learn exactly what robot you have.

Condition is critical. Damaged lithographed tin is almost impossible to repair and repaint. Toys in mint condition in the original box are the most desirable. The price difference between a mint robot and one in very good condition may be as high as 200%.

Working condition is important, but not critical. Many robots never worked well, and larger robots stripped their gearing quickly. The rarer the robot, the less important the working condition.

Finally, if you play with your robot, do not leave the batteries in the toy. If they leak or rust, the damage may destroy the value of the toy.

**History:** Atomic Robot Man, made in Japan between 1948 and 1949, is the grandfather of all robot toys. He is an all-metal windup toy, less than five inches high and rather crudely made. Japanese robots of the early 1950s tended to be the friction or windup variety, patterned in brightly lithographed tin and made from recycled materials.

By the late 1950s, robots had entered the battery-powered age. Limited quantities of early models were produced; parts from one model were used in later models with slight or no variations. The robot craze was enhanced by Hollywood's production of movies such as "Destination Moon" (1950) and "Forbidden Planet" (1956). Robby the Robot came from the latter movie.

Many Japanese manufacturers were small and remained in business only a few years. Leading firms include Horikawa Toys, Nomura Toys, and Yonezawa Toys. Cragstan was an American importer who sold Japanese-made toys under its own label. Marx and Ideal entered the picture in the 1970s. Modern robots are being imported from China and Taiwan.

The TV program "Lost in Space" (1965-1968) inspired copies of its robot character. However, the quality of the late 1960s toys began to suffer as more and more plastic was added; robots were redesigned to reduce sharp edges as required by the United States government.

Modern robots include R2D2 and C3PO from the Star Wars epics, Twiki from NBC's Buck Rodgers, and V.I.N.CENT from Disney's "The Black Hole." Robots are firmly established in American science fiction and among collectors.

**References:** Teruhisa Kitahara, *Tin Toy Dreams*, Chronicle Books, 1985; Teruhisa Kitahara, *Yesterday's Toys, & Robots, Spaceships, and Monsters*, Chronicle Books, 1988; Crystal and Leland Payton, *Space Toys,*

Collectors Compass, 1982; Maxine A. Pinksy, *Marx Toys: Robots, Space, Comic, Disney & TV Characters*, Schiffer Publishing, 1996; Stephen J. Sansweet, *Science Fiction Toys and Models*, Starlog Press, 1980; Stuart W. Wells, III, *Science Fiction Collectibles: Identification & Price Guide*, Krause Publications, 1999.

**Periodical:** *Robot World & Price Guide*, P.O. Box 184, Lenox Hill Station, New York, NY 10021.

Astro Boy, Mighty Atom, tin wind-up, Biliken, Japan, 8-1/2" h, MIB........ 225.00
Attacking Martian, tin, green circles and squares dec, door opens and closes, double barrel tin guns shooting with blinking, walks and stops .............................................. 175.00
Atomic Robot Man, Japan, litho tin, pressed tin arms, windup, orig box, 5" h........................................ 1,800.00
Batman, tin wind-up, Biliken, Japan, MIB........................................ 175.00
Big Loo, Your Friend From The Moon, Marx, 1950s, 38" h ................. 785.00
Cone Head, Yonezawa, Japan, tin, plastic eyes, rubber antennae, windup, 8-1/4" h .......................... 2,750.00
Dingaling Boxer, Topper, MIB ....... 35.00
Durham Industries, battery operated, plastic, silver colored, 9-1/2" h .............................................. 35.00
Dux Astroman, Dux, Germany, tin and plastic, battery operated, orig box, 12" h.................................... 1,650.00
Earth Man, Kitahara #144, TN, Japan, litho tin, battery operated, remote control, 9-1/4" h..................... 625.00

Gear Robot, 9" h, battery operated, tin, Japan...................................... 500.00
Joker, tin wind-up, Biliken, Japan, 8-1/2" h, MIB .................................. 240.00
Lost in Space, Remco, 1966 ..... 800.00
Marvelous Mike, tractor, USA, orig box .............................................. 600.00
Mr. Atom, Advance Toy, West Haven, CT, plastic, battery operated, orig box, 18" h............................. 750.00
Mr. Machine, take-apart, MIB ..... 375.00
Nando Robot, Italy, tin, air powered, gray unpainted finish, decal facial features, 1950s, orig box, 5" h .............................................. 550.00
NASA Robot, 1960s, tin litho, 6" h, mkd "Japan" ................................... 350.00
Planet Robot, KO, Japan, tin and plastic, windup, orig box, 9" h ....... 325.00
Radar Robot, Kitahara #8, Japan, tin, battery operated, primitive style, walking mechanism, orig box and insert, 9" h ............................. 750.00
Robby, 16" h .............................. 250.00
Robert Robot, Ideal, orig box ..... 275.00
Robocon, 16" h, vinyl, MIB ......... 100.00
Robot R-35, Modern Toys, Japan, 1950s, 8" h, remote control.... 590.00
Robot 2500, silver, blinking lighted eye and chest, moving arms and legs .............................................. 175.00
Rock'em Sock'em, full color display box, 1960s ........................... 250.00
Silver Warrior, battery operated, Amico, storm trooper action, unused, orig box, 1970s ............................. 95.00
Smoking, lighted see-thru piston action, emits smoke, walks................ 175.00
Space Man, 6-1/2" h, tin litho, litho face in astronaut space helmet, air tanks, regulator, large space rifle, 1950s, mkd "Japan" ....................... 1,800.00

**Marvelous Mike, tin litho and plastic, made by Saunders, Aurora, IL, 1954, $250.**

Takra, Japanese, 190s, 8-1/4" h, litho tin wind-up ................................... 150.00
Television Spaceman, Alps, Japan, tin, battery operated, orig box, 11" h ............................................................. 750.00
Ultra 7, tin wind-up, Biliken, Japan, 8-1/2" h, MIB ........................ 300.00
Video, all tin body, scene of moon and space on TV big screen, walks ............................................................. 175.00
Walk, wind-up, illustrated window box ............................................................... 25.00
Zeroid Zintar, Ideal...................... 125.00
Zoomer, Japan, 1950s, 10" h, battery operated................................. 485.00

# Rock 'n' Roll

**Collecting Hints:** Many rock 'n' roll collections are centered around one artist. Flea markets and thrift shops are good places to look for rock 'n' roll items. Prices depend on the singer or group, and works by stars who are no longer living usually command a higher price.

**History:** Rock music can be traced back to early rhythm and blues. It progressed and reached its golden age in the 1950s. The current nostalgia craze for the 1950s has produced some modern rock 'n' roll which is well received. Rock 'n' roll memorabilia exists in large quantities, each singer or group having had many promotional pieces made.

**References:** Tony Bacon, *Classic Guitars of the '50s*, Miller Freeman Books (6600 Silacci Way, Gilroy, CA 95020), 1996; Mark A. Baker, *Goldmine Price Guide to Rock 'N' Roll Memorabilia*, Krause Publications, 1997; Anthony Curtis, *Lyle Film & Rock 'n' Roll Collectibles*, Berkley Publishing, 1996; Marty Eck, *The Monkees Collectibles Price Guide*, Antique Trader Books, 1998; Karen and John Lesniewski, *Kiss Collectibles*, Avon Books, 1993; Stephen Maycock, *Miller's Rock & Pop Memorabilia*, Millers Publications, 1995; Barbara Crawford, Hollis Lamon and Michael Stern, *The Beatles, A Reference & Value Guide, 2nd Edition*, Collector Books, 1998.

**Periodicals:** *Kissaholics Magazine*, P.O. Box 22334, Nashville, TN 37202; *New England KISS Collector's Network*, 168 Oakland Ave., Providence, RI 02908; *Tune Talk*, P.O. Box 851, Marshalltown, IA 50158.

**Collectors' Club:** American Bandstand 1950's Fan Club, P.O. Box 131, Adamstown, PA 19501; Kissaholics, P.O. Box 22334, Nashville, TN 37202;

**Additional Listings:** Beatles, Elvis Presley, Records.

Action Figure, KISS, ©1978 Mego, 12" h, set of Ace, Gene, Peter, and Paul, MIB, price for set ................... 500.00
Book, *Woodstock 69, Summer Pop Festivals, A Photo Review*, Joseph J. Sia, Scholastic Book Services publisher, ©1970, 70 pgs,. 5-1/4" x 7-1/2" ............................................................. 30.00
Bracelet, gold chain link, burnished gold disc with raised Monkees guitar symbol, orig retail card, ©1967 ............................................................. 27.50
Cuff Links, pr, Dick Clark, MIB ...... 35.00
Doll
    Boy George, LJN, 1984, 12" h, MIB ..................................... 125.00
    Donny Osmond, Mattel, ©1976, MIB .......................................... 35.00
    Michael Jackson, LIN, ©1984 MIJ Productions, Thriller outfit, MIB ............................................ 35.00
Finger Puppet, Monkees, MOC .... 95.00
Folder, 4-1/2" x 6", Swamp Notes, beige vinyl cover, emb image, note pad, reply cards ............................. 50.00
Game, The Elvis Presley Board Game ......................................... 1,850.00
Gum Card Box, KISS ................... 75.00
Handkerchief, Buddy Holly, silk, red and gold paisley, authenticity card ............................................................. 450.00
Lunch Box, Monkees, plastic, Canadian, 1967 ............................ 375.00
Microphone, toy, Michael Jackson 15.00
Nodder, 4-1/2" h, man, gold base, "Let's Twist" decal, Japan stick, c1960 ............................................................. 75.00
Paper Ephemera, pinback button vending machine insert, 1967, shows Monkee buttons ....................... 75.00
Pinback Button
    James Dean, 2-1/2" d, color photo ............................................... 60.00
    Monkees, vending machine type, 1967, set of 6 .......................... 75.00
    Pat Boone, 3-1/2" d, blue "Swoon with Pat Boone" inscription, white background, red rim .................. 7.50
    Rock-Ola, 3" d, red, white, and blue illus c1950 .............................. 17.50

**Monkees, tambourine, $35.**

Poster
    Amboy Dukes, 1968 ............. 235.00
    Badfinger, April 1971, Fond du Lac, WI................................................ 495.00
    Barry Manilow, December 1979 ............................................... 185.00
    Beach Boys, Ike & Tina, Alice Cooper, Moby Grape, Chuck Berry, Wilson Pickett, and others, June 1972 ............................................... 200.00
    Bob Dylan, November 1978, Oakland............................................ 115.00
    Bobby "Blue" Band, March 1973, Fort Worth, TX ...................... 295.00
    Charlie Pride, April 1971, Waterloo, IA .......................................... 200.00
    Conway Twitty, July 1973, Wellsville, OH ....................................... 300.00
    Devo, November 1981, Paramount Theater..................................... 75.00
    Dinah Washington, early 1950s ............................................... 995.00
    Dottie West, Homer & Jethro, Bill Anderson, blank for Grand Old Opry traveling show, 1965 ............. 325.00
    Eagles, Dan Fogelberg, Ozark Mountain Daredevils, July 1975, Iowa State Fair ...................... 145.00
    Eric Clapton, Delaney & Bonnie, German tour, 1970................. 295.00
    Eric Clapton, Stevie Ray Vaughn, August 1990, Alpine Valley WI ............................................... 250.00
    Everly Brothers, Aug 1966, Colorado Springs ......................... 395.00
    Fats Domino, Gerry & Pacemakers, March 1967, London............. 245.00
    Fleetwood Mac, Sept 1972, Wilmington NC ............................... 225.00
    Flying Burrito Brothers, Linda Ronstadt, Savory Brown, March 1970, Grateful Dead, June 1966, Filmore West (Bill Graham)................. 375.00
    Joan Baez, April 1962, Santa Monica ............................................... 400.00
    John Prine, October 1976, Portland, OR............................................ 245.00
    Johnny Cash, May 1965, Des Moines, IA ............................... 455.00
    Kansas, Jan 1978, Seattle ..... 295.00
    King Crimson, May 1971, Plymouth, UK ........................................... 295.00
    Led Zeppelin, February 1970, Swedish tour ................................... 595.00
    Led Zeppelin, Jethro Tull, August 1969, San Antonio, TX .......... 995.00
    Los Angeles........................... 400.00
    Lovin' Spoonful, November 1966, Houston ............................... 395.00
    Neil Sedaka, Adam Faith, April 1962, London Palladium.................. 295.00
    Peter, Paul & Mary, May 1964, San Diego ..................................... 350.00
    Ray Charles, May 1967, Santa Barbara, CA ............................... 225.00
    Sly & The Family Stones, December 1972, San Francisco............. 345.00
    Steve Miller Band, May 1973, Geneva, NY .......................... 125.00
    Stevie Wonder, Beach Boys, November 1972, Greenville SC......... 365.00
    Tanya Tucker, June 1975, Portland, OR......................................... 265.00

Tom Jones, April 196, London Palladium .......................................... 365.00
Tony Bennett, Duke Ellington, March 1963, Philharmonic Hall, NY .. 395.00
War, November 1973, Memorial Coliseum ...................................... 345.00
Who, November 1973, Cow Palace .................................................... 295.00
Promotion Kit, 1993 "Riders in the Sky" concert, media releases, concert releases, post card, bumper sticker, two 8" x 10" glossy photo, product catalog ..................................... 10.00
Puzzle
  Bee Gees, frame tray .............. 20.00
  Gene Simmons, Milton Bradley, 200 pcs, missing one piece, orig box .............................................. 45.00
  KISS, frame tray, 1974 ............. 25.00
  Shaun Cassidy, frame tray ....... 20.00
Radio, KISS, 1977 ...................... 100.00
Record, KISS, I Was Made For Loving You, 33 RPM, Casablanca, 1978, one-sided ................................... 35.00
  Record Case, 7-1/2" x 9", red vinyl, emb design, Ponytail, 1950s.... 55.00
Sheet Music
  Green Tree Boogie, Bill Haley and the Comets, greentone photo, ©1955 Meyers Music .............. 22.00
  Substitute, The Who, bluetone photo, ©1966, Fabulous Music Ltd..... 15.00
Ring, Monkees, club, flicker ......... 50.00
Store Display, Jackson 5, Meagus, 27" x 22" .......................................... 295.00
Tour Book, Bob Dylan, 28 pgs, c1977 ...................................................... 30.00
Toy
  Car, Monkees, tin ................... 300.00
  Guitar, Monkees, plastic, full color diecut litho paper label, ©1966 .............................................. 80.00
  Saxophone, Spike Jones, hard plastic, mkd "A Trophy Product," c1950 .............................................. 30.00
Trading Cards Box, unopened, Nu-Card, 1960, 36 unopened cello packs ...................................... 360.00
Window Card, 22" x 14", Rolling Stones, Gimme Shelter, blue, yellow, and white.................................... 165.00

# Norman Rockwell

**Collecting Hints:** Learn all you can about Norman Rockwell if you plan to collect any of his art. His original artworks and illustrations have been transferred onto various types of objects by clubs and manufacturers.

**History:** Norman Rockwell, the famous American artist, was born on Feb. 3, 1894. When he was 18, he did his first professional illustrations for a children's book, *Tell Me Why Stories*. His next projects were done in association with *Boy's Life*, the Boy Scout magazine, and after that his work appeared in many other magazines. By his death in Novem-

ber 1978, he had completed more than 2,000 paintings, many of which were done in oil and reproduced as magazine covers, advertisements, illustrations, calendars, and book sketches. More than 320 of these paintings became covers for the *Saturday Evening Post*.

Norman Rockwell painted everyday people in everyday situations with a little humor mixed in with the sentimentality. His paintings and illustrations are well loved because of this sensitive nature. He painted people he knew and places with which he was familiar. New England landscapes are seen in many of his illustrations.

Because his works are so popular, they have been reproduced on many objects. These new collectibles, which should not be confused with the original artwork and illustrations, make Norman Rockwell illustrations affordable for the average consumer.

**References:** Denis C. Jackson, *Norman Rockwell Identification and Value Guide*, 2nd ed., published by author (P.O. Box 1958, Sequim, WA 98392), 1985; Mary Moline, *Norman Rockwell Collectibles Value Guide*, 6th ed., Green Valley World, 1988.

**Collectors' Club:** Rockwell Society of America, 597 Saw Mill River Rd., Ardsley, NY 10502.

**Museums:** Museum of Norman Rockwell Art, Reedsburg, WI; Norman Rockwell Museum, Northbrook, IL; Norman Rockwell Museum, Philadelphia, PA; The Norman Rockwell Museum at Stockbridge, Stockbridge, MA.

Bell, Triple Self Portrait, Danbury Mint, 1979, 7-1/2" h .......................... 98.00
Book
  *Norman Rockwell Christmas Book*, Mary Rockwell Consulting Ed., Harry Abrams, 1977, hardcover, 222 pgs, carols, stories, poems, recollections, illus ............................... 40.00
  *Norman Rockwell Illustrator*, Arthur Guptil, Watson-Guptil Publishing, 1946, dj ...................................... 10.00
Calendar, 1976, 12 illus ............. 5.00
Canister, Snickers, 1997, boy and Dad with Christmas tree, c1949 scene .............................................. 6.50
Christmas Ornament, 1983, 50th Anniversary, designed for McDonald's and Coca-Cola.......................... 4.00
Christmas Plate, orig box
  Angel With A Black Eye, 1975, 2nd ed............................................. 35.00
  Golden Christmas, 1976, 3rd ed. .............................................. 35.00

Puppies for Christmas, 1976, Royal Devon ...................................... 60.00
Santa's Helpers, 1979, Gorham .............................................. 24.00
Scotty Gets His Tree, 1974, 1st ed. .............................................. 90.00
Snow Queen, 1979, Lynell, 1st ed. .............................................. 35.00
Figure
  Bride and Groom, Rockwell Museum, 1979 ...................... 60.00
  Cradle of Love, Lynell Studios, 1980 .............................................. 85.00
  First Haircut, Dave Grossman, ©1995, MIB............................ 65.00
  Music Maker, Rockwell Museum, 1981 .......................................... 95.00
  New Arrival, 1st ed., Dave Grossman, 6" h, orig box ................. 35.00
  New Swimming, Dave Grossman, 1973 .......................................... 50.00
  Saying Grace, Gorham, 1976 .......................................... 150.00
  Triple Self-Portrait, Gorham, bisque, 8-1/4" h, 1978 ...................... 300.00
First Day Cover, Clown Poodle, issued 1994, Stockbridge, MA, watercolor by Irv Pope .......................... 10.00
Magazine
  *American Artist*, July, 1976, self portrait and article........................ 20.00
  *Look*, June 14, 1966, JFK's Legacy, The Peace Corps...................... 7.50
  *Post*
    October 1960, JFK portrait .............................................. 22.50
    December 1963, JFK portrait .............................................. 20.00
  *Saturday Evening Post*
    Dec. 14, 1963, In Memoriam, A Senseless Tragedy, The New President........................... 7.50
    September 1975, J. F. Kennedy .............................................. 12.50

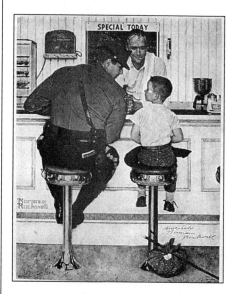

**Print, The Runaway,** *Saturday Evening Post***, Sept. 20, 1958, 11" x 14", $40.**

December 1975 ................... 25.00
October 1976, football issue
.......................................... 28.00
Magazine Cover
*American Boy,* April, 1920 ....... 32.00
Boy's Life
    February 1947 ..................... 48.00
    June, 1957 ........................... 45.00
*Collier's,* March, 1919 ............. 28.00
*Family Circle,* December 1967,
Santa ....................................... 15.00
*Literary Digest,* April, 1922 ...... 20.00
*Parents,* May, 1951 ................. 12.00
Saturday Evening Post
    March, 1945 ........................ 80.00
    August, 1952 ....................... 40.00
    October, 1959, A Family Tree
    .......................................... 12.50
    February, 1960 ..................... 60.00
*Scouting,* October, 1953 .......... 12.50
Mother's Day Plate
A Mother's Love, 1st ed., 1976, orig
box .......................................... 55.00
Faith, 1977, 2nd issue, orig box
.......................................... 40.00
Mug, Memories ............................... 5.00
Plate, orig box
Dreams of Long Ago, Dave Gross-
man, 1981 ............................... 55.00
Lighthouse Keeper's Daughter, 3rd,
1979 ........................................ 40.00
Spring Flowers, 1979, River Shore
.......................................... 110.00
Take Your Medicine, Dave Gross-
man, 1977 ............................... 45.00
The Cobbler, 1978 ................... 40.00
Toy Maker, 1st ed., 1977 .......... 65.00
Tribute to Norman Rockwell, 1979,
Norman Rockwell Museum, 10-3/8"
d, ............................................. 25.00
Young Love, Gorham, 1972 ... 200.00
Poster, taken from *Look* covers, full
color, 31" x 22-1/2"
Hubert Humphrey ..................... 20.00
Lyndon Johnson ....................... 20.00
Richard Nixon .......................... 25.00
Print
Four Seasons, with children, 11" sq,
matte stock .............................. 40.00
The "Tatooist," 14" x 11", framed
.......................................... 45.00
Program, 1957 Inauguration, Rockwell
portraits of Eisenhower and Nixon on
cover ....................................... 30.00
Puzzle, hand made from 1943 Thanks-
giving magazine cover .............. 5.00
Stein, S. P. Gerz, licensed by Curtis
Publishing Co., mkd "Made in Ger-
many"
The Fireman ........................... 55.00
The Graduate .......................... 60.00
The Juror ................................ 55.00
The Teacher ............................ 60.00

# Roseville Pottery

**Collecting Hints:** The prices for Roseville's later commercial ware are stable and unlikely to rise rapidly because it is readily available. The prices are strong for the popular middle-period patterns, which were made during the Depression and produced in limited numbers. Among the most popular patterns from this middle period are Black-berry, Cherry Blossom, Falline, Fer-ella, Jonquil, Morning Glory, Sunflower, and Windsor.

The Art Deco craze has increased the popularity of Futura, especially the more angular-shaped pieces. Pine Cone pieces with a blue or brown glaze continue to have a strong following as do the earlier lines of Juvenile and Dona-tello.

Desirable Roseville shapes include baskets, bookends, cookie jars, ewers, tea sets, and wall pock-ets.

Most pieces are marked. How-ever, during the middle period, paper stickers were used. These often were removed, leaving the piece unmarked.

Roseville made more than 150 different lines or patterns. Novice collectors would benefit from read-ing one of the several books about Roseville and should visit dealers who specialize in art pottery. Collec-tions generally are organized around a specific pattern or shape.

**History:** In the late 1880s, a group of investors purchased the J. B. Owens Pottery in Roseville, Ohio, and made utilitarian stoneware items. In 1892, the firm was incorpo-rated, and George F. Young became general manager. Four generations of Youngs controlled Roseville until the early 1950s.

A series of acquisitions began: Midland Pottery of Roseville in 1898, Clark Stoneware Plant in Zanesville (formerly used by Peters and Reed), and Muskingum Stoneware (Mosaic Tile Company) in Zanesville. In 1898, the offices also moved from Roseville to Zanesville.

In 1900, Roseville developed its art pottery line—Rozane. Ross Purdy designed a line to compete with Weller's Louwelsa. Rozane became a trade name to cover a large series of lines by designers such as Christian Neilson, John J. Herold, and Gazo Fudji. The art lines of hand-decorated underglaze pot-tery were made in limited quantities after 1919.

The success of Roseville depended on its commercial lines, first developed by John J. Herald and Frederick Rhead in the early decades of the 1900s. Decorating techniques included transfers, pouncing (a method which pro-duced the outline of a pattern which could then be used as the basis for further decorating), and air brush-ing or sponging over embossed motifs. Dutch, Juvenile, Cameo, and Holland are some of the lines from this early period.

George Young retired in 1918. Frank Ferrell replaced Harry Rhead, who had replaced Frederick Rhead, as art director. Ferrell developed more than 80 lines, the first being Sylvan. The economic depression of the 1930s caused Roseville to look for new product lines. Pine Cone was introduced in 1935, made for 15 years, and issued in more than 75 shapes.

In the 1940s, a series of high-gloss glazes were used to try to revive certain lines. Other changes were made in response to the fluctu-ating contemporary market. Mayfair and Wincraft date from this period. In 1952, Raymor dinnerware was produced. None of these changes brought economic success back to Roseville. In November 1954, Roseville was bought by the Mosaic Tile Company.

**References:** John and Nancy Bomm, *Roseville In All Its Splendor,* L-W Book Sales, 1998; Virginia Hill-way Buxton, *Roseville Pottery for Love or Money,* updated ed., Tymbre Hill Publishing Co. (P.O. Box 615, Jonesborough, TN 37659), 1996; John W. Humphries, *Price Guide to Roseville Pottery by the Numbers,* published by author, 1993; Sharon and Bob Huxford, *Collectors Ency-clopedia of Roseville Pottery,* 1st Series (1976, 1997 value update), 2nd Series (1980, 1997 value update), Collector Books; James S. Jenkins, Jr., *Roseville Art Pottery, 1998-1/2 Price Guide, Volume II,* Clinical Pharmacology Consultants, 1998; Randall B. Monsen, *Collector's Compendium of Roseville Pottery,* Monsen and Baer (Box 529, Vienna, VA 22183), 1995; —, *Collector's Compendium of Roseville Pottery,* Volume II, Monsen and Baer, 1997; Leslie Piña, *Pottery,* Schiffer Publish-ing, 1994.

**Collectors' Clubs:** American Art Pottery Association, 125 E. Rose Ave., St. Louis, MO 63119; Roseville's of the Past Pottery Club, P.O. Box 656, Clarcona, FL 32710.

**Reproduction Alert:** Reproductions of several Roseville patterns have plagued the marketplace in the late 1990s.

Basket
    Bittersweet, 810-10 ............... 185.00
    Monticello, brown, 632 .......... 555.00
    Pine Cone, brown .................. 365.00
    Poppy, pink, 347-10 .............. 425.00
Bookends, pr
    Gardenia, gray ..................... 300.00
    Silhouette ............................ 150.00
    Zephyr Lily, green ................ 195.00
Bowl
    Blueberry, blue, 412-6 ........... 130.00
    Florentine, 7"d ...................... 85.00
    Lombardy, dark teal ............... 85.00
    Mauve, matte, 3 1/2" h, 5" w, orig paper label............................ 75.00
    Moss Blue, high sides, #294-12
    ................................................ 275.00
    Nursery Rhyme .................... 150.00
    Peony, yellow, 428-6 .............. 95.00
    Pine Cone, green ................. 115.00
    Water Lily, brown, 437-4 .......... 95.00
Bowl and Flower Frog, Clematis, mkd "Roseville USA 458-10," c1944
    ................................................ 195.00
Bud Vase, Dahl Rose, double ..... 175.00
Candleholders, pr
    Carnelian II ............................ 70.00
    Gardenia, 652-4-1/2" ............. 150.00
    Zephyr Lily, 1162-2 ............... 115.00
Candlesticks, pr
    Carnelian I .......................... 140.00
    Pine Cone, #451-4 ................ 325.00
Child's Feeding Plate, rolled edge
    Nursery Rhyme .................... 150.00

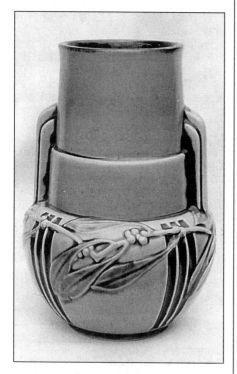

**Vase, Laurel, stamped "S," 9-3/16" h, $165.**

Tom Tom............................. 90.00
Compote, Magnolia, 13" h .......... 110.00
Conch Shell, Peony, blue ........... 185.00
Console Bowl
    Bushberry, #414-10 ............... 180.00
    Freesia, brown .................... 115.00
Cornucopia, mkd "Roseville U.S.A. 321-6", rim chips, repairs............... 85.00
Creamer
    Juvenile, duck.................... 100.00
    Wincraft, 271-C, glossy, 1940s
    ................................................ 75.00
    Zephyr Lily, blue.................... 80.00
Cup and Saucer, Zephyr Lily, blue
    ................................................ 125.00
Ewer
    Clematis, 5" h ...................... 165.00
    Silhouette, maroon, #716-6 .... 175.00
Flower Frog, Clematis, #50........... 90.00
Flower Pot, matching underplate, Thorn Apple, blue ......................... 215.00
Jardiniere
    Bushberry, brown, 657-3.......... 95.00
    Clematis, blue, 667-4 .............. 90.00
    White Rose, 653-3 .................. 95.00
Mug
    Duck with boots ................... 150.00
    Dutch .................................. 110.00
    Rabbit ................................. 140.00
Pitcher
    Blended Landscape, 7-1/2" h 140.00
    Carnelian II, mottled green and cream, rough bottom ............. 175.00
    Forget-Me-Not, old rim flakes ....95.00
Planter
    Magnolia, 388-6 .................... 110.00
    Pine Cone, 12-1/2" x 4-1/2" .... 125.00
    Poppy, blue ........................... 85.00
Plate, Juvenile, rabbit, rolled edge, 7" d
    ................................................ 155.00
Tea Set, Bushberry, damage to cup and saucer .................................. 250.00
Vase
    Bushberry, brown, 28-4............ 95.00
    Dahl Rose, 4" x 10"................ 190.00
    Donatello, 10" h .................... 230.00
    Failine #648, 7" h, brown........ 700.00
    Freesia, #128-16, brown, rim defect
    ................................................ 400.00
    Futura, pink and green, 384-8
    ................................................ 675.00
    Iris, blue, #927-10, restored base chip ..................................... 285.00
    Ivory II, 740-10, white, 2 repaired chips .................................... 90.00
    Laurel, 6" h, brown ................ 185.00
    Magnolia, blue, 86-4 ............... 95.00
    Peony, 14" h, yellow, small base repair .................................. 325.00
    Pine Cone, brown, 279-9 ....... 230.00
    Poppy, 872-9, base chips ...... 120.00
    Primrose, blue....................... 175.00
    Rozane, 8" h, honeycomb, pastel roses .................................. 375.00
    Russco, 7" h ........................ 160.00
    Silhouette, blue, nude, fan, #783-7, small base repair .................. 400.00
    Sunflower, 5" h...................... 695.00
    Wincraft, panther, 10-1/2" h, 4-3/4" w
    ................................................ 800.00
Wall Pocket
    Carnelian............................. 185.00
    Clematis, green..................... 180.00

Cosmos, blue........................ 375.00
Gardenia, green..................... 265.00
Snowberry............................. 145.00
White Rose, pink ................... 325.00

# Royal China

**Collecting Hints:** The dinnerware has become very collectible and increasingly popular. It can be found at flea markets and antiques malls across the country. Prices are steadily increasing, and it is becoming more difficult to find some of the serving pieces.

The backs of pieces usually contain the names of the shape, line, and decoration. In addition to many variations of company backstamps, Royal China also produced objects with private backstamps. All records of these markings were lost in a fire in 1970.

The following are some of the items that are considered scarce: the lug soup/cereal bowl in several different patterns, many items with tab handles, coffee mugs, and some glasses and pitchers.

**History:** The Royal China Company manufactured dinnerware in Sebring, Ohio, from 1934 to 1986. The original officers were Beatrice L. Miller, William H. Hebenstreit, and John Briggs.

The firm produced a large variety of dinnerware patterns, the most popular being the blue and white Currier and Ives. Other patterns made by the company include Bucks County, Colonial Homestead, Fair Oaks, Memory Lane, Old Curiosity Shop, and Willow Ware. Gordon Parker, art director at Royal China, was credited with designing the border on the Currier and Ives pattern as well as some of the other popular dinnerware lines which were made in four basic colors: blue, pink, green, or brown.

Royal China was sold through retail department stores, catalog mail-order houses, and supermarket chains. Numerous serving pieces, as well as advertising and decorative items to compliment the dinnerware, were available.

In the last few years that it was in business, Royal made many different cake plates, pie bakers, and holiday related items, including Christmas items. These items are becoming very collectible and sought after.

In 1948, Kenneth Doyle developed a new machine, the underglaze stamping machine, that allowed the dinnerware to be mass produced at a very reasonable cost.

The company had various owners including the Jeanette Glass Corporation from 1969 to 1976. In 1970, the building and records were destroyed by fire and the operation was moved to the French Saxon China Company building. In 1976, the company was purchased by Coca-Cola and was operated by them until 1981, when it was sold to the J. Corporation. It was sold for the last time in 1984. The new owner, Nordic Capital, filed for bankruptcy in 1986 and ceased production in March of that year.

**References:** Eldon R. Aupperle, *Collector's Guide for Currier & Ives Dinnerware by Royal China Co.*, published by author (27470 Saxon Rd., Toulon, IL 61483), 1996; Susan and Al Bagdade, *Warman's American Pottery and Porcelain*, Wallace-Homestead, 1994; Jo Cunningham, *Collector's Encyclopedia of American Dinnerware*, Collector Books, 1982, 1995 value update; Harvey Duke, *Official Identification and Price Guide to Pottery and Porcelain*, 8th ed., House of Collectibles, 1995; Lois Lehner, *Lehner's Encyclopedia of U.S. Marks on Pottery, Porcelain & Clay*, Collector Books, 1988.

**Collectors' Club:** Currier & Ives Dinnerware Collectors Club, RR 2, Box 394, Holidaysburg, PA 16648.

**Advisor:** David J. and Deborah G. Folckemer.

**Willow Ware, snack plate with cup, 9" d, $50. Photo courtesy of David Folckemer.**

**Bucks County**: Introduced c1950; prices given are for yellow pieces with a dark brown print.

### Accessories
Juice Tumbler ................................. 15.00
Old Fashion Tumbler..................... 15.00
Promotional Jug, 2" x 2-3/4" ........ 100.00
Tidbit
    2 tier, wood legs...................... 125.00
    3 tier ........................................ 60.00

### Dinnerware
Bread and Butter Plate, 6-3/8" d ..... 3.00
Breakfast Plate, 9" d .................... 12.00
Butter Dish, cov, 1/4 lb ................ 45.00
Casserole, cov, angle handles ..... 75.00
Cereal Bowl, 6-1/4" d ..................... 8.00
Coffee Mug .................................. 40.00
Creamer.......................................... 4.00
Cup and Saucer ............................. 3.50
Dinner Plate, 10-1/4" d ................... 4.00
Fruit Bowl ...................................... 3.00
Gravy Boat, underplate ................ 25.00
Grill Plate, 3 sections ................... 15.00
Lug Soup/Cereal Bowl .................. 20.00
Platter
    Lug, meat, 11-1/2" l.................. 20.00
    Oval, 10" x 13"......................... 20.00
    Round, 12" d ............................ 22.00
    Round, 13" d ............................ 25.00
Rim Soup Bowl, 8-3/8" d ................. 9.00
Salad Plate, 7-3/8" d ...................... 8.00
Salt and Pepper Shakers, pr ........ 20.00
Sugar Bowl, cov
    Angle handles.......................... 20.00
    Tab handles ............................. 15.00
Teapot, cov ................................. 100.00
Vegetable Bowl
    9" d............................................ 15.00
    10" d......................................... 20.00

**Colonial Homestead**: Introduced c1950; prices given are for white pieces with a green print.

### Accessories
Ashtray ........................................ 10.00
Batter Set, large waffle pitcher and smaller syrup pitcher ............. 150.00
Beverage Set, frosted pitcher and 6 tumblers................................. 200.00
Juice Set, frosted pitcher and 6 tumblers...................................... 125.00
Juice Tumbler .............................. 14.00
Old Fashion Tumbler ................... 14.00
Tidbit
    2 tiers, wood legs ................. 100.00
    3 tiers....................................... 50.00
Tile and Rack............................... 75.00

### Dinnerware
Bread and Butter Plate, 6-3/8" d ..... 2.50
Breakfast plate, 9" d .................... 12.00
Butter Dish, cov, 1/4 lb ................ 25.00
Casserole, cov
    Angle handles......................... 65.00
    Tab handles .......................... 200.00
Cereal Bowl, 6-1/4" d ................... 10.00
Coffee Mug .................................. 20.00
Creamer.......................................... 4.00
Cup and Saucer ............................. 3.00
Dinner Plate, 10-1/4" d ................... 4.00
Fruit Bowl, 5-1/2" d ........................ 2.00
Gravy Boat, underplate ............... 25.00
Gravy Ladle ................................. 40.00
Lug Soup/Cereal Bowl.................. 20.00
Pie Plate, 10" d ........................... 20.00
Platter
    Lug, meat, 11-1/2" ................... 20.00
    Oval, 10" x 13"......................... 25.00
    Round, 12" d ............................ 20.00
    Round, 13" d ............................ 30.00
Rim Soup, 8-3/8" d.......................... 8.00

**Currier & Ives, wall plaque, very rare, $500. Photo courtesy of David Folckemer.**

**Colonial Homestead, casserole, tab handle, very rare, $200. Photo courtesy of David Folckemer.**

Salad Plate, 7-3/8" d ......................8.00
Salt and Pepper Shakers, pr.........20.00
Sugar Bowl, cov, angle handles ... 10.00
Teapot, cov ...................................90.00
Vegetable Bowl
   9" d .........................................15.00
   10" d .......................................20.00

**Currier and Ives:** Introduced late 1940s; prices given are for white pieces with a blue print. Prices are 25% higher for pieces with a pink print.

### Accessories

Ashtray.........................................12.00
Beverage Set, frosted pitcher and 6 tumblers ......................................250.00
Candle Lamp, with globe............300.00
Clock Plate
   10-1/4" d................................400.00
   12" d .....................................450.00
Juice Set, frosted pitcher and 6 tumblers .......................................125.00
Juice Tumbler ...............................12.00
Old Fashion Tumbler....................12.00
Placemats, vinyl, foam back, set of 4
   ..........................................100.00
Tidbit
   2 tiers, wood legs..................125.00
   3 tiers ....................................75.00
Tile and Rack .............................150.00
Wall Plaque, 5-1/4" x 6-3/4".........500.00

### Dinnerware

Bread and Butter Plate, 6-3/8" d .....3.00
Breakfast plate, 9" d .....................15.00
Butter Dish, cov, 1/4 lb
   Fashionable Turnouts...............45.00
   Road Winter ...........................30.00
Casserole, cov
   Angle handles..........................75.00
   Tab handles...........................200.00
Cereal Bowl, 6-1/4" d ...................12.00
Creamer
   Regular.....................................5.00
   Tall..........................................20.00
Cup, flared, round handle.............10.00
Cup and Saucer.............................4.00
Dinner Plate, 10-1/4" d ...............4500
Fruit Bowl, 5-1/2" d ........................3.00
Gravy Boat, underplate
   Regular...................................35.00
   White tab handles ..................125.00
Gravy Ladle .................................40.00

Lug Soup/Cereal Bowl..................35.00
Mug
   Coffee .....................................25.00
   Train scene..............................30.00
Pie Plate, 10" d, 9 different scenes
   ..........................................25.00
Platter
   Lug, meat, 11-1/2".................20500
   Oval, 10" x 13"........................25.00
   Round, 11" d, Getting Ice ........30.00
   Round, 11" d, Rocky Mountains
   ..........................................50.00
   Round, 12" d ...........................25.00
   Round, 13" d ...........................75.00
Rim Soup, 8-3/8" d.......................10.00
Salad Plate, 7-3/8" d ....................12.00
Salt and Pepper Shakers, pr ........25.00
Snack Plate with Cup, 9-1/8" ......125.00
Sugar Bowl, cov
   Angle handles..........................15.00
   Flared handles ........................35.00
   Handleless ..............................25.00
Teapot, cov ................................135.00
Vegetable Bowl
   9" d.........................................20.00
   10" d .......................................25.00

### Hostess Set

Cake Plate, 10" d
   Flat .........................................50.00
   Footed....................................150.00
Candy Bowl, 7-3/4" d ...................40.00
Dip Bowl, 4-3/8" d ........................40.00
Egg Plate, 10-3/4" d....................150.00
Pie Baker, 11" d............................75.00
Serving Plate, 7-3/4" d .................12.00

**Fair Oaks:** Introduced 1950s; prices given are pieces with a multicolored print.

### Dinnerware

Bread and Butter Plate, 6-3/8" d .....4.00
Butter Dish, cov, 1/4 lb ................35.00
Casserole, cov, angle handles .....75.00
Creamer..........................................6.00
Cup and Saucer.............................5.00
Dinner Plate, 10-1/4" d .................5.00
Fruit Bowl, 5-1/2" d ........................4.00
Gravy Boat, underplate ................25.00
Gravy Ladle ..................................40.00
Lug Soup/Cereal Bowl..................25.00
Platter
   Lug, meat, 11-1/2" l..................45.00

**Fair Oaks, platter, oval, 11-1/4" l, $35. Photo courtesy of David Folckemer.**

**Memory Lane, sugar bowl, tab handles $50. Photo courtesy of David Folckemer.**

Oval, 8-3/4" x 11-1/4" ...............35.00
Oval, 10" x 13"..........................30.00
Rim Soup Bowl, 8-3/8" d.............10.00
Salad Plate, 7-3/8" d ...................8.00
Salt and Pepper Shakers, pr ........25.00
Sugar Bowl, cov, angle handles ... 15.00
Teapot, cov ................................125.00
Tidbit, 3 tier................................60.00
Vegetable Bowl
   9" d.........................................15.00
   10" d .......................................25.00
   Divided ....................................35.00

**Memory Lane:** Introduced 1965; prices given are for white pieces with a pink print.

### Accessories

Ashtray.........................................10.00
Juice Tumbler ...............................12.00
Old Fashion Tumbler ....................12.00
Serving Tray, 19" d, metal ............45.00

### Dinnerware

Bread and Butter Plate, 6-3/8" d .....3.00
Breakfast Plate, 9" d .....................15.00
Butter Dish, cov, 1/4 lb ................35.00
Casserole, cov, angle handles .....75.00
Cereal Bowl, 6-1/4" d ...................10.00
Coffee Mug ...................................25.00
Creamer..........................................5.00
Cup and Saucer.............................4.00
Dinner Plate, 10-1/4" d .................4.00
Fruit Bowl, 5-1/2" d ........................3.00
Gravy Boat, underplate ................25.00
Gravy Ladle ..................................40.00
Pie Plate, 10" d ............................30.00
Platter
   Lug, meat, 11-1/2" l..................25.00
   Oval, 10" x 13"........................30.00
   Round, 12" d ...........................25.00
Rim Soup Bowl, 8-3/8" d ................9.00
Salad Plate, 7-3/8" d ....................10.00
Salt and Pepper Shakers, pr ........25.00
Sugar Bowl, cov
   Angle handles..........................12.00
   Tab handles ............................50.00
Teapot, cov ................................125.00
Vegetable Bowl
   9" d.........................................20.00
   10" d.......................................25.00

**Old Curiosity Shop, tile and rack, very rare, $150.**

**Old Curiosity Shop**: Introduced early 1950s; prices given are for white pieces with a green print.

### Accessories

Ashtray............................................. 10.00
Beverage Set, frosted pitcher and 6 tumblers ................................. 300.00
Juice Set, frosted pitcher and 6 juice tumblers ................................. 150.00
Juice Tumbler ............................... 18.00
Old Fashion Tumbler..................... 18.00
Tidbit
    2 tier, wood legs..................... 150.00
    3 tier .......................................... 75.00
Tile and Rack.............................. 150.00

### Dinnerware

Bread and Butter Plate, 6-3/8" d ..... 3.00
Breakfast Plate, 9" d...................... 15.00

Butter Dish, cov, 1/4 lb ................. 35.00
Casserole, cov, angle handles ..... 75.00
Cereal Bowl, 6-1/4" d ................... 12.00
Coffee Mug ................................... 40.00
Creamer.......................................... 4.50
Cup and Saucer ............................. 4.00
Dinner Plate, 10-1/4" d................... 5.00
Fruit Bowl, 5 1/2" d........................ 3.00
Gravy Boat, underplate ................ 25.00
Gravy Ladle .................................. 40.00
Lug Soup/Cereal Bowl.................. 25.00
Pie Plate, 10" d............................. 25.00
Platter
    Lug, meat, 11-1/2" l.................. 25.00
    Oval, 10" x 13"......................... 25.00
    Round, 12" d ........................... 25.00
    Round, 13" d ........................... 40.00
Rim Soup Bowl, 8-3/8" d............... 10.00
Salad Plate, 7-3/8" d ................... 10.00
Salt and Pepper Shakers, pr ........ 25.00
Sugar Bowl, cov, angle handles ... 15.00
Teapot, cov ................................ 125.00
Vegetable Bowl
    9" d........................................... 20.00
    10" d......................................... 25.00

**Willow Ware**: Introduced 1940s; prices given are for white pieces with a blue print.

Ashtray.......................................... 20.00
Batter Set, large waffle pitcher, smaller syrup pitcher.......................... 125.00
Beverage Set, frosted pitcher and 6 tumblers .............................. 175.00
Juice Tumbler .............................. 15.00
Old Fashion Tumbler..................... 15.00
Tidbit
    2 tier, wood legs..................... 125.00
    3 tier .......................................... 60.00

### Dinnerware

Bread and Butter Plate, 6-3/8" d..... 4.00
Breakfast Plate, 9" d ..................... 15.00
Butter Dish, cov, 1/4 lb ................. 30.00
Casserole, cov
    Angle handles.......................... 75.00
    Tab handles ........................... 200.00
Cereal Bowl, 6-1/4" d ................... 12.00
Coffee Mug................................... 20.00
Creamer.......................................... 4.00
Cup and Saucer ............................. 4.00
Dinner Plate, 10-1/4" d................... 4.00
Fruit Bowl, 5-1/2" d ....................... 3.00
Gravy Boat, underplate
    Regular .................................... 25.00
    Tab handle ............................... 75.00
Gravy Ladle .................................. 40.00
Grill Plate, 3 section..................... 15.00
Lug Soup/Cereal Bowl.................. 25.00
Pie Plate, 10" d ............................ 25.00
Platter
    Lug, meat, 11-1/2" l................. 20.00
    Oval, 8-3/4" x 11-1/4" .............. 30.00
    Oval, 10" x 13"......................... 25.00
    Round, 11" d ........................... 30.00
    Round, 12" d ........................... 25.00
    Round, 13" d ........................... 50.00
Rim Soup Bowl, 8-3/8" d.............. 10.00
Salad Plate, 7-3/8" d .................... 10.00
Salt and Pepper Shakers, pr ........ 25.00
Snack Plate, with cup, 9-1/8" d..... 50.00
Sugar Bowl, cov
    Angle handles.......................... 12.00
    Handleless ............................... 30.00
    Tab handles ............................. 20.00
Teapot, cov .................................. 95.00
Vegetable Bowl
    9" d........................................... 20.00
    10" d......................................... 25.00

# S

# Saloon Collectibles

**Collecting Hints:** Collectors concentrate on material that predates prohibition (i.e., before 1918), and many collectors recreate the decor of an old-time saloon in one room of their house. This material also is extremely popular with decorators. The field still is in its infancy and little information is available. Many bargains can be found by the more-experienced collector.

**History:** Throughout American history, the saloon has been a refuge and playground for off-duty males. Women and children often were forbidden to enter this masculine turf. Gambling, cursing, drinking, smoking, and fighting were the primary forms of entertainment at the saloon. Today the illusion exists that life was much more exciting in a yesteryear saloon than in a modern bar.

The saloon consisted of many units—the back bar, the front bar, and the room itself. All types of material—from bottles to spittoons—was made, as needs demanded.

**Reference:** George J. Baley, *Back Bar Breweriana*, L-W Book Sales, 1992.

Ashtray, porcelain, triangular, red, white, and blue adv "CinZano Vermouth," 1960s ........................... 7.50
Bottle
    8" h, Burke's Union Club, clear
    ................................................ 37.50

**Tip Tray, Straus, Gunst & Co., black and white, 1907, 12" d, $115.**

11" h, Westminster Rye, gold emb
    .................................................. 100.00
Bottle Opener, loop top, brown plastic whiskey bottle-shaped handle, full color label of Lord Calvert Whiskey, 4-7/8" l ................................... 10.00
Brochure
    A Message from Gandier, 8 pgs, issued by California Anti-Saloon League, promoting candidacy of a. J. Wallace for US Senator .......... 5.00
    Light Wines and Beers, issued by Anti-Saloon League of South Dakota, temperance era ......................... 6.00
    The Anti-Saloon League Indispensable, by Nolan R. Best, encouraging fight to hold Prohibition, undated
    .................................................... 5.00
Cigarette Card
    Frazier-Nash B.M.W. Saloon, 1936
    .................................................... 5.00
    Wolsley Super Six Sportsman's Saloon, 1936 ............................. 5.00
Decanter
    Belle of Kentucky, clear, ribbed, gold emb letters, orig stopper ....... 120.00
    Maryland Club, cut glass, fluted neck, cut glass stopper ........... 65.00
Display, adv, place for full bottle
    6-1/2" h, 11" l, Tuaca Milk Brandy, porcelain Guernsey cow, laying down, head up in air, porcelain banner in front with emb grapes and blue printing 'Tuaca demi sec liqueur Milk Brandy" ........................... 90.00
    8" h, 13-3/4" l, Early Times Bourbon Whiskey, chalkware Pierce Arrow, 1975, some damage ................ 50.00
    17" h, Beefeater Gin, composition statue of Beefeater with staff, green wooden base, some repairs .... 70.00
    25-1/4" h, 13" l, Old Forester Straight Bourbon Whiskey, cast plaster, sailboat, two cloth sails, blue base, c1970 ...................................... 65.00
    29" l, Wurzburger Hofbrau, 8-1/2" h driver, bright red vest, brown pants, black boots, Alpine hat, 11" horses, wooden wagon with rubber wheels holding 12 wooden barrels, each with "Wurzburger Hofbrau" on end, 11" chard board sign on back, c1950
    .................................................. 500.00
Key Chain, bronze, round medallion, emb "Jim Beam 1795-1995 200th Anniversary," orig box .............. 10.00
Lamp, 20" h overall, 14" h metal shade, 6-1/2" h statue of Johnny Walker, red, metal, search light tower base. 75.00
Photograph, 8" x 6", interior scene, bartender, fixtures, bar ................ 125.00
Pouring Spout, plastic, cork base
    Gallagher & Burton's, carriage on top, black and yellow ................ 8.50
    Gilbey's, red and white .............. 5.00
    Old Sunny Brook, black and yellow
    .................................................... 5.00
Salt and Pepper Shakers, pr, figural, western stagecoach and saloon, Arcadia, 1-1/4" h, 1-1/2" w ....... 90.00
Shot Glass
    Just a Swallow, clear glass, yellow and red painted design of swallow bird ............................................. 5.00

Lord Calvert, The Whiskey of Distinction ............................................. 5.00
Old Crow, the Greatest Name in Bourbon ..................................... 5.00
Old Kentucky Tavern ................... 5.00
Reagan, full color illus of Ronald Reagan, black lettering "Ronald W. Reagan 40th President" ............ 8.00
Universal Studios Tour, black glass, white lettering, two horizontal bands
    .................................................... 7.50
Sign, reverse painting on glass
    9" d, Overholt Pennsylvania Rye, gold, silver, and red, wood frame
    .................................................. 500.00
    15" x 8", Ginger Cordial, Clayton and Russel ..................................... 425.00
Token, brass, Deer Lodge, Montana
    .................................................. 20.00
Whiskey Dispenser, 15-1/2" h, etched "Ask for Sanderson's Whiskey"
    .................................................. 500.00

# Salt and Pepper Shakers, Figural

**Collecting Hints:** Collect only sets in very good condition. Make certain the set has the proper two pieces, and base if applicable. China shakers should show no signs of cracking. Original paint and decoration should be intact on all china and metal figurals. All parts should be present, including the closure.

Collectors compete with those in other areas, e.g., advertising, animal groups, Blacks, and holiday collectors. Many shakers were stock items to which souvenir labels were later affixed. The form, not the label, is the important element.

**History:** The Victorian era saw the advent of elaborate glass and fine-china salt and pepper shakers. Collectors were attracted to these objects by the pioneering research work of Arthur Goodwin Peterson that was published in *Glass Salt Shaker*. Figural and souvenir shakers, most dating from the mid-20th century and later, are gaining in popularity.

More and more people are collecting the figural and souvenir shakers, especially since prices are lower. Many of these patterns were made by Japanese firms and imported heavily after World War II.

Some forms were produced for decades; hence, it is difficult to tell an early example from a modern one. This is one of the factors that keeps prices low.

**References:** Gideon Bosker and Lena Lencer, *Salt and Pepper Shak-*

*ers*, Avon Books, 1994; Larry Carey and Sylvia Tompkins, *1003 Salt and Pepper Shakers*, Schiffer Publishing, 1997; Melva Davern, *Collector's Encyclopedia of Salt & Pepper Shakers*, 1st Series (1985, 1991 value update), 2nd Series (1990, 1995 value update), Collector Books; Helene Guarnaccia, *Salt & Pepper Shakers*, Vol. I (1985, 1996 value update), Vol. II (1989, 1993 value update), Vol. III (1991, 1995 value update), Vol. IV (1993, 1997 value update), Collector Books; Mildred and Ralph Lechner, *World of Salt Shakers*, 2nd ed., Collector Books, 1992, 1995 value update; Arthur G. Peterson, *Glass Salt Shakers*, Wallace-Homestead, out of print; Irene Thornburg, *Collecting Salt and Pepper Shakers,* Schiffer, 1998.

**Collectors' Clubs:** Antique and Art Glass Salt Shaker Collector's Society, 2832 Rapidan Trail, Maitland, FL 32751; Novelty Salt and Pepper Shakers Club, P.O. Box 3617, Lantana, FL 33465.

**Museum:** Judith Basin Museum, Stanford, MT.

### Advertising

| | |
|---|---|
| Budweiser, miniature bottles | 7.50 |
| Coca-Cola, miniature bottles | 15.00 |
| Dairy Queen | 32.00 |
| GE Refrigerators, 1930-style refrigerator, milk glass | 30.00 |
| Hormel, hash and egg | 15.00 |
| Pillsbury Dough Boy | 12.00 |
| Planters Peanuts | 30.00 |
| RCA Nipper, plastic | 15.00 |
| Rice-A-Roni | 7.50 |
| Schlitz Beer, miniature bottles | 7.50 |

### Ceramic

| | |
|---|---|
| Amish Couple | 5.00 |
| Barber shaving pig | 70.00 |
| Barn and Silo | 10.00 |
| Baseball and Glove | 12.00 |
| Birds on Nest | 10.00 |

**Toby's, blue coats, red britches, Czechoslovakian, 2-1/2" h, $24.**

| | |
|---|---|
| Birds, standing, white, gold trim, mkd "Made in Japan" | 6.50 |
| Bugs Bunny and Taz with football | 15.00 |
| Chicks emerging from egg-shaped cups, script mark "Japan," 4-1/2" h | 60.00 |
| Chicks, salt and pepper, mustard inside egg box, luster, Japanese | 45.00 |
| Cowboys, Vandor | 10.00 |
| Cows | 15.00 |
| Dachshund and Tire | 18.00 |
| Donald Duck and BBQ | 15.00 |
| Duck and Egg | 7.50 |
| Feet | 5.00 |
| Frogs | 7.00 |
| Kettles, hand painted | 5.00 |
| Lawn Mower, moving wheels and pistons, 1950s | 30.00 |
| Lemons | 5.00 |
| Mickey and Piano | 15.00 |
| Minnie Mouse and Vanity | 15.00 |
| Pigs, Otagiri | 10.00 |
| Pluto and Doghouse | 15.00 |
| Poodles | 40.00 |
| Puss N' Boots | 30.00 |
| Rabbits, yellow, snuggle type, Van Telligen | 42.00 |
| Rooster and Hen | 7.50 |
| Skunks, Enesco | 12.00 |
| Thermos and Lunch Pail | 35.00 |
| Thread and Thimble | 30.00 |
| Toilets | 10.00 |
| Tomatoes | 5.00 |
| Willie and Millie | 10.00 |

# Santa Claus

**Collecting Hints:** The number of Santa Claus-related items is endless. Collectors are advised to concentrate on one form (postcards, toys, etc.) or a brief time period. New collectors will find the hard-plastic 1950s Santas easily accessible and generally available at a reasonable price.

**History:** The idea of Santa Claus developed from stories about St. Nicholas, who lived about 300 A.D. By the 1500s, "Father Christmas" in England, "Pere Noel" in France, and "Weihnachtsmann" in Germany were well established.

Until the 1800s, Santa Claus was pictured as a tall, thin, stately man wearing bishop's robes and riding a white horse. Washington Irving, in *Knickerbocker's History of New York* (1809), made him a stout, jolly man who wore a broad-brimmed hat and huge breeches and smoked a long pipe. The traditional Santa Claus image came from Clement C. Moore's poem "An Account of a Visit from St. Nicholas" (*Troy Sentinel*, NY, 1823) and the cartoon characterizations by Thomas Nast which

appeared in *Harper's Weekly* between 1863 and 1886. The current appearance of Santa Claus is directly attributable to the illustrations of Haddon Sundblom for the Coca-Cola Company.

**References:** Beth Dees, *Santa's Guide to Contemporary Christmas Collectibles*, Krause Publications, 1997; Lissa Bryan-Smith and Richard Smith, *Holiday collectibles, Vintage Flea Market Treasures Price Guide*, Krause Publications, 1998.

Reproduction Alert.

**Additional Listings:** Christmas Items.

**Advisor:** Lissa Bryan-Smith and Richard Smith.

Advertising Trade Card, 3" x 5", "Santa Claus Soap, Gifts for Wrappers," N. K. Fairbanks Co, Chicago, St. Louis, New York, 1899 .......................... 12.00

Bank
   3" h, red hard plastic, egg shaped, Santa mask, mkd "Firestone Bank, Lisbon, Ohio" ............................. 8.00
   4" h, cardboard, Santa and box-shaped sleigh, 1960s ................ 8.00
   11" h, chalkware, Santa sitting on chimney, waving, 1960s .......... 32.00

Book
   *Night Before Christmas,* Samuel Gabriel Sons & Co., NY, 1947, linenette, 12" h ................................. 20.00
   *Santa Claus In Storyland,* pop-up, Doechia Greeting Cards, Fitchburg, MA, 1950, 11" h ...................... 25.00

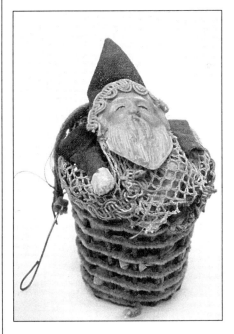

**Candy container, Santa in chenille basket, fabric netting, celluloid face, Japan, c1930, 4" h, $75.**

**Candy mold, tin, $85.**

Candy Box
   3" x 4-1/2" x 1-3/4", Santa face, cotton string handle, USA, 1970s ... 6.00
   3-1/2" x 5-1/2" x 2", Merry Christmas, picture of Santa and his workshop, cloth handle, USA, 1940s ........ 10.00
Candy Container
   4-1/2" h, red hard plastic, green skis, lollipops in open back on back, USA ............................................. 10.00
   5-1/2" h, glass, Father Christmas in chimney, metal base, Victory Candy Co............................................ 100.00
   8-1/2" h, papier-mâché, Father Christmas, white mica coat, holding feather tree, early 1900s ........ 500.00
Chromolithograph, 10" h, standing Santa, tinsel trim, Germany, 1920s ............................................. 45.00
Clicker, 1-1/2" l, green, red, black, and white, Grant's Toy Department, 1930s ...................................... 40.00
Figure
   3" h, composition face, red chenille body, Japan ............................. 15.00
   4" h, hard plastic, Santa on bike, USA, 1960s ............................. 10.00
   6-1/2" h, composition face, skier, red cloth coat, blue pants, wood skis and poles, Japan ..................... 70.00
   10" h, papier-mâché................. 35.00
   13-1/2" h, hard plastic, small pack in hand, hole for light in back, Union Products, Leominster, MA ........ 20.00
Game, 10" h, Santa Claus Ring Toss, cardboard, First National Bank of Berwick giveaway ................... 12.00
Greeting Card, Santa riding plane over world, Merry Christmas, 1940s .. 8.00

Lantern, 24" h, two piece hard plastic, Santa face fits over outdoor light, early 1960s ............................. 35.00
Ornament
   3-1/4" h, blown glass, holding tree, German, 1930s ........................ 35.00
   4" h, cotton batting, paper face, chenille hanger ............................. 15.00
   6" h, blown glass, holding sack, metal clip base, Germany, 1920s ................................................. 55.00
Paint Book, Santa's Surprise Paint Book, Merrill Co, 1949, flocked Santa with pack on cover .......................... 15.00
Postcard
   Christmas Greetings, Father Christmas with candlelit tree and toys, German, 1908 ......................... 12.00
   Merry Christmas, Santa wearing emb green outfit, red ground, carrying presents and tree.............. 15.00
Push Puppet, Santa, holding bell, mkd "Made in Hong Kong for Kohner" ................................................. 60.00
Ramp Walker, 6-1/2" h, hard plastic, cloth coat, orig paper label, Germany....................................... 35.00
Tin, 4" d, Santa face surrounded by poinsettias, early 1900s ........... 24.00
Toy, 12" h, battery operated, Happy Santa, 5 actions, Japan ......... 235.00

# Scouting

**Collecting Hints:** Nostalgia is one of the principal reasons for collecting Scouting memorabilia; individuals often focus on the period during which they themselves were involved in the Scouting movement. Other collectors select themes, e.g., handbooks, jamborees, writings by scout-movement leaders or Eagle Scout material. Jamboree ephemera is especially desirable. The greatest price fluctuation occurs in modern material and newly defined specialized collecting areas.

Scouting scholars have produced a wealth of well-researched material on the Scouting movement. Many of these pamphlets are privately printed and can be located by contacting dealers specializing in Scouting memorabilia.

Girl Scout material is about five to ten years behind Boy Scout material in respect to collecting interest. A Girl Scout collection can still be assembled for a modest investment. While Boy Scout uniforms have remained constant in design throughout time, the Girl Scout uniform changed almost every decade. This increases the number of collectibles.

**History:** The Boy Scout movement began in America under the direction of William D. Boyce, inspired by

a helping hand he received from one of Baden-Powell's English scouts when he was lost in a London fog in 1910. Other American boys' organizations, such as the one organized by Dan Beard, were quickly brought into the Boy Scout movement. In 1916, the Boy Scouts received a charter from the United States Congress. Key leaders in the movement were Ernest Thompson-Seton, Dan Beard, William D. Boyce, and James West.

One of Norman Rockwell's first jobs was editor of *Boys' Life* in 1913, and this began the famous American illustrator's lifelong association with the Boy Scouts.

The first international jamboree was held in England in 1920. America's first jamboree was in 1937 in Washington, D.C. Manufacturers, quick to recognize the potential for profits, issued a wealth of Boy Scout material. Local councils and Order of the Arrow lodges have added significantly to this base, especially in the area of patches. Around the time of the 1950 National Jamboree, everything from patches to lizards were traded.

The Girl Scout movement began on March 12, 1912, under the direction of Juliette Gordon Low of Savannah, Georgia. The movement grew rapidly, and in 1928 the Girl Scout manual suggested cookies be sold to raise funds. The Girl Scout movement received wide recognition for its activities during World War II, selling more than $3 million worth of bonds in the fourth Liberty Loan drive.

**References:** George Cuhaj, *U. S. Scouting Collectibles,* Krause Publications, 1998; Fred Duersch, Jr., *Green Khaki Crimped-Edge Merit Badges*, Downs Printing, 1993; Franck, Hook, Ellis & Jones, *Aid to Collecting Selected Council Shoulder Patches*, privately printed, 1994.

**Periodicals:** *Asta Report,* Doug Krutilek, 9025 Alcosta Blvd., #230, San Ramon, CA 94583-4047; *Fleur-de-Lis,* 5 Dawes Ct., Novato, CA 94947; *Scout Memorabilia Magazine*, c/o Lawrence L. Lee Scouting Museum, P.O. Box 1121, Manchester, NH 03105; *Scouting Collectors Quarterly,* 806 E. Scott St., Tuscola, IL 61953.

**Collectors' Clubs:** American Scouting Traders Association, P.O. Box 92, Kentfield, CA 94914; International Badgers Club, 7760 NW 50th St., Lauder Hill, FL 33351; National Scouting Collectors Society, 806 E. Scott St., Tuscola, IL 61953; Scouts on Stamps Society International, 7406 Park Dr., Tampa, FL 33610.

**Museums:** Girl Scout National Headquarters, New York, NY; Juliette Gordon Low Girl Scout National Center, Savannah, GA; Lawrence L. Lee Scouting Museum and Max J. Silber Scouting Library, Manchester, NH; Lone Scout Memory Lodge, Camp John J. Barnhardt, New London, NC; Murray State University National Museum of the Boy Scouts of America, Murray, KY; Western Scout Museum, Los Angeles, CA; World of Scouting Museum, Valley Forge, PA.

**Advisor:** Richard Shields.

**Reproduction Alert:** Boy Scout jamboree patches, rare Council Shoulder patches, and rare Order of the Arrow patches.

### Boy Scouts

Backpack, canvas, New York City logo ........................................... 15.00
Bolo Tie, Southeast Region ............. 8.00
Book, 1960-80s
    Bear Cub Scout .......................... 1.00
    Wolf ............................................. 1.00
Booklet, Philadelphia Enquirer, National Jamboree, 1950 ......................... 8.00
Campaign Hat (Smokey Bear), felt, leather band, chin strap ........... 50.00
Handbook
    Boys, 1950s ............................... 8.00
    Scoutmaster, 6th ed. .................. 3.00
Hat Pin, National Jamboree, 1993 .. 3.00
Key Chain, Cub Scout, "Be Square" in promise ...................................... 3.00
Key Chain Medallion, National Jamboree, 1953 ................................... 8.00

**Neckerchief, emblem in center, activities in corners, brown and red dec, 14-5/8" sq, $20.**

**Song Book, C. C. Birchard and Co., Boston, MA, 1930, 46 pgs, $10.**

Magazine Tear Sheet, Cross-X-Knit, Scouts in scene ....................... 10.00
Medal
    Ad Altare Dei ........................... 20.00
    Eagle, blue casket shaped box
    ................................................. 100.00
    Eisenhower War Service .......... 20.00
    God and Country, blue ribbon
    ................................................... 20.00
Mug, ceramic, white ..................... 2.50
Neckerchief, National Jamboree, 1964 ............................................... 7.50
Neckerchief Slide
    New York World's Fair, 1964-65
    ................................................... 25.00
    Philmont brand, ceramic ............ 3.00
Pamphlet, Merit Badge, full picture, 1950-60s ..................................... 1.00
Paperback, *The Scout Law in Action,* MacPeek, 1966 .......................... 5.00
Patch
    Activity, 1960s ........................... 1.00
    Camporee, 1960s ...................... l.00
    Historic Trails Award .................. 1.00
    National Jamboree, 1977, pocket
    ..................................................... 5.00
    National Office, Irving, TX .......... 3.00
    New York World's Fair, 1939 ..... 40.00
    Rank, Bear Cub, black on red felt
    ..................................................... 3.00
    Scout Show, 1960s ................... 1.00
Pin
    First Class, thin metal, World War II era, 2" l ................................... 50.00
    Fleur-de-lis, universal ................. .50
Plate, Our Heritage, Rockwell ....... 45.00
Pocket Coin, You Make The Difference
    ..................................................... 1.00
Post Card, World Jamboree, US, 1967
    ..................................................... 1.00
Poster, Scout Week, cardboard, 1930s-40s ......................................... 20.00

Shampoo Bottle, Snoopy Beagle Scout, plastic ...................................... 20.00
Shirt, Explorer, dark green, circle v design emblem ........................ 8.00
Sundial, pocket, metal, orig box ... 50.00
Utensil Set, 3 pc, fits together, plastic case .......................................... 5.00
Wash Basin, clear plastic, orig box
    ................................................... 15.00

### Girl Scouts

Belt, dark green web, trefoil emblem, metal buckle ........................... 15.00
Beret, dark green wool, with patch
    ..................................................... 8.00
Book, *World's to Explore,* 1980s ..... 3.00
Camera, Herbert George Co., model 620 ............................................. 50.00
Guide Book, leader's, nature, 1942
    ................................................... 12.00
Handbook, Brownie, 1964 ............. 3.00
Photo Album, dark green cover, small size .......................................... 25.00
Pin, World Association, crude clasp
    ..................................................... 2.00

# Dr. Seuss Collectibles

**Collecting Hints:** The characters made famous by Dr. Seuss are alive and well and appearing on numerous items from children's bandages to clothing at many major department stores. Many Seuss collectors look for both new and vintage items. With the opening of the Seuss Landing Theme Park at Universal Studios Islands of Adventure in Orlando, Florida, there will be even more new items with Seuss characters on the market. Before buying newer Seuss merchandise, check around at your local retail stores. Many items being offered as "hard to find" at online auctions are sometimes still on store shelves. Common older Dr. Seuss items include red plastic bookends and plastic and canvas book bags. Many Dr. Seuss records are currently hard to sell even though they have great graphics. Watch for terms like "rare" at online auctions or on antique dealer's price tags. Many Dr. Seuss items are not rare. Savvy collectors should watch for copies of 1930s and '40s magazines with Dr. Seuss artwork on the cover or inside. Also, become familiar with which firms Seuss did advertising work for and look for advertising pieces with his artwork. While Seuss did some artwork for Flit insecticide, he did not do all of the firm's art. Some Flit sprayers are being sold as Dr. Seuss items, even though the artwork looks nothing like the good Doctor's work.

Book Club editions of all of Dr. Seuss' books are common. Determining a first edition of his books takes some homework. Know the order his books were published in, as well as their original prices. Your homework will pay off if you have a first. Many of his first-edition titles sell in the $100 to $500 range.

**History:** The collector of Dr. Seuss memorabilia has far more to search for than children's books. Long before the Cat in the Hat first stepped onto the mat, Dr. Seuss had been busy producing cartoons, films, and advertising campaigns.

Dr. Seuss was born Theodor Seuss Geisel in 1904. In the 1920s, he started using his middle name and added the Dr. to the front. He began his career as a freelance illustrator and sent humorous pieces and cartoons to newspapers and magazines. Soon he began to get work in advertising. One of his first accounts was Flit insecticide, a product of Standard Oil of New Jersey. Other advertising work was done for Essolube Motor Oil, Essomarine Products, Ford Motor Co., National Broadcasting Co., Holly Sugar, Narragansett Lager and Ale, Brevo Shaving Cream, and Hankey Bannister Scotch Whiskey. Dr. Seuss won Academy Awards for the documentaries *Hitler Lives* in 1946 and *Design for Death* in 1947 and for the animated cartoon *Gerald McBoing-Boing* in 1951. In 1953, *The 5,000 Fingers of Dr. T* was released by Columbia. Seuss wrote the story, and those familiar with his work will recognize his characters in the movie.

*Boners* was the first book linked with the name Dr. Seuss. Published in 1931, it was a collection of humorous writings by children which Seuss illustrated. His first children's book was *And to Think I Saw It on Mulberry Street*, published in 1937 after it had been rejected by 28 publishing houses. *The Cat in the Hat* was published in 1957. Another famous Seuss work, *Green Eggs and Ham*, is the third-largest-selling book in the English language.

Many of the creatures which would later become famous in his children's works made their first appearance in the advertisements and cartoons that Seuss drew. The forerunner to Horton the kindly elephant first appeared in a 1929 *Judge* magazine.

Dr. Seuss died in 1991. Most of his children's books are still in print and his characters are still licensed to new products including toys and clothing items.

**References:** Richard Marschall (ed.), *The Tough Coughs as He Ploughs the Dough*, William Morrow and Co. Inc./Remco World Service Books, 1987; Neil and Judith Morgan, *Dr. Seuss and Mr. Geisel: A Biography*, Random House, 1995; *Dr. Seuss from Then to Now*, a catalog of the retrospective exhibition organized by the San Diego Museum of Art, 1986, Random House, 1986; *The Secret Art of Dr. Seuss*, with introduction by Maurice Sendak, Random House, 1995.

**Web sites of interest:** Random House has an interactive Dr. Seuss web site where children will find activities and can even write a letter to the Cat in the Hat. Events related to the famous cat and Dr. Seuss are often listed: http://www.randomhouse.com/seussville. Another good source is an online listing of the holdings of the University of California, San Diego, Geisel Library, Mandeville Special Collections. The URL is http://orpheus.ucsd.edu/speccoll/collects/seuss.html.

**Advisor:** Connie Swaim.

Beer Tray, 12" d, Narragansett Beer, picturing Chief Gansett and Cat, slight rubbing on edges........... 95.00
Booklet, *The Log of the Good Ship*, Esso, 37 pgs, Seuss illustrations throughout, excellent condition
................................................. 175.00
Coaster, 4-1/4" d, Chief Gansett on front, Narragansett Beer advertising on back................................... 20.00

**Coaster, 4-1/4" d, Chief Gansett on front, Narragansett Beer advertising on back, $20.**

Drinking Glass, Esso Seuss Navy, "Official When Hen," 5-1/4" h.......... 45.00
Figure, stuffed, Cat in the Hat,
    Impulse Items Original, 24", slight stains ........................................ 40.00
    Macy's, 1995, excellent, no book
    ................................................. 30.00
Lunch Box, 1970, metal, Aladdin Industries, Seuss characters on all sides, plastic handle, light wear consistent with use.................................... 85.00
Magazine
    *Judge,* March 23, 1929, color illustration by Seuss on the cover
    ................................................. 160.00
    *McCall's,* October, 1970, 4 pages inside, Mr. Brown Can Moo Like a Cow, Can You?........................ 20.00
Magazine Tear Sheet, talking Seuss toys adv, 1970........................... 5.00
Model, Revell, Gowdy, circa late 1950s, complete with box and instruction sheet ...................................... 190.00
Plush figure, Coleco, 1983
    Cat in the Hat, no box, with umbrella, 24", excellent condition............ 25.00
    Cat in the Hat, with original box, all tags and excellent condition
    ................................................. 100.00
    Cat in the Hat, 48", excellent condition, body tag........................... 80.00
    Grinch, no box, excellent......... 75.00
    The Lorax, no box, excellent ... 50.00
    Thidwick, no box, no tags, excellent
    ................................................. 25.00
Premium Booklet, 8" x 11", paper, McElligot's Pool, given away by Crest, Wonder or Prell, 1975 ............. 10.00
Puzzle, "Foiled by Essolube," Esso advertising, paper mailing envelope, complete, 150 pieces, very good condition........................ 90.00
Thermos, plastic, for lunch box, excellent condition .......................... 40.00

# Sewing Items

**Collecting Hints:** Collectors tend to favor sterling silver items. However, don't overlook pieces made of metal, ivory, celluloid, plastic, or wood. Before buying anything which is metal-plated, be sure the plating is in very good condition.

Advertising and souvenir items are part of sewing history. Focus on one of these aspects to develop a fascinating collection. Other collectors may specialize in a particular instrument, i.e., tape measures. Figural items of any sort have a high value because of their popularity.

Most collectors concentrate on material from the Victorian era. A novice collector might look to the 20th century, especially the Art Deco and Art Nouveau periods, to build a collection.

**History:** Sewing was considered an essential skill of a young woman of the 19th century. The wealth of early American samplers attests to the talents of many of these young seamstresses.

During the Victorian era, a vast assortment of practical, as well as whimsical, sewing devices appeared on the market. Among these were tape measures, pincushions, stilettos for punchwork, and crochet hooks. The sewing birds attached to table tops were a standard fixture in the parlor.

Many early sewing tools, e.g., needle holders, emery holders and sewing boxes, were made of wood. However, the sterling silver tool was considered the height of elegance. Thimbles were the most popular of these, although sterling silver was used in other devices, particularly the handles of darning eggs, stilettos, and thread holders.

Needle cases and sewing kits were important advertising giveaways in the 20th century. Plastic sewing items are available, but they have not attracted much collector interest.

**References:** *Advertising & Figural Tape Measures*, L-W Book Sales, 1995; Elizabeth Arbittier et al., *Collecting Figural Tape Measures*, Schiffer Publishing, 1995; Carter Bays, *Encyclopedia of Early American Sewing Machines*, published by author, 1993; Lori Hughes, *A Century of American Sewing Patterns, 1860-1959,* C & B Press, 1998; Frieda Marion, *China Half-Figures Called Pincushion Dolls*, published by author, 1974, 1994 reprint; Averil Mathias, *Antique and Collectible Thimbles and Accessories*, Collector Books, 1986, 1995 value update; Bridget McConnel, *The Story of Thimble: An Illustrated Guide for Collectors*, Schiffer Publishing, 1997; Wayne Muller, *Darn It!, History and Romance of Darners*, L-W Book Sales, 1995; James W. Slaten, *Antique American Sewing Machines*, Singer Dealer Museum, 1992; Glenda Thomas, *Toy and Miniature Sewing Machines*, Book I (1995), Book II (1997) Collector Books; Helen Lester Thompson, *Sewing Tools & Trinkets*, Collector Books, 1997; Debra J. Wisniewski, *Antique & Collectible Buttons*, Collector Books, 1997; Estelle Zalkin, *Zalkin's Handbook of Thimbles & Sewing Imple-*

*ments,* Warman Publishing, 1988, distributed by Krause Publications.

**Collectors' Clubs:** International Sewing Machine Collectors Society, 1000 E. Charleston Blvd., Las Vegas, NV 89104; National Button Society, 2723 Juno Road, Apt. 4, Akron, OH 44313; Toy Stitchers, 623 Santa Florita Ave., Millbrae, CA 94030.

**Museums:** Fabric Hall, Historic Deerfield, Deerfield, MA; Sewing Machine Museum, Oakland, CA; Shelburne Museum, Shelburne, VT; Smithsonian Institution, Museum of American History, Washington, DC.

**Additional Listings:** Thimbles.

Basket, wicker, round, beaded lid .................................................. 27.50
Bodkin, 2-1/2" to 3-3/8" l, sterling silver, mkd with intertwined B and U, "Sterling" and "925 fine," set of three .................................................. 85.00
Book
  *American Needlework, 1776-1976,* Leslie Tillett, NY Graphic Society, 1975 .......................................... 15.00
  *Designs in Patchwork,* Dianne Logan, Oxmoor House, 1987, 143 pgs .............................................. 15.00
  *Gloria Vanderbuilt designs for your Home,* 1977, 1st edition, dj ...... 10.00
  *Terrace Hill Needlepoint Designs, Orig Designs from Iowa Governor's Mansion,* Billie Ray, 1980, sgd .................................................. 10.00
Button
  Bakelite, all colors, 12 on orig card .................................................. 85.00
  Figural, bowling, plastic, self shank, navy blue, 1/2" d, set of 6 ........ 10.00
  Figural, grape cluster, celluloid, plastic shank, purple, blue, and green grapes, blue-green leaves ......... 5.00
  Figural, orange, celluloid, plastic shank, brown leaf, orange body .................................................. 4.50
  Knot, plastic, metal stems, gray, 3/4" d, five buttons on orig card mkd "Costumakers Trade Mark, Made in

**Advertising Trade Card, Singer Sewing Machine, adv on back, 5-1/2" x 4", $9.**

U.S.A.," number stamped on back .................................................. 10.00
Rhinestone, black plastic backing, orig card with 4 buttons mkd "B. Blumenthal & Co., New York, NY" ...... 8.00
Catalog
  Davis Sewing Machine Co., Watertown, NY, 1881, 64 pgs, 5-1/2" x 8-3/4", cover wear ................... 24.00
  New Home Sewing machine, New York, NY, c1900, 12 pgs, 3-3/4" x 6-1/4" .......................................... 12.00
  Ormond Manufacturing Co., Baltimore, MD, 1878, 96 pgs, 4-1/2" x 5-3/4" .......................................... 73.00
  United Thread Mills, New York, NY, c1930, 7 pgs, 6-3/4" x 10" ........ 18.00
  White Sewing Machine, Cleveland, OH, c1923, 16 pgs, 3-1/2" x 6" .................................................. 24.00
  Wilson Sewing Machine Co., Chicago, IL, pre-1900, 26 pgs, 6" x 9" .................................................. 38.00
Clamp, wood, painted, pin cushion, cupid decal ........................... 115.00
Crochet Hook, metal, capped ...... 15.00
Darner Combination, 6-7/8" l, varnished wood, mkd "California Big Tree," combination darning egg, glove darner, needle case, and thimble .................................................. 35.00
Darning Egg, 4-1/4" l, 1-1/2" w egg, ebony, sterling silver handle, stamped "Sterling" on both sides .................................................. 90.00
Hem Gauge, 4-3/4" l, poinsettias dec, mkd "Sterling," some corrosion on back .......................................... 95.00
Magazine
  *McCalls,* 1969, 8-1/4" x 11-1/4" .................................................. 8.00
  *Workbasket and Home Arts Magazine,* 1976, 12 issues .............. 10.00
Needle Book
  Liberty National Life Insurance Company, Birmingham, Alabama, Statue of Liberty on front, 1 needle packet .................................................. 7.50
  Sears Roebuck and Co, A Gift to you from Kenmore - Fine Needlework, Japan ......................................... 9.00
  Sewing Circle, 4 ladies sewing, 6 needle packets and threader .................................................. 10.00
  Sewing Susan, Japan, 4 needle packets and threader, Japan... 10.00
  Sew Smart, Japan ..................... 9.00
  The National Life and Accident Insurance Company Shields You, int. reads "A Stitch in Time Saves Nine - Presented by The Shield Man," 3" x 3" shield shape ......................... 9.00
  Traveler, illus of 2 children and mother sewing, 6 needle packets and threader ........................... 9.00
Needle Case
  2" h, Adv, Formamint, metal, adv "Wulfing's Formamint for Sore Throat" on side, mkd "Germany" on bottom .................................... 10.00
  2-3/4" h, plastic, yellow thimble top, ivory colored base, yellow tassel .................................................. 22.00

**Pin Cushion, trapezoid, black and red velvet, jet bead trim, 4" d, $27.50.**

3" h, 1-1/4" d, arrel Shape, Piccadilly, wood .......................................... 85.00
Needle Gripper, Nimble Thimble, orig package .................................... 20.00
Needle Sharpener
   Cat ............................................... 50.00
   Strawberry .................................... 9.00
Pin Cushion
   1-1/2" h, 5" l, Dutch shoe, thimble and thread holder, wood burned picture of Dutch windmill on one side and "Galveston, Texas" on other side ................................................ 12.00
   2-1/2" h, 3" d, apple, satin, red and yellow, green leaves and stem ................................................ 65.00
   4-1/2" h, Black boy leaning on green watermelon ................................ 80.00
   5" h, 3" w, strawberry, red velvet, green felt leaves, c1870 ........... 90.00
   5" h, 5-1/2" w, doll face, bisque, blue glass eyes, blond hair, open mouth with teeth, mounted on purple orchid, orig box, German ......... 90.00
Pin Holder, adv, Prudential ............ 10.00
Scissors, emb florals on handle, German ........................................ 30.00
Sewing Bird, hand held, sgd "Turner" ................................................ 80.00
Sewing Box, 6-1/2" x 4" box, cats playing on lid and sides, 24 Belding Heminway Corticelli mini spools of thread, plastic thimble, some wear ................................................ 35.00
Sewing Caddy
   4" x 3-1/2", wood, red stain, three spools ........................................ 28.00
   8-1/2" h, figural chair, hand made, plywood, drawer in front, scissors holder on back of chair, thimble holders on side, pin cushion seat ................................................ 48.00
Sewing Kit, 2-1/4" h, silver-colored metal capsule, holds thimble, thread bobbin, incised "Lydia Pinkham's Vegetable Compound" ............. 18.00
Sewing Machine, full size, working condition
   Singer Featherweight ............. 300.00

**Tape Measure, multicolored litho, young girl with flowers on each side, 1-1/2" d, $55.**

Wheeler & Wilson, treadle, c1871, flat belt, partial instruction manual, accessories ............................ 800.00
Sewing Machine, toy, working condition
   Gateway Junior, Model NP-1, mkd "Gateway Engineering Company, Chicago, 51, Ill," stamped metal, some wear, needle missing, orig instruction sheet and box ........ 85.00
   Kay-an-EE, pink, mkd "Made in Germany, Berlin, US Zone" ............ 90.00
   Singer, Little Touch & Sew, battery operated, plastic base cabinet, 26" h, 22-1/2" w, 12-1/2" d, some minor parts missing, wear ................. 90.00
Spool Cabinet, JP Coats, metal, black, glass slant front ...................... 125.00
Tape Measure, figural
   Apple, hard plastic, red, leaf pull ................................................ 24.00
   Clock, metal, hands turn, mkd "Germany" .................................... 125.00
   Dress form ............................... 50.00
   Fish, celluloid ........................... 30.00
   Little Boy, clown hat, mkd "Germany" ................................................ 45.00
Thimble Case
   Brass, walnut .......................... 25.00
   Crocheted ............................... 10.00
   Sweet Grass ........................... 30.00
Thread Holder, 3-1/2" h, thimble top, red celluloid top, hand painted floral pattern ........................................ 40.00
Tracing Paper, Singer, unopened back, c1960 ....................................... 4.00
Travel Kit, 2" l, metal case, thimble as lid, wooden tube with needs and thread on outside, adv "J. B. Best & Co., Clothing & Shoes Since 1919, Woodville, Texas, Patent No. 2084780" ................................. 18.00

Zipper Pull
   1-1/8" h, tassel, Bakelite, butterscotch, orig metal attachment ... 8.50
   1-1/2" d, Mexican Hat, wood, hole at edge of brim, brightly colored ... 8.50

# Shawnee Pottery

**Collecting Hints:** Many Shawnee pieces came in several color variations. Some pieces were both painted and decorated with decals. The available literature indicates some, but not all, of the variations.

Shawnee also produced artware and dinnerware lines. These include Cameo, Cheria (Petit Point), Diora, and Touche (Liana). New collectors might consider concentrating in one of these areas.

Shawnee pieces were marked "Shawnee," "Shawnee U.S.A.," "USA #___," "Kenwood," or with character names, e.g., "Pat. Smiley" and "Pat. Winnie."

**History:** The Shawnee Pottery Co. was founded in 1937 in Zanesville, Ohio. The company acquired a 650,000-square-foot plant that had previously housed the American Encaustic Tiling Company. Shawnee produced as many as 100,000 pieces of pottery a day until 1961, when the plant closed.

Shawnee limited its production to kitchenware, decorative art pottery, and dinnerware. Distribution was primarily through jobbers and chain stores.

**References:** Jim and Bev Mangus, *Shawnee Pottery*, Collector Books, 1994, 1998 value update; Mark Supnick, *Collecting Shawnee Pottery*, L-W Book Sales, 1989, 1997 value update; Duane and Janice Vanderbilt, *Collector's Guide to Shawnee Pottery*, Collector Books, 1992, 1996 value update.

**Collectors' Club:** Shawnee Pottery Collectors Club, P.O. Box 713, New Smyrna Beach, FL 32170.

Bank
   Smiley, brown ...................... 550.00
   Winnie, butterscotch ............. 600.00
Bookends, pr, cattails and ducks ................................................ 75.00
Bowl, 8-3/4" l, oval, Corn King, #95 ................................................ 45.00
Butter Dish, cov, Corn King, #72 .. 50.00
Casserole, cov
Casserole, cov
   Corn King, large, mkd "Shawnee USA Oven Proof 74" ............... 90.00
   Lobster, 4-3/4" h, 11-1/4" l, 8" w, mkd "Oven Proof, USA Kenwood" ... 70.00

**Cookie Jar, basket of fruit, mkd "Shawnee, USA 83," 7-3/8" d, $90.**

Cookie Jar
　Lucky Elephant, gold trim ...... 600.00
　Mugsy ................................. 450.00
　Owl ...................................... 175.00
　Puss n' Boots, gold trim, decals, white bow ........................... 495.00
　Smiley Pig, shamrock trim ..... 325.00
　Winnie Pig, blue collar .......... 325.00
Corn Dish, Corn King, oval .......... 25.00
Creamer
　Cat, yellow and green ............. 55.00
　Corn King, #70 ........................ 25.00
　Elephant ................................. 35.00
　Puss N Boots .......................... 90.00
Creamer and Sugar, Corn King .... 85.00
Cup, Corn King, #90 .................... 20.00
Fruit Dish, 6" d, Corn King, #92 .... 40.00
Incense Burner, 5" h, Chinaman, blue base, mkd "USA" .................. 30.00
Jardiniere, 3-3/4" h, 4-1/4" w, muted orange, orig silver and red Shawnee sticker .................................... 15.00
Lamp, Oriental motif, pr .............. 75.00
Marmalade, cov, Fruits ................ 40.00
Mixing Bowl, Corn King
　5" d, #5 ................................... 40.00
　6-1/4" d ................................... 45.00
Mug, Corn King, 8 oz, #69 ........... 45.00
Pie Bird, 5-1/2" h, yellow, made for Pillsbury ..................................... 75.00
Pitcher
　Bo Peep, blue bonnet ............ 145.00
　Chanticleer ........................... 110.00
　Corn King, #71 ........................ 65.00
　Fruits, juice ............................ 50.00
　Smiley Pig, red flower ........... 145.00
　Sunflower, large ...................... 95.00
Planter
　Dog and Jug ........................... 22.00
　Giraffe and baby, brown and rust ............................................ 65.00
　Pixie Boot, green, gold trim ...... 15.00
　Polynesian Girl, 5-3/4" h, #896 ............................................ 35.00
　Pup, three button shoe, ivory ... 18.00
　Train, 3 pc, caboose, coal car, and engine .................................. 150.00
　Wishing Well, Dutch boy and girl ............................................ 20.00

Plate
　8" d, Corn King ........................ 40.00
　9-1/2" d, Corn King, #68 .......... 37.50
Platter, 12" l, Corn King, #96 ........ 50.00
Range Shakers, pr
　Boy and Girl, 5" h .................... 50.00
　Dutch Boy and Girl, large ........ 95.00
　Mugsy .................................. 140.00
　Pig, green bib ....................... 125.00
　Rooster, 5-1/2" h ..................... 50.00
Relish Tray, Corn King, #79 .......... 40.00
Salad Plate, Corn King, #93 ......... 40.00
Salt and Pepper Shakers, pr
　Bo Peep and Sailor ................. 45.00
　Cats, orig paper labels ............ 85.00
　Corn King, tall ......................... 35.00
　Dutch Boy and Girl .................. 95.00
　Mugsy
　　Large ............................... 175.00
　　Small ................................. 90.00
　Owls ...................................... 75.00
　Puss n' Boots ......................... 75.00
　Smiley and Winnie, 3-1/4" h, red heart on Winnie's hat and pocket ............................................ 95.00
　Swiss Children, 5" h, gold trim . 75.00
　Watering Can, 2-1/4" ............... 45.00
Saucer, Corn King, #91 ............... 20.00
Soup Bowl, Corn King, #94 .......... 55.00
Spoon Holder
　Flower Pot, patent pending ...... 15.00
　Window Box, patent pending .. 15.00
Sugar, Bowl, cov, Corn King ......... 42.00
Sugar Shaker, White Corn ........... 55.00
Teapot, cov
　Corn King ............................... 98.00
　Granny Anne, peach apron ... 150.00
　Tom The Piper's Son ............. 115.00
Vase
　Bowknot, green ...................... 20.00
　Dove, yellow, #829 .................. 32.00
Wall Pocket, wheat ..................... 40.00

# Sheet Music

**Collecting Hints:** Pick a theme for your collection: show tunes, songs of World War I, Sousa marches, Black material, songs of a certain lyricist or composer—the list is endless.

Be careful about stacking sheets on top of one another because the ink on the covers tends to bleed. The ideal solution is to place acid-free paper between each cover and sheet.

Unfortunately, tape was often used to repair tears in old sheet music, resulting in discoloration. This detracts from value. Seek professional help in removing tape from rarer sheets.

**History:** Sheet music, especially piano scores, dates to the early 19th century. The early music contains some of the finest examples of lithography. Much of this music was bound into volumes.

The covers of sheet music chronicle the social, political, and historical trends of all eras. The golden age of the hand-illustrated cover dates to around 1885. Leading artists such as James Montgomery Flagg used their talents to illustrate sheet music. Cover artwork was critical to helping a song sell.

Once radio and talking pictures became popular, covers featured the stars. A song sheet might be issued in dozens of cover versions, each picturing a different personality. By the 1950s, piano playing no longer was popular and song sheets failed to maintain a high quality of design.

**References:** Debbie Dillon, *Collectors Guide to Sheet Music*, L-W Book Sales, 1988, 1995 value update; Anna Marie Guiheen and Marie-Reine A. Pafik, *Sheet Music Reference and Price Guide*, 2nd ed., Collector Books, 1995; Marion Short, *Covers of Gold: Collectible Sheet Music*, Schiffer Publishing, 1998; —, *Hollywood Movie Songs: Collectible Sheet Music,* Schiffer, 1999; ---, *The Gold in Your Piano Bench,* Schiffer Publishing, 1997.

**Periodical:** *The Rag Times,* 15522 Ricky Court, Grass Valley, CA 95949.

**Collectors' Clubs:** City of Roses Sheet Music Collectors Club, 13447 Bush St. SE, Portland, OR 97236; National Sheet Music Society, 1597 Fair Park Ave., Los Angeles, CA 90041; New York Sheet Music Society, P.O. Box 354, Hewlett, NY 11557; Remember That Song, 5623 N. 64th St., Glendale, AZ 85301; Sonneck Society for American Music & Music in America, P.O. Box 476, Canton, MA 02021.

*Ain't You Coming Out Malinda?* 1921, by Andrew Sterling, Edward Moran, and Harry Vontilizer, cover photo of Gus Van and Joe Schonck ...... 10.00
*America I Love You,* 1915, Tom Ward and Dolly McCue on cover with sketches of Statue of Liberty, Indian chief, covered wagon, Liberty Bell, pilgrims, farmer, New York City ................ 12.00
*Archie's Little Love Song,* Hoagy Carmichael and Ed "Archie" Gardner, ©1946 ...................................... 10.00
*Carioca,* 1933, movie "Flying Down to Rio," Fred Astaire and Dolores Del Rio cov ...................................... 9.00
*Childhood Days Are Dear to Me,* 1910, man looking into mirror with reflection as young boy, insert oval photo of Paulina Parks ....................... 10.00
*Comin' In On A Wing And A Prayer,* 1943, Eddie Cantor and plane on cover ...................................... 10.00

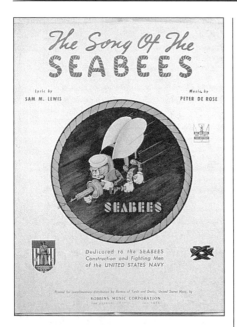

**The Song of the Seabees,** WWII era, Robbins Music Corp., $10.

*Country Style,* Bing Crosby, Joan Caulfield, and Barry Fitzgerald on cover, 1947, Paramount, "Welcome Stranger" ................................. 10.00
*Der Furherer's Face,* Donald Duck ................................. 35.00
*Down in Jungle Town,* African hut, 1908 ................................. 9.00
*Enjoy Yourself* (It's Later Than You Think), 1948, Guy Lombardo cover ................................. 9.50
*Ev'rybody Shimmies Now,* 1918, sepia photo cover of Sophie Tucker and her 5 Kings of Syncopation ........ 8.50
*Everybody Two-Step Rag,* by Wallie Herzer, published by Jerome H. Remick & Co; 1912, caricature of black man in checked suit, top hat, banjo, framed .......................... 20.00
*For Once in My Life,* Stevie Wonder on cover, 1965 ................................. 9.00
*Happy Go Lucky,* Mary Martin, Dick Powell, Betty Hutton, Eddie Bracken, and Rudy Vallee ...................... 18.00
*Harold Teen Songsheet,* movie poster graphics cover, 1934 .............. 45.00
*Hop Scotch Polka,* 1949, Gene Rayburn and Dee Finch in nightcaps, radio mike WNEW, caricature of two children in plaid playing hop scotch ................................. 10.00
*Humpty Dumpty Heart,* 1941, Kay Kyser, John Barrymore, Lupe Velez, Ginny Simms on cover dancing ................................. 9.25
*If You Were But A Dream,* Frank Sinatra on cover, 1941 .......................... 10.00
*I Got The Sun In The Morning,* Ethel Merman cover ........................... 9.00
*I'm Drifting Back to Dreamland,* 1922, Benson Orchestra, Chicago ...... 8.50
*I'm Sitting High On A Hill Top,* Dick Powell, Fred Allen, Paul Whiteman, Ann

Dvorak, Rubinoff, and Patsy Kelly, 1935, 20th Century Fox Production "Thanks A Million" .................... 10.00
*It Takes A Little Rain,* boy and girl cover, 1913 .......................... 8.00
*I Won't Dance,* 1935, RKO Picture "Roberta," Fred Astaire, Ginger Rogers and Irene Dunn on cov ........... 10.00
*Just You, Just Me,* 1929, soldiers and Marion Davies on cover, MGM "Marianne" ........................................ 9.00
*Lavender Blue (Dilly Dilly),* Morey & Daniel, 1948 ...................... 10.00
*Little Old Lady,* 1936, Beatrice Lillie and Bert Lahr on cover ..................... 9.50
*Lullaby Land,* 1919, little girl, standing in surf ........................................ 8.50
*Muddy Waters, (*A Mississippi Moan,) 1926, Nora Baves on cover, lagoon background ............................ 10.00
*Old Black Joe,* Beaux Arts edition, 1906 ................................................ 9.00
*Old Folks at Home,* composed by Stephen C. Foster, published by National Music Co., bluetone sketch on cover of old home, wear and soiling ................................................. 8.50
*Piccolino,* 1935, RKO Picture "Top Hat," Fred Astaire and Gingor Rogers on cover ........................................ 9.00
*Pick Yourself Up,* 1936, RKO "Swing Time," Fred Astaire and Ginger Rogers cov ...................................... 10.00
*Plantation Echoes,* Otto M. Heinzman, c1899, "Respectfully dedicated to Misses Drislane," Southern river plantation scene, Rosenthall litho ................................................. 90.00
*Plantation Melodies,* arranged by Eugene Walter, 1905, several songs ................................................. 8.50
*Please,* 1932, by Leo Robin and Ralph Ringer, Paramount "The Big Broadcast," cover montage with Bing

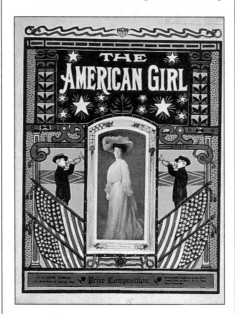

**The American Girl, Miss Alice Roosevelt,** $10.

**You're A Grand Old Flag,** George M. Cohan, $12.

Crosby, Burns & Allen, Cab Calloway, Boswell Sisters, Mills Brothers, Vincent Lopez, Kate Smith, Leila Hyams, Stuart Erwin, and Arthur Tracy ........................................ 12.00
*Rudolph the Red-Nosed Reindeer,* 1949, sketch of Santa, sleigh, and reindeers .................................... 8.50
*San Fernando Valley, I'm Packing My Grip,* 1953, Bing Crosby cover .. 9.50
*Seventh Heaven,* 1937, Simone Simon and Jimmy Stewart .................. 10.00
*Something To Remember You By,* 1930 ................................................. 9.00
*Sound Off,* Duckworth Chant, Willie Lee Duckworth, 1950, sketch of army sergeant yelling on cover, *Vaughn Monroe* insert photo ............... 10.00
*Tam O'Shanter,* 1909 ..................... 8.50
*The Army Air Corps,* Official Song of the United States Army Air Corps, 1939, logo, red, white and blue, "Buy War Bonds" stamp on cover .......... 10.00
*There's A Girl in the Heart of Maryland,* 1913 ........................................... 9.00
*There's a Mother Old and Gray Who Need Me Now,* Harold Rossiter Music Co .................................... 20.00
*The Waltz In Swing Time,* 1936, RKO "Swing Time," Fred Astaire and Ginger Rogers on cover ................. 9.00
*Victory Polka,* 1943, red, white, and blue cover with stars and "V" symbol ................................................. 8.00
*Waiting For the Robert E. Lee,* 1912 ................................................ 10.00
*We've Only Just Begun,* 1970, full color cover of the Carpenters ............ 9.00
*When the Daisies Bloom,* 1909, field of daisies cover, insert photo of young girl ........................................... 9.00
*Will You Remember,* 1944, Nelson Eddy & J. McDonald ........................ 10.00
*Yip-i-addy-i-ay,* 1908 ..................... 9.50

*You Belong To My Heart,* 1945, Disney movie "The Three Caballeros," by Agustin Lara and Ray Gilbert, Aurora Miranda, Carmen Molina, and Dora Luz on front cover, back cover with signed photo of Andy Russell..... 12.00

# Shelley China

**Collecting Hints:** The familiar Shelley mark—a script signature in a shield—was used as early as 1910 even though the firm's name was still Wileman & Co. Dainty White was one of the company's most popular shapes, and pieces are, therefore, relatively easy to acquire.

**History:** While the Shelley family has been producing pottery since the mid-1880s, it wasn't until 1925 that the company bore the family name. Joseph Shelley and James Wileman became partners in 1872, operating their pottery under the name Wileman & Company. Joseph's son, Percy, joined the company in 1881 and assumed full control after his father's death in 1896. It was under Percy's direction that the company introduced its most popular shapes—Dainty White, Intarsio, Queen Anne, and Vogue.

Percy's three sons became involved in the business following World War I. During the 1920s and 1930s the pottery produced miniatures, heraldic and souvenir china, Parian busts of military figures, tea wares, and nursery items, in addition to its fine dinnerware lines. Percy retired in 1932. After World War II the company concentrated solely on its dinnerware lines. In 1965 the firm's name was changed to Shelley China Ltd. The Shelley family ties to the company were severed in 1966 when Allied English Potteries took control. Allied merged with the Doulton Group in 1971.

**References:** Chris Davenport, *Shelley Pottery, The Later Years,* Heather Publications, 1997; Robert Prescott Walker, *Collecting Shelley Pottery,* Francis Joseph Publications, 1997.

**Collectors' Club:** National Shelley China Club, 5585 NW 164th Ave., Portland, OR 97229.

Bowl, 10" d, 3" h, satin glaze, abstract design .................................... 150.00
Cake Plate, Charm, pattern #13752, Richmond shape, 10" x 9", tab handles trimmed in gold ................ 90.00

Child's Plate, "Little Blue Bird, How He Sings, So Happy on My Plates and Things," Mabel Lucie Attwell illus, 7" d............................................ 150.00
Creamer and Sugar, Meisenette... 95.00
Cream Soup, Sheraton, pattern #13291, double handles, 6-1/2" d saucer
............................................. 85.00
Cup and Saucer
  Anemone, pattern #12879, Henley shape ...................................... 75.00
  Country Garden, pattern #2500, Ludlow shape .......................... 85.00
  Crochet pattern, Henley shape, mauve, reverse white dec...... 100.00
  Dainty Blue................................ 85.00
  Daffodil, pattern #13677, Henley shape ...................................... 85.00
  Lily of the Valley, Athol shape
    ............................................. 95.00
  Maytime, pattern #13452, Henley shape, beige trim.................. 155.00
  Morning Glory, Dainty shape ... 85.00
  Orange pattern ...................... 170.00
  Primrose, pattern #13430, Richmond shape, oversized ..................... 80.00
  Scilla, pattern #2511 ................ 85.00
  Shamrock pattern ................... 85.00
  Syringa, Dainty shape............. 85.00
Demitasse Cup and Saucer
Begonia, pattern #13427, Dainty shape, tall ............................................. 85.00
Dainty Blue, tall cup..................... 95.00
Duchess........................................ 80.00
Red Rose and Daisy, pattern #12425, tall ............................................. 85.00
Rosebud, pattern #13291, Dainty shape, tall ................................ 85.00
Sheraton, pattern, #13291 ........... 90.00
Eggcup
  Charm, pattern #13752, ftd ..... 95.00
  Rose............................................. 18.00
Gravy Boat and Underplate, Dainty Blue........................................ 525.00
Luncheon Plate, Blue Rock, 8-1/4" d
  ................................................. 75.00
Mocha Cup and Saucer, Primrose, pattern #13430, 2-1/2" h cup ........ 90.00
Pin Dish, 4-3/4" d, Primrose, pink edge trim............................................ 95.00
Plate
  Harebell, 10-3/4" d ...................... 70.00
  Rock Garden, 6" d ..................... 115.00
  Woodland, pattern #13348, 8" d ... 80.00
  Teapot, Begonia........................... 175.00
Trio, cup, saucer, and plate
  Charm, pattern #13752, Richmond shape, 6" plate ........................ 75.00
  Wileman, pattern #3730, 6-1/2" d plate, c1898 ........................ 275.00
Vase, 8-1/4" h, hand painted storks, c1930, backstamp "Shelley, Made in England" ................................ 125.00

# Slot Machines

**Collecting Hints:** Check the laws in your state. Some states permit the collecting of slot machines manufactured prior to 1941, while other states allow the collecting of all machines

25 years old or older provided that they are not used for gambling. A few states prohibit ownership of any gambling machine.

A complete slot machine is one that is in working order, has no wood missing on the case and no cracked castings. Restoration work to improve appearance can cost from $100 to more than $1,000. The average restoration includes plating of all castings, refinishing the cabinet, repainting the castings to the original colors, rebuilding the mechanism, tuning up the operation of the mechanism, and adding new reel strips and award card. A quality restoration will increase the value of a machine by $400 to $800. A guarantee usually is given when a restored machine is purchased from a dealer.

Most collectors stay away from foreign machines, primarily because foreign coins are hard to find. Machines that have been converted to accept American coins frequently jam or do not pay out the correct amount.

Condition, rarity, and desirability are all very important in determining the value of a machine. Try to find one that is in as close to new condition as possible since "mint original" machines will resell for at least the same amount as restored machines.

**History:** The Liberty Bell, the first three-reel slot machine, was invented in 1905 by Charles Fey in San Francisco. Only three of these can be accounted for, and one of them is housed at the Liberty Bell Saloon, the inventor's grandson's restaurant in Reno, Nevada.

In 1910, the classic fruit symbols were copyrighted by Mills Novelty Company. They were immediately copied by other manufacturers. The first symbols still are popular on contemporary casino machines. The wood cabinet was replaced by cast iron in 1916. By 1922, aluminum fronts were the norm for most machines, and in 1928, the jackpot was added.

Innovations of the 1930s included more reliable and improved mechanisms with more sophisticated coin entry, and advanced slug detection systems. In the 1940s, drill-proof and cheat-resistant devices were added. Electronics, including electronic lighting, were introduced in the 1950s.

Although the goosenecks of the 1920s and 1930s often are more intricate and rarer than the models of the 1930s and 1940s, the gimmickry and beauty of machines of the latter period, such as Rolatop, Treasury, Kitty or Triplex, bring more money.

**References:** Jerry Ayliffe, *American Premium Guide to Jukeboxes and Slot Machines*, 3rd ed., Books Americana, 1991; Richard M. Bueschel, *Collector's Guide to Vintage Coin Machines*, Schiffer Publishing, 1995; —, *Lemons, Cherries and Bell-Fruit-Gum*, Royal Bell Books (5815 W. 52nd Ave., Denver, CO 80212), 1995; Marshal Fey, *Slot Machines: A Pictorial History of the First 100 Years*, 4th ed., published by author; David L. Saul and Daniel R. Mead, *Slot Machine Buyer's Handbook*, 2nd ed., Mead Publishing Co., 1998.

**Periodicals:** Antique Amusements, Slot Machines & Jukebox, 909 26th St. NW, Washington, DC 20037; Chicagoland Program, 414 N Prospect Manor Ave., Mt. Prospect, IL 60056; Chicago Land Slot Machine & Jukebox Gazette, 909 26th St., NW, Washington, DC 20037; Coin Drop International, 5815 W. 52nd Ave., Denver, CO 80212; Coin-Op Classics, 17844 Toiyabe St., Fountain Valley, CA 92708; Coin-Op Newsletter, 909 26th St., NW, Washington, DC 20037; Coin Slot, 4401 Zephyr St., Wheatridge, CO 80033; Loose Change, 1515 South Commerce St., Las Vegas, NV 89102.

**Museum:** Liberty Belle Saloon and Slot Machine Collection, Reno, NV.

**Notes:** All machines listed are priced as if they are in good condition, meaning the machine is complete and working. An incomplete or non-working machine is worth only 30% to 70% of the listed price.

Machines listed are those which accept nickels or dimes. Quarter- and 50¢-piece machines can run several hundred dollars more. A silver-dollar machine, if you are lucky enough to find one, can cost $400 to $800 more than those listed.

**Advisor:** Bob Levy.

Bally Reliance, c1937, classic slot machine that throws dice and pays as real "craps," horse heads on both sides................................. 4,500.00
Buckley, Criss-Cross, c1948, revamp of 1946 Mills "Golden Falls," Art Deco styling, guaranteed jackpot window ........................................... 1,200.00
Caille
   Centaur, c1904, single wheel upright floor model, superb cast iron feet and dec.............................. 13,000.00

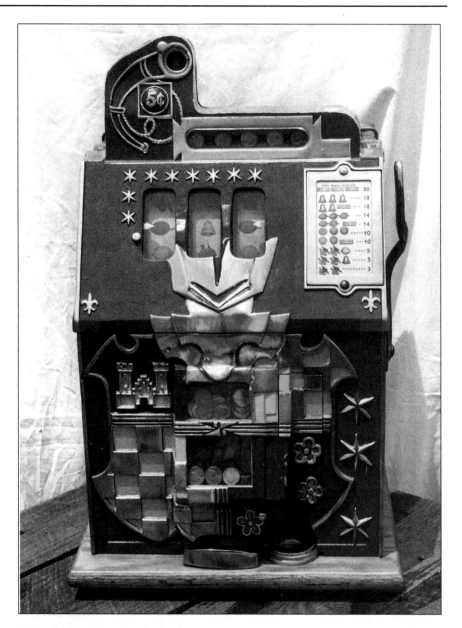

**Mills, Jackpot, 1930s, $1,700.**

Silent Sphinx, c1934, design celebrates discovery of King Tut's tomb ........................................... 1,600.00
Superior Jackpot, c1928, first countertop machine during Depression to make a jackpot ................. 1,200.00
Jennings
   Little Duke, c1932, most unusual in that reels spin concentrically, Art Deco style .......................... 1,500.00
   One Star Chief, c1936, large bronze Indian head on front, hunting Indian scene at bottom .................. 1,400.00
   Standard Chief, c1946, chrome face, first basic slot after WWII .... 1,250.00
   Sun Chief, c1948, illuminated colored front panels, introduced for the glitz of Las Vegas................ 1,800.00

Mills
   Blue Bell Hightop, c1948, colorful, bright, wrinkle-painted design in car-like style.............................. 1,500.00
   Castle front, c1939, golden age machine............................. 1,500.00
   Diamond front, c1938, ten raised diamonds on front.............. 1,300.00
   Golden Falls, c1946, gold and black painted, raised red cherries ........................................... 1,600.00
   Operator Owl, c1925, classic gooseneck coin entry ................... 1,200.00
   War Eagle, c1931, very colorful, often reproduced, price for vintage model................................. 1,700.00
Pace
   Comet, c1935, fancy front, Art Deco style ..................................... 1,400.00

Harrahs Club Special, c1962, all chrome plated .......................... 900.00

Watling

Owl, upright, c1925, floor model, large ornate bronze feet and hardware ................................... 11,000.00

Rolatop Cherry Front, c1937
........................................... 4,000.00

Treasury, c1936, extremely ornate, raised gold coins top and front castings ...................................... 4,000.00

# Soakies

**Collecting Hints:** Some Soakies come in several variations, like Bullwinkle and Top Cat. Sometimes the variations are subtle or it might the color of clothing, etc.

**History:** Colgate Palmolive introduced a figural plastic bubble bath container, called "Soaky" in the early 1960s. Because these figures soon caught on with children and moms alike, other companies such as Purex and Avon soon started to develop their own characters. Today collectors refer to these figural type of containers as Soakies.

Most of the figures are about 10" high. These colorful containers represent the most popular cartoon characters and other characters designed to appeal to young children.

**Reference:** Greg Moore and Joe Pizzo, *Collector's Guide to Bubble Bath Containers,* Collector Books, 1998.

Alvin Chipmunk, red ..................... 20.00
Atom Ant ....................................... 50.00
Auggie Doggie ............................. 55.00
Babalooie ...................................... 15.00
Bamm-Bamm, cap on head .......... 25.00
Barney Rubble ............................. 10.00
Bozo Clown .................................. 35.00
Bugs Bunny ................................. 25.00
Bullwinkle, arms crossed ............. 48.00
Caspcr Ghost ............................... 45.00
Chewbacca ................................... 10.00
Chipmunks
    Alvin, cap on head ................... 25.00
    Simon, full head ....................... 30.00
Cinderella, moving arms ............... 30.00
Creature from the Black Lagoon ... 90.00
Deputy Dawg
    Cap head ................................. 30.00
    Large head ............................... 40.00
Dick Tracy, hairline in neck ........... 35.00
Donald Duck ................................. 30.00
Dopey ........................................... 30.00
Dum Dum, Hanna-Barbera ........... 65.00
Elmer Fudd .................................. 35.00
Felix the Cat, sealed .................... 45.00
Fred Flintstone, cap on head ........ 35.00
Goofy, cap on head ...................... 16.00
Huckleberry Hound ...................... 30.00
Magilla Gorilla .............................. 20.00
Mickey Band Leader ..................... 35.00

Mighty Mouse, small ..................... 25.00
Mr. Jim's ....................................... 10.00
Pinocchio ...................................... 35.00
Pluto, with hat .............................. 25.00
Punkin Puss, reprint ..................... 55.00
Santa ............................................ 25.00
Speedy Gonzales ......................... 45.00
Spouty Whale ............................... 10.00
Squiddly Diddly ............................ 75.00
Superman ..................................... 40.00
Sylvester the Cat .......................... 35.00
Tennessee Tuxedo ....................... 45.00
Topcat, blue vest .......................... 45.00
Touche Away Turtle, laying down
...................................................... 60.00
Tweety Bird on Cage .................... 35.00
Wendy ........................................... 35.00
Winsome Witch ............................. 40.00
Woody Woodpecker ...................... 30.00
Yacky Doodle ................................ 10.00

# Soda Fountain Collectibles

**Collecting Hints:** The collector of soda fountain memorabilia competes with collectors in many other categories—advertising, glassware, ice cream, postcards, food molds, tools, etc. Material still ranges in the 25¢ to $200 range.

When buying a tray, the scene is the most important element. Most trays were stock items with the store or firm's name added later. Always look for items in excellent condition.

**History:** From the late 1880s through the end of the 1960s, the local soda fountain was the social center of small-town America, especially for teen-agers. The soda fountain provided a place for conversation and gossip, a haven to satisfy the mid-afternoon munchies, and a source for the most current popular magazines.

**References:** Douglas Congdon-Martin, *Drugstore and Soda Fountain Antiques,* Schiffer Publishing, 1991; Ray Klug, A*ntique Advertising Encyclopedia,* Vol. I (1978, 1993 value update), Vol. II, (1985, 1990 value update), L-W Book Sales; Tom Morrison, *Root Beer,* Schiffer Publishing, 1992.

**Collectors' Club:** Ice Screamers, P.O. Box 5387, Lancaster, PA 17601; National Assoc. of Soda Jerks, PO Box 115, Omaha, NE 68101.

**Museums:** Greenfield Village, Dearborn, MI; Museum of Science and Industry, Finigan's Ice Cream Parlor, Chicago, IL; Smithsonian Institution, Washington, DC.

**Reproduction Alert.**

**Additional Listings:** Ice Cream Collectibles.

Ashtray, Breyers, 90th Anniversary, 1866-1956 ............................... 22.00
Blackboard, Frostie Root Beer, tin, 1950s ........................................ 75.00
Can, Abbott's Ice Cream, half gallon, Amish girl, c1940 ................. 15.00
Catalog
    Bastian-Blessing Co, Chicago, IL, Soda Fountain Parts & Carbonators, 1955, 65 pgs, 8-1/2" x 11" ........ 30.00
    Foot & Jenks, Jackson, MI, c1935, 8 pgs, 5-3/8" x 7", "Start the Season Right With These 3 Proven Winners, Killarn Ginger-Ale, CXC Cherrystone & CXC Lemon & Limes Combined," picture of bottle, return post card ............................................... 14.00
    National Licorice Co, New York, NY, early 1900, 19 pgs, 3-1/4" x 6-1/4", licorice specialties, lozenges, penny sticks, cigars, pipes, etc .......... 65.00
    Stanley Knight Corp, Chicago, IL, Soda Fountains, Instructions and Specifications, c1944, 52 pgs, 7" x 10" ............................................ 32.00

**Flyer, Grand Opening, Ice Cream Parlor and Soda Fountain, Georges, black and white newsprint, 4" w, 9-3/4" h, $10.**

Container, Lutted's S. P. Cough Drops, house shaped, name engraved on door, 7" x 7 3/4" ..................... 400.00

Counter Bin, 9" x 13-3/4" x 4-1/4", Quaker Brand Salted Peanuts ................................................... 42.00

Display Rack
    Beech-Nut Chewing Gum, c1920 ............................................... 300.00
    Lance Candy, four shelves ...... 25.00

Dispenser, white ceramic body
    13-1/2" h, Drink Dr. Swett's The Original Root Beer, On The Market Seventy Five Years," picture of boy holding glass of root beer, silhouette shows older profile, picture on front and back, replaced pump ........... 3,200.00
    13-1/2" h, Hires Root Beer, hourglass shape, "Drink Hires It Is Pure" on front and back, orig pump mkd "Hires" ..................................... 800.00
    14" h, Birchola, birch leaves around "Drink Birchola" on front and back, not orig pump....................... 1,800.00
    14" h, Ward's Lemon Crush, lemon shape, porcelain ball pump, minor paint loss to base................ 2,200.00
    14" h, Ward's Lime-Crush, lime shape, porcelain ball pump, some staining............................... 2,800.00
    14-1/2" h, Cherry Smash, round, trio of cherries on stem on front and back, "Always Drink Fowler's Cherry Smash Our Nation's Beverage," orig pump.................................... 1,800.00
    14-1/2" h, Fowler's Root Beer, bulbous, "Drink Fowler's Root Beer The Best" on two sides, orig pump mkd "Fowler's Root Beer" .............. 700.00
    14-1/2" h, Ward's Orange-Crush, orange shape, porcelain ball pump, some paint loss, hairline cracks ................................................. 950.00

Festoon, diecut cardboard, Hires
    11" h, 49-1/2" l, full bottles of Hires on each end, logo in center........ 800.00
    14" h, 52" l, lady in winter scene reaching for bottle, c1940...... 400.00

Hat, soda jerk style ........................ 5.00

Hot Plate, commercial, Nestle's Hot Chocolate, 8" x 12", standing metal sign, red and white snowman graphics, late 1940s.......................... 95.00

Ice Chipper, Gilchrist, 1930s ........ 95.00

Ice Cream Scoop
    Dover, brass........................... 70.00
    Erie, round, size 8, aluminum ................................................. 180.00
    Gilchrist, #30, size 8, polished ................................................. 70.00

Jar, Borden's Malted Milk, glass label ................................................. 175.00

Magazine Cover, *Saturday Evening Post,* young soda jerk talking to girls at counter, Norman Rockwell, Aug. 22, 1953 ................................... 15.00

Malt Machine
    Arnold #15 ............................ 145.00
    Dairy Bar, metal, white Bakelite canister, logo.............................. 115.00

Milkshake Machine
    Gilchrist, orig cup, c1926....... 100.00

Hamilton Beach, push-down type ................................................. 150.00

Paper Cone Dispenser, 11" l, glass tube, metal holder, "Soda Fountain Drinks & Ice Cream Served in Vortex," gold label, wall mount...... 40.00

Pinback Button
    1" d, Sanderson's Drug Store, blue and white, soda fountain glass illus, "Ice Cream, Soda/Choice Cigars/ Fine Candies," 1901-12 ........... 28.00
    2-1/4" d, Hi-Hat Ice Cream Soda, 10¢, McCory's, c1940 .............. 15.00

Post Card
    Bodie's Ice Cream Store, diecut ................................................. 12.00
    Gunther's Soda Fountain, Chicago ................................................. 15.00

Poster, 24" h, 57-1/2" w, heavy paper, Hires R-J Root Beer, So Good With Food, lady with bottle in glass in hand, bottle and glass beside finger sandwiches, framed .............. 225.00

Pretzel Jar, 10-1/2" h, Seyfert's Original Butter Pretzels, glass, orig lid .. 60.00

Seltzer Bottle, Sun Shine, 11" h ................................................. 150.00

Set, black and chrome, Art Deco styling, price for 11 pcs............... 495.00

Sign
    12-1/4" x 22", Purity Butter Pretzels, diecut cardboard, easel-back, multicolor, smiling blond boy carrying giant pretzel against black ground, white lettered company logo, bright red and gold ground, Harrisburg, PA, early 1930s ..................... 68.00
    24" x 18", Orange County Fountain, porcelain on steel, yellow oval center, blue and white lettering, dark blue ground .......................... 100.00
    27" h, 13" w, Kayo, Specials Today, enameled tin, Donaldson Art Sign Co ................................................. 100.00

Straw Jar, glass
    Frosted panel........................ 225.00
    Green panel .......................... 410.00
    Pattern glass, Illinois pattern, orig lid ................................................. 450.00
    Red, metal lid, 1950s ............ 175.00

Syrup Dispenser Pump, hires..... 135.00

Tin, Schrafft's Marshmallow Topping, 25 lbs ............................................. 35.00

Tray, 13" x 11", Schuller's Ice Cream, ice cream sodas and cones ........ 200.00

Tumbler, Grapette ........................ 10.00

Wafer Holder, Reliance.............. 175.00

# Soft Drink Collectibles

**Collecting Hints:** Coca-Cola items have dominated the field. Only recently have collectors begun concentrating on other soft drink manufacturing companies. Soft drink collectors compete with collectors of advertising, bottles, and premiums for the same material.

National brands such as Canada Dry, Dr. Pepper, and Pepsi-Cola are best known. However, regional soft drink bottling plants do exist, and their products are fertile ground for the novice collector.

**History:** Sarsaparilla, a name associated with soft drinks, began as a medicinal product. When carbonated water was added, it became a soft drink and was consumed for pleasure rather than medical purposes. However, sarsaparilla was only one type of ingredient added to carbonated water to produce soft drinks.

Each company had its special formula. Although Coca-Cola has a large market share, other companies provided challenges in different historical periods. Moxie was followed by Hire's, which in turn gave way to Pepsi-Cola and 7-Up.

In the 1950s, large advertising campaigns and numerous promotional products increased the visibility of soft drinks. Regional bottling plants were numerous and produced local specialties such as Birch Beer in eastern Pennsylvania. By 1970, most of these local plants had closed.

Many large companies had operations outside of the United States, and there is a large quantity of international advertising and promotional material. The current popularity of diet soda is a response to the modern American lifestyle.

**References:** Tom Morrison, *Root Beer*, Schiffer Publishing, 1992; —, *More Root Beer: Advertising and Collectibles,* Schiffer Publishing, 1997; Allan Petretti, *Petretti's Soda Pop Collectibles Price Guide*, Antique Trader Books, 1996.

**Collectors' Clubs:** Club Soda, P.O. Box 489, Troy, ID 83871; Dr. Pepper 10-2-4 Collectors Club, P.O. Box 153221, Irving, TX 75015; Moxie Enthusiasts Collectors Club of America, Route 375, Box 164, Woodstock, NY 12498; National Pop Can Collectors, P.O. Box 7862, Rockford, IL 61126; New England Moxie Congress, 445 Wyoming Ave., Millburn, NJ 07041.

**Museums:** Clark's Trading Post, North Woodstock, NH; Matthews Museum of Maine Heritage, Union, ME.

**Additional Listings:** Coca-Cola, Pepsi, Soda Bottles, Soda Fountain Collectibles.

Advertising Trade Card, Hire's Root Beer, late 1800s ...................... 12.00
Badge, Dad's Root Beer, Finest Draw in the West ................................... 35.00
Baseball Counter, 3" h, 2-1/2" w, Hires Root Beer, celluloid, Josh Slinger face, changeable eyes and scoring numbers, 1915 ...................... 450.00
Book, adv, *1940 Football Book,* Hire's Root Beer, schedules and rules, 40 pgs.......................................... 30.00
Bottle
   3-1/2" h, Canada Dry, c1950 ...... 7.50
   7" h, Ting, Wild Cherry ............... 2.00
   7-1/2" h, Hire's, Old Homemade Root Beer from Hires Extract, brown and white stoneware, half pint size, minor crazing and pitting ................. 125.00
   10" h, Hire's Root Beer Concentrate, glass, paper label, orig seal and contents, slight damage to paper label ........................................ 25.00
Bottle Carrier
   7-Up, aluminum, holds 12 bottles ................................................ 10.00
   Spur Cola, unused, 1940s ....... 10.00
Calendar, 1927, Nehi, woman leaning on boat at beach..................... 125.00
Card, Drink Squirt, 5" x 6-1/2", diecut, scalloped border, full color art, ©1947 Squirt Co. ..................... 30.00
Charm, 1" h figural plastic soda bottle, multicolored paper label wrapper, 1940s-50s
   Canada Dry Ginger Ale, orange ................................................ 12.00
   Royal Crown Cola, orange ....... 10.00
   White Rock Crown Cream, yellow ................................................ 12.00
Clock
   7-Up, oak frame, c1950 ......... 100.00
   Sprite, wood frame, quartz, c1980 ................................................ 30.00
Doll, Sparky, 7-Up, vinyl head, cloth body........................................ 45.00
Door Push, 9" h, 3" w, emb tin litho, Canada Dry Ginger Ale ................ 170.00
Fan
   7" x 8", Moxie Man, "Frank Archer says...," ©1922, girl in pigtails on back........................................ 50.00
   13-1/2" x 8", cardboard fan, wood handle, Cherry Smash, black waiter serving George and Martha Washington on lawn of Mt. Vernon ........ 300.00
Glass, 4" h, Vernors Ginger Ale, Deliciously Different ...................... 40.00
Lamp, 7-Up, metal bottle.............. 45.00
Match Holder, Dr. Pepper ............... 6.50
Mobile Store Display
   Cheer Up, green bottle, red label, double sided cardboard, unused ................................................ 20.00
   Quiky Soda Pop ....................... 40.00
Mug, ceramic
   5" h, Hires Root Beer, older trademark boy holding identical mug with his likeness of it, Mettlach, very minor crazing ...................... 375.00
   5-1/2" h, Hires Root Beer, blue and gray, emb intertwined roots encircling mug at top and bottom, handle simulates a tree branch ........ 150.00

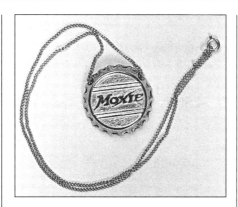

**Pendant, Moxie, $18.**

6" h, Dr. Swett's Root Beer, highly emb, likeness of Dr. Swett against brown ground on front, back with emb cupids among fancy filigree ................................................ 200.00
6" h, Dr. Swett's Root Beer, highly emb, likeness of Dr. Swett against green ground on front, back with emb water greenery.............. 225.00
Pin
   1" h, diecut tin, Moxie, boy's head ................................................ 75.00
   1-3/4" h, diecut thin celluloid, flipper type, Gold Label Ginger Ale, youngster with brimmed hat .............. 40.00
Pinback Button, Orange Crush, orange and black figure, white ground, c1930 ...................................... 25.00
Pocket Mirror
   3" d, Dr. Swett's Original Root Beer, celluloid, earthenware bottle, American Art Works litho, very light scratch to celluloid................. 200.00
   3" h, 1-3/4" w, Hires Root Beer, oval, celluloid, titled "Put Roses in Your Cheeks Drink Hires Root Beer," young girl with rosy cheeks, holding armful of roses ...................... 200.00
Puppet, hand, Bubbles, Booth Soda ................................................ 250.00
Radio, Royal Crown, can shape, late 1970s ...................................... 40.00
Salt and Pepper Shakers, pr
   Squirt, bottle shape, unused, MIB ................................................ 30.00
   7-Up, bottle shape, unused, MIB ................................................ 25.00
Sign
   5-1/2" h, 19-3/4" l, Drink Hires The Genuine Root Beer, emb tin, white letters ...................................... 375.00
   13-3/4" h, 41-3/4" l, Diamond Beverages, porcelain, some edge chipping ...................................... 100.00
   20-1/2" h, 9-1/4" w, paper banner, offering 18" h Squirt vinyl doll, fabric outfit, ©1962 Squirt Co., folded ................................................ 40.00
   29" h, 13-1/2" l, Dad's Old Fashioned Root Beer, emb tin, oversized bottle ................................................ 200.00
   29-1/2" h, 23-1/2" l, Sparketta Up, cardboard, lady holds bottle, titled "California's Favorite," framed ................................................ 350.00

**Pinback Button, Drink Cherry Cheer, blue, red and green on white background, gold band, $22.**

Thermometer
   Dr. Pepper, round..................... 90.00
   Frostie Root Beer, illus of Frostie ................................................ 85.00
   Hire's, diecut bottle shape ....... 90.00
   Moxie, 25-1/2" h, 9-1/2" w, "Drink Moxie take home a case tonight," Moxie man points to viewer, green, red, and black, unused, orig box ............................................. 1,100.00
Tip Tray, Royal Crown Cola........... 40.00
Toy, truck, Canada Dry-Special Sparkle, 4" l.............................................. 27.50
Tray, 13" x 10", Ace-Hy, blue, orange, and white ................................. 40.00
Uniform Patch, 10" d, Dr. Pepper, Good for Life........................................ 27.50
Watch Fob, Hire's Root Beer, octagonal, emb image, early 1900s .......... 75.00

# Soldiers, Dimestore

**Collecting Hints:** Figures of soldiers are preferred over civilians. The most valuable figures are those which had short production runs, usually because they were less popular with the youthful collectors of the period. Even though many figures produced had manufacturer reference numbers, reference books by Richard O'Brien have become so common that when communicating with other collectors it is simplified by using O'Brien's numbering system. Newcomers to the field should study these books, taking note of the many style and color variations in which these soldiers were made.

Condition, desirability, and scarcity establish the price of a figure. Repainting or the presence of rust severely reduce the value.

Auction prices often mislead the beginning collector. While some rare figures have sold in the $150 to $300 range, most sell between $10 and $25.

**History:** Three-dimensional lead, iron, and rubber soldier and civilian figures were produced in the United States by the millions before and after World War II. These figures are called dimestore soldiers because they were sold in the "five and dime" stores of the era, and usually cost a nickel or dime. Although American toy soldiers can be traced back to the early 20th century, the golden age of the dimestore soldier lasted from 1935 until 1942.

Four companies—Barclay, Manoil, Grey Iron, and Auburn Rubber—mass produced the three-inch figures. Barclay and Manoil dominated the market, probably because their lead castings lent themselves to more realistic and imaginative poses than iron and rubber.

Barclay's early pre-war figures are identifiable by their separate glued-on and later clipped-on tin hats. When these are lost, the hole in the top of the head identifies the piece as a Barclay.

The Manoil Company first produced soldiers, sailors, cowboys, and Indians. However, the younger buyers of the period preferred military figures, perhaps emulating the newspaper headlines as World War II approached. Manoil's civilian figures were made in response to pacifist pressure and boycotts mounted before the war began.

Figures also were produced by such companies as All-Nu, American Alloy, American Soldier Co., Beton, Ideal, Jones, Lincoln Log, Miller, Playwood Plastics, Soljertoys, Tommy Toy, Tootsietoy, and Warren. Because most of these companies were short-lived, numerous limited production figures command high prices, especially those of All-Nu, Jones, Tommy Toy, and Warren.

From 1942-1945, the wartime scrap drives devoured tons of dimestore figures and the molds that produced them.

In late 1945, Barclay and Manoil introduced modernized military figures, but they never enjoyed their pre-war popularity. Military operations generally were phased out by the early 1950s. Similarly, the civilian figures could not compete with escalating labor costs and the competition from plastic products.

**References:** Bertel Bruun, *Toy Soldiers*, Avon Books, 1994; Norman Joplin, *Great Book of Hollow-Cast Figures*, New Cavendish Books, 1992; Norman Joplin, *Toy Soldiers*, Running Press, 1994; Richard O'Brien, *Collecting Toy Soldiers*, No. 3, Krause Publications, 1996.

**Periodicals:** *Mini Soldier Gazette*, P.O. Box 15, Eatontown, NJ 07724; *Old Toy Soldier*, 209 N. Lombard, Oak Park, IL 60302; *Plastic Figure & Playset Collector*, P.O. Box 1355, LaCrosse, WI 54602; *Toy Soldier Review*, 127 74th Street, North Bergen, NJ 07047.

**Reproduction Alert:** Some manufacturers identify their newer products; many do not. To help with identification in the following lists, we have used the original makers' mark (where available) which was included on the castings.

**Notes:** Prices listed are for figures in original condition with at least 95% of the paint remaining. Unless otherwise noted, uniforms are brown.

**Advisor:** Barry L. Carter.

**Mailman, Barkley, B189, $10.**

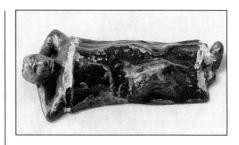

**Sleeping Soldier, 3" l, $7.50.**

## Civilian Figure

### Auburn Rubber
Baseball...................................... 30.00
Football....................................... 30.00

### Barclay
Cowboy
    Mounted, firing pistol (190)...... 22.00
    With lasso (752) ...................... 18.00
Indian
    Standing, bow and arrow (757)....9.00
    Tomahawk and shield (754)....... 9.00
Miscellaneous
    Girl Skater (636)...................... 10.00
    Mailman (853)......................... 10.00
    Newsboy (621) ........................ 10.00
    Pirate (714) ............................. 12.00
    Policeman, raised arms (850).. 10.00
    Redcap with bag (614)............ 15.00
    Santa Claus on skis (500)........ 45.00
    Woman passenger with dog (610)
    ............................................... 10.00

### Grey Iron
American Family Series, 2-1/4" h
    ................................... 5.00-25.00
Western
    Bandit, hands up ..................... 55.00
    Cowboy, hold-up man.............. 25.00
    Cowboy, standing ...................... 9.00

### Manoil
Happy Farm Series
    Blacksmith, horseshoes (41/7)
    ............................................... 20.00
    Blacksmith, wheel (41/22) ....... 21.00
    Farmer sowing grain (41/10) .... 18.00
    Man chopping wood (41/18) ... 18.00
    Man with barrel (41/36)............ 20.00
    Watchman with lantern (41/16)
    ............................................... 25.00
    Woman with pie (41/35)........... 20.00
Western
    Cowboy, arms raised (18a)...... 17.00
    Cowboy, one gun raised (18) .. 14.00
    Cowgirl riding horse (2 pieces)
    ............................................... 25.00
    Indian with knife (22) .............. 10.00

## Military Figure

### Auburn Rubber
Charging with tommy gun ............ 15.00
Grenade thrower.......................... 15.00
Machine gunner, kneeling ........... 11.00
Marching with rifle ...................... 15.00
Motorcycle with sidecar............... 55.00
Motorcyclist ................................. 37.00
Kneeling with binoculars ............. 11.00
Searchlight................................... 25.00

## Barclay

Podfoot Series, 2-1/4" h
Bugler (909) .................................. 7.00
Flag bearer (901) ..................... 10.00
Gunner, prone (928) .................. 8.00
Machine gunner charging (937)
................................................. 7.00
Nurse (962) .............................. 18.00
Officer standing (908) ................ 8.00
Sailor, blue (920) ...................... 10.00
Soldier, charging (906) .............. 6.00
Soldier, marching, with rifle (977)
................................................. 7.00

Post War, pot helmet
Flag bearer (701) ..................... 18.00
Machine gunner, prone (728)
................................................. 18.00
Officer with sword (708) ........... 18.00
Rifleman, standing (747) .......... 18.00

Pre-War
AA gunner (774) ....................... 18.00
At attention (707) ..................... 14.00
Aviator (741) ............................ 15.00
Bugler, tin helmet (709) ........... 15.00
Cameraman, kneeling (758) .... 35.00
Cook holding roast (769) ........ 25.00
Crawling, tin hat (750) ............. 18.00
Dispatcher with dog (952) ....... 38.00
Doctor, white, with bag (745) ... 16.00
Lying wounded (761) ............... 12.00
Machine gunner, kneeling (702)
................................................. 15.00
Marching, with rifle, tin hat (704)
................................................. 12.00
Marine officer, marching (708)
................................................. 35.00
Mortar, two-man (791) ............. 20.00
Nurse, kneeling, cup (767) ...... 18.00
Parachutist (784) ..................... 18.00
Peeling potatoes (771) ............ 22.00
Prone with binoculars (729) ..... 18.00
Releasing pigeons (737) .......... 18.00
Running with rifle (748) ............ 18.00
Sailor, marching (179) .............. 12.00
Sailor with flag (756) ............... 15.00
Sailor with signal flags (730) .... 22.00
Searchlight (776) ..................... 25.00
Stretcher bearer (759) ............. 15.00
Telephone operator (732) ......... 15.00
Wireless operator with antenna (951)
................................................. 30.00
Wounded crutches (775) ......... 18.00
Wounded, sitting, arm in sling (752)
................................................. 15.00

## Grey Iron

Cavalryman .................................. 25.00
Colonial Soldier ........................... 20.00
Doctor, white, with bag ................ 20.00
Doughboy, crawling ..................... 15.00
Drum Major .................................. 17.00
Drummer ...................................... 15.00
Ethiopian
Charging ................................. 25.00
Marching ................................. 28.00
Flag bearer .................................. 15.00
Kneeling, with rifle ....................... 15.00
Machine gunner
Kneeling .................................. 10.00
Prone ...................................... 15.00
Marching ...................................... 10.00
Nurse ........................................... 18.00
Radio Operator ............................ 45.00

Sailor marching ............................ 14.00
Sentry .......................................... 15.00

## Manoil

Post-War
Bazooka (45/13) ....................... 25.00
Marching with rifle (45/8) ......... 18.00
Mine detector (45/19) .............. 30.00
Tommy-gunner, standing (45/12)
................................................. 22.00

Post-War, 2-1/2" h, mkd "USA"
Aircraft spotter (527) ............... 25.00
Aviator with bomb (525) ........... 24.00
Bazooka (528) ......................... 18.00
Flag bearer (521) .................... 20.00
Grenade thrower (535) ............. 24.00
Machine gunner, seated (531)
................................................. 20.00
Observer, with binoculars (526)
................................................. 27.00

Pre-War
At searchlight (47) ................... 20.00
Bicycle rider (50) .................... 30.00
Bomb thrower, with 3 grenades (31)
................................................. 14.00
Boxer (68) ............................... 70.00
Cameraman with overhead flash (61)
................................................. 45.00
Cannon loader (24) .................. 14.00
Charging with bayonet (36) ..... 28.00
Cook's helper with ladle (60) ... 30.00
Deep-sea diver (65) ................. 15.00
Doctor, white (20) .................... 12.00
Firefighter, Hot Papa, gray (92)
................................................. 75.00
Flag bearer (7) ........................ 18.00
Gas mask with flare gun (63) ... 20.00
Hostess, green (35) ................. 45.00
Machine gunner, prone (12) .... 15.00
Marching (8) ............................ 16.00
Navy deck gunner (48) ............. 30.00
Navy signalman with 2 flags (17)
................................................. 24.00
Nurse, white, red dish (21) ...... 16.00
Observer with periscope (45) .. 30.00
Radio operator, standing (88)
................................................. 35.00
Rifleman, standing (26) ............ 15.00
Running with cannon (94) ........ 30.00
Sailor (14) ............................... 18.00
Sharpshooter, camouflage (57)
................................................. 20.00
Sitting, eating (54) ................... 26.00
Stretcher carrier, with medical kit
(32) .......................................... 17.00
Wounded (30) .......................... 15.00
Writing letter (59) .................... 50.00

# Soldiers, Toy

**Collecting Hints:** Consider three key factors: condition of the figures and the box, the age of the figures and the box, and the completeness of the set.

Toy soldiers were meant to be playthings. However, collectors consider them an art form and pay premium prices only for excellent to mint examples. They want figures with complete paint and intact parts, including the moving parts.

The box is very important, controlling 10% to 20% of the price of a set. The style of the box is a clue to the date of the set. The same set may have been made for several decades, the earlier the date of manufacture, the more valuable the set.

Sets have a specific number of pieces or parts. These must all be present for full value to be realized. The number of pieces in each set, when known, is indicated in the listings below.

**History:** The manufacture of toy soldiers began in the late 18th century by individuals such as the Hilperts of Nuremberg, Germany. The early figures were tin, pewter, or composition. By the late 19th century, companies in Britain (Britain, Courtenay), France (Blondel, Gerbeau, and Mignot), and Switzerland (Gottschalk, Wehrli) were firmly established. Britain and Mignot dominated the market into the 20th century.

Mignot established its French stronghold by purchasing Cuperly, Blondel, and Gerbeau who had united to take over Lucotte. By 1950, Mignot had 20,000 models representing soldiers from around the world.

Britains developed the hollow cast soldiers in 1893. Movable arms also were another landmark. With concern for lead in children's toys in the 1960s, Britains went into plastic production. Outcries from collectors and a declining market eventually brought Britains back into production of metal figures. This past year Britains have been purchased by an American toy company, Ertles, which will continue production of the 54 mm. Model soldiers.

Between 1930 and 1950, the English toy soldier was challenged in America by the dimestore soldiers made by Barclay, Manoil, and others. Nevertheless, the Britains retained a share of the market because of their high quality. The collecting of toy soldiers remains very popular in the United States as is evidenced by the emergence of specialized toy soldier shows.

**References:** Bertel Bruun, *Toy Soldiers*, Avon Books, 1994; *Elastolin, Miniature Figures and Groups from the Hausser Firm of Germany* (1990), Vol. 2 (1991), Theriault's;

Norman Joplin, *Great Book of Hollow-Cast Figures*, New Cavendish Books, 1993; Norman Joplin, *Toy Soldiers*, Running Press, 1994; Richard O'Brien, *Collecting Toy Soldiers*, No. 3, Krause Publications, 1996; —, *Collecting Foreign-Made Toy Soldiers*, Krause Publications, 1997; James Opie, *Collecting Toy Soldiers*, Pincushion Press, 1992; Joe Wallis, *Armies of the World*, published by author, 1993; —, *Regiments of all Nations,* published by author, 1992;

**Periodicals:** *Mini Soldier Gazette,* P.O. Box 15, Eatontown, NJ 07724; *Old Toy Soldier,* 209 North Lombard, Oak Park, IL 60302; *Plastic Figure & Playset Collector,* P.O. Box 1355, LaCrosse, WI 54602; *Toy Soldier Review,* 127 74th St., North Bergen, NJ 07047.

**Collectors' Club:** American Model Soldier Society, 1528 El Camino Real, San Carlos, CA 94070; Military Miniature Society of Illinois, 7230n W. Balmoral, Chicago, IL 60656; Northeast Toy Soldier Society, 12 Beach Rd., Gloucester, MA 09130; Toy Soldier Collectors of America, 5340 40th Ave., St Petersburg, FL 3309.

**Reproduction Alert.** Beware of repainted older examples and modern reproductions. Toy soldiers still are being manufactured, both by large companies and private individuals.

**Advisor:** Barry L. Carter.

**Authenticast,** Russian Infantry, advancing with rifles at the ready, 2 officers, carrying pistols and swords, 8 pcs ........................................ 75.00

**Bienheim**, sets only, mint, orig excellent box

B2, Coldstream Guards Colors, 1812, 2 color bearers, escort of 4 privates, 6 pcs ......................................... 115.00

B17, Royal Marines, 1923, marching at the slope, officer, sword at carry, 6 pcs .......................................... 75.00

B63, Royal Co of Archers Colors, 2 color bearers, escort of 4 privates, 6 pcs .......................................... 100.00

C13, 17th Lancers, 1879, foreign service order, officer, bugler and trooper with lance, 6 pcs .................... 130.00

US Naval Academy Color Guard, 2 standard bearers, escort of 2 midshipmen .............................. 100.00

**Britains**, sets only

28, Mountain Gun of the Royal Artillery, with gun, gunners, mules, and mounted officer, 14 pcs, mint, orig good box ................................. 250.00

33, 16th/5th Lancers, mounted at the half in review order, officer turned in the saddle, excellent orig illus box .................................... 170.00

44, 2nd Dragoon Guards, The Queen's Bays, mounted at the gallop, lances and trumpeter, c1940, 5 pcs, excellent, good orig Whisstock box .................................... 135.00

117, Egyptian Infantry, at attention in review order, c1935, 8 pcs, good, orig Whisstock box ................ 150.00

122, The Black Watch, standing, firing, tropical service dress, officer holding binoculars, c1930, 8 pcs, good orig Whisstock box ........................ 150.00

136, Russian Cossacks, mounted at the gallop with officer, 5 pcs, excellent, orig box ................................. 135.00

138, French Cuirassiers, mounted at the walk, review order with officer, 5 pcs, excellent, orig box ................. 140.00

167, Turkish Infantry, standing on guard, review order, d1935, 5 pcs, good/fine, orig Whisstock box .............................................. 150.00

190, Belgian 2nd Regiment Chasseurs a Cheval, mounted in review order, officer, 5 pcs, good, orig box ................................................. 140.00

201, Officers of the General Staff, comprising Field Marshal, General officer and 2 Aides-de-Camp, 4 pcs, good ................................................ 120.00

216, Argentine Infantry, marching at the slope, review order, c1940, 8 pcs, excellent, good orig "Types of the Argentine Army" box ............. 275.00

217, Argentine Cavalry, mounted in review order, lances and officer, 8 pcs, excellent, orig box ......... 225.00

1323, The Royal Fussilers, The Royal Sussex Regiment and the Seaforth Highlanders, marching at the slope, mounted and foot officers, 23 pcs, excellent, orig box ................. 300.00

1339, The Royal Horse Artillery Khaki Service Order, 6-horse team, lumber, gun, drivers with whips, 4 mounted outriders on trotting horses, officer on galloping horse, 13 pcs, excellent, good orig "Types of the British Army" box with gold and black label .......................... 1,700.00

1343, The Royal Horse Guards, mounted in winter cloaks, officer, c1940, 5 pcs, good orig "Armies of the World" box ...................... 130.00

1631, The Governor General's Horse Guards of Canada, mounted in review order, officer on prancing horse, 5 pcs, mint, orig excellent box .................................................. 110.00

1632, The Royal Canadian Regiment, marching at the slope, officer, c1940, 8 pcs, good, fine orig "Soldiers of the British Empire" box ................ 400.00

1836, Argentine Military Cadets, marching at the slope, review order, officer, c1940, 8 pcs, excellent, orig "Armies of the World" box ................ 1,250.00

1935, Argentine Naval Cadets, marching at the slope, review order, officer, 1948-49, excellent, good orig box ............................................. 1,800.00

2009, Belgian Grenadier Regiment, marching in review order, officer, 8 pcs, excellent, orig box ......... 180.00

2028, Red Army Cavalry, mounted at the halt in parade uniforms, officer, 5 pcs, excellent, orig box ......... 120.00

2035, Swedish Life Guard, marching at the slope, officer, 8 pcs, mint, tied in excellent, orig box ................. 200.00

2059, Union Infantry, action poses, with officer holding sword and pistol, bugler and standard bearer, 87 pcs, excellent, orig box ................... 90.00

9217, 12th Royal Lancers, mounted in review order, officer, 5 pcs, mint, good orig window box ............. 80.00

9265, Egyptian Camel Corps, mounted on camels, detachable riders, 5 pcs, mint, tied in excellent orig window box ........................................ 180.00

9291, Arabs of the Desert on Horses, with jezalls and scimtars, excellent, good orig window box .............. 80.00

9402, State Open road Landau, drawn by 6 Windsor Grays, with 3 detachable positions, attendants, Queen Elizabeth and Prince Philip as passengers, 13 pcs, mint, tied in excellent orig box .......................... 375.00

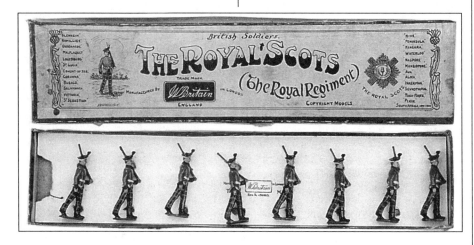

**Britians, The Royal Scots, #450,003, $365.**

9407, British Regiments on Parade, comprising General Officer, Royal Horse Artillery at the walk, 17th Lancers in review order on trotting and cantering horses with officer, Life Guard with trumpeter and officer, Royal Norfolk Regiment at the slope with officer, Scots Greys on trotting and walking horses with officer, The Black Watch marching at the slope with piper and officer, Band of the Line, 67 pcs, excellent, orig 2-tray display box ........ 2,500.00

### Elastolin/Lineol

Flak Gunner, blue and gray uniform, kneeling with shell, very good .................................................. 40.00

Medic, walking, helmet, back pack with red cross ................................. 35.00

Nurse, attending wounded, kneeling, olds foot of soldier sitting on keg, excellent .................................. 40.00

Staff Officer, pointing, field glasses, aristocratic pose ...................... 35.00

### Heyde

Chicago Police, 1890s, on foot, with billy clubs, policeman with dog, standard bearer, and mounted policeman, very good ............ 225.00

French Ambulance Unit, horse-drawn ambulance, 2-horse team, rider with whip, stretcher bearers, stretchers, casualties, mounted and foot medical officers, medical orderly, very good, fair orig box .................. 275.00

German Infantry, World War I, attacking with fixed bayonets, officer with extended sword, very good ..... 90.00

Heissan Infantry, 1777, marching at the slope, officers, standard bearer, 4 mounted dragoons, movable reins on horses, good ..................... 375.00

### Mignot

15, French Muskeeters Period of King Louis XIII, marching with muskets at shoulder arms, officer and standard bearer, c1960, 12 pcs, excellent, orig box ................................. 275.00

17, Infantry of King Louis XIV, marching at the slope, officer, standard bearer, drummer, c1950, 12 pcs, excellent, orig box ................................. 400.00

28/C, Napoleon's Imperial Guard Band, 1812, marching will full instrumentation, band director with baton, 12 pcs, excellent ........................... 350.00

36, French Napoleonic Skirmishers of the 17th Line Regiment, 1809, marching in blue and white uniforms, faced in red, tall plumed shakos, gloss paint, c1965, mint 4-piece set in excellent orig window box and outer cardboard box ................ 80.00

39, Italian Light Infantry, Regiment de Beauhamais, 1810, marching at the slope, green uniforms, pale blue facings, plumed shakos, drummer and officer, 12 pcs, excellent, orig box .................................................. 225.00

43/H, Austrian Infantry, 1805, standing at attention, shoulder arms, officer, drummer, and standard bearer, 12 pcs, limited issue, mint, tied in excellent orig box ........................... 225.00

45/A, Bavarian Infantry, 1812, marching at the slope, blue and white uniforms, yellow facings, plumed light infantry caps, standard bearer and bugler, excellent 8-pc set in orig box ................................................. 250.00

200, Ancient Gaul Cavalry, mounted with swords, spears, and shields, 5 pcs, excellent, orig box ......... 275.00

200/8, Ancient Greek Cavalry, mounted with swords, spears and shields, 5 pcs, excellent, orig box ......... 250.00

231/B, Austrian Cavalry, 1814, mounted in review order, officer, trumpeter and standard bearer, 6 pcs, mint, excellent orig box .................. 250.00

255, Spanish Hussars, 1808, mounted in green uniforms, red facings, tall plumed shakos, officer, trumpeter, and standard bearer, mint, excellent orig box ................................ 375.00

1016, Drum Majors of the Empire, French Napoleonic regiments, including Orphans of the Guard, Marines of the Guard, St. Cyr Academy and various line infantry regiments, special limited edition, all mint, excellent orig boxes ...... 475.00

### Militia Models

Gatling Gun Team of 3rd London Rifles, Gatling gun and gunner, 2 ammunition carriers, officer holding binoculars, mint, excellent orig box ............... 90.00

The Pipes and Drums of 1st Battalion Royal Irish Rangers, pipe major and 4 pipers, 2 snare and 2 tenor drummers, drum major, limited edition, mint, excellent orig box .......... 125.00

### Nostalgia, mint, excellent orig box

1st Gurkha Light Infantry, 1800, red and blue uniforms, marching with slung rifles, officer with sword at the carry ............................. 80.00

Kaffrarian Rifles, 1910, gray uniforms, plumed pith helmets, marching at the trail, officer with sword at the carry, mint ............................. 125.00

New South Wales Irish Rifles, 1900, marching at the trail, officer holding sword at the carry ................... 95.00

New South Wales Lancers, 1900, marching, carrying lances on the shoulder, khaki uniforms, trimmed in red and plumed campaign hats, officer holding swagger stick... 65.00

### S.A.F., mint, excellent orig box

1358, Royal Horse Guards, 1945, mounted at the halt, officer ...... 50.00

1761, French Cuirassiers, mounted at the walk, ................................. 85.00

3310, 1st Bengal Lancers, mounted at the half ................................. 115.00

# Souvenir and Commemorative Items

**Collecting Hints:** Most collectors of souvenir and commemorative china and glass collect items from a region which is particularly interesting to them—their hometown or birthplace, or place of special interest such as a President's home. This results in regional variations in price because a piece is more likely to be in demand in the area it represents.

When collecting souvenir spoons, be aware of several things: condition, material, subject, and any markings, dates, etc. Damaged spoons should be avoided unless they are very rare and are needed to complete a collection. Some spoons have enamel crests and other decoration. This enameling should be in mint condition.

**History:** Souvenir and commemorative china and glass date to the early fairs and carnivals when a small trinket was purchased to take back home as a gift or remembrance of the event. Other types of commemorative glass include pattern and milk glass made to celebrate a particular event. Many types of souvenir glass and china originated at the world's fairs and expositions.

The peak of souvenir spoon collecting was reached in the late 1800s. During that time, two important patents were issued. One was the Dec. 4, 1884, patent for the first flatware design, and it was issued to Michael Gibney, a New York silversmith. The other important patent was the one for the first spoon design which commemorated a place. That patent was given to Myron H. Kinsley in 1881 for his spoon, which showed the suspension bridge at Niagara Falls. This was the first of many scenic views of Niagara Falls, which appeared on spoons over the years.

Spoons depicting famous people soon followed, such as the one of George Washington which was issued in May 1889. That was followed by the Martha Washington spoon in October 1889. These spoons, made by M. W. Galt of Washington, D.C., were not patented but were trademarked in 1890.

During the 1900s, it became popular to have souvenir plates made to memorialize churches and local events such as centennials and homecomings. These plates were well received in their respective communities. Collectors search for them today because they were made in a limited number. They are especially interesting as an indication of how an area changed architecturally and culturally over the years.

**References:** Patricia EW. Apkarian-Russell, *A Collector's Guide to Salem Witchcraft & Souvenirs*, Schiffer Publishing, 1998; Wayne Bednersch, *Collectible Souvenir Spoons: Identification and Values*, Collector Books, 1998; Arene Burgess, *Collector's Guide to Souvenir Plates*, Schiffer Publishing, 1996; Monica Lynn Clements and Patricia Rosser Clements, *Popular Souvenir Plates*, Schiffer Publications, 1998; George B. James, *Souvenir Spoons (1891)*, reprinted with 1996 price guide by Bill Boyd (7408 Englewood Ln., Raytown, MO 64133), 1996; Dorothy T. Rainwater and Donna H. Fegler, *American Spoons*, Schiffer Publishing, 1990; —, *Spoons from around the World*, Schiffer Publishing, 1992; *Sterling Silver, Silverplate, and Souvenir Spoons with Prices*, revised ed., L-W Book Sales, 1987, 1994 value update.

**Collectors' Club:** American Spoon Collectors, 7408 Englewood Lane, Raytown, MO 64133; Antique Souvenir Collectors News, Box 562, Great Barrington, MA 01230; Northeastern Spoon Collectors Guild, 52 Hillcrest Ave., Morristown, NJ 07960; The Scoop Club, 84 Oak Ave., Shelton, CT 06484.

Booklet
　Cathedral of Commerce, Woolworth Building, 8" x 11", gray softcover, relief gold accent lettering, 32 pgs, black and white photos and text, ©1917, Broadway Park Place Co .................................................. 22.00
　Souvenir of Coney Island, Brighton, and Manhattan Beaches, 1904, 40 pgs with black and white illus, 8" x 5" .................................................. 65.00
　Views of Coney Island, 7-3/4" x 9-3/4", green softcover, gold accent title, 32 pgs, photos and text of Luna Park, Dreamland, and bathers, © 1906, LH Nelson Co ................................... 35.00
　Steel Pier, Atlantic City, NJ, summer program, 32 pgs, pictures and ads .................................................. 45.00
Bottle Opener, San Diego, 1912 .................................................. 25.00

Calling Card Receiver, Philadelphia, 1907, copper, moose, tree, lake, and mountains ................................. 40.00
Card Game, Excursion to Coney Island, Milton Bradley, c1885 .............. 20.00
Cup, china, white
　St Charles Hotel, New Orleans .................................................. 15.00
　Souvenir of the Midget's Palace, Montreal, well-dressed male and female midgets illus, late 1800s .................................................. 65.00
Cup and Saucer, Niagara Falls, marked "Carlsbad, Austria" ................. 18.00
Demitasse Cup and Saucer, Hotel Roosevelt, New Orleans .......... 35.00
Doll, Luray Caverns, VA, Skookum, boy and girl, 3-1/2" h, price for pr ... 70.00
Figure, 3-1/2" h, Chinatown, NY, Chinese couple ............................. 25.00
Guide Book, 7" x 10", New York, softcover, full color, airships and planes flying over city skyline and Statue of Liberty, 64 black and white pgs, ©1932 Manhattan Card Co Publishing Co. ................................... 24.00
Hatchet, 6" l, Hazelton, PA, white milk glass, red letters ..................... 40.00
Medal
　Coney Island, steeplechase face, orig ribbon, 1924 .................... 90.00
　Souvenir of Wisconsin, green with gold.......................................... 30.00
Mug
　Hardwick, VT, custard glass, gold trim............................................ 35.00
　Lincoln Hotel, Reading, PA, white ceramic................................... 10.00
　New Rockford, ND, custard glass .................................................. 35.00
Paperweight, glass, round
　Brainard, MN, lake scene, 3" d .................................................. 40.00
　New Salem State Park, 2-3/4" d .................................................. 35.00
Pennant, felt
　Coney Island, maroon, white title, yellow, green, orange, and white scene of Steeplechase Pool, amusement rides, Luna Mill Sky Chaser building, c1930 ........................ 30.00
　Hershey Park, brown ground, white letters, c1950 .......................... 25.00
Photo Album, New Orleans, various scenes, 1885 .......................... 45.00
Pinback Button, 1-1/4" d
　Asbury Park, black and white, bathing beach scene, c1900 ......... 12.00
　Coney Island, multicolored, bathing beauty scene, rim reads "Citizens Committee of Coney Island," c1915 .................................................. 35.00
　Dreamland, NY, white lettering, red ground, 1900s........................ 10.00
　Hershey Park, multicolored, child emerging from cocoa bean, c1905 .................................................. 35.00
　New Virginia Reel, Luna Park, two men and four ladies on ride, Bastian Brothers back label............... 125.00
　Wonderland Stamford, CT, multicolored, c1900........................... 90.00

**Plate, Pennsylvania Turnpike & Twin Tunnels, Kittatiny and Blue Mountain, full color decals, 10" d, $15.**

Pinback Button Name Tag, attached ribbon
　Charter Day Celebration, July 5-6-7, MCMIX, 1884-1909, North Plainfield, Plainfield, Member of Citizen Committee, 1-3/4" d........................ 42.00
　18th Annual Saengerfest, Philadelphia, Pa, June 21-24, 1897, Aurora Singing Society, New Brunswick, NJ, double sided, 1-1/2" d ............. 45.00
Pitcher, Bar Harbor, ME, custard glass, gold trim, beaded base .......... 95.00
Plate
　Alabama, state capital in center, blue, Vernon Kilns.................... 22.00
　Albany, Minnesota ................... 40.00
　Along 101 The Redwood Highway, maroon, Vernon Kilns............... 25.00
　Baltimore & Ohio Railroad, Harpers Ferry, blue and white, 10-1/2" d .................................................. 95.00
　Birmingham, AL, The Industrial City, maroon, Vernon Kilns............... 22.00
　Boston, MA, Filene's, brown, Vernon Kilns......................................... 22.00
　Carlsbad Caverns, White's City, New Mexico ................................... 25.00
　Chicago, clock in center, maroon .................................................. 22.00
　Daytona Beach, FL, World's Most Famous Beach, maroon, Vernon Kilns......................................... 22.00
　Delaware Tercentenary Celebration, 1938, black and white, Spode .................................................. 35.00
　Denver, CO, state capital in center, blue, Vernon Kilns.................... 22.00
　Greenville, SC, blue, Vernon Kilns .................................................. 22.00
　Hollywood, CA, NBC Studios, Hollywood Bowl, Ciro's, Graumann's, Earl Carroll's, Brown Derby, blue, Vernon Kilns......................................... 35.00
　Jacksonville, FL, Gateway to Florida, maroon.................................. 22.00
　Laguna Beach, CA, Festival of Arts .................................................. 25.00

Maine, state capital in center, multicolored, Vernon Kilns .............. 30.00
Mississippi, blue, Vernon Kilns
............................................... 22.00
My Old Kentucky Home, 10" d, cobalt blue, Adams ...... .......... 75.00
Nevada, The Silver State, Hoover Dam in center, brown, Vernon Kilns
............................................... 22.00
New Mexico, picture map ........ 22.00
Northwestern University, multicolored, Vernon Kilns .................... 35.00
Our West, Vast Empire, maroon, Vernon Kilns ................................. 35.00
Portsmouth Virginia Bicentennial, 1752-1952, light brown, Vernon Kilns
............................................... 22.00
Saint Augustine, FL, brown, Vernon Kilns ......................................... 22.00
San Diego County Fair, Delmar, CA, Don Diego Welcomes You, blue
............................................... 35.00
SE Missouri State College, Diamond Jubilee, brown, Vernon Kilns .... 25.00
Sonoma, CA, Cradle of California, maroon, Vernon Kilns .............. 35.00
South Dakota, state capital in center, maroon, Vernon Kilns .............. 22.00
Spokane, Washington, The Inland Empire, blue, Vernon Kilns ....... 25.00
SS Grand View Hot4el, A Steamboat in the Allegheny Mountains, 10" d, cobalt blue, Adams ................. 95.00
Statue of Liberty, mkd "Made expressly for James Hill, Bedloe's Island, NY, The New Colossus by Emma Lazarus" on back, blue, Vernon Kilns ................................. 35.00
Vermont, Green Mountain State, brown, Vernon Kilns ................. 22.00
Washington, state capital in center, brown, Vernon Kilns ................. 22.00
West Virginia, state capital in center, brown ...................................... 22.00
Program
    Ice Follies of 1953, Shipstads & Johnson ................................... 25.00
    Radio City Music Hall Pictorial, 1945
    .............................................. 20.00
    Sonja Henie and Her Hollywood Ice Review, 1940 ............................ 25.00
    The Eighth World Championship Rodeo, Boston, Garden Area Sports News, Vol. VII, No. 1, c1939 ..... 25.00
Salt and Pepper Shakers, pr
    Alscar de Segovia, emblem, Limoges ............................................ 32.00
    Penn State, ceramic, blue logo .. 5.00
    World's Fair, 1939, Trylon and Perisphere, 3" h, gold trim ............ 60.00
Spoon, sterling silver
    Athens, PA, engraved high school bowl .......................................... 35.00
    Battle Monument, Trenton, NJ
    .............................................. 35.00
    Ben Franklin, Philadelphia ....... 55.00
    Bethesda Springs, Waukesha, WI
    .............................................. 55.00
    Bismarck, ND, post office bowl
    .............................................. 45.00
    Brooklyn, NY, 13th Regiment ... 35.00
    Calumet, MI, mining, Helco Shaft #2
    .............................................. 35.00

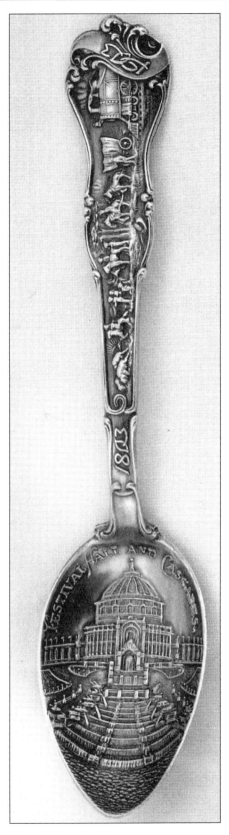

**Spoon, Louisiana Purchase Exposition, 1904, Festival Hall and Cascades in bowl, demitasse, sterling silver, $20.**

Chicago, IL, US Government Building, Fort Dearborn ................... 40.00
Columbus, OH, Lancaster pattern handle ...................................... 35.00
Cuba, Morro castle ................. 50.00
Detroit Skyline ........................ 70.00
Elgin Watch Factory ................ 85.00
Eureka, CA, courthouse ........ . 30.00
Fredericton, New Brunswick, spiral handle, gold wash bowl ........... 60.00
Girard College, Irian pattern handle
............................................... 45.00
Golden Gate, San Francisco ... 45.00
Grant Monument, Chicago ...... 45.00
Hope, Idaho ............................ 30.00
Hot Springs, Arkansas, Indian head, corn ...................................... 45.00
Inclined Plane, Cincinnati, OH
............................................... 35.00
Kansas City, Missouri, Convention Hall ....................................... 45.00
Lake Worth, Palm Beach, FL ... 65.00
Madison, WI ............................ 35.00
McDermott Falls, Glacier National Park bowl ............................. 45.00
Michigan City, IN, ornate Art Nouveau handle ............................ 50.00
Mt. Vernon .............................. 20.00
Old Hickory, Jackson monument
............................................... 75.00
Paul Revere, Midnight Ride ..... 95.00
Prairie de Chien, WI ................ 28.00
Quebec, open work handle ..... 35.00
Reading, PA, Mt. Penn Tower, demitasse ...................................... 40.00
Salt Lake City, UT, Mormon Temple handle, demitasse .................. 45.00
San Francisco, Mission Dolores 1776, bear on dec handle, gold bowl
............................................... 45.00
Sioux City, IA, Corn Palace, 1891
............................................... 80.00
Springfield, IL, Abraham Lincoln
............................................... 60.00
Statue of Liberty, Tiffany .......... 75.00
Texas, enameled star, demitasse
............................................... 25.00
Union Station, Dayton, OH, picture bowl ........................................ 35.00
Vassar, MI, high school engraved in bowl ........................................ 35.00
Waseca, MN, grape pattern .... 55.00
Washington's Tomb ................. 30.00
Wilmington, NC, floral handle, gold wash bowl, demitasse ............ 35.00
Yellowstone Park, etched falls bowl, bear, stag's head, and buffalo head on handle ............................. 45.00
Tape Measure, New York City, celluloid, pig .......................................... 25.00
Teapot, Morrison Hotel, Chicago
............................................... 35.00
Tip Tray, Hotel Coronado, china ... 15.00
Toothpick Holder
    Glen Ullen, ND, ruby stained glass, gold ........................................ 35.00
    Lewistown, ME, Georgia Gem pattern, custard glass, gold trim ... 45.00
    Providence, Shamrock pattern, ruby stained glass ........................ 40.00
Trowel, Acme Portland Cement, engraved eagle, 5-1/2" l .......... 40.00

Vase

Camp Lake View, Lake City, MN
.................... 20.00
Opera House, What Cheer, IA, china, multicolored scene ................... 45.00

# Souvenir Buildings

**Collecting Hints:** Collectors look for rarity, architectural detail, and quality of material, casting, and finishing. As in real estate, location affects price: European and East Coast buildings are more expensive on the West Coast and vice versa.

Many souvenir buildings are now sold via Internet auction sites. Common items sell at low prices, often under $15. Rare and unusual buildings can command prices in the $500 to $700 range.

**History:** Small metal replicas of famous buildings and monuments first became popular souvenirs among Victorian travelers returning from a Grand Tour of Europe. In the 1920s and 1930s, metal replicas of banks and insurance company headquarters were made as promotional give-aways to new depositors and clients. In the 1950s and 1960s, Japanese-manufactured metal souvenir buildings were the rage for motorists visiting attractions across America.

Souvenir buildings are still being manufactured and sold in cities around the world. They depict churches, cathedrals, skyscrapers, office buildings, capitols, TV and radio towers, castles, and museums. They can often be found in gift or souvenir shops located in or near the structure. Desirable souvenir buildings are made of white (or pot) metal with a finish of brass, copper, gold, silver, or bronze. They have also been made in sterling silver, brass, silvered lead and plastic and ceramic. Today many are made of resin mixed with marble dust, ground pecans, or metal dust. Although these often have fine detail, some collectors do not consider them desirable. Many resin miniatures are hand painted and made in China.

**Collectors' Club:** Souvenir Building Collectors Society, P.O. Box 70, Nellysford, VA 22958.

**Advisor:** Dixie Trainer.

Alamo, San Antonio, TX, 2" x 4" x 3-1/2", copper finish ............................. 17.00
Alder Planetarium, Chicago, IL, incense burner, 3" x 4" d, copper finish
.................................................. 65.00
Arc de Triomphe, Paris, 1-3/4" x 1-1/2" x 1", copper finish ......................... 8.00
Brandenberg Gate, Berlin, 4" x 4-3/4" x 2", antique bronze, wood base
.................................................. 50.00
Bunker Hill Monument, Boston, MA, copper finish ............................. 14.00
Capitol, Washington, DC
2-1/4" x 3-1/2" x 2", souvenir ...... 6.00
4-1/4" x 5" x 3-1/2", jewelry box, gold, mkd "JB" on bottom ................. 55.00
Coit Tower, San Francisco, 6-1/2" h, 2-1/4" sq base, antique bronze finish .......................................... 78.00
Cologne Cathedral, Germany, 4-1/8" x 3-3/4" x 1-1/2", antique pewter or silver finish ................................. 15.00
Coliseum, Rome, 1-1/2" x 2-/4" x 2", copper finish ............................. 15.00
Dollar Savings Bank, Pittsburgh, PA, 3-1/8" x 4" x 3", silvered lead bank
.................................................. 88.00
Easton National Bank, Easton, PA, 4-1/2" x 3-3/4" x 2-1/2", copper finish bank
.................................................. 78.00
Eiffel Tower, Paris
3" x 1" x 1", copper, antique brass or silver finish ................................. 8.00
6" x 2-1/2" x 2-1/2", copper, antique brass or silver finish ................. 13.00
Empire State Building, New York City
3-1/2" x 1-1/4" x 3/4", postwar, with radio antenna spire, gold plastic
.................................................. 3.00
3-1/2" x 1-1/2" x 1", prewar, no spire, antique brass finish .................. 28.00
5" x 1-3/4" x 1-1/4", postwar, with radio antenna spire, antique brass finish ............................................ 7.00
5-3/4" x 2-1/2" x 2", prewar, no spire, silver finish ................................. 65.00
7-1/2" x 2-3/4" x 1-1/4", postwar, with radio antenna spire, copper finish
.................................................. 14.00
Field Museum of Natural History, Chicago, IL, 1" x 4-1/4" x 3", silver or copper finish ............................. 50.00
Flatiron Building, New York City, 5-1/2" h, cast iron bank, silvery finish
.................................................. 160.00
Ft. Dearborn, Chicago, IL, 4" x 3-1/8" x 2", green or tan paint, souvenir of 1933 Chicago World's Fair ....... 50.00
General Motors Building, Detroit, MI, 3-3/4" x 6-1/4" x 4", antique bronze finish ...................................... 350.00
La Giralda, Seville, Spain, 7-1/2" h, antique brass, 2-1/4" black marble base ............................................ 55.00
Havoline Tower, thermometer, souvenir of 1933 Chicago World's Fair, 4-5/8" h
Cast iron, ivory paint ............... 37.00
Plastic, marble base ............... 22.00
Immaculate Conception National Shrine, Washington, DC, antique copper finish
3" x 3" x 2" ............................. 16.00
5" x 5" x 4" ............................. 38.00

Ivan's Bell Tower, Moscow, 3-1/2" x 2" x 1-1/4", solid brass, marble base
.................................................. 125.00
Jefferson Memorial, Washington, DC, 1-1/2" x 2" x 2", copper finish ... 16.00
Kraft International Headquarters, Chicago, IL, 3-1/8" x 2-3/4" x 3-1/4", silvered lead paperweight, cast by A. C. Rehberger ............................. 95.00
Leaning Tower of Pisa, Italy
3-1/2" h, silver finish, metal ashtray
.................................................. 34.00
5" x 1-3/4" d, white alabaster ... 28.00
Lincoln Memorial, Washington, DC, 1-1/2" x 3" x 2", copper finish ............ 8.00
Louisiana State Capitol, Baton Rouge, LA, 7" x 5-1/2" x 2-3/4", antique copper finish ................................. 88.00
Metropolitan Life Insurance Co., New York City, 5-1/4" x 3-3/4" x 2-1/4", silver or gold finish ..................... 150.00
Miami Beach Federal Savings, Miami, FL, 5-1/2" x 3-1/2" x 3-1/4", brass finish, Banthrico Bank ............... 125.00
Mormon Temple, Salt Lake City, UT, 4" x 2-1/4" x 3-3/8", copper finish .... 30.00
Notre Dame, Paris, 2" x 3" x 1-1/2", bronze finish ........................... 16.00
Parthenon, Athens, Greece, 3-1/4" x 6" x 3-1/2", copper, marble base ... 98.00
Pilgrim Memorial Monument, Provinceton, MA, 4-3/4" h, 2-1/4" d base
.................................................. 22.00
Rockefeller Center (RCA Building), New York City
2-5/8" x 2" x 1", copper finish ...... 27.00
4-1/4" x 3" x 1-3/8", silver finish
.................................................. 90.00
Sacre Couer, Paris, 4-1/2" x 4-1/4" x 2-1/2", antique brass ............... 32.00
Singing Tower, Bok Tower, Lake Wales, FL, 5" h, 1-3/4" d base ............ 21.00
Space Needle, Seattle, WA, 6" h, revolving turret, silver or copper finish
.................................................. 22.00
Statue of Liberty, New York City
2" h .......................................... 3.00
4-1/2" h ................................... 5.50
6" h .......................................... 8.00
St. Basil's Cathedral, Moscow, 4" x 3-1/2" x 3-1/2" h, solid brass, marble base
.................................................. 300.00
St. Mary's Cathedral, Florence, Italy, 2-1/2" x 3-1/2" x 2-1/2", silver finish
.................................................. 27.00
St. Peter's Cathedral, Rome, 3-1/2" x 3-1/2" x 2-1/2", silver finish ....... 28.00
Syracuse Savings Bank, Syracuse, NY, 5-1/2" x 4" x 3", copper finish ...... 68.00
Taj Mahal, Agra, India, 8" x 7" x 7", white marble, night-light ................... 65.00
United Nations Building, New York City, 3" x 4" x 2-1/2", antique brass
.................................................. 22.00
US Fidelity & Guaranty Co., 5-3/4" x 7-1/4" x 6", building as combination cigar humidor, inkwell, and clock, cast by Art Metal Works, NJ, antique bronze finish ...................................... 190.00
Washington Monument, Washington, DC
3-1/2" h, silver, salt and pepper shakers, pr ...................................... 28.00
6" h, copper, thermometer ......... 9.00

Woolworth Building, New York City, 4" x
1-3/4" x 1-1/4", gold finish ........26.00
Zembo Museum, Harrisburg, PA, 2-1/2"
x 4-1/2" x 1-3/4", antique copper fin-
ish...............................................63.00

# Space Adventurers and Exploration

**Collecting Hints:** There are four distinct eras of fictional space adventurers: Buck Rogers, Flash Gordon,
the radio and television characters
of the late 1940s and 1950s, and the
"Star Trek" and "Star Wars" phenomenon. Because Buck Rogers material is rare, condition is not as much
of a factor as it is for the other three
areas. Beware of dealers who break
apart items, especially games, and
sell parts separately.

In the early 1950s, a wealth of tin,
battery-operated, friction, and
windup toys not associated with a
specific Space Adventurer were
marketed. The popularity of these
robots, space ships, and space
guns is growing rapidly.

Trekkies began holding conventions in the early 1970s. They issued
many fantasy items which must not
be confused with items issued during the years the TV show was
broadcast. The fantasy items are
numerous and have little value
beyond the initial selling price.

The American and Russian space
programs produced a wealth of souvenir and related material. Beware of
astronaut-signed material; it may
have a printed or autopen signature.

**History:** In January 1929, "Buck
Rogers 2429 A.D." began its comic
strip run. Buck, Wilma Deering, Dr.
Huer, and the villain Killer Kane,
were the creation of Phillip Francis
Nowlan and John F. Dille. The heyday of Buck Rogers material was
1933-1937, when premiums were
issued in conjunction with products
such as Cream of Wheat and Cocomalt.

Flash Gordon followed in the mid-
1930s. Buster Crabbe gave life to
the character in movie serials.
Books, comics, premiums, and other
merchandise enhanced the image
during the 1940s.

The use of rockets at the end of
World War II and the beginning of
the space research program gave
reality to space travel. Television
quickly capitalized on this in the

early 1950s with programs such as
"Captain Video" and "Space Patrol."
Many other space heroes, such as
Rocky Jones, had short-lived popu-
larity.

In the 1950s, real-life space pioneers and explorers replaced the
fictional characters as the center of
the public's attention. The entire
world watched on July 12, 1969, as
man first walked on the moon.
Although space exploration has suffered occasional setbacks, the public remains fascinated with its
findings and potential.

"Star Trek" enjoyed a brief television run and developed a cult following in the early 1970s. "Star Trek:
The Next Generation" has an established corps of watchers. "Star
Wars" (Parts IV, V, and VI) and "ET"
also initiated a wealth of merchandise which already is collectible.

**References:** Dana Cain, *UFO &
Alien Collectibles Price Guide,*
Krause Publications, 1999; Christine
Gentry and Sally Gibson-Downs,
*Greenberg's Guide to Star Trek Col-
lectibles,* Vols. I–III, Greenberg Pub-
lishing, 1992; John Marshall, *Action
Figures of the 1980s,* Schiffer Pub-
lishing, 1998; Rex Miller, *The Inves-
tor's Guide to Vintage Character
Collectibles,* Krause Publications,
1999; Toy Shop, *Star War Collecti-
bles,* Krause Publications, 1999; Stu-
art W. Wells, III, *Science Fiction
Collectibles: Identification & Price
Guide,* Krause Publications, 1999;
Bruce Lanier Wright, *Yesterday's
Tomorrows: The Golden Age of Science Fiction Movie Posters*, Taylor
Publishing, 1993.

**Periodicals:** *Starlog Magazine,* 475
Park Ave. S., New York, NY 10016;
*Strange New Worlds,* P.O. Box 223,
Tallevast, FL 34270; *Star Wars Collection Trading Post,* 6030 Magnolia, P.O. Box 29396, St. Louis, MO
63139; *Trek Collector,* 1324 Palm
Blvd., Dept. 17, Los Angeles, CA
90291.

**Collectors' Clubs:** Galaxy Patrol, 22
Colton St., Worcester, MA 01610;
International Federation of Trekkers,
P.O. Box 3123, Lorain, OH 44052;
Lost in Space Fan Club, 550 Trinity,
Westfield, NJ 07090; Society for the
Advancement of Space Activities,
P.O. Box 192, Kent Hills, ME 04349;
Star Trek: The Official Fan Club, P.O.
Box 111000, Aurora, CO 80011;
Starfleet, P.O. Box 430, Burnsville,
NC 28714; Starfleet Command, P.O.
Box 26076, Indianapolis, IN 46226.

**Museums:** Alabama Space &
Rocket Center, Huntsville, AL; Inter-
national Space Hall of Fame, The
Space Center, Alamogordo, NM;
Kennedy Space Center, Cape
Canaveral, FL.

**Additional Listings:** Robots, Space
Toys.

## Space Adventurers

### Battlestar Galactica

Figure, Cylon Centurian, Mattel, MIB
.................................................150.00
Magazine, glossy periodical unfolds to
33" x 22"
#1, Boxey & Muffey poster.......20.00
#2, Battlestar Spacecraft poster
.................................................20.00
#3, Cyclon Warriors poster ......20.00
Script, 1970s ...............................20.00

### Buck Rogers

Atomic Disintegrator, Hubley, 1930s,
missing holding pin ...............290.00
Badge, Solar Scouts...................100.00
Battle Cruiser..............................100.00
Big Little Book, CocoMalt.............80.00
Book, Kelloggs ............................450.00
Comics, orig Sunday Funnies ....100.00
Figure, lead...................................15.00
Membership Kit
1938, Rocket Rangers, card, letter,
orig mailer.............................200.00
1945, letter, card, and ship poster,
envelope................................500.00
Whistle Badge, Spaceship Commander
.................................................275.00

### Captain Video

Decoder, 1-1/2" d, Capt Video Mysto-
Coder, brass, plastic wheels, lightning bolt design.....................165.00
Gun, 2-1/2" x 3-1/2", Captain Video
Secret ray Gun, red plastic flashlight,
secret message instructions, glow-
in-the-dark card, Power House
Candy premium ......................85.00
Magazine, *TV Star Parade,* 2 pg photo
article, Ideal Publishing Co., 1953
.................................................20.00
Pen Rocket ...................................30.00
Press Book, 12" x 18", black, white, and
blue cover, newspaper headline
style .........................................90.00
Rocket Sled, orig rockets ..........125.00

**Bubble Gum Cards, Jets, Rockets,
Spacemen, Bowman Gum, Card #4
Final Check Before Blast-Off, $5.**

**Child's Book and Record Set,** *Star Trek, Passage to Moauv,* **$15.**

Space Figure, rubber.................... 20.00
Spaceship, all parts..................... 50.00

### Flash Gordon

Bank, metal, rocket...................... 35.00
Better Little Book, *Flash Gordon And The Perils of Mongo,* Whitman, 1940 .................................................. 45.00
Big Little Book, *Flash Gordon and the Tournament of Mongo* ............. 55.00
Comics, Sunday Comics Page, 1935 .................................................. 15.00
Book, pop-up, *Tournament Of Death,* Blue Ribbon Press and Pleasure Books, ©1935, 20 pgs ........... 145.00
Figure, Defender of the Earth
  Flash Gordon, MIP .................. 15.00
  Ming, MIP ............................... 15.00
Gun, Radio Repeater, 1935, slight wear .................................................. 800.00
Pencil Case, 1951...................... 160.00
Playset, Tootsietoy, figures, 1978, MIB .................................................. 100.00
Water Pistol, holster, King Features, 1975, MOC.............................. 45.00

### Lost in Space

Blueprint Set .............................. 20.00
Comic Album, 7-3/4" x 10-1/4", Space Family Robinson/Lost In Space, stiff cover comic album, English reprints of Western Publishing Co. full-color comic book stories, ©1965 by World Distributors Ltd, 64 pgs ........... 18.00
Game .......................................... 180.00

### Space Cadet, Tom Corbett

Binoculars................................... 125.00
Book, *Tom Corbett Space Cadet/Sabotage In Space,* Grosset & Dunlap, hardcover, 212 pgs, dj............. 15.00
Decoder, 2-1/2" x 4", Tom Corbett Space Cadet Code, black, white, and red cardboard, membership card printed on back .............. 45.00

Flashlight, 7" l, Space Cadet Signal Siren Flashlight, full color illus, orig box, c1952.............................. 65.00
Lunch Box, 7" x 8" x 4", litho metal, full color space scene, dark blue galaxy background, ©1954 Rockhill Radio .................................................. 95.00
Membership Kit Fan Photo, 3-1/2" x 5-1/4", glossy black and white photo, Tom with Space Rangers, facsimile blue ink signature, c1952 .................................................. 28.00
Patch, 2" x 4", cloth, Space Cadet, red, yellow, and blue, Kellogg's premium .................................................. 35.00
Photo, 3-1/2" x 5-1/2", black and white glossy, blue signature "Spaceman's Luck/Tom Corbett/Space Cadet," early 1950s .............................. 45.00
Viewmaster Reel, set of 3, orig story folder and envelope................ 45.00
Wrist Watch................................. 250.00

### Space Patrol

Belt and Buckle, 4" brass buckle, rocket, decoder mounted on back, glow-in-the-dark belt, Ralston premium, early 1950s.................. 175.00
Coin Album, 3" x 7-3/4", thin cardboard black, white, and blue folder, spaceship landing and men rushing toward it, diecut slots for plastic Ralston premium or Schwinn Bicycle dealer coins, c1953 .............. 175.00
Film Projector, pocket ................ 185.00
Gun, Satellite ............................... 40.00
Handbook................................... 165.00
Microscope, orig slides ............. 195.00
Paper Cup, package of 6, rocket ships, stars, and planets motif, orig cellophane and company label....... 70.00
Premium Card, 2-1/2" x 3-1/2", full color scene on front and back, text, ad for Wheat and Rice Chex Cereal, Rockets, Jets, and Weapons Series, seven cards from 40 card set, early 1950s ...................................... 135.00
Space Helmet, diecut cardboard, six sided, yellow, green, red design, black top with printed red lightning flashes................................ 1,230.00

**Patch, Kennedy Space Center, Florida, space shuttle, MISP, $2.50.**

Watch, silvered chrome, stainless steel back, black leather straps, "Space Patrol" inscription on dial, black numerals, US Time, early 1950s .................................................. 165.00

### Star Trek

Action Figure
  Andorian, 8" h
    Carded............................. 700.00
    Loose ............................... 400.00
  Chekov, 9" h ........................... 15.00
  Cheron, 8" h, carded............. 250.00
  Gorn, 3rd Series, 8" h, carded
    ..................................... 500.00
  Guian, 9" h ............................. 50.00
  Jem Hadar, 9" h ..................... 25.00
  Keeper, loose.......................... 75.00
  Kira, 9" h ................................ 15.00
  Kirk, 8" h, carded ................... 60.00
  Kirk and Spock, #1, Piece of the Action, Kayhee Set ............... 200.00
  Klingon, 8" h, carded ............. 60.00
  McCoy, 8" h, carded ............. 125.00
  Mugato, loose ........................ 300.00
  Neptuneman, loose .............. 100.00
  O-Brien, 9" h ......................... 15.00
  Q, Judge's robe, flesh, 9" h...... 25.00
  Riker, 9" h .............................. 50.00
  Romulan, loose ...................... 700.00
  Scotty, 8" h, carded ............. 125.00
  Sisko Dress, 9" ...................... 15.00
  Spock, 8" h, carded ............... 60.00
  Talos, 8" h
    Carded............................. 400.00
    Loose ............................... 200.00
  Ulhura, 8" h, carded............. 125.00
  Warrior Worf, 9" h .................. 50.00
Children's Book, *The Truth Machine,* hardcover, 1977 ...................... 10.00
Christmas Ornament, Hallmark
  1991, Enterprise ................... 325.00
  1992, Shuttle.......................... 35.00
  1993, 1701-D, 1993 ................ 30.00
  1994, Bird of Prey .................. 30.00
  1995, Warbird ........................ 30.00
  1996, Voyager........................ 30.00
  1997, Defiant ......................... 30.00
  1998, 1701-E .......................... 40.00
  Store display for 1992 ornament
    ..................................... 100.00
Classic Communicator, lights and sounds
  Calculator .............................. 40.00
  Recorder................................. 40.00
  Universal Garage Door Opener
    ....................................... 50.00
Cup, plastic, Deka, 1701 ship and crew, 1975........................................ 30.00
Doll, Commander Sulu, 15" h, MIB .................................................. 135.00
Drinking Glasses, set of 4, orig Taco Bell display, Star Trek 3........... 60.00
Halloween Costume, Mr. Spock, 1975 .................................................. 85.00
Inflatable Enterprise, Star Trek 5, Kraft Foods promo, 24" l.................. 15.00
Limited Edition Figure, Franklin Mint, pewter, orig stand, MIB
  Borg Ship............................... 155.00
  Space Station ........................ 145.00
  U. S. S. Enterprise ................ 160.00

Lunch Box, Borg, head, talking, 1992 ..................................................... 40.00
Manual, *Star Fleet Technical Manual*, hardcover, 1975 ....................... 60.00
Model
　Galileo 7 Space Ship, AMT, 1974, orig contents sealed in box ............. 150.00
　Klingon Battle Ship, AMT, 1968, orig contents sealed in box ........... 150.00
　Mr. Spock, AMT, 1968, orig contents sealed in box ......................... 250.00
　USS Enterprise, AMT, 1968, orig contents seated in box ........... 200.00
　USS Enterprise Command Bridge, AMT, 1975, orig contents sealed in box ...................................... 150.00
Playset, Mego
　Bridge, 1975, sealed, MIB ..... 300.00
　Command Console ................ 250.00
　Communicators, carded ........ 200.00
　Mission to Gamma VI ............. 400.00
　Trekulator................................. 250.00
　Tricarder ................................. 250.00
Puzzle, boxed, Canadian.............. 20.00
Stamp Cachet, Trek Artwork, Shuttle, 1991, limited edition................. 50.00
Record, book and record, MIP ....... 5.00
Towel, Voyager Promo, Fritts Candy, full color .......................................... 50.00
Vehicle and Accessories
　Borg Cube............................... 50.00
　Communicators, loose, pr........ 85.00
　DS9 Station ............................ 70.00
　Enterprise B .......................... 140.00
　Excelsior................................ 140.00
　Insurrection Phaser ................. 15.00
　Klingon Disruptor ..................... 25.00
　Pikes Laser Pistol ................... 20.00
　Romulan Warbird .................... 50.00
　Shuttlecraft, Goodard, battle sounds, MIB....................................... 75.00
　Voyager ................................. 140.00
Wall Clock, 1701-E Ship, Wesco... 50.00
Watch, Timex, Cloaking Romulan, 1993, orig case ................................. 75.00

## Space Exploration

Autograph, envelope, inked Jack Swigert signature on back, Man on Moon stamp, canceled Kennedy Space Center, April 11, 1970............... 50.00
Bank, Apollo Astronaut in Space Suit, ceramic .................................... 40.00
Book
　*First American Into Space,* Robert Silverberg, Monarch Books, 142 pgs, 1961................................. 20.00
　*NASA Astronauts Biography Book,* NASA, 1968, 8" x 10-1/4", softcover ................................................ 40.00
Clock, 4" x 4-1/2" x 2", Apollo 11, animated wind-up, ivory case, red, white, and blue diecut, metallic blue dial, Apollo craft illus, gold colored numerals, brass hands, mkd "Lux Clock Mfg Co."....................... 145.00
Dish, 8" d, Apollo II Commemorative, iridescent glass, raised design, inscription "One Small Step," 1970s ................................................ 18.00
Glass
　Astronaut Neil Armstrong, 5-1/2" h, clear glass, brown and white graphics of Armstrong wearing suit, gold lettering "Wapakoneta Astronaut Neil Armstrong," list of 1961-1966 manned space flights on reverse ............. 37.00
　Columbia Space Shuttle, 4-1/2" h, clear, weighted bottom, black and white facsimile of NY times, April 15, 1981, Wendy's........................... 15.00
Gyroscope, Gemini, plastic, 1960s, MOC............................................ 30.00
Letter Opener, 7" l, Apollo 11, gold colored metal, insignia on handle, grained black leather-like scabbard ................................................ 30.00
Magazine
*Life*
　1966, July 1, Moon Shot cover ................................................. 5.00
　1969, July 25, Leaving for Moon cover, article on Armstrong ................................................ 10.00
　1969, Aug. 8, On the Moon with Flag cover, color photos...... 12.00
*Look,* 1960, Feb. 2, The Lady Wants To Orbit, cov article, 6 pgs, Betty Skelton article and photos ....... 17.50
*Newsweek*
　1969, Jan. 6, Apollo, Anders, Lovell, Borman cover .................. 8.00
　1969, July 28, Moonwalk cover, black and white.................... 9.00
　1969, Aug. 11, Moonwalk cover, color ..................................... 9.00
*Time*
　1962, March 2, John Glenn cover ................................................ 6.00
　1962, Aug. 24, Russian Astronauts cover .......................... 5.00
　1969, Jan. 3, US Astronauts cover ................................................ 5.00
Medal, 1-1/2" d, commemorative, SS, astronaut descending from landing module onto moon, "One Small Step" inscription, plaque left on moon on reverse, acrylic case................. 40.00
Mug, 3" h, china, black St Louis Globe-Democrat newspaper design of July 20, 1969, moon landing ........... 35.00
Patch, 9" x 9", cloth, Apollo 16, white background, full color 3-1/2" d astronaut patch in center of red, white and blue shield, eagle at top against lunar background, blue and white star border, astronaut names Young, Matlingly, and Duke ................. 24.00
Pennant, 29" l, felt, red and white, blue trim, First Man On Moon .......... 20.00
Photograph, Space Program, 1965/66, set of 5 UPI and WW photos ...... 20.00
Pinback Button
　1-1/4" d, New Frontier, Man of the Year, Astronaut John Glenn, blue and white ................................. 35.00
　3" d, Challenger 7, black and white photo, purple background....... 15.00
　3-1/2" d, Gemini 4, black and white photos of McDivitt and White, red, white, and blue ground, June 3-7, 1965 walk in space mission..... 35.00
Plate
　7-1/2" d, Apollo 13, glass, brown and tan lunar landscape, white silhouette of astronaut on moon surface, rim inscribed "General Electric" and "United States Atomic Energy Commission," back and white NASA symbol.......................................... 40.00
　9-1/4" d, John Glenn, white china, black and white illus, stylized gold patter, Feb. 20, 1962 flight....... 30.00
Poster, Apollo Astronaut, set of 3, large ................................................ 35.00
Press Pass, 3" x 4-1/4", laminated, ABC News, June 18-24, 1983, Challenger Mission, black and white photos, blue, white, and orange design........... 60.00
Puzzle, Apollo 11, 1969, MIB ....... 25.00
Record, America's First Man In Orbit, John Glenn, 33-1/3 rpm, orig envelope.......................................... 35.00
Rug, 19-1/2" x 37-1/2", woven, full color moon landing scene, red, white, and blue stars and stripes motif border, made in Italy, orig label............. 60.00
Ruler, 6", Space Shuttle 3-D Picture Ruler, blue, red, and white, illus 4-1/2" x 7" card, diecut opening, five images of space shuttle in flight, Vari-Vue, Mt. Vernon, NY, unopened, orig display bag ..................................... 8.00
Salt and Pepper Shakers, pr, 3" h, china, blue symbol and Columbia shuttle design, inscription "Johnson Space Center, Houston, TX," early 1980s ..................................... 20.00
Tie Clip, 1-1/2", Apollo 11, brass, black accents, raised moon landing design, landing date and astronaut names on rim, orig plastic display case ........................................ 40.00

## Space Related

Bank, Satellite, Duro, mold diecast rocket, 11" h........................... 100.00
Birthday Card, 1950s, 6" x 7"........ 20.00
Book
　*Rockets to Explore The Unknown*, 1964......................................... 20.00
　*Science Fiction Films Pictorial History*, Jeff Rovin, 1975 .............. 25.00
Cap
　Beacon Beanie, signal cap, 1950s, orig box.................................. 100.00
　Junior Astronaut, 1950s........... 45.00
Costume, child's
　Space Commander, uniform and hat ................................................ 100.00
　Space Man, 1950s................. 250.00
Flashlight
　Alien head, green plastic......... 30.00
　Johnny Astro Explorer, Topper, 1960s, MIB............................. 95.00
Folder, Mead, colorful.................. 20.00
Globe, moon, tin ......................... 45.00
Little Golden Book, *Exploring Space,* 1958......................................... 20.00
Nodder, Martian couple, plastic, 4" h ................................................ 65.00
Pinback Button, Space Angel ...... 40.00
Planter, Space Shuttle and Astronaut, Inarco....................................... 75.00
Poster, Space Age Brand Fireworks, 24" x 10", 1960s ........................ 15.00
Radio, Star Command, Calfax, 1970s, AM ................................................
Robark, mascot robot, MIB...... 60.00

Space Ship, yellow, MIB .......... 50.00
Record, child's, Space: 1999, book and record, MIP ........................ 5.00
Store Display
   Atomic Jet Flying Saucer, helicopter ................................. 50.00
   Spaceman Air Freshner, 1950s space outfit ..................... 150.00
Toy, Space Alien, pop-up, green plastic, 3" h .................................. 20.00
Writing Tablet, Frontiers of Space, 8-1/2" x 11", 1950s, unused ............... 20.00

# Space Toys

**Collecting Hints:** The original box is an important element in pricing, perhaps controlling 15% to 20% of the price. The artwork on the box may differ slightly from the toy inside; this is to be expected. The box also may provide the only clue to the correct name of the toy.

The early lithographed tin toys are more valuable than the later toys made of plastic. There is a great deal of speculation in modern toys, e.g., Star Wars material. Hence, the market shows great price fluctuation.

Collect toys in very good to mint condition. Damaged and rusted lithographed tin is hard to repair. Check the battery box for damage. Don't ever leave batteries in a toy when it is not in use.

**History:** The Hollywood movies of the early 1950s drew attention to space travel. The launching of Sputnik and American satellites in the late 1950s and early 1960s enhanced this fascination. The advent of manned space travel, culminating in the landing on the moon, further increased interest in anything space-related, and the toy industries of Japan and America. Lithographed tin and plastic models of astronauts, flying saucers, spacecraft, and space vehicles became quickly available. Some were copies of original counterparts; most were the figments of the toy designer's imagination.

During the 1970s, there was less emphasis on the space program and a corresponding decline in the production of space-related toys. The earlier Japanese- and American-made products gave way to less-expensive models from China and Taiwan.

**References:** Dana Cain, *UFO & Alien Collectibles Price Guide,* Krause Publications, 1999; Toy

Shop, *Star War Collectibles,* Krause Publications, 1999; Stuart W. Wells, III, *Science Fiction Collectibles: Identification & Price Guide,* Krause Publications, 1999.

**Periodical:** *Robot World & Price Guide,* P.O. Box 184, Lenox Hill Station, New York, NY 10021.

**Reproduction Alert.**

**Additional Listings:** Robots, Space Adventurers and Explorers.

Astronaut
   Astro-Scout, 9-1/2" h, Yonezawa, Japan, litho tin, advances using crank friction lever, separate litho tin chest plate with #3, clear plastic helmet visor over litho tin face .......... 2,500.00
   Man in Space, 8" l, Alps, Japan, battery operated, litho tin and plastic, orig box ............................ 950.00
   Mark Apollo Astronaut, 7-1/2" h, Marx, jointed plastic, orange space suit, white helmet, plastic accessories, orig instructions and box ................ 175.00
Cap Gun
   Jet Jr. Space, chrome, MIB.... 425.00
   Strato Gun, chrome, mint ....... 465.00
Chalk, rocket ship illus, Creston ... 10.00
Colored Pencils, Dixon, space graphics ................................... 25.00
Colorforms, Battlestar Galactica .. 35.00
Doll, Mars Attack, Spygirl, talking, MIP ................................... 65.00
Drafting Set, Space Scientist, 1950s ................................... 80.00
Eagle Lunar Module, Daishin, Japan, battery operated, 1969, MIB ................................... 300.00
Figure
   A-OK Astronaut, helmets, plastic, 1950s, MIP ........................... 10.00
   Astronaut, 6" h, Marx, set of six different poses ........................... 100.00
   Close Encounter of the Third Kind, Alien, bendee, MOC ............... 45.00

Snoopy the Astronaut, Knickerbocker Preschool, 1958, vinyl, orig box, $27.50.

Space Alien, 11" l, suction cup walker ...................................... 40.00
Spaceman, plastic, Hong Kong, MIP ................................... 15.00
Firecrackers, Chinese, Rocket brand ................................... 20.00
Flying Saucer
   Air Commanders, sling powered glider, MIP .............................. 25.00
   Atomic Jet, Flying-O-Saucer, 1950s, orig instructions ..................... 20.00
   Blue, clear plastic and tin, 5" d ................................... 75.00
   Flying Saucer and Pilot, Cragston, Japan, 1950s, battery operated, 7-1/2" d ............................... 285.00
   Jupiter, litho tin, clear dome, sparks, mkd "K, Japan" ....................... 45.00
   King, tin, battery operated, MIB ................................... 140.00
   Z-101, litho tin, friction, 1950s, 6-1/2" l ................................... 225.00
Game
   Astro Launch, Ohio Art ......... 110.00
   Blast Off, 1960s, MIP .............. 35.00
   Countdown Arithmetic Space Game, Whitman, 1962 ....................... 30.00
   Moon Blastoff, Schaper, unused, sealed, MIB ........................... 48.00
   Planet Patrol, interplant space game, 1950s .............................. 75.00
   Space-O, card ........................ 30.00
Gumball Machine, Rocket to the Stars, rocketship shape ................... 225.00
Gun
   Astroray, tin friction, Japan, 10" l, MIB ........................................ 100.00
   Cosmic Ray Space Gun, 1950s ................................... 100.00
   Cosmic Space Rifle, tin, Korea, 13" l ................................... 75.00
   Dan Dare Planet Gun, Eagle Toys, England, 1950s, unplayed with ................................... 165.00
   Jet Ray Gun, friction, graphic box ................................... 35.00
   Jet Space Gun, KO, Japan, tin litho, 1960s, 10" l ........................... 55.00
   Junior Jet Play Gun, open faced box with Space Girl graphics ......... 45.00
   Rocket Jet Space Gun, silver plastic, 7" l ................................... 45.00
   Space Fazer, Kusan, 12" l ....... 65.00
   Space Flash, battery operated, plastic, 6" l, MIB .......................... 65.00
   Space Gun, litho tin, friction window, yellow, Toy Hero, Japan ........... 30.00
   Space Gun, Mickey Mouse, green plastic, Young Epoch Co., Japan, 1928 ................................. 90.00
   Space Gun, plastic, 6" l .......... 60.00
   Space Gun, western style, red plastic, M&L Toys, 9" l ................. 75.00
   Space Jet, litho tin, Japan, 10" l ................................... 75.00
   Space Pilot Jet Ray Gun, Hong Kong, friction, 1970s, 10" l ....... 45.00
   Space Pistol, Arco, ©1982, MOC ................................... 15.00
   Space 1999, stun gun, MIB, some damage to box ..................... 100.00
Kite, Gayla Space Craft, unused, MIP ................................... 35.00

Lunar Bug Mooncraft, battery operated, 1960s, unused, MIB .............. 150.00
Missile Launcher, 1950s, MIB ....... 45.00
Model Kit, Cyclops with Chariot, Lost in Space, Aurora, MIB ............. 2,350.00
Moon Platoon, rubber robot figures, Japanese, Imperial, 1969, on card .................................................... 70.00
Pinball Game, bagatelle, space scene, 1950s, 14" l .................................. 45.00
Playset
    ID4 Los Angeles Invasion, buildings, tanks, men, MIB ....................... 35.00
    Space: 1999 Adventure Playset, unpunched, mint .................... 145.00
    Space: 1999 Moonbase Alpha .................................................... 125.00
    Star Station Seven, Marx #4115, 1978, MIB ................................ 75.00
Puzzle
    Moon map, Rand McNally, 1960s, unused, sealed ........................ 25.00
    Rip Foster, frame tray, 1953 ..... 35.00
Satellite, Orbiters, Frisbee type, 1950s, unused, MOC .......................... 55.00
Space Car, Pyro, plastic, 4" l, played with condition ........................... 30.00
Space Helmet, metal, bullet shaped, 1950s, 10" h ............................ 75.00
Space Rocket, Marx, 11" h ........... 70.00
Space Ship
    Space 1999 Eagle 1 Spaceship, 30" l, MIB ..................................... 225.00
    Space Ship X-5, battery operated, tin and plastic, 1970s, orig box .... 95.00
    Transcontinental Rocket Ship, Buck Rogers, 4" l, 1930s .................. 95.00
Space Tank, Robby, China, 1980s, MIB .................................................... 145.00
Space Vehicle, plastic, red, yellow, and blue, Irwin, 1950s, 9" l ............ 200.00
Spinner, Space Patrol .................. 20.00
Squeeze Toy, Space Boy in rocket, figural, unused ............................. 40.00
Target Game, tin
    Rocket and spaceship, 1950s, 15" x 23" ......................................... 100.00
    Rocket Patrol, magnetic, 14" x 16" ............................................ 100.00
Transformer, Space Mummy, Ultraman, diecast, 1980, MIB ................. 225.00
Whistle, Space Signal, rocket shape, red and yellow plastic, 5" l ....... 25.00

# Sports Collectibles

**Collecting Hints:** The amount of material is unlimited. Pick a favorite sport and concentrate on it. Within the sport, narrow collecting emphasis to items associated with one league, team, individual, or era, or concentrate on one type of equipment. Include as much three-dimensional material as possible.

Each sport has a hall of fame. Make a point to visit it and get to know its staff, an excellent source of leads for material that the museum

no longer wants in its collection. Induction ceremonies provide an excellent opportunity to make contact with heroes of the sport as well as with other collectors.

**History:** Individuals have been saving sports-related equipment since the inception of sports. Some material was passed down from generation to generation for reuse. The balance occupied dark spaces in closets, attics, and basements.

In the 1980s, two key trends brought collectors' attention to the sports arena. First, decorators began using old sports items, especially in restaurant decor. Second, card collectors began to discover the thrill of owing the "real" thing. Although the principal thrust was on baseball memorabilia, by the beginning of the 1990s all sport categories were collectible, with automobile racing, boxing, football, and horse racing especially strong.

**References:** Mark Allen Baker, *All Sport Autograph Guide*, Krause Publications, 1994; —, *Complete Guide to Boxing Collectibles*, Krause Publications, 1995; David Bushing, *Sports Equipment Price Guide*, Krause Publications, 1995; Jeanne Cherry, *Tennis Antiques & Collectibles*, Amaryllis Press (Box 3658, Santa Monica, CA 90408), 1996; Duncan Chilcott, *Miller's Soccer Memorabilia*, Millers Publications, 1994; Ralf Coykendall, Jr., *Coykendall's Complete Guide to Sporting Collectibles*, Wallace-Homestead, 1996; Chuck Furjanic, *Antique Golf Collectibles, A Price and Reference Guide,* Krause Publications, 1997; Alice J. Hoffman, *Indian Clubs*, Abrams, 1996; Michael McKeever, *Collecting Sports Memorabilia*, Alliance Publishing, 1966; Tom Mortenson, *2000 Standard Catalog of Sports Memorabilia,* Krause Publications, 1999; Sports Collectors Digest, *1998 Sports Collectors Alamanac,* Krause Publications, 1998.

**Periodical:** *Sports Collectors Digest,* 700 E. State St., Iola, WI 54990.

**Museum:** National Bowling Hall of Fame & Museum, St. Louis, MO; New England Sports Museum, Boston, MA; University of New Haven National Art Museum of Sport, W Haven, CT.

**Additional Listings:** Baseball Collectibles, Basketball Collectibles,

Boxing Collectibles, Fishing Collectibles, Golf Collectibles, Hunting Collectibles, Olympics Collectibles, Racing Collectibles; Wrestling Collectibles.

Autograph
    Agassi, Andre, photograph ..... 40.00
    McEnroe, John ......................... 40.00
    Navrailova, Martina ................. 40.00
    Perry, Fred, canceled check .... 50.00
    Sabatina, Gabriella ................. 40.00
    Witt, Katarina, photograph ....... 40.00
Bank, 4-1/2" d, metal, emb enameled fishing, golf, and travel scenes, changing date feature, 1950s, Cada Co., Chicago .......................... 60.00
Book, *Giant Book of Sports,* 185 pgs, 8-1/2" x 11-3/4", some wear ........ 20.00
Calendar Plate, 1967, bowling, football, water skiing, tennis, gold trim, 10" d .................................................... 5.00
Figure, 6-1/2" h, caricature, zealous lady bowler who rocks back and hits male bowler, ©1941 L. Ritgers, painted plaster ...................... 195.00
Game, Bowling A Board Game, Parker Bros, orig box, 1896 ............... 60.00
Hair Bow, 3" x 8" x 7-1/2" orig package, "Queen of the Roller Derby," 12 orig cellophane packages with rayon fabric hair bow and roller skating theme, each also includes black and white photo of female roller derby star, Gerry Murray, Toughie Brasuhn, or Mary Gardner, by Burlington Mills, 1950s ...................................... 60.00
Magazine
    *Life,* November, 1971 ................ 7.50
    *Sport Revue,* Quebec publication, February 1956, Bert Olmstead, Hall of Fame cov ........................... 15.00

**Greeting Card, Hallmark, c1980, $1.**

*Sports Illustrated,* July 15, 1974, Jimmy Connors and Chris Evert ................................................ 10.00

*Sports Illustrated,* Sept. 6, 1954, sailing ................................................ 17.50

Nodder, 6" h, "You're Right Down My Alley," composition, man holding bowling ball, mounted on wood block base .............................. 50.00

Pencil Sharpener, 1-1/4" x 1-3/4" x 2", green had plastic, portable TV shape, full color flicker as screen, Kohner Products, c1950 .......... 25.00

Pinback Button

American Bowling Congress, 1932, 32nd Annual Tournament, Detroit, silver dollar size, red, blue, and blue, large luxury car in center ......... 80.00

Congressional Country Club Caddie, red and white center, blue and gold trim, c1930 .............................. 20.00

Dallas Turnverein Bowling Club, "There's No Use Crying Baby Houston, You Can't Have This Cup," blue, white, and black, 1901-10........ 42.00

Devil's Lake Regatta, blue and white, speedboat races, July 1934, 1-3/4" d ................................................ 15.00

National Association of Amateur Oarsmen, black and white illus, competition roaring crews, late 1890s ................................................ 30.00

Outboard Regatta, black lettering, tan ground, 1930s, 2-1/8" d ..... 15.00

US Open Tennis Championship, 1975, 2-1/8" d........................... 15.00

Poster, Play Helps Study, colorful tennis motif, 1924 .............................. 30.00

Program, United States Lawn Tennis Championships, 9" x 12", official souvenir program, men's singles, women's singles, mixed doubles, September 1947, West Side Tennis Club, Forest Hills, NY, 56 pages, photos and player profiles, ads .................... 40.00

Snow Dome, 3" d pale transparent amber glass globe, 1-1/2" x 3" x 3" hard plastic black base, gold lettering on front "York County Lions/ Team-High Average 1959," 3 miniature golden bowling pins and black ball in center with gold granules ................................................ 40.00

Telephone, *Sports Illustrated,* speakerphone ...................................... 25.00

Tennis Racket, 27" l, Maureen Connolly, full color portrait on handle, Wilson Sporting Goods, 1950s ............ 20.00

Wire Service Photo, Chicago Bulls Scottie Pippen and Detroit Pistons Vinnie Johnson, 1989............................ 3.50

# Stangl Pottery

**Collecting Hints:** Stangl Pottery produced several lines of highly collectible dinnerware and decorative accessories, including the famed Stangl birds. The red-bodied dinnerware was produced in distinctive shapes and patterns. Shapes were designated by numbers. Pattern names include Country Garden, Fruit, Tulip, Thistle, and Wild Rose. Special Christmas, advertising, and commemorative wares also were produced.

Bright colors and bold simplistic patterns make Stangl pottery a favorite with Country collectors. Stangl sold seconds from a factory store long before outlet malls became popular. Large sets of Stangl dinnerware currently command high prices at auctions, flea markets, and even antiques shops.

As many as ten different trademarks were used. Dinnerware was marked and often signed by the decorator. Most birds are numbered; many are artist signed. However, signatures are useful for dating purposes only and add little to value.

Several of the well-known Stangl birds were reissued between 1972 and 1977. These reissues are dated on the bottom and are worth approximately half as much as the older birds.

**History:** The origins of Fulper Pottery, the predecessor to Stangl, are clouded. The company claimed a date of 1805. Paul Evans, a major American art pottery researcher, suggests an 1814 date. Regardless of which date is correct, by the middle of the 19th century an active pottery was located in Flemington, New Jersey.

When Samuel Hill, the pottery's founder, died in 1858, the pottery was acquired by Abraham Fulper, a nephew. Abraham died in 1881, and the business continued under the direction of his sons, Edward, George W., and William.

In 1910, Johann Martin Stangl began working at Fulper as a chemist and plant superintendent. He left Fulper in 1914 to work briefly for Haeger Potteries. By 1920, Stangl was back at Fulper serving as general manager. In 1926, Fulper acquired the Anchor Pottery in Trenton, New Jersey, where a line of solid-color dinnerware in the California patio style was produced.

William Fulper died in 1928, at which time Stangl became president of the firm. In 1920, Johann Martin Stangl purchased Fulper, and Stangl Pottery was born. During the 1920s, production emphasis shifted from art pottery to dinner and utilitarian wares.

A 1929 fire destroyed the Flemington pottery. Rather than rebuild, a former ice cream factory was converted to a showroom and production facility. By the end of the 1930s, production was concentrated in Trenton with the Flemington kiln used primarily for demonstration purposes.

Stangl's ceramic birds were produced from 1940 until 1972. The birds were made in Stangl's Trenton plant, then shipped to the Flemington plant for hand painting. During World War II the demand for these birds and Stangl pottery was so great that 40 to 60 decorators could not keep up with it. Orders were contracted out to private homes. These pieces were then returned for firing and finishing. Different artists used different colors to decorate these birds.

On Aug. 25, 1965, fire struck the Trenton plant. The damaged portion of the plant was rebuilt by May 1966. On Feb. 13, 1972, Johann Martin Stangl died. Frank Wheaton, Jr., of Wheaton Industries, Millville, New Jersey, purchased the plant in June 1972 and continued Stangl production. In 1978, the Pfaltzgraff Company purchased the company's assets from Wheaton. Production ceased. The Flemington factory became a Pfaltzgraff factory outlet. One of the original kilns remains intact to commemorate the hard work and to demonstrate the high temperatures involved in the production of pottery.

**References:** Susan and Al Bagdade, *Warman's American Pottery and Porcelain,* Wallace-Homestead, 1994; Harvey Duke, *Stangl Pottery,* Wallace-Homestead, 1993; Mike Schneider, *Stangl and Pennsbury Pottery Birds,* Schiffer Publishing, 1994.

**Collectors' Club:** Stangl/Fulper Collectors Club, P.O. Box 64-A, Changewater, NJ 07831.

**Advisor:** Peter Meissner.

**Additional Listings:** See *Warman's Antiques and Collectibles Price Guide* for prices of bird figurines.

## Dinnerware

Blueberry

Coffeepot .............................. 100.00

Creamer .................................. 15.00

Platter, 14" d ......................... 75.00

Salt and Pepper Shakers, pr ... 24.00

Vegetable Bowl, 8".................. 50.00

Brittany, plate, 10-1/2" d ............ 125.00

Colonial, #1388
   Candleholders, pr, blue ........... 40.00
   Carafe, pottery stopper, wooden handle ...................................... 65.00
   Cigarette Box ........................... 60.00
   Creamer and Sugar, green ...... 20.00
   Cup and Saucer, green ............ 12.00
   Dinner Plate, 10"d, yellow ........ 12.00
   Salad Bowl, Round, 10" d ........ 35.00
   Salad Plate, 8" d, tangerine ........ 8.00
   Salt and Pepper Shakers, pr .. 20.00
   Teapot ....................................... 75.00
   Teapot, individual .................... 45.00

Fruit
   Casserole, 8" d ........................ 85.00
   Chop Plate, 14" d ..................... 75.00
   Creamer, individual ................. 25.00
   Cup and Saucer ....................... 18.00
   Dinner Plate, 10" d ................... 25.00
   Eggcup ..................................... 18.00
   Salt and Pepper Shakers, pr .... 24.00
   Sherbet ..................................... 20.00
   Teapot ..................................... 100.00
   Teapot, individual .................... 60.00

Jeweled Christmas Tree
   Chop Plate, 14" d ................... 175.00
   Cigarette Box ......................... 250.00
   Creamer .................................... 40.00
   Cup and Saucer ....................... 50.00
   Dinner Plate, 10" d ................... 65.00
   Pitcher, 2 qt. ........................... 100.00
   Punch Bowl, 12" d ................. 200.00
   Punch Cup ................................ 25.00
   Salad Plate, 8" d ...................... 40.00
   Sugar ........................................ 40.00

Kiddieware
   Bowl, Goldilocks .................... 150.00
   Child's Feeding Dish, 3 compartments
      Ducky Dinner .................... 125.00
      Kitten Capers ................... 100.00
      Playful Pups ..................... 125.00

Cup
   Goldilocks ............................. 150.00
   Little Bo Peep ....................... 150.00
   Little Boy Blue ......................... 50.00
   Ranger Boy ............................ 100.00

Plate
   Little Quakers ....................... 110.00
   Mary Quite Contrary .......... 200.00
   Peter Rabbit ......................... 175.00
   Pony Trail .............................. 200.00

Magnolia
   Bread and Butter Plate .............. 6.00
   Coffeepot, individual size ...... 100.00
   Creamer and Sugar ................. 20.00
   Cup and Saucer ....................... 12.50
   Dinner Plate ............................. 15.00
   Fruit Bowl ................................ 10.00
   Salt and Pepper Shakers, pr .... 25.00
   Vegetable, round
      8" d ..................................... 24.00
      10"d ..................................... 28.00

Thistle
   Coffeepot, cov ....................... 100.00
   Cup and Saucer ....................... 13.50
   Dinner Plate, 10" d ................... 20.00
   Eggcup ..................................... 15.00
   Fruit Dish ................................. 12.00
   Gravy Boat ............................... 20.00
   Pitcher, 1qt. ............................. 35.00
   Platter, oval ............................. 35.00

Town and Country
   Bowl, blue, 10"d ....................... 60.00
   Butter Dish, cov ....................... 45.00
   Candlesticks, pr, 7-1/2" h ......... 60.00
   Coffeepot, yellow ................... 100.00
   Creamer .................................... 20.00
   Cup and Saucer ....................... 20.00
   Dinner Plate, 10-1/2" d, brown .. 20.00
   Mug, blue ................................. 40.00
   Salad Plate, 8-1/2" d, brown ......... 15.00
   Salt and Pepper Shakers, pr, handles ...................................... 35.00
   Spoon Rest ............................... 35.00
   Sugar, cov ................................ 30.00
   Wash Pitcher and Basin, large, blue ...................................... 175.00

Tropic, # 3338
   Carafe, wood handle .................. 5.00
   Chop Plate, 14" d ..................... 75.00
   Cup and Saucer ....................... 15.00
   Dinner Plate, 10"d ................... 25.00
   Salad Plate, 7" d ...................... 12.00
   Salt and Pepper Shakers, pr, figural ...................................... 60.00
   Vegetable Bowl, oval ................ 40.00

### Miscellaneous and Artware

Christmas Coasters
   Carolers ................................. 125.00
   Holly & Bells .......................... 125.00
   Snowman ............................... 125.00

Cigarette Boxes, cov
   Double Boxes
      Daisy, #3666 ....................... 50.00
      Tropic Flower, #3781 ........... 75.00
   Pagoda Lid, Marsh Rose, #3799 ...................................... 75.00

Sunburst Artware ("Rainbow")
   Planter, swan, large ............... 400.00
   Vase
      Acanthus Leaf, #1540 ....... 125.00
      Deco, #1185, 9" h ............. 150.00
      Twist, #1124, 3 handles .... 125.00

Terra Rose Artware
   Bowl
      Lily of the Valley, green, #3620 ...................................... 75.00
      Seahorse, handles, green, #3671 ...................................... 50.00
   Candleholders, pr, Starfish, mauve, #3712 ........................................ 75.00
   Candy Jar, cov, bird finial, #3676 ...................................... 60.00
   Nautilus Shell, blue #3705 ...... 75.00
   Vase
      Butterfly, blue #3701 ......... 300.00
      Gazelle Head, blue #3708 ...................................... 400.00
   Watering Can, yellow tulip, #3511 ...................................... 150.00
   Watering Pitcher, blue tulip, #3211 ...................................... 50.00

Wigstand
   Female ................................... 250.00
   Male ..................................... 1,000.00

# Star Wars

**Collecting Hints:** With the 1999 release of *Star Wars, Episode I, The Phantom Menace*, many Star War collectibles are being offered for sale. Look for completeness when collecting vintage toys and figures.

When Kenner originally introduced Star War figures in 1977, the line contained only 12 figures. One way to identify those early figures when mint on the card is by the 12 photographs on the back. Collectors have nicknamed these "12 backs" to be able to tell the difference from "20 backs" and later issues.

If buying new release items, be aware their value is speculative and also be prepared to store them carefully for several years. Remember that the anticipated revenue from the new release is estimated to be $4 billion in sales. That should give collectors many buying opportunities.

**History:** *Star Wars*, 1977; *Empire Strikes Back*, 1980, and *Return of the Jedi*, 1983, have delighted movie-goers with special effects and stunning music as George Lucas has created a classic for all times. The new release, *Episode I, The Phantom Menace*, successfully takes the story line back in time to reveal the origins of Anakin Skywalker who later becomes that dastardly villian, Darth Vader.

While most collectors know the details of each of the movies, hopefully they will not be disappointed with the wide range of collectibles being offered for this release. The first three movies have yielded many collectibles and rare items now going to auction are showing signs of high prices and keen collector interest.

Besides the toys and collectibles licensed by Hasbro and Kenner, the fast food companies have also created items which collectors eagerly seek. So strap yourself down in the old Land Speeder and enjoy the collecting ride of the millennium.

**References:** Sharon Korbeck and Elizabeth Stephan, *Toys & Prices 2000*, 7th ed., Krause Publications, 1999; *Toy Shop Presents Star Wars Collectibles;* Stuart W. Wells, III, *Science Fiction Collectibles Identification & Price Guide*, Krause Publications, 1999.

**Periodical:** *The Star Wars Collector*, 20982 Homcrest Court, Ashburn, VA 22011.

**Collectors' Clubs:** Alabama Star Wars Club, eformatt@traveller.com; Carolina Star Wars Collector Club, rlcox@uncg.edu; clubtokyo.simplenet.com/cswee/; Chicago Area

Collectors Club, cesba@aol.com; members.aol.com/cesba/club.htm; Houston Star Wars Club, abrower@argohoustom.com; users.argolink.net/abrower/sw/index.html; Long Island's Network of Collectable Star Wars, Robot-Fan@aol.com; members.aol.com/robotfan/LINCS.html; Ohio Star Wars Collectors Club, webster@oswcc.com; www.osmcc.com; Official Star Wars Fan Club, P.O. Box 111000, Aurora, CO 80042-1000; Pennsylvania Star Wars Club, guzpro@ezonline.com; ajmay@postoffice.ptd.net; Seattle Area Lucasfilm Artifact Collectors Club, lopez@halcyon.com; www.tosrgus.com/seattle.html; The Wisconsin Collector Page, heybtbm@aol.com; members.aol.com/heybtbm/index.html.

**Note:** Loose, mint condition (LMC) means accompanied by all small accessory pieces, but not in orig package.

### Action Figure

Blue Snaggletooth, Kenner, 1977, only issued with playset............... 150.00
Bobba Fett, 3" h, 1978, MIP........ 920.00
C-3PO, Kenner, 1980, removable limbs
   LMC............................................. 8.00
   MIP............................................. 50.00
Chewbacca, Kenner, 1977, 3-3/4" h, MIP............................................. 220.00
Darth Vader, Kenner, 1977, 3-3/4" h, MIP............................................. 235.00
Death Squad Commander, Kenner, 1977, 3-3/4" h, MIP................. 175.00
Death Star Droid, 3" h, 1978, MIP ............................................. 155.00
Emperor's Royal Guard, loose ..... 14.00
*Empire Strikes Back,* six figures, MIP ............................................. 1,000.00
FX-7, Kenner, 1980
   LMC............................................. 8.00
   MIP............................................. 55.00
Greedo, Kenner, 1977
   LMC............................................. 15.00
   MIP............................................. 135.00
Greedo, JC Penney ...................... 45.00
Hammerhead, Kenner, 1977
   LMC............................................. 15.00
   MIP............................................. 135.00
Han & Tauntaun, Kenner, 1997, Toys R' Us exclsuive
   LMC............................................. 65.00
   MIP............................................. 185.00
Han Solo, Kenner, 1980, Hoth outfit
   LMC............................................. 10.00
   MIP............................................. 80.00
Imperial Commander, loose............ 8.00
Jawa, Kenner, 1977, 3-3/4" h
   Cloth cape, MIP ................... 220.00
   Vinyl cape, MIP ...................3,200.00
Lando Calrissian, Kenner, 1980
   LMC............................................. 10.00
   MIP............................................. 40.00
Luke Skywalker, Kenner, 1977, 3-3/4" h, MIP............................................. 320.00

Obi-Wan Kenobi, Kenner, 1977
   LMC............................................. 30.00
   MIP............................................. 300.00
Power Droid, loose ...................... 10.00
Princess Leia, Kenner, 1977, Benspin outfit
   LMC............................................. 20.00
   MIP............................................. 100.00
Red Snaggletooth, Kenner, 1977
   LMC............................................. 24.00
   MIP............................................. 140.00
R2-D2, Kenner, 1980, retractable sensor-scope
   LMC............................................. 10.00
   MIP............................................. 50.00
R5-D4, 3" h, 1978, MIP .............. 130.00
Sand Trooper, Diamond Exclusive, 12" h ............................................. 75.00
Snaggletooth, 3" h, 1978
   Blue body, Sears Exclusive, MIP ............................................. 200.00
   Red body, MIP ...................... 160.00
Snow Trooper, loose...................... 10.00
Stormtrooper, Kenner, 1977, 3-3/4" h, MIP............................................. 220.00
Tusken Raider, Kenner, 12" h
   With blaster rifle ...................... 50.00
   With gafi stick........................... 50.00
Walrus Man, Kenner, 1977
   LMC............................................. 25.00
   MIP............................................. 135.00
Wequay, loose........................... 7.50
Wicket, loose........................... 25.00
Yak Face, *Power of the Force,* MIP ............................................. 1,700.00
Yoda, loose ........................... 25.00
Zuckuss, loose........................... 12.00
**Activity Book,** Darth Vader, Black Falcon, Ltd., 1970, some pages completed in pencil ............................. 5.00
**Backpack,** Yoda, Sigma.............. 30.00

### Bank

Darth Vader, Leonard Silver, 1981, silver plated......................................... 95.00
Yoda, litho tin, combination dials ............................................. 25.00

**Book and Record Set, *Star Wars, Droid World, The Future Adventures,* ©MCMLSSSIII Lucasfilm Ltd., 33-1/3 rpm, $18.50.**

**Gum Card Wrapper, Topps, left, #5, $2.50; right, #4, $3.**

**Box,** Star War Cookies, no contents ............................................. 50.00
**Child's Book,** *Princess Leia*........ 25.00
**Carrying Case**
Empire Strikes Back
   Darth Vader, 1982................... 35.00
   Mini figure, 1980 ................... 30.00
Return of the Jedi
   C-390, 1983........................... 40.00
   Darth Vader, 1983................... 210.00
Star Wars ................................. 45.00
**Clock,** Bradley, 1980-84.............. 45.00
**Coat Rack,** Jedi ......................... 400.00
**Doll,** 12" h, sealed in orig box
Ben Kanobi................................. 550.00
Chewbacca ............................. 150.00
Darth Vader ............................. 450.00
Han Solo ................................. 800.00
Jawa ......................................... 350.00
Lea ......................................... 450.00
Luke Skywalker......................... 550.00
R2D2......................................... 300.00
**Gum Card Box,** 1st issue .......... 25.00
**Halloween Costume,** Darth Vader, 1977......................................... 45.00
**Light Saber,** inflatable, 1977, MIB ............................................. 250.00
Mailer
Han Solo, Fruit Loops ................. 35.00
Spirit Obi................................. 20.00
**Pencil Tray,** C-3PO, Sigma......... 50.00
Playset
Endor Ambush, 1997.................... 20.00
Ewok Village, Kenner, 1983
   LMC............................................. 30.00
   MIP............................................. 90.00
Hoth Battle, 1997...................... 20.00
Ice Planet Hoth Action Fleet, Galoob, 1996
   LMC............................................. 10.00
   MIP............................................. 25.00
Land of the Jawas, Kenner, 1978
LMC............................................. 50.00
MIP............................................. 200.00
Snowspeeder, Action Fleet, Galoom, 1995
LMC............................................. 8.00
MIP............................................. 16.00

### Poster

Boba Fett, 10th anniversary ....... 195.00
Burger King, 1978-80 .................. 10.00
Empire Strikes Back
   Advance ................................. 100.00
   Re-release, 1981-82 ............... 35.00
**Nestea**, 1980............................. 10.00

Revenge of the Jedi
   With date ................................ 150.00
   Without date ........................... 200.00
Return of the Jedi
   1986 re-release ........................ 80.00
   Special edition ........................... 20.00
Star Wars
   Advance, mylar ................... 1,200.00
   Second advance .................... 175.00
**Portfolio,** art, Darth Vader, sealed with medallion and two prints, 1979 ............................................. 250.00
**Press Kit,** first movie ................... 90.00
**Print,** lithograph, Willitts, framed
   Death Star Scene ................... 150.00
   Jabba's Throne Room ............ 150.00
   Rancor Creature ..................... 150.00
   Speeder Bike Chase .............. 150.00
**Pulltoy,** R2-D2, talking ............... 400.00
**Puppet,** Chewbacca, 40" h, plush, Regal Limited ...................... 1,925.00
**Robot,** R2 D2, remote controlled ............................................... 30.00
**String Dispenser,** R2-D2, Sigma ............................................... 45.00
**Store Display**, designed to hold orig 12 action figures ......................... 575.00
**Tape Dispenser,** C-3PO, Sigma... 80.00
**Vehicle**
Darth Vader's TIE Fighter, Kenner, 1978
   LMC ......................................... 60.00
   MIP .......................................... 150.00
Empire Rebel Transport, MIB ...... 150.00
Jawa Sandcrawler, contents sealed, MIB ...................................... 1,000.00
Jedi AT-AT Walker, MIB ............... 325.00
Jedi Millennium Falcon .............. 250.00
Jedi Speederbike, MIB ................. 35.00
Landspeeder, Kenner, 1978, 5" l, diecast
   LMC ......................................... 30.00
   MIP .......................................... 70.00
Landspeeder, Kenner, 1978
   LMC ......................................... 20.00
   MIP .......................................... 75.00
Landspeeder, Kenner, 1996
   LMC ........................................... 6.00
   MIP .......................................... 15.00
Millennium Falcon, lights, orig sealed box ....................................... 100.00
X-Wing Fighter, Kenner, white, 1978
   LMC ......................................... 50.00
   MIP .......................................... 320.00
**Weapon,** Blaster, Kenner, 1977
   LMC ......................................... 25.00
   MOC ........................................ 85.00

# Stereo-Viewers

**Collecting Hints:** Condition is the key to determining price. Undamaged wooden-hood models are scarce and demand a premium price if made of bird's-eye maple. The presence of all-original parts increases the value. Plentiful engraving adds 20% to 30%.

Longer lenses are better than smaller ones. Lenses held in place by metal are better than those shimmed with wood.

Because aluminum was the same price as silver in the late 19th century, aluminum viewers often are the more collectible.

**History:** There are many different types of stereo viewers. The familiar table viewer with an aluminum or wooden hood was jointly invented in 1860 by Oliver Wendell Holmes and Joseph Bates, a Boston photographer. This type of viewer also was made in a much scarcer pedestal model.

Three companies—Keystone, Griffith & Griffith, and Underwood & Underwood—produced hundreds of thousands of hand viewers between 1899 and 1905.

In the mid-1850s, a combination stereo viewer and picture magnifier was developed in France and eventually was made in England and the United States. The instrument, which was called a Graphascope, usually consisted of three pieces and could be folded for storage. When set up, it had two round lenses for stereo viewing, a large round magnifying lens to view cabinet photographs, and a slide, often with opaque glass, for viewing stereo glass slides. The height was adjustable.

A rotary or cabinet viewer was made from the late 1850s to about 1870. Becker is the best-known maker. The standing floor models hold several hundred slides; the table models hold 50 to 100.

From the late 1860s to 1880s, there were hundreds of different viewer designs. Models had folding wires, collapsible cases (Cortascope), pivoting lenses to view postcards (Sears' Graphascope), and telescoping card holders. The cases, which also became ornate, were made of silver, nickel, or pearl and were trimmed in velvets and rosewood.

**Reference:** John Waldsmith, *Stereo Views*, Wallace-Homestead, 1991.

**Collectors' Clubs:** National Stereoscopic Association, P.O. Box 14801, Columbus, OH 43214; Stereo Club of Southern California, P.O. Box 2368, Culver City, CA 90231.

Corte-Scope, folding aluminum or metal, came in box with views, c1914 ...................................... 50.00
Hand, common maker
   Aluminum hood, folding handle ............................................... 65.00

**Walnut base and standard, teak top, 15-3/4" h, $95.**

Bird's eye maple hood, folding handle ............................................. 85.00
Walnut, screw on handle, velvet hood ........................................ 85.00
Wide hood for people who wear glasses, dark brown or green metal ............................................. 80.00
Hand, scissors device to focus, groove and wire device to hold card ............................................. 120.00
Pedestal
   Foreign, French or English, nickel plated with velvet hood .......... 300.00
   Keystone, school and library type, black crinkle metal finish with light ............................................. 85.00
Sculptoscope, Whiting, counter top style, penny operated ............ 500.00
Stand, Bates-Holmes, paper or wood hood ...................................... 150.00
Stereographascope, Sears Best, lens rotates to allow viewing of photos or postcards ................................ 90.00
Telebinocular, binocular style, black crinkle metal finish, excellent optics, came with book-style box ........ 50.00

# Stereographs

**Collecting Hints:** Value is determined by condition, subject, photographer (if famous), rarity, and age—prior to 1870 or after 1935. A revenue stamp on the back indicates the item dates between 1864 and 1866, the years a federal war tax was imposed. Lithograph printed cards have very little value.

Collect stereographs that are in good condition or better, unless the image is extremely rare. Very good condition means some wear on the mount and a little dirt on the photo. Folds, marks on the photo, or badly worn mounts reduce values by at least 50%. Faded or light photos are worth less than bright ones.

Don't try to clean cards or straighten them. Curved cards were made to heighten the stereo effect, an improvement made in 1880.

It pays to shop around to get the best price for common cards, but it is a good idea to buy rarer cards when you see them since they are harder to find and values are increasing annually. Dealers who are members of the National Stereoscopic Association are very protective of their reputation and their establishments are good places for the novice collector to visit.

Using the resources of the public library to thoroughly study the subject matter you are collecting will help you assemble a meaningful collection.

**History:** Glass and paper stereographs, also known as stereo views, stereo view cards, or stereoscope cards, were first issued in the United States in 1854. From the late 1850s through the 1930s, the stereograph was an important visual record of every major event, famous person, comic situation, and natural scene. It was the popular news and entertainment medium until replaced by movies, picture magazines, and radio.

The major early publishers were Anthony (1859-1873), Kilburn (1865-1907), Langeheim (1854-1861), and Weller (1861-1875). Between 1880 and 1910, the market was controlled by large firms, including Davis (Kilburn), Griffith & Griffith, International View Company, Keystone, Stereo Travel, Underwood & Underwood, Universal Photo Art, and H. C. White.

**References:** William C. Darrah, *Stereo Views*, published by author, out of print; —, *World of Stereographs*, published by author, out of print; John S. Waldsmith, *Stereo Views*, Wallace-Homestead, 1991.

**Collectors' Clubs:** National Stereoscopic Association, Box 14801, Columbus, OH 43214; Stereo Club of Southern California, P.O. Box 2368, Culver City, CA 90231.

**Notes:** Prices given are for cards in very good condition, i.e., some wear and slight soiling. Pieces in excellent condition bring 25% more; those with a perfect image and mount are worth twice as much. Reverse the mathematical process for fair, i.e., moderate soiling, some damage to mount, minor glue marks, some foxing (brown spots) and poor folded mount, very dirty and damage to tone or both images.

**Animal**

Birds, Hursts', 2nd series, #7, birds in tree ............................................. 5.00
Cat
    Keystone #2314 ......................... 6.50
    Keystone #9651, man and cat ................................................. 5.00
    Soule, The Pickwickian Ride .... 20.00
Dog
    Kilburn #1644, "Home Protection," dog close up ............................. 6.50
    U & U, the puppies singing school ................................................. 5.00
    Universal #3231 ........................ 5.00
Farm Yard, Kilburn #739, sheep and cows, 1870s .............................. 5.00
Horses, Schreiber & Sons, Jarvis and sulky, early .............................. 18.00
Walrus, Keystone #V21232, Bronx Zoo ................................................. 4.50
Zoo, London Stereo Company, animals in London Zoo .......................... 10.00

**Astronomy**

Comet, Keystone #16645, Morehouse's ................................................. 9.50
Mars, Keystone #16767T, the planet ................................................. 6.50
Moon
    Beer Bros. 1866, photo by Rutherford ................................................. 15.00
    Kilburn #2630, full moon ............ 6.50
    Soule #602, last quarter ............. 8.00
Planetarium, Keystone #32688, Adler's, Chicago .................................. 10.00

**Aviation**

Air Mail Plane
    Keystone #29446, at Cleveland ................................................. 30.00
    Keystone #32372, Inaugural, Ford Tri-motor, air-rail service NY to LA, 7/2/29 ...................................... 20.00
Aviators, Keystone #26408t, 6 men who first circled earth ..................... 25.00

Keystone View Co., #P239, Christopher Columbus Flagship, history on back, $6.50.

Keystone View Co., #2201, "As Good As Gold" poem in German on back, $3.50.

Balloon, Anthony #4114, Prof. Lowe's flight from 6th Ave. in NYC..... 100.00
Dirigibles, and Zeppelins, Keystone
    #17397, *Los Angeles* at Lakehurst ............................................. 45-50.00
    #17398, *The Los Angeles* ........ 45.00
    #18000, flying over German town ................................................. 6.50
    #32277, *Gray Zeppelin* in hanger at Lakehurst, NJ ........................... 35.00
    #32740, framework of *ZRS-4, Akron* ................................................. 65.00
    #V19216, 1918, *R-34* at Mineola, from WWI set ......................... 15.00
Doolittle, Keystone #28031, Major Doolittle, 1931 ......................... 65.00
General View, Keystone #32785, five biplanes fly over Chicago's field museum .................................. 20.00
Lindbergh, Keystone
    #28029, in plane with wife ....... 55.00
    #30262T, next to Spirit of St. Louis ................................................. 30.00
Plan, Keystone
    #18920, Michelin bomber ........ 20.00
    #19049, Nieuport ..................... 10.00
    #V18921, twin seat fighter ......... 9.00
Wright Bros., Keystone #V96103, in flight at Ft. Meyers .................. 85.00

**Blacks**

Keystone #9506, "We done all dis'a'morning," picking cotton ... 6.50
Kilburn #14317, boy and mule ....... 3.00
Singley
    #10209, "One never came up," swimmers ................................. 12.00
    #10217, "One got an upper cut," fighting ................................... 10.00
U & U, "Cotton is King," picking ..... 5.00
U & U, "Keystone, Kilburn," Whiting, etc., cheating at cards, stealing millions, infidelity, etc. ................... 15.00

Wm. G. Preston, World's Peace Jubilee, coliseum, 1872, $5.

Whiting
#960, "There's a watermelon smiling on the vine" .................. 10.00
#961, "Happiest Coon" ............. 8.00

### Cave

Keystone
#9586, man in front of Great Oregon Caves ..................... 6.50
#33516, int. of Crystal Springs Cave, Carlsbad ..................... 4.50
U & U, Luray Caverns .............. 8.00
Waldack, 1866, Mammoth Cave, typical early magnesium light view...... 15.00

### Christmas

Brownies & Santa, Universal #4679, Graves, sleigh in foreground ..... 20.00
Children with Tree
Griffith #16833, children's Christmas dinner ........................ 18.00
Keystone, 1895, #987, Santa in front of fireplace ................. 15.00
Santa coming down chimney, Keystone #11434, Santa with toys ........... 25.00
Santa with Toys, Keystone 1898, #9445, Santa loaded with toys............. 15.00

### Comics

Bicycle Bum, Graves #4551-58, "Weary Willie," 4 card set ..................... 20.00
Drinking
Kilburn 1892, #7348, "Brown just in from the club".................. 3.00
R.Y. Young 1901,woman drinking, two cards .................. 16.50
U & U, 1897, man sneaks in after drinking, 2 card set ................... 7.50
English, boy carves roast, "The Attack," ivory mount, hand tinted ............ 5.00
Humor
Keystone #2346-7, before (cuddling) and after (reading) marriage.... 70.00
U & U, 1904, "Four queens and a jack," 4 girls and a jackass........ 6.50
Infidelity
"Foolin-around," 1910, husband fools around with his secretary, 12 cards ...................... 48.00
Keystone #12312-22, The French Cook-Communist version .................. 50.00
U & U
Sneaking-in, 1897, caught by wife after night on the town........... 8.00
The French Cook, 10 card set ...................... 50.00
Romance
U & U, Going with Stream," hugging couple ....................... 6.50
Weller #353, "Unexpected," necking ...................... 5.00
Rumors, H. C. White, 5576-5578, quickest way to spread news: "Tell a graph, tell a phone, tell a woman," 3 card set ..................... 20.00
Sentimental, American Stereo, #2001-2012, He goes to war; wounded; returns; reunited, etc., 12 card set ...................... 60.00
Wedding Set, White #5510-19, getting ready, wedding, reception, alone in bedroom................... 45.00

### Disaster

Boston Fire, 1872, Soule, ruins ....... 8.00

Chicago Fire, 1871, Lovejoy & Foster, ruins .................. 9.00
Galveston Flood, 1900, Graves, ruins ..................... 20.00
Johnstown Flood, ruins
Barker ....................... 9.00
U & U ....................... 7.00
Mill Creek Flood, 1874, popular series, house ...................... 5.00
Portland Fire, 1866, Soule #469, ruins ...................... 8.00
St. Pierre Eruption, Kilburn #14941, ruins ...................... 3.00
San Francisco Earthquake Scenes
Keystone #13264, Market St...... 9.00
U & U #8180, California St....... 16.50
White #8713, wrecked houses. 20.00
Train Wreck, Dole.................... 50.00
Worcester, MA, Flood, 1876, Lawrence ...................... 5.00

### Doll

Graves #4362, Sunday School Class ...................... 20.00
Kilburn
#15, tired of play ..................... 15.00
When will Santa come?........... 12.00
U & U
#6922, playing doctor.............. 15.00
#6952, girl asleep with cat and doll ...................... 9.00
Webster & Albee #160, doll's maypole ...................... 20.00

### Entertainer

Actress, J. Gurney & Son, 1870s, Mrs. Scott or Mrs. Roland, etc. ........ 10.00
Dancers, Keystone #33959, Bali, Dutch Indies ...................... 2.00
Natives, Keystone #16423, Java, good costumes .................. 3.00
Singer
J. Gurney & Son, Annie Cary... 15.00
James Cremer, opera, studio pose in costume .................. 12.00

### Exposition

NY Sanitary Fair, Anthony #1689-2864, fountain view .................. 15.00
1872, World Peace Jubilee, Boston Pollock, interior view .................. 8.00
1876, U.S. Close Up Centennial, Centennial Photo Co
Common view of grounds and buildings ...................5.00-10.00
Corliss Engine.................... 12.00
Monorail ...................... 65.00
Statue of Liberty..................... 85.00
1894
California Mid-Winter, Kilburn #9474-2984 ...................... 12.00
Columbian Chicago, Kilburn
Most views .................. 7.00
Ferris Wheel.................. 10.00
1901, Pan American Buffalo, Kilburn
Most views .................. 6.50
President McKinley .................. 9.00
1904, Louisiana Purchase Exposition, St. Louis
Graves for Universal Photo or U & U ...................... 8.00
White #8491, Education & Manufacturing buildings .................. 8.00

Whiting, #620, Missouri Fruit Exhibit ...................... 12.00
1905, Lewis & Clark Centennial, Portland, Watson Fine Art #34, building ...................... 9.00
1907, Jamestown Exposition, Keystone #14219, life saving demonstration ...................... 7.00
1908, West Michigan State Fair, Keystone #21507 ...................... 12.00
1933, Century of Progress, Chicago, Keystone #32993, Lief Ericksen Dr. ...................... 20.00

### Hunting and Fishing

Bass, Ingersoll #3159, string of bass ...................... 10.00
Deer, Keystone #26396, hunters and kill ...................... 5.00
Halibut, Keystone #22520, commercial fishing ...................... 5.00
Moose, Keystone #9452, 1899, big game kill ...................... 6.50
Trout, Kilburn, #115, a day's catch . 5.00
Wildcat, Keystone 312264, man shoots sleeping wildcat...................... 6.50

### Indian

Burge, J.C., Apaches bathing.... 125.00
Continental Stereo Co., Pueblo eating bread ...................... 65.00
Griffith #11873, Esquimau at St. Louis Fair...................... 8.00
Hayes, F. J.
#865, Crow burial ground........ 25.00
#1742, Sioux ...................... 30.00
Jackson, Wm. H., #202, Otoe, with bow ...................... 100.00
Keystone
#23095, Chief Black Hawk ...... 12.00
#23118, Indian girl ...................... 5.00
#V2181, Blackfeet...................... 9.00
Montgomery Ward, squaw ............ 6.50
Soule #1312, Pieute squaw .......... 60.00
U & U
Hopi ...................... 12.00
Wolpi...................... 10.00
White #12279, pueblo .................. 15.00

### Mining

Alaska Gold Rush
Keystone
#9191, men with supplies getting ready to climb the "golden stairs" at Chilkoot Pass ............... 9.00
#9195, preparing to climb the golden stairs ..................... 9.00
#21100, panning for gold ... 12.00
U & U #10655, looking into glory hole ...................... 15.00
Universal, Graves, 1902, man working sluice, scarce card by scarce publisher...................... 40.00
Easter, Anthony #474, working gold chute...................... 45.00
Gold Hill, Housewerth #743, city overview...................... 75.00
Hydraulic, Housewerth #799, water spraying...................... 70.00
Virginia City
Housewerth #713, street view . 95.00
Watkins
Opera House ...................... 95.00
Panorama, new series ...... 125.00

## Miscellaneous

Auto
Keystone #22143, employees leaving Ford.............................8.00
U & U, early auto in Los Angeles, 1903..........................20.00

Beach scenes, H. C. White, #476, bathers, Atlantic City.....................5.00

Bicycles
Kilburn #11924, women and bike .............................................6.50
Thorne, big two wheeler, early 1870s ...........................................45.00

Circus
U & U, Chicago.......................20.00
Windsor & Whipple, Olean, NY, people with elephant...................40.00

Crystal Palace, yellow mount, outside general view..........................25.00

Firefighting
Early 18702, unknown maker, close view of pumpers....................40.00
Keystone #11684, action view of pumpers..............................25.00

Glass Stereos
Foreign Scenes.......................75.00
United States Scenes...............80.00

Groups, various, Rogers statuaries ...............................................9.00

Gypsies, unknown maker, in front of tent ......................................20.00

Hawaii, Keystone
#10156, hula girls.....................9.00
#10162, Waikiki Beach...............9.50

Lighthouses
Keystone #29207.......................5.00
Williams, Minot Ledge Light.....20.00

New York City, Anthony #3938......20.00

Opium Dens
X82, 1900................................25.00
Unknown Maker, two tier bed, pipe for smoking opium ...................60.00

Prisons, Pach, view of cabinets of rifles .............................................15.00

Tinted Views
Foreign...................................6.50
United States..........................10.00

Toy Train, Keystone P-21329, boy playing with Lionel trains ................25.00

Tunnel, Ward #808 Hoosac tunnel, just completed ................................15.00

## National Park

Death Valley, Keystone #32666, pool ...............................................9.00

Garden of the Gods, Rodeo McKenney, Pike's Peak ...............................5.00

Grand Teton, Wm. H. Jackson, #503, average for this prized photographer ...............................................20.00

Yellowstone
Jackson, Wm. H., #422............15.00
Universal, peak view..................5.00

Yosemite
Keystone #4401, Nevada Falls ..5.00
Kilburn #9284, Bridal Veil Falls ..5.00
Reilly, tourists at Yosemite Falls .8.00
U & U, Glacier Point ..................5.00

## Niagara Falls

Anthony #3731, falls.....................5.00
Barker, ice bridge .......................2.00
U & U
Tourist....................................4.00

Whirlpool rapids........................2.00
White #7, tourists, 1903.................5.00

## Occupational

Blacksmith, Keystone #18206, many tools in picture .........................5.00

Cowboys, Keystone
#12465, Kansas.......................7.00
#13641, Yellowstone, Montana .............................................7.50

Farming, Kilburn #1796, hay, 1870s .............................................7.00

Fireman
G. K. Proctor, Mid-distance hook & ladder, horse drawn ...............35.00
1870s, good view of steam pumper .............................................45.00

Milkman, Keystone #P-26392, horse-drawn wagon .........................10.00

Mill, U & U, linen factory, typical industrial view ...............................3.00

Store, Keystone #18209, grocery store int...................................15.00

## Oil

Pennsylvania
Detlor & Waddell, #76, burning tanks .............................................15.00
Keystone #20352T, shooting a well .............................................5.00
Robbins #32, Triumph Hill........13.00
Robbins #88, gas well ..............8.00
Wilt Brothers, Allegheny area.....8.00
Texas, Keystone #34864, tanks near Kilgore.................................6.50

## Person, Famous

Barton, Clara, Keystone #28002, founder of American Red Cross .............................................60.00

Buffalo Bill, American Scenery #1399, on horseback in New York City .............................................50.00

Buntline, Ned, J. Gurney, portrait .............................................150.00

Burbank, Luther, Keystone #16746, with a cactus ................................8.00

Bryan, W. J., Keystone #15539, on way to hotel in NYC .......................30.00

Coolidge, President, Keystone
#26303, President and Cabinet50.00
#26303 .................................30.00
#28004, at desk .......................12.00

Custar, General
Lovejoy & Foster, with bear he killed .............................................350.00
Taylor #2438, with his dog in camp .............................................500.00

Czar of Russia, U & U, with President of France...............................10.00

Edison, Thomas
Keystone, #V28007, in lab.....100.00
U & U, in lab..........................150.00

Edison, Ford and Firestone, Keystone
#18551 ............................75-125.00
#45612 ............................75-125.00

Eisenhower, President, Keystone, at table with microphones, about 1954 .............................................250.00

Farqutt, Admiral, Anthony, from Prominent Portrait Series...................40.00

Ford, Henry, Keystone #28023 .....60.00

Gandhi, Mahatma, Keystone #33852, portrait.................................35.00

Gehrig, Lou, Keystone #32597, baseball player .............................200.00

Grant, President, Bierstadt Bros., on Mount Washington .................75.00

Hayes, B., President, party at Hastings .............................................100.00

Harding, W., President, addressing boy scouts ...............................20.00

Hoover, President, Keystone #28012, close portrait ..........................35.00

Kettering, C. F., Keystone, inventor of auto self starter .....................60.00

Kingman, Seth, no maker, famous California Trapper .....................120.00

Lincoln, Abraham, Anthony
Funeral, #4596....................50-65.00
President, #2969, scarce, highly prized view .........................900.00

Marconi, Keystone #V11969, radio inventor ...............................45.00

McKinley, President, Keystone, Kilburn, U & U, most views ..................15.00

Morse, Samuel, J. Gurney .........225.00

Queen Victoria, U & U 1897, having breakfast with Princesses .......35.00

Rockefeller, J.D., Keystone #V11961, world's richest man.................25.00

Rogers, Will, Keystone #32796, at 1932 Chicago Democratic Convention .............................................75.00

Roosevelt, Theodore, President
Keystone, Kilburn, U & U .......30.00
U & U, on horseback ...............15.00

Ruth, Babe, Keystone #32590.......250.00

Sarazen, Gene, Keystone #32436, golfer....................................35.00

Schmeling, Max, Keystone #28028, boxer.....................................75.00

Shaw, Dr. Anna, Keystone #V26151, suffrage leader .......................25.00

Shaw, George Bernard, Keystone #34505, on ship ......................60.00

Strauss, Johann, Gurney .............90.00

Taft, President, U & U #10062, at desk .............................................20.00

Thomas, Lowell, Keystone #32812, world travel expert and newsman .............................................50.00

Twain, Mark
Evans & Soule.......................350.00
U & U #8010 or White #13055, in bed writing..........................250.00

Washington, Booker T., Keystone #11960, with Andrew Carnegie .............................................70.00

Wirewalkers, Barker
Bellini on wire..........................10.00
Blondin on rope .......................15.00

Young, Brigham, C. W. Carter, bust portrait....................................20.00

## Photographer, Famous

Brady, Anthony
1863, Tom Thumb Wedding... 125.00
#428, Captain Custer with Confederate prisoner..........................900.00
#3376, Jeff Davis Mansion.......50.00

Houseworth, San Francisco, e.g.,
#150, show photo studio .......150.00
#429, Golden Gate ...............45.00

Langenheim, 1856, Trenton Falls, typical view, but scarce, on glass .............................................135.00

Muybridge
#318, The Golden Gate............ 80.00
#880, Geyer Springs................ 45.00
#1623, Indian scouts............. 250.00
O'Sullivan, T.H., Anthony #826, Men's
Quarters................................... 60.00
Pond, C.L., #786, Mirror Lake....... 30.00
Watkins, C.E.
Panoramic, #1338, from Telegraph
Hill.......................................... 55.00
San Francisco street scene, e.g.,
#767, panorama from Russian Hill
................................................ 55.00
Trains..................................... 150.00
Virginia City, NV, Panorama, new
series........................................ 90.00
Yosemite series, #1066, Yosemite
Falls....................................25-30.00

### Photographica

Camera, Houseworth #1107, wet plate
camera in Yosemite................75.00
Comic, Keystone #423, many viewers
and cards in this comic "mouse" rou-
tine .......................................... 15.00
Gallery, American scenery, street with
gallery sign visible ................... 50.00
Photo Wagon, Weitfle's Photograph Van,
close view with sign on wagon
................................................ 125.00
Photography with stereo camera above
street, Keystone #8283 ............ 65.00
Viewing, Keystone #11917, looking
through viewer ......................... 10.00

### Railroad

American stereo, view in Penn Station
................................................ 15.00
Centennial, 1876 Monorail, World's Fair,
scarce ....................................... 65.00
Keystone
#2367, loop at Georgetown ....... 5.00
#7090, interior of Baldwin Works
................................................ 8.00
#37509, The Chief, 1930s........ 75.00
Kilburn
#135, pushing car up Jacob's Lad-
der................................................ 7.00
#432, large side view of locomotive
................................................ 35.00
#779, train with engineer posed,
1870........................................ 65.00
#2941, silver ore train................. 5.00
U & U
#52, train going through Pillars of
Hercules...................................... 7.00
#6218, Royal Gorge................... 5.00
Universal Photo Art #2876, Columbian
Express ..................................... 20.00
Unknown Maker, dramatic close-up of a
1870 locomotive....................... 75.00

### Religious

Bates, open Bible, St. Luke ........... 3.00
Keystone, Billy Sunday, evangelist
................................................ 20.00
Keystone, Kilburn, U & U, Holy Land
................................................ 2.00
Pope............................................... 7.50
Life of Christ, unmarked, usually set of
photos of drawings or lithographed
set, per set of 10-12................ 10.00
Shakers, Irving, view of people..... 65.00

### Risque

1820's, unmarked, typical "Peek-a-boo"
................................................ 20.00
Griffith #2427, two girls, arms around
each other, lightly clad............. 20.00
Keystone, #9489, school girls retiring, in
nightgowns ................................ 7.00
Nude, early, bare breast ............... 45.00
Nude, 1920s or 1930s ................. 40.00

### Sets

Boxer Rebellion, U & U 1901, 72 cards
................................................ 200.00
Bullfight, U & U, set of 15 ........... 100.00
China, Stereo Travel, set of 100,
unusual subject....................... 400.00
Egypt, U & U set of 100 .............. 310.00
France
Stereo Travel, set of 30 ............ 70.00
U & U, set of 100.................... 250.00
Glacier Park, Forsyth, set of 30
................................................ 150.00
India, U & U, set of 100 .............. 250.00
Italy, U & U, set of 100 ............... 200.00
Jerusalem, U & U, set of 30.......... 40.00
Switzerland, U & U, set of 100, guide-
book and maps....................... 200.00
United States, U & U, set of 100, good
U.S. tour ................................. 350.00
Wild Flowers, Keystone, 100, hand
tinted ...................................... 400.00
World Tour, Keystone
Set of 200, trip from U.S. around
world and back ...................... 350.00
Set of 400.............................. 700.00
Set of 600, trip from U.S. around
world and back, oak cabinet
................................................ 950.00
Yellowstone, U & U, set of 30........ 95.00
Yosemite, U & U, set of 30 .......... 125.00

### Ship

Battleships
Griffith #2535, 1902, *USS Brooklyn*
................................................ 8.00
Universal Photo Art, *USS Raleigh*
................................................ 9.00
Cruiser, White #7422, 1901, *USS New
York*........................................ 10.00
Deck View, American Stereo, 1899, *USS
Iowa* ........................................ 8.00
Foreign, Keystone #16090, *HMS Albe-
marie* ...................................... 6.50
Riverboat, Anthony #7567, sternwheeler
at Cincinnati ............................ 25.00
Sailboat, Anthony #22................... 20.00
Steamships
Anthony #8691, *Bristol,* good aver-
age early view......................... 15.00
London Stereo, *Great Eastern*, early
view.......................................... 75.00
Submarine, Keystone #16667, at San
Diego ......................................... 8.00

### Survey

Amundsen, Keystone, #13327, at
Antoretie Glacier, 1911 ............. 7.00
Gerlache, Keystone #13328, hunting
seals at South Pole .................... 6.50
Hayden, Jackson #796, people view
................................................ 25.00
Lloyd, Grand Canyon, U & U, at work on
mountain, 1903 ....................... 25.00

Perry, Greenland, Keystone #13325,
ships ......................................... 6.50
Powell, #13, the wall .................... 20.00
Wheeler, William Bell
#14, Canon de Chelle, wall, 1873
................................................ 40.00
#15, Canon de Chelle, wall, 1872
................................................ 25.00
Tissue, French
Balloon, close view ................... 70.00
Diablo, 1870s, devils, skeletons,
etc., good shape with lots of "evil"
................................................ 30.00
Interior scene, 1870s, minor dam-
age, viewable ............................ 7.50
Interior scene, 1870s, nice stereo,
pinpricked, no tears................. 20.00
Wedding, Young #7 ................. 10.00

### War

Boer, U & U, artillery firing............. 9.00
Boxer Rebellion, U & U, 1901......... 9.00
Civil War
Anthony
#3031, Dunlop Home.......... 20.00
#3365, Brady, Libby Prison, yel-
low mount........................... 25.00
#3406, chair in which Lincoln was
shot .................................... 60.00
Gardner, #237, home of Rebel
sharpshooter.......................... 50.00
Taylor & Huntington
#458, Confederate fortifications
................................................ 25.00
#2557, pontoon boats......... 25.00
#6705, powder magazine..... 35.00
Russo-Japanese, U & U #4380, general
view of Port Arthur .................... 5.00
Spanish American, U & U............. 12.00
World War I
Set of 100............................. 175.00
Set of 200............................. 300.00
Set of 300............................. 400.00

### Whaling

Freeman, beached whales........... 50.00
Keystone
#14768T, floating whale station
................................................ 10.00
#V27198T, whalers cruising....... 8.00
Nickerson, beached whales......... 70.00
Unknown maker, beached whale
................................................ 30.00

# Sterling Silver Flatware

**Collecting Hints:** Focus on one pattern by one maker. The same pattern
names were sometimes used by
several makers for similar pattern
designs. Always check the marks
carefully; several thousand patterns
were manufactured. Popularity of
pattern, not necessarily age, is the
key to pricing.

A monogram on a piece may
reduce its value slightly. Monograms
on sterling occasionally can be
removed. Some owners of sterling

silver start their collections by inheriting family silver and often treasure monograms denoting special family members. Silver flatware sold in sets often brings less than pieces sold individually. The reason is that many buyers are looking to replace pieces or add place settings to a pattern they already own. Sterling silver sets certainly retain their value better than silver-plated sets. A number of dealers specializing in replacement services have evolved over the past several years. Many advertise in The Antique Trader Weekly and on the Internet.

**History:** The silver table service became a hallmark of elegance during the Victorian era. In the homes of the wealthy, sterling silver services made by Gorham, Kirk, Tiffany, and Towle were used. Silver place settings became part of a young girl's hope chest and a staple wedding gift. Sterling silver consists of 925 parts silver and 75 parts copper per 1,000 parts sterling.

When electroplating became popular, silver-plated flatware allowed the common man to imitate the wealthy. Silver-plated flatware has a thin layer of silver which has been plated onto a base metal by a chemical process known as electrolysis. The base metal is usually britannia (an alloy of tin, antimony, and copper) or white metal (an alloy of tin, copper, and lead or bismuth). Leading silver-plate manufacturers are Alvin, Gorham, International Silver Co. (a modern company created by a merger of many older companies), Oneida, Reed & Barton, William Rogers, and Wallace.

**References:** Maryanne Dolan, *1830s-1990s American Sterling Silver Flatware*, Books Americana, 1993; Marilyn E. Dragowick (ed.), *Metalwares Price Guide*, Antique Trader Books, 1995; Tere Hagan, *Silverplated Flatware*, Revised 4th ed., Collector Books, 1990, 1995 value update; Joel Langford, *Silver: A Practical Guide to Collecting Silverware and Identifying Hallmarks*, Chartwell Books, 1991; Dorothy T. and H. Ivan Rainwater, *American Silverplate*, Schiffer Publishing, 1988; *Sterling Silver, Silverplate, and Souvenir Spoons with Prices*, revised ed., L-W Book Sales, 1987, 1994 value update; Charles Venable, *Silver in America 1840-1940*, Chronicle Books, 1994.

**Periodicals:** *Silver Magazine*, P.O. Box 9690, Rancho Santa Fe, CA 92067; *Silver News*, 1112 16th St. NW, Ste 240, Washington, DC 20036; *Silver Update*, P.O. Box 960, Funkstown, MD 21734.

**Collectors' Club:** New York Silver Society, 242 E. 7th St., #5, New York, NY 10009; Society of American Silversmiths, P.O. Box 3599, Cranston, RI 02910.

Abbreviations: fb = flat blade
fh = filled handle
gw = gold washed
hh = hollow handle
ind = individual
mono = monogram
Place Setting = fork, knife, salad fork, and teaspoon

### Bridal Rose, Alvin

| | |
|---|---|
| Baked Potato Fork, mono | 95.00 |
| Beef Fork, pierced, mono | 195.00 |
| Berry Spoon, large | 300.00 |
| Berry Spoon, medium | 250.00 |
| Bouillon Soup Spoon, mono | 50.00 |
| Butter Knife, master | 50.00 |
| Cake Server | 145.00 |
| Cheese Scoop, mono | 250.00 |
| Citrus Spoon | 35.00 |
| Cocktail Fork, gw, mono | 50.00 |
| Coffee Spoon, mono | 24.00 |
| Dinner Fork, mono | 100.00 |
| Dinner Knife, mono | 100.00 |
| Gumbo Spoon | 40.00 |
| Jam Spoon | 55.00 |
| Pickle Fork, long | 195.00 |
| Pie Server | 595.00 |
| Salad Fork, mono | 120.00 |
| Sauce Ladle, mono | 100.00 |
| Serving Spoon, mono | 100.00 |
| Soup Spoon, mono | 80.00 |
| Sugar Spoon, mono | 80.00 |
| Teaspoon, mono | 35.00 |

### Buttercup, Gorham

| | |
|---|---|
| Asparagus Fork | 250.00 |
| Baby Fork | 40.00 |
| Baked Potato Fork | 70.00 |
| Beef Fork, not pierced | 80.00 |
| Beef Fork, pierced | 100.00 |
| Bouillon Spoon | 24.00 |
| Butter Knife, ind, fb | 40.00 |
| Butter Pick, twisted | 40.00 |
| Candle Snuffer | 70.00 |
| Casserole Spoon, stainless bowl | 50.00 |
| Cheese Knife, with pick | 90.00 |
| Cheese Scoop, large | 130.00 |
| Coffee Spoon | 20.00 |
| Cold Meat Fork | 80.00 |
| Confection Spoon, gw, pierced | 300.00 |
| Cream Soup Spoon, mono | 40.00 |
| Crumber, 11-3/4" | 500.00 |
| Cucumber Server | 350.00 |
| Demitasse Spoon, gw | 25.00 |
| Dessert Spoon | 30.00 |
| Dinner Bell | 65.00 |
| Dinner Fork | 40.00 |

| | |
|---|---|
| Entree Server, flat, stainless blade | 50.00 |
| Fish Fork | 100.00 |
| Fish Fork, gw | 95.00 |
| Fruit Knife, plated blade | 50.00 |
| Fish Slice, mono | 200.00 |
| Grapefruit Spoon | 40.00 |
| Gumbo Soup Spoon | 60.00 |
| Ice Cream Fork | 35.00 |
| Ice Cream Slice | 145.00 |
| Ice Cream Slice, hh, plated blade | 250.00 |
| Ice Cream Spoon | 70.00 |
| Iced Tea Spoon | 35.00 |
| Junior Set, 2-pc | 120.00 |
| Letter Opener | 60.00 |
| Luncheon Fork | 20.00 |
| Luncheon Knife | 24.00 |
| Macaroni Server | 185.00 |
| Napkin Clip | 40.00 |
| Napkin Ring | 50.00 |
| Olive Spoon, long | 245.00 |
| Pasta Server, part stainless | 50.00 |
| Pastry Server, part stainless | 50.00 |
| Pickle Fork | 45.00 |
| Pie Server, mono | 350.00 |
| Punch Ladle, stainless bowl | 90.00 |
| Ramekin Fork | 35.00 |
| Roast Holder | 250.00 |
| Salad Fork | 27.50 |
| Sardine Fork | 120.00 |
| Serving Spoon | 80.00 |
| Soup Ladle, mono | 300.00 |
| Soup Ladle, gw, small | 350.00 |
| Soup Spoon | 40.00 |
| Steak Carving Knife | 60.00 |
| Strawberry Fork | 48.00 |
| Sugar Tong, large | 75.00 |
| Teaspoon | 12.00 |
| Tea Strainer | 395.00 |
| Terrapin Fork | 35.00 |
| Vegetable Serving Fork | 250.00 |
| Vegetable Serving Spoon | 200.00 |
| Wedding Cake Knife, serrated | 500.00 |

### Chippendale, Towle

| | |
|---|---|
| Baked Potato Fork | 60.00 |
| Bottle Opener | 35.00 |
| Bouillon Soup Spoon | 40.00 |
| Butter Knife, ind, fb, hh | 20.00 |
| Butter Knife, master, fh | 35.00 |
| Butter Pick, twisted | 35.00 |
| Candle Snuffer | 70.00 |
| Cheese Plane | 50.00 |
| Cheese Scoop | 50.00 |
| Citrus Spoon | 26.50 |
| Cocktail Fork | 25.00 |
| Cold Meat Fork | 70.00 |
| Cracker Scoop | 120.00 |
| Cream Soup Spoon | 35.00 |
| Dinner Bell | 70.00 |
| Dinner Knife | 35.00 |
| English Server | 24.00 |
| Fruit Spoon, flat | 40.00 |
| Grapefruit Spoon | 25.00 |
| Gravy Ladle | 70.00 |
| Ice Cream Fork | 27.50 |
| Iced Tea Spoon | 35.00 |
| Jelly Server | 35.00 |
| Junior Fork | 25.00 |
| Lemon Fork | 30.00 |
| Letter Opener | 40.00 |
| Lobster Fork | 40.00 |

Luncheon Fork................................ 26.00
Luncheon Knife............................. 27.50
Magnifying Glass........................... 50.00
Olive Fork..................................... 24.00
Olive Spoon.................................. 60.00
Pasta Server, stainless bowl ........ 50.00
Pickle Fork, 2 tine ........................ 27.50
Pie Server.................................... 50.00
Roast Carving Set, 2 pcs............ 245.00
Salad Fork.................................... 38.00
Serving Spoon .............................. 70.00
Soup Spoon.................................. 36.00
Steak Carving Set ...................... 130.00
Strawberry Fork ........................... 25.00
Teaspoon ..................................... 22.00
Tomato Server, stainless bowl..... 245.00

### Classic Bouquet, Gorham

Butter Knife, master, hh ............... 50.00
Dinner Fork .................................. 50.00
Iced Tea Spoon............................ 60.00
Roast Carving Set, 2 pcs............ 395.00
Salad Fork.................................... 70.00
Steak Knife .................................. 70.00
Sugar Spoon................................. 60.00

### Classic Rose, Reed & Barton

Butter Knife, ind, fb...................... 32.00
Butter Knife, master, hh ............... 25.00
Cheese Knife, with pick ............... 50.00
Cheese Server ............................. 40.00
Dinner Fork .................................. 50.00
Dinner Knife ................................. 50.00
Gravy Ladle .................................. 80.00
Jam Spoon.................................... 45.00
Luncheon Fork.............................. 16.00
Pickle Fork ................................... 28.00
Place Fork.................................... 40.00
Place Knife................................... 28.00
Place Spoon................................. 22.00
Salad Fork.................................... 42.00
Soup Spoon.................................. 40.00
Teaspoon ..................................... 25.00

### Colonial, Tiffany

Cocktail Fork................................. 42.00
Cold Meat Fork ........................... 150.00
Dessert Fork, 3-tine ..................... 80.00
Dinner Fork .................................. 80.00
Dinner Knife ................................. 70.00
Fish Fork ...................................... 90.00
Ice Cream Spoon.......................... 70.00
Salad Fork, 4-tine......................... 90.00
Salt Spoon, master, gold wash bowl
..................................................... 110.00
Serving Spoon ............................ 120.00

### Columbia, Lunt

Dinner Fork .................................. 25.00
Salad Fork.................................... 21.00
Teaspoon ..................................... 15.00

### Copenhagen, Manchester

Baked Potato Fork ........................ 36.00
Berry Spoon, large, 8-1/2" ........... 90.00
Berry Spoon, small, 7" ................. 70.00
Citrus Spoon ................................ 20.00
Cocktail Fork................................. 25.00
Cold Meat Fork ............................ 60.00
Dinner Fork .................................. 40.00
Dinner Knife ................................. 20.00
English Server............................... 25.00
Gravy Ladle .................................. 70.00
Gumbo Soup Spoon ..................... 40.00
Ice Cream Fork ............................ 20.00

Luncheon Fork.............................. 22.00
Pie Server .................................... 50.00
Place Fork.................................... 32.00
Place Knife................................... 25.00
Salad Fork.................................... 35.00
Sugar Spoon................................. 32.00
Teaspoon ..................................... 22.00

### Country Manor, Towle

Butter Knife, master, hh ............... 30.00
Cream Soup Spoon ...................... 35.00
Iced Tea Spoon............................ 35.00
Lemon Fork................................... 25.00
Place Fork.................................... 26.75
Place Knife................................... 25.00
Salad Fork.................................... 36.00
Sugar Spoon................................. 32.00
Teaspoon ..................................... 22.00

### Courtship, International

Baked Potato Fork ........................ 30.00
Butter Knife, ind, fb...................... 17.00
Butter Knife, master, hh ............... 20.00
Citrus Spoon ................................ 22.00
Cocktail Fork................................. 25.00
Cream Soup Spoon ...................... 35.00
Demitasse Spoon ........................... 2.00
Dinner Fork .................................. 40.00
Dinner Knife ................................. 38.00
Gravy Ladle .................................. 45.00
Ice Cream Fork ............................ 22.50
Luncheon Fork.............................. 22.75
Luncheon Knife............................. 28.00
Salad Fork.................................... 32.75
Serving Spoon .............................. 40.00
Soup Spoon.................................. 36.00
Sugar Spoon................................. 30.00
Teaspoon ..................................... 20.00

### Craftsman, Towle

Baby Fork ..................................... 22.00
Baked Potato Fork ....................... 70.00
Butter Knife, ind, fb...................... 22.00
Butter Knife, master, hh ............... 20.00
Butter Pick, twisted ...................... 40.00
Butter Spreader, hh ...................... 24.00
Candle Snuffer.............................. 70.00
Cheese Knife, pick ....................... 40.00
Cheese Plane ............................... 40.00
Cheese Server ............................. 40.00
Cocktail Fork................................. 25.00
Cold Meat Fork ............................ 45.00
Corkscrew..................................... 70.00
Cream Soup Spoon ...................... 35.00
Demitasse Spoon ......................... 20.00
Dinner Bell ................................... 70.00
Dinner Fork .................................. 40.00
Dinner Knife ................................. 38.00
English Server............................... 34.00
Grapefruit Spoon .......................... 40.00
Gravy Ladle .................................. 70.00
Gumbo Soup Spoon ..................... 42.00
Horseradish Scoop ....................... 48.00
Ice Cream Fork ............................ 30.00
Iced Tea Spoon............................ 35.00
Jam Server ................................... 25.00
Lemon Fork................................... 25.00
Luncheon Fork.............................. 22.00
Luncheon Knife............................. 28.00
Nut Spoon..................................... 40.00
Olive Fork..................................... 22.00
Olive Spoon.................................. 55.00
Pickle Fork, 2 tine ....................... 25.00
Pie Server, hh.............................. 47.50

Place Fork.................................... 30.00
Place Knife................................... 25.00
Salad Fork.................................... 32.00
Sauce Ladle ................................. 42.00
Serving Spoon, pierced................ 60.00
Soup Spoon.................................. 40.00
Steak Knife .................................. 40.00
Sugar Shovel ............................... 38.00
Sugar Spoon................................. 28.00
Teaspoon ..................................... 24.00

### Eloquence, Lunt

Baked Potato Fork ........................ 80.00
Butter Pick, twisted ...................... 45.00
Butter Spreader, hh ...................... 30.00
Cake Knife ................................... 50.00
Candle Snuffer.............................. 80.00
Corkscrew..................................... 80.00
Cracker Scoop ............................ 100.00
Dinner Bell ................................... 75.00
Dinner Fork .................................. 60.00
Dinner Knife ................................. 50.00
Fish Fork ...................................... 70.00
Fish Knife, stainless blade........... 55.00
Fish Serving Fork ....................... 145.00
Grapefruit Spoon .......................... 48.00
Gravy Ladle .................................. 90.00
Iced Tea Spoon ........................... 40.00
Magnifying Glass.......................... 80.00
Pickle Fork ................................... 35.00
Pie Server .................................... 48.00
Place Setting, 4 pcs ................... 110.00
Salad Fork.................................... 32.00
Salad Serving Fork ...................... 80.00
Salt Spoon ................................... 12.00
Serving Spoon .............................. 90.00
Soup Spoon, oval ......................... 48.00
Steak Carving Set ...................... 120.00
Stuffing Spoon ............................ 145.00
Sugar Sifter................................. 100.00
Sugar Spoon................................. 50.00
Teaspoon ..................................... 27.00

### Embassy Scroll, Lunt

Fish Serving Fork.......................... 55.00
Place Setting, 4 pcs ................... 130.00
Soup Spoon.................................. 50.00
Teaspoon ..................................... 24.00
Tomato Server............................... 48.00

### Evening Rose, Lunt

Butter Knife, ind, fb...................... 12.00
Cream Soup Spoon ...................... 35.00
Place Setting, 4 pcs ..................... 55.00
Salad Fork .................................... 40.00
Sugar Spoon................................. 35.00
Tablespoon ................................... 30.00
Teaspoon ..................................... 25.00

### Fairfax, Durgin

Baby Fork ..................................... 30.00
Baby Knife.................................... 50.00
Baked Potato Fork ....................... 70.00
Bonbon, mono .............................. 25.00
Bouillon Soup Spoon .................... 30.00
Butter Pick, 2 tines, pierced ......... 70.00
Butter Spreader, hh ...................... 24.00
Candle Snuffer.............................. 70.00
Casserole Spoon, stainless bowl
..................................................... 50.00
Cheese Scoop ............................ 110.00
Chocolate Spoon.......................... 50.00
Cocktail Fork................................. 25.00
Coffee Spoon................................ 20.00
Cream Soup Spoon ...................... 35.00

Cucumber Server, mono ............. 130.00
Demitasse Spoon .......................... 20.00
Dinner Fork ................................... 40.00
Dinner Knife ................................. 38.00
Fish Fork ...................................... 80.00
Fish Knife, stainless blade .......... 60.00
4 O'clock Spoon .......................... 20.00
Grapefruit Spoon ......................... 40.00
Gumbo Soup Spoon .................... 40.00
Horseradish Scoop ...................... 50.00
Ice Cream Spoon ......................... 40.00
Iced Tea Spoon ........................... 35.00
Lemon Fork, mono ....................... 24.00
Letter Opener .............................. 48.00
Luncheon Fork ............................. 24.00
Luncheon Knife ............................ 24.00
Macaroni Knife ............................ 90.00
Magnifying Glass ......................... 65.00
Napkin Ring ................................. 50.00
Olive Spoon, pierced ................... 75.00
Pie Server ................................... 48.00
Place Fork ................................... 35.00
Place Knife .................................. 40.00
Poultry Shears ........................... 200.00
Punch Ladle, stainless bowl ........ 90.00
Ramekin Fork ............................... 38.00
Salad Fork, 6" .............................. 35.00
Salt Spoon, ind. ........................... 18.00
Salt Spoon, master ...................... 60.00
Seafood Fork ............................... 25.00
Serving Spoon ............................. 70.00
Serving Spoon, pierced ............... 80.00
Soup Spoon ................................. 50.00
Steak Carving Set ...................... 100.00
Sugar Spoon ................................ 35.00
Tea Infuser Spoon ...................... 275.00
Teaspoon ..................................... 20.00
Terrapin Fork ............................... 40.00
Tomato Server, pierced ............... 90.00

### Grande Baroque, Wallace

Baby Set, 2 pcs ........................... 55.00
Berry Shell, hh ............................ 40.00
Butter Knife, master, hh .............. 27.00
Butter Spreader, hh ..................... 32.00
Cocktail Fork ............................... 35.00
Cold Meat Fork .......................... 100.00
Cranberry Server ......................... 40.00
Cream Soup Spoon ..................... 45.00
Demitasse Spoon ......................... 28.00
Dessert Spoon, oval bowl ............ 45.00
Dinner Fork, large ....................... 65.00
Dinner Knife ................................. 45.00
Fruit Spoon .................................. 45.00
Gravy Ladle ............................... 100.00
Iced Tea Spoon ........................... 42.00
Lasagna Server ........................... 22.00
Pasta Scoop ................................ 35.00
Pie Server ................................... 50.00
Place Fork ................................... 40.00
Place Knife .................................. 30.00
Rice Spoon, hh ............................ 40.00
Roast Carving Fork .................... 150.00
Salad Fork ................................... 42.00
Salad Serving Fork ..................... 190.00
Salad Serving Set ...................... 350.00
Salt Spoon ................................... 12.00
Serving Spoon, pierced ............. 100.00
Soup Ladle, hh ............................ 45.00
Soup Spoon ................................. 40.00
Steak Carving Fork ...................... 50.00
Steak Carving Knife ..................... 50.00
Strawberry Fork ........................... 22.00

Sugar Spoon ................................ 40.00
Teaspoon ..................................... 30.00
Tomato Server ........................... 120.00
Wedding Cake Knife ..................... 38.00

### Imperial Queen, Whiting

Baked Potato Fork ....................... 70.00
Banquet Knife, 10-1/2" l, mono ... 100.00
Beef Fork, mono ........................ 100.00
Berry Spoon, gw, 8-3/4" l, mono
................................................... 245.00
Bonbon Server ............................ 50.00
Bouillon Soup Spoon, gw, mono ... 40.00
Breakfast Fork ............................. 50.00
Butter Pick, 2 tines ..................... 70.00
Cheese Scoop, mono ................. 125.00
Cocktail Fork ............................... 45.00
Cold Meat Fork, mono ............... 130.00
Crumber ..................................... 350.00
Cucumber Server ....................... 250.00
Demitasse Spoon, gw ................. 40.00
Dessert Spoon, mono .................. 30.00
Dinner Fork, mono ....................... 85.00
Dinner Knife, 9-1/4" l ................... 80.00
Fish Fork, gw, mono ................... 100.00
Fish Serving Set, 12" server, 9-3/4" 3 tine
   fork, mono ............................... 650.00
Gravy Ladle ................................. 60.00
Grapefruit Spoon ......................... 70.00
Gumbo Soup Spoon .................... 70.00
Ice Cream Fork ............................ 72.00
Ice Cream Server, 9-1/2", mono
................................................... 375.00
Jelly Slice, mono ........................ 100.00
Junior Fork .................................. 50.00
Lettuce Fork, mono .................... 145.00
Macaroni Knife ........................... 115.00
Olive Spoon ............................... 145.00
Pie Server ................................. 300.00
Place Knife, mono ....................... 80.00
Ramekin Fork, mono .................... 65.00
Roast Carving Set, 2 pcs, mono
................................................... 395.00
Salad Fork ................................. 140.00
Salad Serving Fork, gw, mono .... 120.00
Salt Spoon ................................... 18.00
Seafood Fork ............................... 24.00
Serving Spoon ............................. 75.00
Serving Spoon, pierced, mono ..... 90.00
Soup Spoon ................................. 65.00
Strawberry Fork, 2 tines, mono .... 55.00
Sugar Sifter ............................... 250.00
Sugar Spoon, mono ..................... 50.00
Tablespoon .................................. 35.00
Teaspoon ..................................... 40.00

### Madrigal, Lunt

Butter Spreader, hh ..................... 25.00
Cheese Server ............................. 40.00
Cocktail Fork ............................... 25.00
Cold Meat Fork ............................ 70.00
Gravy Ladle ................................. 75.00
Lemon Fork .................................. 30.00
Nut Spoon .................................... 48.00
Pie Server ................................... 50.00
Place Fork ................................... 22.00
Place Setting, 4 pcs .................. 100.00
Salad Fork ................................... 40.00
Serving Spoon ............................. 75.00
Soup Spoon ................................. 40.00
Sugar Spoon ................................ 30.00
Tablespoon .................................. 55.00
Tablespoon, pierced .................... 58.00
Teaspoon ..................................... 20.00

### Modern Victorian, Lunt

Butter Knife, ind, fb ..................... 12.00
Butter Spreader, hh ..................... 24.00
Cocktail Fork ............................... 20.00
Cold Meat Fork ............................ 80.00
Cream Soup Spoon ..................... 35.00
Dinner Knife ................................. 38.00
Gravy Ladle ................................. 65.00
Iced Tea Spoon ........................... 35.00
Jam Server .................................. 30.00
Lemon Fork .................................. 25.00
Nut Spoon .................................... 35.00
Pickle Fork .................................. 25.00
Pie Server ................................... 50.00
Place Setting, 4 pcs .................... 95.00
Salad Fork ................................... 40.00
Salad Serving Set ...................... 225.00
Salt Spoon ................................... 12.00
Sauce Ladle ................................. 40.00
Serving Spoon ............................. 70.00
Sugar Spoon ................................ 30.00
Teaspoon ..................................... 20.00
Tomato Server, pointed .............. 110.00
Salad Serving Set ...................... 225.00

### Normandie, Wallace

Bouillon Soup Spoon ................... 30.00
Cocktail Fork ............................... 25.00
Coffee Spoon .............................. 20.00
Cream Soup Spoon ..................... 32.00
Demitasse Spoon ......................... 20.00
Dinner Fork .................................. 35.00
Gravy Ladle ................................. 70.00
Luncheon Fork ............................. 20.00
Mayonnaise Ladle ....................... 48.00
Nut Spoon .................................... 35.00
Pickle Fork, 2 tines ..................... 25.00
Place Fork ................................... 35.00
Place Knife .................................. 25.00
Salad Fork ................................... 35.00
Salad Serving Set ...................... 235.00
Serving Spoon ............................. 65.00
Sugar Spoon ................................ 32.00
Sugar Tong .................................. 40.00
Tablespoon .................................. 15.00
Teaspoon ..................................... 22.00

### Old Maryland, plain, Kirk

Baby Food Pusher ....................... 50.00
Baby Fork .................................... 27.50
Baked Potato Fork ....................... 80.00
Butter Pick, twisted ..................... 35.00
Candle Snuffer ............................ 75.00
Coffee Spoon .............................. 12.00
Cream Soup Spoon ..................... 42.00
Egg Spoon ................................... 40.00
Dinner Fork .................................. 40.00
Dinner Knife ................................. 45.00
Fish Fork ...................................... 75.00
Fish Knife .................................... 70.00
Horseradish Scoop ...................... 48.00
Ice Cream Slice, stainless blade
................................................... 125.00
Ice Tong .................................... 380.00
Mayonnaise Ladle ....................... 42.00
Pickle Fork .................................. 45.00
Pie Server ................................... 50.00
Place Setting, 4 pcs .................... 95.00
Salad Fork ................................... 45.00
Serving Spoon, pierced ............... 95.00
Soup Spoon ................................. 40.00
Steak Carving Knife ..................... 50.00
Sugar Spoon ................................ 40.00
Tablespoon .................................. 52.00

Tablespoon, pierced......................54.00
Teaspoon ......................................25.00
Tomato Server.............................125.00

### Orchid, International

Berry Spoon..................................90.00
Bouillon Soup Spoon.....................30.00
Butter Knife, ind, fb.......................24.00
Butter Knife, master, hh................35.00
Cocktail Fork................................24.00
Coffee Spoon................................10.00
Cream Soup Spoon.......................35.00
Demitasse Spoon..........................20.00
Dinner Fork..................................40.00
Gravy Ladle.................................70.00
Grill Fork.....................................30.00
Grill Knife....................................25.00
Iced Tea Spoon............................35.00
Jam Spoon...................................40.00
Lemon Fork..................................25.00
Luncheon Fork.............................20.00
Nut Spoon...................................40.00
Pie Server...................................48.00
Place Setting, 4 pcs.....................48.00
Salad Fork...................................38.00
Serving Spoon.............................70.00
Sugar Spoon................................30.00
Teaspoon ....................................20.00

### Queen's Lace, International

Baked Potato Fork.........................70.00
Butter Knife, ind, fb.......................20.00
Butter Knife, master, hh................24.00
Cheese Knife, with pick.................50.00
Cheese Scoop..............................50.00
Corkscrew...................................70.00
Cream Soup Spoon.......................35.00
Dinner Bell...................................70.00
Dinner Fork..................................35.00
Dinner Knife.................................25.00
Horseradish Scoop........................50.00
Ice Cream Fork.............................40.00
Iced Tea Spoon............................35.00
Napkin Clip..................................40.00
Olive Spoon.................................70.00
Pie Server...................................50.00
Salad Fork...................................40.00
Salt and Pepper Shakers, pr.......250.00
Serving Spoon.............................70.00
Serving Spoon, pierced.................70.00
Sugar Spoon................................22.00
Teaspoon ....................................20.00

### Violet, Wallace

Aspic Slice, mono.......................115.00
Baked Potato Fork.........................70.00
Berry Spoon, 9" l, mono..............125.00
Bonbon, mono..............................65.00
Bouillon Soup Spoon, mono..........30.00
Butter Spreader, hh......................25.00
Cake Saw, mono.........................100.00
Candle Snuffer.............................65.00
Cocktail Fork................................25.00
Cold Meat Fork............................95.00
Cream Soup Spoon.......................35.00
Demitasse Spoon, mono...............25.00
Dinner Fork..................................30.00
Dinner Knife.................................25.00
Gumbo Spoon, mono....................24.00
Iced Tea Spoon............................45.00
Pickle Fork, 3 tines.....................110.00
Pie Server...................................60.00
Place Fork...................................32.00
Place Knife..................................28.00

Roast Carving Set, 2 pcs, mono
...................................................175.00
Salad Fork, mono.........................45.00
Salad Serving Set, mono.............250.00
Serving Spoon, mono....................75.00
Serving Spoon, pierced.................95.00
Soup Spoon.................................45.00
Sugar Tongs, mono.......................48.00
Teaspoon, mono...........................25.00

### Warwick, Wallace

Butter Knife, ind, fb.......................30.00
Olive Spoon, pierced.....................40.00
Pickle Fork...................................25.00
Pie Server...................................50.00
Salad Fork...................................40.00
Toast Fork..................................280.00

### Wedding Bells, International

Baby Fork....................................30.00
Butter Knife, ind, fb.......................12.00
Cocktail Fork................................25.00
Cream Soup Spoon.......................35.00
Infant Spoon................................30.00
Junior Fork...................................30.00
Place Setting, 4 pcs.....................55.00
Serving Spoon.............................70.00
Sugar Spoon................................15.00
Teaspoon ....................................24.00

### Wedgwood, International

Bouillon Soup Spoon.....................30.00
Butter Knife, ind, fb.......................22.00
Butter Knife, master, hh................20.00
Cocktail Fork................................25.00
Demitasse Spoon..........................20.00
Dinner Fork..................................40.00
Dinner Knife.................................40.00
Gravy Ladle.................................75.00
Grill Fork.....................................70.00
Grill Knife....................................70.00
Iced Tea Spoon............................35.00
Jam Spoon...................................45.00
Pie Server...................................50.00
Place Fork...................................34.00
Place Knife..................................28.00
Salad Fork...................................40.00
Salad Serving Set.......................295.00
Serving Spoon.............................70.00
Soup Spoon.................................50.00
Steak Carving Set.......................100.00
Steak Carving Fork.......................50.00
Steak Knife..................................30.00
Sugar Spoon................................35.00
Tablespoon..................................40.00
Teaspoon ....................................25.00

### Wild Rose, International

Baked Potato Fork.........................70.00
Butter Knife, master, fh.................35.00
Butter Pick, twisted......................35.00
Butter Spreader, fh.......................27.00
Butter Spreader, hh......................24.00
Candle Snuffer.............................65.00
Cocktail Fork................................25.00
Cold Meat Fork............................75.00
Cream Soup Spoon.......................35.00
Demitasse Spoon..........................16.00
Dinner Bell...................................65.00
Dinner Fork..................................40.00
Dinner Knife.................................40.00
Fish Server, stainless blade...........45.00
Grapefruit Spoon..........................40.00
Horseradish Scoop........................45.00
Iced Tea Spoon............................35.00

Jam Server..................................35.00
Lemon Fork..................................18.00
Letter Opener...............................48.00
Lobster Fork.................................40.00
Napkin Clip..................................40.00
Olive Spoon.................................70.00
Pasta Server, stainless bowl.........48.00
Pie Server...................................50.00
Place Setting, 4 pcs....................112.00
Salad Fork...................................35.00
Salad Serving Set, part stainless
.....................................................95.00
Serving Spoon.............................65.00
Serving Spoon, pierced.................75.00
Sugar Spoon................................32.00
Sugar Tong..................................35.00
Tablespoon..................................30.00
Teaspoon ....................................24.00

# Stock and Bond Certificates

**Collecting Hints:** Some of the factors that affect price are: 1) date (with pre-1900 more popular and pre-1850 most desirable), 2) autographs of important persons (Vanderbilt, Rockefeller, J. P. Morgan, Wells and Fargo, etc.), 3) number issued (most bonds have the number issued noted in text), and 4) attractiveness of the vignette.

Stocks and bonds are often collected for the appeal of their graphics or as a record of events or people which have impacted American history, such as gold and silver mining, railroad development, and early automobile pioneers.

**History:** The use of stock to raise capital and spread the risk in a business venture began in England. Several American colonies were founded as joint-venture stock companies. The New York Stock Exchange on Wall Street in New York City traces its roots to the late 18th century.

Stock certificates with attractive vignettes date to the beginning of the 19th century. As engraving and printing techniques developed, so did the elaborateness of the stock and bond certificates. Important engraving houses which emerged include the American Bank Note Company and Rawdon, Wright & Hatch.

**References:** Gene Utz, *Collecting Paper*, Books Americana, 1993; Bill Yatchman, *Stock & Bond Collectors Price Guide*, published by author, 1985.

**Periodical:** *Bank Note Reporter* 700 E. State St., Iola, WI 54990.

**Collectors' Club:** Bond and Share Society, 26 Broadway, New York, NY 10004.

**Museum:** Museum of American Financial History, New York, NY.

## Bonds

Cairo & Norfolk RR co., Kentucky, 1908, issued, not canceled, orange, speeding train vignette, coupons ............................................... 45.00

Chicago & Wisconsin Valley Street Railways Co., 1912, $1,000, issued and canceled, first mortgage gold, black and white .................................. 25.00

Columbus & Southern Ohio electric co., issued and canceled, blue, engraved ..................................... 7.50

Consolidated Edison Co., New York, $1,000, issued and canceled, engraved, blue or purple .......... 8.00

Long Island Lighting Co., issued and canceled, orange, engraved, woman, child, generator, and light vignette ..................................... 7.50

New Paltz, & Highland Electric RR, 1893, $500, issued and canceled, trolley car vignettes, gold seal, two pages of coupons .................... 95.00

New York, New Haven & Hartford, 1920, $10,000, issued and canceled, engraved, electric train vignette ............................................... 48.00

Pennsylvania Canal Company, issued and canceled, 1870, canal and surrounding area vignette, two revenue stamps ................................... 125.00

Sacramento & Woodland RR, California, 1911, issued, not canceled, rust-brown, logo around capitol building vignette, coupons ................. 165.00

Southern Indiana, 1908, $1,000, issued and canceled, green ............... 28.00

Sovereign Gold Mining, issued and canceled, $5,000, Canadian, 1903, peach borders, coupon ........... 10.00

Union Pacific RR, 1946, $1,000, issued and canceled, two engraved angels and company logo ................... 15.00

## Stocks

American Express Co, issued and canceled, 1860s, bulldog vignette, sgd "Henry Wells" and "William Fargo" ................................................... 750.00

Broadway Joe's, issued and canceled, green or blue border, sports figure's restaurant ............................... 10.00

California Street Cable RR Co., San Francisco, CA, 1884, unissued, cable car vignette ................... 35.00

Cambridge Railroad Co, MA, 1880s, unissued, black and white ........ 8.00

Chico Gold & Silver Mining Co., 1867, sgd by company president John Bidwell ................................. 310.00

Colorado Milling & Elevator Co., issued and canceled, gold border, company buildings vignette, 1890s ........................................................... 25.00

Communications Satellite Corp., 1960s, issued and canceled, green or blue, space vignette ........................... 5.00

Edison Portland Cement Co., issued and canceled, engraved, rust or green, Thomas Edison vignette, 1900s ..................................... 35.00

F. W. Woolworth Co., eagle over two hemispheres vignette, brown ..... 8.00

General Foods, issued and canceled, green, brown, or orange, engraved, vignette scene on right .............. 2.50

Gulf, Mobile & Ohio, issued and canceled, engraved, blue or brown, two women and diesel train vignette ........................................................... 3.50

Heppner Railroad & Coal Co., Oregon, 1904 ....................................... 165.00

Hornell Airways Inc., issued and canceled, NY, two women and sun rising over mountains vignette, 1920s ........................................................... 65.00

Illinois, Central, issued and canceled, engraved, orange or brown, diesel train vignette ............................ 3.50

International Business Machines Corp., issued, brown ........................... 5.00

International Immigration & Colonization Assn., Hawaii, 1911, issued, not canceled, map vignette ............... 100.00

International Telephone & Telegraph, 1930s, blue, engraved, goddess and globe vignette ..................... 8.00

Isabella, Gold Mining, Co., Colorado, 1890s, issued and canceled, engraved, eagle vignette .......... 8.00

Jantzen Knitting Mills, 1930s, issued and canceled, engraved, swimmer vignette, orange or green ........ 20.00

Kelly-Springfield Motor Truck Co., issued and canceled, 1910-20 seated woman, anvil, and gears vignette, green or purple, American Bank Note Company ............... 35.00

Maryland Telecommunications, issued and canceled, green, drawn 1957 TV and TV camera vignette ..... 10.00

Nashville & Decatur, 1880s, issued and canceled, green border, train vignette ..................................... 25.00

Omaha & Council Bluffs Street Railway, 1906, issued and canceled, blue, green, or pink ........................... 20.00

Penn-Yan Mining Co., Montana Territory, 1888, colorful vignette of gold and silver coins ........................... 195.00

Philippine Long Distance Telephone Co., 1950s, issued and canceled, blue, engraved, woman on two globes vignette ......................... 5.00

Raleigh & Gaston, 1870s, issued and canceled, two vignettes ........... 65.00

Rochelle & Southern, Illinois, 1900, unissued, black and white ....... 12.00

Rock Island & Eastern, Illinois, 1900, black and white, curved company name ...................................... 15.00

Sentinel Radio Corp., issued and canceled, green or brown, goddess and two radio towers vignette .......... 5.00

Sheba Gold & Silver Mining, Humboldt County, Nevada, issued, not canceled, three mining vignettes, gold seal ..................................... 20.00

Solid Gold & Silver Mining Co., Colorado, 1884 ........................... 135.00

Texas Oil, 1901, sgd by A. M. Britton ........................................................... 140.00

Tuolumne County Water Co., 1850s, issued and canceled, mining methods vignette ........................... 75.00

Uncas National Bank of Norwich, 1900, green, gray and white, Indian, blacksmith, and sailing ship vignette ........................................................... 15.00

**Chenango Canal, Rawdon, Wright, Hatch & Co., NY, engravers, 1837, 9-3/4" x 7-1/2", $24.**

Wells Fargo Bank & Union Trust, 1940s, issued and canceled, green pony express ride vignette .............. 25.00

# Stuffed Toys

**Collecting Hints:** Collectors tend to focus on one type of animal and to collect material spanning a long time period. The company with the strongest collector following is Steiff.

Collectors are mainly interested in items in very good to mint condition. Often stuffed toys had ribbons or clothing. All accessories must be intact for the toy to command full value.

**History:** The stuffed toy may have originated in Germany. Margarete Steiff GmbH of Germany began making stuffed toys for export beginning in 1880. By 1903, the teddy bear had joined Steiff's line and quickly worked its way to America. The first American teddy bears were made by the Ideal Toy Corporation. Not much is known about earlier manufacturers since companies were short-lived and many toys have lost their labels.

The stuffed toy has always been an American favorite. Some have music boxes inserted to enhance their appeal. Carnivals used stuffed toys as prizes. Since the 1960s an onslaught of stuffed toys have been imported to America from Japan, Taiwan, and China. These animals often are poorly made and are not popular among serious collectors.

**References:** Dottie Ayers and Donna Harrison, *Advertising Art of Steiff*, Hobby House Press, 1990; Ann Gehlbach, *Muffy VanderBear: Identification & Price Guide,* Hobby House Press, 1997; Dee Hockenberry, *Big Bear Book*, Schiffer Publishing, 1996; —, *Enchanting Friends: Collectible Poohs, Raggedies, Golliwogs & Roosevelt Bears*, Schiffer Publishing, 1995; Margaret Fox Mandel, *Teddy Bears and Steiff Animals*, 1st Series (1984, 1997 value update), 2nd Series (1987, 1996 value update), 3rd Series (1990, 1996 value update), Collector Books; Linda Mullins, *American Teddy Bear Encyclopedia*, Hobby House Press, 1995; Linda Mullins, *4th Teddy Bear and Friends Price Guide*, Hobby House Press, 1993; —, *Teddy Bears Past & Present*, vol. II, Hobby House Press, 1992; Sue Pearson and Dottie Ayers, *Teddy*

*Bears: A Complete Guide to History, Collecting, and Care*, McMillan, 1995; Christel and Rolf Pistorius, *Steiff*, Hobby House Press, 1991; Cynthia Powell, *Collector's Guide to Miniature Teddy Bears*, Collector Books, 1994; Gustav Severin, *Teddy Bear*, Running Press, 1995; Carol J. Smith, *Identification & Price Guide to Winnie the Pooh Collectibles*, Hobby House Press, 1994.

**Periodicals:** *National Doll & Teddy Bear Collector*, P.O. Box 4032, Portland, OR 97208; *Soft Dolls & Animals*, 30595 Eight Mile, Livonia, MI 48152; *Teddy Bear and Friends*, 6405 Flank Dr., Harrisburg, PA 17112; *Teddy Bear Review*, 170 Fifth Ave., New York, NY 10010.

**Collectors' Clubs:** Collectors Club for Classic Winnie the Pooh, 468 W Alpine #10, Upland, CA 91786; Good Bears of the World, P.O. Box 13097, Toledo, OH 43613; Steiff Collectors Club, PO Box 798, Holland, OH 43528; Teddy Bear Boosters Club, 19750 SW Peavine Mt. Rd., McMinnville, OR 97128.

Alligator, 9-1/2" l, vinyl, green and brown, glass eyes, c1950 ........ 35.00
Bambi, Gund, c1953 .................... 65.00
Beagle, plush, glass eyes, 9" h .... 28.00
Beaver, mohair, brown, Steiff ........ 45.00
Boa Constrictor, plush, multicolored, felt eyes and tongue, c1958 .......... 12.00
Camel
   4-1/2" h, leather, tan, single hump, straw saddle, c1955 ................ 12.00
   8" h, plush, tan, single hump, glass eyes, c1950 ............................ 65.00
Cat
   4" h, Tabby, orig bell, Steiff 60.00
   5" l, sleeping, mohair, 5" l ....... 100.00
   5-1/4" h, mohair, green plastic eyes, movable head and legs, Steiff, c1950 ...................................... 45.00
   11" h, Diva, long white fur, sitting, orig Steiff tag and button ....... 110.00
Cow, 5-1/2" h, felt, brown and white, glass eyes, wooden wheels ..... 65.00

**Cat, Siamese, R. Dankin Co., 14" l, $20.**

Deer, 15" h, Bambi, plush, Gund, c1953 ................................................. 60.00
Dog
   4-1/2" h, Scottie, cotton, plaid, embroidered features and collar, hand made, c1950 ................... 5.00
   6" h, Boxer, Steiff ...................... 75.00
   7" h, Dalmatian, sitting, mohair, swivel head, orig collar, Steiff .................................................... 75.00
   8" h, plush, amber, swivel neck, oversized head, milk glass and amber bead eyes, embroidered nose and mouth, stitched tail and ears, early 20th C .................................... 75.00
   8-1/2" h, Poodle, pink, standing, glass eyes ................................ 18.00
   9" h, Beagle, plush, glass eyes .................................................. 25.00
   10" h, Snoopy, black and white .................................................. 15.00
   11" h, Terrier, white plush, black spots, swivel head, white muzzle, yellow glass eyes, embroidered features, red ribbon, c1925 .......... 50.00
   12" h, Poodle, curly, gray, plaid coat, hat, and boots, c1960 ............. 15.00
   16" h, Huckleberry Hound ....... 14.00
Donkey, gray plush body, brown glass eyes, brown yarn mane, gray tail, wheeled base, c1950 ............ 110.00
Duck, 8" h, plush, standing, yellow, straw hat, blue suspender pants .................................................. 45.00
Elephant
   4" h, gray mohair, black glass eyes, red saddle, Steiff, c1953........ 100.00
   6-1/2" h, standing, gray, red suspender pants .......................... 65.00
Frog, green velvet back, white satin underside, c1960.................... 15.00
Giraffe, 4" h, plush, yellow, brown spots, brown button eyes, brown yarn tail, c1957 ..................................... 20.00
Goat, 6-1/2" h, standing, white, brown felt horns, Steiff ....................... 50.00
Hedgehogs, 22" h, Micky & Mecky, vinyl swivel heads, pressed mask face, tan, squinting eyes, smiling mounts, bristly hair, felt bodies sewn on shoes, checkered costumes, c1950, price for pr ........................... 475.00
Hen, 7" h, gold and black spotted feathers, yellow plush head, felt tail, black button eyes, Steiff, c1949 ........ 75.00
Hippo, plush, purple, plastic eyes and teeth, c1962 ............................ 18.00
Horse, 15" h, amber hopsacking, straw stuffing, reinforced stitching, pale yellow underbelly, amber glass eyes, stitched smiling mouth, applied ears, black fur mane, horsehair tail, velvet and leather saddle and harness, c1890 .................................... 85.00
Kangaroo, 11" h, plush, glass eyes, two plastic Joeys, Steiff button in ear marked "Linda" ......................... 65.00
Lamb, 9" h, white, fluffy, glass eyes, embroidered features, bell, flowers and ribbon at neck, paper label .................................................. 90.00
Leopard, 15" l, silver button, Steiff .................................................. 185.00

Llama, 11" h, standing, white, brown spots, Steiff ............................ 100.00

Monkey
  11" h, mohair, jointed, felt paws and face, Steiff ................................ 85.00
  36" h, Curious George, plush, knit yellow sweater, red cap, c1975 ................................................ 48.00

Mother Goose, 22" h, muslin, white, yellow felt feet, white cotton bonnet, blue floral apron, c1962 ........... 30.00

Owl, 10" h, Steiff ............................. 70.00

Owl, 8-1/2" h, Steiff Wittie Owl, Marguerite Steiff's nephew's signature on bottom of foot ............................... 70.00

Panda, 47" h, plush, black and white, jointed, humpback, pie shaped eyes, straw filled ................... 225.00

Parrot, 9" h, Lora, glass eyes, Steiff ................................................ 75.00

Penguin, 10" h, black and white, black plastic wings, c1960 ................. 10.00

Pig, 6" h, plush, pink, pink felt cork screw tail, black and white felt eyes ................................................ 20.00

Rabbit
  6-1/2" h, mohair, jointed, Steiff ................................................ 100.00
  12" h, plush, glass eyes, embroidered features, jointed body, paper label ............................... 70.00
  15" h, felt, eating carrot, Lenci ................................................ 24.00

Raccoon, Gund ............................ 20.00

Seal, 10" h, fur, black, glass eyes ................................................ 85.00

Squirrel, plush, Perri, Steiff .......... 42.00

Teddy Bear
  4" h, plush, dark brown, jointed ................................................ 40.00
  5" h, plush, standing, swivel head, "Character" label ...................... 40.00
  6" h, plush, jointed, fully dressed orig clothes, "Berg" label ................ 65.00
  9" h, plush, blonde, black shoe button eyes, shoulder hump, small tail, straw filled, c1905 ................. 165.00
  9-1/2" h, 13-3/4" l, brown curly hair bear on all fours, mohair, early 20th C, unjointed, glass eyes...... 1,380.00
  11" h, brown woven mohair, black shoe button eyes, embroidered features and claws ...................... 115.00
  12" h
    Mohair, blond, c1910, black shoe button eyes, fully jointed ...... 275.00
    Plush, amber, swivel head, jointed arms and legs, stitched on ears, felt paws, functioning grower, straw filled, c1915 ............. 200.00
  14" h
    Knickerbocker, 1950s ......... 26.00
    Zotty, Hermann, platinum frosted mohair ............................... 155.00
  15" h, mohair, brown, black shoe button eyes, black embroidered nose, mouth, and claws, fully jointed, label "Bruin Mfg. Co.," c1907 ......... 250.00
  16" h, Steiff
    Molly Koala bear, gray and tan ................................................ 135.00
    1903 Anniversary Bear, 1980s, #3026, yellow mohair, peach felt pads, certificate, orig box ............................................ 275.00

17" h
  Mohair, blond, 1910, black steel eyes ..................................... 517.50
  Plush, brown, tan paws, molded muzzle, Ideal Toy .................. 50.00

18" h, gold mohair, unmarked, brown glass eyes, applied ears, felt pads on paws .................................. 375.00

20" h, mohair, brown, jointed, flat face, Knickerbocker ............... 100.00

24" h, mohair, brown, glass eyes, black cloth nose, fully jointed, c1925 ................................................ 600.00

25" h, Ideal, light yellow mohair, c1905, black shoe button eyes ........................................ 13,800.00

Tiger
  6" h, plush, Steiff ...................... 60.00
  8" h, Tony, Esso Tiger, orange and black, felt trim ......................... 45.00
  13" h, plush, Shere Khan, black-green eyes, 8" l tail, button in ear, Steiff ...................................... 175.00

Turtle, 5-1/2" l, plush and felt, Steiff ................................................ 40.00

Walrus, pink, Gund ...................... 25.00

Weasel, 7-5/8" h, Steiff, 1970's, "Wiggy," synthetic white winter fur, black plastic eyes, ear button and chest tag ................................................ 258.75

Zebra, 7" h, belt and white, button in ear, Steiff ................................ 75.00

# Super Heroes

**Collecting Hints:** Concentrate your collection on a single super hero. Because Superman, Batman, and Wonder Woman are the most popular, new collectors are advised to focus on other characters or on one of the modern super heroes. Nostalgia is the principal motivation for many collectors; hence, they sometimes pay prices based on sentiment rather than true market value.

Comics are a fine collectible but require careful handling and storage. An attractive display requires inclusion of a three-dimensional object. Novice collectors are advised to concentrate on these first before acquiring too much of the flat paper material.

**History:** The super hero and comic books go hand in hand. Superman made his debut in 1939 in the first issue of *Action Comics*, six years after Jerry Siegel and Joe Shuster conceived the idea of a man who flew. A newspaper strip, radio show, and movies followed. The popularity of Superman spawned many other super heroes, among them Batman, Captain Marvel, Captain Midnight, The Green Hornet, The Green Lantern, The Shadow, and Wonder Woman.

These early heroes had extraordinary strength and/or cunning and lived normal lives as private citizens. A wealth of merchandising products surround these early super heroes. Their careers were enhanced further when television chose them as heroes for Saturday morning shows as well as for prime time broadcasts.

The Fantastic Four—Mr. Fantastic, The Human Torch, The Invisible Girl, and The Thing—introduced a new type of super hero, the mutant. Other famous personalities of this genre are Captain America, Spiderman, and The Hulk. Although these characters appear in comic form, the number of secondary items generated is small. Television has helped to promote a few of the characters, but the list of mutant super heroes is close to a hundred.

**References:** John Bonavita, *Mego Action Figure Toys*, Schiffer Publishing, 1996; Bill Bruegman, *Superhero Collectibles*, Toy Scouts (137 Casterton Ave., Akron, OH 44303), 1996; Les Daniels, *Superman: the Complete History,* Chronicle Books, 1998; Tom Heaton, *The Encyclopedia of Marx Action Figures,* Krause Publications, 1999; Paris & Susan Manos, *Collectible Action Figures*, 2nd ed., Collector Books, 1996; Rex Miller, *The Investor's Guide to Vintage Character Collectibles*, Krause Publications, 1999; Jeff Rovin, *Encyclopedia of Super Heroes*, Facts on File Publications, 1985.

**Collectors' Clubs:** Air Heroes Fan Club, 19205 Seneca Ridge, Gaithersburg, MD 20879; Batman TV Series Fan Club, P.O. Box 107, Venice, CA 90291.

**Additional Listings:** Action Figures, Comic Books, Radio Characters and Personalities.

## Aquaman

Action Figure, MOC ..................... 35.00

Bathtub Toy, Burger King Kids Meal premium .................................. 12.00

Costume, Ben Cooper, 1967 ...... 200.00

Glass, 1973 ................................. 15.00

Puzzle, Whitman, action scene, 1967 ................................................ 40.00

Tattoo, 1967, unused, orig wrapper ................................................ 50.00

## Batman & Robin

Bank, plastic, full color, arms crossed ................................................ 75.00

Batmobile
  Animated ................................. 90.00
  Radio controlled, Richman's Toys, 1989, some damage to remote ................................................ 350.00

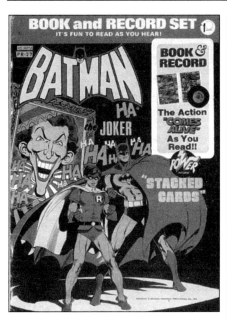

**Batman, child's book and record set, ©National Periodical Publications, Inc., 1975, $15.**

Tin, red, Taiwan, some damage to orig box ..................................... 300.00
Batmobile Gift Pack, batmobile and boat, Corgi, 1979, MOC ......... 395.00
Coloring Book, 1963, used ........... 20.00
Cosmetics, Robin goes to a Weekend, Travel Time Cosmetics, Hasbro, 1960s, unused, MIB ................. 65.00
Costume, Switch & Go, orig box ............................................. 150.00
Desk Set, calendar, stapler, and pencil sharpener, MIB ....................... 150.00
Doll, Batman, 15" h, 1992, DC Comics ................................................. 85.00
Figure, McDonald's Happy Meal, never removed from plastic bag
   Batman, press and go car, ©1991 .............................................. 6.00
   Ridler, ©1993 .............................. 5.00
Halloween Mask
   Batgirl, 1977, Ben Cooper, unworn, orig elastic.............................. 25.00
   Ratman, 1960s, tears on lower chin section..................................... 36.00
License Plate, Batmobile, 1966 .... 45.00
Lunchbox and Thermos, plastic, ©1997 DC Comics ............................ 10.00
Model, MPC Super Powers, Aurora ................................................. 75.00
Movie Viewer, cassette, Galoob, 1984, MIB............................................ 20.00
Napkins, Batman and Robin, 7" sq, MIP ................................................. 10.00
Pez Dispenser, European, Dark Knight, TAS, MOC ............................... 20.00
Plane, friction, plastic, MIB .......... 65.00
Playset, Ideal, Sears Mail Order, 1966, orig box opened from bottom, mint condition box and all accessories, one figure neatly trimmed, rest unplayed with...................... 4,000.00
Puppet
   Hand, Robin, vinyl, Ideal, 1966 ............................................. 185.00

Marionette, hard plastic, Hazelle, c1966
   Batman.............................. 195.00
   Robin................................. 195.00
Puzzle, jigsaw
   Casse-tete, 1975...................... 75.00
   Whitman, 1966 ........................ 35.00
Ring, Nestle, 1977 ...................... 65.00
Statue, WB Resin, Batgirl............ 100.00
Watch, Fossil, MIB ...................... 60.00

### Bionic Woman
Bank, figural, wearing running suit, pile of rocks base ......................... 42.00
Card Set, 44 color cards, colorful wrapper with Jamie...................... 40.00
Model, Repair Kit, Jamie on operating table, computerized medical equipment, Oscar Goldman, snap together, 1976......................... 30.00

### Buck Rogers
Action Figure, 12" h, Mego, NRFB ................................................. 30.00
Rubber Stamp Kit, MIB................ 35.00
View-Master Set, Battle of the Mon, cartoon version, 1978, MISP ......... 24.00

### Captain Action
Doll, red shirt, fully dressed, complete accessories, orig box ........... 225.00
Outfit, cap, chains ....................... 95.00

### Captain America
Action Figure, 12" h, Mego, MIB ................................................. 125.00
Badge, Sentinels of Liberty, very good condition ............................... 750.00
Doll, 8" h, Super Baby, vinyl head, white hair, stuffed body, uniform, shield, gloves, Amsco, 1970s, orig box ................................................. 85.00
Game, Captain America game, Milton Bradley, 1966...................... 60.00
License Plate, 2-1/4" x 4", metal, full color graphics, green background, ©1967 Marvel Comics Group, Louis Marx & Co, Japan ................... 28.00
Transfer Sheet, 11" x 12-1/4", white sheet, colorful day-glow image, © 1971 Marvel Comics Group ..... 18.00
Tricycle, worn............................... 95.00
Wrist Watch, figural, digital, MIP... 30.00

### Captain Marvel
Christmas Card........................... 150.00
Code Wheel................................ 350.00
Figure, lead, British, set of Captain Marvel, Captain Marvel Jr., and Mary Marvel ................................... 275.00
Magic Blotter.............................. 225.00
Magic Flute, MOC....................... 125.00
Membership Kit, card, pin, letter, code sheet ................................... 300.00
Pencil Clip.................................... 75.00
Pennant, blue felt, name and drawing in red and white, 1940s ............. 125.00
Pinback Button, club ................. 100.00
Power Siren................................ 250.00
Puzzle, boxed, incomplete .......... 75.00
Shoulder Patch, multicolored ..... 150.00
Slurpee Cup, 7-11 ....................... 15.00
Toy, helicopter, MIP.................... 125.00
Wrist Watch, Mary Marvel, Shazam, wear ..................................... 140.00

### Captain Midnight
Book, Joyce of the Secret Squadron ................................................. 35.00
Brochure, Smithsonian ................ 45.00
Decoder, 1946 ............................ 95.00
Manual
   1941................................... 200.00
   1946................................... 125.00
   1949................................... 150.00
   1955................................... 200.00
Medal, membership ..................... 25.00
Order Form for Flight Commander Ring ................................................. 35.00
Patch
   Secret Squadron...................... 30.00
   Wings................................. 200.00
Ring
   Flight Commander, signet...... 900.00
   Secret Compartment ............. 150.00
Salt and Pepper Shakers, pr, full color, plaster..................................... 75.00
Service Ribbon, letter, orig mailer ................................................. 395.00
Shake-Up Mug, orig box, 1957 .. 250.00
Whistle Decoder, 1947 ................ 75.00

### Fantastic Four
Action Figure, Mego, set of four figures, MOC ................................... 200.00
Puzzle, Marvel, 1970s ................ 120.00

### Green Hornet
Annual, British, hardbound, 1966, some ink marks ................................. 75.00
Big Little Book ............................. 75.00
Cutlery Set, MOC......................... 85.00
Halloween Costume, Ben Cooper, c1966, MIB ........................... 275.00
Magic Rub-Off Slate, Whitman, 1966 ................................................. 200.00
Puzzle, frame tray, 1966, set of 4 ................................................. 95.00
Ring, seal/secret compartment ................................................. 850.00
Spoon ........................................ 20.00
Trading Card................................. 8.00
Walkie Talkies, Remco, ©1966, MIB ................................................. 800.00
**Incredible Hulk**, utility belt, Remco, 1978, MIB ............................... 45.00
**Legion of Super Heroes,** gold tone, MIB ......................................... 55.00
**Mr. Fantastic,** Marvel, flashlight, 1978, unused ..................................... 55.00

### Spiderman
Action Figure, 9-1/2" x 14-3/4", diecut card, Spiderman on rope, red, blue, and black costume, Fly Away Action version sticker, Mego, ©1979 Marvel Comics, MOC................... 90.00
Figure, Mego, 12" h ..................... 85.00
Halloween Candy Container, plastic, black and white eyes, AJ Renzy Corp., Leominster, MA, 1979 Marvel Comic copyright ................... 20.00
Model Kit, MPC, 1978.................. 50.00
Motorcycle, Super Moto, MIP ....... 40.00
Patch, iron-on, set of six different poses, Marvel ...................................... 5.00
Race- Car, Ricochet, 1974 .......... 85.00
Ring, nickel plated, color face, 1972 ................................................. 175.00

Sign, adv Spider-Man comic strip in Bee Comics, autographed by Stan Lee, 1977 ............................... 150.00
Toy, Helicopter, NRMIB ................. 95.00
Wrist Watch, figural, digital, MIP ... 35.00

### Super Heroes, DC Comics

Activity Set, Prestofix, Tarco, 1977, MIB ............................................. 50.00
Beverage Napkins, 5" sq, 16 in pack, MIP ........................................... 10.00
Plaster Set .................................... 25.00
Record Case, white, multicolored lithos of Super Heroes, 1977 ............. 25.00

### Superman

Animation Art, cel, Superman with three lava monsters, flying to left, matted and framed ........................... 300.00
Catalog, Superman at the Gilbert Hall of Science, toy catalog, Superman cover, illus, 8-1/2" x 5-1/2", 1948 ................................................. 175.00
Cake Topper, Wilton, set in orig box, 1979 ......................................... 20.00
Cartoon Slide, Kenner See A Show, "The Eyes Have It" .................... 5.00
Coloring Book, Saalfield, 11" x 15", 1940, 52 pages, some colored ................................................. 120.00
Comic Book, *Amazing World of Superman, Official Metropolis Edition,* 14" x 12", 1973, NPP ......................... 30.00
Cookie Jar, ceramic, brown telephone booth ........................................ 595.00
Figure, rubber, flexible, Ben Cooper, 1978 ......................................... 65.00
Game, 9" x 14" x 1-3/4", Electronic Question and Answer Game, lid with graphics of Superman flying past angry dictator on telephone, green plastic and silver foil insert, four diecut 8-1/2" x 10" colorful tin cardboard cards, holes for insertion of green plastic pens, Lisbeth Whiting Co ©1966 National Periodical Publications Inc ............................. 38.00
Hair Brush, 2-1/4" x 4" x 1-1/2" tan wooden brush, curved top surface, black and brown bristles, 1-1/4" x 2" red and dark blue image of flying Superman carrying red, white, and blue stars and stripes banner reading "Superman America" gold background, c1942 ......................... 90.00
Movie Viewer, cassette, Galoob, 1984, MIB ............................................ 20.00
Record Player, child's, 1970s ........ 40.00
Ring
    Logo, DC Comics, sterling silver ............................................... 100.00
    Superman of America, silver, diamond, metal tin container, membership kit .................................... 375.00
Squirt Gun ..................................... 65.00
Valentine ....................................... 40.00
Wallet, Standard Plastic/Mattel, 1966 ................................................... 15.00

### Wonder Woman

Action Figure, MOC ..................... 25.00
Animation Art, cel, Wonder Woman and Firestore, 3/4 poses, matted and framed ....................................... 50.00

Book and Record Set, 33-1/3 rpm, Peter Pan, 16 pg comic story, 1977, orig cardboard sleeve ..................... 20.00
Cake Pan Set, Wilton, 16" h figural aluminum pan, orig plastic Wonder Woman face, MIB ................... 40.00
Coloring and Fun Activity Book, mask ................................................. 12.00
Doll, 12" h, Steve Trevor, orig box with small tape tear ........................ 75.00
Drinking Cup, Burger King Kid's Meal premium ................................... 12.00
Drinking Glass, Pepsi, yellow boots, 1978 ......................................... 30.00
Light Switch Cover ....................... 15.00
Puzzle, 15 pc ................................. 8.00
Skates .......................................... 20.00
Squeeze Toy, rubber ..................... 24.00
Sticker, 3-D, unused sheet ............. 3.00
Sunglasses .................................... 4.00

# Swankyswigs

**Collecting Hints:** Ideally, select glasses whose pattern is clear and brightly colored. Rarer patterns include Carnival, Checkerboard, and Texas Centennial. Look-alike patterns from other manufacturers include the Rooster's Head, Cherry, Diamond over Triangle, and Circus. The look-alike patterns date from the 1930s to the 1960s.

**History:** Swankyswigs are decorated glass containers that were filled with Kraft Cheese Spreads. The first Swankyswigs date from the early 1930s. Production was discontinued during the last days of World War II because the paint was needed for the war effort. After the war, production resumed and several new patterns were introduced, including Posy or Cornflower No. 2 (1947), Forget-Me-Not (1948), and Tulip No. 3 (1950). The last colored pattern was Bicentennial Tulip (1975).

In the mid-1970s, several copycat patterns emerged. These include Wildlife Series (1975) and Sportsman Series (1976)—most likely Canadian varieties—Rooster's Head, Cherry, Diamond over Triangle, and Circus. Kraft Cheese Spread is still available but is sold in crystal-type glass.

Swankyswigs were very popular with economy-minded ladies of the Depression era. After the original contents had been consumed, the containers, which could be used as tumblers or to store juice, served as perfect companions to Depression glass table services. Their cheerful designs helped to chase away the Depression blues.

The first designs were hand applied. When the popularity of Swankyswigs increased, more intricate machine-made patterns were introduced. Designs were test marketed and those that did not achieve the desired results are hard to identify and find.

The lack of adequate records about Swankyswigs makes it very difficult to completely identify all patterns. Since 1979, quite a few look-alikes have appeared. Although these glasses were similar to the originals, only Kraft glasses are considered Swankyswigs.

**References:** Gene Florence, *Collectible Glassware from the 40s, 50s, 60s,* 3rd ed., Collector Books, 1996; Ian Warner, *Swankyswigs,* Revised, The Daze, 1988, 1992 value update.

**Periodical:** *The Daze,* P.O. Box 57, Otisville, MI 48463.

**Advisor:** M. D. Fountain.

**Notes:** If a Swankyswig retains its original label, add $4 to the value of the glass.

Antiques, 3-3/4" h
    Churn and cradle, orange ......... 5.00
    Coffee Grinder and Plate, green ................................................. 5.00
    Spinning Wheel and Bellows, red ................................................. 5.00
    Teapot and lamp, blue .............. 5.00
Band #2, red and black ................. 2.50
Band #3, 3-3/8" h ......................... 3.00
Bear and Pig, light blue, 3-3/4" h .... 5.00
Bird and elephant, red, 3-3/4" h ..... 5.00
Bustlin' Betsy, 3-3/4" h
    Brown ...................................... 6.00
    Orange ..................................... 2.75
    Red .......................................... 2.75
    Set, red, blue, brown, yellow, and green ..................................... 25.00
Carnival, 3-1/2" h
    Blue ......................................... 4.25
    Green ....................................... 4.50
    Red .......................................... 3.00
Cars and Wagon, black and white, 3-3/4" h ..................................... 4.00
Checkerboard, 3-1/2" d, red and white ................................................. 16.00
Circle and Dot, black, blue, or red ................................................. 4.25
Cornflower
    #1, light blue
        3-1/2" h .............................. 9.00
        3-3/4" h ............................ 15.00
        4-1/2" h ............................ 18.00
    #2
        3-1/4" h
            Dark Blue ................... 12.75
            Light Blue .................. 12.50
            Yellow ........................ 12.00
        3-1/2" h
            Dark Blue ................... 2.75
            Light Blue .................. 2.50

**Cornflower No. 2., dark blue, 3-1/2" h, $2.50.**

| | |
|---|---|
| Red | 2.50 |
| Yellow | 2.00 |

Daisy
  3-1/4" h
    Red and white ..................... 35.00
    Red, white, and green ......... 15.00
  3-1/2" h, red and white ......... 25.00
  3-3/4" h, red, white, and green
    ............................................... 2.00
  4-1/2" h, red, white, and green
    ............................................. 17.50
Davy Crockett, 3-1/2" h ................... 8.50
Dog and rooster, orange, 3-3/4" h
  ............................................... 5.00
Dots, red, 3-1/2" h .......................... 3.00
Duck and horse, black, 3-3/4" h ..... 5.00
Flying Geese, red, yellow, and blue,
  3-1/2" h ...................................... 4.00
Forget Me Not
  3-1/4" h
    Dark Blue ........................... 15.00
    Light Blue .......................... 12.75
    Red .................................... 14.00
    Yellow ................................ 13.00
  3-1/2" h
    Dark or light blue .................. 2.75
    Red ...................................... 4.00
    Yellow .................................. 3.00
Horizontal Lines, black and red, 3-1/4" h
  ............................................... 3.00
Kiddie Cup
  3-1/4" h
    Black .................................. 13.50
    Brown, green, or orange ..... 12.75
  3-3/4" h
    Black .................................... 3.50
    Brown, green, or orange ....... 2.75

4-1/2" h
  Black ................................... 20.00
  Brown, green, or orange ..... 18.00
Posy
  Jonquil, yellow
    3-1/4" h ............................... 18.00
    3-1/2" h ................................. 6.00
    4-1/2" h ............................... 20.00
  Tulip, red
    3-1/4" h ............................... 15.00
    3-1/2" h ................................. 4.00
    4-1/2" h ............................... 12.00
  Violet, purple
    3-1/4" h ............................... 18.00
    3-1/2" h ................................. 5.00
    4-1/2" h ............................... 20.00
Scotty, red dog, blue fence, 3-1/2" h
  ............................................... 6.00
Squirrel and Deer, brown, 3-3/4" h
  ............................................... 5.00
Spaceships, blue, 3-1/2" d ............. 6.00
Stars, 3-1/2" h
  Black ..................................... 2.00
  Green .................................... 3.00
  Red ....................................... 4.00
Tulip
  #1
    3-1/4" h, green ..................... 14.00
    3-1/2" h
      Black ................................ 3.00
      Dark blue or green ............ 2.75
      Red ................................... 3.50
    4-1/2" h
      Blue or red ...................... 15.00
      Green .............................. 14.00
  #2
    3-1/4" h, dark blue ............... 15.00
    3-3/4" h, dark blue ................. 4.00
    4-1/2" h, dark blue ............... 18.00
  #3
    3-1/4" h, yellow .................... 14.00
    3-3/4" h, dark blue, light blue, or
    red ........................................ 2.75
    3-3/4" h, yellow ..................... 3.00
    4-1/2" h, red ........................ 15.00

# Swarovski Crystal

**Collecting Hints**: Sophisticated design and custom fabricated components of the clearest crystal are some of the criteria that distinguish Swarovski crystal from other collectible crystal figurines. The most popular array of Swarovski items falls within the Silver Crystal line, which has included animals, candlesticks, paperweights, and decorative accessories since 1977. Most items are marked, and this is helpful to collectors. The first mark for Silver Crystal items was a block style "SC," sometimes accompanied by the word "Swarovski." Since 1989, an impressionistic swan has been used as the Swarovski symbol. The logo accompanied by a small copyright symbol indicates that the piece was manufactured for the American market.

Other items produced by the Swarovski company are also of interest to collectors, and these include Trimlite, Savvy, Swarovski Selections, Daniel Swarovski Collection, Ebeling & Reuss, and Giftware Suite assortments.

Swarovski crystal collecting has attracted a worldwide following, with a vigorous secondary market. New collectors will find the Swarovski company's Product Listing leaflet very helpful as a beginning checklist of retired and current items. Condition is critical when contemplating an item for resale, and presence of original packaging with enclosures, where applicable, is important. Also desirable is an artist's autograph, occasionally found on the underside of a figurine. Some figurines were produced in more than one version, and the pursuit of various configurations of a design is one type of collection pursued by some Swarovski enthusiasts.

Some crystal figurines have metal trim, usually in one of two colors: shiny silvertone is called "Rhodium" and usually predates the goldtone version of the same item. Examples include the In Flight series of Bee, Butterfly, and Hummingbird, which were produced with both types of trim.

In addition to stunningly clear crystal, color appears in some Swarovski items. For a number of years paperweights were produced in assorted colors, few of which were sold at retail in the United States. These paperweights, which were colored by applying a vaporized chemical coating to the bottom, have sparked interest among collectors. Recently, the company has introduced several figurines with integrally colored glass.

Few Swarovski pieces are serially numbered, and the items that are numbered have attracted considerable interest. In 1995 the Eagle was produced in an edition of 10,000 pieces. In 1995 and 1996, the company collaborated with perfume makers to create serially numbered perfume flacons in limited quantities.

**History**: The Swarovski family has been perfecting the glassmaker's art in Wattens, Austria, since 1895, and is responsible for many technical advances in the glass industry. For decades, this company has been a leading producer of colored and faceted stones for the costume jewelry and fashion industry, and also is widely respected for its industrial abrasives and quality optics.

Silver Crystal collectible figurines and desk accessories were introduced in 1977, with the creation of a sparkling crystal mouse, followed soon after with a spiny crystal hedgehog. Formed of crystal with lead content of at least 30%, these crystal critters have unmistakable sparkle, and were immediately popular.

Sophisticated design and custom fabricated components of the clearest crystal are some of the criteria that distinguish Swarovski crystal from other collectible crystal figurines. The most popular array of Swarovski items falls within the Silver Crystal line, which has included animals, candlesticks, paperweights, and decorative accessories since 1977. Most items are marked, and this is helpful to collectors. The first mark for Silver Crystal items was a block style "SC," sometimes accompanied by the word "Swarovski." Since 1989, an impressionistic swan has been used as the Swarovski symbol. The logo accompanied by a small copyright symbol indicates that the piece was manufactured for the American market.

Other items produced by the Swarovski company are also of interest to collectors, and these include Trimlite, Savvy, Swarovski Selections, Daniel Swarovski Collection, Ebeling & Reuss, and Giftware Suite assortments.

Swarovski crystal collecting has attracted a worldwide following, with a vigorous secondary market. New collectors will find the Swarovski company's Product Listing leaflet very helpful as a beginning checklist of retired and current items. Condition is critical when contemplating an item for resale, and presence of original packaging with enclosures, where applicable, is important. Also desirable is an artist's autograph, occasionally found on the underside of a figurine. Some figurines were produced in more than one version, and the pursuit of various configurations of a design is one type of collection pursued by some Swarovski enthusiasts.

Some crystal figurines have metal trim, usually in one of two colors: shiny silvertone is called "Rhodium" and usually predates the goldtone version of the same item. Examples include the In Flight series of Bee, Butterfly, and Hummingbird, which were produced with both types of trim.

In addition to stunningly clear crystal, color appears in some Swarovski items. For a number of years paperweights were produced in assorted colors, few of which were sold at retail in the United States. These paperweights, which were colored by applying a vaporized chemical coating to the bottom, have sparked interest among collectors. Recently, the company has introduced several figurines with integrally colored glass.

Few Swarovski pieces are serially numbered, and the items that are numbered have attracted considerable interest. In 1995 the Eagle was produced in an edition of 10,000 pieces. In 1998, the Peacock was issued, again limited to 10,000.

The Swarovski Collectors Society, which was formed in 1987, extends exclusive offers to members to purchase annual limited editions. The first SCS series, called Caring and Sharing, features three different pairs of birds. The second series, entitled Mother and Child, focuses on three sets of sea mammals with their young. The third SCS series, with the Inspiration Africa theme, offers three different African wildlife figurines. A fourth series, called Fabulous Creatures, was launched in 1997, and offered mystical creatures. The new series, Masquerade, debuted in 1999 with the introduction of "Pierrot." All SCS figurines are limited to one per member during the year it is offered, and each piece comes with special packaging and a certificate of authenticity.

**References:** Swarovski, *Swarovski, The Magic of Crystal*, Harry N. Abrams, 1995; Jane and Tom Warner, *Warner's Blue Ribbon Book on Swarovski Silver Crystal*, 3rd ed. (separate pocket guide included), published by authors (7163 W. Frederick-Garland Rd., Union, OH 45322), 1996.

**Periodical**: *Swarovski Collector*, General Wille Strasse 88, SH-8706, Feldmeilien, Switzerland.

**Collectors' Clubs:** Swan Seekers, 9740 Campo Rd., #134, Spring Valley, CA; Swarovski Collectors Society, 2 Slater Rd., Cranston, RI 02920.

**Reproduction Alert:** Nefarious reproductions haven't been a problem, but copycats are widespread.

Collectors who are alert to correct proportions and quality material rarely are mistaken about a piece of Swarovski crystal, and the presence of the maker's mark and correct packaging make acquisition almost foolproof. Replica mouse, replica hedgehog, and replica cat were issued by the company in 1995. Although similar to early figurines, these reissues are clearly marked with the swan logo and also have design distinctions that will keep collectors from becoming confused.

**Advisor:** Jimer De Vries.

**Notes:** All prices shown are approximate retail replacement cost for items in perfect condition with correct original packaging and enclosures. Deduct 15% for missing boxes or certificates.

### Accessories

Apple, photo, apple hinged at side, when top is tilted back, it reveals a photograph
#7504NR030R, 30 mm d, rhodium, SC logo ................................. 275.00
#7504n050, 50 mm d, gold, SC or swan logo .............................. 275.00
#7504NR060, 60mm d, SC logo, gold ......................................... 690.00
Ashtray, #7641NR100, sculpted crystal, 3-3/8" d, SC or swan logo
............................................. 350.00
Bell, #7467NR071000, 5-3/4" h, SC or swan logo ............................. 210.00
Candleholder
#7600NR116, for 5 candles, found with sockets or pickets, SC logo
............................................. 3,850.00
#7600NR131, pickets, set of six, 15/16" h, SC logo .................. 300.00
#7600NR136001, gold metal foliage, pineapple, SC logo ........ 600.00
Christmas Ornament
1981, not dated, crystal snowflake, hexagonal metal trim ring and neck chain, hexagonal ring is stamped "SC" at top on back side, orig blue velour pouch, silver logo box, called the "First Annual Edition," only ornament produced in the Silver Crystal Line ...................................... 525.00
1987, dated, Giftware Suite, etched baroque teardrop shape, first in "Holiday Etching" series, no mark
............................................. 375.00
1991, dated, Giftware Suite, star/snowflake series .................... 350.00
Cigarette Holder, #7463NR062, sculpted crystal, 2-3/8" h, SC or swan logo ............................. 175.00
Cigarette Lighter, #7462NR062, 3-1/2" h, chrome lighter in crystal base, SC or swan logo ......................... 410.00
Eagle, 1998, edition of 10,000
............................................. 6,000.00

Grapes, #7550NR30015, cluster of fifteen 1-1/8" d clear grapes, gold stem, SC logo, USA only ..... 2,700.00

Paperweight

#7451NR60095, Carousel, 2-3/4" h, flared sides, vertical facets, clear, SC logo, often found without logo, sometimes paper label on felted bottom ........................................... 1,200.00

#7452NR600, Cone, 3-1/8" h, facets that spiral around cone, Bermuda Blue, shades from dark to light blue, SC or swan logo ..................... 575.00

#7452NR600, Cone, 3-1/8" h, facets that spiral around cone, Volcano color, SC or swan logo .......... 700.00

#7452NR600878, Cone, 3-1/8" h, facets that spiral around cone, clear, SC or swan logo ..................... 300.00

#7453NR60088, Barrel, 2-5/8" h, rect facets that line up vertically, Bermuda Blue, shades from dark to light blue, SC logo, often found without logo, sometimes paper label on felted bottom .......................... 800.00

#7453NR60095, Barrel, 2-5/8" h, rect facets that line up vertically, clear, SC logo, often found without logo, sometimes paper label on felted bottom ................................. 450.00

#7454NR600, Atomic, 2-3/4" h, hexagonal facets, Bermuda Blue, shades from dark to light blue, SC logo, often found without logo, sometimes paper label on felted bottom ......................................... 2,875.00

#7454NR600, Atomic, 2-3/4" h, hexagonal facets, clear, SC logo, often found without logo, sometimes paper label on felted bottom .............................................. 1,500.00

#7454NR600, Atomic, 2-3/4" h, hexagonal facets, Vitrail, medium color, SC logo, often found without logo, sometimes paper label on felted bottom ..................................... 2,100.00

Perfume Bottle, Lancome Tresor, 1994 edition of 5,000 serially numbered, full, with box ........................... 450.00

Picture Frame

#7505NR75G, oval, 3" h, gold trim, SC or swan logo ................., 500.00

#7506NR60, square, gold or rhodium trim, SC or swan logo ...... 400.00

Pineapple, rhodium metal foliage

#7507NR060002, 2-1/2" h ...... 200.00

#7507NR105002, 4-1/8" h, SC logo ............................................. 600.00

Salt and Pepper Shakers, pr, #7508NR068034, 2-3/8" h, rhodium screw on tops, SC logo .......... 500.00

Schnapps Glass, #7468NR039000, approx. 2" h, SC or swan logo

Europe, set of 3 ..................... 200.00

USA, set of 6 .......................... 625.00

Treasure Box, removable lid

#7464NR50, round shape, flowers on lid, SC or swan logo ......... 300.00

#7464NR50/100, round shape, butterfly on lid, SC logo ............... 300.00

#7465NR52, heart shape, flowers on lid, SC logo ..................... 600.00

#7465NR52/100, heart shape, butterfly on lid, SC or swan logo ............................................. 350.00

#7466NR063000, oval shape, flowers on lid, SC or swan logo .... 350.00

#7466NR063100, oval shape, butterfly on lid, SC logo .................. 425.00

Vase, #7511NR70, 2-7/8" h, sculpted crystal, three frosted crystal flowers, SC or swan logo ..................... 220.00

**Figurine**

Angel, #7475NR000600 ............. 210.00

Baby Lovebirds, #7621NR005 ... 115.00

Bear

#7636NR112, 4-1/2" h, SC mark only, USA only, SC logo .............. 3,500.00

#7637NR92, 3-3/4" h, USA only, SC logo ..................................... 2,650.00

#7670NR32, 1-1/8" h, SC logo ............................................. 375.00

Bee, crystal and metal bee feeding on crystal lotus flower, 4" w, SC logo

#7553NR100, gold metal bee ..................................... 2,250.00

#7553NR200, silver metal bee ..................................... 5,225.00

Butterfly

#7551NR100, 4" w, crystal and metal butterfly feeding on crystal lotus flower, gold metal butterfly, SC logo ..................................... 1,400.00

#7551NR200, 4" w, crystal and metal butterfly feeding on crystal lotus flower, silver metal butterfly, SC logo ..................................... 5,150.00

#7671NR30, 1" h, crystal, metal antennae, no base, USA only SC logo ...................................... 225.00

Cat

#7634NR52, 2" h, flexible metal tale, SC logo ................................... 700.00

#7634NR70, 2-7/8" h, SC or swan logo ..................................... 150.00

#7659NR31, 1-1/4" h, flexible metal tail, SC or swan logo ............... 75.00

Cheetah, #7610NR000001 ......... 500.00

Dachshund, metal tail

#7641NR75, 3" l, rigid, limp, or gently arched, SC or swan logo... 150.00

#7642NR42, 1-1/4" l, SC logo ............................................. 200.00

Dog (Pluto on European list), SC or swan logo ............................. 150.00

Dolphin, #7644NR000001 .......... 210.00

Duck

#7653NR45, 1-7/8" l, silver beak, SC logo ................................... 100.00

#7653NR55, 2-1/8" l, silver beak, USA only, SC logo ................. 225.00

#7653NR75, 3" l, crystal beak, USA only, SC logo ......................... 600.00

Eagle, #7607NR000001, 1995, edition of 10,000 serially numbered, gray train case type box, wood display pedestal .............................. 8,100.00

Elephant

#7640NR60, 2" h, frosted tail, swan logo ..................................... 150.00

#7640NR55, 2-1/2" h, flexible metal tail, SC logo ........................... 275.00

#7640NR100, Dumbo, 1990, black eyes, clear hat, only 3,000 made, most have swan logo, few unmarked ........................................... 1,150.00

#7640NR1000001, Dumbo, 1993, blue eyes, frosted hat, swan logo and Disney copyright symbol ......................................... 1,500.00

Falcon Head, SC or swan logo

#7645NR45, 1-3/4" h ............. 230.00

#7645NR100, 4" h ............... 3,500.00

Frog

#7642NR48, black eyes, clear crown, SC or swan logo ........ 150.00

#7642NR48, clear eyes, clear crown, usually found with SC logo .... 350.00

Grand Piano, with stool, #7477NR000006 .................. 260.00

Hedgehog, silver whiskers

#7360NR30, 1-1/4" h including spines, 30mm body, SC logo, USA only ........................................ 565.00

#7360NR40, 1-3/4" h including spines, 40mm body, found only with SC mark, worldwide distribution ............................................. 180.00

#7360NR50, 2" h including spines, 50mm body, SC logo, worldwide distribution ................................... 200.00

#7630NR60, 2-3/8" h including spines, 60mm body, SC logo, USA only ....................................... 1,150.00

Hummingbird, crystal and metal hummingbird feeding in crystal lotus flower, 4" w, SC logo

#7552NR100, gold metal hummingbird, green stones on wings ................................................ 1,500.00

#7552NR200, silver metal hummingbird, red stones on wings ... 6,500.00

Mallard, #7647NR80, 3-1/2" l, frosted beak, SC or swan logo .......... 225.00

Mouse, silver whiskers, metal coil tail

#7631NR23, 13/16" h, SC logo ................................................ 100.00

#7631NR30, 1-3/4" h to top of ears, 30mm body, octagonal base, SC or swan logo .............................. 130.00

#7631NR50, 2-7/8" h to top of ears, 50mm body, sq base, USA only, SC mark ...................................... 1,500.00

#7631NR60, 3-3/4" h to top of ears, 60mm body, sq base, USA only, SC logo ...................................... 2,200.00

Peacock, #7607NR000002, 1998, edition of 10,000 ...................... 6,000.00

Pig, #7638n65, 1-3/4" l, crystal "J" shaped tail, SC logo ............. 500.00

Rabbit, ears lay flat on top of head, SC logo

#7652NR20, 1" h .................... 110.00

#7652NR45, 1-1/2" h .............. 550.00

Rose, #7478NR000001 ............. 155.00

Santa Maria, #7473NR000003 ... 375.00

Shell with Pearl, #7624NR055000 ................................................ 175.00

Sparrow, silver metal open beak

#7650NR20, 3-/4" h, SC or swan logo ....................................... 75.00

#7650NR32, 1-1/4" h, SC logo ................................................ 80.00

Swan, #7658NR27, 1" h, delicate crystal neck connected to body, two wings, tail, SC logo ........................... 190.00

Turtle, #7632NR75, 3" l, green eyes, SC logo ...................................... 800.00

# T

## Taylor, Smith and Taylor

**Collecting Hints:** Collector interest focuses primarily on the Lu-Ray line, introduced in 1938 and named after Virginia's Luray Caverns. The line actually utilized forms from the Empire and Laurel lines. Lu-Ray was made from the 1930s through the early 1950s in coordinating colors, which has encouraged collectors to mix and match sets.

Pieces from the Coral-Craft line are very similar in appearance to pink Lu-Ray. Do not confuse the two.

Vistosa, introduced in 1938, is another example of the California patio dinnerware movement that featured bright, solid-color pieces. Unfortunately, the number of forms was restricted. As a result, many collectors shy away from it.

Pebbleford, a plain colored ware with sandlike specks, can be found in gray, dark blue-green, light blue-green, light tan, and yellow. When in production, it was the company's third most popular line, but it is only moderately popular among today's collectors.

Taylor, Smith, and Taylor used several different backstamps and marks. Many contain the company name as well as the pattern and shape names. A dating system was used on some dinnerware lines until the 1950s. The three-number code identifies month, year, and crew number.

**History:** W. L. Smith, John N. Taylor, W. L. Taylor, Homer J. Taylor, and Joseph G. Lee founded Taylor, Smith, and Taylor in Chester, West Virginia, in 1899. In 1903, the firm reorganized and the Taylors bought Lee's interest. In 1906, Smith bought out the Taylors. The firm remained in the family's control until it was purchased by Anchor Hocking in 1973. The tableware division closed in 1981.

Taylor, Smith, and Taylor started production with a nine-kiln pottery. Local clays were used initially; later only southern clays were used. Both earthenware and fine-china bodies were produced. Several underglaze print patterns, e.g., Dogwood and Spring Bouquet, were made. These prints, made from the copper engravings of ceramic artist J. Palin Thorley, were designed exclusively for the company.

During the 1930s and through the 1950s, competition in the dinnerware market was intense. Lu-Ray was designed to compete with Russel Wright's American Modern. Vistosa was Taylor, Smith, and Taylor's answer to Homer Laughlin's Fiesta.

**References:** Susan and Al Bagdade, *Warman's American Pottery and Porcelain*, Wallace-Homestead, 1994; Jo Cunningham, *Collector's Encyclopedia of American Dinnerware*, Collector Books, 1982, 1995 value update; Lois Lehner, *Lehner's Encyclopedia of U.S. Marks on Pottery, Porcelain & Clay*, Collector Books, 1988; Kathy and Bill Meehan, *Collector's Guide to Taylor, Smith & Taylor Lu-Ray Pastels U.S.A.*, Collector Books, 1995.

**Beverly**, platter .............................. 12.00
**Delphian**, cup and saucer ............. 7.50

### Empire

Butter Dish, cov ............................ 20.00
Dinner Plate, 10" d ........................ 12.00

### Fairway

Casserole ...................................... 20.00
Dinner Plate, 9-1/2" d .................... 8.50
**Laurel**, cake plate, 10-1/4" d ........ 12.00

### Lu-Ray

Berry Bowl, Chatham Grey ........... 14.00
Bowl, c1936
    Persian Cream ......................... 60.00

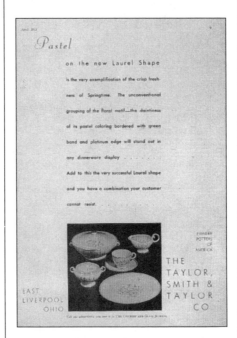

**Magazine Tear Sheet, *Crockery and Glass Journal*, April, 1933, Pastel on Laurel Shape, black and white, $3.**

Surf Green .............................. 60.00
Windsor Blue ........................... 60.00
Bread and Butter Plate, 6" d, Windsor
    Blue................................. 6.00
Breakfast Plate, 9" d, Persian Cream
    ........................................ 7.50
Bud Vase
    Surf Green ....................... 150.00
    Windsor Blue ................... 135.00
Butter Dish, Persian Cream ......... 35.00
Cake Plate
    Persian Cream ................... 110.00
    Sharon Pink...................... 110.00
Casserole, cov
    Sharon Pink...................... 150.00
    Surf Green ....................... 140.00
    Windsor Blue ................... 140.00
Chop Plate, 14" d
    Sharon Pink........................ 30.00
    Surf Green ......................... 25.00
Creamer, Persian Cream ............... 6.00
Cream Soup and Underplate
    Persian Cream ................... 125.00
    Sharon Pink...................... 125.00
    Windsor Blue ................... 125.00
Demitasse Creamer, Sharon Pink
    ........................................ 50.00
Demitasse Cup and Saucer
    Persian Cream ..................... 20.00
    Surf Green ......................... 45.00
Dinner Plate, 10" d
    Sharon Pink........................ 20.00
    Surf Green ......................... 20.00
Egg Cup
    Persian Cream ..................... 20.00
    Surf Green ......................... 20.00
    Windsor Blue ..................... 20.00
Epergne
    Sharon Pink...................... 145.00
    Windsor Blue ................... 145.00
Fruit Bowl, Persian Cream ............. 8.00
Gravy Boat, attached underplate, Windsor Blue................................... 50.00
Grill Plate
    Persian Cream ..................... 30.00
    Surf Green ......................... 30.00
Juice Pitcher, Windsor Blue........ 225.00
Juice Tumbler
    Persian Cream ..................... 70.00
    Sharon Pink........................ 70.00
Luncheon Plate, 8" d, Sharon Pink
    ........................................ 20.00
Nappy, Sharon Pink ...................... 15.00
Nut Dish
    Persian Cream ................... 125.00
    Surf Green ....................... 125.00
Pickle Dish, Persian Cream .......... 45.00
Pitcher
    Persian Cream ................... 135.00
    Sharon Pink........................ 65.00
Platter, 12" l, Surf Green.............. 20.00
Relish, 4 sections, Surf Green .... 220.00
Salad Bowl, Sharon Pink............... 45.00
Salt and Pepper Shakers, pr
    Persian Cream ..................... 18.00
    Windsor Blue ..................... 15.00
Sauceboat, underplate, Persian Cream
    ........................................ 18.00
Soup, flat, Windsor Blue .............. 15.00
Teapot, Sharon Pink...................... 50.00
Tidbit Tray, Chatham Grey ........... 80.00
Tumbler, Windsor Blue................. 98.00

Vegetable Bowl, 8" d
 Sharon Pink.............................20.00
 Windsor Blue...........................17.50

**Marvel**
Cup and Saucer............................6.00
Salad Bowl...................................17.50
**Paramount**, gravy boat...............12.50
**Pebbleford**, dinner plate, 10" d....10.00
**Plymouth,** chop plate .................20.00
**Versatile**, Salt and Pepper Shakers, pr
 ....................................................6.00

**Vistosa**
Bowl
 8" d, Cobalt Blue......................65.00
 12" d, ftd, Mango Red............115.00
Chop Plate, 12" d, Light Green.....85.00
Creamer
 Cobalt Blue.............................20.00
 Light Green.............................20.00
Cup and Saucer
 Deep Yellow ...........................15.00
 Light Green.............................17.50
Demitasse Cup and Saucer, Deep Yel-
 low...........................................45.00
Dinner Plate, Cobalt Blue..............20.00
Eggcup, Cobalt Blue ....................25.00
Luncheon Plate, 9" d, Light Green
 ................................................17.50
Salad Bowl, 12" d, ftd, Light Green
 ..............................................195.00
Salt and Pepper Shakers, pr
 Deep Yellow ...........................22.00
 Mango Red ..............................20.00
Sauce Boat, Light Green .............145.00
Soup, coupe, Mango Red.............25.00
Soup, flat, Deep Yellow.................24.00
Sugar, cov
 Light Green.............................25.00
 Mango Red ..............................25.00
Teapot
 Deep Yellow ...........................85.00
 Light Green.............................95.00
 Mango Red ..............................85.00
Vegetable Bowl, Cobalt Blue........45.00
Water Jug, Deep Yellow................75.00
Water Pitcher, Mango Red............85.00
**Vogue,** cup and saucer..................6.50

# Teapots

**Collecting Hints:** Most collectors
focus on pottery, porcelain or china
examples. Much attention has been
given recently to the unglazed pottery teapots referred to as Yixing.
These teapots are small in size and
feature earthy designs such as lotus
flowers, handles of twig, and insects
shaped on the body or lid finial. Yixing (traditionally Vis-Hsing or I
Hsing) is a Chinese province that
has been known for these artistic
wares since the 16th century. Since
they are still being produced, collectors need to learn to differentiate the
antique from the modern.

**History:** The origin of the teapot has
been traced back to the Chinese
province of Yixing in the late 16th
century. The teapots, similar to ones
still being produced today, were no
bigger than the tiny teacups used at
that time.

By the 17th century, tea drinking
had spread throughout the world.
Every pottery or porcelain manufacturer from Asia, Europe and America
has at one time produced teapots.
Forms range from the purely functional, such as the English Brown
Betty, to the ornately decorative and
whimsical, such as individual artist
renditions or popular figurals depicting shapes of people, animals, or
things. The majority of teapots available in today's market date from
1870 to the present.

**References:** Edward Bramah, *Novelty Teapots*, Quiller Press (available
from John Ives, 5 Normanhurst Dr.
Twickenham, Middlesex, TW1 1NA,
London, England), 1992; Tina M.
Carter, *Teapots*, Running Press
(available from author, 882 S. Mollison Ave., El Cajon, CA 92020),
1995; Robin Emmerson, *British Teapots and Tea Drinking*, distributed
by Seven Hills, 1996.

**Periodicals:** *Tea Talk*, P.O. Box 860,
Sausalito, CA 94966; *Tea Time
Gazette*, P.O. Box 40276, St Paul,
MN 55104.

**Museum:** Arthur Wood Teapot
Showroom, Los Angeles, CA;
Greater Gibson County Area Cham-
ber of Commerce, P.O. Box 464,
Trenton, TN 38382, sponsors an
annual Teapot Festival.

**Reproduction Alert:** New and modern Yixing teapots mimicking the vintage pots. This category requires
extra study. Watch for teapots and
other porcelain with a celadon color
and cobalt design similar to flow
blue. These reproduction teapots
often have a blurred mark, including
a lion, unicorn and shield, which is
similar to many pottery marks from
England.

**Advisor:** Tina M. Carter.

**American**
Ford, pottery, pink glaze, small.....22.00
Fraunfleter, ribbed body, marked "Ohio"
 in diamond...............................32.00
Harker, Royal Gadroon pattern, floral
 ................................................25.00
McCormick, by Hall China, mkd "Balto,
 Maryland"..................................40.00
Monterey, CA, pink, speckled glaze
 ................................................42.00
Tin, Ohio Art, Blue Willow pattern,
 child's set...............................125.00

**Chinese, Yixing, modern, cloth cov-
ered box, Chinese writing on body,
chop mark on bottom, $55. Photo
courtesy of Tina Carter.**

Weil Ware, CA pottery, rose pattern,
 1954........................................35.00
**Chinese**
Brass, hammered design, matching
 warming stand, mkd "China"...85.00
China, white, large 8-cup teapot, rattan
 handle, no mark.......................18.00
Floral, tiny spout, unmarked.........25.00
Set, teapot and 2 cups, in padded basket, mkd "China"....................125.00
Yixing
 Gourd shape, leaves and insects
 dec, chop mark (Chinese manufacturer's mark) under cover.......125.00
 Modern, Chinese writing on body,
 chop mark (Chinese manufacturer's
 mark) on bottom, cloth covered box
 ................................................55.00

**English**
Abrams, cozy pot, pitcher shape, patents.........................................50.00
Crown Dorset, florals, cabbage roses
 dec, modern ...........................40.00
Ellgreave, Wood & Sons, floral.....32.00
Sadler, floral, raised mark.............30.00
Staffordshire, coralene raised decoration, black ground, lion and Staffordshire knot mark, made as fundraiser
 for wartime efforts, c1948........40.00
Wade, majolica style, basket and fruit
 ................................................35.00

**Figural**
Colonial man and woman, Tony Wood,
 England ...................................40.00

**English, coralene raised decoration,
lion and Staffordshire knot mark,
c1948, $40. Photo courtesy of Tina
Carter.**

**Comical, pastels, 1950s, made in Japan, $32. Photo courtesy of Tina Carter.**

Dickens characters, Beswick, England ........................................ 75.00
House, Cottage Ware, Price, Kensington, England ............................ 32.00
Jim Bean Club, collector's edition, Wade, 1995 ............................ 50.00
Santa, white glaze, Price Bros., England, 1960s ...................... 30.00
Sherlock Holmes, Hall China, 1988, 12" h .................................. 125.00
Snow White, dwarves around base, holds 1-1/2 cups, music box base plays "Hi Ho, Hi Ho," c1940, 6" h ........................................ 130.00

**German**

Large, chocolate pot, scroll handle, ftd ........................................ 85.00
Small, hand painted china, Royal Hanover ................................ 75.00

**Japan**

Brown luster, square, 2 cup .......... 15.00
Comical style, pastel dec, spout as nose, cover as hat, 1950s, mkd "Made in Japan" ...................... 32.00
Cube shape, hand painted, c1930 ........................................ 25.00
Majolica style, twin tea, two pots on a tray, mkd "Japan" ...................... 25.00
Miniature Set, hand painted, matching tray, 1-3/4" h .............................. 25.00

**Snow White, music box base, c1940, $130. Photo courtesy of Tina Carter.**

Rebekah at the Well, orange luster, relief design, mkd "Japan" ...... 22.00
Violets dec, china, c1950 ............. 22.00

**Miniature**

Aluminum, Swans Brand, 2 cup, England, 4" h ............................. 15.00
China
    Hand painted, dragonflies, Chinese mark, 2-1/2" h ...................... 12.00
    Peking Duck, teapot on stand, 2" h ........................................ 18.00
Copper, mkd "Italy," 1-3/4" h ......... 10.00
Porcelain
    Children playing dec, no mark, attributed to Germany, 4" h ...... 25.00
    Floral, lid screws on, Germany, 3" h ........................................ 25.00
    Relief flowers, white porcelain, England, 2" h ...................... 15.00
Precious Moments, Taiwan, 1992, 2" h ........................................ 12.00
Thimble, pewter mouse peaks out of teapot, 1" h ............................. 10.00

**Porcelain**

Lipton's Tea, Hall China, various colors ........................................ 35.00
Mermaid, Eliza Hurdle, modern .. 350.00
Simple Yet Perfect, teapot on side, floral ........................................ 185.00

**Pottery**

Brown Betty, colored rings, various sizes ........................................ 28.00
Granny Woods, English ............... 40.00
Torquay, motto ware, small, Watcombe, England ................................. 38.00

# Television Personalities & Memorabilia

**Collecting Hints:** Collectors of television memorabilia fall into two categories. One includes those who specialize in acquiring items from a single television series: "Star Trek," "Hopalong Cassidy," "Howdy Doody," "Roy Rogers," or "Leave It To Beaver" are the most popular series. The other category of collector specializes in TV memorabilia of one type such as *TV Guides*, model kits, films, or cards.

There have been more than 3,750 series on television since 1948. Therefore, an enormous number of artifacts and memorabilia relating to television are available. Pop-culture collectors eagerly seek premiums from the early space shows and cowboy adventure series. As a result, these items are beginning to command high prices at auction.

Systematic scheduling of television programs developed a new type of publication called *TV Guide*.

The early guides are avidly sought. The first schedules were regional and include titles such as *TV Today in Philadelphia*, *TV Press in Louisville*, and *Radio-Television Life in Los Angeles*. The first national *TV Guide* was published on April 3, 1953. Collectors enjoy these older magazines because they are good sources for early stories about the stars of the time.

**History:** The late 1940s and early 1950s was the golden age of television. The first TV programming began in 1948. Experimentation with programming, vast expansion, and rapid growth marked the period. Prime-time live drama series were very successful, and provided the start for many popular stars, such as Paul Newman, Steve McQueen, Rod Steiger, Jack Lemmon, and Grace Kelly. The stars signed autographs and photographs to promote the dramas. These items, plus scripts and other types of articles, have become very collectible.

When the period of live drama ended, the Western assault began. In 1959, there were 26 Western series, many of which were based on movie or radio heroes. The Western era continued until the early 1960s when it was replaced by the space adventure series and science fiction.

The 1970s are remembered for their situation comedies, including "All In The Family" and "M*A*S*H*." The collectibles resulting from these series are numerous.

**References:** Paul Anderson, *The Davy Crockett Craze: A Look at the 1950s Phenomenon and Davy Crockett Collectibles*, R & G Productions, 1996 (P.O. Box 605, Hillside, IL 60162); Tim Brooks and Earle Marsh, *The Complete Direction to Prime Time Network and Cable TV Shows, 1948-Present*, 6th ed., Ballantine Books, 1995; Dana Cain, *Film & TV Animal Star Collectibles*, Antique Trader Books, 1998; Greg Davis and Bill Morgan, *Collector's Guide to TV Memorabilia 1960s & 1970s*, Collector Books, 1996; Robert W. Getz, *The Unauthorized Guide to The Simpsons Collectibles*, Schiffer, 1998; David R. Greenland, *Bonanza, A Viewer's Guide to the TV Legend*, R & G Publications (P.O. Box 605, Hillside, IL 60162); Ted Hake, *Hake's Guide to Character Toys*, 2nd ed., Avon Books, 1998; Jim Harmon, *Radio & TV Premiums*,

Krause Publications, 1997; Jack Koch, *Howdy Doody*, Collector Books, 1996; Cynthia Boris Liljeblad, *TV Toys and the Shows That Inspired Them*, Krause Publications, 1996; Rex Miller, *The Investor's Guide to Vintage Character Collectibles*, Krause Publications, 1999; Kurt Peer, *TF Tie-Ins: A Bibliography of American TV Tie-In Paperbacks*, Neptune Publishing, 1997; Maxine A. Pinksy, *Marx Toys: Robots, Space, Comic, Disney & TV Characters*, Schiffer Publishing, 1996; Neil Summers, *Official TV Western Book*, Vol. 4, Old West Shop Publishing, 1992; Ric Wyman, *For the Love of Lucy*, Chronicle Books, 1995; Alan Young, *Mister Ed and Me*, St. Martin's Press, 1994; Dian Zillner, *Collectible Television Memorabilia*, Schiffer Publishing, 1996; Stuart W. Wells III, *Science Fiction Collectibles: Identification & Price Guide*, Krause Publications, 1999.

**Periodicals:** *Autograph Times*, 2303 N. 44th St., #225, Phoenix, AZ 85008; *Big Reel*, P.O. Box 83, Madison, NC 27025; *Celebrity Collector*, P.O. Box 1115, Boston, MA, 02117; *Collecting Hollywood*, 2401 Broad St., Chattanooga, TN 37408; *Norm's Serial News*, 1726 Maux Dr., Houston, TX 70043; *Television History Magazine*, 700 E. Macoupia St., Staunton, IL 62088; *TV Collector*, P.O. Box 1088, Easton, MA 02334.

**Collectors' Club:** TV Western Collectors Fan Club, P.O. Box 1361, Boyes Hot Springs, CA 95416.

**Museum:** Smithsonian Institution, Washington, DC.

**Additional Listings:** Cowboy Heroes, Space Adventurers & Explorers, Super Heroes, Western Americana.

Action Figure
  A-Team, 6" h, Galoob, Murdock, MOC ............................... 25.00
  A-Team, 6" h, Galoob, Templeton Peck, MOC .......................... 25.00
  Dukes of Hazzard, 3-1/2" h, Bo, MOC ............................... 25.00
  Dukes of Hazzard, 3-1/2" h, Luke, MOC ............................... 25.00
Alarm Clock, Mr. T., A-Team, metal, blue, silvered metal bells, Zeon, ©1973 Ruby-Spears Enterprises ............................... 27.50
Autograph, color photo, Lost in Space, Jonathan Harris ................ 50.00
Book Bag, Dukes of Hazzard ....... 30.00
Car
  Dick Dastardly, Corgi ............. 75.00

**Book and Record Set,** *Knight Rider, Highway to Danger,* **Kid Stuff, ©1982, 1984 University City Studios, Inc., 33-1/3 rpm, $7.50.**

Magnum PI, Burnin' Key Car Action Set, Kidco, 1981, MIB .............. 40.00
Muppet Show, die-cast, Corgi, complete set of four, 1979, MOC ............................... 135.00
Colorforms
  Flipper, 1966 ........................... 55.00
  Tammy ..................................... 40.00
  Welcome Back Kotter, ©1976 ............................... 30.00
Coloring Book
Addams Family, ©1965, Saalfield, used ............................... 25.00
I Love Lucy, ©1954, Whitman, unused ............................... 75.00
Jackie Gleason, ©1956, Abbott, unused ..................................... 75.00
Ozzie & Harriet, ©1973 Filmways Television Corp., Saalfield, unused ............................... 45.00
Wagon Train, ©1959, Whitman, unused ............................... 35.00
Comic Book
  Gidget, Dell, December 1966 ............................... 15.00
  I Love Lucy, 1956 ...................... 5.00
Cookbook, Granny's, Beverly Hillbillies, orig dust jacket ............... 100.00
Cookie Jar, Howdy Doody, Purinton Pottery, 9-3/4" h .............. 900.00
Display Box, Welcome Back Kotter, for pinback buttons, Canadian, 1976, slight wear ............................... 60.00
Doll
  Bart Simpson ........................... 35.00
  Flying Nun, Hasbro, 1967, MIB ............................... 1,000.00
  Herman Munster ...................... 35.00
  Ricky Jr., 1950s ...................... 275.00
  Tabitha, Bewitched, MIB ..... 2,420.00
Drawing Set, Laugh-In, 1969 ........ 70.00
Fan Club Kit, Banana Splits ........ 295.00
Figure, Magilla Gorilla, Playtime Toys, 7" h, 1979 ............................... 20.00
Fire Helmet, child's, Emergency, color photo on front with show stars ............................... 50.00

**Game, I Dream of Jeannie, Milton Bradley, 1965, $12.**

Game
  Columbo ................................. 27.50
  Dick Van Dyke, Standard Toykraft, 1964 ....................................... 500.00
  Gilligan's Island, Game Gems, 1965 ............................... 570.00
  Kukla, Fran & Ollie .................. 27.50
  Laverne and Shirley ................ 27.00
  Merv Griffin's Word for Word Game, Mattel, ©1963 NBC, orig box .. 37.50
  Perry Mason, Missing Suspect, 1959 ............................... 42.00
Halloween Costume
  Beany, 1960s, some wear ...... 175.00
  Dukes of Hazzard, Bo, 1982.... 40.00
Hat, My Favorite Martian, 1963 .... 45.00
Ice Cream Spoon, Howdy Doody ............................... 50.00
Keychain, Lost in Space, robot .... 10.00
Lunch Box
  Family Affair, King-Seeley, ©1969, no thermos .................................. 95.00
  Happy Days, orig thermos ....... 85.00
  Wagon Train, King Seeley, ©1964, no thermos ........................... 160.00
Magazine
  Bewitched, *TV Guide,* June 18, 1966 ............................... 25.00
  Charlie's Angels, *Star,* 1977 ..... 20.00
  Farrah Fawcett, *Bananas,* complete with mini poster ...................... 20.00
  Flintstones, *Chicago* ............... 40.00
  Jackie Gleason, *TV Spotlight,* 1953 ............................... 38.00
  Laugh-In, *Post* ...................... 15.00
  Our Miss Brooks, *Philadelphia News* ............................... 30.00
Magic Slate, Sea Hunt, 1960 ........ 60.00
Magic Transfers, Fall Guy, Rub-A-Doos, Imperil, 1982 ............................. 5.00
Mittens, pr, Howdy Doody and Clarabell, wool, red .......................... 40.00
Night Light
  Church Lady, Saturday Night Live, 1991 ....................................... 30.00
  Howdy Doody, figural, Leadworks, Inc., 1988, 8" h ...................... 150.00
Paint by Number, Dukes of Hazzard, acrylic, MIB ............................ 50.00
Paint Set, Winky Dink, 1950s, 12" x 18" x 2" box, slight use .................... 70.00
Paper Dolls
  Hee-Haw, punch-out type, 1972, unused ................................... 25.00

Welcome Back Kotter, ©1976 Wolper Organization, Toy Factory, diecut figure, orig box .............. 50.00
Paramedic Kit, Emergency, MOC ................................................ 40.00
Party Hat, A-Team, mint in orig bag ....................................................... 5.00
Pencil By Number Set, Buccaneers ................................................ 40.00
Pinback Button, 3-1/2" d, America's Foist Family/The Bunkers, red, white, and blue, black and white photo, ©1972 Tandem Productions, Inc. .................................................. 17.50
Placemat, Howdy Doody, set of 8 . 50.00
Playset, Detective, tommy gun, leather holster, pistol, badge, handcuffs, orig box, 1958 .................... 375.00
Portfolio, cardboard, Dukes of Hazzard ................................................ 15.00
Poster, Partridge Family, unopened pack ........................................... 30.00
Produce Bag, clear plastic, Howdy Doody, 1950s, red, white, and blue graphics of 6 characters, 7" x 12" .................................................. 22.00
Punch Out Book, unused
   Beverly Hillbillies, Whitman ...... 85.00
   Dr. Kildare, 1962 ..................... 22.00
   Heckle & Jeckle, 1978 ............. 18.00
Puppet
   Flintstone's, Bam Bam.............. 45.00
   Flintstone's, Pebbles ................ 45.00
   Pokey ..................................... 35.00
Puzzle
   Beany & Cecil, frame tray, c1960 .................................................. 95.00
   Charlie's Angels, Farrah, sealed, orig box ........................................ 25.00
   Chicken Charlie, Jaymar, boxed .................................................. 90.00
   Dukes of Hazzard, boxed, Canadian .................................................. 25.00
   Emergency, canned, sealed .... 32.00
   Flipper, frame tray, 1965 .......... 20.00
   Gene Autry, Whitman, No. 261029, 1957, frame tray ...................... 54.00
   Gumby, frame tray ................... 20.00
   Happy Days, HG Toys, 1976, boxed
      Fonz, Ritchie and Potsy around motorcycle, #45-02 ............. 23.00
      Fonz, Ritchie and Potsy sitting in luncheonette, #465-03 ........ 23.00
      The Fonz, #465-01 .............. 23.00
   Highway Patrol, Broderick Crawford, boxed ...................................... 75.00
   Lassie, Bilt Rite, 1950s, 6" x 9", real photo of Lassie and friend on dock fishing, frame tray ................... 24.00
   Rootie Kazootie, 10" x 14", 1950s, frame tray, set of two ............... 85.00
   Six Million Dollar Man, British... 50.00
   Super Six, Whitman, 1959, boxed .................................................. 27.00
   Zorro, Whitman No, 4417, 1957, frame tray ............................... 40.00
Radio
   A-Team, MIB............................. 40.00
   Knight Rider, car ...................... 55.00
   Six Million Dollar Man, Kenner, 1973, unused .................................... 45.00
Ring, Howdy Doody, raised face .................................................. 75.00

**Straw Holder, Howdy Doody, 50 cellophane straws, orig box, 2" x 2" x 8-1/4", $27.50.**

Scrapbook, Dr. Kildare, 11" x 14", photo type, 1962, unused .................. 65.00
Sheet Music, theme song
   Jackie Gleason ....................... 35.00
   S.W.A.T. ................................... 20.00
Slide Puzzle, Knight Rider, Michael with K.I.T.T., 1982 ........................... 18.50
Stethoscope, Thumpy the Heart Beat Stethoscope, picture of Richard Chamberlain on package, MIP .................................................. 40.00
Sticker Book, Flipper ................... 25.00
Store Display, Beverly Hillbillies, Buddy Ebsen, adv flyswatters, 30" x 24" .................................................. 225.00
Stuffed Animal, Scooby Do, 13" h, orig tab, 1980 ................................. 35.00
Tablecloth, paper, I Dream of Jeannie, MIB ...................................... 30.00
T-shirt, Lost in Space ................... 20.00
Thermos, Partridge Family, metal .................................................. 38.00
Toy
   A-Team Great Escape Stunt Set, motorized van, Lin, 1983, played with condition .......................... 30.00
   Howdy Doody Power Tools, MIB .................................................. 20.00
   Knight Rider, K.I.T.T. dashboard, MIB .................................................. 175.00
   Yogi, squeeze toy..................... 35.00
Walkie Talkie, Six Million Dollar Man Porta Communicator Set, Kenner, 1975, unused .......................... 48.00
Wallpaper, Howdy Doody, 36" section .................................................. 30.00
Waste Can, litho tin, 13" h
   Grizzly Adams, 1977 ................ 45.00
   Laugh-In................................... 55.00
   Welcome Back Kotter, 1976..... 48.00
Wrist Watch, Dukes of Hazzard, Unisonic, 1981, orig case, unused .................................................. 25.00
Writing Tablet, Hogan's Heroes .... 35.00

# Televisions

**Collecting Hints:** There are two distinct types of early television sets: mechanical and electronic. Mechanical televisions, the earliest, look nothing like their modern counterparts. Mechanical sets from the 1920s typically have a motorized 12-inch-diameter metal disc with a "glow tube" in back and a magnifier in front. Starting in 1938, sets used picture tubes, as they do today. Generally, the earlier the set, the smaller the screen. The easiest way to gauge the age of a television set is by the numbers found on the channel selector. Pre-1946 television sets will tune a maximum of five stations, usually channels 1 to 5. In 1946, channels 7 to 13 were added, thus sets made between 1946 and 1948 will show channels 1 to 13 on the station selector.

In 1949, Channel 1 was dropped, leaving all 1949 and newer sets with V.H.F. channels 2 to 13, as we have them today. The U.H.F. band was added in 1953.

Brand and model number are essential in determining a set's worth. However, physical condition of the cabinet is much more important than the operating condition of the set.

**History:** Early television sets can be divided into three distinct eras. The first, the mechanical era, was from 1925 to 1932. Sets often were known as "radiovisors," since they were visual attachments to radios. Many mechanical television sets did not have cabinets and resembled an electric fan with a round metal disk in place of the blades. These units were most prevalent in the New York City and Chicago areas.

Manufacturers of mechanical sets included Jenkins, Baird, Western Television, Insuline Corp. of America, Short-Wave and Television Corp., Daven, See-All, Rawls, Pioneer, and Travler Radio & Television Corp. A complete mechanical set is worth several thousand dollars.

The second time frame, known as the pre-World War II era, includes sets made between 1938 and 1941. Televisions made during this period were the first all-electronic sets and usually were combined with a multiband radio in a fancy cabinet. A favorite design of the era was a mirror-in-the-lid arrangement, whereby a mirror in the underside of a lift lid reflected the picture tube, which was pointed straight up. Production, which totaled no more than 2,000 sets, was concentrated in those areas with pre-war television stations: New York City, Albany/Schenectady/Troy, Philadelphia, Chicago, and Los Angeles. Depending on model and condition, these sets usually start at $1,000 and can exceed $5,000 in the collecting market.

The final era of television started in 1946 with the resumption of post-war television production when output rapidly increased. Few sets after 1949 have collectible value. Some notable exceptions include the first color wheel sets (1951), the giant Dumont 30-inch screen sets (1953), and limited production or oddball sets.

**References:** *Classic TVs, Pre-War thru 1950s*, L-W Book Sales, 1997; Harry Poster, *Poster's Guide to Collectible Radios and Televisions*, Wallace-Homestead, 1994.

**Periodicals:** Antique Radio Classified, P.O. Box 802,Carlisle, MA 01741; Radio Age, 636 Cambridge Rd, Augusta, GA 30909.

**Collectors' Club:** Antique Wireless Association, 59 Main St., Bloomfield, NY 14469.

**Caution:** If a set has been in storage for many years, do not plug it in without first having it inspected by a qualified serviceman. Components

can go bad and short-circuit, causing a fire. Many early sets had no fuses for protection.

### 1925-1932, Mechanical

| | |
|---|---|
| Daven, kit of parts | 500.00 |
| Insuline Corp. of America (ICA), Bakelite cabinet model | 3,000.00 |
| See-All, open frame | 1,500.00 |
| Short-Wave and Television Corporation, drum scanner | 3,000.00 |
| Western Television Corp., "Ship's wheel," cabinet type | 2,200.00 |

### 1938-1941, Electronic

| | |
|---|---|
| Andrea | |
| 1-F-5 | 4,000.00 |
| KTE-5 | 2,500.00 |
| Dumont, 180 | 2,000.00 |
| General Electric | |
| HM-171 | 2,500.00 |
| HM-225 | 4,000.00 |
| HM-275 | 5,000.00 |
| R.C.A. | |
| TRK-5 | 4,000.00 |
| TRK-12 | 5,000.00 |
| TRK-120 | 3,500.00 |

### 1946 and Later

| | |
|---|---|
| CBS/Columbia, 12CC2, color wheel set | 5,000.00 |
| Dumont, RA-119, 30" screen | 1,000.00 |
| Ferneshgerät, Sobell 107, combination radio and television, tall floor model, c1949 | 800.00 |
| Leningrad T2, combination radio and television, table top | 1,200.00 |
| Motorola, VT-71 | 225.00 |
| Philco | |
| Predicta, table model | 225.00 |
| Safari | 250.00 |
| Pilot, TV-37, magnifier | 200.00 |
| R.C.A. | |
| 630TS | 250.00 |
| 648PTK | 200.00 |
| 8TS30 | 100.00 |

# Shirley Temple

**Collecting Hints:** Dolls are made out of many materials—composition, cloth, chalk, papier-mâché, rubber, and vinyl. Composition dolls are the earliest. When Shirley Temple's popularity was boosted by television in the 1950s, a new series of products was issued.

**History:** Shirley Jane Temple was born on April 23, 1928, in Santa Monica, California. A movie scout discovered her at a dancing school. The 1932 film, "Pie Covered Wagon," was her screen test, and during that decade she made 20 movies, earning as much as $75,000 per film.

Her mother supervised the licensing of more than 15 firms to make Shirley Temple products, including dolls, glassware, china, jewelry, and

soap. The Ideal Toy Company made the first Shirley Temple dolls in 1934. These composition (pressed wood) dolls varied in height from 11 to 27 inches. Ideal made the first vinyl dolls in 1957.

**References:** Edward R. Pardella, *Shirley Temple Dolls and Fashion*, Schiffer Publishing, 1992; Patricia R. Smith, *Shirley Temple Dolls and Collectibles*, Vol. I (1977, 1992 value update), Vol. II (1979, 1992 value update), Collector Books.

**Videotape:** Shirley Temple Dolls & Memorabilia, Sirocco Productions, 1994.

Reproduction Alert.

| | |
|---|---|
| Advertisement, 4-1/4" x 6", for Shirley Temple Sewing Kit | 8.00 |
| Arcade Card, Educational Pictures, black and white | 2.50 |
| Book, *Shirley Temple, My Life & Times*, 1936 | 50.00 |
| Candy Mold | 35.00 |
| Carriage, handle height 27", brown wicker carriage on metal frame, excellent condition | 900.00 |
| Cereal Bowl, cobalt blue glass, white portrait image | 50.00 |
| Cereal Box, Quaker Puffed Wheat, c1930 | 110.00 |
| Clothing | |
| Coat, cashmere, label, Bambury orig, c1937 | 285.00 |

**HMV Model 900, c1937, pre-war mirror type, $2,046. Photo courtesy of Auction Team Breker.**

**Post Card, black and white, inscribed "Sincerely, Shirley Temple Agar," Vanguard Studio, Culver City, CA, $17.50.**

Dress, child's, satin, pink, ruffled, blue and white tag .................. 50.00

Cereal Box, Quaker Puffed Wheat, c1930 ..................................... 110.00

Doll, Ideal, composition

16" h, Ideal, Glad Rags to Riches, 1984, orig box ....................... 195.00

19" h, Ideal, vinyl head, hazel flirty sleep eyes, real lashes, feathered brows, open-closed mouth, 6 upper teeth, dimples, rooted hair in orig set, 5 pc vinyl body, tagged pink and blue nylon dress, orig underclothes, socks and black shoes, orig wrist tag, mkd "Ideal Doll, ST-19" on back of head and on back, box label "Shirley Temple Doll, Made in U.S.A. by Ideal Toy Corporation, Hollis 23, N.Y.," worn orig box, unplayed with condition .................................. 650.00

Embroidery Set, tablecloth, four napkins, hoop, needle, threads, plastic thimble, unused, Gabriel, 1960s ................................................. 50.00

Fan, teen-age Shirley, with RC Cola, "I'll Be Seeing You" movie ............. 24.00

Figure, 8-1/2" h, rubber, black Scottie dog under one arm, marked "Made in Czechoslovakia," mid-1930s .................................................... 90.00

Game, The Little Colonel, board, diecut figure pieces, box with Shirley's picture, Selchow & Righter, 1935 ................................................. 70.00

Jewelry

Charm, 5/8", brass rim, cut out center, 1930s ............................. 75.00

Necklace, 14", brass, 5/8" cut out head disk, 1930s ..................... 100.00

Ring, celluloid, red, black and white diecut head of Shirley, marked "Made in Japan" ...................... 25.00

Movie Still, 8" x 10", Little Miss Marker, Shirley on horse with Adolphe Menjou, Paramount Film, 1934 ....... 20.00

Mug .............................................. 55.00

Paper Dolls, uncut ....................... 18.50

Pinback Button, 1" d, enamel on brass, "Sunday Referee/Shirley Temple League," English newspaper issue ................................................. 110.00

Pitcher, 4-1/2" h, cobalt blue glass, white portrait image, Wheaties offer, c1938 ........................................ 65.00

Pocket Mirror, Quaker Puffed Wheat adv, 1937 ................................. 18.00

Post Card, 3-1/2" x 5-1/2", glossy sepia picture, "Captain January" scene, unused, 1936 ........................... 15.00

Scrapbook, 11" x 15", Saalfield, 1937 copyright ................................. 25.00

Sewing Cards, six black and white cards, yarn, 5" x 7" box, marked "Made by Saalfield 1936" ........ 45.00

Sheet Music

Good Night My Love, 1936 ...... 18.50

Pigskin Parade, Shirley on back ................................................. 10.00

Slipper Box, child's, 6" x 10-1/2" x 3-1/4", gray and blue design, marked "Restful," mid-1930s ................... 75.00

Song Album, 9" x 12", 36 pgs, words and music, pink tinted films scenes ................................................. 35.00

Souvenir Book, 9" x 12", 32 pgs, Tournament of Roses Parade, Shirley as Grand Marshal, 1939 ............. 22.00

String Holder, 7" h, chalkware, orig scissors ........................................ 375.00

# Thermometers

**Collecting Hints:** These are collectibles we can all identify. Ranging from the small ones kept in the medicine cabinet, to the readily found color advertising examples, thermometers are plentiful and represent a hot collectible.

Thermometer collectors divide their collections into advertising, science/medicine, souvenir types, and miscellaneous. Souvenir types are especially numerous since many were produced. Some are unusual and whimsical. Science/medicine thermometers range from industrial usage models to the type often tucked away in the medicine cabinet.

**History:** Galileo invented The first practical thermometer, about 1593. It wasn't until the Celsius and Fahrenheit scales were accepted that measurement became standardized; early Americans had used as many as 18 different scales to measure temperature. New Englanders used devices with alcohol, rather than expensive mercury. Southerners were known to favor a bi-metallic spring device. Thermometers are found mounted on metal, wood, silver, and gold, but brass seems to have been the favorite.

Thousands of advertising thermometers were made, running the gamut of products from beverages to home heating contractors. One of the more unusual types of thermometers is the kind known as a bathtub floater. Long before the advent of hot water and indoor plumbing it was used to check the bath water temperature. Desk and more decorative room thermometers became an important home accessory.

**Collectors' Club:** Thermometer Collectors Club of America, 6130 Rampart Drive, Carmichael, CA 95608.

**Museum:** Richard Porter's Thermometer Museum, Box 944, Onset, MA 02558-0944.

**Reproduction Alert:** Reproduction advertising thermometers exist. Many of these counterfeits use a paper label, whereas the original was painted and has the maker's name stamped on the back in ink. Modern metal thermometers lack the natural aging resulting from long exposure to the weather.

**Advisor:** Richard Porter.

Bradley & Hubbard, desk/wall

Brass rococo frame, st Fahrenheit scale, mercury, 1890, 11" ...... 1,850.00

Iron rococo frame, iron Fahrenheit scale, mercury, 1905, 11" x 3" ................................................. 680.00

C. J. T., wall, brass frame, brass Fahrenheit scale, blue permacolor tube, 1895, 8" h ............................. 850.00

Fairbanks & Co., wall, brass, round frame, Fahrenheit dial scale, 1900, 8" x 8" ........................................ 750.00

Harris P., Birmingham, wall, rosewood frame, Centigrade/Reaumur/Fahrenheit scales, mercury, 1905, 8" x 4" ................................................. 750.00

Kendall, J., New Lebanon, desk, iron column frame, Fahrenheit scale, square base, mercury, 1875, 8" ................................................. 1,900.00

Philadelphia Therm Co., wall, wood frame, Fahrenheit brass scale, mercury, 1900, 8" x 4" .................. 850.00

Thermodial, Newark, desk, brass beehive frame, radial scale, 1923, 6" x 3" ................................................. 700.00

Tycos

Desk, hygrometer, wood frame, two blue enamel Fahrenheit scales, mercury, 1900, 8" x 4" .................. 800.00

Desk/wall, hygrometer, Lloyd's, iron frame, Fahrenheit iron scale, mercury, 1915, 10" x 7" ................. 950.00

Unknown Maker

Desk, bronze frame with flower border, mercury, 1885, 6" x 2" ......... 1,125.00

Desk, granite obelisk, Fahrenheit brass scale, mercury, 1920, 4" ........ 250.00

Desk, painted woodcut, priest walking pig, wood scale, permacolor tube, 1880, 9" ............................. 2,800.00

Desk, tin frame with butterflies, Fahrenheit brass scale, mercury, 1885, 4" x 2" ........................................ 1,750.00

Ormolu frame with dragon, Fahrenheit black scale, mercury, 1901, 7" x 5" ................................................. 1,200.00

Wall, wood battle ax, Reaumur/Centigrade scales, mercury, 1920, 18" ................................................. 450.00

Unknown Maker, France, wood, engine turned base, Reaumur sterling scale, mercury, 1890 ...................... 850.00

Unknown Maker, Great Britain, desk

Brass, blue enamel, Fahrenheit ivory scale, mercury, 1890, 6" x 2" ................................................. 1,350.00

Sterling twin inkwells, Fahrenheit and Reaumur porcelain scales, mercury, 1900, 5" x 6" ................... 1,200.00

# Thimbles

**Collecting Hints:** There are many ways to approach thimble collecting. You can collect by material (metal or porcelain), by design (cupids or commemorative), by types (advertising or political), or limited editions (modern collectibles). However, in reality, there is only one philosophy that applies: collect what you like.

There are thousands of thimbles. The wise collector uses a narrow approach, thereby saving money and enabling a meaningful collection to be assembled.

The wonderful thing about thimble collecting is that there is something for every budget. The person with a limited budget might look at advertising or modern collectible thimbles, while the more prosperous could focus on gold examples.

**History:** Silver thimbles were imported from England during the colonial period, and only the wealthy could afford to buy them. By the late 18th century, advertisements appeared in the *New York Weekly Post*, *New York Gazette*, and *Philadelphia Directory* offering American-made thimbles. These were gold, silver, or pinchbeck thimbles, some with steel caps.

The 19th-century Industrial Revolution brought about the golden age of thimble production because of the availability of machinery, which could produce fine thimbles. By the end of the 19th century, world production of thimbles was about 80 million per year.

Before the sewing machine became a permanent household fixture, all sewing and mending was done by hand. The frontier homemaker guarded her thimble. Replacing it meant a visit to the general store, which was often miles away, or waiting until a traveling peddler came along. City ladies had no problem replacing a lost thimble. A selection was always available at the local dry good stores. The name "dry goods" assured a lady that no "wet goods," or alcoholic beverages were sold in that store, and it was perfectly proper for her to shop there.

Needlework can be divided into two kinds: plain and fancy. Plain sewing required a utilitarian thimble made of steel, brass, or celluloid. A process for making celluloid thimbles was patented by William Halsey in 1880. Eugene Villiers patented a thimble-molding process in the same year. Because aluminum was a costly metal during the 19th century, it was not used to make thimbles until the 20th century, when it became less expensive and more practical to use the metal in such applications.

Fancy sewing was considered a parlor or social activity. Ornate thimbles made of precious metals were saved for this purpose. Many gold and silver thimbles were received as gifts. In years past, proper etiquette did not permit a young man to give his lady any gift that was personal, such as jewelry or clothing. Flowers, books, or sweets were considered proper gifts. The thimble somehow bridged this rule of etiquette. A fancy gold or silver thimble was a welcomed gift. Many of these do not show signs of wear, probably because either they did not fit the recipient or were considered too elegant to use for mundane work.

An extensive array of goods and services are advertised on thimbles, and many collections are built around these advertising thimbles because they are easy to find and inexpensive to buy. Advertising thimbles made of celluloid or metal are older than the modern plastic examples. These little advertising ploys helped salesmen open the door. Tradesmen knew that these tokens would constantly remind the customer of their product. There was no standard method of distributing advertising thimbles, although most were handed to a potential customer by a salesman. Others were packaged with a product, such as flour or bread.

The history of thimbles advertising political campaigns began with the amendment giving the vote to women, ratified on Aug. 20, 1920, just in time for the political campaign that year. The first presidential candidate to use the advertising thimble was Warren Harding. Political thimbles are higher priced than other advertising thimbles because of competition from political memorabilia collectors.

**References:** Averil Mathis, *Antique and Collectible Thimbles*, Collector Books, 1986, 1995 value update; Bridget McConnell, *The Story of Thimbles: An Illustrated Guide for Collectors,* Schiffer Publishing, 1997; Gay Ann Rogers, *An Illustrated History of Needlework Tools,* Needlework Unlimited, 1983, 1989 Price Guide; —, *Price Guide Keyed to American Silver Thimbles,* Needlework Unlimited, 1989; Helen Lester Thompson, *Sewing Tools & Trinkets,* Collector Books, 1997; Estelle Zalkin, *Zalkin's Handbook of Thimbles & Sewing Implements,* Warman Publishing, 1988, distributed by Krause Publications.

**Periodical:** *Thimbletter,* 93 Walnut Hill Rd, Newtown Highlands, MA 02161.

**Collectors' Clubs:** Empire State Thimble Collectors, 8289 Northgate Dr., Rome, NY 13440; Thimble Collectors International, 6411 Montego Bay Rd, Louisville, KY 40228; Thimble Guild, P.O. Box 381807, Duncanville, TX 75138.

**Reproduction Alert:** As soon as thimble collecting became popular, recast reproductions appeared on the market. Antiques shows and shops across the country have been known to carry a cast reproduction of an enamel thimble originally made before the Russian revolution. The "84" Russian silver mark is clear, but the maker's mark is deliberately smeared. The rim of the reproduction is thick and the inside of the thimble is rough.

American thimbles also have been reproduced. An artisan is casting many of the popular patterns, including the cottage scene, harbor scene with lighthouse, anchors and chains, cupid and garlands, the teddy bear, and two birds on a branch. No maker's mark appears inside the cap and the "Sterling" mark is stamped on the band. This is the first clue that these are recast reproductions. It is illegal to use the word "sterling" on any silver piece without the manufacturer's name or trademark. These cast thimbles are thick, rough inside, and much heavier than the genuine machine-drawn antique thimbles. The casting process does not duplicate the fine engraved designs of the originals.

**Advertising**

Aluminum
  Colored Band
    Stone Top ............................. 4.00
    Threader Attachment ............ 4.00
  No Colored Band
    Inked Message ..................... 3.00
    Inscribed Message ............... 3.50
  Brass, advertisement or inscription
    .................................................. 6.50

Plastic, old, 1930-1950
  One color ............................... 3.00
  Two colors, red top ............... 4.00
Sterling Silver ......................... 20.00

## Gadgets

Magic Thimble, "M.T.," thread cutter and needle threader ............. 15.00
Thread Cutter, lip on band ........... 15.00
Thimble Holder
  Basket, lid magnetized to hold thimble, mkd "Florenza" .................. 50.00
  Cat, 1-1/4" h, 4-1/4" l, rect base, mkd "John Wanamaker, Phila, New York, Quadruple Plate" .................... 150.00
  French child standing on round base, fancy hat, big bow in back, base imp "Pour Mon De" ....... 250.00
  Frog, gold colored metal, green glass eyes, 1" h, 2" l ............... 95.00
  Sterling silver, needle and thimble holder, size 2-3/8", hallmarked "WH," Birmingham, England, 1907 date code .......................................... 80.00
  Walnut on branch, cast metal, matching thimble mkd "Sterling" .................................................. 190.00

## Political

Coolidge and Dawes, metal ..... 20.00
Elect Ike, Beall, Hyde ............... 25.00
Hoover & Curtis, metal, red or blue rim ............................................... 20.00
Hoover Home Happiness, metal blue rim ............................................... 20.00
Nixon for U. S. Senator ............. 75.00
Safeguard the American Home, Nixon for US Senator, red and off-white plastic ............................. 75.00

## Thimbles

Avon, Fashion Silhouettes series, shows fashionable woman, 2" h, orig box and felt bag
  1890 style dress, mkd, 1982 .... 25.00
  1900 style dress, mkd, 1982 .... 25.00
  1925 style dress, mkd, 1983 .... 25.00
  1927 flapper style, mkd, 1983 ... 25.00
  1942 style dress, mkd, 1984 .... 25.00
  1947 style dress, mkd, 1984 .... 25.00
Gold, 1900-40
  Plain band ............................... 75.00
  Scenic band ........................... 100.00
  Semi precious stones on band .................................................. 200.00
Ivory
  Modern scrimshaw ................. 20.00
  Vegetable ivory ....................... 65.00

**Statue of Liberty, left: French, $60; right: Simons, $20.**

Metal, common
  Brass
    Enameled, colorful abstract design, lined in blue enamel .................................................. 55.00
    Fancy band ......................... 15.00
    Cloisonné design, China ..... 20.00
  Cast Pot Metal, "For a Good Girl" .................................................. 15.00
  Silver, 1900-40
    Applied wire work, Mexico . 20.00
    Continental, synthetic stone cap .................................................. 25.00
    Cupid in high relief ........... 100.00
    Enameled ............................ 60.00
    English, steel core
      DORCAS ........................ 50.00
      DREEMA ...................... 125.00
      DURA ........................... 125.00
    Engraved, two birds on branch .................................................. 30.00
    Flowers in high relief .......... 35.00
    Italian, stones on band, modern .................................................. 35.00
    Paneled band ..................... 32.00
    Raised design ..................... 35.00
    Scenic Band ....................... 35.00
    Simons Brothers, sterling, size 9 .................................................. 30.00
    Sterling, mkd "Sterling 9," some old surface scratches, 1/2" h .................................................. 22.50
  Souvenir
    Liberty Bell, 1976 issue ....... 75.00
    Palm Beach ........................ 75.00
  Statue of Liberty, France .......... 35.00
  World's Fairs
    1892, Colombian, buildings .................................................. 225.00
    1904, St. Louis World's Fair .................................................. 200.00
    1933, Chicago World's Fair . 75.00
Porcelain
  Bing & Grondhal, seagull, mkd "B & G 4831, Made in Denmark" ..... 20.00
  Flow Blue, windmill dec, mkd "Mosa Holland," 1-1/4" h ..................... 18.00
  Lefton, set of 12, white ground, each with different flower dec, gold trim, orig box .................................... 45.00
  Meissen, hp, modern, Germany .................................................. 125.00
  Partridge, 1986, 9th in series, hand made, orig box and wrapping . 30.00
  Royal Copenhagen, mkd "Denmark," 1" h ...................................... 20.00
  Royal Worcester, hp, modern, artist sgd, England ......................... 25.00
  Staffordshire, Charles Dickens .................................................. 18.00
  Wedgwood, jasper, blue and white
    Josiah Wedgwood, anniversary collection, 1980, MIB ......... 40.00
    Woman by spinning wheel .. 30.00
Scrimshaw, antique, whalebone or whale tooth ............................... 90.00

# Tinsel Art

**Collecting Hints:** Look for those pieces which contain different-colored foil and have an elaborate design. Signed pictures often are viewed as folk art and may be higher priced.

Nineteenth-century material is preferred over the nondescript 20th-century examples. However, collectors seek Art Deco and Art Nouveau designs of quality from these fields.

**History:** Tinsel pictures (or paintings) were both a "cottage art" and a commercial product, which enjoyed popularity from the late 19th century through the 20th century. The "painting" took two forms. The first was similar to a reverse painting on glass. A design was placed on the glass and colored foil was placed behind to accent the piece. The second form consisted of a silhouette or cutting, separate from the glass, placed over a layer of crumpled foil.

Reverse-painted examples were highly personalized; a mother and her children could work on tinsel pictures as a family project. This handiwork often contained presentation remarks and was artist signed and dated. The silhouette type appears to be related to the Art Deco and Art Nouveau periods and may have been a form of souvenir available at carnival games and the seashore. The similarity of many designs, e.g., flamingos in a swamplike setting, denotes commercial production.

**Reference:** Shirley Mace, *Encyclopedia of Silhouette Collectibles on Glass*, Shadow Enterprises, 1992.

**Flamingoes, multicolored, black ground, framed, 10-3/4" x 8-3/4", $75.**

Basket of flowers, multicolored, black ground, 17-3/4" x 13-1/2" ....... 150.00

Birds drinking from stylized fountain, trees, 23" x 27", 19th C ........... 200.00

Flamingos, pink, palm tree, reeds, yellow sun, black ground, 10-3/4" x 8-1/4" .................................... 85.00

Flower arrangement in bowl, brightly colored ...................................... 30.00

Fountain, surrounded by garland of flowers, multicolored, 15-3/4" x 15-1/2" .................................... 100.00

Lilacs, black ground, gilt frame, 10-1/2" x 7-1/2", 19th C ...................... 145.00

Motto
   Home Sweet Home, houses and trees, reverse painted, 12-1/4" x 18" ................................................ 65.00
   The Lord Is My Shepherd, floral border, reverse painted, 12-1/4" x 18" ................................................ 50.00

Silhouettes, girl and boy, facing pr, framed .................................... 45.00

Statue of Liberty, multicolored, reverse painting on glass highlights, oval wooden frame .......................... 75.00

Titanic, multicolored, reverse painting on glass highlights, wooden frame ................................................ 150.00

# Toys

**Collecting Hints:** Condition is a critical factor. Most collectors like to have examples in very fine to mint condition. The original box and any instruction sheets add to the value.

Sophisticated collectors concentrate on the tin and cast iron toys of the late 19th and early 20th centuries. However, more and more collectors are specializing in products made between 1940 and 1970, including those from firms such as Fisher-Price.

Many toys were characterizations of cartoon, radio, and television figures. A large number of collectible fields have some form of toy spin-off. The result is that the toy collector is constantly competing with the specialized collector.

**History:** The first cast-iron toys began to appear in America shortly after the Civil War. Leading 19th-century manufacturers include Hubley, Dent, Kenton, and Schoenhut. In the first decades of the 20th century, Arcade, Buddy L, Marx, and Tootsie Toy joined these earlier firms. Wooden toys were made by George Brown and other manufacturers, who did not sign or label their work.

Nuremberg, Germany, was the European center for the toy industry from the late 18th through the mid-20th centuries. Companies such as Lehman and Marklin produced high-quality toys.

**References:** E. Ackerman and F. Keller, *Under the Big Top with Schoenhut's Humpty Dumpty Circus*, published by author (P.O. Box 217, Culver City, CA 90230), 1997; Linda Baker, *Modern Toys*, Collector Books, 1985, 1993 value update; William M. Bean and Al M. Sternagle, *Greenberg's Guide to Gilbert Erector Sets, Vol. 1, 1913-1932*, Greenberg Publishing, 1993; John Bonavita, *Mego Action Figure Toys*, Schiffer Publishing, 1996; Bob Chartain, *Hot Wheels Price Guide and Collector's Handbook*, Krause Publications, 1996; Wallace M. Chrouch, *Mego Toys*, Collector Books, 1995; John A. Clark, *HO Slot Car Identification and Price Guide*, L-W Book Sales, 1995; *Collector's Digest Price Guide to Pull Toys*, L-W Book Sales, 1996; Christopher Cook, *Collectible American Yo-Yos*, Collector Books, 1997; Don Cranmer, *Collectors Encyclopedia: Toys-Banks*, L-W Book Sales, 1986, 1994-95 value update; C. Lee Criswell and Clarence L. Criswell, Sr., *Criswell's Pedal Tractor Guide*, Criswell Press, 1999; Henry René D'Allemagne, *Antique Playing Cards*, Dover, 1996; Don and Barb DeSalle, *Collector's Guide to Tonka Trucks 1947-1963*, L-W Book Sales, 1996; —, *The DeSalle Collection of Smith-Miller & Doepke Trucks*, L-W Book Sales, 1997; Charles F. Donovan, Jr., *Renwal, World's Finest Toys*, Vol. 2, published by author (11877 US Hwy 431, Ohatchee, AL 36271), 1996; Elmer Duellman, *Elmer's Price Guide to Toys*, Vol. 1 (1995), Vol. 2 (1996), L-W Book Sales; James L. Dundas, *Collecting Whistles*, Schiffer Publishing, 1995; *Evolution of the Pedal Car*, Vol. 1 (1996 values), vol. 2 (1993 values), Vol. 3 (1992 values), Vol. 4 (1997 values); Edward Force, *Classic Miniature Vehicles: Made in Italy*, Schiffer Publishing, 1992; —, *Corgi Toys*, Schiffer Publishing, 1984, 1997 value update; —, *Dinky Toys*, 3rd ed., Schiffer Publishing, 1996; —, *Lledo Toys*, Schiffer Publishing, 1996; —, *Solido Toys*, Schiffer Publishing, 1993;

Ted Hake, *Hake's Price Guide To Character Toys*, 2nd ed., Avon Books, 1998; Bill Hanlon, *Plastic Toy*; Morton Hirschberg, *Steam Toys*, Schiffer Publishing, 1996; Daniel E. Hodges, *Marionettes and String Puppets Collector's Reference Guide*, Antique Trader Books, 1998; Don Hultzman, *Collector's Guide to*

*Battery Toys, Identification & Values*, Collector Books, 1998; Ken Hutchison & Greg Johnson, *Golden Age of Automotive Toys*, Collector Books, 1996; Sharon and Bob Huxford, *Schroeder's Collectible Toys Price Guide: Antique to Modern*, 5th ed., Collector Books, 1999; Charles M. Jacobs, *Kenton Cast Iron Toys*, Schiffer Publishing, 1996; Alan Jaffe, *J. Chein & Co.*, Schiffer Publishing, 1997; Dana Johnson, *Collector's Guide to Diecast Toys & Scale Models*, 2nd ed., Collector Books, 1998; —, *Matchbox Toys*, 2nd ed., Collector Books, 1996; Michele Karl, *Composition & Wood Dolls and Toys: A Collector's Reference Guide*, Antique Trader Books, 1998; Douglas R. Kelly, *Die Cast Price Guide*, Antique Trader Books, 1997; Lisa Kerr, *American Tin-Litho Toys*, Collectors Press, 1995; Raymond R. Klein, *Greenberg's Guide to Tootsietoys 1945-1969*, Greenberg Publishing, 1993; Sharon Korbeck and Elizabeth Stephan, eds., *Toys & Prices, 2000*, 7th edition, Krause Publications, 1999; David Longest, *Antique & Collectible Toys*, Collector Books, 1994; —, *Toys*, Collector Books, 1990, 1995 value update; Charlie Mack, *Lesney's Matchbox Toys*, Vol. 1 (1992), Vol. 2 (1993), Vol. 3 (1993), Schiffer Publishing; L. H. MacKenzie, *Squeaky Toys: A Collector's Handbook & Price Guide*, Schiffer Publishing, 1998; Neil McElwee, *McElwee's Collector's Guide #1: Smith-Miller*, published by author, 1994; —, *McElwee's Collector's Guide #3: Tonka Toys*, published by author, 1992; —, *McElwee's Collector's Guide #5: Postwar Buddy "L,"* published by author, 1992; —, *McElwee's Collector's Guide #6: Ny-Lint*, published by author, 1993; —, *McElwee's Collector's Guide #7: Big Ertl, Cast Commercial Trucks & Construction Vehicles*, published by author, 1993; —, *McElwee's Collector's Guide #8: Gasoline Company Toys...Trucks & Automotive*, published by author, 1994; —, *McElwee's Collector's Guide #9: Structo*, published by author, 1993; —, *McElwee's Collector's Guide #10: Postwar Big Metal Classics*, published by author, 1994; —, *McElwee's Small Motor News Annual*, published by author, 1994.

Rex Miller, *The Investor's Guide to Vintage Character Collectibles*, Krause Publications, 1999; John J. Murray and Bruce Fox, *Fisher-Price*, 2nd ed., Books Americana, 1991;

Richard O'Brien, *Collecting Toy Cars & Trucks*, 2nd ed., Krause Publications, 1997; —, *Collecting Toys*, 8th ed., Krause Publications, 1997; Robert M. Overstreet, *Overstreet Toy Ring Price Guide*, 2nd ed., Collector Books, 1996; John Ramsay, *British Diecast Model Toys*, 6th ed., available from Tim Arthurs (109 Glover Ave., Norwalk, CT 06850), 1996; R & B Collectibles & Marketing, *Texaco Collectors 1997 Price Guide*, published by authors, 1997; Mike and Sue Richardson, *Diecast Toy Aircraft: An International Guide*, New Cavendish, 1998; David Richter, *Collectors Guide to Tootsietoys*, 2nd ed., Collector Books, 1996; *Riding Toys*, L-W Book Sales, 1992, 1996 value update; Carole and Richard Smith, *Pails by Comparison*, published by authors (P.O. Box 2068, Huntington, NY 11743), 1996; Ron Smith, *Collecting Toy Airplanes*, Books Americana, 1995; Gerhard G. Walter, *Tin Dream Machines: German Tin Toy Cars and Motorcycles of the 1950s and 1960s*, New Cavendish, 1998; Stuart W. Wells, III, *Science Fiction Collectibles: Identification & Price Guide*, Krause Publications, 1999; Harry A. and Joyce A. Whitworth, *G-Men and FBI Toys and Collectibles, Identification & Values*, Collector Books, 1998; Neil S. Wood, *Evolution of the Pedal Car, Volume 5*, L-W Book Sales, 1999.

**Periodicals:** *Action Toys Newsletter*, P.O. Box 31551, Billings, MT 59107; *Antique Toy World*, P.O. Box 34509, Chicago, IL 60634; *Canadian Toy Mania*, P.O. Box 489, Rocanville, Saskatchewan SOA 3LO Canada; *Collecting Toys*, P.O. Box 1989, Milwaukee, WI 53201; *Die Cast & Tin Toy Report*, P.O. Box 501, Williamsburg, VA 23187; *Die Cast Digest*, P.O. Box 12510, Knoxville, TN 37912; *Matchbox USA Newsletter*, 62 Saw Mill Rd, Durham, CT 06422; *Model and Toy Collector Magazine*, 137 Casterton Ave., Akron, OH, 44303; *Plane News*, P.O. Box 845, Greenwich, CT 06836; *Plastic Figure & Playset Collector*, Box 1355, La Crosse, WI 54602; *Spec-Tacular News*, P.O. Box 324, Dyersville, IA 52040; *Toy Cannon News*, P.O. Box 2052-N., Norcross, GA, 30071; *Toy Collector and Price Guide*, 700 E. State St., Iola, WI 54990; *Toy Collector Marketplace*, 1550 Territorial Rd, Benton Harbor, MI 49022; *Toy Farmer*, HC 2, Box 5, LaMoure, ND 58458; *Toy Shop*, 700 E. State St., Iola, WI 54990; *Toy Trac-tor Times*, P.O. Box 156, Osage, IA 50461; *Toybox Magazine*, 8393 E. Holly Rd, Holly, MI 48442; *Tractor Classics*, P.O. Box 191, Listowel, Ontario N4H 3HE Canada; *Turtle River Toy News & Oliver Collector's News*, RR1, Box 44, Manvel, ND 58256; *US Toy Collector Magazine*, P.O. Box 4244, Missoula, MT 59806; *Wheel Goods Trader*, P.O. Box 435, Fraser, MI 48026; *Yo-Yo Times*, P.O. Box 1519, Herndon, VA 22070.

**Videotape:** David Pressland, *Magic of the Tin Toy*, Antique Toy World.

**Collectors' Clubs:** AC Gilbert Heritage Society, 594 Front St., Marion, MA 02738; American Game Collectors Association, P.O. Box 44, Dresher, PA 19025; American International Matchbox Collectors & Exchange Club, 532 Chestnut St., Lynn, MA 01904; Anchor Block Foundation, 980 Plymouth St., Pelham, NY 10803; Antique Engine, Tractor & Toy Club, 5731 Paradise Rd, Slatington, PA 18080; Antique Toy Collectors of America, Two Wall Street, 13th Floor, New York, NY 10005; Capitol Miniature Auto Collectors Club, 10207 Greenacres Dr., Silver Spring, MD 20903; Diecast Exchange Club, P.O. Box 1066, Pineallas Park, FL 34665; Ertl Collectors Club, Hwys 186 & 120, Dyersville, IA 52040; Farm Toy Collectors Club, P.O. Box 38, Boxholm, IA 50040; Fisher-Price Collector's Club, 1442 N. Ogden, Mesa, AZ 85205; Girder and Panel Collectors Club, P.O. Box 494, Bolton, MA, 01740; HO Slot Car Collecting & Racing Club, 284 Willets Ln, West Islip, NY 14795; Majorette Diecast Toy Collectors Association, 1347 NW Albany Ave., Bend, OR 97701; Matchbox Collectors Club, P.O. Box 278, Durham, CT 06422; Matchbox International Collectors Association, 574 Canewood Crescent, Waterloo, Ontario N2L 5P6 Canada; Miniature Piano Enthusiast Club, 633 Pennsylvania Ave., Hagerstown, MD 21740; San Francisco Bay Brooklin Club, P.O. Box 61018, Palo Alto, CA 94306; Schoenhut Collectors Club, 45 Louis Ave., West Seneca, NY 14224; Schoenhut Toy Collectors, 1916 Cleveland St., Evanston, IL 60202; Southern California Meccano & Erector Club, 9661 Sabre Ave., Garden Grove, CA 92644; Southern California Toy Collectors Club, Ste. 300, 1760 Termino, Long Beach, CA 90804.

**Museums:** American Museum of Automobile Miniatures, Andover, MA; Eugene Field House & Toy Museum, St. Louis, MO; Evanston Historical Society, Evanston, IL 60201; Forbes Magazine Collection, New York, NY; Hobby City Doll & Toy Museum, Anaheim, CA; Margaret Woodbury Strong Museum, Rochester, NY; Matchbox & Lesney Toy Museum, Durham, CT; Matchbox Road Museum, Newfield, NJ; Museum of the City of New York, New York, NY; Smithsonian Institution, Washington, DC; Spinning Top Exploratory Museum, Burlington, WI; Toy & Miniature Museum of Kansas City, Kansas City, MO; Toy Museum of Atlanta, Atlanta, GA; Washington Dolls' House & Toy Museum, Washington, DC; Western Reserve Historical Society, Cleveland, OH.

**Additional Listings:** Battery Operated Automata, Cartoon Characters, Disneyana, Dolls, Games, Paper Dolls, Radio Characters, Dimestore Soldiers, Toy Soldiers, Toy Trains, and many other categories.

## Alps

Alps Shoji Ltd., located in Tokyo, Japan, was founded in 1948. The company manufactured windup and battery-powered toys made from tin and plastic. Toys are marked "ALPS."

Butterfly, litho tin friction, Alps, 1950s, 4" l .............................. 100.00

Chimpee The One Man Drummer, 1970s, orig box ...................... 45.00

Hot Rod Custom "T" Ford, battery operated, litho tin and plastic, stop-and-go action, lighted engine, orig box, 10-1/2" l ......................... 200.00

Merry Go-Round, windup, litho tin, four cars and celluloid balls rotate around base, child rider in each car, orig box, 10" l ......................... 265.00

School Bus, battery operated, doors open and close, flashing headlights, MIB ...................................... 125.00

Television Car, Alps, 1950s, 6-1/4" l ................................................. 125.00

## Arcade

The Arcade Manufacturing Company first produced toys in 1891. In 1919, the firm began to make the yellow cabs for the Yellow Cab Company of Chicago. The exclusive advertising rights were sold to the cab company with Arcade holding the right to make toy replicas of the cabs. This idea was popular and soon was used with Buick, Ford, etc., and McCormack and International Harvester farm equipment. The company remained in business until 1946 when it was sold to Rockwell Manufacturing Company of Pittsburgh.

Harvester, cast iron, 1/12 scale, 1930 .............................................. 300.00

Model T Sedan, 4 doors, cast iron, nickel-plated spoke wheels, 6-1/2" l .............................................. 565.00

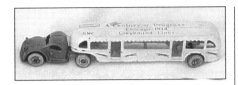

**Arcade, Greyhound Bus, A Century of Progress, Chicago, 1934, cast iron, painted white and blue, green lettering, 10-1/2" l, $265.**

Plow, McCormick-Deering, cast iron, red and yellow wheels, 1932 ................................................ 100.00
Road Roller, cast iron, wood roller, 5-3/4" l .......................................... 300.00
Stake Truck ............................ 195.00
Threshing Machine, John Deere, cast iron, c1930 ................... 150.00
Tractor, cast iron, 3-1/2" l ........ 125.00

## Auburn Toys
Car, yellow, rubber ...................... 20.00
Farm Tractor, red, orig driver, 7" l ................................................ 75.00
Fire Truck, red, rubber .................. 25.00
Pick-Up Truck, red, rubber .......... 20.00
Pistol, black vinyl, western-type ... 15.00
Take-Apart Hot Rod, 1960s, unplayed with, orig bag on header card ................................................ 35.00
Telephone Repair Truck, rubber ................................................ 25.00
Truck, rubber .............................. 22.00
**Bachman,** miniature planes, store display, set of 6, mint on sealed card ................................................ 125.00

## Bandai Co.
Bandai Co., one of the many toy manufacturers that began production in Japan after World War II, started with tin toys and later changed to plastic and steel. Bandai Toys have friction action or are battery operated. They are often marked "Bandai Toys, Japan." Bandai still produces toys

and is a major Japanese exporter to the U.S. and other foreign countries.
Batmobile, MIB .................. 2,500.00
Citreon D5-19, friction, tin, detailed litho tin int., "DS" on hubs, 8-1/4" l ............................................ 120.00
Family House Trailer, 1950s, 12" l, 7" h .............................................. 195.00
Ford Falcon Licensed Plated Model Car, tin, detailed litho tin int., black rubber tires, orig windshield, orig box, 1961, 8-3/4" l ............... 110.00
Isetta 700, litho tin friction, 1950s ............................................ 185.00
MG Magnetta Convertible ........ 90.00
Ocean Boat, litho tin, crank handle, driver wearing goggles, orig box, 12" l ............................................. 165.00
Rocket Racer, 7" l ................... 175.00
Vespa Scooter, friction, tin, Vespa license plate, 9" l ................... 275.00
Volkswagen Beetle, friction, tin, plastic steering wheel and windshield, 6" l ............................................. 125.00

## Buddy L
Fred Lundahl founded the Buddy L Company in 1921. It produced high-quality, finely detailed toys. Many were large enough to ride on. Production changed from steel to lighter-weight, smaller toys in the 1930s. A limited number of wooden toys were made during World War II. The firm still operates today.
Airplane, orange wings, 2" d aluminum propeller, decals, c1930 .......... 95.00
Baggage Truck ......................... 165.00
Dairy Transport Truck, Duo-Tone slant design paint, red and white, opens in back, orig decal, 26" l .............. 75.00
Dump Truck, winch, A-frame ...... 500.00
Fast Freight Truck, pressed steel, white cap, orange truck, black rubber tires, c1940, 20" l ................... 150.00
Flat Tire Wrecker, yellow ............. 125.00
Merry Go Round Truck ................. 95.00
Repair It Wrecker, 1957 ............. 200.00

**Buddy L, Coca-Cola truck, with conveyor, 1950s, $185.**

Steam Shovel, orig red and black paint, orig decals ............................. 150.00
Texaco Tanker, red, white letters ................................................ 75.00

## Chein
The Chein Company was in business from the 1930s through the 1950s. Most of their lithographed tin toys were sold in dimestores. Chein toys are clearly marked.
Alligator, windup, native on back ................................................ 315.00
Bear, litho tin wind-up, 1938, 4" h ................................................ 65.00
Disney Top, litho tin, Walt Disney Productions, c1950, 5-1/2" d ....... 100.00
Duck, litho tin wind-up, 1930, 4" h ................................................ 45.00
Ferris Wheel, Hercules, 1930s ................................................ 350.00
Navy frogman, lint litho, 1950s, mint sealed package with battleships and jets ......................................... 400.00
Sand Pail, nursery rhyme characters, 4" h .......................................... 60.00
Three Little Pigs Wringer Washer, crank, litho tin tub, wood and tin ringer attachment, 1930s, 8" h ................................................ 225.00
Troop Transport ...................... 450.00
Truck, Hercules Motor Express, red and green, 1936, 15" l ........... 575.00
Windmill Sand Toy, litho tin ...... 90.00
**Chilton Toys,** Kool-Aid Dispenser, plastic body, glass container, 1950s, 11" h, orig box ......................... 75.00
**Con-Cor,** USA, bus, red, orange stripe, 24" l ................................... 1,250.00

## Corgi
Playcraft Toys introduced Corgi miniature vehicles in 1956. This popular line soon became Corgi Toys. The first cars were made on a scale from 1:45 to 1:48. Corgi cars were the first miniature cars to have clear-plastic windows. Other design features included doors that opened and interiors. In 1972, the scale of 1:36 was introduced. This scale was more durable for play but less desirable to collectors. Finally, the company added other types of cars and trucks, including character representations.
Austin Cambridge Saloon, #201, MIB ....................................... 100.00

**Bandai, motorbike, BMW 500, c1952, $1,119. Photo courtesy of Auction Team Breker.**

Bedford Daily Express Van, #403, MIB........85.00
Buick Riviera, #245, MIB........100.00
Captain American Jet Mobile, #263, MIB........85.00
Car Transporter, #1101, MIB ........250.00
Charlie's Angels Van, MIB........75.00
Chevrolet Caprice, #325, MIB..55.00
Chevrolet Corvair, #229, MIB...85.00
Chevrolet New York Taxi Cab, #221, MIB........90.00
Circus land Rover and Animal Trailer, #30 MIB........220.00
Citroen DS 19, #210S, MIB......70.00
Construction Set, #GS-24, MIB ........250.00
Corgi Club Land Rover and Horse Box, #GS-15........100.00
Corgi Motor School Car, #238, MIB ........90.00
Disc Harrow, #71, MIB
Dodge Kew Fargo Tipper, #483 ........65.00
Ford Consol Saloon, #200M, MIB ........100.00
Ford Cortina Police Car, #402, MIB ........15.00
Ford Escort Delivery Car, #498, MIB ........30.00
Ford T-Bird, #214, MIB........70.00
Ford Tractor, #67, MIB........80.00
Ford Transit Tipper, #1121 ........75.00
Horse Transporter, #1105........90.00
Hyster 800 Stratcatruck, #1113, MIB ........75.00
Jaguar XJ12C, #286........200.00
Jean Richard's Human Cannon, #1163, MIB........75.00
Karrier Dairy Van, #435, played with condition........40.00
Kennel Service Wagon, #486, MIB ........75.00
London Routemaster Bus, #468, MIB ........80.00
Lotus Elite, #301, MIB........35.00
Mack Exxon Tanker, #1151, MIB ........75.00
Massey Ferguson 65 Tractor, #50, MIB........135.00
Mazda Camper, #415, MIB......40.00
Mercedes Benz 220 SE Coupe, #230 ........75.00
Mercedes Bonna Ambulance, #306, MIB........65.00
Monkee Mobile, #277, MIB....250.00
Renault 16TS, #202, MIB........50.00
Rice's Pony Trailer with Pony, #102, MIB........75.00
Rover 90 Saloon, #204, MIB ........100.00
US Racing Buggy, #167, MIB ........35.00
Vegas T-Bird, #348, MIB........85.00
Yardley McLaren M19A, #151, fair ........30.00

### Cragston, Japan

Crap Shooter, battery operated, vinyl face, MIB........150.00
Freight Train Set, battery operated, working, some tears to orig box ........145.00

Pet Shop Truck, litho tin, friction, swivel bed doors, black rubber tires, orig 11" l........125.00
Police Chief Car, battery operated, fires caps, Chevrolet, 12" l, never used........545.00
Star of the Circus Clown, litho tin, friction, clown driving red and yellow car, 6-1/2" l........190.00

### Dinky

Frank Hornby first created dinky Toys, made by the Meccano Toy Company of England, in 1933. The Dinky series of die-cast cars and trucks continued until World War II precluded the use of metal for toys. In 1945, production of die-cast metal toys again began with the introduction of a military line, as well as new cars and trucks. Production continued in factories in England and France until competition from Corgi, Tootsietoy, and Matchbox caused a decline in sales. The Dinky line was discontinued in 1979.

Airport Fire Tender, #276, MIB......90.00
Austin Somerset Saloon, #161, MIB ........70.00
Beachcraft S35 Bonanza, #710, MIB ........120.00
Bently Coupe, #194, MIB........125.00
Brinks Truck, #275, MIB........100.00
Bristol Helicopter, #715, MIB........65.00
Cadillac Eldorado, #131, played with condition........45.00
Caravan, #117, MIB........60.00
Cinderella's Coach, #111, MIB ........55.00
Coles Hydra Truck, #980, MIB ........100.00
Engineering Staff, #4, MIB.....450.00
Farm Produce Wagon, #343, MIB ........75.00
Fiat 600, #183, MIB........70.00
Fire Chief's Land Rover, #195, MIB ........50.00
Ford Consul Corsair, #130, MIB ........65.00
Fork Lift Truck, #404, MIB........55.00
Happy Cab, #130, MIB........50.00
Heinz 57 Varieties Bedford Van, #923, MIB........400.00
International Road Signs, #771, MIB ........180.00
Jaguar Mark X, #142, MIB........100.00
Jeep, #405, MIB........40.00
Johnston Road Sweeper, #451, MIB ........80.00
Leopard Recovery Tank, #699, MIB ........60.00
London Taxi, #284, MIB........50.00
Mercury Cougar, #174, MIB........95.00
Michigan Tractor Dozer, #976.....100.00
Passengers, #3, MIB........350.00
Plymouth Stockcar, #201, MIB......50.00
Pontiac Parisienne, #173, MIB......75.00
Range Rover Ambulance, #268, MIB ........60.00
Refuse Wagon with Cars, #978, MIB ........75.00
Rolls Royce Silver Wraith, #150, MIB ........80.00

**Ertl, International Tractor, metal and plastic, red body, rubber tires, 1:32 scale, $70.**

Rover 75 Saloon, #156, MIB.......100.00
Sam's Car, #108, MIB........120.00
Shovel Dozer, #977, MIB.......100.00
Telephone Service Van. #261, MIB ........100.00
Train and Hotel Staff, #5, MIB ........270.00
Triumph Spitfire, #114, MIB...100.00
UFO Interceptor, #351, MIB...125.00
VW Beetle, #181, MIB........95.00

### Doepke

Airport Tractor........125.00
Baggage Trailer, yellow or green ........50.00
MG........75.00
Road Grader, orange........275.00
Unit Crane........250.00

### Ertl

Fred Ertl, Sr., founded Ertl in 1945. Blueprints obtained from companies such as John Deere and International Harvester were used as patterns, thus insuring a high level of similarity to the originals. Ertl produces a fill line of wheeled vehicles and is recognized as the world's largest manufacturer of toy farm equipment.

Car, Dukes of Hazzard, General Lee, 1981, MOC........25.00
Chevy Bel Air, 1/18 scale, 1957, hard-top, green and ivory........30.00
Coke Beverage Truck, 1/64 scale ........15.00
Farmall Tractor, 1586, MIB.......55.00
Ford F150 Pickup Truck, 1/16 scale ........24.00
Manure Spreader, New Holland, high sides........65.00
Papa Smurf Car, MIP........10.00
Rumley #6 Tractor, 1/16 scale ........50.00
Smurfette Car, MIP........10.00
Tractor, diecast, 1/16 scale, Agri King, Case, white, 1974........185.00
Truck, semi, American Hardware ........100.00
Wagon, diecast, 1/16 scale, John Deer, metal wheels, 1960........95.00

### Fisher-Price

Fisher-Price Toys was founded in East Aurora, New York, in 1930. The original company consisted of Irving L.

Price, retired from F. W. Woolworth Co., Herman G. Fisher, who was associated with the Alderman-Fairchild Toy Co. in Churchville, New York, and Helen M Schelle, a former toy store owner. Margaret Evans Price, wife of the company president, was the company's first artist and designer. She had been a writer and illustrator of children's books. The company began with sixteen designs. Herman Fisher resigned as president in 1966. In 1969 the Quaker Oats Company acquired the company. Black and white rectangular logos appeared on all toys prior to 1962. The first plastic part was used after 1949.

Donald Duck Xylophone .......... 65.00
Dr. Doodle, #132, 1940, 10" h
.................................................. 95.00
Hickory Dickory Dock, radio and clock.......................................... 30.00
Little Snoopy, wood and plastic 18.50
Magic Key Mansion, six rooms, furnishings, 125 pc set............... 245.00
Mickey Mouse Drummer .......... 60.00
Miss Piggy, puppet, 1978 ........ 25.00
Molly Mop, #190..................... 250.00
Pony Express, #733 ................. 80.00

### Gabriel, Tricky Trapeze
Bozo the Clown ........................ 25.00
Disney Dancer, 1975................ 20.00
Donald Duck ............................ 25.00
Mickey Mouse ......................... 25.00
Santa Claus............................. 20.00

**Gay Products,** Texaco Star Indy Car
.................................................. 120.00

### Gilbert, A. C.
The first Mysto-Erector set was introduced at the 1913 Toy Fair and was an immediate hit. By 1915, Alfred Gilbert had refined the sets, added electric motors and expanded the line. The company continued to prosper until the Depression, when downsizing occurred. By 1967, the company was acquired by Gabriel Industries.

Mysto Magic Set, late 1930s, wood box, some items missing ....... 130.00
Set #0, 1913, cardboard box, some play wear.................................. 90.00
Set #1, 1914-15, cardboard box, some play wear........................ 85.00
Set #1-1/2, 1935-42, cardboard box, excellent condition.................... 65.00
Set #2, 1914-21, cardboard box, some play wear........................ 75.00
Set #2-1/2, 1945-56, cardboard box, excellent condition.................... 70.00
Set #3-1/2, 1935, cardboard box, some play wear..................... 125.00
Set #4, 1915, wood box, excellent condition ............................... 215.00
Set #4-1/2, 1936-42, cardboard box, excellent condition.................... 85.00
Set #5, 1915, wood box, excellent condition ............................... 265.00
Set #5-1/2, 1936-38, metal box, some play wear........................ 90.00
Set #6, 1915-16, wood box, excellent condition ............................... 275.00

Set #6-1/2, 1945-57, metal box, played with condition.............. 50.00
Set #7, 1914-32, wood box, played with condition......................... 185.00
Set #7-1/2, 1934-37, metal box, excellent condition................. 160.00
Set #8, 1933, metal box, excellent condition ............................... 245.00
Set #8-1/2, 1931-32, wood box, excellent condition.............. 3,150.00
Set #9, 1929-32, wood box, played with condition..................... 2,850.00
Set #9-1/2, 1935, metal box, played with condition......................... 275.00
Set #10, 1920-26, wood box, played with condition..................... 4,600.00
Set #10-1/2, 1938-42, metal box, excellent condition................. 475.00
Set #12-1/2, 1945-50, metal box, played with condition............. 725.00
Set #10021, 1956-61, cardboard box, excellent condition......... 100.00
Set #10026, 1958, cardboard box, played with condition.............. 50.00
Set #10062, 1958, metal box, played with condition.......................... 85.00
Set #10093, 1959, metal box, excellent condition ..................... 1,275.00
Set #10128, 1963-65, metal box, excellent condition................. 185.00
Set #10251, 1954, cardboard box, excellent condition.................. 45.00
Set #10351, 1965-68, cardboard box, excellent condition......... 220.00

### Hasbro
Hasbro Industries, Inc., an American toy manufacturer, is well known for several lines. One of the most popular toys produced by this company is Mr. Potato Head. It was introduced in 1948 and is still being made today. Another popular Hasbro line is GI Joe along with all the accessories made for this series of action figures.

Amazamatic Chevrolet Astro Vet, 1969, MIB................................. 95.00
Brothers Grimm School Kit, 1962
.................................................. 48.00
Buick Century, Amaz-A-Matics, 1969, MIB............................... 48.00
Casper Stitch a Story, 1967, sealed, MOC......................................... 48.00

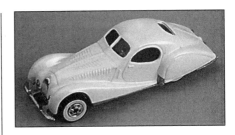

**Talbot Lago, 1986, $4.**

Junior Police Kit, cars, plastic scenery, 1960s, MOC ..................... 48.00
Mr. Potato Head Funny Face Kit, Set #2000, Hassenfield Bros., 1950s, 9" sq box.................................... 110.00
Mr. Potato Head Masquerade Playset, © 1968, MIB..................... 145.00
Transformer Mircomaser Patrols, Military Patrol, 1989, MIP............. 35.00
Wacky Wheel, 1960s, MOC ..... 40.00

### Hot Wheels
Corvettes, Micro Chrome Racers, four pack, MOC ...................... 35.00
Ferrari 312P, copper, Redlines, MOC
.................................................. 165.00
Flying Colors, Packin' Pacer, yellow, MOC ...................................... 45.00
GMC Hauler, #1917 ................. 45.00
GMC Van, #1970 .................... 45.00
Kenworth Hauler, #1915 .......... 45.00
Porsche P-11, chrome with red and green trim, Redlines, MOC, unpunched top ...................... 95.00
Racing Team Delivery Truck, yellow
.................................................. 95.00
Racing Team Truck and Trailer, white, Steering Rigs .......................... 95.00
Sand Crab, Redline ................. 30.00
Seasider, yellow-green, Redlines, MOC, unpunched top........... 285.00
Showcase Plaque, Custom Shop, MOC ...................................... 150.00
Simpsons, Family Camper, 1990, MOC ...................................... 15.00
Sizzlers Race Case, for Juice machine and race cards, vinyl, unused, orig tag ..................... 48.00
Speed Machines, Packin' Pacer, blue, MOC ............................... 45.00

**Hubley, horse drawn ladder wagon, repaired, $260.**

Steering Rig, 1980, MIB ........... 45.00
Talbot Lago, white, 1990, loose
.................................................. 5.00
Twin Mill, one wheel missing .... 60.00

## Hubley

John Hubley founded the Hubley Manufacturing Company in 1894 in Lancaster, Pennsylvania. The first toys were cast iron. In 1940 cast iron was phased out and replaced with metals and plastic. By 1952, Hubley made more cap pistols than any other type of toy. Gabriel Industries bought Hubley in 1965.

Bell Telephone Truck, pot metal, hoist and tools, 9" l ................ 195.00
Boat Tail Racer, cast iron, 6-1/2" l
.................................................. 200.00
Bus, cast iron, 5-3/4" l, new tires
.................................................. 125.00
Earth Mover, #354, plastic, automatic dumping auction, spare tire, orig box, 14" l ................ 110.00
Kiddie Toy Race Car, metal, nickel plated driver, red, black rubber tires, 1950s, 7" l .................................. 30.00
Motorcycle, cast iron, replaced handle bars, 60% orig paint ........ 200.00
Surf 'n' Sand, jeep and boat with trailer, blue and white, orig window box, 15" l ................................. 95.00

## Ideal

Lewis David Christie owned the Ideal Toy Company. It was located in Bridgeport, Connecticut. Among the toys it produced were dolls, cars, trucks, and even a line of toy soldiers produced for a short time span in the 1920s.

Bomber, B-25 Mitchell, plastic, 9" wing span ................................. 65.00
Cadillac, Fix-It Convertible, hard plastic, one pc missing, 13" l
.................................................. 195.00
Car, XP-600 Fix-It ..................... 75.00
Evel Knievel Precision Miniature, Formula 5000 race car replica, diecast metal, white, orig box, 1977 ..... 24.00
Flintstones Cave House, 1964
.................................................. 65.00
Jeep, plastic, brown, star stick, 1950s, 4" l ................................. 24.00
Mickey Mouse Pirate Ship Playset, missing several figures ......... 365.00
Washing Machine, windup, MIB
.................................................. 50.00

## Japanese, Post War

Following World War II, a huge variety of toys produced in Osaka and the Koto District of Japan flooded the American market. The vast majority of these toys are marked only with the country of origin and a trademark, usually consisting of a two- or three-letter monogram. It is virtually impossible to trace these trademarks to a specific manufacturer. Also, many toys were assembled from parts made by several different factories. To make matters even more confusing, names found on

boxes are often those of the agent or distributor, rather than the manufacturer.

Boxing Dog, wind-up, plush and litho tin, sign around neck reads "Next 4th Round," Yonezama, orig box, 6" h
.................................................. 115.00
Bunny on Tricycle, tin wind-up, orig box ............................................. 45.00
Bus
  Airport Service, opening doors, battery operated, 10" l ........ 60.00
  Continental Bus, tin friction, 8-1/2" l ................................. 135.00
  Continental Trailways, tin friction, 10-1/2" l ................................. 95.00
  Cross Country, hard plastic, friction, mkd "Hong Kong," 12" l
  .............................................. 85.00
  Greyhound Express, tin friction, 3-1/4" l ................................. 90.00
  Greyhound Lines Highway Traveler Express, tin friction, 1960s, 10" l, MIB ......................... 115.00
  Greyhound Scenicrusier, General Motors, tin friction, 7-1/2" l ... 65.00
Chevrolet Camaro, tin plate, battery operated, MIB ....................... 100.00
Fire Chief, KKK, red, tin friction, 9" l
.................................................. 35.00
Ford, battery operated, 7-1/2" l
.................................................. 145.00
Ford, Model T, tin friction, black and cream, 6-1/2" l ......................... 24.00
Ford Fairlane, tin friction, station wagon ..................................... 295.00
Gun, G-Men, sparking machine gun, litho tin, 8" h, MIB ................... 160.00
Jaguar, tin, battery operated, TT, orig box ............................................. 120.00
Jet, tin friction, Daiya ............. 395.00
Jumpy Rudolph, Asahi Toys, cable, 6" ........................................... 155.00
Main Street Bakery van, tin litho, Marusan ................................. 395.00
Police Helicopter, tin wind-up, MTU, orig box ..................................... 20.00
Racer, Blue Bird Land Racer, hard plastic, friction, orange, mkd "Hong Kong," 8-1/2" l, MIB ............... 165.00
Spin Turn Racer, wind-up, tin, plastic tires, Yone, orig box, 5" l ....... 115.00
Super Express, 3 train cars, K, 21" l
.................................................. 55.00
Tractor Trailer, Union Sheep, litho friction, Daiya Co., 13" l .......... 175.00
Tumbling Bear, tin face, plush and vinyl, orig box ......................... 60.00
Turtle, Go-Go Turtle, plastic wind-up, Daito, 1960s, MIB ................... 35.00
Volkswagen, Taiyo, all tin, 8-1/2" l, MIB ....................................... 140.00
Wales Gasoline Truck, tin, friction, orange and white, 10" l, 1950s
.................................................. 95.00

## Kenner

Easy Bake Oven, Betty Crocker, 1969 ........................................ 48.00
Fast III's, diecast, Dirt Digger, 1980, MOC ........................................ 15.00
Girder and Panel Building Set, #8
.................................................. 110.00

Give-A-Show Projector Set, Frankenstein Jr., Hanna-Barbera, orig slides with other Hanna-Barbera characters, working projector, orig box, 1967 ....................................... 175.00
Give-A-Show Projector Set, Glow-A-Show, 16 full color slides, 1960, orig box, some damage to slides, projector not working ....................... 65.00
Mold Master Road Builder Set, 1964, unused, MIB ......................... 115.00
Sky Rail Girder and Panel Set, #17, 1963, MIB ............................... 65.00
Spiroman, #432, 1968 .............. 25.00

## Knickerbocker

Dukes of Hazzard, finger racer crash car, General Lee or Sheriff, 1981, MOC, each ............................. 25.00
Fred Flintstone, pushbutton marionette, 1960s .......................... 185.00
Pixie and Dixie, stuffed, pair .. 300.00
Snooper and Blabber Mouse, stuffed, pair ......................... 180.00
Spare darts, 2 per card, MOC ... 6.00

**Lincoln Toys, Canada,** Lincoln Van Lines Trans Canada Service Truck, 18 wheeler, 23" l ................... 150.00

## Line Mar (Linemar)

Line Mar is a subsidiary of Marx. Linemar toys are manufactured in Japan.

Dino the Dinosaur, litho tin wind-up, Hanna Barbera, 1961, walks, growls
.............................................. 1,000.00
Fire Chief Car, battery operated, Chevrolet, 1956, MIB ............ 175.00
G-Man Machine Gun, green metal gun, black perforated barrel, 1950s, 13" l, MIB ............................. 100.00
Mechanical Cat, litho tin wind-up, ribbon collar, swirling rubber tail, 1950s, orig box, 3-1/2" h ........ 160.00
Patsy the Pig, litho tin wind-up, pink, blue, and yellow, 1960s, orig box, 4" h ........................................... 65.00
Playtime Airlines, tin friction, four metal propellers, 7-1/2" l wingspan
.................................................. 170.00
Popeye Lantern, litho tin battery operated, 1950s, 7-1/2" h ...... 245.00
Pull Back Donald Duck and Huey, litho tin, orig box, 5-1/2" h ...... 895.00
Touchdown Pete, the Football Player, litho tin wind-up, 1950s, 6" l ... 240.00

## Marx

Louis Marx founded the Marx Toy Company in 1921, stressing high quality at the lowest possible price. His popular line included every type of toy except dolls. The company was sold to Quaker Oats Company, who sold it in 1976 to the European company of Dunbee-Combex-Marx.

Archie & Veronica's Jalopie, litho tin wind-up, 1960s, 7-1/2" l ........ 600.00
Batmobile, child's ride-on type, green, silver hubcaps, plastic, 1960s, 24" l ......................... 185.00
Blue Bird Garage, gas station, 1930s, tin, MIB ..................... 650.00
British Soldier, walking, plastic, wind-up, orig box, 3" h ................... 55.00

Cape Canaveral Missle Set, 1950s, nearly complete .................... 225.00
Coca-Cola Truck, repainted, 20" l .............................................. 225.00
Combine, tin friction, MIB ........ 35.00
Dick Tracy Nora the Nursemaid, litho tin ramp walker, Baby Bonnie in carriage ...................................... 345.00
Dick Tracy Squad Car, 20" l, missing parts ...................................... 100.00
Dog and Doghouse, tin litho, 1920s .............................................. 100.00
Fire Chief Car, hard plastic, red and yellow, 5-1/2" l, MIB ................ 60.00
Fire Truck
   Aerial ladder, plastic, wind-up, electric lights .................... 125.00
   Hose and ladder ............... 350.00
Great Garloo, orig medallion, 1960s, 23" h ..................................... 275.00
Hans and Hop, ramp walker .... 48.00
Hill Climbing Dump Truck, battery operated, bright green and white plastic, 1960s ......................... 65.00
Intercity Delivery Truck, 18" l, played-with condition ........................... 55.00
Jaguar XKE, friction ................ 45.00
Laser Rifle, 2 action sounds, 1970s, MOC ........................................ 45.00
Marx-O-Matic All Star Basketball, metal and plastic, some water damage to box ............................. 125.00
Military Battleground, mechanical tank, 33" fold out tin ramp, 5" tin wind-up tank, 1950s.............. 115.00
Security Pistol, 2 action sounds, 1970s, MOC ........................... 35.00
Tinykins, Flintstone Cop .......... 45.00
Tractor, orig white rubber treads, partial box, pre-war ............... 250.00
Train Set, #532, 4 cars, 10 pcs of track, 2 keys, torn orig box .... 200.00

**Matchbox**

Matchbox cars were first manufactured by Lesney Products, an English company founded in 1947 by Leslie Smith and Rodney Smith. Their first die-cast cars were made in 1953 on a scale of 1:75. The trademark "Matchbox" was registered in 1953. In 1979, Lesney Products Corp. made more than 5.5 million toys a week. The company was sold to Universal International in 1982.

Airport Fire Fighting Crash Tender, #63, 1964, MIB ....................... 35.00
Army Saracen Personnel Carrier, #54, 1959, MIB ....................... 30.00
Austin Taxi, #17, 1960, MIB ..... 60.00
Beach Buggy, #30, 1971, MIB ... 9.00
Bedford Low-Loader, #27, metal wheels, MIB .......................... 415.00
Blue Shark, #61, 1971, MIB ..... 10.00
Case Tractor Bulldozer, #16, 1969, MIB ............................................ 18.00
Caterpillar Tractor, No. 8, 1955 .............................................. 40.00
Citreon DS19, #66, 1959 .......... 30.00
Coca-Cola Truck, #37, 1956, MIB .............................................. 80.00
Daimler Ambulance, #14, 1955 .............................................. 25.00

Dennis Refuge Truck, #15, 1963 .............................................. 20.00
Dodge Wreck Truck, BP Label, #13, green body, yellow cab, MIB ... 30.00
Flying Bug, #11, 1972, MIB ..... 14.00
Flat Car and Container, #25, 1979, MIB.............................................. 8.00
Formula 1 Racing Car, #34, 1971, MIB............................................ 15.00
Ford Pickup, #6, 1969.............. 15.00
Ford Zephyr 6, MKIII, #33, 1963, MIB .............................................. 38.00
Freeway Gas Tanker, #63, 1973, MIB .............................................. 20.00
General Army Lorry, #62, 1959, MIB .............................................. 28.00
Harley Davidson Motorcycle, #50, 1971, played-with condition ...... 3.00
Honda Motorcycle with Trailer, #38, 1968, MIB ............................... 24.00
Horse Box, #40, 1977, MIB ........ 8.00
House Trailer Caravan, #23, 1967, MIB .............................................. 40.00
Jaguar XK 140 Coupe, #32, 1956, MIB .............................................. 55.00
Lamborghini Countach, #27, 1974, MIB .............................................. 10.00
London Bus, #5, 1954, MIB ..... 45.00
Mercury Cougar, #62, 1969, MIB .............................................. 15.00
Merryweather Marquis Fire Engine, #9, 1959, MIB....................... 30.00
MGA Sports Car, #19, 1969, MIB .............................................. 70.00
Military Scout Car, #61, 1959, MIB .............................................. 32.00
Mobile Home, #54, 1981, MIB ... 8.00
Playset, Slip Stream Racing, slot car racing, 3 cars, 1980 ............. 100.00
Pontiac Convertible, #39, 1962, MIB .............................................. 65.00
Scaffolding Truck, Mercedes, #11, 1969 ........................................ 10.00

**Matchbox, Land Rover Fire Truck, #57, $5.**

Sugar Container Truck, No. 10, 1961, MIB ........................................ 55.00
Swamp Rat, #30, 1977, MIB ...... 8.00
Taxi Cab, Chevrolet Impala, #20, 1965, MIB ............................... 35.00
Tractor, #4, 1954 .................... 45.00
Truck, Ken Worth, made in Macau .............................................. 500.00
Volkswagen 1500 Saloon, #15, 1968, MIB ......................................... 25.00
Wild Life Truck, #57, 1973, MIB .............................................. 12.00

**Mattel**

Mattel, formed by Harold Mattson and Ruth and Elliot Handler in 1945, originated in a garage in Los Angeles. From its humble beginnings as a manufacturer of picture frames, the company evolved into making dollhouse furniture, burp guns, and eventually the Barbie doll, its most-famous product.

Beany and Cecil, Beany Copter, 1950, MOC .......................... 150.00
Beany and Cecil Disguise Kit .. 75.00
Crackers, The Talking Parrot, 1960s, on stand ............................... 195.00
Doctor Dolittle, talking, MIB ... 175.00
Incredible Edibles, 1966.......... 35.00
Jack in the Box, tin, clown, 1971 .............................................. 48.00
Jack in the Box, tin, Winnie the Pooh .............................................. 100.00
Mother Goose, pull string talker .............................................. 150.00
Rocket Set, H20, MIB ........... 125.00
Vic-A-Farm Set, 1962............. 125.00
V-Rrooom Racer, guide-whip, orig box ....................................... 125.00

**Mego**

Amazing Spider-Car, orig box .............................................. 125.00
Dukes of Hazzard Boss Hogg Caddy, 1981, 10-1/2" l .......... 385.00

**Nylint**

ABC Olympic Truck ................. 75.00
Fire Truck, ladder, 30" l ......... 100.00
Ford Camper, with radio ........ 250.00
Guided Missile Launcher, 1957 .............................................. 125.00
Grand Prix Special, racer and trailer .............................................. 50.00
Horse Van ............................. 160.00
Jungle Wagon...................... 135.00
Michigan Shovel, bucket tips when raised to boom, 10 wheels, yellow .............................................. 165.00
Payloader, red, rubber tires, 1955 fs............................................. 125.00
Street Sweeper, litho tin wind-up .............................................. 195.00
Tournarocker, yellow, adjustable front blade, pivoted rear low bar, 1955 .............................................. 100.00
U-Haul Ford Truck and Trailer 145.00

**Occupied Japan**

Dancing Black Man .............. 395.00
Friction Car, Alps, red metal, white rubber tires, 5" l, box missing end flap ...................................... 160.00

Merry Car, Sinsei Toys, tin litho key-wind, 5-1/2" l, MIB .................. 300.00
Stork, celluloid, figural, set of 12 in orig box, "Grade A, Made in Occupied Japan" ............................. 500.00

## Playsets

Black Goucho, Zorro, Nadel & Sons Toy Corp, 1950s ...................... 35.00
Blue Knight, George Peppard, MOC .................................................... 15.00
Charles Bronson's Commander, MOC ................................................ 15.00
CHiPs Highway Patrol, MOC .... 15.00
Dr. Kildare Doctor Playset, 1960s, MIB .................................................. 50.00
Early Settlers Log Set, Walt Disney, MIB ................................................ 125.00
Getaway Chase Game, DX, orig box ................................................... 85.00
Green Giant, Child Guidance, one truck missing ........................... 95.00
Handy Dandy Any Mechanical Drawing Set, MIB ..................... 85.00
Johnny Astro ......................... 135.00
Los Angeles Invasion Set, 104 pcs, MIB ................................................ 45.00
Motorific Alcan Hiway Torture Tract, Ideal, orig cars ........................ 85.00
Movieland Drive In Theatre, Remco, few pcs missing ..................... 235.00
Shell Oil Playset, Playmobile, 1992 ................................................... 35.00
Supercity Skyscraper, Ideal, 307 pcs ................................................ 85.00
Walton's, Amsco, figures missing ................................................... 125.00

## Remco

Remco Industries, Inc., was founded by Sol Robbins and was the first company to advertise its products on television. A unique aspect of the firm was that many of their products were related to television and promotional character dolls. The company closed in January 1974.

Lone Ranger Bazooka, shells, orig box, 1961 ................................. 75.00
Mighty Magee, aircraft carrier, hard plastic, gray and blue, 12 plastic planes, one truck, 1960s, 4" x 18" x 4-1/2" ................................ 60.00
Project Yankee Doodle, complete set ................................................ 110.00
Shark Race Car, 19" l ............. 70.00
Viking Ship, played with condition ................................................... 225.00
Voyage to the Bottom of the Sea, 1960s, near mint condition, orig box ............................................... 2,800.00

## Schuco

Clown Violinist, 1950s ........... 125.00
Convertible, Examico 4001, litho tin wind-up, black ....................... 195.00
Dump Truck, orig key ............ 125.00
Espresso Snack Bar, Coca Cola sign, #3068 ......................... 395.00
Gas Pump, Shell, 4" h ........... 295.00
Highway Patrol Squad Car, set, 1958 ................................................. 110.00
Mercedes Simplex, litho tin wind-up, 1902 model, 8-1/2" l ............ 125.00

Mercer, litho tin wind-up, 1913 model, 7-1/2" l ...................... 100.00
Monkey, lifting and dancing with bear ...................................... 275.00
Radio 412 Car, built-in music box, maroon ................................. 320.00
Renault, two seater, open, 7" l ................................................... 125.00
Sedan, litho tin wind-up, c1950, 4-1/2" l .................................. 200.00
Shell Gas Station, #3055, MIB ................................................... 395.00
Telesteering 3000, orig key .... 245.00
Van, battery operated ............. 75.00
Slinky, Hippo, MIB .................. 50.00

**Slinky,** Hippo, MIB ..................... 50.00

## Structo

Airplane, Lone Eagle, monoplane, spring motor, orange wings, 1928 ................................................... 800.00
Ambulance, green, 1928, 17" l ................................................... 600.00
American Airlines Sky Chief Lift Truck ..................................... 210.00
Auto Builder, Racer, red, 1919, 12-1/2" l ............................... 620.00
Bearcat Car, 1919, 16" l ........ 850.00
Caterpillar Tractor, 1921, 9" l ................................................... 325.00
Dump Truck, orange, black fenders, 1924, 12-1/2" l .................... 225.00
Emergency Van, blue and white, 1962 ........................................ 100.00
Excavator, 1931 .................... 325.00
Fire Insurance Patrol Car, 1928 ................................................... 200.00
Fire Truck
    Hook and ladder, 1930, 24" l ............................................... 425.00
    Pumper, red, orange water tank, 1928, 21" l ........................ 700.00
Hi Lift Dump Shovel, tin wind-up ................................................... 50.00
Hydraulic Dumper .................... 65.00
66 Gas Truck ........................ 175.00
Motor Dispatch Truck, blue, orange wheels, black tires, orig decals, 1929, 24" l ......................... 900.00
Moving Van, orange body, green wheels, black tires, 1928, 17" l ................................................... 375.00
Pile Driver, blue crane, red roof, 1924, 10-3/4" l ...................... 150.00
Road Grader, green, 1922, 16" l ................................................... 200.00
Sanitation Truck, #178, pressed steel, lever action dumping, rubber tires, plastic windows, side decals, orig window box, 11-1/4" l ...... 115.00
Tank, climbing, green tank, chain link treads, 1929 ........................ 550.00
US Mail Truck, green, red wheels, white tires, 1928, 17" l ........... 500.00

## Sun Rubber

The Sun Rubber Company was located in Barberton, Ohio. During the 1930s, it produced a number of character dolls and Disney items in addition to a general line. It was forced to cease production during World War II because of the scarcity of rubber. Production was revived

after World War II and continued through the 1950s.

Coupe, white, faded red, c1935, 4-1/4" l ................................... 35.00
Horse Van, yellow, red, 1935 ... 40.00
Station Wagon, white, red, c1939, 4" l ............................................... 65.00

## Tonka

In 1946, Mound Metal Crafts Inc., Mound, Minn., manufactured the first Tonka Toys. The name Tonka was derived from the firm's proximity to the banks of Lake Minnetonka. The company introduced a full line of trucks in 1949. In 1956, it changed it's name to Tonka Toys.

Ace Hardware, semi trailer, red, orig decals, 1955 ........................ 250.00
Airport Service Truck, 1962 ... 175.00
Allied Van Lines Truck, orange, black etters, 1963 ....................... 150.00
Army Jeep ............................. 45.00
Army Troup Carrier, 1964 ........ 80.00
Backhoe, 1963 ...................... 90.00
Baggage Tractor, trailer ......... 50.00
Bulldozer, 100, steel version ................................................... 175.00
Camper, pickup truck, 1963 .... 90.00
Car Carrier, blue, orig cars ... 175.00
Carnation Milk Van, white, decals, 1955 ...................................... 135.00
Cement Mixer ....................... 250.00
Coast to Coast Stores Truck, red cab ................................................. 100.00
Crane, with clam, yellow, tracks, 1949 ...................................... 125.00
Dragline, #514, orig box ........ 250.00
Dump Truck, red and blue ..... 175.00
Eibert Coffee Van, 1954 ........ 150.00
Fire Department Rescue Van, 1963 ................................................... 70.00
Fire Truck
    Ladder, red, 1954 ............ 175.00
    Pumper, red, 1957 ........... 190.00
    Tanker, T. F. D., white, red decals, 1958 ............................... 400.00
Gasoline Tanker, red, 1957 .... 220.00
GI Joe Striker, orig box .......... 75.00
Grain Hauler, red cab, 1952 .... 75.00
Hi-Way Mobile Clam, orange, 1961 ................................................... 125.00
Horse Trailer, 2 horses ........... 45.00
Jeep, horses, trailer, plastic top ................................................... 85.00
Jeep with snowplow, needs paint ................................................... 25.00
Livestock Van, red, 1952 ........ 90.00
Log Hauler, red cab, orig logs ................................................... 110.00
Minute Maid Van, white, decals ................................................... 245.00
Parcel Delivery Van, brown, 1954 ................................................... 120.00
Pickup Truck, stake sides, horse, 1957 ...................................... 150.00
Road Grader, yellow ............. 185.00
Sportsman Pick-Up ................. 75.00
Star-Kist Tuna Van, red cab, blue body, 1954 ........................... 220.00
Steam Shovel, red, 1948 ....... 120.00
Thunderbird Express, semi truck, red, 1959 .............................. 120.00

Tonka Marine Express, 1961
............................................. 125.00
Tonka Toy Transport Truck, red, silver
roof, 1949 ............................... 165.00
Trencher, yellow, 1963............. 60.00
Wrecker Truck, blue, 1950 ..... 110.00

## Tootsietoy

The first Tootsietoys were made in 1911, although the name was not registered until 1924, and it was not until after 1930 that the name appeared on the toys. Tootsie was an early manufacturer of prizes for Cracker Jack. Production of real vehicles began in 1914 and continued until World War II. After the war, cars were made as toys rather than models.

Airplane
  Atlantic Clipper, 2" l ............... 8.00
  Beechcraft Bonanza, orange
  .............................................. 7.50
  Bi-Wing Seaplane, yellow, 1926
  .............................................. 35.00
  F-94 Spitfire, green, 4 engines,
  1970s................................... 12.00
  Low Wing Piper Club........... 20.00
  Navy Jet, red, 1970s ............. 4.00
  P-38, WWII, blue props ..... 225.00
  Snow Skids, rotating prop, 4"
  wings .................................. 40.00
  Supermainliner ..................... 20.00
  Transport Plane, orange, 1941
  .............................................. 45.00
  TWA Electra, two engines ... 12.00
  US Army, 1936 .................... 35.00
  Waco Bomber, blue base, silver
  top ....................................... 55.00
Ambulance, Chevrolet, 4" l....... 18.00
Army Cannon, six wheels, 1950s
.................................................. 12.00
Army Tank, 1941 ...................... 35.00
Auburn Roadster, red, white rubber
tires ......................................... 20.00
Austin Healy Roadster, 6" l....... 22.00
Battleship, silver, red top, 6" l... 12.00
Bluebird Daytona Race Car ..... 24.00
Boat Trailer .............................. 10.00
Buick
  Coupe, blue, white tires, 1924
  .............................................. 30.00
  Delivery Van ........................ 25.00
  Estate Wagon, yellow and
  maroon, black tires, 1948.... 25.00
  LaSabre, red, open top, black
  tires, 1951........................... 28.00
  Sedan, 1947 ........................ 20.00
  Station Wagon, green, yellow top,
  black tires, 1954.................. 25.00
  Touring Car........................... 40.00
Cadillac
  Brougham............................ 40.00
  Coupe, blue and tan ........... 40.00
  Sedan, rubber wheels ......... 42.00
  Touring Car, 1925 ............... 45.00
Caterpillar Dozer, orig treads, 4"
.................................................. 85.00
Chevrolet
  Corvette, metallic copper color,
  black wheels ........................ 35.00
  Coupe, green, black wheels
  .............................................. 20.00
  Delivery Van ........................ 25.00

El Camino, red .................... 20.00
Fastback, blue, black wheels, 3" l,
1950 .................................... 20.00
Panel Truck, green, 3" l ....... 18.00
Roadster............................... 22.00
Touring Car........................... 55.00
Chrysler
  Convertible, blue-green, black
  wheels, 1960 ...................... 18.00
  New Yorker, blue, black wheels,
  1953 .................................... 20.00
  Windsor Convertible, 1960
  .............................................. 45.00
Contractor Set, pickup truck and 3
wagons ..................................... 60.00
Cross Country Bus................... 32.00
Cruiser, silver, 6" l .................... 12.00
DeSoto Airflow, green, white wheels
.................................................. 22.00
Destroyer, 1939, 4" l................. 10.00
Dirigible, USN Los Angeles, silver
.................................................. 45.00
Federal Van, black, cream wheels,
1924
  Bakery ................................. 50.00
  Florist................................... 75.00
  Grocery ................................ 45.00
  Laundry ................................ 55.00
  Market .................................. 60.00
  Milk....................................... 60.00
Fire Department Set, 1947 Mack pumper, ladder, and hose attachments, 1947 Mack fire trailer, Pontiac fire chief sedan, 1950 Chevy panel truck ambulance, fire hat and shovel, orig box, 1950s ...................... 250.00
Fire Truck
  American LaFrance Pumper, red,
  1954 .................................... 18.00
  Hook and Ladder, red and blue,
  side ladders ........................ 25.00
  Hose Car, orig driver and figure
  standing by water gun, 1937
  .............................................. 40.00
  Mack Fire Pumper, red, side ladders ..................................... 40.00
  Water Tower Truck, blue and
  orange, red water tower ...... 30.00
Ford
  Army Stake Truck, yellow radar
  unit, 6" l............................... 20.00
  Convertible Coupe, 1934 .... 32.00
  Customline, blue, black wheels,
  1955 .................................... 18.00
  Falcon, red, black wheels, 3" l
  .............................................. 12.00
  Oil Tanker, red, 1962 .......... 15.00
  Pickup, F1, orange, 4" l....... 12.00
  Station Wagon, blue, black
  wheels, 3" l, 1960 .............. 10.00
Graham, rubber wheels, 1933-35
  Convertible Coupe, rear spare tire
  .............................................. 50.00
  Coupe, side spare tire......... 50.00
  Sedan, side spare tire......... 50.00
  Towncar, rear spare tire....... 50.00
Greyhound Bus, silver and blue,
1950s, 6" l ................................ 90.00
Horse Trailer, red, white top ..... 12.00
House Trailer, powder blue, 2 black
wheels...................................... 15.00
International
  Panel Truck, blue, 4" l.......... 24.00

Standard Oil Truck, 6" l ....... 35.00
Station Wagon, red and yellow,
white tires, 1939 ................. 15.00
Jacquar XK 120 Roadster, green,
black wheels ............................ 12.00
LaSalle Convertible, red, black rubber wheels ............................... 15.00
Mack Truck
  Cement Mixer, red, yellow mixer,
  1955 .................................... 25.00
  Coal Truck, orange cab, blue
  bed, 1925.......................... 100.00
  Dump Truck, L-Line, yellow, light
  green dump body, 6" l......... 25.00
  Oil Tanker, B-Line, red........ 20.00
  Searchlight Truck, c1931 ... 35.00
  Stake Truck, B-Line, red tractor,
  orange trailer...................... 20.00
  Wrigley's Spearmint Gum, green,
  white rubber tires ............... 75.00
Mercury Custom, blue, black
wheels, 4" l, 1949.................... 15.00
MG TF Roadster, red, black wheels,
6" l, 1954 ................................. 18.00
Milk Trailer Set, tractor, 3 milk tankers
.................................................. 60.00
Oil Tanker, red, silver detailing, orig
box, 1950s, 9" l ....................... 90.00
Oldsmobile
  88 Convertible, bright green,
  black wheels, 6" l ............... 22.00
  98 Staff Car, red body, yellow top,
  open fenders, black wheels, 4" l,
  1955 .................................... 24.00
  Coupe .................................. 25.00
  Roadster, orange and black, 1924
  .............................................. 30.00
Plymouth, dark blue, black wheels,
two door, 3" l, 1957 ................. 12.00
Pontiac
  Fire Chief, red, black wheels,
  1950 .................................... 22.00
  Sedan, green, black wheels, 2
  door, 1950 .......................... 18.00
  Star chief, red, black wheels, 4" l,
  1959 .................................... 15.00
Racer, orange, black wheels, 3" l,
1950s ....................................... 10.00
Rambler Wagon, dark green, yellow
top, black wheels, yellow int., 1980s
.................................................. 10.00
Restaurant Trailer, yellow, black
tread wheels ............................ 35.00
Shell Oil Truck.......................... 50.00
Studebaker
  Coupe, green, black wheels, 3" l,
  1947 .................................... 55.00
  Lark Convertible, lime green,
  black wheels, 3" l, 1980 ...... 12.00

**Tootsietoy, submarine, metal and plastic, black body, red deck, gray tower, $70.**

Texaco Oil Truck........................60.00
Thunderbird Couple, powder blue, black wheels, 4" l, 1958 ...........15.00
Tootsietoy Dairy, semi trailer truck
..............................................85.00
Triumph TR3 Roadster, green, black wheels, 3" l, 1956 ....................12.00
U-Haul trailer, red, black tread wheels, logo ............................10.00
US Army Armored Car, camouflage, 1935 .......................................30.00
VW Bug, metallic gold, black tread wheels, 6" l ...............................15.00
Yacht, 1940, 4" l .......................12.00

## Winross Trucks

AACA Library and Research Center
..............................................60.00
Acme Printing........................30.00
Almond Joy ..............................48.00
Alpo .......................................30.00
American Red Cross ..............55.00
Anderson Windows ................50.00
Antique Car Show, Hersey .......55.00
Bon Ton Potato Chips..............35.00
Borden ...................................85.00
Bubble Yum ............................55.00
Busch .....................................85.00
California Raisins ....................60.00
Cherry Hill Orchard ................45.00
Cola-Cola ...............................100.00
Coors .....................................185.00
Cracker Jack...........................225.00
Dannon Yogurt .......................35.00
Eastman Kodak .......................55.00
Emergency Fire, 1500 cab.....100.00
Firestone ................................55.00
Georgia Pacific ......................250.00
Girl Scout Cookies ..................60.00
Goodwill .................................35.00
Great American Van Lines .......35.00
Hanover Brands .....................125.00
Hawaiian Punch .....................100.00
Hershey's Chocolate, ford cab
..............................................75.00
Iceland Seafood......................75.00
Jeno's Pizza ...........................55.00
Kraft........................................65.00
Lancaster Farm Toy Show......175.00
Londonderry Fire Co. .............45.00
Mack Truck..............................125.00
Morton Salt.............................100.00
Mountain Dew ........................35.00
Mrs. Paul's ..............................65.00
Nabisco ..................................85.00
Nestle's Quik ..........................75.00
Pepsi ......................................150.00
Quaker Oaks...........................115.00
Reading Railroad ....................75.00
Red Hawk Racing ...................95.00
Schmidt's Beer .......................115.00
Snyder's of Hanover ...............95.00
TMI ........................................115.00
Tyson Foods............................85.00
US Mail....................................50.00
Union Carbide .........................50.00
Watergate ...............................20.00
Wilbur Chocolate....................65.00
Winston Motor Sports..............45.00
Wonder Bread .........................75.00
Wyler's ...................................30.00
Y & S Candies .........................60.00
Yoplait Yogurt .........................35.00

Zeager Brothers .....................115.00

## Wolverine

The Wolverine Supply & Manufacturing Company was founded in 1903 and incorporated by Benjamin F. Bain in 1906. The first type of toys it produced were lithographed tin sand toys. The company began to make girls' housekeeping toys and action games by the 1920s. Production of toys continued and expanded in 1959 to include children's appliances, known as "Rite-Hite." The name was changed to Wolverine Toy Co. in 1962. The company was originally located in Pittsburgh, Pennsylvania, but relocated to Booneville, Arkansas, in 1970 after being acquired by Spang and Company.

Camping Trailer.......................95.00
Capt. Sandy Andy, sand toy, orig box
..............................................195.00
Drum Major, round base, c1930, 13-1/4" h..................................225.00
Express Bus ............................315.00
Farm Wagon, plastic wind-up, orig box, 10" l ..............................115.00
Icebox, tin ..............................50.00
Kitchen Cabinet, No. 280, toy groceries, orig box, 1949 .............195.00
Jet Roller Coaster, one car, orig box
..............................................145.00
Lunar Landing, marble game ..55.00
Merry Masons, automatic sand toy, litho tin, building shape, 3 litho tin masons, 1950s, orig box, 16" h
..............................................145.00
Mustang, white........................75.00
Snow White Ironing Board, tin, white ground, 8" x 27" l top, 21" h
..............................................150.00
Sunny Suzy, electric iron, orig box
..............................................18.00

## Wyandotte

All Metal Products Company, located in Wyandotte, Michigan, was in business by the early 1920s. The company, better known as Wyandotte Toys, originally produced wood and steel toy weapons. In 1935, it introduced an innovative line of streamlined wheeled vehicles. The firm ceased operations in 1956.

Ambulance, "Red Cross" on one side, other with "Wyandotte Toys," 11-1/4"..................................185.00
Autogyro Plane, 9-1/4" l ..........85.00
Auto Hauler Set, sedan, trailer, dump truck .......................................195.00
Battleship, rubber wheels, 6" l
..............................................40.00
China Clipper Airplane, 9-1/4" l
..............................................90.00
Chrysler Airflow, some damage to orig paint.................................100.00
Circus Truck and Wagon, red, and yellow, cardboard animals .....750.00
Coast to Coast Bus ..................315.00
Engineer Corps Truck, wood wheels
..............................................75.00
Gasoline Service Station, Shell Oil, two orig cars ..........................275.00

Giant Construction Dump Truck, 1950s .....................................195.00
Medical Corps Truck, pressed steel, wood tires, c1939, 12" l.........200.00
Pickway Pasture Truck............95.00
Rocket Racer, 6" l ...................50.00
Sambo, tin target board..........70.00
Sand Hopper Set, orig shovel
..............................................35.00
Soap Box Derby Racer, 6-1/4" l
..............................................45.00
Stake Truck, wood wheels .......40.00
Station Wagon, woody, 21" l
..............................................250.00
Steam Shovel, pressed steel
..............................................150.00
Stratoship Mystery Plane, 4-1/4" l
..............................................12.00
Tipper Truck, 1950s ..............195.00
Touring Sedan, #220, 1930s, 6" l, professional restoration ..........45.00
USA Medical Corps Truck, 11-3/4" l
..............................................100.00
Zephyr Racer, 10" l ................75.00

# Trains, Toy

**Collecting Hints:** Prices do fluctuate—those from mail order houses and stores generally are higher than those found at train swap meets.

Condition is critical. Items in fair condition (scratched, chipped, dented, rusted or warped) and below generally have little value to the collector. Restoration is accepted and can enhance the price by one or two grades, provided it has been done accurately. Spare parts are actively traded and sold among collectors to assist in restoration efforts.

Exterior condition often is more important than operating condition. If you require a piece that works, you should test it before you buy it.

Collecting toy trains is a very specialized field, and collectors tend to have their own meets. A wealth of literature is available but only from specialized book, railroad, or toy-train dealers. Novice collectors should read extensively before buying.

**History:** Railroading has always been an important part of childhood, largely because of the romance associated with the railroad and the prominence of toy trains.

The first toy trains were cast iron and tin; windup motors added movement. The golden age of toy trains was 1920 to 1955, when electric-powered units and high-quality rolling stock were available and names such as Ives, American Flyer, and Lionel were household words.

The advent of plastic in the late 1950s resulted in considerably lower quality.

Toy trains are designated by a model scale or gauge. The most popular are HO, N, O, and standard. Narrow gauge was a response to the modern capacity to miniaturize. Its popularity has decreased in the last few years.

**References:** Paul V. Ambrose, *Greenberg's Guide to Lionel Trains, 1945-1969, Vol. III, Sets*, Greenberg Publishing, 1990; Paul V. Ambrose and Joseph P. Algozzini, *Greenberg's Guide to Lionel Trains 1945-1969*, Vol. IV (1992), Vol. V. (1993), Greenberg Publishing; Tom Blaisdell and Ed Urmston, St., *Standard Guide to Athearn Model Trains*, Krause Publications, 1998; Pierce Carlson, *Collecting Toy Trains*, Pincushion Press, 1993; W. Graham Claytor, Jr., Paul A. Doyle, and Carlton Norris McKenney, *Greenberg's Guide to Early American Toy Trains*, Greenberg Publishing, 1993; Joe Deger (ed.), *Greenberg's Guide to American Flyer S Gauge*, Vol. I (4th ed., 1991), Vol. II (1991), Vol. III (1992), Greenberg Publishing; Cindy Lee Floyd (comp.), *Greenberg's Marx Train Catalogues*, Greenberg Publishing, 1993 John Glaab, *Brown Book of Brass Locomotives*, 3rd ed., Chilton, 1993, distributed by Krause Publications; *Greenberg's Pocket Price Guide, American Flyer S Gauge,* 14th ed., Kalmbach Publishing, 1997; Bruce C. Greenberg, *Greenberg's Guide to Ives Trains, 1901-1932*, Vol. I (1991) Vol. II (1992), Greenberg Publishing; —, *Greenberg's Guide to Lionel 1901-1942, Pre War, Vol. I: Standard and 2 7/8" Gauge*, Greenberg Books, 1994; —, *Greenberg's Pocket Guide, Lionel Trains, 1901-1998*, Kalmbach Publishing, 1997; —, *Greenberg's Guide to Lionel Trains 1945-1969*, Vols. 1 and 2, Greenberg Publishing, 1993; Greenberg Publishing, *Greenberg's Lionel Catalogues, Vol. V: 1955-1960*, Greenberg Publishing, 1992; George J. Horan, *Greenberg's Guide to Lionel HO Vol. II, 1974-1977*, Greenberg Publishing, 1993; George J. Horan and Vincent Rosa, *Greenberg's Guide to Lionel HO Vol. I, 1957-1966*, 2nd ed., Greenberg Publishing, 1993; Roland La Voie, *Greenberg's Guide to Lionel Trains, 1970-1991*, Vol. I (1991), Vol. II (1992), Greenberg Publishing; Roland E. La Voie, Michael A. Solly, and Louis A. Bohn, *Greenberg's Guide to Lionel Trains, 1970-1991*, Vol. II, Greenberg Publishing, 1992; Dallas J. Mallerich III, *Greenberg's American Toy Trains from 1900 with Current Prices*, Greenberg Publishing, 1990; Eric J. Matzke, *Greenberg's Guide to Marx Trains*, Vol., I (1989), Vol. II (1990), Greenberg Publishing; *Greenberg's Pocket Price Guide, Marx Trains*, 6th ed., Kalmbach Publishing, 1996; Tom McComas and James Tuohy, *Lionel: A Collector's Guide & History*, 6 vols., Chilton Books, 1993; Richard O'Brien, *Collecting Toy Trains*, No. 4, Krause Publications, 1997; Rick Ralston, *Cast Iron Floor Trains*, Ralston Publishing, 1994; Bob Roth, *Greenberg's Pocket Price Guide, LGB, 1968-1996*, 3rd ed., Kalmbach Publishing, 1996; Robert Schleicher, *Fun with Toy Trains*, Krause Publications, 1999; John David Spanagel, *Greenberg's Guide to Varney Trains*, Greenberg Publishing, 1991; Elizabeth A. Stephan, *O'Brien's Collecting Toy Trains*, 5th ed., Krause Publications, 1999; Alan Stewart, *Greenberg's Guide to Lionel Trains 1945-1969, Vol. VI: Accessories*, Greenberg Books, 1994; Robert C. Whitacre, *Greenberg's Guide to Marx Trains Sets*, Vol. III, Greenberg Publishing, 1992.

**Periodicals:** *Classic Toy Trains*, P.O. Box 1612, Waukesha, WI 53187; *LGB Telegram*, 1571 Landvater, Hummelstown, PA 17036; *Lionel Collector Series Marketmaker*, P.O. Box 1499, Gainesville, FL 32602; *O Scale Railroading*, P.O. Box 239, Nazareth, PA 18064; *S Gaugian*, 7236 Madison Ave., Forest Park, IL 60130.

**Collectors' Clubs:** American Flyer Collectors Club, P.O. Box 13269, Pittsburgh, PA 15243; Lionel Collector's Club of America, P.O. Box 479, La Salle, IL 61301; LGB Model Railroad Club, 1854 Erin Dr., Altoona, PA 16602; Lionel Operating Train Society, 18 Eland St., Fairfield, OH 45014; Marklin Club-North America, P.O. Box 51559, New Berlin, WI 53151; Marklin Digital Special Interest Group, P.O. Box 51319, New Berlin, WI 53151; The National Model Railroad Association, 4121 Cromwell Rd., Chattanooga, TN 37421; Toy Train Operating Society, Inc., 25 W. Walnut St., Ste 308, Pasadena, CA 91103; Train Collector's Association, P.O. Box 248, Strasburg, PA 17579.

**Note:** All prices given are for items in very good condition, meaning that the piece shows some signs of use but all parts are present and any damage is minor.

### American Flyer O Gauge
Set
Burlington Zephyr Streamliner, passenger, #9900 power car, coach, baggage car, #9900 tail car ............................................. 700.00
Freight, 2-6-4 locomotive, 8 wheel tender, flat bed car, box car, derrick car, tank car, gondola, caboose, 1930s ...................................... 450.00
Passenger, #253 locomotive, two #610 cars, #612, dark green, maroon inserts, 1924 .......................... 295.00

### American Flyer S Gauge
Accessories
Billboard, #566, whistling, 1951-55 ............................................. 20.00
Eureka Diner, #275, 1952-53 ............................................. 45.00
Gabe The Lamplighter, #23780, controller, orig decal, 1958 ......... 585.00
Hotel, #168, roof reattached, 1953 ............................................. 225.00
Log Loader, #164, gray, vermilion roof, controller, wiring bad, 1940 ............................................. 400.00
Magnetic Crane, #165, controller, 1940 ...................................... 600.00
Station and Terminal, #795, 1954 ............................................. 400.00
Truss Bridge, #571, 1955-56 ..... 7.50
Locomotive
#303, 4-4-2, Atlantic, 1954-56, steam ............................................. 25.00
#316, 4-6-2, K-5, Pennsylvania, 1946, steam ........................... 45.00
#345, 4-6-2, Pacific, 1954, steam ............................................. 50.00
#405, Silver Streak, 1952, Alco PA ............................................. 85.00
#499, New Haven, 1956-57, GE Electric .................................. 150.00
#21551, Northern Pacific, 1958, Alco PA .......................................... 110.00
Rolling stock
Box Car, #24047, GN, plug door ............................................. 85.00
Caboose
#607 .................................. 10.00
#907 .................................. 18.00
#24526, 1957 ..................... 15.00
Coal Car, #752, Seaboard, 3 button controller, 1946 ..................... 475.00
Flat Car, #24516, New Haven, 1957-59 .......................................... 10.00
Gondola, #24125, Bethlehem Steel, 3 rails, 1960 .......................... 40.00
Hopper and Dump Car
#719, CB & Q, 1950-54 ....... 30.00
#940, Wabash, 1953-56 ...... 15.00
Passenger Car
#653, Pullman, 1946-53 ...... 25.00
#662, Vista dome, 1950-52 ............................................. 27.50
#961, Jefferson, 1953-58 .... 30.00
#24773, Columbus, 1957-58 ............................................. 45.00

Reefer, #24191 Canadian National, 1958 ........................................250.00
Tank Car
#24313, Gulf, 1957-60.........20.00
#24330, Baker's Chocolate, 1961-72 .......................................25.00
Set
American Legion Ltd., #4019 locomotive, #4040 box car, American pullman, Pleasant View observation car, maroon litho and roofs ....660.00
Century, #9915, locomotive, integral tender, two #3178 coaches, #3179 observation car ......................850.00
Eagle, #21920 MP Alco PA, #24856 combine, #24863 vista dome, #24866 observation car, 1963, MIB ...................................1,600.00
Minnie Ha-Ha, locomotive, three coaches, orange and gray, minor wear ........................................295.00
Nation Wide, #1093 locomotive, green and black, brass trim, combine and coach ......................575.00
Northwestern Freight, #4677 diecast locomotive and tender, #3207 sand car gondola, #3025 wrecker car, #3211 caboose, 10 pcs curved track, 1938, some wear from use ...................................400.00
Passenger, #21927 engine, #24773, #24813, #24833 cars, 1960 ...450.00
Post Office, #1270 locomotive, coach, Railway Post Office car, 8 pcs track, orig box, uncataloged, cars unnamed, 1927, some wear ....................................250.00
Washington, #21089 locomotive and tender, #24055 box car, #24565 flat bed car with replica cannon, #24750 coach ......................................600.00

**Ives**

Accessories
Bridge, 91, O gauge, 1912-30 ....................................25.00
Platform, cov, 119, 1905-14 ...................................100.00
Locomotive
#17, 0-4-0, 1908....................300.00
#1118, 0-4-4-, 1913-14 .........275.00
#1661, 2-4-0, steam, 1932.....125.00
#3218, 0-4-0,1917................125.00
Rolling stock
#52, Passenger Car, 1915-25 ....................................45.00
#57, Lumber, O gauge, 1915-30 ....................................40.00
#121, Caboose, 1929..............75.00
#130, Buffet, 1930...................75.00
#136, Observation, 1926-30 ....40.00
#198, Gravel Car, 1930..........200.00
#1813, Baggage, 1931-32.......20.00
Set, #3250 tinplate locomotive with repainted body, #53 box car with white body, gray roof, #57 log car with brown body, 1908-30, assembled set, some wear..............300.00

**Lionel O Gauge**

Accessories
Block Signal, red base, #99N, 1932 ...................................200.00

Lionel, Silver Streak, #616 engine, #617 passenger cars, #618 caboose, $450.

Diesel Fueling Station, #415, 1955-57, MIB..................................250.00
Light Tower, 11" h...................110.00
Milk Car Platform.....................75.00
Power Station, #435, mustard, terra cotta, and green, 1926 .........275.00
Railroad Crossing Station ......125.00
Street Sign, Main Street/Broadway, 7" ....................................60.00
Locomotive
#60, Lionelville, trolley type, aluminized paper reflector, 1955-58 ...................................175.00
#203, 0-6-0, steam, 1940-42 ...................................325.00
#212, US Marine Corps, Alco A, 1958-59..................................50.00
#665, 41-6-4, steam, 1954-59 ...................................75.00
#706, 0-4-0, Electric, 1913-16 ...................................250.00
#3927, Lionel Lines, 1956-60 ...................................65.00
Rolling stock
#530, Observation, 1926-32 ....17.50
#605, Pullman, 1925-32 ..........65.00
#801, Caboose, 1915-26 ........17.50
#638-2361, Van Camp's Pork & Beans, 1962...........................20.00
#1007, Lionel Lines, SP Die 3, 1948-52 ....................................17.50
#1514, Baby Ruth.....................35.00
#1717, gondola, 1933-40........25.00
#1887, flat car, fence and horses, 1959....................................125.00
#2400, Maplewood, green and gray ...................................25.00
#2454, Sunoco tank car, 1946 ...................................10.00
#2816, hopper and dump car, 1935-42....................................50.00
#3356, Santa Fe Railway Express, 1956-60..................................35.00
#3360, Burro Crane, 1956, MIB ...................................275.00

#3413, Mercury Capsule Launching, 1962, MIB .....................325.00
#3444, Erie, gondola, 1957-59 ...................................30.00
#3461, flat car, log, dump, 1949-55 ...................................25.00
#3494-150, MoPac, box car, 1956, MIB ......................................300.00
#6025, Gulf, tank car, 1956-57 ...................................10.00
#9116, hopper, Domino Sugar, dome tank car, blue, black vertical stripe and center dome, blue and white logo........................................25.00
#9422, box car, EJ & E, green, orange, black..........................20.00
#9705, box car, D & RGW, orange and silver ...............................27.50
#17203, box car, Cotton Belt, double doors, red, large white letters ...................................35.00
#19835, box car, Fedex, animated, blue and white .........................40.00
Set
Blue Streak, #265, #265WX, #617 coach, #618 observation car, #619, 1936........................................700.00
City of Denver, #636W locomotive, two #617 coaches, #618 observation car, 1936..............................550.00
Flying Yankee, #616 locomotive, three #617 coaches, #618 observation car, gunmetal and chrome, 1935 ...................................275.00
Hiawatha, #250E locomotive, #250W tender, #782 coach, #783 coach, #784 observation car, 1935 ..........................................12,500.00

**Lionel S Gauge**

Accessories
Animated Circus Clown Car, #16651, MIB ..........................................30.00
Christmas Car/Seasons Greetings #7806, 1976, MIB................75.00

#7813, 1977, MIB...............75.00
#7814, 1978, MIB...............80.00
#9491, 1986, MIB...............50.00
#9778, 1975, MIB.............145.00
#19908, 1989, MIB.............35.00
#19929, 1994, MIB.............30.00
Passenger Train Station, Lionelville, c1923, some scratches and paint chips, chimneys missing........175.00
Locomotive
#1912, square cab, 1910-12
............................................250.00
#2035, steam locomotive, tinplate, #6466W tender, sq firebox, high headlight, repainted, smoke, whistle in tender, c1950 ....................225.00
Rolling stock
#6814, Billboard Reefer, Perrier, MIB
.............................................32.00
#9115, Billboard Hopper, Planters, MIB.......................................30.00
#9156, Plated Tank, Mobilgas, MIB
.............................................35.00
#9319, Buillon Car, Silver TCA, MIB
...........................................170.00
#9809, Reefer, Clark, MIB........36.00
#9863, Reefer, Nabisco, MIB ...55.00
#9916, Hopper, Domino, MIB ..25.00
#16800, Ore Car, Railroad Club, MIB
.............................................75.00
#17873, Conv Car, L.C.C.A., 1988, MIB..........................................48.00
#17890, Conv Car, L.O.T.S., 1991, MIB..........................................88.00
#17900, Unibody Tank Car, Sante Fe, MIB.......................................40.00
#17901, Unibody Tank Car, Chevron, #17901, MIB............................36.00
#19531, Billboard Reefer, Rice Krispies, MIB...........................36.00
#19963, Conv Car, T.T.O.S., MIB
.............................................50.00
#52047, Caboose, Southwest T.T.O.S., wood-side, MIB..........70.00
Set
Freight, #33, #35, #36, olive green, 1920 ......................................350.00
Freight, #41, #38 locomotive, #114 box car, #112 Lakeshore gondola, #113 stock car, #116 hopper, #117 caboose, 1913-24....................325.00
Passenger, #352E, #10E locomotive, #332 baggage car, #339 coach, #341 observation car, 1926, orig box, minor fatigue to locomotive
............................................500.00
Special Set No. 5006X, uncatalogued, 248 electric, two #629 passenger cars, #630 observation car, 1935, some wear from usage
............................................350.00

**N Gauge**
Atlas
Locomotive, EMD E8, diesel, Santa Fe..............................................25.00
Rolling Stock
Box Car, #2204, Great Northern
..............................................5.00
Pullman, #2601, Santa Fe .....9.00
Lone Star
Locomotive, EL-65, F-7, Kansas City
............................................17.50

Rolling Stock
EL-70, coach, British Main Line
.............................................5.00
El-141, caboose, Canadian Pacific ....................................7.50
Tyco, locomotive, car, Santa Fe
...........................................100.00

# Typewriters

**Collecting Hints:** Patent dates marked on frames are not accurate indicators of age, as these identify the date of the mechanical innovation's patent, not necessarily the date of manufacture. A machine with an 1890s patent date may have been made much later. The serial number is a far more useful tool in dating a machine. However, there are many manufacturers' numbering systems that are unknown, extremely confusing, or illogical.

In quite a number of cases, the only way to date a particular machine is through the use of old advertisements and catalogs. These references can also reveal particular models, colors, and unusual features.

Most manual typewriters produced after 1920 have little value, albeit some later models with unusual features have attracted collector interest. Some Electromechanical (or electric) typewriters manufactured before 1933 are scarce and, hence, valuable.

Domestic typewriter collectors are a small but steadily growing group. There is a well-established and active international typewriter collecting community, especially in Europe where mechanical objects and typewriters are eagerly sought. American collectors have generally swapped and traded among themselves, thus keeping prices low. This is changing as international collectors become more interested in American machines.

**History:** The first commercially manufactured American typewriter was the Sholes & Glidden Typewriter, manufactured by E. Remington & Sons in 1874. This typewriter produced a row of tiny, uneven capital letters. In 1876, Remington exhibited an example of the Sholes & Glidden at the United States Centennial Exhibition in Philadelphia. Souvenir messages were typed and sold for 25¢, and these are highly collectible today. Mark Twain was one of the first to purchase a Sholes & Glidden.

Although his review of it was rather mixed, his book *Life on the Mississippi* is thought to have been the first typewritten manuscript.

In 1878, Remington produced the Perfected Type Writer #2, later named the "Standard Remington Typewriter #2." This model, which was far more reliable and useful than its predecessor, typed on paper wound on a platen suspended over a circular type basket. Because the carriage had to be lifted away from the basket to view the typed material, this type of machine was known as a blind typewriter. It was the most common typewriter style for the next 30 years.

Like so many other manufacturers of the time, five major typewriter companies joined together in 1893 to form the Union Typewriter Company, in essence a trust created to limit competition and fix prices. Members of the trust produced thick, squat, blind-writing office machines exclusively, with little impetus for innovation. Two companies formed in competition to the Union Typewriter trust, Underwood Typewriter Company (1895) and L. C. Smith & Brothers Typewriter Company (1903), manufactured machines with a visible writing surface. These companies became the powerhouses of the typewriter industry for the next 30 years.

The first American-made electric machines appeared and quickly disappeared just after the turn of the century. The famous Blickenderfer Electric and little-known Cahill Electric are two of the earliest examples. The first successful electric typewriter was the IBM Model 01, introduced in the early 1930s.

Early typewriters generally have a glossy black finish, sometimes decorated with colored pinstripes or, less frequently, with highly detailed painted designs and inlays. This was the general trend until the 1920s when various bright colors were used, generally on portable machines. Many examples had a wood-grain finish. Black typewriters with a two-tone finish of glass and crackle panels were exclusively produced during the 1930s. Starting in the 1940s, typewriters and other office equipment was manufactured in "designer" colors to match office interiors.

The electronic typewriter is light, has few moving parts, and many additional features, but personal computers are quickly making type-writers obsolete.

**References:** Michael Adler, *Antique Typewriters from Creed to QWERTY*, Schiffer Publishing, 1997; Wilfred A. Beeching, *Century of the Typewriters*, William Heinemann, 1974; Richard N. Current, *The Typewriter and the Men Who Made It*, University of Illinois Press, 1954; Darryl Matter, *Simplex Typewriters from the Early Twentieth Century* Green Gate Books, 1984; Dan R. Post, *Collector's Guide to Antique Typewriters*, Post-Era Books, 1981.

**Periodical:** *Typewriter Times*, 1216 Garden St., Hoboken, NJ 07030.

**Collectors' Clubs:** Early Typewriter Collectors Association, 2591 Military Ave., Los Angeles, CA 90064; Internationales Forum Historische Burowelt, Postfach 50 11 68, D-5000 Koln-50, Germany.

**Museums:** Henry Ford Museum, Dearborn, MI; Milwaukee Public Museum, Milwaukee, WI; Onandaga Historical Society, Syracuse, NY; Smithsonian Institution, National Museum of American History, Washington, DC.

American Flyer, child's, 1935, orig box, MIB.......................................... 250.00
Bennett, 1901, small ................... 550.00
Blickensderfer
    No. 5, orig oak case.............. 150.00
    No. 7, cylinder case, Stanford, CT, oak case .............................. 125.00
Corona, #3, folding, patent 1904 and 1910 ....................................... 65.00
Hall, 1881................................... 700.00
Hammond
    No. 12, 1893 .......................... 225.00
    Varityper, 1927 ...................... 250.00
IBM, Selectric, electric, interchangeable ball type face .................. 25.00
Imperial, Model D, 1919 ............. 600.00
Keystone...................................... 75.00
L. C. Smith, 10" carriage, black case ................................................. 75.00

Merritt, linear index mechanism, plunger type selector, double shift, inking by roller, wooden base, orig oak case, c1900, 12-1/2" l ..... 175.00
Olivetti, portable, manual ............. 35.00
Olympia Robust, 1941 ............... 225.00
Remington
    No. 2 ..................................... 550.00
    No. 5, 1888 ........................... 400.00
    No. 6, orig tin cov ................. 175.00
Rheinmetall................................. 125.00
Royal, portable, manual, 1930s.... 90.00
Sears, portable, manual, 1950s ... 20.00
Simplex, Model I, index type, red, white, and blue, orig box .................. 50.00
Smith-Corona, portable, manual, 1950s ................................................. 20.00
Tip-Tip, 1936 ............................. 125.00
Underwood
    1895-1923.............................. 95.00
    1922....................................... 50.00
Valentine, orig case ................... 150.00

# U

## Uhl Pottery

**Collecting Hints:** Miniatures remain in strong demand, especially those pieces that double as souvenirs or advertising items. Uhl's Christmas jugs also continue to be popular with buyers, although prices have stabilized on all but the hardest-to-find examples. Remaining undervalued are a small number of unusual and one-of-a-kind items designed by Jane Uhl.

**History:** Two German immigrants, August and Louis Uhl, founded their pottery company, A.&L. Uhl, in 1854 in Evansville, Indiana. The company went through a number of owners and name changes over the next 90 years. Toward the end of the 19th century, the firm was known as Uhl Pottery Works, which later become Uhl Pottery Co. Although the office remained in Evansville, the production facility was moved to Huntingburg, Indiana, in 1908, in order to be closer to good clay deposits.

Names and addresses weren't the only things to change. During the first quarter of the 20th century, Uhl shifted away from its dependence on utilitarian stoneware like crocks and jugs, focusing instead on pottery dinnerware and household goods such as vases. Uhl also found success with a large line of miniature novelty items, including a series of Christmas jugs.

The company closed its doors in 1944 following a labor dispute. Family members brought the company back to life in the late 1980s, and a small number of miniatures and Acorn Wares crocks have been made since then.

**Reference:** F. Earl and Jane A. McCurdy, *A Collector's Guide & History of Uhl Pottery*, Ohio Valley Book, 1988.

**Collectors' Clubs:** Uhl Collectors Society, 801 Poplar St., Boonville, IN 47601.

**Advisor:** Don Johnson.

Acid Measure, brown, 1 gallon ... 130.00
Ashtray
　Dog at fire hydrant, marked ... 550.00
　Shell gasoline logo, embossed
　................................................. 175.00
Bank, pig
　Hitler image, "Cents 4 Defense, US Navy, Botay, KC Mo." ............ 500.00
　Large, white ........................... 450.00

**Dog at fire hydrant, marked, $550. Photo courtesy of Don Johnson.**

Medium, black ....................... 400.00
Batter Bowl, blue, marked ......... 110.00
Beater Jar, pink, marked.............. 85.00
Book, *A Collector's Guide & History of Uhl Pottery* by F. Earl and Jane A. McCurdy
　Hardcover ............................. 230.00
　Softcover............................. 100.00
Bottle, hand-turned, green ........ 400.00
Bowl
　Basketweave, pink.................. 40.00
　Pond lily, blue, 5" d.................. 45.00
Candleholder, hand-turned, green
　................................................. 180.00
Casserole
　#175, light blue ....................... 50.00
　#528, blue, marked................. 70.00
Catalog, Uhl Pottery Company Catalogue No. 15, original............. 100.00
Christmas Jug
　Bellied jug, brown over white, "Greetings from Uhl Pottery Co., Huntingburg, Ind." ................. 400.00
　Shoulder jug, brown over white, "A

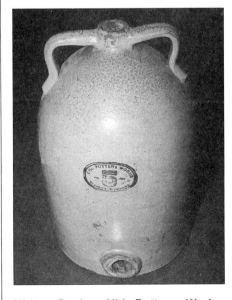

**Water Cooler, Uhl Pottery Works, Evansville, IN, 5 gallons, $200. Photo courtesy of Don Johnson.**

Merry Christmas" ink stamp
　........................................ 1,100.00
Prunella jug, brown over white, "Greetings from Uhl Pottery Co., Huntingburg, Ind." ink stamp
　............................................. 350.00
1930, shoulder jug, brown over white, Acorn Wares logo and "Christmas Cheer 1930" .................. 975.00
1933, demijohn, brown, "Christmas Cheer from Uhl Pottery Company 1933" flanked by Santas........ 700.00
1937, globe jug, brown over white, "Merry Christmas 1937"........ 300.00
1939, beehive jug, brown over white, "Merry Xmas 1939" ............... 250.00
1940, double-handled jug, red over green, "Merry Christmas 1940"
　............................................. 275.00
1941, double-handled jug, red over green, "Merry Christmas 1941"
　............................................. 275.00
1942, squat jug, brown over white, "Merry Christmas 1942"......... 250.00
1943, pitcher, brown, paper label
　........................................ 1,100.00
Churn, Acorn Wares, 6 gallons
　............................................. 150.00
Coffeepot, with lid and bail handle, blue
　............................................. 710.00
Cookie Jar, globe, yellow, marked
　............................................... 60.00
Creamer, hand-turned, green....... 80.00
Crock, Acorn Wares
　1/2 gallon ............................... 85.00
　1 gallon ................................. 30.00
　5gallons ................................ 50.00
Dog Dish, pink ........................... 165.00
Egyptian Jug, #162, purple ......... 75.00
Figurine, Scottie dog, black ....... 500.00
Flour Jar, Acorn Wares, blue stripes
　............................................. 600.00
Jug
　Acorn Wares
　　Pint .................................... 525.00
　　1/2 gallon .......................... 100.00
　　2 gallons ............................ 50.00
　　5 gallons ............................ 60.00
　Dillsboro Sanitarium
　　2 gallons, blue over white
　　................................................. 650.00
　　5 gallons, blue over white
　　................................................. 675.00
　Uhl Pottery Works, Evansville
　　2 gallons .......................... 125.00
　　4 gallons .......................... 135.00
　　5 gallons .......................... 150.00
　　10 gallons, double handles
　　................................................. 250.00
Mug, plain barrel
　"Big Boonville Fair," tan .......... 80.00
　Blue....................................... 150.00
Lawn ornament, turtle, 13" l, marked
　........................................... 1,400.00
Match Holder, #25, teal, marked
　............................................. 140.00
Miniature
　Acorn Jug
　　Brown over tan .................... 35.00
　　Pink over tan ..................... 180.00
　Baby Shoes
　　Pink, pair ........................... 400.00
　　White, marked, pair........... 170.00

Baseball Jug, white.................. 70.00
Basketball Trophy, Happy Hunters
.............................................. 2,200.00
Boots
   Cowboy, green, marked, pair
   .................................................. 375.00
   "Kentucky State Fair," yellow, pair
   .................................................. 150.00
Canteen, Botay ...................... 200.00
Cat Jug
   Black ................................. 170.00
   Blue, Meier paper label..... 225.00
Churn, with lid and dasher, blue over
white, acorn mark on base
................................................ 1,200.00
Cookie Jar
   #522, brown ...................... 90.00
   Globe, souvenir of "Indiana State
   Fair 1940," pink ................ 625.00
Football Jug
   Large size, brown.............. 365.00
   Small size, brown .............. 40.00
Horsehead jug, white............ 260.00
Jug
   Bellied
      Double handled, blue over
      white, Meier's paper label
      ............................................ 300.00
      Single handle, blue over white,
      "Great Smoky Mountains
      National Park" .............. 275.00
      Demijohn, purple ........... 65.00
      Globe, blue and white
      ........................................ 130.00
   Shoulder
      Brown over white, marked, 1" h
      ........................................ 115.00
      Brown over white, "State Fair
      1910" ............................ 100.00
      Purple............................. 90.00
      Square, brown over white,
      marked "Jug of corn from Cudjo's
      Cave, Cumberland Gap, Tenn-
      VA-KY:.............................. 325.00
   Pitcher, teal, marked ............. 175.00
   Ring Jug, blue....................... 500.00
   Slipper
      Blue................................... 40.00
      Black, pair ......................... 70.00
   Stein
      Brown, marked.................... 55.00
      Pink, marked ................... 100.00
   Tank, brown ......................... 750.00
   Tank jug, "Red Boiling Springs" ink
stamp...................................... 650.00
Mixing Bowl, inverted pyramid and
picket fence, blue, 5" d ........... 80.00
Mug, Dillsboro logo..................... 400.00
Pitcher
   #182, peach............................ 60.00
   #184, light blue ....................... 65.00
   Bellied, blue and white spongeware,
marked.................................... 400.00
   Grape, blue and white, 1 qt
.................................................. 110.00
   Hall Boy, "Dillsboro Health Resort"
ink stamp............................. 1,000.00
   Hand-turned, green, marked, 14" h
.................................................. 275.00
   Ice, black ............................... 60.00
   Jane Uhl, marked.................... 300.00
   Lincoln, 1/2-pint, "Hill-Top Gift Shop"
ink stamp.............................. 290.00
   Lincoln, 1 pint, diffused blue and
white exterior......................... 350.00

Squat grape with lid, blue...... 270.00
Planter
   Elephant, pink ...................... 175.00
   Pig, blue............................... 500.00
   Rabbit, blue .......................... 120.00
Refrigerator Jug
   #190 with stopper, pink.......... 100.00
   Polar Bear, no stopper, marked
.................................................. 375.00
Roaster, with lid, blue................. 200.00
Salad Bowl
   Blue, marked, 11" d .............. 140.00
   Pink, S-9............................... 50.00
Steam Table Jar, size A, fits 5" opening
.................................................. 200.00
Sugar Bowl, hand-turned, green,
marked..................................... 140.00
Teapot, #131, 2 cup, blue, marked
.................................................. 270.00
Thieves Jar, #136, teal, marked, 7" h
.................................................. 170.00
Vase
   #117, black, marked............... 55.00
   #123, blue, marked................ 70.00
   Hand-turned, aqua, marked, 9" h
.................................................. 275.00
   Hand-turned, blue................. 625.00

# Universal Pottery

**Collecting Hints:** Not all Universal pottery carried the Universal name as part of the backstamp. Wares marked "Harmony House," "Sweet William/Sears Roebuck and Co.," and "Wheelock, Peoria" are part of the Universal production. Wheelock was a department store in Peoria, Illinois, that controlled the Cattail pattern on the Old Holland shape.

Like many pottery companies, Universal had many shapes or styles of blanks, the most popular being Camwood, Old Holland, and Laurella. The same decal might be found on several different shapes.

The Cattail pattern had many accessory pieces. The 1940 and 1941 Sears Roebuck and Company catalogs listed an oval wastebaskel, breakfast set, kitchen scale, linens, and bread box. Calico Fruits is another pattern with accessory pieces. Because the Calico Fruits decal has not held up well over time, collectors may have to settle for less than perfect pieces.

**History:** Universal Potteries of Cambridge, Ohio, was organized in 1934 by The Oxford Pottery Company. The firm purchased the Atlas-Globe plant properties. The Atlas-Globe operation was a merger of the Atlas China Company (formerly Crescent China Co. in 1921, Tritt in 1912, and Bradshaw in 1902), and the Globe China Company.

Even after the purchase, Universal retained Oxford ware, made in Oxford, Ohio, as part of their dinnerware line. Another Oxford plant was used to manufacture tiles. The plant at Niles, Ohio, was dismantled.

The most popular Universal lines were Ballerina and Ballerina Mist. The company developed a detergent-resistant decal with permacel, a key element in keeping a pattern bright. Production continued until 1960, when all plants were closed.

### Ballerina

Bread and Butter Plate, 6" d, Pink
.................................................... 3.50
Cup and Saucer, Pink..................... 7.50
Dinner Plate, 10" d, Dove Gray..... 14.00
Eggcup, Jade Green.................... 12.00
Platter, 10" d, Pink....................... 15.00
Relish, Dove Gray.......................... 5.00

### Bittersweet

Drip Jar, cov ................................. 25.00
Mixing Bowl ................................. 30.00
Platter .......................................... 35.00
Salad Bowl.................................... 24.00
Stack Set ..................................... 35.00

### Calico Fruit

Custard Cup, 5 oz ......................... 6.50
Milk Jug, 3 quart.......................... 30.00
Plate, 6" d .................................... 5.00
Refrigerator Set, three jars, 4", 5", and 6"
d........................................... 45.00
Salt and Pepper Shakers, pr ........ 20.00
Utility Pitcher, cov ....................... 40.00
Utility Plate, 11-1/2" d .................. 20.00

### Cattails

Bread Box, double compartment
.................................................. 40.00
Butter Dish, cov, 1 pound............ 40.00
Canteen Jug ................................. 30.00
Casserole, cov, 8-1/4" d................ 20.00
Cookie Jar, cov ............................ 45.00
Gravy Boat.................................... 20.00
Milk Pitcher, 1 quart..................... 20.00
Pie server..................................... 20.00
Platter, oval ................................. 24.00
Range Set, 5 pcs.......................... 40.00
Refrigerator Pitcher, Cattails........ 40.00
Tea Set, 4 pcs.............................. 27.50
**Circus,** batter bowl set, 4-1/2" d, 5-1/2" d, 6-1/2" d, 3 matching lids, one with nick ...................................... 25.00

### Rambler Rose

Dinner Plate ................................. 10.00
Gravy Boat.................................... 12.00
Milk Pitcher.................................. 20.00
Plate, 9" d .................................... 7.50
Salt Shaker .................................. 5.00
Soup Bowl, flat.............................. 6.50

### Woodvine

Creamer and Sugar, cov ............. 20.00
Cup and Saucer ........................... 12.00
Gravy Boat.................................... 10.00
Plate, 9" d .................................... 5.00
Utility Jar, cov .............................. 20.00
Vegetable Bowl, oval .................... 9.50

# V

# Valentines

**Collecting Hints:** Unless the design is unique, the very simple, small penny cards given by school children are not of interest to collectors. Most collectors tend to specialize in one type of card, e.g., transportation theme cards, lacy, or honeycomb.

Condition of the card is very important—watch out for missing parts, soil, etc.

Keep cards out of direct sunlight to prevent fading and to keep them from becoming brittle. Store them in layers with acid-free tissue between each one, and use moth crystals or silverfish packets to protect them from insect infestation.

**History:** Early cards were often handmade and included both hand-written verses and hand-drawn design or border. Many cards also had some cutwork and hand-colored designs.

Among the prettiest collectible cards found today are the early hand-done lace paper valentines made between 1840 and 1900. Lace paper cards are folded in half, the front is covered with one or more layers of lace paper—either white, silver, or gold—with colored scraps or lithos filling the center. A printed verse is found inside, and the card may come in a matching embossed lacy envelope. The older the paper-lace, the fine the quality of the paper. The period from 1840 to 1860 is considered the golden age of lace paper valentines.

Most of the collectible valentines found today were made between 1900 and 1914 and are freestanding and consist of layers of die cuts. These include pull-downs, pullouts, pop-ups, and foldouts.

Pull-downs are made of cardboard die cut into fancy, lacy, colored shapes that create multi-dimensional images such as boats, ships, cars, planes, or gardens. Early examples pulled down from the middle; later pieces, which are not quite as elaborate as their predecessors, come down from the front.

Honeycomb tissue was used a great deal on pullouts, which open out and are free standing on a honeycomb base or easel back. Some of these open to form a whole circu-

lar design. The most valuable ones are those with a center column and a honeycomb base and canopy top. Tissue used on the early pieces was usually white, soft pink, blue, or green; during the 1920s red or soft red tissue was used.

Along with tissue paper valentines, we see lots of mechanical cards from the 1920s. Mechanicals have moving parts that are set in motion by pulling at tabs or moving wheels that are part of the card.

Two other popular styles are flats and hangers. Flats—easy to find and among the most reasonable to collect—often have fancy die-cut borders, embossing, and an artist-designed center of a pretty girl. Hangers are cards with silk ribbon at the top for hanging. A string of pretty die-cuts on a ribbon is called a charm string.

Bitter comic valentines were made as early as 1840, but most are from the post-1900 period. These cards make fun of appearance, occupation, or personality, and also embraced social issues of the day. Comic character valentines feature comic strip characters or the likes of Snow White, Mickey Mouse, Superman, or Wonder Woman.

**References:** Robert Brenner, *Valentine Treasury,* Schiffer Publishing, 1997; Dan and Pauline Campanelli, *Romantic Valentines,* L-W Books, 1996; Katherine Kreider, *Valentines with Values,* Schiffer Publishing, 1996.

**Collectors' Club:** National Valentine Collectors Association, P.O. Box 1404, Santa Ana, CA 92702.

**Advisor:** Evalene Pulati.

### Animated

Children with bear, seesaw, 1920s ................................................. 18.00
Girl playing piano, 1920s, 6" h... 15.00
Walking Doll, small, 4" h, 1923...... 14.00
World War II sailor boy in boat, 5" x 8" ................................................. 20.00
World War II soldier boy, stand-up ................................................. 18.00

### Comic

McLoughlin
    4" x 6" ........................................ 9.50
    8" x 10", sheet, sgd CJH, 1914 ................................................. 9.50
    10" x 15", sheet, occupational ................................................. 18.00
Unknown maker, 8" x 10", sheet, 1925 ................................................. 7.50

### Diecut, small

Brundage, artist sgd ...................... 9.00
Clapsaddle, artist sgd ................. 10.00

Heart shapes, girls ........................ 5.00

### Flat

Art Nouveau, embossed
    Fancy, 4" x 4" ............................ 7.50
    Girls, 3" x 5" .............................. 5.00
Heart Shape, child, 1920s .............. 3.50

### Folder

Fancy borders, blrds, 1914 ........... 9.50
Lacy cutwork edges, verse ......... 12.50
Tied with silk ribbon, 1920 ............. 7.50

### Hanger and String

Hanger
    Art Nouveau, heart, silk ribbon, 5" x 5" ....................................... 15.00
    Cutwork edge, litho, 1910, 3" x 4" ................................................. 9.50
    Fancy, artist sgd, 8" x 8", 1905 ................................................. 18.00
String
    Artist sgd, 3" x 3", 4 pcs........... 35.00
    Sweet children, 2" x 4", 5 pcs ................................................. 45.00

### Honeycomb Tissue

Beistle
    Early 1920s, pale red .............. 15.00
    Honeycomb base and top, red, 1926 ................................................. 10.00
Temple Love
    Honeycomb base only ............. 18.00
    Honeycomb base and top ....... 25.00
    Wide-eyed children playing house ................................................. 25.00

### Paper Lace

American
    McLoughlin, layered folder, 1890 ................................................. 15.00
    3" x 5", orig envelope, c1900 ................................................. 25.00
    6" x 9", 2 added lace layers ..... 25.00
    8" x 10", 2 layers, c1910 .......... 35.00
    Boxed, fancy scraps, ribbons ...... 45.00
    Early, hand done, scraps, ribbons ................................................. 55.00
Simple lace folder
    c1870, 5" x 7" .......................... 20.00
    c1885 ........................................ 15.00

### Parchment

Children, umbrella ........................... 5.00
Layered, ribbons ........................... 35.00
Silk, cherubs ................................. 45.00

### Pull-Down

Artist diecut, 1920s ...................... 45.00
Auto, layered, large, c1910 ........ 125.00
Auto, large, cute children, 1920s ................................................. 75.00
Children, 1930s
    Fancy background ................... 27.50
    Two layers ................................ 20.00
    Windmill background .............. 35.00
Dollhouse, large, elaborate, 1920s ................................................. 85.00
Floral, large, children, 4 layers, 1920s ................................................. 55.00
Flowers, three layers, 1920s ......... 25.00
Garden, large, layered, fancy, 1920s ................................................. 75.00
German Auto, pre-World War I, 5" x 8" ................................................. 75.00
Hearts, 1930s .............................. 45.00
Horse-drawn wagon, 1910 ........ 165.00

**Pullout**

Flowers in vase, opens out, 1920s
.................................................20.00
Garden scene, children, 7" x 10"
.................................................45.00
Gondola, children, honeycomb base,
  1930s .........................................55.00
Lighthouse, opens out, 1920s ...... 45.00
Sea plane, opens out, 1920s ........ 45.00
Ship, honeycomb base, 7" x 12"
.................................................95.00
Tunnel of Love
  Honeycomb base......................28.00
  Honeycomb base and top .......35.00

**Silk Fringed**

Prang
  Double-sided, 1880s, 3" x 5"....22.00
  Fancy, padded front, 5" x 7".....35.00
Tuck
  Artist-signed, c1890, 5" x 7".....25.00
  Double-sided, c1900, 3" x 5"....15.00
  Unmarked, small, 1900...............7.50

**Standup with Easel Back**

Airport scene, children traveling
.................................................18.00
Automobile, windows open, small
.................................................15.00
Cherub with heart ...........................5.00
Children
  Diecut, fancy...........................12.50
  Dollhouse, 1925 ......................15.00
  Figural .......................................5.00
  School room scene ...................8.50
  Sledding, flat.............................7.50
Fancy, silk inserts, 1900, 10" x 14"
..................................................9.50
Flat, flapper, c1920, 8" ...................7.50
Flower Basket
  Cherub .....................................15.00
  Pasteboard, 1918........................7.50
Layered Parchment, c1910, 5" x 8"
.................................................18.00
Sports Figure, 7" h ........................10.00
World War I, doughboy, 6" h ...........9.50
World War II, soldier and sailor boys,
  flat pcs, 8" h ..............................9.50

**Victorian Novelty**

Animated, doll, head reverses, large,
  rare............................................150.00
Diecut
  Children, fancy, boxed..............25.00
  Musical instruments, large.......75.00
  Musical instruments, small.......35.00

**Wood, telephone, boxed**

  Large.........................................85.00
  Small .........................................55.00

# Vending Machines

**Collecting Hints:** Since individual manufacturers offered such a wide range of models, some collectors choose to specialize in a particular brand of machine. Variations are important. Certain accessories, porcelain finish, colors, or special mechanical features on an otherwise common machine can add greatly to value.

Original paint is important, but numerous machines, especially peanut vendors with salt-damaged paint, have been repainted. Most vendors were in service for 10 to 20 years or more. Repainting normally was done by the operator as part of routine repair and maintenance. Repaints, recent or otherwise, if nicely done, do not necessarily lessen the value of a desirable machine. However, original paint should be retained if at all possible.

Decals add substantially to the appearance of a vendor and often are the only means of identifying it. Original decals, again, are the most desirable. Reproduction decals of many popular styles have been made and are a viable alternative if originals are not available.

Some reproduction parts also are available. In some cases, entire machines have been reproduced using new glass and castings. Using one or two new parts as a means of restoring an otherwise incomplete machine is generally accepted by collectors.

Collecting vending machines is a relatively new hobby. It has increased in popularity with other advertising collectibles. Previously unknown machines constantly are being discovered, thus maintaining the fascination for collectors.

**History:** Some of us still remember the penny gumball or peanut machine of our childhood. Many such vendors still survive on location after 30 years or more of service, due in part to the strength and simplicity of their construction.

The years between 1910 and 1940 were the heyday of the most collectible style of vendor, the globe-type peanut or gumball machine. Throughout this period machine manufacturers invested a great deal of money in advertising and research. Many new designs were patented.

The simple rugged designs proved the most popular with the operator who serviced an established route of vendors as a means of making a living. Many operators made their fortunes "a penny at a time," especially during the Depression when dollars were hard to come by. Fifty years later, the vendors that originally cost between $4 and $15 command a much higher price.

In addition to the globe-style variety of vendor, cabinet-style machines were also made. These usually incorporate a clockwork mechanism and occasionally mechanical figurines to deliver the merchandise. The earliest examples of these were produced in the 1890s.

**References:** Richard M. Bueschel, *Collector's Guide to Vintage Coin Machines*, Schiffer Publishing, 1995; —, *Lemons, Cherries and Bell-Fruit-Gum*, Royal Bell Books, 1995; —, *Guide to Vintage Trade Stimulators & Counter Games*, Schiffer Publishing, 1997; Richard Bueschel and Steve Gronowski, *Arcade 1*, Hoflin Publishing, 1993; Herbert Eiden and Jurgen Lukas, *Pinball Machines*, Schiffer Publishing, 1992; Bill Enes, *Silent Salesmen Too, The Encyclopedia of Collectible Vending Machines*, published by author (8520 Lewis Dr., Lenexa, KS 66227), 1995; Eric Hatchell and Dick Bueschel, *Coin-Ops on Location*, published by authors, 1993; Bill Kurtz, *Arcade Treasures*, Schiffer Publishing, 1994.

**Periodicals:** *Antique Amusements Slot Machines & Jukebox Gazette*, 909 26th St. NW, Washington, DC 20037; *Around the Vending Wheel*, 54217 Costana Ave., Lakewood, CA 90712; *Coin Drop International*, 5815 W. 52nd Ave., Denver, CO 80212; *Coin Machine Trader*, 569 Kansas SE, P.O. Box 602, Huron, SD 57350; *Coin-Op Classics*, 17844 Toiyabe St., Fountain Valley, CA 9270; *Coin-Op Newsletter*, 909 26th St., NW, Washington, DC, 20037; *Coin Slot*, 4401 Zephyr St., Wheat Ridge, CO 80033; *Gameroom*, 1014 Mt. Tabor Rd, New Albany, IN 47150; *Loose Change*, 1515 S. Commerce St., Las Vegas, NV 89102; *Pin Game Journal*, 31937 Olde Franklin Dr., Farmington, MI, 48334; *Scopitone Newsletter*, 810 Courtland Dr., Ballwin, MO 63021.

**Museum:** Liberty Belle Saloon and Slot Machine Collection, Reno, NV.

**Advisor:** Bob Levy.

Arcade Cards, Exhibit Supply, c1925, 2
  column, 1¢ ............................. 150.00
Aspirin, Reeds, Kayem Products,
  c1940, package of six for 10¢
................................................. 175.00
Candy/Gum
  Advance #11, c1925 ............. 175.00
  Ajax Deluxe Nut, c1947 ........ 350.00

Canteen, c1933...................... 425.00
Columbus, Model B, c1912 ... 450.00
Dean, c1972........................ 50.00
Hershey, c1950, 1¢ ................. 75.00
Mills, automatic, c1936 ......... 100.00
Norris, Master Novelty, c1923
........................................ 175.00
Northwestern, merchandiser, c1931
........................................ 175.00
Oak, Acorn, c1947................. 50.00
Pulver, short, clown, c1940 .... 550.00
Victor, Topper, c1950 .............. 90.00
Cigarettes, Dial-A-Smoke, Elde, Inc.,
c1940, circular ..................... 200.00
Cigars, Roi-Tan, c1940 ............. 125.00
Combs, Advance, Unit-e, c1950, 10¢
........................................ 75.00
Lighter Fluid, Van-Lite, c1933 ..... 700.00
Matches, Diamond books, c1928
........................................ 250.00
Pens, Servend, c1960.................. 40.00
Perfume, Silent Night, c1950 ...... 200.00
Prophylactic, Advance, c1923...... 75.00
Stamps
American Postmaster, c1930 . 125.00
National Postage, c1940.......... 75.00
Shipman Stamp, c1960........... 45.00

# Vernon Kilns

**Collecting Hints:** Vernon Kilns used 48 different marks during its years of operation. Collect examples which are in very good condition and concentrate on the specialty items rather than dinnerware.

**History:** During the Depression, many small potteries flourished in southern California. One of these, Poxon China, which was founded in Vernon, California, in 1912 was sold to Faye G. Bennison in 1931. It was renamed Vernon Kilns and also was known as Vernon Potteries, Ltd. Under Bennison's direction, the company became a leader in the pottery industry.

High quality and versatility made its wares very popular. Besides a varied dinnerware line, Vernon Kilns also produced Walt Disney figurines and advertising, political, and fraternal items. Their popular historical and commemorative plates were made in several different series featuring scenes from England, California missions, and the West.

Vernon Kilns survived the Depression, fires, earthquakes, and wars. However, it could not compete with the influx of imports. In January 1958, the factory was closed. Metlox Potteries of Manhattan Beach, California, bought the trade name and molds along with the remaining stock.

**Periodical:** *Vernon View*, P.O. Box 945, Scottsdale, AZ 85252.

**Brown-Eyed Susan**
Creamer.................................. 6.00
Mug...................................... 25.00
Pitcher, 2 qt, ice lip ................. 40.00
Plate, 6" d............................... 5.00
Platter, 12" d, round .................. 12.00
Salt and Pepper Shakers, pr ........ 15.00
Sugar..................................... 6.00
Teapot................................... 45.00
Tumbler, 4 oz ........................... 18.00

**Calico**, pink and blue plaid, blue border
Berry Bowl ............................... 8.50
Bread and Butter Plate, 6" d ........ 10.00
Creamer and Sugar ..................... 42.00
Cup and Saucer .......................... 45.00
Dinner Plate, 10" d ..................... 12.00
Relish..................................... 25.00
Salt and Pepper Shakers, pr ........ 35.00

**Chatelaine**
Cup and Saucer
Jade.................................... 24.00
Topaz................................. 40.00
Dinner Plate, 10" d, Jade ............. 20.00
Salad Plate, Topaz ....................... 25.00

**Chintz**
Bread and Butter Plate, 6" d .......... 8.00
Chowder Bowl ........................... 15.00
Creamer................................... 14.00
Cup....................................... 22.00
Dinner Plate, 9-1/2" d.................. 48.00
Salad Plate, 7-1/2" d .................. 18.00
Saucer.................................... 4.00
Sugar.................................... 12.00

**Gingham**, green and yellow plaid with green border
Bowl, 5" d............................... 15.00
Carafe................................... 30.00
Casserole, handle........................ 25.00
Chop Plate, 12" d ...................... 30.00
Creamer and Sugar ..................... 18.00
Cup....................................... 7.50
Dinner Plate, 10-1/2" d................. 8.00
Eggcup................................... 18.50
Luncheon Plate, 9-1/2" d ............... 6.50
Pitcher, ice lip ......................... 45.00
Salt and Pepper Shakers, pr ........ 35.00
Serving Bowl, 9" d...................... 17.50
Soup Bowl, 8-1/2" d .................... 15.00
Syrup Pitcher ........................... 85.00
Teapot................................... 20.00
Tumbler, 5-1/2" h ....................... 22.00

**Hawaiian Flowers**
Bread and Butter Plate, 6" d, pink
........................................ 20.00
Chop Plate, 14" d
Blue.................................... 90.00
Maroon................................ 95.00
Coffeepot, blue ......................... 125.00
Creamer and Sugar, blue ............. 50.00
Cup and Saucer ......................... 60.00
Dinner Plate, 9" d, blue................ 32.00
Dinner Service, maroon, 91 pcs
........................................ 850.00
Luncheon Plate, 8" d, maroon ...... 24.00
Salt and Pepper Shakers, pr, maroon
........................................ 40.00

**Homespun**, green, rust, and yellow plaid with rust border
Bowl, 9" d............................... 14.00
Bread and Butter Plate ................. 3.00

Butter Dish, cov ......................... 35.00
Carafe................................... 42.50
Chop Plate, 12" d....................... 25.00
Coffee Server ........................... 75.00
Creamer, lid ............................. 17.00
Cup and Saucer .......................... 5.50
Dinner Plate ............................. 5.00
Flowerpot................................ 30.00
Gravy.................................... 16.00
Jug, small ............................... 25.00
Mixing Bowl, 8" d ...................... 17.50
Platter, 12-1/2" l....................... 9.00
Salt and Pepper Shakers, pr ......... 8.00
Sauceboat, 6-1/2" l .................... 10.00
Soup Bowl, rim .......................... 10.00
Saucer.................................... 3.00
Tidbit, 3 tiers, metal handle ......... 30.00
Tumbler, 5-1/2" h ....................... 18.00
Vegetable Bowl, divided............... 22.00

**Moby Dick**
Bread and Butter Plate, dark blue
........................................ 30.00
Chowder Bowl, dark blue ............ 30.00
Creamer, brown.......................... 15.00
Cup and Saucer, brown................. 20.00
Dinner Plate, 10-1/2" d, dark blue
........................................ 60.00
Fruit Bowl, dark blue.................... 25.00
Luncheon Plate, maroon............... 40.00
Mug, maroon ............................ 95.00
Pitcher, brown........................... 435.00
Sauceboat, brown ....................... 25.00
Sugar, cov, brown ....................... 30.00
Teapot, dark blue........................ 175.00
Tumbler, dark blue ...................... 80.00

**Organdie**, brown and yellow plaid
Berry Bowl ............................... 9.50
Bowl, 7-1/4" d .......................... 5.00
Butter Dish, cov ......................... 35.00
Cake Plate, 12" d ....................... 20.00
Casserole, 8" d .......................... 65.00
Chop Plate, 12" d ....................... 15.00
Creamer................................... 5.00
Cup and Saucer .......................... 7.50
Demitasse Cup and Saucer ........ 20.00
Dinner Plate, 10-1/2" d................. 12.00
Eggcup................................... 27.50
Flowerpot................................ 40.00
Fruit Bowl, 5-1/2" d .................... 4.00
Mug, 9 oz................................. 15.00
Jug....................................... 65.00
Platter, 12-3/4" l, oval ................. 10.00
Salt and Pepper Shakers, pr ......... 15.00
Tea Set, round cov teapot, creamer,
sugar.................................. 45.00
Tidbit Tray, 2 tiers........................ 25.00

**Raffia**
Butter Dish, cov ......................... 30.00
Casserole, cov........................... 24.00
Chop Plate................................ 20.00
Coffee Server ........................... 65.00
Creamer and Sugar ..................... 22.00
Eggcup................................... 20.00
Pitcher, 2 qt............................. 40.00
Syrup.................................... 48.00

**Tam O'Shanter**, chartreuse, green, and rust plaid with green border
Bread and Butter Plate, 6" d ........... 6.50
Butter Dish, cov ......................... 40.00
Demitasse Cup and Saucer ......... 20.00
Dinner Plate, 10-1/2" d................. 15.00
Eggcup................................... 30.00

Luncheon Plate, 9-1/2" d................8.50
Pitcher, 2 quart.....................95.00
Platter, 12" l.......................17.50
Ramekin, cov.......................25.00
Salad Bowl.........................25.00
Tidbit Tray, 3 tiers, wood handle
...................................45.00
Tumbler, 14 oz......................15.00
Vegetable Bowl, divided.............20.00

**Winchester 73**

Chop Plate, 14" d..................200.00
Demitasse Cup and Saucer..........65.00
Mug...............................250.00
Platter, 12-1/2" l, oval............130.00
Salt Cellar and Pepper Mill........125.00
Set, service for 8...............1,200.00
Tumbler...........................250.00

# View-Master Products

**Collecting Hints:** Condition is the key price determinant. Because this collecting category is relatively new and large quantities of material were made, viewers and reels in mint or near-new condition can still be found.

Original packaging is sought by collectors. Many viewers and reels were removed from boxes and envelopes, used excessively, and damaged.

**History:** The first View-Master viewers and reels were made available in 1939. Invented by William Gruber, View-Master products were manufactured and sold by Sawyer's, Inc., of Portland, Oregon. The early growth of View-Master was cut short by World War II. Shortages of film, plastic, and paper would have crippled the operation and possibly ended the existence of View-Master had not the Army and Navy recognized the visual training potential of this product. Between 1942 and the war's end, about 100,000 viewers and 5 to 6 million reels were ordered by the military.

After the war, public demand for View-Master products soared. Production barely satisfied the needs of the original 1,000-dealer network. The Model C viewer, introduced in 1946, was practically indestructible, making it the most common viewer found by collectors today.

In October 1966, General Aniline & Film Corporation (GAF) bought Sawyer's and revamped the View-Master line. GAF introduced new 2-D projectors and the 3-D Talking View-Master.

In late 1980, GAF sold the View-Master portion of its company to a limited partnership headed by businessman Arnold Thaler. Further acquisition resulted in the purchase of Ideal Toys. Today the 3-D viewers and reels are manufactured by View-Master Ideal, Inc.

**Reference:** Roger T. Nazeley, *View-Master Single Reels*, published by author, 1987; John Waldsmith, *Stereo Views*, Wallace-Homestead, 1991.

**Collectors' Club:** Many View-Master collectors are members of the National Stereoscopic Association, P.O. Box 14801, Columbus, OH 43214.

A Christmas Carol, B380, 3 reels, sealed..........................15.00
Alaska, 49th State, Sawyers.........15.00
Alex................................4.50
Alf................................8.50
Annie..............................5.00
Annie Oakley......................15.00
Archie.............................8.00
Auto Racing, Phoenix 200, ABC Sports
...................................35.00
Banana Splits......................10.00
Barnaby In Space, 1972, GAF........20.00
Baseball, 3 reels..................85.00
Batman.............................15.00
Battle of the Planets..............15.00
Beverly Hillbillies.................15.00
Big Blue Marble....................10.00
Birds of the World, 1968, GAF......15.00
Black Beauty.......................10.00
Black Hole.........................15.00
Bon Voyage Charlie Brown, 1980, GAF
...................................10.00
Bonanza, B47, 1964, GAP............34.00
Bozo...............................15.00
Brady Bunch, 1960s, GAF............38.00
Brooklyn USA, 3 reels..............40.00
Buck Rogers, 1960s, GAF............10.00
Buffalo Bill Jr....................24.00
Bugs Bunny.........................10.00
Bugs Bunny and Tweety...............4.00
Bugs Bunny-Road Runner Show.........4.00
Bullwinkle.........................12.50
Captain America.....................5.00
Captain Kangaroo...................10.00
Care Bears..........................5.00
Casper, 1961, GAF..................25.00
Charlie Brown, Bon Voyage...........5.00
Charlotte's Web.....................5.00
CHiPs..............................15.00
Cisco Kid, single reel..............2.50
Cowboy Stars.......................25.00
Daktan, 1968, GAF..................35.00
Dale Evans.........................27.50
Daniel Boone.......................15.00
Dark Shadows.......................32.00
Dennis the Menace...................4.00
Deputy Dawg........................30.00
Detroit, A583, 3 reels.............18.00
Dick Tracy..........................7.50
Disneyland, 1962, Sawyers
  Adventureland....................20.00
  Fantasyland......................25.00
  Frontierland.....................25.00
  Mainstreet USA...................20.00

Tomorrowland.......................25.00
Donald Duck, 1960s, Sawyers........25.00
Dr. Who............................35.00
Dracula............................15.00
Duck Tales..........................5.00
Dukes of Hazzard, MOC..............15.00
Dumbo...............................7.50
Emergency..........................10.00
E.T................................15.00
Expo, 1967, 3 reels
  A071.............................24.00
  A073.............................24.00
  A074.............................27.00
Family Affair......................24.00
Fantastic Four.....................10.00
Fat Albert & Cosby Kids............10.00
Flintstones, View-Master International, 1980 copyright, MOC.....15.00
Fraggle Rock........................3.50
France, Sawyers, sealed pack.......15.00
Frankenstein, 1976, GAF............15.00
Full House..........................3.00
Germany, GAF, sealed pack..........15.00
Ghostbusters........................5.00
GI Joe Adventures, GAF.............20.00
Godzilla...........................14.00
Goonies.............................7.50
Great Muppet Caper..................4.50
Grizzly Adams......................10.00
Grotto of Redemption West Bend, IA, GAF............................10.00
Gunsmoke, 1972, GAF................30.00
Happy Days..........................9.00
Hawaii Five-O......................20.00
Hopalong Cassidy
  No. 955, Hopalong Cassidy and Topper, 1950......................12.00
  No. 956, The Cattle Rustler, 1950
  .................................12.00
Howard the Duck.....................8.00
Huckleberry Hound and Yogi Bear
  ..................................5.00
Incredible Hulk, 3 reels, booklet, envelope, GAF Viewmaster Cartoon Favorites, J26, 1981...........12.00
Inspector Gadget....................6.00
International Swimming and Diving, ABC Sports.....................60.00
Iowa, Sawyers......................15.00
Ironman.............................3.50
Isis, MIP..........................25.00
Italy, Sawyers, sealed pack........15.00
James Bond, Live & Let Die.........12.00
Jaws................................3.50
Jetson's, 1981, sealed pack........24.00
John Travolta, 1979, MIP...........35.00
Julia, three reels, story booklet, no envelope, 1969................40.00
King Kong...........................9.00
Kiss Me Kate......................125.00
Knight Rider........................5.00
Korg, sealed.......................10.00
Kotter, sealed.....................18.00
Kung Fu.............................9.00
Lake Tahoo, A161, 3 reels..........14.00
Land of the Giants, Sawyer, B484, 3 reels, 1968....................45.00
Land of the Lost, #2, The Abominable Snowman, 1971, orig booklet, damage to envelope................15.00
Lassie and Timmy, 1958, GAF........20.00
Lassie Look Homeward, 1965, GAF
  .................................20.00
Last Starfighter....................7.50

Laugh-In, three reels, orig envelope, 1968 .......................................... 45.00
Legend of the Lone Ranger ............ 7.50
Little Mermaid ................................. 2.50
Lost Treasures of the Amazon
.......................................... 120.00
Love Bug ........................................ 10.00
Mannix, sealed .............................. 15.00
Mary Poppins .................................. 8.00
M*A*S*H ........................................ 10.00
Mexico, 1973, GAF, sealed pack
............................................ 15.00
Michael .......................................... 25.00
Mickey Mouse Club ....................... 25.00
Mighty Mouse ................................ 20.00
Mission Impossible ........................ 15.00
Mod Squad, B478, 3 reels ............. 38.00
Monkees, talking, illus box ............ 80.00
Mount Rushmore, 1966, GAF ....... 15.00
Movie Stars, 1 reel ........................ 15.00
Munsters, orig book .................... 200.00
Muppets Go Hawaiian ..................... 5.00
Naval Aviation Training, World War II, test reel #13, hand lettered, plane identification ............................. 25.00
NCAA Track & Field Championships, ABC Sports .............................. 55.00
New Mickey Mouse Club ................. 4.50
New Zoo Revue .............................. 12.00
Old Mexico, B206, 3 reels, sealed
............................................ 15.00
One of Our Dinosaurs is Missing
............................................ 12.00
Partridge Family talking, illus box, MIB
............................................ 50.00
Pee Wee's Playhouse, Tyco, 1987, MOC
............................................ 15.00
Pete's Dragon ................................. 8.00
Pinocchio, B311, 3 reels, sealed
............................................ 16.00
Planet of the Apes, master set, orig envelope ................................. 30.00
Pluto ................................................ 5.00
Polly in Venice ............................... 18.00

Popeye, 1962, Sawyers ................ 20.00
Poseidon Adventure ...................... 24.00
Quick-Draw McGraw, 1961, Sawyers
............................................ 25.00
Red Riding Hood, 1 reel ................. 3.00
Return to Witch Mountain .............. 7.50
Rin-Tin-Tin ..................................... 15.00
Road Runner, 1967, GAF, ............ 20.00
Robin Hood .................................... 24.00
Romper Room .................................. 8.00
Roy Rogers .................................... 25.00
San Diego Zoo, A173, 3 reels ....... 15.00
Scenic USA, GAF, sealed pack
............................................ 15.00
Scooby Doo ..................................... 5.00
Sebastian ....................................... 28.00
Secret Squirrel & Adam Ant .......... 10.00
Sesame Street, Follow That Bird ..... 4.50
Silver Dollar City, 1971 ................. 15.00
Silverhawks ..................................... 5.00
Smurf, Flying ................................... 3.50
Snoopy and the Red Baron ............. 8.00
Snow White and the Seven Dwarfs
............................................ 10.00
Snowman ......................................... 6.50
Space Mouse, 1964, Sawyer ........ 25.00
Space: 1999, 1975, GAF .............. 28.00
Spider-Man .................................... 10.00
Star Trek, Mr. Spock's Time Trek, 1974, GAF ..................................... 20.00
Strange Animals of the World, 1958, GAF ..................................... 18.00
Superman Movie, sealed .............. 18.00
S.W.A.T., sealed ........................... 15.00
Tailspin ........................................... 5.00
Tarzan, B444, 3 reels ................... 48.00
Teenage Mutant Ninja Turtles ......... 2.50
Thomas the Tank Engine ............... 7.50
Thor ................................................ 2.00
Thunderbirds ................................. 45.00
Time Tunnel, Sawyer, 1966 ........ 165.00
Toby Tyler ...................................... 30.00
Tom & Jerry ................................... 10.00
Tom Sawyer ..................................... 9.00

Top Cat, 1962, MIP ...................... 40.00
Tournament of Thrills, ABC Sports
............................................ 35.00
TV Stars, 1 reel ............................. 20.00
Tweety and Sylvester ...................... 9.00
20,000 Leagues Under The Sea, 1962, Sawyers ................................. 30.00
U.N.C.L.E., three reels, story booklet, no envelope, 1965 ................... 36.00
U.F.O. ............................................ 40.00
US Spaceport, GAF ....................... 15.00
Universal Studios Scenic Tour, 1974, GAF, sealed pack ................... 25.00
Virgin Islands, B036, 3 reels ........ 16.00
Voyage to the Bottom of the Sea, 1966, Sawyers ................................. 30.00
Walt Disney
Mickey Mouse in Clock Cleaners, 1971, GAF ............................. 20.00
The Love Bug, 1968, GAF ....... 25.00
World Adventureland, GAF ..... 20.00
Waltons .................................. 10.00
Washington DC, Sawyers, sealed pack
............................................ 15.00
Water Ski Show, Cypress Gardens
............................................ 15.00
Welcome Back Kotter, three reels, story booklet, color photo cover, 1977
............................................ 24.00
Wild Animals of Africa, 1958, GAF
............................................ 15.00
Wild Animals of the World, 1958, GAF
............................................ 12.00
Wild Bill Hickcock & Jingles ......... 30.00
Wind in the Willows ........................ 8.00
Winnetou ....................................... 25.00
Wizard of Oz ................................. 15.00
Woody Woodpecker ....................... 15.00
World Bobsled, Championships, ABC Sports ..................................... 60.00
Yellowstone, Sawyer ..................... 15.00
Young Indiana Jones ....................... 7.50
Zorro .............................................. 35.00

# W

# Watch Fobs

**Collecting Hints:** The most popular fobs are those related to old machinery, either farm, construction, or industrial. Advertising fobs are the next most popular group.

The back of a fob is helpful in identifying a genuine fob from a reproduction or restrike. Genuine fobs frequently have advertising or a union trademark on the back. Some genuine fobs do have blank backs; but a blank back should be a warning to be cautious.

**History:** A watch fob is a useful and decorative item which attaches to a man's pocket watch by a strap and assists him in removing the watch from his pocket. Fobs became popular during the last quarter of the 19th century. Companies such as The Greenduck Co. in Chicago, Schwabb in Milwaukee, and Metal Arts in Rochester produced fobs for companies that wished to advertise their products or to commemorate an event, individual, or group.

Most fobs are made of metal and are struck from a steel die. Enamel fobs are scarce and sought after by collectors. If a fob was popular, a company would order restrikes. As a result, some fobs were issued for a period of 25 years or more. Watch fobs still are used today in promoting heavy industrial equipment.

**Reference:** John M. Kaduck, *Collecting Watch Fobs*, Wallace-Homestead, 1973, 1995 value update.

**Collectors' Clubs:** Canadian Assoc. of Watch Fob Collectors, P.O. Box 787, Caledonia, Ontario, N0A IA0 Canada; International Watch Fob Association, Inc., RR5, P.O. Box 210, Burlington, IA 52601; Midwest Watch Fob Collectors, Inc., 6401 W. Girard Ave., Milwaukee, WI 53210.

Reproduction Alert.

## Advertising

Anheuser-Busch, 1-1/2" d, diecut silvered brass, enameled red, white, and blue trademark.................60.00
Brown Gin and Liquors, 1-1/2" d, brass, raised moose head, reverse "Sold by H Obernauer & Co., Pittsburgh, PA" ..................................................60.00
Caterpillar, relief tractor on front, reverse mkd "Smith Tractor & Equip Co., Union, NJ," 1-3/4" x 1-1/2"........30.00

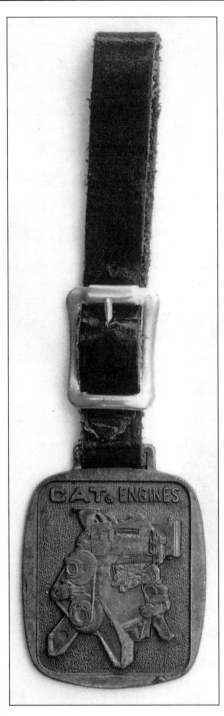

**Advertising, Foley Machinery Co., Leavers Mfg. Co., Ahaboro, MA, cat engines, $25.**

Chapman Drug Co., White Lion Drugs, Knoxville, silvered metal ..........35.00
Engeman-Matthew Range, diecut range ..................................................85.00
Evening Gazette, baseball shape, scorecard back, 1912..............95.00
Gardner-Denver Co., jackhammer, silvered brass, tool replica, symbol and name on back, c1950 ..............25.00

General Motors Diesel Engine, bronze luster metal, detailed engine image, block inscription "GM/General Motors Diesel Power," block logo on back, engraved dealer name ...............................................15.00
Green River Whiskey ....................45.00
Huntingdon Pianos, dark white metal, 7/8" black, white, blue, and gold celluloid with Paderewski, inscription "Paderewski Bought One," early 1900s.....................................65.00
Ingersoll-Rand, bronze luster, construction worker using pneumatic jackhammer beside "IR" logo, name and "Carset Jack Bits" on back......25.00
Kellogg Switchboard & Supply Co./The Service Of The Telephone Proves The Worth Of The Line, dark copper luster brass, raised image of candlestick phone with receiver off the hook, "K" circular logo, 1920s ................................................60.00
Kelly Springfield Tires, 2" d, white metal, raised illus of female motorist, "Kelly Springfield Hand Made Tires" on back..........................................75.00
Lima Construction Equipment, copper luster, large excavation tractor, world continents background, inscribed "Lima/Move The Earth With a Lima," back text for shovels, draglines, clamshells, and cranes............25.00
Lorain Construction Equipment, silvered brass, truck crane used to fill bed of pickup truck, inscribed "Loraine Cranes-Shovels/Draglines/Moto-Cranes," back inscribed "Freeland Equipment Co., Baltimore, orig strap ......................30.00
Martin-Senour Paints, 1-1/2" d, silvered brass, 1" d multicolored celluloid insert, hand holding dripping paint brush, text on back..................65.00
Moose Club Whiskey, silvered brass, center celluloid insert, inscribed "Moose Club Whiskey, The Best in The Land, The Adler Co., Cincinnati, O," early 1900s .....................125.00
Old Dutch Cleanser, porcelain center with Dutch lady ......................75.00
Red Bird Coffee, silver luster finish, brass, black, white, and red celluloid disk, blank reverse...................50.00
Red Goose Shoes, enameled red goose.......................................95.00
Rosenthal Bros., NY, Adamant Suit, boy holding knickers, sitting on box holding extra pants.........................40.00
Schramm Tractors .......................60.00
Studebaker, enameled tire design ................................................50.00
Ward's Fine Cakes, white porcelain, bluebird, silvered beaded rim ................................................45.00
Zeno Means Good Chewing Gum, brass.......................................95.00

## Fraternal

American Legion, Cleveland State Convention, 1946, diecut brass .....30.00
Elk's Tooth, gold filled ...................65.00

## Political

Bryan, Our Next President............ 40.00
Democratic National Convention, Baltimore, 1912, silvered brass, center shield with eagle standing atop .................................................. 20.00
Hughes, Charles F, 1908, silvered brass, head and shoulder portrait, from governor's campaign....... 60.00
Republican National Convention, brass, 1920, bust of Lincoln................ 40.00
Taft, brass, figural, padlock, "White House Lock, Taft 1908/Holds The Key"............................................ 50.00

## Souvenir

Magnetic Club, NY, enameled, 1913 .................................................. 45.00
Mormon Temple, Salt Lake City .... 50.00
Princeton University, brass, 1908 .................................................. 45.00
World Championship Rodeo Contest, Chicago.................................... 45.00

# Watt Pottery

**Collecting Hints:** Since Watt pottery was hand painted, there is a great deal of variation in patterns. Look for pieces with aesthetically pleasing designs which have remained bright and cheerful.

Watt had a strong regional presence in New England and New York, where more than 50% of its production was sold. Little of the output made its way West. Beware of placing too much emphasis on availability as a price consideration when buying outside the New England and New York areas.

Watt made experimental and specialty advertising pieces. These are eagerly sought by collectors. In addition, Watt made pieces to be sold exclusively by other distributors, e.g., Ravarino & Freschi Company's "R-F Spaghetti" mark.

**History:** Watt Pottery traces its roots back to W. J. Watt who founded the Brilliant Stoneware Company in 1886 in Rose Farm, Ohio. Watt sold his stoneware company in 1897. Between 1903 and 1921, W. J. Watt worked at the Ransbottom Brothers Pottery owned by his brothers-in-law.

In 1921, W. J. Watt purchased the Crooksville, Ohio, Globe Stoneware Company, known briefly as the Zane W. Burley Pottery between 1919 and 1921, and renamed it Watt Pottery Company. Watt was assisted by Harry and Thomas, his sons, C. L. Dawson, his son-in-law, Marion Watt, his daughter, and numerous other relatives.

Between 1922 and 1935, the company produced a line of stoneware products manufactured from clay found in the Crooksville area. The company prospered, exporting some of its wares to Canada.

In the mid-1930s, Watt introduced a kitchenware line with a background of off-white and tan earth tones. This new ware was similar in appearance to dinnerware patterns made by Pennsbury, Pfaltzgraff, and Purinton. It also can be compared to English Torquay.

Most Watt dinnerware featured an underglaze decoration. On pieces made prior to 1950, decoration was relatively simple, e.g., blue and white banding. Patterns were introduced in 1950; the first was a pansy motif. Red Apple began in 1952 and Rooster in 1955. Floral series, such as Starflower and Tulip variations, were made. New patterns were introduced yearly.

Watt sold its wares through large chain stores such as Kroger's, Safeway, and Woolworth, and grocery, hardware, and other retail merchants. Most of their output was sold in New England and New York. The balance was sold in the Midwest, Northwest, and South.

In the early 1960s, Watt was grossing more than three-quarters of a million dollars. Future prospects were promising, but on Oct. 4, 1965, fire destroyed the factory and warehouse. The pottery was not rebuilt.

**References:** Susan and Al Bagdade, *Warman's American Pottery and Porcelain*, Wallace-Homestead, 1994; Sue and Dave Morris, *Watt Pottery*, Collector Books, 1993, 1996 value update; Dennis Thompson and W. Bryce Watt, *Watt Pottery*, Schiffer Publishing, 1994.

**Periodical:** *Watt's News*, P.O. Box 708, Mason City, IA 50401.

**Collectors' Club:** Watt Pottery Collectors USA, Box 26067, Fairview Park, OH 44126.

**Reproduction Alert:** A Japanese copy of a large spaghetti bowl marked simply "U.S.A." is known. The Watt example bears "Peeddeeco" and "U.S.A." marks.

## Apple

Bean Pot.................................... 200.00
Bowl
   #6, ribbed, adv ........................ 70.00
   #8.......................................... 50.00
   #63........................................ 60.00
   #66........................................ 85.00
#601, cov, ribbed three leaves .................................................. 125.00
Canister, cov, #72..................... 265.00
Casserole, cov, individual size, two leaves, hairline...................... 100.00
Cereal Bowl ................................ 24.00
Coffee Server, cov, #115.......... 2,400.00
Cookie Jar, #503......................... 375.00
Creamer, #62 ............................ 175.00
Dinner Plate, #29, 10" d.............. 250.00
Ice Bucket ................................. 295.00
Mug ........................................... 65.00
Nappy, #64 ................................. 65.00
Pie Plate.................................... 150.00
Pitcher
   #16........................................ 65.00
   #17...................................... 175.00
Salad Bowl, #73........................... 65.00
Salt and Pepper Shakers, pr ...... 175.00
Spaghetti Bowl, #39 .................. 150.00
Sugar, #98 ................................. 400.00
Vegetable Bowl, cov.................... 50.00

## Autumn Foliage

Baker, cov ................................. 90.00
Bean Pot, #76 ............................ 50.00
Cookie Jar, #76............................ 95.00
Creamer, #62 ............................ 200.00
Sugar, cov, #98 .......................... 150.00
Teapot, #505 ............................. 995.00

## Bleeding Heart

Bean Pot.................................... 125.00
Bowl, #7 ...................................... 30.00
Creamer...................................... 75.00
Pitcher, #15................................ 55.00

## Cherry

Baker, #53 ................................. 100.00
Berry Bowl, #4 ............................ 25.00
Bowl, #89 .................................... 50.00
Pitcher, #15................................. 60.00
Platter ...................................... 150.00
Salt Shaker ................................ 50.00
Spaghetti Bowl, #39 .................... 50.00

## Pansy

Creamer, 3-1/2" h....................... 100.00
Pie Plate, #33, adv....................... 60.00
Pizza Plate ................................ 275.00
Spaghetti Bowl, #39 .................... 80.00

## Rooster

Baker, cov, #67........................... 165.00
Bowl, adv..................................... 55.00
Casserole, cov, #18 ................... 425.00
Cheese Crock, #80................... 1,500.00
Creamer, #62 ............................ 275.00
Ice Bucket ................................. 125.00
Mixing Bowl, #5 ........................... 85.00
Pitcher, #15............................... 165.00
Salt and Pepper Shakers, pr ...... 300.00
Vegetable Bowl, adv..................... 55.00

## Starflower

Baker, #67 ................................. 165.00
Bowl, #15, four petal flower .......... 95.00
Casserole, cov, #67 ................... 110.00
Cookie Jar, #21 .......................... 165.00
Creamer, #62 ............................ 185.00
Dinner Plate, 10" d ...................... 15.00
Grease Jug, #1 .......................... 350.00
Mixing Bowls, nesting, set of four, #4, #5, #6, #7............................. 185.00
Mug, #501 ................................... 95.00
Pitcher, #15................................. 50.00

Platter, #31 ......................................50.00
Salt and Pepper Shakers, pr, barrel
.................................................160.00
Tumbler ........................................300.00

**Tulip**
Baker, #600 ..................................350.00
Bean Pot, #76 ..............................100.00
Bowl, #73 .....................................115.00
Casserole, cov, #600 ..................125.00
Cookie Jar, #503 ..........................375.00
Mixing Bowl, #62 ..........................85.00
Pitcher, #17 .................................295.00
Salad Bowl, #73 ...........................145.00
Spaghetti Bowl, #39 ....................100.00

# Weller Pottery

**Collecting Hints:** Because pieces of Weller's commercial ware are readily available, prices are stable and unlikely to rise rapidly. Forest, Glendale, and Woodcraft are the popular patterns in the middle price range. The Novelty Line is most popular among the lower-priced items.

Novice collectors are advised to consider figurals. There are more than 50 variations of frogs, and many other animal shapes also are available.

Pieces made during the middle production period are usually marked with an impressed "Weller" in block letters or a half-circle ink stamp with the words "Weller Pottery." Late pieces are marked with a script "Weller" or "Weller Pottery." Many new collectors see a dated mark and incorrectly think the piece is old.

There are well more than 100 Weller patterns. New collectors should visit other collectors, talk with dealers, and look at a large range of pieces to determine which patterns they like and want to collect. Most collections are organized by pattern, not by shape or type.

**History:** In 1872, Samuel A. Weller opened a small factory in Fultonham, near Zanesville, Ohio. There he produced utilitarian stoneware, such as milk pans and sewer tile. In 1882, he moved his facilities to Zanesville. Then in 1890, Weller built a new plant in the Putnam section of Zanesville along the tracks of the Cincinnati and Muskingum Railway. Additions to this plant followed in 1892 and 1894.

In 1894, Weller entered into an agreement with William A. Long to purchase the Lonhuda Faience Company, which had developed an art pottery line under the guidance of Laura A. Fry, formerly of Rook-

wood. Long left in 1895, but Weller continued to produce Lonhuda under the new name "Louwelsa." Replacing Long as art director was Charles Babcock Upjohn who, along with Jacques Sicard, Frederick Hurten Rhead, and Gazo Fudji, developed Weller's art pottery lines.

At the end of World War I, many prestige lines were discontinued and Weller concentrated on commercial wares. Rudolph Lorber joined the staff and designed lines such as Roma, Forest, and Knifewood. In 1920, Weller purchased the plant of the Zanesville Art Pottery and claimed to produce more pottery than anyone else in the country.

Art pottery enjoyed a revival when the Hudson Line was introduced in the early 1920s. The 1930s saw Coppertone and Graystone Garden wares added. However, the Depression forced the closing of the Putnam plant and one on Marietta Street in Zanesville. After World War II inexpensive Japanese imports took over Weller's market. In 1947, Essex Wire Company of Detroit took control through stock purchases, but early in 1948 operations ceased.

**References:** Susan and Al Bagdade, *Warman's American Pottery and Porcelain*, Wallace-Homestead, 1994; Sharon and Bob Huxford, *Collectors Encyclopedia of Weller Pottery*, Collector Books, 1979, 1998 value update.

**Collectors' Club:** American Art Pottery Association, 125 E. Rose Ave., St. Louis, MO 63119.

**Note:** For pieces in the middle and upper price ranges see *Warman's Antiques and Collectibles Price Guide.*

Ashtray
  Coppertone, frog seated at end
  ...................................................115.00
    Roma, 2-1/2" d .........................35.00
    Woodcraft, 3" d ........................75.00
Basket
    Melrose, 10" ...........................155.00
    Sabrinian ................................165.00
    Silvertone, 8" ..........................350.00
    Wild Rose, 6" h, 5" d ...............65.00
Bowl
    Cameo, 6" d .............................95.00
    Claremont ...............................325.00
    Claywood, 4" d .........................40.00
    Knifewood, swans, dark ground
    ...................................................255.00
    Marbleized, 5-3/4" d, 1-5/8" d, shades of rose, pink and mauve
    .....................................................55.00
    Sabrinian, 6-1/2" x 3" h ..........240.00
    Scandia, 6-1/2" d .....................75.00

**Wall Pocket, Roma, 10-1/4" l, $195.**

    Squirrel on rim ..........................95.00
Candlesticks, pr
    Euclid, 12-1/2" h, orange luster
    .....................................................85.00
    Lorbeek, 2-1/2" h, shape #1
    ...................................................125.00
    Pumila .......................................65.00
    Silvertone ...............................175.00
Children's Ware
    Feeding Dish, Strutting Duck
    ...................................................125.00
    Milk Pitcher, 4" h, Zona ...........75.00
    Plate, Zona, 7" d ......................70.00
Cigarette Holder, figural, frog, Coppertone ...................................200.00
Compote, Bonito, 4" ...................75.00
Console Set, Warwick, 10-1/2" d bowl, pr candlesticks .....................175.00
Cornucopia
    Softone, light blue ....................45.00
    Wild Rose ..................................75.00
Ewer
    Cameo, 10" h, white rose, blue ground .......................................65.00
    Etna, 9" h ................................150.00
    Forest, 8" h .............................175.00
    Greenbrier, 11-1/2" h .............200.00
    Louwelsa, red and orange clover dec, 5-1/2" h, artist sgd .........190.00
    Panella .....................................55.00
Figure
    Brighton Kingfisher ...............350.00
    Elephant, bug-eyed, Cactus line, yellow ......................................145.00
    Turtle, Coppertone, 5-1/2" l ......95.00

Flask, Take a Plunge ................... 135.00
Flower Frog
   Kingfisher, 6" ........................... 475.00
   Silvertone, 1928 ..................... 100.00
   Woodcraft, figural lobster, c1917
   ............................................. 120.00
Hanging Basket
   Ivory Ware, marked with half kiln ink
   stamp ..................................... 110.00
   Marvo, 7" ................................ 145.00
   Woodcraft, 9" .......................... 225.00
Jardiniere
   Claywood, 8", cherries and trees
   ............................................... 95.00
   Ivory, 5" .................................... 45.00
   Marvo, rust, 7-1/2" ................... 85.00
   Roma, cat chasing canary ..... 175.00
Jug, Louwelsa, small .................. 140.00
Mug
   Claywood, star shaped flowers
   ............................................... 75.00

## Why Not a Sun Dial?

For years the bird bath has been the leader in garden ware. Now is the time to feature something new for the garden, particularly as we are in a position to turn out an attractive sun dial to retail for less than $5.00. Made of stoneware with sun dial in excellent bronze finish.

Also Art Pottery, Garden Ware Lines and Kitchen Pottery.

## S. A. Weller Company
### ZANESVILLE, OHIO
*"Buy American Pottery"*

**Magazine Tear Sheet, Pottery, Glass & Brass Salesman, March, 1933, showing sun dial, retail for less than $5, black and white, $3.**

Ivory, brown accents, cream ground
................................................... 55.00
   Souevo, #30 .......................... 150.00
Pitcher
   Bouquet, 6" h, ruffled top, lavender flower, white ground, artist sgd "M"
   ............................................... 60.00
   Pansy, 6-1/2" h ...................... 110.00
   Pierre, 5" h .............................. 50.00
   Zona, 8" h, kingfisher dec, green glaze, c1920 ........................ 140.00
Planter
   Blue Drapery .......................... 60.00
   Duck ....................................... 75.00
   Klyro, small ............................ 45.00
   Sabrinian, 5" x 5" ................. 170.00
   Woodrose, 9" h ...................... 60.00
Tub, Flemish, 4-1/2" d ................. 75.00
Tumbler, Bonito, multicolored flowers, 4-1/4" h .................................. 70.00
Umbrella Stand, Ivory, 20" h ....... 225.00
Urn, sculpted handles, matte blue, unmarked, 5-1/2" h ................... 50.00
Vase
   Art Nouveau, 9-3/4" h ............. 225.00
   Bonito, blue flowers, 2 small handles, 5" h ................................. 70.00
   Burntwood, pin-oak dec, 11" h
   ............................................. 150.00
   Chase, 9" h ........................... 350.00
   Claremont, 5" h, 2 handles ....... 60.00
   Coppertone, 8-1/2" h ............. 265.00
   Eocean, 10-1/2" h .................. 250.00
   Floretta, 7-1/2" h, grapes dec, high-gloss glaze ........................... 175.00
   Forest, 6" h ........................... 165.00
   Genova .................................. 95.00
   Glendale Thrush ................... 250.00
   Hudson, floral dec, 7" h
      Sgd "D England" .............. 200.00
      Sgd "Timberlake" ............. 375.00
   Ivory, peacocks, 11" h ............. 85.00
   Knifewood, 5-1/2" h, canaries, high glaze, nick on inside rim ........ 125.00
   Louella, gray, hp, nasturtiums
   ............................................. 220.00
   Louwelsa, 10" h ..................... 210.00
   Muskota, boy fishing, c1915, 7-1/2" h
   ............................................. 200.00
   Oak Leaf, 7" h, double bud type, green and brown accents, blue ground .................................. 85.00
   Paragon, gold, base chip, 6-3/4" h
   ............................................. 145.00
   Roma, grape, dec, 6" h
   Scenic ................................... 65.00
   Souevo, 7" h .......................... 115.00
   Turquoise, round, low, handled
   ............................................... 35.00
   Tutone, 4" h, 3-legged ball shape
   ............................................... 75.00
   Viola, fan shape ..................... 65.00
   Woodcraft, 1917, smooth tree-trunk shape, molded leafy branch around rim, purple plums, 12" h ........ 195.00
Wall Pocket
   Roma ..................................... 195.00
   Squirrel .................................. 375.00
   Souevo .................................. 195.00
   Sydonia, blue ......................... 225.00
   Woodcraft, 10" h .................... 300.00

# Western Americana

**Collecting Hints:** The collecting category of Western Americana is as vast and as wide ranging as the West itself. Western art and books are collected, along with well-used cowboy gear like saddles and spurs. Western-theme furniture, decorative items, and dinnerware have become very collectible and are often priced as high as their antiques that are 100 years older.

Western memorabilia has a strong regional following. For example, memorabilia from the early years of the Grand Canyon National Park has a stronger following in Arizona, while "Let 'er Buck" souvenirs of the Pendleton Rodeo are more eagerly sought out by Oregon collectors.

Look for a hot spot in the market to be ethnic collectibles. Memorabilia from the black "Buffalo Soldiers" calvary units is sought after by Western and military collectors for its rarity as well as for the contribution to black Western history. Hispanic cultural influence in the settlement of the West cannot be overlooked. After all, it has been more than 400 years since the first Spanish settlers arrived in modern day New Mexico. Souvenirs from Mexico continue to be popular today, as more collectors come to recognize the fine craftsmanship involved in their manufacture of sterling silver jewelry, weavings and pottery.

Cowgirl memorabilia has long been a "sleeper" in this category and is now becoming a vibrant, exciting part of the Western Americana market. This is due, in part, to a growing number of books and short stories chronicling the role of women in settling the West. Just check out the auction prices for a signed Annie Oakley cabinet card! Posters, sheet music, or postcards featuring a cowgirl in vintage clothing is a hot item. Cowboy and cowgirl toys remain a good buy. Western-themed toys, especially Japanese tin lithographed toys from the 1950s and 1960s are relatively inexpensive and sure to appreciate.

With popularity comes imitation, and Western memorabilia is no exception. Beware of the many "new" items of Western memorabilia that are in reality cheaply made imports. Be especially wary of spurs marked "Korea" or those that have scratch marks where the country of origin has been ground off. Most contemporary Western artists, whether their medium is leather, metal or oils, market their products honestly—as a new work of art.

**History:** Western American was sought out and preserved even before the turn of the century when astute historians saw their way of life disappearing before their eyes and made an effort to save all that they could through oral histories and artifacts. Much regional Western memorabilia is available in tiny local museums and historical societies. Early collectors were often ranchers, cowboys, and the descendants of early residents trying to keep their own family history intact. Today, collectors are more varied and you can find Western memorabilia on display in barns, high-class restaurants and attorney's offices. As the American West has become more popular, prices have risen and the fine line between the "real" old West and that of story, song and movie has blurred. Today, you can find a fine pair of woolly chaps displayed beside a vintage Gene Autry movie poster or a Red Ryder BB gun mounted on a gun rack right next to a Winchester.

The 150th anniversary of California's Gold Rush was in 1998 and further such celebrations continue to foster interest in the American West. Such enthusiasm is not strictly an American phenomenon, as collectors are scattered all over the globe.

**References:** Warren R. Anderson, *Owning Western History*, Mountain Press Publishing, 1993; Robert W. D. Ball, *Western Memorabilia and Collectibles*, Schiffer, 1993; Judy Crandall, *Cowgirls*, Schiffer, 1994; William C. Ketchum, Jr. *Collecting the West*, Crown Publisher, 1993; Ned & Jody Martin, *Bit and Spur Makers in the Vaquero Tradition*, 1998; McMenamin, *Popular Arts of Mexico*, 1997; William Manns with Elizabeth Flood, *Cowboys and the Trappings of the Old West*, Zon Publishing, 1998; Joice I. Overton, *Cowboy Bits and Spurs*, Schiffer, 1997; —, *Cowboy Equipment*, Schiffer, 1998; Jim and Nancy Schaut, *Collecting the Old West*, Krause Publications, 1999; James W. Wojtowicz, *Buffalo Bill Collectors Guide with Values*, Collector Books, 1998.

**Periodicals:** *American Cowboy*, P.O. Box 54555, Boulder CO 80322; *Cowboy Magazine*, Box 126, La Veta, CO 81055; *Cowboys*, P.O. Box 6459, Santa Fe, NM 87502; *Lone Prairie Roundup*, 2931 South St., Lincoln NE 68502; *Persimmon Hill*, 1700 NE 63rd St., Oklahoma City OK; *Wild West*, 6405 Flank Dr., Harrisburg, PA 17112.

**Collectors' Club:** American Barbed Wire Collectors Society, 1023 Baldwin Rd, Bakersfield, CA 93304; National Bit, Spur, and Saddle Collectors Association, P.O. Box 3035, Colorado Springs, CO 80904.

**Museums:** Autry Museum of Western Heritage, Los Angeles, CA; Buffalo Bill Historical Center, Cody, WY; Cowgirl Hall of Fame, Hereford, TX; Cowboy Museum of the West, Sheridan, WY; National Cowboy Hall of Fame, Oklahoma City, OK; Wells Fargo History Museum, Los Angeles, CA; Rockwell Museum, Corning, NY.

**Advisors**: Jim and Nancy Schaut.

Advertising
    Banner, 19-1/2" by 29", Winchester horse and rider in center, "Headquarters for Winchester Rifles and Shotguns," fringed hem ......... 250.00
    Figure, cowboy with saddle, rope, Stetson cologne, composition
    .................................................... 35.00
    Sign, Moccasin Agency, fierce Indian with headdress, emb tin
    .................................................... 95.00
Artwork
    Buffalo Bill, pyrography, drawn and burnt of Albert J. Seigfried, NY, 1907
    .................................................... 150.00
    Wells Fargo Depot and Office Building, Moron Taft, CA, 1910, original ink drawing, 20" by 30" framed
    .................................................... 750.00
Autograph, photo card, "Louise from W. F. Cody, 1906," (Buffalo Bill)
    .................................................... 1,500.00
Belt Buckle, Heston, Rodeo, 1985
    .................................................... 25.00
Bit
    Iron, rusted, marked "CSA," often used by former Confederate soldiers in the West .................... 500.00
    Silver inlay spade bit, full engraving of kissing birds, J. F. Echaverria, minor restoration .................... 2,000
    G. S. Garcia, silver inlay, curved snake cheeks, large 2" domed conchos .................................. 1,500.00
Bolo, 3" diameter figural turtle, crushed turquoise inlay, marked ".925" (sterling silver) and "Taxco" ............ 55.00
Book, Elizabeth B. Custer, *Tenting on the Plains*, 1893 ...................... 35.00
Bookends, pr, "End of the Trail," tired Indian on pony, cast metal ....... 75.00

**Bookends, pr, Saguaro cactus, wagon wheel and steer head motif, $95. Photo courtesy and Jim and Nancy Schaut.**

Buckskin Jacket, beaded, w/fringe, 1920s ...................... 250.00
Cabinet Card, Butch Cassidy & Sundance Kid ........................... 2,200.00
Chaps
    Black woollies ........................ 500.00
    Edward Bohlin, batwing style, black, engraved sterling silver buckle mounted with eight 1878 silver dollars ...................................... 2,800.00
    Shotgun (narrow leg) style, well-worn leather, initials "JS" ................ 450.00
Cuffs, pr
    Plain leather, brass studs form star design, unmarked.................. 250.00
    Tooled leather, fancy floral engraving, no maker's mark.............. 150.00
Dinnerware, Wallace China
    Boots & Saddles, cup & saucer set
    .................................................... 45.00
    Rodeo, salad plate, 7" d ......... 75.00
    Westward Ho, ashtray.............. 55.00
Glass, frosted, painted cowboy on bucking bronco, 1950s era...... 25.00
Holster and belt, tooled leather, floral design, marked Mexico .......... 95.00
Holster w/running iron (portable branding iron), crudely handmade ... 75.00
Magic Lantern Slides, set of 60, "Colorado by a Tenderfoot," shows mining towns, Pike's Peak, waterfalls, 1907 Denver .................................. 300.00
Neckerchief, bucking bronco motif, "Let 'er Buck" rodeo souvenir, 1920s
    .................................................... 125.00
Parade Outfit, Bohlin, silver mounted, made 1937 for Eleanor Montana
    .......................................... 22,000.00
Party Set, Covered wagon bean pot, ceramic coffeepot, beverage barrel, chip and dip bow with cowboy hat lid, ranch scenes, McCoy pottery, set ...................................... 1,200.00
Pennant, Grand National Livestock Show and Rodeo, San Francisco, 1960s .................................. 35.00
Pinback Button, "Let 'er buck," celluloid, cowboy on bucking horse, 1" d
    .................................................... 25.00

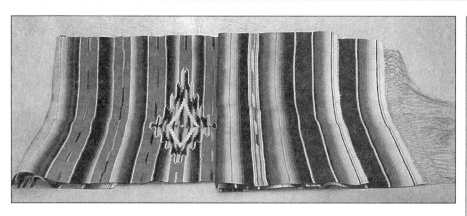

**Serapes, Mexican, 1950s, finely woven wool with cotton knotted fringe, each $75. Photo courtesy and Jim and Nancy Schaut.**

Pitcher, plastic, figural cowboy with gun, 1950s ............................... 45.00
Post Card, cowboys & cowgirls on picnic, by "Dude" Larsen .............. 15.00
Poster
    Yosemite National Park, 1931, Jo Mora ...................................... 200.00
    101 Ranch Wild West Show, 28" by 42", 1915 ............................ 2,700.00
Program, Texas Prison Rodeo, 1970s ................................................. 15.00
Rope
    Braided horsehair .................. 225.00
    Braided rawhide, "riata" ......... 150.00
Rope box, tooled leather with initials "FS" ........................................ 450.00
Saddle
    Calvary, McClellan military issue ................................................ 800.00
    Charo style, mother of pearl inlay, marked "La Moderna" ......... 2,500.00
    Child's, Roy Rogers imprint ................................................ 1,250.00
    Hamley, Pendleton, OR, exc condition ...................................... 2,800.00
    Pack saddle, wood frame for burro ................................................ 75.00
Saddle Bags
    Embossed floral leather, black, marked "Garcia, Mexico" ....... 125.00
    R. T. Frazier marked, woolly angora trim ...................................... 2,000.00
    "US" military saddle bags, fair condition ...................................... 250.00
Saddle Blanket
    Navajo, densely woven, few stains, 1960s ..................................... 475.00
    Pendleton, Indian style print, 1970s tag ......................................... 125.00
Spittoon
    Brass and iron turtle .............. 650.00
    Copper, 13" d, saloon-type, 1870s ................................................ 275.00
Spurs
    Buerman, marked "Hercules Bronze," gal leg, old leathers ................................................ 650.00
    Child's, marked "Made in USA," good leather ............................ 40.00
    Mexican style, silver inlay, large rowels ........................................ 450.00

Crockett, large conchos on leathers ........................................... 1,500.00
Prison made, Thunderbird design ............................................... 950.00
Tobacco Felt, Indian rug design, "rolling logs" (swastikas) good luck motif ................................................ 25.00
Toy Chest, cowboy and Indian motif, burnt-wood designs, 1950s ... 250.00
Trunk, Miller Bros. Rawhide cov., "101" and "MB" in brass nailheads, from the 101 Ranch show ........... 1,200.00
Vase, Wagon Wheel shape, stamped "Frankoma" ............................. 35.00
Watch Fob, sterling, 101 Ranch, shows the Miller Bros. ...................... 650.00

**Watch Fob, 101 Ranch Wild West Show, sterling, $650. Photo courtesy and Jim and Nancy Schaut.**

# Westmoreland Glass Company

**Collecting Hints:** The collector should become familiar with the many lines of tableware produced. English Hobnail, made from the 1920s to the 1960s, is popular. Colonial designs were used frequently, and accessories with dolphin pedestals are distinctive.

The trademark, an intertwined "W" and "G," was imprinted on glass beginning in 1949. After January 1983, the full name, "Westmoreland," was marked on all glass products. Early molds were reintroduced. Numbered, signed, dated "Limited Editions" were offered.

**History:** The Westmoreland Glass Company was founded in October 1899 at Grapeville, Pennsylvania. From the beginning, Westmoreland made handcrafted high-quality glassware. During the early years the company processed mustard, baking powder, and condiments to fill its containers. During World War I candy-filled glass novelties were popular.

Although Westmoreland is famous for its milk glass, other types of glass products were also produced. During the 1920s, Westmoreland made reproductions and decorated wares. Color and tableware appeared in the 1930s; but, as with other companies, 1935 saw production return primarily to crystal. From the 1940s to the 1960s, black, ruby, and amber objects were made.

In May 1982, the factory closed. Reorganization brought a reopening in July 1982, but the Grapeville plant closed again in 1984.

**References:** Lorraine Kovar, *Westmoreland Glass*, Vols. I and II, The Glass Press, 1991; Hazel Marie Weatherman, *Colored Glassware of the Depression Era, Book 2*, Glassbooks, Inc., 1982; Chas West Wilson, *Westmoreland Glass*, Collector Books, 1996, 1998 value update.

**Collectors' Clubs:** National Westmoreland Glass Collectors Club, P.O. Box 372, Westmoreland City, PA 15692; Westmoreland Glass Collectors Club, 2712 Glenwood, Independence, 64052; Westmoreland Glass Society, 4809 420th St. SE, Iowa City, IA 52240.

**Museum:** Westmoreland Glass Museum, Port Vue, PA.

Animal, covered dish type, white milk glass
    Camel, kneeling ....................... 75.00
    Cat, blue eyes .......................... 75.00
    Chick on eggs, iridized ........... 85.00
    Fox, brown eyes, lacy base ..... 75.00
    Swan, raised wing ................. 115.00
Appetizer Canape Set, Paneled Grape, milk glass ................................. 80.00
Ashtray, 5" d, Beaded Grape ....... 15.00
Basket, Pansy, milk glass ............ 20.00
Bon Bon, Waterford, #1932, ruby stained, 6" d, heart shaped, handle ............................................... 70.00
Bowl, cov, 5" d, flared, Beaded Grape ............................................... 55.00
Bowl, open
    9" w, sq, ftd, Beaded Grape, milk glass ..................................... 55.00
    9" d, 6" h, ftd, Paneled Grape, milk glass ..................................... 60.00
    10-1/2" d, ftd, Paneled Grape, milk glass ................................... 100.00
Bud Vase, 10" h, Paneled Grape, milk glass, orig label ...................... 30.00
Butter Dish, cov, 1/4 lb
    Old Quilt, milk glass ............... 28.00
    Paneled Grape, milk glass ....... 24.00
Cake Salver, Paneled Grape, milk glass, skirted, ftd ................................. 80.00
Candlesticks, pr
    Old Quilt, milk glass ............... 30.00
    Paneled Grape, milk glass, 4" h ............................................... 25.00
    Ring & Petal ........................... 22.00
    Waterford, #1932, ruby stained, 6" h, 1-lite ...................................... 130.00
Candy Dish, cov
    Beaded Bouquet, blue milk glass ............................................... 35.00
    Beaded Grape, 9" d, ftd .......... 40.00

**Candy Dish, cov, Bramble, milk glass, sgd in lid, 1953, 3-3/4" h, $12.**

Paneled Grape, milk glass, 3 legs, crimped ................................. 35.00
Wakefield, crystal, low ............ 45.00
Waterford, ruby stained, 9" d ... 35.00
Cheese, cov, Old Quilt, milk glass ............................................... 52.00
Children's Dishes
    Creamer, File & Fan, ruby carnival ............................................... 20.00
    Mug, chick, milk glass, #603, dec, orig label ............................... 30.00
    Pitcher, Flute, cobalt blue, white floral dec ............................... 40.00
    Sugar, cov, File & Fan, ruby carnival ............................................... 30.00
    Table Set, cov butter, creamer, cov sugar, File & Fan, milk glass .... 45.00
    Tumbler, Flute, green, white floral dec ....................................... 15.00
Compote, Waterford, #1932, ruby stained, ruffled, ftd ................. 120.00
Cordial, Waterford, #1932, ruby stained ............................................... 50.00
Creamer, 6-1/2 oz, Paneled Grape, milk glass, orig label ...................... 16.00
Cruet, stopper
    Old Quilt, milk glass ............... 30.00
    Paneled Grape, milk glass ....... 30.00
Cup and Saucer, Paneled Grape, milk glass ............................................... 22.00
Dinner Plate, Daisy Decal, #1800, 10-1/4" d, dark blue mist, scalloped edge ................................. 45.00
Dish, heart shape, handle, Della Robia, stained ................................. 70.00
Epergne, 8-1/2" h, Paneled Grape, milk glass ................................. 70.00
Flower Pot, Paneled Grape, milk glass ............................................... 48.00
Fruit Cocktail, Paneled Grape, milk glass ............................................... 25.00
Fruit Cocktail Underplate, Paneled Grape, milk glass ...................... 9.00
Goblet, 8 oz
    Della Robia, stained ................ 40.00
    Paneled Grape, milk glass ....... 18.00
Gravy Boat and Underplate, Paneled Grape, milk glass ...................... 58.00
Honey, cov, 5" d, Beaded Grape, milk glass, roses and garland dec ............................................... 45.00
Ice Tea Tumbler, Paneled Grape, milk glass, 12 oz ............................... 25.00
Jardiniere, Paneled Grape, milk glass, 6-1/2" h, ftd ............................. 42.00
Jelly, cov, Paneled Grape, milk glass ............................................... 30.00
Mint Compote, Waterford, #1932, ruby stained, crimped ...................... 60.00
Pitcher
    Old Quilt, milk glass ............... 40.00
    Paneled Grape, milk glass
      16 oz ................................ 45.00
      32 oz ................................ 35.00
Planter, 5" x 9", Paneled Grape, milk glass ............................................... 48.00
Plate, 7" d, Beaded Edge
    Goldfinch center ..................... 13.00
    Red edge ............................... 10.00
Puff Box, cov, Paneled Grape, milk glass ............................................... 30.00
Punch Bowl Base, Paneled Grape, milk glass ............................................. 115.00

**Magazine Cover, China Glass & Tablewares, August 1967, several white opaque patterns, $4.50.**

Punch Cup, Fruits, milk glass ......... 6.00
Punch Set
    Fruits, milk glass, 12 pc set ... 150.00
    Paneled Grape, milk glass, red hooks and ladle, 13" d, 15 pc set ............................................. 595.00
Rose Bowl, 4" d, Paneled Grape, milk glass, ftd ................................. 30.00
Salad Plate, Della Robia, dark stain ............................................... 22.00
Salt and Pepper Shakers, pr
    Della Robia, stained ............... 70.00
    Old Quilt, milk glass ............... 25.00
    Paneled Grape, milk glass ...... 25.00
Sauceboat and Underplate, Paneled Grape, milk glass ...................... 70.00
Saucer, Paneled Grape, milk glass 8.50
Sherbet, 10-3/4" h, Della Robia, light stain ................................. 26.00
Slipper, figural, almond milk glass ............................................... 20.00
Spooner, Old Quilt, milk glass, 6-1/2" h ............................................... 28.00
Sugar
    Beaded Grape, milk glass, individual size ........................................... 10.00
    Old Quilt, milk glass, large, open ............................................... 15.00
Sweet Meat, Waterford, #1932, ruby stained, ftd, crimped ............... 40.00
Torte Plate, 14" d, Della Robia, light stain ................................. 125.00
Tumbler, flat
    Della Robia, dark stain, 8 oz.... 28.00
    Paneled Grape, milk glass ...... 12.50
Vase
    6" h, ftd, bell-shape, Paneled Grape, milk glass ................................. 15.00
    7" h, horn-shape, Lotus, #9 ...... 35.00
    9" h, Paneled Grape, milk glass, bell shape, ftd ................................. 30.00

15" h, swung-type, Paneled Grape, milk glass .................................. 20.00
Water Set, 1776 Colonial, amber, flat water pitcher, six goblets, price for 7 pc set ............................................. 70.00
Wedding Bowl, Roses & Bows, milk glass, 10" d ............................. 130.00

# Whiskey Bottles, Collectors' Special Editions

**Collecting Hints:** Beginning collectors are advised to focus on bottles of a single manufacturer or to collect around a central theme, e.g., birds, trains, or Western. Only buy bottles that have a very good finish (almost no sign of wear), no chips, and intact original labels.

A major collection still can be built for a modest investment, although some bottles, such as the Beam Red Coat Fox, now command more than $1,000. Don't overlook miniatures if you are on a limited budget.

In many states, it is against the law to sell liquor without a license; hence, collectors tend to focus on empty bottles.

**History:** The Jim Beam Distillery began the practice of issuing novelty (collectors' special edition) bottles for the 1953 Christmas trade. By the late 1960s, more than 100 other distillers and wine manufacturers followed suit.

The Jim Beam Distillery remains the most prolific issuer of the bottle. Lionstone, McCormick, and Ski Country are the other principal suppliers today. One dealer, Jon-Sol, Inc., has distributed his own line of collector bottles.

The golden age of the special edition bottle was the early 1970s. Interest waned in the late 1970s and early 1980s, as the market became saturated with companies trying to join the craze. Prices fell from record highs, and many manufacturers dropped special edition bottle production altogether.

A number of serious collectors, clubs, and dealers have brought stability to the market. Realizing that instant antiques cannot be created by demand alone, they have begun to study and classify their bottles. Most importantly, collectors have focused on those special edition bottles which show quality workmanship and design and which are true limited editions.

**References:** Hugh Cleveland, *Bottle Pricing Guide*, 3rd ed., 1988, 1993 value update; Ralph and Terry Kovel, *Kovels' Bottles Price List*, 12th ed., Crown Publishers, 1998; Michael Polak, *Bottles*, 2nd ed., Avon Books, 1997.

**Collectors' Clubs:** Cape Codders Jim Beam Bottle & Specialty Club, 80 Lincoln Rd, Rockland, MA 02370; Hoffman National Collectors Club, P.O. Box 37341, Cincinnati, OH 45222; International Association of Jim Beam Bottle & Specialties Clubs, 5013 Chase Ave., Downers Grove, IL 60515; National Ski Country Bottle Club, 1224 Washington Ave., Golden, CO 80401; Space Coast Jim Beam Bottle & Specialties Club, 2280 Cox Rd, Cocoa, FL 32926.

**Museum:** American Outpost, James B. Beam Distillery, Clermont, KY.

### ALPA, Warner Bros. Characters
Bugs Bunny, 1977 ........................ 10.00
Tweety Bird, 1978 ......................... 20.00
**Anniversary**, Lincoln, 1973 .......... 15.50

### Ballantine
Golf Bag, 1969 .............................. 9.50
Mallard, 1969 ............................... 18.00
Zebra, 1970 ................................. 14.00

### Jim Beam
Ahepa, 1972 .................................. 5.00
Akron, Rubber Capital, 1973 ........ 24.00
Barney's Slot Machine, 1978 ........ 20.00
Bing Crosby, 1970s ...................... 15.00
BPO Does, 1971 ............................ 5.00
Buffalo Bill, 1970s ........................ 10.00
Cable Car, 1983 ........................... 66.00
Churchill Downs, Kentucky Derby
............................................... 15.00
Civil War, 1961, South ................... 50.00
Cowboy, 1981 .............................. 15.50
Ducks Unlimited ........................... 50.00
Ernie's Flower Car, 1976 .............. 35.00
Evergreen State Club, 1974 ......... 15.50
Harolds Club, Covered Wagon, green, 1969 ............................................. 6.00
Hawaiian Open ............................. 10.00
Horse, brown, 1967-68 ................. 21.50
Kansas City Convention Elephant, 1976
............................................... 15.00
Katz Cat, black, 1968 ................... 13.00
Key West, FL ................................. 6.00
John Henry, 1972 ......................... 72.00
London Bridge, Regal China, 1971
................................................. 7.50
Louisiana Superdome, 1975 .......... 9.00
Marine Corps ............................... 35.00
New Jersey .................................. 40.00
New York World's Fair, 1964 ........ 12.00
Ohio, 1966 ................................... 18.00
Opera Series
    Don Giovanni ......................... 170.00
    Figaro ................................... 185.00
    Madame Butterfly, 1977 ......... 200.00
Pennsylvania Dutch Club, 1974 ... 12.00
Pony Express ............................... 10.00

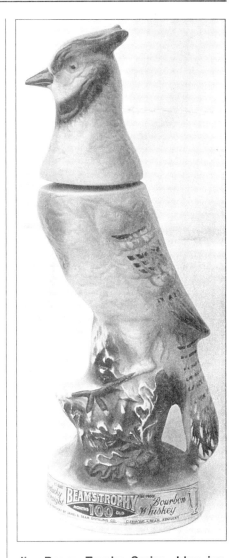

**Jim Beam, Trophy Series, blue jay, Royal China, 1969, $15.**

Rabbit, 1971 ................................. 12.00
San Diego, 1968 ............................ 7.00
Saturday Evening Post, 1970s ...... 15.00
Stutz Bearcat ............................... 50.00
Train Caboose .............................. 50.00
Travelodge Bear ........................... 25.00
Twin Bridges Club, 1971 .............. 50.00
Volkswagen ................................. 55.00
Yellowstone ................................... 8.00
Yosemite ....................................... 8.00
Zimmerman Liquors ...................... 10.00

### Beneagle
Alpine Pitcher, 1969 ..................... 25.00
Amphora, 2 handles, 1950 .......... 20.00
Barrel, thistle ................................. 4.50
Bell House, 1960 .......................... 12.00
Chess Pawn, John Knox, black, miniature ............................................. 12.00
Fruit, canteen, 1969 ..................... 18.00

### Bischoff
Chinese Boy, 1962 ....................... 36.00
Grecian Vase, 1969 ..................... 15.50
Pirate .......................................... 20.00

## Ezra Brooks

Basketball Players, 1974 .............. 10.00
Card, Jack of Diamonds, 1969 ..... 10.00
Casey at Bat, 1973 ....................... 16.00
Clown with balloons, 1973 ............ 22.00
Club Bottle #1, Distillery, 1970 ...... 12.50
Clydesdale, 1974 .......................... 10.00
Dummy Gallon, 1969 ..................... 90.00
Elephant, Big Bertha, 1970 ............. 8.00
FOE Eagle, 179 ............................ 15.00
Fresno Grape, 1970 ...................... 12.00
Go Big Red #3, 1972 .................... 12.00
Greensboro Open, cup, 1975 ....... 50.00
Hereford, 1971 ............................. 14.00
Iowa Farmers Elevator, 1978 ........ 36.00
Lion on Rock, 1971 ...................... 10.00
Masonic, fez, 1976 ...................... 10.00
Max "The Hat" Zimmerman, 1976
............................................... 32.00
Mr. Merchant, 1970 ...................... 10.00
Motorcycle, 1971 ......................... 13.50
Oliver Hardy, 1976 ....................... 17.50
Ontario Racer, #10, 1970 ............. 21.00
Panda, 1972 ................................ 18.00
Penguin, 1973 ............................. 15.00
Phoenix Bird, 1975 ...................... 18.00
Spirit of St. Louis, 1977 ............... 12.00
Stonewall Jackson, 1974 ............. 32.00
Tank, 1972 .................................. 30.00
Train, Iron Horse, 1969 ................ 12.00
Vermont Skier, 1973 .................... 12.00
Whitetail Deer, 1974 .................... 20.00
Wichita Centennial, 1970 .............. 7.50

## Collector's Art

Basset Hound, miniature .............. 25.50
Cardinal, miniature ....................... 30.00
Poodle, white, miniature ............... 21.00
Texas Longhorn, 1974 ................. 35.00

## Cyrus Noble

Buffalo Cow & Calf, Nevada ed, 1977
............................................... 85.00
Burro, 1973 ................................. 50.00
Carousel Series, pipe organ, 1980
............................................... 45.00
Harp Seal, 1979 .......................... 50.00
Moose & Calf, 2nd ed, 1977 ........ 80.00
Sea Turtle, 1979 .......................... 50.00
Snowshoe Thompson, 1972 ....... 150.00
Whitetail Deer, 1979 .................... 35.00

## J.W. Dant

American Legion, 1968 ................. 10.00
Boeing 747 .................................. 14.00
Boston Tea Party .......................... 12.00
Field Bird
 #2, 1969, Chukar partridge ...... 12.00
 #4, 1969, mountain quail ........... 9.00
Mt. Rushmore, 1968 .................... 12.00
Patrick Henry, 1969 ....................... 5.00

## Early Times, 1976

Cannon Fire
 Delaware ................................. 22.00
 Nevada .................................... 22.00
 New Mexico ............................. 28.00
Drum and Fife
 Florida .................................... 17.00
 Kansas ................................... 20.00
Minuteman
 Alaska .................................... 35.50
 Oklahoma ................................ 24.00
Paul Revere, Arizona ................... 21.00

Washington Crossing the Delaware,
 South Dakota .......................... 17.00

## Famous Firsts

Balloon, 1971 .............................. 65.00
Bears, miniature, 1981 ................. 36.00
Bucky Badger Mascot .................. 10.00
China Clipper, 1989 ................... 120.00
Circus Lion, 1979 ........................ 20.00
Corvette, 1963 Stingray, white, minia-
 ture, 1979 ............................... 13.50
Fireman, 1980 ............................. 50.00
Golfer, 1973 ................................ 30.00
Hippo, baby, 1980 ....................... 50.00
Hurdy Gurdy, miniature, 1979 ....... 15.50
Minnie Meow, 1973 ..................... 17.50
National Racer, No. 8, 1972 ......... 70.00
Panda, baby, 1980 ...................... 50.00
Pepper Mill, 1978 ........................ 20.00
Phonograph, 1969 ....................... 36.00
Porsche Targa, 1979 ................... 44.00
Sewing Machine, 1979 ................. 35.00
Swiss Chalet, 1974 ..................... 20.00
Winnie Mae, large, 1972 .............. 85.00
Yacht America, 1978 .................... 25.00

## Garnier (France)

Baby Foot, 1963 .......................... 15.00
Bullfighter .................................... 18.00
Cat ............................................. 70.00
Christmas Tree, 1956 .................. 65.00
Diamond Bottle, 1969 .................. 15.00
Inca, 1969 .................................. 15.00
Locomotive, 1969 ........................ 14.00
Meadowlark, 1969 ....................... 12.00
Parrot ......................................... 30.00
Soccer Shoe, 1962 ...................... 30.00
Trout .......................................... 24.00
Young Deer ................................. 28.00

## Grenadier

American Revolution Series
 Second Maryland, 1969 .......... 37.50
 Third New York, 1970 .............. 22.00
British Army Series, Kings African Rifle
 Crops, 5th, 1970 ..................... 20.00
Civil War Series, General Robert E. Lee,
 1/2 gal, 1977 ......................... 150.00
George Washington, on horseback
............................................... 20.00
Jester Mirth King, 1977 ................ 56.00
San Fernando Electric Mfg. Co., 1976
............................................... 66.00
Santa Claus, blue sack ................ 30.00

## Hoffman

Aesop's Fables Series, music, 6 types,
 1978 ....................................... 30.00
Canada Goose Decoy .................. 15.00
Cheerleaders, Rams, miniature, 1980
............................................... 20.00
Doe and Fawn ............................. 40.00
Fox and Eagle, 1978 .................... 45.00
Kentucky Wildcats, football, 1979
............................................... 38.00
Mr. Lucky Series, music
 Barber, 1980 ........................... 38.00
 Cobbler, 1973 ......................... 25.00
 Fiddler, 1974 ........................... 25.00
 Mailman, miniature, 1976 ......... 12.50
Pistol, Dodge City Frontier, framed,
............................................... 25.00
Stage Coach Driver ...................... 30.00
Tennessee Volunteers .................. 28.00
Wood Duck, decoy ...................... 15.00

## Japanese Firms

House of Koshu
 Geisha, chrysanthemum, 1969
........................................... 23.50
 Sake God, white, 1969 ........... 14.00
Kamotsuru, treasure tower, 1966
............................................... 18.00
Kikukawa
 Eisenhower, 1970 ................... 17.00
 Royal couple, pr ...................... 32.00

## Lewis and Clark

Clark, miniature, 1971 .................. 15.50
General Custer, 1974 ................... 70.00
Grandfather, 1978 ........................ 10.00
Indian, 1978 ................................ 65.00
Lewis, 1971 ................................ 85.00
Major Reno ................................. 25.00
Sheepherder ............................... 40.00
Trader ........................................ 50.00

## Lionstone

Annie Oakley, 1969 ...................... 60.00
Barber, 1976 ............................... 40.00
Bartender, 1969 .......................... 30.00
Baseball Player, 1974 .................. 27.50
Cherry Valley .............................. 20.00
Dance Hall Girl, 1973 ................... 60.00
Dove of Peace, 1977 ................... 40.00
Eastern Bluebird, 1972 ................ 20.00

**Luxardo, basket of fruit, 1969, $30.**

Fireman, #8, fire alarm box, 1983
................................................. 50.00
Hockey Player, 1974 ..................... 20.00
Indian, squaw, 1973..................... 25.00
Riverboat Captain, 1969 .............. 14.00
Stutz Bearcat, miniature, 1978...... 15.00
Telegrapher, 1969 ........................ 20.00
Tennis Player, male, 1980 ............ 45.00
Turbo Car STP, red, 1972.............. 27.50

### Luxardo

Apple, figural .............................. 14.00
Apothecary Jar ............................ 20.00
Bizantina .................................... 26.00
Babylon, 1960.................................
Calypso Girl, 1962 ........................ 15.50
Coffeepot .................................... 12.00
Mayan, 1960................................. 50.00
Tower of Flowers, 1968 ................ 18.00
Venus, 1969 ................................ 20.00
Zodiac, 1970................................ 30.00

### McCormick

Betsy Ross, miniature, 1976 ......... 48.00
Bluebird ...................................... 20.00
Centurion, 1969 ........................... 20.00
Chair, 1979.................................. 40.00
Eleanor Roosevelt......................... 20.00
FOE, 1985 ................................... 50.00
Henry Ford................................... 30.00
Kit Carson, 1975 .......................... 15.00
Mark Twain, 1977......................... 32.00
Merlin ......................................... 30.00
Nebraska Football Player, 1972.... 24.00
Oregon Duck ............................... 20.00
Robert E. Lee, 1976...................... 40.00
Sir Lancelot................................. 40.00
Texas Longhorn, 1974 .................. 36.50
Train Series, wood tender, 1969
................................................. 22.00
Ulysses S. Grant, 1976 ................ 25.00
Victorian, 1964 ............................ 20.00
Wood Duck, 1983 ......................... 28.00

### OBR

Caboose, 1973 ............................. 21.00
River Queen, 1967........................ 10.00
W.C. Fields, top hat, 1976............. 16.00

### Old Commonwealth

Apothecary Series, North Carolina University, 1979 ............................ 30.00
Coal Miners, #5, coal shooter, 1983
................................................. 40.00
Fireman, #5, lifesaver, 1983......... 72.50
Indian Chief Illini, University of Illinois, 1979 ................................ 60.00
Irish at the Sea, 1989................... 24.00
Lumberjack, old time, 1979 .......... 20.00
Kentucky Peach Bowl.................... 30.00
Kentucky Thoroughbreds, 1977
................................................. 40.00
Sons of Erin................................. 25.00
Symbols of Ireland, 1985 ............. 12.00

### Old Crow

Chess Set, 32 pcs....................... 450.00
Crow, 1974.................................. 14.00

### Old Fitzgerald

America's Cup, 1970 ..................... 27.00
Blarney, Irish toast, 1970 ............. 16.00
Candlelite, 1963........................... 10.00
Classic, 1972 .............................. 10.00
Davidson, NC, 1972...................... 40.00
Hospitality, 1958 ........................... 9.00

Old Ironsides ................................. 9.00
Rip Van Winkle, 1971.................... 34.50
West Virginia Forest Festival, 1973
................................................. 22.00

### Old Mr. Boston

Black Hills Motor Club, 1976 ........ 12.00
Concord Coach, 1976 ................... 17.00
Dan Patch .................................... 25.00
Deadwood, SD, 1975 .................... 16.00
Eagle Convention, 1973 ............... 10.00
Hawk, 1975.................................. 18.00
Lion, sitting ................................. 12.00
Nebraska, #1, gold, 1970 ............. 20.00
Paul Revere, 1974 ....................... 15.50
Town Crier, 1976 ......................... 10.00
Wisconsin Football....................... 25.00

### Pacesetter

Camaro, Z28, yellow, 1982 .......... 42.00
Coca-Cola Truck.......................... 135.00
Corvette, red, 1975 ...................... 40.00
Mack Pumper ............................. 140.00
Pontiac Firebird............................ 35.00
Tractor Series, No. 2, Big Green Machine, International Harvester, 1983 ........................................... 66.00
Vokovich, #2, 1974 ...................... 30.00

### Ski Country

Antelope, pronghorn..................... 70.00

**Old Mr. Boston, Amvet, No. 44, 1975, $15.**

Bassett, miniature, 1978.............. 20.00
Blackbird ..................................... 40.00
Bull Rider .................................... 15.00
Ceremonial Indian, Falcon.......... 110.00
Chickadee ................................... 50.00
Cigar Store Indian, 1974.............. 40.00
Clown, bust, 1974, miniature ...... 18.00
Eagle, paperweight ..................... 190.00
Ebenezer Scrooge, 1979, miniature
................................................. 24.00
Jaguar, miniature ........................ 30.00
Koala, 1973 ................................. 42.00
Labrador with mallard, 1977, miniature
................................................. 40.00
Mallard Drake .............................. 40.00
Mill River Country Club, 1977....... 44.00
Mountain Lion, 1973, miniature .... 30.00
Ringmaster, 1975, miniature......... 26.50
Salmon........................................ 40.00
Submarine, 1976, miniature.......... 29.00
Tom Thumb .................................. 30.00
Woodpecker, ivory bill, 1974 ....... 66.00

### Wild Turkey

Crystal Anniversary, 1955........ 2,000.00
Mack Truck .................................. 20.00
Series #1
   No. 2, female, 1972 .............. 150.00
   No. 3, on wing, miniature, 1983
   ........................................... 65.00
   No. 5, with flags, 1975 ........... 40.00
   No. 8, strutting, 1978 ............. 45.00
Series #2, No. 2, lore, 1980 ......... 30.00
Series #3
No. 5, with raccoon, 1984 ........... 40.00
No. 7, with fox, 1984, miniature .... 30.00
No. 12, with skunk, 1986 ............. 90.00
Series #4, No. 2, habitat, 1989..... 90.00

# World War I Collectibles

**Collecting Hints:** Be careful. Uniforms and equipment from World War I were stockpiled at the end of the war and reissued in the early years of World War II. Know the source of the items before you buy, and scrutinize all materials. Some research and investigation might be necessary to correctly identify an item as an actual war artifact.

Collectors' clubs and re-enactment groups are among the best sources of information. These groups also are very knowledgeable about reproductions, copycats, and fantasy items.

**History:** Power struggles between European countries raged for hundreds of years. As the 20th century dawned, leading European countries became entangled in a series of complex alliances, many sealed by royal marriages, and a massive arms race. All that was needed to set off the powder keg was a fire. The assassination of Austrian Archduke Franz Ferdinand by a Serbian national ignited the fuse on June 28, 1914. Germany invaded Belgium and moved into France. Russia, England, and Turkey joined the war. Italy and the United States became involved by mid-1917.

In 1918, Germany sued for peace. A settlement was achieved at the Versailles Conference, January-June 1919, during which time the United Sates remained in the background. President Wilson's concept for a League of Nations failed to gain acceptance in his own country, opening the door to the events which culminated in World War II.

**References:** W. K. Cross, *Charlton Price Guide to First World War Canadian Infantry Badges*, The Charlton Press, 1995; *Windrow & Greene's Militaria Directory and Sourcebook 1994*, Motorbooks International, 1994.

**Periodicals:** Men at Arms, 222 W. Exchange St., Providence, RI 02903; Military Collector Magazine, P.O. Box 245, Lyon Station, PA, 19536; Military Collectors' News, P.O. Box 702073, Tulsa, OK 74170; Military History, 6405 Flank Dr., Harrisburg, PA 17112; Military Trader, P.O. Box 1050, Dubuque, IA 52004; Wildcat Collectors Journal, 15158 NE 6 Ave., Miami FL 33162.

**Collectors' Clubs:** American Society of Military Insignia Collectors, 526 Lafayette Ave., Palmerton, PA 18701; Association of American Military Uniform Collectors, P.O. Box 1876, Elyria, OH 44036; Company of Military Historians, North Main St., Westbrook, CT 06498; Orders and Medals Society of America, P.O. Box 484, Glassboro, NJ 08028.

**Museums:** Liberty Memorial Museum, Kansas City, MO; National Infantry Museum, Fort Benning, GA; The Parris Island Museum, Parris Island, SC; Seven Acres Antique Village & Museum, Union, IL; US Air Force Museum, Wright-Patterson AFB, Dayton, OH; US Army Transportation Museum, Fort Eustis, VA; US Navy Museum, Washington, DC.

Advertising, drawing book, Old Reliable Coffee, patriotic edition .............. 8.00
Badge, American Red Cross-Military Welfare, cap, enamel .............. 20.00
Bayonet, orig case ........................ 20.00
Belt, web ...................................... 254.00
Book
   *Building the Kaiser's Navy*, Gary Weir, 289 pgs .......................... 27.00

*Newton D. Baker-America At War Based On Personal Papers of Secretary War Baker, Confidential Correspondence and Cablegrams*, F. Palmer, 1931, 2 volumes .......... 35.00
Candleholder, Germany, sword handle fits into candleholder, silver inlay reads "To Mom & Dad from Gordon" just above handle, no blade .... 85.00
Canteen, Army ............................... 15.00
Flip Book, 2" x 2-1/2" x 1/4", soldier, sailor, and Uncle Sam presenting the colors, pledge of Allegiance, Liberty Bone promotion, ©1917 .......... 30.00
Gas Mask, carrying can, shoulder strap, canister attached to bottom, German ...................................... 50.00
Handkerchief, 11" sq, "Remember Me," soldier and girl in center, red, white, and blue edge ........................... 20.00
Helmet, US, 3rd Army insignia ..... 65.00
Key Chain Fob, Kaiser Bill's Bones, 1-1/4" l replica of shell casing holding miniature celluloid die set, inscription on firing cap end of brass cartridge, removable silver bullet head, loop for key chain .................................... 72.00
Medal, Iron Cross ......................... 45.00
Paperweight, weighted celluloid, full color image of 12 "Flags of the Allies-United For The Cause Of Liberty," white center, black letters, mirror base .................................... 40.00
Pinback Button
Australia Day
   1916, light sepia portrait of English naval officer Lord Kitchener, white ground, blue letters, 1916 Unley event ................ 20.00
   1918, red, white, blue, and black, aborigine young lady puffing pipe, wearing red bandanna, blue and black rim depiction of tiny boomerangs ........................ 40.00
Lloyd George, black and gray portrait of British Prime Minister, Welsh rim inscription ........... 30.00
On Active Service, multicolored image of English bulldog staunchly positioned on nationality flag, blue lettering ........... 30.00
Our Heroes Welcome Home, blue letters, white bordered by red victory wreath .......................... 20.00

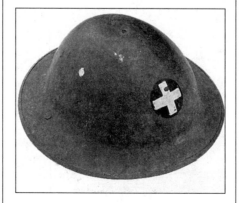

**Helmet, American, orig liner, $50.**

Port Pirie Repatriation, black cat on lower yellow ground, shaded blue top, black lettering, Australian, c1916 ......................... 35.00
78th Division, red, white and blue, Welcome Home, issued for "The Fighting Demons" ............... 35.00
World Peace, multicolored, Allied flags around white dove carrying olive branch ........................ 60.00
Pin Holder, 2-1/4" d, celluloid, full color image of 12 Allies flags around white center, blue letters, perimeter ring holds glass mirror .................... 35.00
Portrait, 5-3/4" x 8", full color celluloid, sepia portrait, surrounding flags and patriotic symbols, inscription "Army and Navy Forever," single star service banner, black velveteen over metal back, wire easel stand ... 65.00
Ribbon, 2" x 5", Welcome Home 26th Division ................................... 25.00
Tobacco Jar, cov, 6-1/2" h, ceramic, brown glaze, General Pershing .............................................. 145.00
Uniform, US Army, Engineer, coat, belt, pants, cap, canvas leggings, wool puttees, and leather gaithers, canteen ...................................... 400.00
Watch Fob, flag on pole, USA, beaded, blue ........................................ 45.00

# World War II Collectibles

**Collecting Hints:** To the victors go the spoils, or so World War II collectors would like to think. Now that the Soviet Block has fallen, a large number of dealers are making efforts to import Soviet Block World War II collectibles into the United States. Be careful when buying anything that has a new or unused appearance. Many Soviet countries continued to use stockpiled World War II equipment and still manufacture new goods based on World War II designs.

The Korean Conflict occurred shortly after World War II. The United States and other armed forces involved in this conflict used equipment and uniforms similar to those manufactured during World War II. Familiarize yourself with model styles, dates of manufacture, and your buying sources.

If you locate a World War II item, make certain to record all personal history associated with the item. This is extremely important. Collectors demand this documentation. If possible, secure additional information on the history of the unit and the battles in which it was engaged. Also make certain to obtain any extras that are available, such as insignia or a second set of buttons.

**History:** With the rise of the German Third Reich, European nations once again engaged in a massive arms race. The 1930s Depression compounded the situation.

After numerous compromises to German expansionism, war was declared in 1939 following Germany's Blitzkrieg invasion of Poland. Allied and Axis alliances were formed.

Although neutral, Americans were very supportive of the Allied cause. The Dec. 7, 1941, Japanese attack on the U.S. Naval Station at Pearl Harbor, Hawaii, forced America into the war. It immediately adopted a two-front strategy.

From 1942 to 1945, the entire world was directly or indirectly involved in the war. Virtually all industrial activity was war related. The resulting technological advances guaranteed that life after the war would be far different from prior years.

Germany surrendered May 7, 1945. Japan surrendered on Aug. 14, 1945, after the atomic bombing of Hiroshima on Aug. 6, 1945, and Nagasaki on Aug. 9, 1945.

**References:** Thomas Berndt, *Standard Catalog of U.S. Military Vehicles*, Krause Publications, 1993; Stan Cohen, *V for Victory*, Pictorial Histories Publishing, 1991; —, *To Win The War: Home Front Memorabilia of World War II*, Motorbooks International, 1995; Robert Heide and John Gilman, *Home Front America: Popular Culture of the World War II Era*, Chronicle Books, 1995; Jon A. Maguire, *Silver Wings, Pinks & Greens: Uniforms, Wings, & Insignia of USAAF Airmen in World War II*, Schiffer Publishing, 1994; Jack Matthews, *Toys Go to War: World War II Military Toys, Games, Puzzles & Books*, Pictorial Histories Publishing, 1994; Ronald Manion, *American Military Collectibles Price Guide*, Antique Trader Books, 1995.

**Periodicals:** *Men at Arms*, 222 W. Exchange St., Providence, RI 02903; *Military Collector Magazine*, P.O. Box 245, Lyon Station, PA, 19536; *Military Collectors' News*, P.O. Box 702073, Tulsa, OK 74170; *Military History*, 6405 Flank Dr., Harrisburg, PA 17112; *Military Trader*, P.O. Box 1050, Dubuque, IA 52004; *Wildcat Collectors Journal*, 15158 NE 6 Ave., Miami FL 33162.

**Collectors' Clubs:** American Society of Military Insignia Collectors, 526 Lafayette Ave., Palmerton, PA 18701; Association of American Military Uniform Collectors, P.O. Box 1876, Elyria, OH 44036; Company of Military Historians, North Main St., Westbrook, CT 06498; Imperial German Military Collectors Association, 82 Atlantic St., Keyport, NJ 07735; Orders and Medals Society of America, P.O Box 484, Glassboro, NJ 08028.

**Museums:** Liberty Memorial Museum, Kansas City, MO; National Infantry Museum, Fort Benning, GA; The Parris Island Museum, Parris Island, SC; Seven Acres Antique Village & Museum, Union, IL; US Air Force Museum, Wright-Patterson AFB, Dayton, OH; US Army Transportation Museum, Fort Eustis, VA; US Navy Museum, Washington, DC.

Arm Band, Civilian Defense Air Raid Warden, 4" w, white, 3-1/2" blue circle, red and white diagonal stripes within triangle .......................... 10.00
Better Little Book, *Fighting Heroes Battle For Freedom*, #1401, ©1942, 1943 ........................................ 18.00
Binoculars, Army, M-17, field type, 7-1/2" l, olive drab, 7" x 50" power, clear, fixed optics ..................... 95.00
Book
*Day of Infamy, Dec. 7, 1941*, Walter Lord, 1957, Henry Holt, 243 pgs, illus, slightly worn dj ................ 12.00
*Europe & the Mediterranean*, Dept. of History, West Point Military Academy, 1978, 366 pgs ................. 35.00

**Badge, US Naval Training Station, Great Lakes, IL, 2-3/4" x 2" oval, $10.**

*Handbook of Hospital Corps, United States Navy*, Government Printing Office, 1939 ............................. 17.00
*History of World War II, Armed Services Memorial Edition*, Francis Trevelyan Miller, Reader's Service Bureau, war photos, official records, maps ...................................... 18.00
*Song & Service Book for Ship & Field, Army & Navy*, Ivan L. Bennett, 1942, A. S. Barnes Pub. .......... 15.00
*The General Was A Spy-The Truth About German General Gehlen, Who Served Hitler, The CIA & West Germany*, Heinzel-Hohne, H. Zolling, c1972, photos, dj .................... 30.00
*World War II Operations in North African Waters, October 1942-June 1943*, Samuel Eliot Morison, Atlantic, Little Brown, 1955, 297 pgs, dj ........................................................ 25.00
Calendar, 6-3/4" x 10", Co-Operative Elevator Co., Gen. Douglas MacArthur, 1943, cream colored diecut sheet, red, and blue sword design at center, browntone portrait of general ....................................................... 45.00
Cap, AAF Officer's, 50-Mission, crash cap, small gilded eagle, front and back straps, soft bill, gabardine, mkd "Fighter by Bancroft, O.D." ................................................... 95.00
Figure, 3-3/4" h, Kilroy Was Here, plastic, wistful pregnant girl ............ 35.00
Flight Suit, Army Air Force, Type A-4, olive drab gabardine, matching belt, zipper front ............................. 95.00
Glass, 4-1/2" h, flying white eagle, blue and red "V" symbol .................. 24.00
Helmet, MI, olive drab sand finish, olive drab chin strap, orig liner, thin mesh helmet net ............................. 145.00
Jacket, A-2 Army Air Force, leather, cowhide, light brown, name tag ............................................... 495.00
Knife, Camillus USN Mark 5 Sheath, black finish blade, light scabbard wear, USN and name marked on guard, gray web belt loop, gray fiber scabbard ................................ 65.00
Magazine
*War Planes*, Dell, 8-1/4" x 11", full color cov, 28 black and white pgs, ©1942 ...................................... 35.00
*Life*, Occupation of Germany, Feb. 10, 1947 ............................. 9.00

**Cap, AAF Officer, small gilded eagle, front and back straps, gabardine, $60.**

*Pin-Up Parade*, 8-1/2" x 11", black and white photo cov, purple and yellow accents, 48 pgs, full page black and white pin-up photos of Hollywood stars such as Lucille Ball, Barbara Stanwyck, Lana Turner, Ginger Rogers centerfold, ©1944 Bond Publishers .................................. 40.00

Mirror and Thermometer Premium Picture, 4-1/2" x 9-3/4", cream colored cardboard mat, diecut opening, blue accent mirror, full color 3" oval art of Gen. MacArthur, 2-1/4" diecut opening with thermometer, c1943 ................................................ 48.00

Patch, AAF, cloth, bombardier wings, embroidered silver and gray, tan cotton, unused ........................... 15.00

Pin, Axe the Axis, hatchet shape, inscription on blade, marked "Sterling Silver" ................................ 85.00

Pinback Button
Battleship USS Washington, green on gold, June 1, 1940 launch from Philadelphia Navy Yard ........... 45.00
Eat To Beat The Devil, red, white, and blue litho, image of clenched fist belting head of devil ............... 55.00
Gen. MacArthur Welcome Home, red, white and blue, bluetone portrait ................................................. 60.00
Gopher Ordnance Works, full color war production cartoon of determined gopher.......................... 35.00
Mothers of World War II, blue and white image.............................. 40.00
Pabst Breweries Bond Buyer, red, white, and blue, 10% salary contributor............................................. 30.00

Post Card, 3-1/2" x 5-1/2", Just A Little Something To Remember Pearl Harbor, full color cartoon showing Navy ship firing on and sinking Japanese ship, 1942 cancellation ............ 18.00

Shovel, fox hole type..................... 15.00

Sign, 18" h, 12" w, Kool Cigarettes, full color, graphics showing Kool penguin as Army sentry on duty, text at top "Keep Alert-Smoke Kools" ................................................. 135.00

# World's Fairs and Expositions

**Collecting Hints:** Familiarize yourself with the main buildings and features of the early World's Fairs and Expositions. Much of the choicest china and textiles pictured an identifiable building. Many exposition buildings remained standing long after the fairs were over, and souvenirs proliferated. Prices almost always are higher in the city or area where an exposition was held.

There have been hundreds of local fairs, state fairs, etc., in the last 100 years. These events generally produced items of value mostly to local collectors.

**History:** The Great Exhibition of 1851 in London marked the beginning of the World's Fair and Exposition movement. The fairs generally featured exhibitions from nations around the world displaying the best of their industrial and scientific achievements.

Many important technological advances have been introduced at world's fairs, including the airplane, telephone, and electric lights. Ice cream cones, hot dogs, and iced tea were first sold by vendors at fairs. Art movements were often closely associated with fairs and exhibitions. The best works of the Art Nouveau artists were assembled at the Paris Exhibition in 1900.

**References:** Robert L. Hendershott, *1904 St. Louis World's Fair Mementos and Memorabilia*, Kurt R. Krueger Publishing (5438 N. 90th St., Ste. 309, Omaha, NE 68134), 1994; Frederick and Mary Megson, *American Exposition Postcards*, The Postcard Lovers, 1992; *New York World's Fair Licensed Merchandise*, World of Tomorrow Co. (P.O. Box 229, Millwood, NY 10546), 1996; Howard M. Rossen, *World's Fair Collectibles: Chicago 1933 and New York 1939*, Schiffer Publishing, 1998.

**Periodical:** *World's Fair*, P.O. Box 339, Corte Madera, CA 94976.

**Collectors' Clubs:** 1904 World's Fair Society, 529 Barcia Dr., St. Louis, MO 63119; World's Fair Collectors' Society, Inc., P.O. Box 20806, Sarasota, FL 34276.

**Museums:** Atwater Kent Museum, History Museum of Philadelphia, Philadelphia, PA; Buffalo & Erie County Historical Society, Buffalo, NY; California State University, Madden Library, Fresno, CA; 1893 Chicago World's Columbian Exposition Museum, Columbus, WI; Museum of Science & Industry, Chicago, IL; Presidio Art Museum, San Francisco, CA; The Queens Museum, Flushing, NY.

## 1893, Chicago, The Columbian Exposition

Belt Buckle, brass, "Landing of Columbus," wheat husk tied with bow, 1492-1892, mkd "Made by Tiffany Studio, NY," 3-3/8" x 2-3/8"..... 100.00

Book, *Harper's Chicago and the World's Fair*, Julian Ralph, NY, Harper and Brothers, 1893, clothbound, 244 pgs, 70 illus............................. 45.00

Brochure, Mammoth Redwood Plank, Owned By The Berry Bros., Ltd., 4 pgs, 4" x 5"............................... 25.00

Comb and Case, 4-1/2" l, gold colored, top of case mkd "1934 Chicago World's Fair," Golden Temple of Jehol, US Building, and Dairy Building, other side shows General Exhibits Building, Travel & Transportation Building and Electrical Building, yellow comb .................................. 60.00

Crumb Tray and Scraper, silverplated ................................................ 30.00

Scarf, 17" x 15", silk, Chicago 1893, Expo, panorama of Expos overlaying American flag .......................... 45.00

Souvenir Book, *Official Guide To The World's Columbian Exposition*, 5" x 7", 192 pgs.............................. 50.00

Table Cloth, 11" sq, Machinery Hall, fringed border, small stain and damage ................................................ 70.00

## 1894, California Mid-Winter Exposition, souvenir spoon, bowl with drawing of ornate pavilion, SP, mkd "AMN Sterling Co." .................. 25.00

## 1901, Pan Am Exposition, Buffalo

Bandanna, 20" sq, silk, Electrical Tower illus.......................................... 195.00

Book, *The Pan American Exposition, Buffalo, N.Y., 1901*, softbound, green cover, gold lettering ................. 25.00

Fan, flowers on front, back "Japan Welcome, Beautiful, Battleship Game, Fishing Game, Lucky Co., On the Zone, Pan. Pac. Int. Expo, San Francisco, 1915"............................. 70.00

Match Holder, hanging type ......... 25.00

Souvenir Spoon
4-1/2" l, SP, Machinery & Transportation Building on bowl ............... 13.00
6" l, SP, buffalo sitting on earth on top of handle, waterfalls on bowl ... 15.00

Tip Tray, King's Puremalt, woman holding tray with bottle, fair emblem at bottom, reads "Panama-Pacific International Exposition-Medal of Award," 6" l, 4-1/4" w, oval .................. 165.00

## 1904 St. Louis, Louisiana Purchase Exposition

Bowl, Grant log cabin................. 165.00

Coffee Tin, Hanley & Kinsella ....... 30.00

Letter Opener, emb buildings on handle ................................................ 45.00

Souvenir Book, *Souvenir Book of the Louisiana Purchase Exposition*, day and night scenes, published by the Official Photographic Company, 11" x 8-1/2".................................... 45.00

## 1915, San Francisco, Panama-Pacific International Exposition

Badge w/Ribbon, top pin "Guest-Los Angeles Produce Exchange," orange ribbon mkd "San Francisco Dairy Produce Exchange, Santa Barbara, May 6-8, 1910," attached hen charm reads "Laying For Panama-Pacific International Exposition" ................................................ 95.00

**Century of Progress, Chicago, 1933, train schedule, Baltimore & Ohio, 18 pgs, folded, 4" x 9", $50.**

Booklet, Panama-Pacific International Exposition, compliments of Remington Typewriter, 30 pgs, 7-1/4" x 11" ............................................ 40.00

Handbook, *The Sculpture & Murals of the Panama-Pacific International Exposition,* Stella S G Perry, 1915, 104 pgs, 5" x 6-3/4", ex-library copy ............................................ 45.00

Tray, 3-1/2" x 5-1/2", hammered metal, bear figural, emb "Tower of Jewels, Panama Pacific International/San Francisco, Cal 1915," dark finish ............................................ 45.00

Watch Fob, brass, orig black leather strap ...................................... 95.00

**1934, Chicago, Century of Progress**

Automobile Accessory, rear view mirror, no glare, orig box ..................... 90.00
Bracelet, copper, scenic .............. 35.00
Brochure
  Baltimore and Ohio Railroad World's Fair Exhibit 1934, 20 pgs, 4-1/2" x 9-3/4" .................................... 25.00
  57 At The Fair, Heinz 57 Exhibit, Agricultural Building, 16 pgs .......... 22.00
  How! And Where! At Chicago and The World's Fair, Chicago and Northwestern (Railroad) Line, 16 pg guide to Chicago ............................. 20.00
  Official Pictures, Rueben H Donnelly, black and white, 7" x 10" .......... 35.00

Sky-Ride, See The Fair From The Air, 4 pg, 3-1/2" x 5-3/4" ................. 12.00
The Why-What-and When of A Century of Progress, 10 pgs .......... 10.00
Certificate of Attendance, Closing Day, Oct. 31, 1934, 3" x 5-1/4" ......... 15.00
Coffee Mug, Stewart's .................. 50.00
Coin, flattened
  1-3/8" l, Fort Dearborn ............. 15.00
  1-1/2" x 3/4", General Motors Exhibit ............................................ 15.00
Good Luck Key, 2" l, Master Lock, pavilions on shank ......................... 20.00
Handkerchief, 11" sq, painted silk, small stains .......................................... 40.00
Magazine, *Marshall Field & Co.,* 9-1/2" x 13", 44 pgs, photos and articles ............................................ 20.00
Map, City of Chicago and Century of Progress fairgrounds, Shell Oil ............................................ 16.00
Needlecase, 6-3/4" x 4-1/2", A Century of Progress ........................... 27.00
Playing Cards, gold leaf edges, orig red leather case ......................... 30.00
Pocket Mirror ............................ 25.00
Puzzle, 16-1/2", aerial view of fair opening, 300 pcs ...................... 50.00
Snowglobe .................................. 50.00
Souvenir Book
  *1933 Century of Progress Souvenir Book,* 8-1/2" x 11-1/2" .............. 20.00
  *Official Guide Book of the Fair,* fold-out map and Firestone colored adv insert ...................................... 25.00
Souvenir Spoon, silverplate
  Electrical Group on bowl, Fort Dearborn on handle, dated 1934 .... 10.00
  Travel & Transport on bowl, Hall of Science on handle, dated 1933. 8.00
Tray, Hall of Science, emb buildings, bridge ...................................... 30.00
View Book, 9" x 12", A Century of Progress Exhibition Official Book of Views, watercolor views and painting reproductions, published by Donnelly ...................................... 30.00
Wings ........................................ 25.00

**1939, New York, New York World's Fair**

Ashtray, 3" x 3-1/2", Trylon and Perisphere, Manuf by Almar, Point Marian, PA ...................................... 60.00
Banner, 10" x 8", multicolored paint on blue felt ................................ 45.00
Belt Buckle, goldtone, enameled Trylon, and Perisphere ...................... 20.00
Bookends, pr, alabaster, figural, Trylon and Perisphere .................... 110.00
Booklet
  General Motors Highway & Horizons, 20 pgs .................................. 24.00
  The Foods of Tomorrow, Birdseye .......................................... 8.00
Bowl, spring, Homer Laughlin Pottery ............................................ 55.00
Brochure, 12 pgs, fold-out, Trylon and Perisphere ......................... 16.00

Cake Server, 10" l, National Silver Co., view of man with 5 stars on handle "New York World's Fair 1939" with symbols and flags surrounding words .................................... 60.00
Cane, 34" l, wood, blue, round wooden knob, Trylon and Perisphere decal ............................................ 85.00
Clock, travel, chrome silver case, Trylon, Perisphere, and fair buildings on cover, blue and orange enamel accents .................................... 125.00
Coin, flattened, World of Tomorrow, Trylon and Perisphere .................. 13.00
Commemorative Plate ................ 150.00
Compact, 2-3/4" d, metal, full color celluloid insert, ivory white enameling ............................................ 40.00
Cuff Links, pr, Trylon, and Perisphere ............................................ 45.00
Cup ............................................ 25.00
Glass, 4-1/4" h
  Business Administration Building, dark blue top and center, orange base, NYWF 39 and row of stars at base .................................... 20.00
  Textile Building, yellow top and center, green base, center shows building .................................... 20.00
Guide Book, *Official Guide to World of Tomorrow,* first edition, 1939 .... 25.00
Hat, employee, wool, navy, orange Trylon and Perisphere, and "1940" on front ........................................ 42.00
Hot Plate, silver, engraved fair scenes ............................................ 15.00
Identification Check, Greyhound Bus, Sightseeing Bus Trip Thru Grounds ............................................ 7.50
Kerchief, 20" sq, deep blue, cluttered yellow, green, and red artwork of Fair buildings, Trylon, and Perisphere ............................................ 65.00
Key Ring .................................... 20.00
Magazine, *Life,* Trylon and Perisphere on cover ................................ 30.00
Map, Transit Map of Greater New York, Compliments of Franklin Fire Insurance Co. ................................ 25.00
Match Case, 1-1/2" x 2", leather, Trylon and Perisphere ...................... 35.00
Music Box .................................. 65.00
Night Light, ceramic, oval base with Trylon and Perisphere, ivory white finish, gold accents .................... 100.00
Photo, 25" x 20", American Jubilee, dry-mounted .................................. 55.00
Pin
  I Have Seen The Future ........... 25.00
  Shield-shaped logo, 5/8" h, 3/8" w, 1-1/2" chain to "39" on smaller shield, blue enamel on brass ............. 25.00
Plate
  7-1/4" d, Joint Exhibit of Capital & Labor, The American Potter, New York World's Fair, 1940, National Brotherhood Cooperative Potteries ........................................ 45.00
  9" d, Homer Laughlin Pottery, potter, turquoise .............................. 38.00
  10" d, Cronin, crazed .............. 85.00
Playing Cards, two decks, orig box, US Playing Card Co. ...................... 50.00

Postcard, set of 10 double faced cards, orig folder, unused .................. 18.00

Postage Stamps, 54 licensed stamps in orig envelope, unused ............ 25.00

Pot Holder, 7-1/2" x 8-1/2", woven terry cloth, blue and white design, inscribed "Macy's Pot Holder" ............................................... 50.00

Program, Opening Day, April 30, 1939 ............................................. 150.00

Ring, 5/8" d, 3/8" x 5/8" top with Trylon and Perisphere, sterling silver .............................................. 45.00

Rug, 9" x 13", woven Oriental-type, image of Trylon and Perisphere surrounded by flowers, shades of green, yellow, red, and orange highlights, Italian ............................. 95.00

Salt and Pepper Shakers, pr, figural, Trylon, and Perisphere, orange and blue ......................................... 25.00

Scarf, 18" x 17", white, orange, yellow, and maroon, blue ground, trees and buildings, Trylon and Perisphere around edge, clouds center .... 45.00

Spoon
    4-1/2" l, flags, Sphere and Trylon, date "1939" and 2 stars on handle, bowl with "New York World's Fair," tarnished silver ......................... 24.00
    6" l, 3 stars, flags, Theme Bldg, date "1939" and 2 more stars on handle, bowl with "New York World's Fair," rim of stars, silverplated .......... 30.00

Table Mat, 11" x 21", red felt, yellow, green, and white graphics, Statue of Liberty, Fair Administration Bldg., Empire State Bldg., Trylon, and Perisphere ...................................... 95.00

Tape Measure, 2-1/2" w, egg shape, metal, blue finish, bee figure on both sides, orange Trylon and Perisphere on one side, mkd "New York World's Fair 1939" ............................... 60.00

Teapot, white glazed china, blue Trylon, and Perisphere ......................... 50.00

Thermometer, 8-1/4" l, key shape, aerial view ........................................... 32.00

Thermos, 10" h, steel, threaded aluminum cap, orange Trylon and Perisphere, Universal Thermos .... 100.00

Ticket, 3" x 4", black and white photo, starched black fabric holder .... 45.00

Tie Clip, 2-3/4" w, brass, raised center emblem of Trylon and Perisphere .............................................. 25.00

Valet Holder, clothes brush holder and tie rack, syrocco wood, raised Trylon and Perisphere, orig brush .... 50.00

View-Master, set of 3 reels, orig booklet and envelope .......................... 40.00

### 1939, San Francisco, Golden Gate International Exposition

Ashtray, 1939 Golden Gate Expo, Homer Laughlin Pottery ........ 125.00

Belt Buckle, silver colored metal, badge emblem in center, aerial view of Treasure Island, name at top, 1-1/2" l 1" w ............................................... 60.00

Handkerchief, 12-1/2" sq, Treasure Island, minor stains ................. 40.00

Labels, set of 5, 1-1/2" d, "1939 Golden Gate International Exposition 1939 - a Pagent of the Pacific" around edge, center with woman arms up, flags at her feet, sunset, Treasure Island in background .............. 30.00

Matchbook Cover, Golden Gate Bridge scenes, pr ............................... 25.00

Pinback Button, 1-1/4" d, yellow, blue, and white .............................. 25.00

Plate, 10" d, Homer Laughlin ...... 125.00

Stamps, set of six, San Francisco, Oakland and Bay Cities Invite the World in 1939, "1939 Golden Gate International Exposition 1939, A Pageant of the Pacific," one stamp stuck to another, orig packaging ........... 45.00

Ticket, 3-1/2" x 2-1/4", general admission, slight glue and paper on back ............................................... 15.00

### 1962, Seattle, Century 21 Exposition

Glass, set of eight ........................ 80.00

Pinback Button, 1-1/4" d, red, white, and blue, Space Needle scene 17.50

Token, gold ................................. 10.00

Tray, metal, Space Needle scene .................................................. 12.00

### 1964, New York, New York World's Fair

Ashtray, 4" x 5", glass, white, orange, and blue graphics, two Fair Kids, Unisphere, 1964 .................... 25.00

Bank, dime register, orig card ...... 40.00

Change Tray ................................ 12.00

Coaster, 4" d, plastic, white, emb gold Unisphere, title and date, price for 4 pc set ...................................... 32.00

Comic Book, Flintstones at the World's Fair ......................................... 22.00

Doll, 8-1/2" h, ©1963 Sun Rubber, New York World's Fair, 1964-1965 .................................................. 85.00

Envelope, Unisphere as Christmas tree ornament, unused ................... 10.00

Flash Card Set, New York World's Fair Attractions
    Full Size, 3-1/2" x 6", 28 cards . 25.00
    Miniature Size, 24 cards ......... 20.00

Fork and Spoon Display, 11" l, mounted on wooden plaque, Unisphere decals on handles ................. 45.00

Hat, black felt, Unisphere emblem, white cord trim, feather, name "Richard" embroidered on front ....... 25.00

New York, 1964-65, Flash Card Set, orig box, $5.

**New York, 1964-65, post card, Astral Fountain, unused, $3.50.**

Mug, 3-1/4" h, milk glass, red inscription .................................................. 17.50

Paperweight, panoramic scenes .. 40.00

Placemat, 11" x 17-1/2", plastic, full color illus, Swiss Sky Ride and Lunar Fountain, price for pr ............. 25.00

Postcard, ten miniature pictures, twenty natural color reproductions, unused .................................................. 20.00

Salt and Pepper Shakers, pr, Unisphere, figural, ceramic .......... 50.00

Souvenir Book, *Official Souvenir Book of the New York World's Fair,* 1965 .................................................. 25.00

Stein, 6" h, ceramic, blue, German-style, emb Unisphere, German village scene, beer drinke .......... 25.00

Thermometer, 6" x 6", diamond shape, metal and plastic, full color fair buildings and attractions ................. 25.00

Ticket
    Belgian Village .......................... 7.50
    General Admission, adult, unused .................................................. 20.00
    Pavilion of American Interiors, unused prepaid ticket, courtesy of International Silver Co ............. 15.00
    Travelers Pavilion, The Travelers Insurance Companies stockholders courtesy card ........................ 12.00

Tray, 10-1/2" x 11-1/2", oval, plastic, raised fair attractions .............. 42.00

Tumbler, Science Hall, 6-1/2" h..... 17.50

### 1967, Montreal, Montreal Expo

Lapel Pin, brass, repeated motif around edge, threaded post fastener on back ......................................... 12.00

Tab, 1-1/2" l, litho tin, blue and white, US Pavilion, Compliments of Avis Car Rental ...................................... 6.00

### 1982, Knoxville, World's Fair

Glass, 5-1/2" h, clear, tapered, Energy Turns The World theme, trademark for McDonald's and Coca-Cola .................................................. 8.00

Sailor Cap, black and red inscription on brim .......................................... 5.00

# Wrestling Collectibles

**Collecting Hints:** When collecting wrestling action figures, be sure to save the card and biographical information presented on each wrestler. If pro-wrestling continues to remain a popular form of entertainment, more and more collectibles will surely be generated.

**History:** The sport of wrestling dates back to the days of Henry VIII and King Francis I of France. During the 1500s, these two royals loved to watch their favorites fight it out and may have even wrestled each other. Soldiers used to wrestle to show their strength as did ordinary folks. The ancient Greeks also apparently enjoyed the sport and included wrestlers in their art work and sculpture. When the first Olympics were held in Athens in 1896, wrestling was one of the events. No weight class structure was adhered to then as the first classes were designated in St. Louis in 1904. Time limits were not set to the present twelve minutes until the 1964 Olympics in Tokyo set that standard.

The sport has been encouraged by high school wrestling programs, where meets are regularly scheduled and good wrestling techniques are taught. Wrestling on the college level is organized into several leagues.

Probably the most recognized form of wrestling in the 1990s is more of an entertainment than actual sport. Through the WWF and other professional organizations, stunts and rehearsed maneuvers, have created a whole segment of wrestlers who take on good or evil personas and entertain live audiences and televised events.

**Periodical:** *Sports Collectors' Digest,* 700 E. State St., Iola, WI 54990.

Action Figure, Tag Team, loose
  British Bulldogs .......................... 45.00
  Hart Foundation ......................... 95.00
  Killer Bees ................................. 45.00
  Strike Force .............................. 75.00
Action Figure, WCW, Galoob, 1990, 5" h
  Butch Reed, orig card, opened pack
  ................................................. 10.00
  Lex Luger, MOC ........................ 20.00
  Ron Simmons, MOC ................... 15.00
  Sting, blue tights, MOC ............. 17.00
Action Figure, WWF, Hasbro, 5" h, MOC
  Brutus Beefcake, 1990 ............. 15.00
  Greg Valentine, 1992 ............... 12.00
  Hulk Hogan, 1990 .................... 20.00
  Macho Man #3, 1992 ............... 20.00
  Million Dollar Man, green, 1991
  ................................................. 17.00
  Mr. Perfect, 1992, card bad ..... 20.00
  Rowdy Piper, 1991 ................... 14.00
  Superfly Jim Snurka, 1991 ....... 12.00

**WCW race cars, $35. Andrew Tincher Collection.**

Action Figure, WWF, LIN, 10" h
  Adrian Adonis, MOC ................. 22.00
  Andre, long hair, loose ............. 12.00
  Animal Steele, loose ................ 12.00
  Ax, loose ................................. 32.00
  Big Boss Man .......................... 95.00
  Billy Jack Haynes, loose .......... 19.00
  Blue Referee, loose .................. 22.00
  Bruno Sammartino, loose ......... 12.00
  Brutus Beefcake, MOC ............. 12.00
  Elizabeth, loose ....................... 20.00
  Fred Classie Blassie, MOC ..... 25.00
  Hulk, no shirt, loose ................. 12.00
  Hulk, red ................................. 95.00
  Hulk, white shirt, loose ............. 45.00
  Jesse Ventura, loose, played-with condition ................................... 12.00
  Johnny V, MOC ........................ 25.00
  King Hanley, loose ................... 70.00
  Mean Gene, MOC ..................... 25.00
  Mr. Fuji, MOC .......................... 25.00
  Outback Jack, loose ................ 20.00
  Roddy Piper, slight damage to card
  ................................................. 25.00
  Sgt. Slaughter, mail order, MOC
  ............................................... 150.00
  Ted Dibiase, MOC ................... 35.00

**Card game, Hulk Hogan's Rock 'n' Wrestling, Golden Toys, $2.50.**

  Terry Funk, loose ..................... 12.00
  Ultimate Warrior, loose ............ 75.00
  Vince McMahon, MOC ............. 35.00
Bendie, LIN, 1985, MOC, typical
  ................................................. 12.00
Colorforms, WWF, Marvel, 1990, MIB
  ................................................. 20.00
Figure, talking, The Undertaker, Playmates, 14" h, 1997, MIB .......... 45.00
Game, Shoot-Out WWF Superstars, 2 teams, 12 players, Remco, 42" x 21"
  ................................................. 80.00
Magazine
  *Wrestling,* Vol. 1, #4, May 1951, full color action photo featuring Gene Stanlee, 52 pgs, articles, photos
  ................................................. 30.00
  *Wrestling Official Magazine,* Champion Sports Publishing, NY, first issue, October 1971 ................ 30.00
Medal, brass, finely detailed image of Greco-Roman wrestlers, small shield engraved "Heavy," reverse engraved "2nd Annual York County Wrestling Tourney," 1927 ......................... 20.00
Photograph, autographed, black and white
  Animal Wrestler, 5" x 7" ............. 2.00
  Bobby Allison, 8" x 10" ............... 9.50
  Stone Cold Steve Austin, 8" x 10"
  ................................................. 27.00
  Stone Cold, Tyson, Michaels, Wrestle Mania, 8" x 10" ........................ 75.00
  Giant, 8" x 10" ......................... 15.00
  Bill Goldberg, 8" x 10" .............. 30.00
  Bret Hart, 8" x 10" ................... 20.00
  Bobby "The Brain" Heenan, 8" x 10"
  ................................................. 12.00
  Thomas "The Hit Man" Hearns, 8" x 10" .......................................... 15.00
  Raye "Zap" Hollitt, 8" x 10" ......... 8.00
  Jeff Jarrett, 8" x 10" ................. 15.00
  Lex Luger, 8" x 10" ................... 18.00
  Mankind, 8" x 10" ..................... 17.00
  Kevin Nash, 8" x 10" ................. 20.00
  Diamond Dallas Page, 8" x 10"
  ................................................... 4.00
  Sable, 8" x 10" ......................... 20.00

Sting, 8" x 10" ............................ 28.00
Task Master, 8" x 10" ................. 10.00
Bad Boy Tony Rumble, 8" x 10"
.................................................... 10.00
Undertaker, 8" x 10" ................... 20.00
Valentine, 8" x 10" ...................... 10.00
Pinball Game, WWF, Playtime, 1991
.................................................... 25.00
Poster, black and white, small ........ 3.00
Ring, blue, Hasbro, 1990, MIB ..... 30.00
Squirt Gun, WWF ........................... 12.00
Valentines, WWF Superstars, 32 cards,
MIB .......................................... 10.00
Wrestling Gear, Hulk Hogan, WWF, 24"
Pythons, Hasbro, 1991, MIB .... 20.00

# Wright, Russel

**Collecting Hints:** Russel Wright worked for many different companies in addition to creating material under his own label, American Way. Wright's contracts with firms often called for the redesign of pieces which did not produce or sell well. As a result, several lines have the same item in more than one shape.

Wright was totally involved in design. Most collectors focus on his dinnerware; however, he also designed glassware, plastic items, textiles, furniture, and metal objects. He helped popularize bleached and blonde furniture. His early work in spun aluminum often is overlooked as is his later work in plastic for the Northern Industrial Chemical Company.

**History:** Russel Wright was an American industrial engineer with a passion for the streamlined look. His influence is found in all aspects of domestic life. Wright and his wife, Mary Small Einstein, wrote *A Guide To Easier Living* to explain their concepts.

Russel Wright was born in 1904 in Lebanon, Ohio. His first jobs included set designer and stage manager under the direction of Norman Bel Geddes. He later used this theatrical flair for his industrial designs, stressing simple clean lines. Some of his earliest designs were executed in polished spun aluminum. These pieces, designed in the mid-1930s, include trays, vases, and teapots. Wright garnered many awards, among which were those he received from the Museum of Modern Art in 1950 and 1953.

Chase Brass and Copper, General Electric, Imperial Glass, National Silver Co., Shenango, and Steubenville Pottery Company are some of the companies that used Russel Wright designs. In 1983, a major exhibition of his work was held at the Hudson River Museum in Yonkers, New York, and at the Smithsonian's Renwick Gallery in Washington, DC.

**References:** Susan and Al Bagdade, *Warman's American Pottery and Porcelain*, Wallace-Homestead, 1994; Ann Kerr, *Collector's Encyclopedia of Russel Wright Designs*, 2nd ed., Collector Books, 1997; Leslie Piña, *Pottery, Modern Wares 1920-1960*, Schiffer Publishing, 1994.

**American Modern** Made by the Steubenville Pottery Company, 1939-1959. Originally issued in Bean Brown, Chartreuse Curry, Coral, Granite Grey, Seafoam Blue, and White. Later color additions were Black Chutney, Cedar Green, Cantaloupe, Glacier Blue, and Steubenville Blue.

Baker, small, Chartreuse Curry ..... 25.00
Bread and Butter Plate, 6" d
   Coral ............................................ 3.00
   Granite Gray ................................. 3.00
Butter, cov
   Black Chutney ........................... 285.00
   Chartreuse Curry ...................... 285.00
   Coral .......................................... 285.00
Carafe, Granite Grey .................... 175.00
Casserole, cov, stick handle, Seafoam
   Blue ............................................ 40.00
Celery
   Bean Brown ................................ 24.00
   Black Chutney ............................. 30.00
   Granite Grey ............................... 20.00
Children's Dish Set, 7" d cov bowl, six sets of chartreuse cups and saucers, 8" rect tray, three 6" d coral plates, three 6" d blue plates, blue, creamer, cov sugar, teapot and lid, made by Ideal ......................... 100.00
Chop Plate
   Chartreuse Curry ....................... 20.00
   Coral ........................................... 20.00
   Granite Grey ............................... 25.00
Seafoam Blue ................................. 25.00
Coaster, White ................................ 24.00
Cocktail, 2-3/4" h, 2-1/2 oz, Seafoam
   Blue, glass .................................. 17.00
Creamer
   Chartreuse .................................... 9.00
   Coral ............................................. 8.00
   Granite Gray ................................. 8.00
Creamer and Sugar, Chartreuse Curry
.................................................... 20.00
Cup, Seafoam Blue ........................... 9.00
Cup and Saucer
   Chartreuse Curry ......................... 9.00
   Coral ............................................. 8.00
   Glacier Blue ................................ 28.00
   Granite Grey ............................... 12.00
Demitasse Cup
   Chartreuse Curry ......................... 8.00
   Granite Grey ............................... 17.00
Demitasse Cup and Saucer, coral
.................................................... 20.00

Demitasse Pot, cov
   Coral ........................................... 70.00
   Granite Grey ............................... 80.00
   Seafoam Blue ............................ 150.00
Dinner Plate, 10" d
   Bean Brown ................................ 18.00
   Black Chutney .............................. 8.00
   Cedar Green ............................... 10.00
   Granite Gray ................................. 6.00
   Seafoam Blue .............................. 11.00
Dinner Service, Seafoam Blue, 74 pcs
.................................................. 600.00
Fruit Bowl, lug handle
   Bean Brown ................................ 19.00
   Chartreuse Curry ......................... 8.00
   Coral ........................................... 12.00
Hostess Plate
   Chartreuse Curry ....................... 75.00
   Granite Grey ............................... 85.00
Iced Tea Tumbler, 5" h, Coral, glass,
   slight use ................................... 24.00
Pickle
   Chartreuse Curry ....................... 12.00
   Granite Grey ............................... 13.00
Pitcher
   Chartreuse Curry ....................... 65.00
   Coral ......................................... 120.00
   Seafoam Blue ............................. 85.00
Platter, oval
   Chartreuse Curry ....................... 17.00
   Coral ........................................... 20.00
Refrigerator Dish, cov
   Coral ......................................... 225.00
   Granite Grey ............................. 175.00
Relish
   Chartreuse Curry, rosette ....... 145.00
   Seafoam Blue ............................. 24.00
Salad Bowl
   Coral ........................................... 75.00
   Granite Grey ............................... 85.00
   Seafoam Blue ............................. 85.00
Salad Plate, 8" d
   Coral ........................................... 15.00

**Pitcher, white, 10-3/4" h, $55.**

Granite Grey............................ 12.00
Salt and Pepper Shakers, pr
Chartreuse ............................... 12.00
Coral........................................ 12.00
Granite Grey............................ 12.00
Seafoam Blue.......................... 15.00
Sauceboat, liner, Coral ............. 45.00
Sherbet, 5 oz, Seafoam Blue, glass
............................ 20.00
Soup Bowl
Bean Brown, lug handle........... 24.00
Coral........................................ 15.00
Granite Grey, lug handle.......... 15.00
Stack Server, Cedar Green......... 250.00
Sugar, cov
Cedar Green ........................... 12.00
Chartreuse Curry .................... 20.00
Seafoam Blue.......................... 12.00
Teapot, Granite Grey.................... 75.00
Tumbler
Black Chutney.......................... 65.00
Cedar Green ........................... 72.00
Coral........................................ 60.00
Granite Grey............................ 65.00
Vegetable Bowl
Chartreuse Curry .................... 15.00
Coral........................................ 20.00
Granite Grey............................ 22.00
Seafoam Blue.......................... 20.00
Vegetable Bowl, divided, Chartreuse
Curry ....................................... 80.00

**Iroquois Casual** Made by the Iroquois China Company and distributed by Garrison Products, 1946-1960s. Initially issued in Ice Blue, Lemon Yellow, and Sugar White. Later colors produced were Aqua, Avocado Yellow, Brick Red, Cantaloupe, Charcoal, Lettuce Green, Oyster, Nutmeg Brown, Parsley Green (later called Forest Green), Pink Sherbet, and Ripe Apricot Yellow.

Bread and Butter Plate, 6-1/2" d
Avocado Yellow.......................... 4.00
Ice Blue..................................... 3.00
Ripe Apricot .............................. 3.50
Sugar White............................... 6.50

Butter, cov
Avocado Yellow........................ 65.00
Ice Blue..................................... 85.00
Lemon Yellow........................... 54.00
Pink Sherbet............................. 75.00
Ripe Apricot ............................. 85.00
Sugar White ............................. 85.00
Carafe
Avocado Yellow........................ 90.00
Ripe Apricot ............................ 175.00
Casserole, cov, 2 qt
Avocado Yellow........................ 35.00
Oyster ...................................... 20.00
Cereal Bowl, 5-1/4" d
Cantaloupe ............................... 15.00
Ice Blue..................................... 8.00
Oyster ...................................... 10.00
Chop Plate, 13" d
Ripe Apricot ............................. 24.00
Sugar White ............................. 30.00
Coffeepot, cov
Ice Blue................................... 135.00
Nutmeg Brown ....................... 125.00
Coffee Service, Nutmeg Brown, 10 pc
set ......................................... 135.00
Creamer and Sugar, cov, stacking
Avocado Yellow........................ 15.00
Ice Blue..................................... 12.50
Sugar White ............................. 27.50
Cup and Saucer
Charcoal .................................. 10.00
Ice Blue, ear handle.................. 8.00
Lemon Yellow........................... 8.00
Pink Sherbet............................. 8.00
Sugar White ............................. 10.00
Demitasse Pot, cov
Avocado Yellow........................ 65.00
Nutmeg Brown ........................ 75.00
Demitasse Cup and Saucer
Avocado Yellow...................... 150.00
Ice Blue................................... 150.00
Dinner Plate, 10" d
Avocado Yellow........................ 8.00
Charcoal .................................. 8.00
Lemon Yellow........................... 8.50
Lettuce Green .......................... 9.00
Oyster ...................................... 10.00
Fruit Bowl
Avocado Yellow........................ 4.00
Oyster ...................................... 4.50

Gumbo
Ice Blue..................................... 35.00
Pink Sherbet ............................ 30.00
Hostess Plate, Ice Blue .............. 85.00
Luncheon Plate, 9" d
Avocado Yellow ....................... 6.00
Ice Blue..................................... 6.50
Oyster ...................................... 8.00
Mug, Ripe Apricot ....................... 75.00
Platter, 14" l, oval, Ice Blue .......... 20.00
Salad Plate, 7-3/8" d
Ice Blue..................................... 6.00
Lemon Yellow........................... 7.00
Oyster ...................................... 8.00
Sugar White ............................. 10.00
Salt and Pepper Shakers, pr, stacking
Oyster ...................................... 15.00
Sugar White ............................. 17.50
Vegetable
8" d, open
Avocado Yellow................... 15.00
Ice Blue.............................. 15.00
Nutmeg Brown ................... 15.00
Pink Sherbet....................... 17.50
10" d, cov
Chartreuse, pinch lid, 2 pt
............................ 30.00
Nutmeg Brown ................... 55.00
Pink Sherbet....................... 50.00

**Iroquois Casual, Redesigned** In 1959, Iroquois Casual dinnerware was produced in patterns and offered in 45 piece sets. Cookware was another later addition in the redesigned style.

Cup, Charcoal .............................. 8.00
Cup and Saucer, Ice Blue ............ 10.00
Gravy, Ice Blue .......................... 220.00
Mug
Apricot Yellow ......................... 80.00
Ice Blue.................................... 75.00
Lemon Yellow........................... 75.00
Pink Sherbet ............................ 70.00
Ripe Apricot............................. 70.00
Sugar White, Christmas dec.... 85.00
Set, Pink Sherbet, 24 pcs ........... 125.00
Teapot, Lemon Yellow................ 185.00

# Index

## A

Abingdon Pottery, 22
Action figures 22, 23
    Charlie's Angels, 23
    Defenders of the Earth, 23
Action figures,
    Alien, 23
    A-Team, 23
    Baseball, 23
    Basketball, 23
    Battlestar Galactica, 23
    Black Hole, 23
    Buck Rogers, 23
    Clash of the Titans, 23
    Comic Book, 23
    DC Direct, 23
    Falcon, 23
    Happy Days, 23
    MAD Magazine, 23
    Monsters, 23
    Our Gang, 23
    Planet of the Apes, 23
    Raiders of the Lost Ark, 23
    S.W.A.T., 24
    Sinthia, 23
    Star Com, 23
    Star Trek, 23
    Star Wars, 23
    Super Powers, 23
    Visionaires, 24
Advertising characters, 29
    AC Spark Plug, 30
    Alka Seltzer, Speedy, 30
    Aunt Jemima, 30
    Borden's, 30
    Buster Brown, 30
    Cadbury Bunny, 30
    Campbell Kids, 30
    Charlie Tuna, 31
    Dutch Boy, 30
    Esso Tiger, 30

Fleischmann's Yeast, 30
Fresh-Up Freddy, 31
Frito Bandito, 30
Green Giant, 30
Hawaiian Punch, 30
Hush Puppy, 30
Joe Camel, 30
Keebler Elf, 30
Kool Cigarettes, 31
Lee Jeans, 31
Michelin Man, 31
Mr. Bubble, 31
Mr. Clean, 31
Nipper, 31
Philip Morris, Johnny, 31
Pillsbury Dough Boy, 31
Red Goose Shoes, 31
Reddy Kilowatt, 31
Sinclair Oil, 31
Tony the Tiger, 31
Trix Rabbit, 31
Tropicana, 31
Advertising, 24
    Ashtrays, 24
    Bill Hook, 24
    Blotter, 24
    Booklet, 24
    Bookmark, 25
    Box, 25
    Brochure, 25
    Clip, 25
    Coffee Tin, 25
    Display Cabinet, 25
    Display, 25
    Fan, 25
    Flipper Pin, 25
    Hat Rack, 26
    Key Holder, 26
    Keychain Fob, 26
    Letter Opener, 26
    Lunch Box, 26
    Memo Booklet, 26
    Mirror, 26

Model, 26
Paperweight, 26
Pencil Sharpener, 27
Pinback Button, 27
Radio, 27
Record Brush, 27
Ruler, 27
Sharpening Stone, 27
Shoe Horn, 27
Sign, 27
Stamp Case, 28
Stickpin, 28
Store Bin, 28
Stove, 28
Stud, 28
Tape Measure, 28
Telephone, 28
Tin, 28
Toothpick Holder, 29
Toy, 29
Tray, 29
Whistle, 29
Advertising-logo watches, 31
    Campbell Soup Co., 32
    Captain Midnight, 32
    Charlie the Tuna, 32
    Chuck Wagon Dog Food, 32
    Coppertone, 32
    Hawaiian Punch, 32
    Icee Bear, 32
    Keebler Elf, 32
    Little Hans, 32
    M&Ms, 32
    Major Moon, 32
    Peter Pan Peanut Butter, 32
    Raid Bug Spray, 32
    Reddy Kilowatt, 33
    Ritz Cracker, 33
    Scrubbing Bubble, 33
    Shell Oil, 33
    Snickers, 33
    Stanley, 33
    Swiss Miss, 33

Tony the Tiger, 33
Toppie the Elephant, 33
Westinghouse, 33
Akro Agate Glass, 33
Children's dishes, 33
Household items, 34
Aluminum, Hand Wrought, 34, 35
American Bisque, 35
Animation Art, 36
Autographs, 36, 37
Cards signed, 37
Document signed, 37
Equipment, 37
First Day Covers, 38
Letters signed, 37
Photographs signed, 38
Aviation Collectibles, 38
Commercial, 38, 39
General, 39
Personalities, 39
Avon Collectibles, 39
Awards and representative gifts, 40
California Perfume Co., 40
Children's items, 40
Men's items, 40
Miscellaneous, 40
Women's items, 41

**B**

Banks, Still, 42
Ceramic, 42
Metal, 42
Plastic and vinyl, 42
Tin, 42
Barbershop and Beauty Collectibles, 43
Barbie, 44, 45
Baseball Cards, 45
Bowman Era, 46
Pre-Bowman/Tops Period, 46
Topps Era, 46, 47, 48
Baseball Collectibles, 48, 49
Basketball Collectibles, 49, 50
Battery Operated Automata 51
Bauer Pottery, 51, 52
Beanie Babies® 52
Advertising, 53
Retired, 53
Beatles, 53, 54
Beer Bottles, 54
Embossed, 54
Painted label, 54

Paper label, 54
Stoneware, 54
Beer Cans, 54
10 oz., 55
11 and 12 oz., 55
12 oz., cone top, 55
15 and 16 oz., 55
7 oz., 55
8 oz., 55
Bells 214
Beswick, 55, 56
Bicycle Collectibles, 56, 57, 58
Big Little Books, 58, 59
Better Little Books, 59
Black Memorabilia, 59, 60, 61
Blue Ridge Pottery, 61, 62, 63
Bookends, 63, 64
Books, Science Fiction, 64, 65
Bottle Openers, Figural, 65, 66
Boxing Collectibles, 66, 67
Brastoff, Sascha, 67
Brayton Laguna Pottery, 67, 68
Breweriana, 68, 69
Bubblegum Cards, Nonsport, 69, 70

**C**

Calculators, 71
Calendars, 71, 72
Cameras, 72, 73
Ansco, 73
Eastman Kodak, 73
Sears, 74
Universal Camera Corp., 74
Voightlander, 74
Zeiss, 74
Candlewick, 74, 75, 76, 77
Candy Containers, 77, 78
Candy Molds, 78
Chocolate molds, 79
Hard candy, 79
Maple sugar, 79
Cap Guns, 79, 80
Carnival Chalkware, 80, 81
Cartoon Characters, 81
Andy Gump, 84
Andy Panda, 82, 83
Archie, 82, 83
Archies, 84
Atom Ant, 83
Barney Google, 83
Beetle Bailey, 83, 84
Betty Boop, 82, 84
Betty Rubble, 84

Blondie, 82, 83
Brownies, 83
Bugs Bunny, 82, 83, 84, 210, 385
Bullwinkle, 82, 83
Casper, 83
Charlie Brown, 83
Daddy Warbucks, 83
Daffy Duck, 83
Dick Tracy, 83, 84
Dixie, 83
Dudley Do-Right, 83
Elmer Fudd, 82
Felix the Cat, 82, 83
Flintstones, 82, 83, 84
Foxy Grandpa, 83
Fred Flintstone, 82, 83
Froggie Gremlin, 83
Garfield, 82, 84
Gasoline Alley, 84
Grape Ape, 82
Gumby and Pokey, 83
Happy Hooligan, 83
Heckle and Jeckle, 82
Hong Kong Phooey, 82
Huckleberry Hound, 83
Jessica Rabbit, 83
Jiggs, 83
Joe Palooka, 83
Just Kids, 82
Lil' Abner, 83, 84
Little Lulu, 83
Lucy, 83
Lulu and Tubby, 84
Maggie and Jiggs, 83
Magilla Gorilla, 82, 84
Mammy Yocum, 83
Mickey Mouse, 215
Moon Mullins, 83
Mutt & Jeff, 82
Olive Oyl, 83, 84
Peanuts, 207, 210, 215
Penelope Pitstop, 84
Pink Panther, 84
Popeye, 82, 83
Porky Pig, 82, 84
Prince Valiant, 82, 84
Quick Draw McGraw, 82, 84
Quick-Draw McGraw, 83
Reg'lar Fellers, 83
Road Runner, 83
Rocky and Bullwinkle, 82
Sally, 83
Scooby Doo, 82, 83, 84

Skippy, 82
Smitty, 84
Snoopy, 82, 84
Snuffy Smith, 83
Sparkle Plenty, 83
Stan Laurel, 82
Sylvester, 83
Tennessee Tuxedo, 82
The Katzenjammer Kids, 83
Tom & Jerry, 82, 83, 84
Tweety and Sylvester, 82
Tweety, 83
Uncle Wiggily, 82
Uncle Willie, 83
Underdog, 83
Woody Woodpecker, 82, 83, 84
Yellow Kid, 83
Yogi Bear, 82, 83, 84
Yogi, 82
Cat Collectibles, 85, 86
Catalina Pottery, 84
Catalogs, 84, 85
Ceramic Arts Studio, 86, 87
Cereal Boxes, 87, 88
Cereal Premiums, 88, 89
Character and Promotional Glasses, 89, 90, 91
Children's Books, 91, 92, 93
Children's Dishes, 93
Aluminum, 94
Cast iron, 94
China, 94
Depression-era glass, 94
Pattern glass, 94
Plastic, 94
Christmas Collectibles, 95
Christmas Village/Garden, 95
Non-tree related items, 95
Tree-related items, 95, 96
Cigar Collectibles, 96, 97
Cigarette Items, 97, 98
Circus Items, 98, 99
Cleminson Clay, 99, 100
Clickers, 100
Advertising, 100
Mechanical, 100
Political, 100
Clocks, 100, 101
Clothing and Clothing Accessories, 101, 102, 103
Coca-Cola Collectibles, 103, 104, 105
Cocktail Memorabilia, 105, 106
Coloring Books, 106, 107
Comic Books, 107, 108, 109

Cookbooks, 109
Cookie Cutters, Plastic 110
Cookie Jars, 110
Abingdon Pottery, 111
Advertising, 111
American Bisque, 111
Avon, 111
Brush, 111
California Originals, 111
Cardinal, 111
Certified International, 111
Clay Art, 111
Cleminsons, 111
Doranne, 111
Enesco, 111
Fitz and Floyd, 111
Hall, 111
McCoy, 111
Metlox, 111
Puriton, 111
Redwing Pottery, 111
Regal, 111
RRP CO, 111
Shawnee, 112
Treasure Craft, 112
Twin Winton, 112
Vandor, 112
Warner Brothers, 112
Coors Pottery, 112
Empire, 112
Mello-Tone, 112
Ram's Head, 112
Rosebud, 112
Cow Collectibles, 112, 113
Cowboy Heroes, 113, 114
Annie Oakley, 114
Bonanza, 114
Buck Jones, 114
Buffalo Bill, 114
Cisco Kid, 114
Davy Crockett, 114
Gabby Hayes, 114
Gene Autry, 114
Gunsmoke, 115
Hopalong Cassidy, 115, 116
John Wayne, 116
Ken Maynard, 116
Kit Carson, 116
Lone Ranger, 116
Maverick, 116
Miscellaneous, 117
Rawhide, 116
Red Ryder, 116
Restless Gun, 116
Rin Tin Tin, 116

Roy Rogers, 116
Straight Arrow, 116
The Rebel, 116
The Rifleman, 116
Tim McCoy, 117
Tom Mix, 117
Wagon Train, 117
Wild Bill Hickok, 117
Wyatt Earp, 117
Cracker Jack, 117, 118

**D**

Degenhart Glass, 119
Depression Glass, 119, 120
Bowknot, 120
Dewdrop, 120
Floragold, 121
Floral and Diamond Band, 121
Forest Green, 121, 122
Georgian, Lovebirds, 122
Jubilee, 122
Moonstone, 122, 123
Patrick, 123
Sunburst, Herringbone, 123
Thistle, 123
Dirigibles, 123, 124
Disneyana, 124
Bambi, 125
Cinderella, 125
Disneyland, 125
Donald Duck, 125
Dumbo, 125
Lady and the Tramp, 125
Mickey Mouse Club, 126
Mickey Mouse, 125, 215
Minnie Mouse, 126, 208, 215
Pinocchio, 126
Pluto, 126, 215
Snow White, 126, 215
Winnie the Pooh, 127
Zorro, 127
Dog Collectibles, 127, 128
Dollhouse Furnishings, 128, 129
Dolls, 129, 130
Advertising, 130
American Character, 130
Annalee 209
Arranbee, 130
Ashton Drake, 209
Character and Personality, 131
Cosmopolitan Doll Company, 131
Deluxe Toys, 131

Eegee , 131
Effanbee, 131, 132
Enesco, 209
Gorham, 209
Hasbro, 132
Horsman, 132
Ideal, 132
Madame Alexander, 133, 134
Mary Hoyer, 134
Mattel, 134
Sun Rubber, 134
Terri Lee, 134
Vogue, 134
Dr. Seuss Collectibles, 305, 306
Drugstore Collectibles, 135
Beauty products, 135
Chemical companies, 135
Cold and cough, 136
Dental, 136
First aid, 136
Herbs, 136
Infants and children, 136
Laxatives, 136
Miscellaneous, 137
Stomach, 137

# E

Electrical Appliances, 138
Blenders, 138, 139
Chafing dishes, 139
Coffe makers and sets, 139
Coffee makers and sets, 140
Egg cookers, 140
Food cookers, 140
Hot plates, 140
Miscellaneous, 140
Mixers, 140, 141
Popcorn poppers, 141
Toaster, 142
Toasters, 141
Waffle irons and sandwich grills, 142
Elephant Collectibles, 142, 143

# F

Farm Collectibles, 144, 145
Fast Food Memorabilia, 145
A&W, 146
Big Boy, 146
Burger King, 146
Dairy Queen, 146
Denny's, 146
Howard Johnson, 146
Kentucky Fried Chicken, 146
McDonald's, 146
Pizza Hut, 146
Taco Bell, 146
Wendy's 146
Fiesta Ware, 146, 147, 148
Fire King, 149, 150
Dinnerware, 150
Kitchenware, 150
Ovenware, 151
Firehouse Collectibles, 148, 149
Fishing Collectibles, 151, 152
Flag Collectibles, 152, 153, 154
Flashlights, 154, 155
Florence Ceramics, 155, 156
Flow Blue China, American, 156, 157
Football Cards, 157
Bowman Card Company, 157
Fleer, 158
Leaf, 158
Philadelphia, 158
Pro-Set, 158
Score, 158
Stadium Club, 158
Topps, 158
Upper Deck, 158
Football Collectibles, 158, 159
Franciscan Dinnerware, 159
Apple, 160
Coronado, 160
Daisy, 160
Desert Rose, 160
Fresh Fruit, 161
Ivy, 161
Magnolia, 161
Meadow Rose, 161
Poppy, 161
Rosemore, 161
Starburst, 161
Wildflower, 161
Willow, 161
Fraternal Organizations and Service Clubs, 161
American Legion, 161
Benevolent & Protective Order of Elks, 161
Fraternal Order of Eagles, 162
Improved Order of Red Man, 162
Independent Order of Odd Fellows, 162
Knights of Columbus, 162
Knights of Pythias, 162
Knights Templar, 162
Lions Club, 162
Loyal Order of Moose, 162
Masonic, 162
Order of Eastern Star, 163
Rotary International, 163
Salvation Army, 163
Shrine, 163
Woodmen of the World, 163
Frog Collectibles, 163
Fruit Jars, 164
Funeral Memorabilia, 164, 165

# G

G.I. Joe Collectibles, 169, 170
Gambling Collectibles, 166, 167
Games,
Board, 167, 168
Card, 168
Frankenstein, 167
Gasoline Collectibles, 168
Golf Collectibles, 170, 171
Gonder Pottery, 171
Graniteware, 172, 173
Griswold, 173
Muffin Pan, 173
Other, 174
Skillet, 173

# H

Haeger Potteries, 175
Hall China, 175
Autumn Leaf, 176
Blue Garden/Blue Blossom, 176
Chinese Red, 176
Crocus, 176
Golden Glow, 176
Orange Poppy, 176
Red Dot, 176
Red Poppy, 176
Rose White, 177
Taverne, 176
Teapots, 177
Wild Poppy, 177
Harker Pottery, 177
Cameo, 177
Petit Point Rose, 177
Red Apple, 178
Hockey Collectibles, 178

Holiday Collectibles, 178
    Christmas, 207, 211, 212, 213, 214, 215
    Easter, 179, 209, 212
    Fourth of July, 212
    Halloween, 179
    St. Patrick's Day, 179
    Thanksgiving, 180, 212
    Valentine's Day, 209, 212, 215
Holt-Howard Collectibles, 180
    Christmas, 180
    Cozy Kittens, 180
    Jeeves, butler, 180
    Merry Mouse, 180
    Miscellaneous, 180
    Red Rooster 180
Homer Laughlin, 181
    Harlequin, 181
    Kitchen Kraft, 181
    Mexicana, 182
    Priscilla, 182
    Riviera, 182
    Virginia Rose, 182
    Wells Art Glaze, 182
Horse Collectibles, 182, 183
    Equipment and related items, 183
    Theme items, 183, 184
Hull Pottery, 184
    Post-1950 patterns, 185
    Pre-1950 patterns, 185
Hummel Items, 185, 186, 187, 207, 210, 212
Hunting Collectibles, 187, 188

**I**

Ice Cream Collectibles, 189, 190
Insulators, 190, 191
Irons, 192
    Charcoal, 192
    Children's, 192
    Flat irons, 192
    Fluters, 192
    Goffering, 192
    Liquid fuel, 192
    Slug, 193
    Special purpose, 193

**J**

Jewelry, Costume, 194
    Bracelets, 194

Brooch/pin, 195, 196
    Clip, 196
    Cuff links, 196
    Earrings, 196
    Necklace, 196
    Pendant, 197
    Suite, 197
Jukeboxes, 197, 198

**K**

Kewpies, 199
Kitchen Collectibles, 199, 200, 201
Kitchen Glassware, 201, 202, 203
Knowles, Edwin M., 203
    Beverly, 203
    Deanna, 203
    Esquire, 203
    Mexican, 203
    Souvenir plates, 203
    Yorktown, 203

**L**

Labels, 204, 205
    Fruit and crate, 204
    Fruit crate, 204
    Miscellaneous, 205
    Tin Can, 205
    Vegetables, 205
Lamps, 205, 206
Limited Edition Collectibles, 206
    Bing & Grondahl, 207, 210
    Currier & Ives, 207
    Danbury Mint, 207, 208
    Dave Grossman Creations, 208
    Department 56, 209
    Enesco, 207, 209
    Ferrandiz, Anri J., 207
    Franklin Mint, 207, 209, 210, 212
    Gorham, 207, 209
    Hallmark, 208
    Haviland, 208
    Hummel, 207, 210, 212
    Lalique, 213
    Lenox, 207, 213
    Lladro, 207, 210, 213
    Lunt, 200
    Pickard, 207
    Reco, 207, 213
    Reed & Barton, 207, 208, 213
    River Shore, 207, 210

    Rosenthal, 213
    Royal Copenhagen, 210, 214
    Royal Doulton, 209, 210, 215
    Schmid, 207, 208, 210, 215
    Towle, 208
    Wallace Silversmiths, 208
    Walt Disney, 208, 210
    Wedgwood, 208, 209, 216
Little Golden Books, 216, 217
Little Red Riding Hood, 217, 218
Lottery Tickets, 218, 219
Lunch Kits, 219, 220

**M**

Magazine Covers and Tear Sheets, 221, 222
Magazines, 222, 223
Marbles, 223
    Akro Agate, 224
    Christensen Agate Co., 224
    End of Day, 224
    Lutz, 224
    M.F. Christensen & Son, 224
    Marble King Co., 224
    Master Marble Co., 224
    Mica, 224
    Other, 224
    Peltier Glass Co., 224
    Swirl, 224
    Transitional, 224
    Vitro Agate/Gladding Vitro Co., 224
Matchcovers, 224
    Special covers, 225
    Topics, 225
McCoy Pottery, 225, 226
McKee Glass, 227
Metlox Pottery, 227
    Antique Grape, 228
    Blue Provincial, 228
    California Ivy, 228
    California Provincial, 228
    California Strawberry, 228
    Camelia California, 228
    Colonial Homestead, 228
    Contempora, 228
    Della Robia, 228
    Homestead Provincial, 228
    Provincial Rose, 229
    Red Rooster, 229
    Sculpted Daisy, 229
    Sculpted Grape, 229
    Sculpted Zinnia, 229

Model Kits, 229, 230
Monsters, 230
    Creature From the Black Lagoon, The, 232
    Dracula, 231
    Elvira, 231
    Exorcist, The, 232
    Frankenstein, 231
    Godzilla, 231
    Hammer, 231
    Musters, 231
    Nightmare Before Christmas, The, 232
    Nightmare on Elm Street/Freddy Krueger, 232
Morton Potteries,
    American Art Potteries, 234
    Cliftwood Art Potteries Inc., 233
    Midwest Potteries Inc., 233
    Morton Pottery Works, Morton Earthenware Co., 232
    Morton Pottery Company, 233
Movie Memorabilia, 234, 235, 236
Movie Personalities, 236, 237
Music Boxes 210, 237, 238
Music Collectibles
    Music Boxes 210

# N

Napkin rings, 239
New Martinsville Viking Glass, 239, 240
Newspapers, 240, 241, 242
Niloak Pottery, 242
Nippon China, 243
Noritake Azalea China, 243, 244
Norman Rockwell 207, 209, 212, 213
Nutcrackers, 244, 245

# O

Occupied Japan, 246, 247
Ocean Liner Collectibles, 247, 248
Olympics Collectibles, 248, 249
Owl Collectibles, 249, 250

# P

Padlocks, 251, 252
    Brass lever, 252

Combination, 252
Commemorative, 252
Dragons, 252
Express, 252
Lever push key, 252
Logo, 252
Pin tumbler, 253
Railroad, 253
Scandinavian, 253
Six lever and eight lever, 253
Story, 253
Warded, 253
Wrought iron lever, 253
Paper Dolls, 254
Paperback Books, 255
Patriotic Collectibles, 255
    Eagle, 256
    Fans and shields, 256
    George Washington, 257
    Liberty Bell 256
    Statue of Liberty, 257
    Uncle Sam, 257
Pennsbury Pottery, 257, 258
Pens and Pencils, 258
    Desk set, 258
    Pen, 258, 259
    Pencil, 259
Pepsi-Cola Collectibles, 259, 260
PEZ, 260, 261
    Dispenser, 261
    Other, 261
Phoenix Bird China, 261, 262, 263
Pig Collectibles, 263, 264
Pinball Machines, 264
    Bally, 265
    Chicago Coin, 265
    Exhibit, 265
    Genco, 265
    Gottlieb, 265
    Mills Novelty Co., 265
    Pacific Amusement, 265
    Rock-Ola, 265
    United, 265
    Williams, 265
Pin-Up Art, 265, 266
Planters Peanuts, 268, 269
Planters, 267, 381
    Figural, 267, 268
    Head types, 268
    Wall pocket, 268
Plastics, 269
    Acrylic, 269, 270
    Bakelite, 270
    Celluloid, 270
Playboy Collectibles, 270, 271

Playing Cards, 271, 272
Pocket Knives, 272, 273
Police Collectibles, 273, 274
Political and Campaign Items, 274
    Bush, George, 276
    Carter, Jimmy, 276
    Clinton, Bill, 276
    Eisenhower, Dwight, 275
    Goldwater, Barry, 276
    Harding, Warren G., 275
    Harrison, Benjamin, 274
    Hoover, Herbert, 275
    Johnson, Lyndon, 276
    Kennedy, John F., 276
    Landon, Alfred, 275
    Lincoln, Abraham, 274
    McKinley, William, 274
    Nixon, Richard M., 275
    Reagan, Ronald, 276
    Roosevelt, Franklin D., 275
    Roosevelt, Teddy, 275
    Truman, Harry S., 275
    Willkie, Wendell, 275
    Wilson, Woodrow, 275
Post Cards, 276
    Advertising, 277
    Artist signed, 277, 278
    Folder, 278
    Greetings, 278
    Humor, 278
    Patriotic, 278
    Photogenic, 278, 279
    Political and social history, 279
    World fairs and expositions, 279
Pottery,
    Beswick, 215
    Goebel, 209, 212
Presley, Elvis, 279, 280
Punchboards, 280, 281
Purinton Pottery, 281, 282

# R

Racing Collectibles, 283
    Auto, 283
    Dog, 284
    Horse, 284
Radio Characters and Personalities, 284
    Allen, Jimmie, 285
    Amos n' Andy, 284
    Armstrong, Jack, 285
    Benny, Jack, 285

Bergen, Edgar and Charlie Mc-
    Carthy, 285
  Captain Midnight, 284
  Fibber McGee and Molly, 285
  Flying Family, 285
  Little Orphan Annie, 285
  Major Bowes, 285
  Penner, Joe, 285
  Quiz Kids, 285
  The Shadow, 285
  Winslow, Don, 284
  Young Explorers Club, 285
Radio Premiums, 285, 286
Radios, 286, 287
  Admiral, 287
  Air King, 287
  Arvin, 287
  Atwater Kent, 287
  Bulova, 287
  Colonial, 287
  Columbia, 287
  Crosley, 287
  Dumont, 287
  Emerson, 287
  Fada, 287
  Federal, 287
  General Electric, 287
  Grebe, 288
  Halicrafters, 288
  Majestic, 288
  Metrodyne, 288
  Motorola, 288
  Olympic, 288
  Paragon, 288
  Philco, 288
  Radiobar, 288
  RCA, 288
  Silverstone, Sears, 288
  Sony, 288
  Sparton, 288
  Stewart Warner, 288
  Stromberg Carlson, 288
  Westinghouse, 288
  Zenith, 288
Railroad Items, 288, 289, 290
Reamers, 290
  China and Ceramic, 291
  Glass, 291
  Metal, 291
Records, 291, 292
Red Wing Pottery, 292, 293
Robots, 293, 294, 295
Rock 'n' Roll, 295, 296
Rockwell, Norman, 296, 297
Roseville Pottery, 297, 298

Royal China, 298
  Bucks County, 299
  Colonial Homestead, 299
  Currier and Ives, 300
  Fair Oaks, 300
  Memory Lane, 300
  Old Curiosity Shop, 301

# S

Saloon Collectibles, 302
Salt and Pepper Shakers, Figural,
302
    Advertising, 303
    Ceramic, 303
Santa Claus 208, 212, 213, 215,
303, 304
Scouting, 304
    Boy Scouts, 305
    Girl Scouts, 305
Sewing Items, 306, 307, 308
Shawnee Pottery, 308, 309
Sheet Music, 309, 310, 311
Shelley China, 311
Slot Machines, 311, 312, 313
Soakies, 313
Soda Fountain Collectibles, 313,
314
Soft Drink Collectibles, 314, 315
Soldiers, Dimestore, 315
    Civilian figure, 316
    Military figure, 316, 317
Soldiers, Toy, 317
    Authenticast, 318
    Bienheim, 318
    Britains, 318, 319
    Elastolin/Lineol, 319
    Heyde, 319
    Mignot, 319
    Militia Models, 319
    Nostalgia, 319
    S.A.F., 319
Souvenir and Commemorative
Items, 319, 320, 322
Souvenir Buildings, 322, 323
Space Adventurers and Exploration,
323
    Battlestar Galactica, 323
    Buck Rogers, 323
    Captain Video, 323
    Flash Gordon, 324
    Lost in Space, 324
    Space Cadet, Tom Corbett, 324
    Space exploration, 325

    Space Patrol, 324
    Space related, 325
    Star Trek, 324, 325
Space Toys, 326, 327
Sports Collectibles, 327
Stangl Pottery, 328
    Dinnerware, 328, 329
    Miscellaneous and artware, 329
Star Wars, 329, 330, 331
Stereographs, 331
    Animal, 332
    Astronomy, 332
    Aviation, 332
    Blacks, 332
    Cave, 333
    Christmas, 333
    Comics, 333
    Disaster, 333
    Doll, 333
    Entertainer, 333
    Exposition, 333
    Hunting and fishing, 333
    Indian, 333
    Mining, 333
    Miscellaneous, 334
    National Park, 334
    Niagara Falls, 334
    Occupational, 334
    Oil, 334
    Person, famous, 334
    Photographer, famous, 334
    Photographica, 335
    Railroad, 335
    Religious, 335
    Risque, 335
    Sets, 335
    Ship, 335
    Survey, 335
    War, 335
    Whaling, 335
Stereo-Viewers, 331
Sterling Silver Flatware,
    Violet, Wallace, 339
Sterling Silver Flatware, 335
    Bridal Rose, Alvin, 336
    Buttercup, Gorham, 336
    Chippendale, Towle, 336
    Classic Bouquet, Gorham, 337
    Classic Rose, Reed & Barton,
        337
    Colonial, Tiffany, 337
    Columbia, Lunt, 337
    Copenhagen, Manchester, 337
    Country Manor, Towle, 337
    Courtship, International, 337

Craftsman, Towle, 337
Eloquence, Lunt, 337
Embassy Scroll, Lunt, 337
Evening Rose, Lunt, 337
Fairfax, Durgin, 337
Grande Baroque, Wallace, 338
Imperial Queen, Whiting, 338
Madrigal, Lunt, 338
Modern Victorian, Lunt, 338
Normandie, Wallace, 338
Old Maryland, plain, Kirk, 338
Orchid, International, 339
Queen's Lace, International, 339
Warwick, Wallace, 339
Wedding Bells, International, 339
Wedgwood, International, 339
Wild Rose, International, 339
Stock and Bond Certificates, 339
Bonds, 340
Stocks, 340, 341
Stuffed Toys, 341, 342
Super Heroes, 342
Aquaman, 342
Batman & Robin, 342
Bionic Woman, 343
Buck Rogers, 343
Captain Action, 343
Captain America, 343
Captain Marvel, 343
Captain Midnight, 343
Fantastic Four, 343
Green Hornet, 343
Incredible Hulk, 343
Legion of Super Heroes, 343
Mr. Fantastic, 343
Spiderman, 343
Super Heroes, DC Comics, 344
Superman, 344
Wonder Woman, 344
Swankyswigs, 344, 345
Swarovski Crystal, 345, 346
Accessories, 346, 347
Figurine, 347

T

Taylor, Smith and Taylor, 348
Beverly, 348
Delphian, 348
Empire, 348
Fairway, 348
Laurel, 348

Lu-Ray, 348
Marvel, 349
Paramount, 349
Pebbleford, 349
Plymouth, 349
Versatile, 349
Vistosa, 349
Vogue, 349
Teapots, 349
American, 349
Chinese, 349
English, 349
Figural, 349
German, 350
Japan, 350
Miniature, 350
Porcelain, 350
Pottery, 350
Television Personalities and Memorabilia, 350, 351, 352
Televisions, 352
1925-1932, mechanical, 353
1938-1941, electronic, 353
1946 and later, 353
Temple, Shirley, 353, 354
Thermometers, 354
Thimbles, 355
Advertising, 355
Gadgets, 356
Political, 356
Thimbles, 356
Tinsel Art, 356, 357
Toys, 357, 358
Alps, 358
Arcade, 358
Auburn Toys, 359
Bachman, 359
Bandai Co., 359
Buddy L 359
Chein, 359
Chilton Toys, 359
Con-Cor, 359
Corgi, 359, 360
Cragston, Japan, 360
Dinky, 360
Doepke, 360
Ertl, 360
Fisher-Price, 360
Gabriel, Tricky Trapeze, 361
Gay Products, 361
Gilbert, A.C., 361
Hasbro, 361
Hot Wheels, 361
Hubley, 362
Ideal, 362

Japanese, Post War, 362
Kenner, 362
Knickerbocker, 362
Lincoln Toys, Canada, 362
Line Mar (Linemar), 362
Marx, 362
Matchbox, 363
Mattel, 363
Mego, 363
Nylint, 363
Occupied Japan, 363
Playsets, 364
Remco, 364
Schuco, 364
Slinky, 364
Structo, 364
Sun Rubber, 364
Tonka, 364
Tootsietoys, 365, 366
Winross Trucks 366
Wolverine, 366
Wyandotte, 366
Trains, Toy, 366, 367
American Flyer O Gauge, 367
American Flyer S Gauge, 367, 368
Ives, 368
Lionel O Gauge, 368
Lionel S Gauge, 368
N Gauge, 369
Typewriters, 369, 370

U

Uhl's Pottery, 371, 372
Universal Pottery, 372
Ballerina, 372
Bittersweet, 372
Calico Fruit, 372
Cattails, 372
Circus, 372
Rambler Rose, 372
Woodvine, 372

V

Valentines, 209, 212, 215, 373
Animated, 373
Comic, 373
Diecut, small, 373
Flat, 373
Folder, 373
Hanger and String, 373

Honeycomb Tissue, 373
Paper Lace, 373
Parchment, 373
Pull-Down, 373
Pullout, 374
Silk Fringed, 374
Standup with Easel Back, 374
Victorian Novelty, 374
Wood, telephone, boxed, 374
Vending Machines, 374
Vernon Kilns, 375
Brown-Eyed Susan, 375
Calico, 375
Chatelaine, 375
Chintz, 375
Gingham, 375
Hawaiian Flowers, 375
Homespun, 375
Moby Dick, 375
Organdie, 375
Raffia, 375
Tom O'shanter, 375
Winchester, 73, 376
View-Master Products, 376, 377

# W

Watch Fobs, 378
Advertising, 378
Fraternal, 378
Political, 379
Souvenir, 379
Watt Pottery, 379
Apple, 379

Autumn Foilage, 379
Bleeding Heart, 379
Cherry, 379
Pansy, 379
Rooster, 379
Starflower, 379
Tulip, 380
Weller Pottery, 380, 381
Western Americana, 381, 382, 383
Westmoreland Glass Company, 383, 384, 385
Whiskey Bottles, Collectors' Special Editions, 385
Anniversary, 385
Ballantine, 385
Warner Bros. Characters, 385
Whiskey Bottles, Collectors' Special Editions,
Beneagle, 385
Bischoff, 385
Collector's Art, 386
Cyrus Noble, 386
Early Times, 386
Ezra Brooks, 386
Famous Firsts, 386
Garnier, 386
Grenadier, 386
Hoffman, 386
J.W. Dant, 386
Japanese Firms, 386
Jim Beam, 385
Lewis and Clark, 386
Lionstone, 386
Luxardo, 387
McCormick, 387

OBR, 387
Old Commonwealth, 387
Old Fitzgerald, 387
Old Mr. Boston, 387
Pacesetter, 387
Ski Country, 387
Wild Turkey, 387
World War I Collectibles, 387, 388
World War II Collectibles, 388, 389, 390
World's Fairs and Expositions, 390
California Mid-Winter Exposition, 390
Century 21 Exposition, 392
Century of Progress, 391
Golden Gate International Exposition, 392
New York World's Fair, 392
New York's World Fair, 391, 392
Pan Am Exposition, 390
Panama-Pacific International Exposition, 390
St. Louis, Louisiana Purchase Exposition, 390
The Columbian Exposition, 390
World's Fair, 392
Wrestling Collectibles, 392, 393, 394
Wright, Russell, 394
American Modern, 394, 395
Iroquois Casual, 395
Iroquois Casual, Redesigned, 395

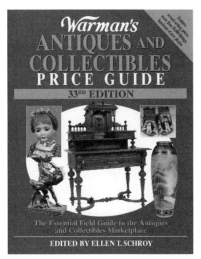
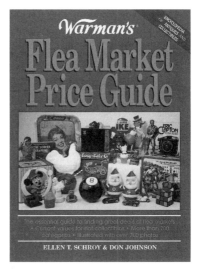

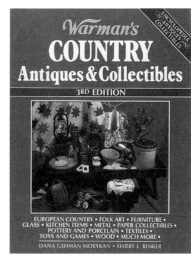
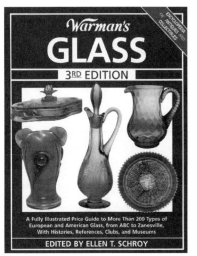
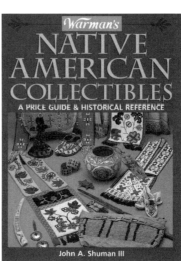

# TRUST THE EXPERTS FOR COLLECTIBLE ADVISE

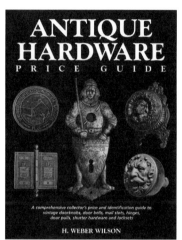

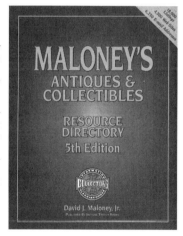